Since we've printed the first copy of PC Intern we've received excellent reviews and comments from reviewers and customers like yourself. The following is a sample of their suggestions and comments:

"This book is a necessity for the serious programmer." J.W., IL

"I'm a high School student taking a pascal course and this informative book has put me miles ahead of the class." G.T., NJ

"This book is the best one I've read this year. "A.W., Syria

"Well done. One of the most used references in my library." B.S., VA

"Best computer book I've ever seen..." B.S., NE

"Just a great book." H.N., CA

"How Comprehensive! So much information in just one book." W.V., TN

"Great book, used the at clock driver right off the bat and save myself a $65.00 service call." E.R., OH

"Looks like a comprehensive single volume reference source...It is like an encyclopedia." A.H., MA

"The secrets finally explained in a thorough and readable manner-the best computer book I have ever seen." S.J., CA

"PC Intern is an awesome book ..." S.T., WA

"This book is full of treasures of knowledge and should be read by every program." Q.A., Netherlands

"PC Intern is the best DOS book I've purchased." P.D., MD

"Valuable Resource for DOS/PC based application programmers." M.R., FL

"Great book! Lots of useful information saved my butt!!" D.R., CA

"This book is exactly what I've been looking for." P.C., UT

"Excellent information source code and companion disk make it a 'must have' for beginning programs." C.X., WA

"An excellent book with hard to find PC information." B.R., WA

"Is an outstanding book. We need more books at this level." W.S., TX

"Excellent! Very informative. Superb examples." P.D., CA

"Great book, it's many in one, thanks!" C.G., VT

"Big book, big price, lots of good stuff." H.C., CT

"Great, detailed book on important topics." M.M., NJ

"I like the combined language support this book has very wide range of information." A.R., TX

"The best book about PC Programming I have ever read! Superb! Excellent." K.A., Finland

"Excellent book, exactly what I was looking for to learn PC System Programming." D.K., NY

"In love with book!!" H.C., MO

"The book is worth its weight. Keep up the good work!" A.P., Argentina

"Excellent reference." F.P., OH

"Great! Infinitely better than the competition." D.F., TX

"Good info without B.S. & fluff" S.B ., HI

"Very good, nice...I should say 'excellent'" G.K, CA

"This looks like it will be the best encyclopedia available." J M, VA

"Interesting... Excellent Book" T.P., OK

"Excellent; Very thorough coverage and extremely readable; the most complete reference on my shelf" D.H., NC

"Extremely pleased...well written and explained topics..." G J, TX

"Great Book! Great Reference!" T.M., AL

"I've been looking for this type of book for a long time. It's very in-depth & and an excellent reference" T.M., MI

"Excellent book. Just what a beginning or intermediate programmer needs to know, well organized" D.S., IL

"I really like this book because it tells you how to do things I've been wanting to know." J.T., CO

"Excellent book!" S.S., NM

"Very informative and useful for programmers working on PC" T.G., Singapore

"An excellent programming book-it covers the two most widely used languages-Pascal & C" R.H., CO

"I appreciate the completeness of this volume & hope to learn much from it" D.A., NE

"I cut the back off 1/8" and installed in a 3 ring note book this makes it better to use as a reference..." R.M., NJ

"This has been a good reference book for me! I like the packaged diskettes. Saves a lot of time for learning rather than typing." G.P., PQ

"I like the in-depth nature of the book!" D.L., CA

"Extraordinary Book ..." D.E., WA

"Excellent book. I've been looking for this for years." E.P., VA

PC INTERN

SYSTEM PROGRAMMING

The Encyclopedia
of Programming
Know How

Michael Tischer

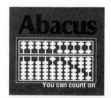

Printed in the U.S.A.

ISBN 1-55755-282-7

10 9 8 7 6 5 4 3 2 1

Table Of Contents

Chapter 5

The Interrupt Controller   *215*

Chapter 9

Keyboard Programming   275

Chapter 10

Joysticks   301

Chapter 11

Mouse Programming   305

Chapter 15

Accessing And Programming The AT Realtime Clock   377

Chapter 16

System Configuration And Processor Types   387

Chapter 17

A Brief History Of DOS   397

Chapter 37

CD-ROM And Its Technology   615

Chapter 38

Sound Blaster And Compatible Cards   665

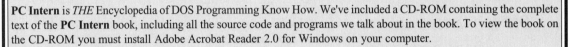

The Companion CD-ROM

PC Intern is *THE* Encyclopedia of DOS Programming Know How. We've included a CD-ROM containing the complete text of the **PC Intern** book, including all the source code and programs we talk about in the book. To view the book on the CD-ROM you must install Adobe Acrobat Reader 2.0 for Windows on your computer.

The Adobe™ Acrobat Reader 2.0 for Windows™ software gives you instant access to documents in their original form, independent of computer platform. By using the Acrobat Reader™, you can view, navigate, print selected files and present Portable Document Format (PDF) files.

System Requirements

➤ 386- or 486-based personal computer (486 or higher recommended)

➤ Microsoft Windows 3.1 or greater

➤ 4 Meg hard drive space and 4 Meg application RAM

Why a companion CD-ROM?

As you look through this copy of **PC Intern**, you'll quickly notice that it includes dozens of assembly language, BASIC, the C language and Pascal programs and routines. However, it would take the average user weeks to type in the listings accurately (there is over three megabytes' worth of program listings in this book).

The companion CD-ROM saves you time because now you won't have to type in the dozens of program listings we talk about in **PC Intern**. The program listings include the actual source codes in QuickBASIC, Turbo Pascal, assembly language, and C (almost all the C source codes are compatible from Turbo C++ and Microsoft C 6.00). For those BASIC, Pascal, and C codes that require separate assembly language modules, the companion CD-ROM has assembler source code and assembled object code for easy compilation.

The program files on this companion CD-ROM demonstrate general interrupt calls, video card access, keyboard operation, disk drive access, parallel port control, mouse support, joystick, support, extended and expanded memory, COM and EXE files, networking, sound, TSRs, and much more.

PLEASE NOTE: We do not include Microsoft QuickBASIC, the Microsoft Macro Assembler (MASM), Turbo C++, Microsoft C Version 6.00 with this book/CD-ROM package. We recommend that you contact Microsoft Corporation and Borland International for information on purchasing these quality program development tools.

Installing Acrobat Reader

Follow these steps to install Acrobat Reader 2.0 on your hard drive (Installation requires approximately 2 Meg of free hard drive space). Insert the CD-ROM in your drive and load Windows. From the Windows Program Manager, choose Run from the File menu. Next, type the following:

```
[drive]:\acroread.exe
```

and press Enter.

Then simply follow the instructions and prompts which appear on your screen.

Double click the Acrobat Reader icon to load it. After the Acrobat Reader is loaded, go to **File/Open...** and select either MAINFILE.PDF to view/read the **PC Intern** book *or* select PRG_MAIN.PDF to view the program pages.

Chapter 1

System Programming Basics

In the first part of this book we'll discuss the basics of system programming. We'll talk about the purpose of system programming and the methods and tools used in system programming. We'll also explain the PC's basic structure and the interaction between hardware, BIOS and DOS.

What Is System Programming?

Some users, regardless if they'e beginners or experienced programmers, believe system programming is a programming technique that converts a problem into a finished program. Others think system programming means developing programs for one particular computer system.

Application programming vs. system programming

Although both answers are incorrect, the second is more accurate than the first. The most accurate description of system programming can be derived from the term application programming. This type of programming refers to information management and presentation within a program. This involves arranging this information into lists, etc., and processing this information. The algorithms used for this are system independent and can be defined for almost any computer.

The way this information is passed to a program, and the way the information is displayed or printed are system dependent. System programming controls any hardware that sends information to, or receives information from, the computer. However, since this information must be processed, developing programs for PCs requires both application programming and system programming.

Programming hardware requires the interaction of system programming, DOS, and the ROM-BIOS (more on this later).

The Three-Layer Model

One of the most important tasks of system programming involves accessing the PC hardware. However, the access doesn't have to occur immediately, with the program turning directly to the hardware, which is similar to accessing the processor on a video card. Instead, the program can use the ROM-BIOS and DOS to negotiate hardware access. The ROM-BIOS and DOS are software interfaces, which were created specifically for hardware management.

Advantages of the DOS and BIOS interfaces

The greatest advantage of using DOS or BIOS is that a program doesn't have to communicate with the hardware on its own. Instead, it calls a ROM-BIOS routine that performs the required task. After the task is completed, the ROM-BIOS returns status information to the program as needed. This saves the programmer a lot of work, because calling one of these functions is faster than directly accessing the hardware.

There's another advantage to using these interfaces. The ROM-BIOS and DOS function interfaces keep a program isolated from the physical properties of the hardware. This is very important because monochrome graphic cards, such as the MDA and Hercules cards, must be programmed differently from color graphic cards, such as the CGA, EGA, VGA, and Super VGA. If you want a program to support all these cards, you must implement individual routines for each card, which is very time-consuming. The ROM-BIOS functions used for video output are adapted to the resident video card, so the program can call these functions without having to adapt to the video card type.

ROM-BIOS

The BIOS offers functions for accessing the following devices:

➢ Video cards   ➢ RAM (extended memory)   ➢ Diskettes   ➢ Hard drives

➢ Serial ports   ➢ Parallel ports   ➢ Keyboard   ➢ Battery-operated realtime clock

The three layer model

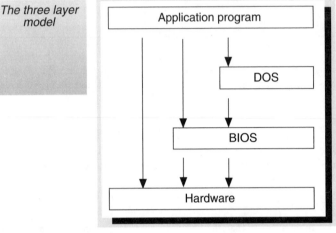

As this illustration shows, the ROM-BIOS can be viewed as a layer overlapping the hardware.

Although you can bypass the ROM-BIOS and directly access the hardware, generally you should use the ROM-BIOS functions because they are standardized and can be found in every PC. The ROM-BIOS, as its name indicates, is in a ROM component on the computer's motherboard. The moment you switch on your computer, the ROM-BIOS is available (see Chapter 3 for more information).

DOS interface

Along with BIOS, DOS provides functions for accessing the hardware. However, since DOS views hardware as logical devices instead of physical devices, DOS functions handle hardware differently. For example, the ROM-BIOS views disk drives as groups of tracks and sectors, but DOS views these drives as groups of files and directories. If you want to view the first thousand characters of a file, first you must tell the ROM-BIOS the location of the file on the drive. With DOS functions, you simply instruct DOS to open a file on drive A:, C:, or whatever device, and display the first thousand characters of this file.

Access often occurs through BIOS functions used by DOS. However, sometimes DOS also accesses hardware directly, but you don't have to worry about this when you call a DOS function.

Which functions should you use?

Later in this chapter we'll show you how to call DOS and BIOS functions. Before doing this, however, we must determine which hardware access to use. We have the option of direct hardware programming, calling BIOS functions, and calling DOS functions. First, you don't always have a choice between direct hardware programming, and BIOS and DOS functions. Many tasks aren't supported by the BIOS or DOS functions. For example, if you want your video card to draw circles or lines, you won't find the appropriate functions in DOS or the BIOS. You must use direct hardware programming or purchase a commercial software library that contains this program code.

Choosing between BIOS and DOS

When either a BIOS function or a DOS function can be used, your decision should be based on the current situation. If you want to work with files, you must use DOS functions. If you want to format a diskette, you must use the appropriate BIOS functions. This is similar to displaying characters on the screen. If you want to redirect your program output to a file (e.g., DIR >list.txt), you must use DOS functions. Only DOS functions automatically perform this redirection. The BIOS functions provide better control of the screen (e.g., cursor placement). So, the situation determines which function you should use.

Slowing access

However, in some instances, both the BIOS functions and DOS functions are at a disadvantage because of slow execution speed. As the number of software layers, which must be negotiated before hardware access occurs, increases, the programs become longer. If the hardware must access a program that reads a file through BIOS and DOS, a hard drive's data transfer rate can decrease a maximum of 80 percent.

This problem is caused by the way the layers are handled. Before the call can be passed to the next level, parameters must be converted, information must be loaded from internal tables, and buffer contents must be copied. The time needed for this passage is called overhead. So, as overhead increases, so does the programmer's work.

As a result, when maximum execution speed is required and direct hardware programming is relatively simple, programmers often use direct access instead of the BIOS and DOS. The best example of this is character output in text mode. Almost all commercial applications choose the most direct path to the hardware because BIOS and DOS output functions are too slow and inflexible. Direct video card access in text mode is quite easy (refer to Chapter 4 for more information), although graphic mode output offers more challenges.

Later in this chapter you'll learn how to call the DOS and BIOS functions and how to directly access the hardware of the PC.

Basics Of PC Hardware

In this section we'll examine some of the basic concepts of PC architecture, which lead all the way to the system programming level. Knowing something about the hardware will make it easier to understand some of the programming problems discussed later in this book.

Birth of the PC

When the PC appeared on the market, much of what PC users take for granted today was inconceivable. The concept of having a flexible computer on a desktop wasn't new; companies much smaller than IBM had already introduced similar computers. IBM had just completed work on its System/23 DataMaster. However, the DataMaster was equipped with an 8085 8-bit processor from Intel, which was outdated. In 1980, the 16-bit processor was introduced and IBM began planning a new, revolutionary machine.

Choosing a processor

The 8086 processor and 8088 processors from Intel were the first representatives of the new 16-bit processors. Both had 16-bit registers. This meant they could access 1 megabyte memory addresses instead of the old 64K memory addresses. A megabyte was an unimaginable amount of memory in 1980, just as 1 gigabyte of RAM is still unimaginable to many today.

Another reason developers were anxious to use the 8086 and 8088 processors was that many support chips already existed. Obviously this saved a lot of development time. Also, both processors were supported by an operating system and an implementation of the BASIC language, which was developed by Microsoft Corporation.

Block diagram of your PC's hardware

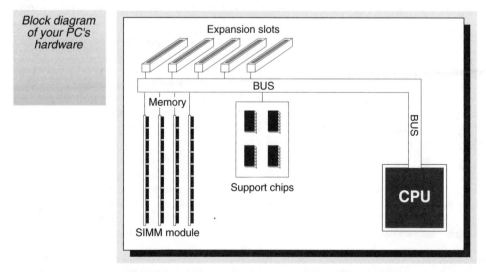

The developers chose the 8088 over the 8086 because, while the 8088 worked on a 16-bit basis internally, it only communicated with the outside world using an 8-bit data bus. Since the 8-bit DataMaster data bus already existed, the 8088 was the obvious choice. This bus connects the motherboard of the PC, where the processor and its support chips are resident, to the memory and the expansion boards, which are plugged into the expansion slots.

The Bus

Although the bus is vital to the operation of the computer system, the development of the PC bus represents one of the darkest moments in the history of the PC. Although IBM tried to create an open system and publish all technical information, it neglected to document the exact sequence of the bus signals, probably assuming that no one would need or want this information.

However, the openness of the PC and the option of easily adding expansion boards and more hardware added to the PC's success on the market. Many users quickly took advantage of this, buying IBM expansion boards and third-party compatible boards. The PC has its entire data and address bus on the outside; the bus connects to RAM, the various expansion boards, and some support chips.

Operating the PC bus

The bus is basically a cable with 62 lines, from which data are loaded into memory by the processor, and through which data can be transported to the processor.

The bus consists of the data bus and the address bus. When memory is accessed, the processor puts the address of the desired memory location on the address bus, with the individual lines indicating a binary character. Each line can be only a 0 or a 1. Together, the lines form a number that specifies the address of the memory location. The more lines that are available, the greater the maximum address and the greater the memory that can be addressed in this way. Twenty lines were available on the original address bus because with 20 bits you can address 1 megabyte of memory, which corresponds to the processor's performance.

The actual data are sent over the data bus. The first data bus was only 8 bits wide, so it could transfer only one byte at a time. If the processor wanted to discard the contents of a 16-bit register or a 16-bit value in memory, it had to split the register or value into two bytes and transfer one byte at a time.

Although theoretically this sounds simple, it's actually a complicated procedure. Along with the data and address buses, almost two dozen other signal lines communicate between the processor and memory. All the boards communicate with the bus. When a board takes responsibility for the specified address, it must send an appropriate signal to the processor. At this point, all the other boards separate from the rest of the communication and wait for the beginning of the next data transfer cycle.

Using expansion boards always leads to problems. This usually occurs when two boards claim the same address range or there are overlapping address ranges. The DIP switches on these boards let you specify the address range. One board must be reconfigured to avoid conflict with the other board.

As a system programmer, you'll never encounter bus signals. Actually, bus performance usually isn't important to system programming. The bus signal timing is very important to expansion board manufacturers. Their products must follow this protocol to function in the PC. However, this is the protocol that IBM never published. So, the manufacturers must measure the signal sequences by using existing cards and then imitate those cards.

AT bus

In 1991, the IEEE (Institute of Electrical and Electronic Engineers) submitted an international standard for the AT bus. The PC bus was limited by its 8-bit width. When the AT appeared on the market, it included a 16-bit bus that was compatible with the older bus. That's why the old PC 8-bit boards can be used with the new 16-bit boards in one device. Obviously, the 16-bit boards are much faster because they can transfer the same data in half the time it would take an 8-bit board.

The address bus was expanded to 24 bits, so the AT can address 16 megabytes of memory. Also, higher clock signal speed increased bus transfer time. From 4.77 MHz on the PC, the AT speed increased to 8 MHz. However, that's as fast as the AT address bus can handle information, although Intel processor speeds have reached the 100 MHz limit. As a result, the bus is a bottleneck, through which the data will never be transferred quickly enough between memory and the processor. Modern hard drives have a higher data transfer rate than the bus.

Wait state

The wait state signals found in some expansion boards give slow boards more time to deliver data to the processor.

This is also one reason why the classic AT bus resulted in more powerful successors like the Micro Channel bus and the EISA bus, which haven't been very successful on the market for other reasons. At first there wasn't a generic name for the AT bus. However, when competition appeared on the market, the bus was assigned the name Industry Standard Architecture bus, or ISA bus.

Problems with 16-bit boards on the AT bus

Since most of the modern 386s and 486s have an ISA bus, many problems in the PC can be traced to this bus. For example, the coexistence of 8-bit and 16-bit expansion boards within a PC causes problems as long as the address range for which these boards are responsible is located within any area of 128K. The problem starts at the beginning of a data transfer, when a 16-bit board has to signal from a control line that it can take a 16-bit word from the bus and, unlike an 8-bit board, doesn't depend on the transfer being split into two bytes.

However, the board must send this signal when it cannot even be aware the address on the data bus is intended for it and requires an answer. Of the 24 address lines that carry the desired address, only lines A17 to A23 have been correctly initialized to this point. This means the board only recognizes bits 17 to 23. These bits cover a complete 128K region, regardless of what might follow in address bits 0 to 16. So for the moment, the board only knows whether the memory address is located in the 0K-127K region, the 128K-255K region, etc.

If the 16-bit board sends the signal for a 16-bit transfer at this moment, it's speaking for all other boards within this region. They experience this in the next moment, because after address bits 0 to 16 have arrived on the bus, the intended board will be determined. If it really is the 16-bit board, no problems occur. However, if an 8-bit board was intended, the 16-bit board will simply separate from the rest of the transfer, leaving the 8-bit board by itself. However, the 8-bit board won't be able to manage the transfer because it's only set for 8-bit transfers. So, the expansion board cannot accept the data as sent.

PC BUS and Vesa Local Bus

In view of the limitations of the AT bus and the inability of the EISA and MCA bus to gain acceptance on the market, developers devised some other bus concepts. The Vesa Local bus (VL bus) came out first, designed and publicized by the independent VESA Committee. The members of the VESA committee made it their business to define standards for graphic cards, so they didn't really have anything at all to do with PC bus design. However, graphic cards suffer from the low speed of the AT bus. That's why the VESA committee made the suggestion for a faster bus, the VESA local bus.

Unlike the EISA, MCA and PCI buses, the VL bus does not replace the ISA bus, instead, it complements it. A PC with a VL bus has a normal ISA bus and the appropriate slots for expansion cards. However, there are also one or two additional slots for cards designed for the VL bus, usually graphic cards. Only these slots are connected to the CPU via the VL bus, so the other slots are left undisturbed and ISA cards can perform their work.

As you might guess from the name, the VL bus is a local bus. Unlike the ISA bus, it is directly coupled to the CPU. On the one hand, that gives the bus a significantly higher clock speed (that of the CPU), but it also makes the bus dependent, both on the control lines of the CPU and on the clock. Along with these drawbacks, the specifications of the VESA committee aren't very well thought out. As a result, the VL bus will not make the grade in the long run. While reasonably priced 486 systems often have this bus type, its heyday is over.

Clearly, the bus of the future is Intel's PCI bus. PCI stands for Peripheral Component Interconnect, and represents a modern bus that is superior to the ISA bus not only with regard to clock speed and a larger bus width. Finally, there is a bus that automatically synchronizes/tunes installed expansion cards regarding their port addresses, DMA channels and interrupts. The user no longer has to deal with this issue.

The PCI bus is independent from the CPU, because a PCI bus controller is always interconnected with the CPU and the PCI bus. That makes it possible to use the PCI bus in systems that aren't based on an INTEL processor, such as an Alpha processor from DEC. In the future, the Power Macintosh with the PowerPC processor is also supposed to be equipped with a PCI bus.

PCI upgrade cards work reliably in all systems equipped with a PCI bus and can be exchanged. Only the software drivers have to be adapted to the host system, i.e., the CPU.

In addition to that, the PCI bus is not dependent on the clock of the CPU, because the PCI bus controller separates it from the CPU. If you add a newer, faster CPU to your computer, you don't have to worry about your installed upgrade cards not being able to handle the higher clock speeds. Because the CPU and PCI bus are separate, the higher clock rates don't even affect them.

Modern Pentium computers are almost exclusively equipped with PCI buses, and the PCI bus is also becoming increasingly popular with 486 boards. Although you cannot operate an ISA card in a PCI slot, this doesn't mean you have to do without ISA cards on most systems with a PCI bus. Often a board with a PCI bus will have a "PCI to ISA bridge". This is a chip that is interconnected to the various ISA slots and the PCI bus controller. Its job is to convert signals from the PCI bus to the ISA bus. This allows you to continue running your ISA cards under the protection of the PCI bus.

Although the future belongs to the PCI bus, the ISA bus and ISA expansion boards will continue to exist. Not all expansion boards require the high transfer rates made possible by the PCI bus. However, in the future, above all graphic, SCSI and network cards will be attached to the PCI bus in ever greater numbers. The speed advantage of this bus system takes full effect on these cards, so the hardware can keep up with the steadily increasing speed of the processor.

Support chips

Developers supplied the processor with some additional chips to handle tasks the processor cannot handle on its own. These support chips, which are also called controllers because they control a part of the hardware for the processor, perform many tasks. This enables the processor to concentrate on other tasks.

The following are descriptions of these support chips and the chips initially selected by IBM. If a support chip is programmable, we'll indicate this later in the book.

DMA controller (8237)

DMA is an acronym for Direct Memory Access. This technique transfers data directly to memory by using a device (e.g., a hard drive). This method seems to work much faster than the normal method, in which the processor prompts the hardware for each word or byte and then sends the word or byte to memory. Actually, the DMA controller's advantages are evident only with slow processors because the DMA is linked to the bus speed.

Modern processors, which work more than five times as fast as their bus, barely benefit from DMA transfer because the DMA controller in the PC is obsolete. Because of this, the DMA controller cannot even be used for one of the most interesting areas of programming, which is moving large amounts of data from conventional RAM to video RAM (RAM on the video card). This chip is still found in all PCs although it isn't used for its original purpose, which is data transfer between disk drives and memory. ATs have two DMA controllers.

The PC is equipped with DRAM (dynamic RAM) instead of SRAM (static RAM). DRAMs lose their contents unless the system continually refreshes the RAM. The DMA controllers in AT systems, instead of the processors, perform this RAM refresh.

Interrupt controller (8259)

The interrupt controller is important for controlling external devices, such as the keyboard, hard drive or serial port. Usually the processor must repeatedly prompt a device, such as the keyboard, in short intervals to react immediately to user input and pass this input to the program currently being executed. However, this continual prompting, also called *polling*, wastes processor time because the user doesn't press a key as often as the processor polls the keyboard. However, the less often the processor prompts the keyboard, the longer it takes until a program notices that a key has been pressed. This obviously defeats the purpose, since the system is supposed to react promptly.

Hardware interrupt

The PC takes another route. Instead of the processor repeatedly prompting the devices, the devices report activity to the processor. This is an example of a hardware interrupt, because at that exact moment the processor interrupts the execution of the current program to execute an interrupt handler. This interrupt handler is a small routine, usually provided by the BIOS, that deals with the event that triggered the interrupt. After the routine ends, the processor continues executing the interrupted program as though nothing happened. This means the processor is called only when something actually happens.

However, the process of triggering an interrupt, halting program execution, and calling the interrupt handler takes a long time. Expansion board and support chip interrupt requests are sent to the interrupt handler first, instead of to the processor. The PC has several interrupt lines, each connected to a device. Each of these devices could trigger an interrupt over its line simultaneously.

Because the processor can only process one interrupt at a time, priorities must be defined so the incoming interrupt requests are handled according to their priority. The interrupt controller is responsible for determining priority.

The interrupt controller in a PC/XT can process up to eight interrupt sources, which enables it to handle eight interrupt requests simultaneously. Since this isn't sufficient for an AT, two interrupt controllers are coupled on the AT. Together they can process up to 15 interrupt requests simultaneously. For more information about hardware interrupts, refer to the "Interrupts" section in this chapter.

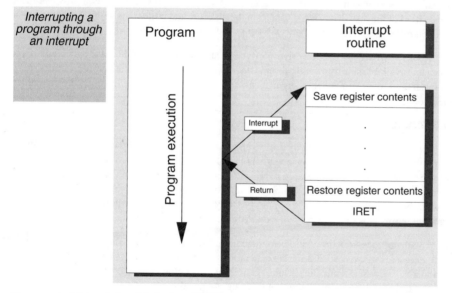

Interrupting a program through an interrupt

Programmable peripheral interface (8255)

This chip connects the processor to peripheral devices, such as the keyboard and speaker. It acts only as a mediator, which is used by the processor to pass given signals to the desired device. (Refer to Chapter 13 for more information on this chip and how it's used to make musical sounds.)

The clock (8248)

If the microprocessor is the brain of the computer, then the clock could be considered the heart of the computer. This heart beats several million times a second (about 14.3 MHz) and paces the microprocessor and the other chips in the system. Since almost none of the chips operate at such high frequencies, each support chip modifies the clock frequency to its own requirements.

The timer (8253)

The timer chip can be used as a counter and timekeeper. This chip transmits constant electrical pulses from one of its output pins. The frequency of these pulses can be programmed as needed, and each output pin can have its own frequency. Each output pin leads to another component. One line goes to the audio speaker and another to the interrupt controller. The line to the interrupt controller triggers interrupt 8 at every pulse, which advances the timer count.

CRT controller (6845)

Unlike the chips we've discussed so far, the CRT (Cathode Ray Tube) controller is separate from the PC's motherboard (main circuit board). This chip is located on the video card, which is mounted in one of the computer's expansion slots. Originally the controller was a Motorola 6845 model controller, which was used on the CGA and MDA video cards first released by IBM. The later EGA and VGA cards superseded these cards because of their more powerful processors. Even though these new chips are no longer compatible with the original Motorola controllers, this doesn't affect the processor. Unlike the other support chips, the processor doesn't come directly into contact with the CRT controller. The ROM-BIOS is specially adapted to working with the CRT controller, which relieves the processor of the task (see Chapter 4 for more information about programming video cards).

Disk controller (765)

This chip is also usually located on an expansion board. It's addressed by the operating system and controls disk drive functions. It moves the read/write head of the disk drive, reads data from the diskette, and writes data to the diskette. Similar to the CRT controller, the disk controller is addressed by the ROM-BIOS instead of by the processor.

The first PCs didn't have disk drives. IBM provided a cassette drive interface, assuming that this would be the preferred storage device. However, disk drives became available shortly afterward, and IBM stopped using the cassette interface. Data storage on a disk drive is much safer, faster, and more convenient than on a cassette. (Refer to Chapter 6 for more information on diskettes, hard drives, and their controllers.)

The math coprocessors (8087/80287/80387/80487)

Until the 80486 was released, Intel processors weren't able to work with floating point numbers. They could only process whole numbers. Depending on the bit width, integers cover a value range of 0 to 255 (8 bit), 0 to 65535 (16 bit) or 0 to 429624976 (32 bit), while floating point numbers cover the range of real numbers. That's why floating point numbers are used wherever it's necessary to calculate with real numbers, for example in a spreadsheet or CAD program. While floating point numbers can be represented with the help of integers and it is possible to base floating point arithmetic on integers via software, calculating floating point numbers is much faster when done directly in the hardware.

That is why Intel offered special math coprocessors that could be plugged into a free socket on the motherboard, next to the CPU. They were adapted to the successors of the Intel 8088, from generation to generation. There is a math coprocessor for each Intel processor up to the 486 SX. The 486 DX and the various versions of the Pentium chip have this coprocessor built in, so they are able to execute floating point calculations without adding a special coprocessor. However, there is one requirement. The software must really make use of the appropriate machine language commands for floating point arithmetic.

We won't discuss programming a coprocessor in this book because this involves normal assembly language processing instead of system programming. (Refer to Chapter 14 for more information about coprocessors.)

Memory layout

The first PCs included 16K of memory, which could be upgraded to as much as 64K on the motherboard. IBM also sold memory expansion boards containing 64K of memory, which could be inserted in one of the five expansion slots. You could install up to three of these boards, upgrading your PC to 256K of memory. In 1981, this was considered a lot of memory.

The PC developers defined a memory layout that allowed RAM expansion to 640K. Along with the RAM expansion, they also planned for additional video RAM, additional ROM-BIOS, and some ROM expansions in the 1 megabyte address space of the 8088 processor.

Whether RAM or ROM is in a given memory location doesn't matter to the processor, except that ROM locations cannot be written. The processor can also address memory locations that don't exist physically. Although the processor can manage up to 1 megabyte of memory, this doesn't guarantee that a RAM or ROM component exists behind every memory address.

As the following table shows, this memory layout is based on 64K segments because the 8088 and its successors manage memory in blocks of this size (more on this in Chapter 12). Sixteen of these blocks comprise an address space of 1 megabyte.

Division of PC RAM		
Block	Address	Contents
15	F000:0000 - F000:FFFF	ROM-BIOS
14	E000:0000 - E000:FFFF	Free for ROM cartridges
13	D000:0000 - D000:FFFF	Free for ROM cartridges
12	C000:0000 - C000:FFFF	additional ROM-BIOS
11	B000:0000 - B000:FFFF	Video RAM
10	A000:0000 - A000:FFFF	Additional video RAM (VGA/EGA)
9	9000:0000 - 9000:FFFF	RAM from 576K to 640K
8	8000:0000 - 8000:FFFF	RAM from 512K to 576K
7	7000:0000 - 7000:FFFF	RAM from 448K to 512K
6	6000:0000 - 6000:FFFF	RAM from 384K to 448K
4	5000:0000 - 5000:FFFF	RAM from 320K to 384K
5	4000:0000 - 4000:FFFF	RAM from 256K to 320K
3	3000:0000 - 3000:FFFF	RAM from 192K to 256K
2	2000:0000 - 2000:FFFF	RAM from 128K to 192K
1	1000:0000 - 1000:FFFF	RAM from 64K to 128K
0	0000:0000 - 0000:FFFF	RAM from 0K to 64K

The first 10 memory segments are reserved for conventional memory, limiting its size to 640K. Memory segment 0 is important because it contains important data and operating system routines.

Memory segment A follows conventional memory. This segment indicates an EGA or VGA card and contains additional video RAM for generating the various graphics modes supported by these cards.

Memory segment B is reserved for a Monochrome Display Adapter (MDA) or Color/Graphics Adapter (CGA). They share the same segment of video RAM. The monochrome card uses the lower 32K and the color card uses the upper 32K. Each video card only uses as much memory as it needs for the display. The MDA uses 4K while the CGA card uses 16K.

The next memory segment contains ROM beginning at segment C. Some computers store the BIOS routines that aren't part of the original BIOS kernel at this location. For example, the XT uses these routines for hard drive support. Since this location isn't completely utilized, this memory range may be used later to store BIOS routines supporting hardware extensions.

ROM cartridges

Segments D and E were originally reserved for ROM cartridges, but they were never properly used. Today this range is used either for additional RAM or EMS memory (see Chapter 12 for more information).

Segment F contains the actual BIOS routines, the original system loader, and the ROM BASIC available on early PCs.

Following this memory layout

The PC hardware isn't limited to any particular memory layout, including IBM's. However, IBM set the standard with its first PC, and suppliers still follow this standard. This usually affects software because the BIOS and DOS have adapted to the locations of certain memory areas (e.g., video RAM). Every software product on the market also complies with IBM's memory structure.

After the PC

Although the original IBM PC wasn't the last development in the PC world, it did establish a series of basic concepts, including the BIOS functions, the memory layout, and the interaction between the processor and the support chips.

However, the XT and the AT brought a few small changes to these concepts. The XT, released in 1983, had the first hard drive with a 10 megabyte capacity. This upgrade barely affected the total system, except the C segment was given an additional hard drive ROM, which added some ROM-BIOS functions for hard drive access.

The AT

The AT (Advanced Technology) computer was released in 1984, only one year after the XT. The most significant improvement involved the processor because developers used the Intel 80286 instead of the 8088. This processor finally gave the PC a 16-bit data bus. So, memory accesses no longer had to be divided into two bytes, as long as the memory and expansion board cooperated. Also, the address lines of the bus were increased from 20 to 24 bits because the 80286 could manage 24-bit addresses, which allowed it to address a memory range of 16 megabytes.

Disk drives

The AT doubled the hard drive capacity to 20 megabytes and introduced the 5.25" HD (high density) disk drive with a capacity of 1.2 megabytes. This disk drive is still used today. Also, the AT had a battery operated realtime clock, which finally made it possible for the clock to continue running even after the computer was switched off. The AT also increased the number of DMA controllers and interrupt controllers to two each.

A few new ROM-BIOS functions, such as functions for accessing the battery operated realtime clock, supported the new hardware.

Although the AT provided many improvements, it signaled the beginning of a trend that favors the current version instead of creating solutions for future upgrades. For example, "downward compatibility" in protected mode (an operating mode that separated the 80286 from its predecessors) wasn't widely used until the 80386 and Windows 3.0 were introduced.

When the 80286 appeared, preparations hadn't been made for protected mode. DOS, BIOS, and software avoided supporting this mode. Users continued working in real mode, in which the 80286 acts like a glorified 8088, performing at a fraction of its total capacity. Unfortunately, this is still happening today; real mode will probably be used until the switch to Windows NT and OS/2.

PS/2

After the AT, IBM attempted to set another standard with its PS/2 systems. These systems were successful mainly because of an improved bus system called the Micro-Channel Architecture (MCA). However, IBM kept the architecture of the new bus secret. It provided the information needed for building expansion cards only to hardware manufacturers that paid the licensing fees. This resulted in a limited supply of expansion boards for a system that wouldn't accept any AT boards. ISA boards cannot be used in systems with an MCA bus because the MCA bus has an entirely different line capacity.

No standards after the AT

Many companies began offering less expensive (and sometimes better) alternatives to the AT and PS/2. Companies like Compaq, which released laptop computers and an AT that had an 80386 processor, kept PC technology moving forward.

However, no company could fill the gap that was left by IBM when it dropped in the market. Once the PC market became fragmented, none of the companies had the power to define new hardware/software standards and push them onto the market. After a few years, committees met to set hardware standards (e.g., the Super VGA standard) that improved system and software compatibility.

After the AT, a new PC based on the ISA bus wasn't defined. So, systems with 80386 or 80486 processors are still generically referred to as ATs because they're based on the technology introduced by IBM when the AT was released.

The Processor

You don't have to become a professional assembly language programmer to understand system programming. You can also use high level languages, such as BASIC, Pascal, or C, for system programming. However, you must understand some concepts of the processor that are important in system programming. These concepts, which overlap into high level language programs, include the processor register, memory addressing, interrupts, and hardware access.

Although these principles haven't changed much since the 8088 was introduced, this chip is in its fifth generation and has capabilities that were unheard of ten years ago. However, these changes relate to the processor's speed instead of its fundamental concept.

The PC's brain

Let's discuss the family of Intel PC processors. The *microprocessor* is the brain of the PC. It understands a limited number of assembly language instructions and processes or executes programs in this assembly language. These instructions are very simple and can't be compared to commands in high level languages, such as BASIC, Pascal, or C. Commands in these languages must be translated into numerous assembly language instructions the PC's microprocessor can then execute. For example, displaying text with the BASIC PRINT statement requires the equivalent of several hundred assembly language instructions.

Assembly language instructions are different for each microprocessor used in different computers. The terms Z-80, 6502, or 8088 assembly language (or machine language) refer to the microprocessor being programmed.

Intel's 80xx series

The PC has its own family of microprocessor chips, which were designed by the Intel Corporation. The following figure shows the Intel 80xx family tree. Your PC may contain an 8086 processor, an 8088 processor (used in the PC/XT), an 80186 processor, an 80286 processor (used in the AT), or even an 80386 processor microprocessor. The first generation of this group (the 8086) was developed in 1978. The successors of the 8086 were different from the original chip. The 8088 is actually a step backward because it has the same internal structure and instructions of the 8086, but is slower than the 8086. The reason for this is the 8086 transfers 16 bits (2 bytes) between memory and the microprocessor simultaneously. The 8088 is slower since it transfers only 8 bits (1 byte) at a time.

The other microprocessors of this family are improved versions of the 8086. The 80186 provides auxiliary functions. The 80286 has additional registers and extended addressing capabilities. However, the 80286's greatest innovation is protected mode (see Chapter 33 for more information). DOS doesn't support protected mode.

The 80386 followed the 80286, and marks a great leap forward in performance. However, it's already outdated, and you will hardly find 386s on the market any more. This processor has advanced protected mode and 32-bit registers. Like protected mode, DOS doesn't support these registers. The 80386 includes SX and DX versions, which differ in clock frequency and data bus width. The SX works with a 16-bit data bus, while the DX can transfer an entire 32-bit word at one time.

The 80486 (often called the "i486" by Intel), is no longer "state of the art", although it is still very popular and selling in high numbers. It differs from the 80386 because it includes the 80387 mathematical coprocessor, a code cache, and faster processing of many assembly language instructions. However, the 80486 also maintains downward compatibility with the 8086.

The Pentium is currently considered the most advanced processor. Compared to the 486, the main improvement in the Pentium is the internal processing speed. In specific situations, this processor is able to process two sequential commands simultaneously, provided the second command doesn't depend on the result of the first command.

The name of the processor, Pentium, is also new. Users were expecting the 80586. Intel preferred to break with tradition, because names such as 8088 or 80586 cannot be protected by copyright. Other chip manufacturers took advantage of this to sell Intel compatible processors under similar names. Intel decided to take the wind out of the competition's sails and came up with "Pentium", which is protected by copyright.

No one knows yet whether the Pentium will by followed by the "Hexium", but we can start looking forward to the next generation of Intel processors, which will be introduced in 1995.

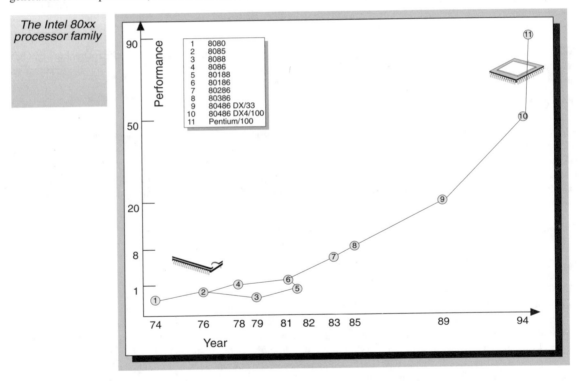

The Intel 80xx processor family

Processor registers

Registers are memory locations within the processor itself instead of in RAM. These registers can be accessed much faster than RAM. Registers are also specialized memory locations. The processor performs arithmetic and logical operations using its registers.

The processor registers are important for system programming because the flow of information between a program and the DOS and BIOS functions that call this program occurs through these registers.

From a system programming viewpoint, nothing has changed in registers since the 8086. This is because the BIOS and DOS were developed in connection with this processor, so they only support this processor's 16-bit registers. The 32-bit registers of an 80386 and i486 cannot be used in system programming under DOS. We'll discuss only 8088 registers, which apply to all later chips.

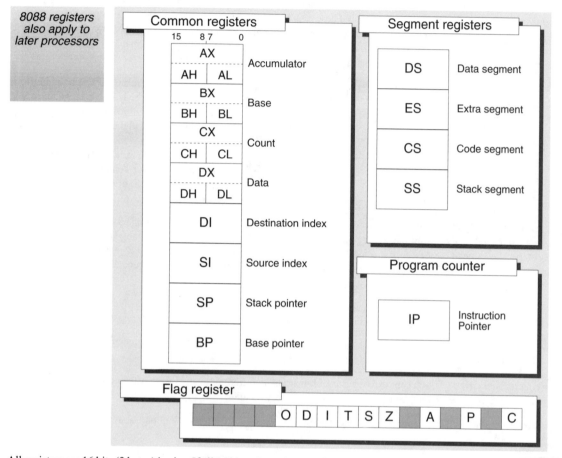

8088 registers also apply to later processors

All registers are 16 bits (2 bytes) in size. If all 16 bits of a register contain a 1, the result, which is the decimal number 65535, is the largest number that can be represented within 16 bits. So, a register can contain any value from 0 to 65535 (FFFFH or 1111111111111111b).

Register groupings

As the illustration above shows, registers are divided into four groups: common registers, segment registers, the program counter and the flag register. The different register assignments are designed to duplicate the way in which a program processes data, which is the basic task of a microprocessor.

The disk operating system and the routines stored in ROM use the common registers extensively, especially the AX, BX, CX, and DX registers. The contents of these registers tell DOS what tasks it should perform and which data to use for execution.

These registers are affected mainly by mathematical (addition, subtraction, etc.) and input/output instructions. They are assigned a special position within the registers of the 8088 because they can be separated into two 8-bit (1 byte) registers. Each common register usually contains three registers: a single 16-bit register and two smaller 8-bit registers.

Common registers

The common registers are important for calling DOS and BIOS functions and are used to pass parameters to a particular function that needs these parameters for execution. These registers are also influenced by mathematical operations (addition, subtraction, etc.), which are the central focus of all software activities at processor level. Registers AX, BX, CX, and DX have a special position within this set of registers, because they can be divided into two 8-bit registers. This means that each of these registers consists of three registers, one big 16-bit register and two small 8-bit registers.

8088 registers also apply to later processors

Bit 15	Bit 8	Bit 7	Bit 0
AH		AL	
Bit 15			Bit 0

The small registers have H (high) and L (low) designators. So, the 16-bit AX register may be divided into an 8-bit AH and an 8-bit AL register. The H and the L register designators occur in such a way the L register contains the lower 8 bits (bit 0 through 7) of the X register, and the H register contains the higher 8 bits (bits 8 through 15) of the X register. The AH register consists of bits 8-15 and the AL register consists of bits 0-7 of the AX register.

However, the three registers cannot be considered independent of each other. For example, if bit 3 of the AH register is changed, then the value of bit 11 of the AX register also changes automatically. The values change in both the AH and the AX registers. The value of the AL register remains constant since it is made of bits 0-7 of the AX register (bit 11 of the AX register doesn't belong to it). This connection between the AX, the AH, and the AL register is also valid for all other common registers and can be expressed mathematically.

You can determine the value of the X register from the values of the H and the L registers, and vice versa. To calculate the value of the X register, multiply the value of the H register by 256 and add the value of the L register.

Example: The value of the CH register is 10 and the value of the CL register is 118. The value of the CX register results from CH*256+CL, which is 10*256+118 = 2678.

Specifying register CH or CL, you can read or write an 8-bit data item from or to any memory location. Specifying register CX, you can read or write a 16-bit data item from or to a memory location.

In addition to common registers, segment registers and the flag register are an important part of system programming.

Flag register

The flag register communicates between consecutive assembly language instructions by storing the status of mathematical and logical operations. For example, after using the carry flag to add two 16-bit registers, a program can determine whether the result is greater than 65,535 and thus present it as a 32-bit number. The sign, zero, and overflow bits perform similar tasks and can be used after two registers have been compared to establish whether the value of the first register is greater than, less than, or equal to the value of the second register.

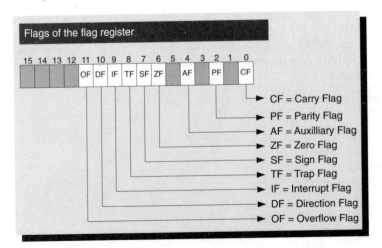

Only the carry flag and zero flag are important for system programming from high level languages. Most DOS and BIOS functions use these flags to indicate errors for insufficient memory or unknown filenames (see Chapter 2 for information on accessing these flags from high level languages).

Memory addresses

How the processor generates memory addresses is especially important for system programming, because you must constantly pass buffer addresses to a DOS or BIOS function. In these instances, you must understand what the processor is doing. The 8088 and its descendants use a complicated procedure. So that you'll understand this procedure, we'll discuss the origins of the 8086.

One of the design goals of the 8088 was to provide an instruction set that was superior to the earlier 8-bit microprocessors (6502, Z80, etc.). Another goal was to provide easy access to more than 64K of memory. This was important because increasing processor capabilities allows programmers to write more complex applications, which require more memory. The designers of the 8088 processor increased the memory capacity or address space of the microprocessor (more than 16 times) to one megabyte.

Address register

The number of memory locations that a processor can access depends on the width of the address register. Since every memory location is accessed by specifying a unique number or address, the maximum value contained in the address register determines the address space. Earlier microprocessors used a 16-bit address register, which enables users to access addresses from 0 to 65535. This corresponds to the 64K memory capacity of these processors.

To address one megabyte of memory, the address register must be at least 20 bits wide. At the time the 8088 was developed, it was impossible to use a 20-bit address register, so the designers used an alternate way to achieve the 20-bit width. The contents of two different 16-bit numbers are used to form the 20-bit address.

Segment register

One of these 16-bit numbers is contained in a segment register. The 8088 has four segment registers. The second number is contained in another register or in a memory location. To form a 20-bit number, the contents of the segment register are shifted left by 4 bits (thereby multiplying the value by 16) and the second number is added to the first.

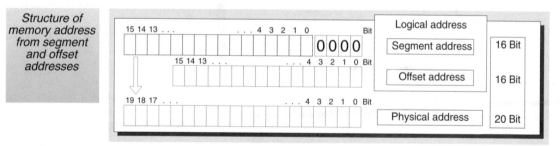

Structure of memory address from segment and offset addresses

Segment and offset addresses

These addresses are the segment address and the offset address. The segment address, which is formed by a segment register, indicates the start of a segment of memory. When the address is created, the offset address is added to the segment address. The offset address indicates the number of the memory location within the segment whose beginning was defined by the segment register. Since the offset address cannot be larger than 16 bits, a segment cannot be larger than 65,535 bytes (64K).

Let's assume the offset address is always 0 and the segment address is also 0 at first. In this case, you receive the address of memory location 0. If the segment address is increased to 1, you receive the address of memory location 1 instead of memory location 16. This happens because the segment address is multiplied by 16 when addresses are formed.

If you continue incrementing the segment address, you'll receive memory addresses of 32, 48, 64, etc., if the offset address continues to be 0. According to this principle, the maximum memory address is 1 megabyte when the segment address reaches 65535 (FFFFH), which is its maximum value. However, if you keep the segment address constant and increment the offset address instead, the segment address will quickly become the base address for a memory segment from which you can reach a total of 65,536 different memory locations. Each memory segment contains 64K. The offset address represents the distance of the desired memory locations from the beginning of the segment.

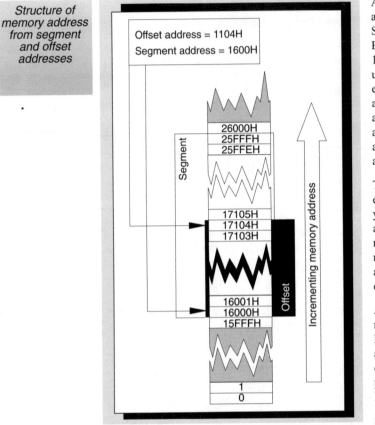

Structure of memory address from segment and offset addresses

Although the individual memory segments are only 16 bytes apart, they contain 64K. So they obviously overlap in memory. Because of this, a memory address, such as 130, can be represented in various ways by using segment and offset addresses. For example, you could specify 0 as the segment address and 130 as the offset address. It's also possible to specify 1 as the segment address and 114 as the offset address or 2 as the segment address and 98 as the offset address, etc.

These overlapping segments are actually easy to use. When you specify an address you can choose the combination of segment address and offset address yourself. You must obtain the desired address by multiplying the segment address by 16 and adding the offset address to it; everything else is unimportant.

A segment cannot start at every one of the million or so memory locations. Multiplying the segment register by 16 always produces a segment address that is divisible by 16. For example, it's not possible for a segment to begin at memory location 22.

Segmented address

The *segmented address* results from the combined segment and offset addresses. This segmented address specifies the exact number of the memory location that should be accessed. Unlike the segmented address, the segment and the offset addresses are *relative addresses* or *relative offsets*.

Combining the segment and offset addresses requires special address notation to indicate a memory location+s address. This notation consists of the segment address, in four-digit hexadecimal format, followed by a colon, and the offset address in four-digit hexadecimal format. For example, in this notation a memory location with a segment address of 2000H and an offset address of AF3H would appear as "2000:0AF3". Because of this notation, you can omit the H suffix from hexadecimal numbers.

The segment register for program execution

The 8088 contains four segment registers, which are important for the execution of an assembly language program. These registers contain the basic structure of any program, which consists of a set of instructions (code). Variables and data items are also processed by the program. A structured program keeps the code and data separate from each other while they reside in memory. Assigning code and data their own segments conveniently separates them. These segment registers are as follows:

CS The CS (Code Segment) register uses the IP (Instruction Pointer) register as the offset address. Then it determines the address at which the next assembly language instruction is located. The IP is also called the Program Counter. When the processor executes the current instruction, the IP register is automatically incremented to point to the next assembly language instruction. This ensures the instructions are executed in the proper order.

DS Like the CS register, the DS (Data Segment) register contains the segment address of the data the program accesses (writing or reading data to or from memory). The offset address is added to the content of the DS register and may be contained in another register or may be contained as part of the current instruction.

SS The SS (Stack Segment) register specifies the starting address of the stack. The stack acts as temporary storage space for some assembly language programs. It allows fast storage and retrieval of data for various instructions. For example, when the CALL instruction is executed, the processor places the return address on the stack. The SS register and either the SP or BP registers form the address that is pushed onto the stack.

When accessing the stack, address generation occurs from the SS register in conjunction with the SP or BP register.

ES The last segment register is the ES (Extra Segment) register. It's used by some assembly language instructions to address more than 64K of data or to transfer data between two different segments of memory.

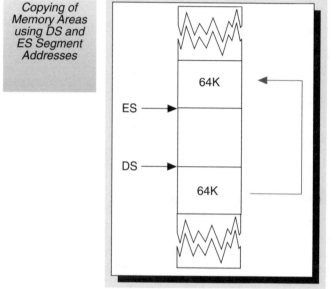

Copying of Memory Areas using DS and ES Segment Addresses

With the help of the ES register, however, it's possible to leave the DS register on the memory segment of the source area while referencing the target area using the ES memory segment. The 8088 and its descendants even have assembly language instructions that can copy an entire buffer by assuming, before their execution, the segment address of the start area has been loaded into the DS register and the segment address of the target area has been loaded into the ES register.

To copy, the instructions also need the start of both areas within their memory segments. They expect the start of the source area in the SI register and the start of the target area in the DI register. Expressed in the notation introduced earlier, these instructions copy data from DS:SI to ES:DI.

Overlapping segments

As the following illustration shows, two segment registers can specify areas of memory that overlap or are completely different from each other. Usually a program doesn't require a full 64K segment for storing code or data. So, you can conserve memory by overlapping the segments. For example, you can store data, which immediately follows the program code, by setting the DS and CS registers accordingly.

Non-overlapping (left) and overlapping (right) segments

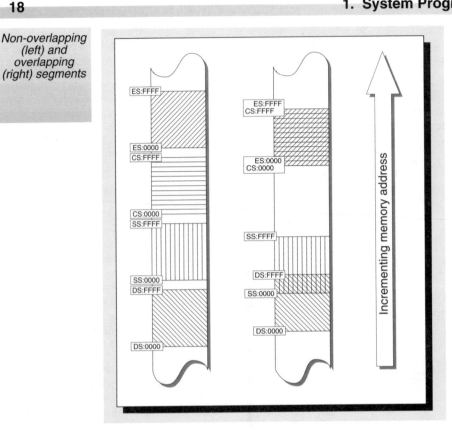

NEAR and FAR pointers

The numbers we've been calling memory addresses are called pointers in high level languages. A pointer in the Pascal or C language receives the addresses of the objects referenced by the pointers. If these addresses change location in memory, the pointers also change. The two types of pointers are NEAR pointers and FAR pointers.

NEAR pointers

NEAR pointers specify the offset address of an object and are only 16 bits wide. Memory cannot be accessed without a segment address. So the compiler prepares the segment address, which it automatically loads, to the appropriate segment register when accessing the object. Because of this, NEAR pointer access is only possible for variables within the 64K segment created by the compiler.

FAR pointers

FAR pointers consist of a segment address and an offset address, so they are saved as two words. The low word receives the offset address and the high word receives the segment address. In Turbo Pascal, pointers are VAR, while in C their type depends on the memory model (see Chapter 2 for more information about pointers).

Data types and their storage

Bytes and words aren't the only data types you'll encounter in system programming. You'll frequently encounter dwords (double words), which are used when the 16 bits of one word aren't enough to store a number. For example, this applies to the internal BIOS clock, which exceeds the 16-bit level of 65535 after a little more than ten hours.

The members of the Intel 80xxx family place dwords in memory so the low word (bits 0 to 15) precedes the high word (bits 16 to 31). This procedure is referred to as the *little endian* format. This is different than the *big endian* format, which reverses the order and is used by processors of the Motorola 68000 family (e.g., the Apple Macintosh¿).

The little endian principle also applies to word storage, in which the low word is placed in front of the high word. Even with qwords (4 words), which are used by the numerical coprocessor, the low-order dword (bits 0 to 31) is stored in front of the high-order dword (bits 32 to 63). Then, within these two dwords, the high word is placed in front of the low word, etc. The following illustration demonstrates this principle:

Storing different data types in little endian format

Offset	0	1			Word
	Low byte	High byte			

	0		2		DWord
	Low word		High word		

	0		2		FAR-PTR
	Offset		Segment		

	0			4	QWord
	Low dword			High dword	

Ports

Ports represent interfaces between the processor and the other system hardware. A port is similar to an 8-bit-wide data input or output connected to a specific piece of hardware. It has an assigned address with values ranging from 0 to 65,535.

The processor uses the data bus and address bus to communicate with the ports. If the processor needs to access a port, it transmits a port control signal. This signal instructs the other hardware the processor wants to access a port instead of RAM.

Although ports have addresses that are also assigned to memory locations in RAM, these addresses aren't related to the memory locations. The port address is placed on the lowest 16 bits of the address bus. This instructs the system to transfer the eight bits of information on the data bus to the proper port. The hardware connected with this port receives the data and responds accordingly.

The 80(x)xx processor series has two instructions that control this process from within a program. The IN instruction sends data from the processor to a port and the OUT instruction transfers data from a port into the processor.

Each hardware device is responsible for an area of port addresses. Therefore, conflicts between expansion boards that allocate the same port address area often occur. So, most expansion boards have DIP switches for setting the port address to which the board will respond. This helps avoid conflicts with other boards.

Standardizing port addresses

The system can set the port address of a certain hardware device. Since this address isn't a constant value, port addressing is similar for the PC, XT, and AT. Although there are only a few differences between the PC and XT, there are many differences between the PC and AT.

The following table shows the port addresses of individual chips in each system.

Component	PC/XT	AT
DMA controller (8237A-5)	000-00F	000-01F
Interrupt controller (8259A)	020-021	020-03F
Timer	040-043	040-05F
Programmable Peripheral Interface (PPI 8255A-5)	060-063	none
Keyboard (8042)	none	060-06F
Realtime clock (MC146818)	none	070-07F
DMA page register	080-083	080-09F
Interrupt controller 2 (8259A)	none	0A0-0BF
DMA controller 2 (8237A-5)	none	0C0-0DF
Math coprocessor	none	0F0-0F1
Math coprocessor	none	0F8-0FF
Hard drive controller	320-32F	1F0-1F8
Game port (joysticks)	200-20F	200-207
Expansion unit	210-217	none
Interface for second parallel printer	none	278-27F
Second serial interface	2F8-2FF	2F8-2FF
Prototype card	300-31F	300-31F
Network card	none	360-36F
Interface for first parallel printer	378-37F	378-37F
Monochrome Display Adapter and parallel interface	3B0-3BE	3B0-3BF
Color/Graphics Adapter	3D0-3DF	3D0-3DF
Disk controller	3F0-3F7	3F0-3F7
First serial interface	3F8-3FF	3F8-3FF

Interrupts

In the "Basics of PC Hardware" section earlier in this chapter we explained that interrupts are mechanisms that force the processor to briefly interrupt the current program and execute an interrupt handler. However, this is only one aspect of interrupts. They are also important for controlling the hardware, and act as the main form of communication between a program and the BIOS and DOS functions.

Software interrupts

Software interrupts call a program, with a special assembly language instruction, to execute a DOS, BIOS, or EMS function. The program execution isn't really interrupted; the processor views the called function as a subroutine. After the subroutine executes, the processor continues with the calling program.

To call a DOS or BIOS function using a software interrupt, only the number of the interrupt, from which the routine can be reached, is needed. The caller doesn't even need to know the address of the routine in memory. These routines are standardized. So, regardless of your DOS version, you know that by calling interrupt 21H you can access DOS functions.

The processor calls the interrupt handler using the interrupt vector table, from which the processor takes the addresses of the desired function. The processor uses the interrupt number as an index to this table. The table is set during system bootup so the various interrupt vectors point to the ROM-BIOS.

This illustrates the advantage of using interrupts. A PC manufacturer who wants to produce an IBM compatible PC cannot copy the entire ROM-BIOS from IBM. However, the manufacturer is allowed to implement the same functions in its ROM-BIOS, even if the BIOS functions are coded differently from within. So, the BIOS functions are called using the same interrupts that IBM uses and expect parameters in the same processor registers. But the routines that provide the functions are organized differently than the routines provided by IBM.

However, these aren't the only advantages of using interrupts. We'll discuss interrupts in more detail in Chapter 2. First, let's look at the interrupt vector table, which represents the key to calling the interrupts.

Interrupt vector table

So far we've discussed a single interrupt and a single interrupt routine. Actually, the 8088 has 256 possible interrupts numbered from 0 to 255. Each interrupt has an associated *interrupt routine* to handle the particular condition. To organize the 256 interrupts, the starting addresses of the corresponding interrupt routines are arranged in the *interrupt vector table*.

When an interrupt occurs, the processor automatically retrieves the starting address of the interrupt routine from the interrupt vector table. The starting address of each interrupt routine is specified in the table in terms of the offset address and segment address. Both addresses are 16 bits (2 bytes) wide. So each table entry occupies 4 bytes. The total length of the table is 256x4 or 1024 bytes (1K). Because the interrupt vector table is in RAM, any program can change it. However, TSR programs and device drivers use the table the most. (See Chapter 35 for more information.)

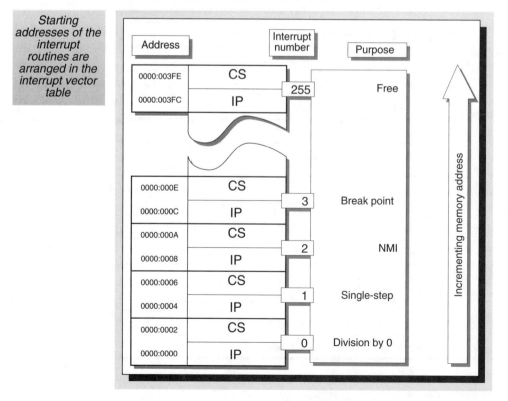

Starting addresses of the interrupt routines are arranged in the interrupt vector table

The following table shows the addresses of the various interrupt vectors, as well as the utilities from which they can be reached. This layout applies to all PCs and is an essential component of the PC standard. A program that uses these interrupts will find these utilities on all PCs. Most of these interrupts and their functions are mentioned throughout this book.

Many of these interrupt vectors are only allocated when the corresponding hardware has also been installed. For example, this applies to interrupt 33H (mouse driver functions) and interrupt 5CH (network functions).

The term "reserved" indicates the interrupt is called by a certain system component (usually DOS), but the interrupt's use was never documented. In other words, we know who is using it, but we don't know why.

General overview of interrupts

No.*	Address*	Purpose
00	000 - 003	Processor: Division by zero
01	004 - 007	Processor: Single step
02	008 - 00B	Processor: NMI (Error in RAM chip)
03	00C - 00F	Processor: Breakpoint reached
04	010 - 013	Processor: Numeric overflow
05	014 - 017	Hardcopy
06	018 - 01B	Unknown instruction (80286 only)
07	01D - 01F	Reserved
08	020 - 023	IRQ0: Timer (Call 18.2 times/sec.)
09	024 - 027	IRQ1: Keyboard
0A	028 - 02B	IRQ2: 2nd 8259 (AT only)
0B	02C - 02F	IRQ3: Serial port 2
0C	030 - 033	IRQ4: Serial port 1
0D	034 - 037	IRQ5: Hard drive
0E	038 - 03B	IRQ6: Diskette
0F	03C - 03F	IRQ7: Printer
10	040 - 043	BIOS: Video functions
11	044 - 047	BIOS: Determine configuration
12	048 - 04B	BIOS: Determine RAM memory size
13	04C - 04F	BIOS: Diskette/hard drive functions
14	050 - 053	BIOS: Access to serial port
15	054 - 057	BIOS: Cassettes/extended function
16	058 - 05B	BIOS: Keyboard inquiry

*= All addresses and numbers in hexadecimal notation

No.*	Address*	Purpose
17	05C - 05F	BIOS: Access to parallel printer
18	060 - 063	Call ROM BASIC
19	064 - 067	BIOS: Boot system (Ctrl+Alt+Del)
1A	068 - 06B	BIOS: Prompt time/date
1B	06C - 06F	Break key (not Ctrl-C) pressed
1C	070 - 073	Called after each INT 08
1D	074 - 077	Address of video parameter table
1E	078 - 07B	Address of diskette parameter table
1F	07C - 07F	Address of character bit pattern
20	080 - 083	DOS: Quit program
21	084 - 087	DOS: Call DOS function
22	088 - 08B	Address of DOS quit program routine
23	08C - 08F	Address of DOS Ctrl-Break routine
24	090 - 093	Address of DOS error routine
25	094 - 097	DOS: Read diskette/hard drive
26	098 - 09B	DOS: Write diskette/hard drive
27	09C - 09F	DOS: Quit program, stay resident
28	0A0 - 0A3	DOS: DOS is unoccupied
29-2E	0A4 - 0BB	DOS: Reserved
2F	0BC - 0BF	DOS: Multiplexer
30-32	0C0 - 0CB	DOS: Reserved
33	0CC - 0CF	Mouse driver functions
34-40	0D0 - 0FF	DOS: Reserved
41	104 - 107	Address of hard drive table 1
42-45	108 - 117	Reserved
46	118 - 11B	Address of hard drive table 2
47-49	11C - 127	Can be used by programs
4A	128 - 12B	Alarm time reached (AT only)
4B-5B	12C - 16F	Free: can be used by programs
*= All addresses and numbers in hexadecimal notation		

	No.*	Address*	Purpose
General overview of interrupts (continued)	5C	170 - 173	NETBIOS functions
	5D-66	174 - 19B	Free: can be used by programs
	67	19C - 19F	EMS memory manager functions
	68-6F	1A0 - 1BF	Free: can be used by programs
	70	1C0 - 1C3	IRQ08: Realtime clock (AT only)
	71	1C4 - 1C7	IRQ09: (AT only)
	72	1C8 - 1CB	IRQ10: (AT only)
	73	1CC - 1CF	IRQ11: (AT only)
	74	1D0 - 1D3	IRQ12: (AT only)
	75	1D4 - 1D7	IRQ13: 80287 NMI (AT only)
	76	1D8 - 1DB	IRQ14: Hard drive (AT only)
	77	1DC - 1DF	IRQ15: (AT only)
	78-7F	1E0 - 1FF	Reserved
	80-F0	200 - 3C3	Used within the BASIC interpreter
	F1-FF	3C4 - 3CF	Reserved
	*= All addresses and numbers in hexadecimal notation		

Hardware interrupts

Hardware interrupts are produced by various hardware components and passed, by the interrupt controller, to the processor. In this section we'll explain the steps involved in this process and the differences between PC/XTs and ATs.

PC/XT hardware interrupts

Hardware interrupts 8 to 15 are called by the interrupt controller. Up to eight devices (interrupt sources) can be connected to the PC interrupt controller using interrupt lines IRQ0 to IRQ7. The device on line IRQ0 has the highest priority. The device connected with IRQ7 has the lowest priority. For example, if two interrupt requests arrive on lines IRQ3 and IRQ5, IRQ3 is addressed first. The number of the interrupt results from adding 8 to the IRQ number (in this case, it's interrupt 11).

Disabling hardware interrupts

It's possible for a program to prevent the execution of hardware interrupts. This is useful when program execution shouldn't be interrupted. The processor will release a hardware interrupt, upon request from the interrupt controller, only if the interrupt flag is set in the processor's flag register. If the software has cleared the flag, the interrupt controller won't receive the requested interrupt.

You can also block single interrupts by programming the interrupt mask register in the interrupt controller.

PC interrupt requests and priorities

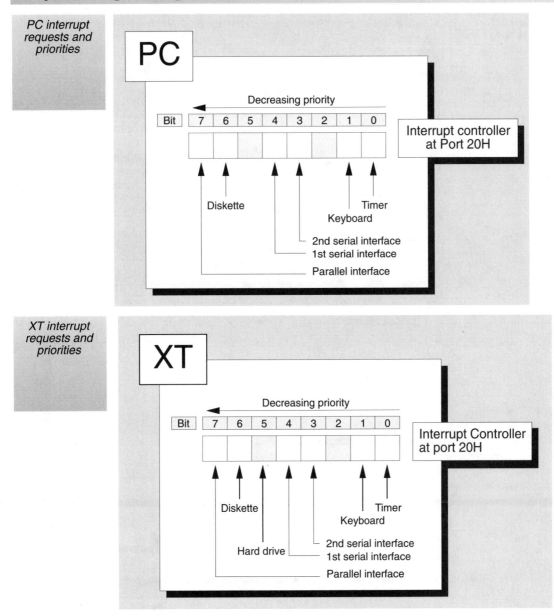

XT interrupt requests and priorities

AT hardware interrupts

ATs have two 8259 interrupt controllers, which provide 16 interrupt sources. The eight additional interrupts are labeled IRQ08 to IRQ15. When an interrupt request addresses the second interrupt controller, it emulates an IRQ2 from the first interrupt controller. All the interrupt requests of the second interrupt controller are assigned a higher priority than lines IRQ4 to IRQ7 of the first interrupt controller.

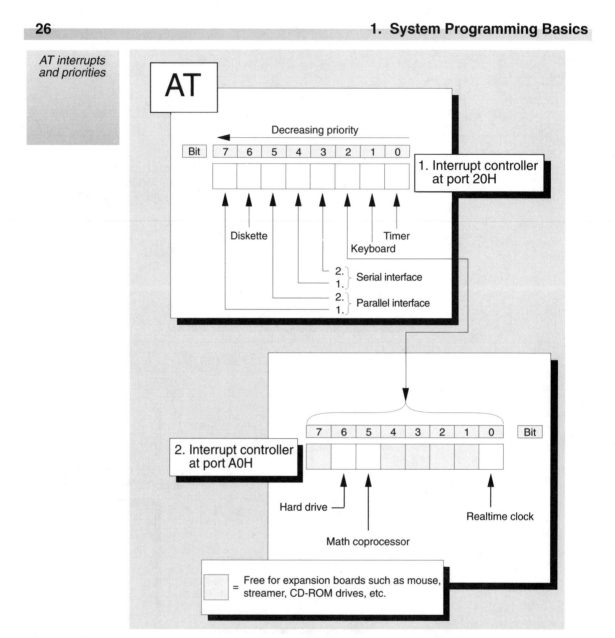

If a request for IRQ2 is granted, the interrupt handler of interrupt 10 is executed. This interrupt handler first reads some of the registers of the second interrupt controller to determine the number of the IRQ. Based on the IRQ number, one of interrupts 70H to 77H is called as a software interrupt. It doesn't matter the call was actually initiated by the hardware because the device is waiting for execution of "its" interrupt handler.

However, as a result of this procedure, the IRQ2 is unavailable to the first interrupt controller. So 15 interrupt sources are supported instead of 16.

System Interaction

Now that we've discussed the essentials of system programming, let's see how DOS, BIOS, and the different levels of hardware communicate to give programs easy access to PC hardware. We'll use the keyboard as an example, since hardware interrupts, DOS, and BIOS functions are all involved. Let's follow the path of a character from the keyboard hardware to the program that reads the entered character and displays it on the screen.

Keyboard hardware

The keyboard hardware consists of the keyboard's processor. It's connected to the PC's processor by a cable. The keyboard processor monitors the keyboard and reports each key that is pressed or released to the system. The keyboard processor assigns a number instead of a character to each key. Control keys, such as Ctrl or Shift, are treated like any other key.

When the user presses a key, the keyboard processor passes the key number to the processor as a make code. (See Chapter 5 for more information on make codes.) When the user releases the key, the processor passes a break code. There is a minor difference between these codes. Although both use numbers between 0 and 127 for the key, the break code includes bit 7.

To initiate the transfer, the keyboard controller first sends an interrupt signal to the interrupt controller, which arrives at line IRQ2. If hardware interrupts are enabled and a higher priority interrupt request doesn't exist, the processor then executes interrupt 09H.

BIOS keyboard handler

Interrupt 09H is a BIOS routine called the keyboard handler. The keyboard processor passes the key code to port 60H using the keyboard cable, then calls the interrupt handler. From there, the BIOS handler reads the number of the key that was pressed or released. The rest of the system cannot use the key number because different keyboards generate different numbers. So, the keyboard handler must convert the code into a character from the ASCII character set, which is a form the system can understand.

When you press a key, this key code is passed to the CPU as a byte. When you release the key, the processor passes the code to the CPU again, along with an added 128. This is the same as setting bit 7 in the byte. The keyboard instructs the 8259 interrupt controller the CPU should activate interrupt 9H. If the CPU responds, we reach the next level because a BIOS routine is controlled through interrupt 9H. While this routine is being called, the keyboard processor sends the key code to port 60H of the main circuit board using the asynchronous transmission protocol. The BIOS routine checks this port and obtains the number of the depressed or released key. This routine then generates an ASCII code from this key code.

This task is more complicated than it first appears because the BIOS routine must test for a control key, such as Shift or Alt. Depending on the key or combination of keys, either a normal ASCII code or an extended keyboard code may be required. The extended key codes include any keys that don't input characters (e.g., cursor keys).

Keyboard buffer

Once BIOS determines the correct code, this code is passed to the 16-byte BIOS keyboard buffer, which is located in the lower area of RAM. If it's full, the routine sounds a beep that informs the user of an overflow in the keyboard buffer. The processor returns to the other tasks that were in progress before the call to interrupt 09H.

BIOS keyboard interrupt

The next level, BIOS interrupt 16H, reads the character in the keyboard buffer and makes it available to a program. This interrupt includes three BIOS routines for reading characters, as well as the keyboard status (e.g., which control keys were pressed), from the keyboard buffer. These routines can be called with an INT assembly language instruction.

DOS level

The keyboard's device driver routines represent the DOS level. These DOS routines read a character from the keyboard and store the character in a buffer using the BIOS functions from interrupt 16H. In some instances, the DOS routines may clear the BIOS keyboard buffer. If the system uses the extended keyboard driver ANSI.SYS, this keyboard driver can translate

*Keyboard
access using
the three-layer
model*

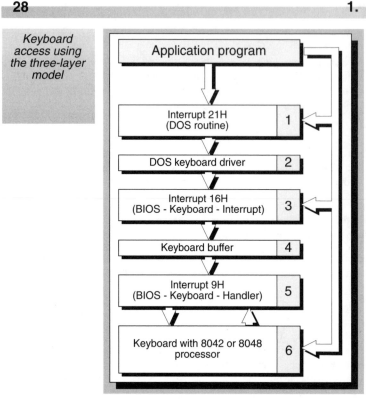

certain codes (e.g., function key F1) into other codes or strings. For example, it's possible to program the F10 key to display the DIR command on the screen. Although, theoretically, you can call device driver functions from within a program, DOS functions usually address these functions.

DOS is the highest level you can go. Here you'll find the keyboard access functions in DOS interrupt 21H. These functions call the driver functions, transmit the results, and perform many other tasks. For example, characters and strings can be read and displayed directly on the screen until the user presses the Enter key. These strings are called by a program and complete a long process.

The Pentium Processor

With the Pentium processor, which was introduced by Intel in 1993, the technical possibilities of a PC have changed again. The Pentium features 100 MIPS (Million Instructions Per Second) at a clock speed of 66 MHz. This makes the Pentium almost twice as fast as a 486 DX2/66 in integer performance. The differences are even more significant in floating-point performance. Depending on the instruction mix, the Pentium beats its predecessor by three to seven times. Also, it's completely binary compatible with the 486, 386, 286, and even the 8086.

When asked about the performance of the Pentium, Intel has a very simple answer: 567. This measurement is a result of the ICOMP test developed by Intel for its own processors. This test, geared entirely to Intel's own processors, flows into the ICOMP index. As the following illustration shows, the measured value for the 66 MHz Pentium surpasses that of an equally fast 486 by almost double.

*The Intel
ICOMP index*

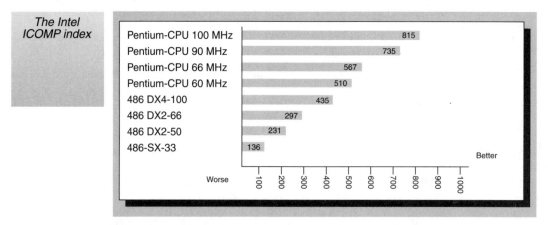

However, be careful when interpreting absolute data, such as the information returned by the ICOMP index. After all, selecting the processor test for such a benchmark is a subjective process, even if the manufacturers claim to be simulating real application conditions. Also remember, each manufacturer is eager to show its product is the best. So, they may downplay the performance areas in which its chip suffers compared to the competition or simply omit these performance areas.

On the whole, however, the direction in which this index is moving compared to the previous Intel processors might be correct, although you can't assume that doubling processor performance from the 486 to the Pentium could be duplicated at the user and software levels. There are numerous hardware and software components between the CPU and the user. These components either benefit only partially from the processor's performance, or they don't benefit at all. For example, this applies to all expansion boards. However, the Pentium has definitely advanced the PC world to previously unattainable dimensions. You're probably wondering what makes the Pentium so fast. Three components are responsible for the Pentium's speed: Superscalar integer execution unit, the first level processor cache, and the superscalar floating-point execution unit. We'll discuss these features in detail in this chapter.

Block diagram of the Pentium processor

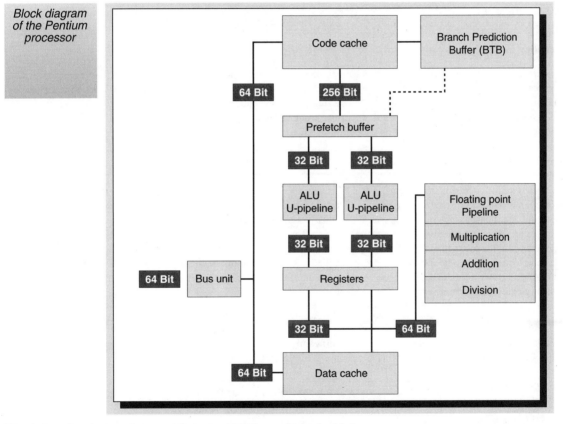

First, let's review the most important facts about Intel's new "miracle chip":

> The Pentium is manufactured in 0.8-micron BiCMOS submicron technology. The traces or signal paths are only 0.8 millionths of a meter wide, or eight thousands of a millimeter wide.

> The processor is completely binary compatible with its predecessors in relation to instruction set, register, addressing modes, and operating modes.

> The processor still works with 32-bit registers and 32-bit addressing, but can be connected to a 64-bit data bus, enabling faster communication with memory.

> A superscalar architecture based on two parallel integer pipelines. In ideal circumstances, this would allow simultaneous execution of 2 machine language instructions in one cycle.

- ➢ The chip has a total of 3.1 million transistors.

- ➢ Two separate 8K data and code caches, in conjunction with the 64-bit bus interface (port), provide fast and continuous memory access.

- ➢ A special protocol called MESI (Modified, Exclusive, Shared, Invalid) ensures that a Pentium processor will work smoothly with other processors in a multiprocessor system.

- ➢ An improved floating-point unit executes commands significantly faster than the 486 and even provides the option of simultaneous execution of two instructions, although this happens on a limited scale.

Program execution

Program execution through the Pentium processor is based on a superscalar architecture with two parallel, five-stage integer pipelines that are connected with the processor cache and a branch target buffer (BTB).

Execution in the pipeline procedure

To understand this efficient, expensive mechanism of program execution, you must first know how a microprocessor executes programs and machine language instructions. Although this process appears as a monolithic block from the outside, in the interior of the processor it is divided into five stages. The 486 and Pentium both have five stages that each instruction undergoes during its execution in a set sequence. These stages are abbreviated to PF, D1, D2, EX and WB. The following table shows the five stages of instruction execution on the 486 and the Pentium:

PF	Prefetch	D1	Decode1	D2	Decode2	EX	Execute	WB	Writeback

The execution of an instruction begins in the PF stage, the "instruction prefetch". In this stage, the machine language instruction is fetched from memory to the processor for execution. Once the instruction reaches the processor, it enters D1 stage, the first phase of instruction decoding. In this phase, the objective is to evaluate (analyze) the instruction, thus determining what kind of action it is supposed to trigger. Depending on the type of instruction, the next job is to determine the operands of the instruction (e.g., for a displacement memory address). This is the task of the second stage of instruction decoding, called D2. In the next pipeline stage, called EX, the execution of the instruction takes place, along with the associated memory accesses. In the WB stage, execution of the instruction concludes, with the contents of the processor register and the internal status register being updated.

The processor requires one cycle per stage to run these stages, while stages D2 and EX can also require one extra cycle, depending on the type of instruction. This provides a minimum of five cycles. However, if you check the Intel manuals, you'll discover that many instructions are executed in significantly fewer cycles. Some instructions even require only one or two cycles. Now we must determine how this is possible, if all the stages of the pipeline are necessary.

Simultaneous execution of several instructions within the pipeline

Program in memory	**Processor Pipeline**					
	PF	**D1**	**D2**	**EX**	**WB**	
	Prefetch	Decode 1	Decode 2	Execute	Write Back	
MOV AX,1	MOV AX,1					**Cycle 1**
ADD AX,BX	ADD AX,BX	MOV AX,1				2
CMP AX,15	CMP AX,15	ADD AX,BX	MOV AX,1			3
INT 123	INT 123	CMP AX,15	ADD AX,BX	MOV AX,1		4
SHL AX,1	SHL AX,1	INT 123	CMP AX,15	ADD AX,BX	MOV AX,1 finished	5
⋮	⋮	SHL AX,1	INT 123	CMP AX,15	ADD AX,BX finished	6
⋮	⋮	⋮	SHL AX,1	INT 123	CMP AX,15 finished	7

Time

The solution is found in a principle used in assembly line production. Instead of only one instruction, as many instructions as the pipeline has stages runs through the various stages of the pipeline. So the subsequent instruction isn't processed after the preceding instruction leaves the last stage of the pipeline. Instead, it is processed immediately after the first stage of the pipeline. This means the different stages of the pipeline are busy at all times, always executing their function on a different instruction.

The instructions still require a minimum of five cycles to run through the complete pipeline, but because the pipeline finishes executing an instruction with each cycle, the instructions seem to require only one cycle for execution.

Superscalar pipelines

While the pipeline procedure of the 486 is already extremely fast, the Pentium multiplies this procedure by setting up a second, parallel pipeline. This is where the phrase "superscalar pipeline architecture" comes from. To keep the two pipelines separate, the first is called the "U pipeline" and the second one is called the "V pipeline."

With the help of these two pipelines, the Pentium should theoretically be able to execute two instructions simultaneously and, as a result, double the execution speed. However, in reality, this process isn't that easy. Frequently two sequential instructions can only be executed in sequence because they are dependent on each other. A simple example of this would be two machine language instructions, the first one describing a processor register on which the second instruction performs a read access. There are many other rules that make simultaneous execution of two sequential commands seem impossible. One such rule is the limitation of parallel execution to "simple" machine language instructions. Some examples of simple machine language instructions are MOV instructions, integer addition and subtraction, PUSH and POP instructions, and others. Only these instructions are actually "threaded" in the processor; all others are executed by Microcode, which is a type of processor operating system. It controls execution of complex machine language instructions through different execution units of the processor.

The second stage of the pipeline, D1, determines whether a parallel execution of both instructions is possible. In the PF stage, the current instruction to be executed and its successor are loaded into two parallel decoding units. This establishes the exact sequence. The current instruction goes to the decoding unit of the U pipeline and its successor goes to the decoding unit of the V pipeline.

If it is determined in D1 that simultaneous execution of the two instructions is possible, each of the two instructions then passes the various stages of its pipeline in parallel. If parallel execution is not possible, the instruction from the U pipeline goes to the next stage, while the instruction from the V pipeline is executed in the U pipeline as the instruction following the current instruction.

So the program code determines whether two instructions can be executed simultaneously or whether they have to pass the various stages of the U pipeline in sequence. Optimizing compilers for the Pentium consider this by organizing the machine code in such a way the sequential machine language instructions permit simultaneous execution as often as possible.

Branch Target Buffer

The efficiency of the pipeline principle is based upon the constant provision of new instructions to the pipeline. Only when the various stages of the pipeline are permanently filled does it seem possible the various instructions can be executed in one cycle. That is why two prefetch buffers are preset to the first stage of both pipelines. These prefetch buffers load the next instruction for the pipeline from memory or the processor-specific cache.

However, even these aren't helpful when the processor has to execute a jump instruction. In this case, instead of continuing with the following instruction, program execution continues with an entirely different instruction. As a result, execution of the following instructions, which are already in the pipeline, must be canceled and the pipeline must be loaded with new instructions. It takes a few cycles before the first instruction leaves the pipeline after the jump instruction.

Pentium uses a Branch Target Buffer (BTB) to avoid the problem of jump instructions. This buffer is used in the D1 stage of instruction execution for all types of NEAR jump instructions (i.e., for conditional and unconditional jumps, as well as for procedure references). If the processor encounters such an instruction in the D1 stage, it uses the address of the instruction in memory to search the BTB for the instruction. Every time the processor executes one of these jump instructions, it stores both the instruction's address and the jump destination's address in the BTB. If the instruction is registered there because it has already been executed, the processor assumes the jump should be executed again. Instead of loading the successor of the jump instruction into the pipeline, the processor loads the command to the target address.

However, if the jump instruction isn't registered in the BTB, the subsequent instruction is loaded in the pipeline. During the EX stage (at the latest), the processor will determine whether to execute the jump. If the processor predicted accurately with the address from the BTB, the instruction that follows the jump instruction will already be in the pipeline. So program execution can immediately continue. Even execution of a conditional jump will only take one cycle in this case.

However, if the processor's prediction is incorrect, this means the wrong commands are in the pipeline. So the pipeline must be "flushed." This involves canceling the execution of the commands currently in the pipeline and completely reloading the pipeline. As a result, instead of only one cycle, at least three cycles are needed to execute the jump command.

The Cache

The Pentium processor has two separate 8K caches: One for data and one for program code. Both of these caches are two-way set-associative caches. Each path consists of 128 entries with a cache line size of 32 bytes. The data cache can be operated in Writethrough and in Copyback mode, and is capable of responding to two accesses from the U and V pipeline of the processor simultaneously. To guarantee this, each cache line of 32 bytes is divided into eight 4-byte blocks.

If you're a computer expert, the previous explanation reveals the most important information about the cache structure of the Pentium processor. However, the explanation is extremely confusing to average computer users. You've probably never encountered the terms "cache lines", "two-way associativity", and "Copyback mode." Therefore, in the following sections we'll discuss how a processor cache operates and discuss Pentium cache in detail. This information may not improve your programming skills. However, if you want to know what makes the Pentium so fast, you must understand the cache.

Also, since the on-chip cache was first used with the 486, we'll also briefly discuss the processor cache of the i486.

Processor cache, hard drive cache, font cache, and CD-ROM cache are different devices that use the term "cache." A cache accelerates access to specific data and information by holding a portion of the data in a reserved section of memory. This process provides faster access than the actual storage device. This means that, for example, a hard drive cache reserves sectors of a hard drive, which have already been read in RAM memory, to deliver the sectors directly from this memory to the caller for a new read request instead of getting the sectors from the hard drive. Because a hard drive is several hundred times slower in access time than RAM, you can use this method to save a great deal of time.

While hard drive, CD-ROM, and font caches use RAM memory as "high-speed memory", this doesn't apply to the processor cache. From the processor's view, it requires a cache because RAM doesn't supply data and program instructions fast enough for its purposes. This cache stores the memory locations the processor addressed during the last memory accesses. As a result, the next time the processor needs to access these memory locations, it doesn't have to get them from RAM. Instead, the processor can take the memory locations directly from high-speed cache memory.

However, not all processor caches are the same. It makes a big difference whether you are dealing with a primary or secondary processor cache. These are sometimes also called "first level cache" and "second level cache."

Currently 128K or 256K caches always refer to secondary cache. This is the cache that is between the processor and RAM and usually consists of SRAM (a form of high-speed RAM). The main memory is equipped with lower-priced DRAM chips, which are three to four times slower in supplying data to the processor than SRAM chips. This is where the speed advantage of a secondary cache becomes important. For comparison, consider that while SRAM is able to produce response times between 20 and 25 nanoseconds (millionths of a second), most PCs use 70ns, 80ns, or 100ns DRAM chips as main memory.

While secondary cache memory is located outside the CPU, the primary cache refers to the memory located directly on the CPU. The CPU can read from primary cache memory just as fast as from its registers. This is why it would be best to place the entire cache memory of a system directory on the processor, or better still, all the RAM memory. However, considering the current status of processor technology, this is impossible.

First level,
second level
and third level
caches

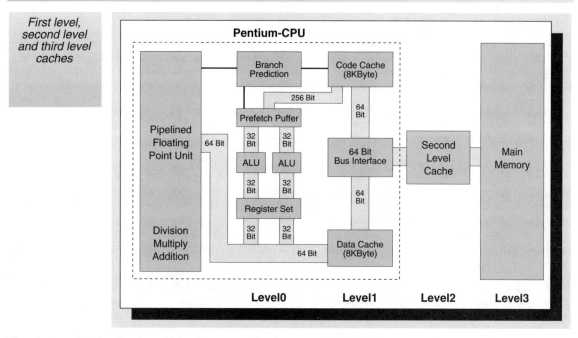

There is also a third level cache, which refers to normal main memory (RAM). This serves cache memory for hard drives and other peripherals. The numbering sequence is intentional, because the higher the number, the farther the cache is from the processor. As the number increases, the cache memory speed decreases, as does the price for 1K of the cache memory.

Cache effectiveness

The quality and effectiveness of a cache is measured from the ratio of cache hits and cache misses. A cache hit occurs when the data requested by the processor is already in a cache. So, the processor doesn't have to access slower memory. A cache miss means the data is not reserved in the cache, so first it must be loaded from memory into the cache, before it can be passed on to the processor. The greater the number of cache hits in comparison with cache misses, the more often the processor can be served from high-speed memory, ultimately causing it to work faster.

The ratio between cache hits and misses mainly depends on three factors: Organization of the cache, the type of program code being executed, and, obviously, the size of the cache. The third factor can be checked off quickly, because a growing cache size also increases the probability the information, for which the processor is searching, is already in the cache.

For the second factor, the type of program code, the "locality" of this code is very important. First, remember that a process cache not only caches the data that a program reads from memory during its execution, but also the executed program code. Regardless of whether the processor reads a variable or the next machine language instruction, they both must be furnished from memory. Also, in both cases, the cache first checks whether the address has already "been there" once.

This is why self-contained program sections, especially loops, that fit in the cache can be executed so quickly. If the execution of programs mainly occurs in blocks that aren't bigger than the cache, the existence of the cache will increase the speed of program execution. However, if a program continually jumps back and forth between different program sections, the cache won't be as noticeable.

There are two other factors that are basic prerequisites for the efficient use of cache memory. These two factors fall into the category of "Cache Organization". The first factor is cache strategy, in relation to read and write accesses, while the second factor is cache architecture, i.e., the way cached information is stored in the cache.

Cache strategies

Writethrough and WriteBack caches are related to the read and write accesses of the CPU. Writethrough is the simpler type, because the cache is addressed only for read accesses of the CPU. The cache transfers write accesses directly to main memory (RAM). Before doing this, however, the cache checks whether the specified memory location is already stored in the cache as a result of a read access. If this is the case, the new value of the memory location must also be entered in the cache.

If this doesn't happen, the cache contents and the contents of conventional memory may be inconsistent, which is the worst thing that can happen to a cache. Because of this inconsistency, the next time you read access the cache, it will return the old contents of the memory location, while conventional memory already contains a completely different value.

Along with the pure Writethrough procedure, Intel 80486 processors and above support a slightly modified procedure called "buffered writethrough." To speed up write accesses to memory, the first-level cache of the processor is equipped with additional write buffers. The 486 has four of these buffers. When data must be written to memory, the cache first places the data in one of these write buffers. This lets the CPU continue working immediately, because this memory can be addressed very quickly, similar to cache memory. While the CPU works, the cache writes the contents of the write buffer to conventional memory on its own, as soon as the bus is free. As long as this buffer doesn't fill up because the CPU is attempting to write data to memory faster than the data can be transported from the write buffer, the CPU's write operations to conventional memory won't be affected.

The Writeback procedure competes with the Writethrough procedure. For read operations, a Writeback cache acts just like a Writethrough cache. However, the two caches handle write operations differently. If the information to be written to conventional memory is already in the cache, it is first updated only in the cache. The information doesn't go to memory until the cache is forced to remove the memory location from cache memory because it needs space for new entries as a result of a read access by the CPU. If a memory location is written over and over again, this saves you the trouble of relatively slow write accesses to conventional memory until the time the memory location has to leave the cache. To keep this from taking too long, a type of write buffer called a castoff buffer is installed. The data are first stored in this buffer and then transferred to conventional memory in parallel with the work of the CPU.

Cache architecture

Cache memory is usually organized into cache lines; each line can receive information from conventional memory that is cached during a read or write operation. The size of a cache line depends on the internal data capacity of the CPU or the capacity of its primary cache. On the 80386 the cache lines are 32-bit (one DWord = 4 bytes), on the 486 they are 128-bit (4 DWord = 16 bytes), and on the Pentium the cache lines are 256-bit (4 QWord = 32 bytes).

For a read access to memory, the entire cache line is always filled, even when the processor requested only a single byte. Modern processors support "burst mode", which dramatically speeds up access to byte sequences in memory. Usually the CPU must place the address on the bus before reading out the desired memory location. However, in a burst access, the data are read as a block. The CPU only has to place the address for the first byte on the bus; the memory automatically furnishes all subsequent memory locations upon request.

For example, the 486 usually requires 2 clock cycles to read a DWord from memory, so 4*2 clock cycles are necessary to fill a cache line. In burst mode, two cycles are required only for the first DWord; the three following words will be furnished in one cycle. That's why burst mode is also called a 2-1-1-1 burst; it takes only five cycles instead of the normal eight. The same procedure can also be used for write accesses.

Along with cached data, the cache must also store the memory addresses for the data. Each cache line is connected with a tag. This is where the cache stores the address of the data, as well as additional status information. (We'll talk about this information later in this chapter.) In secondary caches, the tags are not included with the cache lines. Instead, they are housed in separate memory components, which work even faster than the actual cache memory. In searching the cache for a memory location, the address not only has to be read out from the tag, but also must be compared with the address of the particular access by using a comparator. Naturally, this is time-consuming but is compensated for by speedier SRAM memory.

Along with cache lines and tags, a cache also always has a cache controller. A secondary cache usually has a microcontroller on the motherboard, while on a primary cache the controller is part of the processor. The controller controls communication with the CPU as well as the comings and goings of the cached information in the cache lines. It is the controller that translates the cache strategy into action and manages the pool of cache lines in accordance with a specific pattern.

Cache line organization

To determine the best possible cache line organization, first you must understand the cached information cannot be saved in any cache line you choose. Otherwise, in a read access the cache controller would be forced to run through all the tags in search of the correct address and compare the addresses stored there with the CPU address. This process would take more time than loading the information directly from conventional memory.

For this reason, cache controllers always connect the addresses of the cached memory locations with the cache lines, in which the addresses are stored. In the simplest type of cache organization, called "direct mapping", each byte from conventional memory has only one cache line in which it can be stored.

The cache controller checks this cache line when the CPU performs a read access. If the address is not listed there, it isn't in the cache.

In a direct mapped cache, mapping between the address and the cache line, in which it is stored, takes place via the memory address. The address is broken down into various components. To describe this process, we'll use a 256K secondary cache for a 486 system as an example.

Direct mapped secondary cache for the 486

Secondary caches for the 486 work with a cache line size of 128 bits (16 bytes). So, a 256K cache provides 16,384 cache lines. The cache controller's task is to clearly map the CPU address to one of the 16,384 cache lines. Since 16,384 is 2 to the 14th power, the lower 14 bits of the CPU address determine the number of the cache line. However, instead of bits 0 to 13, these are bits 4 to 17. Bits 0 to 3 are needed to form the offset in the cache line; these four bits contain precisely the value between 0 and 15 that is needed for addressing the desired byte within the specific cache line.

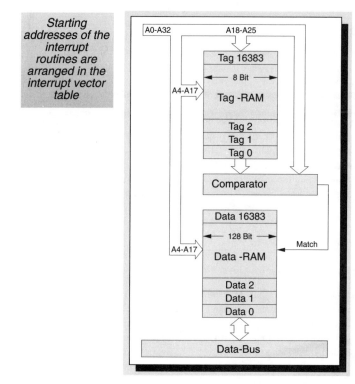

Bits 0 to 3 make up the index in the cache line and bits 4 to 17 are used as an index in the cache line pool. So bits 18 to 31 remain. Actually, these bits are supposed to be stored in the tag of a cache line. However, instead of the 14 bits, frequently only eight bits (bits 18 to 25) are stored there. This means the cache can manage only the lower 64 Meg (2^{26}) of RAM memory, since there usually aren't even enough sockets provided on the motherboard for this much memory.

While its simplicity makes this procedure appealing, it does have a big disadvantage. Because the 64 Meg of RAM are mapped only to 16,384 cache lines, 256 memory locations share the same cache line. These memory locations are always 256K apart. However, once an address is loaded into the cache, whose cache line is already loaded with another one of these 256 addresses, it forces the old address out of the cache.

Associative caches

To prevent memory addresses from excluding each other in advance, associative cache memory refines the direct mapping process. Instead of assigning a single cache line to each memory location, it assigns each memory location two, four, or even eight possible cache lines. These are also called twofold, fourfold, or eightfold associative caches. An example of such a cache is the primary, fourfold associative cache of the 486, which holds 8K.

An associative cache requires much more circuitry than a direct mapped cache. In searching for a memory location, the cache controller must read two, four, or eight tags (depending on associativity), rather than one tag. Then the controller uses a comparator to compare them with the specific CPU address (or part of it).

The four-way associative 8K first level cache of the 486

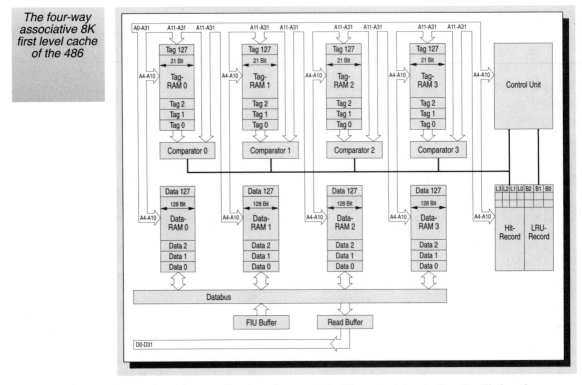

In addition, for a read access, the cache controller must choose which of the potential cache lines it will place the memory location(s) in, since it can be assumed that all imaginable cache lines are already occupied. Instead of randomly forcing one of the filled cache lines out of the cache, most cache controllers implement an LRU (Last Recently Used) algorithm. LRU means the cache line which hasn't had a read hit for the longest time is removed from the cache. Next to the address in the tag, a couple of bits are also stored; the bits contain the sequence of the last accesses. On the whole, these measures significantly increase the effectiveness of an associative cache compared to a direct mapped cache.

Paging and interleaving

Paging or interleaving are other terms that are frequently used to describe the architecture of a cache. Both terms refer to the same concept, describing the distribution of the contents of various cache lines to different pages in memory. A page is a continuous block of memory; it's not the different cache lines that are divided, but their contents.

For example, the first level data cache of the Pentium is interleaved eightfold, meaning that eight DWords of a 256-bit cache line are also placed in eight separate pages. The first DWords from all cache lines are stored in the first page, the second DWords are stored in the second page, etc. This is done on the Pentium to enable simultaneous access to the cache from the U and V pipeline of the processor. As long as the U and V pipeline want to read different DWords from one of the cache lines, they access different pages so they can both be operated at the same time.

MESI protocol

The cache's greatest difficulties are caused by external memory accesses that bypass the processor and cache controller. What is written to memory during such accesses could destroy the consistency of the cache (i.e., the information stored in the cache would no longer match the actual contents of RAM). DMA controllers can cause such inconsistencies by bypassing the processor to write data to memory from an external device, such as a hard drive controller. However, bus masters on bus systems, such as EISA and MCA, can also destroy the consistency of a cache. In the bus mastering design, the CPU briefly passes bus control to the bus master. Usually the bus master is a component of an add-in board and it uses the control over the bus to shift data within RAM as quickly as possible, or to transfer data from its own memory to RAM.

To eliminate inconsistencies resulting from such accesses in advance, the cache controllers of secondary caches are linked to the system in such a way they handle DMA transfers and bus master accesses. However, in multiprocessor systems, which will become more important in the era of the Pentium and Windows NT, this is not possible, because the CPUs are directly on the bus. Therefore, they cannot be connected to the bus from the cache controller.

Also, with multiprocessor systems, each processor has its own first level cache and consistency between these different caches (and RAM) must be preserved. INTEL solves this problem with the Pentium processor by using Pentium:MESI protocol, which the Pentium supports for synchronization of caches in a multiprocessor system. MESI protocol has a feature called bus snooping, which is a procedure that helps a processor and other system components prompt for and manipulate the status of cached information in the caches of other processors.

We'll use the following example to illustrate this:

Two Pentium processors running in parallel cache a specific memory location simultaneously. One of the two processors modifies this memory location. Since the cache is operating in write-back mode, the memory location doesn't get updated in RAM until later. This makes the memory location in the cache of the second processor invalid, since it still has the old value. If the processor doesn't realize this, it will inevitably result in a conflict if the processor continues processing this memory location.

However, when the different processors communicate with each other by using MESI protocol, such inconsistencies are avoided. The acronym MESI stands for the four different states that a cache line of the processor cache can have, M, E, S and I. Each cache line has a tag containing the appropriate flags for identifying this state. The following is an explanation of each letter:

M - Modified

The cache line is only in this cache, but it has been modified and not yet written back to RAM. As a result, the contents in RAM no longer match the current contents of the memory location.

E - Exclusive

The cache line is exclusively in this one cache and hasn't been modified. The contents of RAM and the contents of the cache line still match.

S - Shared

The cache line may still be in other caches and hasn't been modified. A write access must take place in write-through mode (i.e, must be passed on directly to RAM). All other caches containing this cache line will recognize the change and automatically update the contents of their cache lines.

I - Invalid

The contents of the cache line are invalid; it is empty and free to receive new data.

First level cache of the Pentium

Now that we've discussed the principle and structure of first and second level caches, you may better understand the information presented at the beginning of this chapter. Now we'll discuss how a first level cache is implemented in the Pentium. Actually the Pentium has two separate first level caches: One for data and one for code. Both caches are 8K and two-way associative. Each path contains 128 cache lines of 32 bytes each (2 paths * 128 cache lines * 32 bits = 8K).

Both caches can be prompted at the same time, while the data cache is capable of responding simultaneously to two requests from the U and V pipeline of the processors. To achieve this purpose, its cache lines are eight-fold interleave, permitting simultaneous access to each DWord in the cache. The tags in the data cache are even triple-ported, which means they can be addressed by three sources at the same time. Two of these sources are the U pipeline and the V pipeline, while the third source is used for bus snooping when it is necessary to determine whether a specific address is in the cache.

You can switch each cache line in the data cache to Writethrough or Writeback mode using software or hardware. While operating the cache in Writeback mode makes sense from a performance standpoint, it can lead to problems with specific memory areas. For example, consider the video RAM on a graphics card. If this memory area is cached in Writeback mode, the cached information takes quite a while to get to video RAM, which, in turn, slows down composition of the screen.

Overall, the cache architecture in the Pentium is much more complicated than that of its predecessor, the 486. The double integer pipeline and the concept of using the Pentium in multiprocessing systems contribute to this factor. Nevertheless, the cache is an important driving force behind the outstanding performance of the Pentium.

Floating-point unit

The floating-point unit of the Pentium is integrated on the chip, just like the 486. However, the performance of this unit has been significantly improved compared to its predecessor. The following table demonstrates this by showing a comparison of execution times for floating-point instructions on a 486 and on a Pentium. Intel claims the execution of floating-point instructions on the Pentium is up to seven times faster than the 486, enabling the Pentium to compete with workstation processors.

Command	486	Pentium
FXCH	4	1
FLD	3	1
FST	3	2
FADD	10	3
FSUB	10	3
FMUL	16	3
FDIV	73	39

The table on the left compares execution times for floating point instructions on a 486 and a Pentium. The FCXH command has a special position, since it is frequently used in floating-point programming. The reason for this has to do with the organization of the eight floating-point registers for all Intel processors and numerical coprocessors. These registers are handled like a stack; most floating-point instructions use the top of the stack as one of their arguments and also place their result there. As a result, a program must always take values to the top of the floating-point stack or move the values from there. Because the FXCH instruction handles this task, it is executed more frequently than all other floating-point instructions.

That is also why developers increased the speed of executing this instruction on the Pentium significantly over the 486's execution speed. The Pentium requires only one cycle, and sometimes doesn't even need any cycle at all. What makes this possible is the floating-point unit's ability to run the FXCH command parallel to another floating-point instruction. However, this is also the only case in which both floating-point pipelines can be occupied simultaneously with the execution of two floating-point instructions.

The superscalar, eight-stage floating-point pipeline forms the foundation for parallel execution of an FXCH instruction and any other floating-point instruction. Like an integer pipeline, the floating-point pipeline consists of two pipelines working in parallel. Actually, the floating-point pipeline shares its first five stages with the integer pipeline, but also requires three additional stages to complete execution of a floating-point instruction.

PF	Prefetch
D1	Decode1
D2	Decode2
EX	Execute
X1	Floating-point Execution Stage 1
X2	Floating-point Execution Stage 2
WF	Write File
ER	Error Report

The table on the left shows the eight stages of the floating-point pipeline. The first three stages are identical to the execution of an integer command, because this is when the CPU finds out that it is dealing with a floating-point instruction. In the fourth pipeline stage (EX), in which the integer commands are executed, depending on the command, the floating-point unit first fetches the operands of the floating-point instruction from memory or a register and converts them into a special floating-point format, with which the floating-point operates internally. The actual execution of the instruction takes place in stages X1 and X2. In the WF stage, the result of the floating-point operation is then rounded off and transferred to the target register on the floating-point stack. Execution of the floating-point is completed in the ER stage, in which any errors that may have occurred in the operation are reported and the floating-point status register is updated.

Other features

In addition to its superscalar architecture, first level cache, and floating-point unit, the Pentium has several other features that distinguish it from its predecessors. They are:

➤ Paging in Protected and Virtual 86 mode is no longer limited to 4K pages, but can also operate with a page size of 2 Meg or 4 Meg. This should help reduce the management time necessary for paging in multitasking systems.

➤ The Pentium has a system management mode, as already implemented in special versions of the 486. It helps integrate a Pentium processor in programs designed to save power.

➤ The "Function Redundancy Check" allows parallel operation of two Pentium processors that check up on each other to ensure correct operation. This should spur the development of error-tolerant systems.

➤ Improvements in debugging support searching for complex errors and debugging with hardware add-ons.

➤ In Performance monitoring, the Pentium measures the progress of program execution.

Chapter 2

System Programming In Practice

Now that you know some fundamentals, we can look at the practical side of system programming: Program development in BASIC, Pascal and C. Each language has its own commands, procedures, and functions for addressing memory, reading ports, or calling interrupts.

QuickBASIC

QuickBASIC isn't the best language to use for system programming because it's more limited than Pascal or C. However, system programming in BASIC is possible even if you cannot do everything that you can in Pascal or C. For example, BASIC doesn't have direct pointer access. In this book, you'll find fewer demonstration programs in BASIC than in Pascal and C. We included any programs that could be translated into BASIC.

The BASIC demonstration programs we list and include on the companion CD-ROM run under the QuickBASIC interpreter Version 4.5. However, these programs don't run under Microsoft's QBasic interpreter (QBasic isn't able to call interrupts). Most of these programs require that you run the QuickBASIC environment while loading a library named QB.LIB:

```
QB /L QB
```

QuickBASIC data types

When you call interrupt functions, you must be familiar with the processor data types. Interrupt functions are written in assembly language and no other data types are available at that level of programming. So, if you want to perform system programming in QuickBASIC, you must copy the QuickBASIC data types to the data types of the processor. The table on the left shows which types correspond.

QuickBASIC Type	Stored as
String * 1	BYTE
Integer	WORD
Long	DWORD

Unlike Pascal and C (the char type), QuickBASIC doesn't recognize single characters. The String * 1 type compensates for this limitation. String * 1 is a string the length of a byte. The QuickBASIC compiler views this string in memory as a single byte.

However, it's more difficult to operate one of these strings than a normal byte. The reason for this is that a numeric value can only be loaded into a variable declared in this way using the CHR$() function, as the following example shows:

```
DIM byte AS STRING * 1
byte = CHR$(5)     'This is O.K.          - Program runs if you enter this
byte = 5           'Error: Type mismatch  - Program does not run
```

You can derive the value of such a byte only by using the ASC function:

```
DIM byte AS STRING * 1
byte = CHR$(13)
IF ASC(byte) = 13 THEN PRINT 13   'This is O.K.          - Program runs if you
                                  '                        enter this
IF byte = 13 THEN PRINT 13        'Error: Type mismatch - Program does not run
```

Working with the integer and long data types is also difficult if you use them to reproduce words and dwords. QuickBASIC views the highest bit as the type of number (positive or negative) and views the number as negative when that bit is set. For example, if you receive a word after the interrupt call and bit 15 is set in this word (indicating that the value is greater than 32,768), QuickBASIC views the number as negative. The same problem occurs with dwords, only less frequently. (A number with bit 31 set is much larger than you'd normally see in system programming.)

You can manage integer types by converting them into floating point numbers with a function. Check the sign bit, make the conversion, and continue processing. The following MakeWord function listed appears under different names, such as GetWord, in some of the BASIC demonstration programs listed on the companion CD-ROM:

```
FUNCTION MakeWord& (ANum AS INTEGER)

IF ANum < 0 THEN
  MakeWord = 65536& + ANum
ELSE
  MakeWord = ANum
END IF
END FUNCTION
```

You pass the integer, which may have a set bit 15, to the function. The function returns a positive long data type because the function assumes that bit 31 specifies the sign.

Strings

Most DOS and BIOS functions expect strings as a sequence of bytes containing the ASCII codes of the individual characters and terminated by a null byte (a byte consisting of the value 0). System programming books often call this type of string an ASCIIZ string (ASCII-Zero) string.

BASIC stores strings in a different format, from which you must distinguish between variable length strings and fixed length strings. System programming always uses fixed length strings because it's easier to calculate their addresses in memory than variable length strings. You need the string addresses to pass them to a DOS or BIOS function (more on this later). If you declare a string of fixed length in your programs, QuickBASIC reserves that many bytes of the string. The following reserves 20 bytes, whose contents are undefined:

```
DIM S as STRING * 20
```

Adding the following loads the contents of the array S in these 20 bytes, padding the remainder of the allocated string with spaces:

```
S = "PC Intern"
```

Adding the null byte to create an ASCIIZ string requires special handling. We need a WHILE+WEND loop to locate the last character of the string, then we must add the null byte to the string using the MID$ statement:

```
DIM S AS STRING * 20
DIM I AS INTEGER

S = ""
INPUT "Please enter a string"; s

I = LEN(S) - 1
WHILE (I > 0) AND (MID$(S, I, 1) = "")
  I = I - 1
WEND
IF I = 0 THEN I = 1
MID$(S, I) = CHR$(0)
```

However, if you know the string and don't want the user to enter it, you can include the null byte in the string allocation:

```
S = "PC Intern" + CHR$(0)
```

Structures and arrays

Similar to applications and other programs, DOS and the BIOS manage much information using structures and arrays. The following table shows an example of a structure returned to the caller by DOS. This information occurs when you browse through directories looking for files.

Directory entry structure as returned by DOS functions 4EH and 4FH		
Address	Contents	Type
00H	Reserved	21 bytes
15H	Attribute byte of the file	1 byte
16H	Time of last modification	1 word
18H	Date of last modification	1 word
1AH	File size	1 dword
1EH	Filename and extension separated by a period but without a path specification (ends with a null byte)	13 bytes
Length: 43 bytes		

The following program listing excerpt shows how this structure can be recreated in QuickBASIC (you'll find this structure in the DIRB.BAS program discussed later in this book):

```
TYPE DirStruct
    Reserved AS STRING * 21
    Attrib AS STRING * 1
    Time AS INTEGER
    Date AS INTEGER
    Size AS LONG
    DatName AS STRING * 13
END TYPE
```

As you can see, the Reserved element at the beginning of the DirStruct structure is represented by a fixed length string. This is the easiest way to reserve a specific number of bytes. The rest of the elements in the DirStruct structure refer to the various components of the DOS structure in their data types. Bytes are reproduced as String * 1, words as INTEGERs, and dwords as LONGs. The names of the individual fields are unimportant. You can choose any name you want because the names don't affect the structure. Obtaining a correct reproduction of the structure is important.

Accessing bit fields

In structures, fields often represent bit fields, in which individual bits or groups of bits have a specific meaning. The attribute byte in the previous directory structure also represents a bit field. As the illustration on the left shows, each single bit represents a

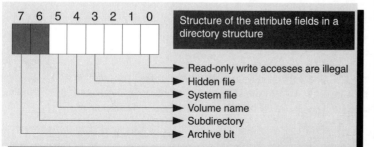

```
7 6 5 4 3 2 1 0
```

Structure of the attribute fields in a directory structure

▶ Read-only write accesses are illegal
▶ Hidden file
▶ System file
▶ Volume name
▶ Subdirectory
▶ Archive bit

certain file attribute. For example, a bit might provide information about whether the file is write/protected, is a system file, or even is a file (a subdirectory). You must know how to read the individual bits.

If you want to read a certain bit, first you must know its value. You know that bit 0 has a value of 1, bit 1 a value of 2, bit 2 a value of 4 and so on, until you reach bit 7, which has a value of 128. To determine whether you're dealing with a subdirectory, you must use the value of bit 4, which is 16.

You want to set all the attribute byte's other bits to 0. From there you can then determine whether bit 4 is set. The AND operator masks all bits not in the AND mask. The following expression unsets all bits except bit 4 (bit 4 = 16):

```
AttributeByte AND 16
```

If bit 4 is set, a result of 16 is returned. Otherwise, the result is 0.

We can apply this expression using IF+THEN+ELSE:

```
IF ( ( AttributeByte AND 16 ) <> 0 ) THEN
     'If the result <> 0 it's a subdirectory
ELSE
     'If the result = 0 there's no subdirectory
ENDIF
```

Unfortunately, checking more than one bit at a time complicates this process. The values of the different bits must be added together. For example, suppose that you want to determine whether the file is both hidden and a system file. The corresponding flags are stored in bits 1 and 2, and have a value of 6 when added together. The following expression returns the contents of both bits:

```
AttributeByte AND 6
```

This time, however, the expression used in the previous example cannot be directly applied to this example:

```
( AttributeByte AND 6 ) <> 0
```

This expression is already TRUE if one of the two bits is set and the result of the AND operation doesn't equal 0. However, if you want to know whether both flags were set, you must modify the process to something similar to the following:

```
IF ( ( AttributeByte AND 6 ) = 6 ) THEN
    'Hidden and System
ELSE
    'Not Hidden, not System
ENDIF
```

Often you'll want to set bits to pass a bit field to a DOS or BIOS function. Again, the main focus is on the values of the bits, but the OR operator performs this task instead of the AND operator. The following statement sets bit 3 of the attribute byte:

```
AttributeByte = AttributeByte OR 8
```

Again, to set multiple bits, the values must be added:

```
AttributeByte = AttributeByte OR ( 8 + 16 )
```

Both of these expressions set the desired bit to 1. Suppose that you want to set a bit to 0. To do this, use an AND operation in a different arrangement to mask the bit you want set to 0. According to the laws of binary logic, you must then invert the value using the NOT operator to achieve the desired result. To set bit 5 to 0, use the following statement:

```
AttributeByte = AttributeByte AND NOT(32)
```

Once again, you can mask more than one bit at a time using the following:

```
AttributeByte = AttributeByte AND NOT( 32 + 8 );
```

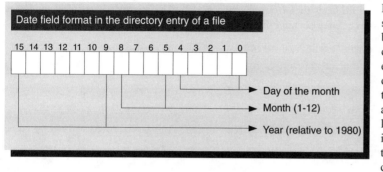

Date field format in the directory entry of a file

```
15 14 13 12 11 10 9 8 7 6 5 4 3 2 1 0
```

► Day of the month
► Month (1-12)
► Year (relative to 1980)

However, bit fields don't always consist of separate bits. Often they are comprised of bit groups, whose individual bits form a certain value when added together. An example of this is the date field in the directory entry of a file. This field contains three bit groups that specify the day, month, and year the particular file was created or last modified. So, to analyze this information, you must determine the value the three bit groups represent instead of checking the status of given bits.

You can easily determine the day by using the described procedure with an AND operator:

```
Day = DateField AND ( 1 + 2 + 4 + 8 )
```

When you want to determine the month, the AND operation is no longer sufficient because the isolated bit group must also be shifted to the right by five bits to obtain the number of the month. In BASIC, the only way to do this is by dividing the value by 2 raised exponentially by the number of bit positions (by which the value is to be shifted to the right). You can determine the month and the year by using the following statements:

```
Month = ( DateField AND ( 32 + 64 + 128 + 256 ) ) \ 32   '2^5 power = 32
Year = ( DateField AND ( 512+1024+2048+4096+8192+16384+32768 ) ) \ 512
```

However, you'll encounter problems again, at least with the second statement, because of the sign bit. This is why you should use the MakeWord function described earlier in this section:

```
Year = ( MakeWord(DateField) AND 65024& ) \ 512
```

To shift bits to the left instead of to the right, use multiplication instead of division. For example, the following will make a DateField out of a given day, month, and year:

```
DateField = Day + ( Month * 32 ) + ( Year * 512 )
```

Calling interrupts from QuickBASIC

The QuickBASIC QB.QLB quick library provides the INTERRUPT and INTERRUPTX statements for calling software interrupts. You can call all 256 Intel processor interrupts with these statements. To access this library, you must start QuickBASIC with the /L QB switch.

INTERRUPT and INTERRUPTX can also access interrupt 21H, which lets you call the DOS API (DOS Application Program Interface) functions. There are more than 200 of these functions, which refer to functions provided by DOS applications. The QB.BI include file lets you access DOS API functions. You must include this file in your programs by using the following:

```
REM $INCLUDE: 'QB.BI'
```

The syntax for both statements is:

```
CALL INTERRUPT(Interruptnum, InReg, OutReg)
CALL INTERRUPTX(Interruptnum, InReg, OutReg)
```

Accessing the processor registers

The InReg and OutReg parameters used by the INTERRUPT statement are of type RegType, which represents a structure defined within QB.BI. The RegType structure makes the various processor registers available to a BASIC program. From the InReg structure, the INTERRUPT command loads the processor registers with the specified values from the InReg structure. After the interrupt call, the OutReg structure contains the contents of the processor registers.

From the definition of RegType you may conclude that the different variables within this structure reflect the processor registers of the same name.

```
TYPE RegType
    ax AS INTEGER
    bx AS INTEGER
    CX AS INTEGER
    dx AS INTEGER
    bp AS INTEGER
    si AS INTEGER
    di AS INTEGER
flags AS INTEGER
END TYPE
```

RegType accesses only the 16-bit registers instead of the 8-bit registers. So, to access an 8-bit register, you must use a 16-bit register. For example, the following lines load the value 1BH (&h1B) into the AH register by multiplying that register's value by 256, and then moving the value eight bit positions to the left:

```
DIM Regs AS RegType
Regs.AX = &h1B * 256
CALL INTERRUPT( &hxyz, Regs, Regs )    'The result of the interrupt call
```

However, this also sets AL to 0. If you don't want this to happen, set the desired value with OR:

```
DIM Regs AS RegType
Regs.AX = Regs.AX OR ( &h1B * 256 )
CALL INTERRUPT( &hxyz, Regs, Regs )    'The result of the interrupt call
```

Write the desired value to the AX register (and ensure that the AH register is empty) to access the AL register. However, if there is already a value in AH, you should use the OR operator to avoid destroying the contents of AH.

```
DIM Regs AS RegType
Regs.AX = &h1B                         'Load AL with 1BH (&h1B), assume AH = 0
Regs.AX = Regs.AX OR &h1B              'AH remains unchanged
CALL INTERRUPT( &hxyz, Regs, Regs )    'The result of the interrupt call
```

You could also use the same principle with all the other general registers. For example, it's just as easy to determine the contents of the various 8-bit registers after an interrupt call. If you're interested in the high byte, simply divide the contents of the 16-bit register by 256. If you're interested in the low byte, you can mask the high byte with an AND operator.

```
DIM Regs AS RegType
CALL INTERRUPT( &hxyz, Regs, Regs )    'Interrupt call (replace &hxyz with
                                       'the interrupt of your choice
PRINT "AH = "; MakeWord(Regs.AX) \ 256
PRINT "AL = "; Regs.AX AND &HFF
```

Including the segment register

Maybe you've already noticed that the segment register is ignored in RegType. Numerous DOS and BIOS functions expect parameters in the DS and ES segment registers or return information to these registers. Because of this, there is a command called INTERRUPTX, which works exactly like INTERRUPT except that it works with structures of the RegTypeX type. Although RegTypeX is similar in structure to RegType, it also contains two fields for the ES and DS registers.

```
TYPE RegTypeX
    ax AS INTEGER
    bx AS INTEGER
    CX AS INTEGER
    dx AS INTEGER
    bp AS INTEGER
    si AS INTEGER
    di AS INTEGER
 flags AS INTEGER
    ds AS INTEGER
    es AS INTEGER
END TYPE
```

Reading the flags in the flag register

In many cases, the flag registers can also return information to the calling program. DOS functions extensively use the carry flag, which is set after the function is called and when the function call fails.

Flag	Bit Pos.	Value
Carry	0	1
Parity	2	4
Auxiliary	4	16
Zero	6	64
Sign	7	128
Overflow	11	2048

You can also access the various processor flags after calling INTERRUPT or INTERRUPTX using the FLAGS variable in the OutReg structure. You can calculate the contents of each flag using an AND operator, with the value of the flag, as the table on the left shows.

So, a test for the carry flag could look like the following:

```
DIM Regs AS RegType
CALL INTERRUPT( &hxyz, Regs, Regs )  'The interrupt call
IF ( Regs.Flags AND 1 ) <> 0 THEN PRINT "Error"
```

Buffers and QuickBASIC

Many functions expect pointers to buffers when they are called. The functions either take information from the buffers or place information in the buffers (e.g., file contents). These pointers are always FAR; they consist of a segment address and an offset address. This FAR pointer data can be anywhere in memory, not necessarily in the current program's memory segment.

Passing pointers to interrupt functions

DOS function 09H is an example of a function that takes pointers. This function displays a string on the screen beginning at the current cursor position. Like all DOS functions, it expects the function number in the AH register and the address of the buffer containing the string to be displayed in the DS:DX register pair. DS takes the segment address of the buffer, and DX takes the offset address.

Although creating a string is easy in QuickBASIC, you may also want to know how to pass the buffer address. QuickBASIC provides the VARSEG and VARPTR functions, which supply the segment and offset addresses of the specified variable. The following program demonstrates how to use these functions with DOS function 09H (&H09) as an example. Unlike other DOS functions, function 09H looks for a $ character, instead of a null byte, at the end of the buffer.

```
'9HDEMOB.BAS

'$INCLUDE: 'QB.BI'                      'Include file for interrupt call

DIM S AS STRING * 20
DIM RegsX AS RegTypeX

CLS
S = "PC Intern" + "$"
RegsX.AX = &H900                       'Function number 09H
RegsX.DS = VARSEG(s)                   'Segment address
RegsX.DX = VARPTR(s)                    'Offset address
CALL InterruptX(&H21, RegsX, RegsX)
```

Receiving pointers from interrupt functions

The following program calls DOS function 1BH, which returns a pointer in the DS:BX register pair. This pointer points to a byte containing the media code of the current drive. DOS uses the media code to describe the different types of drives, with codes between F0H and FFH. The value F8H (248) characterizes all types of hard drives.

Since QuickBASIC doesn't recognize FAR pointers, you must use the PEEK() command to read the media ID. Although this command can be used to read the contents of any memory location, it accepts only one offset address and always accesses the "current" segment. Fortunately, you can define this segment with the help of the DEF SEG command, as the following program demonstrates.

```
'MEDIAIDB.BAS

'$INCLUDE: 'QB.BI'                          'Include file for interrupt call

DIM RegsX AS RegTypeX
DIM MediaID AS INTEGER

CLS
RegsX.AX = &H1B00                          'Function number
CALL interruptx(&H21, RegsX, RegsX)
DEF SEG = RegsX.DS                         'Define segment
MediaID = PEEK(RegsX.BX)                    'Read media ID
PRINT "Media ID = "; MediaID
```

Turbo Pascal

Our discussion of Pascal is based on Borland's Turbo Pascal. Although Turbo Pascal compatible Pascal compilers (e.g., Pascal+ from Stony Brook Software) are available, we'll concentrate on Turbo Pascal. All the Pascal programs we describe were developed using Turbo Pascal Version 5.5, but they will also run under the succeeding versions of Turbo Pascal or Borland Pascal. Since the demonstration programs illustrate system programming, we omitted all the OOP (Object Oriented Programming) enhancements that are available in Turbo. Once you understand the logic of each demonstration program, you can add any extras, such as OOP objects, to suit your own needs.

Turbo Pascal data types

Similar to other compilers, Turbo Pascal's data types mostly correspond with processor data types, which allow fast and easy processing. The table at the top of the following page shows how Turbo Pascal stores the different data types.

In Turbo Pascal, pointers are always FAR, regardless of whether they point at data or are procedural pointers, which refer to program code.

Pascal Type	Stored as
CHAR	BYTE
BYTE	BYTE
BOOLEAN	BYTE
INTEGER	WORD
WORD	WORD
LONGINT	DWORD
POINTER	DWORD

Strings

Most DOS and BIOS functions expect strings as a sequence of bytes, containing the ASCII codes of the individual characters, and terminated by a null byte (a byte consisting of the value 0). In system programming, this type of string is called an ASCIIZ (ASCII-Zero) string. Pascal also saves a string as a sequence of bytes, with each byte representing the ASCII codes of the characters. However, unlike ASCIIZ strings, the first byte indicates the string's length instead of the string null byte at the end of the string. Although this method is more practical for processing strings, it's incompatible with DOS and BIOS functions.

The following program listing shows how Pascal strings can be easily converted into ASCIIZ strings by simply adding a null byte. However, when passing such a string to a DOS or BIOS function using its address, you must specify the address of the first character (string[1]), instead of the address of the length byte (string[0]). We'll discuss this in detail after the program listing.

```
{*   ASZDEMO.PAS   *}

program ASZDemo;

var ASCIIZ : string[100];
    i : integer;

begin
  write ( 'String: ' );
  readln( ASCIIZ );
  ASCIIZ := ASCIIZ + chr(0);
  for i := 0 to ord( ASCIIZ[0] ) do
    begin
      write( i:2, '    ', ord( ASCIIZ[i] ):3 );
      if ( ASCIIZ[i] > ' ' ) then
        write( '   ', ASCIIZ[i] );
      writeln;
    end;
end.
```

The following shows the screen output that's created by the previous program after it's compiled and called. The program prompted the user for a string. After the user typed the string and pressed Enter, the program added a null byte and displayed the string on the screen, including the length byte and null byte.

Output of the ASZDEMO program

```
String: ASCIIZ string       <---- Prompt and input
   0    14                   <---- Length byte
   1    65 A
   2    83 S
   3    67 C
   4    73 I
   5    73 I
   6    90 Z
   7    32
   8   115 s
   9   116 t
  10   114 r
  11   105 i
  12   110 n
  13   103 g
  14     0                   <---- Added null byte
```

Structures and arrays

Similar to applications and other programs, DOS and the BIOS manage much information using structures and arrays. The most important factor lies in the compiler's creating the information in the sequence specified, aligning each field on a word boundary. Although Turbo Pascal has a compiler directive for aligning data (the {A$} directive), this directive usually doesn't work on structures and arrays.

The following table shows an example of a structure returned to the caller by DOS.

Directory entry structure as returned by DOS functions 4EH and 4FH		
Address	**Contents**	**Type**
00H	Reserved	21 bytes
15H	Attribute byte of the file	1 byte
16H	Time of last modification	1 word
18H	Date of last modification	1 word
1AH	File size	1 dword
1EH	Filename and extension separated by a period but without a path specification (ends with a null byte)	13 bytes
Length: 43 bytes		

The following program listing excerpt shows how this structure can be recreated in Pascal (you'll find this structure in the DIRP1.PAS program which we'll discuss later):

```
type DirBufTyp = record       { Data structures of functions 4EH and 4FH }
                   Reserved : array [1..21] of char;
                   Attr     : byte;
                   Time     : integer;
                   Date     : integer;
                   Size     : longint;
                   Name     : array [1..13] of char
                 end;
```

As you can see, the Reserved element at the beginning of the DOS structure is represented by an array. This can be either a char or byte array. The fields within this structure must have the same offset address, which means that these elements are the same distance from the beginning of the structure as in the DOS structure.

The rest of the elements in the DirBufType structure refer to the various components of the DOS structure in their data types. Bytes are reproduced as bytes, words as integers, and dwords as longints. The individual field names are unimportant. You can choose any name you want because the names don't affect the structure. Obtaining a correct reproduction of the structure is all that matters.

Accessing bit fields

In structures, fields often represent bit fields, in which individual bits or groups of bits have a specific meaning. The attribute byte in the previous directory structure also represents a bit field. As the following illustration shows, each single bit represents a certain file attribute. For example, a bit may provide information about whether the file is write/protected, is a system file, or even is a file (a subdirectory). You must know how to read the individual bits.

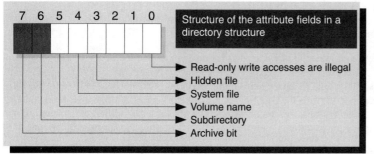

Structure of the attribute fields in a directory structure

▶ Read-only write accesses are illegal
▶ Hidden file
▶ System file
▶ Volume name
▶ Subdirectory
▶ Archive bit

If you want to read a certain bit, first you must know its value. You know that bit 0 has a value of 1, bit 1 a value of 2, bit 2 a value of 4, and so on until you reach bit 7, which has a value of 128. To determine whether you're dealing with a subdirectory, you must use the value of bit 4, which is 16.

You want to set all the attribute byte's other bits to 0. From there you can then determine whether bit 4 is set. The AND operator masks all bits not in the AND mask. The following expression unsets all bits except bit 4 (bit 4 = 16):

```
AttributeByte and 16
```

If bit 4 is set, a result of 16 is returned. Otherwise, the result is 0.

This expression can be used as follows within an if loop:

```
If AttributeByte and 16 <> 0 then
  { If the result <> 0 it's a subdirectory }
else
  { If the result = 0 there's no subdirectory }
```

Checking more than one bit at a time complicates this process. The values of the different bits must be added together. For example, suppose that you want to determine whether the file is both hidden and a system file. The corresponding flags are stored in bits 1 and 2, and have a value of 6 when added together. The following expression returns the contents of both bits:

```
AttributeByte and 6
```

This time, however, the expression used in the previous example cannot be directly applied to this example:

```
AttributeByte and 6 <> 0
```

This expression is already TRUE if one of the two bits is set and the result of the AND operation doesn't equal 0. However, if you want to know whether both flags were set, you must modify the process to something similar to the following:

```
If AttributeByte and 6 = 6 then
  { Hidden and System }
else
  { not Hidden, not System  }
```

Often you'll want to set bits to pass a bit field to a DOS or BIOS function. Again, the main focus is on the values of the bits, but the OR operator performs this task instead of the AND operator. The following statement sets bit 3 of the attribute byte:

```
AttributeByte := AttributeByte or 8;
```

Again, to set multiple bits, the values must be added:

```
AttributeByte := AttributeByte or ( 8 + 16 );
```

Both expressions set the desired bit to 1. Suppose that you want to set a bit to 0. Use an AND operation in a different arrangement to mask the bit you want set to 0. According to the laws of binary logic, you must then invert the value using the NOT operator to achieve the desired result. To set bit 5 to 0, use the following statement:

```
AttributeByte := AttributeByte and not( 32 );
```

Once again, you can mask more than one bit at a time using the following:

```
AttributeByte := AttributeByte and not( 32 + 8 );
```

However, bit fields don't always consist of separate bits. Often they are comprised of bit groups, whose individual bits form a certain value when added together. An example of this is the date field in the directory entry of a file. This field contains three bit groups that specify the day, month, and the year the particular file was created or last modified. So, to analyze this information, you must determine the value the three bit groups represent instead of checking the status of given bits.

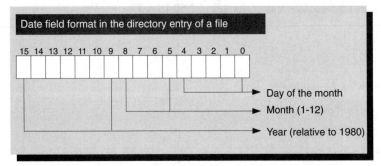

Date field format in the directory entry of a file

You can easily determine the day by using the described procedure with an AND operator:

```
Day := DateField and ( 1 + 2
+ 4 + 8 );
```

When you want to determine the month, the AND operation is no longer sufficient because the isolated bit group must also be shifted to the right by five bits to obtain the number of the month. The SHR operator in Turbo Pascal shifts an expression to the right by any number of bits. You can determine the month and the year by using the following statements:

```
Month := ( DateField and ( 32 + 64 + 128 + 256 ) ) shr 5;
Year := ( DateField and ( 512+1024+2048+4096+8192+16384+32768 ) shr 9;
```

The SHL operator, which is the opposite of the SHR operator, shifts a value to the left bit by bit. For example, you can use this operator to create a date field from a given day, month, and year:

```
DateField := Day + ( Month shl 5 ) + ( Year shl 9 );
```

Calling interrupts from Turbo Pascal

Turbo Pascal provides the Intr and MsDos procedures, which are defined in the DOS unit. This unit also contains some type and constant declarations that are needed for calling types and constants.

The syntax for Intr is as follows:

```
Intr(InterruptNumber : byte, Regs : Registers);
```

The InterruptNumber parameter specifies the number of the interrupt to be called. Since every value between 0 and 255 is accepted for this parameter, you can call all available interrupts, including hardware interrupts.

The MsDos procedure is a special form of the Intr procedure. You can call it the same way you call Intr:

```
MsDos(Regs : Registers);
```

Notice that unlike Intr, MsDos doesn't have an InterruptNumber parameter. MsDos accesses interrupt 21H, which lets you call the DOS API (DOS Application Program Interface) functions. There are over 200 of these functions, which refer to functions provided by DOS applications.

Accessing the processor registers

As you may conclude from the definition of RegType, the different variables within this structure reflect the processor registers of the same name.

Both procedures expect a variable of type Registers, which is defined in the DOS unit. Registers accepts the values loaded in the processor registers before the interrupt call. Then these values are supposed to be passed to the called interrupt. After returning from MsDos or Intr, these variables contain the values that were in the various processor registers after the called interrupt function ends.

To simplify register addressing, Registers provides a variant record, in which the registers are listed with their normal names. Registers is defined as follows in the DOS unit:

```
type Registers = record
                 case integer of
                     0 : (AX, BX, CX, DX, BP, SI, DI, DS, ES, Flags : word);
                     1 : (AL, AH, BL, BH, CL , CH, DL, DH : byte);
                 end;
```

The 16-bit processor registers AX to ES are represented by the word variables of the same name. The 8-bit processor registers AL to DH are represented by variables of type byte.

The divisions of 8-bit and 16-bit registers into half registers results in overlapping between both register groups in memory (i.e., two 8-bit variables overlap the corresponding 16-bit variable). So, AL and AH share the same memory space as AX BL and BH share the same memory space of BX. This also applies to the CL/CH and DL/DH variables.

Notice the order in which 8-bit registers are specified. This order must mirror the format in which the 16-bit register is placed in memory above them. Since, in memory, the low byte of a word precedes the high byte, the L register must be declared before the corresponding H register.

If Regs is a variable of type Registers, you can easily address the single processor registers by the different components of this variable:

Regs.ax,	Regs.bx,	Regs.cx,
Regs.ah,	Regs.dl	etc.

To pass the value D3H to the DL register during an interrupt call, do the following:

```
Regs.DL := $D3;
```

Before calling an interrupt using Intr or MsDos, load the registers, which are used by the function you'll call, with the information you want passed to the function. The interrupt ignores all registers except those on which it directly relies.

Reading the flags in the flag register

In many cases, the flag registers can also return information to the calling program. DOS functions extensively use the carry flag, which is set after the function is called and when the function call fails.

To simplify checking the flags, the DOS unit defines different constants, which reflect the bit values of the processor flags:

You can use an AND operator to check whether one of these bits is set. The following expression sets the Boolean variable to TRUE when the carry flag is set.

```
Error := ( ( Regs.Flags and FCarry ) <> 0 );
```

Constant	Bit Pos.	Bit Value
FCarry	0	1
FParity	2	4
FAuxiliary	4	16
FZero	6	64
FSign	7	128
FOverflow	11	2048

Buffers and Turbo Pascal

Many functions expect pointers to buffers when they're called. The functions either take information from or place information in the buffers (e.g., file contents). These pointers are always FAR; they consist of a segment address and an offset address. This FAR pointer data can be anywhere in memory, not necessarily in the current program's memory segment.

Passing pointers to interrupt functions

DOS function 09H is an example of a function that takes pointers. This function displays a string on the screen, beginning at the current cursor position. Like all DOS functions, it expects the function number in the AH register and the address of the buffer containing the string to be displayed in the DS:DX register pair. DS takes the segment address of the buffer and DX takes the offset address.

Although creating a string in Pascal is easy, you may also want to know how to pass the buffer address. Turbo Pascal provides the Seg() and Ofs() functions, which supply the segment and offset addresses of any memory object. It doesn't matter whether you're working with a local or global variable or a typed constant.

The following program demonstrates how to use these functions with DOS function 09H ($09) as an example. The program uses DOS function 09H to display the string from the Message variable on the screen. Unlike other DOS functions, function 09H looks for a $ character, instead of a null byte, at the end of the buffer.

```
'9HDEMOP.PAS

program 9HDemoP;

uses DOS;

var Regs    : Registers;
    Message : string[20];

begin
  Message := 'DOSPrint' + '$';

  Regs.AH := $09;
  Regs.DS := seg( Message[1] );
  Regs.DX := ofs( Message[1] );
  MsDos( regs );
end.
```

Receiving pointers from interrupt functions

The following program calls DOS function 1BH, which returns a pointer in the DS:BX register pair. This pointer points to a byte containing the media code of the current drive. DOS uses the media code to describe the different types of drives, with codes between F0H and FFH. The value F8H (248) characterizes all types of hard drives.

To determine the media ID from the returned pointer, the MediaPtr type is defined as a pointer to a byte at the beginning of the program. Since pointers are always FAR in Turbo Pascal, you can be certain that you've created a FAR pointer. The program defines MP as a variable of this type. After calling the DOS $1B function, the program loads MP with the returned pointer from the register pair DS:BX. The program uses Turbo Pascal's Ptr function to do this. This function receives a segment and offset address and forms a generic pointer from them.

This pointer can be used to access the referenced information as in any normal pointer operation. The Writeln statement at the end of the program demonstrates this.

```
{*   MEDIAIDP.PAS        *}

program MediaIdP;

uses Dos;                                             { Add Dos unit }

type MediaPtr = ^byte;                         { Create a byte pointer }

var Regs : Registers;         { Processor registers for interrupt call }
    MP   : MediaPtr;                        { Variable for media pointer }

begin
  Regs.AH := $1B;                         { Pass 1BH to AH register }
  MsDos( Regs );                           { Call DOS interrupt 1BH }
  MP := ptr( Regs.DS, Regs.BX );                 { Read pointer }
  writeln( 'Media ID = ', MP^ );                 { Display media ID }
end.
```

Accessing memory with Mem, MemW, and MemL

Turbo Pascal has three predefined arrays, called Mem, MemW, and MemL, that are used to access bytes, words, and longints (dwords). A special syntax is used to access these arrays within brackets and the segment address is separated from the offset address by a colon.

You could have accessed the media ID using the following in the MEDIAIDP.PAS program:

```
mem[ Regs.DX : Regs.BX ];
```

When accessing multiple pointers, Mem, MemW, and MemL will need a more complex syntax than the one previously shown.

Port access in Turbo Pascal

Turbo Pascal recognizes PC ports as a predefined array. However, Turbo Pascal also supports two arrays for port access: Port (for 8-bit ports) and PortW (for 16-bit ports). PortW allows you to send 16-bit values to ports, while Port only accepts 8-bit values. The array you select will depend on the expansion board or support chip you want to access. If the board or chip is 16-bits, you can use PortW; otherwise, you must use Port for access.

You can read information from ports and write information to ports using normal array syntax. For example, both of the following statements dump the contents of port 3C4H, which is part of the graphics controller on an EGA/VGA card:

```
XByte := port[ $3C4 ];
XWord := portw[ $3C4 ];
```

The following statements allow you to send a byte or word just as easily:

```
port[ $3C4 ] := XByte;
portw[ $3C4 ] := XWord;
```

Examples of these statements are located in Chapter 4.

The C Language

Unlike Pascal, the market for C compilers is characterized by the rivalry between Microsoft and Borland. Both companies have several products on the market: Microsoft QuickC and Microsoft C 6.0, Borland Turbo C++ and Borland C++. Both C++ compilers preserve the compatibility with the standard (Turbo C) implementation.

The C programs in this book can be compiled under all the compilers we just named, although some warning messages may appear on the screen. All the programs were compiled under Microsoft C 6.00, with warning levels changed as needed. We also test-compiled programs using Borland's Turbo C++ and the default settings of the Turbo C++ environment.

These programs are affected by the differences between the libraries found in the Microsoft and Borland compilers. Because of this, some programs contain constructs like the following, which is taken from the DIRC2.C demonstration program listed later in this book. The differences between the two libraries are intercepted by defining macros.

```
#ifdef __TURBOC__                                    /* Turbo C Compiler? */
  #define DIRSTRUCT                     struct ffblk
  #define FINDFIRST( path, buf, attr )  findfirst( path, buf, attr )
  #define FINDNEXT( buf )               findnext( buf )
  #define NAME                          ff_name
  #define ATTRIBUTE                     ff_attrib
  #define TIME                          ff_ftime
  #define DATE                          ff_fdate
  #define SIZE                          ff_fsize
#else                                                /* No --> Microsoft C */
  #define DIRSTRUCT                     struct find_t
  #define FINDFIRST( path, buf, attr )  _dos_findfirst(path, attr, buf)
  #define FINDNEXT( buf )               _dos_findnext( buf )
  #define NAME                          name
  #define ATTRIBUTE                     attrib
  #define TIME                          wr_time
  #define DATE                          wr_date
  #define SIZE                          size
#endif
```

Since the demonstration programs in this book illustrate system programming, we omitted all the OOP (Object Oriented Programming) enhancements available in Turbo C++. Once you see the logic of each demonstration program, you can add any extras, such as OOP objects, to suit your own needs.

C data types

Like all compilers, the C data types mainly correspond with processor data types, which allows fast and easy processing. The table on the right shows how various C compilers store the different data types.

Since C doesn't have a byte type or word type, you'll find typedef functions, similar to the following, at the beginning of many of the C programs we use:

```
typedef unsigned char BYTE;
typedef unsigned int WORD;
```

These lines define the two types that are very important to system programming. In C, the memory model that's used governs the use of NEAR and FAR pointers. The programs in this book were developed using the SMALL memory model. So they work exclusively with NEAR pointers. When FAR pointers are needed for system programming, the far modifier is used in the variable declaration:

C Type	Stored as
unsignedchar	BYTE
char	BYTE
int	WORD
unsigned int	WORD
near *void	WORD
long	DWORD
far *void	DWORD

```
int far *p;        /* P is a FAR pointer */
```

We found that Microsoft QuickC doesn't like working with FAR pointers while the Options/Compiler Flags/Pointer Check option is enabled. Disable this option to avoid problems while executing the demonstration programs from this book.

Strings

Most DOS and BIOS functions expect strings as a sequence of bytes, containing the ASCII codes of the individual characters, and terminated by a null byte (a byte consisting of the value 0). In system programming, this type of string is called an ASCIIZ (ASCII-Zero) string. Since C stores strings in ASCIIZ format, they don't have to be converted.

Structures and arrays

Similar to applications and other programs, DOS and the BIOS manage much information using structures and arrays. The most important factor lies in the compiler's creating the information in the sequence specified, aligning each field on a word boundary.

All C compilers are familiar with compiler directives that can influence this structure. Microsoft C compilers support the / Zp directive, which ensures that the fields within structures aren't separated. Borland compilers have an option called Word alignment in the Options/Compiler.../Code generation... dialog box within the integrated development environment. Ensure that this option is disabled; otherwise the compiler will separate the fields.

The following table shows an example of a structure returned to the caller by DOS:

Directory entry structure as returned by DOS functions 4EH and 4FH		
Addr.	Contents	Type
00H	Reserved	21 bytes
15H	Attribute byte of the file	1 byte
16H	Time of last modification	1 word
18H	Date of last modification	1 word
1AH	File size	1 dword
1EH	Filename and extension separated by a period but without a path specification (ends with a null byte)	13 bytes
Length: 43 bytes		

The following excerpt from a program listing (DIRC1.C) which we'll describe later demonstrates how this structure can be reproduced in C.

```
typedef unsigned char BYTE;                          /* Create a byte */
typedef struct {           /* DIR structure for functions 4EH and 4FH */
             BYTE          Reserved[21];
             BYTE          Attribute;
             unsigned int  Time;
             unsigned int  Date;
             unsigned long Size;
             char          Name[13];
           } DIRSTRUCT;
```

As you can see, the Reserved element at the beginning of the DOS structure is represented by an array. You can use either a CHAR array or BYTE array. The various fields within the C structure must have the same offset addresses so they are the same distance from the beginning of the structure as in the DOS structure.

The remaining elements in the DIRSTRUCT structure correspond to the various components of the DOS structure in reference to their data types. Bytes are reproduced as bytes, words as unsigned ints, and dwords as unsigned longs. The names of the individual fields are unimportant. Since the names don't affect the structure, you can choose any name you want. Obtaining a correct reproduction of the structure is all that matters.

Accessing bit fields

In structures, fields often represent bit fields, in which individual bits or groups of bits have a specific meaning. The attribute byte in the previous directory structure also represents a bit field. As the following illustration shows, each single bit represents a certain file attribute. For example, a bit may provide information about whether the file is write/protected, is a system file, or even is a file (a subdirectory). You must know how to read the individual bits.

If you want to read a specific bit, first you must know its value. You know that bit 0 has a value of 1, bit 1 a value of 2, bit 2 a value of 4, etc., until you reach bit 7, which has a value of 128. To determine whether you're working with a subdirectory, you must use the value of bit 4, which is 16.

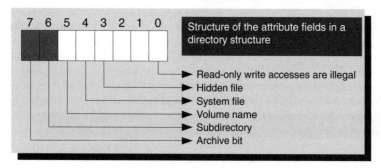

Structure of the attribute fields in a directory structure

➤ Read-only write accesses are illegal
➤ Hidden file
➤ System file
➤ Volume name
➤ Subdirectory
➤ Archive bit

You want to set all the attribute byte's other bits to 0. Then you can then determine whether bit 4 is set. The AND operator (the & character in C) masks all bits that aren't in the AND mask. The following expression unsets all bits except bit 4 (bit 4 = 16):

```
AttributeByte & 16
```

If bit 4 is set, a result of 16 is returned. Otherwise, the result is 0. This expression can be used within an if loop as follows:

```
if ( ( AttributeByte & 16 ) != 0 )
  /* If the result <>0 it's a subdirectory */
else
  /* If the result = 0 there's no subdirectory */
```

Checking more than one bit at a time complicates this process. The values of the different bits must be added together. For example, suppose that you want to determine whether the file is both hidden and a system file. The corresponding flags are stored in bits 1 and 2, and have a value of 6 when added together. The following expression returns the contents of both bits:

```
AttributeByte & 6
```

This time, however, the expression used in the previous example cannot be directly applied to this example:

```
( AttributeByte & 6 ) != 0
```

This expression is already TRUE if one of the two bits is set and the result of the AND operation doesn't equal 0. However, if you want to know whether both flags were set, you must modify the process to something similar to the following:

```
If ( ( AttributeByte & 6 ) == 6 )
  /* Hidden and System */
else
  /* Not Hidden, Not System ) */
```

Frequently you'll want to set bits to pass a bit field to a DOS or BIOS function. Again, the main focus is on the values of the bits, but the OR operator (the | character in C), instead of the AND operator, performs this task. The following statement sets bit 3 of the attribute byte:

```
AttributeByte = AttributeByte | 8;
AttributeByte |= 8; /* Abbreviated version */
```

Again, to set multiple bits, the values must be added:

```
AttributeByte = AttributeByte | ( 8 + 16 );
```

Both of these expressions set the desired bit to 1. Suppose you want to set a bit to 0. Use an AND operation in a different arrangement to mask the bit you want set to 0. According to the laws of binary logic, you must then invert the value using the NOT operator (the ! character in C) to achieve the desired result. To set bit 5 to 0, use the following statement:

```
AttributeByte = AttributeByte & !32;
```

Once again, you can mask more than one bit at a time using the following statement:

```
AttributeByte = AttributeByte & !( 32 + 8 );
```

However, bit fields don't always consist of separate bits. Often they are comprised of bit groups, whose individual bits form a certain value when added together. An example of this is the date field in the directory entry of a file. This field contains three bit groups that specify the day, month, and year the particular file was created or last modified. So, to analyze this information, you must determine the value the three bits represent instead of checking the status of the given bits.

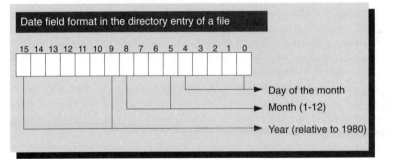

Date field format in the directory entry of a file

You can easily determine the day by using the described procedure with an AND operator:

```
Day = DateField & ( 1 + 2 + 4 + 8 );
```

However, when determining the month, the AND operation is no longer sufficient because the isolated bit group must also be shifted to the right by five bits to get the number of the month. In C, the >> operator shifts an expression to the right by any number of bits. You can determine the month and the year by using the following statements:

```
Month = ( DateField & ( 32 + 64 + 128 + 256 ) ) >> 5;
Year = ( DateField & ( 512+1024+2048+4096+8192+16384+32768 ) ) >> 9;
```

The << operator, which is the opposite of the >> operator, shifts a value to the left bit by bit. For example, you can use this operator to create a date field from a given day, month, and year:

```
DateField = Day + ( Month << 5 ) + ( Year << 9 );
```

Calling interrupts from C

Both Borland and Microsoft compilers provide the int86(), int86x(), intdos(), and intdosx() functions for calling software interrupts. While the int86() and int86x() functions can call all 256 interrupts of the Intel processor, the intdos() and intdosx() functions direct their attention to interrupt 21H (0x21), which lets you call the DOS API (DOS Application Program Interface) functions. There are over 200 of these functions, which refer to functions provided by DOS applications.

The declarations of these functions are in the DOS.H include files of both compilers, which must be linked to a C program to work with these functions. These declarations are as follows:

```
int intdos(union REGS *inregs, union REGS *outregs);
int intdosx(union REGS *inregs, union REGS *outregs, struct SREGS *sreg);
int int86(int, union REGS *inregs, union REGS *outregs);
int int86x(int, union REGS *inregs, union REGS *outregs, struct SREGS *sreg);
```

Accessing processor registers

All four procedures expect pointers to structures of type REGS, while the two functions that end with "x" expect a variable of type SREGS. These are structures that reproduce the processor registers.

From the first passed structure (inregs), the functions load the various processor registers before the interrupt call, while they load the contents of the processor registers in the second passed structure (outregs) after the call.

To make it easier to address both the 8-bit and the 16-bit registers, REGS represents a union in which two structures of WORDREGS and BYTEREGS type can be placed on top of each other:

```
union REGS {
          struct WORDREGS x;
          struct BYTEREGS h;
          };

struct WORDREGS {
                unsigned int ax;
                unsigned int bx;
                unsigned int cx;
                unsigned int dx;
                unsigned int si;
                unsigned int di;
                unsigned int cflag;
                };

struct BYTEREGS {
                unsigned char al, ah;
                unsigned char bl, bh;
                unsigned char cl, ch;
                unsigned char dl, dh;
                };
```

The 16-bit processor registers AX to ES are represented by the unsigned int variables of the same name in the WORDREGS structure. The 8-bit processor registers AL to DH are represented by the variables in the BYTEREGS structure.

The variant record applies to the 8-bit registers, which are as important as the 16-bit registers for carrying information during the interrupt call. Dividing the 8-bit and 16-bit registers into two variants results in an overlapping of both register sets in memory, with two 8-bit variables overlapping "their" 16-bit variable. So, AL and AH share the same memory space as AX BL, and BH share the same memory space of BX. This also applies to the CL/CH and DL/DH variables.

Notice the order in which 8-bit registers are specified. This order must mirror the format in which the 16-bit register is placed in memory above them. Since, in memory, the low byte of a word precedes the high byte, the L register must be declared before the corresponding H register.

If pregs is a variable of the REGS type, you can easily address the processor registers from the various components of this variable:

> pregs.x.ax, > pregs.x.bx, > pregs.x.cx,

> pregs.h.ah, > pregs.h.dl, etc.

If you want to pass the value D3H (0xD3) to the DL register during an interrupt call, do the following:

```
pregs.h.dl = 0xD3;
```

Before calling an interrupt using Intr or MsDos, load the registers, which are used by the function you'll call, with the information you want passed to the function. The interrupt ignores all other registers except those on which it directly relies.

Including the segment register

As the definitions of BYTEREGS and WORDREGS show, these structures ignore the various segment registers and duplicate only the general registers. This occurs because segment registers aren't needed in most function calls. If a function call requires a segment register, use the int86x() and intdosx() functions, which expect a pointer to a variable of the SREGS type, as well as two pointers to variables of the REGS type. The two functions load the various segment registers from this variable before the interrupt call, and save their contents there after the interrupt call.

Here's the definition of SREGS:

```
struct SREGS {
            unsigned int es;
            unsigned int cs;
            unsigned int ss;
            unsigned int ds;
            };
```

Reading the flags in the flag register

In many cases, the flag registers can also return information to the calling program. DOS functions extensively use the carry flag, which is set after the function is called and when the function call fails.

To simplify checking the flags, the WORDREGS structure contains a field named CFLAG, which is loaded with the contents of the carry flag after a function call. This field shows a value of 1 if the carry flag is set and a value of 0 if it isn't set. Before the function call, the contents of this variable are ignored because the carry flag isn't important for working with interrupt functions until after the interrupt call.

The following program excerpt shows that after the interrupt call it's easy to determine whether the carry flag is set. This program also demonstrates that it's definitely possible to specify a single variable for the inregs and outregs parameters, which will be loaded before the interrupt call with the desired parameters, and accept the contents of the processor register afterwards.

```
#include <dos.h>

void test( void )
{
 union REGS pregs;
 pregs.h.ah = 0x13;            /* Function number */
 pregs.h.dl = 0;               /* Any value */
```

```
intdos( &pregs, &pregs );
if ( pregs.x.cflag )
    ;                              /* Carry flag set */
else
    ;                              /* Carry flag unset */
}
```

However, you'll encounter problems if you want to read other flags because some BIOS functions use the zero flag for returning information. In these instances, you can't accomplish anything on Microsoft compilers with the int...() functions. However, the developers at Borland were clever enough to expand the WORDREGS structure by a FLAGS variable, which reflects the contents of the entire flag register after the function call.

```
struct WORDREGS {                        /* Borland only! */
                unsigned int ax, bx, cx, dx, si, di, cflag, flags;
            };
```

Constant	Bit Pos.	Bit Value
Carry	0	1
Parity	2	4
Auxiliary	4	16
Zero	6	64
Sign	7	128
Overflow	11	2048

With Borland compilers, you can determine whether one of the flags is set in the flag register. This is done after calling an int...() function through a binary combination of the flags variable with the value of the particular flag.

The table on the left shows the values of the various processor flags.

Buffers and the C language

Many functions expect pointers to buffers when they're called. The functions either take information from the buffers or place information in the buffers (e.g., file contents). These pointers are always FAR; they consist of a segment address and an offset address. This FAR pointer data can be anywhere in memory; it doesn't have to be in the current program's memory segment.

Passing pointers to interrupt functions

DOS function 09H (0x09) is an example of a function that takes pointers. This function displays a string on the screen beginning at the current cursor position. Like all DOS functions, it expects the function number in the AH register and the address of the buffer containing the string to be displayed in the DS:DX register pair. DS takes the segment address of the buffer, and DX takes the offset address.

Although creating a string is easy in C, you may also want to know how to pass the buffer address. At first this may seem quite simple because both the Borland and the Microsoft compilers define two macros named FP_SEG() and FP_OFF(), which help determine a segment and offset address. However, because these manufacturers define FP_OFF() and FP_SEG() differently, there are some problems:

Borland:

```
#define FP_SEG(fp) ((unsigned)(void _seg *)(void far *)(fp))
#define FP_OFF(fp) ((unsigned)(fp))
```

Microsoft:

```
#define FP_SEG(fp) (*((unsigned _far *)&(fp)+1))
#define FP_OFF(fp) (*((unsigned _far *)&(fp)))
```

Although the Borland definition's macros can contain the variables whose segment or offset addresses you want to determine, the Microsoft macros must be passed a FAR pointer that refers to the appropriate variable.

The following programs also show the differences. Both programs use DOS function 09H (0x09) to display the string from the Message variable on the screen. Unlike other DOS functions, function 09H looks for a $ character, instead of a null byte, at the end of the buffer. The Borland version is as follows:

```
/**************** 9HDEMOBC.C ******************/

#include <dos.h>              /* Borland Version */

void main( void )
{
 union REGS pregs;
 struct SREGS sregs;
 char Message[20] = "PC Intern$";

 pregs.h.ah = 0x09;
 sregs.ds = FP_SEG( Message );   /* Get the var. */
 pregs.x.dx = FP_OFF( Message ); /* addresses    */
 intdosx( &pregs, &pregs, &sregs );
}
```

As you can see, the FP_SEG() and FP_OFF() functions specify the address at which the message can be found. However, the Microsoft version of the same program requires a FAR pointer that points to the string:

```
/**************** 9HDEMOMC.C *******************/
#include <dos.h>                 /* Microsoft Version */

void main( void )
{
 union REGS pregs;
 struct SREGS sregs;
 char Message[20] = "PC Intern$";
 void far *mesptr = Message; /* FAR pntr to string */

 pregs.h.ah = 0x09;
 sregs.ds = FP_SEG( mesptr );   /* Pass address to */
 pregs.x.dx = FP_OFF( mesptr ); /* FAR pointer     */
 intdosx( &pregs, &pregs, &sregs );
}
```

Receiving pointers from interrupt functions

The following program calls DOS function 1BH (0x1B), which returns a pointer in the DS:BX register pair. This pointer points to a byte containing the media code of the current drive. DOS uses the media code to describe the different types of drives, with codes between F0H (0xF0) and FFH (0xFF). The value F8H (248) characterizes all types of hard drives.

A FAR pointer, from which the media ID can be read, must be generated. Borland implementations of C provide the MK_FP() macro defined in the DOS.H include file. This macro expects two parameters describing the segment and offset addresses to which the desired pointer should refer. This pointer results from this macro and the void far type *.

Although the Microsoft compilers don't define this type of macro, you could easily make your own MK_FP, as shown in the following program listing. MK_FP is defined here, in case it hasn't already been defined by the include files.

After the interrupt call, a FAR pointer is formed by MK_FP() and assigned the mp variable. In the printf() call at the end of the program, this pointer "de-references" the media ID so it can be displayed on the screen.

```
/******************** M E D I A I D C . C ********************/

#include <dos.h>
#include <stdio.h>

#ifndef MK_FP                          /* Macro MK_FP already defined */
  #define MK_FP(seg,ofs) ((void far *) ((unsigned long) (seg)<<16|(ofs)))
#endif

void main( void )
{
 union REGS pregs;
 struct SREGS sregs;
 unsigned char far *mp;

 pregs.h.ah = 0x1B;
 intdosx( &pregs, &pregs, &sregs );
 mp = MK_FP( sregs.ds, pregs.x.bx );
 printf( "Media ID = %d\n ", *mp );
}
```

If you examine the definition of the MK_FP() macro, you'll notice that it's quite simple despite the many parentheses and keywords. Within the definition, the segment is cast into a long type, shifted to the left by 16 bits and the offset address is then set in the lower 16 bits of the resulting new long type. The result corresponds exactly to the desired FAR pointer in its composition, so it only has to be accessed by a cast.

Port access in C

Both the Microsoft and Borland compilers offer various functions for accessing ports. However, they have different names and are declared in different include files. Borland has its declarations in DOS.H, while Microsoft has its declarations in CONIO.H. Port Access:C language

The following shows the different routines and declarations of the two compiler manufacturers:

Microsoft: Include file <conio.h>

```
int      inp( unsigned port );
unsigned inpw( unsigned port );
int      outp( unsigned port, int databyte );
unsigned outpw( unsigned port, unsigned dataword );
```

Borland: Include file <dos.h>

```
int           inport (int __portid);
unsigned char inportb(int __portid);
void          outport (int __portid, int __value);
void          outportb(int __portid, unsigned char __value);

#define inp(portid)    inportb(portid)
#define outp(portid,v) outportb(portid,v)
```

As you can see, theoretically the same functions are available from both manufacturers. Each has two functions for reading and writing to ports; one is for 8-bit ports and one is for 16-bit ports.

The Borland compiler demonstrates some cooperation with Microsoft with its inp() and outp() macros, which the Borland functions copied from the names of the two Microsoft functions. Unfortunately, Borland did this only for the two 8-bit functions. However, it's easy to do the same for the two 16-bit functions within a program:

```
#ifdef __TURBOC__                                /* Compiling with Turbo C? */
  #define inpw(portid)     inport(portid)
  #define outpw(portid,v)  outport(portid,v)
#endif
```

This enables you to use the names of the Microsoft functions in your programs even if you're working with a Borland compiler. For example, the following statements read the contents of port 3C4H (0x3C4), which is part of the graphics controller on an EGA/VGA card:

```
XByte = inp( 0x3C4 );
XWord = inpw( 0x3C4 );
```

The following statements allow you to send a byte or word as easily:

```
outp( 0x3C4, XByte );
outpw( 0x3C4 XWord );
```

You'll find examples of these statements in Chapter 4.

Chapter 3

The BIOS (Basic Input/Output System)

Most users associate the term operating system with DOS. However, DOS isn't the only operating system on a PC. Before hard drives became standard equipment, the PC searched the BIOS (Basic Input/Output System (BIOS)) for the basic input and output routines needed for communicating between software and hardware. The BIOS can be found on a ROM chip, which is usually placed on the PC's main circuit board. The BIOS is accessed every time you switch on your PC.

This BIOS contains all the essential routines needed by the PC for communication between hardware and peripheral devices. These routines include instructions for handling screen output, printed output, fonts, date, and time.

Why the BIOS is important

Since these routine calls are standardized, the programmer doesn't have to fit programs to one particular PC hardware configuration. This means you can develop a program on one PC or compatible, and run it on another compatible PC without errors, although neither the hardware nor the individual BIOS routines are completely compatible.

The BIOS is an integral part of the PC. It doesn't matter whether a system contains a 20 megabyte hard drive or a 20 gigabyte hard drive or whether the system is made by IBM or a smaller manufacturer, the BIOS hard drive functions are identical in both instances. This hardware independent concept is mainly responsible for the PC's popularity. It enables computer manufacturers to develop PCs that aren't identical to a true IBM PC, but can still run popular software. Except for additions to accommodate the AT system, few changes have been made to the BIOS since the PC's introduction on the market.

Over a dozen companies manufacture BIOS chips. (These companies include AMI, Phoenix, Award, and Quadtel.) Although there are differences in each BIOS, they all perform the same essential tasks.

The BIOS Standard

Let's begin with the basics of BIOS: How it works, its ground level functions and how it contributes to starting your PC.

IBM defined the types of different BIOS functions and parameters needed in a PC. There are 256 BIOS interrupts, which are divided into functions. This provides a wider selection than that provided by one function per interrupt. These functions provide the communication with the hardware. The table on the left shows the different BIOS interrupts. BIOS views some interrupts as variables, such as video and hard drive functions. (We'll discuss these in more detail later.)

Number	Meaning
10H	Video card access
11H	Configuration test
12H	RAM test
13H	BIOS disk functions
14H	Serial interface functions
15H	Cassette and extended AT functions
16H	Keyboard functions
17H	Parallel interface functions
1AH	Date/time/realtime clock functions

BIOS architecture

The BIOS itself is located in PC ROM, which makes it resident even after the computer has been switched off. It's stored very high in the processor's address space. The ROM chip that contains the BIOS code is always located in the highest area of memory segment F000H. The exact starting location of BIOS varies depending on the BIOS, the system, and sometimes the memory capacity. For example, the original IBM BIOS started at offset address E000H, while Phoenix BIOS may start at offset address C000H.

The starting point of the BIOS ROM varies with the size of the BIOS ROM. It usually ends at the last memory location of the F segment, at offset address FFFFH. This is the last memory address accessible to Intel processors running in real mode. Some manufacturers add little extras to their BIOS designs so they can beat their competition. For example, VGA cards often bypass ROM-BIOS. These cards include such features as shadow RAM, hard drive parameters, independent setup, and password protection. Let's examine these items individually.

Shadow RAM

Shadow RAM is hidden at the same memory addresses as ROM-BIOS. Since double memory allocation isn't permitted in RAM, the ROM-BIOS keeps this shadow RAM hidden from the operating system and applications. Many BIOS systems copy their ROM-BIOS code to shadow RAM, from which BIOS data is accessed. This generally improves execution speed in the PC, because the shadow RAM data bus is 16 bits wide, and the ROM-BIOS data bus is only 8 bits wide. NEAT chips from Chips & Technologies support shadow RAM.

Hard drive parameters

BIOS often has trouble communicating with the many hard drives on the market. This problem is caused by the different type numbers assigned to each hard drive. Before BIOS can communicate with a hard drive, it must know the number of tracks and sectors available, the number of sectors per track, and other hard drive data.

The original solution to this problem was a table of hard drives from which the user could select the drive information using a SETUP program. This information would then be passed to the ROM-BIOS. However, because of the numerous hard drives currently on the market, this solution has become obsolete. Instead, with the SETUP program, the user can manually enter the hard drive parameters. This information is then passed to battery operated RAM (sometimes called CMOS) for access from BIOS.

SETUP

The SETUP program enables the user to configure elements of the ROM-BIOS according to his/her own needs. These elements include date, time, and drive types. Some BIOS systems offer the option of configuring part of RAM as expanded memory, if the PC supports EMS. Laptop computers include an option for blanking LCD screens and disabling hard drives after a period of keyboard inactivity. This saves battery power on the laptop.

Most SETUP programs support adjustments to the processor's timer frequency. The user can make this adjustment by holding the [Alt] key, and pressing the [+] and [−] keys on the numeric keypad.

Password entry

ROM-BIOS is the best place to include BIOS:password protection. Password access can then be requested before the system starts, and before DOS is loaded. Many BIOS manufacturers permit password entry through the SETUP program. The password is then stored in battery operated RAM (CMOS) or on the hard drive.

POST

Program execution in a computer based on the Intel 8088 (or one of its successors) starts after the computer is switched on at memory location F000:FFF0. This memory location is part of the ROM-BIOS and contains a jump instruction to a BIOS routine, which takes system testing and hardware component initialization. This routine is called the POST (Power-On Self-Test).

The tests

The POST consists of many tests for checking onboard PC hardware (the processor, memory, the interrupt controller, DMA, etc.), as well as the ability to initialize expansion cards (e.g., video cards). If an error occurs during these tests, the POST displays an error message or error number on the screen and instructs the computer to beep.

The following list shows the different tests performed by the POST and the sequence in which these tests are executed. This sequence isn't absolute and can change depending on the manufacturer.

➤ Function check of CPU (coprocessor, real mode, protected mode, etc.)

➤ BIOS ROM checksum

➤ CMOS RAM (battery operated RAM) checksum

➤ Test/initialize DMA controller

➤ Test/initialize keyboard controller

➤ Check first 64K of RAM

➤ Test/initialize interrupt controller

➤ Test/initialize cache controller (AT only)

First, the POST tests individual functions of the processor, its registers, and some instructions. If an error occurs during this test, the system stops without displaying an error message (since the processor is defective, screen display would be impossible). If the processor passes the test, a checksum is computed for each of the BIOS ROM's contents and compared with the various ROMs to determine whether a defect exists there. Each chip on the main circuit board (such as the 8259 interrupt controller, the 8237 DMA controller, and the RAM chips) undergoes tests and initialization.

➤ Video controller   ➤ RAM above 64K

➤ Serial and parallel interfaces   ➤ Disk and hard drive controllers

Peripheral testing

After determining that the main circuit board is fully functional, the POST tests the peripherals (keyboard, disk drives, etc.). In addition to these hardware related tasks, the BIOS variables and the interrupt vector table must be initialized.

Searching for ROM extensions

Once these tests are completed, the search for ROM extensions begins. These ROM extensions originate either from the main circuit board or an expansion card, and augment or replace onboard BIOS functions. For example, EGA, VGA, and Super VGA cards have their own BIOS functions to replace the old BIOS interrupt 10H, which was designed specifically for handling MDA and CGA cards. Also, SCSI controllers, which are used for controlling hard drives, don't use BIOS disk interrupt 13H.

Initialization of ROM Module		
Offset	Contents	Type
00H	ID byte #1 (55H)	1 byte
01H	ID byte #2 (AAH)	1 byte
02H	Module length in 512-byte blocks	1 byte
	Initialization routine	. . . .

The POST tests for ROM extensions by checking offset 00H and 01H in the memory range allocated for BIOS functions. A BIOS extension exists if the contents of these two bytes are 55H and AAH respectively. Offset 02H indicates the size of the ROM module in blocks of 512 bytes. The module's initialization routine begins at offset 03H.

ROM modules

These ROM modules have the option of replacing existing BIOS routines with their own routines, and integrating these new routines with the system. The module routines must be placed in memory ranges specifically allocated for such routines.

C000H:0000H - C000H:7FFFH: EGA and VGA BIOS extensions

This range is usually reserved for the BIOS extensions provided by EGA, VGA, and Super VGA cards. BIOS divides this range into 2K increments because most extensions accept this division.

C000H:8000H - D000H:FFFFH: Hard drive extensions

This range is usually reserved for the BIOS extensions provided by many hard disk controllers. BIOS divides this range into 2K increments. The D segment of this range (D000H:0000H - D000H:FFFFH) is often used for the page frame by EMS cards. If an EMS card is being used, this range is unavailable for ROM extensions.

E000H:0000H - E000H:FFFFH: Miscellaneous

This range is reserved for BIOS systems that require more memory than is provided by memory segment F. Few BIOS extensions recognize this range.

After POST

Once ROM initialization ends, the boot process directly applying to BIOS also ends. Interrupt 19H, known as the bootstrap loader, tries to load some form of the basic operating system on startup or on system reset (when you press the [Alt] [Ctrl] [Del] key combination), from a predetermined place on the diskette.

This bootstrap process may fail for various reasons:

➤   There is no disk in the disk drive.

➤   There is a non system disk in the drive (the DOS files are not available on the diskette). If this occurs, the bootstrap routine attempts to find the routine on the other disk drives connected to the PC, or on a predetermined location on an existing hard disk.

If the system still cannot find the bootable system disk, there are two other reasons that may be causing the problem:

➤   Some older systems switch to ROM BASIC, a BASIC interpreter stored in PC ROM directly beneath the BIOS, starting at memory location F000H:6000H. Newer PCs display a message on the screen requesting that the user insert a system diskette and press a key.

➤   BIOS doesn't care what operating system it loads, so it may attempt to load a non-DOS operating system if one exists on the disk. This makes it possible to load other operating systems, such as XENIX.

Determining BIOS Version

Next to the BIOS code and some static variables (e.g., the hard drive parameter table), you'll find information describing the BIOS brand and the type of PC. You can access this information.

The previous section described memory location F000H:FFF0H with the system startup and POST. A 5-byte-long jump instruction to the POST routine is usually found at this location. After this instruction, an additional 11 bytes are available (to F000:FFFF) in the ROM chip normally used to store the BIOS version or release date. You can examine the contents of these memory locations to determine which BIOS version your PC uses. Call the DEBUG program from the DOS prompt:

```
debug
```

Enter the following line to display the bytes at the end of the ROM-BIOS (the character following the memory location is a lowercase "l", not the number "1"):

```
d f000:fff0 l 10
```

The next line displays the contents of this memory location as a hexadecimal number; the characters to the right of the hex display are the corresponding ASCII codes. Day, month, and year appear as two digits separated by "/" characters.

BIOS date display in DEBUG

```
C>debug
-d f000:fff0 l 10
F000:FFF0  EA 5B E0 00 F0 30 32 2F-30 36 2F 38 36 00 FC 00  [...02/06/86...
-q
C>_
```

Determining the PC Type

Certain BIOS functions are used more for model identification than for BIOS version identification. They indicate the type of PC being used. They also indicate when the BIOS has additional functions (e.g., AT BIOS is better equipped than the PC and XT BIOS). These extra functions essentially handle string output on the screen, realtime clock access (standard on the AT), and additional RAM beyond the 1 megabyte memory limit (also standard on the AT).

Model identification byte codes	
Code	Meaning
FCH	AT
FEH	XT
FBH	
FFH	PC

A program that calls these functions must first ensure that the computer being used is actually an AT, and that the functions addressed are available. The programmer can use the model identification byte located in the last memory location of the ROM-BIOS at address F000:FFFE. This byte can contain the codes listed in the table on the left.

Note: These values aren't entirely accurate. Many PC/XT compatibles indicate completely different values in the model identification byte. Use the following guideline: A model identification byte of FCH identifies an AT; any other number indicates a PC/XT.

Only IBM computers have guaranteed reliable model identification numbers at memory location F000:FFFE. This may not apply to compatibles because the BIOS varies slightly with each manufacturer. Chapter 14 discusses processor types in more detail.

BIOS Variables

The preceding sections described different BIOS interrupts and their functions. These functions require a segment of memory for storing variables and data. Therefore, the BIOS variable memory reserves over 256 bytes of memory, starting at address 0040H:0000H, for storing internal variables. This range is called the *BIOS variable range* or *BIOS variable segment*.

This memory range's allocation is standardized because many DOS programs directly access the BIOS variables and BIOS manufacturers don't provide alternate ways of accessing these variables. This standardization refers to the BIOS variables developed for the PC and PC/XT models, which stands in this range up to offset address 0071H. Memory beyond this point is used by EGA and VGA cards, as well as AT and PS/2 systems. The contents change after 0071H depending on the BIOS, PC type, and video card available.

The following list describes the individual variables, their purposes, and addresses. The address indicated is the offset address of segment address 0040H. For example, a variable with the offset address 10H has the address 0040H:0010H or 10H.

00H   Serial interface port addresses   4 words   INT 14H

During the POST (Power On Self Test), a BIOS routine determines the configuration of its PC. Among other things, this routine determines the number of installed serial (RS-232) interfaces. These interface numbers are stored as four words in memory. Each word represents one of the four cards that can be installed for asynchronous data transmission. First the low byte is stored, followed by the high byte. Since few PCs have four serial cards at their disposal, the words that represent a missing card contain the value 0.

08H   Parallel interface port addresses   4 words   INT 17H

During the POST (Power On Self Test), a BIOS routine determines the configuration of its PC. It determines the number of installed parallel interfaces. These card numbers are stored as four words in memory. Each word represents one of the four cards that can be installed for parallel data transmission. First the low byte is stored, followed by the high byte. Since few PCs have four parallel cards at their disposal, the words that represent a missing card contain the value 0.

10H Configuration 1 word INT 11H

This word represents the hardware configuration of the PC as called through BIOS interrupt 11H. Similar to the previous two words, this configuration is determined during the booting process. The purposes of individual bits of this word are standardized for the PC and the XT, but can differ in other computers.

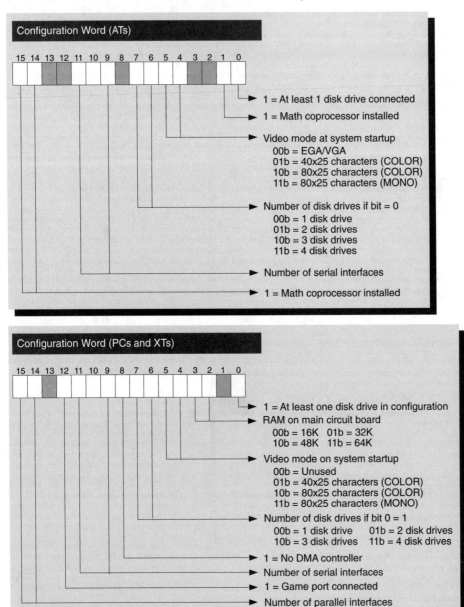

12H POST status #1 1 byte POST

This byte provides storage for information gathered during the POST, and executed during the booting process and after a warm start. BIOS routines also use this byte for recognizing active keys. It has no practical use for the programmer.

13H   RAM size 1 word   INT 12H

This word indicates the RAM capacity of the system in kilobytes (not counting expanded memory). This information is also gathered during the booting process, and can be read using BIOS interrupt 12H.

15H   POST status #2   1 word   POST

These two bytes test the hardware during the booting process. How this test is performed varies with the BIOS.

17H   Keyboard status byte   1 byte   INT 16H

This is called the keyboard status byte because it contains the status of the keyboard and different keys. Function 02H of BIOS keyboard interrupt 16H reads this byte. Accessing this byte allows the user to toggle the ⟨Ins⟩ or ⟨Caps Lock⟩ key on or off. The upper four bits of this byte may be changed by the user; the lower four bits must remain undisturbed.

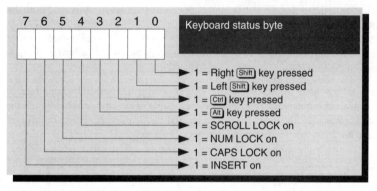

18H   Extended keyboard status byte   1 byte   INT 16H

This byte is similar to byte 17H above, except that this byte indicates the active status of the ⟨Sys Req⟩ and ⟨Break⟩ keys. Bit 3 indicates the status of pause mode.

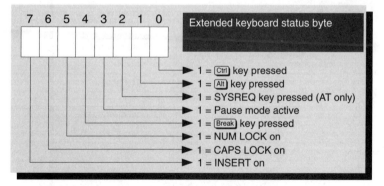

19H   ASCII code entry   1 byte   INT 16H

This byte isn't used in older systems. Newer systems use this byte for storing ASCII codes produced from the numeric keypad and the ⟨Alt⟩ key.

1AH   Next character in keyboard buffer   1 word   INT 16H

This word contains the offset address of the next character to be read in the keyboard buffer (see also 1EH).

1CH   Last character in keyboard buffer   1 word   INT 16H

This word contains the offset address of the last character in the keyboard buffer (see also 1EH).

1EH   Keyboard buffer   16 words INT 16H

These 16 words contain the actual keyboard buffer. Since every character stored in the keyboard buffer requires 2 bytes, its 32-byte capacity provides space for a maximum of 16 characters. For a normal ASCII character, the buffer stores the ASCII code and then the character's scan code (the number of the key that generated the ASCII character). If the character in the keyboard buffer uses an extended code (e.g., a cursor key), then the first byte contains the value 0 and the second byte contains the extended key code.

The computer constantly reads characters from the keyboard buffer. If the buffer isn't full, characters can be added. The address of the next character to be read from the keyboard buffer is stored in the word at offset address 001AH. When a character is read, the character moves 2 bytes toward the end of the buffer in memory. When a character was read from the last memory location of the buffer, this pointer resets to the beginning of the buffer. This also applies to the pointer in offset address 001CH, which indicates the end of the keyboard buffer. If you add a new character, it is stored in the keyboard buffer at the location indicated by this pointer. Then the pointer is incremented by 2, moving toward the end of the buffer. If a new character is stored at the last memory location of the buffer, this pointer resets to the beginning of the buffer.

The relationship between the two pointers is an indication of the buffer's status. Two conditions are especially important. In one condition, both pointers contain the same address (no characters are currently available in the keyboard buffer). In the other condition, a character should be appended to the end of the keyboard buffer, but adding 2 to the end pointer would point it to the start pointer. This means the keyboard buffer is full, (no other characters can be accepted).

Keyboard buffer with start, end pointers and ring buffer

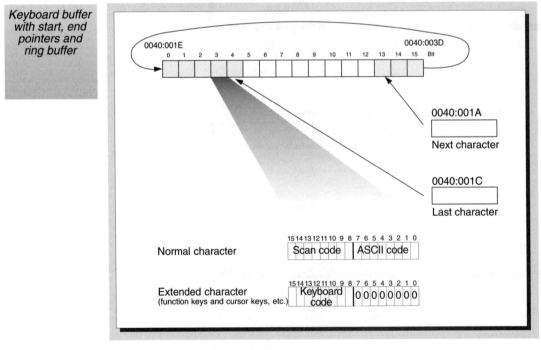

3EH   Disk drive recalibration   1 byte   INT 13H

The lowest four bits correspond to the number of installed PC disk drives specified by BIOS (you can use a maximum of four drives). These bytes also indicate whether the connected drives must be calibrated. Usually this is necessary after an error occurs during read, write, or search access. Bit 7 is set to 1 when a disk drive releases the disk hardware interrupt.

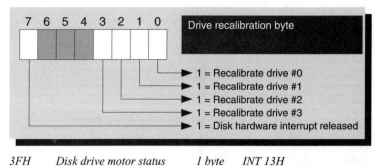

3FH   Disk drive motor status   1 byte   INT 13H

The four lower bits of this byte indicate whether the current disk drive motor is running. A 1 in the corresponding bit indicates this. Bit 7 is always set during write access or formatting, and unset during read access or a search.

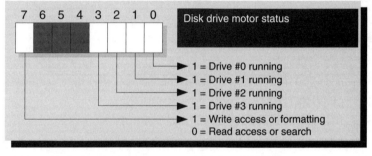

40H   Disk drive motor timer   1 byte   INT 13H

This byte contains a numerical value that indicates the number of calls made to the timer (interrupt 08H) until a disk drive motor switches off. Since BIOS can only access one disk drive at a time, this value refers to the last drive that was accessed. Following access to this drive, BIOS places the value 37 (25H) into this register, indicating a duration of about two seconds. During each timer interrupt (which occurs about 18.2 times per second), the value in this byte is decremented by 1. When it finally reaches 0, the disk motor is switched off. This occurs after about two seconds.

41H   Disk error status   1 byte   INT 13H

This byte contains the status of the last disk access. When the byte contains the value 0, the last disk operation was performed in an orderly manner. Another value signals that an error code was transmitted by the disk controller.

42H   Disk controller status   7 bytes   INT 13H

These seven bytes indicate the status of the disk controller. They also indicate hard disk controller status on hard disk systems.

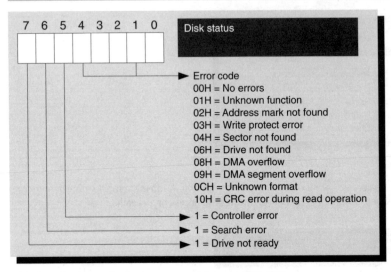

49H   *Current video mode*   *1 byte*   *INT 10H*

This byte contains the current video mode as reported by the BIOS. This is the same value indicated when the user activates a video mode through function 0H of BIOS video interrupt 10H.

4AH   *Number of screen columns*   *1 word*   *INT 10H*

This word contains the number of text columns per display line in the current display mode.

4CH   *Screen page size*   *1 word*   *INT 10H*

This word contains the number of bytes required for the display of a screen page in the current display mode, as reported by the BIOS. In the 80x25 character text mode, this is 4,000 bytes.

4EH   *Offset address of current screen page*   *1 word*   *INT 10H*

This word contains the address of the current screen page now on the monitor, relative to the beginning of video RAM.

50H   *Cursor position in eight screen pages*   *8 words*   *INT 10H*

These 8 words contain the current cursor position for each screen page. BIOS can control a maximum of 8 screen pages and reserves two bytes for each screen page. The low byte indicates the screen column; the high byte indicates the screen line.

60H   *Starting line of screen cursor 1 byte*   *INT 10H*

This byte contains the starting line of the blinking cursor, which can have values ranging from 0 to 7 (color card) or from 0 to 14 (monochrome card). Changing the contents of this byte doesn't change the cursor's appearance, because first it must be transmitted by BIOS to the video controller.

61H   *Ending line of screen cursor 1 byte*   *INT 10H*

This byte contains the ending line of the blinking cursor, which can have values ranging from 0 to 7 (color card) or from 0 to 14 (monochrome card). Changing the contents of this byte doesn't change the cursor's appearance, since it must first be transmitted by BIOS to the video controller.

62H   *Current screen page number 1 byte*   *INT 10H*

This byte contains the number of the currently displayed screen page.

63H   *Port address of video controller*   *1 word*   *INT 10H*

This word contains the address of the video card port. If a PC contains several video cards, the value stored will be the address of the currently active video card's port. This address is 3B4H in monochrome video cards, and 3D4H on CGA, EGA, and VGA video cards.

65H   *Mode selector register contents*   *1 byte*   *INT 10H*

The contents of a video controller card's mode selector determines the current video mode. The current value is stored in this memory location.

66H   *Palette register contents*   *1 byte*   *INT 10H*

A color card in medium-resolution CGA compatible graphic mode can display 320x200 pixels in four different colors. This byte indicates the currently active color palette.

67H   *Miscellaneous*   *5 bytes*   *POST*

The early PC BIOS versions could use a cassette recorder for data storage. Those early versions of BIOS used these five bytes for cassette access when storing data. XT and AT models, which don't have this interface, use these memory locations for other purposes.

6CH   *Timer*   *1 dword* *INT 1AH*

These four bytes act as a 32-bit counter for both BIOS and DOS. The counter is incremented by 1 on each of the 18.2 timer interrupts per second. This permits time measurement and time display. The value of this counter can be read and set with BIOS interrupt 1AH. If 24 hours have elapsed, it resets to 0 and counts up from there.

70H   *24-hour flag*   *1 byte*   *INT 1AH*

This byte contains a 0 when the timer routine is between 0 and 24 hours. Byte 70H changes to 1 when the time counter routine exceeds its 24-hour limit. If the BIOS timer interrupt 1AH is used to set the time, this byte resets to 0.

71H   *CTRL-Break flag*   *1 byte*   *INT 16H*

This byte indicates whether a keyboard interrupt occurs after the user presses Ctrl C or Ctrl Break. If bit 7 of this byte contains the value 1, a keyboard interrupt has occurred.

XT BIOS variables

The hardware configurations of the XT permit the introduction of additional variables. The following is a list of BIOS variables found in the XT and AT.

72H   *POST test*   *1 word*   *POST*

During the POST, a reset command is sent to the keyboard controller, whether a cold or warm start has occurred. For the duration of this reset, this location assumes the value 1234H. No memory test occurs when a warm start is executed.

74H   *Last hard drive operation (AT)*   *1 byte*   *INT 13H*

This byte indicates the status of the last hard drive operation.

01H	Function not available, or invalid drive specification
02H	Address marker not found
04H	Sector not found
05H	Controller reset error
07H	Controller initialization error
09H	DMA transfer error: Segment overflow
0AH	Bad sector
0BH	Bad track
0D	Invalid number of sectors in track
0EH	Address mark not found
0FH	DMA overflow
10H	Read error
11H	Corrected ECC read error
20H	Controller defect
40H	Seek failed
80H	Drive time out
AA	Drive not ready
CC	Write error

75H   Number of hard drives (AT)   1 byte   INT 13H

This byte indicates the number of hard drives connected to the system.

76H   Hard drive control byte (AT) 1 byte   INT 13H

This byte controls the hard drive from BIOS interrupt 13H. Its exact purpose is unknown.

77H   Hard drive port (AT)   1 byte   INT 17H

This byte contains the base address of the hard drive controller.

78H   Parallel interface time out counter   4 bytes   INT 14H

These 4 bytes correspond to the time out counters for the four parallel interfaces. Each byte indicates the number of times a parallel time out error occurs.

7CH   Serial interface time out counter   4 bytes   INT 16H

These 4 bytes correspond to the time out counters for the four serial interfaces. Each byte indicates the number of times a serial time out error occurs.

80H   Keyboard buffer starting address (AT) 1 word   INT 16H

This word contains the beginning of the keyboard buffer as the offset address to segment address 0040H. Since the keyboard buffer normally starts at address 0040H:001EH, this memory location usually contains the value 1EH.

82H   Keyboard buffer ending address (AT) 1 word   INT 10H

This word contains the end of the keyboard buffer as the offset address to the segment address 0040H.

84H   Number of screen lines (EGA/VGA)   1 byte   INT 10H

This byte contains the number of screen lines being used by the EGA or VGA card.

85H   Character height (EGA/VGA) 1 word   INT 10H

This byte indicates EGA/VGA character height in pixels, as well as the number of visible text lines.

87H   EGA/VGA status range (EGA/VGA)   4 bytes   INT 10H

These 4 bytes indicate the status of the EGA or VGA card.

8BH   Disk drive/hard drive parameters (PS/2) 11 bytes INT 13H

These bytes describe PS/2 disk drive and hard drive information.

96H   MF II status (AT)   1 byte   INT 16H

This byte indicates the status of an MF II model keyboard. Bit 4 of this byte indicates whether the system includes an MF II American (101-key) or European (102-key) keyboard. Applications that use the additional keys found on the MF II keyboard (e.g., F11 and F12) check 96H and adjust to the keyboard.

97H   LED status (AT)   1 byte   INT 16H

This byte indicates the status of the keyboard LEDs. MF II keyboards include three LEDs, which correspond to the three toggled keyboard modes (Num Lock, Caps Lock, and Scroll Lock). Function 02H returns keyboard status without reading characters from the keyboard.

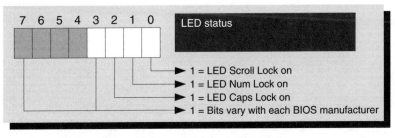

98H   Wait flag pointer (AT)   1 dword INT 15H

You can define a BYTE variable whose bit 7 will be set to 1 after a specific amount of time has elapsed (see the description of interrupt 15H, function 83H in the Appendices for more information). The address of the BYTE variable is stored at this location in the BIOS variable segment.

9CH   Timer (AT)   1 dword INT 15H

This dword represents the variable in which the timer duration can be placed before passing the duration to the caller (see the descriptions of interrupt 15H, functions 83H and 86H in the Appendices for more information).

A0H   Wait status (AT)   1 byte   INT 15H

This variable states whether the system is waiting, and whether interrupt 15H, function 86H is active.

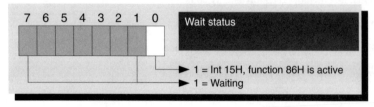

A1H   Reserved 95 bytes ---------

This range is reserved for BIOS extensions and programs.

100H   Hardcopy recursion flag   1 byte   INT 05H

All PC types have a variable in common, at memory location 0050H:0000H. This location is used by the hardcopy routine (interrupt 05H) as a recursion flag. The recursion flag prevents the user from printing more than one hardcopy at a time. When the hardcopy routine is executing, this flag is set to 1; otherwise it is set to 0. Output errors set this flag to 255.

Chapter 4

A Closer Look At Video Cards

Since there are several graphic standards (MDA, CGA, EGA, VGA and Hercules), a single standard hasn't been established for video cards. Even the new Super VGA and TIGA card types don't have a single standard. We'll describe all these video graphic cards in this chapter.

History And Highlights

Let's begin with an overview of the history of the different video standards used in PCs. Significant advancements have been made in two areas of computer hardware technology. Processor speeds have increased and video cards have been improved. The video card improvements have resulted in higher resolutions and a larger spectrum of colors.

A few years ago, advancements in video cards dramatically improved the capabilities and performance of video displays. The original idea was to take the burden of drawing lines and figures away from the 80x86 processor.

As you probably already know, graphical user interfaces have become the preferred way to interact with the computer. Therefore, video technology has become even more important because software places more demands on the processor. If the application seems to operate quickly, the video card is probably sharing some of the work with the 80x86 processor. Most modern graphic cards with the popular S3 chip or a different graphic processor perform especially well in these situations. (We'll discuss these cards later.)

In the following sections we'll discuss the history of hardware development and describe the highlights of various types of video cards.

Monochrome Display Adapter (MDA)

Besides the CGA card, the IBM Monochrome Display Adapter or MDA, is the oldest graphics adapter available for the PC. The MDA was the standard when IBM released the first PCs in 1981. The MDA card supports only one operating mode. This is a text mode consisting of 80 screen columns and 25 screen rows. Unlike other graphics cards, the MDA contains very little video RAM. So, it can store only one screen page in RAM.

Although this card cannot display graphics, many users preferred the MDA over the CGA card because it was the only alternative at the time. Compared to CGA, the MDA actually has a higher screen resolution, which reduces eye-strain. Few PCs use MDA cards today and IBM stopped manufacturing them years ago. The Hercules Graphics Card (HGC) has replaced the MDA. The Hercules card has all the attributes of the MDA but can also display graphics.

Color/Graphics Adapter (CGA)

The CGA (Color/Graphics Adapter) standard was also introduced in 1981. This card, which can display graphics, offered users an alternative to the MDA card. Users who could afford a CGA card could actually save money. Instead of using a monitor, these users could connect a standard television set to a special connector on the CGA card. Also, a CGA card can produce RGB output, in which electrical lines send different signals for the colors red, green and blue. However, the CGA graphics quality wasn't as good as the MDA's because of the larger three color pixels that were generated.

Similar to the MDA card, the CGA card also has a text mode consisting of 80 columns and 25 rows. The individual characters are based on a smaller pixel matrix. However, a CGA card can also display graphics with a resolution of 320x200 pixels, in four colors. Color suppressed mode produces graphics with a resolution of 600x200 pixels, in only two colors.

Although CGA and MDA differ, they are based upon the same video controller (the Motorola MC6485).

Hercules Graphics Card (HGC)

A year after the PC was introduced, a company called Hercules released a new graphics card that immediately made them famous. The Hercules Graphics Card (HGC), which is based on the Motorola MC6485, is completely MDA compatible. This card can display two 720x348 graphic screen pages. The Hercules card combines the readability of the MDA card and the graphic output of the CGA card. However, it also has the resolution to display high quality graphics and text.

The Hercules card is still considered the standard among monochrome graphics cards. Whenever monochrome cards must be used instead of the more popular color cards, the Hercules card is used. Although today only a few firms manufacture CGA or MDA cards, many firms produce Hercules Graphics Cards.

Unfortunately both the original HGC and its clones have a flaw. Since IBM won't support third party video cards, Hercules cards have incomplete BIOS support. However, the system tolerates Hercules cards because they are compatible with the old MDA card and because of ROM BIOS support in text mode.

When discussing the graphics mode on this card, you must remember that it doesn't support BIOS. This applies to graphics mode initialization and screen pixel access. This isn't actually a problem because the BIOS would only slow down screen display. As you'll see in this chapter, it's easy to access Hercules pixel information.

Since the Hercules Graphics Card represents a fixed standard in the ever-changing PC market, the card has undergone the miniaturization applied to many PC components. While the first Hercules cards required a full card's length and 40 ICs, newer Hercules cards now require half a card and use as few as 10 ICs. Some of these cards also include a parallel printer interface.

Although the Hercules Corporation has manufactured new video cards (the Hercules Graphics Card Plus and the Hercules InColor Card), they haven't achieved the success of the original Hercules Graphics Card.

Enhanced Graphics Adapter (EGA)

After the release of the Hercules Graphics Card, IBM tried to design a card to replace the CGA card and surpass the capabilities of the Hercules card. The result was the EGA (Enhanced Graphics Adapter), which was released in 1985.

Due to the many technological advances that occurred between 1981 and 1985, the EGA started a minor revolution in PC computing. Since the EGA was more powerful than the CGA and MDA cards combined, it set a new standard for screen resolution and price. This card placed high resolution graphics in a price range most users could afford.

The EGA card has its own video modes, as well as fully compatible MDA and CGA modes. This is useful for programs that support multiple video modes. Because of its ability to display monochrome graphics on a monochrome monitor, the EGA is similar to the Hercules card. The EGA card was the first graphics card for the PC that could handle both monochrome and color screens.

The EGA is most effective when it's combined with an EGA monitor. This monitor is similar to a CGA monitor except the graphics mode resolution is much higher (640x350 pixels) and more color options are available (16 colors at a time, from a total palette of 64 colors). Also, the EGA card contains increased video RAM (some EGA cards can hold up to 256K of video RAM) for displaying different graphic screen pages.

Instead of the MC6845 video controller, the EGA card uses highly integrated VLSI chips for handling video display. All screen information is stored in video RAM, which makes this standard dramatically different from earlier methods.

Because of its smaller pixel size, the EGA's screen resolution is sharper than the CGA's resolution. Also, the EGA offers more options for generating custom fonts than the earlier cards. The EGA card also gives users the power needed to create computer animation and other applications, such as arcade-style games.

Unlike MDA and CGA cards, the EGA isn't supported by the IBM ROM BIOS. So, the EGA has its own ROM BIOS. The EGA ROM BIOS replaces the original BIOS and allows access to all the features of the EGA card.

As the EGA became more popular, manufacturers began developing compatible cards with additional video modes, which weren't supported by many programs. Even though IBM sued manufacturers for marketing EGA compatible cards, it couldn't stop the flow of compatible cards from the Far East.

Many EGA cards are still being used although VGA cards have replaced EGA cards as the standard for video display. However, many VGA cards include EGA modes.

Video Graphics Array (VGA)

The VGA (Video Graphics Array) card was released in 1987, which was the same year IBM introduced its PS/2 systems. This card combines new technology and the features found in the EGA card. So, it maintains compatibility with all predecessors and offers more colors, higher resolution and better text display.

Although today most VGA cards are inexpensive, the monitor needed for VGA graphics is expensive. Although users may not want to view VGA display in monochrome, many computer systems are equipped with only VGA monochrome monitors. The VGA standard was originally designed for IBM's PS/2 machines and the Micro Channel bus. However, since many manufacturers sell VGA cards for the ISA bus, almost any system can use a VGA card.

The VGA's advantages over EGA is its higher integration density and an entire control logic that's packed into a single chip. Unlike the EGA card, the VGA card sends analog color signals to its monitor instead of digital signals. This means that VGA cards can generate more than 260,000 different colors when modes 2, 4, 16 or 256 are active.

The highest resolution VGA mode provides 640x480 pixels, with either 2, 4 or 16 colors, depending on the mode selected. The extended 320x200 pixel mode is more versatile, offering up to 256 colors on the screen at a time. Higher resolution or more colors means that some video RAM will be needed to handle screen information. So, VGA cards frequently contain a minimum of 256K of video RAM; this can easily be increased to 512K.

Like an EGA card, a VGA card has its own BIOS, which replaces the standard BIOS video output functions. The VGA hardware is often downwardly compatible with EGA BIOS. So, all the programs intended for the EGA BIOS will also operate without problems under the VGA card.

Third party VGA cards encounter the same problems faced by the EGA cards (added video modes and different color capabilities). Although it may be tempting for the system programmer to use one of these additional modes or color sets, we'll concentrate on standard VGA modes in this book. An extended VGA standard will make it possible to standardize the extended video modes with access to any program.

Super VGA

Super VGA cards have the same hardware as normal VGA cards, but they display pixels faster, in more colors and with higher resolutions than their predecessors. These cards support all VGA modes.

While a normal VGA card can display 256 colors in 320x200 mode, Super VGA cards can display the same amount of colors in three other modes (640x200, 640x350 and 640x480 pixels). Other graphics modes can display 800x600 and 1024x768 pixels on a compatible VGA or multiscan monitor, if sufficient video RAM is available.

Again, different manufacturers have added their own extended modes and hardware registers to Super VGA cards. The largest VGA chip manufacturers (Tseng, Paradise and Video Seven) formed a consortium, called Video Electronic Standard Association (VESA). Its goal was to present a standard for Super VGA modes and video BIOS that was based on the chips developed by these three manufacturers. TSR programs can be used to add the new BIOS functions to older Super VGA cards.

Unfortunately, this consortium wasn't formed until 1990, so a lot of time passed before the VESA standard became effective. Until then, every program had to directly access the hardware of different Super VGA cards to use the extended VGA modes.

Memory Controller Gate Array (MCGA)

While VGA cards were designed for the IBM's upscale PS/2 models, the MCGA; (Memory Controller Gate Array) cards were designed for the lower end PS/2 machines. This card was intended to replace almost every previous standard.

The MCGA's text mode, which is similar to the CGA card's, provides a 80x24 character display. The foreground and background colors can be selected from a 16 color palette. Unlike the CGA card, the MCGA's palette can be selected from a group of 262,000 colors (similar to VGA). The MCGA's vertical resolution in text mode is 400 pixels rather than 200 pixels, which provides a higher quality display.

For a hybrid, the MCGA card handles various graphics modes. In addition to two VGA compatible modes, the MCGA supports both CGA modes (320x200 and 640x200 pixels). Because the card uses a vertical resolution of 400 pixels, the vertical pixels in the CGA modes are doubled. Otherwise, the image on the screen would appear in only half its height.

A major disadvantage of the VGA modes on this card is the color selection. Although the MCGA can display the necessary VGA resolution, the card is limited in its color palette because of the small amount of video RAM that's available (only 64K).

MCGA cards are so named because they will operate only on Micro Channel systems. This means that only low end PS/2 systems can use the MCGA.

8514/A

Still trying to set video standards, IBM presented a successor to the VGA standard in 1987. This card, ambiguously named the 8514/A video card, caused a revolution in video cards. While earlier video controllers relied upon the main processor for information (i.e., they were "dumb" controllers), this video card had its own processor.

With this feature, graphics functions could be delegated to the graphics processor on the card, instead of requiring the PC's 80x86 processor to calculate these functions. So the graphics are drawn from the video card itself, which frees the PC's processor for other tasks.

So far, the 8514/A hasn't been able to replace the VGA. This may have been caused by poor development and marketing decisions. For instance, this graphic standard was intended for only the PS/2 models and Micro Channel. This immediately reduced the market share. Also, IBM kept the technical details of this card confidential, so third party manufacturers couldn't build compatible copies of the card. This strategy is quite different from IBM's earlier "open system" attitude. Finally, this video card requires a software interface developed by IBM, which developers have avoided. Although this software interface is powerful, sometimes it hinders the hardware's performance. Consequently, the 8514/A has a small following.

The Video BIOS

The PC's ROM BIOS performs many actions for different screen display tasks. These actions are grouped as functions of interrupt 10H (video interrupt functions). Although there are other interrupt 10H functions, we'll discuss only the video BIOS functions.

In this section, we'll describe the video BIOS functions, how you can access them and why direct access to video hardware is usually the best method.

The video BIOS and its extensions

Originally, the functions of interrupt 10H applied only to MDA and CGA cards. These functions also support Hercules cards in text mode because the Hercules cards are fully compatible with the MDA standard. The original BIOS doesn't support EGA and VGA cards or their extended features in text and graphics modes. So, EGA and VGA cards include their own BIOS extensions on a ROM chip. These extensions are enabled when you boot the system.

This set of BIOS extensions interact with interrupt 10H to add EGA and VGA functions to the existing BIOS. Although they contain the same extensions, the EGA BIOS has fewer capabilities than the VGA BIOS. EGA and VGA cards are manufactured by several manufacturers, but they have the same BIOS extensions as IBM's EGA and VGA cards. Only a few cards are incompatible with these functions.

Some top-of-the-line PCs are packaged with VGA cards directly on the motherboard. In these instances, the VGA and EGA BIOS functions are added to the ROM BIOS, which eliminates the extensions. However, this doesn't change how the cards are programmed.

Speed and BIOS functions

Using the video BIOS functions isn't the only way to handle tasks such as positioning the cursor or drawing characters on the screen. The DOS screen output functions and any BIOS functions used for direct video hardware programming can also be used. If listed according to effectiveness, the BIOS functions would be located between the DOS functions and direct hardware programming. These functions are used when execution speed, compatibility, device independence and flexibility are important to program development.

The DOS functions offer the most device independence because the output can be sent to the screen, the printer or a disk as a file. However, DOS functions execute slowly and aren't very flexible. Direct hardware programming provides the highest possible execution speed and flexibility because the programmer has absolute control over execution. However, direct hardware programming is extremely hardware dependent. For example, a character output routine written for a CGA won't work when on an MDA.

The BIOS functions aren't as fast as direct access routines, but they will work with the currently installed video card. So, the programmer doesn't have to make a distinction between cards; the BIOS always performs the tasks. You may be wondering why the BIOS functions are slower than direct hardware access. There are two reasons for this. First, the mechanism used to call these BIOS functions is slow. Second, the call to an interrupt takes much longer than a routine within a program. All BIOS routines use this latest technique, called the interrupt programmer.

Many video cards are 8-bit cards, which slow down access to the ROM BIOS. Remember, 80286, 80386 and 80486 processors "think" in 16-bit and 32-bit units. If you consider the PC must execute every assembly language instruction in the BIOS routines as an 8-bit instruction, you can see why the routines are so slow.

With many PCs, you can relocate their ROM BIOS to a range of RAM between video RAM and the 1 Meg memory limit, called shadow ROM. This makes the BIOS routines run considerably faster since the processor can make 16 and 32-bit accesses. However, the disadvantages of direct hardware programming also apply in this instance.

While the BIOS functions perform many useful services, most PC applications use a combination of BIOS functions and direct access routines, especially for fast screen output in text and graphics modes. Control tasks, such as video mode initialization, text cursor placement and screen page selection should be handled by the BIOS.

The video BIOS services

In this section we'll describe the most important control functions and the services used in text output. We'll discuss other functions in later chapters and in the Appendix. Let's begin with an overview of the different services available from the BIOS video interrupts and their sub-functions.

Video BIOS functions and support from EGA, VGA and standard BIOS					
No.	Meaning	BIOS*	No.	Meaning	BIOS*
00H	Determine video mode	SEV	0EH	Terminal character output	SEV
01H	Define cursor size	SEV	0FH	Determine video mode	SEV
02H	Set cursor position	SEV	10H	EGA/VGA color options	EV
03H	Read cursor position	SEV	11H	Character generator access	EV
04H	Read light pen	SEV	12H	Set/read video configuration	EV
05H	Define current screen page	SEV	13H	Write string (AT only)	SEV
06H	Scroll screen up	SEV	14H	Reserved	---
* S = Standard BIOS E = EGA BIOS V = VGA BIOS					

\multicolumn{6}{l}{Video BIOS functions and support from EGA, VGA and standard BIOS (continued from previous page)}					
No.	Meaning	BIOS*	No.	Meaning	BIOS*
07H	Scroll screen down	SEV	15H	Reserved	---
08H	Read character and attribute	SEV	16H	Reserved	---
09H	Write character and attribute	SEV	17H	Reserved	---
0AH	Write character to cursor position	SEV	18H	Reserved	---
0BH	Set color palette for graphics mode	SEV	19H	Reserved	---
0CH	Set screen pixel in graphics mode	SEV	1BH	Toggle between video cards	V
0DH	Read screen pixel in graphics mode	SEV	1CH	Save/restore video card status	V ⋮
\multicolumn{6}{l}{* S = Standard BIOS E = EGA BIOS V = VGA BIOS}					

The first step in calling these functions is to load the AH register with the function number. If a sub-function exists, this number is loaded into the AL register. However, we will mention exceptions to this rule in this book. One exception to the rule are the functions that alter the contents of the registers because most functions usually change registers.

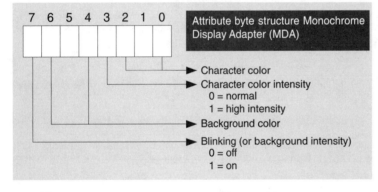

Selecting character and background colors

Some character display functions expect foreground and background colors from the caller. Some video cards have separate systems for setting foreground and background colors.

Unfortunately, monochrome and color video cards determine these colors differently. In both cases, each character has a color or attribute byte divided into two nibbles. The least significant nibble (bits 0-3) defines the foreground color, while the most significant nibble (bits 4-7) defines the background color.

MDA cards divide the nibbles into bits for foreground intensity and character blinking, as you can see in the illustration above. The following illustration shows how the intensity bits for foreground and background colors interact through bit combination:

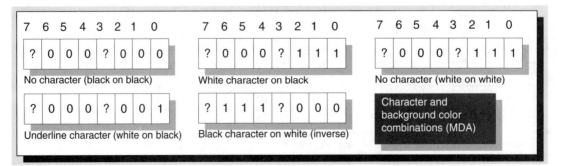

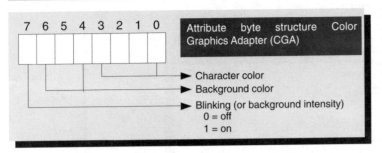

Frequently selected monochrome video card colors are 07H (light text on dark background) and 70H (dark text on a light background). These codes also work with color cards for color combinations such as light gray on black and black on light gray.

Selecting 0 or 7 as text or background color changes the status of bit 7 in the attribute byte. This byte determines whether the character blinks or the background appears in high intensity color. The illustration above shows the structure of the color attribute bytes.

The color card lets you specify colors for foreground and background from a palette of 16 colors. The following shows the structure of the color palette.

Color/Graphics Adapter color palette							
Decimal	Hex	Bin	Color	Decimal	Hex	Bin	Color
0	00H	0000(b)	Black	8	08H	1000(b)	Dark gray
1	01H	0001(b)	Blue	9	09H	1001(b)	Light blue
2	02H	0010(b)	Green	10	0AH	1010(b)	Light green
3	03H	0011(b)	Cyan	11	0BH	1011(b)	Light cyan
4	04H	0100(b)	Red	12	0CH	1100(b)	Light red
5	05H	0101(b)	Purple	13	0DH	1101(b)	Light purple
6	06H	0110(b)	Brown	14	0EH	1110(b)	Yellow
7	07H	0111(b)	Light gray	15	0FH	1111(b)	White

The ASCII character set

The PC uses a character set based on 256 symbols, numerals, letters and special characters. Many of these special characters are foreign language characters, mathematical symbols and linedrawing characters.

For more information and examples of these characters, refer to the Appendix. We've included a complete ASCII table which displays these codes.

The screen coordinate system

Many BIOS functions require screen coordinates as a parameter. These coordinates specify the location on the screen where you want to display the character. You must understand this coordinate system before you can call many of the functions.

Whether in text or graphics mode, the origin of this coordinate system is the upper-left corner of the screen. Moving to the right increments the X-coordinate, while moving down increments the Y-coordinate. In 80x25 character text mode, the lower-right screen corner is coordinate 79/24, while the lower-right corner of a CGA card's 640x200 pixel graphics mode is coordinate 639/199.

Screen row and column numbering

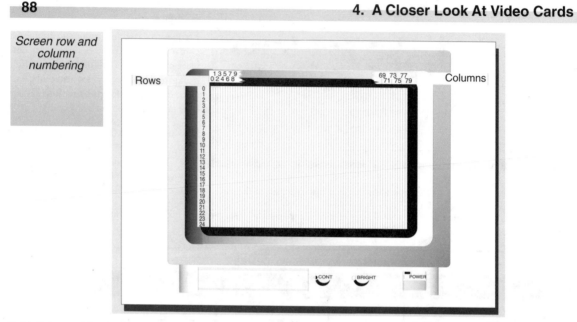

Initializing a video mode

Using function 00H initializes the video mode of a graphics card. Placing 00H in the AH register and a sub-function code in the AL register initializes the standard video mode in text or graphics mode (except graphics mode on the Hercules card).

Initializing a video mode assumes the corresponding video card is installed. If you initialize a video card or mode that doesn't exist, the system may crash. When you call function 00H, the contents of video RAM are cleared and the selected video mode is initialized. The contents can be retained on EGA and VGA cards by adding 128 to the mode number (i.e., by setting bit 7 in the mode number). Calling function 00H in this way keeps the contents of video RAM intact and displays these contents on the screen after initialization.

You can immediately set 80x25 character text mode as active when a program starts. This is mode 7 on MDAs and mode 3 on CGAs. You don't need to call function 00H when you want your program to operate in 80x25 text mode. Function 0FH reads the current video mode. Call this function by passing 0FH in the AH register. After you call the function, the AL register returns a value. Use the table previously listed to determine the currently active video mode. The number of columns per screen line is returned in the AH register (if this mode is a text mode). The number of current screen pages, if applicable, is returned in the BH register.

Video mode sub-functions from video BIOS function 00H		
Code	Mode	Card
00H	40x25 character text, 16 colors, no color display	CEV
01H	40x25 character text, 16 colors	CEV
02H	80x25 character text, 16 colors, no color display	CEV
03H	80x25 character text, 16 colors	CEV
04H	320x200 pixel graphics, 4 colors	CEV
EGA card on MDA monitor M = MDA H = Hercules C = CGA E = EGA V = VGA		

Video mode sub-functions from video BIOS function 00H (continued)		
Code	Mode	Card
05H	320x200 pixel graphics, 4 colors, no color display	CEV
06H	640x200 pixel graphics, 2 colors	CEV
07H	80x25 character text, mono	MHE*
08H	Reserved	
0CH	Reserved	
0DH	320x200 pixel graphics, 16 colors	EV
0EH	640x200 pixel graphics, 16 colors	EV
0FH	640x350 pixel graphics, mono	E*
10H	640x350 pixel graphics, 16 colors	EV
11H	640x480 pixel graphics, 2 colors	V
12H	640x480 pixel graphics, 16 colors	V
13H	320x200 pixel graphics, 256 colors	V
* EGA card on MDA monitor M = MDA H = Hercules C = CGA E = EGA V = VGA		

Programming the text cursor

In text mode, every video card from MDA to VGA has a blinking cursor. This cursor indicates the current input or output position. The video BIOS controls both the appearance and screen position of this cursor.

Function 02H handles cursor positioning. Place the function number (02H) in the AH register. Place the row where you want to locate the cursor in the DH register and place the column where you want to locate the cursor in the DL register. Also, place the number of the screen page, at which you want the cursor located, in the BH register. This is applicable only if each page has its own cursor available. The blinking cursor only appears when the value in the BH register corresponds to the current screen page.

This function call determines the next location at which screen input and output will occur. Refer to the Appendix for more information about this function.

Function 03H reads the current cursor position in a specified screen page and returns this position to the program that called the function. Place the function number (03H) in the AL register and the screen page that should be read in the BH register. This function returns the cursor position in the CH register (starting pixel line of the cursor) and the Cl register (ending pixel line of the cursor), instead of the actual position.

To understand these values, remember that a character in text mode on a color card is eight pixels high and that a character in text mode on a monochrome card is 14 pixels high (not screen rows). These values tell the programmer where the blinking cursor begins and ends.

These values also provide information about the height of the character matrix, from which you can determine the sizes of the characters. Since the CGA card generates characters that are eight pixels high, the starting and ending lines should be from 0 to 7. Since a Hercules and an MDA card generate characters that are 14 pixels high, the cursor values range from 0 to 13.

Starting and ending line of a text cursor

The EGA and VGA cards use even higher values, but the CGA measurement of 0 to 7 is used here. The actual character matrix can be recalculated from these values.

Greater values for the starting and ending lines can occur when the cursor disappears from the screen.

Function 01H defines the appearance of the cursor. To do this, place 1 in the AH register, the starting line in the CH register and the ending line in the CL register. Be sure the starting line is less than or equal to the ending line; otherwise the cursor will no longer be visible.

Selecting the screen page

Although we've mentioned the current screen page, we haven't explained how to activate a screen page. Function 05H of the video BIOS performs this task. Place the value 05H in the AH register and the number of the screen page you want activated in the AL register. The screen page number will vary depending on the number of pages available in the video card. For example, since the MDA has only one page, calling this function for an MDA card is useless.

Number of available screen pages depends on video card and video mode			
Mode	Resolution	Card	Pages
7	80x25	MDA/Hercules	1
0/1	40x25	CGA	8
2/3	80x25	CGA	4
0/1	40x25	EGA/VGA	16
2/3	80x25	EGA/VGA	8

The table on the left show values apply to the video cards that support multiple screen pages with their video modes. Screen page numbering always begins at 0. So, an EGA or VGA card in mode 2 can access screen pages 0 to 7.

Character output and BIOS

The video BIOS contains various character output functions. Each function handles control codes differently. These control codes consist of ASCII codes 7, 8, 10 and 13. Although the IBM system views them as normal characters, data processing history considers these characters text controls (see the table on the lower left).

PC ASCII control characters		
ASCII code	Name	Purpose
7	Bell	Sounds beep
8	Backspace	Deletes character left of cursor and moves cursor right one character
10	Linefeed	Moves cursor to next line
13	Carriage Return	Moves cursor to beginning of current line

Some functions view these codes as normal ASCII characters and display them as such. Other functions execute the controls specified by these codes. For example, code 7 instructs the computer to sound a beep. The function you select determines the actions performed by these codes.

Remember, all text output functions operate in both text mode and graphics mode. Character output in graphics mode isn't directly accessible because a character set isn't available. However, BIOS compensates for this limitation by setting the ASCII character patterns as graphic pixels. While the character patterns for ASCII codes 0 to 127 are already stored in ROM, codes 128 to 255 are taken from a table in RAM, which is installed by the GRAFTABL command from MS-DOS.

BIOS removes the address of this table as a FAR pointer (you'll find the table starting at 0000:007C). Although these memory addresses lie within the interrupt vector table, interrupt 1FH, which normally uses this address, cannot be used.

The condition that stores this table in RAM enables you to design your own table. With a user-defined table, special characters, which aren't found in the standard character table, can be displayed on the screen. Each character requires eight bytes. The first eight bytes in the table define ASCII code 128, the second eight bytes define ASCII code 129, etc. Each byte represents the bit pattern for one of the eight lines used in each character. Bit 0 represents the right border of each character matrix, while bit 7 represents the left border of each character matrix. If a bit is set as 1, the corresponding pixel appears on the screen.

Although functions 09H and 0AH both display characters, there is a difference between them. Function 0AH displays the character in the color established for that position on the screen and function 09H displays the color (the attribute) set by the character itself. After character output, both functions keep the cursor at the same cursor position so the next call of either function places character output at that same location.

Function 02H moves the cursor to the next screen position.

Both functions interpret control codes as normal characters and display these characters as such. Place the function number in the AH register and the ASCII code you want displayed in the AL register. The BH register contains the screen page, on which the character should be displayed (where applicable). The CX register contains a number that indicates how often the output should follow. This enables you to display a single character several times in one function call. If the character in the AL register should be displayed only once, the CX register should contain the value 1.

Because of an error in BIOS, the repeat factor during the call of this function in graphics mode should be limited to the maximum number of characters that can be displayed in one line.

Function 09H passes the character and its color. Place the character color number in the BL register.

Both functions have a disadvantage. The cursor remains at the same cursor position, unlike function 0EH, which increments the cursor to the next screen position. It simulates a terminal; this process is often referred to as the TTY routine (teletype routine) routine. Calling function 0EH displays the character and increments the cursor to the next character. If the cursor reaches the end of a screen line, the cursor jumps to the beginning of the next screen line.

If the cursor reaches the lower-right corner of the screen (column 79, line 24), the entire contents of the screen scroll up one line and the cursor moves to the first column of line 24.

Unlike functions 09H and 0AH, the TTY function handles the control codes as control codes instead of as normal ASCII characters. The TTY function displays the character in the color previously defined for that screen location. This function applies only to text mode. In graphics mode, the TTY function must have the character color stored in the BL register.

Place the function number 0EH in the AH register, the code you want displayed in the AL register and the screen page, in which the character should be displayed, in the BH register.

String output

When the AT was introduced, the video BIOS included a new function (13H), which was also found in the BIOS versions included on EGA and VGA cards. This function displays a character string on the screen with a single function call.

Place the function number in the AH register and the screen page to be displayed in the BH register. Place the starting position of the string in the DH register (row) and the DL register (column). The CX register should contain the number of characters to be displayed in the string.

The AL register contents define one of four available modes, in which the string can be displayed. Modes 0 and 1 specify the format in the first screen page and modes 2 and 3 specify the format in other screen pages. Modes 0 and 1 contain only the characters to be displayed, but modes 2 and 3 include both characters and attribute bytes for each character. The BL registers should contain the attribute bytes for all characters. Whatever buffers are allocated, the ES:BP register pair must contain a FAR pointer to the buffer.

Modes 2 and 3 contain two bytes (character byte and attribute byte) for every character in the string. So, a string that's four characters long actually contains eight characters. However, the CX register should contain the number 4 (i.e., the number of bytes in the actual string). There's another difference between modes 0 and 2 and modes 1 and 3. After screen output in modes 1 and 3, the cursor moves to the next screen position so BIOS output continues at this point. However, in modes 0 and 2, the cursor position isn't updated.

Reading characters from the screen

While functions 09H, 0AH and 0EH display characters, function 08H reads characters currently on the screen. The function senses which character is at a particular screen position and which attribute applies to that character. Place the function number in the AH register and the screen page number in the BH register. The screen position is the current cursor position.

Although the character code can be read directly from video RAM in text mode, in graphics mode, the character pattern at the current cursor position must be compared with all available character patterns. However, since this doesn't always work, you shouldn't rely on this function in graphics mode.

The function returns the attribute (color) in the AH register and returns the ASCII code of the character in the AL register.

Screen scrolling

In the description of the TTY output function (0EH) we mentioned the screen scrolls (moves up) when the cursor reaches the last column and line on the screen.

Function 0EH executes an internal call to function 06H to perform the scrolling. Function 06H scrolls the screen area one

CH	Upper-left window corner (line)
CL	Upper-left window corner (column)
DH	Lower-right window corner (line)
DL	Lower-right window corner (column)

or more lines up, displaying a blank space at the bottom of the screen. Only the currently displayed screen page is affected by this operation. Place the function number 06H in the AH register and the number of lines you want scrolled in the AL register. If you place a value of 0 in this register, instead of being scrolled, the line(s) will be filled with spaces. In this case, the BH register contains the color you want assigned to the blank line(s). The CH, CL, DH and DL registers define the screen range.

Function 07H scrolls the screen window down rather than up. The same parameters are used for function 07H and function 06H.

Demonstration programs

The following programs demonstrate how to use the BIOS video interrupt functions that are available from higher level languages. In Pascal and C, you'll find that using BIOS display functions works much faster than the standard procedures and functions, which use the slower DOS functions, that are included in these languages.

Advantage

An advantage of accessing BIOS video interrupt functions instead of using onboard graphics commands in higher level languages is the BIOS function can be accessed at any time.

Disadvantage

However, there is a disadvantage to using BIOS functions for screen output. The higher level language display commands can accept numeric variables, which are then converted to ASCII characters. These higher level commands can format the variables according to decimal places (or a certain degree of precision) and then display them. However, if numeric variables are displayed using the BIOS functions, first they must be converted into a character string that must be transferred to the BIOS output function. Obviously, this procedure is very time-consuming.

Both programs operate the same way. Each fills the screen with continuous characters from the PC character set, then opens two windows in which two arrows move up and down. You'll understand how this was done and how it will actually appear on the screen, after you've studied the program codes. The programs limit their access to one screen page because of incompatibility problems that could occur between monochrome and color cards. Also, they don't present subroutines, functions or procedures for calling the BIOS graphics functions.

Once you understand this section you should be able to add the missing functions and even write a short demonstration program of your own. Using the BIOS video interrupt ensures the computer won't crash and that you won't encounter serious problems.

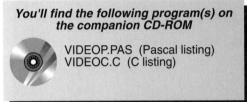

You'll find the following program(s) on the companion CD-ROM

VIDEOP.PAS (Pascal listing)
VIDEOC.C (C listing)

The individual functions and procedures of the VIDEO.PAS and VIDEOC.C programs which you'll find on the companion CD-ROM are fully documented and should be self-explanatory. These programs look similar because the procedures, functions and variables have the same names.

Determining Video Card Type

Whenever you want to access the video card hardware or use a BIOS function that's only available in special versions of the BIOS, first you must ensure the card is actually installed in the system. If you don't do this, the image that appears on the screen may look different than what you expected.

Combinations of PC video cards					
	VGA	EGA	HGC	CGA	MDA
VGA					
EGA					
HGC					
CGA					
MDA					

If the program is supposed to be compatible with all types of cards, it's especially important that it recognize the type of video card that's installed, while still directly accessing video hardware. The output routines need this information to use the special properties of the given card effectively.

Remember the PC can have both a monochrome video card (MDA, HGC or EGA with a monochrome monitor) and a color video card (EGA, VGA or CGA) installed. However, only one of the cards can be active at a time.

We must determine which video cards are installed. BIOS or DOS functions cannot be used to do this and variables cannot be read. So, we must write an assembly language routine that checks for the existence of different video cards.

Refer to the documentation for the various cards. Manufacturers usually include a procedure for determining whether their card is being used. It's important to keep the test specific (i.e., it doesn't return a positive result if a certain type of video card isn't installed). This is difficult to do with EGA and VGA cards, which can emulate CGA or MDA cards with the appropriate monitor and are difficult to distinguish from true CGA or MDA cards.

However, not all registers can be described and read in this case. Registers 14 and 15, which determine the address of the blinking cursor, don't cause any problems.

All the tests we present are located at the end of this section in the form of two assembly language programs. These programs are intended to be used with C and Pascal programs. The functions place the type of video card installed and the type of monitor connected to it into an array. The function is passed a pointer to this array. If two video cards are installed, their order in the array indicates which one is active.

The following cards can be detected by the assembly language routine:

➢ MDA cards   ➢ CGA cards   ➢ HGC cards

➢ EGA cards   ➢ VGA cards

Since the assembly language routine checks for the existence of a specific video card, there is a separate subroutine for each type of card. The name of the subroutine is the same as the video card for which it tests. For example, these routines could be called TEST_EGA, TEST_VGA, etc.

Although these tests can be called sequentially, certain tests can be excluded if you know they would return a negative result. For example, this applies to the CGA test if an EGA or VGA card has already been detected and is connected to a high resolution color monitor. Since a CGA card cannot be installed along with this type of card, you don't need to test for it.

A flag for each test determines whether the test will be performed. Before the first test (the VGA test), all the flags are set to 1 so all the tests will be performed sequentially. During the testing, certain flags can be set to 0 so the corresponding tests won't be performed.

VGA test

Return Code of Function 00H of Function 1AH	
Code	Meaning
00H	No video card
01H	MDA card/monochrome monitor
02H	CGA card/color monitor
03H	Reserved
04H	EGA card/high resolution monitor
05H	EGA card/monochrome monitor
06H	Reserved
07H	VGA card/analog monochrome monitor
08H	VGA card/analog color monitor

The tests begin with the VGA test. A special function in the VGA BIOS, sub-function 00H of function 1AH, returns the information needed by the assembly language routine. The information is available only if a VGA card and a VGA BIOS are installed. This is the case if the value 1AH is found in the AL register after the call. If the test routine encounters a different value there, the VGA test will be terminated and the other tests will be performed. This indicates that a VGA card is not installed. Based on this information, the sequence of both entries is exchanged in the last step of the assembler routine.

After this function is called, the BL register contains a special device code for the active video card and the BH register contains a code for the inactive card. The table on the left shows which errors can occur.

These codes are separated into values for the video card and the monitor connected to it and loaded into the array whose address is passed to the assembly language routine. Since this routine already has information about both video cards, the following tests don't have to be performed. However, the routine executes the monochrome test if the functions discover a monochrome card, because it cannot distinguish between an MDA and HGC card.

EGA test

After the VGA test, the EGA test is performed only if the VGA test was unsuccessful and, consequently, the EGA flag wasn't cleared. This test uses a function that's found only in the EGA BIOS, called sub-function 10H of function 12H. If an EGA card isn't installed and this function isn't available, the value 10H will still be found in the BL register after the function call. In this case, the EGA test ends.

If an EGA card is installed, the CL register will contain the settings of the DIP switches on the EGA card after the call. These switches indicate which type of monitor is connected. They are converted to the monitor codes the assembly language routine uses and placed in the array along with the code for the EGA card. The CGA or monochrome test flag is cleared, depending on the type of monitor connected. The EGA routine ends.

CGA test

If the CGA flag hasn't been cleared by the previous tests, the CGA test follows the EGA test. As with the monochrome test, there aren't any special BIOS functions that can be used and we must check for the presence of the appropriate hardware. In both routines this is done by calling the routine TEST_6845, which tests to determine whether the 6845 video controller found on these cards is at the specified port address. On a CGA card this is port address 3D4H, which is passed to the routine TEST_6845.

The only way to test the existence of the CRTC at a given port address is to write some value (other than 0) to one of the CRTC registers and then read it back immediately. If the value read matches the value written, then the CRTC and, therefore, the video card are present.

Before writing a value into a CRTC register, you should remember these registers have a major impact on the makeup of the video signals. So, carelessly accessing them can not only thoroughly confuse the CRTC, but also harm the monitor. Registers 00H to 09H cannot be used for this test, so only registers 0AH to 0FH are available. All these registers affect the screen contents. We can use registers 0AH and 0BH, which control the starting and ending lines of the cursor.

The assembly language routine first reads the contents of register 0AH before it loads any value into this register. After a short pause so the CRTC can react to the output, the contents of this register are read back. Before the value read is compared to the original value, the old value is first written back into the register so the screen is disturbed as little as possible. If the comparison is positive, then a CRTC is present and so is the video card (CGA in this case). The CGA routine responds by loading the code for a color monitor into the array because this is the only type of monitor that can be used with a CGA card.

Monochrome test

The last test is the monochrome test, which also checks for the existence of a CRTC; except this time port address 3B4H is checked. If it finds a CRTC there, then a monochrome card is installed and we must determine whether it's an MDA or HGC card. The status registers of the two cards, at port address 3BAH, are used to determine this. Since bit 7 of this register is meaningless on the MDA card, its value is undefined. However, it contains a 1 on an HGC card whenever the electron beam is returning across the screen. Since this isn't permanent and occurs only at intervals of about two milliseconds, the contents of this bit constantly alternate between 0 and 1.

Hercules

The test routine first reads the contents of this register and masks out bits 0 to 6. The resulting value is used in a maximum of 32,768 loop passes, in which the value is read again and compared with the original value. If the value changes, which means the state of bit 7 changes, then an HGC card is probably installed. If this bit doesn't change over the course of 32768 loop passes, then an MDA card is being used.

Again, we place the appropriate code for the video card in the array. The monitor code is also set to monochrome, since this is the only monitor that can be connected to an MDA card or an HGC card.

Primary and secondary video systems

The tests are now complete. Next we must determine which card is active (primary) and which is inactive (secondary). If the outcome of the VGA test was positive, we can skip this because the VGA BIOS routine determines the active card automatically.

In other instances, we can determine the active video card from the current video mode, which can be read with the help of function 0FH of the BIOS video interrupt. If the value seven is returned, then the 80x25 text mode of the monochrome card is active. All the other modes indicate that a CGA, EGA or VGA card is active. This information is used to exchange the order of the two entries in the array if it doesn't match the actual situation.

The assembly language routine returns control to the calling program.

We've included C and Pascal programs that call the function GetVIOS from the assembly language module and demonstrate how GetVIOS works. You'll find the source code and programs and modules on the companion CD-ROM.

You'll find the following program(s) on the companion CD-ROM

VIOSP.PAS (Pascal listing)
VIOSPA.ASM (Assembler listing)
VIOSPC.C (C listing)

Anatomy Of A Video Card

Regardless of whether a card is an old MDA or the newest Super VGA card, all video cards operate under the same principles. Before we discuss each video standard in detail, we'll look at the general design of video cards. You'll learn how a monitor generates a video image and how to control the CRT controller. We'll also discuss the CRT controller's registers.

This section also contains information about video RAM and how you can use it for creating a video image. In addition, you'll learn the basics of video RAM programming.

Getting to the screen

The character generator first accesses video RAM and reads each characters individually. It uses a character pattern table to construct the bitmap that will later form the character on the screen. The attribute controller also receives information about the display attributes (color, underlining, reverse, etc.) of the character from the video RAM.

Both the character generator and the attribute controller prepare this information and send it to the signal controller. This controller converts the information to the appropriate signals, which are sent to the monitor. The signal controller itself is controlled by the CRT controller, which is the central point of video card operations. Besides the monitor and the video RAM, this CRT controller is one of the most important components of a video system. We'll discuss all these components in detail.

The monitor

The monitor is the device on which the video data is displayed. Unlike the video card, the monitor is a "dumb" device. This means that it has no memory and cannot be programmed. All monitors used with PCs are raster-scan devices, in which the picture consists of many small dots arranged in a rectangular pattern or raster.

When forming the picture, the electron beam of the picture tube touches each individual dot and illuminates it if it's supposed to be visible on the screen. This is done by switching on the electron beam as it passes over this dot, which causes a phosphor particle on the picture tube to light up.

Color monitors

While monochrome monitors need only one electron beam to create a picture, color monitors; use three beams that scan the screen simultaneously. Here a screen pixel consists of three phosphor particles in the basic colors of light: Red, green and blue. Each color has a matching electron beam. Any color in the spectrum can be created by combining these three colors and varying their intensities.

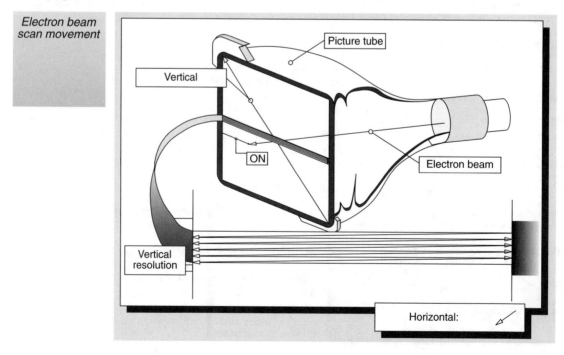

Electron beam
scan movement

However, since an ionized phosphor particle emits light for only a very brief period of time, the entire screen must be scanned many times per second to create the illusion of a stationary picture. PC monitors perform this task 50 to 70 times per second. This repeated re-scanning is called the *refresh rate*. Generally, the quality of the picture improves as the refresh rate increases.

Each new screen image begins in the upper-left corner of the screen. From there, the electron beam moves to the right along the first raster line. When it reaches the end of this line, the electron beam moves back to the start of the next line down, similar to pressing the [Return] key on a typewriter. The electron beam then scans the second raster line. At the end of this line it moves to the start of the next raster line, etc. Once it reaches the bottom of the screen, the electron beam returns to the upper-left corner of the screen and the process restarts. The illustration on page 96 shows the path of the electron beam.

Resolution on different monitor types		
Monitor	Raster lines	Raster columns
MDA/Hercules	350	720
CGA	200	640
EGA	350	640
VGA*	350	640
Super VGA*	600	800
Multisync	Varies to 800	Varies to 1200
*Available in monochrome and color versions		

Remember the video card and not the monitor, controls the movement of the electron beam. The resolution of the monitor naturally controls the number of raster lines and columns, which the electron beam scans when creating a display. So, a monitor that has only 200 raster lines of 640 raster columns each cannot handle the high resolutions of an EGA card at 640x350 pixels. The table on the left shows the resolutions on different monitor types used with a PC.

The CRT controller

The CRT controller or CRTC, is the heart of a video card. It controls the operation of the video card and generates the signals the monitor needs to create the image. Its tasks also include controlling light pens, generating the cursor and controlling the video RAM. To inform the monitor of the next raster line, the CRTC sends a display enable signal at the start of each line. This signal activates the electron beam. While the beam moves from left to right over each raster column of the line, the CRTC controls the individual signals for the electron beam(s) so the pixels appear on the screen as desired. At the end of the line, the CRTC disables the display enable signal so the electron beam's return to the next raster line doesn't produce a visible line on the screen. The electron beam is directed to the left edge of the following raster line by the output of a horizontal synchronization signal. The display enable signal is again enabled at the start of the next raster line and the generation of the next line begins.

Overscan

Since the time the electron beam needs to return to the start of the next line is less than the time the CRTC needs to receive and prepare new information from the video RAM, there is a short pause. However, the electron beam cannot be stopped, so overscan; occurs, which is visible as the left and right borders of the actual screen contents. Although this is an undesirable side effect, it's useful because it prevents the edges of the screen contents from being hidden by the edge of the monitor. If the electron beam is enabled while it's traveling over this border, a color screen border can be created.

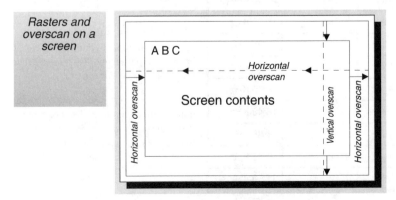

Rasters and overscan on a screen

Once the electron beam reaches the end of the last raster line, the display enable signal is disabled and a vertical synchronization signal is sent. The electron beam returns to the upper-left corner of the screen. Again the display enable signal is re-enabled and scanning begins again.

As with the horizontal electron beam return, a pause occurs. This pause is displayed in the form of overscan, which creates a vertical screen border.

The registers of the CRT controller

The timing of individual signals varies depending on the video mode. Therefore, the CRTC has numerous registers that describe the signal outputs and their timing. The structure of these registers and how they are programmed will be discussed in the remainder of this section. Many of these registers originate from the registers of the 6845 video controller from Motorola. This controller is used in the MDA, CGA and Hercules graphics cards. The EGA and VGA cards use a special VLSI (very large scale integration) chip as a CRTC and its registers are slightly more complicated. The techniques described here are intended as general descriptions for all video cards.

Motorola 6845 video controller registers		
Register	Meaning	Access
0CH	Starting address of screen page (high byte)	Write
0DH	Starting address of screen page (low byte)	Write
0EH	Character address of blinking screen cursor (high byte)	Read /Write
0FH	Character address of blinking screen cursor (low byte)	Read /Write
10H	Light pen position (high byte)	Read
11H	Light pen position (low byte)	Read

These registers, like all the other registers on the video card, are accessed using I/O ports with the assembly language instructions IN and OUT. Instead of being accessed directly from the address space of the processor, the registers of the CRTC are accessed through a special address register. The number of the desired CRTC register is written to the port corresponding to this address register. Then the contents of this register can be read into a special data register with the IN assembly language instruction. If a value must be written to the addressed register, it must be transferred to the data register with the OUT instruction. Then the CRTC automatically places it in the desired register. Although these two registers are actually found at successive port addresses, these addresses vary among video cards.

Monochrome video card port addresses are 3B4H and 3B5H and color card port addresses are 3D4H and 3D5H.

Throughout this chapter we've included tables to describe the contents of individual CRTC registers under the various video modes. The following example shows how the contents of these registers are calculated and how the individual registers are related to each other. If you try some of these calculations with your calculator or PC, you'll notice that some of them do not work out evenly. But since the registers of the CRTC hold only integer values, they will be rounded up or down.

The basis for the various calculations are the bandwidth and the horizontal and vertical scan rates of a monitor. As the following table shows, MDA, CG and Hercules cards operate with a single bandwidth, while EGA and VGA cards have two or more different bandwidths. Although Super VGA cards use normal VGA bands, they can operate with more bandwidths.

The bandwidths in the table on the left specify the number of points the electron beam scans per second. This is also called the *point rate* or *dot rate*.

The *vertical scan rate* specifies the number of screen refreshes per second, while the *horizontal scan rate* refers to the number of raster lines the electron beam scans per second.

Bandwidths and scan rates of different video cards				
Video card	Resolution	Bandwidth	Vertical scan rate	Horizontal scan rate
MDA	720 x 350	16.257 MHz	50 Hz	18.43 KHz
CGA	640 x 200	14.318 MHz	60 Hz	15.75 KHz
HGC	640 x 200	14.318 MHz	50 Hz	18.43 KHz
EGA	640 x 350	16.257 MHz	60 Hz	21.85 KHz
	640 x 200	14.318 MHz	60 Hz	15.75 KHz
	720 x 350	16.257 MHz	50 Hz	18.43 KHz
VGA	640 x 350	16.257 MHz	60 Hz	21.85 KHz
	640 x 200	14.318 MHz	60 Hz	15.75 KHz
	720 x 480	28.000 MHz	70 Hz	31.50 KHz

Starting with these values, let's practice calculating the individual CRTC register values for the 80x25 character text mode on a CGA card.

Occasionally you can determine the number of bands supported by a video card by looking at the circuitry of the card. The video card needs a quartz crystal for each bandwidth and for keeping the CRT controller as accurate as possible. You can easily identify the crystal components on the board by looking for a component or set of components that are silver instead of black. The timing rate should be printed on these crystals.

If you want to look at the Hercules card's graphics mode, you can activate it by directly accessing the different CRTC registers. Function 00H initializes these registers. However, it's interesting to look at the different values that apply to each CRTC register, such as the values needed to produce 80x25 character text mode on a CGA card.

Since a CGA card has an 8x8 character matrix, a screen resolution of 80x25 characters corresponds to a "graphic" resolution of 640x200 pixels. This mode amounts to a bandwidth of 14.318 MHz, a screen refresh frequency of 60 Hz and a horizontal scan rate of 15.740 KHz.

	Bandwidth	14.318 MHz
÷	Horizontal scan rate	15.570 KHz
	Pixels per line	919

To obtain the number of pixels (screen dots) per raster line, divide the bandwidth by the horizontal scan rate. Since the CRTC registers usually refer to the number of characters instead of pixels, this value must be converted to the number of characters per line. This is done by dividing the number of pixels per line by the width of the character matrix (see illustration on the left). This is eight pixels on the CGA card.

	Raster lines	262
÷	Pixels per character	8
	Lines per screen	32

This value, decremented by one, is placed in the first register of the CRTC and specifies the total number of characters per line. In the second register we load the number of characters that will actually be displayed per line. The 80x25 character text mode usually provides 80 characters.

The difference between the total and the number of characters actually displayed per line is the number of characters that can be displayed between the horizontal return and the overscan. In this instance, the difference is 34 characters.

The duration of the horizontal beam return must be entered in the fourth register of the CRTC. This register stores the number of characters that could be displayed during this time, rather than the actual time duration. The monitor specifications define this instead of the video card itself. Usually this number is between 5% and 15% of the total number of characters per line. A color monitor uses exactly ten characters.

This leaves 24 characters for the overscan (the horizontal screen border). The third CRTC register specifies how these characters are divided between the left and right screen borders. This register specifies the number of character positions that will be scanned before the horizontal beam return occurs. The BIOS specifies the value 90 here or after ten characters have been displayed for the screen borders. The remaining 14 characters are placed at the start of the next line and form the left screen border.

The calculations for the vertical data, the number of vertical lines, the position of the vertical synchronization signal, etc., follow a similar scheme. The first calculation is the number of raster lines per screen. This results from the division of the number of lines displayed per second by the number of screen refreshes per second:

Since the characters in CGA text mode are eight pixels high by eight pixels wide, again we divide by eight to obtain the number of text lines per screen.

This result must be decremented by 1 and loaded into the fifth CRTC register (resulting in 7). The seventh register receives the number of lines

	Pixels per line	919
÷	Pixels per character	8
	Characters per line	114
	Horizontal scan rate	15.750 KHz
÷	Screen refreshes	60 Hz
	Raster lines	262

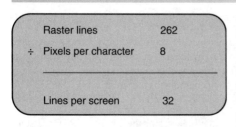

Raster lines	262
÷ Pixels per character	8
Lines per screen	32

to be displayed per screen (25). Seven lines less are displayed on the screen. So after overscan, the vertical rescan occurs after the 28th line.

The character height must be decremented by one and loaded into CRTC register 9. The decrement result is 7 in this example. This value also determines the range for the values loaded into registers 0AH and 0BH. They specify the first and last raster lines of the screen cursor. The cursor position is determined by the contents of registers 0EH and 0FH. They refer to the distance of the character from the upper-left corner of the screen, instead of line and column. This value is calculated by multiplying the cursor line by the number of columns per line and then adding the cursor column. The high byte of the result must be loaded into register 0EH and the low byte in register 0FH.

Structure of a video card

The CRT controller provides many tasks for screen design, but these tasks cannot work on their own. A video card consists of additional function levels which interact with the CRT controller. The following illustration shows the block diagram of a video card.

Block diagram of a video card

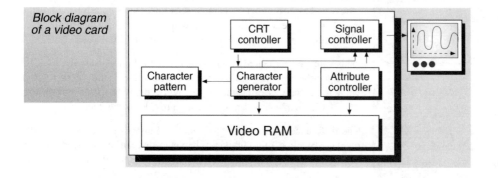

The video RAM is the most important starting point for creating a graphic. Video RAM is a memory range directly connected to the video card (more on this later). When the video card operates in text mode, video RAM contains the ASCII character codes and the character colors, while in graphic mode, video RAM is used to store individual pixels and the number of bits needed for colors.

Video RAM accessed the character generator and attribute controller from text mode. First, an instruction from the CRT controller loads a character from video RAM and generates the character from pixels. A ROM chip containing all the character patterns found in the ASCII character set converts the patterns into table form. The result of this conversion is then passed directly to the signal controller, which is driven by the CRT controller. This signal controller instructs the lines in the monitor cable to display the character pattern.

The signal controller and attribute controller prepare for output. In text mode, the CRT controller is responsible for conveying the character color and reading the signal controller. Although other orders aren't needed for graphics mode, the alternate structure of video RAM must be remembered.

If you look at an early video card, you'll see that it's easy to visually divide it into function units. One reason this is possible is because of the different ICs scattered around the card. Because of advances in miniaturization, almost all components in modern video cards can be packed into a single IC. This applies to EGA and VGA cards, which have a more complicated design than older cards, but still closely match the previous block diagram.

In the following sections we'll present detailed information about the design of specific video cards.

Video RAM

Video RAM is a location common to all video cards (from MDA to Super VGA), whether in text mode or graphics mode. Before you can directly program a graphics card (i.e., communicate with the card's ROM BIOS), you must know the design and position of video RAM. While video RAM is organized differently in different video cards when in graphics mode, the structure is virtually identical for all video cards in text mode.

In this section you'll learn about video RAM organization in different graphics modes. You'll find descriptions of different video cards, as well as how to set and read different graphics modes.

Video RAM in the PC's address space

You may already know that a PC's RAM doesn't always have to be on the motherboard: It can also exist on an expansion card. Video cards often use this expansion RAM as address space and video RAM. Although the video cards themselves are established, the video RAM found in a PC's address range isn't completely flexible. Much of this space is already committed to other tasks. Remember the early PCs had to store RAM, ROM and any system extensions into one megabyte. Video cards only need memory segments A and B, starting at segment addresses A000H and B000H, which requires only 64K.

For the user to use these features, both a monochrome card and color card must be running simultaneously. The B segment would be divided into two equal parts. Monochrome video cards (i.e., MDA and Hercules) use video RAM in the range B000:0000 to B000:7FFF. Color cards (i.e., CGA, EGA and VGA) use video RAM starting at B800:0000.

The locations of video RAM in EGA and VGA cards isn't always clear. For example, an MDA monitor can be connected to an EGA card and the EGA card will then emulate an MDA card. Then video RAM begins at B000H (which would also apply to an MDA) instead of B800H. The case is similar with VGA cards. You cannot connect an MDA monitor to a VGA card, but you can run a VGA monitor from the MDA. In either case, the video RAM begins at B000H.

However, a video card won't always use the entire 32K that's allocated for it. So, the MDA card uses only the first 4K of video RAM, the CGA card uses the first 16K (one half of the available address range) and the Hercules card uses 32K and may extend into the second half of the B segment. The range beginning at B800:0000 acts as the second screen page. Changing DIP switches on the video card may be required, if range B800:0000 is being used by a color card. Also, EGA and VGA cards use a large portion of video RAM. Generally, these cards use up to 256K of video RAM; most of the first 32K of the B segment is used frequently. Section 4.8.2 demonstrates how to access the remaining portion of video RAM.

Addressing video RAM

Since video RAM is part of the PC's normal address space, usually it can be accessed just like normal RAM. The entire video RAM can be read with a screen refresh rate of 70 times per second by different components of the video card, which generates a video image.

While this access isn't possible during an application or during ROM BIOS access, most video cards include options for avoiding memory conflict while accessing video RAM. The only exception is the older IBM CGA cards, which required some foresight in ROM BIOS or program access. (We'll discuss this in more detail in "The IBM Color/Graphics Adapter (CGA)" section later in this chapter.)

Video RAM structure in text mode

Most programs operate in text mode. However, some characters can be written directly to video RAM, regardless of the type of video card installed. Many programs, such as Lotus 1-2-3 and dBASE IV, use this option, with the help of equivalent BIOS functions. At the end of this section you'll find programs in Pascal and C. Both programs demonstrate direct access to video RAM in text mode. You could improve the speed even more by writing the code in assembly language. However, the routines are already quite fast. To understand how these routines work, you'll need a visual idea of how video RAM works, as demonstrated in the figure on the next page.

As you can see from the following illustration, in video RAM each screen position is represented as two bytes. The ASCII code of the character to be displayed is placed in the first of these two bytes (the one with the even address). By using eight bits per character code, a maximum of 256 characters can be displayed. See "The Video BIOS" section earlier in this chapter for more information on the PC character set.

The attribute byte (which defines the appearance of the character on the screen) follows the ASCII code. The attribute byte always appears at the odd offset address. The attribute controller subdivides this byte into two nibbles. The most significant nibble (bits 4 to 7) contains the character background and the least significant nibble (bits 0 to 3) describes the character foreground. These nibbles contain two values between 0 and 15, depending on the type of monitor involved. A color monitor (CGA or EGA) can display up to 16 possible colors on the screen. Each character has its own foreground and background.

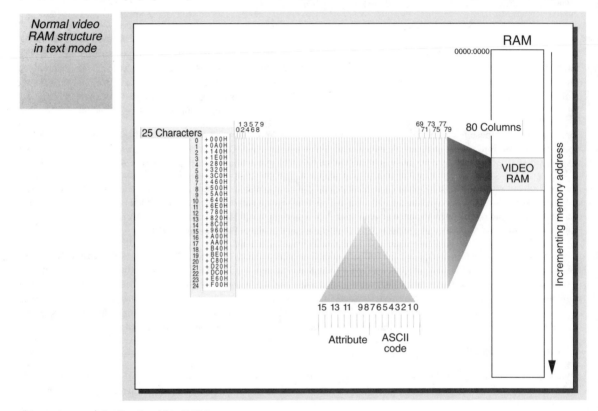

Normal video RAM structure in text mode

Character organization in video RAM

To access video RAM, you must know how the individual characters are organized within this memory. This organization is similar to character display on the screen.

The first character on the screen (the character in the upper-left corner) is also the first character in video RAM, located at offset position 0000H. The next character to the right is located at offset position 0002H. All 80 characters of the first screen line follow in this manner. Since each screen character requires two bytes of memory, each line occupies 160 bytes of RAM. The first character of the second screen line follows the last character of the first line, etc.

Finding character locations in video RAM

You can easily find the starting address of a line within video RAM by multiplying the line number (starting with zero) by 160. To get from the beginning of the line to a character within the line, the distance of the character from the start of the line must be added to this value. Since each character requires two bytes, this is done by simply multiplying the column number (also starting at zero) by two. Add both products together to obtain the offset position of the character in the video RAM. These calculations can be combined into a single formula:

```
Offset_position(row, column) = row * 160 + column * 2
```

The RAM memory of the video card is integrated into the normal RAM of the PC system, so you can use normal memory access commands to access video RAM. You must know the segment address of video RAM, which is used together with the previous formula to find the offset position. Later we'll show you how this can be done easily in assembly language, Pascal and C.

> **NOTE**
>
> Since only 40 characters per line are displayed in 40-column video modes, you must use the value 80 instead of 160.

Now that we've discussed the most important similarities between video cards, in the following sections we'll describe the capabilities of these cards. Also, we'll explain how these capabilities can be used for optimal screen output.

Extended text modes

CGA, EGA and VGA cards recognize more than 80x25 text mode. CGA cards also have 40x25 text mode and EGA and VGA cards have 80 character text mode with more than 25 lines. The standard for EGA is 43 lines and the standard for many VGA cards is 50 lines. We can also include tricks for displaying 43 lines on VGA. If that isn't sufficient, Super VGA cards have various text modes, with resolutions of up to 132x80 characters.

However, these modes don't affect the video RAM structure. The more lines that we want displayed, the more calculations are involved in the offset address for adapting a character to video RAM. It should be sufficient to adapt a factor of 160, change the line width to characters and multiply that number by 2. However, 40x25 character text mode on a CGA card should use a factor of 80 instead of 160.

Occasionally, you won't have to program the video card. For example, a program run from DOS will usually start in 80x25 character text mode.

Access to different screen pages

As we mentioned, Hercules, CGA, EGA and VGA cards support multiple screen pages because video RAM offers much space for allocating a video page. To access multiple screen pages, use the formula discussed earlier and add the respective page to the offset address and starting offset.

We can organize the different screen pages in 40x25 text mode in 4K (4096 byte) units. Since a single screen page occupies 4000 bytes (80*25*2), 96 bytes are unused and ready for other applications. The offset formula for screen pages and 80x25 text mode is similar to the following:

```
Offset_position(column, row) = row * 160 + column * 2 + page * 4096
```

The first screen page contains a value of 0. Since the screen pages will be placed in 2K units, 40x25 text mode requires a factor of 2048 instead of 4096. If you're working with EGA and VGA text modes of 43 or 50 lines, then you must use a factor of 8K.

Demonstration programs

The following programs implement the above formula as a routine to transmit a string directly from video RAM to the screen. This is a small example, as many applications use multiple routines for direct video RAM access. These routines can include coloration of a screen range, storing screen contents in a window and restoring these contents later.

The three programs in BASIC, Pascal and C contain the same general components, but you'll notice there are some major differences in the way these programs are coded because of language differences.

You'll find the display routine itself, as well as an initialization routine for accessing the segment address of video RAM. The program determines whether a monochrome card or color card is installed in the system, by examining one of the BIOS variables (see Chapter 3). So at first glance, the video RAM segment address doesn't seem to have anything to do with it, because it contains the address of the CRTC address register. Upon closer examination, however, you will notice a direct connection between these two bits of information:

On monochrome cards this register is always located at port address 3B4H and the video RAM is always at segment address B000H. This connection between the port address of the address register and the segment address of the video RAM also applies to color cards, where the address register of the CRTC is always found at port address 3D4H and the video RAM is at segment address B800H. By determining the port address of the CRTC data register then, you find a statement about the segment address of the video RAM at the same time. Once you have determined this address, it is placed in a global variable and the initialization routine ends.

Along with this routine, all three programs have the actual output routine, which uses the segment address previously determined to access the video RAM. On top of that, the routine determines the start address of the screen page being displayed on the screen every time it is called. This is supposed to guarantee the output also appears on the screen and is not redirected to a screen page that doesn't get displayed on the screen. The routine also uses a variable from the BIOS variable area. The variable CRT_START is located at the address 0040:004E and registers the offset address of the displayed screen page relative to the first screen page at offset address 0000H.

After determining this address, the video RAM can finally be accessed. However, if this is done within the program, it is dependent on the particular language to a great extent. Let's take a look at the programs.

The BASIC implementation

The BASIC version of this program performs the required task. The execution of this program is slow, because of the alternative means of display. However, this program is a good example of how BASIC can take full advantage of the 80x86 memory system. DEF SEG, PEEK and POKE perform much of this memory access.

While DEF SEG always defines the segment address of the "current" 64K segment, PEEK and POKE lets you read the contents of a byte (PEEK) and write new contents to a byte (POKE). The InitDPrint routine uses this technique to define the current segment as the BIOS variable segment. After defining the segment, two PEEK commands read the port address of the CRTC address register and changes the contents of the VSEG variable to the segment address of video RAM.

Once the current video RAM segment is defined, the offset address of video RAM must be defined as well. From this address the program takes the screen page from the BIOS variable range and adds this page to the offset of the display position within video RAM. The row coordinates (the ScRow% variable) are multiplied by 160 and the column coordinates (the Column% variable) are multiplied by 2.

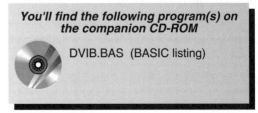

You'll find the following program(s) on the companion CD-ROM

DVIB.BAS (BASIC listing)

The Pascal implementation

The ABSOLUTE statement and assembler routines allow Turbo Pascal to handle video RAM as a normal variable. Turbo Pascal provides a simpler method.

Turbo Pascal's MEM and MEMW functions allow Turbo to access memory ranges with known offset and segment addresses outside the Turbo Pascal data segment MEM handles bytes, while MEMW handles words. The two arrays are virtual (i.e., they don't really exist) and cover the entire memory range.

Values can be read from and written to these arrays, using the following syntax:

```
MEMW[ Segmentaddr. : Offsetaddr. ] := Expression
```

or

```
Variable := MEMW[ Segmentaddr. : Offsetaddr. ]
```

We use the MEM array in a display procedure which takes converted ASCII characters and a constant attribute. The DPrint procedure uses the MEMW array, as one 16-bit access on a 16-bit PC runs much more quickly than two consecutive 8-bit accesses on the same machine.

The MEMW array in DPrint takes the video RAM segment address from the VSeg variable initialized at the beginning of the program in the InitDPrint procedure. This procedure checks the contents of the BIOS variable contained in the port address of the CRTC address register. This is declared like other BIOS variables, called from within DPrint. Turbo's ABSOLUTE function prepares both variables, then handles them as global variables.

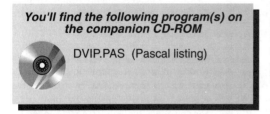

You'll find the following program(s) on the companion CD-ROM

DVIP.PAS (Pascal listing)

During DPrint's access to video RAM, the screen page number and coordinates are taken from the offset address of the MEMW array. From this information, the row coordinates are multiplied by 160 and the column coordinates are multiplied by 2. The string being processed is incremented by 2, shifting the paired ASCII attribute bytes to the right.

The Write statement and corresponding procedures write the text to the screen, provided the Crt unit is linked to the program and provided that DIRECTVIDEO is not set to FALSE.

The C implementation

This is the neatest of the three solutions, because the video RAM is treated as a normal variable. First, the VELB structure is defined, which describes the ASCII attribute pair as found in the video RAM. A new data type called VP is formed as pointers to this structure. It is important these be FAR type pointers, since these structures are within the video RAM, placing them outside of the C data segment. It is impossible to reach them in smaller memory models with their NEAR addressing without explicitly specifying the command word FAR.

The VPTR global variable within the INIT_DPRINT initialization routine is created as a pointer to the first ASCII attribute pair in page 0 of the video RAM. Within the actual output routine, it serves the DPRINT function as a basis for addressing the characters within the video RAM.

The LPTR pointer is loaded in the DPRINT output function with the address of the passed output position in the screen. First, the pointer is loaded with the contents of the VPTR global variable, with the offset address of the displayed screen page (from the variables in the BIOS region) being added to it.

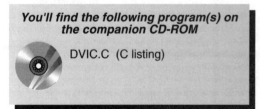

You'll find the following program(s) on the companion CD-ROM

DVIC.C (C listing)

Don't forget the LPTR pointer must first be cast in a BYTE pointer, since the contents of the BIOS variables don't refer to the VELB structure, but rather to Byte. Without the appropriate CAST operator, the C compiler would generate a code that multiplied the contents of the BIOS variables by the length of the VELB structure (2 bytes) before the addition, giving us the wrong result.

The actual output position, transmitted to the DPRINT function in the form of a Y- and an X-coordinate, must be added to the pointer. The video RAM is viewed as a kind of vector, whose 2000 components consist of the VELP structure. Since you have already determined the base address of this vector in LPTR, all that's left is to determine the index in this vector. Multiply the X-coordinate times 80 (columns per line) and then add the Y-coordinate. As an end result, you get a pointer to the output position in the video RAM, which can be treated like any other C pointer.

This pointer executes the specified string by pointing to the next VELB structure on each loop run. On each execution of the loop, the next ASCII attribute pair is placed in video RAM. The DPRINT function writes the ASCII code and character color to the specified string. This process repeats until the last character in the string is reached.

The IBM Monochrome Display Adapter (MDA)

The IBM Monochrome Display Adapter (or simply, MDA) is probably the oldest video card. This card is based on the Motorola 6845 video controller, which is an intelligent peripheral chip. The 6845 controller constructs a display by generating the proper signals for the monitor from video RAM.

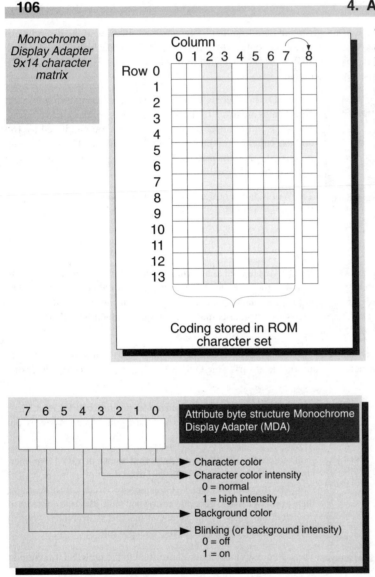

Monochrome Display Adapter 9x14 character matrix

Coding stored in ROM character set

This card is excellent for text display because of its 9x14 character matrix, which permits high resolution character display. The format of this matrix is unusual since a character generator containing the bit pattern of each character can only produce characters that are 8 pixels wide. Characters from the IBM character set may not connect with each other (e.g., using box characters to draw a box). A circuit on the graphics card avoids this problem by copying the eighth pixel of the line into the ninth pixel for any characters whose ASCII codes are between B0H and DFH. This enables the horizontal box drawing characters to connect.

The character generator requires one byte for each screen line: one bit per pixel, eight bits per line. Each character requires 14 bytes. The complete character set has a memory requirement of almost 4K, which is stored in a ROM chip on the card. For some reason the card has an 8K ROM, so the second bank of 4K remains unused.

Video RAM on the MDA

The video RAM of the card starts at address B000:0000 and extends over 4K (4,096 bytes). Since the screen display only has space for 2,000 characters and requires only 4,000 bytes of memory for those characters, the unused 96 bytes at the end of video RAM are available for other applications.

The illustration on the left shows the meanings of the different values representing the attribute byte.

7	6	5	4	3	2	1	0

Attribute byte structure Monochrome Display Adapter (MDA)

➤ Character color
➤ Character color intensity
  0 = normal
  1 = high intensity
➤ Background color
➤ Blinking (or background intensity)
  0 = off
  1 = on

Any combination of bits can be loaded into this byte. However, the MDA only accepts the following combinations:

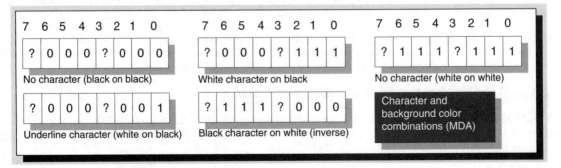

7	6	5	4	3	2	1	0
?	0	0	0	?	0	0	0

No character (black on black)

7	6	5	4	3	2	1	0
?	0	0	0	?	1	1	1

White character on black

7	6	5	4	3	2	1	0
?	1	1	1	?	1	1	1

No character (white on white)

7	6	5	4	3	2	1	0
?	0	0	0	?	0	0	1

Underline character (white on black)

7	6	5	4	3	2	1	0
?	1	1	1	?	0	0	0

Black character on white (inverse)

Character and background color combinations (MDA)

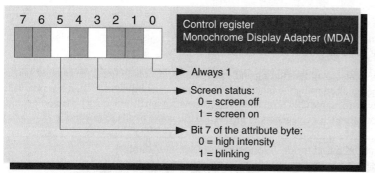

Besides these bit combinations, bits 3 and 7 of the attribute byte can be set or unset. Bit 3 defines the intensity of the foreground display. When this bit is set, the characters appear in higher intensity. Bit 7's purpose varies with the contents of the control registers (more on this later). For now, all you need to know is that bit 7 can either enable blinking characters or enable an intensity matching the background color.

The control register and the status register are also available for monochrome cards.

MDA control register

The MDA control register, which is located at port 3B8H, controls the monochrome display adapter's various functions. As the following figure shows, only bits 0, 3 and 5 are important. Bit 0 controls the resolution on the card. Although the card only supports one resolution (80x25 characters), this bit must be set to 1 during system initialization. Otherwise, the computer goes into an infinite wait loop. Bit 3 controls the creation of a visible display on the monitor. If bit 3 is set to 0, the screen is black and the blinking cursor disappears. If bit 3 is set to 1, the display returns to the screen. Bit 5 has a similar function.

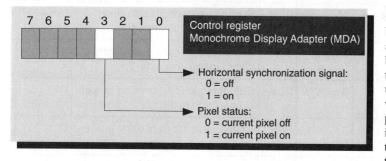

If bit 7 in the attribute byte of the character is set to 1, it enables blinking characters. If bit 7 contains the value 0, the character appears, unblinking, in front of a light background color. This means that bit 7 of the attribute byte acts as an intensity bit for the background. This register can only be written. This makes it impossible for a program to determine whether the display is switched on or off. The normal value for this register is 29H, which indicates that all three relevant bits default to 1.

MDA status register

Only bits 0 and 3 are used in the MDA status register; all the other bits must contain the value 1. Unlike the control register, programs can read this register, but register contents cannot be changed by program code.

Horizontal synchronization

Bit 0 indicates whether a horizontal synchronization signal is being sent to the screen. The video card sends this signal after creating a screen line (which is different than a text line, which consists of 14 screen lines) on the screen. This signal informs the electron gun, which "draws" the picture on the screen, that it should return to the left border of the current screen line. In this case, the bit has the value 1. Bit 3 contains the value of the pixel where the electron beam is currently located. A 1 signals the pixel is visible on the screen and 0 indicates the screen remains black at this location.

Accessing the CRT controller

The 6845's address register in the MDA card lies at port address 3B4H and the data register lies at port address 3B5H. Although these exist as consecutive port addresses, the number of registers to be addressed and the new contents of this register aren't output through port 3B4H by a 16-bit OUT instruction (this is the case with the other video cards). Also, the output must follow with the help of two 8-bit OUT instructions, between which a brief (5 or 6 cycles) pause is added to give the CRTC a chance to react to the output in the address register. Within an assembly language program, this pause executes and, after the OUT instruction, is followed by a jump instruction.

```
JMP $+2
```

The transfer of program execution to the instructions that follow takes some time, but doesn't change the actual program execution. This time can be used by the CRTC to prepare access to the desired register.

Programming the CRTC register on this card consists of the starting and ending line of the blinking cursor and its position on the screen. These tasks can be easily accomplished using the function 10H sub-functions from the BIOS interrupts. This keeps hardware calls to a minimum. If you want to juggle CRTC registers and create different displays, such as an 81 column or 26 line screen, you can do this by manipulating CRTC registers in the MDA card while in 80x25 text mode.

CRTC registers in 80x25 text mode (Monochrome Display Adapter)					
Reg.	Meaning	Content	Reg.	Meaning	Content
00H	Total horizontal character	7	09H	Number of scan lines per screen line	13
01H	Display horizontal character	80	0AH	Starting line of blinking screen cursor	11
02H	Horizontal synchronization signal after ...char	82	0BH	Ending line of blinking screen cursor	12
03H	Duration of horiz. synchronization signal in char	15	0CH	Starting address of displayed screen page (high byte)	0
04H	Total vertical character	25	0DH	Starting address of displayed screen page (low byte)	0
05H	Adjust vertical character	6	0EH	Character addr. of blinking screen cursor (high byte)	0
06H	Display vertical character	25	0FH	Character addr. of blinking screen cursor (low byte)	0
07H	Vertical synchronization signal after ...char	25	10H	Light pen position (high byte)	*
08H	Interlace mode	2	11H	Light pen position (low byte)	*
*not available on MDA					

You'll find the following program(s) on the companion CD-ROM

VMONO.ASM (Assembler listing)

The VMONO.ASM program which you'll find on the companion CD-ROM uses all the Monochrome Display Adapter's capabilities. It was written in assembly language.

The individual routines are completely documented and require no additional explanation. The demonstration program that's built into the listing demonstrates some practical ways to use the individual routines.

The Hercules Graphics Card (HGC)

In 1982, only a year after the IBM PC was released, Hercules Computer Technology made their contribution to the PC market by releasing the Hercules Graphics Card or HGC. Until then, only two video systems existed for the IBM: the MDA card for reading only text and the CGA for graphics display and fuzzy text. The Hercules card was intended for excellent text and graphics display. This card can drive a normal monochrome monitor in 80x25 text mode, with a 720x348 pixel graphics mode. The Hercules Graphics Card was an immediate success.

Non-BIOS support

Since the IBM BIOS supports only the MDA and CGA cards, the Hercules card isn't supported by BIOS. This doesn't present a problem in text mode because the Hercules text mode is completely compatible with the MDA card. However, this non-support is noticeable in graphics mode because in this mode BIOS functions cannot set or read pixels. In this chapter you'll find some assembly language routines that solve these problems.

Video RAM on a Hercules Graphics Card

The Hercules card contains 64K of RAM, allowing it to operate in a memory intensive graphic mode. This RAM can be divided into two screen pages. Each of the two pages is 32K in length and can comprise either a text page requiring only 4K or a graphic page. The first screen page lies in the address range from B000:0000 to B000:7FFF. The second screen page follows, lying in the range from B000:8000 to B000:FFFF. Since this range matches those normally used by color video cards (CGA, EGA and VGA), this range can be adjusted by setting the DIP switches on the card. You can reconfigure the card to provide only one screen page.

Unlike the MDA card, you can communicate with the configuration register through port 3BFH. You can write to this port, but you cannot read from it. This register has two bits (0 and 1). Bit 0 specifies whether graphic mode is enabled (1) or disabled (0). Bit 1 specifies whether the second screen page is available (0 if not, 1 if so).

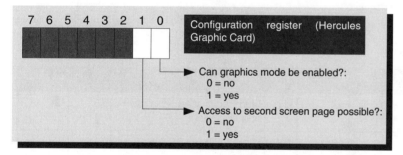

To avoid conflicts with other video cards (color cards) both bits must be set to 0 so a graphic won't be displayed and the second screen page won't be used. If you want a program with these features to continue accessing the card, the control register must be changed accordingly.

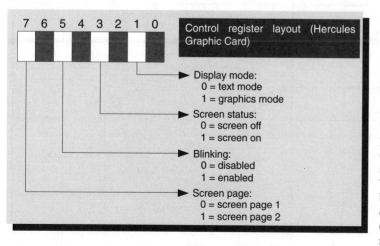

The control register of the Hercules card differs from the control register of the MDA, which we've discussed.

Unlike the IBM monochrome display adapter, bit 0 is unused and doesn't have to be set to 1 during the system boot. Bit 1 determines text or graphics mode: 0 enables text mode or 1 enables graphics mode. As you'll see in the following examples, changing these bits isn't enough for switching between text and graphics modes. The internal registers of the 6845 must also be reset. During this process, the screen display must be switched off to prevent the 6845 from creating garbage during its reprogramming.

The Hercules card has a seventh bit in this register. The contents of this bit determine which of the two screen pages appear on the screen. If this bit is 0, the first screen page appears and if it is 1, the second screen page appears. The user can write to or read from either page at any time. You can only write to this register; if you try to read this register, the value FFH is

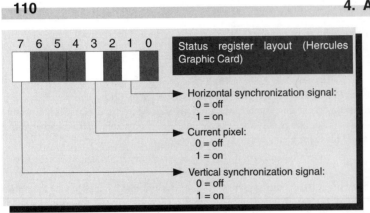

Status register layout (Hercules Graphic Card)

Horizontal synchronization signal:
0 = off
1 = on

Current pixel:
0 = off
1 = on

Vertical synchronization signal:
0 = off
1 = on

returned. Because of this, it's impossible to switch off the display simply by reading the contents of the status register and erasing bit 3, regardless of the display mode and the screen page selected.

Unfortunately, the control register cannot be read. This means that you won't know the card's current mode or when the card has initialized itself. This is a serious problem in TSR programs.

Unlike the MDA card, the meaning of bit 7 in the Hercules status register has changed. In the Hercules card this bit always contains a 0 when the 6845 sends a vertical synchronization signal to the screen, to generate a new screen structure.

The Hercules CRT controller

Similar to the MDA and CGA cards, the Hercules Graphics Card has a 6845 CRT controller as its main processor. Its address register is at port address 3B4H and its data register is at port address 3B5H. Unlike the MDA, the Hercules CRTC can be accessed by loading a 16-bit OUT instruction with the contents of the AX register. The output follows through the address register, where the processor register AL must contain the number of CTRC registers to be addressed and the AH register must contain the new contents of these registers. The following table lists the values that must be loaded into individual registers to initialize text or graphics mode.

No.	Meaning	Text	Graphic	No.	Meaning	Text	Graphic
0H	Total horizontal character	97	53	9H	Number of scan lines per line	13	3
1H	Horizontal character displayed	80	45	AH	Starting line of blinking cursor	11	0
2H	Horiz. synchronization signal after character	82	46	BH	Ending line of the blinking cursors	12	0
3H	Horiz. synchronization signal width	15	7	CH	High byte of screen page starting address	0	0
4H	Total vertical character	25	91	DH	Low byte of screen page starting address	0	0
5H	Vertical character justified	6	2	EH	High byte of blinking cursor char. address	0	0
6H	Vertical character displayed	25	87	FH	Low byte of blinking cursor char. address	0	0
7H	Vert. synchronization signal after character	25	87	10H	Light pen position (high byte)	?	?
8H	Interlace mode	2	2	11H	Light pen position (low byte)	?	?
? = depends on light pen's position							

Starting and programming graphics mode

You cannot switch to graphics mode using BIOS, although text mode automatically starts on bootup through the BIOS.

As we mentioned, the Hercules card in graphics mode provides 348x720 resolution. Each pixel on the screen corresponds to one bit in the video RAM. If the corresponding bit contains the value 1, the dot is visible on the screen; otherwise it remains hidden. The following illustration shows how video RAM is arranged in graphics mode.

Arrangement of video RAM in graphics mode

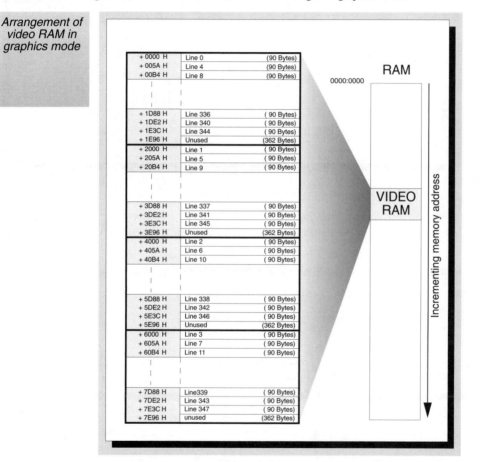

The bit patterns of the individual lines in the video RAM aren't arranged sequentially. Instead, the 32K of video RAM is divided into four 8K blocks. The first block contains the bit pattern for any lines divisible by 4 (0, 4, 8, 12, etc.). The second block contains the bit patterns for lines 1, 5, 9, 13, etc. The third block contains the bit patterns for lines 2, 6, 10, 14, etc. and the last block contains lines 3, 7, 11, 15, etc.

When the 6845 generates a display, it obtains information for screen line zero from the first data block and screen line one from the second data block, etc. After it has obtained the contents of the third screen line from the fourth data block, it accesses the first data block again for the structure of the fourth line. Each line requires 90 bytes within the individual data blocks and each pixel requires a bit (720 pixels divided by 8 bits (per byte) equals 90). The first 90 bytes in the first memory area provide the bit pattern for screen line zero and the next 90 bytes provide the bit pattern for the fourth screen line. The zero byte of one of these 90-byte sets represents the first eight columns of a screen line (columns 0-8). The first byte represents columns 8-15, etc. Within one of these bytes, bit 7 corresponds to the left screen pixel and bit 0 corresponds to the right screen pixel.

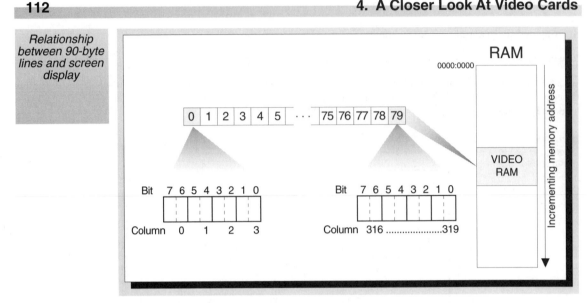

Relationship between 90-byte lines and screen display

If the screen pixels of a line (0 to 719) and the screen pixels of a column (0 to 347) are sequentially numbered, an equation indicates the address of the bytes relative to the beginning of the screen page. This address contains the information for a pixel with the coordinates X/Y.

To determine the bit within the byte that represents the pixel, the following formula can be used:

```
Address = 2000H * (Y mod 4) + 90 * int(Y/4) + int(X/8)
```

To send the number of desired bits within this byte, use the following formula:

```
Bitnumber = 7 - (X mod 8)
```

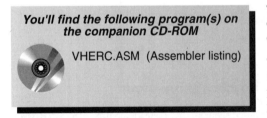

You'll find the following program(s) on the companion CD-ROM

VHERC.ASM (Assembler listing)

The VHERC.ASM program which you'll find on the companion CD-ROM demonstrates the capabilities of the Hercules Graphics Card.

The individual routines within this program differ from the routines in the Monochrome Display Adapter demo program from the previous section. The routines here enable access to both screen pages and support the Hercules graphics mode.

The IBM Color/Graphics Adapter (CGA)

Similar to the MDA card, the CGA card was introduced in the early days of the PC. It was the standard for graphics output for many years until the EGA card replaced it. Unlike any other card, you cannot access the video RAM without the help of the CRT controller, without causing grainy pictures or snow.

CGA text modes

The CGA card recognizes two text modes, which comprise 40x25 characters and 80x25 characters. In reference to the video BIOS initialization function, these modes are assigned codes 1 (40x25) and 3 (80x25). These modes include two variants, which let you select the foreground and background colors from a palette of 16 colors. BIOS modes 0 (40x25) and 2 (80x25) send no color signal to the monitor, where the color codes are automatically converted to gray scales.

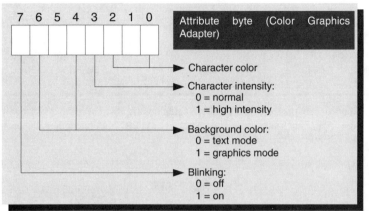

Each 80x25 text page requires 4,000 bytes of video RAM. 16K allows a total of four text pages. The first page starts at address B800:0000, the second at B800:1000, the third at B800:2000 and the last at B800:3000. The 40x25 mode allows storage of eight screen pages because, in this mode, each screen page only requires 2,000 bytes. The first screen page starts at address B800:0000, the second at B800:0800 and the third at B800:1000.

Attribute bytes

The lower four bits of the attribute byte indicate one of the 16 available colors. The meanings of the upper four bits depend on whether blinking is active. If it's active, bits 4 to 6 indicate the background color (taken from one of the first eight colors of the color palette), while bit 7 determines whether the characters blink. If blinking is disabled, bits 4 to 7 indicate the background color (taken from one of the 16 available colors).

Color/Graphics Adapter color palette							
Dec	Hex.	Binary	Color	No.	Meanin	Text	Graphics
0	00H	0000(b)	Black	8	08H	1000(b)	Dark gray
1	01H	0001(b)	Blue	9	09H	1001(b)	Light blue
2	02H	0010(b)	Green	10	0AH	1010(b)	Light green
3	03H	0011(b)	Cyan	11	0BH	1011(b)	Light cyan
4	04H	0100(b)	Red	12	OCH	1100(b)	Light red
5	05H	0101(b)	Magenta	13	0DH	1101(b)	Light magenta
6	06H	0110(b)	Brown	14	0EH	1110(b)	Yellow
7	07H	0111(b)	Light gray	15	0FH	1111(b)	White

Graphics modes

The CGA supports three different graphics modes, of which only two are normally used. The color-suppressed mode; displays 160x100 pixels with 16 colors. The 6845 supports this resolution, but the rest of the hardware doesn't offer color-suppressed mode support. The remaining two graphic modes have resolutions of 320x200 and 640x200 respectively. The 320x200 resolution permits four-color graphics, while 640x200 resolution only allows two colors.

320x200 resolution

The CGA uses all 16K of its video RAM for displaying a graphic in 320x200 resolution with four colors. This limits the user to one screen page at a time. Of the four colors permitted, the background can be selected from the 16 available colors. The other three colors originate from one of the two user-selected color palettes, which contain three colors each.

Palette 1:	Color 1	Cyan	Palette 2	Color 1	Red
	Color 2	Violet		Color 2	Green
	Color 3	White		Color 3	Yellow

Since a total of four colors are available, each screen pixel requires two bits. Four bits can represent the color numbers (0 to 3). The following values correspond to the various colors:

0	00(b) = freely selectable background color	1	01(b) = color 1 of the selected palette	2	10(b) = color 2 of the selected palette	3	11(b) = color 3 of the selected palette

The video RAM assignment in this mode is similar to that of the Hercules card during graphics display. The individual graphic lines are stored in two different blocks of memory. The first block, which begins at address B800:0000, contains the even lines (0, 2, 4...); the second block, which begins at B800:2000, contains odd lines (1,3,5).

Arrangement of video RAM in graphics mode (blocking)

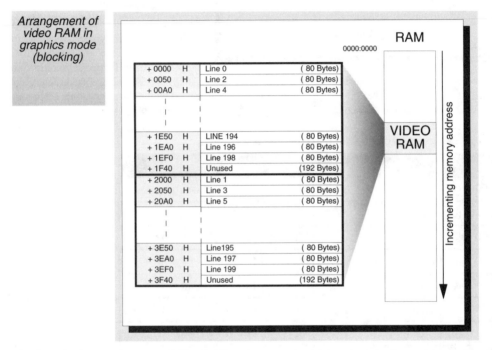

The desired palette can be accessed either by direct programming of the color selection registers or by calling a special BIOS function (interrupt 10H, function 0BH, sub-function 01H). Load the AH register with the function number (0BH), the BH register with the sub-function (01H) and the BL register with the number of the desired palette (0 or 1).

Each graphic line within the two blocks requires 80 bytes, since the 320 pixels in a line are coded into four pixels to a byte. The first byte in a graphic line (an 80-byte series) corresponds to the first four dots of the graphic on the screen. Bits 7 and 8 contain the color information for the leftmost pixel, while bits 0 and 1 contain the color information for the rightmost pixel of the byte.

With this information, you can derive a formula for determining the byte in video RAM, similar to the Hercules card. This byte is relative to the starting address of the screen page, which contains the color information for a pixel. The screen column (0-319) is designated as X and the screen line (0-199) as Y:

```
Address = 2000H * (Y mod 2) + 80 * int(Y/2) + int(X/4)
```

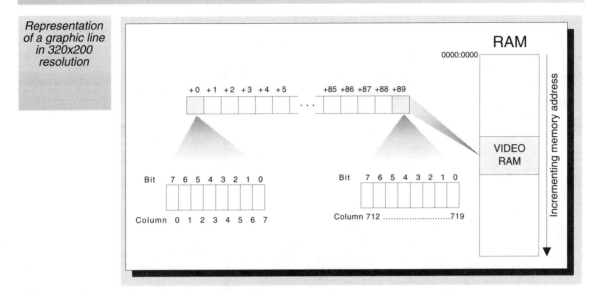

Representation of a graphic line in 320x200 resolution

To determine the number of the two bits within this byte that represents the pixel, use the following formula:

```
Bit number = 6 - 2 * (X mod 4)
```

For example, if this formula returns 4, the color information for the dot is coded into bits 4 and 5. The 320x200 pixel graphics mode can also suppress the color signal, converting colors to gray scales using mode code 5.

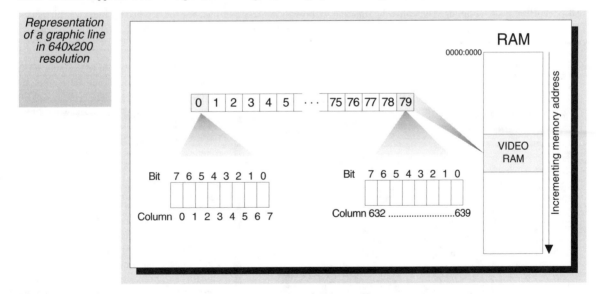

Representation of a graphic line in 640x200 resolution

640x200 resolution

The 640x200 pixel mode (BIOS code 6) is similar to the 320x200 pixel mode previously described. The doubled resolution makes only one bit per graphic pixel available, limiting the display to two colors. However, this mode has both odd and open lines in two different memory blocks and the width of a graphic line in video RAM is 80 bytes. Addressing a pixel is identical to the 320x200 pixel mode.

```
Address = 2000H * (Y mod 2) + 80 * int(Y/2) + int(X/8)
Bit_number = 7 - (X mod 8)
```

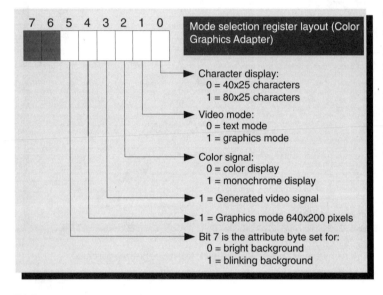

CGA registers

The CGA has a selection register at address 3D8H, which is comparable with the control register of the monochrome display adapter. You can write to this register but you cannot read it. Pixels that represent bits with values of 0 appear in this mode as black pixels. However, if a bit is set, the corresponding pixel appears on the screen as coded in one of the bottom four bits of the color selection register (more on this register later).

The desired color can be implemented without direct programming using a video BIOS function (interrupt 10H, function 0BH, sub-function 00H). Place the function number (0BH) in the AH register, the sub-function (00H) in the BH register and the color (0 to 15) in the BL register.

Bit layout

Bit 0 of this register determines the text mode display of 80 or 40 columns per line. A 1 in bit 0 displays 80 columns, while a 0 in bit 0 displays 40 columns. The following illustration shows how these bits must be programmed to obtain certain modes. The status of bit 1 switches the CGA from text mode to the 320x200 bit-mapped graphics mode. A 1 in this register selects graphics mode, while a 0 selects text mode.

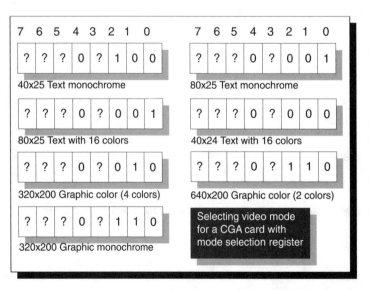

Bit 2 is useful if you want to use your CGA with a monochrome monitor. If this bit contains the value 1, the 6845 suppresses the color signal, displaying monochrome mode only. Bit 3 is responsible for creating screens. If this bit contains the value 0, the screen remains black. This suppression is useful when changing between display modes; it prevents sudden signals, which could cause damage, from reaching the monitor.

Bit 4 enables and disables 640x200 bitmapped graphics mode. A 1 in bit 4 enables this mode, while a 0 disables it. Bit 5 has the same significance as in the monochrome card. If it contains a 0, blinking stops and bit 7 returns one of the 16 available background colors. This bit contains a default value of 1, which causes blinking characters.

The various text or graphics modes and the color or monochrome display can be selected in these modes with this register. Bits 0, 1, 2 and 4 are used for this for purpose.

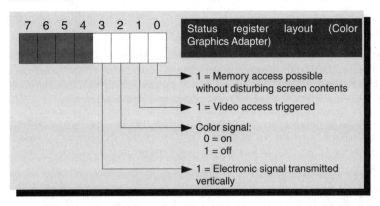

Status register layout (Color Graphics Adapter)

► 1 = Memory access possible without disturbing screen contents

► 1 = Video access triggered

► Color signal:
0 = on
1 = off

► 1 = Electronic signal transmitted vertically

The CGA also has a status register; similar to the status register in the monochrome display adapter. The illustration on the left shows the construction of this register, which can be found at address 3DAH. It's a read-only register.

Bit 0 of this register always contains the value 1 when the 6845 sends a horizontal synchronization signal to the monitor. This signal is transmitted when the creation of a line ends and the CRT's electron beam reaches the end of the screen line. The electron beam then jumps back to the left corner of the screen line. This bit is significant because the CGA doesn't always allow data reading or writing within video RAM.

Flickering and the CGA

Flickering occurs because the 6845 must continuously access video RAM to read its contents for screen display. If a program tries to transmit data to video RAM, problems can arise when the 6845 accesses video RAM simultaneously. The result of this memory conflict is an occasional flickering on the screen.

To avoid this problem, you should only access video RAM when the 6845 isn't accessing it. This only occurs when a horizontal synchronization signal travels to the screen because it needs some time until the electron beam has executed this instruction. Therefore, the status register must be read before every video RAM access on a CGA. This process must be repeated until bit 0 contains the value 1. When this happens, a maximum of two bytes can then be transmitted to video RAM.

Demonstration program

The program at the end of this section demonstrates how this process works. This delay in video RAM access doesn't occur with monochrome cards because they are equipped with special hardware logic and fast RAM chips. This is also true of most of the newer model color cards. Before waiting for the horizontal synchronization signal, which results in a delay of the display output, the user should try direct access to video RAM to test the color card's reaction time.

If many accesses to video RAM occur within a short period of time (e.g., scrolling the screen), the electron beam doesn't respond fast enough. The screen should be switched off using bit 3 of the mode selection register. This prevents the 6845 from accessing video RAM, which allows unlimited user access to video RAM. When data transfer ends, the screen can be switched on again. BIOS uses this method during scrolling, which results in the flickering "strobe effect".

Color selection register

The color selection register is located at address 3D9H. This register is write-only (cannot be read). The meanings of the individual bits in this register depend on the display mode. Text mode uses the lowest four bits for assigning the background color from the 16 available colors. In 320x200 graphics mode, these four bits indicate the color of all pixels represented by the bit combination 00(b) (background color).

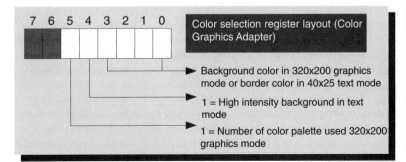

Color selection register layout (Color Graphics Adapter)

► Background color in 320x200 graphics mode or border color in 40x25 text mode

► 1 = High intensity background in text mode

► 1 = Number of color palette used 320x200 graphics mode

Synchronizing screen access

To minimize flickering, the CRT controller and video RAM must be synchronized. Bit 0 in the CGA card's status register helps you do this. If bit

0 contains a value of 1, the electron beam is performing a horizontal scan. If pixels aren't currently being displayed on the screen, the CRT controller isn't accessing video RAM. So, it can place a program in video RAM undisturbed.

To use this mechanism, every CGA access to video RAM should start with a short code sequence, consisting of two loops and end when the CRTC performs a horizontal rescan. The first loop reads the contents of the status register as long as a horizontal rescan doesn't occur (i.e., bit 0 contains 0). If this condition occurs, the second loop, which reads the contents of the status register, executes. This continues until bit 0 contains 1 and the system performs a horizontal rescan.

At first this procedure may seem very complicated. Although it's not immediately clear why the first loop waits for a horizontal rescan, it's important to know what happens when the rescan occurs. This loop ensures the second loop ends at the beginning of a horizontal retrace. If the first loop failed, then the second loop would end before it was supposed to end. However, then a conflict with the CRTC may occur during video RAM access.

Linking this routine doesn't guarantee access to video RAM because when the horizontal retrace ends, the video RAM access ends about 4 microseconds later. How many bytes can be transferred between video RAM and the processor in that time depends on the processor speed and other factors, such as data bus width. Let's see how this works on a basic PC with a system timer of 4.77 MHz. Exactly two bytes (an ASCII character and its attribute) can be transferred during the horizontal retrace.

In addition to horizontal retrace, you can also use the 7 millisecond pause during vertical retrace; to access video RAM. Up to 800 bytes can be transferred during this period. However, vertical retraces are much less frequent than horizontal retraces. So, the best method is to simply transfer data during horizontal retraces.

Both procedures hinder screen output. However, many CGA cards don't even need these procedures. When video RAM is available, it can be used by both the CRTC and the processor. Your program code should be constructed so the code sequence mentioned can be suppressed by a flag. Although the possibility of flickering caused by the card cannot be tested by the program itself, the user can be given the option of calling the program using a switch to control this flickering. You'll see how we did this in the demonstration program at the end of this section.

We can also minimize screen flickering by completely suppressing video RAM access. This method is successful only if multiple video RAM accesses can occur sequentially (e.g., when scrolling the screen). So, a program could suppress video RAM access until it called BIOS video interrupt functions 06H (scroll up) or 07H (scroll down). To realize this, bit 3 of the mode select register would have to be switched off before the access and switched on after the access. The result is a "strobe effect" that occurs during scrolling or other functions.

Bit 5 selects the color palette for 320x200 mode. If this bit contains the value 1, the first color palette (cyan, violet, white) is selected. A value of 0 selects the second color palette (green, yellow, red).

The CGA card's CRT controller

The CGA card uses the 6845 CRT controller from Motorola (see Section 4.4 for more information on this controller). This controller accesses the 18 internal registers exactly like the MDA card, using two consecutive 8-bit OUT instructions. A single 16-bit OUT instruction (used in Hercules cards) isn't permitted. Unlike the MDA, the CGA's registers are at port address 3D4H and 3D5H. The following table shows the contents of the CRT register in different display modes:

Reg.	Meaning	Txt	Txt	Grf	Reg.	Meaning	Txt	Txt	Grf
	CGA CRTC register contents in 40x25 text mode (Txt1), 80x25 text mode (Txt2) and graphics mode (Grfx)								
0H	Horiz. character total	56	11	56	9H	Number of scan lines per line	7	7	1
1H	Horiz. characters displayed	40	80	40	AH	Starting line of blinking cursor	6	6	6
2H	Horiz. synchronization signal to	45	90	45	BH	Ending line of blinking cursor	7	7	7
3H	Horiz. synchronization signal in chars.	10	10	10	CH	Screen page starting address (high byte)	0	0	0
4H	Vert. character total	31	31	12	DH	Screen page starting address (low byte)	0	0	0
5H	Vert. characters justified	6	6	6	EH	Cursor character address (high byte)	0	0	0
6H	Vert. characters displayed	25	25	10	FH	Cursor character address (low byte)	0	0	0
7H	Vert. synchronization signal to chars.	28	28	11	10H	Light pen position (high byte)	?	?	?
8H	Interlace mode	2	2	2	11H	Light pen position (low byte)	?	?	?
? = depends on light pen's position									

These registers are useful because they define the position and appearance of the cursor on the screen. In the "History And Highlights" section we described how to program these registers. The CGA adds registers 0CH and 0DH. These registers indicate the start of the video page, that must be displayed on the screen, as offset of the beginning of the 16K RAM on the card (B800:0000), divided by 2. Register 0CH contains the most significant 8 bits of this offset, while register 0DH contains the least significant 8 bits. Usually both registers contain the value 0, displaying the first screen page (beginning at the address B800:0000) on the screen. To display the first screen page, which begins at location B800:1000 in the 80x25 text mode, the value 1000H divided by 2 (800H) must be entered in both registers.

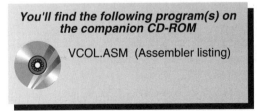

You'll find the following program(s) on the companion CD-ROM

VCOL.ASM (Assembler listing)

The VCOL.ASM demonstration program which you'll find on the companion CD-ROM accesses the Color/Graphics Adapter. The only significant difference between this program and the previous programs is the video controller can synchronize video RAM access and screen construction. This is necessary on all video cards where direct access to video RAM causes a flickering on the screen. The WAIT constant, defined directly after the program header, switches synchronization on or off. Its contents decide during the assembly of the program, whether to assemble the program lines for synchronization listed in the source listing. Since these lines would slow down the screen considerably, they should be included only if it's absolutely necessary.

EGA And VGA Cards

In this section we'll discuss the features of EGA and VGA cards that separate them from their predecessors. Later in this section we'll discuss sprites because EGA and VGA cards can be used in animation programming. The most important feature in text output is the ability to work with different fonts. We'll discuss both the 16 color and 256 color VGA graphics modes and some tricks you can use to double VGA resolution in 256 color mode.

Although IBM set the standards with its original EGA and VGA cards, the newer cards from third party manufacturers surpass the performance and capabilities of the originals. While all cards adhere to IBM standards, there still isn't a standard for the expanded modes with resolutions up to 1024x768 pixels. So, each manufacturer has its own idea of what works best. We'll discuss this in more detail later in this book, try to find some common features and suggest some ways you can use them.

The complexity of EGA/VGA cards makes the direct programming of different controllers and registers more complicated. Programming becomes even more involved when manufacturers don't adhere to the standards set by IBM. As you'll see in this section, you won't always have to rely on direct programming to fully use these cards. Instead, programming can access the special functions supported by the special EGA/VGA BIOS.

Some of the subsections describe how individual registers are programmed for performing certain tasks. The last section summarizes all standard functions of the EGA and VGA registers. This section also includes a listing of expanded EGA and VGA BIOS functions. Before programming a register, check references to ensure the appropriate EGA/VGA BIOS function actually exists.

Monitors and cards

The kind of monitor used can significantly affect the performance of an EGA or VGA card. If your video card's capabilities exceed the physical capabilities of your monitor, you won't get the 800x600 resolution and billions of colors that may have been advertised. You'll need a more sophisticated monitor to use all the capabilities of your video card.

This applies to all the applications using your EGA or VGA card. Matching the capabilities of the video card and monitor is extremely important.

First, you must determine whether the monitor is color or monochrome. There are several possibilities with EGA and VGA cards.

EGA monitors

An EGA card may be connected to a CGA, EGA, multisync or monochrome MDA monitor. Depending on the type of monitor connected, the card behaves like either a normal EGA card or like an expanded MDA card. Switching between these modes affects the internal registers of the EGA card and video RAM. In monochrome mode, video RAM begins at B000H instead of B800H. Also, the attribute bytes of the characters in video RAM are interpreted in monochrome mode as they are with an MDA card. The CRT controller's index and data registers change to conform to the MDA standard.

Since an EGA card connected to a monochrome monitor behaves like an MDA card, we won't discuss this configuration in detail. When we mention an EGA card, we're referring to an EGA card with a high resolution monitor attached. This is usually the case because many EGA compatible cards don't even support monochrome monitors, even though the original IBM EGA card offered such support. Compatible cards work only with EGA or multisync monitors.

Another accessory that has almost vanished is the IBM EGA card with 64K of video RAM. These cards could be expanded to 128K, 192K and 256K. All newer EGA cards include 256K of RAM as standard equipment and we assume this standard configuration in the following sections.

VGA monitors

VGA cards operate differently. A VGA card can be connected to a monochrome monitor, but it must be an analog monochrome VGA monitor instead of a simple MDA monitor. Although analog VGA monitors cost less than color VGA monitors, they can still use the high resolution VGA modes.

An analog VGA monitor isn't able to produce the entire VGA palette of 256 colors because it can display only 64 shades of gray. Usually this won't make a difference as long as you avoid colors that differ slightly in green components. Analog VGA monochrome monitors ignore the red and blue components of the RGB signal and use only the green component.

One advantage the monochrome VGA monitor has over its color counterpart is the VGA card can be switched into a monochrome mode, in which it behaves like a very powerful MDA card. Just as with the EGA card, the video RAM begins at B000H instead of B800H and the addresses of the various registers conform to the MDA standard.

Code	EGA/VGA video mode	MONO	CGA	EGA/VGA
00H	40x25 character text, 16 colors		■	■
01H	40x25 character text, 16 colors			■
02H	80x25 character text, 16 colors			■
03H	80x25 character text, 16 colors			■
04H	320x200 pixel graphics, 4 colors		■	■
05H	320x200 pixel graphics, 4 colors		■	■
06H	640x200 pixel graphics, 2 colors		■	■
07H	80x25 characters, monochrome	■		■
0DH	320x200 pixel graphics, 16 colors			■
0EH	640x200 pixel graphics, 16 colors			■
0FH	640x350 pixel graphics, monochrome	■		■
10H	640x350 pixel graphics, 16 colors+			■
11H	640x480 pixel graphics, 2 colors			*
12H	640x480 pixel graphics, 16 colors **			*
13H	320x200 pixel graphics, 256 colors			*

* only possible with VGA card
** EGA Cards with 64K of RAM can only display 4 colors

You can switch modes on the card using the MODE MONO and MODE CO80 DOS commands or by using function 00H of the BIOS video interrupt. Only video mode 07H (which is also used by the MDA card) gives you monochrome operation. All other modes enable color operation on a VGA card. The large table on the left summarizes which monitors can display which EGA and VGA video modes.

Throughout this section we assume that your VGA card has already been switched to color mode for the demonstration program. For EGA cards, we'll always assume 256K of RAM and an EGA or a multisync monitor are being used.

Identifying EGA and VGA cards

If your programs use features that are unique to EGA or VGA cards and the performance depends on a certain monitor type, then your programs should include a query routine that checks for the required hardware before proceeding.

Our routine, called IsEgaVga, is listed as a function in both the C and Pascal versions of the demonstration program. The routine calls two BIOS functions that are found only in EGA and VGA cards. One of these functions immediately determines whether you have an EGA/VGA card or an older card (from MDA to CGA). The function fails if the card is a CGA or an MDA (i.e., the function doesn't exist on these cards).

The other function is available only on the VGA card, which then lets you distinguish between EGA and VGA. This is function 1AH, which has two sub-functions. We're interested in sub-function 00H, which returns information on active and passive video cards.

Active and passive video cards refer to a PC that may have a second video card, such as an MDA or a Hercules card, installed in addition to a VGA card. However, this doesn't apply to most PS/2 models because MDA or Hercules cards aren't available for the MCA bus on these systems.

When you call the 1AH function with the function number in the AH register and the sub-function number in the AL register, you can tell by the contents of the AL register if the function is supported by the BIOS and if a VGA card is installed. A normal BIOS will simply leave the value 00H unchanged in the AL register, indicating the requested function isn't supported. The VGA BIOS loads the function number 1AH in the AL register to acknowledge the function call. The code returned to the BL register indicates the active video card and the code returned to the BH register indicates the passive video card. These codes are described in the following table:

Code	Meaning	Code	Meaning
00H	No video card	07H	VGA card with analog monochrome monitor
01H	MDA card with MDA monitor	08H	VGA card with analog color monitor
02H	CGA card with CGA monitor	09H	Reserved
03H	Reserved	0AH	MCGA with CGA card
04H	EGA card with EGA color monitor	0BH	MCGA with analog monochrome monitor
05H	EGA card with MDA monitor	0CH	MCGA with analog color monitor
06H	Reserved		

If the call to function 1AH fails, then we assume that a VGA card doesn't exist. In the next step, we check for an EGA card. Sub-function 10H of function 12H is supported only by EGA cards. Unlike many other BIOS functions, the sub-function number is passed in the BL register instead of the AL register. If the sub-function number 10H remains in this register after the function call, the system contains an EGA card.

Code	EGA Video RAM	Code	EGA Video RAM
00H	64K	02H	192K
01H	128K	03H	256K

The contents of the BH register indicate if the EGA card is connected to an MDA or EGA color monitor. The value of this register is 1 for MDA and 0 for EGA. Also, the contents of the BL register indicates how much RAM is available, as indicated by the table above left.

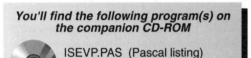

You'll find the following program(s) on the companion CD-ROM

ISEVP.PAS (Pascal listing)
ISEVC.C   (C listing)

The demonstration programs ISEVP.PAS and ISEVC.C each contain an IsEgaVga function and demonstrate its use within a program. You'll also find other slightly modified versions of this function in other demonstration programs later in this section. These programs and program listings are on the companion CD-ROM.

Selecting and programming fonts

Unlike earlier video cards, EGA and VGA cards aren't limited to the fonts present in the ROM chips on the card. Instead, they use a powerful character generator that relates the characters in an area of the video RAM to the corresponding bitmaps used to display the characters. In this section we'll discuss the structure of the character table and explain how to use it.

Loading and defining fonts with the BIOS

The expanded EGA and VGA BIOS has several functions that allow you to manipulate character tables. There are more than a dozen sub-functions available through function 11H of the BIOS video interrupt. As usual, you must place the function number in the AH register and the sub-function number in the AL register when making the call.

In addition to working with predefined character tables, these functions also allow you to load your own character tables, display a character table on screen or switch between different character tables. The predefined character tables are stored in a ROM chip on the EGA or VGA card and copied from there to a portion of the video RAM. The character generator then accesses the information about the appearance of certain characters. EGA cards have only two fonts in ROM and VGA cards have three fonts. The third font on the VGA card can be activated through the BIOS.

Character structure within a matrix

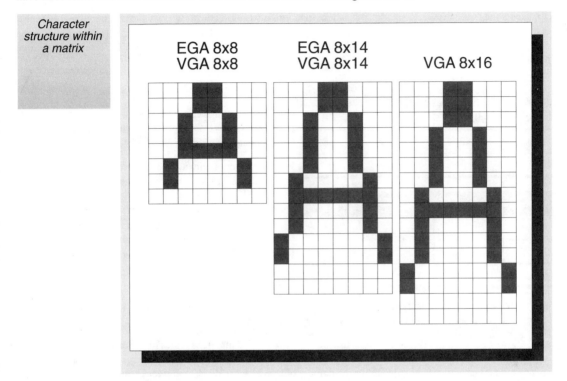

The structure of the video fonts is different than the fonts that are used on a printer. The difference lies in the size of the characters (i.e., the matrix; size on which the characters are based). The EGA card normally uses an 8x14 pixel matrix for the first ROM font. The second ROM font uses a smaller matrix that squeezes the characters into an 8x8 pixel box. The pixels remain the same size, although the font changes in size. Since this means the characters in the 8x8 matrix are smaller and harder to read, you may be wondering why you would select a smaller font.

A smaller font occupies less space on the screen, which enables you to display more characters. The 8x8 font lets you display 43 lines of text instead of the usual 25, allowing you to display more information on a single screen.

EGA vertical resolution:	350 pixels	350 pixels
Character matrix height:	÷ 14 pixels	÷ 8 pixels
Number of text lines:	25 lines	43.75 lines

The number of text lines actually depends on the vertical resolution of the EGA card, which is always 350 pixels in text mode. From the calculations listed below, we see there are actually 43.75 lines available on the screen. But since displaying 3/4 of a line isn't possible, the number is rounded down to 43.

The horizontal resolutions for the two character matrices are the same. The EGA card always contains 640 pixels per line. Since each character matrix is 8 pixels wide, there are 80 characters per line.

The VGA card is slightly different in both horizontal and vertical resolution. The vertical resolution in text mode is 400 pixels instead of 350 pixels. So, the normal text screen of 80x25 characters is obtained with a special VGA character matrix. This character matrix has a height of 16 pixels. The two EGA fonts are also available on the VGA card and these fonts permit text resolutions of 28 and 50 lines.

The horizontal resolution of the VGA card is also higher with 720 pixels per line instead of 640 pixels per line. However, we still get only 80 characters per line in VGA text modes because the horizontal dimensions of the character matrices increase from 8 to 9 pixels. The ninth pixel has a special purpose, which we'll discuss later.

First, let's discuss the functions used to load a font. These functions also automatically specify the number of text lines that will be displayed on screen. The numbers of these functions are 11H, 12H and 14H. To call these functions, place the function number in the AX register and an additional argument in the BL register. This gives the number of the character table into which the selected font will be loaded and activated.

Sub-function	Matrix	EGA lines	VGA lines
11H	8x14	25	28
12H	8x8	43	50
14H	8x16		25

If you don't want to work with several character tables simultaneously, enter a value of 0 for the first character table. EGA cards can use values from 0 to 3 and VGA cards can use values from 0 to 7. The following sections provide additional information on the different character tables.

Sub-function	Matrix	EGA	VGA
1H	8x14		
2H	8x8		
4H	8x16		

These functions always load a certain font and then set the registers of the video card to display the corresponding number of text lines. It's also possible to simply load a font into a character table. If you want to work with a character table other than the one currently active, this won't affect the screen display because the font isn't activated and the number of text lines doesn't change. Calling this function is identical to the three functions we just described except for the contents of the registers.

You aren't limited to the character tables stored in ROM; the BIOS also lets you load your own fonts. You can leave certain characters undefined or select different fonts, just as you can with a printer.

One feature allows you to set the character height from 1 to 32 pixels. The number of lines of text displayed on the screen is set accordingly. However, remember that characters less than 6 pixels high can't be read on the screen. Characters greater than 16 pixels high are easy to read, but this limits the number of lines you can display on screen simultaneously. Generally character heights should be from 8 to 16 pixels; otherwise an unusual looking screen display may be produced.

The BIOS lets you specify any number as the character height. Place the character height in the BH register when calling function 10H. The character width cannot be altered in any way; it remains fixed at 8 pixels for EGA mode and 9 for VGA mode.

You can also select any character table for your font. The character table number is loaded in the BL register. The CX register is passed the number of characters to be loaded. This allows you to load only selected characters, if desired. In the DX register, you're expected to enter the ASCII code of the first character you want to load. This may be a number from 0 to 255.

The BIOS retrieves the pixel pattern data for the characters from a buffer. This buffer must be created and initialized by the function caller. The address of the buffer is expected as a FAR pointer in the ES:BP register pair.

As the previous figure shows, the buffer must have an entry for each character to be defined. The size of the entry in bytes corresponds to the character height. For example, if an 8x12 matrix has been defined, each buffer entry consists of 12 bytes. The total buffer size is then 12 times the number of characters to be defined, since the entries follow each other. The first entry has the offset address of 0000H. The data for the first character is found here, followed by the data for subsequent characters.

Within each entry, each byte represents the pixel pattern for one pixel line of the character. The bytes correspond to lines in ascending order from the first to the last line of the character. Within each byte, the individual bits indicate the status of each pixel in the line, from left to right. If the bit is set, then the corresponding pixel is displayed using the text foreground color. If the bit's off, then the pixel is displayed in the background color.

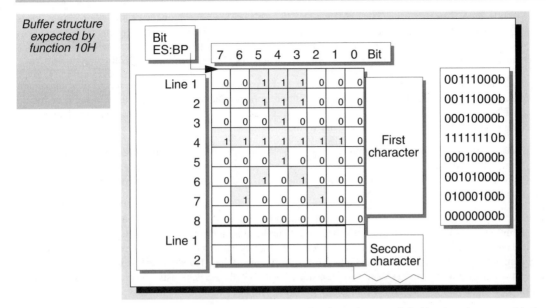

Buffer structure expected by function 10H

Sub-function 00H works the same as 10H. This function loads the given character definition in a character table, but doesn't activate the font or change the number of text lines on the screen. Function 00H corresponds to function 10H just as we saw functions 01H, 02H and 04H correspond to 11H, 12H and 14H.

When using characters and fonts that you've designed, don't forget they can be displayed only on your screen. Your printer won't be able to reproduce them. So, don't be surprised if your printer uses a completely different font if you try to print a screen displaying a custom font.

Changing from 9 pixel to 8 pixel display

The programs we'll discuss on the next few pages are examples of user-defined fonts applied to company logos and compound characters. However, this program has a problem with VGA cards because of the width of the characters. With an EGA card, each character has an actual width of 8 pixels. VGA characters are 9 pixels wide. This produces horizontal screen resolutions of 640 (EGA) and 720 (VGA).

You're probably wondering why there is a ninth pixel when the standard ROM fonts, as well as any font you can load with the BIOS, are 8 pixels wide. The ninth pixel is usually left blank. The only exceptions are characters with ASCII codes between C0H and DFH. This range contains various characters used for drawing frames and borders. These characters must be connected, without any space between them, to create unbroken horizontal lines. So, these characters simply copy the eighth pixel to the ninth to fill the empty space.

By adding the ninth pixel, VGA achieves higher resolution even though only 8 of the pixels are coded. This is possible because EGA actually uses only seven of the eight pixels. The eighth remains empty to ensure spacing between characters. VGA can use eight pixels and leave the ninth free.

As long as you define individual characters that have spaces between them, this characteristic of the VGA card doesn't usually cause any problems. But if you want to create a logo or a compound character (with two or more characters joined together), you'll encounter problems because you cannot control the ninth pixel. To work with such a font, you must sacrifice the additional resolution of the 9 pixel mode and use one of the normal 8 pixel modes as they are used with the EGA card.

This mode change involves several registers of the VGA card. Unfortunately, not all these can be addressed through the BIOS. Some must be programmed directly. First we'll discuss the miscellaneous output register. This register can be read using port address 3CCH and written using port address 3C2H. It contains two bits (bits 2 and 3) that set the VGA clock, which in turn determines the horizontal resolution.

In normal text mode, the VGA card runs at 28.322 MHz with 720 pixels per line. The frequency with 640 pixels per line is 25.175. This is the resolution we want to create a screen with 80 characters per line using 8 pixel characters. To switch your VGA card to the desired 640 pixel mode, we must modify bits 2 and 3 and then return the new register values. However, since the characters in VGA fonts are nine pixels wide, we must also switch to a character width of 8 pixels.

This is done by changing the contents of the clocking mode register. This register is part of the sequencer controller and cannot be directly addressed like the miscellaneous output register. Before and after the sequencer controller register is accessed, it is reset using its reset register. This is done before a sequencer register, such as the clocking register, can be changed. Bit 0 of the clocking register is responsible for the character width.

The last step is to modify the horizontal pel panning register. We've already encountered this register in a description of smooth scrolling. After switching to the 8 pixel width, this register is loaded with the value 0. This moves the picture one pixel to the left. If you don't do this, the first pixel column on the screen would flicker. We don't have to access this register directly, since there is a BIOS function available.

The three steps required to change from a 9 pixel character width to an 8 pixel character can also be reversed to revert to 9 pixel width. Simply switch the horizontal resolution back to 720 in the miscellaneous output register and set the character width back to 9 pixels in the clocking mode register. Don't forget to set the horizontal pel panning register back to 8 so the first pixel column is visible again. If you want to know the exact structure of these registers, refer to the end of this chapter. You'll find detailed descriptions of all EGA and VGA registers. The LOGOP.PAS demonstration program in the following section contains a routine for executing these changes.

Logos

Now let's discuss creating logos. Logos are an attractive way to introduce your software on screen. They give your software a professional look. For example, a logo, instead of a simple copyright message, can be displayed on the screen. However, it's difficult to create an interesting logo using only the standard characters available in the normal ASCII set. But both the EGA and VGA cards allow you to change the appearance of individual characters. Remember, if you have a VGA card, you must reduce the character width to 8 pixels.

Usually, you need more than one character to create an interesting logo. Each character consists of 128 pixels on a VGA card (8x16) and only 112 on an EGA card (8x14). We'll explain how you can create logos by combining several characters into complex patterns.

Logos from compound characters

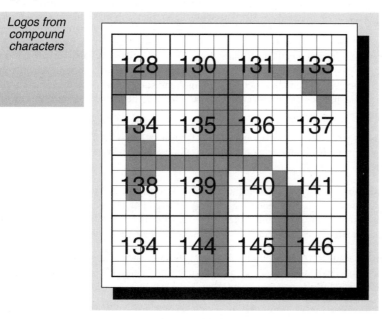

Combining characters to create logos provides more pixels to work with and allows you to create a larger logo, which in turn demands more detail. However, you shouldn't use too many characters in your logo. Otherwise, you may lose too many useful characters from the ASCII character set. Also, you should ensure that all the characters continue to appear correctly so subsequent text is readable. Remember, to create the logo, we're redefining only a few characters instead of the entire font.

You should select characters that aren't used elsewhere in your program. Characters with ASCII codes less than 32, the foreign language characters and characters with ASCII codes greater than 224 are good choices. Depending on which characters your program needs, up to 100 characters are usually available for creating a logo. This allows you to create a 10x10 character logo with a resolution of more than 12,000 pixels.

We've included an ASCII table in the Appendix (located on the companion CD-ROM) which displays the possible choices. You'll see examples of the ASCII codes, including those described above, in this ASCII table.

To help you create your own logos, we've included the LOGO program in both C (LOGOC.C) and Pascal (LOGOP.P) versions. The main feature of each program is a function called BuildLogo function, which is responsible for the structure of the logo and for displaying it on screen. Data about the desired position of the logo on screen, the logo's height in pixels, its color and the string array that defines how the logo looks is required by this function.

In this array, each string represents one pixel line of the logo. Each character in the string represents a pixel in the line. If the character for a certain pixel is a space, then this pixel is blank. If any other character is used, the pixel is set. Although this method of storing the information for creating the logo uses a lot of memory, it also allows you to edit the appearance of the logo in the source code easily, without using a special editor. Also, since the logo's width is taken directly from the length of the string array, it doesn't have to be passed as an extra parameter.

Depending on the size of the logo and the video card that's installed (EGA or VGA), BuildLogo calculates the number of characters required and defines the pixel patterns for each individual logo character using sub-functions 00H and 10H of the BIOS video interrupt (previously described). If the logo doesn't completely fill the rectangle reserved for it, it is centered within it.

BuildLogo uses the foreign language characters to create logos. These are the characters with ASCII codes from 128 to 167; this provides a total of 39 characters. You can easily modify the BuildLogo function so you can also use other ASCII characters.

This function also switches the VGA character width from 9 pixels to 8 pixels. The IsEgaVga function determines whether the current system has a VGA card. The SetCharWidth function makes the switch. The steps required to switch the character width were already described.

BuildLogo defaults to character heights of 14 pixels on EGA cards and 16 pixels on VGA cards. The normal fonts are used, which produces a screen resolution of 25 lines by 80 columns. If you want to use BuildLogo in a program that uses a smaller font (resulting in better screen resolution), then you must change the value of the CharHeight variable in the LOGO programs. If you use a smaller font, remember that you'll need more characters to create the same logo because each character will have fewer pixels in its height.

If you no longer need a logo, the ..ResetLogo function; can restore all the characters of the original font and set the character width back to 9 pixels for VGA systems. Both LOGO demonstration programs use the BuildLogo function to create a small logo and display it on the screen. The ASCII character set is displayed in the portion of the screen above the logo. The characters that were redefined to form the logo will be highlighted with a different color. This allows you to see each redefined character and how they fit together like the pieces of a puzzle to form the logo.

You'll find the following program(s) on the companion CD-ROM

LOGOP.PAS (Pascal listing)
LOGOC.C (C listing)
LOGOCA.ASM
(Assembler listing)

The Pascal version LOGOP.PAS doesn't require any assembler routines, but the LOGOCA.ASM assembly language module supports the C version LOGOC.C. This assembly language module supplies character definition information because the BIOS function that defines characters cannot access character information in the BP register using the int86() C input function. The defchar routine in the assembler module handles character definition.

Character table structure and location

You don't need to worry about the structure and location of character tables as long as you use only the BIOS to access them. However, occasionally you'll have to access them directly. Let's examine when this occurs and see how to access character definitions directly from character tables by using BIOS functions.

Using bitplanes in text mode

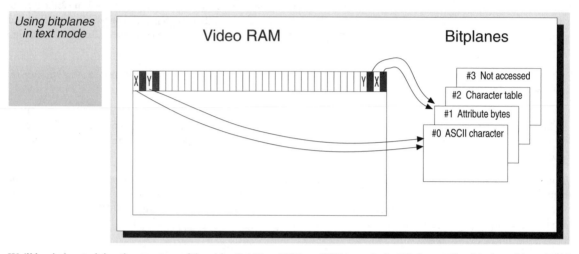

We'll begin by studying the structure of the video RAM on EGA and VGA cards. In "Understanding bitplanes" later in this section we note that EGA and VGA cards divide their video RAM into four large areas called bitplanes. These areas serve different purposes in text and graphics modes. A fully populated video card (with 256K) allocates 64K per bitplane.

The first two bitplanes (0 and 1) contain character codes and attribute bytes in text mode. The ASCII character codes are stored in bitplane 0. Accessing the video RAM above B800H at an even offset address is directed to this bitplane. Accessing the video RAM at an odd offset address is directed to bitplane 1, which contains the attribute bytes. The other bitplanes are also used in text mode. EGA and VGA cards normally use the third bitplane for the character table. In a fully populated video card, each bitplane has 64K of RAM. Since each character table requires 8K, this allows you to store 8 different character tables. But only the VGA card fully uses this bitplane. Since the EGA card uses only four character tables, 32K of memory remains unused.

Location of character tables within bitplane 2

EGA	Offset	VGA
Unused		Character table #7
	E000h	
Character table #3		Character table #3
	C000h	
Unused		Character table #6
	A000h	
Character table #2		Character table #2
	8000h	
Unused		Character table #5
	6000h	
Character table #1		Character table #1
	4000h	
Unused		Character table #4
	2000h	
Character table #0		Character table #0
	0000h	

Each character table needs 8K because 32 bytes are reserved for each of the 256 characters (32 x 256 = 8192 bytes or 8K). Remember, 32 pixels is also the maximum character height for EGA and VGA fonts. The character tables are organized for the maximum font size. If a smaller font is used, then the extra bytes at the end of each entry simply remain unused.

The bytes that are used are coded in connection with the BIOS functions for character definitions. Each byte represents the bit pattern for one pixel line of the character. The individual bits in each byte indicate whether the corresponding pixel is on or off. You can easily determine the starting address for a specific character or a pixel line within a character if you know the starting address for the character table. Simply multiply the ASCII code number for the character by 32, then add the starting address for the table and the number of the desired pixel line.

Character table structure

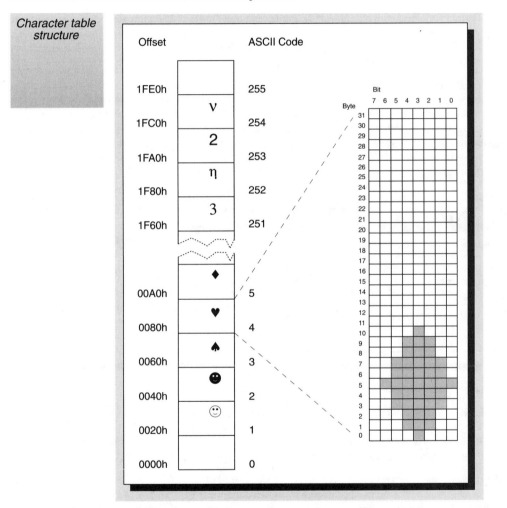

Before accessing a character table, we must perform one more step. Since direct access to bitplane 2 isn't allowed, its contents must first be loaded into memory, from which it can be accessed from segment address A000H. Unfortunately, a BIOS function doesn't do this. So, again we must program the EGA and VGA registers.

Specifically, we'll be working with various registers of the sequencer and graphics controllers. Registers 2 and 4 of the sequencer controller; are known as the map mask register; and the memory mode register. The first register determines which bitplane is accessed. Each bit in this register represents a bitplane. In this case, we want bit 2 to be set for bitplane number 2. All other bits should be cleared. This ensures that only bitplane 2 is accessed.

To ensure that only the bitplanes indicated in the map mask register are accessed, you must also load the value 7 in the memory mode register. In normal text modes, this register contains the value 3. This means that when the B800H video RAM is accessed, all even memory addresses (ASCII codes) go to bitplane 0 and all odd memory addresses (attribute codes) go to bitplane 1. Changing the value to 7 changes the memory addressing method.

We must also reset the sequencer registers by accessing the reset register, like we did when changing from a 9 pixel to an 8 pixel character width. So before accessing the map mask and memory mode registers, we load the value 1 and the value 3 in the reset register. A reset isn't required to access the graphics controller registers. We need to manipulate registers 4, 5 and 6 to access bitplane 2. These are called the read map select register, the graphics mode register and the miscellaneous register.

The read map select register; is loaded with the value of the bitplane we want to read (2, in this case). This means that read access to the video RAM is also directed to bitplane 2. The graphics mode register requires a value of 0. This is accomplished by simply clearing bit 4, since all other bits pertain only to graphics mode. Clearing this bit ensures the odd and even memory addresses won't be split into different bitplanes.

This information is repeated in bit 1 of the miscellaneous register. We're also interested in bits 2 and 3 of this register. These bits indicate where we can find the video RAM and where the bitplanes should be stored. In text mode, the video RAM is located at segment address B800H and extends for 32K. Bitplane 2 begins at segment address A000H, allowing access to the entire 64K. Setting up the registers in this way destroys the normal text mode settings. So, now you're able to access bitplane 2, but you can no longer access the normal video RAM at B800H. Any character output that occurs during access to bitplane 2 is ignored by the video RAM. The picture on your screen appears unchanged because the video card can directly access the video RAM internally.

Remember, for your program or the BIOS to access the video RAM again, you must reset of the registers to their original values. The table on the left shows the proper register values for access to bitplane 2 and for access to video RAM at B800H.

Register	Bitplane	Video RAM
Map mask register (sequencer controller)	04H	03H
Memory mode register (sequencer controller)	07H	03H
Read map select register (graphics controller)	02H	00H
Graphics mode register (graphics controller)	00H	10H
Miscellaneous registers (graphics controller)	04H	0EH

The demonstration program MIKADO (listed later in this chapter) contains two routines used for toggling access between video RAM and bitplane 2. Also, at the end of this chapter, you'll find additional information about the registers we just discussed.

Switching between fonts: 512 different characters simultaneously

We've seen that bitplane 2 can store four different fonts on an EGA card and eight different fonts on a VGA card and that BIOS access isn't limited to the first font. Now we must determine how to switch between fonts to display the desired one on the screen. We must use register number 4 (the character map select register) of the sequencer controller. This register is responsible for selecting the current character table, as the illustration below shows.

As you can see, the character map select register works with two fonts instead of only one. The order of the bits that specify the two fonts is confusing. Instead of using three consecutive bits to identify the font, each font has a group of two bits and one additional bit that's separate from the other two. The single bit is the highest bit of the group. The reason for this can be traced back to the development of EGA and VGA cards. Since EGA cards have only four fonts, they only need to represent the numbers 0 through 3, which can be done with 2 bits.

VGA cards have eight available fonts, so we need to represent the values 0 through

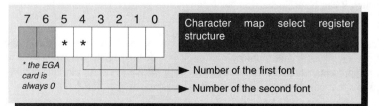

7. To maintain compatibility, the VGA card was developed to imitate the original two bit configuration of the EGA card. A single extra bit was then added to accommodate the extra fonts. Since this extra bit was never used in the EGA card, it doesn't interfere with its operations.

The fonts listed in the previous figure are called first font and second font. However, this doesn't represent a hierarchical relationship. Instead, this is what gives the EGA and VGA cards the ability to display 512 characters on the screen simultaneously, unlike their predecessors, which can display only 256 characters. You may be wondering how to select characters from one of these fonts. Since there are only 256 ASCII codes, this isn't the answer.

At first, you might think the attribute byte for a character doesn't have enough space for this kind of information. The two nibbles of this byte select a background and a foreground color for the character. However, this is the key to working with 512 characters simultaneously.

The highest bit of the foreground color (bit 3 in the attribute byte) is used to select the first or second font. If this bit is set to 0, then the foreground color is less than 8 and the video card will use the corresponding character from the first font. If this bit is set, then a foreground color greater than or equal to 8 is indicated and the character is taken from the second font.

Although the user may not notice, a distinction is always made between the first and second font. This is because the same font is specified twice in the character map select register. Once two numbers are entered in this register, the difference between the fonts immediately becomes apparent on the screen.

Access this register if you want to display two fonts on the screen simultaneously or if you just want to switch to another font. You can produce some very interesting visual effects by simply switching between two fonts in your application.

You don't have to program the character map select register directly because the video BIOS uses sub-function 03H of function 11H to do this. This sub-function expects the two function numbers in the AH and the AL registers. When sub-function 03H is called, an additional parameter must be passed to the BL register. This parameter is the value that you want to load in the character map select register to indicate a desired font. The following section contains an example of how this function is used. This example uses the second font to create a graphic window within a text screen.

Selecting fonts from the character map select register and attrribute byte

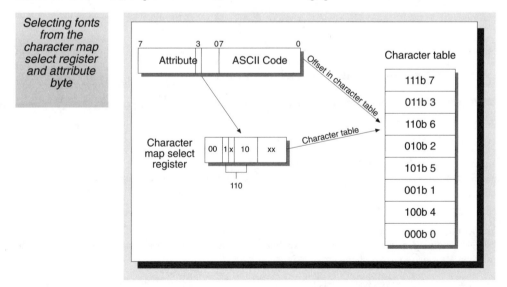

One problem you may encounter when using a second font is the characters of the second font may appear lighter on screen. This occurs because bit 3 of the attribute byte is set, which results in a foreground color number of 8 or greater being used for characters of the second font. This problem can easily be solved by simply changing the palette registers to set foreground colors 8-15 equal to those assigned to 0-7.

Since the BIOS has many functions for handling this type of manipulation, this operation can easily be performed. Although this limits the number of foreground colors to eight, few programs would use that many foreground colors simultaneously. You could program the palette registers yourself to obtain additional colors if necessary.

A graphics window in text mode

Suppose that instead of displaying 512 characters, you need mathematical symbols or other special characters. There's an alternative to using the character select map register. Instead, you can use the second font to create a graphics window in your text screen. Then you can display small graphics or images without switching to the more complicated graphics mode.

The technique for creating a graphics window is similar to the technique for creating a logo. Simply piece together a number of specially defined characters to form the desired image. Each character from the second font appears once in the graphics window. This is important because it limits the size of the graphics window to 256 characters. The resulting block may be as large as 16x16 characters, but you aren't limited to any particular shape of window.

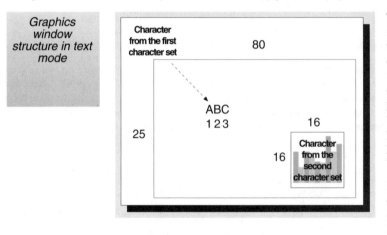

Graphics window structure in text mode

The second font is considered an array of individual pixels relating to coordinates within the graphics window. To set or clear a pixel within the graphics window, first you must calculate which character contains the appropriate pixel. The pixel position is determined relative to the upper-left corner of the character. The pixel is then set or cleared in the bit pattern for the character in the character table.

For example, suppose that a VGA character comprises 16 pixel lines, each consisting of eight pixels. If we take the lower-left corner of the screen as the point of origin for our graphics window, then all pixels with X-coordinates less than 8 and Y-coordinates less than 16 are considered part of the first character, which is in the lower-left corner of the graphics window. As the previous figure indicates, this character is always ASCII code 0. The number of each character in our window remains fixed.

The next step calculates which pixel line within the character we want to manipulate. This structure is the same as that found in the character table. So, a pixel with a Y-coordinate of 15 would be in the top pixel line of the character with ASCII code 0 and a pixel with a Y-coordinate of 0 would be in the bottom line of the character. This enables us to easily calculate the location of any pixel.

The final step determines the location of the desired pixel within the pixel line. The bit positions of the pixels are numbered 7 to 0 from left to right. By knowing the character number, pixel line and bit number, any pixel can be switched on or off by passing the corresponding information to the character table in video RAM.

Redefining an entire character every time you want to set or clear a single pixel may seem inefficient. However, if you're using the BIOS functions for defining characters, there's no alternative. Also, since these functions aren't very fast, you'll notice problems when you want to process pixels in rapid succession (e.g., when drawing a line). For these reasons, both programs presented in this section access bitplane 2 directly. This allows you to manipulate the graphics window effectively.

Unfortunately, there is a problem with VGA because of the ninth pixel. We've already encountered this problem while using the LOGO program. As you may remember, the ninth pixel always remains blank, so we must limit the VGA character width to 8 pixels so the characters will flow together smoothly and without an empty space between them. We described the procedure for changing VGA character width from 9 pixels to 8 pixels earlier in this chapter.

The demonstration program discussed in this section is called MIKADO. Again, we've included both Pascal (MIKADO.PAS) and C (MIKADO.C) versions. The highlight of these programs is a routine called InitGraphArea routine, which configures the graphics window. The programs also include a routine called SetPixel, which allows you to set or delete individual pixels. This routine acts as the basis of the Line function, which draws a line within the graphics window.

The InitGraphArea procedure accepts data about the location of the graphics window, its size and the colors to be used. You can also select the font number that you want to use to create the graphics window. The maximum X and Y coordinates are calculated from the character resolution and the window's size. These values are then stored in the xmax and ymax global variables.

Bitplane 2 is accessed using the procedure we described (in the GetFontAccess routine). The ReleaseFontAccess function performs the opposite task; it restores access to the video RAM at B800H. These routines aren't called very often because "snow" appears on your screen while they are executing.

The SelectMaps procedure is also important to the MIKADO program. This routine enters the desired fonts in the character map select register, using the BIOS function we described earlier. This prevents direct hardware access to the video card. Bypassing hardware access makes the program more compatible with all types of VGA cards because different manufacturers may assign different uses to the registers.

Several procedures in the MIKADO programs use the BIOS to program the palette registers. Any element of the 16 color palette can be changed, the entire palette can be redefined or the current contents of the palette can be queried. The procedures that set the colors for the text and graphics windows are called SetPalCol, SetPalAry, GetPalCol and GelPalAry.

When considering colors for the graphics window, remember that color must be assigned by character instead of by pixel, which is possible in graphics mode. A character consists of 14x8 pixels with EGA and 16x8 pixels with VGA. Usually it's best to assign one background color and one foreground color to the graphics window. However, the MIKADO programs do something entirely different. These programs assign a successive color code to each character in the graphics window. This gives the illusion of gradually changing bands of color.

These two programs also clarify the order in which the various routines must be called. First, IsEgaVga determines whether an EGA card or VGA card is available. Only then can the graphics window be opened with InitGraphArea. Before the window can be accessed, GetFontAccess must be called. Then you can draw lines or pictures within the window using SetPixel.

If you want to send text to the screen, you must call ReleaseFontAccess first, then call GetFontAccess again to return to graphics output. ClearGraphArea clears the graphics window, then restores access to video RAM and the default font (font 0). MIKADO fills the screen around the graphics window with ASCII characters, showing the complete ASCII character set is still available with the graphics window in place.

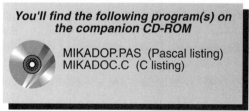

You'll find the following program(s) on the companion CD-ROM

MIKADOP.PAS (Pascal listing)
MIKADOC.C (C listing)

The MIKADO programs contain of the tools you'll need to work with a graphics window in text mode. After studying the listing, you'll be able to modify or expand these routines according to your own needs. Having a graphics window open in the middle of a text screen can be very useful. Now you can add this feature to your own applications.

Fonts for graphics mode

Character tables also display characters in EGA and VGA graphics modes by using the corresponding BIOS functions. Since it's already being used to store pixel information for the graphics screen, bitplane 2 won't be available for storing character tables in graphics mode. So, the pixel pattern for each character must be passed to the BIOS. This can be done either directly from the ROM chip or from a RAM buffer. However, you must determine which font to access.

If you don't tell the BIOS which font you want to use, it defaults to the font enabled for 80x25 character text mode. EGA cards default to the 8x14 font and VGA cards default to the 8x16 font. To determine the number of text lines that will fit on the graphics screen, divide the vertical resolution by the pixel height of a character. Dividing the character width (8) by the horizontal resolution determines the number of characters per line.

You don't have to use the default font for text output in graphics mode. The BIOS allows you to access any font available in ROM. To do this, use sub-functions 22H, 23H and 24H of video BIOS function 11H. The system documentation indicates that in addition to the function numbers in the AL and AH registers, you must also pass two other items of information in the BL and DL registers. Based on our experiences with the original IBM cards, the information passed in these registers doesn't affect text output in graphics mode and can be ignored. You only need the function numbers to call these functions.

You can also use sub-function 21H to load your own character table for graphics mode. This character table must include all 256 characters. This call requires the function numbers in the AH and AL registers and the individual character height in the CX register. As with all other BIOS functions used to define characters, this function requires a pointer to the character table in the ES:BP register pair. The structure of this pointer corresponds to that of the character table pointers used by sub-functions 00H and 10H.

Sub-function.	Matrix	EGA	VGA
22H	8x14		
23H	8x8		
24H	8x16	(n.a.)	

Smooth scrolling

Prior to EGA and VGA, it was impossible to create a smoothly moving picture with video cards. It was possible to scroll one character at a time in a single direction in text mode. But to scroll in graphics mode, you had to recopy the entire video RAM, even if you only wanted to move the screen by one pixel. This was one of the reasons why the PC lagged so far behind other computers in pixel animation.

EGA and VGA cards offer some relief. The video hardware on these cards contains the ability to move the screen pixel by pixel and perform smooth scrolling. This made the first convincing animated graphics possible on the PC and opened new horizons in text mode.

Smooth scrolling using the pel panning register

In the EGA and VGA cards, two registers are used to move the screen display pixel by pixel. These two registers control different parts of the video hardware, but they work together to perform basically the same task, which is setting the screen origin (the horizontal and vertical starting points of the screen). The vertical pel panning register is part of the CRT controller and the horizontal pel panning register is part of the attribute controller.

The horizontal and vertical starting points of the screen

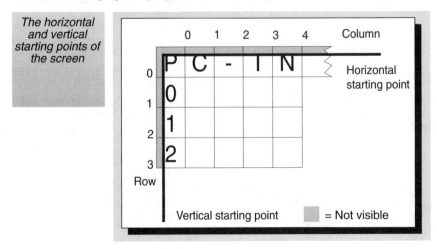

Let's first look at the horizontal pel panning register. In its normal state, this register contains a value of either 0 or 8. These values indicate the character width in text mode, ensuring the correct horizontal proportions in characters. A value of 8 is the default setting for all video modes with a character width of nine pixels. This applies to the VGA card and the EGA card when emulating an MDA card (i.e., when the EGA is attached to a monochrome monitor). The default value for an EGA card attached to a color monitor is 0.

Incrementing the value in the horizontal pel panning register moves the contents of the entire screen to the left, pixel by pixel. For an EGA card with color monitor, the values would be 1, 2, 3, etc. The larger the number, the further to the left the screen scrolls. The maximum value is 7, which scrolls the screen the width of one entire character. You cannot use the horizontal pel panning register to scroll more than the width of one character.

This procedure works differently for VGA cards and EGA cards in MDA emulation mode. As we mentioned, the default value is 8. The numbers 0 to 7 perform scrolling to the right. Unlike left scrolling, you must begin with the maximum number (7) and decrement the value to 0. With VGA cards and EGA cards with MDA monitors, you can skip up to a value of 8 for the final step.

The horizontal pel panning register can be applied to text mode and graphics mode. There are two different cases to consider in graphics mode: The VGA card's 256 color mode and all other modes. In 256 color mode, the starting point is 0. You can scroll the screen up to three pixels to the left, instead of entering 1, 2 or 3 as you might expect. However, using the horizontal pel panning register in graphics mode requires values of 2, 4 or 6 to scroll.

All other graphics modes also have a starting point of 0. The horizontal pel panning register will accept values from 1 to 7 to scroll the screen a maximum of seven pixels to the left.

You can load the horizontal pel panning register either by programming the attribute controller directly or by using subfunction 00H of BIOS video interrupt function 10H. This BIOS function was originally intended for loading a specific palette register. However, since the pel panning register is found in the attribute controller just like the palette registers, it can also be accessed using this function. Enter the number of the horizontal pel panning register instead of one of the palette registers. When calling this function, enter the two function numbers as usual. Then pass the number of the horizontal pel panning register (13H) to the BL register and the value you want to pass to the BH register.

If speed isn't an important requirement, you should use this method instead of accessing the attribute controller. To access the attribute controller directly, your program should be able to distinguish between EGA and VGA cards. However, since most manufacturers of EGA and VGA cards have adhered to the standards for assigning registers, you shouldn't have any problems if you want to program the horizontal pel panning register directly.

If you prefer the direct route, first the number of the horizontal pel panning register (13H) must be passed to the combined data/index register of the attribute controller at port address 3C0H. When doing this, remember to set bit 5 in this register. This bit enables and disables the attribute controller. If this bit isn't set, the attribute controller remains disabled and the screen will be black.

After sending value 33H (register number 13H plus bit 5) to port 3C0H, you can pass the new value that should be placed in the horizontal pel panning register. This value is the pixel counter that controls the degree of screen scrolling.

Vertical scrolling

Vertical scrolling using the vertical pel panning register is less complicated because the starting point is always 0, regardless of the mode or video card type. Any value greater than 0 scrolls the screen the corresponding number of pixels up and any value less than 0 scrolls the screen down. In the normal 80x25 character text mode, the maximum values for vertical scrolling are 13 for EGA and 15 for VGA.

In graphics mode, the vertical pel panning register accepts values from 0 to 31, where 31 (not 0) is the starting point. Any smaller value moves the screen the corresponding number of pixels down. If you want to scroll up, set the starting point from 31 to the minimum scroll value, then increment that value.

To scroll down in text mode, the procedure is the same as horizontal scrolling to the right. Start with the highest value and decrement the value until you reach the starting point. The vertical pel panning register must be accessed directly using the CRT controller; there are no BIOS functions available. First pass vertical pel panning register number (08H) to the CRT controller's index register.

The port address of this index register depends on the video card's current operating mode. In color mode, the port address is 3D4H. In monochrome mode, it is 3B4H. The data register, which immediately follows the index register, must be loaded with the new value for the vertical pel panning register. Instead of two 8-bit operations, you can perform a single 16-bit operation and load both the index and data registers simultaneously.

In practice, the pel panning registers are rarely used for scrolling the screen. A developer usually wants to scroll continuously instead of one character at a time. You could scroll the screen in this way, reset the pel panning registers to their starting points, move the entire contents of video RAM and repeat the procedure to obtain continuous scrolling. However, moving the characters in video RAM takes too much time and results in a slower execution time.

The technique described in the following paragraphs is usually preferable. It involves moving the screen display's point of origin and changing the line length in video RAM.

Moving the screen origin and changing the line length in video RAM

One way to scroll the screen contents up by one text line is to move the contents of the video RAM up by 160 bytes (160 bytes is equivalent to one line in 80x25 character text mode). You could also simply increment the starting address of the current screen page by 160 bytes. The CRT controller will begin the display with what was originally the second line when the screen is repainted. Regardless of which method you use, the result is the same to the user.

Instead of moving everything in the video RAM, it's much easier, from a programmer's point of view, to change the contents of the CRT controller registers and move the starting address of the current screen page. This same register also allows you to jump directly from one screen page to another. This method also stores the lines you've scrolled past in video RAM so they can be recalled later.

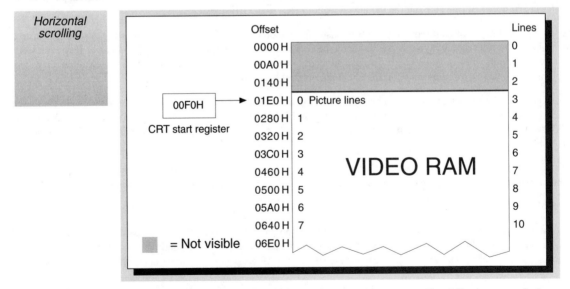

Changing the starting address of the video RAM is similar to using your arrow keys to scroll to different pages of a document in a word processing program. Instead of using arrow keys, we use the CRT starting registers. And instead of the text in a document, we're scrolling the contents of the video RAM.

The numbers of the two registers we use are 0CH and 0DH. These registers contain the starting address of the portion of the video RAM that's currently visible on the screen. These registers cannot be reached directly using the BIOS, so again we must program the CRT controller directly. You should remember two important points when doing this. First, the starting address is given in the form of a 16-bit offset address with its high byte in register 0CH and its low byte in register 0DH. The order is reversed from what you would normally expect because the high byte appears before the low byte. Also, this offset is counted in words rather than bytes, so you must divide by two before writing the address to the register.

You can easily scroll vertically by accessing the pel panning register and changing the screen origin. However, this method has some unpleasant surprises if you try to use it to scroll horizontally. For example, suppose that you scroll one character to the left and then increment the starting address from 0000H to 0002H. The character from the second column of the first line is now in the first column. But the first character from the second line now appears in the last column of the first line and so on down the screen. This is known as character wrapping.

Character wrapping when moving the screen origin

The character wrapping problem is related to video RAM organization; this problem can't be solved using the CRT start registers. Fortunately, we don't have to move the entire contents of the video RAM. The CRT controller has another register called the offset register. This register stores the length of a text line in video RAM. The normal value for this register is 80 words, which corresponds to a line length of 160 bytes.

Increasing this value doesn't instruct your system to display more characters per line on the screen. Instead, the CRT controller's internal address counter increments to make more room per line in the video RAM. For example, if you placed a value of 82 (52H) in this register instead of the normal value of 80 (50H), then each line in video RAM would contain 82 characters. Only the first 80 are visible on the screen until you scroll. Once you scroll, the last two characters in the line become visible and the first two characters move beyond the left border of the screen.

The offset register (register 13H in the CRT controller) is 8 bits wide. So, it can accommodate line lengths of up to 255 characters, which gives each line a length of 510 bytes in video RAM.

Remember this when you're addressing a certain line within the video RAM. Before, you would always multiply by 160 to access a certain line. Now, you must multiply by 510, 320 or whatever the video RAM line length is at the time. In all cases, this number will be twice the number of characters per video RAM line.

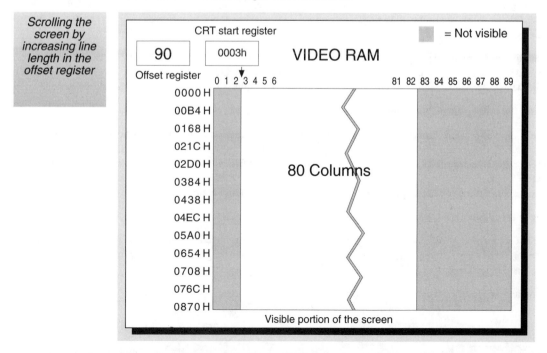

Scrolling the screen by increasing line length in the offset register

Once you've increased the internal line length using the offset register, you can easily scroll the screen by using the pel panning register and changing the screen origin. Another important point to consider when scrolling (both vertically and horizontally) is the synchronization of events. If you aren't careful with synchronization, the result on the screen may be completely different from what you had intended.

Synchronization with the CRT controller

Scrolling the screen by manipulating the pel panning register and screen origin must always be coordinated with the CRT controller. First, the pel panning register should be accessed only during vertical synchronization of the electron beam (i.e., when visual information isn't being sent to the screen). This ensures the changes to these registers won't affect any parts of the screen that are created with different values in these registers.

If the pel panning register; and the CRT start register must be programmed simultaneously (e.g., to return the pel panning register to its starting value and to move the screen origin), then you must be very careful. While the changes to the pel panning register are considered immediately as the next screen is built, the change to the CRT start register takes longer to process.

This occurs because a program usually hesitates after starting vertical synchronization, even if the hesitation is only a fraction of a second. The hesitation occurs because of querying the vertical synchronization. This query is usually done using bit 3 of the input status register, which shows the vertical synchronization status. It's on during synchronization and off at all other times. The query takes place in a program loop that constantly checks the status and the hesitation occurs because the assembly language instructions in this query need some time to execute. The delay is worse if you program in a high level language, in which the query code will be even slower.

Once the program recognizes the vertical synchronization, it may already be a fraction of a second into its execution and the CRT controller may have already loaded the starting address for the next screen refresh from the CRT start register. So, any change to the contents of this register won't be considered until the subsequent screen refresh.

Changes to the pel panning register take effect with the next screen refresh. This results in internal inconsistencies that are visible on screen. To avoid these problems, you must follow a specific procedure when programming the pel panning register and the CRT start register simultaneously.

This procedure uses input status register 1 to wait for a vertical synchronization to start and finish. Then the new screen origin is loaded in the proper register of the CRT controller. This won't disturb the next screen refresh because the CRT controller has already loaded the screen origin address into its internal address counter before the screen refresh and doesn't have to access the register again.

Now, wait for the screen to regenerate and for the next vertical synchronization. After this event, you can program the pel panning register. The change to this register is then taken into account with the next screen refresh. Now we can be sure the address of the new screen origin is correctly loaded into the internal address counter for this screen refresh as well.

Algorithms for setting the pel panning register and CRT start register

Waiting for the vertical synchronization also synchronizes your program with the video frequency of the video card, regardless of the CPU speed. This is very useful, especially with games. If you continuously call the routine for setting the pel panning register and the CRT start register, you can move the screen contents by a few pixels each time the picture regenerates. This involves 50 to 70 movements per second, depending on whether you have an EGA or VGA card. Since the human eye cannot follow so many rapid changes, it interprets this as smooth animation.

Scrolling in text mode

The SOFTSCRP.PAS and SOFTSCRC.C programs which you'll find on the companion CD-ROM are examples of this combined control of the pel panning register and the CRT start register. Each program scrolls text printed in a large font, from right to left across the screen.

These programs are based on two routines called ShowScrlText and SetOrigin. ShowScrlText takes the text to be displayed and stores it in the video RAM so it's not completely visible at once. The program divides the text into three sections, each

216 characters long by 25 characters high. Each section uses 10,800 bytes (or a total of 32,400 bytes), leaving only 368 bytes of video RAM unused.

After the text is placed in video RAM, ShowScrlText begins the display. The SetOrigin procedure is important because it sets the starting point for the screen. The section of text, the starting row and column and the number of pixels to move must be specified. The number of pixels is entered directly in the pel panning register. The number of the text section and the starting column and row are linked to a starting address of the visible screen and loaded in the CRT start register.

First SetOrigin is called from within ShowScrlText using constant values for the starting column and row. Only the pixel counter increments to create the horizontal movement. Then when the maximum value for the horizontal pixel counter is reached, the counter resets to 0 or 8 and the starting column increments.

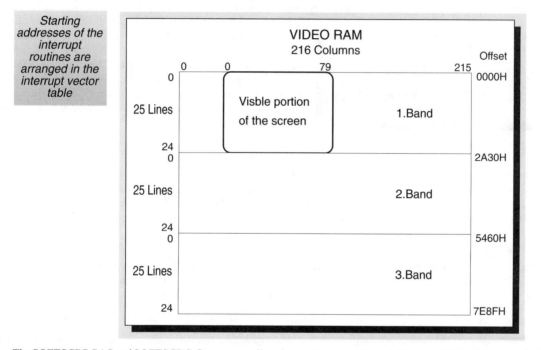

Starting addresses of the interrupt routines are arranged in the interrupt vector table

The SOFTSCRP.PAS and SOFTSCRC.C programs allow the user to control the scrolling speed. The differences in character width between EGA and VGA are also taken into account. To control this, the ShowScrlText routine accepts two parameters. One parameter is used for the scrolling speed and the other is used for the video card type. Speed is determined by selecting either the FAST, MEDIUM or SLOW constant and the video card type is determined by entering either EGA or VGA.

While the screen origin is being moved in ShowScrlText, these two constants are converted to an index in the array step table. This table is declared within the routine. Depending on the speed and video card type, a series of values for the horizontal pixel counter is selected. The value 255 indicates the end of each row of values in the array, which means that scrolling continues in the next column.

Different scrolling speeds are obtained with different intervals in the value of the horizontal pixel counter. In SLOW mode, each pixel in each character is scrolled. In MEDIUM mode, every other pixel is skipped, which doubles the scrolling speed. The speed is doubled again for FAST mode, in which only two pixels in each character are scrolled.

The value 216 indicates the limit for incrementing the starting column. This value refers to the last column in a section. The program must switch to the next section of text and start again with column one. But since the contents of the last screen in the previous text section can no longer be scrolled left off the screen, the next section must begin with the same characters found at the end of the previous section. This allows you to program a completely smooth transition between sections of text.

The speed at which the user can comfortably read the characters that are scrolling by depends mostly on the character width. The PrintChar routine; is responsible for building the characters in video RAM. The arguments PrintChar requires are the character code and the column number and text section number where the character should appear. The row number is given by the constant STARTR, so it doesn't have to be passed again. The routine obtains the bit pattern for the characters from the 8x14 pixel font, which is included in ROM on both EGA and VGA cards. This font is accessed using sub-function 30H of BIOS video interrupt function 11H.

This routine is also the reason why the C version of this program requires the small assembler routine called SOFTSCCA.ASM. The BIOS function mentioned returns information to the BP register, which cannot be accessed by normal C interrupt functions.

PrintChar sends the 8x14 character matrix to the screen by mapping each pixel in the pattern to a character position on the screen. This means that one character will occupy 8 screen columns and 14 screen rows. So, one section of the text contains 27 characters (216/8). Any 10 characters (80/8) are visible at a time. However, remember the second and third sections of the text must repeat the last screen of the previous section. This means that sections 2 and 3 can only contain 17 new characters instead of 27. Therefore, the total number of characters that can be loaded in video RAM is 61 (27 + 17 + 17).

> **You'll find the following program(s) on the companion CD-ROM**
>
> SOFTSCRP.PAS (Pascal listing)
> SOFTSCRC.C (C listing)
> SOFTSCCA.ASM (Assembler listing)

Disabling the screen

Occasionally the screen display of your video card must be disabled. Screen saver programs do this to prevent the screen image from burning into your monitor. EGA:Disabling screen; The EGA and VGA cards offer capabilities for disabling screen display, which we'll discuss in this section. Specifically, we'll look at the attribute controller, its role in generating the video picture and how this can be used to disable the screen display.

The attribute controller's role

The four basic control components in EGA and VGA cards are the CRT controller, the graphics controller, the attribute controller and the sequencer controller. The attribute controller assigns color information to the picture. If its operation is interrupted, then no color information will reach the screen and the result is a black screen.

It's much easier to interrupt the attribute controller than the other controllers found on EGA and VGA cards. When bit number 5 in the index register is set to 0, the attribute controller is switched off and color information doesn't reach the screen.

This bit is only significant to the attribute controller. To the other controllers, the index register only accepts the number of the register being addressed. The reason for the difference in the attribute controller involves the palette register (the attribute registers most frequently addressed). Before accessing a palette register, the attribute controller must be temporarily stopped. Since accessing a palette register requires access to an index register anyway, it makes sense to put the bit used for suspending the attribute controller in the index register also. And since there are only 21 registers available to the attribute controller, only bits 0 to 4 of the index register are needed for accepting a register number.

However, before we can disable the attribute controller by clearing bit 5, we must first read the CRT controller's status register. This makes the attribute controller reset effective and must be done before enabling or disabling the attribute controller.

Demonstration programs

The VONOFFP.PAS and VONOFFC.C programs demonstrate how to enable or disable the screen display using the attribute controller. First, these programs check to ensure the system is using an EGA or VGA card. If it isn't, an error message is displayed and the program ends. If an EGA or VGA card is found, a different message is displayed. The user is given five seconds to read this message, then the ScrOff routine disables the screen display.

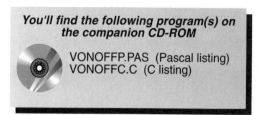

The ScrOff routine starts by reading the status register of the CRT controller. To make this routine work with both color and monochrome monitors, a double reset occurs: Once using the monochrome address of the status register (3BAH) and once using the color address (3DAH). This won't cause any problems, since only one of these two ports will be used.

Next, the value 0 is written to the attribute controller's index register at port address 3C0H, bit 5 is set to 0 and attribute controller activity is suspended. The screen display goes black. The ScrOn routine executes after the user has pressed a key. This routine writes the value 20H to the attribute controller's index register. This activates the controller again and enables screen display.

Understanding bitplanes

The technological progress of PC video cards has produced higher resolutions and increasing numbers of colors. As resolution increases, so does the amount of video RAM required. As the need to display more colors increases, more than one bit is needed to represent each pixel. For example, VGA cards with 256 colors require 8 bits per pixel. As a result, almost all EGA and VGA cards manufactured today include 256K of RAM as standard equipment. Depending on the video mode and the number of screen pages stored, this memory is often used to capacity.

Although the 64K limitation of early video cards no longer exits, we can't continue to add more video RAM. Remember, PCs are limited to 1 megabyte of addressable memory. In this section, we'll discuss how the PC's addressable memory handles the 256K of video RAM and how this affects programming EGA and VGA cards.

Dividing video RAM into bitplanes

In the total addressable memory of the PC, only segments A (from A000:0000) and B (from B000:0000) are available to the video card. Segment B is already reserved for the video RAM in MDA, CGA and Hercules cards. So, only segment A can be used for EGA and VGA cards. This means the developers of the first EGA card had to address 256K of video RAM in a 64K area.

The solution resulted in the development of bitplanes, which divide the video RAM of EGA and VGA cards into equal sections. On a card with 256K of video RAM, each bitplane has 64K that is completely addressable using memory segment A, starting at A000:0000. If your video card has less video RAM, such as the first EGA cards that had only 64K, then each bitplane is correspondingly smaller.

This memory addressing technique, which was developed in 1984, is valid for all EGA and VGA cards. This includes the Super VGA card, although the addressing is used in a slightly expanded form (more on this later).

Latch registers

Use different bitplanes in text modes only if you want to use more than one font simultaneously. Bitplanes are always used when graphics modes are active. Pixel information is spread out among the bitplanes in various ways for different modes. Regardless of this, EGA and VGA cards manage communications between the processor and video RAM using four 8-bit registers known as the latch registers. Each latch register corresponds to one of the four bitplanes.

Latch registers cannot be directly accessed by programs. If a program wants to access a byte in video RAM, then the four latch registers receive this byte from the four corresponding bitplanes using the same offset address. For example, if the offset address is 9, then the tenth byte (byte 0 is the first) from the first bitplane will be loaded into the first latch register, the tenth byte from the second bitplane will be loaded into the second latch register and so on for the third and fourth.

The same procedure is used for a write access to video RAM. The contents of the four latch registers are written to the corresponding bitplanes at the specified offset address.

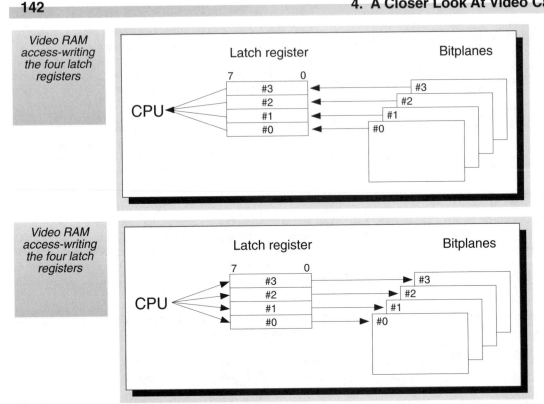

Video RAM access-writing the four latch registers

Video RAM access-writing the four latch registers

This process involves more than simply reading or writing to the latch register. A read access of video RAM must result in a byte being sent to the processor and a write access must result in a byte being transferred from the processor to the video RAM. However, during a read access, only one byte can be sent to the processor at a time. So, we must determine which of the four bytes in the latch registers is sent. This also applies to writing to video RAM because four different bytes (one for each bitplane) must be transferred from the processor.

The graphics controller's role in graphics programming

The answer to all these questions comes from the nine registers of the graphics controller, which is an important component of every EGA and VGA card. These registers determine how and where all read and write accesses to the video RAM occur. This applies not only to the different graphics modes, but also to the text modes. You may frequently use these registers in graphics programming by assigning them different values, depending on the desired operation. However, this isn't the case in text mode. In text mode, during initialization of the mode through the BIOS, the various registers are set so additional accesses aren't necessary after initialization. However, all input and output to or from the video RAM in text mode is conducted through the four latch registers, even if this process is transparent for a program. The nine registers of the graphics controller for the EGA card and their defaults:

Reg	Meaning	Default	Reg	Meaning	Default
00H	Set / Reset	00H	05H	Mode	00H
01H	Enable Set / Reset	00H	06H	Miscellaneous	various
02H	Color Compare	00H	07H	Color Don't Care	0FH
03H	Function Select / Data Rotate	00H	08H	Bit Mask	FFH
04H	Read Map Select	00H			

Programming the registers of the graphics controller is similar to accessing the CRTC register of the Hercules graphics card. These registers can also be used on other controllers of an EGA and VGA card. Port address 3CEH has an address register, in which the number of the register within the graphics controller that's being accessed must be loaded first. The value for this register can then be output to the data register next to the address register, which has a port address of 3CFH.

However, access to these two ports doesn't have to be separate. Instead, you can use a 16-bit OUT command on the address register. The AX register sent to this port in the course of the machine language command, OUT DX,AX must contain the register number in the AL register and the value to be loaded for this register in the AH register.

Although values can be loaded in the individual registers of the graphics controller in this way, a read access is only possible with VGA cards; you cannot read these registers on EGA cards.

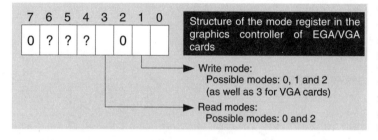

The mode register, number 5, is important to the graphics controller during read and write accesses to the video RAM. This register sets one of two read modes and one of three write modes. These modes affect read or write accesses to the video RAM. The other registers are only accessories, which specify given parameters depending on the set read and write mode.

In the following sections we'll discuss how the various read and write modes operate, their tasks and how other registers of the graphics controller affect these modes. However, you will quickly realize that you need to use only a few of these modes because the other modes are too difficult to use.

Read mode 0

Read mode 0 gives a program the option of reading a byte from a specific bitplane. This is practical, for example when a part of the video RAM must be saved, for which purpose the four bitplanes are executed sequentially in a loop and the desired area from each bitplane is loaded and placed in main memory.

During a read access to the video RAM in read mode 0 all four latch registers are loaded with the addressed byte of their plane. However, only one of these four bytes gets by its latch register and reaches the CPU. Which bitplane the byte comes from is determined by the contents of the read map select register, which is number 4 within the graphics controller.

Only the lower two bits in this register are allocated. These two bits decide on the number of the latch register, whose contents can advance up to the CPU. When programming this register, ensure the first bitplane is set to 0 (i.e., don't set it to 1 if you want to access the first bitplane).

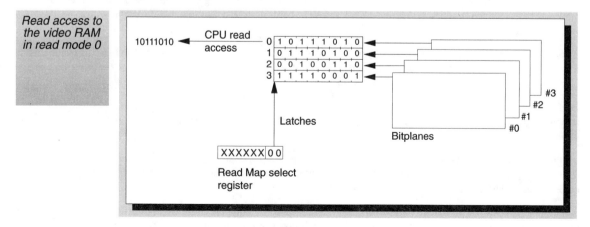

The following sequence of assembly commands demonstrates how read mode 0 is used. The first 8K from the second bitplane are loaded into the main memory. First read mode 0 is set and then the read map select register is loaded with the value 1 so the second bitplane can be read. With the help of the assembly command REP MOVSB, the first 8K are then loaded byte by byte from the video RAM and copied to a buffer.

```
mov ax,ds              ;ES:DI to target buffer
mov es,ax
mov di,offset buffer
mov ax,0A000h          ;DS:SI to starting address of bitplane
mov ds,ax              ;in video RAM
xor si,si
mov cx,8*1024          ;Copy 8K

mov dx,3CEh            ;Address graphics controller
mov ax,0005h          ;Write read mode 0 in mode register
out dx,ax             ;
mov ax,0104h          ;Write 1 (plane number in read map
out dx,ax             ;register

rep movsb             ;Copy 8K
```

After studying the assembly sequence, you may think that you could speed up the copying process by simply copying 4096 words instead of 8192 bytes. To do this you would have to convert REP MOVSB to REP MOVSW and load the CX register with 4096 instead of 8192. This would work for copying memory areas within the main memory. However, in this case, it would result in some unpleasant consequences.

Because 16-bit accesses aren't possible in video RAM, the CPU would first execute two read accesses at byte level before executing the write access. The second read access would overwrite the results of the first read access within the latch register before these results could even reach the CPU. As a result, in the target buffer, you would find only words whose low and high byte have the same value. Only the high byte would correspond to the actual contents of the video RAM. For this reason, 16-bit read accesses to video RAM should be avoided in all forms on EGA and VGA cards.

Read mode 1

Although it's relatively easy to understand the operation and purpose of read mode 0, read mode 1 is more complicated. This mode involves more than sending the contents of one of the latch registers to the CPU. Instead, in this mode numerous logical operations, which affect the contents of all four latch registers, occur.

This mode is responsible for determining whether the bits from the four latch registers contain a specific value. Later, this mode can be used in the graphics modes of the EGA and VGA cards with 16 colors to search for pixels with a specific color value. As a rule, however, this mode is rarely used.

After the four latch registers are loaded, eight groups, each consisting of four bits, are formed. The four bits occupying an identical bit position within the four different latch registers are located in one group. For example, all the bits at bit position 0 are in one group, all the bits from bit position 1 are in another group, etc.

Each of these eight groups of four bits is now compared with the value from the color compare register, which was loaded into this register before the read access. The result of this comparison determines the byte that is sent to the CPU as the result of the read operation.

All the bits, whose group showed the value from the color compare register, are set to 1, while the other bits contain the value 0. So, after the read access, it's possible to determine not only whether one of the groups corresponded to the value from the color compare register, but also which groups correspond.

Although it may be difficult to believe, this isn't the entire process. Actually, the Color Don't Care register is also involved. Only when this register contains the value 00001111b are the various groups of four bits completely compared with the comparison value from the Color Compare register. Each of the lower four bits in the Color Don't Care register represents one of the four bitplanes: Bit 0 for the first, bit 1 for the second, etc. Only if one of these bits contains the value 1 is the corresponding bitplane also included in this comparison of the four bit groups with the value from the Color Compare register.

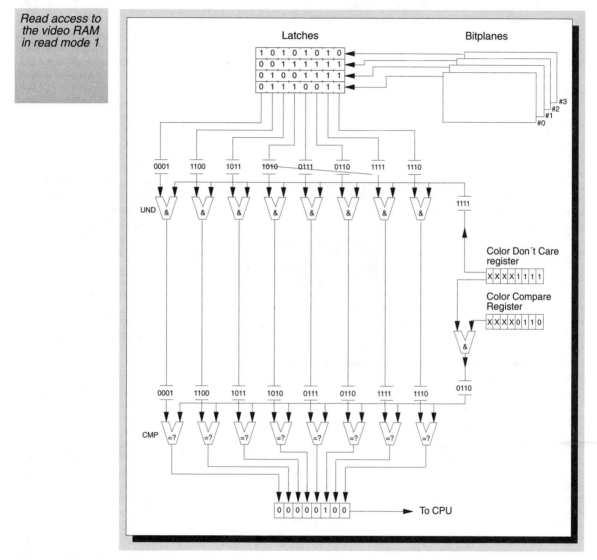

Read access to the video RAM in read mode 1

However, if the value is 0, it's as if the value from this bitplane matches the corresponding bit from the Color Compare register in all eight groups. So, specifying the value 0 in the Color Don't Care Register always returns the value 11111111b to the CPU, regardless of the contents of the four latch registers and Color Compare register. This is possible because the eight groups are no longer compared with the comparison value. Instead, all the groups are considered to be appropriate.

The following assembly sequence demonstrates the use of read mode 1. This assembly sequence establishes which of the groups of four, from the first byte in the four bitplanes in video RAM, has the value 5. The Color Don't Care register isn't explicitly programmed, because it's assumed that its default value is 00001111b. So, all the bitplanes will be included in the comparison.

```
mov ax,0A000h            ;Set ES to video RAM
mov es,ax

mov dx,3CEh              ;Address graphics controller
mov ax,0805h            ;Write read mode 1 in mode register
out dx,ax
mov ax,0502h            ;Write color value 5 in color compare
out dx,ax               ;Register

mov al,es:[0]           ;Read and compare pixels,
                        ;return result in AX
or  al,al              ;No bit to 1?
je  AllUnequal         ;No
```

Write mode 0

In accessing the video RAM in write mode 0, several operations, which depend on the contents of several registers, occur. The contents of the bit mask register decide whether the contents of a bit in the four latch registers will go to the four bitplanes unchanged or will be manipulated beforehand. The individual bits in the bit mask register correspond to the bits in the four latch registers. If a bit in the bit mask register contains the value 0, the matching bit in the four latch registers is taken, unchanged, in the four bitplanes. An operation occurs if the bit contains the value 1 instead. Which operation is determined by the contents of the function select register. As the illustration on the left shows, the bits can simply be replaced or manipulated with the help of one of the logical operators AND, OR or EXCLUSIVE OR.

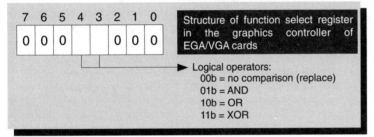

The contents of the Enable Set/Reset register determine what will be the partner of these bits in the operation. If the lower four bits each contain the value 1, the operation takes place through the contents of the lower 4 bits of the Set/Reset register. Each of these bits is used in the operation with the four bits of a bit position from the four latch registers, whose type is described by the contents of the function select register.

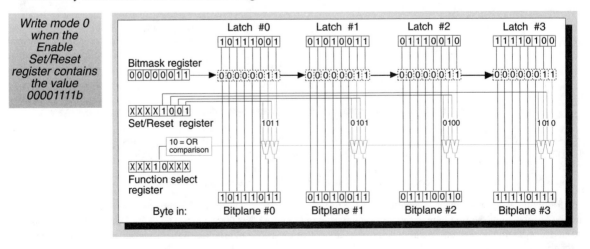

All the bits to be manipulated from latch register 0 are then linked with bit 0 of the Set/Reset register by the selected operator. In the same way, all the bits to be manipulated from latch registers 1, 2 and 3 are linked with bits 1, 2 and 3 from the Set/Reset register. The CPU byte, which is transferred to the graphics controller during a write access, is unimportant here. The write access is reduced to a trigger, which cannot have any direct influence on the contents of the latch register (or the bitplanes).

The following assembly language sequence assigns code 1011b to the group of four with bit 2 from the first byte in the video RAM, without disturbing the contents of the other groups. As you'll see in the next section, this is a technique that's frequently used in setting pixels in the 16 color graphics modes of EGA and VGA cards.

Since the color of the other groups of four shouldn't be changed, their contents are first loaded into the latch register through a read access to the video RAM. Which of the various read modes is active is unimportant. After all, the value returned to the processor is not important; it simply fills the latch register.

Since only the group of four at bit position 2 must be manipulated and the other groups return to the bitplanes unchanged, the value 00000100b (04H) is loaded into the bit mask register first. Then, the value 0 is written in the Function Select register because the bits to be manipulated should be replaced by a new bit combination. After that, the color for the group of four at bit position 2 (1011b = 0BH) is loaded into the Set/Reset register.

To remove the color from this register when writing to the video RAM, write the value 1111b (0FH) to the Enable Set/Reset register as the last access to the register of the graphics controller. Then execute the write access to the video RAM, in which the transferred processor byte is unimportant.

```
mov ax,0A000h        ;Video RAM segment address
mov ds,ax            ;to DS
mov al,ds:[0]        ;Load byte 0 in latch register
mov dx,3CEh          ;Address graphics controller
mov ax,0005h         ;Read mode 0, write mode 0
out dx,ax            ;to mode register
mov al,03h           ;Write 0 to function select
out dx,ax            ;register
mov ax,0408h         ;Write bit masks in bit mask register
out dx,ax
mov ax,0B00h         ;Write new color value to
out dx,ax            ;Set/Reset register
mov ax,0F01h         ;Write 1111b to Enable Set/Reset
out dx,ax            ;register
mov ds:[0],al        ;Manipulate & return latch register
```

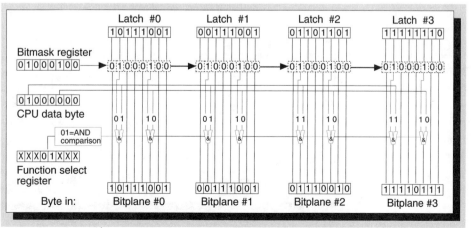

Write mode 0, when the Enable Set/Reset register contains the value 00000000b

This process is different when the Enable Set/Reset register contains the value 0. In this case, all the bits to be manipulated from the four latch registers are linked to the CPU byte latch by latch. Again, the operator depends on the contents of the Function Select register. For example, if you choose OR and want to manipulate bits 1, 2, 4 and 6, then these bits in all four latch registers are individually linked by a logical OR with bits 1, 2, 4 and 6 in the CPU byte.

In this mode the single bit positions in the four latch registers are linked with the same value from the CPU byte. So, this mode isn't used as much as the operation through the Set/Reset register as described.

Write mode 1

Compared to the complex operations in write mode 0, write mode 1 seems very simple. The contents of the various registers of the graphics controller and the passed CPU byte are no longer important here, since the contents of the four latch registers are written to the specified offset address within the four bitplanes in unchanged form.

For example, it makes sense to use this write mode to copy a specific area from the video RAM to another area. Simply run this area in the video RAM, fill the contents of the four latches through a read access in any read mode and then write the latch register to video RAM through a write access in write mode 1. This allows you to copy four bytes at a time, which saves a lot of time.

```
mov ax,0A000h          ;Segment address of video RAM
mov ds,ax              ;to DS and ES
mov es,ax
mov si,0000h           ;Source begins at 0000H
mov di,0200h           ;Target begins at 0200H
mov cx,100h            ;Copy 256 bytes
cld                    ;Increment on string inst.

mov dx,3CEh            ;Address graphics controller
mov ax,0105h           ;Read mode 0, Write mode 1.i).Video RAM:Write mode 1 ;
out dx,ax             ;to mode register

rep movsb              ;Copy all four bitplanes
```

Write mode 2

Write mode 2 is like a combination of the different modes in write mode 0. Like write mode 0, in write mode 2, the bit mask register decides which bits are sent unchanged to the latch registers and which ones are to be manipulated.

Write access to the video RAM in write mode 2

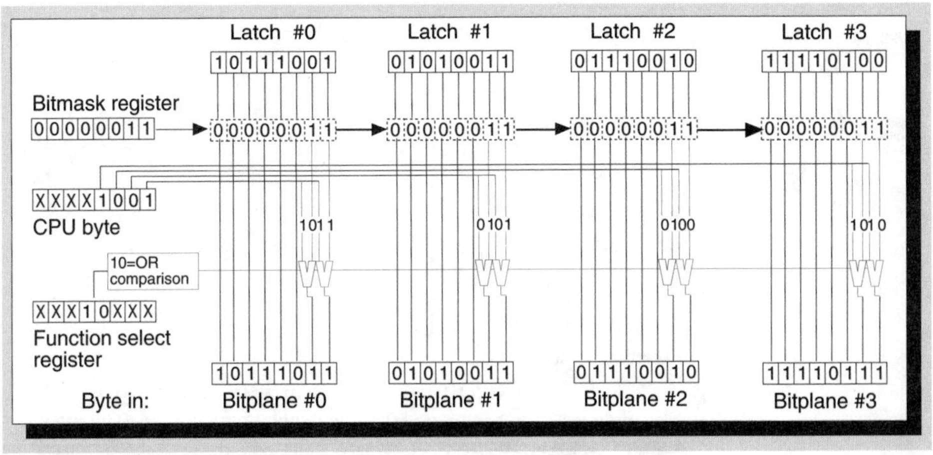

The linking mode recorded in the Function Select register determines the manner in which the single bits are manipulated. Regardless of the contents of the Enable Set/Reset register, the lower 4 bits of the CPU byte are linked with the latch registers within write mode 2. Bit 0 of the CPU byte is linked with all bits in latch register 0 that are to be manipulated. The same applies for CPU bits 1, 2 and 3, which are linked individually with all the bits in latch registers 1, 2 and 3.

This mode is well-suited for setting the color of single pixels in 16 color graphics mode on EGA and VGA cards. While this is also possible in write mode 0, the appropriate assembly sequence is shorter in write mode 2, since neither the Enable Set/ Reset register nor the Set/Reset register must be programmed.

Here's the same example for write mode 2:

```
mov ax,0A000h          ;Segment address of video RAM
mov ds,ax              ;to DS
mov al,ds:[0]          ;Load byte 0 to latch register
mov dx,3CEh            ;Address graphics controller
mov ax,0205h           ;Write read mode 0, write mode 2
out dx,ax              ;to mode register
mov ax,0003h           ;Write REPLACE mode (0) to
out dx,ax              ;function select register
mov ax,0408h           ;Write bit mask to bit mask register
out dx,ax
mov byte ptr ds:[0],0Bh ;New color value in video RAM
```

Write mode 3

In addition to the three write modes of the EGA card, the developers of the VGA card added a fourth mode. This mode is selected in the same way as the others; enter the corresponding mode number in the mode register of the graphics controller.

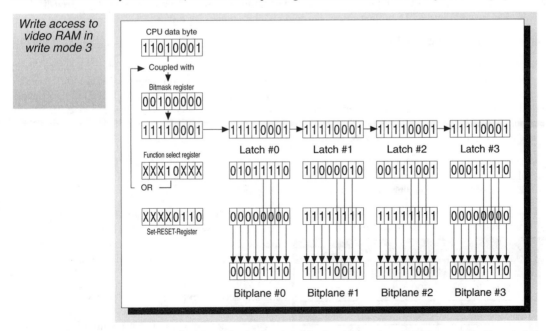

Write access to video RAM in write mode 3

During a read access to video RAM in this mode, the four low bits from the set/reset register must first be coupled with the bits from the four latch registers. Unlike write mode 0, the contents of the enable set/reset register are included in this operation. However, the type of coupling is determined by the Function select register as usual.

In this mode, a logical AND combines the CPU byte with the contents of the bit mask register. The result then determines which bits from the latch registers are written to the bitplanes unchanged and which are taken as the combination of the set/reset register and the latch bits. The CPU byte is helping in the task the bit mask register performs alone in modes 0 and 2.

Since we have yet to find a meaningful application for this mode, we couldn't provide a practical example.

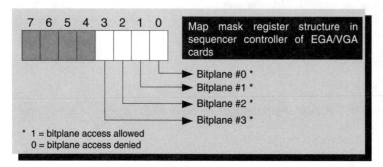

The map mask register

Another register we'll discuss is the map mask register of the sequencer controller. It's used to lock individual bitplanes which then prevents them from being written to or read. This is useful when you want to manipulate the contents of only one specific bitplane.

Each bitplane's status is represented in this register by the four low bits. Each bit corresponds to a bitplane. The bit must be set to 1 to allow access to the corresponding bitplane.

The following sections describe how to implement the various read and write modes to perform tasks such as setting and querying pixels in graphics modes or copying areas of the screen from video RAM to main memory.

The 16 color EGA and VGA graphics modes

The most important feature of EGA and VGA cards is the 16 color graphics modes. These modes are available with resolutions from 320x200 to 640x350 pixels. For those used to working with the four colors of the CGA card, the 16 color modes are a definite improvement. Although EGA and VGA are still far from the ultimate goal of photographic quality screen displays, which would require approximately 16 million colors, the color graphics modes are a start.

Why multiple 16 color graphics modes?

The development of PC video cards includes a steady progression of higher resolutions with more colors. Why then would the EGA card want to include two lower resolution 16 color graphics modes in addition to the high resolution 640x350 mode? As you'll see in the following table, the lower resolution modes require less memory per screen page. This allows more pages to be stored in video RAM simultaneously. In many user applications, a greater number of screen pages in video RAM may be more important than higher resolution. One example of this is sprite programming, which we'll discuss in "Sprites" later in this section. This section also explains how the remaining video RAM can be used.

As you can see in the table, the 16 color graphics modes are also fully supported by the VGA card. The VGA card also has an additional 640x480 mode. Although this resolution is exceeded on the Super VGA card, it remains the highest resolution mode for the standard VGA card and has been widely used by many applications.

Video RAM structure in 16 color graphics modes				
Mode	Resolution	Memory	Pages	Remaining bytes
0DH	320x200	32,000	8	6,144
0EH	640x200	64,000	4	6,144
10H	640x350	112,000	2	38,144
12H*	640x480	153,600	1	108,544
*VGA only				

Although we have different modes with different resolutions, the color information for each pixel in all modes is encoded in basically the same way, except for a few minor differences. These differences involve the way video RAM is organized.

Each byte of video RAM contains color information for eight consecutive pixels in the same pixel line of the screen. This means that each pixel is represented by one bit. In the 16 color modes this isn't sufficient because each pixel needs four bits to identify the color. These bits are obtained by using one bit from each of the four bitplanes, as shown in the following illustration.

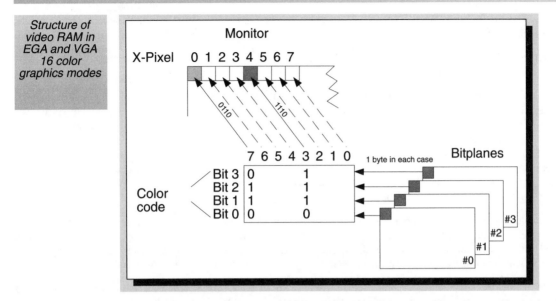

Structure of video RAM in EGA and VGA 16 color graphics modes

Let's look at a practical example. The first eight pixels in the upper-left corner of the screen are represented by the four bytes found at offset address 0000H in each of the four bitplanes. The four bits required to encode the color information are obtained by combining the bits at the same bit position in the first byte of each bitplane. The procedure creates eight groups of four bits, each of which determines the color of a single pixel.

The bit from bitplane 0 becomes bit 0 of the color code. The bit from bitplane 1 is bit 1 of the color code and so on for bits 2 and 3. The color code is then interpreted as a color, just as with the CGA card: black (0), blue (1), green (2), etc.

We've discussed how the division of video RAM into bitplanes works in the various read and write modes. The same groups of four bits are at work with the read and write modes, accessing individual pixels using the latch registers in 16 color graphics modes.

In addition to the structure of each byte, the order in which these bytes are stored in video RAM is an important aspect of programming the graphics modes. EGA and VGA cards use a very simple procedure for this in the 16 color modes. Starting at offset address 0000H (the start of video RAM), each pixel line is represented by a certain number of consecutive bytes. For graphics modes with a horizontal resolution of 640 pixels, this is 80 bytes. Mode 0DH (320x200) uses 40 bytes per pixel line.

Pixel lines follow one another sequentially in memory, so you can use the following formula to calculate the offset address of the byte that contains any given pixel:

```
Offset = Y * (horizontal_resolution / 8 ) + int( X / 8)
```

The byte found at this address contains information for eight consecutive pixels. To find the specific bit that contains the color information for the desired pixel, use the following formula:

```
Bit = 7 - (X mod 8)
```

The difference between the various 16 color graphics modes lies in the length of a graphic line in RAM, the number of lines per screen and the amount of memory required per screen page instead of in how the color information is encoded. This information must be considered when programming each of the various graphics modes.

Accessing individual pixels in 16 color graphics modes

The V16COL.PAS, V16COLPA.ASM, V16COLC.C and C16COLCA.ASM demonstration programs which you'll find on the companion CD-ROM show how these formulas are used to access individual pixels through read and write modes. The programs, named V16COLP.PAS and V16COLC.C, can be used with of the EGA/VGA 16 color graphics modes. As we'll see in the "Super VGA Cards" section of this chapter, this also applies to the Super VGA card's 16 color 800x600 mode.

Assembler routines improve both programs' performance. These routines, called V16COLPA.ASM and V16COLCA.ASM, access individual pixels and work with different screen pages.

The high level language and assembler modules use the same global variable and routine names. Both versions of the program work almost identically, so our discussion will apply to both versions. Let's begin with the assembler module, since this is where the work actually occurs. The PUBLIC declarations at the beginning of the module lists the routines used to support the C or Pascal program. You'll find four routines called INIT640480, INIT640350, INIT640200 and INIT320200. One of the four EGA/VGA 16 color graphics modes can be selected using these routines. In addition to these, the routines GETPIX routine; and SETPIX routine; set or read individual pixels in the selected graphics mode. The last two routines in the assembler module are SETPAGE; and SHOWPAGE. These routines are responsible for setting the screen page that is accessed by GETPIX and SETPIX and selecting the page that is displayed.

The assembler module for the C program has another routine called GETFONTPTR. This routine actually has nothing to do with graphics programming. It simply returns a pointer to the 8x8 font stored in the EGA/VGA ROM chip. This pointer is required by the C or Pascal module to display characters on screen in graphics mode. The Pascal version of the program gets this pointer without using an assembler routine, so GETFONTPTR isn't used in V16COLPA.ASM.

The INIT routines for initializing the graphics mode perform two basic tasks. First, function 00H of the BIOS video interrupt sets the desired video mode and clears the screen. Then three global variables are declared for use in accessing individual pixels and screen pages.

The three variables are VIO_SEG, LNWIDTH and PAGEOFS. The first variable, VIO_SEG, stores the segment address of video RAM. This variable also represents the current screen page because the offset of the current screen page is included in this segment address. This means that SETPIX and GETPIX don't have to consider the starting address of the current screen page when addressing a pixel; the segment address in VIO_SEG already reflects this information.

For example, in 640x200 pixel graphics mode, each screen page requires 64,000 bytes, which is spread across the four bitplanes. This means that a new screen page starts every 8000 bytes within a bitplane. In hexadecimal mode, this interval is 1F40H bytes.

The first screen page begins at A000:0000, the second at A000:1F40, the third at A000:3E80, the fourth at A000:5DC0, etc. Using the segment address, the first pages starts at A000:0000, the second at A1F4:0000, the third at A3E8:0000 and the fourth at A5DC:0000. You must consider the screen size before calculating the start of each screen page for each video mode. The INIT routines store this information in the global variable PAGEOFS, which represents the offset address divided by 16. This division allows easy merging with the segment address.

The global variable LNWIDTH calculates individual pixel addresses. It stores the width of a single pixel line in bytes. This value is plugged into the "horizontal_resolution / 8" expression in the equation previously listed.

With the information stored in the global variables VIO_SEG and LNWIDTH, routines such as SETPIX and SHOWPAGE can perform their tasks. With SETPIX and GETPIX, the screen coordinates specified by the caller are converted into an offset address for accessing video RAM. This is done by multiplying the Y-coordinate by LNWIDTH, dividing the X-coordinate by eight and adding the two results.

Then the bit position of the desired pixel is calculated from the X-coordinate. In addition to the MOD operation in the equation already listed, the assembler instruction AND is used to ignore all but the three lowest bits of the X-coordinate. This performs the same task as a MOD operation with 8, but runs faster.

Until now, GETPIX and SETPIX are identical in their execution. With SETPIX, the next step is to convert the bit position into a bit mask, which is needed later to access the pixel using write mode 2. This is done by shifting the value 1 to the left by the number of the bit position. For example, by using bit position 4 you would end up with the value 0010000(b).

This value is then loaded into both the bit mask register of the graphics controller and the mode register for write mode 2 and read mode 0. Next, the segment address of the video RAM, including the offset address of the current screen page, is loaded in the ES register so video RAM is addressable.

Although we're going to set the pixel without reading it, the next step is to load the byte that contains the pixel to be accessed. The value passed to the CPU is actually meaningless. The purpose of this operation is only to load the four latch registers with the four bitplane bytes that contain the color code for the pixel we want to access. The pixel color is then set by writing the desired color code to video RAM.

According to write mode 2, the EGA or VGA card then writes this bit value in all the latch register groups of four that have a value of 1 in the corresponding bit position of the bit mask register. In our case, this applies only to the bit position of the pixel we're accessing, so all other groups of four remain unaffected by the write access. In the four bitplane bytes, only the four bits that determine the pixel we're accessing are changed in the write operation that automatically follows.

This completes the task of SETPIX. Before returning to the caller, however, the changed graphics controller registers are set back to their default values. This should always be done whenever these registers are manipulated so the next routine that uses them can assume they contain the default values. This allows you to change only the appropriate registers; the others can be left with their default values.

The same applies to GETPIX. However, here only one register of the graphics controller must be programmed. This is the read map register. At the end of the routine, this register is set back to its default value. It's more difficult for GETPIX to read a pixel than for SETPIX to set one. Unfortunately, there is no corresponding read mode in the EGA and VGA cards, so GETPIX must manage with read mode 0.

This mode returns only one byte per read access of the video RAM. This byte comes from the bitplane indicated by the number in the read map register of the graphics controller. So, GETPIX must run through a loop four times, reading a byte from one of the four bitplanes each time. Before this bit can be read, GETPIX programs the read map register within the loop.

Access proceeds from bitplane 3 to bitplane 2, bitplane 1 and finally bitplane 0. At the end of the loop, the read map register is loaded again with its default value of 0. Within the loop, the color of the desired pixel is represented using the four bytes read. All the bits in each byte that don't apply to the desired pixel are hidden using a previously defined bit mask. The result is a byte with either only one bit set or with none. The latter case indicates the corresponding bit from the color code of the pixel wasn't set in the bitplane currently being processed.

The status of this bit is obtained by executing the NEG instruction when other bits have been blanked out with the bit mask. The result of this instruction is the status of the bit not affected by the bit mask is reflected in bit 7 of the register. If the isolated color bit was set, then bit 7 of this register is set after the NEG operation. Similarly, bit 7 is off if the corresponding color bit isn't set.

The bit 7 obtained in this way is moved from the BH register to the BL register with the ROL instruction. This operation is executed four times. The previous result is moved one place to the left to a lower position with each execution of the loop, which then loads the color of the desired pixel in the lower four bits of the BL register. This is why it's important to process the bitplanes from number 3 to number 0; otherwise, if you switched this, you would invert the color code.

This is how GETPIX returns the actual color code of the selected pixel. This method works, even if it's slower and more complicated than the procedure for setting a pixel.

The SETPAGE and GETPAGE routines are much simpler than SETPIX and GETPIX. This is especially true for SETPAGE, which sets the current page number in video RAM. SETPIX and GETPIX operate within this routine. The SETPAGE routine works by multiplying the screen page number by the page length as stored in the PAGEOFS variable. The base segment address of A000H is added and the result is stored in the global variable VIO_SEG.

All subsequent calls of SETPIX and GETPIX are then based on this screen page. Remember, a screen page isn't displayed on screen simply by selecting it with SETPAGE. This enables you to select a page in the background and work on it with SETPIX and GETPIX while a different page is displayed.

SHOWPAGE actually displays a page. SHOWPAGE accepts a page number as input and begins by converting this page number into an offset address in video RAM. This operation also multiplies the value of PAGEOFS by the page number. This time, however, the result is also multiplied by 16, because the value in PAGEOFS is a segment address and not an offset address as is required here.

To display a screen page on screen, the offset address of the screen origin is loaded into two registers of the CRT controller. Theoretically, you can load any value you want in these registers. However, for the display to be understandable, the screen origin and the starting address(es) used by routines, such as SETPIX and GETPIX, must be specified. So, the page number is also multiplied by PAGEOFS here.

From the assembler modules V16COLPA.ASM and V16COLCA.ASM we move on to the main program modules, from which the routines previously described are called. Both programs can work in all EGA and VGA 16 color graphics modes, as long as the mode is set before the program is compiled.

In the declaration of constants, we find a constant called MODUS, which must be assigned a value of A320200, A640200, A640350 or A640480. These values indicate the various graphics modes.

At runtime, the main program uses the IsEgaVga function to determine if the mode indicated by the value of VMODE can be initialized. For the 640x480 mode, this means that a VGA card must be installed. All other modes will run with either VGA or EGA.

If the installed video card passes this test, the global variables MAXX, MAXY and PAGES are loaded with values that depend on the selected video mode. These variables indicate the maximum X-coordinates and Y-coordinates on the screen and the total number of screen pages available.

This information is very important for the DEMO routine, which is called next. DEMO uses the various assembler module routines for running through each screen page in a loop, defining each page with SETPAGE, using each page in conjunction with SETPIX and GETPIX and finally displaying each page with SHOWPAGE. Finally (also within the loop), the COLORBOX, DRAWAXIS and GRFXPRINT or GRFXPRINTF (in the C version) routines are called to fill the screen.

COLORBOX essentially draws a box filled with lines drawn by the LINE routine. LINE is based on the Bresenham algorithm that draws lines without complicated floating point mathematics. Each pixel in the line is drawn with SETPIX.

You'll find the following program(s) on the companion CD-ROM

V16COLP.PAS (Pascal listing)
V16COLPA.ASM (Assembler listing)
V16COLC.C (C listing)
V16COLCA.ASM (Assembler listing)

Because of the way it works, this routine isn't very fast. However, it is intentionally written in the high level language instead of assembly language. Of course, you can rewrite this routine in assembly language. To do so, you need routines for filling areas, drawing circles and polygons, etc. You'll quickly realize that this requires a lot of work. We didn't think the added performance was worth the extra programming effort, so the C and Pascal LINE routines are suitable for demonstration purposes. In addition to LINE, the GRFXPRINT and GRFXPRINTF functions also use SETPIX. These routines print letters and numbers in graphics modes. Each character is read pixel by pixel from the 8x8 ROM resident font and transferred to video RAM using SETPIX.

Although it's not extremely fast, this program demonstrates how assembler routines can be used in the EGA/VGA 16 color graphics modes. The routines in this demo program serve as a starting point for your own 16 color graphics programs.

The VGA 256 color graphics modes

One of the biggest advantages of the VGA card over its predecessor, the EGA card, is its ability to display 256 different colors on the screen simultaneously. This group of 256 is selected from a palette of 262,000 colors. This was a milestone in the development of PC graphics.

But the 256 color mode has a resolution of only 320x200 pixels, which is much less than the 640x480 high resolution 16 color mode. However, display quality is based on more than resolution. For example, it can also be based on the wide variety of colors in this mode. This section discusses how to select this graphics mode, address individual pixels and increase the actual resolution.

Setting the 256 color mode and addressing pixels

To programmers, the 256 color mode with a resolution of 320x200 pixels is the easiest VGA graphics mode to use. This is especially evident in the way the pixels are addressed. Pixel addressing is similar to text mode access in some ways.

Before we can access any pixels, we must enable this mode. You can use function 00H of the BIOS video interrupt to do this. The number for this mode (13H) is passed in the AL register and function number 00H is passed in the AH register. These are the only requirements for setting 256 color graphics mode. This single operation also sets the graphics controller's read and write modes and the corresponding registers. This prepares the video card for access to the 320x200 pixels.

The four bitplanes that were so bothersome in the 16 color graphics modes aren't used; 256 color mode uses a much simpler video RAM organization. Each pixel is represented in video RAM by a single byte, just as in text mode. This byte represents the color as a value between 0 and 255. This color value acts as a direct index to the DAC color table, from which the actual color representing the pixel on screen is taken.

Since a single byte describes each pixel, a screen line consists of 320 contiguous bytes in video RAM. These bytes represent pixels in a row, from left to right. As in text mode, each succeeding line (row) begins immediately after the end of the previous line in the video RAM. So the offset address of a pixel is calculated from its screen coordinates as follows:

```
Offset = y * 320 + x
```

All pixels are therefore located within the 64K segment of video RAM that begins at segment address A000H in this mode. This makes it easy to access every pixel.

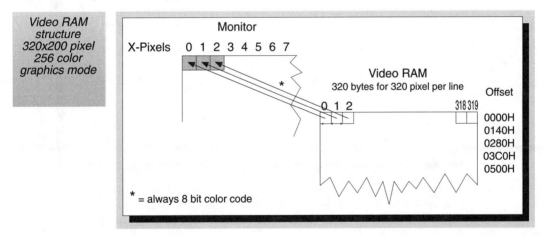

Video RAM structure 320x200 pixel 256 color graphics mode

Since it's easy to access any pixel in this mode, a special demo program isn't required. However, there's another reason for not including a demo program. Since each pixel is represented by one byte, this only requires 320x200 bytes or 64K. In a fully populated VGA card, this leaves 192K of unused video RAM.

So, why can't we simply include three additional screen pages in the remaining video RAM? Although this is theoretically possible, the video RAM structure previously described won't allow it. This may have something to do with the MCGA card, which is related to the VGA card. The MCGA card has the same 256 color mode the VGA card uses, but it's limited to 64K of video RAM (i.e., one screen page). Perhaps IBM wanted to maintain compatibility between the two cards in this mode.

Four graphic pages in one

To overcome this limitation, you can use a few tricks to store and access four graphics pages in video RAM while in VGA 256 color graphics mode.

To manage four graphics pages in the 256 color mode, you must understand how pixel information can be divided among bitplanes. As in text mode, the contiguous video RAM model beginning at A000H is only an illusion that's created to make it easier for the programmer to address individual pixels.

The pixels are actually managed in four bitplanes, just as we saw earlier, using the Chain4 mode. This mode is an extension of the odd/even mode the VGA card uses in text mode to move information from video RAM to bitplanes 0 and 1. In this mode, the lower two bits of a specific offset address determine the number of the bitplane to which the value is sent. These two bits are then internally set to 0 and are used as the offset address to access the selected bitplane. Three bytes remain unused between each occupied byte in each bitplane.

Instead of distributing this information among all four bitplanes, like the 16 color modes, a single byte within the bitplane contains the color information for a pixel. So, four pixels can be found at the same offset address, but in different bitplanes.

Let's consider the first line on the screen. The information for the first four pixels in this line is set at offset address 000H in each of the four respective bitplanes. The pixel with X-coordinate 0 is in bitplane 0, the pixel with X-coordinate 1 is in bitplane 1, etc. According to this scheme, we also find the pixels with X-coordinates 4 through 7 at the same offset address, which is the fourth byte in each bitplane. The information for the pixels is spread over the four bitplanes in the same way.

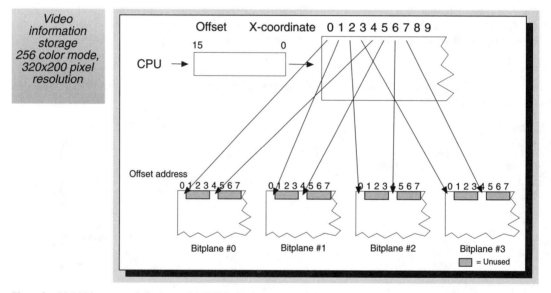

Video information storage 256 color mode, 320x200 pixel resolution

Since the 64,000 bytes needed to store 320*200 pixels are spread out across the four bitplanes, only 16K of each bitplane is actually used. However, there still isn't room for additional screen pages in video RAM. This occurs because the bytes are stored across the entire bitplane with permanent "gaps" of three bytes between each byte that's actually used.

To store more than one page in the video RAM at a time, we must have a way to move the occupied bytes closer together so we don't waste three bytes for every byte used. To do this, you must reprogram several VGA registers.

However, to do this, we must omit Chain4 mode. This means that we must write the color information to the various bitplanes "by hand". The demonstration programs V3220C.C, V3220P.PAS, V3220CA.ASM and V3220PA.ASM control VGA 320x200 pixel graphics mode. The assembler modules contain various routines for initializing video mode and accessing individual pixels. They are specially developed to be called from the accompanying high level language module.

Both programs use the init320200 assembler routine to configure the 320x200 256 color graphics mode that allows four screen pages in video RAM.

This operation begins by setting the video mode as usual with BIOS function 13H. Then the routine changes the registers that are needed to restructure the video RAM according to our needs.

The first step is to switch off the Chain4 and the odd/even modes. This activates a sort of linear mode, which means the offset addresses aren't grouped into bitplanes when video RAM is accessed. This affects read and write access to video RAM only from the CPU's point of view. To the CRT controller, nothing has changed yet.

The CRT controller must be informed the color bytes in the bitplanes are adjacent, rather than spaced in four byte intervals. Next, we switch from doubleword to byte mode, which means that word mode must also be disabled. The program listings document the registers involved with each change. Refer to the end of this chapter for detailed descriptions of the EGA and VGA registers.

After completing this operation, the CRT controller views video RAM as follows:

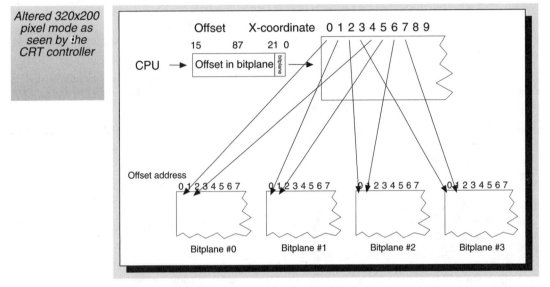

Altered 320x200 pixel mode as seen by the CRT controller

Now, since only the first 16K in each bitplane are occupied, it's possible to store three additional screen pages in the video RAM. The first screen page begins at offset address 0000H in each bitplane, the second at 4000H, the third at 8000H and the fourth at C000H.

In this mode, it's more difficult to address each pixel because all the pixels aren't available in the 64K of video RAM at A000H. Each bitplane is addressed individually. The setpix routine; in the assembler modules performs this task. It expects the X- and Y-coordinates and the pixel color as its arguments.

Setpix starts by creating the offset required to access the desired pixel. According to the new video RAM structure, each bitplane represents 80 pixels instead of 320. So, we begin by multiplying the Y-coordinate by 80. Then, the X-coordinate is divided by four because there are still four consecutive pixels located at each offset address. The sum of these two calculations can then be used to access the proper bitplane.

The number of the bitplane to be accessed is taken from the two lowest bits of the X-coordinate. These two bits represent the number of bits the value 1 is moved to the left to create the bit mask for the map mask register. After this bit mask is passed to the proper register, all subsequent write accesses are addressed to the correct bitplane.

The offset address previously calculated is then used to access the desired pixel and assign the given color to it. Now, all we have to do is determine how the different screen pages are selected.

Instead of being selected by setpix, the screen page is selected by a previous call to setpage. The ..setpage routine; determines the screen page, to which all subsequent calls of setpix will apply. Another setpage call is required to change the page.

The current page is passed to setpix using the segment address stored in the vio_seg variable. This variable stores the video RAM segment address of the page selected by setpage. This is A000H for the first page, A400H for the second, A800H for the third and AC00H for the fourth. Since the segment address already contains the screen origin, it doesn't have to be considered again in calculating the offset address in setpix.

To determine the color of a given pixel, the getpix routine is included in the assembler module. The arguments for this routine are the X- and Y-coordinates for the desired pixel. The pixel color is returned as the result.

The getpix routine works similar to setpix, except that we don't have to program the map mask register of the sequencer to determine the bitplane to be accessed. Instead, we're interested in the read map register of the graphics controller. This register determines the contents of which latch register and therefore which bitplane, is read and sent to the CPU during a read access to video RAM in read mode 1. Unlike the map mask register, the input for this register is only the value of the desired bitplane, instead of a bit mask.

After the offset address of the desired pixel has been calculated and the read map register has been programmed, the pixel color can be read from video RAM. Again, the segment address is taken from the contents of the vio_seg variable so the screen page determined by the last setpage call is used.

One more routine is needed to display the selected page on screen. This is the showpage routine. Its argument is the number of the page to be displayed. Showpage then sends the desired page to the screen by loading the offset address 0000H, 4000H, 8000H or C000H in the starting register of the CRT controller.

The demo program shows what you can do with the routines in the assembler module. Each of the four screen pages is loaded with a very similar pixel pattern, consisting of a coordinate grid, a copyright message and an object drawn with various lines. These lines use a series of colors with color numbers from 0 to n.

The ColorBox routine; draws this object. The variable n represents the upper limit of the color number. This is set to 16 on

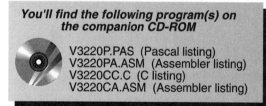

You'll find the following program(s) on the companion CD-ROM

V3220P.PAS (Pascal listing)
V3220PA.ASM (Assembler listing)
V3220CC.C (C listing)
V3220CA.ASM (Assembler listing)

page 0, 64 on page 1, 128 on page 2 and 256 on page 3. ColorBox uses a routine called Line to draw the various lines. This routine accesses setpix from the assembler module to draw lines according to the Bresenham algorithm.

The four different screens are identical except for minor details. The main program quickly switches between them to create interesting optical effects.

320x400 pixels with two screen pages

Although the 256 colors of the 320x200 mode are impressive, the resolution of this mode doesn't compare well with that of other VGA graphics modes. VGA Mode 12H, the highest of the standard VGA modes, uses almost five times as many pixels on screen. Although the many colors of the 256 color mode give the impression of higher resolution, as with a television, it still would be nice to have more pixels with which to work.

When you consider that a single screen page requires only 64K of video RAM in this mode, you may start to wonder if it isn't possible to use more memory per screen page and increase the number of pixels per page. As we'll see later, the VGA card can be programmed to display 400 pixel lines per screen instead of 200. Actually, this is easy to do because the 320x200 mode doesn't actually use 200 horizontal pixel lines.

Even in the 320x200 pixel mode, the VGA card actually has 400 horizontal lines on screen. Since the lines are joined in pairs, it appears as if only 200 lines are on the screen. So, instead of having to double the number of lines, we must simply address each pixel line separately.

The CRT registers responsible for the horizontal and vertical timing don't have to be reprogrammed to change the 320x200 mode to 320x400. Although this results in a rather unusual ratio between the horizontal and vertical axes, the doubled resolution makes this a problem we can tolerate.

The 128,000 pixels in a single screen cannot all be addressed in the usual way. This would require 128K of video RAM, which is too much for the Chain4 mode. So, we use the same method described in the last section to address the pixels in this mode. Each screen page requires 128K, so there is enough room for two pages in video RAM. For most applications, this is sufficient.

Two demonstration programs on the companion CD-ROM (V3240C.C and V3240P.PAS) show you how graphics programming works in this mode.

These programs are very similar to the ones discussed in the previous subsection. Each program also uses an assembler module (V3240CA.ASM and V3240PA.ASM). Compared to those already presented, these modules needed only slight modifications. These changes reflect the differences between the 320x200 and 320x400 modes.

You'll find the following program(s) on the companion CD-ROM

V3240P.PAS (Pascal listing)
V3240PA.ASM (Assembler listing)
V3240C.C (C listing)
V3240CA.ASM (Assembler listing)

One difference is immediately noticeable. The init320200 routine has been replaced with a routine called init320400. The routine itself has changed very little. Video mode 13H is still initialized using the BIOS. The linear mode for addressing video RAM is selected and doubleword mode is replaced with byte mode.

A new step in the routine is the access to the maximum scan line register of the CRT controller. Two changes occur: the bits that indicate the number of pixel lines and the character height. The 200 line bit is disabled so all 400 lines are displayed. The other bit must be set from 1 to 0 to indicate that each pixel line will be processed individually instead of in groups of two.

These are the only changes required to switch from 320x200 mode to 320x400 mode.

The change in screen resolution also affects the setpage and showpage assembler routines. These routines are changed to reflect the new screen page size. Also, the second (and last) screen page now begins at 8000H instead of 4000H.

Surprisingly, setpix and getpix don't have to be changed at all. The line length remains the same and the lines are still stored contiguously in video RAM. Now there are twice as many lines as before and they can be accessed by the correspondingly greater Y-coordinates.

The main programs are also similar. A coordinate grid is drawn on screen along with a copyright message. A box filled with colored lines appears below this.

You can immediately tell there are 400 pixel lines on screen by looking at the coordinate grid. You can also tell that more than one screen page is in memory because of the interesting effects that result from quickly switching the two pages.

Finally, we should mention that some (not all) VGA cards have another 256 color mode, with a resolution of 360x480 pixels. This mode exceeds the limit of 128K per screen page, so only one page can be stored in video RAM at a time.

For these reasons we won't discuss this mode in detail. The practical resolution limit of the VGA card with 256 colors lies with the 320x400 mode. If you really need greater resolution in a 256 color mode, you should consider using the Super VGA card, which offers higher resolution modes as a standard feature.

Freely selectable colors

An important difference between the EGA/VGA cards and their predecessors is the ability to work with more than just the 16 basic colors. The EGA card has 64 colors from which to choose and the color palette of the VGA card exceeds 262,000 different colors. Of course, not every available color can be displayed on screen at one time. Depending on which text or graphics mode you're using, you'll be limited to a set of 16 or 256 colors that can be used at any given time.

What are palette registers?

The 16 palette registers are part of the attribute controller. These registers are important for the color display in all text and graphics modes with 16 or fewer colors. When the CRT controller is building a screen, it receives the color information for a given pixel as a value between 0 and 15. This value is used as an index into the palette register table. The color information is taken from the index palette register and sent directly to the monitor by the EGA card.

This process shows how the EGA and VGA cards still have a strong connection between the different color codes and the colors that appear on the screen, similar to the earlier video cards. So the programmer has the option of freely selecting the colors that should appear on the screen. This global color selection must occur without changing the contents of video RAM. For example, if all pixels in 640x350 pixel graphics mode were black and a program abruptly changed these pixels to another color, changing the palette register contents from 0 to another value is all that's needed.

If you allow for the palette registers, VGA and EGA color selection isn't different than CGA color selection. The color values are identical to CGA after initializing the palette registers by calling BIOS video interrupt function 00H. The palette registers can then be controlled using the sub-functions of BIOS video interrupt 10H, function 12H, after video mode initialization using function 00H.

To call this function, place the function number 12H in the AH register and the sub-function number (31H) in the BL register. The AL register, which normally contains the sub-function number, is used here to determine whether the palette registers are automatically initialized. If this register contains a value of 1, the palette registers aren't initialized with each subsequent call of function 00H. A value of 0 switches on the automatic initialization feature.

With this feature switched on, you can use the expanded color capabilities of the EGA and VGA cards by programming the palette registers. Before doing this, you must understand the structure of the palette registers. With an EGA card and an EGA or multisync monitor, the individual bits in a palette register directly correspond to the different monitor leads that encode the colors. The basic colors red, green and blue (RGB) each have two leads available. One represents a brighter, more intense display and the other is for a normal display. This makes a total of six bits involved in color programming, which allows for a maximum of 64 (26) colors; 16 of these colors can be loaded in the 16 palette registers at a time.

The attribute controller's color plane enable register plays a vital role in color selection and the palette registers. Before every access to one of the 16 palette registers, the EGA/VGA video controller executes a logical AND between the color index and the lower four bits of this register.

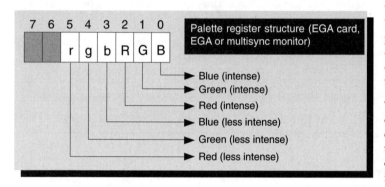

This operation is usually transparent because the lower four bits of the color plane enable register contain a default value of 1111(b). The AND operation with the color index doesn't change the value and the desired color appears on screen.

This is quite different if the value in the color plane enable register changes. For example, if a value of 0111(b) is stored in the color plane enable register, the AND operation with the color value would result in the highest bit from the color value being switched off. This means that all pixels (or characters) with color codes from 8 to 15 would be reassigned to color codes from 0 to 7. Actually, this capability is seldom used and the default value of the color plane enable register is rarely changed.

The DAC color table

The palette register contents can be passed directly from the EGA card to the monitor, through the monitor cable's six color leads. However, this is impossible with the VGA card. The VGA card produces an analog signal for the monitor, which works under a completely different premise.

So, the contents of the VGA card's 16 palette registers are added to the DAC (Digital to Analog Converter) color table before color information can be sent to the monitor. As the name suggests, this table converts the digital color information from the palette registers to an analog signal the monitor can understand.

The DAC color table has 256 registers, each of which stores the information for one color selected from the total VGA palette of over 262,000 colors. This impressive number of colors is a result of 18-bit color coding ($2^{18} = 262,144$). Each entry in the DAC color table consists of three 6-bit color values: one each for the red, green and blue color components.

To select a register in the DAC color table, the video controller interprets the contents of the palette register as an index to the DAC color table instead of as a color value. The following illustration shows how the contents of several other registers determine various ways of organizing the DAC color table into groups.

Creating color codes with the VGA card

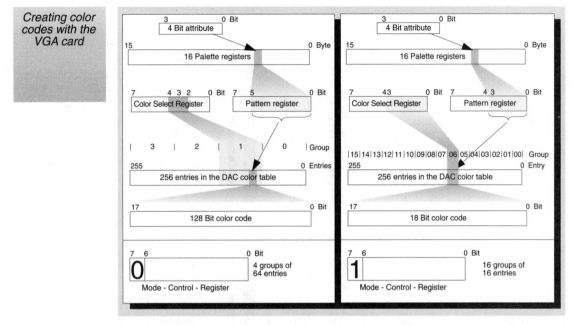

The mode control register of the video controller plays an important part in this process. If this register contains the value 0, then the index to the DAC color table is created from bits 0 through 5 of the corresponding palette register and bits 2 and 3 of the color select register. This means the DAC color table is divided into four groups of 64 consecutive registers and that bits 2 and 3 of the color select register determine which of the four groups is currently active.

It's slightly different if bit 7 from the mode control register contains a value of 1. In this case, the DAC color table is divided into 16 groups of 16 consecutive registers. The index to the table is then created from bits 0 through 3 of the palette register and bits 0 through 3 from the color select register. Again, the value from the palette register is an index and the value in the color select register determines the currently active group in the DAC color table.

This type of coding can create fast and continuous color changes for entire groups of characters or pixels on screen. This is done by loading the color groups of the DAC color table with series of colors that have increasing or decreasing intensities. Then simply change the current DAC color group using the color select register.

To emulate default CGA colors, the VGA card is initialized so the 16 palette registers point to the first 16 registers of the DAC color table. These registers in the DAC color table are loaded with the color information for the standard CGA colors from black (0) to white (15). The other DAC color table registers aren't set when a text mode is initialized with video BIOS function 00H. In a graphics mode, all 256 registers of the DAC color table are initialized as long as the initialization isn't switched off by sub-function 31H of function 12H.

The following illustration shows the scheme used to initialize the DAC registers. There is also a short program at the end of this section that shows the initialization of the DAC registers on screen and allows you to make changes to individual registers.

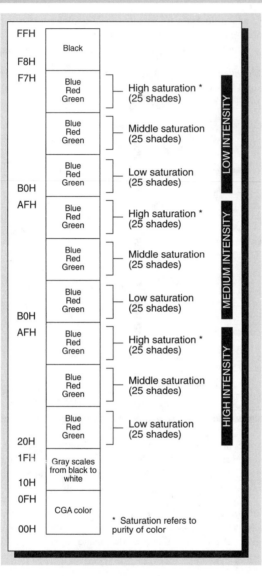

Initialization of 256 DAC color table registers (VGA graphics modes)

The palette registers themselves are the actual color sources in text and 16 color graphics modes. In the 256 color modes of the VGA card, however, this scheme would require 256 different palette registers. This is why the palette registers store index values to the DAC color table in these modes.

The 256 entries in the DAC color table determine the 256 different colors that can be displayed on the screen at any one time. So, programming the palette registers directly in these modes won't have the desired effect on the screen colors.

Setting colors using the BIOS

The expanded EGA/VGA BIOS has several functions for manipulating the contents of the palette registers and the DAC registers. The other register of the attribute controller can also be set. These tasks are accomplished with sub-functions of function 10H of the BIOS video interrupt. When calling one of these sub-functions, load function number 10H into the AH register and place the sub-function number in the AL register.

The first of these sub-functions is 00H, which enables you to load any color value into one of the 16 palette registers. To call this sub-function, load function number 10H into the AH register and the sub-function number 00H into the AL register. Also, load the palette register number (00H-0FH) into the BH register and the color number into the BL register.

The register number passed to this sub-function isn't checked. So, you can also use it to access the overscan register, which is found immediately after the last palette register. Since this register determines the color of the screen frame and background color in the CGA compatible graphics modes, it also has its own sub-function (01H).

Since there are only two or three raster lines available for a screen frame, you should only use black as a background color, especially for the EGA text modes. Also, the contents of the overscan register are meaningless when a monochrome monitor is attached.

To call this function for accessing the overscan register, load the function number 10H into the AH register and sub-function number 01H into the AL register. Load the screen border color into the BH register. This is passed to the overscan register when the function is called.

Sub-function 02H loads both the palette registers and the overscan register in one operation. In addition to the usual function number and sub-function number, load the 17-byte address of a table that contains values for all 17 registers (16 palette registers plus the overscan register) into the ES:DX register pair. When the function executes, the 17 values from this table are loaded into the 17 registers.

Although we have two functions for changing the contents of the palette registers, the expanded EGA BIOS doesn't have any functions for reading the contents of these registers. The EGA card doesn't allow the contents of the attribute controller registers (and almost all other registers) to be read. This situation worsens when working with TSR programs because they aren't able to restore the palette registers to their original contents when the interrupted program is reactivated.

Many programs solve this problem by diverting the results of sub-functions 00H and 02H to a custom routine that stores the values in the palette registers before writing new values. This method doesn't work, however, if you attempt to bypass the BIOS functions and program the palette registers directly. So, you should always use the BIOS functions, even though Section 4.8.10 shows you how to manipulate the palette registers directly.

The last sub-function of function 10H in the expanded EGA BIOS defines the meaning of bit 7 in the attribute byte of a character in text mode. Just as with the CGA and MDA cards, this bit can be used with the EGA/CGA card to make a character blink or to display a character with an intense background color. The CGA and MDA cards require direct programming to define the meaning of this bit, but the EGA/VGA BIOS has a special function (sub-function 03H of function 10H).

Place the function number (10H) in the AH register and the sub-function number (03H) in the AL register. The BL register specifies the degree of intensity. Loading 0 into this register produces a high intensity background color and 1 enables character blinking when bit 7 of the attribute byte is set.

Other sub-functions of the expanded VGA BIOS

The VGA BIOS video interrupt has some functions that aren't included in the EGA BIOS. These apply to the DAC color table and palette register reading. Unlike the EGA card, the VGA card can easily read palette register contents. This also applies to several other registers that are inaccessible on the EGA card.

The contents of the DAC color registers can be modified with sub-function 10H. Place the function number (10H) in the AH register and the sub-function number (10H) in the AL register. Also, place the number of the desired DAC color register (0 - 255 [00H - FFH]) in the BX register and the desired color code in the CH, CL and DH registers. 18-bit VGA color codes consist of three 6-bit components, one for each color component (red, green and blue). Like many of the other sub-functions we'll describe, 10H expects the red component in DH, the green component in CH and the blue component in DL. Only the first six bits (0 - 5) are significant.

The DH, DL and CL registers are also used by sub-function 15H to return the contents of a DAC color register. Place the function number (10H) in the AH register and the sub-function number (15H) in the AL register. Also, place the DAC color register number in the BX register.

Sub-function 12H loads a number of DAC color registers in one operation. The BX register expects the number of the first DAC color register to be loaded and the CX register expects the total number of registers to load. Instead of processor registers, a buffer is used to pass the new values for the given DAC color registers. The address of this buffer is loaded in the ES:DX register pair. Each DAC color register receives three consecutive bytes from this buffer. In each group of three bytes, the first byte provides the green component, the second byte provides the red component and the third byte provides the blue component.

Sub-function 17H allows you to read the contents of a range of DAC color registers. The number of the first register to read is loaded in the BX register and the total number of registers is loaded in the CX register. The VGA BIOS then copies the contents of these registers to the buffer with the segment and offset address specified in the ES:DX register pair. The structure of this buffer is the same as that described for sub-function 12H. Remember, each register from the DAC color table contains three bytes instead of one, so be sure that you have a large enough buffer.

You can determine the way the DAC color table is organized and which color group is active with sub-function 13H. This sub-function has two sub-functions of its own. If this function is passed the value 0 in the BL register, then bit 0 of the BH register is copied to bit 7 of the mode control register of the VGA controller and the DAC color table is divided into 4 or 16 groups. If the BL register contains the value 1, then the content of the BH register is copied to the color select register and the active color group of the DAC color table is selected.

The contents of these two registers can be determined by calling sub-function 1AH. After this function call, the BL register contains the contents of bit 7 of the mode control register and the BH register contains the contents of the color select register.

There is also a sub-function for converting the color codes of the DAC color table to gray scales. This is sub-function 1BH. This is helpful for displaying a black and white picture on a color VGA monitor. If you have a monochrome VGA monitor, the conversion of colors to gray scales takes place in the monitor itself.

To use sub-function 1BH, load the first register number into the BX register and the total number of registers to convert into the CX register. The actual conversion or gray scale summing, is done by weighting each color component to obtain a gray scale value between 0 (black) and 1 (white). The color component values are weighted so the red component is 30% of the final gray scale value, the green component is 59% and the blue component is 11%.

In addition to the selective conversion of the certain DAC registers to gray scales, you can use sub-function 33H of BIOS function 12H to convert the contents of the entire table. Before calling the BIOS video interrupt, the sub-function number is loaded in the AL register and the function number is loaded in the AH register as usual. In this case, the AL register determines whether the conversion occurs. A value of 0 tells the BIOS to convert the color values to gray scales. A value of 1 leaves the color values intact.

In addition to the sub-functions for manipulating the DAC color table, the VGA BIOS also has several sub-functions for reading the palette registers using function number 10H. Sub-function 07H reads the contents of any palette register. The number of the desired palette register is loaded in the BL register and its contents are returned to the BH register. The contents of the overscan register are also read with this sub-function, but the BIOS has also dedicated sub-functions 08H for this purpose. As with sub-function 07H, the result is returned to the BH register.

Sub-function 09H returns a copy of the contents of all 16 palette registers and the overscan register. This sub-function writes the contents of these registers to a 17-byte buffer. The segment address of this buffer is loaded into the ES register when the sub-function is called and the offset address is loaded into the DX register.

Demonstration programs

The BIOS functions make it easy to set the available colors. It's more difficult to select from these colors the actual colors your program will display on screen for a given character or pixel. This is especially true for the VGA card. The EGA card is limited to a choice of 64 colors, but the VGA's palette of 256 simultaneous colors makes this process more complicated. So, we'll conclude this section with a demo program called VDAC. The companion CD-ROM includes C and Pascal versions of this program called VDACC.C and VDACP.PAS.

The program works in the VGA 256 color graphics mode with a resolution of 320x400 pixels. The assembly language modules V3240PA.ASM and V3240CA.ASM, which were described in "The VGA 256 color graphics modes" in this section, are also used. Other routines, which you may remember from previous chapters, such as ISVGA, LINE and GRAFXPRINT, are also used.

The heart of the program consists of the routines SETDAC, GETDAC and DEMO. SETDAC and GETDAC are ports to sub-functions 12H and 17H of function 10H. They read and write any number of DAC color registers. The DEMO routine frequently uses these to load all the DAC registers and allows you to read or change the contents of individual registers.

On screen, you'll see a collection of 256 color blocks that are arranged in a square. Each color block consists of pixels of a certain color. The block in the upper-left corner starts with color value 0. The next block to the right uses color value 1 and its neighbor uses color value 2 and etc. to the lower-right block, which uses color value 255.

In this way, all 256 colors in the DAC color table are displayed on screen. First, you'll see the colors the BIOS automatically assigns when the graphics mode is initialized. In addition to the actual colors, the program also displays the numerical data for the color in the status line. When the program begins, the numbers of the red, green and blue color components for the upper-left color block will be displayed. You can then use the arrow keys to view the color component values for the other color blocks.

As you scroll through the color values, you'll notice the current color block is indicated by a white frame. The copyright message across the top of the screen will also be displayed in the color of the current color block. At first you cannot see the copyright message because it's initialized with the color black.

To change the color of the copyright message, it is initialized with color code 255, which starts out as black. Then, each time you move the cursor, the color of the current block is copied to DAC color register number 255. This means the color of the lower-right color block and the color of the copyright message change with each cursor movement.

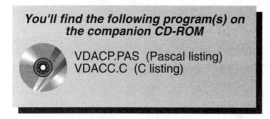

You'll find the following program(s) on the companion CD-ROM

VDACP.PAS (Pascal listing)
VDACC.C (C listing)

The program also allows you to change the red, green and blue components for the current color block with the Ⓡ, Ⓖ and Ⓑ keys. Pressing one of these keys increments the value of the corresponding color component by one. The change is reflected immediately in the color of the color block, the color of the copyright message and the contents of the status line. To decrease the value of a color component, hold down the Shift key while pressing the corresponding letter. You can also press Spacebar to return a color to its original value.

Press the Enter key to end the program. The program restores the original color table and returns you to text mode.

Sprites

Nothing dazzles computer users more than slick graphics. Whether it's a PacMan character zipping across the screen, a starship defending its homeworld from evil invaders or a dinosaur emerging from the jungle, good graphics and animation always catch the user's attention. However, behind every successful animation lie dozens of hours of development. This is especially true for PC software development because most home based PCs contain video hardware that has limited capabilities for graphics programming. So, a lot of coding must be done from scratch.

In this section, we'll show you how to create convincing graphics on the PC despite these limitations. The technique involves using sprites, which are graphics objects that are used in almost all computer games and many animation applications.

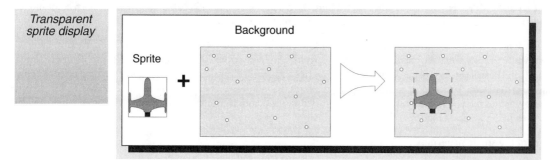

Transparent sprite display

What are sprites?

A sprite is a rectangular block of pixels grouped together to form an object. You can then move this object across the screen. The colors used must be selected carefully. Many programmers assign a single color to the object and then assign the screen background color to all the pixels in the sprite block that don't represent the object itself. Although this simplifies development, it limits your animation options.

In addition to the basic image represented by the sprite, you should also be able to replace it with another image while the program is running. For example, the basic image may be a starship, but the second image may be an exploding starship.

Programming an application then involves coordinating the movement of sprites on the screen to create the desired animation. We won't discuss that here, but we'll cover all the routines you'll need for basic sprite programming. These include routines for sprite definition, movement, removal and image change.

The demonstration programs show examples of sprite programming on EGA and VGA cards. First, we'll look at the two VGA 256 color modes described in "The VGA 256 color graphics modes" in this section. Then, we'll explore the EGA/VGA 16 color modes with 640x350 pixel resolution. This mode is more difficult to program than the 256 color modes.

Each demonstration program exists in C and Pascal implementations. They all begin by filling the screen with the PC character set to create a background for sprite movements. Six sprites appear as spaceships, moving vertically on the screen. These ships bounce off the top and bottom screen borders, changing their appearances to point in a different direction when this occurs. Assembly language modules help increase the speed of sprite movement.

The two-page concept

Switching between two screens produces smooth animation. Sprite animation with only one screen page results in flickering as your objects move. This occurs because of the way sprites are displayed and moved on the screen.

There are several steps to this procedure. The screen area containing the sprite is processed several times. First, the background of the area on which the sprite is overlaid is saved for later restoration, after the sprite has moved to another location. This process is invisible to the user, because only a certain portion of the video RAM is being read.

In the next step, the sprite is copied to its location in video RAM and displayed on the screen. These steps themselves don't cause screen flickering. The critical point is when you move the sprite again to create the illusion of motion. In this case, the background of the sprite must first be restored by copying the old pixels from the buffer back to video RAM.

Although this process is fast, it's visible on the screen. The sprite disappears momentarily and then reappears in its new location. Then the entire cycle of saving the background, writing the sprite and restoring the old background is repeated.

The flickering effect cannot be avoided if you're working with only a single screen page. This is why we use two screen pages when programming sprites; this allows you to switch smoothly between screens. The processing always occurs on the hidden screen. When the processing is complete, the next scene in the animation is displayed and the cycle begins again.

The need for two screens also explains why we don't use the high resolution 640x480 VGA mode. A single screen page in this mode requires 150K, leaving only 106K. So, we limit the resolution to 640x350 in the EGA and VGA 16 color modes. This mode is adequate for most games, which are the most common applications for sprites.

Regardless of the video mode and how we choose to write sprites in video RAM and store their old backgrounds, there are certain universal problems that we must address when programming with sprites. The solutions to these problems are similar in both the C and Pascal versions of the demonstration programs. So, we'll discuss common aspects of the two versions before viewing the differences. These occur primarily in the modules that address video RAM, which is organized differently for the various graphics modes. These modules can be modified so the demonstration programs work with other types of video cards or even in the graphics modes of the Super VGA card.

Structure of the sprite programs

The sprite demo begins by determining the video card type. Next, a routine named DEMO is called from the main program or the MAIN() function. The DEMO routine fills screen pages 0 and 1 with characters from the PC character set using the GRAFXPRINTF (C version) and PRINTCHAR (Pascal version) routines (see "The 16 color EGA and VGA graphics modes" and "The VGA 256 color graphics modes" in this section for descriptions of these routines). These routines in turn access assembler modules, such as V3220CA.ASM and V3240PA.ASM to enable various video modes (see "The VGA 256 color graphics modes" in this section). The assembler modules contain routines for reading and writing pixels, switching between and displaying screen pages and initializing a specific graphics mode.

After the characters form the background for the sprite display, a copyright message appears in the middle of the screen. Then the COMPILESPRITE routine defines the sprites.

The sprites aren't actually created by COMPILESPRITE. A routine called CREATESPRITE later creates the sprites in each program. A string array conveys the appearance of a sprite. The COMPILESPRITE routine converts this array to a binary format that is later used to display the sprite on the screen. COMPILESPRITE begins by creating a bit pattern that can later be assigned to a number of sprites. COMPILESPRITE accepts a different number of parameters, depending on the version of the program. The first two parameters are always the same, however. The first parameter contains the string array that describes the appearance of the sprite and the second parameter contains the number of strings in the array.

This second parameter also defines the height of the sprite. A sprite can have a height ranging from one to hundreds of pixels. Each pixel line is represented by one string in the array. The first string is the top line of the sprite, the next string is the second line from the top, etc. Each character in a string represents a pixel. Since a sprite is a rectangular object, all strings in the string array have identical widths. So it's unnecessary to pass the width of the sprite, since this can be obtained from the width of the first string in the array.

The following is an example of how a sprite may be coded in a C array:

```
static char *STARSHIPUP[20] =
                { "                    AA                  ",
                  "                   AAAA                 ",
                  "                   AAAA                 ",
                  "                    AA                  ",
                  "                  GGBBGG                ",
                  "                 GBBCCBBG               ",
                  "                GBBBCCBBBG              ",
                  "               GBBBBBBBBBBG             ",
                  "               GBBBBBBBBBBG             ",
                  " G             GBBBBBBBBBBBG          G ",
                  "GCG          GGDBBBBBBBBBBBDGG        GCG",
                  "GCG    GGBBBDBBB    BBBDBBBGG         GCG",
                  "GCBGGGBBBBBDBB       BBDBBBBBGGGBCG",
                  "GCBBBBBBBBBBBDB       BDBBBBBBBBBBBCG",
                  "BBBBBBBBBBBBBDB BB BDBBBBBBBBBBBBB",
                  "GGCBBBBBBBDBBBBBBBBBBBDBBBBBBBCG ",
                  "   GGCCBBBDDDDDDDDDDDDDBBBCCG     ",
                  "      GGBBDDDDGGGGGDDDDDDBBG      ",
                  "        GDDDDGGG    GGGDDDDG      ",
                  "          DDDD        DDDD       " };
```

The sprite demonstration programs were intended for use with color monitors, so each pixel must have a color associated with it instead of a simple "on/off" status. The programs read the @ character as black (color code 0), A as blue (color code 1), B as green (color code 2) and so on.

Pixels that aren't associated with the sprite appear in the background color (blank spaces).

The COMPILESPRITE routine; always returns a pointer to a structure of type SPLOOK, which is placed on the heap by the COMPILESPRITE routine. This structure contains all the important information needed about the sprite. Sprite creation requires this structure in the following steps. After COMPILESPRITE is finished, the string array initially used to define the sprite is no longer needed.

Two types of sprites are defined within the programs. They are represented by the string arrays STARSHIPUP and STARSHIPDOWN. One sprite displays the ship going up and the other displays it going down. Using the pointer to the SPLOOK structure, the sprites are generated within a program loop.

The SPRNUM constant controls the number of times the loop is processed, which is set to a value of 6 in each demonstration program. Each time the loop is processed, a new sprite is created with a call to the CREATESPRITE routine. If you want to experiment with the program, you can easily set this constant to a higher value to create more sprites on the screen. The sprites will be crowded closer and closer together until they overlap. This will cause problems with your display, since these demonstration programs aren't written to handle collisions between sprites.

When experimenting with the number of sprites displayed on screen, you'll notice the sprite movement suddenly becomes jerky and hesitant. Reduce the number of sprites by one until smooth movement returns. The number of sprites that can be smoothly processed depends on the processor speed and graphics card type in your system. The reason for this problem will become clear as we discuss sprite movement in more detail.

The CREATESPRITE routine creates sprites through recursive calls. The first parameter required by this routine is the pointer to the sprite description, as returned by COMPILESPRITE. This is how the size and appearance of the sprite are defined. The rest of the parameters passed to CREATESPRITE depend on the sprite program and will be discussed along with the individual details of each program as we encounter these details.

In all the sprite demonstration programs, the CREATESPRITE routine returns a pointer to a structure of type SPID. This structure stores all the relevant data for the sprite that was just created. This information includes the pointer to the appearance of the sprite, its current position in both screen pages and other information that will vary with the program version. This data structure is also placed on the heap, just as with COMPILESPRITE.

The loop used to create sprites also determines their initial position on screen and the speed at which they will move. This information is generated by a random number function. The speed of movement in the X direction is always set to 0 in the local variable DX, which ensures the sprites will move only up or down, but never right or left. When experimenting with these programs, you may want to set this variable to a value other than 0 and watch what happens to the sprites.

The pointer to the sprite (or its SPID structure) and its speed of movement are stored in a local variable called SPRITES. This variable is a simple array.

The SETSPRITE procedure displays the sprite on the screen. The first parameter required is the pointer to the sprite description that was returned by CREATESPRITE. Then the X- and Y-coordinates for the sprite in screen page 0 are passed, followed by the X- and Y-coordinates in screen page 1.

The two coordinate pairs are passed separately because they cannot be identical. This is the basis of the two-page concept. If the sprite were located at the same position in both screen pages, it would not appear to move at all when you switch pages. The speed of the sprite's movement is determined by the distance between the sprite's positions in the two screen pages.

Independent movement

Imagine a sprite that you want to move vertically on the screen from the top edge (Y-coordinate = 0) to the bottom edge. Each time the screen is redrawn, the sprite moves down by one pixel. We can initialize the program with the sprite at Y-coordinate 0 in the first screen page and at Y-coordinate 1 in the second page. Then when the display switches from page 0 to page 1, the sprite appears to move down one pixel.

Now, while screen page 1 is being displayed, the sprite in screen page 0 is moved to a new location. The new location will be two pixels below its original position, so when screen page 0 reappears, the sprite appears at Y-coordinate 2 (one pixel below its previously displayed position). This means that if you want the sprite to appear to move by a certain number of pixels when each new screen is drawn, you must move it by twice as many pixels when internally building a new screen page.

The same is also true for changes in the X-coordinate to make your object move horizontally.

After the sprites are created and initially displayed, a loop processes their movements until the user presses any key on the keyboard. Inside the loop, the program constantly switches between the two screen pages and the sprite is moved on the screen page that isn't displayed.

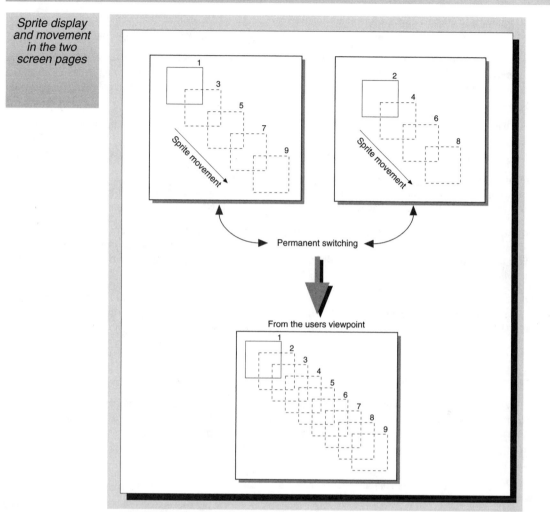

Sprite display and movement in the two screen pages

This is accomplished with the MOVESPRITE function. This is one of the few sprite routines that appears unchanged in all the sprite demonstration programs. That is because this routine is based on the lower level routines that reflect the actual differences between the programs.

The arguments for this routine are a pointer to the sprite description, the page number in which you want to move the sprite and the number of pixels to move in the X- and Y-directions. The current sprite position and the movement increment ("speed") calculate the new position. Collisions with the edge of the screen are also taken into consideration. If the new sprite position is different from the old position, the movement executes.

The RESTORESPRITEBG routine; deletes the sprite from its current position by restoring the background. The background of the sprite's new location is stored in a buffer using the GETSPRITEBG routine. Finally, the sprite itself is copied to its new location using the PRINTSPRITE routin;e.

The result of the MOVESPRITE function is a byte that reflects any collisions with the edge of the screen. The constants OUT_LEFT, OUT_TOP, OUT_RIGHT, OUT_BOTTOM and OUT_NO can determine whether any collisions have occurred.

The DEMO routine also uses the information in this byte. Remember, when the sprite collides with the edge of the screen, it changes its appearance as well as its direction. This keeps the nose of the ship pointing in the correct direction.

The execution speed of the sprite movement loop within DEMO (and the speed of the sprite on screen) varies with your processor's speed, your video card and the bus that connects the two. The frequency of your screen picture also makes a difference because the rate at which screen pages are changed to create movement must be synchronized with the picture frequency.

A query loop within the assembler routine SHOWPAGE handles this. SHOWPAGE returns to its caller after a screen redraw has begun. The new screen page is selected and displayed only after this occurs. This prevents the caller of the SHOWPAGE routine from accessing a screen page that is still visible for a short time because the next screen redraw hasn't begun yet.

Because of this, it's possible that up to 1/50 of a second is lost, depending on the picture frequency and whether SHOWPAGE is called immediately after a screen redraw has begun. Once you've accumulated a certain number of sprites on the screen, it starts taking too long to switch screen pages. This shows up on the screen as a hesitation in the movement of the sprites.

The speed at which the sprites appear to move is determined by the number of pixels the sprite moves each time the movement loop is processed. There are practical limits here. If you move the sprite too far in a single screen change, it will appear to jump and the impression of fluid movement is lost. The speed with which your system can process the movement loop is also a determining factor.

To limit these problems, the most important routines that connect the program and the video card are written in assembly language. These assembler routines are called by the routines GETVIDEO and PUTVIDEO, which in turn are called by high level language routines, such as PRINTSPRITE, GETSPRITEBG and RESTORESPRITEBG.

PUTVIDEO and GETVIDEO store an area of the screen in a buffer or fill a screen area with a pixel pattern that has already been stored in a buffer. These routines are used by PRINTSPRITE, GETSPRITEBG and RESTORESPRITEBG to display a sprite on screen, save a background area and restore a background area.

The assembly language routines called by GETVIDEO and PUTVIDEO differ significantly depending on the graphics mode being used. In the next section, we'll focus on these routines when we discuss the differences caused by the various graphics modes. We'll start with the VGA 256 color modes. This mode isn't available on the EGA card, but the program is actually simpler in this mode than in the 16 color modes. A discussion of the 640x350 pixel mode for both EGA and VGA appears at the end of this section.

Sprites with 320x200 pixels and 256 colors

Graphics programming requires many compromises. For example, although the 320x200 pixel mode with 256 colors has low resolution, the numerous colors and the ability to program with four screen pages can be great advantages for many applications. Although only two screen pages are needed to animate with sprites, the other 128K of video RAM can be used to store screen backgrounds and bit patterns for sprites.

This is not just a matter of using less of the main memory. Keeping this information in video RAM can significantly increase the execution speed of your program. Remember, only one byte can be passed from the bitplanes to main memory at once, so this also taxes the system bus. Such limitations are removed if you move these memory areas around exclusively within video RAM.

Not only can we avoid I/O operations between the CPU and the video card over the system bus, but we can also enable four bytes to be copied using the four latch registers of the VGA card at once with a single MOVSB command. The REP MOVSB assembly language instruction allows an entire graphics line to be copied in one operation. This is a sufficient reason to put the unused portion of the video RAM to work doing things besides storing complete screen pages. Unfortunately, there is a problem with this procedure, as we'll see later.

First, let's discuss the programs. In the C version, the modules S3220C.C, S3220CA.ASM and V3220CA.ASM generate sprites in the 320x200 pixel 256 color mode. We've already seen V3220CA.ASM in "The VGA 256 color graphics modes" in this section. The S3220C.C. and S3220CA.ASM modules are new. The S3220C.C module contains the C routines COMPILESPRITE through GETVIDEO, which we've already discussed.

The assembly language module 3220CA.ASM contains only the BLOCKMOVE routine, which moves a rectangular block of pixels within video RAM. The Pascal version isn't much different. The modules are called S3220P.PAS, S3220PA.ASM and V3220PA.ASM. V3220PA.ASM was also discussed in "The VGA 256 color graphics modes" in this section.

Storing sprite information in video RAM itself allows us to move this information quickly to different locations. But the structure of video RAM in the 320x200 pixel mode imposes certain limitations on your program. The width of each sprite must always be rounded to a multiple of four. This is because four pixels (i.e., four bytes) are always copied simultaneously using the four latch registers.

If the sprite width isn't a multiple of four, then you would always have to ensure that you copied only the bytes belonging to the current line. This means one or more latch registers would have to be excluded from the copy operation of the last group of bytes in a line. We always round the width of each sprite to a multiple of four, if only to save some development time.

There's another issue involved in those multiples of four. If the information for the sprite's appearance begins at an X-coordinate that is a multiple of four, then it can only be copied to another X-coordinate that is a multiple of four. A sprite starting at X-coordinate 0 can only be copied to coordinates such as 4, 8, 96, 224, etc., but never to coordinates such as 1, 2, 5, 13 or 182. This is simply because any read access to the video RAM in 320x200 pixel mode must begin with an X-coordinate that is a multiple of four. You must do this if you want to use all four latch registers together. The same is true if you would like to write data with all four latch registers in one operation.

There is only one way to move the copies of the four latch registers one pixel to the right, to X-coordinates such as 1, 2 or 25. You cannot simply move the contents from one latch register to the next. For example, you cannot move latch register 0 to latch register 1 or latch register 1 to 2 or 2 to 3, etc. Likewise, you cannot save the contents of latch register 3 and write it to latch register 0 as part of the next copy operation. However, it's possible to mask latch register 0 before the write operation, so its contents aren't copied to an X-coordinate in video RAM that is divisible by four.

Even this last possibility would require too much effort. So instead of this, we simply store four copies of the sprite with the first one starting at an X-coordinate that is a multiple of four. The second copy is stored starting with the next pixel to the right. This keeps the far left pixel column of the sprite unused. For now, this column takes on the background color and is seen as transparent. The third and fourth sprites are stored in the same way, with two or three pixel columns remaining transparent.

Sprite definition in video RAM: 320x200 pixel mode with 256 colors

Before a sprite can be displayed on the screen, a sprite must first be moved to an X-coordinate that is divisible by four. The difference between the starting X-coordinate and the target X-coordinate equals the number of empty columns at the start of the sprite. This also gives the number that identifies the sprite to be copied. The following formula can be used:

```
TargetX =  int(X / 4) * 4
       [or] X and not(4)
Sprite  =  X - int(X / 4) * 4
       [or] X and 3
```

However, the problem of the transparent pixel columns still exists. As long as you use the four latch registers together and copy in groups of four pixels, the complete sprite is copied exactly as it was stored and the blank columns will remain blank. So before the write operation we must use the map mask register of the sequencer controller to mask the latch registers that would otherwise be overwritten with background pixels.

Since there is a different latch register for each group of sprite pixels, the map mask register must be specially programmed for each case before writing to the latch registers. This is done using a value calculated while the sprite description was being compiled with COMPILESPRITE. This value is passed to the BLOCKMOVE routine as part of an array.

Although this makes the procedure more complicated, it's unavoidable if you want to store the sprites directly in video RAM. Fortunately, this is only required when writing the sprite itself. It's not necessary to program the map mask register when saving or restoring a sprite background.

This method of storing sprites in video RAM and copying them as part of an array containing values for the map mask register plays a major role in the S3220C.C and S3220P.PAS modules, as well as the BLOCKMOVE procedure; used in the S3220CA.ASM and S3220PA.ASM assembly language modules.

This starts with the COMPILESPRITE routine. The string array that defines the sprite and the sprite's height are the first two parameters passed to this routine. There are four others. The first of these specifies the screen page that is used to store the sprite description. Since pages 0 and 1 are being used for the display, this must be either 2 or 3.

The next parameter is the pixel line in which the sprite definition will begin. This can be any value from 0 to 200 (the sprite height). Be careful not to overlap sprite descriptions in video RAM.

Within the given line, the four copies of the sprite are stored right next to one another. You can actually see what this looks like by displaying the screen page with SHOWPAGE after compiling the sprite with COMPILESPRITE in the DEMO routine.

The next parameter for COMPILESPRITE is a character that represents the smallest color value in the string array used to define the sprite. Usually, you use the letter 'A' for this. Of course, you can also use lowercase letters or numbers to code the pixel colors within the string array, in which case you would enter 'a' or '0' for this parameter.

The last parameter also handles pixel colors. It gives the color number assigned to the sprite pixel with the smallest color code ('A', 'a' or '0'). This defines the meanings of all the other characters in the string array, since 'B', 'b' or '1' corresponds to the next color value in the palette.

In this way, more than 128 colors can also be reached without using foreign or special characters in your string array. Regardless of the values in the last two parameters, an empty space always represents a transparent pixel. When the sprite is displayed, the transparent pixel turns to the background color.

COMPILESPRITE uses the information passed to it to build the sprite four times in the given page, as previously described. Background pixels are assigned color code 255 so they can be distinguished from the non-transparent pixels in what follows.

Next, the four sprites are processed again to fill the array that is later used to program the map mask register when BLOCKMOVE is called. The memory for this array is allocated on the heap. Each pixel in the four sprites gets a nibble containing the corresponding value for the map mask register.

The pointer to this array is stored in the sprite description (SPLOOK) along with all other relevant information. A pointer to this structure is returned to the calling routine.

CREATESPRITE also requires more information. In addition to the obligatory pointer to the sprite description, the locations of the two areas in video RAM used to store sprite backgrounds from screen pages 0 and 1 must be passed. This requires the screen page (2 or 3) and the X- and Y-coordinates. Remember, you need an area twice as wide as the sprite area itself. This is because the two buffers from both page 0 and page 1 are stored next to each other.

Once a sprite is created with this procedure, you can use the SETSPRITE routine to display it on screen and MOVESPRITE to animate it. PRINTSPRITE, GETSPRITEBG and RESTORESPRITEBG support the BLOCKMOVE assembly language routine.

BLOCKMOVE expects a number of parameters, including the starting coordinates of the source and target areas. These locations are represented by the combination of the screen page plus the X- and Y-coordinates. The width and height of the rectangular block are also required. Finally, BLOCKMOVE receives a pointer to the array that contains the values for programming the map mask register.

If all pixels in the rectangular sprite should be copied regardless of the background pixels, then the array isn't required. You can pass a NULL pointer for this parameter. In the Pascal version, this is represented by the predefined NIL constant and in the C version by the NOBIT MASK constant.

If BLOCKMOVE encounters a NULL pointer, it copies an entire pixel line from the specified area in one move. This is much faster than the normal copy routine, in which the map mask register is programmed before each four byte transfer.

In either case, write mode 1 is set before the copy loop begins. Only this mode allows simultaneous transfer of the latch registers' contents to the four bitplanes. The routine restores the original write mode and ends.

You'll find the following program(s) on the companion CD-ROM

S3220P.PAS (Pascal listing)
S3220PA.ASM (Assembler listing)
S3220C.C (C listing)
S3220CA.ASM (Assembler listing)

Sprite programs using the 256 color 320x200 pixel graphics mode run faster than the other demonstration programs in this section because they can use video RAM for storing sprite descriptions and sprite backgrounds. Unfortunately, a screen resolution that is lower than what PC users are accustomed to is used. We believe that if 256 colors are needed, the 320x400 pixel mode is better, (even despite the slower execution speed).

Sprites in 320x400 pixel mode with 256 colors

When using the higher resolution 320x400 pixel graphics mode, we must sacrifice the advantage of sprite background and sprite description storage in video RAM. Instead, we must move this information from conventional memory to video RAM. These routines take longer to execute than those used to copy structures directly within the video RAM, but the user shouldn't notice the change in speed.

However, this mode simplifies creating and displaying sprites because the transfer from conventional RAM to video RAM occurs one byte at a time. We can also remove our artificial limitation of making sprite widths divisible by four and the need for maintaining four copies of each sprite. So, a sprite of any width can be copied to any X-coordinate. Also, this mode eliminates the need for the map mask register.

The different method for storing sprite information and for moving the information to video RAM can be seen in the sprite modules required for programming in this mode. These are S3240C.C, S3240CA.ASM and V3240CA.ASM in the C version and S3240P.PAS, S3240PA.ASM and V3240PA.ASM in the Pascal version.

The PUTVIDEO and GETVIDEO routines used by the modules previously listed contain the interface between conventional RAM and video RAM. GETVIDEO transfers the contents of a rectangular screen area from video RAM to conventional RAM, as in cases where you would save a sprite background to a buffer. PUTVIDEO then restores an area saved by GETVIDEO from the conventional RAM buffer to a specified location in video RAM.

These routines are based on two routines called COPYBUF2PLANE and COPYPLANE2BUF from the S3240CA.ASM and S3240PA.ASM assembly language modules. These routines transfer a rectangular area of pixels either from a specified bitplane to conventional RAM or from conventional RAM to a bitplane.

The four bitplanes, used to store pixels in all 256 color modes, are each handled separately. This is why these routines are called four times when they are used within GETVIDEO or PUTVIDEO. This works faster than trying to take four pixels (one from each bitplane) in a single move, in which case the read map register of the graphics controller or the map mask register of the sequencer controller would also have to be programmed before each move. Using the method previously described, these registers need to be programmed only once with each COPYBUF2PLANE or COPYPLANE2BUF call, because these routines access only one bitplane at a time.

GETVIDEO and PUTVIDEO are able to work with rectangular blocks of any width, not just multiples of four. So, the areas to be processed within each bitplane may not always be the same width. Imagine a GETVIDEO call where you want to load an area from video RAM with a width that extends from the X-coordinates 0 to 6. In this area, each pixel line has two pixels from the first bitplane (at X-coordinates 0 and 4), two pixels from the second bitplane (at 1 and 5) and two pixels from the third (at 2 and 6). The fourth bitplane therefore contains only one pixel, the one at X-coordinate 3.

Since GETVIDEO is called separately for each bitplane, the routine must keep track of how many pixels are involved and other information that is needed when GETVIDEO is recalled. This information is stored in a data block allocated on the heap by GETVIDEO when it is called. A pointer to this data block is passed back to the caller.

The data block is of type PIXBUF, which begins with an array of four pointers that point to the four buffers that contain the screen areas represented by the four bitplanes. This is followed by another array with four entries that indicate the number of pixels per bitplane. The last entry in this structure is the height of the screen area or the number of pixel lines.

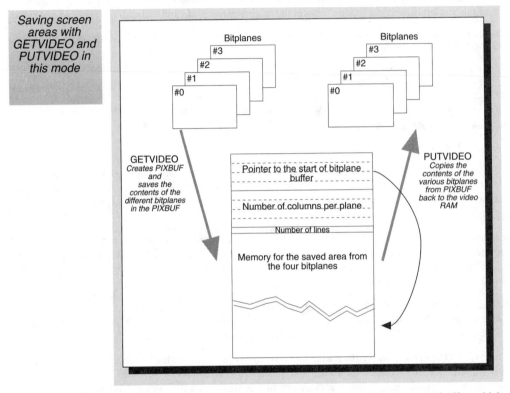

Saving screen areas with GETVIDEO and PUTVIDEO in this mode

The screen area's height is the last entry in the PIXBUF structure. GETVIDEO places the buffer, which stores the pixel information from the individual bitplanes, after this structure. Space for this additional buffer is created when GETVIDEO allocates the PIXBUF buffer. The buffer size required for the information from the four bitplanes is added directly to the size of the PIXBUF structure. The result is a block of memory containing the PIXBUF structure, followed by the pixel information from the four bitplanes as loaded by COPYPLANE2VIDEO.

GETVIDEO returns a pointer to its caller, pointing to the pixel buffer. This pointer can then be passed on to subsequent PUTVIDEO calls. This allows the saved screen area to be copied to any position in video RAM, as often as desired.

The GETVIDEO function serves another purpose. If GETVIDEO is passed a pointer as its last parameter with a value other than NIL (in Pascal) or the ALLOCBUF constant (in C), then the information is loaded into an existing buffer (indicated by the pointer) that was created in a previous call to GETVIDEO. This saves time by allowing you to reuse buffers without having to create a new buffer on the heap each time you call GETVIDEO. When doing this, you must be sure the new screen area to be saved fits within the existing buffer.

The sprite demo programs for the 320x400 pixel mode use this feature for tasks such as saving a sprite background. This works because the size of a given sprite and consequently the size of its background, remains constant, so the pixel buffer needs to be allocated only once.

GETVIDEO and PUTVIDEO aren't only used for saving and restoring sprite backgrounds. These routines also compile the sprite description in COMPILESPRITE. Using the information in the string array that defines the sprite, this routine builds the sprite at screen coordinates 0/0 in the specified screen page (the screen page is passed as a parameter).

Then the area occupied by the sprite is simply copied to a pixel buffer by calling GETVIDEO. Any time you want to display the pixel on screen, simply pass this pixel buffer to the PUTVIDEO routine, with the screen page and the desired coordinates. The pointer to the pixel buffer is stored under the name PIXBP in the SPLOOK structure.

Sprite backgrounds are handled in a similar way. The CREATESPRITE routine uses GETVIDEO to create two pixel buffers of the same size as the corresponding sprite. The first buffer stores the sprite background from the first screen page and the other buffer stores the background from the second page. The pointers to these two pixel buffers are stored in an array called HGPTR within a structure of type SPID. CREATESPRITE configures this structure for identifying and working with sprites.

The pixel buffers for the sprite description and the two background areas are then used by routines such as PRINTSPRITE, GETSPRITEBG and RESTORESPRITEBG, to display the sprite and save or restore its background. You'll see these routines are simpler than those from the sprite demonstration programs for 320x200 pixel mode.

We haven't explained how background pixels are handled yet. The PUTVIDEO routine uses a Boolean variable called BG. This variable is passed on to the assembler routine COPYBUF2PLANE to determine whether the background should be taken into consideration when copying the buffer to each bitplane.

If this parameter contains the value TRUE, then COPYBUF2PLANE checks each byte to determine whether it represents a background pixel when copying the contents of the specified buffer to video RAM. Background pixels are assigned color code 255. This color code was assigned, within the CREATESPRITE routine, to all pixels represented by a space in the string array. If COPYBUF2PLANE encounters such a pixel, it skips it and doesn't write its color to video RAM. The routine then continues with the next pixel in the buffer.

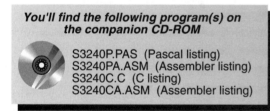

You'll find the following program(s) on the companion CD-ROM

S3240P.PAS (Pascal listing)
S3240PA.ASM (Assembler listing)
S3240C.C (C listing)
S3240CA.ASM (Assembler listing)

This represents a rather simple solution to the problem of background pixels, even if it does add some time to the copy procedure between main memory and video RAM. However, the added time isn't really noticeable to the user.

Now we've covered the major points in the 320x400 pixel sprite programs. If you need additional information about how these demo programs work, the listings are fully documented.

Sprites in EGA and VGA 640x350 16 color graphics modes

If you'd rather have higher resolution at the expense of fewer colors, then you should use 16 color 640x350 pixel mode. Another advantage of this mode is that it's compatible with both EGA and VGA cards. The 640x480 pixel VGA mode cannot be used for sprite programming because it doesn't allow two screen pages to be stored in video RAM simultaneously.

The 640x350 pixel mode uses only 219K of the available 256K of video RAM for screen page storage. So 38,144 bytes remain; these bytes can be used for more than 76,000 additional pixels in a 640x120 pixel block. This extra video RAM can be used to store sprite descriptions and sprite backgrounds, as we did in the 320x200 pixel mode demonstration programs.

Depending on the number of sprites you define and the number of sprites actually displayed on screen, this extra video RAM can be used up rather quickly. As we'll see later, the main reason for this is that you must maintain eight copies of each sprite description instead of four.

Because of this potential limitation, the sprite demonstration programs in 640x350 pixel mode store their sprite descriptions and sprite backgrounds in conventional RAM. Although this is the same method used in the 320x400 pixel mode, the sprite creation and data transfer routines in these programs are quite different from the 320x400 mode programs. The main reason is the video RAM is organized in a completely different way for 16 color modes than for 256 color modes. We saw that eight pixels are represented by a single byte in 16 color modes, as opposed to one pixel per byte in 256 color modes. But one bit isn't sufficient for representing a color code between 0 and 15. This is why the video RAM is organized into bitplanes, allowing the group of four corresponding bytes from each bitplane to define the color information for all eight pixels.

Organizing video RAM into bitplanes can make accessing a specific pixel slow and awkward. This affects the routines found in the S6435C.C (C version) and S6435P.PAS (Pascal version) modules, which display sprites on screen in the 640x350 pixel mode.

The sprite widths are rounded to multiples of eight pixels. If you don't do this, you must isolate only those desired bits from the last byte, save them and then write them back to ensure that only those bits belonging to the sprite are copied. This also applies to programming the map mask register, which is an alternative method for allowing sprites of any width.

This rounding is done internally and is transparent to routines, such as COMPILESPRITE, CREATESPRITE and MOVESPRITE. The fact that eight copies of the sprite description are kept is also transparent. Eight copies are required because of a problem similar to that found in 320x200 pixel mode.

For example, if the binary coding of a sprite description begins in bit 7 of the first byte, it can be copied only to a screen area with an X-coordinate that is a multiple of eight if you want the description to remain unchanged. If you copy to any screen area that starts at an X-coordinate whose value mod 8 is unequal to zero, you must then shift all bits to the right by a value equal to the result of the mod 8 operation. This would actually take too much time to execute.

So, the COMPILESPRITE routine used in S6435C.C and S6435P.PAS creates eight copies of each sprite description, where each copy is shifted one bit to the right. Whenever you must move a sprite to a certain screen position, simply select the copy that matches the desired X-coordinate.

The eight copies of a given sprite description are stored in the form of a pixel buffer. Just as we saw in the 320x400 pixel demonstrations, the sprite description is built in video RAM and then loaded into a pixel buffer with GETVIDEO. Unlike the 320x400 mode, however, this operation is repeated eight times instead of four. This requires much space in conventional RAM.

For example, imagine a sprite consisting of 20x30 pixels, which is a small object for such a high resolution screen mode. After you increase the width by seven pixels and round the width off to make it a multiple of eight, the result is 32 pixels:

```
int( ( 20 + 7 + 7 ) / 8 ) * 8 = 32
```

Each pixel requires four bits, so this sprite requires 16 bytes per pixel line. This amount multiplied by 20 equals 640 bytes for the pixel buffer, not including the status information in PIXBUF. This must be repeated eight times for each sprite description, which increases the number to 5K. When we include the two background buffers required for each sprite, we must add another 1K to the total.

An AND buffer must also be created for each sprite description. This makes the background transparent so the sprite doesn't appear as a rectangular block on the screen. Because of the way video RAM is organized in this mode, this isn't a simple task. It requires a three step process repeated for each byte to write a sprite to video RAM. This process involves loading the byte to be processed, programming the bit mask register to affect only the desired pixels and finally writing the value.

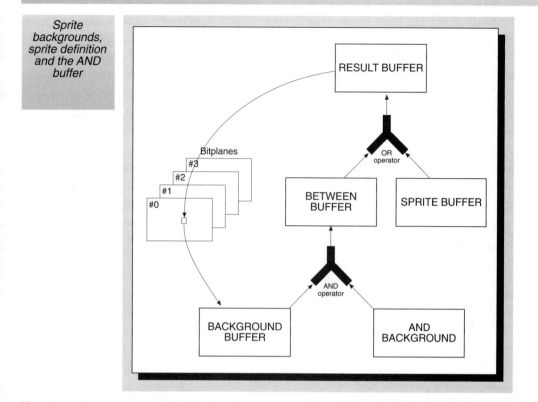

Sprite backgrounds, sprite definition and the AND buffer

Since the previous process would take too long to execute, you should use another method. Remember the sprite background is already available before we write the sprite to its new location. This means that we can merge the buffers containing the sprite description and the background information. This creates the desired pattern of background pixels and pixels before we access video RAM. This process results in the bytes that we actually want to write to video RAM, without having to mask certain bits.

This process involves taking the contents of the background buffer and changing only those bits that don't correspond to background pixels in the sprite description. This leaves the background pixels undisturbed and overwrites all other pixels with pixels from the sprite. This is accomplished with the AND mask.

Imagine a byte from the sprite description and the eight pixels it describes. Suppose that in this byte, the last pixel (represented by bit 7) should be transparent or part of the background. The AND mask for this byte would have all bits set to 0 except for bit 7, which would be set to 1. Then, when merging the buffers, the background byte combines with the corresponding byte from the AND buffer using a logical AND operation.

The result is that only the background bit, bit 7, remains unchanged. All other bits are set to 0. In the next step of the process, the result is combined with the corresponding byte from the sprite description using a logical OR operator. This byte contains a 0 in all bit positions that represent transparent background pixels. All other bits contain values that make up part of the four bit color code for a sprite pixel.

The result of this operation is that all pixels needed to display the sprite are changed to the colors given in the sprite description and all background pixels remain unchanged. This entire operation must be repeated for each bitplane. The AND mask is always the same, however, since the bit positions that represent sprite pixels and background pixels are the same for all bitplanes. The size of the AND buffer in bytes, which is only good for one of the eight copies of the sprite description, is:

```
width * height / 8
```

The AND buffers for each sprite description are created with COMPILESPRITE, in the same way as the sprite descriptions themselves. As the sprite array is processed, a 1 is placed in each bit that describes a transparent background pixel. A 0 represents a sprite pixel that overwrites its background.

The S6435CA.ASM and S6435PA.ASM assembly language modules perform the combination of the sprite background, the sprite description and the AND buffer. This routine is called MERGEANDCOPYBUF2VIDEO. As its name suggests, this routine merges the necessary buffers to create the desired pixel pattern and copies the buffers from conventional RAM to video RAM. Actually, these operations are done in parallel, byte by byte. First, a byte from the three buffers is merged, then it's copied to video RAM; the process continues with the next byte.

This process repeated four times in MERGEANDCOPYBUF2VIDEO for each of the four bitplanes. This also applies to the COPYBUF2VIDEO and COPYVIDEO2BUF assembly language routines which appear instead of the COPYBUF2PLANE and COPYVIDEO2PLANE routines which are found in the assembler module used in 320x400 pixel mode.

These routines can process all four bitplanes automatically because the width of the screen area is limited to multiples of eight in this mode. So, it's unnecessary for the calling routine to specify the number of bytes to process. So COPYVIDEO2BUF copies the given screen area from all four bitplanes to the specified buffer and COPYBUF2VIDEO copies the specified buffer's contents to all four bitplanes.

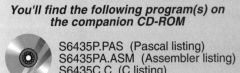

You'll find the following program(s) on the companion CD-ROM

S6435P.PAS (Pascal listing)
S6435PA.ASM (Assembler listing)
S6435C.C (C listing)
S6435CA.ASM (Assembler listing)

This concludes our discussion of conceptual differences in the 640x350 mode sprite demonstration programs. Many features have been documented in the earlier programs in this chapter.

EGA and VGA card registers

EGA and VGA cards are based on several different controllers that share the work of generating a video signal. These are the CRT controller, the attribute controller, the graphics controller, the sequencer controller and the digital to analog controller (DAC), which is found only on VGA cards. In addition to these, EGA and VGA cards use several general registers. We'll discuss these controllers and registers in this section.

Originally, you could actually see which component on the card was responsible for which function because each was performed by a different chip. However, because of advancements in computer chip technology, all functions are now handled by one or two integrated controller chips.

In many instances, these integrated chips perform functions and graphics modes that far exceed the original EGA/VGA standard. To maintain compatibility, however, the register assignments are kept as similar to the original IBM EGA and VGA registers as possible. You'll find the registers described in this section on almost all EGA/VGA cards. Any registers that have different functions in EGA and VGA cards are discussed in detail.

WARNING

You should not change some registers. The most important of which are the CRT controller registers that manage the video signal and synchronize horizontal and vertical rescans. The interaction of these registers is very complex and improper programming could cause monitor damage.

There are many other bits and registers that you can manipulate without problems. However, you should be careful because sometimes there are small but important differences between the EGA and VGA cards. We'll document these differences in this section when possible.

This section doesn't cover registers that don't follow the EGA/VGA standard. Once we look past standard EGA and VGA functions and registers, standards don't exist. For example, there are no register standards for Super EGA or Super VGA. The three most popular Super VGA cards differ significantly in register assignments and expanded functions.

The registers we'll examine here show how many options haven't been explored yet in the expanded EGA/VGA BIOS.

General registers

In addition to the special controller registers, other EGA and VGA registers transfer more general information, which is used in the operation of the card. These are known as the *general registers*.

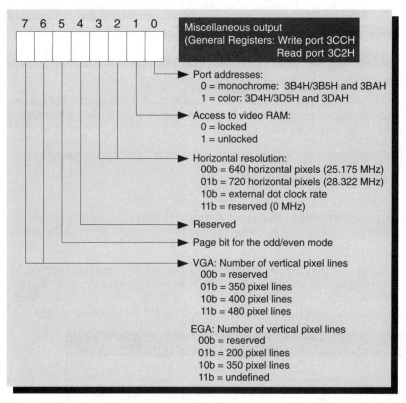

0   For MDA card emulation, this bit specifies the port address of the CRT data and index registers and the input status register 1. These registers normally occupy ports 3D4H/3D5H and 3DAH, but this allows you to switch them to 3B4H/3B5H and 3BAH.

2+3   This bit field selects the active clock. This also specifies the horizontal resolution of a pixel line because the dot clock rate is directly related to the number of pixels that can be displayed.

         The dot clock rate of 0 MHz is reserved because it may only be used during a reset of the VGA card.

         A reset using the sequencer's reset register must always be executed immediately after changing this register.

5   In the Odd/Even video modes (0, 1, 2, 3 and 7), this bit acts as the low bit for memory access. It determines whether odd or even addresses will be accessed in each bitplane. If this bit is 1 (default), then all bytes at even offset addresses are accessed. If it is 0, then odd addresses are accessed.

         This bit loses its meaning if bit 1 in register 6 of the graphics controller sets chain mode or if bit 3 in register 4 of the sequencer controller sets chain4 mode.

6+7   These two bits specify the polarity between the horizontal and vertical rescan signals. This usually results in setting the specified vertical resolution.

Remember the VGA card's 200 pixel emulation mode cannot be set using this bit field because it's actually a 400 pixel mode that displays only half of the lines.

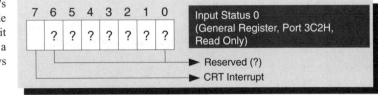

7	6	5	4	3	2	1	0
	?	?	?	?	?	?	?

Input Status 0
(General Register, Port 3C2H,
Read Only)

→ Reserved (?)
→ CRT Interrupt

7   This bit indicates when a vertical rescan of the electron stream occurs in cases where this event triggers an interrupt. After a rescan, the value of this bit remains 1 until it is reset using bit 4 in the vertical rescan end register of the CRT controller.

1+2   These bits act as the light pen port on the EGA card. They aren't used on the VGA card. Bit 2 indicates the presence of a light pen and bit 1 indicates whether the button has been pressed. The position of the light pen can be read using registers 10H and 11H of the CRT controller.

3   This bit indicates the vertical rescan status, which allows a program to determine when certain register changes can safely be made.

CRT controller

The CRT controller is responsible for the picture displayed on your screen. It generates video signals for the monitor using the electron stream generated by the picture tube. It contains a number of registers that manage the timing of the electron stream's horizontal and vertical rescans.

Programmers usually aren't interested in these registers because the interactions between them are very complex. So, programming them should be left to the BIOS, which handles this automatically when you switch video modes. Registers, such as the offset register or the line compare register, are more useful to programmers. These can be used to create special video effects that aren't accessible using the BIOS. The following is an overview of the 25 CRT controller registers:

Number	Register Name	Number	Register Name
00H	Horizontal Total	0EH	Cursor Location High
01H	Horizontal Display End	0FH	Cursor Location Low
02H	Start Horizontal Blanking	10H	Start Vertical Rescan
03H	End Horizontal Blanking	11H	End Vertical Rescan
04H	Start Horizontal Rescan	10H	Light Pen Low (EGA only)
05H	End Horizontal Rescan	11H	Light Pen High (EGA only)
06H	Vertical Total	12H	Vertical Display End
07H	Overflow	13H	Offset
08H	Vertical Pel Panning	14H	Underline Location
09H	Maximum Scan Line	15H	Start Vertical Blank
0AH	Cursor Start	16H	End Vertical Blank
0BH	Cursor End	17H	Mode Control
0CH	Start Address High	18H	Line Compare
0DH	Start Address Low		

The CRT controller registers are addressed by an index register and a data register, which are located at port addresses 3D4H and 3D5H when the EGA or VGA card is in color mode. If the card is in monochrome mode, these registers are accessed at port addresses 3B4H and 3B5H.

As usual, the register number must be written to the index register prior to access. With a read access, the contents of the specified register can then be read in the data register. This doesn't apply to most of the registers on the EGA card, however. Only the two light pen registers can be read on this card; all other registers are write-only. All of these VGA registers can be read.

You can write to the index and data registers in a single 16-bit operation during a read access. The value for the index register must be in the low byte and the value for the data register must be in the high byte.

Once you've placed the register number in the index register, it remains valid for subsequent read or write operations. So, you don't have to enter the register number each time if you perform several consecutive operations on the same register.

Remember the first eight registers of the CRT controller on VGA cards can only be written if bit 7 in register 11H is set to 0. The BIOS will generally set this value to 1, prohibiting access to the first eight CRT registers.

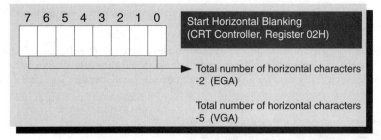

0-7   This specifies the total number of "characters" per screen line. The term "character" indicates an actual ASCII character in text mode. In graphics mode, "character" refers to a group of eight pixels. The total number of characters is calculated as the quotient of the bandwidth and the horizontal scan rate divided by the number of pixels per "character".

        On an EGA card, the value in this register must be the number of total characters minus 2. For a VGA card, it's the total number minus 5.

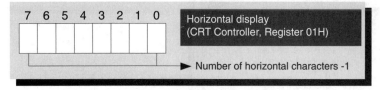

0-7   This register specifies the actual number of horizontal "characters". The value in this register must be reduced by 1 with both EGA and VGA cards.

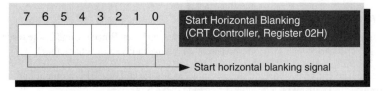

0-7   When the horizontal blanking signal starts, no more characters will be output because the electron stream from the picture tube has been shut off. Once again, the value is given in units of "characters." The first character at the left of the screen is assigned the number 0.

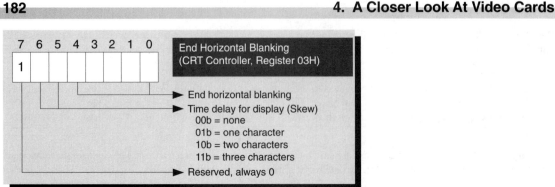

0-7   The end of the horizontal blanking is also described in terms of "characters." The first character output at the left of the screen is counted as 0. The end of the horizontal blanking always occurs before the start, so a maximum of six bits instead of eight are required. The sixth bit is in the end horizontal rescan register, which is number 05H in the CRT controller.

The value in this register is calculated as the sum of the values from the horizontal blanking register and the width of the horizontal blanking in "characters."

5+6   In certain instances, it may be necessary to build in a time delay (skew) to give the CRT controller enough time to read a character and its attributes from video RAM and then generate the corresponding pixel pattern with the character generator. The EGA card typically requires a skew of one character, but this usually isn't necessary with a VGA card.

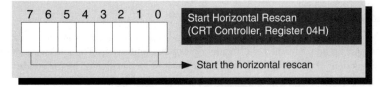

0-7   This register determines the "character" that triggers the rescan. This is used to center the picture horizontally.

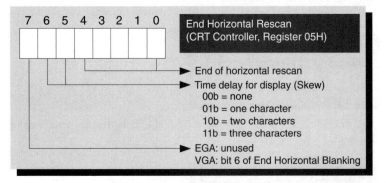

0-4   This specifies the number of characters where the end of the horizontal rescan is set. Since the end of the rescan is always before the start, only 5 bits are needed to code it. The units are again given in "characters".

5-6   A skew or time delay, can set for the end of the horizontal rescan just as for the end of the horizontal blanking. Since the skew will vary from card to card, you should never change these bits.

7   This bit is an expansion of bits 0 through 4 of the end horizontal blanking register. It's the highest bit of the group.

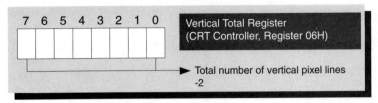

0-7　　This register contains the number of pixel lines processed during a screen build. This includes those lines processed during the vertical rescan.

For both EGA and VGA, the total number of pixel lines exceeds 256, so this register stores only the lower eight bits of the value. The ninth bit is found in the overflow register, which is number 07H. VGA cards also have a tenth bit, which is found in bit 5 of this same register. For both EGA and VGA cards, the value in this register must always be the actual total number of lines minus two.

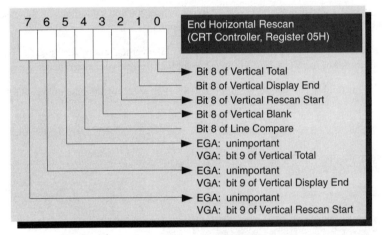

EGA and VGA cards need an overflow register because the number of vertical pixel lines exceeds 256 and therefore cannot be represented in a single eight bit register. The extra bit is kept in the overflow register for the registers that need nine bits. Additional overflow bits for the VGA card are stored in the maximum scan line register (index number 09H).

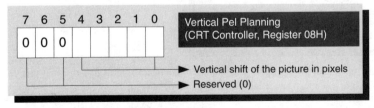

0-4　　These bits are used to create smooth vertical scrolling by moving the entire picture up by a specified number of pixels. A value of 0 represents the normal picture location. Larger values indicate a corresponding upward shift.

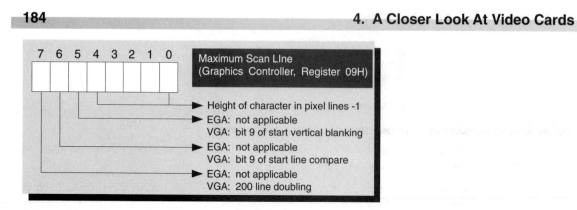

0-4   These bits determine the height of a character in text mode. The unit of measure is pixel lines. The value stored in this register must be the actual height minus 1.

       This bit field normally contains a value of 0 in graphics mode unless it's using a 200 line VGA mode. In this case, the display of each line is doubled and this register will contain a value of 1.

5   This bit isn't used on the EGA card. On the VGA card, it's used as bit 9 of the vertical blank start register. This bit also isn't used on the EGA card. For the VGA card, it is used as bit 9 of the line compare register.

7   The VGA card uses this bit for line doubling to obtain 400 lines in modes that are really 200 line modes. It's not used on the EGA card.

CAUTION

Do not change this bit when programming any registers involved in the vertical timing of the screen build.

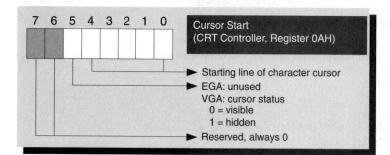

0-4   This specifies the starting line for the cursor; it begins with line 0. It can be a value from 0 to 31. If this value exceeds the actual character height, then the cursor will not be visible on screen.

       If the starting line is greater than the end line (CRT register 0BH), then the EGA card will display a two-part cursor, but the VGA card won't display a cursor.

5   On the VGA card only, this bit can be used to explicitly hide the cursor. This bit isn't used on the EGA card.

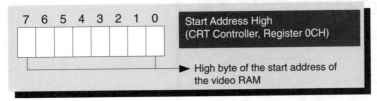

0-4   This bit field contains the last pixel line of the cursor. This value can also be from 0 to 31, but it may not exceed the character height.

If the end line is less than the starting line (CRT register 0AH), then a two-part cursor will appear on an EGA card and a cursor won't appear on a VGA card.

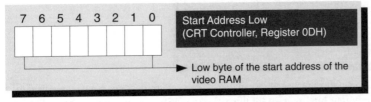

0-7   Together with register 0DH, this register represents the offset address at which the CRT controller will start to read the screen contents from the video RAM. This is the same as the start of the current screen page in video RAM. In odd/even mode, this value must be the actual offset value divided by two. In chain4 mode, it's the actual offset divided by four.

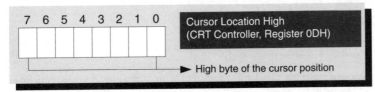

0-7   This register contains the low byte of the start address of the current screen page in video RAM. See also register 0CH.

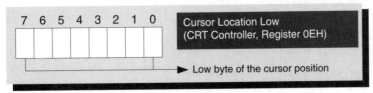

0-7   This register defines the current cursor position as an offset in the current screen page. The address given in this register must be the actual address divided by two. The high byte of the address is stored in this register and the low byte is stored in the next register.

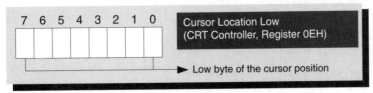

0-7   This register contains the low byte of the cursor position in the current screen page. See also register 0DH.

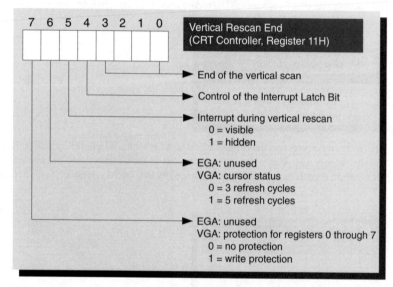

0-7   This contains the pixel line where the vertical rescan will begin. Since EGA and VGA cards manage over 256 lines, eight bits isn't enough room to store this number. The overflow register (register number 07H) contains a ninth bit and tenth bit (for VGA cards).

0-3   These bits contain the pixel line where the vertical rescan ends. The synchronization signal is switched off and a new screen build begins. Only four bits are used for this value, so the maximum line number is 15.

4   When a vertical interrupt is executed, bit 7 of the input status register is set to 1 to indicate the start of the vertical rescan. The interrupt bit remains active until it is reset by a value of 1 in this bit, which prohibits a new vertical interrupt.

5   This bit can be used to execute interrupt 2 with the start of every vertical rescan. However, you should remember that many VGA cards cannot generate a vertical interrupt.

6   Only VGA cards are able to change the refresh cycles per line from 3 to 5. Since this requires more time for each refresh of the video RAM, the VGA card operates with a smaller line frequency, which allows the use of monitors that cannot work with the normal VGA line frequency.

7   This bit locks and unlocks access to the first eight registers of the CRT controller on the VGA card. If this bit is set, these registers can be read but not written.

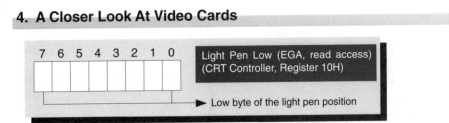

7 6 5 4 3 2 1 0   Light Pen Low (EGA, read access)
(CRT Controller, Register 10H)

➤ Low byte of the light pen position

0-7   As we've already seen, the EGA card handles register 10H differently for read and write accesses. During a write access, it contains the start of the vertical rescan. With a read access, it returns the low byte of the current light pen position. As with the cursor position, this value represents the low byte of this address divided by two.

VGA cards, which don't support the use of a light pen, return the contents of the vertical rescan start register during a write access.

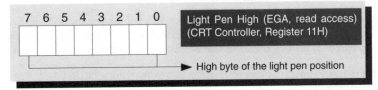

7 6 5 4 3 2 1 0   Light Pen High (EGA, read access)
(CRT Controller, Register 11H)

➤ High byte of the light pen position

0-7   On EGA cards, this register returns the high byte of the light pen position with a read access. See also the description of register 10H.

7 6 5 4 3 2 1 0   End Vertical Display
(CRT Controller, Register 12H)

➤ Number of pixel lines - 1

0-7   This register sets the number of the last pixel line in the screen build. This must be a nine bit number for EGA screens and a ten bit number for VGA. The additional bits required are found in the overflow register 07H.

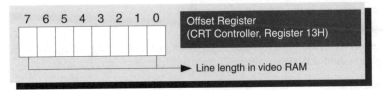

7 6 5 4 3 2 1 0   Offset Register
(CRT Controller, Register 13H)

➤ Line length in video RAM

0-7   The offset the CRT controller adds to the offset of the previous line at the start of each line is stored in this register. Depending on the address mode, this offset must be divisible by a certain factor. This factor is 2 in odd/even mode, 4 in chain4 mode and 1 in byte mode.

Normally, the value in this register corresponds to the length of a line in video RAM. In text mode, which is handled internally in odd/even mode, this value is 80 because a text line uses 160 bytes or 80 words. Larger or smaller values can also be given.

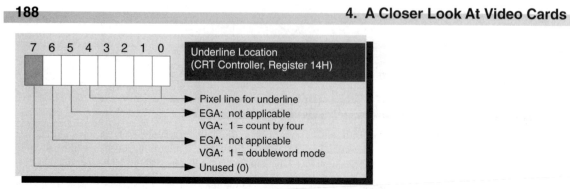

0-4   EGA and VGA cards working in monochrome modes can display characters on screen with underlining. This bit field indicates the pixel line in which the underlining will appear.

5   For VGA cards only, this bit determines whether the internal address counter will be incremented with every fourth tick of the character clock. If so, this bit must be set to 1 and bit 3 of the CRT mode register (count by two) must be set to 0. If the count by two bit is set to 1, then doubleword mode is ignored in any case.

6   This bit switches on the doubleword mode for VGA cards. It causes the access mode bit of the CRT mode register to be ignored.

                 In doubleword mode, the address in the internal address counter is pushed up by two bits during the screen build. This moves bits 14 and 15 to bit positions 0 and 1. As long as the address counter is less than 4000H, all memory locations between 0000H and FFFCH where modulo 4 = 0 are addressed.

                 If the internal address counter reaches a value between 4000H and 7FFFH, then all memory locations between 0001H and FFFDH where modulo 4 = 1 are addressed. The same is true for the regions 8000H - BFFFH and C000H - FFFFH. The memory locations are then addressed where modulo 4 = 2 and 3, respectively.

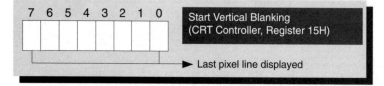

0-7   This register contains the number of the last pixel line plus 1. The ninth bit required for EGA and VGA cards is found in the overflow register (number 07H).

                 VGA cards require a tenth bit, which is found in the maximum scan line register (register number 09H).

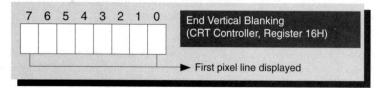

0-7   This register contains the number of the first pixel line. When this line number is reached, the vertical blanking signal is switched off again so a new screen build can begin.

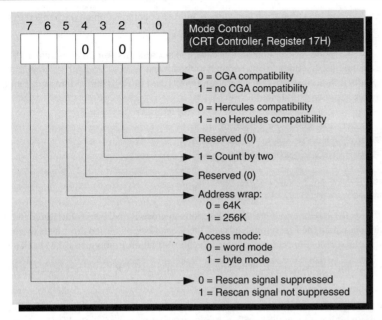

Mode Control
(CRT Controller, Register 17H)

Bits: 7 6 5 4 3 2 1 0 (with 0 in positions 4 and 2)

- ▶ 0 = CGA compatibility
  1 = no CGA compatibility
- ▶ 0 = Hercules compatibility
  1 = no Hercules compatibility
- ▶ Reserved (0)
- ▶ 1 = Count by two
- ▶ Reserved (0)
- ▶ Address wrap:
  0 = 64K
  1 = 256K
- ▶ Access mode:
  0 = word mode
  1 = byte mode
- ▶ 0 = Rescan signal suppressed
  1 = Rescan signal not suppressed

0   If a program sets this bit to 0, other registers can be set to emulate the CGA four color 320*200 pixel mode and CGA video RAM structure. The video RAM is divided into two blocks starting at offset addresses 0000H and 2000H. The first block contains the even-numbered lines and the second block contains the odd-numbered lines.

     To emulate this process, setting this bit causes bit 0 of the internal row scan counter to be transferred to bit 13 of the internal address counter during the screen refresh. The counter contains the addresses in video RAM from which the CRT reads the screen information.

     Bit 13 starts with a value of 2000H. So the CRT alternates between the address blocks starting at 0000H and 2000H, because bit 0 of the internal row scan counter alternates between 0 and 1. A requirement for this is the character height must be set to two by entering a value of 1 in the maximum scan line register.

1   This bit is an extension of bit 0. It must be set to 0 when emulating a foreign video mode that divides the video RAM into four blocks. This includes the Hercules graphics card and other CGA modes with 16 colors and 320*400 pixel resolution.

     In these modes, the video RAM is divided into four blocks starting at offset addresses 0000H, 2000H, 4000H and 6000H. The block that contains a given line is determined by the modulo of the line number with 4. Line 0 is in the first block, the second line in the second block, the third line in the third block and the fourth line in the fourth block.

To emulate this structure, a procedure similar to that used with bit 0 copies bit 1 of the internal row scan counter to bit 14 of the internal address counter. Before doing this, you must be sure the character height has been set to four in the maximum scan line register. This ensures that bit 1 of the row scan counter will have a value of 1 so bit 14 in the address counter will be set to 1. The value in the address counter will be greater than 4000H in any case, so blocks two and three can be addressed.

3   If this bit is set to 0, then the internal address counter increments with each beat of the character clock. If assigned a value of 1, however, the counter only increments with every other beat of the character clock.

5   On EGA cards with only 64K of video RAM, this bit must be set to 0 to prevent overruns in word mode (see bit 6). Then bit 0 will be copied to bit 13, instead of bit 15 of the address bus.

6   Normally byte mode will be active and the value from the internal address counter is copied unchanged to the 16 address leads that determine which byte in video RAM will be addressed.

If this bit is set to 0, however, word mode is activated. In this case, the address bits from the internal address counter are moved one bit to the left and the highest bit is copied to the lowest address lead A0. As long as the address counter is less than 8000H, then the even bytes between 0000H and 0FFFEH are addressed. Larger values will address the odd bytes between 0001H and FFFFH.

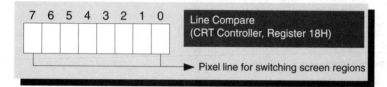

0-7   This register can be used to divide the screen into two different regions in video RAM. The value stored in this register represents the line number where the first region ends and the second begins. When this line is reached, the CRT controller sets the internal offset address for querying screen information from video RAM back to 0.

When a new screen refresh begins, the screen region with the addresses indicated in CRT registers 0CH and 0DH is displayed.

Since both EGA and VGA cards are able to display more than 256 lines on screen, eight bits isn't sufficient to represent the line number. A ninth bit is stored in the overflow register (07). A tenth bit is stored for VGA cards in the maximum scan line register (09).

Sequencer controller

The registers of the sequencer controller are accessed in the usual way using a data register and an index register. The index register is located at port address 3C4H. This is immediately followed by the data register, which is located at port address 3C5H.

Number	Register Name
00H	Reset
01H	Clocking Mode
02H	Map Mask
03H	Character Map Select
04H	Memory Mode

As opposed to the other EGA and VGA controllers, the sequencer controller handles a number of miscellaneous tasks and cannot be easily categorized. Its responsibilities range from video RAM memory access and the management of bitplanes to selecting the currently active character table. It's also responsible for refreshing the video RAM.

The sequencer controller on EGA and VGA cards has five different registers, as shown in the table on the left. Remember, the contents of the register can only be read with VGA cards. This isn't possible with an EGA card.

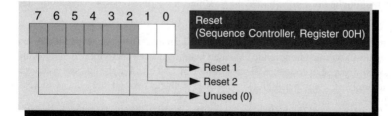

0   This bit usually contains a value of 1. It can be set to 0 to execute a sequencer controller reset, which ends its activity. This ends the generation of horizontal and vertical synchronization signals, causing the screen to go black. Also, the character map select register is set to 0 and the video RAM refresh is switched off. To avoid losing the contents of the video RAM, this bit should be set back to 1 after a maximum of 20 or 30 microseconds. This brings the sequencer controller back to life.

A reset of the sequencer controller is required prior to programming bits 0 and 3 of the clocking mode register of the sequencer controller, as well as bits 2 and 3 of the miscellaneous output register.

1   This bit is also used to reset the sequencer controller, except that it doesn't also reset the character map select register. So, you can use this bit instead bit 0 to reset the sequencer controller, but both bits 0 and 1 must be set back to 1 for the sequencer controller to be able to continue its work.

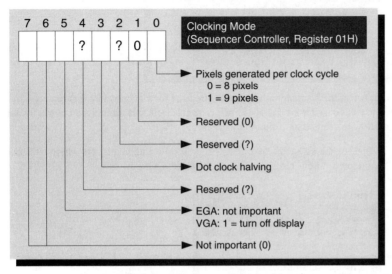

0   This bit sets the number of horizontal pixels that are generated by the CRT controller during each clock cycle. In the graphics modes and with the color text modes of the EGA card, this is always eight. For VGA text modes and for the use of an MDA monitor with an EGA card, this bit must be set to 1 to generate nine pixels per clock cycle.

3   Setting this bit to 1 results in halving the dot clock rate. This happens automatically when the BIOS is used to switch on the 320*200 pixel mode for CGA emulation. This bit will be 0 for all other modes (including the 320*200 256 color mode).

5   On a VGA card, setting this bit to 1 will switch off the video signal. This makes the screen go black and allows the CPU unlimited access to the video RAM.

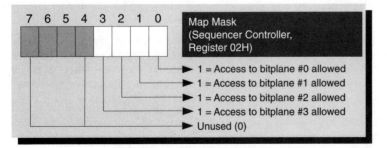

0-3   Each of these bits either blocks or enables access to a bitplane. This is important for accessing the video RAM with the various read and write modes. During a read access, the status of this bit determines whether a byte in the bitplane should be filled with the contents of the corresponding latch register. Conversely, during a read access, this bit determines whether the byte in question should be copied from the bitplane to the latch register or if the contents of the latch register should remain unchanged.

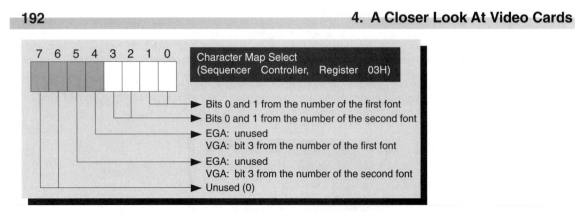

0+1+4   These bits determine the number of the character table that will be used for all characters that have a value of 0 for bit 3 in their attribute byte. Bit 4 isn't used on EGA cards, so font selection is limited to numbers 0 - 3. Bit 4 is used on VGA cards to allow the selection of font numbers from 0 - 7.

2+3+5   These bits determine the number of the character table that will be used for all characters where bit 3 in the attribute byte is set to 1. Again, the third bit (bit 5) is only needed for VGA cards.

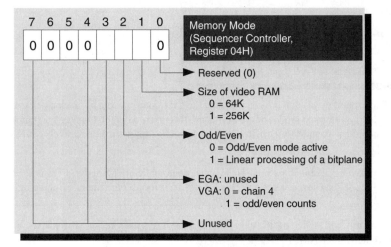

1   This bit applies only to EGA cards because all VGA cards come with 256K of video RAM. You can also safely assume that few, if any, EGA cards with only 64K are still being used.

2   This bit is used to set the division of odd and even memory addresses into different bitplanes. This is known as odd/even mode. In this mode, access to even addresses in video RAM are automatically routed to bitplanes 0 and 2. Access to odd addresses go to bitplanes 1 and 3. In both cases, the low bit of the offset address will be expanded by the page bit (bit 5 in the miscellaneous output register) before this occurs. As always, access to the various bitplanes can be suppressed using the map select register of the sequencer controller.

         If this bit contains a value of 1, the memory addresses aren't divided into odd and even groups and the bitplanes can be processed in a linear fashion. Remember the contents of this bit should always correspond with the odd/even bit in register 5 of the graphics controller.

3   The VGA card uses an expansion of the odd/even mode known as chain4 mode. This is a sort of doubled odd/even mode. It's primarily used in 256 color graphics modes to create a linear video RAM starting at A000H. This is from a program's point of view only and in reality the video RAM is still divided into four bitplanes. This only pertains to access to the video RAM using the CPU. It has no effect on video RAM access through the CRT controller.

As with odd/even mode, access to the video RAM is based on the addresses of memory locations within one of the four bitplanes. The two low bits of the offset address are masked (set to 0) so only locations within the bitplanes that are divisible by four can be accessed. The number of the bitplane to be accessed is determined by the value of two bits that were masked, which is the same as module 4 of the offset address.

A bitplane can be accessed only if it's freed using the map mask register of the sequencer controller. If chain4 mode is active, the bits used to control the odd/even mode are ignored. They become valid again when chain4 mode is switched off.

Attribute controller

The attribute controller prepares the color signals for the screen. It manages the palette registers and the other registers needed for generating color signals. The registers of the attribute controller are accessed using a combined address and data register. The register located at port address 3C0H is used for write operations. For read operations, which are only possible on the VGA card, the register at port address 3C1H is used.

To access an attribute register, first the number of the desired register must be written to port 3C0H or 3C1H. With a read operation, the result can then be read directly from port 3C1H. For a write operation, the new contents of the register must be sent using port 3C0H.

Number	Register Name
00H-0FH	Palette Register
10H	Mode Control
11H	Overscan Color
12H	Color Plane Enable
13H	Horizontal Pel Penning
14H	Color Select (VGA only)

For read access to a register, the combined index and data register at port address 3C1H requires only the register number. The register for write operations requires an additional bit to determine the status of the attribute controller. If this bit is set to 0, then the connection between the attribute controller and the CRT controller is broken and the screen is black or whatever color is contained in the overscan register of the attribute controller. Separate color signals for the characters or pixels on screen will no longer be produced.

The attribute controller on an EGA card has 20 different registers and the VGA card has one additional register. The assignments for some registers differ between EGA and VGA cards because VGA cards require using the DAC color table to generate color signals. EGA cards don't have the DAC color table.

Like the sequencer controller, the registers can only be read on a VGA card. These same registers on an EGA card are write-only.

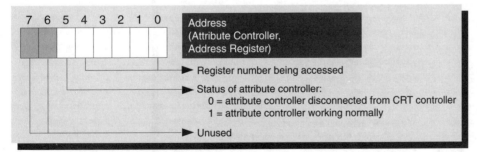

0-4   These bits address the various registers of the attribute controller. This is done in the same way as with other EGA and VGA controllers.

5   If this bit contains 1, the attribute controller works normally. If it contains 0, then the attribute controller is disconnected from the CRT controller, which causes the screen to go black or to become the color stored in the overscan register.

This is the only time when the palette registers can be accessed directly by the CPU to be read or written.

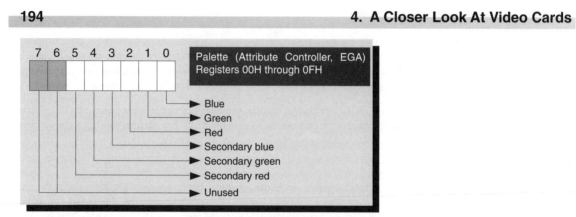

0-5   On an EGA card, the 16 palette registers contain actual 6-bit color codes. This allows for 64 different colors.

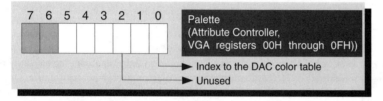

0-5   On a VGA card, a palette register stores an index to the DAC color table instead of an actual color code. The attribute controller uses this index value to load the color assigned to a character or pixel from the DAC color table and send the appropriate color signal to the monitor.

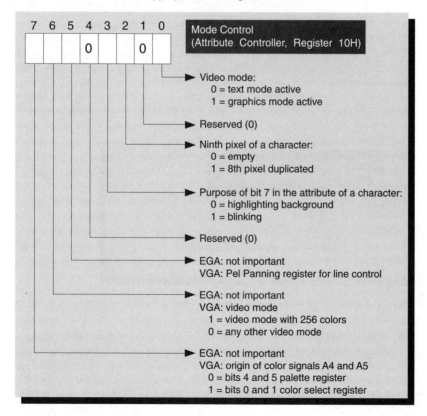

0   This bit is used to tell the attribute controller whether a text mode or a graphics mode is active.

2   This bit is only meaningful for text modes that use a nine pixel character width. This bit determines the meaning of the ninth pixel. The character tables in ROM only store eight pixels per line for each character.

            If this bit is 0, then the ninth pixel remains empty. This creates a space of one pixel between two subsequent characters. If this bit is set to 1, then the contents of this pixel is determined on a character by character basis. If the character is a special border or frame character (ASCII codes between C0H and DFH), then the contents of the eighth pixel are copied to the ninth. The ninth pixel remains empty with all other characters.

3   When this bit is set to 1, a cursor will appear in text mode. The cursor will remain visible for 16 screen generations and then invisible for the next 16. Depending on the frequency of the screen regenerations, this results in a cursor that blinks every 1/3 to 1/4 second.

5   If the line register has been used to split the screen into two halves, this bit determines whether the horizontal and vertical panning should pertain to only the first screen region or to both. Both screen regions are affected with a value of 0. This applies only to VGA.

6   When this bit is set to 1, the attribute controller is set for a 256 color graphics mode. The color information is no longer read directly from the palette register, but rather with an index to the DAC color table.

7   In color modes with 16 or fewer colors, this bit determines whether the color signals A4 and A5 for addressing the DAC color register should be taken as signals A0 through A3 from the palette register or as constants from bits 0 and 1 of the color select register of the attribute controller.

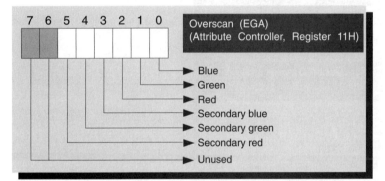

0-5   On EGA cards, the color for the screen border is stored here in the same format used with the palette registers.

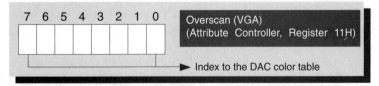

0-7   On a VGA card, the frame color is selected from the DAC color table. Any of the 256 colors in the table can be accessed using this register.

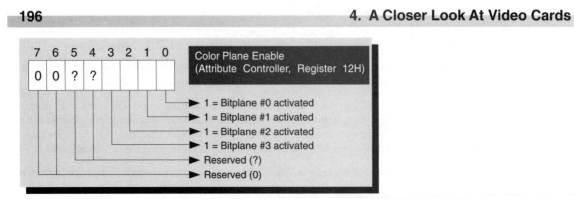

0-3   The four bits in this bit field turn each bitplane on and off for the transfer of color information from the video RAM to the attribute controller. This can be used together with programming the palette or DAC color registers to exclude certain pixels from being displayed.

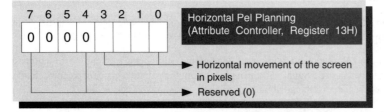

0-3   This is where the counter for horizontal pel panning is stored. This value is used when moving the visible screen display to the left.

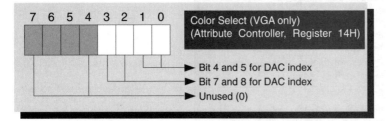

0+1   These two bits are used as bits 4 and 5 of the DAC index number when bit 7 in the mode control register of the attribute controller is set. They then replace bits 4 and 5 from the corresponding palette register.

2+3   These two bits are bits 6 and 7 of the DAC color table index in all graphics modes with less than 256 colors, regardless of the contents of other registers or bit fields.

Graphics controller

The graphics controller is used in all read and write accesses between the CPU and the video RAM using the latch registers. The registers of this controller therefore determine the current read/write mode and store the various parameters for each mode.

The nine registers of the graphics controller are accessed using a data register and an index register, which are found at port addresses 3CFH and 3CEH. As usual, the number of the

Number	Register name	Number	Register name
00H	Set/Reset	05H	Graphics Mode
01H	Enable Set/Reset	06H	Miscellaneous
02H	Color Compare	07H	Color Don't Care
03H	Function Select	08H	Bit Mask
04H	Read Map Select		

desired register must first be loaded in the index register (3CEH). This determines the index that will then be read or written using the data register (3CFH).

As with the registers of the other controllers, read access is only possible with VGA cards. EGA graphics controller registers are write-only. The following is an overview of the graphics controller registers:

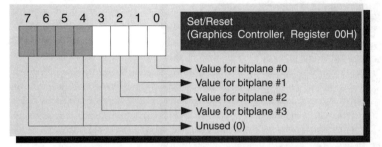

0-3   These bits are used for video RAM access in write mode 0. They determine the value to be written to bit 8 in each bitplane if the source for this bit has been selected as the set/reset register. The source for bit 8 is determined by the enable set/reset register (number 02H).

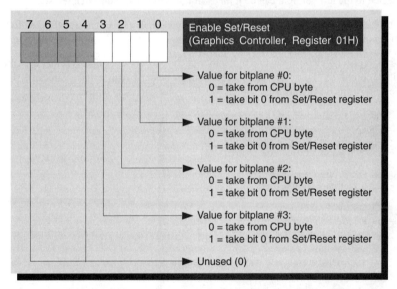

0-3   When working with write mode 0, these bits determine whether the value of bit 8 in the bitplane being accessed should be taken from the CPU byte or from the set-/reset register (number 00H).

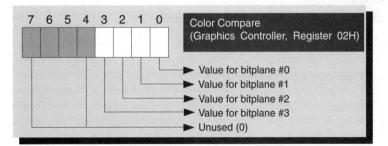

0-3   These bits are important for read access to the video RAM in read mode 1. In this mode, the four bytes read from the four video RAM bitplanes are organized into eight groups of four bits, each of which represents the color of one pixel. The eight resulting color codes are compared individually with the contents of this register and the result of this comparison is sent to the CPU.

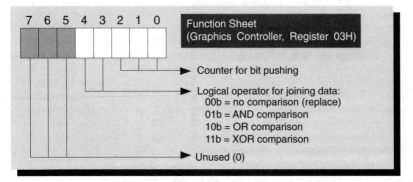

0-2   For write access to the video RAM in write modes 0 and 3, this bit field determines the number of bit positions the CPU byte must be pushed to the left before it can be joined with the contents of the latch register.

3+4   In write modes 0 and 2, this bit field determines the logical operator used to join a CPU byte and the data from one of the four latch registers before it's written to one of the bitplanes.

        The four bits in the bit mask register which correspond to the four latch registers determine whether the CPU byte and latch register will be combined. If the corresponding bit from the bit mask register has a value of 1, then the logical operator indicated by this bit field is used. Otherwise, the values are not combined.

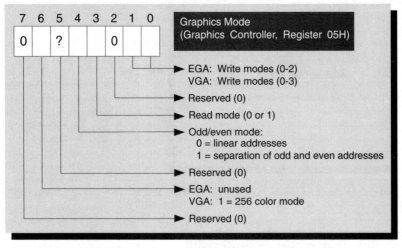

0+1   These bits store the number of the write mode used for write access to the video RAM, regardless of the current video mode.

2   This bit stores the number of the currently active video mode.

3   This bit tells the graphics controller whether an odd/even mode is active or if the bitplanes are to be addressed in a linear fashion. This bit must be loaded with the same value found in bit 2 of the memory mode register of the sequencer controller.

5   For VGA, this bit indicates whether a 256 color mode is active. If it is, the graphics controller must use a different method for passing color information on to the attribute controller.

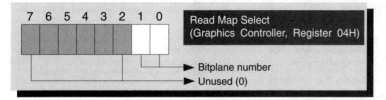

0+1   For read access in read mode 0, these two bits store the number of the latch register (which is the same as the number of the associated bitplane) that will be copied to the CPU. Read accesses in read mode 1 and chain4 mode are not affected.

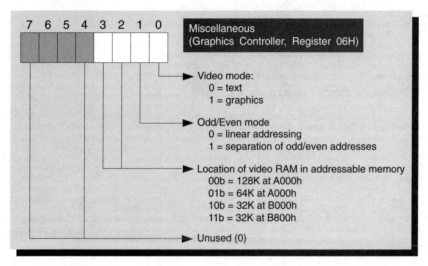

0   This bit indicates whether a text or graphics mode is currently active. This is so the graphics controller will know whether to use the internal latch registers for converting ASCII codes into pixel patterns for text modes.

1   This bit also indicates whether an odd/even mode is active or if linear addressing of the bitplanes is being used.

2+3   This bit field determines where the video RAM will be located in the processor's addressable memory. The BIOS sets this value correctly depending on the video mode and the type of monitor being used.

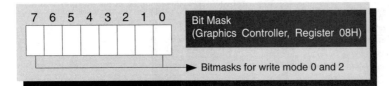

| 7 | 6 | 5 | 4 | 3 | 2 | 1 | 0 | Color Don't Care
(Graphics Controller, Register 07H) |

➤ 0 = Bitplane #0 Don't Care
1 = Bitplane #0 Compare

➤ 0 = Bitplane #1 Don't Care
1 = Bitplane #1 Compare

➤ 0 = Bitplane #2 Don't Care
1 = Bitplane #2 Compare

➤ 0 = Bitplane #3 Don't Care
1 = Bitplane #3 Compare

➤ Unused (0)

0-3   These bits are important for read accesses to the video RAM in read mode 1. They indicate which bitplanes will be included in the color comparison.

| 7 | 6 | 5 | 4 | 3 | 2 | 1 | 0 | Bit Mask
(Graphics Controller, Register 08H) |

➤ Bitmasks for write mode 0 and 2

0-7   For write access to the video RAM in write modes 0 and 2, these bits determine which bits from a given bitplane should be written unchanged to the corresponding latch register and which must first be combined with other data (from the CPU or the set/reset register) using the function select register. This happens in all four latch registers to those bits for which the corresponding bit in this register is set to 1.

Digital to Analog Converter (DAC)

The DAC is found only on VGA cards. Its job is to convert the digital color values into analog color signals for the monitor. The DAC is the last step in color generation for VGA. Each palette register contains an index to one of the 256 color registers in the DAC.

A DAC color register consists of 18 bits: Six bits for each of the basic colors red, green and blue (RGB). This allows for 262,144 different colors. The color registers of the DAC are accessed using the registers listed in the following table. Unlike other EGA and VGA controllers, a single port address is used instead of separate index and data registers.

Number	Register Name
3C8H	Pel Write Address
3C7H	Pel Read Address
3C7H	DAC State
3C9H	Pel Data
3C6H	Pel Mask

To write to one of the DAC color registers, first you must enter its number (0 - 255) in the pel write address register. Then send the data for the new color to the pel data register. The pel data register is only eight bits wide and cannot receive all 18 bits needed to define a color at once. Therefore, the six bits of the red color component are sent first, followed by the six green bits and finally the six blue bits.

Within a program, usually all 256 DAC color registers (or at least a good number of them), instead of only one or two, are loaded. So, the value in the pel write address register is automatically incremented after the data for the three color components has been sent to the pel data register. This allows you to proceed directly with the color components for the next DAC color register without having to access the pel write address register again.

The automatic incrementing of the DAC color register number stops when you enter a new register number in the pel write address register. This starts a new load operation. The number of the DAC color register that is currently being processed can be queried in the pel address register.

This procedure is used for both write and read access to the DAC color registers. For reading, simply load the pel read address register with the number of the first DAC color register that you want to read. The red, green and blue components of each DAC color register can then be read from the pel data register. There must be a slight pause between the three read accesses to the pel data register. In an assembler program, this can be done with a jump to the next command.

As we've described, the contents of the pel read address register are also incremented after the contents of the current DAC color register have been read. The attribute controller has no access to the DAC color registers while they are being read or written. So, the display must be switched off during this time so a blizzard doesn't appear on screen.

The following pages describes each DAC register:

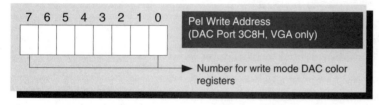

0-7   This register stores the number of the DAC color register that is to be written. The value from the pel data register is copied to this DAC color register in the next step of the write operation. This value is automatically incremented so all (or a large portion) of the DAC color registers can be loaded without having to access this register again.

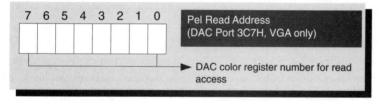

0-7   This register stores the number of the DAC color register that is to be read. The color component values from the DAC color register can be read from the pel data register in the next step of the read operation. This value is also automatically incremented.

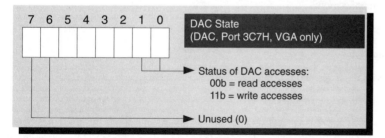

1+2   These bits indicate whether the DAC is currently in read or write mode.

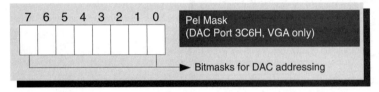

During a write operation on one of the DAC color registers, this register must be loaded with the three color components in sequence: first red, then green and finally blue. Each color component requires only six bits, so it is the lower six bits that are actually copied to the DAC color register.

During a read access to a DAC color register, this register will first have the six bits of the red, then the green and finally the blue color components available for querying.

| 7 | 6 | 5 | 4 | 3 | 2 | 1 | 0 | Pel Mask (DAC Port 3C6H, VGA only) |

        ➤ Bitmasks for DAC addressing

0-7   If the attribute controller wants to read the contents of a DAC color register while generating colors during a screen refresh, the contents of this register must be combined with the number of the desired DAC color register using a logical AND operator. When animating, for example, this allows you to create entire color groups using certain DAC color registers at a low level.

Normally, this register contains the value FFH, so accesses to the DAC color registers aren't changed.

Super VGA Cards

Although it took more than a year for chip manufacturers to unlock the secrets of the IBM VLSI chips to create EGA-compatible video cards, it was only a few months before the first VGA-compatible cards arrived on the market. Just as with EGA cards, a battle for the market share of VGA-compatible video cards began. Prices decreased and manufacturers were pressured to come up with new features that set their card apart from the others. This is how the Super VGA cards were developed. Although these cards are compatible with the IBM VGA standard, they use many hardware registers that aren't defined in this standard to provide extra features and performance. Some of the enhanced capabilities of Super VGA are:

➢   More colors in the normal VGA graphics modes

➢   Higher resolution graphics modes

➢   Text modes with more columns and lines

➢   Hardware cursors in graphics modes

➢   Hardware zooming displayed on the screen in graphics modes

Unfortunately, the manufacturers of these cards didn't develop standards for these advanced features. With a standard, these features could be accessed from the ROM-BIOS. As developers of the expanded capabilities of Super VGA cards know, one program won't work the same way with two different cards. So, to ensure that a program will run with all Super VGA cards, separate routines, which are designed to meet each card's requirements, must be created.

In this section we'll discuss some important aspects of Super VGA cards. Instead of discussing the many cards that are available, we'll end this chapter talking about the VESA Super VGA Standard. This standard was created in 1990 by the major manufacturers of Super VGA cards in an attempt to create a practical tool for Super VGA programming. This standard enables your program to work with Super VGA cards from several different manufacturers.

Although hundreds of companies make Super VGA cards, only about twelve suppliers provide the chips needed for building Super VGA cards. The most important suppliers include the following:

➤ ATI
  ATI manufactures the VGAWONDER which emulates all earlier graphics standards (including Hercules).

➤ Chips & Technologies
  This company manufactures the NEAT chip set.

➤ Genoa
  This is the one company that actually uses the name "SuperVGA" on its Super VGA line of cards.

➤ Headland
  (also known as VideoSeven).

➤ Tseng
  Probably the leading manufacturer or supplier, Tseng supplies the ET30000 and ET4000 VGA chips which are installed in several VGA cards.

➤ Paradise
  A division of Western Digital, a manufacturer of hard drives and other mass storage systems.

Although there are only six major manufacturers of VGA and Super VGA chip sets, the differences between Super VGA cards aren't limited to the use of six different chip sets. Nearly every chip set allows a card manufacturer some freedom in mode selection and addressing BIOS functions.

Super VGA text modes

Of all the various Super VGA text modes, the 25 line by 132 column mode that's supported by many cards is one of the most interesting. There are also other text modes that have 132 columns and higher numbers of lines. Several 80 and 100 column modes, with varying numbers of lines, are also supported. The highest resolution text mode supports 160 columns and 50 lines. Whether you can read any of the characters on the screen is another matter.

Expanded text modes of various Super VGA cards			
Columns	Rows	Columns	Rows
80	30	132	25
80	34	132	28
80	43	132	30
80	60	132	43
100	37	132	44
100	43	132	50
100	60	160	50
100	75		

The table on the left shows a sampling of some of the text modes available on various Super VGA cards.

Generally all these text modes can be initialized with function 00H of the BIOS video interrupt, but different cards may have different code numbers for each mode. This is unfortunate because the video RAM in these modes is structured as it is in the normal text modes. This would make it possible to use the expanded modes simply by setting a wider line length in video RAM.

If you want your DOS programs to have flexible screen resolution, you should use the functions of the VESA BIOS. Or, you can let the user decide. Some configuration programs allow the user to set the screen resolution at the DOS level. Then the user can simply pass the screen resolution, as a parameter, to the program when starting it from DOS or enter the value in a configuration file the program reads after it starts.

Super VGA graphics modes

Super VGA graphic modes also offer a wide variety. The standard VGA modes are supported with more colors, for example 256 instead of only 16. However, there are new graphics modes with higher resolutions, up to 1024x768 pixels.

Unfortunately these higher resolutions are slower. For example, a 640x480 pixel mode uses about 300,000 pixels and an 800x480 mode uses almost 500,000. The processor still must process each pixel, which prevents it from performing other tasks. This is why many Windows users prefer the old standard VGA 640x480 pixel mode. The Super VGA modes simply take too long to paint the screen.

In addition to modes with resolutions like 720x396 or 960x720, the same three modes are included on almost all Super VGA cards:

➢ 640x400 pixels with 256 colors

➢ 800x600 pixels with 16 or 256 colors

➢ 1024x768 pixels with 16 colors

The following table shows these modes represent only a portion of the various Super VGA graphics modes available on different cards:

Expanded graphic modes of various Super VGA cards							
Resolution	Colors	Pixels	Memory	Resolution	Colors	Pixels	Memory
512x480	256	245,760	256K	720x540	256	388,800	512K
640x400	256	256,000	256K	752x410	16	308,320	256K
640x480	256	307,200	512K	800x600	16	480,000	256K
720x396	16	285,120	256K	800x600	256	480,000	512K
720x512	16	368,640	256K	960x720	16	691,200	512K
720x512	256	368,640	512K	1024x768	16	786,432	512K
720x540	16	388,800	256K	1024x768	256	786,432	1 Meg

Regardless of which graphics modes a Super VGA card supports, a given mode can be used only if the proper monitor and sufficient video RAM are available. A normal fixed-frequency VGA monitor is sufficient for the 640x480 modes, but the higher resolution modes require a multisync monitor. When you reach resolutions as high as 1024x768, you'll need an XL monitor. This is a special kind of multisync monitor; that's often used with CAD/CAM applications. A resolution of 1024x768 would represent the lower end of its capabilities.

Structure of the video RAM in Super VGA modes

When you look at all the Super VGA graphics modes, they can be divided into modes that use either 16 or 256 colors, just like the standard VGA graphics modes. In both cases, the structure of the video RAM is the same as in the related standard VGA modes. This means the color of a pixel is determined by four bits from the four bitplanes in the 16 color modes. The 256 color modes use an entire byte to define the color of a pixel. The address of a pixel is the result of multiplying the line number by the line length and adding the column number. The only difference between these modes and the standard VGA modes is the length of each line in video RAM. This makes each screen page longer, which results in a higher resolution.

However, a problem arises. Any mode that requires more than 256K per screen page cannot use standard methods for accessing video RAM. In the 16 color modes, the 64K segment starting at A000:0000 can be used to address only 256K of video RAM using the four bitplanes. This situation is even worse with the 256 color modes. These have only 64K available, although earlier in this chapter we showed a way to address the entire 256K (see "The VGA 256 Color Graphics Modes" information in the "EGA And VGA Cards" section).

<table>
<tr><td>

The 64K limit at A000:0000 is unavoidable for all graphics modes which need to address more than 256K of video RAM

</td><td>

</td></tr>
</table>

Therefore, all Super VGA cards use a mechanism that allows the entire video RAM of the card to be addressed using the memory segment at A000H. Unfortunately, this access can only occur in 64K chunks for 256 color modes or in 256K chunks for 16 color modes. Various cards use different hardware registers to make a piece of the video RAM available at A000H. These registers aren't found on standard VGA cards. The same mechanism manages EMS memory (see Chapter 12 for more information).

Copy a section of video RAM to the 64K window at A000:0000 by dividing the offset address into page and offset components. This process doesn't simplify the routines to set or read a pixel, because you now must know which 64K memory window, as well as the offset in video RAM, to access the desired byte. You also must remember that your 64K window can be moved only in certain increments (granularities), such as 1K, 2K, 4K, 8K, etc. You can also think of the video RAM as being divided into "pages" under this scheme. The page size corresponds to the granularity of the 64K window. If you choose 1K, then the 64K window at A000H will have 64 pages. The number of the first page is set by a hardware register called the page select register.

The visible memory region at segment A000H cannot begin at just any offset address. It must be a multiple of the granularity. For example, suppose that you want to access the address 65539 (64K + 3) with a granularity of 1K. You would load 64 into the page select register. Then you could access the desired location at A000:0003. In this case, there are 63 other possible combinations for the value in the page select register and offset address for accessing the segment A000. Another example would be to load 63 in the page select register to access the byte at 1024 + 3 relative to memory segment A000H.

Because of this scheme, graphics routines must convert offset addresses in video RAM to the combination of a page number plus the offset relative to memory segment A000H. This isn't a difficult task, once we consider the binary nature of these components.

The starting point is the offset for access to the video RAM, which must be 20 bits wide to address 1 megabyte of video RAM. If it's only 512K, then 19 bits will be sufficient. For our example, we'll assume 20 bits. If you're using a granularity of 1K, then this offset must always be divided by 1024 to obtain the value for the page select register. In binary terms, "divide" always means the dividend must be moved to the right the number of bits needed for binary representation of the divisor. Since 1K corresponds to a value of 210, the 20 bit offset address must be moved 10 bits to the right to obtain the desired number. The digits that are moved to the right of the "decimal" then become the offset in memory segment A000H.

The paging mechanism also has other tasks besides calculating page numbers and offsets. It becomes difficult when you must copy pieces of the video RAM that are more than 64K apart from one another. This makes it impossible to fit everything in the segment at A000 at the same time. So, the copy procedure must be divided into three time-consuming steps. First, the source is loaded into the segment at A000 so it can be copied to a buffer in main memory the program creates. Then the destination region must be loaded at A000 so the contents of the buffer can be loaded there.

This type of operation is fairly common, especially with animation applications. So, many Super VGA cards divide the memory segment at A000H into two 32K blocks, each of which has its own page select register. This allows the segment at A000H to handle two different regions of video RAM simultaneously. The regions can then be copied directly via the video RAM without having to use a buffer.

There are also no Super VGA standards for the process that controls page switching. Different cards use different registers and different granularities in segment A000H. Also, you cannot assume that all cards divide the A000H segment into two paging regions.

This causes a lot of problems for any programmer who wants to use a Super VGA mode that requires more than 256K. So it's obvious why the manufacturers of some programs, such as AutoCAD or Windows, let the card manufacturers develop software drivers for their products.

However, the VESA standard represents a solution to this problem. This standard represents a hardware independent interface for programming Super VGA modes. We'll discuss the VESA standard starting on the next page.

Doing it yourself

If, despite all the problems that may occur, you still want to write a program using a Super VGA graphics mode, you should use the 800x600 pixel mode with 16 colors for several reasons. This mode is available on most Super VGA card and it requires only 256K of video RAM. This eliminates having to program the page select register and will ensure that all Super VGA cards, regardless of how much memory they have, will be able to use your program. This mode will also allow you to use a lot of the routines that we've already seen work with the standard VGA 16 color modes.

Demonstration programs

We'll demonstrate how to do this in the following programs which you'll find on the companion CD-ROM. The Pascal (V8060P.PAS) and C (V8060C.C) versions are based on routines from "The 16 color EGA and VGA graphics modes" in the "EGA And VGA" section of this chapter. Initializing the 800x600 mode and setting or querying pixels are all accomplished with the various assembler routines found in the modules V8060CA.ASM and V8060PA.ASM.

The initialization routine INIT800600 performs the most difficult task. This routine must determine which code number the 800x600 pixel graphics mode uses on the installed video card. One way the routine can do this is by trying different code numbers until it finds one the BIOS accepts. There is a kind of array within the assembler program that stores six code numbers that are often used to identify the 800x600 pixel graphics mode. This array is called MODENO.

The most widely used code numbers are first put in the array. These code numbers are 6AH, 58H and 29H. The code numbers 54H, 16H and 79H are also in the array, but these are less common. We encountered these codes frequently while testing various Super VGA cards. They should work for most of the Super VGA cards on the market. If you find a particular card with a different code, you can easily add this code number to the MODENO array.

The INIT800600 routine recognizes the proper code number after it uses one of the codes to successfully initialize a graphics mode with function 00H of the video BIOS. Function 0FH of the video BIOS is used to return the code number of the currently active video mode. If this code number doesn't match the code number the program sent to initialize the mode, then the desired mode wasn't initialized and another code must be tried.

As long as the call to function 0FH doesn't return a match of the code number, the INIT800600 routine will continue to run through the array. This occurs until a code is accepted by the BIOS or until all codes in the array have been tried. In this case, the routine returns a value of 0 to its caller in the C version or a value of FALSE in the Pascal version. If the mode could be successfully initialized, however, the C version returns 1 and the Pascal version returns TRUE.

You'll find the following program(s) on the companion CD-ROM

V8060P.PAS (Pascal listing)
V8060PA.ASM (Assembler listing)
V8060C.C (C listing)
V8060CA.ASM (Assembler listing)

According to our tests, this method can be used to set the proper video mode with several Super VGA cards. However, this method isn't completely foolproof; the entire process can fail if the video card uses one of the codes in the MODENO array for a video mode other than the 16 color 800x600 pixel mode. In this case, the INIT800600 routine will return a value of 1 or TRUE, but the rest of the program won't work properly because a different video mode than expected will be functioning. However, this didn't occur in any of our tests, so this doesn't seem likely.

The VESA standard

The history of the PC has shown hardware manufacturers how the lack of standards can hurt business. Without standardization, manufacturers can develop features that give their products advantages over the competition. However, a video card that has great features but cannot work with any programs is useless. Software developers aren't going to risk developing products that will work only on one manufacturer's video card. This has been the case in the Super VGA market. Manufacturers are offering different cards with different features and no standard methods for addressing video RAM or using the hardware registers. The result is that software developers have been very reluctant to produce programs that use the expanded Super VGA modes. The card manufacturers must therefore deliver software drivers for their cards so at least some programs can use the additional modes.

In an attempt to solve this problem, several VGA manufacturers established the VESA committee (Video Electronic Standards Association) in 1989. ATI, Chips & Technologies, Everex, Genoa, Intel, Phoenix Technologies, Orchid, Paradise, Video Seven and many other companies are part of this association.

This committee's goal was to develop a BIOS expansion that would give programmers hardware independent access to the Super VGA features found on many manufacturers' cards. This BIOS expansion, called the VESA standard, was released in 1990. The BIOS expansion described by this standard will be incorporated in the expanded VGA-BIOS found in the ROM chips on these manufacturers' cards. There will be software drivers for older cards. These drivers will be run as TSR programs to add the VESA functions to the existing BIOS. For the first time, this will give programmers the freedom to develop applications that work with many Super VGA cards, without having to consider the various hardware differences.

The VESA standard graphics modes

First, the VESA committee members had to decide which graphics modes to support. Obviously each manufacturer wanted their own modes in the standard. After some compromise, they came up with a list of nine modes, which are listed in the following table.

Code numbers were assigned to the graphics modes so the VESA BIOS could identify them the same way the normal VGA BIOS does. Codes over 100H (256) were selected, however, because the individual manufacturers had already used many of the codes under 100H for their own special modes. So, Super VGA modes are represented with 16 bit codes under the VESA standard. The one exception to this is the 16 color 800x600 pixel mode, which many manufacturers had already assigned the code 6AH. The VESA standard keeps this code for this mode and supports it as one of the expanded VESA modes.

The VESA BIOS Graphics Modes							
Code	Resolution	Colors	Memory*	Code	Resolution	Colors	Memory*
101H	640x 480	256	512K	105H	1024x 768	256	1 Meg
102H	800x 600	16	256K	106H	1280x1024	16	1 Meg
103H	800x 600	256	512K	107H	1280x1024	256	1.25 Meg
104H	1024x 768	16	512K	6AH	800x 600	16	256K

* This number is given in increments of 256, 512 or 1024K and does represent the actual memory needed for a single screen page.

Calling the VESA BIOS functions

The VESA BIOS functions can be accessed with the BIOS video interrupt 10H, like the normal functions of the VGA BIOS. There are six subfunctions under function 4FH. Before the function call, the function number 4FH must be placed in the AH register and the desired subfunction number (0 - 5) must be placed in the AL register.

The VESA BIOS functions	
No.	Description
00H	Query capabilities of Super VGA card
01H	Query identifying information for a certain mode
02H	Set a VESA mode
03H	Query current video mode
04H	Save/restore status of the Super VGA card
05H	Set/query access window to video RAM

The AH and AL registers are also used to read the results of the function after it has been called. If the VESA BIOS functions are supported by the installed video card, then the value 4FH will be returned to the AL register. The AH register receives a status code. A value of 0 indicates the function was successfully executed and a value of 1 indicates that something went wrong. All other return values (01H - 0FFH) are reserved, but should be handled as error messages if they are encountered. The contents of the registers other than AH and AL aren't changed by these function calls, unless they are used to return specific information.

Usually it isn't necessary to query the contents of the AH and AL registers after every VESA function call to check for errors. But you should always check the results returned to the AH and AL registers after your first VESA function call to ensure the VESA functions are supported by the installed video card.

Checking a Super VGA card's capabilities

Although the VESA standard provides an interface to the most important video modes of the new Super VGA cards, there is no guarantee that a particular card will support all the VESA modes. So, at run time (before working with any of the VESA functions), you must call subfunction 00H so the capabilities of the installed Super VGA card can be queried. For this function call, the function and subfunction numbers are expected in the AH and AL registers, respectively. A FAR pointer to a 256K buffer is also expected in the ES:DI register pair. Subfunction 00H stores information about the capabilities of the installed Super VGA card in this buffer.

Structure of the Subfunction 00H Buffer					
Ofs.	Contents	Type	Ofs.	Contents	Type
00H	VESA Signature ("VESA")	4 BYTE	06H	FAR pointer to an ASCII string containing the name of the card manufacturer	1 DWORD
04H	VESA Version, main version number	1 BYTE	0AH	Flag that indicates the capabilities of the card currently not used, therefore 0000h	1 DWORD
05H	VESA Version, secondary version number	1 BYTE	0EH	FAR pointer to the list of code numbers for the supported video modes	1 DWORD

The most important information for the programmer is obtained via the last pointer in this table. This points to a list of the code numbers, for the video modes, supported by the installed card. This list may be either in the ROM-BIOS of the card or in main memory. It consists of several words. Each word indicates the number of a supported mode. Both the standard VESA modes and the manufacturer's custom modes are listed. The manufacturer's own modes can be easily distinguished from the VESA modes because their code numbers are less than 100H and therefore contain a value of 00H in the high byte of the corresponding entry in this list.

This list can be a different length for each card, depending on the modes it supports and how much RAM it has. The end of the list is indicated by a word containing the value FFFFH, which doesn't represent any video mode.

Reading a specific video mode

Just knowing that a certain mode exists doesn't mean that you can use this mode. Subfunction 01H is used to query all the information needed to program a given video mode. The function and subfunction numbers are expected in registers AH and AL, respectively. Also, the number of the appropriate mode must be passed in the CX register. This number must correspond to one of the entries in the list that is queried with subfunction 00H. The ES:DI register pair expects a pointer to a buffer that will store this information. This buffer must be able to store 29 bytes.

The subfunction 00H mode list includes both the VESA modes and the manufacturer's own modes. This allows you to use subfunction 01H to retrieve information about the expanded Super VGA text modes as well as the standard VESA modes.

The following table shows the structure of the information as it's entered in the buffer by subfunction 01H.

Structure of the subfunction 01H buffer		
Ofs.	Contents	Type
00H	Mode flag, see below	1 word
02H	Flags for the first access window, see below	1 byte
03H	Flags for the second access window, see below	1 byte
04H	Granularity of the two access windows, in K,	1 word
06H	Size of the two access windows, in K	1 word
08H	Segment address of the first access window	1 word

Structure of the subfunction 01H buffer (continued)		
Ofs.	Contents	Type
0AH	Segment address of the second access window	1 word
0CH	FAR pointer to routine for setting the visible region in the two access windows	1 dword
10H	Number of bytes required by each pixel line in video RAM word	1 byte
Optional information, see mode flag		
12H	X resolution in pixels/character	1 word
14H	Y resolution in pixels/character	1 word
16H	Width of character matrix in pixels	1 byte
17H	Height of character matrix in pixels	1 byte
18H	Number of bitplanes	1 byte
19H	Number of bits per screen pixel	1 byte
1AH	Number of memory blocks	1 byte
1BH	Memory model	1 byte
1CH	Size of memory blocks in K	1 byte

The mode flag (the first bit field in the block) provides information on the queried mode. As shown in the following figure, the mode flag indicates if the mode is a text or graphics mode, if color is supported, if text can be output with the BIOS functions and, most importantly, if this mode can even be used with the available monitor and memory. It's also important to determine whether the information in the optional fields of the data block are filled. These fields contain important information for working with a given video mode. This information is usually available.

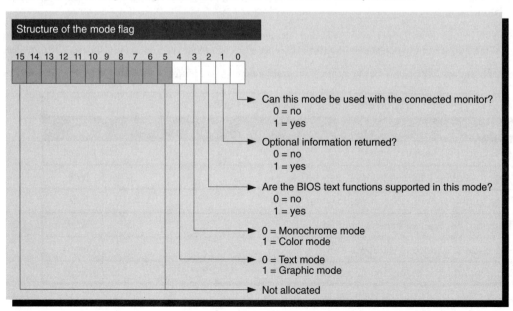

The two flags that describe the access windows to the video RAM are also represented by bit fields. Since not all Super VGA cards have two access windows, these flags must be used to determine whether a second window is available. Also, these flags will indicate which window is for reading and which is for writing.

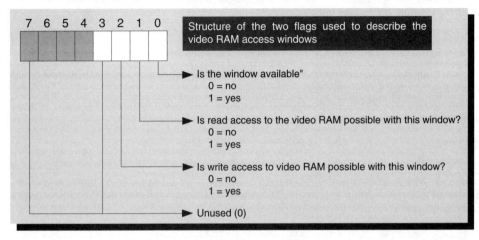

In addition to the flags that describe the video RAM access windows, some other important information about using the access windows is also given in the subfunction 01H data block. This includes the segment addresses of the two access windows. Obviously the entry for the second window is only valid if the second window actually exists. The size and the granularity of the two windows are also given. Remember the granularity is the interval with which the window can be "moved" through the video RAM.

The VESA-BIOS has a routine for moving the window through video RAM. This routine protects programmers from the incompatibilities between different Super VGA cards. You'll find more information about this routine when we discuss subfunction 05H at the end of this section.

The optional information in the block begins with the X and Y resolution of the video mode. If the mode is a text mode, this information will pertain to text lines and columns; otherwise, the resolution is given in pixels. The next two fields, which give the size of the character matrix in pixels, are used only for text modes.

The number of bitplanes used by the mode and the number of bits required to code a single pixel are listed after these fields. These two fields are only required for graphics modes. The next field, which gives the number of memory blocks, is only required for use with the graphics modes of CGA and Hercules graphics cards. This is because these cards store graphics lines in video RAM using memory blocks of different sizes. The last field of the data structure gives the size of the memory block used.

Prior to this field, however, the memory used for direct access to video RAM is given. The memory models are coded as listed in the table on the left.

Valid codes for describing memory models	
Number	Description
00H	Text mode
01H	CGA format, 2 or 4 memory blocks
02H	Hercules format with 4 memory blocks
03H	Normal EGA/VGA format for 16 color graphics modes
04H	Compact format - 2 pixels (4 bits each) per byte
05H	Normal EGA/VGA format for 256 color graphic modes
06H-0FH	Reserved
10H-FFH	Manufacturer-specific codes, currently unused

Setting a mode

Once you've used subfunction 00H to activate the list of supported video modes and subfunction 01H to read the requirements of the various modes, you can select the mode that meets your program's needs. Then you can use subfunction 01H to set this mode.

Before the function call, the function number and subfunction number must be supplied as usual. Also, the code number of the desired mode must be placed in the BX register. If you want to keep the currently existing contents of the video RAM when the new mode is set, bit 15 of the BX register must be set to 1.

After the function call, you should always check to ensure the correct mode was set. To do this, read the contents of the AH and AL registers. If you find values of 00H in AH and 4FH, then the mode was successfully set.

Subfunction 03H can be used to query the current video mode. This function call doesn't require any arguments besides the function and subfunction numbers. After the function has run, the number of the current video mode can be read from the BX register. As usual, values greater than 100H are for the standard VESA modes and values less than 100H are for standard VGA or manufacturer-specific modes.

Saving and restoring a setup

When TSR programs such as SideKick are activated, they must save the current setup of the video card before they can switch to the mode they will use. Also, these programs must be able to restore the contents of the screen to its original state. Some of the video RAM must be saved to accomplish this. This is very difficult to do with Super VGA cards. So, the VESA standard has three sub-subfunctions under subfunction 04H that help a program manage these tasks.

Subfunction 00H must be called before the current video card setup is saved because this function indicates how much memory is needed to save this information. In addition to the function and subfunction numbers, this function also requires the value 00H (sub-subfunction number) in the DL register. In the CX register, a bit field, which describes the components

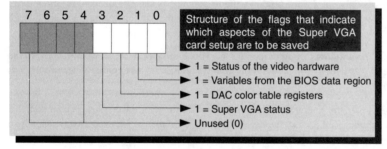

of the video card setup that must be saved, is needed. The structure of this bit field is shown in the illustration to the left.

The entire contents of the video RAM doesn't have to be saved. Only the portion overwritten by the TSR program must be saved. For example, a TSR program that switches from a graphics mode to a text mode must save only the first 4K of video RAM, which will be overwritten for displaying text. It's not necessary to save the entire graphics screen, which could take up to 1 megabyte of memory.

As a result, sub-subfunction 00H returns the number of 64 byte blocks, which are needed to save the indicated status information, to the BX register. The calling routine must prepare a buffer to store this information. The size of the buffer to create is 64 * BX bytes.

Once a program has created this buffer, the setup can be saved with sub-subfunction 01H. This function call requires three parameters in the processor registers in addition to the function and subfunction numbers. The DL register expects the sub-subfunction number 01H. The CX register must contain a bit field that describes which components of the setup should be saved, as we saw with sub-subfunction 00H. It's important that this bit field doesn't contain more components than that of the 00H sub-subfunction call; otherwise the buffer may not be large enough.

The address of the buffer itself must be passed to sub-subfunction 01H as a FAR pointer in the ES:BX register pair.

The same registers are used to restore the saved setup. This is done with a call to sub-subfunction 02H. For this function call, the sub-subfunction number is placed in the DL register. The CX register again must contain a bit field with the components of the setup to be restored and the ES:BX register pair must contain a FAR pointer to the buffer with the stored information.

Moving the access window

Since the entire video RAM can be accessed through the 64K segment at A000:0000, you can easily work with Super VGA modes that use less than 256K of memory per screen page. This process becomes more complicated when more than 256K must be addressed, which applies to most of the modes we're discussing. In these instances, you muse use access windows. These windows allow you to use the 64K segment at A000:0000 (together with the four bitplanes) to access a total of 256K of video RAM simultaneously. Earlier we saw that setting the access window involves programming registers that aren't standardized in Super VGA cards.

The VESA-BIOS solves this problem by providing subfunction 05H. This function is used to set up the access window independent of the hardware on your Super VGA card. In addition to the function and subfunction numbers, this function call requires the value 00H in the BH register and the number of the access window (either 0 or 1) in the BL register. Remember the second access window can be moved only if the subfunction 01H call has indicated the installed video card actually has a second access window.

The last parameter is placed in the DX register. This is related to the granularity of the access window and indicates the start of the addressable region in video RAM. For example, if the granularity is 1K, then a value of 256 would make the second 256K of the video RAM on a Super VGA card available using the 64K segment at A000:0000.

This function call is often needed in the high resolution Super VGA modes. Since calling it as an interrupt function would take too much time, the VESA-BIOS calls this function directly with a FAR call. Subfunction 01H returns the address of this routine as a FAR pointer in its data block. Remember, support of the FAR call method isn't necessary for every VESA BIOS, in which case the address of the routine would be returned as 0000:0000.

But if subfunction 05H is available as a FAR call routine, then you should definitely call it if you're concerned with your program's execution speed. One difference between the FAR call and the interrupt call is the FAR call doesn't return a status code to the AX register. This method still reserves the ability to change the contents of the AX and DX registers during a function call.

Subfunction 05H can also determine the position of the access window in video RAM. To call the function in this way, you must start with the function number and subfunction number as usual. The value 1 must also be entered in the BH register. As a result, the DX register will contain the location of the window, in relation to its granularity.

Chapter 5

The Interrupt Controller

Like other components of the computer system, the CPU is scarce resource. If it is busy performing one task, then it can't handle another. To relieve the CPU of some of the frequent and routine tasks associated with input and output devices, the original PC design includes an interrupt controller.

When first used by Intel in 1985, the 8259A Programmable Interrupt Controller, more commonly know as the PIC, is found between the CPU and the peripheral devices. The controller has since been superseded by "chip sets" which also handle additional chores which were previously performed by other discrete components.

Nonetheless, the function of the 8259A and its successor remains the same. The PIC is the computer's connection to the outside world. Interestingly enough, the 8259A has several capabilities which are not completely used by the PC - namely the "rotation of priorities", which we'll talk about later. The new replacement chip sets do not have this capability.

The inner life of the interrupt controller

Basically, the interrupt controller acknowledges an interrupt from a peripheral device and passes it on to the CPU. The CPU can then activate the corresponding program or routine to handle this particular interrupt.

A computer system has many peripherals, all of which require handling by the CPU. The keyboard, hard drive, printer and timer all require attention of the CPU. But at any given moment, the CPU can attend to only one at a time. The interrupt handler's job is to present the various interrupts to the CPU in sequence.

Some peripheral devices must be serviced quickly and others can tolerate a slight delay.

The PIC can handle eight interrupts. These are assigned a number ranging from 0 to 7. These numbers also represent the interrupt priority. IRQ0 has the highest priority while IRQ7 has the lowest priority. There are no standards which dictate which interrupt sources are connected to a given PIC interrupt line. These are determined by the board designer.

The following table lists the eight interrupt priorities of the original IBM-PC/XT. Note that the timer has a substantially higher priority than the printer, and the keyboard is subordinate to the timer.

Interrupt	Device
IRQ0	Timer
IRQ1	Keyboard
IRQ2	Free
IRQ3	Second serial interface
IRQ4	First serial interface
IRQ5	Hard drive
IRQ6	Disk drive
IRQ7	Printer

One of the special features of the PIC is its ability to "cascade" interrupts. If more than eight different interrupt sources need to be served, you can cascade or combine multiple PICs. Since the early days of the PC/AT, this method has been used so 16 different hardware interrupt devices can be handled.

	The AT hardware interrupts		
Priority	**Interrupt master**	**Slave**	**Device**
0 (highest)	IRQ0		Keyboard
1	IRQ1		Keyboard
2		IRQ0	Realtime clock
3		IRQ1	Unused
4		IRQ2	Unused
5		IRQ3	Unused (i.e., sound card or CD-ROM drive)
6		IRQ4	Unused
7		IRQ5	Math coprocessor
8		IRQ6	Hard drive
9		IRQ7	Unused
10	IRQ2		Realtime clock
11	IRQ3		Second serial interface (COM2:)
12	IRQ4		First serial interface (COM1:)
13	IRQ5		Second parallel interface (LPT2:)
14	IRQ6		Hard drive
15 (lowest)	IRQ7		First parallel interface (LPT1:)

If several PICs are operating together, one always acts as the master and the others are slaves. Only the master is connected directly to the CPU. The slaves pass their interrupt demands to the master. We'll see how this works shortly.

The PIC connections

To understand how the PIC works and how it interacts with the CPU, let take a look at the connections. The original PIC, the Intel 8259A is connected to other components through its 28 pins:

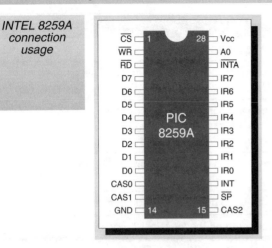

INTEL 8259A connection usage

An interrupt source is connected to one of the eight pins identified as IR0 through IR7. To trigger an interrupt, the source sets the pin to high.

Based on its priority and whether another interrupt is already in progress, the PIC determines if it can transfer the interrupt to the CPU. If so, it sets INT to high. This line is in turn connected to the processor's INTR pin and signals that a hardware interrupt has occurred. If the CPU is ready to accept the interrupt, it responds to the PIC on pin INTA. The PIC in turn responds by sending the interrupt number over pins D0 through D7. These lines serve as the data bus for transmitting the individual bytes of information between the PIC and the CPU.

Following this dialog, the CPU is now ready to call the appropriate interrupt handler. The PIC interrupt number is an index into the table of interrupt vectors. The corresponding interrupt handler is selected by simply extracting its address from the table.

On the hardware side, the communication between the CPU and the PIC is finished for the time being. When the interrupt handler has completed its work and before it returns control to the CPU, the interrupt handler contacts the PIC. In doing so, the PIC can then allow other interrupts access to the CPU. The exact procedure is discussed in a later section on PIC programming.

The following table describes the line on the PIC.

Wire	Pin	Name	Task
-CS	1	Chip-Select	Used in connection with -RD and -WR signals for communication between the PIC and CPU over the data bus.
-WR	2	Write	If this signal is low, the CPU can write data over the data bus to the internal PIC register.
-RD	3	Read	If this signal is low, the CPU can read data from the internal PIC registers over the data bus.
D0-D7	4-11	Data bus	Data is transferred between the PIC and the CPU over these pins.
CAS0-CAS2	12,13, 15	Cascade	A master PIC communicates with its slave over these pins.
GND	14	Ground	Ground

Wire	Pin	Name	Task
-SP	16	Slave Program	Indicates if the PIC is a master or slave.
INT	17	Interrupt	This pin is connected to the CPU INTR pin and signals a hardware interrupt to the CPU.
IR0-IR7	18-25	Interrupt request	Each line is connected to an interrupt source, which signals an interrupt. IR0 indicates the interrupt IRQ0 and is of the highest priority, IRQ7 represents the lowest.
-INTA	26	Interrupt Acknowledge	Indicates that that the CPU is ready to accept the interrupt number from the PIC.
A0	27	Address	Register number to be used during read and write.
Vcc	28		Voltage source (depending on the system +3.3 or +5 Volt)

To keep track of which interrupt is being serviced and which is waiting to be serviced, the PIC has the following three internal registers:

> ➤ Interrupt Request Register (IRR)

> ➤ In Service Register (ISR)

> ➤ Interrupt Mask Register (IMR)

These three registers are all eight bits wide. Each bit corresponds to one of the eight hardware interrupts. The Interrupt-Request-Register is connected directly to the eight interrupt lines - IR0 through IR7. To request an interrupt, the interrupt source sets its line to high. The corresponding bit in the IRR is simultaneously set.

In this way, the PIC knows which source requested the interrupt.

The Interrupt Mask Register can be used to mask or ignore one or more interrupt sources. If a bit in the IMR is set, then an interrupt from the corresponding interrupt source is ignored.

Block diagram of the PICs with the internal registers IRR, ISR and IMR

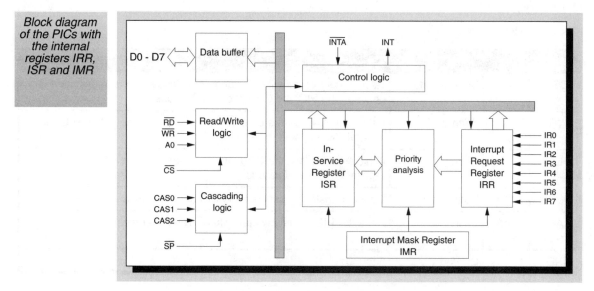

For non-masked interrupts, the PIC has to determine if it should present that interrupt to the CPU. Since additional interrupts may be awaiting service, the PIC selects the bit from the IRR having the lowest value and therefore the highest priority. This is compared to the contents of the ISR which indicates the source of the most recent interrupt. If the IRR has a higher priority interrupt awaiting service, then the PIC passes this onto the CPU - a process which effectively preempts the lower priority interrupt. The PIC continues this watchdog operation until all interrupts having a higher priority have been serviced.

When the PIC passes an interrupt onto the CPU, it sets the corresponding bit in the ISR register. At the same time the corresponding bit is cleared from the IRR register. This way, it keeps track of which interrupt is being handled and won't try to service this interrupt again.

Cascading

Recall that a single PIC is limited to handling only eight interrupt sources. To overcome this limitation, "cascading" is used. Simply stated, cascading is a way of linking together several PICs. Line EN determines if the PIC operates as a master or a slave. When voltage is applied to line EN, the PIC acts as a master. Otherwise, it functions as a slave. Three of the slave's lines (CAS0, CAS1 and CAS2) are connected to the corresponding lines on the master and the INT line on the slave is connected to the IRQ2 line of the master.

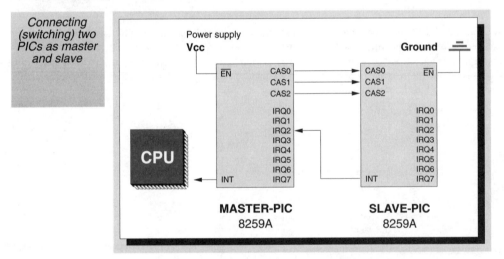

Interrupts on the master that do not involve cascading are handled the same as described above.

Let's see how they're handled on a slave. We'll talk about the similarities first. Devices are connected to one of the slaves eight IRQx lines. Based on the interrupt's priority and whether another interrupt is in progress, the slave determines whether it can pass this interrupt onto the CPU. If so, the slave sets INT to high.

Now we must talk about the differences. By setting INT to high, the slave is actually triggering IRQ2 on the master. The master recognizes that a slave is attached and treats the interrupt the same as if it originated directly from the hardware device.

IRR register bit 2 is set in the master If the IMR and ISR registers allow it, the interrupt is passed onto the CPU. Concurrently, it sets the number of the slave that sent the interrupt request on its lines CAS0, CAS1 and CAS2. These lines are connected to the lines of the same name on the slave.

Since CPU line INTA is connected to both the master and the slave, the CPU lets the slave know that it's ready to accept an interrupt by setting line INTA. The slave passes the interrupt number onto the CPU, which then initiates the call of the appropriate interrupt handler.

Both master and slave then clear the respective bit in their internal IRR registers and set the corresponding bit to one in the ISR registers to keep track of interrupts in progress.

When the PC is first booted, the BIOS initializes the registers of both PICs so they work correctly.

Initializing a PIC

As its name suggests, the PIC is programmable and responds to various commands. Basically there are two categories of PIC commands: initialization commands and operational commands. In fact, these categories have their own acronyms: ICW for Intialization Command Words and OCW for Operational Command Words.

ICWs are sent to the PIC in a very precise order since they're interdependent. OCWs can be sent to the PIC in any order.

Two port addresses are used to talk to the PICs. The port for the master is located at 20h and 21h; the port for the slave is at A0h and A1h.

Iinitialization always begins by writing the first initialization command word, ICW1 to port 20h or A0h, depending on whether the PIC is to be initialized as master or slave.

ICW1 is composed of eight bits. Only certain bits are significant to this discussion: ICW1 bit 0 specifies whether three additional initialization command words are to be sent to the PIC. These are ICW2, ICW3 and ICW4. If bit 0 is set, then the PIC can expect these three additional ICWs.

ICW1 bit 1 specifies whether the PIC is to be used alone or if several PICs are to be cascaded. If bit 1 is clear, then several PICs are to be cascaded. ICW1 bit 3 specifies how PIC lines IRQ0 to IRQ7 respond to the source devices. If bit 3 is clear, the PIC responds as an pulse-triggered device in which the interrupt is triggered by briefly setting IRQx to high and then letting it return to low. If bit 3 is set, the PIC responds as a edge-triggered device in which the interrupt is triggered by setting IRQx to high and leaving it there until the interrupt source drops it to low.

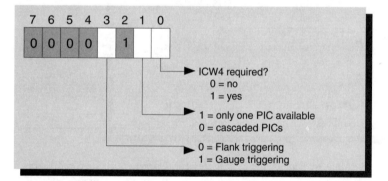

The BIOS sets ICW1 to the value 00010001b. This means that three additional initialization control words are to be sent, that cascading PICs are to be used and that flank triggering is to be used:

```
mov   al,00010001b
out   20h,al  ;ICW1 sent to master
out   0A0h,al ;ICW1 send to slave
```

ICW2 always follows ICW1. ICW2 defines the base address for the first interrupt (IRQ0). The second interrupt (IRQ1) then triggers the interrupt at the base address +1; the third interrupt (IRQ2) triggers the interrupt at the base address + 2, etc.

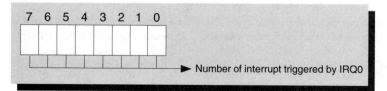

The BIOS sets the base address in ICW2 to 08h for the master and to 70h for the slave.

This means that hardware interrupts handled by the master activate the interrupt handler for the interrupts 08h to 0fh. Hardware interrupts handled by the slave activate the interrupt handler for interrupts 70h to 77h. It's important that ICW2, ICW3 and ICW4 be sent over the second PIC port.

```
mov    al,08h       ;08h is base interrupt for the master
out    21h,al       ;send ICW2 to the master
mov    al,70h       ;70h is the base interrupt for the slave
out    0a1h,al      ;send ICW2 to the slave
```

ICW3 follows ICW2 and must be sent to the PIC if the PICs are to be cascaded. If ICW1 bit 1 is clear, then the PIC expects ICW3. ICW3 has the task of informing master and slave through the interrupt control, to which they are connected. The ICW3's task depends on whether it is directed to the master or to the slave. The following appears with the master appears:

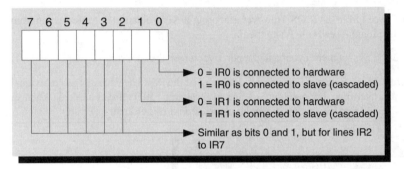

For the master, each bit in this register corresponds to one of the interrupt lines from IRQ0 to IRQ7, regardless of whether the line is connected directly to the hardware or to a slave. The BIOS sets only bit 2 to indicate that a slave PIC is cascaded over line IRQ2.

```
move   al,00000100b         ;cascading over IR2
out    21h,al               ;ICW3 send to the master
```

For the slave, ICW3 contains the interrupt control number.

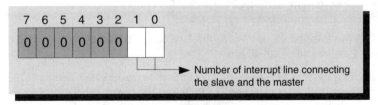

The BIOS sets ICW3 for the slave to the value 2.

```
mov    al,2         ;cascading over IR2
out    0A1h,al      ;ICW3 send to the slave
```

ICW4 is indicates how the end of an interrupt is to be handled. A PIC can be programmed to automatically signal an end of an interrupt or to signal it by software. In a PC, the PIC requires software assistance, so bit 1 is set to 0. This has certain implications for the interrupt handler, which we'll talk about soon.

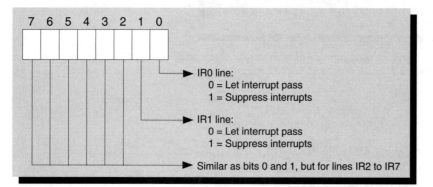

```
7  6  5  4  3  2  1  0
0  0  0  0  0  0
                    └──► 1 = PIC works with a processor from
                         the Intel 80x86 series
                 ──────► 0 = Manual interrupt termination through EOI
                         1 = Automatic interrupt termination
```

```
mov    al,00000001b       ;Intel environment, manual EOI
out    21h,al             ;send to the master
```

Control and inquiry of PICs - OCWs

As a rule, ICWs are sent only to the PIC once - from the BIOS. However user programs can obtain status information from or make changes to a PIC. To do this, the program sends OCWs to the PIC.

A PIC distinguishes between the various OCWs by their layout and the port over which they are sent.

OCW1 lets you change the PIC's Interrupt-Mask-Register. Changing the contents of the IMR lets you suppress individual hardware interrupts or reactivate them at a later time. If a bit is set to 1, the corresponding IRQx line is masked. When an interrupt line is masked, the device attached to that line cannot trigger an interrupt until it is cleared.

```
7  6  5  4  3  2  1  0

                    └──► IR0 line:
                           0 = Let interrupt pass
                           1 = Suppress interrupts
                 ──────► IR1 line:
                           0 = Let interrupt pass
                           1 = Suppress interrupts
              ─────────► Similar as bits 0 and 1, but for lines IR2 to IR7
```

OCW1 is be sent to the second PIC port - port 21h for the master and port A1h for the slave. Normally, all interrupts are enabled and therefore none of the interrupts are masked, so the value 0 is used here.

In the PIC master/slave combination, all slave interrupts may be suppressed if the bit 2 of the master's IMR is set to 1. The actual contents of this register can be obtained at any time by reading port 21h for the master or port A1h for the slave.

OCW2 is primarily used to signal the end of an interrupt handler. It also has other features such as priority rotation and automatic EOI handling. For PC's, neither of these features are enabled, so we'll talk about them only briefly in the following section.

The PIC recognizes OCW2 only if it is sent to the first PIC port, either 20h for the master or A0h for the slave.

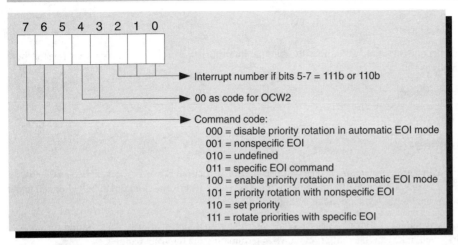

Of the various commands that can be sent using OCW2, only one is relevent for PC programming - code 001b. This is used to indicate the end of an interrupt. We'll talk more about this in the following section.

OCW3 lets you select the internal IRR and ISR PIC registers. Like OCW2, this command is sent to the first port. The PIC distinguishes between OCW2 and OCW3 by the setting of bits 3 and 4. For OCW3, these bits are set to 01b; for OCW2 they are 00b.

By writing the register number to the first port, the status of the desired register can be queried in the next step by reading the port. Therefore, a program can determine which interrupt handler is being serviced at that time and which are still awaiting service.

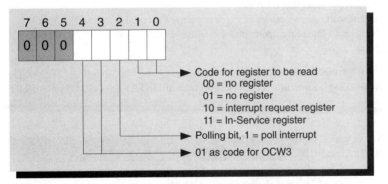

The polling bit has a special attribute if the PIC is operated in polling mode rather than interrupt mode. In polling mode, the INT PIC control is not connected to the INTR processor control. Therefore the PIC is not automatically notified of interrupts. Instead, the operating system ensure that the CPU checks the PIC status on a regular basis so as to recognize pending interrupt requests. With PC's, polling mode is not used.

Communication between the PIC and an interrupt handler

When the CPU sets line INTA, this tells the PIC that the interrupt has been accepted for processing by the CPU. But when the processing has been completed by the interrupt handler, the PIC has to be notified before it executes the IRET instruction.

The interrupt handler notifies the PIC by writing an OCW2 command to the first PIC port. The command code, 0001b means "unspecific EOI", where EOI stands for "End-Of-Interrupt". When combined with the other bits, the resulting command code is 20h.

For interrupts that are handled directly by the master, the corresponding machine language routine reads as follows:

```
mov    al,20h  ;EOI command
out    20h,al  ;send to master
```

For a slave, the interrupt handler must also notify the slave PIC that "its" interrupt has also ended. The corresponding machine language routine for this reads as follows:

```
mov    al,20h  ;EOI command
out    0A0h,al ;send to slave, and also
out    20h,al  ;to master
```

Unused PIC capabilities

We mentioned a PIC feature called *priority rotatation*. The purpose of priority rotation is to give the each line on the PIC an equal chance of service over an extended period of time. After a line is serviced, its priority is automatically dropped to the lowest level, while the ones at the lowest level are move up higher.

If the same interrupt happens again, it is serviced unless another interrupt with a higher priority isn't waiting for service. Although this method works well, it has an inherent problem when terminating the interrupt handler.

IF an EOI command is passed to the PIC, normally it knows from which interrupt it originated, namely from the interrupt handler with the highest priority. But if the priorities can be changed, this simple arrangement no longer works. In addtion to the unspecified EOI, you can send a specific EOI to the PIC using OCW2, which contains the number of the respective interrupt. In this way, the PIC recognizes precisely which interrupt handler was terminated and can clear the corresponding bit in its ISR register. With PC programming, priority rotation is not used.

Sample program

The IRQSTAT program is an example of interrupt controller programming. This program, which you'll find on the companion CD-ROM, is designed to be a resident program that wedges itself into all hardware interrupts. You can execute many things from the DOS level, release the hardware interrupts, for example press the keyboard or access the floppy disk or hard drive. IRQSTAT notifies you of the respective hardware interrupts by displaying the status of the PIC's ISR and IRR registers in the upper right corner of the screen.

In this way, you can recognize which interrupts have just been executed and which are waiting to be executed. Because the interrupt is handled so quickly, the screen displays the information for only a short time. IRQSTAT displays a counter which is incremented for each hardware interrupt. In this way, you get a sense of when and how often a hardware interrupt is triggered.

IRQSTAT is based on the module IRQSTAT.C, which works with two additional modules; IRQUTIL.C and WIN.C. WIN.C is a collection of routines for the management of text windows and the display of text. IRQUTIL.C., on the other hand, is different. It contains routines for many important tasks, which fall into the same category as PIC management and query. Therefore, you'll be able to adapt the code from this module into your own programs. The table on the right lists the functions from the IRQUTIL.C module.

Function	Task
irq_Enable	Hardware-Interrupt admit
irq_Disable	Hardware-Interrupt conceal
irq_SendEOI	"End Of Interrupt" signal
irq_SetHandler	install new Interrupt-Handler
irq_ReadMask	read Interrupt-Mask-Register
irq_ReadISR	read In-Service-Register
irq_ReadIRR	read Interrupt-Request-Register

IRQSTAT works quite simply. The main program calls function InstallIRQ which redirects each of the 16 interrupts to the C-function IRQ by using function irq_SetHandler function. In other words, it creates a new interrupt-handler for all of the hardware-interrupts.

If InstallIRQ is called as the interrupt handler for the keyboard, timer or for one of the other devices, it then uses the PrintIRQ function. PrintIRQ displays the status of the PIC registers on the screen and the currently serviced interrupt number.

Because IRQ is called as the interrupt handler for all hardware interrupts, it must determine the interrupt for which it's currently performing its services. Otherwise, it would be impossible for it to call the original handler, which would quickly result in a system crash. PrintIRQ returns the number of the interrupt since it has to fetch the contents of the ISR register from which the current interrupt results.

Using this information, IRQ can determine the address of the old interrupt handler from a previously loaded array and then call it. Since the old handler is being accessed, IRQ doesn't need to transmit the EOI command to the PIC because that already occurs in the orignal handler.

To keep IRQSTAT as simple as possible we didn't build a deactive feature. To deactivate IRQSTAT, you can simply reboot the computer. However, it's easier if you just start IRQSTAT in a Window's DOS box. This lets you deactivate IRQSTAT simply by closing the box. In any case, you'll be able to see that not all interrupts can slip through from Windows to a DOS box. For example, the timer, keyboard and disk drive can slip through from Windows to a DOS box but the hard drive interrupt cannot.

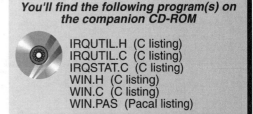

You'll find the following program(s) on the companion CD-ROM

IRQUTIL.H (C listing)
IRQUTIL.C (C listing)
IRQSTAT.C (C listing)
WIN.H (C listing)
WIN.C (C listing)
WIN.PAS (Pacal listing)

To install IRQUTIL.H in your own programs, you'll need files IRQUTIL.H and IRQUTIL.C.

Chapter 6

The DMA Controller

The DMA controller has been a standard component in the PC from day one. DMA is an acronym for *Direct Memory Access*. DMA is either specialized circuitry or a dedicated microprocessor which transfers data between from memory and a peripheral device without using the CPU. Although DMA may periodically steal cycles from the CPU, data is transferred much faster than if the CPU has to transfer every byte.

The transfer is usually directed by a program which continuously reads a byte using the I/O port of the respective peripheral device into a CPU-register and writes it to the memory from there. Since the CPU is not involved in a DMA transfer, the speed of the transfer is increased. In fact, the DMA controller was a great performance feature in the early days of the PC because a disk drive, for example, delivered data faster than could be read by software in the 8088 or 8086 CPU.

Although the processing speed of the CPU is now 100 times faster than the original 8088, the DMA controller's performance ability has not kept pace. Like the 8088-CPU, it was originally made to operate at a clock speed of 4.77 MHz. Today's CPUs have achieved clock speeds of 100 MHz but the DMA controller has never surpassed 6 MHz. The original AT design use a clock speed of 3 MHz, which was slower than the one in the PC/XT. With the AT, the DMA controller's decline began and it became less important.

Although the functional capabilities of the original DMA-controller 8237A still remain today, it no longer plays a major role in system design. Several PC add-ons, such as sound cards, for example, still support the DMA controller but can also read the data from the CPU through an I/O port. This method is considerably faster than using the DMA and which is why the DMA controller is now considered a "non-factor" in PC design.

Other DMA controller design weaknesses include the following:

➢ It limits the transfer to memory areas within the 64K size pages

➢ It supports the 16-bit transfer only with a great deal of effort

➢ It's never attained the level of performance for today's CPUs

Therefore, the DMA controller is only used in system programming when communicating with hardware extensions, which accept or return data exclusively through DMA. These are becoming increasingly rare.

Hardware and software interaction during DMA transfers

One of the few peripheral devices that still uses the DMA controller is the disk drive. This is one of the best examples of hardware and software interaction during a DMA-transfer.

The starting point is using one of the operating system's BIOS functions for Interrupt 13h from a user program. These BIOS functions let you read or write one or more sectors from/to a floppy disk.

The BIOS function works in two phases: First, it commands the floppy disk controller to seek to the desired sector and read the contents of that sector into a buffer. Concurrently, the BIOS "programs" the DMA controller and the channel connecting the hardware to the disk drive. This program instructs the DMA controller where in main memory the data is to be transferred to and how many bytes are to be transferred.

When the floppy disk controller finds the sector, it activates the line to request that the DMA controller start the tranasfer. The DMA controller accepts the specified number of bytes from the floppy disk controller and transfers them sequentially into the buffer beginning at the main memory address programmed through the BIOS function.

During this process the DMA controller assumes control of the PC bus. The CPU remains uninvolved. The DMA controller directs the bus controls so the individual bytes are transferred directly from the disk drive to main memory without having to temporarily store them in a DMA controller internal register. Once all data has been transferred, the DMA controller again releases the bus, while the disk controller simultaneously executes a hardware interrupt.

Through this hardware interrupt, the BIOS is notified that the data is now available in the designated buffer and returns to the BIOS function.

The DMA controller, however, is not only able to transfer data from a peripheral device into memory (and in the opposite direction), it's also able to copy memory areas within the main memory. It's unfortunate the original design of the DMA limits the transfer to a 64K block. For that reason, many modern PC's no longer support memory-to-memory transfers using DMA

To eliminate some of the limitations of the DMA controller, IBM added an enhanced DMA controller into their PS/2 machines. Unfortunately, the BIOS of the PS/2 machines does not support these extended capabilities.

Channels and priorities

Since the DMA controller has four channels it can serve 4 different devices. However, only one of these channels can be active at a time, and therefore, a DMA transfer is performed on only one channel at any one time. Due to this limitation, a priority mechanism analogous to the interrupt controller is necessary. This is the only way the DMA controller can determine, which one request will be served first when concurrent requests are pending.

Like the interrupt controller, the DMA controller supports, in terms of priorities, two different operational methods: One with static and the other with dynamic (rotating) priorities. PC's basically work with static priorities where channel 0 represents the highest priority and channel 3 the lowest. This order is established by a chip and cannot be changed. It is up to the board designer, however, to connect each peripheral device at board level to a channel via hardware. Each device has its own connection available to the controller, which we'll talk about in the next section on DMA connections.

When multiple DMA devices simultaneously request a DMA transfer, the device at channel 0 always receives top priority. The device on channel 3 always receives the lowest priority. However, you can also disable individual channels using an internal mask register. In this case, the DMA controller ignores the DMA commands from the respective device.

The DMA controller connections

The original 8237A DMA controller was designed as a 40 pin chip. Today, there are several variations including integrated chip sets. Regardless of changes in the "packaging", the function of the DMA has not changed.

The following table shows the different connections of the DMA controller.

DMA controller connections			
Line	Pin	Name	Task
-IOR	1	IO-Read	Depending on the condition of the DMA controller, this signal has different meanings. In the wait state, the CPU activates this line when it reads data from one of the controller's internal registers. During a DMA transfer, the DMA controller activates this line when it transfers data to main memory.
-IOW	2	IO-Write	This signal works analogous to -IOR. It refers, however, to writing procedures. In the wait state, the CPU activates this line when it writes data into one of the internal DMA controller registers. During a DMA transfer, the DMA controller activates this signal when it transfers data to a peripheral device.
-MEMR	3	Memory	The DMA controller activates this line when data from the main memory needs to be read.
-MEMW	4	Memory Write	The DMA controller activates this line when data needs to bewritten to the main memory.
Voc	5		Voltage supply (depending on the system+3,3V or +5V)
Ready	6		Main memory and peripheral devices activate this line to indicate that they have received data from or are ready to initiate a DMA transfer. This line allows slow peripheral devices or memory a way to lengthen the reading or writing access to the DMA controller.
HLDA	7	Hold Acknowledge	The CPU or another controller activates this line when it has released the local bus. This indicates that the DMA controller can assume control of the bus for transfer.
ADSTB	8	Address Strobe	The DMA controller uses this line to load the most significant byte of a transfer address into the external DMA latch register. It activates this line as soon as it has placed this address on lines DB0 to DB7. 12.5 cm 0 frame
AEN	9	Address Enable	The DMA controller activates this line during a DMA transfer to command the external DMA latch register to write its contents as part of the memory address on the lines A8- A15 of the address bus.
HRQ	10	Hold Request	The DMA controller activates this line to request control of the bus from the CPU or from a bus master. Line HLDA is activated when the request is satisfied.
-CS	11	Chip Select	The CPU activates this line when it wants to read from or write to the DMA controller internal registers. The data is passed on lines DB0-DB7, which then functions as local data bus.
CLK	12	Clock	This is the clock speed for the DMA controller.
Reset	13		The CPU activates this line to return the DMA controller to its initial status.

DMA controller connections (continued)			
Line	Pin	Name	Task
DACK0-DACK3	14,15,2	DMA-Acknowled	After a DMA request on one of the DREQ lines, the DMA controller informs the peripheral over one of these lines that it is ready to start the DMA transfer. Since only one device can be served at a time, the DMA controller activates this signal only when there is no DMA request of a higher priority. In addition, activating this signal is always preceded by assuming control over the bus using the HRQ andHLDA lines to insure that the DMA controller has unimpeded access to the bus. Since only one channel is active at a time, only one of these lines is set at any one time.
DREQ0-DR	16-19	DMA Request 0-3	Each of these lines is connected to one of a maximum of four peripeheral devices, served by the DMA controller. If one of these devices initiates a DMA transfer, it activates the DREQ line and, in doing so, informs the DMA controller of an intended transfer.
GND	20	Ground	
DB0-DB7	21-23, 26-30	Bus 0-7	The CPU accesses the DMA controller registers over these lines which form a two-way data bus. Inaddition, the controller uses these lines to write the high order of the address (bits 8-15) to the external DMA latch register.
Vcc	31		Power supply (depending on the system+3.3 or +5 Volt)
AO-A3	32-35	Address 0-3	Depending on the mode of the DMA controller, these lines have different purposes. In the wait state, during a read or write access of the DMA controller's internal registers, the CPU places the register number on these lines (maximum of 16 registers). During a DMA transfer, the DMA controller writes the least significant four bits of the memory address (bits 0 to 3) to the bus.
-EOP	36	End of process	The DMA controller activates this line to indicate to the device the end of the current DMA transfer. A connected deivce can also activate this line to terminate a transfer. In this case, the transfer is terminated and the respective flags in the DMA controller's internal registers are reset.
A4-A7	37-40	Address 4-7	During a DMA transfer, the DMA controller passes bits 4-7 of the memory address to the bus over these lines.

The DMA controller registers

The DMA controller has 27 internal registers - an ample supply for a simple device. Certain registers appear four times to accomodate each of the four DMA channels.

DMA Controller Registers		
Register	Number	Width/bit
Starting address	4	16
Counter	4	16
Current address	4	16
Current counter	4	16
Temporary address	1	16
Temporary counter	1	16
Status	1	8
Command	1	8
Intermediate memory	1	8
Mode	4	8
Mask	1	8
Request	1	8

The counter register specifies the number of bytes to be transferred for a channel. A 16-bit register holds a maximum value of 0FFFFh. This corresponds to a maximum transfer or 64K - the number of bytes transfered is one more than the value in the counter. The reason for this is that the DMA controller decrements the contents of the counter register after each byte and continues until the value in the counter changes from 000h to 0FFFFh. Therefore, to tranfser a single byte, you load the counter register with the value 000h. The cycling of the counter register from 000h to 0FFFFh has a special name in DMA terminology: "Terminal Count" abbreviated TC. We'll see this term again in the next section.

Similarly, the registers which specify the base address for the DMA transfer on their respective channels are also 16-bits wide. The DMA controller can address only the first 64K of main memory if a channel has not been assigned an additional external DMA page register. With the DMA page register, the controller can address bits beyond A15 and thus provide unlimited access to the entire address space.

On the PC/XT with its 20-bit wide address bus, the DMA page register contain address bits A16 to A19. On an AT with its 24-bit address bus, the DMA page register contains address bits A16 to A23.

To complicate matters even more, the DMA controller specifies only address signals A0 to A7 on its lines directly. Address bits A0-A7 are generated by the DMA controller and address bits A16-A19 (or A16-A23 on an AT bus) from the DMA page register. But note that there's a gap in the address. Address bits A8-A15 are missing.

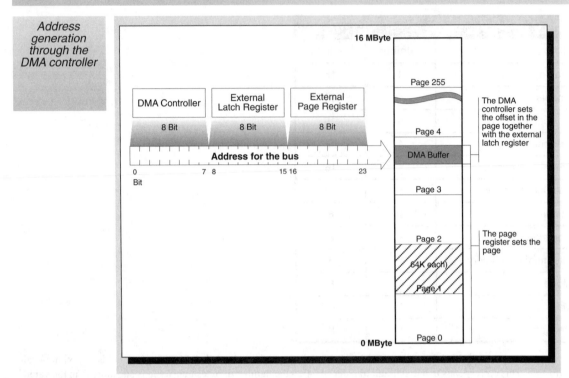

Address generation through the DMA controller

This gap is filled by the DMA address latch. This is an external 8-bit register connecting the DMA controller to its data bus DB0-DB7 through the directional line ADSTB. The DMA controller writes address bits A8-A15 to this register over line DB0-DB7, which are then placed on the address bus by the DMA address latch as soon as a transfer is initiated.

DMA-segment overflow

Because the DMA controller keeps address bits A0-A15 separated from the address bits A16-A19 (or A16-A23 on an AT), there is always the danger of a DMA segment overflow during a DMA transfer. This happens when the lower address bits A0-A15 cycle from 0FFFFh to 000h, meaning a change from the last byte of the current 64K page to the first byte of the following 64K page is taking place. The DMA controller should increment address bits A0-A15 and also increment the contents of the DMA page register. But this does not happen. Instead, the next byte is transferred to the same 64K page, but at offset 000h.

This example illustrates the overflow: Assume that you allocate a buffer in memory to accept data from a DMA transfer at memory address 0000:E000. This is within the first 64K page of the main memory. The buffer is 16K in length (4000h). Therefore the buffer extends to address 1000:2000. The first 8K of the buffer are within the first 64K page of the memory. The second 8K of the buffer are in the second 64K page.

During the DMA transfer, the DMA controller writes the first 8K of data into the buffer. Immediately thereafter, the problem begins. As the offset changes from 0FFFFh to 000h, the DMA controller "forgets" to increment the DMA page register and begins to transfer the second 8K of data. However, this data isn't transferred into the second 8K of the buffer as expected, but rather winds up at the beginning of the first 64K page. A problem like this will soon cause the system to crash since the DMA controller can overwrite data or program code.

As a programmer, you have to prevent this from happening. If the dividing line between two 64K pages is transgressed, the transfer must be split into two blocks. It's therefore important to first program the DMA controller so it is dedicated to the first part of the buffer below the 64K byte limit. Upon completing this transfer, the DMA controller is again be programmed to execute the transfer into, or out of, the second buffer beyond the 64K limit. How the DMA controller is programmed is the subject of "Accessing the DMA controller via software".

DMA architecture in the PC/XT or AT

If the basic functions of the DMA controller are not easy to understand, programming the DMA controller can be even more difficult. The main reason for this is that we're dealing with different DMA architectures for a PC/XT and an AT. On an PC/XT, a single DMA controller performs only 8-bit transfers. On an AT, a second DMA controller can perform 16-bit transfers.

The two DMA controllers in the AT are cascaded (connected to a larger unit, as is also commonly done with the interrupt controller). The slave is then connected to one of the master channels by connecting the HRQ and HLDA connections with the master's DREQ and DACK connections. To be more precise, in the master these are the connections DREQ0 and DACK0, because with the AT, the slave DMA controller is always connected to the master channel 0. Cascading through channel 0 results in all the slave channels having a higher priority than those of the master. According to this priority ranking, the slave channels on the AT are labeled DMA channels 0 to 3, while the master channels are labeled 4 to 7.

Cascading two DMA controllers on the AT

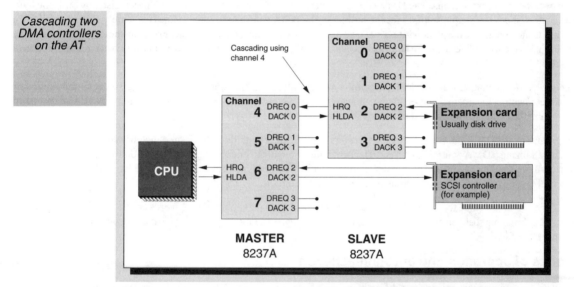

Master channels 4 to 7 on the AT are designed for 16-bit transfers. The slave, as with the PC/XT, can perform only 8-bit transfers. The tables below and to the right show how each channel is used.

Using the DMA channels in the PC/XT		
Channel	Width	Application/use
0	8 bit	memory refresh
1	8 bit	free
2	8 bit	disk drive
3	8 bit	hard drive

Use/application of the DMA channels with the AT			
Channel	Master /slave	Width	Use/application
0	Slave	8 bit	memory-refresh
1	Slave	8 bit	unused
2	Slave	8 bit	disk drive
3	Slave	8 bit	unused
4	Master	16 bit	cascading the slave
5	Master	16 bit	unused
6	Master	16 bit	unused
7	Master	16 bit	unused

16-bit transfers

Although you can refer to 16-bit transfers in the master DMA controller in an AT, you should note that controller itself can peform only 8-bit transfers. This is best illustrated, by the fact that for each transfer, the internal address registers are incremented or decremented by one only byte and not two, which happens in 16-bit transfers.

Nevertheless, 16-bit-transfers can occur by carefully interconnecting the DMA controller channels with the address and data bus. First, remember the DMA controller never reads the bytes or words that are to be transferred, but only directs the signals on the data, address and directional or control buses so the data are transferred from a peripheral device into the memory (or in the opposite direction). Therefore, when changing from an 8-bit to a 16-bit-transfer, the internal register do not have to be expanded.

For 16-bit-transfers, the DMA controller then needs only to be interconnected to the control bus master so the connected units recognize, through a signal, that words instead of bytes are to be transferred.

However, one problem remains: The DMA controller increases or decreases the internal address register by only one byte. Fortunately, there is a simple solution for the problem: The DMA controller's address lines are simply shifted one line (or one bit) from the address line of the address bus. The line A0, by which the DMA controller prints out the lower valued address bit, is connected to the line A1 at the address bus, and the same is true for A1 of the DMA controller with A2 of the address bus, etc.

The addresses originating from the DMA controller are all shifted one bit to the left, which is equivalent to multiplying by two. Incrementing the internal address register means the address is incremented by one word. This method "steps through" the data in the area to be transferred one word at a time.

Programming the DMA controller for 16-bit transfers is a little different. First, the desired memory address must be halved when initializing a DMA controller register. The hardware automatically doubles this address. Additionally, the buffer must start at an even memory address. The transfer length is specified as words and not as bytes. To transfer 160 bytes, for example, specify 80 words. Is isn't possible to transfer an odd number of bytes.

Since the maximum value for this 16-bit-register remains 0FFFFh, a maximum of 64K words can be transferred (equivalent to 128K). Providing that you start at the beginning of a 64K page in memory, you won't have to be concerned about a DMA segment overflow.

Modes of operation and auto-initialization

The DMA-controller recognizes three different modes of operation which determine the type of transfer:

> Single transfer

> Block transfer

> Demand transfer

What is commonly called a DMA transfer is actually a block transfer. Once triggered by a signal on one of the DREQx lines, the DMA controller executes the data transfer within a block transfer until either the respective counter register jumps from 000h to 0FFFFh (Terminal Count) or the initiating peripheral device stops the transfer with a signal on the -EOP line. During the transfer, the bus remains under the control of the DMA controller, so the CPU cannot access the bus. In certain situations, it's not desirable to isolate the CPU from the bus for the duration of a complete transfer, so the DMA controller also supports single transfers.

For a single transfer, only one byte (or word in 16-bit-channels) is transferred before the DMA controller automatically terminates the transfer. Although the counter register is simultaneously decremented and the address register is incremented, a new command has to initiate the next single transfer. In this manner, the CPU has time after each individual transfer to assume control of the bus before the next single transfer in initiated.

Demand transfer is similar to block transfer, but the DREQx-line has a somewhat different purpose here. Although an short signal on the DREQx line is sufficient to initiate a transfer in a normal block transfer, this line is stay active during a demand transfer. When the respective peripheral device reassumes the line, the DMA controller temporarily halts the transfer until the line is reactivated. When this happens, the transfer restarts at the place where it left off.

This mode is important for devices that independently want to indicate the end of a transfer by signalling on -EOP line in a normal block transfer.

Regardless of the mode of operation, the DMA controller can perform write, read and verify transfers. Data are written from a peripheral device to main memory during a read transfer. Data are written from main memory to a peripheral device during a write transfer. During a verify transfer, no data are moved.

An extremely practical feature of the DMA controller is "auto initialization". This is also available in all three modes of operation. With auto initialization on, when Terminal Count is reached or -EOP line is active, the DMA controller will put the address and length of transfer that was last programmed in the respective channel. This saves the programmer from having to continually set the respective registers when a block having a constant length is transferred to fixed location in memory.

Programming the DMA controller

The following table shows the different DMA controller registers which are used to determine the status of the controller or define the parameters:

DMA register in the PC/XT (or AT) which directs the DMA controller				
Register	Port*	Port**	Read	Write
Status	08h	ODOh		
Command	08h	ODOh		
Request	09h	OD2h		
Masking	10Ah	0D4h		
Mode	0Bh	0D6h		
ByteWord-FlipFlop	0Ch	0D8h		
Intermediate memory	0Dh	0DAh		
Reset	0Dh	0DAh		
masking reset	0Eh	0DCh		
masking	0Fh	0DEh		
* slave in an AT / only one DMA in a PC/XT				
** master in an AT / not present in a PC/XT				

Before you access one of these registers, decide if you're addressing the master or the slave. If you have a PC/XT that has only one DMA controller, it's not possible to access a second DMA controller (master in the AT).

The status register lets you determine if there is a hardware request (a signal on the respective DREQx line), or a Terminal Count for one of the different channels. The latter indicates that a DMA transfer has been completed on that channel. A special feature of this register is to reset the initial values of the four TC flags. By selecting the register, these flags are cleared.

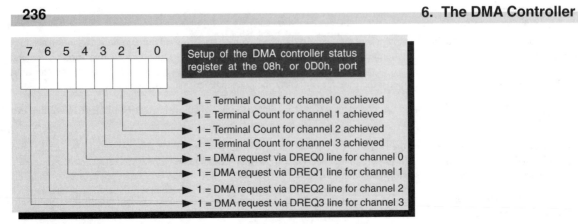

The command register is located at the same port address as the status register. It goes through several settings on the DMA controller. Some of these settings, especially the 5 bit, are interesting in certain situations for DMA programming using software. The problem with this register, however, is that it cannot be selected and used due to the status of the other bits. In regard to the other bits, you must depend on the fact the BIOS has selected the standard setting for the PC when the system was booted and that you can take over these default settings without causing any damage.

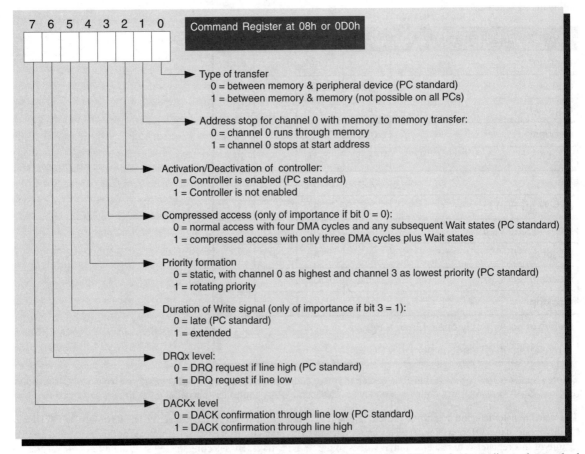

The 7 and 6 bits of the command register determine the polarity of the DREQx and DACK signals. According to the standard PC settings, both bits should be set to 0. The DMA controller recognizes a DMA request in DREQx if this connection is set to high and the corresponding DACKx line is set to low, providing it follows the DMA request. Bits 5 and 3 determine the signal length for read and write impulses and are not important for programming.

Bit 4 determines the priority selection. In the PC, the DMA controller uses static priorities, where channel 0 is assigned the highest priority and channel 3 the lowest. Therefore, always set this bit to zero.

Bit 2 activates and deactivates the DMA controller. For example, you can set the controller to a state in which the CPU can read and write to the registers, but doesn't respond to any DMA requests. A typical use for this is for changing the controller settings and but want to prevent a DMA transfer at the same time. Since channel 0 and the memory refresh are blocked when the DMA controller is deactivated, use this for as brief a time as possible. An alternative is to use the mask register to mask only the channel that you wish to change.

The request register is used to initiate a DMA transfer under software control. This is done by simulating the activation or clearing of one of the DREQx lines The request register is also used to initiate a memory to memory transfer, since a peripheral device is not involved and therefore cannot send a signal over a DREQx line.

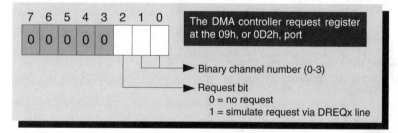

If a DMA request is simulated over the request register, its response depends on whether other, higher priority DMA requests are pending. If so, the DMA request must until for its turn to be serviced. During this time, the request can again be turned off using the request register. This is done by setting the 2, called the request bit, for the respective channel number.

There are two mask registers. Mask register 1 is organized similarly to the request register. It is used to either turn off or reactivate a channel. If a DMA channel is to be deactivated, the preferred option is to turn off the channel since the channel register (start address, length, etc.) would have to be reset. In such an instance, the consequences would be fatal if a DMA transfer were released on this channel while the register indicates piece by piece its old contents and has already been reinitialized.

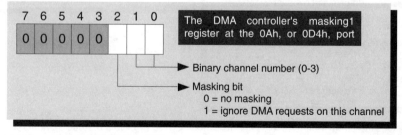

Another way to mask or make a channel receptive to DMA requests is provided by mask register 2. In contrast to the mask register 1, all four channels are affected. Use this register only to change the status for all four channels simultaneously.

As its name suggests, the mode register determines a channel's operating mode. You can specify if the next DMA transfer will happen as a single transfer, a block transfer, or a demand transfer. It also specifies if the channel is to cascade two DMA controllers. In most cases you won't have to change this later setting since this happens when the computer is booted.

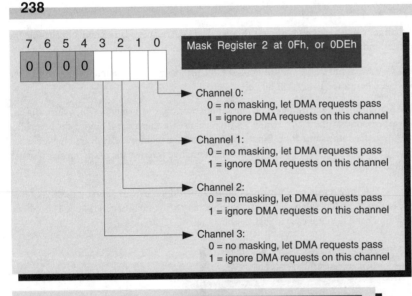

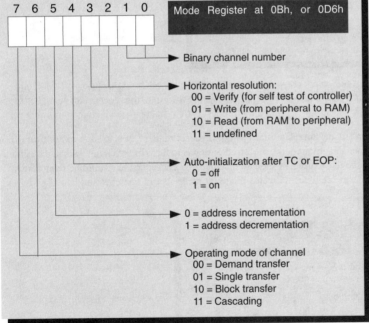

Bit 5 of the mode register, determine the "direction" of a transfer. This "direction" isn't to or from a peripheral, rather it's forward or backward direction in memory. So you can decrement instead of increment the memory address during a DMA transfer. In his case, a data block is read backwards to forwards by the peripheral. Also the ending address of the buffer is loaded into the proper register before starting the transfer.

The mode register also lets you can auto-initialize a channel after reaching Terminal Count, or after receiving a signal on the -EOP line. The channel number is specified by bits 0 and 1 and the operating mode by bits 2 and 3.

Three of the ports on the DMA controller - 0Dh, 0Eh and 0Fh and the corresponding 0D8, 0DAh and 0DCh - are not essentially don't have a register, but are used to receive specialized commands. When the CPU writes to one of these ports, it releases a particular function in the DMA controller (regardless of the contents of the data that was written). By writing to port 0Eh (or 0DCh), masking for all channels is removed and the controller again responds to DMA requests on these channels. The same is true for the 0Dh port (or 0DAh); however, the DMA controller is completely reset so the command, status and request registers are returned to their original settings.

The third "command port", 0Ch (or 0D8h), is used to set the 16-bit register with the starting address for a DMA transfer and for the length of the transfer. This is shown in the following table:

DMA register in the PC/XT or AT for setup and query of the DMA channel					
Channel	Register	Port*	Port**	Read	Write
0	Start address	00h	0C0h		
0	Current address	00h	0C0h		
0	Transfer length-1	01h	0C2h		
0	Remaining length-1	01h	0C2h		
1	Start address	02h	0C4h		
1	Current address	02h	0C4h		
1	Transfer length-1	03h	0C6h		
1	Remaining length-1	03h	0C6h		
2	Start address	04h	0C8h		
2	Current address	04h	0C8h		
2	Transfer length-1	05h	0CAh		
2	Remaining length-1	05h	0CAh		
3	Start address	06h	0CCH		
3	Current address	06h	0CCh		
3	Transfer length-1	07h	0CEh		
3	Remaining length-1	07h	0CEh		
*Slave in an AT / only one DMA in a PC/XT					
**Master in an AT / not present in a PC/XT					

To set up one of these registers to determine the start address or the length of a DMA transfer, you must output to port 0Ch or 0D8h. An internal FlipFlop, lowered to zero, shows the state of a 16-bit transfer. After the FlipFlop is lowered to zero, it sends the low-order byte of the address to the port, for example port 0C4h for channel 1 of the AT master DMA controller (AT channel 5). This output trips the internal FlipFlop. The port now knows that the most signficant byte of the address is coming.

This procedure is necessary because access to the different 16-bit registers has to fit into the 8-bit wide DMA hardware. Therefore, a 16-bit value has to be divided into a low byte and a high byte. And since the low and high bytes are transferred at the same port, the DMA controller needs the FlipFlop to differentiate between the two.

Selecting a 16-bit register proceeds in the same manner: First, the FlipFlop is lowered. Next the port is read to get the low-order byte. Finally, read the port to get the high-order significant byte.

After the mode register, the start address and the transfer length, one other task remains. So as not to be limited to the first 64K of memory for the transfer buffer (128K for a 16-bit channel), the DMA page register for the respective channel must also be set. The following table shows the position of the DMA page register which accepts the address bits 16-23 of the transfer area. Remember, the page register for channels 4 to 7 are only available for AT's having a second DMA controller.

The following table lists the DMA page register for address bits 16-23 of the transfer area:

Channel	Port	Channel	Port
0	87h	4	8Fh
1	83h	5	8Bh
2	82h	6	89h
3	81h	7	8Ah

A special feature is found in the PC/XT page register. For channels 0 and 1, there is only one page register available, but it can be addressed over both of the port addresses.

DMA utility

The module DMAUTIL is an example of programming the DMA controller. You'll find both the listing and the program on the companion CD-ROM. DMAUTIL contains all the important functions that you'll need to set up channel parameters and to initiate a DMA transfer. You'll find an example program with the DMA utility functions in Chapter 38 on how to program Sound Blaster or compatible cards.

You'll find the following program(s) on the companion CD-ROM

DMAUTIL.C　(C listing)
DMAUTIL.H　(C listing)

DMAUTIL.C Functions	
Function	Task
dma_Masterclear	Initiate DMA controller reset
dma_SetRequest	Initiate DMA transfer on the specified channel
dma_ClrRequest	Halt DMA transfer on the specified channel
dma_SetMask	Mask (block) specified channel
dma_ClrMask	Clear specified channel
dma_ReadStatus	Read DMA controller status
dma_ClrFlipFlop	Clear FlipFlop for 16 bit register access
dma_ReadCount	Read channel transfer counter
dma_SetChannel	Set DMA channel for transfer
dma_Until64kPage	Determine the numberof bytes within the buffer, which lie on a 64K-Page
dma_AllocMem	Allocate DMA capable memory
dma_FreeMem	Free DMA capable memory

Chapter 7

Serial Ports

Like the parallel port, the serial port is basic to the PC. Every PC has at least one, and usually two, one with a small connector and another with a large connector. Serial ports are most commonly used to attach a modem or a mouse to the computer, but they can also communicate with more exotic devices such as clock radios, model trains, and other devices. Even subnotebook computers have a serial port.

A serial port is much slower than a parallel port. Instead of eight bits at a time, the serial port sends each bit through a line individually. Given the same clock speed, the serial port is eight times slower than the parallel port. What is responsible for this speed disadvantage however is precisely what gives the serial port its superior cabling properties. This port operates "serially" - instead of eight data lines plus control lines, the serial port consists of just one line for grounding and one for data (data transmission in both directions at the same time requires two data lines, but this is still a total of only three lines). For this reason parallel port cables are heavier and more expensive.

When devices are in close proximity, the cable cost is not a significant factor. When devices are distant, cable costs are a much more important factor.

With only two lines (in its simplest form), the serial port can do some remarkable things. Telephone cables are potential serial transmission cables for a PC. To connect a PC in New York, Buenos Aires or London with a PC in Bombay, you don't have to run a parallel cable halfway around the world - you simply dial the computer in Bombay. Serial ports have been used since the 1960's to connect terminals and printers with their host computers, using the existing telephone cables already in office buildings.

Even today, the serial port is by far the best way to link remote devices with a PC. Connecting a modem or a mouse to the serial port also has historic origins. Early IBM/PC computers included both a parallel and a serial port, even though in most cases only the parallel one was used (for the printer). When modems and mice arrived, the obvious choice for them was the serial port - this way the user didn't have to invest an additional interface cards.

While a new standard has already become necessary for the parallel interface (see Chapter 8), the standard for the serial interface has remained the same since 1969. It was at this time that the EIA (Electronic Industries Association) established the RS-232C standard. This standard defines the data transfer protocol, cables, electrical signals, and connectors for an RS-232 connection. So anywhere in the world if you see a device with the written characters "RS-232", you can hook it up to your PC! Your PC is guaranteed to have an RS-232 interface, although it is usually referred to as the "serial" interface.

As one user types characters on a terminal (or PC with a terminal program), they appear almost immediately on the screen of another user hundreds of miles away. This interaction requires more than just a serial port. You also need:

➤ The terminal program to instruct the serial interface controller to send and receive characters.

➤ The controller to convert a character to be sent into bit sequences, sends them over the appropriate lines and in the opposite direction, interprets incoming signals, converts them to bits and combines them into bytes.

➤ The modem to receive characters through the serial interface and sends them over the telephone network in the form of acoustical signals. At the same it converts incoming signals back to bits and transmits them to the serial interface.

➤ The connector and cable to link one serial port with another serial port or modem.

The following sections describe in detail the steps needed for data to travel from one PC to another. Before we continue however, we'll briefly talk about modems.

Although, telephone lines can theoretically connect two serial ports directly, the technology used by the phone system presents a certain obstacle. The analog telephone network, which still prevails today, is not designed to transmit voltage signals. First +12 volts for a logical zero and then -12 volts for a logical one - such signals are not suited to the telephone network. The telephone system demands the transmission of tones, and this is where the modem comes in.

The modem converts signal sequences from the serial port to acoustical signals of defined frequencies, and sends them through the telephone line. The modem at the other end receives these "tones" and converts them back to the signal sequences expected by the serial port. In this way two serial ports appear to be directly connected.

Modulators and demodulators within the modem are responsible for converting (modulation) of electric signals to tones and tones to signals. This is how a modem gets its name: From mod(ulation) and dem(odulation).

PCs connected through a telephone network

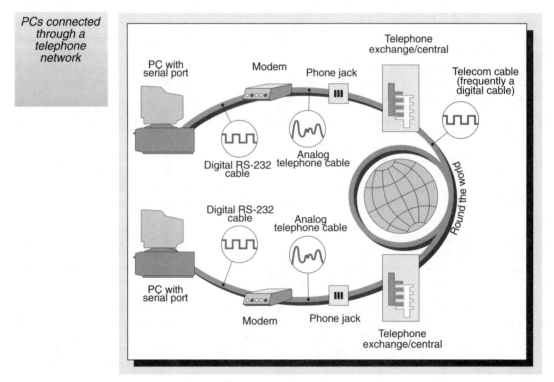

Synchronous And Asynchronous Communication

The two types of communication we'll talk about are *synchronous* and *asynchronous* communication. Synchronous communication occurs when sender and receiver share a common signal pulse. This common signal pulse helps to synchronize their actions. For example, the sender always sends the next bit over the line immediately prior to a new clock pulse and the receiver knows that when the clock pulse occurs it can now retrieve this bit. Sender and receiver are therefore "synchronized".

Synchronization always requires an extra line. The sender and receiver exchange the signal pulse through this extra line. Such a line, however, does not exist in serial transmission through a two-line cable. Both available lines are used one for grounding and the other for data.

Therefore, synchronization for serial transmission must occur on the data line through the data itself. A "data word" to be sent will have status information placed before it and after it, in accordance with the RS-232 protocol. The data words, which can consist of 5-8 bits, are therefore encapsulated. The exact number of bits is set by the two sides upon establishing the connection, depending on how their serial ports are programmed. The two sides must agree about the number of bits, otherwise the communication will fail.

The following illustration shows that the only applicable line states are 0 (low) and 1 (high) in a serial transmission. When no character is being sent, the line is high, or in "marking condition". When the line state changes to low, it marks the beginning of the data transmission. Depending on the agreement, between five and eight data bits are now be sent over the line. During the transmission, when the line goes low a 0-bit is sent, when it goes high a 1-bit is sent. The lowest-order bit of a character always goes first and the highest-order bit last.

Asynchronous serial transmission

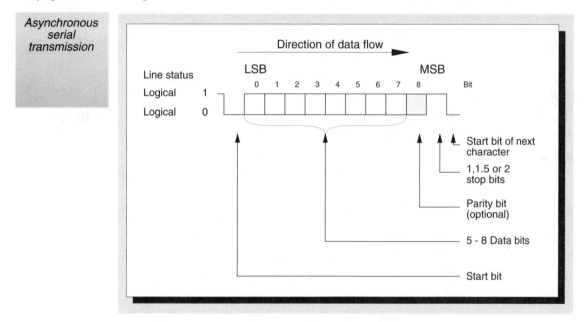

Besides the data bits, a parity bit detects transmission errors. The two types of parity are even parity and odd parity. The parity bit in even parity supplements the data word being transmitted so the number of set bits (those with a value of 1) is even. For example, if the data word contains three bits with the value 1, the parity bit will also be 1. The extra 1 from the parity bit raises the number of 1-bits to four, thereby producing an "even parity". On the other hand, if the word contained an even number of 1-bits, the parity bit would be 0. The opposite occurs with odd parity - the value of the parity bit is such that the total number of 1-bits is odd.

Although parity recognition is well-designed, it often fails because errors are found only when one data bit or an odd number of data bits are "lost" in the transmission, arriving as a 0 instead of a 1 (or vice versa). When an even number of data bits disappears, the parity check still works out despite the underlying transmission error.

In mailbox communication therefore, automatic insertion of parity bits is bypassed. This is easily done by programming the serial interface controller accordingly. Instead, by using checksums, high-level protocols exist which detect errors in the transmission of larger data blocks.

Unlike the parity bit, the stop bit is not optional. A stop bit signals the end of transmission of a data word. The communication protocol allows 1, 1.5 or 2 stop bits (depending on word length).

The option of 1.5 stop bits may at first seem strange, but it does bring up a question not yet answered. How does the receiver know when it should interpret the current line state as a data bit? To answer this we need to return to synchronous transmission.

For example, if the receiver is reading a bit at the same time the sender sends the next signal down the line, whether the bit arrives correctly is strictly a matter of chance.

The solution is in the transmission speed, which must be identical for both sender and receiver. This transmission speed is measured in baud, or "bits per second". A typical rate of 9600 baud means 9600 bits in one second. The "length" of a bit is, therefore, 1/9600th of a second. The receiver reads the current status of the data line every 1/9600 second and converts it - depending on whether it is high or low - to a 1-bit or a 0-bit.

However, this is not enough to synchronize the sender with the receiver. As in the above case, the receiver can still read the line at the same time the sender places the next bit on the line. This is where the start bit is used. Upon detecting the start bit, the receiver knows the transmission is starting and it must now read the line at fixed time intervals (according to the baud rate). To avoid eventual disruption due to small differences in "time counting", the sender and receiver are resynchronized with the transmission of each data word, through the initial start bit.

We can now answer the question of how a stop bit can be 1.5 bits long. The line is simply set to high or low for 1.5 times the normal "bit-transfer time".

The stop bit ends the transmission of a character. The line now remains in "marking condition" (high) until a new character is sent and the line transmitting the start bit changes to low.

There are also interfaces that work with negative logic. In this case you would switch the 0's and 1's in the above illustration (which corresponds to positive logic). The basic principles of serial transmission remain the same.

Data transmission is successful only if the various protocol parameters are the same for both sender and receiver. The first item that must be set is the baud rate, or number of bits per second. This value ranges from 75 baud to 144,000 baud, the highest transmission rate supported by a PC interface.

The number of data bits transmitted each time depends on the data being sent. Seven data bits are enough for normal ASCII data since the ASCII character set contains only 128 characters. However, eight-bit data words are required for both the full PC character set of 256 characters.and binary data. You can also define whether a parity check should occur, and if so, whether parity is odd or even. Both processes yield the same (un)certainties.

Finally, the number of stop bits must be defined. With one stop bit the next character can be sent faster than with two stop bits. Therefore, this setting is very rare in practice. We'll explain later how you can set these parameters either through the BIOS or through direct programming of the serial interface controller.

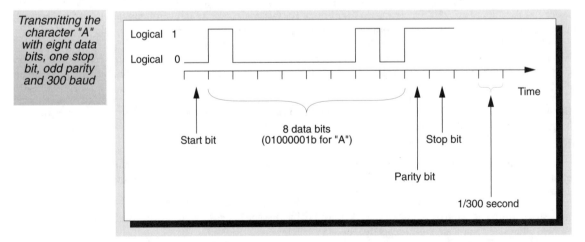

Transmitting the character "A" with eight data bits, one stop bit, odd parity and 300 baud

The illustration shows the character "A" with a protocol of eight data bits, odd parity and one stop bit. We're assuming positive interface logic and a transmission rate of 300 baud. Since the ASCII code of the letter A is 65 (01000001b) and contains only two 1-bits, the parity bit in this case is 1 in order to produce an odd number of 1-bits.

RS-232 Standard

Upon leaving the serial port, the bits enter the domain of the RS-232 standard. This standard governs the physical dimensions of the connectors, the number and configuration of ports and several electrical parameters. More specifically, we're talking about the RS-232C interface on the PC. Several versions of the RS-232 were designed by the EIA committee until the "C" version finally became official.

The EIA, however, was not the only organization to adopt the RS-232 standard. Another was the CCITT (Comitè Consultatif International Télégraphic et Téléfonique), which divided it into two separate standards. The first was V.24 which specified the asynchronous transfer protocol, allocation of individual ports and connector formats. The other standard is V.28 which handles the remaining RS-232 specifications. These specifications include the electrical signal values such as signal level, terminating resistor and circuit stability. The signal level can range from +3 volts to +15 volts for a logical zero and -3 volts to -15 volts for a logical one.

Since RS-232 was intended as a comprehensive standard, there is no mention in the specifications of a particular computer type. Instead they refer to the two poles of the "Data Terminal Equipment" (DTE) and the "Data Communication Equipment" (DCE). In the PC/modem environment, the PC represents the DTE and the modem the DCE. These two devices are connected by an RS-232 cable, as it is commonly known in the industry. The cable becomes unnecessary of course if the PC has a built-in modem card. In this case the card itself functions as the serial port, which is directly connected with the modulator/demodulator (the essence of the modem).

RS-232 connectors and ports

Serial transmission in one direction requires just two lines (grounding and data), while simultaneous transmission in two directions requires just three (an extra data line for the opposite direction). In addition to these, the EIA and CCITT have introduced 17 more lines, which are used for checking and control functions. Luckily not all of these lines need to be implemented for an RS-232 serial data transfer, otherwise an important advantage over parallel cables would be lost.

The following illustration shows the PC version and the wiring inside the 25-pin Submin-D connector. This is a male connector on the PC which connects to the cable leading to the modem.

Implementation of RS-232 lines on the PC, including 25-pin Submin-D connector pin assignments

One of the reasons this connector so large are the six additional lines through which the DTE (PC) and the DCE (modem) communicate. RTS, CTS, DSR and DTR basically involve "handshaking" between PC and modem when they are communicating in both directions (full-duplex mode), as is usually the case. On many modems the state of several of these control lines can be monitored on the front panel of the modem. The state of the control lines can also appear in terminal programs which you'll then see on the screen. These give you the current status of the connection. Frequently, however, the LED designations do not match the line names given by the RS-232 standard. Instead of RLSD for example, you will often see CD.

Control line definitions for RS-232 cables		
Line	Abbreviation	Definition
Transmitted Data	TxD	The line over which data travels. The DTE (PC) can send data only when all four control lines RTS, CTS, DSR and DTR are logical 1. This line is in "marking condition" (logical 1) when no data is being transmitted according to V.24 protocol.
Received Data	RxD	Data line from DCE (modem) to DTE (PC).
Request To Send	RTS	By setting this line to logical 1, the DTE (PC) asks the DCE (modem) if it is ready to receive data.
Clear To Send	CTS	The DCE (modem) sets this line to logical 1 following an RTS when it's ready to receive the data.
Data Set Ready	DSR	By setting this line to logical 1, the DCE (modem) indicates to the DTE (PC) that a connection has been established with the other side (dialed successfully) and that data can now be sent to the remote DCE (another modem).
Date Terminal Ready	DTR	The DTE (PC) sets this line to logical 1 when it is ready for communication with the DCE (modem). The modem thereby recognizes that it is connected to an active DCE.
Ring Indicator	RI	Through this line the DCE (modem) indicates to the DTE (PC) that there is a call on the telephone line to which the modem is connected.
Received Line Signal Detector	RLSD	Through RLSD the DCE (modem) indicates to the DTE (PC) that it has received a carrier signal from the other end of the phone line. RLSD is also called "Carrier Detect". This does not imply an actual connection however, because the two DCEs (modems) may be unable to find a common transfer protocol for the modulation/demodulation.

Modem communication protocol

Before the PC can send data to the modem, it must set various signals and wait for the desired response from the modem. First, the PC sets the DTR line to high. This tells the modem that the DTE (PC) is ready to communicate with it. The modem responds by setting the DSR line to high. This shows it's ready to communicate. Both lines must remain high during the entire communication.

If the DTR line falls back to low, for example if the PC is turned off, the modem resets its DSR line. It then accepts new data only when DTR again goes high. The switching off of DTR by the PC is basically a signal the line should be interrupted. It's used by the telecommunications software on the PC solely for this purpose.

A line refers not only to the connection between modem and PC, but also to the telephone line which the modem opens by dialing. So, if you turn off your PC during a connection but the modem remains switched on, you won't be charged by the telephone company for an open line.

Once DTR and DSR are set, it's still a long way before the computer can actually begin sending characters to the modem. Two handshaking lines are also involved here: RTS and CTS.

The PC is the device that first sets the RTS line to high, to signal its readiness to send data. When the modem is ready to receive, it signals back by setting the CTS line. The communications devices are, in a sense, "extending their hands". Once the handshaking is complete, a byte can now be sent. If the PC wishes to send additional data, it simply leaves the RTS line on high and observes the CTS line. Additional bytes can be sent as long as the CTS line also remains high. If it goes back to low, the PC must wait until the modem again signals its readiness to receive by setting the line.

In this process the PC "pumps" data into the modem faster than the modem can output it over the telephone line. The modem collects the data in an internal buffer until it is full. When no more data can be accepted, the modem resets the CTS line until enough data has left the buffer and there is room for more. However if the PC resets RTS because all desired data has been sent, the modem CTS will immediately go "low".

Unlike sending, there is no handshaking for receiving characters. When the PC sets the DTR line, the modem recognizes it as ready and begins sending, whether it is receiving the data or generating it itself. This is also why the above is called a "sender-oriented protocol".

RI and RLSD are two lines which are unrelated to handshaking. RI is required when the PC wants to accept incoming calls. The modem uses the RI line to indicate the telephone is ringing (RI = ring); the PC can then instruct the modem to answer, thereby opening the line.

RLSD is better known as "Carrier Detect". The carrier is the tone you hear when a modem answers at the other end of the line. The reception of this carrier indicates that although a modem is present, communication may not necessarily occur. Remember, not all modems are compatible due to differences in baud rates or transfer protocols or both. When RLSD is set, however, you at least know you have connected with the other modem.

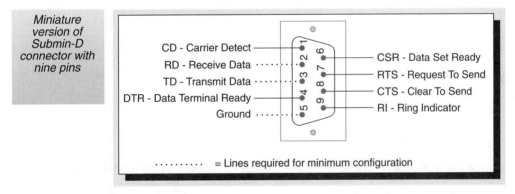

Without further embellishments the above signal lines represent the nine-pin stripped version of the Submin-D connector. This is equally common on PC's as the large version, and contains all the lines necessary to connect a modem with a PC.

Inside The Serial Port

The serial port contains a special chip responsible for input and output of characters, as well as conversion of data words to their corresponding serial interface signals. This chip is called UART (Universal Asynchronous Receiver Transmitter). Another common name for it is SIO for "Serial Input/Output".

The chip is marked 8250, reminiscent of the Intel DMA and Interrupt Controller. Actually however, it was originally made by the National Semiconductor Corporation (NSC). In the meantime, pin-compatible and function-compatible chips are being offered by a number of other manufacturers such as Siemens and UMC. Today's PCs have an easily expanded and improved version called 16550, which we'll discuss later in this section. Now we'll concentrate on the structure, function and registers of the UART chip.

UART registers

The UART chip contains a total of ten registers that are accessible externally (through software). A few additional registers, such as the receiver shift register and the transmitter shift register, can only be accessed internally. These registers are crucial for sending and receiving characters. When the UART receives a character, the incoming bits first "pile up" in the receiver shift register until a complete data word has arrived. If no error has occurred, the byte is then routed to the receiver data register, where it can be read by the software.

In the opposite direction, the software first writes the data word to be sent to the transmitter holding register. From there the UART moves it into the internal transmitter shift register, from which the individual bits can be sent sequentially down the line. Therefore, the transmitter holding and receiver data registers are the most important in UART data transmission. However, we cannot ignore the other registers because they're needed to initialize the UART and to check the transmission status and line status.

Block diagram of the UART chip

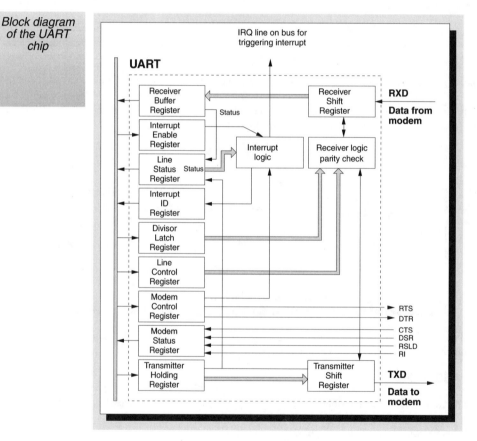

Internal UART 8250 Registers					
Register	Abbreviation	Read	Write	Base port +	Bit 7 in Line Controil Register
Transmitter Holding	THR			0	0
Receiver Data	RBR			0	0
Baud Rate Divisor LSB	DLL			0	1
Baud Rate Divisor MSB	DLM			1	1
Interrupt Enable	IER			1	0
Interrupt ID	IIR			2	-
Line Control	LCR			3	-
Modem Control	MCR			4	-
Line Status	LSR			5	-
Modem Status	MSR			6	-

Polling or interrupt

Communication between software and UART can occur either in polling mode or interrupt mode. In polling mode the software is responsible for checking the UART status at regular intervals through the line control register. This is the only way it can tell whether a new character was received or whether the last character sent was actually transmitted. The corresponding program loops are very easy to write, although they share the disadvantage common to all polling processes: The CPU is occupied with the device the entire time, although relative to CPU speed, characters arrive and depart very slowly.

Depending on your task therefore, you might decide to work in interrupt mode. Although more difficult to program, interrupt processing has several advantages. The CPU devotes itself to the serial port only when a character has actually been received or sent, or when an error has occurred. Only then does the UART initiate an interrupt and activate the interrupt handler, which then deals with the situation. The UART supports this mode through two interrupt registers which we'll discuss later.

Access to registers

The UART registers can be accessed through different ports according to the base address of the serial port. Theoretically, this base address can be freely chosen, but in practice the first two serial ports on a PC (COM1 and COM2) generally use base addresses 3F8h and 2F8h respectively. COM3 and COM4 - if present - normally use base addresses 3E8h and 2E8h.

Base addresses of serial ports and BIOS variables in which they are recorded		
Port	Address in BIOS Variable	Standard Port
COM1	0040:0000	3F8h-3FFh
COM2	0040:0002	2F8h-2FFh
COM3	0040:0004	3E8h-3EFh
COM4	0040:0006	2E8h-2EFh

To ensure that for some reason you "miss" a serial port, you should not use fixed port addresses in your programs. It's better to query one of the four BIOS variables, in which the base addresses of the four ports (maximum supported by the BIOS) are recorded. This way you always get the current address of the desired port.

In reviewing the table with the various UART registers, you can see that two port addresses (base port +0 and base port +1) are reserved by several registers. To differentiate among the various registers when accessing the corresponding port, use the high-order bit in the line control register. Before accessing any register using the first or second port of the serial interface, load this bit with the value given in the table.

Initializing the UART

To establish a connection with another serial port, the UART must first be initialized. Specifically, you must set the various communication parameters, i.e., baud rate, data word length and number of stop bits. It's also good practice to perform a read access on the receiver data register. Otherwise if a previous program has left a character there, it may be misinterpreted as the first transmitted character of the new connection. On the other hand if there are no characters there, the read won't have any effect. You should not have any problems in either case.

You should start by setting the baud rate because when the UART writes to the corresponding registers, it will reset the other communication parameters in the line control register. So, if you set the register prior to setting the baud rate, you will be forced to repeat the process.

The two registers for setting the baud rate are DLL and DLM. The desired baud rate is not entered directly, however, but is expressed as a quotient with respect to the clock frequency of the UART. This is equal to 1.8432 Mhz. The baud rate tells the UART how fast it should generate individual bits in relation to its clock frequency. The following is the actual formula:

```
register value = 1.8432 Mhz / (16  *  baud rate )
```

The equation shows the UART multiplies the clock pulse duration by 16, and after N of these pulses (N = baud rate) sends the next bit through the line.

This formula produces a 16-bit register value, whose low-order byte is written to the DLL register and whose high-order byte is written to the DLM register. Theoretically you can set any baud rate, from 1.75 baud (register value = 0FFFFh) to 115200 baud (register value = 1). In practice however only certain baud rates are used, as listed in the following table. The table also lists their corresponding values in the DLL and DLM registers.

Since the highest transmission rate is 115,000 bits per second (115200 baud), and for each 8-bit data word at least two additional bits must be transferred (1 start bit, 1 stop bit), the maximum throughput is approximately 1.4 KB per second. However this transfer rate is possible only with direct linkage of two computers and only then with the more modern ones. A 16-Mhz 386SX would have a hard time achieving such a high rate - eventually the computer would fall behind.

Common baud rates and their divisor settings in the UART DLM and DLL registers							
Baud rate	Divisor	DLM Reg	DLL Reg	Baud rate	Divisor	DLM Reg	DLL Reg
50	2304	09h	00	2000	58	00h	3Ah
75	1536	06h	00h	2400	48	00h	30h
110	1047	04h	17h	4800	24	00h	18h
134.5	857	03h	59h	7200	16	00h	10h
150	768	03h	00h	9600	12	00h	0Ch
300	384	01h	80h	19200	6	00h	06h
600	192	00h	C0h	38400	3	00h	03h
1200	96	00h	60h	57600	2	00h	02h
1800	64	00h	40h	115200	1	00h	01h

All other parameters such as word length, number of stop bits and use of parity bits are set through the line control register (LCR), located at address 3 relative to the base address of the serial port. Not only can you write to this register to enter new settings, you can also read from it to obtain current settings.

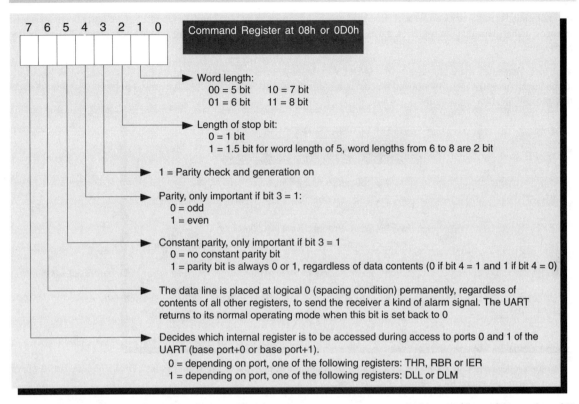

Both bits 5 and 6 have some interesting features. Bit 5 lets you generate a constant parity bit, regardless of the number of 1's in the current data word. This option is not used in practice, however, since it's increasingly being replaced with higher-level software protocols.

Bit 6 allows you to send an alarm to the opposite end. Some programs use this option when sender and receiver need to resynchronize on the software protocol level or when a large data block transmission must be interrupted for some reason. The line is then permanently (until bit 6 is again cleared) set to logical 0. This corresponds to a "spacing condition", which is the exact opposite of the "marking condition" (logical 1) which would otherwise occur when no characters are being sent. The UART at the other end recognizes this and sets a corresponding flag in one of its status registers. Upon checking this register the receiver then becomes aware of the alarm.

It's therefore possible to send information (the alarm information) even when transmission of individual characters or data blocks seems to have gone off track or must be spontaneously interrupted.

Finally, bit 7 is the bit (already mentioned) required to access the registers that share addresses 0 and 1 relative to the base port on the card. To avoid changing the communication parameters in the other bits, you should first read the contents of this register and set or clear bit 7 as needed. The byte obtained in this manner can then be written back to the register.

Current UART status

The line status register (LSR) contains the line status as well as the most critical information regarding sending and receiving of characters.

Bit 0 indicates whether a received character is waiting in the receiver register (RBR). This bit is automatically reset as soon as you retrieve the character from the RBR. Sometimes if this does not happen fast enough, another character comes in before the old one has been read. In such cases the old character is simply overwritten and gets lost. This condition is flagged by bit 1 of the LSR.

Two additional errors, parity errors and "overrun" errors, are covered by bits 2 and 3 of the LSR. The latter occur when the protocol (either data-bits, stop-bits or parity bits) is not maintained while receiving a character, generally due to line interference.

All errors, incidentally, are recorded by the UART without any corrective action being taken. It is the responsibility of the communications software, protocol and mechanism to inform sender and receiver of transmission errors and prompt them to retransmit the data in question.

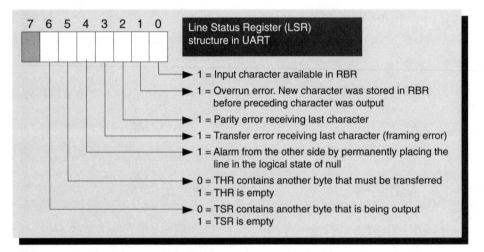

When the sender issues an alarm through bit 6 in its line control register, it's reflected in bit 4 of the receiver's line status register. The receiver can then immediately respond.

Bits 5 and 6 in the LSR give information about the current send status. They pertain to the two send registers, the transmitter holding register and the transmitter shift register. Bit 5 indicates whether the transmitter holding register is empty. If yes, the next character to be sent can be loaded into this register; if no, the software must wait until the bit goes to zero.

Also important is whether the transmitter shift register (TSR) is empty. If yes, it means the last character to be sent has been completely transmitted; if no, the character is still in the TSR and has not yet reached the receiver.

Control through interrupts

When interrupts are used to feed characters to the UART or to read incoming characters, the two interrupt registers are crucial. The interrupt enable register (IER) determines in which situations an interrupt should occur. The interrupt identification register (IIR) tells the serial port interrupt handler what event prompted the interrupt.

You must make the interrupt handler available yourself through software. The sample program SERIRQ which we've included on the companion CD-ROM and talk about at the end of this chapter shows how to build such an interrupt handler. To ensure proper calling of the handler, its address must be recorded in the interrupt vector for that particular serial port. For the first serial port this is IRQ4 with interrupt vector 0Ch, for the second IRQ3 with interrupt vector 0Bh. Not so well-defined are the third and fourth serial ports, where various settings are possible for the port address as well as the interrupt used. The software referring to serial ports above COM2 should always be designed so the user can tell it the port address and the interrupt. Unfortunately there is no fixed mechanism for detecting a serial interface with its port and interrupt.

7	6	5	4	3	2	1	0	Structure of UART Interrupt Enable Register (IER)
0	0	0	0					

▶ 1 = Trigger interrupt as soon as a new character is ready

▶ 1 = Trigger interrupt as soon as the THR register is empty and ready to transfer more characters

▶ 1 = Trigger interrupt as soon as the line status in the LSR changes

▶ 1 = Trigger interrupt as soon as the modem status in MSR changes

You selectively enter the events through the IER that will initiate a call to the interrupt handler. Set bit 0, for example, if the receiving of characters should follow through the interrupt handler and the handler is to be called whenever a new character is in the RBR. If the sending of characters will also occur within the interrupt handler, set bit 1 as well. In this case an interrupt will also occur whenever the transmitter holding register is empty.

It makes no difference whether you have set one or several interrupt sources using the IER. When calling the serial interrupt handler you should always check the interrupt ID register (IIR) first. Most important, you should inspect bit 0 of this register. Bit 0 indicates whether the serial port has actually executed an interrupt (which of course you can assume because the interrupt handler was called). What happens, however, when several serial ports use the same interrupt? First, you must determine which port has requested the interrupt. To do this, sequentially check the interrupt ID registers of the known ports and stop when you get to the port with a 1 in bit 0 of the IIR. You now have the port that has actually executed the interrupt.

Bits 1 and 2 in the IIR tell you why the UART executed the interrupt, so you can respond accordingly. For example, if code 01b is given, this tells the interrupt handler the next character can now be output to the THR. Note that we said "can" and not "must". UART simply sets the line to marking condition if it does not immediately need more characters. This indicates to the other side that at present it has no more characters to transmit.

On the other hand if bits 1 and 2 contain the code 10b when the interrupt handler is called, the handler should immediately read the receiver buffer register to obtain the received character.

With an error or alarm (code 11b) the line status register should be read to determine the cause of error, which can then be routed through internal variables to the main program outside the interrupt handler. Code 00b is similar, except in this case the cause of the interrupt is determined through the modem status register.

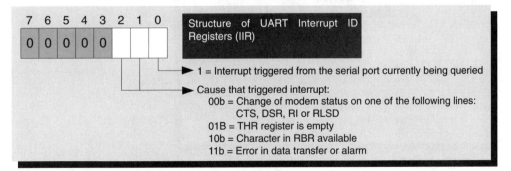

7	6	5	4	3	2	1	0	Structure of UART Interrupt ID Registers (IIR)
0	0	0	0	0				

▶ 1 = Interrupt triggered from the serial port currently being queried

▶ Cause that triggered interrupt:
   00b = Change of modem status on one of the following lines: CTS, DSR, RI or RLSD
   01B = THR register is empty
   10b = Character in RBR available
   11b = Error in data transfer or alarm

Before the UART starts generating interrupts in the situations desired, you must not only set the IER, but also set a bit in the modem control register.

Modem registers

Just as the line status register and line control register oversee the connection between two serial ports, the modem status register and modem control register are responsible for the connection between a serial port and its attached modem.

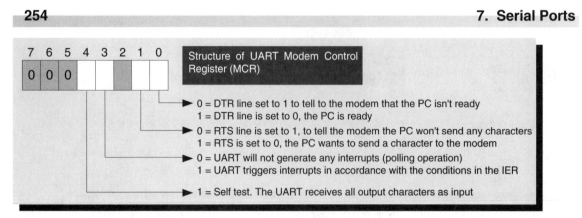

We've mentioned the modem control register contains a flag (bit 3), which can enable or disable interrupts through the UART. Also, communication between serial port and modem occurs through four control lines. Included in these four lines are the DTR (Data Terminal Ready) and RTS (Ready To Send) lines, which lead from PC to modem. These can be controlled through bits 0 and 1 of the modem control register.

According to the RS-232 protocol, the PC must first set the DTR flag to 1 so the DTR line goes to logical 0 and the modem knows the PC is ready. The PC must then set the RTS flag to 1 so the RTS line goes to logical 0 and the modem is made aware of the desired character transfer. In both cases the modem should answer by setting the appropriate handshaking signals.

Apart from the DTR and RTS, the UART can be switched to "loopback mode" through bit 4 of the modem control register. This mode helps in the development of programs that communicate through the UART with other devices. When this flag is on, the UART reroutes all output using THR directly to the RBR. An attached device is no longer required to test your program and respond to characters received. All you need to do is output characters to simulate receiving them. Even the interrupts will occur if interrupt mode is active.

When the DTR and RTS lines are set the modem generally responds through the DSR and CTS lines. You can check this using bits 4 and 5 in the modem control register, which always reflect the status of these two lines.

The modem status register can also be used to check the status of the RLSD and RI lines. Here bits 6 and 7 indicate whether a call is being received by the modem (RI) or whether a modem is present at the other end of the line (Carrier Detect).

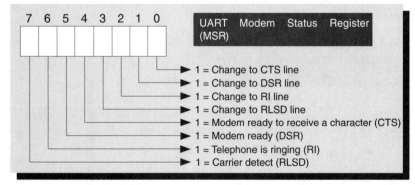

In addition to bits 4 to 7, bits 0 to 3 also refer to the CTS, DSR, RI and RLSD lines. Rather than the current line status however, these bits indicate a potential change since the last read on the modem status register. By checking this register you can tell immediately if action is necessary - normally the case only when the status of one of the four lines has changed since the last inquiry.

Successors to the 8250

Microprocessor and controller manufacturers often suffer the same fate as software companies. They may be so anxious to release new products, the new chip may be released before it has been thoroughly tested. Bugs soon appear which result in grief, expensive recalls and public relations nightmares. This is what happened to National Semiconductor with its INS8250 chip, the original UART for PC's.

Shortly thereafter came a debugged version of the INS8250, the INS8250A, which was fully pin-compatible and function-compatible with its predecessor. Unfortunately however some developers of communications software had already based their products on the errors of the 8250, and their software no longer functioned with the A-version. National Semiconductor, therefore, felt obligated to develop another version of the chip. This new chip, called INS8250-B, intentionally included some of the bugs from the original version to guarantee compatibility with software already in use.

The NS16450 followed the INS8250-B. It was released with the AT. Although it was desgined for the AT's expanded bus and interrupt capabilities, it remained fully compatible with previous versions. Today, however, most PCs have an NS16550A or NS16C552 instead of the 16450. The distinct advantage the NS16550A and NS16C552 have over their predecessors are two buffers for sending and receiving characters.

Send and receive buffers

The lack of such buffers severely limited the chip at high baud rates, especially in processing interrupts. Rates above 9600 baud were rarely achieved because the chip often received characters faster than it could route them to the software using interrupt. Computers were generally not yet fast enough and interrupt requests from the UART could not always be granted immediately. Finally, the serial interface being assigned to IRQ3 or IRQ4 does not have a high interrupt priority in the system as a whole.

Consequently, characters just received were frequently overwritten in the receiver data register by the next character. This resulted in an overrun error. In such cases the baud rate had to be reset to a lower value.

This was a much less serious problem with the NS16550A and its successor, the NS16C552. These chips have two 16-byte buffers, for the receiver buffer register (receive) and the transmitter holding register (send). These two buffers, which operate on the FIFO principle (first in, first out), have also given the 16550 its nickname of the "FIFO chip".

The send buffer is of lesser importance of the two buffers. When sending, the computer itself sets the pace and will not overburden itself. The receive buffer on the other hand is very important. You also need to involve the software of course to use this buffer. First, initialize the UART so the buffer will actually be used. Next, configure the character-reading routine.

When polling the port, little will change because normally here you would be checking the line status register to see if a character is available in the RBR. If so, you would read the character and begin a new pass through the loop. Then if any unread characters exist in the internal buffer, the UART will reset the corresponding bit in the line status register immediately after reading the character from the RBR. This way the character will automatically be captured in the next pass through the loop.

This is the type of loop missing from most serial interrupt handlers. As long as the UART had no characters in an internal buffer, it was enough to read the RBR once after an interrupt call and then wait for the next interrupt to retrieve the next character. With the buffer, a loop must be implemented within the interrupt handler, which continually reads characters from the RBR until the line status register indicates that no more characters are there. At this point all characters have been read from the internal buffer, because otherwise after reading the previous character the UART would have immediately moved any remaining characters from the buffer to the RBR.

To remain compatible with its predecessors, the internal buffers of the 16550 are disabled unless specifically instructed otherwise. A new register located at port address 2 relative to the base port of the interface is responsible for this task. Taking another look at the table on page 249 you'll see the interrupt ID register already exists at this address. Whereas the interrupt ID register is read-only, the new FIFO register can only be written to. This is why they can both share the same register address. The UART knows which register is meant based on the type of access.

Bit 0 of this register activates the FIFO buffers. In the meantime if you need to clear one of the two buffers, enter a value of 1 in bit 1 (for the receive buffer) or bit 2 (for the send buffer). Remember also to set bit 0 or the FIFO buffer will be activated at the same time.

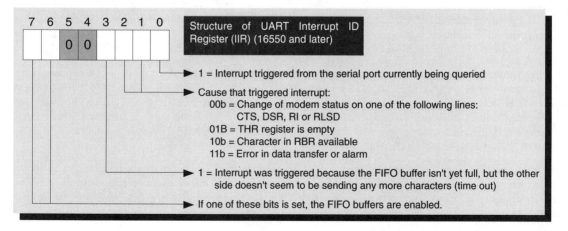

Bits 6 and 7 set the number of received characters after which an interrupt occurs if enabled through the interrupt enable register. The values 4, 8 or 14 in these bits stop the UART from generating an interrupt each time a character is received. This has a positive effect on software performance because interrupts take a relatively long time. The inquiry loop within the interrupt routine (discussed above) then sees to it that all characters are read from the buffer, not just the first.

Unfortunately, however, there is a "catch" to this method. Suppose the other side sends three characters and then stops the transmission because these three characters are telling the receiver to send back certain information. The receiver might not receive these characters because the buffer does not yet contain the required four, eight or fourteen characters after which only then an interrupt occurs. The sender could conceivably wait forever for the receiver's reply.

To prevent this from happening the UART always executes an interrupt even when the buffer is not yet full, but no new characters have arrived within the transfer-time for three characters. This "time-out" is communicated to the interrupt handler using an additional new bit in the interrupt ID register. This bit can normally be ignored however, because the UART also gives the reason for the interrupt - the availability of characters in the RBR.

When developing a communication program for the serial port, you should always include the FIFO options if they are available. The sample programs at the end of this chapter include a routine for identifying the type of UART installed.

Accessing The Serial Port From The BIOS

Since the serial port has become an essential component of the PC, the BIOS must deal with it as well. Unfortunately, built-in support for the programmer is weak. A total of four functions are available:

➢ Setting transmission parameters

➢ Checking line status

➢ Sending/receiving characters in polling mode

However, both support for interrupt-driven control of the serial port and functions to access the expanded capabilities of the 16550 and its successors are missing. In practice then, you're forced to program the various serial interface registers directly as we discussed in the previous section. The BIOS functions are included here only for completeness.

All BIOS functions for serial port access are called using interrupt 14h, with the number of the desired function passed in the AH register. In addition the DX register receives the port number, where 0 represents COM1, 1 for COM2, etc.

BIOS Functions For Serial Port Access	
Number	Task
00h	Set communication parameters
01h	Output characters
02h	Read in characters
03h	Query port status

Setting communication parameters and status check

In addition to the arguments in AH and DX, you must pass a value to function 00h in the AL register, whose structure is shown in the following illustration. Notice the BIOS permits only some of the settings directly supported by the UART. Word length for example can only be 7 or 8 bits, and the range of available baud rates lags far behind the capability of the UART.

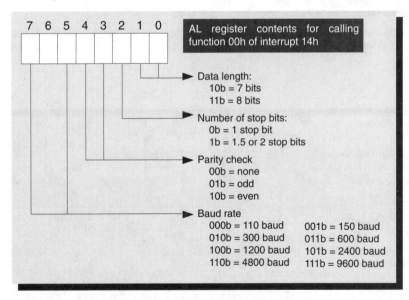

As its return value, function 00h returns in the AH register the line status from the UART line status register, and in the AL register the modem status from the modem status register.

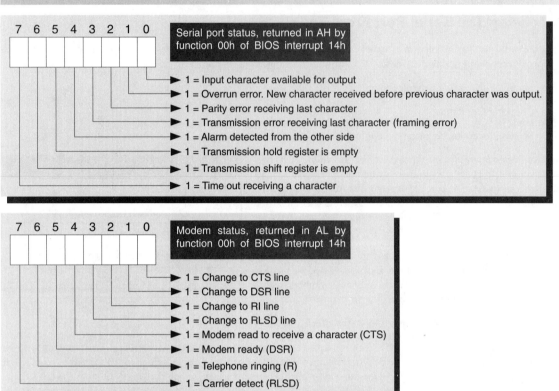

The line status (returned here in the AH register) can also be checked at any time by function 03h. Other than the function number in AH and the port number in DX this function requires no further parameters. As indicated above, it returns the port status in the AH register.

Sending and receiving characters

To send characters, use function 01h. In addition to function and port number, you must also pass the character to be transmitted in the AL register. If successful, bits 7 of the AH register is set to zero. A value of one means the character could not be transmitted. The remaining bits correspond to the line status.

Function 02h receives characters. After the function call the character received will be in the AL register. AH contains a value of zero if no error has occurred, otherwise its value corresponds to the line status.

You'll find the following program(s) on the companion CD-ROM

SERUTIL.H (C listing)
SERUTIL.C (C listing)
SERUTIL.PAS (Pascal listing)
SERIRQ.C (C listing)
ARGS.C (C listing / see Chapter 37)
WIN.C (C listing / see Chapter 38)
IRQUTIL.C (C listing / see Chapter 38)
SERIRQ.PAS (Pascal listing)
SERTRANS.H (C listing)
SERTRANS.C (C listing)
SERUTIL.PAS (Pascal listing)
ARGS.PAS (Pascal listing / see Chapter 37)
SERTRANS.PAS (Pascal listing)

Chapter 8

The Parallel Port

There are three ways to access the parallel port: Direct hardware programming, through the ROM-BIOS or with DOS function calls. In this chapter we'll discuss direct programming and using ROM-BIOS functions to access the parallel port. The first section describes the BIOS functions used in printing. The ROM-BIOS functions offer an advantage over equivalent DOS functions because they allow better control over printer status. DOS immediately fails when a printer triggers the critical error interrupt, but BIOS offers other options.

In the second section of this chapter ("Direct Programming And The Parallel Port") we'll talk about direct programming of the parallel port. We'll show you how to connect two computers through their parallel ports and transfer data quickly between these computers using a file transfer program.

Accessing The Parallel Port From BIOS

BIOS interrupt 17H is reserved exclusively for communication with the parallel port. Most users call interrupt 17H the BIOS printer interrupt, although other peripheral devices could also be connected to this port.

The BIOS printer interrupt

A maximum of three different parallel ports can be connected to the PC (refer to the next section for more information). Interrupt 17H provides three different functions for addressing these ports. These functions perform three specialized tasks and can control all three parallel ports.

Function	Task
00H	Display characters
01H	Initialize printer
02H	Request printer status

About these functions

These functions are superior to the equivalent DOS functions in the choice of the addressed port. The DOS functions only control the first parallel port (PRN or LPT1). The three BIOS functions are more flexible in this respect and, when you call them, expect to find the number of the parallel port to be addressed in the DX register. You can specify values of 0, 1, and 2 for the ports: 0 corresponds to LPT1, 1 corresponds to LPT2, and 2 corresponds to LPT3.

Printer status

These functions have something else in common besides being passed the port number. After being called, each function returns the current printer status in the AH register. The bits of this status byte convey information about whether the printer is currently busy, still has paper, or has encountered an error while receiving characters. This status is very important to the communication with the parallel port.

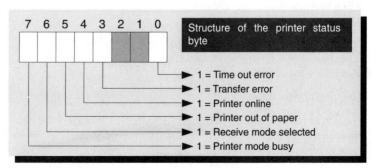

Time out error

A time out error, signaled by bit 0 of the status byte, always occurs when the BIOS attempts to send data to the printer over a certain period of time and the printer is BUSY (bit 7=0) or not accepting the data. This often happens because a parallel port can send up to 100,000 characters per second but no printers on the market can keep up with that pace.

The number of failures that occur before a time out occurs varies with the contents of a BIOS variable. Each parallel port has a byte allocated at a memory range beginning at address 0040:0078H. These bytes specify the number of unsuccessful attempts allowed.

BIOS time out counter for parallel ports	
Address	Meaning
0040:007	Time out counter: first parallel port
0040:007	Time out counter: second parallel port
0040:007	Time out counter: third parallel port

Instead of referring to a given period of time, the values contained in these variables refer to the number of failed attempts that are allowed before BIOS reports a time out error. The program code of the ROM-BIOS continually prompts the parallel port within a program loop. Since this loop consists of only a few assembly language instructions running in cycles of a few microseconds, the time out value from each BIOS variable acts as a factor used in the loop's counter, instead of as the loop counter itself. This factor is multiplied by the constant 262,140 (4 * 65535). The value 20, which the BIOS enters in all three memory locations after the system boots, corresponds to more than five million attempts.

If you use a loop counter instead of a time unit, the period of time that can elapse before a time out occurs depends on the processing speed of the computer. This means that the time span varies with the system's CPU and clock speed. That's why the loop counter must be increased on faster systems, because there isn't a connection between the printer speed and the CPU speed. If you don't make this adjustment, you'll discover, after purchasing a 486, that the system will suddenly send a time out error message during printing.

The BIOS manufacturers usually make this adjustment by using a larger constant instead of a larger default value. For example, if your new computer is twice as fast as a normal AT, instead of 4*65535, you might multiply 8 by 65535.

This is done because applications also access the three BIOS variables to change the time out rate for one of the ports. This is possible because these variables are accessible to any program as part of RAM. This gives the programmer the option of setting a higher time out rate for situations in which the printer would otherwise send a time out error. However, increasing the time out rate wouldn't work on a faster system, unless a large enough constant factor is also chosen.

Other printer status flags

Other bits provide more information about the printer's status. Bit 3 shows a transfer error (a data error in the line), while bit 4 indicates whether the printer is currently online or offline. This bit is the equivalent of the online button found on printers, with an LED indicating its status.

Bit 5 indicates whether the printer has any paper. Bit 6 confirms the printer's receipt of the last character. To determine whether a printer is connected to a particular port, simply prompt for this bit. If it contains a value of 1, then a printer exists.

Bit 7 represents the BUSY signal, which is used by the printer to indicate that it's busy and cannot accept any characters. This bit is also important to the time out error. This signal instructs the ROM-BIOS to repeat the output loop because a character cannot be sent to the printer. This is negative logic: If this bit is set to 0, the printer is busy, and if it is set to 1, the printer is not busy.

Different states of the printer can also result in changes to a series of bits in the status byte. For example, if the printer is ready to print and is online, bits 7 and 4 are set. If you switch the printer offline, not only are bits 7 and 4 cleared, but bit 3 is also set, which signals a transfer error.

Checking printer status

You may be wondering how you can use this status byte in programs. First, the status byte can prompt for the various states that correspond to the single bits before or after transferring a character. This means that you can determine whether the printer is out of paper, switched offline, or connected to the parallel port.

The status byte can also be used to check for printer access. If bit 1 (time out error), 3 (transfer error), or 5 (out of paper) is set, or bit 4 (printer online) or 7 (printer busy) is cleared, you cannot send characters to the printer. The following pseudocode demonstrates how this is done:

```
pstatus = PrinterStatus;
if ( ( (pstatus and 29h) <> 0 ) or
      ( (pstatus and 80h) = 0  ) or
      ( (pstatus and 10h) = 0  ) ) then
   PrinterOK = FALSE
else
   PrinterOK = TRUE;
```

Now let's return to the three BIOS printer interrupt functions.

Function 00H: *Write character*

Function 00H writes a character to the printer. Place the function number (00H) in the AH register and the ASCII code of the desired character in the AL register. After the function call, the AH register receives the status byte.

Function 01H: *Initialize parallel port*

Function 01H initializes the parallel port and printer. Always execute this function before sending data to the printer. Place the function number (01H) in the AH register. After the function call, the AH register receives the status byte.

Function 02H: *Get status byte*

Function 02H reads the status byte. With this function, a printing job and the initialization of the parallel port aren't involved. After the function call, the AH register receives the status byte.

Calling the BIOS functions

Each of these functions can be called from a high level language program in the same way you would call any interrupt. Some C compilers support these functions through their runtime libraries. The table on the right shows the corresponding routines with Borland and Microsoft compilers.

Although QuickBASIC and Turbo Pascal also have printer support, this support uses DOS output functions instead of BIOS functions. If an output error occurs, the DOS functions call critical error interrupt 24H instead of returning an error code to the program. However, this error can be intercepted (e.g., by Turbo Pascal).

QuickBASIC contains the LPRINT statement for transmitting printed output. Turbo Pascal uses Write and WriteLn for the same purpose, provided that the programmer opens a file variable, directs this variable toward the printer, and specifies the printer before calling Writeln or Write. The PRINTER.TPU unit included with Turbo Pascal performs this task for you (refer to your Turbo Pascal documentation for more information).

C Compiler Support for Printer Functions	
Compiler	Function
Turbo C	
Borland C	
Borland C++	biosprint
Microsoft C	
QuickC	bios_printer

Redirecting the BIOS printer interrupt

TSR programs redirect the BIOS printer interrupt to their own routines to suit the needs of these TSRs. This allowed the development of print spoolers (programs that intercept characters sent by the original BIOS functions and store these characters in a buffer for later printing).

Demonstration program

The PRCVT.ASM assembly language program on the companion CD-ROM will help users whose printers uses a different character set than their PCs. For example, if you attempt to print a program listing or file containing PC linedraw characters on some older model Epson printers, the printout may look different than you expected. If the data on the screen looks as follows:

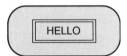

```
| HELLO |
```

an older Epson printout may look like the following:

```
IMMMMMMMMMMMMMMMMMM;
: HELLO         :
HMMMMMMMMMMMMMMMMMM(
```

The PRCVT.ASM program converts some linedraw characters to ASCII equivalents. This enables you to see how the printout will look on printers that have IBM mode:

```
/------------------\
| HELLO            |
\------------------/
```

PRCVT converts these characters before transferring them to the printer by deflecting the BIOS printer interrupt to its own routine, which is called whenever the BIOS printer interrupt is called. This eliminates the need for a definition of the conversion tables provided by many word processing programs.

Automatic character conversion

The new interrupt handler, which is the focus of the PRCVT.ASM TSR program, first checks whether function 00H should be called. This is the only function to be changed. If another function is called, the call is passed to the old printer interrupt.

If a character should be output, the program checks a table called CODETAB to determine whether it contains this character. This table, which you can see at the beginning of the program listing of PRCVT.ASM, consists of 2-byte entries, with the first byte (the low byte) containing the new code of a character that will be converted, while the subsequent byte reflects the character's old code. The table is closed by a byte with the value 0.

This new function 00H checks the second byte of a table entry to determine whether it's identical to the character to be printed. If the character isn't found in the table, then it's passed, unchanged, to the old printer interrupt for output. If it's detected in the table, it's replaced by the first byte of the table entry and then passed on for output.

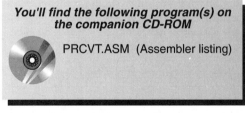

You'll find the following program(s) on the companion CD-ROM

PRCVT.ASM (Assembler listing)

The rest of the program is structurally related to other TSR programs documented in this book. PRCVT was created as a COM program and doesn't require any parameters when called from the command line. After being called, it first checks whether it has been installed. If it hasn't been installed, it installs itself; otherwise it removes the installed copy from memory.

This program can be used for both BIOS and DOS printed output.

Direct Programming And The Parallel Port

If the receiver can keep up with the sender, the BIOS functions for parallel port character output work efficiently. Communicating with a printer is the safest method, but linking two computers through their parallel ports is more complicated. This often requires data transfer rates that extend beyond the capabilities of the BIOS functions. A special type of cable with different pin assignments (called a parallel transfer cable) is needed to connect two computers. The BIOS functions cannot be used with this type of cable because they assume that the normal assignments are being used for each line in the cable.

The I/O ports

Up to three parallel ports can easily be installed in your computer. The I/O address space reserves three ranges for parallel interfaces (see the table on the right).

The port addresses in the previous table are listed in the sequence in which BIOS examines them on startup, instead of in numerical order. From this table, BIOS determines which port addresses are LPT1, LPT2 ,and LPT3.

Port	Interface
3BCH - 3BFH	Parallel interface on MDA card
378H - 37FH	Parallel interface 1
278H - 27FH	Parallel interface 2

The BIOS begins by checking the block at address 3BCH-3BFH. This is part of a large address block that extends from 3B0H to 3BFH, and is reserved for a Monochrome Display Adapter (MDA) or Hercules Graphics Card. During the 1980s most PCs were delivered with this type of video card. In addition to the video logic, these cards included a parallel port.

If the BIOS finds a video card with a parallel port, the BIOS addresses that parallel port as LPT1. The next parallel port found will then be LPT2. If the video card doesn't have a parallel port, then the first parallel port located will be identified as LPT1.

The other two address blocks listed in the table are for additional parallel ports. These ports may exist on two different cards, or on a single I/O card.

Regardless of how the hardware for the parallel port is detected, the BIOS checks for the existence of parallel ports according to the previous table. Suppose that only one parallel port is installed, but it's using the address block reserved for the second. This port will still be recognized by the BIOS as LPT1.

Assigning LPT1, LPT2, and LPT3

The BIOS assigns the names LPT1, LPT2 and LPT3 to the parallel ports by entering their base addresses as variables in the BIOS variable segment. A four-word array starting at offset address 0008H of this segment retains the port addresses of the parallel ports (see the table on the right).

The variable segment can accommodate four parallel ports, even though the BIOS will only look for three parallel ports when you start your system. The BIOS functions will also let you work with a fourth parallel port if you enter its base

Address	Contents
0040:0008H	Base address of LPT1
0040:000AH	Base address of LPT2
0040:000CH	Base address of LPT3
0040:000EH	Base address of LPT4

address by hand at offset address 000EH in the BIOS variables segment. The BIOS then addresses it as interface 3.

The LPT terminology originates from DOS rather than BIOS. LPT1 represents interface number 0, LPT2 represents interface number 1, etc. (DOS doesn't recognize LPT4).

If you want to change interface numbers (e.g., have DOS send output intended for LPT2 to LPT1), you must change the port addresses in these three BIOS variables. The pseudocode for this example would look similar to the following:

```
DummyWord = MEM[ 0040H: 0008H ]
MEM[ 0040H: 0008H ] = MEM[ 0040H: 000AH ]
MEM[ 0040H: 000AH ] = DummyWord
```

Port registers

Regardless of their locations in the addressable memory, all parallel ports use the same register interface, which consists of three ports. These ports occupy the first three port addresses of the card (e.g., 378H, 379H and 37AH) for the first parallel port.

The following illustrations show the meanings of each bit in the port registers. When you compare the assignments of each bit in the tables to the structure of a parallel cable, you'll see that they mainly coincide. A direct connection exists between the bits of the port registers and the lines in a parallel cable. When a bit in one of the registers is set to 1, then an electrical signal is immediately sent over the corresponding line. If the bit value is set to 0, then the current in the line returns to "low" status. The current in the line will always reflect the status of the corresponding register bit as it is manipulated by the software.

Some of the lines in the cable use negative logic. These lines have names preceded by minus signs. The condition associated with this type of line will be executed if the corresponding bit has a value of 0. For example, the ERROR line indicates a problem with printer output only if the corresponding bit is 0. As long as this bit remains set to 1, no error will be indicated.

Data lines

The eight bits of the first parallel port register use positive logic. This register stores the eight data bits that will be carried along data lines D0 to D7 and transferred to the receiver. Remember that this register was intended to be only an output register on a parallel port. It wasn't designed to receive data.

Remember that printers don't send data back to their hosts, and this type of port was never intended to be used for connecting two computers. This will cause some problems when you're developing a communications program because you must deal with communication between two computers as sender and receiver (more on this later).

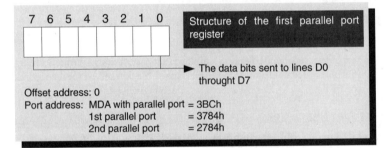

Printer status

The second register is responsible for the current printer status and is read-only. This register reflects the condition of the status lines coming from the printer. The following illustration names the pins from the host's point of view.

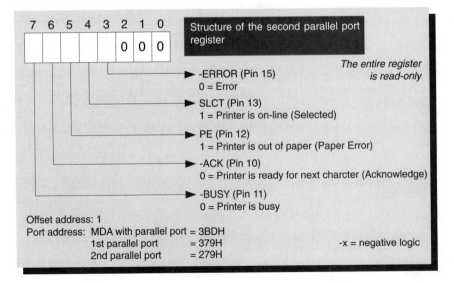

Printer control

The third register controls the printer and its hardware, and plays an important role in transferring characters. Except for bit 4, all bits are connected to corresponding pins of the parallel port.

A bit hidden in this register can execute a hardware interrupt as soon as the ACK signal switches to low, which indicates that the printer has received the last character. You can usually determine which interrupt will be executed by setting some DIP switches on the port. You can choose between IRQ 7 and 5, which are associated with interrupts 0FH and 0DH. Unlike serial ports, this option is rarely used with parallel ports because these ports work on the polling principle instead of the interrupt principle. This also applies to the BIOS, which doesn't use this interrupt vector.

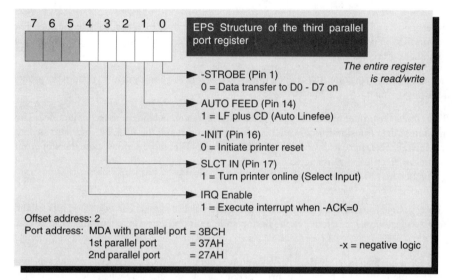

```
 7  6  5  4  3  2  1  0      EPS  Structure  of  the  third  parallel
                             port register

                                              The entire register
                                                  is read/write
                      ► -STROBE (Pin 1)
                        0 = Data transfer to D0 - D7 on
                      ► AUTO FEED (Pin 14)
                        1 = LF plus CD (Auto Linefee)
                      ► -INIT (Pin 16)
                        0 = Initiate printer reset
                      ► SLCT IN (Pin 17)
                        1 = Turn printer online (Select Input)
                      ► IRQ Enable
                        1 = Execute interrupt when -ACK=0
Offset address: 2
Port address:  MDA with parallel port = 3BCH
               1st parallel port      = 37AH
               2nd parallel port      = 27AH          -x = negative logic
```

Communication between printer and host

The assignment of each pin in the port and the meanings of the corresponding register bits become apparent when you take a "behind the scenes" look at communication between host and printer. First, the byte sent out by the host passes to the first parallel port register and is transmitted through data lines D0 through D7. This signal immediately arrives at the printer but more information is needed before this first byte can be processed. Since there is always some sort of signal coming in on data lines D0 through D7, the printer doesn't know whether this is the first character to print or simply a stray byte from the last transmission.

The -STROBE line

The -STROBE line is important for keeping track of data. When the host sets this bit to 0 (and thus setting the current in the corresponding line to low), the printer knows that a character is coming over the data lines. The host must then disable the -STROBE signal quickly; otherwise the printer may read the character twice. The printer hardware needs only a microsecond to read the character from the data lines.

The BUSY line

Since a microsecond isn't a very long time, the printer would never be able to keep up with this kind of data transfer rate, even if it stored the characters in an internal buffer. The BUSY line pauses the communication long enough to process the character it has just received. A BUSY signal is generally sent immediately after a -STROBE signal.

The software or ROM BIOS must then wait until the printer removes the BUSY signal before it can send the next character. The BUSY line is the only pin in the parallel port that inverts the signal when it's received. In order for the host to receive 0, the printer must send a value of 1 over the BUSY line.

The -ACKnowledge line

The printer must also send an -ACK signal of 0 on the -ACKnowledge line. Because of the negative logic of this line, the host will receive this as a value of 1, which indicates that the printer received the character that was sent.

The durations of all signals needed to transmit one character add up to about 10 microseconds. Theoretically, this would produce a data transfer rate of 100,000 characters per second. However, in reality, processor overhead adds a lot of extra time. Real transfer rates are actually about 1/100th of this (1000 characters per second), even if the printer has its own buffer for storing characters as they are received.

The printer responds

Although communication between a host and a printer is mostly unilateral, the printer does offer feedback to the host. The printer uses three pins to send information back to the host: -ERROR, SLCT, and PE. All three of these pins have their corresponding bits in the first parallel port register.

SLCT represents "Select". This corresponds to the ONLINE switch found on the front of your printer. If you turn the printer offline, the printer will signal the host using the SLCT line.

PE represents "Paper Error". This allows the printer to tell the host that it's out of paper or that the paper feed is jammed. This type of error is separated from normal data transfer errors, which are transmitted through the ERROR line. This is done because paper errors can be immediately corrected by the user but data transfer errors are more serious. Data transfer errors are usually caused by cable failures or electrical disturbances.

Host control

Obviously, the host has some control signals that it uses to command the printer. These signals are -AUTO FEED, -INIT, and -SLCT IN. The bits that receive these signals are found in the third parallel port register, where the values can be read or manipulated by software.

-AUTO FEED tells the printer to add a linefeed to every CR (carriage return) character (ASCII code 13) it receives as long as this signal is set to high (1). This line is included because all printers don't react the same way when they receive a CR (carriage return) character. Many printers simply return to the start of the current line without adding the linefeed, which moves the print head down to the next line. So, the LF (linefeed) character must be added separately.

The host can use the -SLCT IN line to turn the printer OFFLINE by sending a signal of 1. Normally, this line will be set to low so the printer stays online.

The host can use the -INIT line to reset the printer. To execute a reset, set the corresponding bit briefly to 0, and then immediately back to 1. If you don't set the value back to 1, the printer will reset itself repeatedly.

The Cable

The entire transfer of data between host and printer will only work if the correct pins on the two ports are connected by a proper cable. Which signals are found at which pins and the way in which the pins are connected is standardized. The Centronics standard describes both the pin assignments at each port and the lines in the cable.

The following table shows how the pins of the host and printer ports are connected. The illustration immediately following the table shows the structure of a parallel cable with the ground line.

Cable connections between parallel port and printer

Computer pin	Printer pin	Signal name	Meaning
1 → 1		-STROBE	Indicates data transfrer
2 → 2		D0	Data line - bit 0
3 → 2		D1	Data line - bit 1
4 → 2		D2	Data line - bit 2
5 → 2		D3	Data line - bit 3
6 → 2		D4	Data line - bit 4
7 → 2		D5	Data line - bit 5
8 → 2		D6	Data line - bit 6
9 → 2		D7	Data line - bit 7
10 ← 10		-ACK	Last character
11 ← 11		-BUSY	received
12 ← 12		PE	Printer busy
13 ← 13		SLCT	Printer has no paper
14 → 14		-AUTO FEED	Printer is online
15 ← 32		-ERROR	Automatic CR after LF
16 → 31		-INIT	Data transfer error
17 → 36		SLCT IN	Reset printer
18-25 ← → 19-30		GND	Turn printer online
			Ground

Structure of a parallel cable

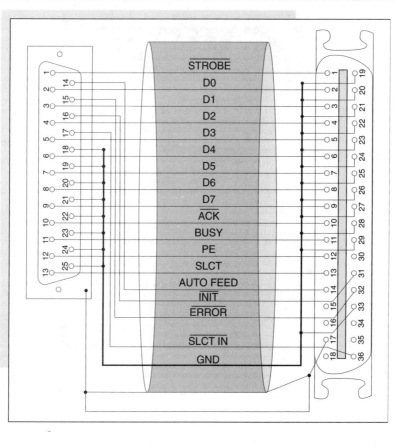

A do-it-yourself parallel transfer cable

If you want to "misuse" your parallel port for transferring data between two computers, a normal parallel cable won't work. One problem is that the parallel ports on both computers have identical female connectors. So, one end of the parallel cable won't plug into a second computer.

Another problem is that normal parallel communications travel in only one direction. One computer can use data lines D0 to D7 to send data, but it cannot receive data over these same lines and the other computer cannot send data over them.

Usually data transfer between two computers requires a bidirectional connection. For example, the receiver will return a checksum of the data it received, so the sender will know whether the data was received without error.

The status lines used by a printer to return status information to the computer can provide a solution. These are the -ERROR, SCLT, PE, -ACK, and BUSY lines, which are associated with the second parallel port register. These lines are connected to data lines D0 to D4. This means that the receiver reads output from the sender through the status lines previously listed. Conversely, data lines D0 to D4 from the receiver are connected to the status lines of the sender, which enables two-way communication.

So, basically we're simply crossing data lines D0 - D4 with the -ERROR, SLCT, PE, -ACK, and -BUSY status lines. So, the following rule applies to both sender and receiver: Any data sent out via the first five bits of the first parallel port register will be received by bits 3 to 7 in the second register of the other communication partner. It doesn't matter which end of the cable is connected to the sender and which end is connected to the receiver.

The following illustration shows which pins to connect at each end of the cable to make a parallel transfer cable.

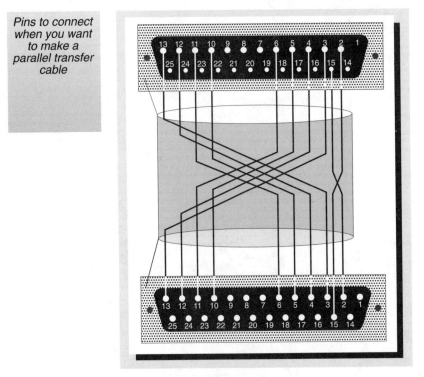

Pins to connect when you want to make a parallel transfer cable

This type of cable is very difficult to find commercially unless you own a LapLink or similar cable. If you want to make your own, you need the following information:

You'll need two male DB-25 connectors and a shielded single-pole cable less than 10 feet in length. Parallel cables longer than this cause data transfer problems.

As the illustration on the right shows, you must connect pins 2 to 6 on one connector with pins 15 and 13 to 10 (leave pin 14 free) on the other. Solder any five lines from the cable to pins 2 to 6 on the first connector. Then connect the other end of each wire to the proper pin on the other connector. Be sure to follow the proper order. For example, D0 must be connected with -ERROR, not SLCT or BUSY.

Pin connections for a parallel transfer cable

Pin		Pin	
2	15	15	2
3	13	13	3
4	12	12	4
5	10	11	6
6	11	10	5

Now you must repeat the entire procedure for the other side of the cable to cross the connections properly. Don't forget to solder the cable shielding to the connectors as a ground.

This type of cable can be used with commercial data transfer programs, such as LapLink. These programs usually work with the same type of cable as our parallel transfer cable. If the cable doesn't work, check your pin connections again. It's also possible that the program assumes the data and status lines are connected in a different order. A parallel transfer cable can be used to connect two PCs and transfer data between them. You can also use this type of cable to control a slave PC from a master PC.

Demonstration programs

The following file transfer programs listed are named PLINKP.PAS and PLINKC.C. Both can act as a sender or receiver in parallel file transfer. The basic syntax for calling either program is as follows:

```
PLINKP
PLINKC
```

The operating mode depends on how you start the program. The previous syntax sets the program in receive mode. The receiver waits until the sender begins transmitting or until the user presses (Esc) to exit. If a sender doesn't appear, the receiver waits until a time out error occurs, then exits.

The following examples start the program in sender mode, and try to send FILENAME.EXE to the receiving computer:

```
PLINKP FILENAME.EXE
PLINKC FILENAME.EXE
```

The sender waits until it senses a receiver. If a receiver exists, file transfer begins. If it doesn't, the sender waits until it recognizes a receiver or until the user presses (Esc) to exit. If a receiver still doesn't appear, the sender waits until a time out error occurs, then exits. You can also use wildcards to specify entire groups of files for transfer. The following examples start the program in sender mode, and try to send all EXE files to the receiving computer:

```
PLINKP *.EXE
PLINKC *.EXE
```

The two optional switches /P and /T can also be entered when you start the program. The /P switch specifies the parallel port through which you want information sent other than the default (LPT1). A number between 1 and 4 must follow the /P. The following examples start the program in receive mode and configure LPT3 as the parallel port for receiving data:

```
PLINKP /P3
PLINKC /P3
```

The /T switch specifies the number of time out intervals. A single time out is 10 seconds; you can enter any group of 10-second intervals. Enter a number after the /T switch. The program multiplies this by 10. The following examples start the program in sender mode, request a 30-second time out, and attempt to send all TXT files:

```
PLINKP /T3 *.TXT
```

```
PLINKC /T3 *.TXT
```

You can get help by typing PLINKC or PLINKP and the /? parameter. Enter the following to see the command syntax:

```
PLINKP /?
PLINKC /?
```

The program lists the switches for interface and time out intervals. Since these programs are coded, we omitted some features, such as checking for existing files. If you try to transfer a file to a receiver containing a file of the same name, the programs overwrite the existing filename, then time out. Check your receiver before sending files or add your own code to check for files.

Transferring data over the parallel transfer cable

With a parallel transfer cable like the one we described, you can simultaneously send five bits through data lines D0 to D4. You can transmit data in both directions simultaneously because the connections are crossed. However, some kind of communications protocol is needed so data can be transferred systematically. We need something similar to the -STROBE line to keep track of the data transfer pace. One of our five data lines must be used for this purpose.

The BUSY bit seems to be best suited for this job. The two outer bits (-ERROR and BUSY) are actually the only possibilities because the four data bits must be next to one another. Of these two, BUSY will be a better -STROBE line because it has no real application of its own for data transfer. Also, this bit is automatically inverted by the hardware. If you used this bit for data, it would have to be inverted after the transfer, which would be time-consuming. The inversion doesn't affect a -STROBE bit. Actually, it's important for the communications protocol. A 0 at one end of the cable must come out as a 1 at the other end. We'll discuss this in more detail later.

Communications protocol refers to the two demo programs described in this section. Although there can be numerous communications protocols, in this instance we're being quite specific. The protocol used here works on two levels, the byte level and the data block level. Each of these levels is handled separately. The data block level is on top of the byte level. The byte level is hardware-oriented, but the block level works with the software.

Data transfer at byte level

First let's discuss the byte level from the sender's point of view. The first thing we must consider is that an entire byte cannot be sent at once. A byte consists of eight bits and we can only send four bits in one direction at one time. So, each byte is divided into two halves called *nibbles*, which are sent one after the other.

First, the low nibble of the byte is written to bits 0 to 3 of the first parallel port register. From here it is sent out through data lines D0 to D3. The bit for data line D4 is set to 0 so the receiver will receive a value of 1 at its BUSY pin. This will tell the receiver that the low nibble of the next byte is ready to be read. This means that the receiver simply waits and reads the status line until the BUSY bit contains a value of 1.

The BUSY bit is then no longer useful, so the receiver proceeds by reading the nibble from the corresponding bits of the second port register. The contents of these four bits are stored in a variable and sent back to the sender through the data lines. The bit for data line D4 is set to 0, so a value of 1 is received back on the other end. This indicates that the returned nibble can be read and saved.

When both nibbles have been returned in this way, the sender can determine whether the byte was properly transferred. The communication is therefore verified at the byte level. However, this isn't the usual procedure. Since it takes too much time to check each byte individually, this type of verification is normally performed only at the block level. In our case, this argument doesn't apply, since the BUSY line must be used to send a -STROBE signal back to the sender with each nibble anyway. It doesn't take any more time to send the entire nibble back.

The transmission of the second nibble is basically the same, except that the value of the status bit is changed to 1. So, the receiver will receive a value of 0 at the BUSY pin. The receiver has been waiting for this as the signal to read the high nibble. The nibble is then returned to the sender and the sender's BUSY bit is reset to 0. The two nibbles can then be combined to form the complete byte, and the transfer is complete from the receiver's point of view. The sender combines the two nibbles sent back by the receiver and checks the complete byte for data transfer errors. The program's send routine alerts its caller of any errors so the appropriate action can be taken and the data block can be re-sent if necessary. Most data transfer error can be detected in this way; exceptions include unusual types of cable interference.

As we saw with normal communication to a printer, successful communication between two computers requires the proper switching of the -STROBE signal over the BUSY line. Remember that because of the way the lines in the cable are crossed, we're dealing with two separate BUSY lines. The same applies to both sender and receiver: For output, the BUSY bit is data line D4. The signal is received, however, at the BUSY status line on the other side.

The communications protocol at the hardware oriented byte level

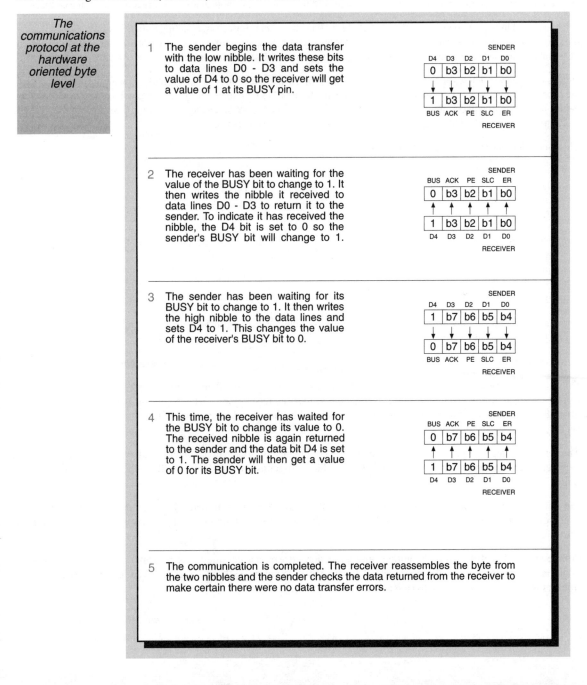

1 The sender begins the data transfer with the low nibble. It writes these bits to data lines D0 - D3 and sets the value of D4 to 0 so the receiver will get a value of 1 at its BUSY pin.

2 The receiver has been waiting for the value of the BUSY bit to change to 1. It then writes the nibble it received to data lines D0 - D3 to return it to the sender. To indicate it has received the nibble, the D4 bit is set to 0 so the sender's BUSY bit will change to 1.

3 The sender has been waiting for its BUSY bit to change to 1. It then writes the high nibble to the data lines and sets D4 to 1. This changes the value of the receiver's BUSY bit to 0.

4 This time, the receiver has waited for the BUSY bit to change its value to 0. The received nibble is again returned to the sender and the data bit D4 is set to 1. The sender will then get a value of 0 for its BUSY bit.

5 The communication is completed. The receiver reassembles the byte from the two nibbles and the sender checks the data returned from the receiver to make certain there were no data transfer errors.

Sender and receiver both use the data lines D0 - D4 for sending information, and each has its own separate -STROBE line. This is shown in the previous illustration.

Time out problems

Communications protocols usually function without error as long as the electrical current isn't interrupted. If an error occurs, either the sender or receiver will be left waiting for the other end to respond to its last message. To prevent a situation in which one of the communications partners is waiting forever for an answer that may never come, a time out value is set. The time out value determines how long one of the systems will wait for an answer from its partner before terminating the connection.

We mentioned in the first section the BIOS also uses a time out counter for communicating with the parallel port. The time out interval is usually measured by executing a read loop a certain number of times. For a program that must run on different PC systems, this isn't easy to manage. The time needed to process the read loop can vary with the system's processor speed.

Here is an example of how the time out counter works. Suppose that the sender has just sent the low nibble of a byte. It sets the time out counter to its maximum value and then waits for its BUSY bit to be set to 1 by the receiver. The read loop then begins to execute. It will continue to run until either the value of the BUSY bit changes to 1 or the time out variable reaches 0. The time out variable will continue to count down as long as its value isn't equal to 0.

This would look as follows in pseudocode:

```
TimeOutCount = MAXVALUE
WHILE ( BUSY-Bit = 0 ) AND ( TimeOutCount > 0 ) DO
  BEGIN
  END

IF TimeOutCount = 0 THEN
  error
ELSE
  o.k.
END
```

The communications protocol is activated along with the time out reading in both demo programs with routines called SendAByte and ReceiveAByte.

Synchronization

Once the communications protocol is activated, it will work without any problems. However, sometimes getting it started can be a problem. Before communications begin, both sender and receiver must have a value of 0 in the BUSY bit. If this is not the case, the receiver will immediately assume that a nibble has already been sent and it will try to read it, although the sender hasn't even sent anything yet.

The sender and receiver must be synchronized before communications can begin. Determining whether the sender or the receiver should be started first is complicated. For the demo programs presented here, we'll use the receiver as our starting point.

For initialization, the receiver waits for the sender to set its BUSY bit to 0. It then sets the sender's BUSY bit to 0. The synchronization is complete when the BUSY bits on both sides are set to 0. In the demo programs, this is done within the PortInit routine.

A time out limit is also used in the initialization procedure. It works according to the principle previously described. In addition, the programs enable the user to quit at any time by pressing the Esc key. Otherwise, you may have to wait several minutes for the time-out interval to be reached.

Stopping the program

Both programs include a keyboard interrupt handler that is activated by pressing the (Esc) key. As with the timer interrupt handler, the program also uses a variable to communicate with the keyboard interrupt handler. In this case, it's a variable of type BOOL, which is set to TRUE when the (Esc) key is pressed.

We can avoid having to read this variable separately in the read loop by coupling it with the time out variable. This is done by setting both the escape variable to TRUE and the time out variable to 0 when the (Esc) key is pressed.

The program will then simply respond as though the time out interval has been reached. A quick check of the escape variable will then allow you to determine the cause of the interrupt.

Block level protocol

The block level is above the byte level. As the name suggests, the block level is used for transferring entire data blocks from sender to receiver. This is strictly a software protocol. It's independent of the hardware because it relies on the send and receive routines from the byte level. In our demo programs, these are the SendABlock and ReceiveABlock routines.

A block always contains the following information: A token that precedes the block and describes its contents, the length of the block, and the block itself. The token is used so the receiver can immediately recognize what is being sent without having to read the data block.

According to this convention, the SendABlock routine expects to be passed the token, the number of bytes in the block, and a pointer to the data block itself. Both the token and the number of bytes are handled as a sort of header and kept separate from the actual data block. The receiver must first correctly receive the header before the first byte of the data block will be sent. Imagine what would happen if the sender wanted to send a 120 byte data block but the receiver was expecting a block of 200 bytes. The receiver would count the next 80 bytes as part of the first data block, and the communication would be hopelessly tangled.

Remember, at the byte level, the receiver is sending every byte it receives back to the sender. So, the block level protocol will immediately know whether the header was properly transferred. Unfortunately, this doesn't let the receiver know whether it received the header correctly. The sender therefore notifies the receiver by sending a standard character. So, the receiver doesn't have to assume that there weren't errors in the header.

As feedback, the sender will send an ACK character (Acknowledge) character if the transfer was successful, or a NAK character (Non-Acknowledge) character if there was an error. The ACK character isn't related to the port pin of the same name; it simply fulfills the same function. The ACK and NAK characters are represented by the codes 00H and FFH in the demo programs, but you can use any codes. These characters also play a part in the communications protocol, since they are also checked at the byte level for successful transfer.

When the receiver has received the header and the subsequent ACK character without errors, the sender can begin to transfer the actual data block. If there was a problem, the sender repeats the transfer of the header. The receiver will know that the header is being sent again because it would have received a NAK character from the previous attempt. Once the receiver has the header and the ACK character, it can concentrate on receiving the data block. As long as you use very different bit patterns for these two characters, it's unlikely that an ACK character could become a NAK character because of a data transfer error.

If it continues to encounter errors, the sender won't keep trying to send the header forever. The constant MAXTRY is set to tell the sender how many errors to count before aborting the attempt to send the current data block. The ACK and NAK characters are also used to confirm receipt of the data block. The feedback character is sent to the receiver only after the entire data block has been sent.

With this method, every type of communication error can be detected. This protocol eliminates the need for checksums, which is a common way of checking for data transfer errors in other communications software.

Reading [Esc] key status

Once the data block is transferred, a final byte is sent to complete the process. But this byte is sent from the receiver to the sender. This also gives the receiver the ability to communicate an ESCAPE signal to the sender. However, this isn't really necessary because the receiver could simply exit the communications software with ESCAPE and then let the sender wait for a time out error.

Since this isn't the best solution, the protocol has the sender wait for an "escape byte" from the receiver after the data block has been completely transferred. If the sender receives a value of TRUE, it exits the program with an appropriate message. Otherwise, the sender continues with normal program execution.

Communicating this type of message must be allowed in both directions, since the sender could also decide to terminate the communication at any time. The procedure for this is different than with the receiver. When it starts, the SendABlock routine determines whether the [Esc] key has been pressed. If it has, it sends a special escape token instead of the actual data block header. This special escape token is known to the receiver. When the receiver recognizes this token, it considers it as a signal to exit the program.

By building this escape mechanism into the block protocol, we can avoid having to make a permanent escape query at a higher level. Both of the demo programs also deal with a file level above the block level. The file level uses the block level protocol to transfer entire files piece by piece. We won't go into detail here about the file level, since the program listings at the end of this section are well documented.

Remember that the routines at the byte and block level can be used to transfer any data between sender and receiver. Also, both the sender and receiver are able to abort the communication at any point. These routines could serve as the basis for your own data transfer programs, which can compete with commercial packages such as LapLink. They may not be quite as fast, however, because this would require all of the byte level routines to be written completely in assembly language.

The higher levels

If an error, such as a time out error at the byte level or the receipt of an escape token at the block level, occurs, this error should be communicated to the highest level as quickly as possible. The various levels (byte, block, and file) in these demo programs use procedures and functions to communicate with each other. Each time a routine ends with an error, it returns to the routine that called it, working its way back to the top level by level.

> **You'll find the following program(s) on the companion CD-ROM**
>
> PLINKP.PAS (Pascal listing)
> PLINKPA.ASM (Assembler listing)
> PLINKC.C (C listing)
> PLINKCA.ASM (Assembler listing)

Modern C compilers support the setjmp() and longjmp() functions in these instances. These functions allow jumps across several program levels. The setjmp() function sets the location in the program code that will be the destination of the jump. If an error occurs, you can change program control to this location by using the longjmp() function. For more information about these functions, refer to your C compiler documentation.

Unfortunately, Turbo Pascal doesn't have similar functions. But you can implement these commands yourself.

Chapter 9

Keyboard Programming

The keyboard is one device that you are always concerned with in DOS programming. Since the keyboard is your computer's main input device, it's at the heart of most applications. TSR programs wouldn't even be possible without the keyboard.

TSR programs use the keyboard differently than normal applications. Usually, a program simply queries the keyboard to determine what keys the user has pressed. However, even this simple task can be filled with hidden complications. For example, the meaning of many keys are changed by the status of the (Caps Lock), (Num Lock) and (Scroll Lock) keys. Other keys, such as the function keys and the cursor keys, change the meaning of a key press without changing the visible characters on the screen.

However, this can easily be managed, as we'll explain in the "Accessing The Keyboard From The BIOS" section. Unfortunately this process becomes more complicated with TSR and ISR routines that capture keyboard entry before the entry can reach the application. We'll explain how to do this in the third section, "The Keyboard Interrupt Handler".

In the "Programming The Keyboard Controller" section we'll show you how to program the keyboard directly. We'll also examine how a program can effect the way the keyboard functions. For example, you can change the key repeat speed or turn on and off the keyboard LEDs.

Keyboard Programming Basics

In Chapter 2 we examined the relationship between the hardware, DOS and the BIOS using the keyboard as our example. In this section we'll discuss this topic in more detail.

Keyboard to program

When the user presses a key on the keyboard, an electric impulse, which identifies the location of the key, is generated. This signal is handled by the keyboard processor, which is located inside the keyboard itself. Generally this processor is an Intel 8048 chip or an equivalent from another manufacturer. On AT class computers the communication is handled by an Intel 8042 chip. With this chip, ATs are capable of bi-directional communication between the keyboard and CPU. The earlier PC's and PC/XT's do not have this bi-directional communication capability.

Converting the scan code

The keyboard processor converts the electric impulse indicating the key position into a number called a *scan code*. There is no relationship between the scan code and the character printed on the key that was pressed or the function the key represents in the currently running program.

The keyboard processor passes the scan code to the computer. On an AT, the keyboard controller accepts the scan code. This transfer is done serially, since the cable that connects the keyboard and the computer has only one data line. This communication is synchronous, unlike the asynchronous communication found on a PC's serial port. Synchronous communication; is achieved by using a clock line and the data line. The clock line; transmits a timing signal by continuously switching from hi to lo (1 to 0). The transmission of the individual bits of the scan code are synchronized to this pulse.

If several keys are pressed simultaneously, the keyboard processor stores them in an internal buffer. The buffer usually has enough space for 10 keystrokes. However, you don't have to worry about this buffer becoming full because the data passes to the CPU much faster than a user can type.

Make and break codes

Scan codes are also generated when the user releases a key. This tells the system whether a key is still being pressed or has already been released. This is very important because it's the only way your computer can correctly interpret the situation when more than one key is pressed at once. Without this capability, you wouldn't be able to perform certain tasks, such as typing uppercase letters or rebooting your computer with [Ctrl]+[Alt]+[Del].

Your system uses make codes and break codes; to distinguish the scan codes for keys that have been pressed ("make") and keys that have been released ("break"). The only difference is that bit 7 is set for a break code.

This leads to two important consequences. First, break codes are always greater than 128 and make codes are always less than 128. Second, a PC keyboard cannot have more than 128 keys; otherwise the make codes would overlap the break codes.

The most obvious example of when more than one key must be pressed simultaneously is to type an uppercase letter. For example, to type an uppercase "A", the user presses and holds the right [Shift] key, then presses [A]. The keyboard controller passes the make code for the [Shift] key (36H), then the make code for the [A] key (1EH) to the computer.

Since the system hasn't received a break code for the [Shift] key yet, it recognizes that both keys are being pressed simultaneously and generates an uppercase character instead of a lowercase one.

The ROM-BIOS keyboard handler

How does the processor receive these scan codes? The hardware interrupt IRQ1 is executed each time the keyboard sends a make code or a break code to the computer. This in turn calls interrupt 09H. This *keyboard handler* routine receives the make and break codes and converts them to the corresponding ASCII character codes, which can then be read by the application currently running (more on this later).

Many other tasks must be performed before the program can read the keyboard. First, the keyboard handler must read the make or break code from the keyboard using an I/O port. The address of this port is 60H for all PC systems. This port reads only make and break codes. The keyboard handler evaluates the codes and determines whether a character has been entered.

As we saw in our uppercase "A" example, not all keystrokes result in characters that are visible on the screen. The keyboard handler generated a character only after receiving the make code for the "A". A character wasn't generated when the make code for the [Shift] key was received. Think of entering the ASCII code for a character using the [Alt] key and the numeric keypad. In this instance, several keys are pressed and released before a character appears on screen.

Once the keyboard handler recognizes the character that was entered, it converts that character to a code the currently running application can understand. The scan codes themselves are unusable, because different keyboards use different sets of scan codes, although most sets are similar.

Scan code/ASCII code conversion

Therefore, scan codes are converted to ASCII codes, which are standard on all computers. Although the normal ASCII character set consists of 128 characters, PCs use an extended ASCII character set, which contains 256 characters. A listing of this character set can be found on the companion CD-ROM in the Appendices.

The converted ASCII character isn't passed directly to the application. First it's stored in a buffer. The structure of this buffer and the way it works are described in the next section.

Now the keyboard handler has completed its work. The application can then read the characters from the keyboard buffer and process them. The ROM-BIOS interrupt 16H has several functions available for this purpose (refer to the "Accessing The Keyboard From BIOS" section later in this chapter for more information).

Using foreign language keyboards

You should know one more thing about the keyboard handler. Although the ROM-BIOS defines which handler to use, DOS can replace this handler with another program. The handler in the ROM-BIOS is configured for the American keyboard by default. To use characters of other languages (such as Ä, Ö, Ü, etc.), you can install another keyboard driver in your AUTOEXEC.BAT file. Installing another keyboard driver on your system will prove that, regardless of the characters printed on your keyboard, the software converts the scan codes to ASCII codes, which determines what characters appear on the screen.

PC Keyboards

Various types of keyboards are available for PCs, but there are really only three standard keyboards. These keyboards were originally introduced by IBM. Although they are standard keyboards, their appearance can vary. This is because these are designed in many different languages, so the keys can be located in different places and contain different symbols. However, the number of keys and the scan codes they produce are standardized. Remember, the symbols printed on the keys don't always apply to what occurs inside the keyboard. The following illustration shows examples of the standard PC keyboards:

Examples of three standard PC keyboards

Original PC/XT - Keyboard with 83 keys

AT - Keyboard (MF-I) with 84 keys

AT - Keyboard (MF-II) with 101 or 102 keys

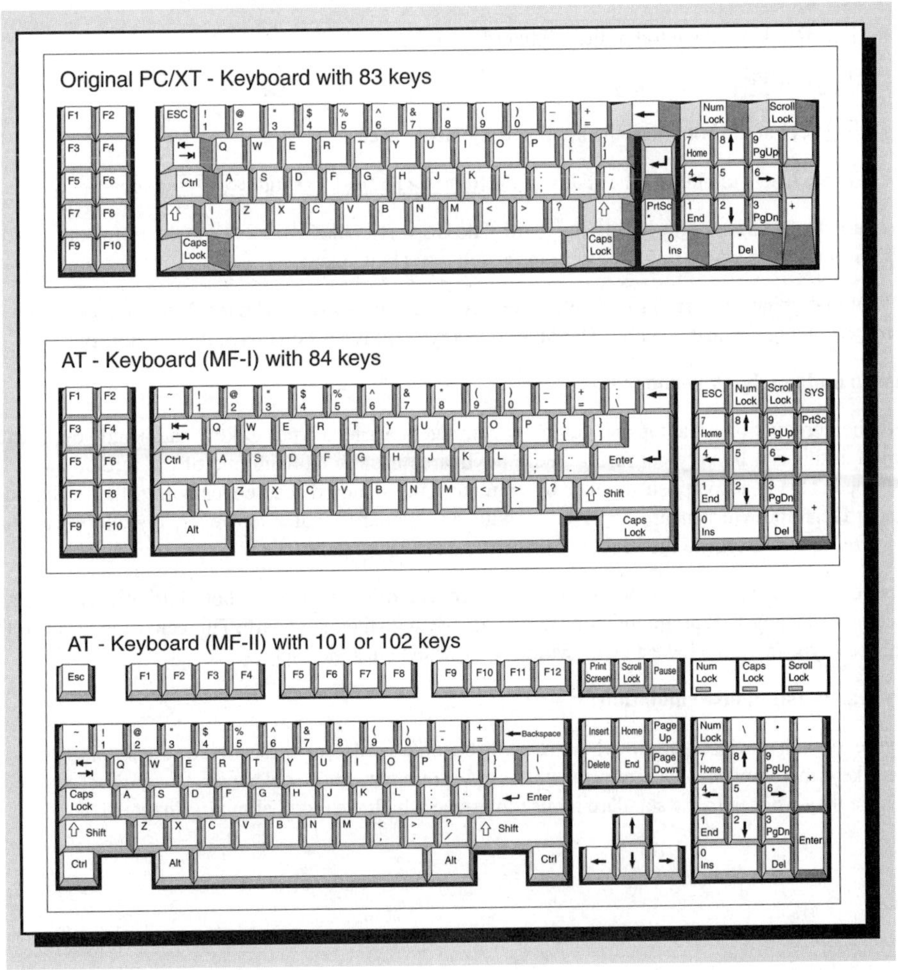

PC/XT and AT keyboards

The PC was first introduced with the PC/XT keyboard, which has 83 keys. The design of this keyboard has small (Enter) and (Shift) keys which were difficult to use.

The AT keyboard, which has 84 keys, solved this problem. The (Enter) key and the two (Shift) keys were larger so you could easily find them, even when typing very quickly. However, since the keyboard itself wasn't larger, some other keys had to be smaller. The (Num Lock), (Scroll Lock) and keypad (+) keys became smaller because they aren't used as frequently as the (Shift) keys.

The (Sys Req) key was also added to the keyboard. Although this key was intended to be used as a function key for calling operating system functions or TSR programs, developers never really adopted it.

The MF-II keyboard

The MF-II keyboard evolved from the MF-I keyboard, which was developed for PCs and XTs but wasn't very popular. Many of the MF-II's features have become keyboard standards:

➤ A group of dedicated cursor keys that are separate from the numeric keypad.

➤ Function keys at the top of the keyboard.

➤ (F11) and (F12) function keys.

➤ (Alt) keys at the bottom of the keyboard for easier access.

➤ Three LEDs to indicate the status of the (Num Lock), (Caps Lock) and (Scroll Lock) keys.

There are two versions of the MF-II keyboard. The US version has 101 keys and the European version has 102. This allows an additional letter key to be added next to the left (Shift) key.

Software (keyboard drivers in particular) can recognize an MF-II keyboard. When checked, the MF-II responds with a corresponding identification code. The other two keyboard types don't have this capability.

Laptop and notebook keyboards

With the introduction of laptop and notebook computers, various types of keyboards and keyboard layouts have appeared. Although this can be very confusing, these keyboards usually emulate one of the three major PC standards previously described. This is accomplished either by emulating the standard scan codes within the keyboard or by converting non-standard scan codes to standard ASCII codes with the keyboard handler. However, this solution isn't used frequently because it also requires changes to the keyboard driver.

Depending on licensing agreements, manufacturers can often modify keyboard drivers. However, the manufacturer may discover that many TSR programs won't work properly with their keyboard. This can occur because TSR programs generally read the keyboard at the lowest level, which is the scan codes themselves.

Keyboards and mouse emulation

Keyboards with mouse capabilities have recently become available. These include trackballs, special mouse pads or separate cursor keys that emulate mouse movements. As a programmer, you do not have to worry about any differences in these devices because they work with the standard mouse interface which we'll talk about in Chapter 11.

Accessing The Keyboard From The BIOS

Interrupt 16H provides three functions to read the keyboard and keyboard status. The BIOS keyboard functions are very limited. For example, there are no BIOS functions for removing characters from the keyboard buffer or renaming keys. DOS functions can perform these operations.

Interrupt 16H functions

The following functions are available to BIOS interrupt 16H:

Function 00H: *Read keyboard*

Interrupt 16H usually receives a call when a program expects user input of one or more characters. If a character was already entered before the function call, this character is removed from the keyboard buffer and is passed to the calling program. If the keyboard buffer is empty, function 00H waits until a character is input and then returns to the calling program. The caller can determine the character or activate a key by examining the contents of the AL and the AH registers.

Control codes

As you already know, any ASCII code can be entered from the keyboard using the ⟨Alt⟩ key and the keys of the numeric keypad. However, it's also possible to use the ⟨Ctrl⟩ key. When used with other keys, this key can enter ASCII codes smaller than code number 32. The figure on the next page shows which keys can be accessed.

ASCII

If the AL register contains a value other than 00H, it contains the ASCII code of the character. The AH register contains the scan code of the active key. The code in the AL register corresponds to the ASCII codes for character output on the screen. Some differences occur in the control keys (see the table to the right).

ASCII codes 8, 9, 10, 13 and 27 have special meanings. This makes it difficult to use them as text characters. For example, the small left arrow character is ASCII code 27. However, most programs interpret ASCII code 27 as an escape command rather than a request to enter this character.

ASCII control codes on PCs			
Code	Meaning	Code	Char.
8	Backspace	BS	
9	Tab	TAB	
10	Linefeed (Ctrl + Enter)	LF	XXX
13	Carriage Return	CR	
27	Escape	ESC	

To avoid this problem in your programs, define a key, such as ⟨F1⟩, that must be pressed before one of these special characters is entered. Then you must ensure that your program saves the last keystroke. So, if ⟨Esc⟩, ⟨Enter⟩ or ⟨Tab⟩ is pressed, simply check to see whether the previous keystroke was ⟨F1⟩. If it was, the keystroke should be interpreted as a text character instead of a control character.

Character input with the [Ctrl] key

Dec	Symbol	Keyboard codes	Dec	Symbol	Keyboard codes
0	Empty (Null)	[Ctrl] + [2]	16	▶	[Ctrl] + [P]
1	☺	[Ctrl] + [A]	17	◀	[Ctrl] + [Q]
2	☻	[Ctrl] + [B]	18	↕	[Ctrl] + [R]
3	♥	[Ctrl] + [C]	19	‼	[Ctrl] + [S]
4	♦	[Ctrl] + [D]	20	¶	[Ctrl] + [T]
5	♣	[Ctrl] + [E]	21	§	[Ctrl] + [U]
6	♠	[Ctrl] + [F]	22	▬	[Ctrl] + [V]
7	•	[Ctrl] + [G]	23	↨	[Ctrl] + [W]
8	◘ BS	[Ctrl] + [H] [Bksp] [Shift] + [Bksp]	24	↑	[Ctrl] + [X]
9	○ TAB	[Ctrl] + [I]	25	↓	[Ctrl] + [Y]
10	● LF	[Ctrl] + [J] [Ctrl] + [Enter]	26	→	[Ctrl] + [Z]
11	♂	[Ctrl] + [K]	27	← ESC	[Ctrl] + [Esc] [Shift] + [Esc] [Esc]
12	♀	[Ctrl] + [L]	28	∟	[Ctrl] + [\]
13	♪ CR	[Ctrl] + [M] [Enter] [Shift] + [Enter]	29	↔	[Ctrl] + []
14	♫	[Ctrl] + [N]	30	▲	[Ctrl] + [6]
15	☼	[Ctrl] + [O]	31	▼	[Ctrl] + [-]
			32	Space	[Spacebar] [Shift] + [Spacebar] [Ctrl] + [Spacebar] [Alt] + [Spacebar]

Extended keyboard codes

In addition to the ASCII codes, the BIOS functions also support the extended keyboard codes. The 256 characters of the PC ASCII character set include certain control characters, such as [Tab], [Enter] and [Esc], but not function keys and cursor keys.

So, the codes for these keys are returned according to a slightly different process, which utilizes ASCII code 0. The real information, the extended keyboard code, is found in the AH register. This is where you would normally find the scan code for the key.

If your program finds the value 00H in the AL register after calling function 00H or 01H of BIOS interrupt 16H, the keyboard code will be found in the AH register. With this method, an additional 256 character codes can be used. The following table lists the extended keyboard codes that can be read with functions 00H and 01H. Key combinations that aren't found in this table, such as all combinations of Ctrl + Shift + a letter key, aren't recognized by the BIOS and don't have their own keyboard codes.

Extended key codes				
Code (hex)	Code (dec)	Key(s)		
0FH	15	Shift	Tab	
10H	16	Alt	Q	(2nd keyboard series)
11H	17	Alt	W	
12H	18	Alt	E	
13H	19	Alt	R	
14H	20	Alt	T	
15H	21	Alt	Y	
16H	22	Alt	U	
17H	23	Alt	I	
18H	24	Alt	O	
19H	25	Alt	P	
1EH	30	Alt	A	(3rd keyboard series)
1FH	31	Alt	S	
20H	32	Alt	D	
21H	33	Alt	F	
22H	34	Alt	G	
23H	35	Alt	H	
24H	36	Alt	J	
25H	37	Alt	K	
26H	38	Alt	L	
2CH	44	Alt	Z	(4th keyboard series)
2DH	45	Alt	X	
2EH	46	Alt	C	
2FH	47	Alt	V	

Extended key codes			
Code (hex)	Code (dec)	Key(s)	
30H	48	Alt	B
31H	49	Alt	N
32H	50	Alt	M
03BH	59	F1	
3CH	60	F2	
3DH	61	F3	
3EH	62	F4	
3FH	63	F5	
40H	64	F6	
41H	65	F7	
42H	66	F8	
43H	67	F9	
44H	68	F10	
47H	71	Home	
48H	72	↑	
49H	73	Page Up	
4BH	75	←	
4DH	77	→	
50H	80	↓	
51H	81	Page Down	
52H	82	Ins	
53H	83	Del	
54H	84	Shift	F1
55H	85	Shift	F2
56H	86	Shift	F3
57H	87	Shift	F4
58H	88	Shift	F5
59H	89	Shift	F6

Extended key codes			
Code (hex)	Code (dec)	Key(s)	
5AH	90	Shift	F7
5BH	91	Shift	F8
5CH	92	Shift	F9
5DH	93	Shift	F10
5EH	94	Ctrl	F1
5FH	95	Ctrl	F2
60H	96	Ctrl	F3
61H	97	Ctrl	F4
62H	98	Ctrl	F5
63H	99	Ctrl	F6
64H	100	Ctrl	F7
65H	101	Ctrl	F8
66H	102	Ctrl	F9
67H	103	Ctrl	F10
68H	104	Alt	F1
69H	105	Alt	F2
6AH	106	Alt	F3
6BH	107	Alt	F4
6CH	108	Alt	F5
6DH	109	Alt	F6
6EH	110	Alt	F7
6FH	111	Alt	F8
70H	112	Alt	F9
71H	113	Alt	F10
73H	115	Ctrl	←
74H	116	Ctrl	→
75H	117	Ctrl	End

Extended key codes			
Code (hex)	Code (dec)	Key(s)	
76H	118	[Alt] [Page Down]	
77H	119	[Alt] [Home]	
78H	120	[Alt] [1]	(1st keyboard series)
79H	121	[Alt] [2]	
7AH	122	[Alt] [3]	
7BH	123	[Alt] [4]	
7CH	124	[Alt] [5]	
7DH	125	[Alt] [6]	
7EH	126	[Alt] [7]	
7FH	127	[Alt] [8]	
80H	128	[Alt] [9]	
81H	129	[Alt] [0]	
82H	130	[Alt]	
83H	131	[Alt] '	

Keystroke combinations not included in this table cannot be read by the BIOS keyboard functions because they don't create keyboard codes. This applies to the function keys and to combinations of keys, such as [Ctrl], [Alt] and [Shift]. Some DOS programs can interpret these keys because they have their own keyboard interrupt handlers that can be programmed to interpret any desired keystroke combinations.

BIOS-proof keys

Some key combinations cannot be read by BIOS as key codes because they execute commands. For example, activating the [Print] key or [Print Screen] calls BIOS interrupt 5H. This starts a routine that copies the current screen display to a printer, to produce a hardcopy.

The [Ctrl]+[Num Lock] keys stop the system completely until the user presses another key. The keyboard buffer ignores the [Ctrl]+[Num Lock] keys and the next key pressed, so programs cannot read these keys.

Pressing the [Ctrl]+[Break] key combination calls interrupt 1BH. Usually the current program stops and returns to DOS. To prevent this from happening, direct this interrupt to a routine, within the application, that continues program execution even if this routine consists only of a single IRET assembly language instruction.

ATs and a few advanced PC/XTs contain the [Sys Req] key. When this key is pressed, interrupt 15H is called by passing the value 8500H to the AX register. When the user releases the key, the AX register then receives the value 8501H. The value 85H in the AH register represents the function number of interrupt 15H. When DOS is first started, function 85H of the BIOS interrupt 15H performs only an IRET instruction; pressing the [Sys Req] key has no visible result. To use this key in your program, you can include your own handler for interrupt 15H and route this function call to this handler.

Function 01H: *Read keyboard*

Function 01H also reads the keyboard. However, unlike function 00H, function 01H leaves the preceding character in the keyboard buffer. Repeated calls to function 01H or function 00H re-read the keyboard. Place the value 01H in the AH register to call function 01H.

Unlike function 00H, after the function call, function 01H immediately informs the calling program, with the zero flag, whether a character is available. If the zero flag equals 1, a character isn't available. If the zero flag is 0, the AL and AH registers contain information about the activated key. As in function 00H, the AL register contains the value 00H if the user activated an extended key and a value unequal to 00H if the user pressed a "normal" key. The AH register contains the scan codes of normal keys; extended keys place their codes in the AH register.

Function 02H: *Read control keys*

Function 02H has a different task. This function reads the status of certain control keys and conditions (e.g., ⎡Insert⎤). Place the number 02H in the AH register to call the function. The keyboard status can be found in the AL register after the function call.

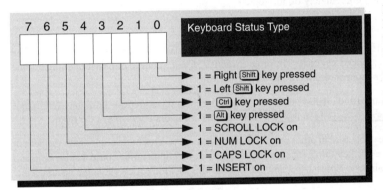

For example, if bit 3 is set, the user is holding down the ⎡Alt⎤ key. If bit 6 is set, then the ⎡Caps Lock⎤ key is on and the user is typing in uppercase mode.

Notice the keyboard status byte is different depending on the left and right ⎡Shift⎤ keys, but not between the two different ⎡Alt⎤ and ⎡Ctrl⎤ keys of the MF-II keyboard. This is because both the keyboard status byte and the BIOS keyboard function 02H were developed with the first PCs, before the MF-II keyboard even existed.

The keyboard status byte is often used by TSR programs to detect when the hotkeys that activate the program are pressed. For more information on this subject refer to Chapter 35 which discusses TSR programming.

Demonstration programs

The following programs demonstrate the various functions of the BIOS keyboard interrupts we've discussed. The four programs can be divided into two groups. The first three programs are written in the higher level languages used throughout this book. They call the various functions of BIOS keyboard interrupts for their own uses. The fourth program is an assembly language program. It modifies the BIOS keyboard interrupt functions and processing and acts as a resident program that can be accessed at a keypress.

Checking key status

The higher level programs provide a subroutine or a function for reading characters from the keyboard. This by itself isn't special because these languages have their own instructions that perform the same task. The important feature of the function is that it accepts other tasks in addition to reading characters. It displays the status of the keyboard functions ⎡Insert⎤, ⎡Caps Lock⎤ and ⎡Num Lock⎤ in the upper-right corner of the screen. This is especially useful for XT and PC owners because most keyboards don't indicate the key status. AT keyboards and some XT keyboards provide light emitting diodes (LED) that indicate the status of these keys. Otherwise, you never really know whether the ⎡Insert⎤ or ⎡Caps Lock⎤ mode is on.

Each program begins with a routine that reads the status of the keyboard functions through function 02H of BIOS keyboard interrupt 16H. Since the program only uses the ⎡Insert⎤, ⎡Caps Lock⎤ and ⎡Num Lock⎤ modes, the program only views the three highest level bits in the keyboard status byte. Based on this status byte, a flag initializes for every keyboard function. These flags indicate the status of one of these functions or modes within the program. The status is reversed when compared with the current mode. For example, if the [Insert] mode is switched off, the flag corresponding changes to OFF. We'll explain this later.

Calling the interrupt function

After initializing the internal flags, the actual routine for keyboard reading can be called. This routine also uses function 2 of the BIOS keyboard interrupt to read the keyboard function status. Then it compares the current status of each individual function with the previous status stored in a flag. During its first call after the initialization routine, it determines whether the status of all three functions has changed since its previous status. The change in status causes the routine to display the new status on the screen.

This explains why the flag is reversed in the initialization routine. This enables the keyboard function status to be displayed on the screen during the first call the keyboard routines instead of after it changed by pressing a key.

Now the routine performs its actual task, which is reading the keyboard. It uses function 01H of the BIOS keyboard interrupt to detect whether a key is available in the keyboard buffer of BIOS. If a key isn't available, the program jumps to the beginning of the routine and reads the keyboard function status again. This creates a loop that runs until a keypress occurs. This loop ensures that any status change is documented immediately on the screen.

Reading the keys

If a character appears in the BIOS keyboard buffer, the loop terminates and BIOS keyboard interrupt function 02H reads the key. The last step of this routine tests for an extended key code. The program adds 256 to the code to inform the calling routine that an extended key code is received. Then control returns to the calling routine.

This routine reads characters from the keyboard and displays them on the screen. This process repeats until the user presses a certain key. If the user presses the [Num Lock], [Caps Lock] or [Insert] key, the screen immediately displays the result.

This type of centralized keyboard routine can be used in other programs for additional tasks. For example, with the help of this routine, a macro conversion can change one key into a string of characters. Another application could display help text on the screen when the user presses a certain key. Lotus 1-2-3 and dBASE use this method for displaying help screens.

NOTE

A small problem occurs with keyboard flag output. Since displaying keyboard flags on the screen changes the cursor's position, subsequent screen output from the program occurs at unexpected locations. These can disrupt the screen display. To avoid this problem, the keyboard routine must determine the current cursor position before the keyboard flag display. Then the routine must restore the cursor position to its previous value after displaying keyboard status.

A similar problem occurs with the color. The flag output assumes a certain color and the original color must be restored after the output. The problem is that none of the three languages has a command to determine the current color. In Pascal programs for keyboard reading, only a special procedure can set the color by recording the colors in a variable and setting it with a command. With these variables, the keyboard routine restores the current color after the individual flags are displayed.

You'll find the following program(s) on the companion CD-ROM

KEYB.BAS (Basic listing)
KEYP.PAS (Pascal listing)
KEYC.C (C listing)

Reading MF-II keyboards

The [F11] and [F12] function keys aren't included in the listing of extended keyboard codes. There is a good reason for this because these keys cannot be read with functions 00H and 01H. The developers of the ROM-BIOS intentionally excluded these keys from being processed by functions 00H and 01H to maintain compatibility.

The keyboard handler writes the scan codes for these keys to the keyboard buffer, like any other keystroke. But functions 00H and 01H simply ignore them and proceed as if the keyboard buffer is empty.

New BIOS functions

Three new BIOS functions detect these codes. These functions were introduced with the AT and can now be found in almost every ROM-BIOS. Also, if these functions are excluded from the ROM-BIOS, DOS Versions 3.3 and up implement these functions with the DOS keyboard driver KEYB.

These new functions are assigned the numbers 10H, 11H and 12H. The way these functions are called and work is similar to functions 00H, 01H and 02H. Function 12H is slightly different from 02H in function results; we'll discuss this difference later.

The new keyboard codes

The differences between 00H and 01H and their counterparts 10H and 11H involve the codes that are returned. This applies almost exclusively to extended keyboard codes that represent keys that aren't found on the PC/XT and AT keyboards or key combinations (such as Ctrl+Tab, Ctrl+↑ or Alt+Esc) that aren't supported by these keyboards.

The following tables show the keys and key combinations that return different codes with functions 00H/01H and 10H/11H (all codes are in hexadecimal notation):

Extended key combinations when calling BIOS functions 10H/11H								
Function keys			Shift		Ctrl		Alt	
	Old AH/AL	New AH/AL	Old AH/AL	New AH/AL	Old AH/AL	New AH/AL	Old AH/AL	New AH/AL
F11	----	85/00	----	87/00	----	89/00	----	8B/00
F12	----	86/00	----	88/00	----	8A/00	----	8C/00
Gray cursor keys in separate cursor block			Shift		Ctrl		Alt	
	Old AH/AL	New AH/AL	Old AH/AL	New AH/AL	Old AH/AL	New AH/AL	Old AH/AL	New AH/AL
Home	47/00	47/E0	47/00	47/E0	77/00	77/E0	-----	97/00
↑	48/00	48/E0	48/00	48/E0	-----	8D/E0	-----	98/00
Page Up	49/00	49/E0	49/00	49/E0	84/00	84/E0	-----	99/00
←	4B/00	4B/E0	4B/00	4B/E0	73/00	73/E0	-----	9B/00
→	4D/00	4D/E0	4D/00	4D/E0	74/00	74/E0	-----	9D/00
End	4F/00	4F/E0	4F/00	4F/E0	75/00	75/E0	-----	9F/00
↓	50/00	50/E0	50/00	50/E0	-----	91/E0	-----	A0/00
Page Down	51/00	51/E0	51/00	51/E0	76/00	76/E0	-----	A1/00
Ins	52/00	52/E0	52/00	52/E0	-----	92/E0	-----	A2/00
Del	53/00	53/E0	53/00	53/E0	-----	93/E0	-----	A3/00

Extended key combinations when calling BIOS functions 10H/11H continued								
Other gray keys	Old AH/AL	New AH/AL	Shift Old AH/AL	Shift New AH/AL	Ctrl Old AH/AL	Ctrl New AH/AL	Alt Old AH/AL	Alt New AH/AL
/	35/2F	E0/2F	-----	E0/2F	-----	95/00	-----	A4/00
*	37/2A	37/2A	-----	37/2A	-----	96/00	-----	37/00
-	4A/2D	4A/2D	-----	4A/2D	-----	8E/00	-----	4A/00
+	4E/2B	4E/2B	-----	4E/2B	-----	90/00	----- 4E/00	
Enter	1C/0D	E0/0D	-----	E0/0D	-----	E0/0A	-----	A6/00
Additional combinations of white keys	Old AH/AL	New AH/AL	Shift Old AH/AL	Shift New AH/AL	Ctrl Old AH/AL	Ctrl New AH/AL	Alt Old AH/AL	Alt New AH/AL
Tab					-----	94/00	-----	A5/00
5					-----	8F/00		
↑					-----	8D/00		
↓					-----	91/00		
Ins					-----	92/00		
Del					-----	93/00		
Esc							-----	01/00
Backspace							-----	0E/00
Tab							-----	A5/00
[							-----	1A/00
]							-----	1B/00
Enter							-----	1C/00
;							-----	27/00
'							-----	28/00
`							-----	29/00
\							-----	2B/00
,							-----	33/00
.							-----	34/00
/							-----	35/00

The codes for the gray cursor keys have been changed. This was done to distinguish them from the cursor keys of the numeric keypad. The gray cursor keys return ASCII code E0H, instead of 00H, to the AL register. When using BIOS functions 10H and 11H, you must have your programs look for ASCII code E0H as well as 00H to be able to read all extended keyboard codes.

If you're only interested in reading the F11 and F12 function keys and don't want to distinguish between the white and gray cursor keys, you can save yourself some work by changing ASCII code E0H to 00H after it's received. This enables you to handle both sets of cursor keys in the same way.

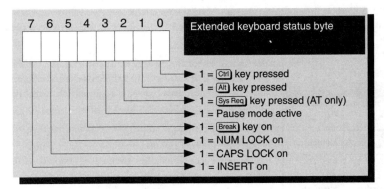

The new status functions

Functions 10H and 11H are identical to their original counterparts, but function 12H differs slightly from 02H in the returned result. In addition to the keyboard status byte, this function returns other information in the AH register. This extra information is known as the extended keyboard status byte. Although this is also a BIOS variable, it's only managed on systems with an MF-II keyboard.

Like the normal keyboard status byte, this byte also contains information on the current status of the various toggle keys. But it also provides the status of both the left and right Alt and Ctrl keys. The normal keyboard status byte doesn't allow you to read these separately.

Are these functions available?

As we mentioned, most BIOS manufacturers now include the extended BIOS keyboard functions or they are provided by DOS 3.3 and higher. However, you can't assume they will be available on all systems.

Because of this, any program that wants to use these functions should first determine whether they are available. This isn't easy to do because no ROM-BIOS function can provide this information.

So you must use a trick. This consists of calling function 12H with the values 12H in the AH register and 00H in the AL register. If the value 1200H is found in the AX register after the function call, you can then be sure that function 12H and therefore the other extended BIOS functions, are unavailable on the system.

This trick relies on an unwritten law of the ROM-BIOS, Under this "law", when an unknown function is called, the function call will end immediately and the contents of the AX register (the function and sub-function numbers) will be returned to the caller unchanged.

Demonstration programs

The MF2B.BAS, MF2P.PAS and MF2C.C demonstration programs listed will demonstrate how easily this test can be implemented in your program code. These implementations in BASIC, Pascal and C perform only one task; they read the keyboard using BIOS function 10H and display ASCII and scan codes entered at the keyboard. The output is in hexadecimal format so you can compare the values with the previous table.

These programs display the codes produced by the extra keys and key combinations available on the MF-II keyboard. This continues until the user presses the Esc key to end the program.

You can easily compare the extended BIOS functions with the normal functions. First, read a few codes with the extended function. Then switch the program to BIOS function 00H and press the same

You'll find the following program(s) on the companion CD-ROM

MF2B.BAS (BASIC listing)
MF2P.PAS (Pascal listing)
MF2C.C (C listing)

keys again. Simply change the line of code in the GetMFKey function where the BIOS function number is loaded in the AX register.

The keyboard query begins only after the TestMF function has determined that an MF keyboard is available. This involves the test previously described using extended BIOS function 12H.

The BIOS keyboard interrupt variables

The BIOS has eight variables in its variable segment for managing the keyboard and communication between the keyboard interrupt handler (interrupt 09H) and the BIOS keyboard functions (interrupt 16H). These are listed in the following table. These variables are useful for TSR programs that change the way the keyboard interrupts work. Even normal programs can find ways to manipulate these variables, as we'll see at the end of this section.

BIOS variables for keyboard management		
Offset	Meaning	Type
17H	Keyboard status	1 byte
18H	Extended keyboard status	1 byte
19H	Code for ASCII input	1 byte
1AH	Next character in keyboard buffer	1 word
1CH	Last character in keyboard buffer	1 word
1EH	Keyboard buffer	16 words
80H	Start address of keyboard buffer	1 word
82H	End address of keyboard buffer	1 word

You should already be familiar with two of these variables: The keyboard status byte and the extended keyboard status byte. These two bytes are returned when calling functions 02H and 12H of interrupt 16H.

Offset address 19H is a byte used when entering ASCII codes with the [Alt] key and numeric keypad. When the number keys are pressed, the code entered is stored in this byte.

Managing the keyboard buffer

The three variables that follow at offset addresses 1AH, 1CH and 1EH manage the keyboard buffer. This is where the keyboard interrupt handler (interrupt 09H) stores keystrokes so applications can read them using the BIOS keyboard interrupt (16H).

Before you can understand the significance of the first two variables, you must know the keyboard buffer is structured as a ring buffer. This kind of buffer is used when characters will be written to the buffer and read from it asynchronously (i.e., not within a specific time span). At first, it may seem that storing characters in sequence (the first character in the first position, the second character in the second position, etc.) is the best way to structure such a buffer. When a character is read, it's taken from the first position and all the other characters move up.

Although this method works, it generates unnecessary work for the processor because each time a character is read, all the characters in the buffer must be moved. So, the ring buffer uses two pointers. One pointer indicates the position from which the next character will be read and the other indicates the position where the next new character will be written.

With this method, the pointers move instead of the entire contents of the buffer. Initially, both pointers point to the beginning of the buffer. They move toward the end of the buffer with every read and write access. When the pointers reach the end of the buffer, they are reset to the beginning of the buffer. The ring buffer's name comes from this circular pointer movement.

For example, suppose the offset address of the next character to be read from the keyboard buffer is 1AH. Once the character is read, the pointer moves two bytes towards the end of the buffer. Each character in the keyboard buffer requires two bytes: One byte for the ASCII code and one byte for the scan code. If the last location in the buffer was read, the pointer is set to the beginning of the buffer.

The same happens with the pointer at 1CH, which points to the position following the last character in the buffer. If the user presses another key, the key is stored at this location. The pointer then moves two bytes towards the end of the buffer. If the new keystroke was stored in the last word of the buffer, this pointer is reset to the beginning of the buffer.

The relationship between the two pointers indicates the buffer's status. Two conditions are important:

1. If both pointers have the same value, this indicates an empty keyboard buffer.

2. If the end pointer tries to occupy the same space as the starting pointer, this indicates a full keyboard buffer.

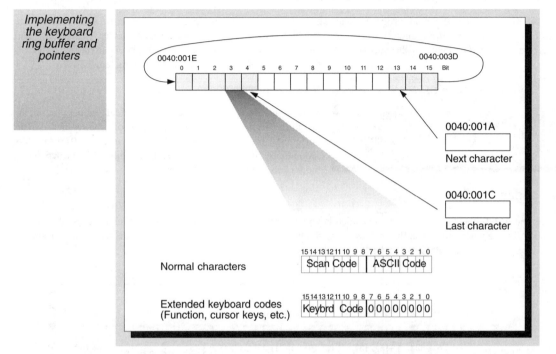

Implementing the keyboard ring buffer and pointers

The BIOS keyboard buffer comprises 32 bytes. Since each character requires two bytes, the buffer can hold up to 16 characters.

With a normal ASCII character, the ASCII code is stored first, followed by the scan code. For extended keyboard codes, the ASCII code will be 0 because the actual character code is in the subsequent byte.

Keyboard buffer location

The concept of the two ring buffer pointers suggests that this is a "mobile" buffer and that its location should be determined by the values of the pointers. However, the keyboard buffer is always located at offset address 1EH. Actually, this was the reason why the two ring buffer was designed; the two pointers would allow the size and location of the keyboard buffer to change as needed.

However, by the time these two variables were introduced with the modified BIOS of the first ATs, there were already numerous TSR programs that expected to find the keyboard buffer in a fixed location at offset address 1EH. So, the original idea never had a chance to be implemented.

Demonstration programs

The NOKEYP.BAS, NOKEYC.PAS and NOKEYB.C programs, which are in BASIC, Pascal and C, demonstrate how to manipulate the BIOS variables. These programs use a function that's very important to basic keyboard programming: Purging the contents of the keyboard buffer.

Occasionally you must purge the contents of the keyboard buffer. For example, if your program involves user prompts for deleting files or formatting disks, you don't want any accidental keystrokes stored in the keyboard buffer. The wrong key may tell your program to proceed before the user has had a chance to confirm the action.

Since the BIOS keyboard interrupt doesn't have a function for this, we must use a user-defined routine. Simply equalize the values of the two ring pointers, which creates the illusion the buffer is empty. It's also important to suppress all interrupts while doing this so new keystrokes aren't added to the buffer.

The NOKEYP.PAS and NOKEYC.C programs listed and stored on the companion CD-ROM in Pascal and C demonstrate how to do this. They begin with a countdown on the screen, which gives you time to enter some characters. Then the keyboard buffer is cleared and BIOS functions 00H and 01H are called to display all characters found in the keyboard buffer. After this, the keyboard buffer is purged and no characters exist.

You'll find the following program(s) on the companion CD-ROM

NOKEYP.PAS (Pascal listing)
NOKEYC.C (C listing)
NOKEYB.BAS (BASIC listing)

BASIC implementation

Since interrupt suppression is more difficult in BASIC, in this version of the program a different method of clearing the keyboard buffer is used. This process calls BIOS functions 01H and 00H sequentially in a loop until the 01H function call indicates that no more characters are in the buffer.

Scan codes

Although the ASCII character set and the extended keyboard codes are standardized, scan codes vary depending on the keyboard. All three keyboard standards work with a different set of scan codes. This is shown in the following illustration. It lists the scan codes for the PC/XT and AT keyboards.

PC/XT and AT scan codess

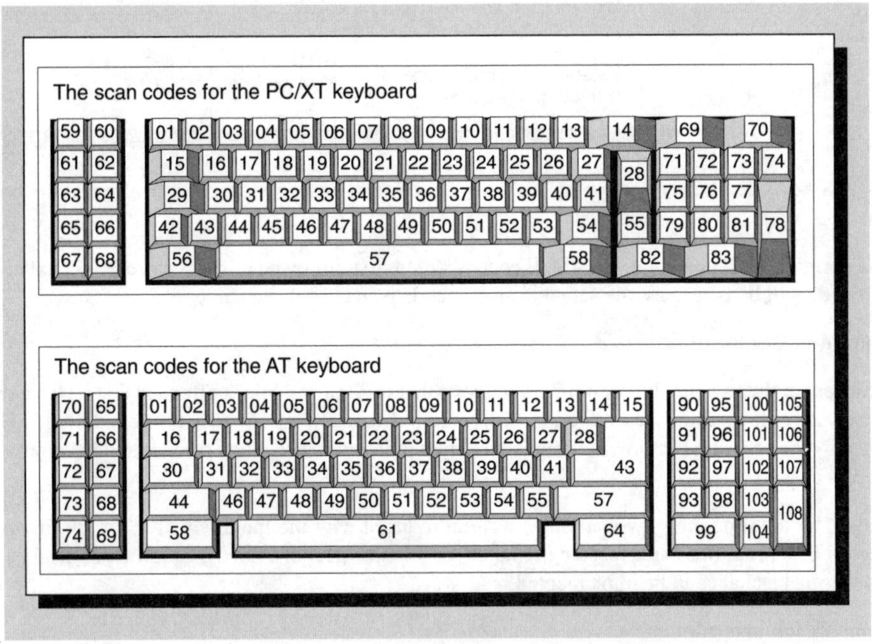

The scan codes for the PC/XT keyboard

The scan codes for the AT keyboard

You cannot always be sure the break code is the scan code plus 80H. For example, the AT keyboard sends two bytes when a key is released: F0H for a break code and then the key's scan code. However, the AT keyboard controller handles such incompatibilities. Anything sent through port 60H to the keyboard driver is converted to the normal format.

MF-II extended scan codes

Because of the AT keyboard controller, the MF-II keyboard also returns the same scan codes at port 60H as the AT keyboard, although they are slightly extended. The MF-II supports three scan code sets that are different from any previous keyboards.

The following table lists the additional MF-II keyboard scan codes. A byte containing the value E0H precedes each code. This byte indicates an extended scan code that must be handled in a special way. This is because most of the scan codes are already reserved and would otherwise be interpreted incorrectly.

In this instance, the break code equals the make code plus 80H and the initial E0H isn't changed. For the cursor keys of the gray cursor block that are used with the Shift key, the Shift key must first be suppressed. So, the break code for the Shift key is sent before this scan code.

For the left Shift key, the prefix of this make code is E0H AAH and the prefix of the break code is E0H D2H. For the right Shift key, the make code is E0H B6H and the break code is E0H D2H.

You'll encounter a problem when programming with scan codes, for example in a TSR program. The only simple solution is to use an installation program in which

Extended Scan Codes on the MF-II Keyboard					
Gray cursor keys in separate cursor block			Function keys		
	Make	Break		Make	Break
Home	E0 47	E0 C7	F11	57	D7
↑	E0 48	E0 C8	F12	58	D8
Page Up	E0 49	E0 C9			
←	E0 4B	E0 CB			
→	E0 4D	E0 CD			
End	E0 47	E0 C7			
↓	E0 50	E0 D0			
Page Down	E0 51	E0 D1			
Ins	E0 52	E0 D2			
Del	E0 53	E0 D3			
All numbers are in hexadecimal notation					

the user actually press the hotkey combinations to be used. Then the program can store the appropriate scan codes. Unless absolutely necessary, don't program with scan codes. Instead, you should use ASCII codes or extended keyboard codes.

Although the scan codes generated by your keyboard or keyboard controller can be listed with the program described in the following section.

The Keyboard Interrupt Handler

The keyboard is the target of many special programs. Macro recorders, utilities for increasing the size of the keyboard buffer, special keyboard drivers and TSR programs activated by special hotkeys all affect the operation of the keyboard with their own interrupt handlers.

Depending on the application, these interrupt handlers replace either BIOS keyboard interrupt 09H or 16H. This section contains examples of both types of programs (refer to Chapter 35) for detailed information about TSR programs).

Accessing BIOS keyboard interrupt 16H

If you want to extend or change the operations of one of the BIOS keyboard interrupts, simply redirect the interrupt to the interrupt handler within your program. Then when the interrupt executes, your own routine will be called. By doing this, you can insert new functions or redirect functions 00H and 01H to 10H and 11H. This is useful in all high level language programs, in which keyboard reading capabilities are based on various library routines.

Often, these routines simply use functions 00H and 01H of the BIOS keyboard interrupt, blocking the user from reading the F11 and F12 keys of the MF-II keyboard. But if you reroute these function calls to the extended functions that support MF-II, you can avoid having to write an extra routine to handle keyboard reading.

A macro utility

The MACROKEY.ASM program is a short macro utility written in assembly language. When you run the executable program from the system prompt, it remains resident in memory until you press the hotkey combination. This version of the program displays the text, "PC Intern published by Abacus" when you press (Alt)+(N). You can easily modify the program to display other text by using any other hotkey combination or even by adding multiple macros.

A new BIOS keyboard interrupt handler

The heart of the MACROKEY.ASM program is a new interrupt handler for BIOS keyboard interrupt 16H. We'll discuss this new BIOS keyboard interrupt handler in detail. This handler, which is a routine called NEWI16, is located at the beginning of the program.

At the start of this routine, the STI assembly language instruction enables hardware interrupts. (It's unnecessary to disable interrupts in this program.)

The JMP instruction following the STI checks for an existing MACROKEY program in memory. The "MT" bytes indicate this.

NI1 reads the function number passed in the AH register. The program is only responsible for functions 00H, 01H, 10H and 11H. Functions 02H and 12H are sent to the old BIOS handler, whose address was stored when the program was started. So, the new handler modifies the old handler instead of completely replacing it.

If a call to one of the desired functions is discovered, the program execution branches to one of two locations, depending on the function required: Label FCT0 for 00H or 10H or FCT1 for 01H or 11H. The functions paired in each group can be handled identically because they both perform the same tasks. In either case, the program checks to see whether the macro has already been called.

If a macro hasn't been called, the new function must determine whether the macro hotkey has been pressed. The specified function is called for the old handler, which returns the function to the AX register if a key has been pressed. The key is compared with the main hotkey code (stored in the MKEY variable at the beginning of the program). The default hotkey is 3100H ((Alt)+(N)).

The new handler returns the result of the old handler to the caller if the hotkey isn't found. Notice the function call to 01H or 11H doesn't end with an IRET assembly language instruction. This would also retrieve the flag register from the stack, which was stored there as part of the calling INT instruction. This in turn would change the zero flag's contents, which indicates the availability of a key. The call ends with the VAR RET 2 instruction, which executes a FAR return to the caller just like IRET, but clears the flag register (2 bytes) from the stack without loading it.

If the hotkey is found, the program begins execution. All subsequent calls to 00H/10H or 01H/11H return a character from the macro buffer, instead of calling the old handler to get a keystroke from the keyboard buffer. This can be located using the MSTART variable, which can contain as many characters as you like. The MEND label must also be available. This indicates the offset address where macro playback ends. When this is reached, the old handler functions are called again and keystrokes are taken from the keyboard buffer.

The macro buffer contains only the ASCII character codes, not the scan codes. The value 0 is always returned as the scan code since most programs ignore this value.

Although this saves a lot of work when defining the macro text, it also makes using the extended keyboard codes in the macro text impossible. If necessary, you can always load both the ASCII code and the scan code in the macro buffer so both will be returned to the caller.

Redirecting keyboard hardware interrupts

If you want to access the keyboard at its lowest level, you must capture and redirect keyboard hardware interrupt 90H. We suggest using the existing handler since writing a completely new keyboard handler is a difficult task (refer to the KEYB.COM program using DEBUG).

Capturing scan codes

The GETSCAN.ASM program is a normal transient program that displays scan codes. It lets you view the scan codes of your keyboard on screen before they are actually routed to the keyboard handler. In this way, you can obtain the two byte make code sequences of the F11 and F12 function keys and the gray cursor keys, which are otherwise masked by the software.

Running the program in normal operating mode displays only make codes. If you start GETSCAN from the system prompt with the /R switch, break codes will also be displayed.

The main section of this program is the new interrupt handler for keyboard interrupt 09H, which executes each time the user presses or releases a key. The make or break code is received through port 60H and stored in the program's internal scan code buffer (the SCANBUF variable). It's managed as a ring buffer with two pointers, just like the BIOS keyboard buffer. These pointers are called SCANNEXT and SCANLAST.

After the scan codes are stored, the program reverts to the old interrupt handler. The address of this handler was noted at the start of the program. This processes the keystrokes in the usual way and stores them in the keyboard buffer.

This is important because the keyboard buffer contents are read within the program using BIOS functions 01H and 00H until the user presses the Enter key. Once Enter is pressed, the program ends. Otherwise, the main program continues to read the internal scan code buffer between two BIOS calls. Whatever the new interrupt handler stores in the scan code buffer is immediately read by the main program and removed. The scan codes and break codes aren't lost until the program displays them on the screen.

This program enables you to read the scan codes that your keyboard uses and check for any differences from the standards. You may find some differences on the less expensive imported keyboards, but these differences usually involve seldom used key combinations.

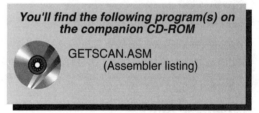

You'll find the following program(s) on the companion CD-ROM

GETSCAN.ASM
(Assembler listing)

Programming The Keyboard Controller

The keyboard is an independent unit in the PC system and has its own microprocessor and memory. The processor informs the system when a key is pressed or released. It does this by sending the system a scan code when a key is pressed or released. In both cases, the key is indicated by a code, which depends on the position of the key. These scan codes aren't related to the ASCII or extended keyboard codes to which the system later converts from the keypresses.

Communication with the system is performed over two bi-directional lines using a synchronous serial communications protocol. In addition to the actual data line used to transfer the individual bits, the clock line synchronizes the periodic transmission of signals. Transfers are made in one-byte increments, whereby a stop bit is transmitted first (with the value 0), followed by the eight data bits, beginning with the least significant bit. A parity bit, calculated using odd parity, follows the eighth data bit. Byte transfer then concludes with a stop bit, which forms the eleventh bit of the transfer. At both ends of the communications line (i.e., in the PC and in the keyboard itself) are devices that convert the signals on the data line to bytes and back again.

Although all types of PCs use this form of communication, we must distinguish between PC/XT and AT models. These systems use different processors as keyboard controllers. The Intel 8048 used in PC and XT keyboards is a relatively "dumb" device, which can only send scan codes to the system. However, the 8042 processor used in AT, 80386 and 80486 keyboards can do much more. With this processor, the communication between the system and the keyboard becomes more complex and the system can even control parts of the keyboard.

For the keyboard, the basis of this communication is represented by a status register and input buffer and output buffers. The buffers transfer the following:

> ➢ Keyboard codes that correspond to pressing or releasing a key.

> ➢ Data the system requests from the keyboard.

These buffers can be accessed at port 60H on the AT.

The input buffer can be written at port 60H as well as port 64H. The port that is used depends on the type of information to be transferred. If the system wants to send a command code to the keyboard, the code must be sent to port 60H, while the corresponding data byte must be sent to port 64H. Both end up in the keyboard input buffer, but a flag in the status register indicates whether a command byte (port 64H) or a data byte (port 60H) is involved.

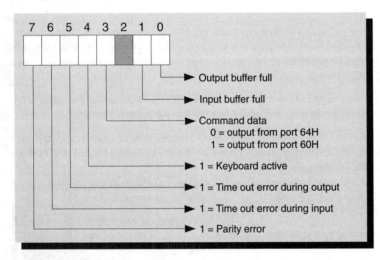

In addition to this flag, bits 0 and 1 of the keyboard status register are especially important for communication with the keyboard. Bit 0 indicates the status of the output buffer. If this bit is 1, then the output buffer of the keyboard contains information that hasn't been read from port 60H yet. Reading from this port will automatically set this bit back to 0, indicating there is no longer a character in the output buffer.

Bit 1 of the status register is always set whenever the system has placed a character in the input buffer, before this character is processed by the keyboard. Nothing should be written to the keyboard input buffer unless this bit is equal to 0, which indicates the input buffer is empty.

Typematic rate

Of the various commands that a system can send to the keyboard, two are important to applications because they also play a role outside a keyboard interrupt handler. The first of these commands sets the typematic (repeat) rate of the keyboard. This is the number of make codes per second the keyboard will send to the system when a key is pressed and held down. It can be between two and 30 codes per second. To prevent the keys from repeating unintentionally, this repeat function doesn't begin until after a certain delay. This delay time can be set by the user and is encoded in binary as follows:

The keyboard will observe these times with a tolerance of 20%.

The repeat rate is also encoded in binary. The following table shows the relationship between the repeat (typematic) rate and the number of repetitions per second.

Coding for AT keyboard delay rate	
Code	Delay rate
00b	1/4 second
01b	1/2 second
10b	1/4 second
11b	1 second

Typematic rate codes for the AT keyboard							
Code	RPS*	Code	RPS*	Code	RPS*	Code	RPS*
11111b	2.0	10111b	4.0	01111b	8.0	00111b	16.0
11110b	2.1	10110b	4.3	01110b	8.6	00110b	17.1
11101b	2.3	10101b	4.6	01101b	9.2	00101b	18.5
11100b	2.5	10100b	5.0	01100b	10.0	00100b	20.0
11011b	2.7	10011b	5.5	01011b	10.9	00011b	21.8
11010b	3.0	10010b	6.0	01010b	12.0	00010b	24.0
11001b	3.3	10001b	6.7	01001b	13.3	00001b	26.7
11000b	3.7	10000b	7.5	01000b	15.0	00000b	30.0
*Repetitions per second							

This relationship may seem somewhat arbitrary at first, but it does follow a mathematical formula. The binary value of bits 0, 1 and 2 of the repeat rate form variable A and the binary value of bits 3 and 4 form variable B:

```
(8 + A) * 2B * 0.00417 * 1/second
```

The delay and repeat rate values are combined into a byte by placing the five bits of the repeat rate in front of the delay value. However, we can't simply send this value straight to the keyboard. First we must send the appropriate command code (34H) and then the repeat parameters. Both bytes must be sent to port 60H, but we cannot send them with an OUT instruction.

We must use a transmission protocol that includes reading the keyboard status and which also accounts for the possibility the transfer might not work the first time. Since we must do this for both bytes, we should write a subroutine to do it. The structure of this subroutine is shown in the flowchart on the following page.

Sending bytes to the keyboard

First we load an error counter that allows the routine to try to send the byte three times before an error is returned. Then the keyboard status port is read in a loop until bit 0 is cleared and the input buffer of the keyboard is empty. Then we can send the character to port 60H. To ensure the character was received (a parity error might have occurred, for example), the keyboard sends back a reply code. This has been received when bit 1 of the keyboard status port is set.

Programming steps for sending a byte to the keyboard

This register is read from port 64H in a loop until this condition is met. Now we can read the reply to our transmission from the keyboard data port. If it is the code 0FAH (acknowledge), the transmission was successful. Any other code indicates an error, which tells the subroutine to decrement the error counter and repeat the entire process, if the counter hasn't reached zero. In this case, the subroutine ends and signals an error to the caller.

*Program
flowchart-byte
transfer from
keyboard*

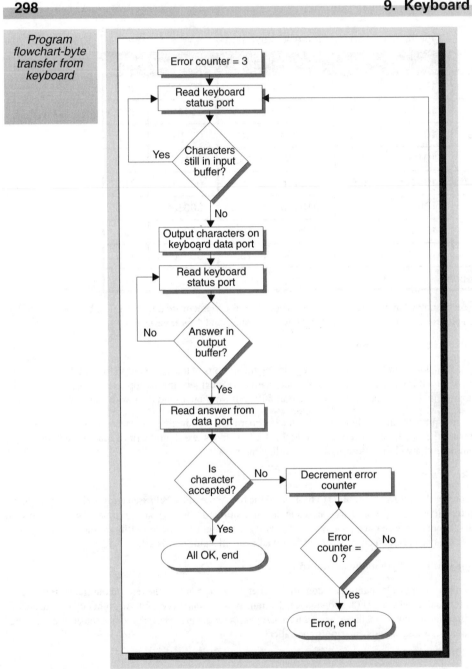

Demonstration programs

To give you an example of how this works, we've included the TYPMP.PAS, TYPMPA.ASM and TYPMC.C programs on the companion CD-ROM. They can be used to set the key repeat parameters on your keyboard. The heart of these programs is an assembly language routine that sends the parameters to the keyboard. This routine contains the subroutine we just discussed, which is first called to send the SetTypm instruction to the keyboard. Another call is used to send the parameters themselves.

The key repeat rate and the delay values are specified as separate parameters, following the program name entered at the DOS prompt.

We also included the listing of the assembly routines for the various programs. The Pascal program includes these with INLINE statements; the linker links these statements to the C version of the program.

You'll find the following program(s) on the companion CD-ROM

TYPMPA.ASM (Assembler listing)
TYPMCA.ASM (Assembler listing)
TYPMP.PAS (Pascal listing)

To see the effect of the key repeat rate, first try setting the smallest repeat rate (0) and then the highest rate (30). Try pressing and holding a key at each of these settings to see the results.

LEDs

We can use this same method to switch the LEDs on the AT keyboard on and off. The corresponding instruction code is number 0EDH and is called the Set/Reset Mode Indicators instruction.

Bit Number	LED
0	Scroll Lock
1	Num Lock
2	Caps Lock
3-7	Unused

After this command code has been successfully transmitted, the keyboard waits for a byte that reflects the status of the three LEDs. One bit in this byte represents one of the three LEDs, which is switched on when the corresponding bit is set. Setting and resetting these bits is useful only when the keyboard mode, which they indicate, is enabled or disabled.

These modes are managed in the BIOS instead of the keyboard. For example, the keyboard doesn't automatically convert all the letters to uppercase in Caps Lock mode. The keyboard can only associate a key with a virtual key number instead of a specific character. This key number is then converted to an ASCII or extended keyboard code by the BIOS. Obviously this also applies to the Caps Lock key, which simply sends a scan code to the computer when it's pressed. The BIOS assigns the Caps Lock function to this key by setting an internal flag that marks this mode as active, then sends the Set/Reset Mode Indicators instruction to the keyboard to switch on the appropriate LED.

Although these keyboard modes are usually enabled and disabled by the user pressing the corresponding keys, it may be useful to set a mode from within a program. This applies to keyboards that have separate cursor keys and a numerical keypad, for example. Since most keyboards can only enter numbers when Num Lock mode is on, it makes sense to set this mode automatically when the system is started.

To do this we simply set the appropriate BIOS flag and then switch on the corresponding LED on the keyboard to inform the user that this mode has been activated.

In practice, a program simply must set the appropriate BIOS mode, since the BIOS automatically controls the keyboard LEDs. Whenever one of the functions of the BIOS keyboard interrupt is called, the BIOS checks to see whether the status of the LEDs matches the keyboard status, as indicated in an internal variable. If an inconsistency is found, the BIOS automatically sets the LEDs to the status given in the keyboard status flag.

Since the position of this flag in the BIOS variable segment and the meaning of the individual bits is completely documented (see Chapter 3), we can easily change these modes.

The LEDB.BAS, LEDP.PAS and LEDC.C programs which you'll find on the companion CD-ROM offer routines that can enable or disable the individual modes. Although PCs and XTs have corresponding LEDs, these programs won't work or change the modes without changing the status of the LEDs on a PC or XT keyboard. This is because these keyboards are equipped with an 8048 processor, which doesn't offer the ability to manage the LEDs. The fact these LEDs do switch on and off according to the modes isn't related to the BIOS and is handled directly by the keyboard.

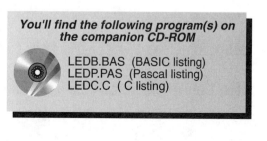

You'll find the following program(s) on the companion CD-ROM

LEDB.BAS (BASIC listing)
LEDP.PAS (Pascal listing)
LEDC.C (C listing)

Chapter 10

Joysticks

Because of the recent improvements in video cards and joysticks, PC versions of many video games have become popular. In this chapter you'll learn how joysticks are connected to the PC, how to "read" the joystick from your own programs, and how the BIOS can help you adapt programs for joysticks.

Three demonstration programs for this chapter (which you'll find on the companion CD-ROM) show how joystick reading works in BASIC, Pascal, and C.

Connecting joysticks

The PC's hardware usually isn't configured to accept joysticks. An additional expansion card provides the hardware needed to implement joystick control. This card, called a *game control adapter* or simply a *game card*, is usually a half-size expansion card that plugs into one of the PC's expansion slots. Although these cards usually contain two connectors for two joysticks, usually you'll need only one.

The PC uses analog joysticks. This means that you can't simply use the joysticks from your old game machine or home computer and plug them into the PC; those joysticks are digital. The analog joystick handles a variety of information that isn't sensed by the digital joysticks, such as intensity. However, you'll see that this feature can sometimes be a disadvantage.

PC joysticks are equipped with two buttons that can be read independently of one another, and can be utilized to fit the software application. A few PC joysticks even have special purpose buttons (e.g., for rapid fire).

Reading Joysticks From BIOS

You don't need software drivers to monitor the joysticks because both the hardware and software interfaces were defined in the early stages of PC design. Hardware ports 200H to 20FH are reserved for a game card. The BIOS refers to the default values provided by these ports.

Two functions are available for software interfacing. These functions (sub-functions 00H and 01H) can be accessed from interrupt 15H, function 84H. They execute a joystick check using the polling method, which takes the current joystick position and joystick button status directly from the hardware ports.

However, the joysticks can be monitored only with the polling method because a special hardware interrupt, which executes when the user moves the joystick or presses a button, is assigned to the joystick cards. So, a program equipped for joystick access continually depends on sub-functions 00H and 01H for joystick movement.

Determining the joystick position

The joystick position can be determined by placing 84H in the AH register and 01H in the DX register, which calls function 84H, sub-function 01H. If the carry flag contains 0 after calling interrupt 15H, the BIOS supports the function (i.e., a game port exists), and joystick position data can be found in the AX, BX, CX, and DX registers.

The first joystick's position is conveyed by the contents of the AX and BX registers (indicating X-position and Y-position, respectively). The second joystick's position is indicated by the contents of the CX and DX registers (again, indicating X-position and Y-position).

The contents of these registers also indicate whether a joystick is connected to the port. If a stick is connected, the corresponding registers return values other than 0. So, if you find the CX and DX registers contain 0 after executing the function, a second joystick is connected. This rule also applies to the first joystick: If the AX and BX registers return 0, there isn't a first joystick.

Values other than 0 represent the joystick's position along the corresponding axis. However, there isn't a standard for these values. The values depend on the *potentiometers* (variable resistors, similar to the volume knob on a radio or television) contained in the joystick, which convert the joystick's position into a voltage. Different joysticks from different manufacturers and even different joystick models made by the same manufacturer return different voltages.

Many joystick oriented programs begin by prompting the user to move the joystick to the upper-right and the lower-left corners of the screen. This helps determine the range of movement offered by the potentiometers. Our in-house joysticks offer a range from 10 to 120 in the X-position, and from 9 to 102 in the Y-position. However, other joysticks may produce different values. It's important to remember that X-position values ascend from left to right, and the Y-position values ascend from top to bottom (not from bottom to top).

Though it would be easy to assume the joystick movement could be transformed into a linear coordinate system after simply determining its value range, this isn't true. The potentiometers in most joysticks operate exponentially rather than linearly.

Exponential operation means the center position of the joystick doesn't correspond to the median value of the value range. The demonstration programs at the end of this chapter will demonstrate this as you run them and test your joystick.

To avoid the problems that result from the exponential measurements of the potentiometers, many programs avoid implementing joystick coordinates in a linear coordinate system. For example, a game such as PacMan needs to recognize only four directions for game object movement (up, down, left, and right).

This type of application checks the joystick's position at the beginning of the program (i.e., the center position). From there, the application needs to compare only the center position with the current joystick values to determine the direction of movement. However, you cannot determine the intensity of the movement by using this method.

Reading the joystick buttons

In addition to the joystick position, the two joystick buttons are important to program operation.

The joystick position can be determined by placing 84H in the AH register and 00H in the DX register, thus calling function 84H, sub-function 00H. If the carry flag contains 0 after calling interrupt 15H, the BIOS supports the function (i.e., a game port exists), and the bits of the AL register indicate the status of the four available buttons on a set of two joysticks. The button being pressed sets the corresponding bit to a value of 1.

If the joystick buttons are arranged one above the other, the top button will be considered the first, and the lower button will be considered the second. When the joystick buttons are arranged side by side, the left one is considered the first, and the right one the second.

The following illustration shows the values of the AL register:

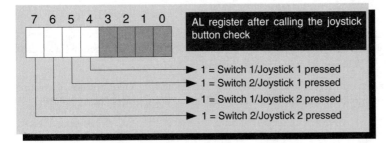

When working with this function, remember that it doesn't have a buffer function. So, it displays only the current joystick button status. If the user briefly presses a button when a joystick button check isn't being performed, the program won't sense the input and won't react to the user's action. So, if your program intends to use these buttons, it's especially important to permanently monitor the joystick button status in your programs using sub-function 00H.

Demonstration Programs

The three demonstration programs in BASIC, Pascal, and C read joystick position and button status using the GetJoyPos and GetJoyButton functions. Within the main program, these functions are used to first determine the joystick's minimum and maximum positions.

The program prompts the user to press the joystick up and right, and press a joystick button while the stick is in this position. This informs the program which joystick is being used (if two joysticks exist).

The program then prompts the user to press the joystick down and left, and press a joystick button while the stick is in this position. The program converts this range into the 80 columns and 25 rows of the text screen, and the current joystick position is calculated and indicated by an uppercase X. The resistance values yielded by the potentiometers are displayed in the upper-left corner of the screen, so the user can see how the joystick operates.

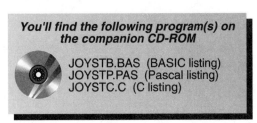

You'll find the following program(s) on the companion CD-ROM

JOYSTB.BAS (BASIC listing)
JOYSTP.PAS (Pascal listing)
JOYSTC.C (C listing)

The program ends when the user presses both joystick buttons simultaneously.

Chapter 11

Mouse Programming

Using a mouse for PC applications was considered a luxury a few years ago. Today, however, most applications require that you use a mouse. One reason for the mouse's popularity is the development of new and more powerful video standards such as EGA, VGA, and Super VGA. These video cards helped advance graphical user interfaces, such as Microsoft Windows. These interfaces are almost unusable without a mouse.

Applications and operating systems benefit from mouse support. Ventura Publisher and Microsoft Works both use the mouse extensively. Also, DOS Version 4.0 accepts mouse as well as keyboard input.

A software interface acts as the connection between a program and the mouse. Although Microsoft Corporation designed this interface for its own mice, other mouse manufacturers accept this interface as a standard. The interface was made available to the industry as a minimum standard to retain compatibility with the Microsoft mouse.

This function interface is usually installed either through a device driver that is loaded during system boot or through a terminate and stay resident (TSR) program, such as MOUSE.COM, that's included with the Microsoft mouse package.

Mouse Functions

Mouse functions can be accessed in the same way as DOS and BIOS functions (refer to Chapters 14 and 8 for more information on the techniques used for addressing DOS and BIOS functions). The individual functions can be called through interrupt 33H. The identification number of the function must be passed to the AX register. The other processor registers are used in various combinations to pass information to a function.

Although 53 different functions can be called in this way, most applications use only a few of these functions. Before we examine each function, let's look at the concepts behind the mouse interface. This will help you understand how the individual functions work. In our discussion, we deliberately concentrated on text oriented mouse control. Pixel oriented applications should use a graphical interface, such as the Windows API, because this interface provides friendlier functions for mouse input than the programming interface found in this chapter.

In the following table we've listed the functions found on mouse drivers up to and including Version 8.0. You'll find more than enough functions needed for mouse control in a text oriented application.

Function	Task	Version
00H*	Reset mouse driver	01
01H*	Display mouse cursor	01
02H*	Hide mouse cursor	01
03H*	Get cursor position/button status	01
04H*	Move mouse cursor	01
05H*	Determine number of times mouse button was activated	01
06H*	Determine number of times mouse button was released	01

Function	Task	Version
07H*	Set horizontal range of movement	01
08H*	Set vertical range of movement	01
09H	Set mouse cursor (graphic mode)	01
0AH*	Set mouse cursor (text mode)	01
0BH*	Determine movement values	01
0CH*	Set event handler	01
0DH	Enable light pen emulation	01
0EH	Disable light pen emulation	01
0FH	Set cursor speed	01
10H*	Exclusion area	01
11H	Undocumented	01
12H	Undocumented	01
13H*	Set maximum for mouse speed doubling	01
14H	Exchange event handlers	01
15H	Determine mouse status buffer size	01
16H*	Store mouse status	01
17H*	Restore mouse status	01
18H*	Install alternate event handler	01
19H	Determine address of alternate event handler	01
1AH	Set mouse sensitivity	01
1BH	Determine mouse sensitivity	01
1CH	Set mouse hardware interrupt rate	01
1DH*	Set display page	01
1EH*	Determine display page	01
1FH	Disable mouse driver	01
20H	Enable mouse driver	01
21H	Reset mouse driver	01
22H	Set language for messages	01
23H	Get language number	01
24H	Determine mouse type	01

Function	Task	Version
25H	Get general driver information	06
26H	Get maximum virtual coordinates	06
27H*	Get masks and mickey counts	7A
28H	Set video mode	07
29H	Count video modes	07
2AH	Get cursor hotspot	7B
2BH	Set acceleration curves	07
2CH	Read acceleration curves	07
2DH	Set/get active acceleration curves	07
2EH	Undocumented	01
2FH	Mouse hardware reset	7B
30H	Set/get ballpoint information	7C
31H	Get minimum/maximum virtual coordinates	7D
32H	Get active advanced functions	7D
33H	Get switch settings	7D
34H	Get MOUSE.INI location	08

Legend:

*= Commonly used function (detailed in this chapter)

01 = Version 1.0 and up   7B = Version 7.02 and up

06 = Version 6.26 and up   7C = Version 7.04 and up

07 = Version 7.0 and up   7D = Version 7.05 and up

7A = Version 7.01 and up   08 = Version 8.0 and up

About mouse buttons

Unlike the keyboard, which has many keys and keyboard codes for each key, a PC mouse usually has two or even three mouse buttons. These buttons enable the user to select data in an application program.

The mouse buttons are also used to move the mouse cursor on the screen. The actual position of the mouse cursor on the screen is important. The mouse driver software always interprets the cursor's location on the screen relative to a virtual graphic screen. This virtual screen's resolution depends on the video mode and video card currently being used.

Since this virtual graphic display screen is also used within the text modes to determine the mouse's position and forms the basis for communication with the mouse interface, a conversion occurs between the graphic coordinates and the mouse cursor's line/column position. Since every column or line corresponds to eight pixels, the graphic coordinates must be either be divided by eight or shifted three places to the left in binary mode, which mathematically produces the same result. However, the processor performs the shifting much faster than it can perform the actual division.

About the mouse cursor

The mouse cursor shows the mouse's relative location on the screen. The cursor's shape can vary depending on the application and it can even change its appearance within an application. Word processors often display the mouse cursor as a block, similar to the text cursor. In text mode, the application can only determine the starting and ending line of the cursor. The cursor's size depends on the current character matrix and video mode. The options for creating a software cursor are more complicated because two 16-bit values, called the screen mask and cursor mask determine the cursor's appearance.

The mouse driver must determine the appearance of the cursor each time the cursor's position on the screen changes. The cursor mask and screen mask values are linked with the two bytes that describe the character code and the character color within video RAM. This linkage occurs in two steps. First, the character code and the attribute byte are combined with screen mask through a binary AND. The result of this connection is then combined with the cursor mask through an exclusive OR. The result then appears on the screen.

This type of combination provides several options for changing the cursor's appearance. Four of the most common cursor options are:

➢ Pointer appears as one specific character in one specific color.

➢ Pointer appears as one specific character, but the color changes when the cursor overlaps a character (e.g., inverse video).

➢ Pointer appears as one specific character, but the character color changes when the cursor overlaps a character.

➢ Pointer appears as one specific character, but character color changes to a variant of the character color when the cursor overlaps a character.

Formation of mouse cursor by combination of current character, cursor and screen mask

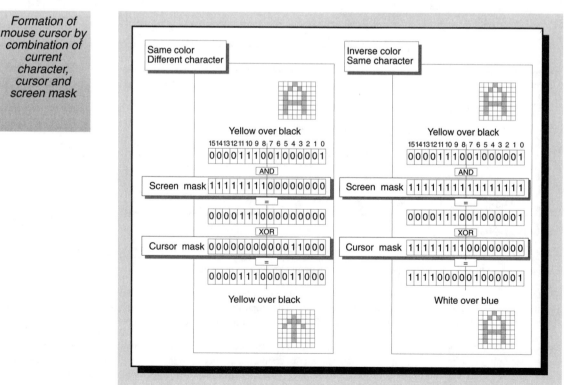

The standard measurement unit in the mouse interface is the *mickey*, which is named after Mickey Mouse. Originally one mickey equaled 1/200". This measurement applies to older systems, which have a resolution of 200 pixels per inch. Newer mice and video cards have mickey measurements of 400 mickeys per inch. Although the mouse driver compensates for additional pixel information, we'll use this as the measurement standard in this chapter.

Function 00H: Reset mouse driver

A program should call the function 00H before calling any of the mouse functions. This function resets the mouse driver. It can also determine whether a mouse and mouse driver exist by examining the content of the AX register after the function call. If the AX register contains the value 0000H after the function call, a mouse driver wasn't installed. Even if a mouse is connected, the mouse driver no longer exists. If a mouse driver and mouse exist, function 00H returns the value FFFFH in the AX register. The BX register contains the number of buttons on the mouse. As we mentioned, PC mice usually have two mouse buttons, although some mice have three buttons. Since very few applications need or use three buttons, usually you'll only need two buttons.

Function 00H resets the numerous mouse parameters to their default values. The mouse cursor moves to the center of the screen. The cursor mask and screen mask are defined so the cursor appears as an inverse video rectangle. Video page 0 is selected as the default page on which the cursor appears. The cursor disappears from the screen immediately.

Function 01H: Display mouse cursor

Function 01H displays the cursor on the screen. Load the function number into the AX register; additional parameters aren't needed. Since the mouse driver follows the movement of the mouse even when the mouse cursor has been disabled, the mouse cursor may not reappear at the position where it was when it disappeared.

Function 02H: Remove mouse cursor

Function 02H removes the mouse cursor from the screen. Load the function number into the AX register; additional parameters aren't required. The calls between functions 01H and 02H must be performed in the proper sequence to be effective. For example, calling function 02H twice in succession means that you must also call function 01H twice in succession to return the cursor to the screen.

Functions 01H and 02H aren't used very often. Usually, you simply must call function 00H and function 01H at the beginning of a program and call function 02H at the end of the program. These functions are frequently used when the application program writes characters directly into video RAM, bypassing the slow DOS and BIOS display routines. Avoid writing characters over the mouse cursor; otherwise the following will occur:

1. The mouse cursor disappears if overwritten by another character.

2. The mouse driver produces the wrong character on the screen when the user moves the mouse cursor. Before the cursor appears at a certain position on the screen, it records the character that occupied this position until now. This character is restored to the old position as soon as the cursor moves to another position on the screen. During a direct write access to video RAM, the driver doesn't record that a new character was output at the position of the cursor. So, the old (and incorrect) character is displayed on the screen while the cursor is moved.

To prevent this from happening, remove the cursor before character output and return the old character to the screen. The new character will be stored when the cursor is restored to the screen. However, don't do this for every character output because it slows the system down and negates the advantages of direct access to video RAM. We recommend removing the cursor once from the screen before extensive output, such as construction of a screen window. After the operation, the cursor can be restored on the screen.

Although the DOS and BIOS character output functions write their output directly to video RAM, you shouldn't worry about programming the cursor when working with these functions. During installation, the mouse driver moved interrupt vector 10H, which handles BIOS and DOS screen output, to its own routine. So, the driver can then display or disable the cursor as needed.

Function 04H: Move mouse cursor

With function 04H you can move the mouse cursor to a specific location on the screen without moving the mouse. Pass the function number to the AX register, the new horizontal coordinate (column) to the CX register, and the new vertical coordinate (line) to the DX register. Remember these coordinates, like all other functions, must be relative to the virtual screen. Text coordinates must be multiplied by eight (or shifted left three binary places) before they can be passed to function 04H. The coordinates must be located inside a screen area designated as the mouse's range of movement.

Function 00H sets the complete range of the mouse's movement to the entire screen area. Functions 07H and 08H limit this range to a smaller area.

Function 07H & 08H: Set range of movement

Function 07H specifies the horizontal range of movement. Pass the function number to the AX register, the minimum X-coordinate to the CX register, and the maximum X-coordinate to the DX register. Function 08H specifies the vertical range of movement. Pass the function number to the AX register, the minimum Y-coordinate to the CX register and the maximum Y-coordinate to the DX register.

After calling these functions, the mouse driver automatically moves the cursor within the range, unless it's already within the indicated borders. The user cannot move the cursor outside this range.

Function 10H: Exclusion area

Besides the area of movement allotted to the cursor, the mouse driver also provides an exclusion area. When the user moves the cursor into this section of the screen, the mouse cursor becomes invisible. The mouse cursor becomes visible again as soon as the user moves the cursor away from the exclusion area. This area is undefined after the call of function 00H. It can be defined at any time by calling function 10H, but the mouse driver can control only one exclusion area at a time. The coordinates of the exclusion area are passed to function 10H in the CX:DX and SI:DI register pairs. These register pairs specify the upper-left corner and lower-right corner respectively. CX and SI accept the X-coordinate, and DX and DI accept the Y-coordinate.

The exclusion area and function 02H perform special tasks during direct access to video RAM. Although function 02H removes the cursor from the screen, this can occur in conjunction with function 10H only if the cursor is already within the exclusion area, or if the user moves the cursor within the exclusion area. This makes function 10H useful when creating large display areas (e.g., a window). This allows the cursor to remain on the screen as long as it isn't within this exclusion area.

The exclusion area can be removed by calling function 01H or function 00H. Function 01H makes the cursor visible automatically if it's already within the exclusion area.

Function 1DH: Set display page

Function 1DH sets the display page on which the cursor appears. This function is needed only if the program switches a display page other than the current one to the foreground through direct video card programming. Pass the number of the display page to the BX register. When BIOS interrupt 10H activates a display page, this function can be omitted because the mouse driver will automatically adapt to the change.

Function 0FH: Set cursor speed

Two parameters determine the speed at which the mouse cursor moves on the screen. These parameters specify the relationship between the distance of a cursor movement and the pixels traversed in the virtual mouse display screen. Function 0FH allows the user to set these parameters for horizontal and vertical movement. The parameters are passed in the CX and DX registers (horizontal and vertical, respectively). These numbers indicate the number of mickeys, which correspond to eight pixels in the virtual mouse display screen. These pixels correspond to one line or column in the text mode display screen.

The default values after calling function 00H are 8 horizontal mickeys and 16 vertical mickeys. In text mode, the cursor moves one column after the cursor is moved 8 mickeys horizontally. A jump to the next line occurs only after the cursor is moved 16 mickeys vertically.

Usually these settings can be used as default values because they work with all resolutions in text mode. This function also enables you to make the cursor movement faster or slower.

Function 0AH: *Set cursor shape*

Function 0AH determines the appearance of the cursor in text mode. The cursor mask and screen mask mentioned earlier are determining factors of the cursor's appearance in text mode. Pass 0AH to the AX register and the value determining the cursor's shape to the BX register.

Software-specific cursor

If the BX register contains the value 0, the mouse driver selects the cursor as specified by the software. The screen mask number must be loaded into the CX register and the cursor mask number must be loaded into the DX register. These numbers indicate the addresses from which the mouse driver can access cursor shape parameters.

Hardware-specific cursor

If the BX register contains the value 1, the mouse driver selects the cursor as specified by the hardware. The starting line of the hardware cursor must be loaded into the CX register, and the ending line must be loaded into the DX register.

Video mode and cursor size

Remember the allowable values for the starting line and ending line depend on the video mode currently in use:

➤ The monochrome display adapter accepts values from 0 to 13.

➤ The color graphics adapter accepts only values from 0 to 7.

➤ EGA and VGA cards accept values from 0 to 7. The EGA/VGA BIOS automatically adapts the number selected to the size of the character matrix currently in use.

The functions we've discussed set the various parameters that control the mouse driver. The mouse driver also supports a group of functions that read the mouse's position as well as the status of the mouse buttons. These functions can be divided into two categories for reading external devices, such as the mouse, keyboard, printer, or disk drives. These categories are the polling method and the interrupt method. The mouse driver supports both of these methods.

Polling method

The polling method constantly reads a device within a loop. This loop terminates only when the desired event occurs. Since the execution of this loop requires the full capabilities of the CPU, usually there isn't enough time left to perform other tasks.

Interrupt method

The interrupt method has an advantage over the polling method because it allows the CPU to execute other tasks until the desired event occurs. Once this happens, the mouse driver calls an interrupt routine that reacts to the event and executes further instructions.

Function 03H: *Get cursor position/button status*

The polling method provides four functions that operate in conjunction with the mouse interface. These functions can be accessed through function 03H, which returns the current cursor position and mouse button status. Function 03H passes the horizontal cursor position to the CX register and the vertical cursor position to the DX register. Since these coordinates also refer to the virtual mouse screen, they must be converted to the text screen's coordinate system by dividing the components by eight, or by shifting the bits three binary places to the right.

The following illustration shows how the mouse button status is returned to the BX register. Only the three lowest bits represent the status of one of the two or three mouse buttons. The bit for the corresponding mouse button contains the value 1 when the user presses that mouse button during the function call.

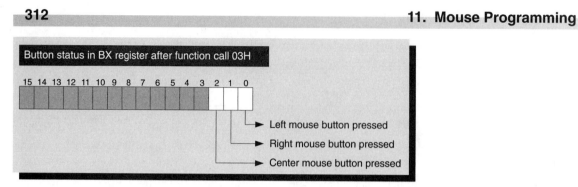

Function 0CH: *Set event handler*

Function 0CH sets the address of a mouse event handler (interrupt routine). The function number must be passed to the AX register. The segment and offset address of the event handler must be passed to the ES:DX register pair. The event mask must be passed to the CX register. The individual bits of this flag determine the conditions under which the event handler should be called. The following illustration shows the CX register coding:

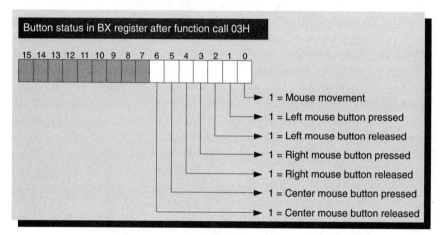

After executing the function, the mouse driver calls the event handler when at least one of the specified events occurs. The call is made using the FAR call instead of the INT instruction. It's important to remember this difference when developing an event handler; the handler must be ended with a FAR RET instruction instead of an IRET instruction. Similar to an interrupt routine, none of the various processor registers can be changed when they're returned to the caller. Therefore, the registers must be stored on the stack immediately after the call and the register contents must be restored at the end of the routine.

Information is passed to the event handler from the mouse driver through individual processor registers. The information about the event can be found in the AX register, in which each bit has the same significance as in the event mask during the call of function 0CH (see the previous table). Individual bits, which have no meaning for the event handler, may be set. For example, if the event handler should be called only when the left mouse button is activated (bit 1), bits 0 and 4 may also be set during the event handler call. This is possible because the mouse was moved and the right mouse button was released simultaneously.

The event handler can obtain the current button status from the contents of the CX register. The coding is identical during the call to the function 03H. Bits 0 to 2 represent the different mouse buttons. The current cursor position can be found in the CX and DX registers, which represent the horizontal and vertical positions. The position can only be set after conversion to the text screen's coordinate system.

During the development of an event handler, the DS register should point to the data segment of the mouse driver during the handler call, instead of the interrupted program. If the event handler accesses its own data segment, it must first load its address into the DS register.

Function 18H: *Install alternate event handler*

Function 18H allows you to install an event handler, which reacts to limited-range keyboard events as well as mouse events. This function signals an event if the Ctrl, Alt or Shift keys are pressed when a mouse button is pressed or released. This function is almost identical in register assignments to function 0CH. The event mask in the CX register has been extended by the three events, as shown in the following illustration:

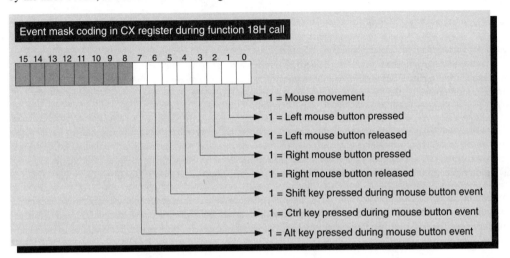

Even during the call of such an alternative event handler, little changes in comparison with the event handlers that were installed by calling function 0CH. Only the content of the AX register must be interpreted differently, since its construction corresponds to the event mask previously shown.

Up to three alternative event handlers can be installed by calling function 18H. During the function 0CH call, the event handler indicated replaces the previously installed handler. Three different event handlers can be installed by calling function 18H three times. This is only valid if the three event handlers are equipped with different event masks. If an event mask passes to function 18H, which is already equipped with a handler, the new handler replaces the existing handler.

Demonstration Programs

This section contains programs in C and Turbo Pascal that demonstrate mouse access functions. These programs show the techniques for developing and installing an event handler, which is the most complicated part of mouse reading. Both programs include functions or procedures that call various mouse functions. These routines require little programming. They load the processor registers with the necessary values, then call interrupt 33H. Since the event handler needs the most programming, we'll discuss this in detail.

Installing an event handler in a higher level language program is difficult because it must meet certain requirements, which usually cannot be controlled by a programmer. The requirements are as follows:

➢ The event handler must be a FAR procedure, and must be terminated with a FAR RET instruction.

➢ The event handler must store the various processor registers during the call and restore them before completion.

➢ The event handler must load the segment address of the higher level language data segment into the DS register to provide access to global variables of the program.

Although these requirements can be met in some versions of Turbo Pascal, Turbo C, and Microsoft C, very complex programming is required. The traditional solution (write a routine in assembly language) is easier and faster to implement. Therefore, we wrote the event handler itself in assembly language, assembled the program, and linked the resulting object module to the higher level language program.

This assembler routine is named AssmHand. It stores the various processor registers on the stack after the call, then calls a C function or Pascal procedure named MouEventHandler. The AssmHand routine passes arguments provided by the mouse driver to the MouEventHandler routine. These arguments include:

➤ The event flag, which describes the event that caused the handler call.

➤ The current mouse button status.

➤ The current position of the mouse cursor.

This information is converted from virtual graphic screen coordinates into text screen coordinates (25 lines x 80 columns). The stack handles parameter passing. The C version of AssmHand must pass the arguments onto the stack in the reverse order of their declaration. After loading the DS register and calling the higher level language routine, these arguments must be taken from the stack again by incrementing the stack cursor by the memory requirements of the arguments (8 bytes). This is only required for the C version of the routine. The Turbo Pascal version performs this task on its own.

After calling this routine, the AssmHand routine returns the processor registers to the stack and passes control to the caller using a FAR RET instruction. The AssmHand instructions execute very quickly, but the handler itself may require more execution time than expected. This introduces the problem of recursion, since an event in connection with the mouse may recur during the handler execution. The AssmHand driver then must be recalled before the previous call is terminated.

To avoid this situation and the complications that can occur, AssmHand maintains a variable named active in its code segment. During execution this variable contains the value 1. Before setting this variable, the program tests if active already contains the value 1. This indicates the last call wasn't completed yet. If this situation occurs, the handler execution terminates immediately, thus avoiding recursion.

Even if this method avoids recursion problems, remember that it can produce its own problems. The suppression of the higher level language handler doesn't notice the event, because the handler wasn't called by the mouse driver. Although we offer the recursion trap as an option, we recommend that you program the higher level language handler as efficiently as possible to avoid using processor time. This will keep call suppression to a minimum.

The AssmHand handler

AssmHand must first be installed through function 0CH, using the MouISetEventHandler procedure/function. MouISetEventHandler is called by the MouInit procedure/function, which initializes the mouse module. This should be called by any application program as the first procedure/function of this module. The number of lines and columns of the display screen must be passed to it as arguments, to determine the size of an internal buffer needed for the various procedure/functions within the module.

This buffer can divide the screen into individual mouse ranges, each equipped with its own code, cursor mask, and screen mask. These mouse ranges are very important in mouse access. They permit the definition of objects such as sliders, command buttons, or menu items. As soon as the user moves the cursor to an object and presses a mouse button, the object executes a particular step in the program.

MouDefRange defines these ranges. The registration of these ranges occurs through the procedure/function MouDefRange, which must receive a cursor to a vector or array, and the number of elements stored there. These elements of the type RANGE describe a screen area and the cursor or screen mask assigned to the cursor as soon as it reaches this area. An area can comprise a single character or the entire screen. The user can define the array with individual area descriptors. The area code depends on the position of the descriptor within the array, and is provided automatically by the procedure/function MouDefRange. The first area has the value 0, the second the value 1, etc. The screen areas not covered by an area descriptor are assigned the code NO_RANGE.

During the creation of this array, especially during the definition of the cursor and screen mask in the PtrMask array, the C implementation provides helpful macros and constants. The Pascal program has functions and constants available for this purpose. The creation of a variable of the type PTRVIEW, stored in the PtrMask field within an area descriptor, is handled by the macro or function MouPtrMask. The cursor and screen mask for the character must be passed to MouPtrMask to define the cursor's appearance on the screen.

If PtrSameChar is indicated, the cursor appears as the character that it covers. If another cursor is desired, the cursor can be defined with PtrDifChar. When the call occurs, enter the ASCII code of the desired character for PtrDifChar. As a second parameter, MouPtrMask receives the cursor's color from the cursor mask and screen mask. Many options for color are possible:

> PtrSameCol ensures the cursor assumes the color of the character currently overlapped by the cursor.

> PtrSameColB creates a cursor that assumes the color of the character currently overlapped. However, bit 7 of the attribute byte is set to 1 so the character either blinks or appears with a high-intensity background color.

> PtrInvCol makes the cursor appear in the inverse color of the character currently overlapped by the cursor.

> PtrDifCol displays the cursor on the screen in the color indicated by the code following PtrDifCol.

In addition to the different mouse areas specified through MouDefRange, a cursor can be assigned to the remaining screen, which is the area carrying the code NO_RANGE. A program can use MouSetDefaultPtr to obtain the cursor and screen mask of the cursor as a parameter of type PTRVIEW. The constants and macros or functions previously described can be used to create this parameter.

Changing the mouse cursor

The MouEventHandler changes the cursor and screen mask for each area. Since it's called for every mouse event (including mouse movement), it can determine the mouse area where the cursor is currently located. To make this happen as fast as possible, it tests if the mouse area contains the position of the cursor.

MouEventHandler uses the internal region buffer that was created by MouInit during the call. It reflects exactly the video RAM structure, and contains one byte for every screen position. Each byte contains the code of the area to which the screen position was assigned. The event handler can use the current position of the cursor as an index to this area buffer. A single memory access is enough to determine the mouse area in which the cursor is located. The area code found is stored in the global variable MouRng, and is used as an index to the array of the mouse descriptor from which it determines the cursor and screen mask for this area.

The higher level language event handler has another assignment that may be even more important. It controls the variable MouEvent, in which the current mouse events are stored. This task cannot be performed by simply copying the mouse events that were passed through AssmHand from the mouse driver. This only shows the current event, but no preceding events. If the user presses and holds the left mouse button, then presses the right mouse button, this results in two event handler calls. This signals each case of an active mouse button. The preceding call (the active left mouse button) is no longer recognized by the call, since it reports only the current event (the depressed right mouse button).

The event handler must isolate the various events that are reflected in the EvFlags variable, and accept only new events in the MouEvent variable. This variable reflects the current status of the mouse buttons, and the cursor's current movement or position. MouEvent can handle the most important mouse sensing tasks, waiting for the occurrence of a certain event (usually a pressed mouse button). MouEventWait waits for the occurrence of an event, which was specified by the bitmask that was passed earlier. This bitmask can be defined through the logical OR function with the following constants:

EV_MOU_MOVE   Mouse movement

EV_LEFT_PRESS   Left mouse button pressed

EV_LEFT_REL   Left mouse button released

EV_RIGHT_PRESS   Right mouse button pressed

EV_RIGHT_REL   Right mouse button released

You'll find the following program(s) on the companion CD-ROM

MOUSEP.PAS (Pascal listing)
MOUSEPA.ASM (Assembler listing)
MOUSEC.C (C listing)
MOUSECA.ASM (Assembler listing)

The procedure/function can be instructed to wait for one or more of these events to occur. The AND or OR correspond to the logical comparisons of the same names. Which events occur can be sensed through the results of a bitmask in which the individual bits represent the various events, and through which the constants previously described can be sensed.

Mouse - PC Communication

Let's briefly look at how the physical movements and button accesses of the mouse are translated into information the computer understands. The method of data transfer depends on the manufacturer of the mouse, and the way the mouse interfaces with the computer. A serial mouse operates differently from a bus mouse. Since the serial mouse is more common than the bus mouse, we'll discuss only the serial mouse.

The mouse driver determines whether a mouse is connected during its initialization. For a Microsoft mouse, the mouse driver sets the serial port's DTR (DTR = Data Transfer Ready) line to 1. The mouse recognizes this signal and sends the ASCII code for the letter M over the data line. The driver doesn't wait very long for this return message. This is why a Microsoft-compatible mouse may not always work with the Microsoft mouse driver. Although the mouse is set up to transfer data according to the Microsoft protocol, the driver may not recognize the mouse if the "M" isn't sent promptly.

Once successful handshaking has been established, the mouse uses the interrupt method to transfer its information to the driver. The mouse executes a hardware interrupt at the serial port as soon as it needs to inform the driver about a movement or button status change. The interrupts used are 0CH (COM1) or 0DH (COM2). The mouse driver diverts the interrupts to a routine of its own so it can read mouse data directly from the serial port. The data transfer for a Microsoft mouse uses the following parameters: 1200 baud, 7 data bits, no parity bit. Each mouse message consists of three bytes that indicate the mouse button status and the relative movement of the mouse since the last data transmission. The distance for mouse movements is measured in mickeys. Depending on the video card and mouse resolution, one mickey can be either be 1/200 or 1/400 of an inch.

As the following illustraton shows, only 7 bits are available to describe mouse movement along the X and Y axes. This allows us to cover distances between -128 and +127 mickeys. At the very latest, the new mouse position must be sent when the mouse moves outside this range. Generally, a new message will be sent much sooner than this.

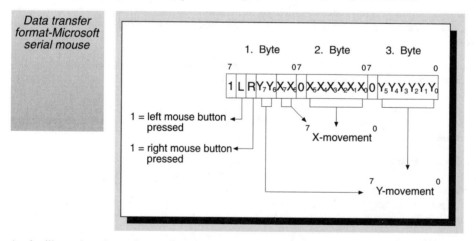

Data transfer format-Microsoft serial mouse

As the illustration above shows, the Microsoft format is limited to two mouse buttons. The highest bit is reserved for synchronization with the mouse driver. This prevents the mouse driver from getting the second or third byte of the message first when the hardware interrupt fails and the first one or two bytes are lost. The high bit in the first byte is always set to 1 and the high bits of the other two bytes are always set to 0.

Other mouse manufacturers that use three buttons use a different communication format (e.g., eight data bits instead of seven). This extra bit allows transmission of the third mouse button's status. The other principles of communication are basically the same; the mouse is still connected to a serial port and the serial port interrupts communicate with the driver.

Chapter 12

Memory Expansion

When the IBM PC was being developed in 1980, its capabilities were quite advanced at the time. This was also true of its main memory size. The maximum size of 640K seemed so large in the early 1980s that no one could imagine what a user would do with so much memory. Thus, the first PCs were equipped with 64K, then 128K, and later 256K of memory. Today memory requirements continue to increase. The minimum amount of RAM for PCs has grown to 640K.

As we enter the age of Pentium microprocessors, graphical user interfaces, and multitasking operating systems, 640K simply isn't enough memory to use the full capabilities of your PC. But we've reached a boundary that cannot be crossed by simply adding more memory chips to the computer. This boundary is the 1 megabyte limit, set by the 8086 microprocessor's addressing capabilities.

Another important factor affecting memory is compatibility. To maintain program compatibility in machines ranging from the simplest XT to a fully equipped Pentium, the processors must be compatible and the memory layouts of each machine must meet certain standards. In this chapter we'll examine ways to access alternate forms of memory.

The following illustration shows the basic memory configuration of the PC. Notice only the first 640K can be used for RAM storage. Any memory beyond that point is reserved for video RAM, hardware enhancements and the BIOS.

Memory can easily be enlarged beyond the one megabyte limit. Today most computers come equipped with 2 megabytes or more of RAM, but this memory cannot be addressed under DOS. Because DOS operates in real mode, memory beyond the 1 megabyte limit cannot be accessed.

There are many solutions for this RAM crisis. Memory needs can be handled by expanded memory and extended memory. These types of memory can increase memory capacity by many megabytes (providing the software can use this capacity).

Before we continue, let's clear up the confusion between expanded memory and extended memory. Since the two terms sound very similar, it's easy to forget which memory performs which task.

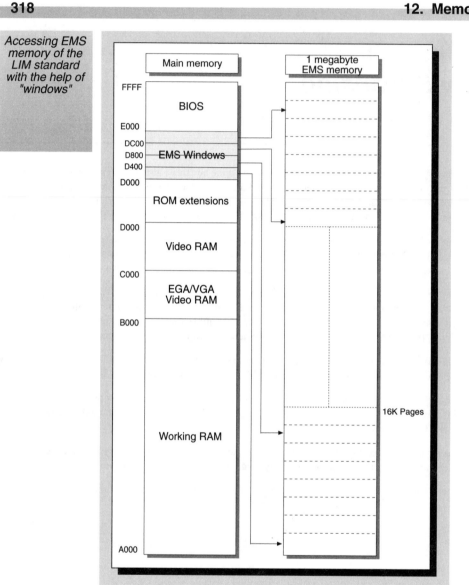

Accessing EMS memory of the LIM standard with the help of "windows"

Expanded memory

Expanded memory is the additional memory you'll find in PC/XT computers. Because of the 8088 processor, these computers are limited to 640K of working RAM. With expanded memory, RAM beyond the 640K boundary can be used. Remember that expanded memory expands RAM beyond 640K.

Extended memory

Extended memory is the additional memory found on 80286 and higher end computers. This memory extends beyond the 1 megabyte boundary.

Let's take a closer look at each memory type.

Expanded Memory

A PC or a PC/XT machine is limited to 640K of conventional memory. 80286 based computers are limited to 16 megabytes of RAM. However, those 16 megabytes are only available when the PC is running in Protected mode (see Chapter 36 for more information), which makes the memory inaccessible to DOS programs.

Several years ago some leading PC firms worked together to devise a way to add more memory, which could also be accessed under DOS, to PCs, XTs, and ATs. These companies were Lotus (the developers of Lotus 1-2-3), Intel (manufacturer of PC processors), and Microsoft (developers of MS-DOS and OS/2). They developed the LIM standard; "LIM" represents the first letters of the company names.

This standard allows up to 8 megabytes to be added to a PC on an expansion card. Only 64K of this 8 megabytes is visible in the 1 megabyte address range of the 8088 processor, in a window called the page frame. Memory installed in this manner is called expanded memory. This memory shouldn't be confused with the extended memory that goes beyond 1 megabyte on an AT. The entire system is referred to as the Expanded Memory System (EMS).

The LIM standard used the reliable trick of bank switching for memory access. Bank switching creates a small memory window, through which a portion of expanded memory can be accessed beyond the address space of the computer. The total addressable memory capacity may extend over several megabytes. The software works with the hardware, moving this window to permit access to the portion of memory currently needed. The remaining memory stays invisible to the program.

Opening the memory window

At least 64K in the 1 megabyte address space of the PC is unused by conventional memory, BIOS, video RAM, or other system expansions. The EMS developers decided to use this as a window into expanded memory. Usually this window lies at segment address D000H, but EMS hardware allows this window to be relocated.

Since this window is under the 1 megabyte memory limit, it can be accessed with normal assembly language instructions, similar to video RAM access. Both read and write accesses are possible. We'll look at specific examples of these accesses later in this chapter.

Page frame division

The page frame is further divided into 16K pages. This allows the programmer to access four completely different pages in EMS memory.

The EMS card's registers allow the programmer to set which pages of the EMS memory will be visible in the page frame. The address lines on the EMS card are programmed so the EMS pages are mapped into the page frame and appear in the 8088's address space. This process is the bank switching we mentioned earlier in this chapter.

Besides the hardware, the EMS also includes a software interface, which handles EMS register programming and other memory management tasks. This software interface, called the EMM (Expanded Memory Manager), provides a standard interface that you can use to access EMS cards from different manufacturers. This also applies to the extended EMS standard (EEMS) developed by AST Research, Quadram and Ashton-Tate, which surpasses the LIM standard.

The best known examples of EEMS are 386-To-The-Max (Qualitas), QEMM-386 (Quarterdeck), and Microsoft Windows. Windows' 386 enhanced mode makes its applications available in expanded memory, where Windows stores extended memory.

The above products are based on a special 80386 operating mode, called the virtual 8086 mode. This mode lets you move memory from above the 1 megabyte barrier into conventional memory, and give this memory the look and feel of a normal page frame. Compared to a conventional hardware implementation, this immediately provides several advantages:

➢ Without EMS emulation, this memory is accessible as extended memory.

➢ Because hardware addressing or I/O addressing isn't required, EMS access and switching between pages occurs very quickly.

➤ Lower cost (EMS cards usually cost more than software emulation).

➤ One more expansion slot is free than there would be with true EMS memory.

This EMS emulation is possible with the 80386 microprocessor and its successors; it's also possible on 80286 machines but speed is decreased. Many Asian AT manufacturers offer the option of using extended memory as expanded memory by using the NEAT (New Enhanced AT) chips available from Chips & Technologies Corporation. These chips allow hardware to view extended memory as expanded memory, without installing a special enhancement card.

The software interface between the EMM and a program resembles many other software interfaces found in the PC environment.

History of the LIM standard

While most programs appear on the market with a starting version number of 1.0, EMS Version 1.0 never existed; actually it never left the laboratory. When Intel and Lotus presented their proposal for an EMS standard in the spring of 1985, Version 3.0 already existed. Microsoft joined the other two firms shortly after this release because they could use a capability of this type for their own products.

Version 3.2 was released in the fall of 1985. The EMS standard became the LIM standard. A few weeks later, a group of firms comprising AST, Quadram, and Ashton-Tate presented their own EMS standard, called the Enhanced Expanded Memory Specification (EEMS). This standard was based on EMS Version 3.2, but offered few advantages over EMS other than the ability to use page frames larger than 64K. EMS 4.0 now supports such capabilities, and EEMS is part of computing's past.

EMS 3.2 became a big success and received support from many well-known manufacturers. Lotus promoted the sale of EMS memory cards because EMS enabled Lotus 1-2-3 to handle very large spreadsheets. TSR (Terminate and Stay Resident) programs, RAM disks, and other utilities also used expanded memory. Microsoft eventually provided EMS support beginning with MS-DOS Version 4.0.

EMS Version 4.0

With its 14 functions, EMS Version 3.2 satisfied all the needs of software developers. EMS Version 4.0, released in the fall of 1987, had 58 functions available for enhanced hardware support. This release included the following features:

➤ Memory support for 32 megabytes instead of 8 megabytes.

➤ Ability to generate EMS windows at any location in addressable memory.

➤ Any size EMS windows, instead of the 64K required by earlier versions.

➤ EMS pages that can be protected from a system crash or an accidental reset, which increased the value of EMS based RAM disks.

Version 4.0 makes greater demands on the EMS hardware than earlier versions. This may be why Version 4.0 hasn't become very popular and Version 3.2 remains the standard for EMS programming. Therefore, we'll concentrate primarily on EMS Version 3.2

EMS Version 3.2

The Expanded Memory Manager (EMM) enables the programmer to access EMS memory. We mentioned the major changes between Versions 3.2 and 4.0 earlier in this chapter. However, you'll probably use only a few Version 3.2 functions in EMS programming.

We'll concentrate on EMS Version 3.2 in this book because this version is considered the standard for expanded memory. If you want more information about Version 4.0, EMS Version 4.0's functions are documented in the Appendices on the companion CD-ROM.

The EMM

Similar to DOS interrupt 21H, which provides a standard interface to the operating system functions, EMM functions can be called through interrupt 67H. Before a program tries to use EMS memory and the corresponding EMM, it should first check to ensure that an EMS is installed. If it doesn't do this and there is no EMM, the results of a call to interrupt 67H are completely unpredictable. The call simply may not work or the system may crash.

To prevent this from happening, a program that uses the EMS must first check to ensure that EMS exists. This can easily be done when you consider the EMM is bound into the system as a normal device driver when the computer is booted. So, it naturally has a driver header that precedes it in memory and defines its structure for DOS. The name of the driver is found at address 10 in the driver header. The LIM standard requires that this name be EMMXXXX0.

The example programs at the end of this chapter test for this name by first determining the segment address of the interrupt handler for interrupt 67H. If the EMM is installed, the segment address points to the segment into which the EMMXXXX0 device driver was loaded. Since the driver header is at offset address 0, relative to the start of this segment, we simply compare the memory locations starting at 10 with the name EMMXXXX0 to determine whether the EMS memory and the corresponding EMM are installed.

Once this is verified, this memory can be accessed in three steps:

1. As conventional memory must be allocated with a DOS function, a program must first allocate a certain number of EMS pages for itself from the EMM. The number of pages to be allocated depends on both the memory requirements of the program and how much EMS memory is available.

2. If the desired number of pages were successfully allocated, the specified pages must first be loaded into one of the four pages of the page frame so data can be written into them or read from them. This results in a mapping between one of the allocated pages and one of the four physical pages within the page frame.

3. When the program ends or it's finished using EMS, the allocated pages should be released again. If this isn't done, the allocated pages will still be owned by the program (even after it ends) and cannot be given to other programs.

As with DOS interrupt 21H, the function number of an EMM call must be loaded into the AH register before the interrupt call. After the function call this register contains the error status of the function. The value 0 signals the function was executed successfully, while values greater than or equal to 80H indicate an error.

About errors

The Appendices on the companion CD-ROM mentions the error codes which are listed in the error descriptions. However, you should be aware of one particular error. If the value 84H is in the AH register after a call to EMM interrupt 67H, this indicates that an invalid function number was passed in the AH register.

The table on the right lists the functions which are needed for a transient program to access the EMS memory.

To ensure the EMS hardware and the EMM operate properly, check the EMM status before allocating EMS memory. This is done with function 40H, which only requires the function number in the AH register. If it returns the value 0 in the AH register, then everything is OK and you can start working with the EMS memory.

Function	Task
40H	Get EMM status
41H	Get segment address of page frame
42H	Get number of pages
43H	Allocate EMS pages
44H	Set mapping
45H	Release EMS pages

Limits to EMS allocation

The number of allocatable EMS pages is limited by the number of free pages. So, you should ensure the memory requirements of the program don't exceed the available memory. Here we can use function 42H, which returns the number of free EMS pages. This function requires only the function number and returns the number of unallocated pages in the BX register. It also returns the total number of installed EMS pages in the DX register.

If enough EMS memory exists for our program, or if the memory requirements are adapted to the available memory, then we can allocate the memory. The number of pages to be allocated must be passed to function 43H in the BX register. If the requested number of pages is successfully allocated (AH register contains 0 after the function call), the caller will find a handle to the allocated pages in the BX register. This handle, which must be used to access the allocated pages, identifies the caller to the EMM. The caller must save this handle. If the handle is lost, the allocated pages cannot be accessed and can no longer be released. A program can call this function several times to allocate multiple logical page blocks.

Once we have the page handle we can start accessing the pages. The handle is passed to the appropriate functions in the DX register. This also applies to function 44H, which maps a logical page to one of the four physical pages of the page frame. The number of the logical page is passed in the BX register and the physical page number in the AL register. Note that both specifications start at zero. So, if you've allocated 15 pages, then the numbers of the logical pages run from zero to 14.

Once the appropriate page is in the page frame, it can be accessed like normal memory. The offset address of the start-of-page is calculated from the physical page number, but the corresponding segment address must be determined with an EMM function. Since this address doesn't change while working with the EMS memory, you can read it once at the beginning of the program and then save it in a variable. Function 41H returns the segment address of the page frame in the BX register.

Function	Task
46H	Get EMM version number
47H	Save current mapping
48H	Reset saved mapping
49H	Get number of EMM handles
4AH	Get the number of pages allocated to a handle
4BH	Get all handles and numbers of allocated pages

When you're finished using the EMS, you must return the allocated pages to the EMM. Simply pass the page handle to function 45H.

In addition to these six functions, which a normal program can use to access EMS memory, the table on the right shows more functions which can be useful under certain circumstances.

Version numbers

Reading the EMM version number is important because the LIM standard has changed slightly since it was introduced. Some functions are no longer supported and new functions have been added. The functions presented here are from Version 3.2, which has been replaced by Version 4.0. Version 3.2 represents a good compromise not only because it's widely used, but also because it's completely compatible with Version 4.0. If you don't want to support earlier or later EMS versions in your program, you should check the version number at the start of the program. The version number will be returned in the AL register after a call to function 46H. It's encoded as a BCD number.

Functions 47H and 48H are important for TSR programs that want to use the EMS memory. When a TSR program interrupts a transient program and places itself in the foreground, it must consider the interrupted program may have been using EMS memory and had created a certain mapping. Since this mapping shouldn't be changed when returning to the interrupted program, it must be saved when the TSR is activated and then restored when the TSR exits. Function 08H saves the current EMM mapping and function 09H resets the saved status. The handle of the function must be passed to both functions. In this case, it's the handle of the TSR program instead of the handle of the interrupted program.

Since the last three functions are only important to the memory manager, we won't discuss them here. More information can be found in the Appendices on the companion CD-ROM.

Demonstration programs

The EMMC.C and EMMP.PAS programs on the companion CD-ROM Show how to use EMS memory. There isn't an assembly language program because, theoretically, calls to the EMM functions simply involve loading variables and constants into registers and calling the EMM interrupt 67H. By using the information in the Appendices (see the companion

CD-ROM), you should be able to write an assembly language program that uses the EMS. There isn't a BASIC program because EMS memory is intended to be used with complex and memory-intensive applications for which BASIC isn't suited.

Since the two programs are almost identical, we'll discuss only the basic program structure. The programs provide several functions and procedures that can be used to access the various EMM functions. Both programs also contain a function called EMS_INST (or EmsInst), which determines whether an EMM is installed.

In Pascal we encounter a problem because a pointer must be loaded with an address consisting of separate segment and offset addresses. Since this isn't possible in Pascal, there is an INLINE procedure, called MK_FP, that (like the C macro of the same name) combines a segment and an offset address into a (FAR) pointer. Since this is a FAR pointer, the page frame isn't in the program's data segment. So, it cannot be addressed by the DS register. This isn't a problem in Turbo Pascal because the code is generated to work with FAR data pointers. In C, we must ensure the program is compiled in a memory model that uses FAR pointers for data. This occurs in compact, large, and huge models.

The main program firsts tests to determine whether EMM is present. Then it uses various functions to obtain status information about EMS memory, which it displays on the screen. Next, a page is allocated and mapped to the first page (page 0) of the page frame. The current contents of video RAM are copied into this page and the video RAM is then erased.

After the copy procedure, a message is displayed for the user and the program waits for a key to be pressed. Then it copies the old screen contents back to video RAM from page 0 of the page frame and the program ends.

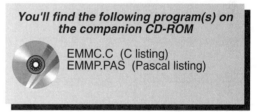

You'll find the following program(s) on the companion CD-ROM

EMMC.C (C listing)
EMMP.PAS (Pascal listing)

This program shows the contents of a page in the page frame can be treated like ordinary data. After you've created a pointer to the corresponding page, you can manipulate the data on this page, including complex objects like structures and arrays, like any other data. It's important to ensure that your objects fit on one page or that you don't forget to change pages or load a new page into the page frame to access larger objects.

Extended Memory

Although EMS access must be performed in portions, placing the PC in protected mode allows access to all of extended memory. In real mode, the extended memory isn't used because the processor cannot address memory beyond the 1 megabyte limit. This explains why 8088 and 8086 based systems cannot use extended memory. These microprocessors recognize only real mode and cannot switch to protected mode.

Changing a single bit in the processor's flag register enables protected mode. Once this is done, a program can access up to 16 megabytes of extended memory, but crashes immediately. This occurs because of the mechanism through which the 80286 and its successors address memory in protected mode. This is completely different from memory access in real mode.

When in protected mode, the processor operates through segment descriptors instead of segment addresses. These segment descriptors point to local and global segment descriptor lists. However, DOS cannot handle this access because it's limited to real mode.

The proper descriptor lists must be created and initialized before you can switch to protected mode. To do this, you must be familiar with assembly language programming and understand how the processor operates in protected mode.

Extended memory address space of a PC

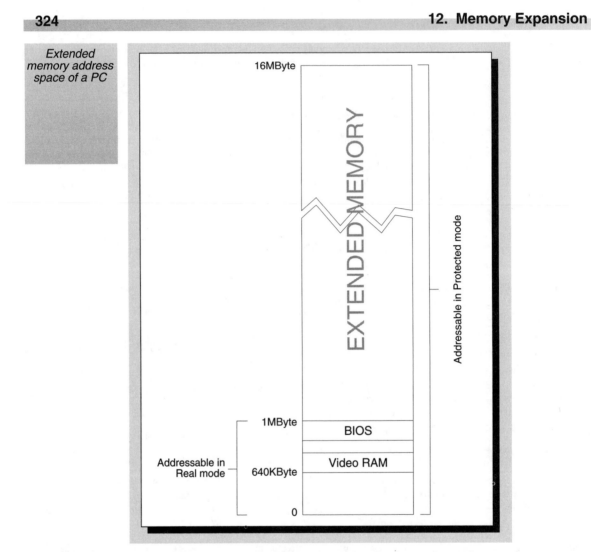

Some BIOS functions and the XMS drivers provide help for extended memory access. The XMS drivers are able to handle extended memory better than the BIOS functions. The drivers can ensure that extended memory is shared instead of limiting all extended memory to a single program.

The fight for access rights to extended memory is a significant problem, which we'll discuss later in this chapter. This problem is especially noticeable if you access extended memory directly. The lowest 64K of extended memory is accessible from real mode (more on this later).

In the following sections, we'll discuss access using BIOS functions, the High Memory Area (HMA), and XMS functions.

Extended memory access from BIOS

Extended memory can be accessed only if it exists. Normally this applies to all computers that have 1 megabyte of RAM because usually only 640K or 512K in the area below the 1 megabyte limit are used. The rest is located immediately above this limit and is therefore available as extended memory.

Function 88H of BIOS interrupt 15H returns the extended memory size. Interrupt 15H was originally intended for the cassette recorder interface (the cassette recorder was the original mass storage device used on the PC). When disk drives replaced the cassette recorder for mass storage, the cassette recorder functions were no longer used.

Interrupt 15H is used for extended memory and joystick reading (see Chapter 10 for information on joysticks). Place function 88H in the AH register. The result, which is placed in the AX register, indicates the extended memory size in kilobytes.

Now that we know extended memory exists on the system, how can we access it? Function 87H moves blocks of memory within the total memory space. This means that blocks of memory can be moved from the area below the 1 megabyte limit to the area above the 1 megabyte limit and vice versa. However, the function shouldn't be used for the latter, since its call is complicated and has other disadvantages. To access memory beyond the 1 megabyte barrier, the processor must be switched to protected mode. Function 87H requires very comprehensive information, since the 80286 processor is more difficult to program in protected mode than in real mode (8086 emulation under DOS). At the end of this section you'll find a program that demonstrates how to use function 87H.

The function number 87H first must be passed to the AH register, then the number of the words to be moved (only words only, not bytes) must be passed to the CX register. A maximum value of 8000H corresponds to a maximum value of 64K.

Global Descriptor Table

The ES:SI register pair receive the address of the GDT (Global Descriptor Table) (Global Descriptor Table (GDT)), which must be installed in the user program. The GDT describes the individual memory segments of the 80x86 in protected mode. The segments in protected mode are exempt from the limitations made in real mode. While segments can only start at memory locations divisible by 16 in real mode, protected mode segments may start at any memory location. Also, protected mode segments may be any size from 1 byte to 64K.

Another protected mode innovation is the access code defined for every segment. This code indicates whether the segment described is a data segment or a code segment (only code segments can be executed). The access code also contains information on access priority and whether access is even permitted. Each segment descriptor consists of 8 bytes. During its call, function 87H expects that six segment descriptors have been prepared in the GDT (i.e., memory space reserved for them). The illustration below shows which segment descriptors are involved and the construction of a segment descriptor.

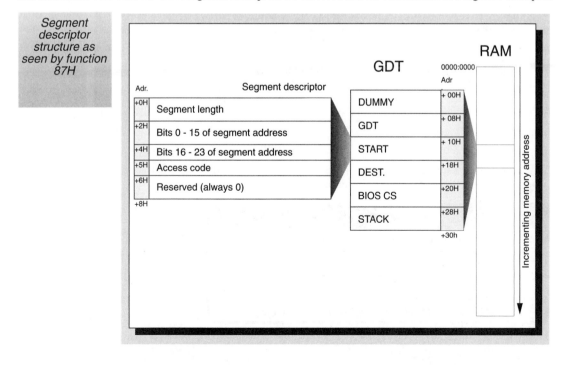

Segment descriptor structure as seen by function 87H

Since the BIOS functions fill out the other descriptors, we're only concerned with the segment descriptors designated as "start" and "destination". The start descriptor describes the segment, from which the data are taken. The destination descriptor describes the segment into which the data are copied.

The length of both segments can be 0FFFFH (64K decimal), even if fewer bytes (or words) copy over in the process. If a lower value is indicated, the number of bytes (number of words multiplied by 2) to be copied cannot exceed this amount. Otherwise, the processor notices an access across a segment boundary during copying, which triggers an error.

The address of the two memory areas must be converted to a (physical) 24-bit address. The lower 16 bits of this address enter the second field of the segment descriptor and the upper 8 bits enter the third field. Access code 92H can be used, which informs the processor the described segment is a data segment with the highest priority, the segment exists in memory, and the segment can be written. The last field of the descriptor maintains compatibility with the 80386 processor this field should always contain the value 0.

Although the address of the user program's buffer remains fixed, the address beyond the 1 megabyte boundary, to which data should be copied, can be freely selected (subject to RAM availability). The following table shows the addresses of the various 1K blocks beyond the 1 megabyte border as 24-bit addresses:

```
0K   = 100000H              124K   = 11F000H
1K   = 100400H              125K   = 11F400H
2K   = 100800H              126K   = 11F800H
3K   = 100C00H              127K   = 11FC00H
4K   = 101000H              128K   = 120000H
5K   = 101400H              129K   = 120400H
6K   = 100800H              130K   = 120800H
7K   = 100C00H              131K   = 120C00H
8K   = 102000H              132K   = 121000H
9K   = 102400H              133K   = 121400H
              . . . . . . . . .
              . . . . . . . . .
              . . . . . . . . .
60K  = 10F000H              252K   = 13F000H
61K  = 10F400H              253K   = 13F400H
62K  = 10F800H              254K   = 13F800H
63K  = 10FC00H              255K   = 13FC00H
64K  = 110000H              256K   = 140000H
65K  = 110400H              257K   = 140400H
66K  = 110800H              258K   = 140800H
67K  = 110C00H              259K   = 140C00H
68K  = 111000H              260K   = 141000H
69K  = 111400H              261K   = 141400H
```

After the function call, the carry flag indicates the success of the function call. If the carry flag is set, an error occurred. The value in the AH register indicates the cause of the error:

Error number	Cause of error
AH = 0	No error (carry flag reset)
AH = 1	RAM parity error
AH = 2	GDT defective at function call
AH = 3	Protected mode could not be properly initialized

A disadvantage of this function is that, while the processor is in protected mode, all interrupts must be suppressed. While in protected mode, BIOS interrupts (e.g., timer or keyboard) can be called, but these routines were designed to be used in real mode only. So, these interrupts may not work properly in protected mode.

This disadvantage is evident when you call the timer. Since its interrupts are suppressed, protected mode doesn't keep track of the time. So time remains frozen for a moment. If programs frequently call function 87H, the clock may slow down by 20 or 30 seconds per day. However, since the clock can be reset to the proper time with software, most of these disadvantages can be avoided.

The execution speed of this function (slow) is more important than interrupt suppression. This is especially true for ATs, which are equipped with an 80286 processor. Although ATs can easily be switched to protected mode, switching back to real mode is more difficult. Since an instruction that smoothly switches the system back to real mode doesn't exist, a processor reset must be used.

An 80286 reset can only be triggered through the keyboard controller. A six millisecond delay occurs between the time the controller receives the reset instruction and the time the controller responds to the instruction. Those six milliseconds can be an eternity in a 10 MHz, 12 MHz, or 16 MHz computer. Unfortunately, this still isn't the solution. Although the processor does change to real mode after the reset, the system begins program execution with the boot code from BIOS.

To prevent this reboot process, a memory location in the BIOS RAM receives a code before triggering the reset. This code informs BIOS of the purpose of the reset. BIOS then returns to the caller of function 87H. However, this process requires a lot of computer time.

PS/2 systems handle this shift more smoothly, even if the systems are equipped with 80286 processors. The PS/2 includes special circuitry that makes a smooth transition from protected mode to real mode.

The 80386, 80486 and Pentium machines switch between modes easily, proving that Intel Corporation made the appropriate improvements to their processors.

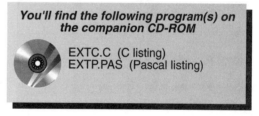

You'll find the following program(s) on the companion CD-ROM

EXTC.C (C listing)
EXTP.PAS (Pascal listing)

Demonstration programs

The EXTP.PAS and EXTC.C programs in Pascal and C copy data between buffers in extended memory.

Conflicts in extended memory

Theoretically, extended memory should be shared by programs. However, some cache programs or other utilities may want to use all existing extended memory. This can cause memory overwriting by other programs and system crashes.

This problem is caused by a lack of control. A program that can help other programs coexist in extended memory is needed. The BIOS causes this problem. BIOS function 88H informs every program that all of extended memory is available. The BIOS cannot allocate single memory blocks.

The XMS standard provides some solutions to this problem (more on this later). This standard, which was developed in 1988, is based on the XMS standard. Two different procedures help avoid collisions in extended memory, but don't always succeed.

The first and most powerful method (the INT 15 method) redirects the interrupt vector of interrupt 15H so it points to its own handler instead of the original interrupt handler in ROM BIOS.

The new interrupt 15H handler should concentrate on controlling function 88h, which checks the size of extended memory. The handler redirects the interrupt call to the original handler as soon as the function number confirms that another function should be called.

If function 88H is called, the caller receives the amount of extended memory currently available (not the current size of extended memory). Function 88H subtracts the amount of extended memory being used from the total extended memory size. This ensures the caller uses only the available extended memory.

Because the caller must also assume the extended memory starts at the 1 megabyte border, the previously installed program must protect itself from the caller. The existing program is located at the end of extended memory instead of at the 1 megabyte limit. The caller views the starting location of the installed program as the end of extended memory.

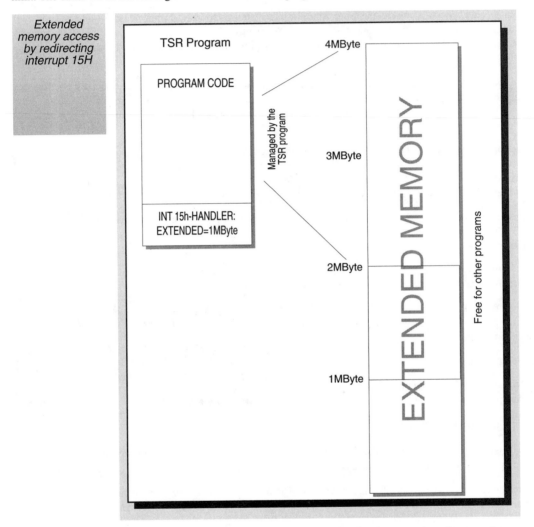

Extended memory access by redirecting interrupt 15H

The second method of extended memory control is frequently used by developers and tends to create new problems in programming.

This VDISK method was first used in the VDISK device driver. VDISK is a RAM disk that can use extended memory for file storage. You'll find VDISK available on MS/PC-DOS starting with Version 3.0. VDISK stores its data starting at the 1 megabyte border, instead of isolating itself from other programs.

VDISK won't overwrite memory reserved using the INT 15 method. However, programs called after VDISK will overwrite VDISK unless the subsequent programs can use the area at the end of extended memory. This is only possible through extensive testing, which are based on a knowledge of memory design under DOS.

The VDISK file header has a structure that's peculiar to all mass memory devices operating under DOS. This header contains status information and a small data structure, which can be designated as a BIOS Parameter Block (see Chapter 14 for more information about BPBs). This block lets you calculate the size of a storage medium and the length of the RAM disk currently in extended memory.

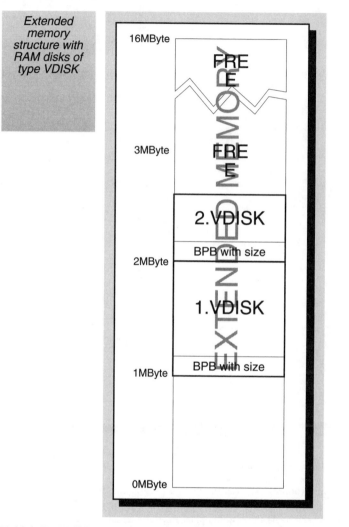

Extended memory structure with RAM disks of type VDISK

Multiple RAM disks complicate the search for available extended memory. We recommend that you always use an XMS driver for extended memory access, because this search doesn't work for every available type of RAM disk (more on this later).

Direct HMA access from real mode

The High Memory Area (HMA) is the first 64K of extended memory. The HMA is the only portion of extended memory that can be accessed (indirectly) from real mode without switching to protected mode. Although various sources credit either Microsoft or Intel with developing the HMA, the additional 64K for real mode is a great discovery.

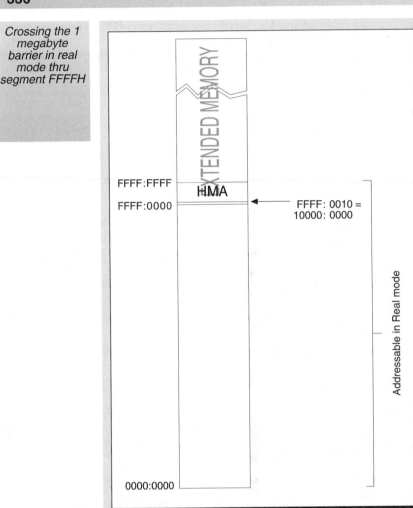

Crossing the 1 megabyte barrier in real mode thru segment FFFFH

How can we access memory locations that actually lie outside the address space of the microprocessor?

The answer lies in the way 80x86 processors form physical addresses, in real mode, from a segment address and offset address. Remember the segment address is multiplied by 16, then the segment and offset addresses are added. If the last segment in the address space of the PC (segment FFFFH) is the segment address, this places offset address 000FH in the physical addresses beyond the 1 megabyte limit. This places you in extended memory in real mode, and you can still access the conventional RAM below the limit.

Since the HMA starts with offset 00010H instead of offset 0000H, you'll find the HMA is smaller than 64K (65,520 bytes). This memory is more than enough to store data and short TSR programs.

Steps required for HMA access

A program that accesses the HMA should first ensure that HMA access is possible. If an 80x86 processor is located, we can continue because this indicates the A20 address line and extended memory exist.

Next, calling BIOS function 88H of interrupt 15H determines how much extended memory exists. HMA access is possible only if a minimum of 64K is available in extended memory.

Address line must be disabled from interfacing with the keyboard controller, and BIOS must enable address line A20 before HMA access can occur. This address line is usually disabled because some programs rely on address overflow at the 1 megabyte limit. This wraparound at address FFFF:0010 usually returns you to the start of conventional memory (address 0000:0000).

Address overflow with address line A20 disabled

Enabling address line A20 affects the keyboard controller as well as the switch from protected mode. On a system reset, the A20 switch occurs through the keyboard controller's output port. Bit 1 of this port must be set to 1 to make the A20 address line transparent, and set to 0 if a memory overflow occurs at the 1 megabyte limit. This bit cannot be easily accessed the keyboard must receive the instruction to disable access to the output port. Also, the controller requires specific parameters in communication. Refer to Chapter 14 for detailed information on how this communication works.

A normal PC with an ISA (Industry Standard Architecture) bus uses the keyboard output port for controlling the status of address line A20. With PS/2 systems and computers upgraded to an 80386 using the Intel InBoard, this line must released using other methods.

A test should confirm the condition of the A20 address line. This is important because if this line isn't free, access to HMA cannot occur. With a small trick this can be determined, without a doubt, because a blocked line indicates an identical memory area through the address overflow at the 1 megabyte limit, such as the memory areas starting at FFFF:0010 and 0000:0000. By comparing the first bytes (e.g., the first 256) in this area, equality can be determined between the two, which proves that A20 is disabled.

Three routines are needed before you can work with the HMA:

➢ A routine to determine the existence of at least 64K of extended memory.

➢ A routine to switch address line A20.

➢ A routine to test address line A20 through memory comparison.

Demonstration programs

The HMAP.PAS and HMAC.C demonstration programs on the companion CD-ROM below contain all three routines for HMA access. These programs, written in Pascal and C, provide a foundation on which you can build other HMA programs. Since all future HMA access should occur through the XMS driver (see Section 12.2.4), these demonstration programs don't test for VDISK compatible RAM disks. If this test doesn't exist, HMA access could overwrite the contents of the RAM disk. So, before starting one of these programs, ensure that a RAM disk doesn't exist in external memory. If a VDISK device or cache program exists, remove them, then run the demonstration program.

Both programs are based on the three routines mentioned above. We call these routines HMAAvail, Gate20, and IsA20On. These programs couldn't be developed in high level languages. So, we wrote them in assembly language and prepared them as INLINE commands (for the Pascal implementation) and as an assembly language module named HMACA.ASM (for the C implementation).

Both programs try to access HMA. If HMA cannot be accessed, the programs display an error message. A pointer of type FAR points to the beginning of the HMA. The Pascal implementation automatically creates FAR pointers, while the C implementation declares a FAR pointer.

If this pointer contains the address FFFF:0010, the HMA is accessible. Both programs perform a simple memory test, in which they fill the HMA with a constant value, then read this memory. Errors (if any) are then documented by the programs. It's unlikely errors will appear because any RAM failure would've been detected by the BIOS during bootup.

After this test, the program disables the A20 address line and suppresses HMA access. This must occur because other programs need the 1 megabyte limit for determining memory overflow.

Remember the following rules for HMA access. First, avoid passing pointers that indicate DOS and compiler runtime library routines that refer to the HMA themselves. If you do this, these routines may normalize the pointer.

Normalization of HMA pointers

	Segment address	Offset address
Original pointer	FFFF	010A
Normalization	+ 0010	− 0100
Normalized pointer (X)	000F	000A

Normalization changes the segment of a pointer so the offset becomes less than 16, but the original memory location is still accessed as before. This results in an overflow of the segment address, which is then set to 0000H. You should avoid the normalization process.

Also, diskette and hard disk operations shouldn't directly access HMA. The software often may cause problems in the DMA controller. This occurs because the DMA controller doesn't know how to properly handle addresses above the 1 megabyte limit.

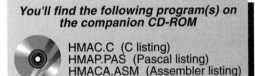

You'll find the following program(s) on the companion CD-ROM

HMAC.C (C listing)
HMAP.PAS (Pascal listing)
HMACA.ASM (Assembler listing)

If you follow these rules, you shouldn't have any problems with direct HMA access. Remember these demonstration programs are simple examples. In the following pages we'll describe the XMS driver and how HMA is used in commercial programs.

The XMS standard

The EMS standard contains a standard software interface, but extended memory existed for years without a software standard. This prompted many software manufacturers to develop their own versions. In 1988, Microsoft, Intel, Lotus and AST Research developed the Extended Memory Specification (XMS).

The XMS standard defines a software interface that allows multiple programs to access extended memory and other memory areas simultaneously. The following types of memory accesses are supported:

> The HMA, which includes the first 64K of extended memory and extends from 1024K to 1088K.

> Four Extended Memory Blocks (EMB), which appear in extended memory starting at 1088K (thus avoiding conflict with the HMA).

> Upper Memory Blocks (UMB), which lie in conventional RAM between 640K and 1024K.

HIMEM.SYS from Microsoft Corporation is probably the most widely known XMS driver. This driver has been included with recent versions of MS-DOS and Windows. The system calls HIMEM.SYS during bootup, through the CONFIG.SYS file.

In addition to MS-DOS and Windows, you can find XMS drivers in some memory management programs designed for 80386, 80486 and Pentium computers. The XMS interface usually supports the LIM standard as well as extended memory.

Some examples of XMS systems are Qualitas' 386-To-The-Max, Quarterdeck's QEMM and Microsoft's EMM386.EXE, which is packaged starting with MS-DOS 5.0. These utilities can designate extended memory as Upper Memory Blocks in the range between 640K and 1024K (provided this range isn't allocated to video RAM, hardware enhancements, or ROM BIOS). The UMBs offer the developer RAM that can be addressed as if the UMBs are conventional RAM.

Few 80286 based systems without this driver can access Upper Memory Blocks, and not all XMS drivers will support 80286 systems. Exceptions to this rule use the NEAT chips from Chips & Technologies. A SETUP program lets the user configure memory, including UMBs.

Before you can access XMS functions, you must determine whether an XMS driver is available. Interrupt 2FH is accessed by the XMS driver, similar to SHARE, APPEND, and PRINT in DOS. Call interrupt 2FH with function code 4300H in the AX register. If an XMS driver exists in the system, this function returns the value 80H to the AL register. Any other value indicates that an XMS driver isn't available and that XMS functions cannot be accessed.

XMS functions are called by a FAR CALL instruction, instead of an actual interrupt. Consequently, the XMS handler's address is needed for the call. This XMS handler is sometimes called the Extended Memory Manager (XMM). Interrupt 2FH releases this address only if an XMS driver is actually installed, and if the first call of this interrupt returned the value 80H in the AL register.

Call interrupt 2FH and place the value 4310H in the AX register. The function returns the XMM's segment register to the ES register, and the XMM's offset register to the BX register. All XMS routines are accessible through this address.

As the following table shows, 18 different XMS functions currently exist, of which the last three aren't available to all XMS drivers.

Function	Task	Function	Task
00H	Determine XMS version number	09H	Allocate Extended Memory Block (EMB)
01H	Allocate High Memory Area (HMA)	0AH	Free allocated Extended Memory Block (EMB)
02H	Free High Memory Area (HMA)	0BH	Move Extended Memory Block (EMB)
03H	Globally enable address line A20	0CH	Lock Extended Memory Block (EMB)
04H	Globally disable address line A20	0DH	Unlock Extended Memory Block (EMB)
05H	Locally enable address line A20	0EH	Get EMB handle information
06H	Locally disable address line A20	0FH	Resize Extended Memory Block (EMB)
07H	Query status of address line A20	10H	Allocate Upper Memory Block (UMB)
08H	Query free extended memory	11H	Free allocated Upper Memory Block (UMB)

Pass the XMS function number in the AH register to call the function. Other information may be placed in the other processor registers, but this differs among functions.

Almost all functions return a status code in the AX register. This status code provides information about the success of the operation. The value 0001H indicates successful execution, while 0000H indicates an error. If an error occurs, the BL register contains the error code, which provides details about the error. See the Appendices of this book for error codes and their meanings.

Next you should check the version number of the XMS driver by using function 00H. This function places the XMS version number in the AX register and the internal revision number in the BX register. The internal revision number indicates minor changes among drivers and is less important than the version number. Both items are returned as BCD numbers; the higher level byte accepts the version number preceding the decimal point and the lower byte accepts the internal revision number (the numbers following the decimal point). For example, 0200H represents Version number 2.0. XMS Version 2.0 is the lowest version you should own. If you have a Version 1 XMS, you should replace it.

Drivers with version numbers of 2.0 are most common, although some Version 3.0 XMS systems exist. We don't know the differences between the two versions, except that Version 3.0 was intended for 80386 memory management.

If you want to use the extended memory in your program as EMBs, use function 08H to determine the size of extended memory. This function returns the total amount of free extended memory (in kilobytes) in the DX register, and the size of the largest free EMB (in kilobytes) in the AX register. Use these values with caution; the HMA (64K in length) is included in calculating both values, but EMB allocation begins after the first HMA.

For example, suppose that you have a 4 megabyte system of which 3 of the 4 megabytes are available as extended memory and no memory has been assigned yet. Calling function 08H returns the number 3072 to both the AX register and the DX register for 3 megabytes. Then the XMM would be able to provide 3 megabytes of extended memory if you later called function 09H, as long as the memory is allocated after the HMA. The last 64K of this area exceed the end of extended memory, so 64K isn't physically available. Always subtract 64K from the value returned by function 08H. This deduction lets the size of the HMA govern the calculation.

Once you've determined the size of the largest available EMB, function 09H lets you request a corresponding amount of extended memory. Place the function number (09H) in the AH register, and the size of the desired block (in kilobytes) in the DX register. The DX register returns the handle needed for addition access to this EMB, unless an error occurred during memory allocation.

Check the AX register for error codes. A memory block allocation may fail, even if enough extended memory is available. The handles returned in the DX register may cause this failure. Since the XMM has only a limited number of these handles available, you may find that free extended memory exists, but all handles have already been assigned to many small EMBs. To prevent this condition, request large EMBs and try to subdivide them internally into various memory areas that are used for different purposes.

We've mentioned the XMM handles several times. You may be wondering why the XMM uses handles, instead of immediately returning the address of the allocated area. The XMM's memory management system was designed to avoid fragmentation of extended memory. This means the XMM will move the various EMBs back and forth in memory, creating a large memory range from smaller EMBs. This large EMB can then be passed to a program that calls function 09H. Another large area can be created from several small and released EMBs. This area can then be passed, as a whole, to a caller of function 09H. The addresses of the already allocated EMBs also change, so the XMM assigns logical handles instead of a physical address.

This handle must be stored safely, since it's required for all future access to an EMB. If the EMB is released, enlarged, or at least partially copied into conventional memory, this handle is required by the XMM to identify an EMB.

Releasing EMBs

It's very easy to release an EMB to make it accessible to other programs. This release doesn't occur automatically at the end of a program because TSR programs can also use EMBs for their own purposes. Function 0AH releases allocated EMBs before terminating a program. If you don't pass this function, the program will continue to access the EMBs until you reset the computer. Place the function number (0AH) in the AH register and the EMB handle's number in the DX register.

Copying EMBs

Since data can be stored in extended memory but not manipulated, complete or partial EMBs must frequently be copied from extended memory into conventional memory, or from conventional memory to extended memory. Function 0BH performs this task. Place the function number (0BH) to the AH register, and a pointer to the extended move structure to the DS:SI register pair. This structure contains all the information needed about the source and target areas, as well as the number of bytes to be copied.

Conveying the handle and offset address information of the two areas must be handled differently, depending on whether the area is in extended memory or conventional memory. If you want to address an EMB, you must then indicate the handle that was returned by function 09H when allocating the EMB. The offset address represents the offset relative to the beginning of the block. However, if you want to address an area in conventional memory, the value 0 must be passed as the handle, and the segment and offset addresses of the beginning of the block must be passed as the offset. Remember the block's address must be passed in the order OFFSET:SEGMENT.

The execution speed of this copy process is slow, especially on 80286 based machines. There's no way to avoid the long and involved switching back from protected mode.

The XMS standard has four additional EMB functions that are rarely used. You'll find information about these functions in the Appendices on the companion CD-ROM.

HMA access

XMM also provides access to the HMA. This minimizes memory conflicts between programs and offers hardware independent control of the A20 address line. This is important because not all PC systems control this line through a bit in the keyboard controller's output port, as we described in the previous section.

Unlike extended memory, HMA access cannot be parceled out to several programs because of its size. If a program requests access rights to the HMA using function 01H, it's an all-or-nothing situation. The program either receives complete access to the HMA, or no access at all. The latter occurs mainly when the HMA was already assigned, or when the size of the required HMA memory is less than the /HMAMIN parameter (an option available when the driver is initially called). This should prevent a TSR program (which may be only a few kilobytes in length) from receiving exclusive access rights to the HMA, while another program is denied access.

For normal purposes, pass FFFFH to the DX register as the amount of HMA memory needed when calling function 02H. For TSR programs, pass the exact number of bytes needed for the TSR to the DX register.

The contents of the AX register indicate whether the access rights were granted. The value 0001H indicates the release of the HMA, while the value 0000H indicates unsuccessful execution.

The A20 address line must be switched before direct access to HMA can occur. The XMM provides a total of four different functions for enabling and disabling this line. Pass the function number to the AH register for calling.

The four functions enable and disable the A20 address line both locally and globally. This distinction is important; global functions always act on the A20 address line, but the local functions rely on an internal counter. This ensures that A20 access occurs only when the calls are balanced (enable/disable). After two consecutive calls of the local enable function (function 05H), the line switches off only if two local disable calls (function 06H) follow.

Displaying and hiding the mouse cursor involves a similar process (see Chapter 11 for more information). Except on rare occasions, you'll use the global functions in HMA access.

Before ending program execution, remember to disable the A20 address using function 04H, and to release the HMA proper using function 04H. If you don't perform these two functions, programs called later will either crash (because a segment overflow was expected at the 1 megabyte limit) or will be denied access to the HMA.

Upper Memory Blocks

Upper Memory Blocks (UMBs) are within the processor's address space, which makes them directly accessible to a program. Unfortunately, RAM seldom exists in the range from 640K to 1 megabyte, unless you have an 80386 computer, in which programs are stored in upper RAM through software.

If the system for which you're developing software has UMBs available, or you just want to keep this memory option open, the XMS standard supports two functions for access to upper memory. MS-DOS Version 5.0 and up support UMB access, although this support merely acts as moderator between a program and the XMS driver (see Chapter 23 for more information).

Unlike the HMA, Upper Memory Blocks provide true memory management, which permits several programs to reside in upper memory. Segment addresses of the allocated blocks are used instead of handles. These segment addresses act as references for identifying a UMB for the XMM.

Allocating UMBs

Function 10H allocates a UMB when possible. Place the function number (10H) in the AH register, and the size of the block you want allocated (in paragraphs [= 16 bytes]) in the DX register. If enough memory isn't available, the DX register returns the size (in paragraphs) of the largest available UMB.

Releasing UMBs

The XMM lets you release a UMB as well as allocate one. Function 11H performs the release. Pass the function number (11H) to the AH register and the segment address of the addressed UMB to the DX register.

Demonstration programs

The following programs present some aspects of the XMS standard. Since these programs contain all the necessary XMS calls, you can adapt these routines to your own needs. Because XMM access is difficult in high level languages, both the Pascal and C implementations include some assembly language programming. C and Pascal libraries include compiler routines for calling almost any interrupt functions, but they don't include provisions for calling and passing register contents to normal subroutines. The C implementation uses an assembly language program (XMSCA.ASM) and the Pascal implementation directly stores the assembly language as INLINE commands.

This routine is similar to commands for calling interrupts. A structure is passed to call an XMM function. This structure contains the required processor register contents. After the function call the structure receives the return values.

The main program checks for the availability of the XMM driver. If this driver exists, two additional procedures check the viability of the HMA and extended memory.

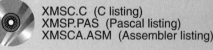

You'll find the following program(s) on the companion CD-ROM

XMSC.C (C listing)
XMSP.PAS (Pascal listing)
XMSCA.ASM (Assembler listing)

Chapter 13

Sound On Your PC

Every PC has a built-in speaker that beeps when certain errors occur or when the keyboard buffer is full. The speaker can also generate other sounds. This chapter demonstrates sound generation through software.

How the PC generates sound

Tones occur when the cone of a speaker *oscillates* (moves back and forth). A single oscillation creates a click instead of a musical sound. If a group of oscillations occur in rapid succession, a tone is produced. The pitch; (the note value) of a tone depends on the number of cycles (oscillations) that occur per second. The pitch of a tone in cycles per second is measured in Hertz. For example, if the speaker oscillates at a rate of 440 times per second, it generates a tone with a frequency of 440 Hertz. Certain pitches have specific note names assigned to them, such as A440 (the note that sounds at 440 Hertz). The following tables show the pitches and frequencies of tones generated by the PC. This range covers 8 octaves (almost the range of a full piano keyboard):

Octave 0		Octave 1		Octave 2		Octave 3	
C	16.35	C	32.70	C	65.41	C	130.81
C#	17.32	C#	34.65	C#	69.30	C#	138.59
D	18.35	D	36.71	D	73.42	D	146.83
D#	19.45	D#	38.89	D#	77.78	D#	155.56
E	20.60	E	41.20	E	82.41	E	164.81
F	21.83	F	43.65	F	87.31	F	174.61
F#	23.12	F#	46.25	F#	92.50	F#	185.00
G	24.50	G	49.00	G	98.00	G	196.00
G#	25.96	G#	51.91	G#	103.83	G#	207.65
A	27.50	A	55.00	A	110.00	A	220.00
A#	29.14	A#	58.27	A#	116.54	A#	233.08
B	30.87	B	61.74	B	123.47	B	246.94

Octave 0		Octave 1		Octave 2		Octave 3	
C	261.63	C	523.25	C	1046.50	C	2093.00
C#	277.18	C#	554.37	C#	1108.74	C#	2217.46
D	293.66	D	587.33	D	1174.66	D	2349.32
D#	311.13	D#	622.25	D#	1244.51	D#	2489.02
E	329.63	E	659.26	E	1328.51	E	2637.02
F	349.23	F	698.46	F	1396.91	F	2793.83
F#	369.99	F#	739.99	F#	1479.98	F#	2959.96
G	392.00	G	783.99	G	1567.98	G	3135.96
G#	415.30	G#	830.61	G#	1661.22	G#	3322.44
A	440.00	A	880.00	A	1760.00	A	3520.00
A#	466.16	A#	923.33	A#	1864.66	A#	3729.31
B	493.88	B	987.77	B	1975.53	B	3951.07

The speaker in the PC can generate frequencies from 1 Hertz up to more than 1,000,000 Hertz. However, most human ears are only capable of hearing frequencies between 20 and 20,000 Hertz. Also, PC speakers don't reproduce music very well because they play some tones louder than others. Since the speaker has no volume control, this effect cannot be changed.

A sound program should oscillate the speaker according to the frequency of the tones desired. The following is a rough outline of a possible sound generation program:

➤ Execute the instruction to move the cone forward, then undo the instruction (i.e., move the cone back to its original position). Repeat these steps in a loop so that it occurs as many times per second as required by the frequency of the tone being generated.

The previous procedure has several disadvantages:

➤ The execution speed of individual instructions depends on the processing speed of the computer.

➤ This program must be adjusted to the processing speed of individual computers.

➤ The tone becomes distorted when the tone production loop ends.

8253 timer

Every PC uses one particular chip for tone generation: The 8253 programmable timer, which actually maintains control of the internal clock. The 8253 can perform both timing and sound because of its ability to enable a certain action at a certain point in time. It senses timing from oscillations it receives from the PC's 8284 oscillator, which generates 1,193,180 impulses per second. The 8253 can then be instructed how many of these impulses it should wait before triggering a certain action. In the case of tone generation, this action consists of sending an impulse to the speaker. Before executing this action, the chip must be programmed for the particular frequency it should generate. The frequency must be converted from cycles per second into the number of oscillations coming from the oscillator. This is done with the help of the following formula:

```
counter = 1,193,180 / frequency
```

The result of this formula, the variable counter, is passed to the chip. As the formula demonstrates, the result for a high frequency is relatively low, and the result for a low frequency is relatively high. This makes sense because it tells the 8253 chip how many of the 1,193,180 cycles per second it must wait until it can send another signal to the speaker. The lower the value, the more often it sends a signal to move the speaker cone back and forth, which produces a higher tone.

Creating a tone on the PC

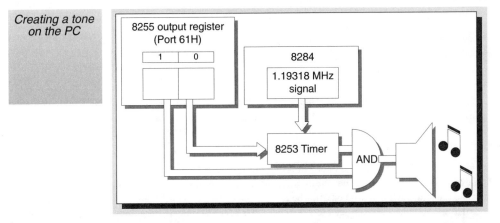

Ports and PC sound

Communication between the CPU and the 8253 chip occurs through ports. First, the value 182 is sent to port 43H. This instructs the 8253 that it should start generating a signal as soon as the interval between individual signals has been passed. This interval is the value that was calculated with the previous formula. Since the 8253 stores this value internally as a 16-bit number (a value between 0 and 65,535), it limits the range of tones generated to frequencies between 18 and 1,193,180 Hertz. This number must be transmitted to port 42H. Since this is an 8-bit port, the 16 bits of this number cannot be transmitted simultaneously. First the least significant eight bits are transmitted, then the most significant eight bits are transmitted.

Now the second step occurs: The 8253 signal is sent to the speaker. The speaker access occurs through port 61H, which is connected to a programmable peripheral chip. The two lowest bits of this port must be set to 1 to transmit the 8253 signal to the speaker. Since the remaining six bits are used for other purposes, they cannot be changed. For this reason, the contents of port 61H must be read, the lowest two bits must be set to 1 (an OR combination with 3), and the resulting value must be returned to port 61H. A tone sounds, which ends only when the bits that were just set to 1 are reset again to 0.

Keyboard setup and timer frequencies

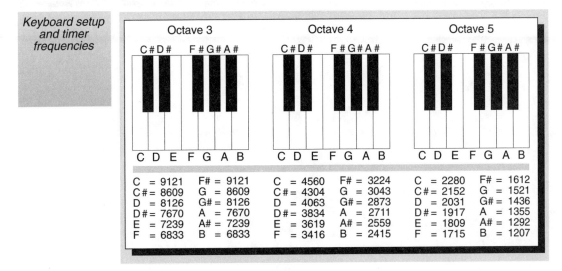

Demonstration programs

GW-BASIC and Turbo Pascal contain resident sound commands. The machine language programmer and C programmer must create their own sound applications.

This chapter contains demonstration programs for both of these languages. These programs can be added to your own C or assembly language programs.

How they work

Both programs produce tones for specific time periods. This is done with the help of the timer interrupt 1CH, which is called by the timer interrupt 8H 18.2 times per second. When the tone generation routine executes, it receives the frequency of the tone and the tone's duration (length). The duration is measured in 18ths of a second, so the value 18 corresponds to a second and the value 9 corresponds to a half-second. This value is stored in a variable.

Immediately before activating the tone output, the interrupt routine of interrupt 1CH turns to a user-defined routine. This routine, called 18.2 times per second, decrements the tone duration in the variable during every call. When it reaches the value, the tone duration ends and the tone must be switched off. The routine allocates a variable to notify the actual sound routine of this end. The sound routine recognizes this immediately because it has been in a constant wait loop since switching on the tone. This loop simply monitors the contents of this variable. After recognizing the end of the tone, it stops the sound output and returns the timer interrupt to its old routine.

The sound routine requires the number assigned to this tone rather than the frequency itself. This number is related to the table containing the frequencies of octaves 3 to 5. The value 0 represents C of the third octave, 1 represents C-sharp, 2 represents D, 3 represents D-sharp, etc.

Both the C program and assembly language program demonstrate the sound routine by playing a scale over the course of two octaves, with each note sounding for a half a second. The machine language demo program and the sound routine are stored in one file. The C versions of these programs are split into two source code files. The C demo program contains the sound function call only, and the machine language program, which creates the sound, must be linked to the demonstration program.

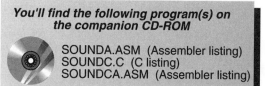

You'll find the following program(s) on the companion CD-ROM

SOUNDA.ASM (Assembler listing)
SOUNDC.C (C listing)
SOUNDCA.ASM (Assembler listing)

Chapter 14

Diskettes And Hard Drives

The main purpose of the BIOS routines is to perform low-level functions on behalf of DOS. For example, BIOS routines can physically format the surface of a floppy diskette or access the sectors of a hard drive. DOS, however, remains the master controller for these processes. Most applications perform disk drive operations at the DOS level instead of the BIOS level. However, there are exceptions. For example, disk utilities, such as PC Tools or Norton Utilities, access the disk drive at the BIOS level. But generally these specialized programs are rare.

In this chapter we'll show you how to access the disk drives using the BIOS functions. Since all disk controllers aren't programmed identically, we won't be programming the disk controller directly. Most of the functions that you can perform at the disk controller level can also be performed at the BIOS level. It's worth using the BIOS functions to avoid hardware-dependent disk controller programming.

In addition to BIOS functions, we'll also discuss a few topics related to the hard drive. We'll explain the different types of hard drive controllers and see how hard drives record data.

We'll end the chapter with a discussion of hard drive partitioning, which lets the user divide the hard drive into several logical drives.

Floppy Diskette And Hard Drive Structure

Let's begin with a look at the common characteristics of floppy diskettes and hard drives. Floppy diskettes and hard drives have similar structures, which is indicated by the number of BIOS functions that apply to both. If you think of a floppy diskette as a two-dimensional version of a hard drive, the similarities are even more apparent.

Floppy diskette structure

A floppy diskette consists of individual tracks arranged as concentric circles at equal intervals over the surface of the diskette's magnetic media. These tracks are labeled from 0 to N; N represents the total number of sectors minus 1 and varies depending on the format. The outermost track is always numbered 0, the next track is numbered 1, etc. This process continues to the innermost track.

Each track is subdivided into a fixed number of sectors. Each sector holds the same amount of data. Sectors are numbered from 1 to N; N represents the number of sectors per track. The maximum number of sectors in a track depends on the type of floppy disk drive and the diskette's format.

Each sector contains 512 bytes and is the smallest amount of data that a program can access. In other words, you must read or write a complete sector at a time. It isn't possible to read or write a single byte from the diskette.

The data in each sector is recorded using either an FM or MFM technique. These are the same recording methods used in hard drives (refer to the "Recording Information On The Hard Drive" section for more information). As a programmer, you don't have to worry about these details to access the data from the disk drive.

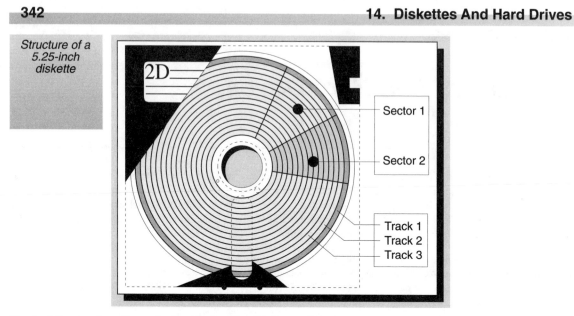

Structure of a 5.25-inch diskette

Use the following formula to calculate the capacity of a floppy diskette:

```
Sectors * tracks_per_sector * 512 [bytes per sector]
```

Remember the above formula is for a single side of a diskette. If the floppy disk drive has two read/write heads (like most recent floppy drives), you must double this value. DOS refers to these sides of a diskette as side 0 and side 1.

The number of sectors per track also affects the data transfer rate. The data transfer rate is the speed of the floppy disk drive electronics and its controller. With a constant rotation speed of 300 revolutions a minute, the more bits per time unit that pass by the read/write head, and the more sectors can be written to a track.

Hard drive structure

Since a hard drive rotates ten times faster than a floppy diskette, its data transfer rate is at least ten times higher than a floppy diskette's. The data transfer rate increases by a second power of ten, because modern 3.5-inch hard drives can store almost 100 sectors per track.

These characteristics don't change the fundamental structure of a hard drive. Think of a hard drive as a group of magnetic plates stacked on top of each other. Each magnetic plate is similar to a floppy diskette; it has two sides, is divided into tracks, and each track is subdivided into sectors. Above the surface of each side of the plate is a read/write head that accesses the data. The plates are aligned so track 0 on one of the plates is exactly above track 0 of another plate.

A read/write arm links all the read/write heads together. To access a particular track on one of the plates, the arm moves all the read/write heads to the specific track. Since this arrangement requires only a single positioning mechanism (the read/write arm), it simplifies the design and lowers the cost of the hard drive. However, with this arrangement, all the read/write heads must be moved to access data on a different track. So, to read data on track 1 of one plate, then data on track 50 of a different plate, and finally data on track 1 of the first plate again, the entire read/write arm must be moved twice. Positioning the arm like this requires a significant amount of time compared to the data transfer time.

To minimize the time needed to access data, you should prevent the data from being spread across multiple tracks. One way to optimize access time to a group of data is to write that data sequentially on a single track. If the data doesn't fit on a single track, then write in on the same track of a different plate. By doing this, the read/write arm doesn't need to be moved. Instead, only the appropriate read/write head needs to be selected to read the desired data. Selecting (changing) heads is much faster than physically moving a mechanical read/write arm to change tracks.

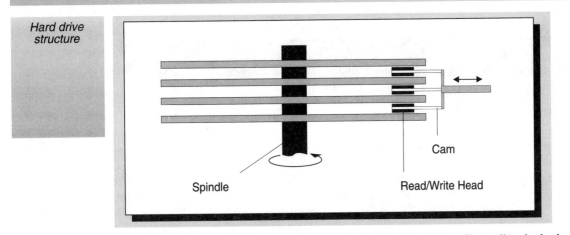

Hard drive structure

Cam

Spindle

Read/Write Head

The term cylinder is used to describe the multiple plates stacked on top of each other. A cylinder refers to all tracks that have the same track number but are located on different disk plates.

Disk Drives And Diskette Formats

Before describing the diskette BIOS routines, let's review the various diskette formats. This format is affected by size and density. PC diskettes come in either 5.25-inch or 3.5-inch sizes. Each size is either single, double, or high density.

5.25-inch floppy disk drives and diskettes

Although DOS is able to use the 8-inch floppy disk drive, this size was never really implemented. The 8-inch floppy disk drive was simply too large to fit into most PC's. The 5.25-inch floppy disk drive became the first PC standard floppy. Even today, more than 10 years later, the 5.25-inch drive is still standard equipment for many PCs. The 5.25-inch drive supports double density diskettes. This term distinguishes the diskettes from the single density diskettes that had been used in earlier microcomputers.

A single density diskette has four sectors per track and 40 sectors on each side. This amounts to a capacity of 80K per side or 160K for floppy disk drives with two read/write heads. With 125 kilobits per second, its data transfer rate was rather slow compared to today's standards.

The double density diskette doubles the number of sectors per track to eight, while retaining the number of tracks per side (40). So, the capacity of the diskette is increased to 160K for a single-sided floppy disk drive and 320K for a double-sided floppy disk drive. The data transfer rate also doubles, yielding 250 kilobits per second.

This 320K format was short-lived. Eight sectors doesn't quite fill up a track on double density diskette. So, there is still room for a ninth sector. Adding an extra sector to each track increases the capacity to 360K. This became the standard double density format, which is still widely used.

When the IBM/AT computer was introduced, a new format was also introduced. The new format, called high density diskette, gives the 5-1/4" floppy diskette a capacity of 1.2 Meg. The number of sectors per track was increased to 15 and the number of tracks per side was doubled to 80. As with double density diskettes, both sides of the diskette are used for this high density format.

Theoretically it's possible to have 16 sectors on each track. But for practical considerations, developers settled on the 15 sectors per track arrangement to ensure a reliable floppy disk drive. High capacity floppy disk drives rotate at 360 RPM.

5.25-inch diskette formats					
Label	Drive	Sectors per track	Tracks per side	Capacity rate	Data transfer
Double Density	PC/XT	8	40	160/320K	250 K/sec
Double Density	PC/XT	9	40	80/360K	250 K/sec
High Density	AT	15	0	1.2 Meg	500 K/sec

Instead of the 40 tracks used by the double density format, the high density format squeezes 80 tracks onto a diskette. So standard double density floppy disk drives cannot read or write this format. Only newer model MF (multi-function) drives are capable of reading and writing this format. A MF drive also adjusts to the standard double density format, which makes it possible to read and write standard 360K diskettes. In MF drives, the data transfer rate can be adjusted and the rotational speed can be reduced to the normal speed of 300 revolutions a minute.

However, the higher number of sectors per track means that earlier PC and XT floppy disk drives cannot read or write to these high density diskettes. These drives cannot achieve the necessary data transfer rate of 500 kilobits per second because they cannot be designed or configured for the task.

Increasing the recording capacity from double density to high density isn't simply a matter of drive electronics. It's also a question of the "granulation" of the magnetic material on the diskette. The smaller the single magnetic particles, the more information can be recorded on a given surface. This is also the reason why double density diskettes can never be formatted error free in AT disk drives at 1.2 Meg; the granulation on those diskettes is simply too coarse.

While it may be possible to format a double density diskette at high density, these diskettes can usually be read only on the PC on which they were formatted. Other PCs will simply give you read errors, making it almost impossible to use the diskette. This is caused by the variances in the positioning of the read/write heads on different floppy disk drives.

The differences between read/write head positioning may only amount to fractions of a millimeter. A single track may actually be wider than the read/write head, allowing the head to be positioned within the track's range. Even allowing for variances in track size, this allows the head to correctly read the information.

However, this causes problems when re-formatting a standard double density diskette using a high density drive, because the high density drive's formatting capabilities may cause problems when a PC/XT double density drive attempts to read the newly formatted disks. The smaller read/write tolerances may cause track skipping and read errors.

Something similar occurs if you try to format a high density diskette in a double density floppy disk drive. Usually this is also doomed to failure or results in read errors on other drives. So, purchasing expensive HD (High Density) diskettes for your PC or XT disk drives isn't necessarily a good idea.

3.5-inch floppy disk drives and diskettes

Although 5.25-inch floppy disk drives are still widely used, they are being replaced by the smaller 3.25" floppy disk drives. These smaller drives first became popular on the laptop computers. Now, 3.5-inch floppy disk drives are also used on most desktop PCs. The 3.5-inch diskettes are preferred because of their convenient size and the sturdiness of their rigid plastic case. The magnetic surface of a 3.5-inch diskette is covered by a sliding metal door to protect the data from damage by dust and dirt particles.

*Structure of a
3.5-inch diskette*

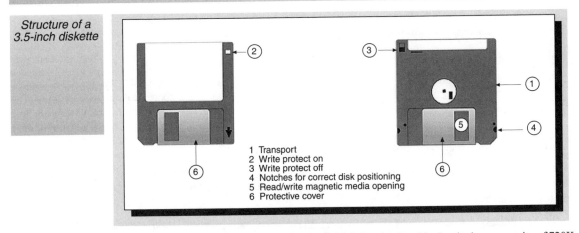

1 Transport
2 Write protect on
3 Write protect off
4 Notches for correct disk positioning
5 Read/write magnetic media opening
6 Protective cover

The 3.5-inch floppy disk drives record data in either double density or high density. Double density has a capacity of 720K, with 9 sectors on a track and 80 tracks on each side of the diskette. A 3.5-inch diskette has a considerably higher track density than a 5.25-inch diskette, especially since the diameter of the magnetic media is much smaller.

The original 3.5-inch floppy disk drives have a double density format with a capacity of 720K. The newer 3.5-inch floppy disk drives have a 1.44 Meg capacity. A 1.44 Meg floppy disk drive is now the standard in 3.5-inch drives today. It also has 80 tracks per side, but has 18 sectors per track. This also doubles the data transfer rate, which makes it impossible to use these diskettes in the double density 3.5-inch floppy disk drives of earlier PCs and XTs.

A 3.5-inch high density floppy disk drive performs like a 5.25-inch MF floppy disk drive in that it can adjust to reading, writing, and formatting double density diskettes.

3.5-inch diskette formats					
Type	Drive	Sectors per track	Tracks per side	Capacity	Data transfer rate
Double Density	PC/XT	9	80	720K	250 K/sec
High Density	AT	18	80	1.44 Meg	500 K/sec
Extra High Density	AT	36	80	2.88 Meg	1 MBit/s

Recently, a new 3.5-inch format was introduced. Diskettes using this format have a capacity of 2.88 Meg. This format is called extra high density (ED). ED diskettes have double the number of sectors (36) and can only be read by the new ED floppy disk drives. Like HD drives, ED floppy disk drives are also downwardly compatible. This means they are able to process both double density and high density diskette formats.

Floppy disk drives that can read and write the different formats must be able to determine the format in which the diskette is written. Then it can pass this information to the BIOS before accessing the data on the diskette. Finding the format of a 5.25-inch diskette isn't easy, because this information can be determined only by reading the data. So, the diskette must already be formatted.

However, the capacity of a 3.5-inch diskette can be determined by a small hole, which is located on the opposite side of the write-protect slider. Within the floppy disk drive itself is a light-sensitive sensor that can detect the presence or absence of the hole. Unlike high density diskettes, double density diskettes don't have this hole. Extra high density diskettes also have a hole, but the hole is located in a different position.

Disk drives and their controllers

A floppy disk drive consists of a motor that rotates the diskette at 300 revolutions per minute (360 RPM for HD 5.25-inch) and a mechanism for moving the read/write head. The drive also has an electronic component, called a data separator. The data separator converts a voltage into a binary data stream as the read/write head passes over the surface of the diskette.

The floppy drive is controlled by a separate diskette controller, which is either part of the computer's motherboard or on an I/O card in one of the computer's expansion slots.

The main functions of the diskette controller are performed by an NEC PD765 or a similar chip from another manufacturer. Only NEC chips or NEC compatible chips are able to work with the ROM-BIOS. After all, it's the ROM-BIOS that uses this chip to control access to the floppy disk drive.

Although it's possible to adapt the ROM-BIOS to work with another diskette controller, most manufacturers of ROM-BIOS systems use the established standard of the NEC PD765.

However, this standard causes problems with the new ED floppy disk drives. These drives have twice the track capacity (36 instead of 18 sectors) and the twice the data transfer rate. But both parameters are unknown to the BIOS. A ROM extension on the controller card can be used to avoid these limitations. The ROM extension wedges itself into the ROM-BIOS when DOS is first started. Then it manages all access to these floppy disk drives. Since the ROM extension is intended to be used only in real mode, it cannot be used if the computer is running protected mode.

Operating systems such as UNIX or OS/2 run in protected mode. These systems rely on the diskette controller to handle all the details of accessing the drives. So, they'll fail with new floppy disk drives unless special device drivers are written into the operating system. Hopefully a BIOS standard for the new ED drives will be developed soon, making ROM extensions unnecessary. Since Windows will be taking over more of the BIOS tasks in the future, this problem will become more prevalent for PC users.

Accessing Floppy Disk Drives With The BIOS

There is a complete set of BIOS functions that access floppy disk drives. Interrupt 13H is used to call these functions. This interrupt is also an interface to the hard drive utilities of the BIOS. Wherever possible, similar floppy and hard drive functions share an identical function number. To differentiate between the drives, the drive specification is passed to the function in the DL register.

For floppy disk drives, either the value 0 (for drive A:) or 1 (for drive B:) is used. A few disk controllers support four floppy drives by providing a BIOS extension that also accepts the values 2 and 3 for the other two floppy disk drives. Hard drives are specified by the values 80H and 81H.

As in several other cases, you must distinguish between the PC/XT-BIOS and the AT-BIOS. For example, there are a few BIOS functions that are specific to MF floppy disk drives.

The following table lists the diskette functions of the BIOS interrupt 13H:

No.	Tasks	PC/XT	AT	No.	Tasks	PC/XT	AT
				Diskette functions of the BIOS interrupt 13H			
00H	Reset	Yes	Yes	08H	Request Format	Yes	Yes
01H	Read status	Yes	Yes	15H	Define drive type	No	Yes
02H	Read	Yes	Yes	16H	Detect diskette change	No	Yes
03H	Write	Yes	Yes	17H	Determine diskette format	No	Yes
04H	Verify	Yes	Yes	18H	Determine diskette format	No	Yes
05H	Format	Yes	Yes				

Notice functions 17H and 18H have the same task. This isn't an error. Function 18H was introduced for the 3.5-inch HD drives. The older function 17H isn't capable of supporting the drive, so it was replaced by a new function. We'll discuss this in more detail later.

Drive status

These BIOS functions also have another similarity. They return a status or error code. This status code is returned to the caller in the AH register. A non-zero value and a set carry flag indicate an error.

Code	Meaning	Code	Meaning
	Status and error codes of the BIOS diskette functions		
00H	No error	08H	DMA overflow
01H	Illegal function number	09H	Data transfer past the segment limit
02H	Address marking not found	10H	Read error
03H	Attempt to write to write-protected diskette	20H	Diskette controller error
04H	Addressed sector not found	40H	Track not found
06H	Diskette was changed	80H	Time out error, drives does not respond

You can also determine the diskette status through function 01H. Simply pass function number 01H in the AH register and the drive specification value in the DL register. After the function call, the drive status is returned to you in the AH register.

Resetting the floppy disk drive

After an error you must reset the floppy disk drive. To do this, use function 00H. Pass function number 00H in the AH register and the drive specification value in the DL register. After the function call, the current drive status is returned to you in the AH register.

It doesn't matter whether you pass 0 or 1 as the drive specification; all the floppy disk drives will be reset. Remember the value in the DL register isn't ignored. Entering a value greater than 80H resets the hard drives.

Prompt for the drive type

A program needs to know the type and format of a floppy disk drive to use it. You can use the 08H and 15H functions to determine this information. Function 08H, which is found in the PC/XT-BIOS, is used to distinguish between the different floppy and diskette formats. Pass function number 08H in the AH register and the drive specification in the DL register. The following illustration shows the information that's returned.

Any error code is returned in the AH register with the carry flag set. By using this function, you can determine whether a given drive is installed to demonstrate, for example, that a second, third, or even fourth drive is present.

Information returned by the 08H function	
Regis	Information
BL	Drive Type 01H = 5.25-inch, 360K 02H = 5.25-inch, 1.2 Meg 03H = 3.5-inch, 720K 04H = 3.5-inch, 1.44 Meg
DH	Maximum number of sides (always 1)
CH	Maximum number of tracks
CL	Maximum number of sectors
ES:DI	Pointers to DDPT

The value in the BL register is especially important. This value not only reveals the floppy disk drive type (3.5-inch or 5.25-inch), but also shows the diskette format (DD or HD). However, this value doesn't necessarily describe the format of the diskette that is located in the drive; it describes only the highest possible density.

This information is taken from the CMOS-RAM, in which this information is stored when the computer is originally setup. The Drive Type value is standardized, but doesn't yet include the new ED 3.5-inch drives. However, in the future these new types will most likely appear under Drive Type 05H.

Although the number of sectors, tracks, and heads can be derived from the Drive Type value, this information is also specified explicitly in the CH/CL, DH/DL registers.

The DDPT, which is referenced by the pointer in the register pair ES:DI, is the Disk Drive Parameter Table. This table contains a parameter the BIOS needs for programming the diskette controller. You'll find a description of this table later on in this chapter.

Function 15H has a different purpose. This function is only supported by ATs and their FM drives. Unlike PC/XT floppy disk drives, these drives are able to detect when a diskette has been changed. This feature is important for programs that depend on the presence of a specific diskette. This is true especially for DOS, which reads the FAT table before it accesses a diskette to determine which sectors of the diskette are occupied and which sectors are still unused.

Drive codes of function 15H	
Code	Meaning
AH = 00H	Drive not present
AH = 01H	Disk drive, does not recognize diskette changes
AH = 02H	Disk drive, recognizes diskette changes
AH = 03H	Hard drive

If the diskette is changed without DOS knowing about it, DOS may continue to use the contents of the original diskette's allocation table (FAT) and may inadvertently overwrite and/or destroy data on the newly inserted diskette. However, if the same diskette is reinserted into the floppy, DOS won't have to reread the FAT again.

Function 15H of the BIOS helps determine if a diskette has been replaced. Pass function number 15H in the AH register and the drive specification in the DL register. The table on the left shows what information is returned after the function call.

Reading diskette sectors

Reading diskette sectors is one of the most basic tasks the BIOS performs. Function 02H reads diskette sectors. Remember that this function can read several sectors through a single call if they're on same track and contiguous.

Register when calling function 02H	
AL	Number of sectors to be read
DL	Drive specification value
DH	Side (0 or 1)
CL	Sector number (1 to N)
CH	Track number (0 to N-1)
ES:BX	Address of the buffer for the data to be read
AH = 03H	Hard drive

Remember the data isn't transferred to a fixed memory location. Instead, the address of a buffer is passed in the register pair ES:BX. Register ES contains the segment address of the buffer and

register BX contains the buffer's offset address.

After the function call, the error status is returned in the AH register and the number of read sectors read is returned in the AL register. If the carry flag is set, it signals an error.

If you're using an MF drive, you can use a trick to determine the format of a diskette. By trying to read a diskette with a sector greater than 9, you can determine whether a diskette is DD or HD. Since the maximum number of sectors per track on a DD diskette is 9, function 15H will return a disk status error. The track number isn't important, but it should be less than 40.

If a disk status error is returned, don't immediately abort the operation. You should repeat all read, write, and format operations at least three times before you give up and assume there is a "real" error. Often an operation fails the first time, but succeeds when you try it a second or third time. Perhaps the read/write head wasn't positioned properly the first time or the floppy drive wasn't synchronized to the electronics yet (see the "Recording Information On The Hard Drive" section in this chapter).

In cases of errors, you don't have to worry about the validity of the data because the drive uses parity checking to ensure the data in each sector is correct.

Writing diskette sectors

Register when calling function 03H	
AL	Number of sectors to be written
DL	Drive specification value
DH	Side (0 or 1)
CL	Sector number (1 to N)
CH	Track number (0 to N-1)
AL	Number of sectors to be read
ES:BX	Pointer to the buffer containing the data

Function 03H is used to write to individual sectors. The parameters are passed according to the table on the left.

Remember the buffer, to which the ES:BX register pair points, must contain the data to be written to the diskette.

Verifying diskette sectors

Function 04H tests whether data have been correctly transferred to the diskette. The data in the memory aren't compared with the data on the diskette. Instead, a CRC value is used to determine whether the data was transferred correctly. CRC, which is an abbreviation for "Cyclical Redundancy Check", is a very reliable procedure for verifying accuracy. This procedure combines the values of each byte within the sector with a checksum through a complicated mathematical formula.

Since most disk drives are very reliable, most programmers consider this routine to be unnecessary and don't use it. DOS uses this function when writing data only if the DOS VERIFY ON command is active.

The parameters for function 04H are the same as for function 02H and 03H except that a buffer address isn't required.

Formatting individual tracks on a diskette

Function 07H is used to format an entire diskette. But it's also possible to format individual tracks on a diskette. To do this, first use function 18H to tell the BIOS which format to use. The function number 18H is passed in the AH register, the drive specification value in the DL register, the number of tracks in the CH register, and the number of sectors per track in the CL register. After the function call, the carry flag signals the specified format is supported by the floppy disk drive. In this case, the register pair ES:DI is a pointer to DDPT, which is required for subsequent formatting functions.

We'll describe the DDPT in more detail later. For now, remember the pointer must be passed to interrupt vector 1EH, in which the BIOS keeps a pointer to the current DDPT.

After function 07H sets the desired format and the DDPT pointer is passed to interrupt vector 1EH, you can start the actual formatting process.

To do this, use function 05H. This function formats a complete track. Although you can format individual sectors with 128, 256, 512, or even 1024 bytes per sector, only a 512 byte format can be used under DOS. This is because DOS supports only this size sector.

To use function 05H, pass the drive specification value in the DL register, the diskette side in the DH register, the number of sectors per track in the AL register, and the track number in the CH register (0 through 39 or 0 through 79).

You'll see the ES:BX register pair points to a "format table". This table represents the formatting attributes. This an array of 4-byte entries (one for each sector to be formatted):

Register when calling function 05H	
AL	Number of sectors in the track
DL	Number of the drive
CH	Number of the track
DH	Side (0 or 1)
ES:BX	Pointer to format table

ES:BX register pair "format table"	
Offset	Meaning
0	Track to be formatted
1	Diskette side (always 0 for one-sided diskettes): 0 = Front side 1 = Back side
2	Number of the sector
3	Number of bytes in this sector:
0	0 = 128 bytes
0	1 = 256 bytes
0	2 = 512 bytes
0	3 = 1024 bytes

Although the track number and diskette side is passed to function 05H, it must be repeated in the table. The sectors are physically created in the same sequence as the table entries. So it's possible to format the first entry as sector number 1 and the second entry as sector number 7. The logical sector number is recorded in the header of each sector on the diskette, so the floppy disk drive can later identify the sector being searched for.

Since the BIOS doesn't define the logical sector numbers, you can change the interleaving. Generally only hard drives use interleaving, as we'll see in Section 6.7. Since interleaving doesn't have any advantages for floppy diskettes, you should number the sectors consecutively when you create the format table.

The number of bytes per sector don't have to be identical either, since these numbers are defined explicitly for each sector in the table. You can change the number of bytes per sector to develop a form of copy protection, for example. We'll soon see how this is done. A program at the end of this chapter shows how to format diskettes using functions 18H and 05H.

Disk Drive Parameter Table

To program the diskette controller, the BIOS needs the physical formatting information described above and some additional information. We've already introduced you to the Disk Drive Parameter Table (DDPT). The ROM BIOS contains a table for every drive and supported diskette format. Also, you can define your own DDPT, since the BIOS always references the current DDPT via a FAR pointer, which is contained in the memory locations in which the interrupt vector 1EH is usually found. Since neither DOS nor the PC hardware use interrupt 1EH, you can change the contents of these memory locations.

Actually DOS creates its own DDPT. This DOS DDPT is designed to speed up access to the diskette.

The table is 11 bytes in size, as shown by the following figure. Not all the parameters can be changed. However, the entries that are marked with an asterisk may be changed.

Diskette functions of the BIOS interrupt 13H					
Offset	Meaning	Type	Offset	Meaning	Type
*00H	Step rate and head unload time	1 BYTE	06H	DTL (Data Length)	1 BYTE
*01H	Head load time	1 BYTE	07H	Length of GAP3 when formatting	1 BYTE
*02H	Post run-time of diskette motor	1 BYTE	*08H	Fill character for formatting	1 BYTE
03H	Sector size	1 BYTE	*09H	Head settle time	1 BYTE
04H	Sectors per track	1 BYTE	*0AH	Time to run up of diskette motor	1 BYTE
05H	Length of GAP3 when reading/writing	1 BYTE			

The first field of the DDPT table actually has two sub-fields: The step rate (bits 4-7) and the head unload time (bits 0-3). The step rate describes the time the controller has to move the read/write head from one track to another. This value is represented as milliseconds, with the value 0FH representing 1 ms, 0EH representing 2 ms, 0DH representing 3 ms, etc. The head unload time describes the time the read/write head has to lift up off of the surface of the diskette, for example when changing tracks. It's specified as a factor of 16 ms. The default value 0FH (240 ms) is extremely conservative and can usually be lowered.

The second field is also two sub-fields: The head load time (bits 1-7) and the DMA flag (bit 0). The head load time is the time the read/write head has to settle to the surface of a track. This value is expressed as a factor of 2 ms. In accessing a diskette, it's usually necessary to wait much longer for the diskette motor to reach its required speed. So it's common to specify a very low value (1 or 2) for the head load time.

The DMA flag is represented by bit 0. This flag must always be set to 0.

The third field is the post run-time of the diskette motor after a diskette operation. This is the period of time that elapses until the diskette motor is switched off when no other diskette operations are being performed. Because it takes a relatively long time to get the motor running, it shouldn't be switched off immediately after each diskette access. This value is related to a cycle of approximately 18 ticks per second (1 tick is approximately 55 ms). So a value of 18 represents a post run-time of about one second. The default value is 25H, which is approximately two seconds.

The forth field specifies the number of bytes per sector that can be used in a read or write operation. This corresponds to the values for formatting a sector, so it usually contains the value 3 for 512 bytes per sector. To read or write to sectors with different sector sizes, you must first enter the appropriate value in this field.

The next field at offset address 04H is the maximum number of sectors per track, which depends on the selected diskette format.

The next three fields refer to the coding and decoding of sector information, which is stored on the diskette along with the actual data. You should never tamper with these values.

However, the field at offset address 08H can be changed. This field contains the ASCII code of the fill character to be used when the diskette is being formatted. During formatting, as the sectors are created, they are also given a fixed contents. The default fill character is a division sign (ASCII code 246).

The next field contains the head settle time. After the read/write head travels from one track to another, a short delay is needed to allow the vibrations from this movement to subside. Only then can the read/write head perform the subsequent data access properly. The value in this field represents a delay in milliseconds. The default value is 25 ms.

The last field in the DDPT specifies the time it takes for the diskette motor to attain its operating speed. The value in this field is a factor of 1/8 seconds. While DOS defaults to a value of 1/4 second, the BIOS equivalent is 1/2 second.

Demonstration programs

Changing the various values in the DDPT won't produce performance miracles. However, you'll probably want to experiment with it. We've developed two small programs in Pascal and C to set the various parameters of the current DDPT. However, the programs won't change all the parameters because this would be too dangerous.

The two programs, DDPTP.PAS and DDPTC.C, both work according to the same principle. You call both programs from the DOS command line without specifying any parameters. Each program displays the contents of the current DDPT (the DDPT of the last accessed disk drive). To address a certain disk drive, use the DIR command before the DDPTP or DDPTC program.

DDPTP and DDPTC programs display the contents of the Disk Drive Parameter Table	Demonstration of DOS File Locking Functions (C)1992 Michael Tischer === DDPTP - (c) 1992 by Michael Tischer Allows users defined changes to current DDPT DDPT contents Step rate (SR): $0D Head unload time (HU): $0F Head load time (HL): $01 Head settle time (HS): $0F Motor postrun time (MP): $25 Motor startup time (MS): $00

You can change the contents of a DDPT field by typing the command with the appropriate parameter. The parameter is a two-letter code (the code that appears on the screen when the fields are displayed), followed by a colon, and then followed by a two digit hexadecimal number that represents the new value.

For example, if you type the following command:

```
DDPTP MA:04 SR:08
```

the starting time of the diskette motor is set to one-half second and the step rate is lowered to 8 ms.

This command will work only if the DDPT is in memory, not the one in the ROM-BIOS. Each program will indicate whether you're trying to change the contents of the ROM.

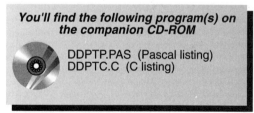

You'll find the following program(s) on the companion CD-ROM

DDPTP.PAS (Pascal listing)
DDPTC.C (C listing)

Do it yourself formatting

Programmers usually don't have to write data directly to or read data directly from a diskette using the BIOS. Generally, your application programs will be working with files. For this purpose, it's better to use the DOS functions.

However, when you're formatting diskettes you must call various BIOS functions.

The following programs, one in Pascal and the other in C, perform this task. These programs are replacements for the DOS FORMAT program. Similar to FORMAT, these programs not only format the diskette, but also create the various data structures that DOS expects. Among these are the boot sector, the root directory of the diskette, which is initially empty, and the FAT. For more information about these data structures and the general structure of mass storage systems under DOS, refer to Chapter 28.

The programs are called DFP.PAS and DFC.C. They can process all known DOS formats (360/1200 on 5.25-inch diskettes and 720/1440 on 3.5-inch diskettes). Use the following model to call them:

```
DFP Drive   Format   [ NV ]
```

```
                 |              |         |
                 |              |         |
  A: or B:       |              |         |
                 |              |         |
   360, 720, 1200, 1440|                  |
                                |         |
                 NV = No Verify |
```

Since both programs are based on the same algorithm and work with the same data types and constants, we'll discuss them together.

Within the main program, the first argument of the DOS command line is analyzed. It's assumed that this argument will be the drive identifier (letter). This value is converted into the drive number (0 or 1). Next, the format of the drive is determined by using the GetDriveType procedure. To do this, we use function 08H of the BIOS disk interrupt, which returns a type code between 0 and 4. Within the program, this code is represented by the respective constants NO_DRIVE, DD_525, HD_525, DD_35, and HD_35.

The older model PCs and XTs don't support function 08H. In this case, the carry flag is set after the function call to indicate an error. The program then defaults to a DD 5.25-inch drive that supports only a 360K format.

After GetDriveType() confirms the specified drive exists, the program then determines the logical and physical formatting parameters through the GetFormatParameter function. The format specified in the command line is passed to GetFormatParameter as a string along with the type code and two variables of type PhysDataType and LogDataType. You can see the organization of the two data structures in the Pascal version:

```
type DdptType = array[ 0..10 ] of byte;        { Structure for DDPT }
     DdptPtr = ^DdptType;                          { Pointer to DDPT }

     PhysDataType = record                 { physical format parameters }
       Seiten,                         { desired side number of diskette }
       Spuren,                               { Number of tracks per side }
       sektoren : byte;                    { Number of sectors per track }
       DDPT     : DdptPtr;    { Pointer to Disk Drive Parameter Table }
     end;

     LogDataType = record                      { DOS format parameters }
       Media,                                          { Media-Byte }
       Cluster,                        { Number of sectors per cluster }
       FAT,                              { Number of sectors for the FAT }
       RootSize : byte;              { Entries in the root directory }
     end;

     SpurBufType = array[ 1..18, 1..512 ] of byte;    { Buffer for track }
```

PhysDataType contains the physical parameters needed for formatting. These are the number of sides, the tracks per side, and the number of sectors per track. Also, a pointer to the DDPT is stored here because both programs work with their own "private" DDPTs to speed up the formatting.

While the information in PhysDataType is needed for physical formatting, the information in LogDataType is needed for logical formatting, which applies to using different DOS data structures. That's why the DOS media ID, the number of sectors per cluster, the size of the FAT in sectors, and the number of entries in the root directory are recorded here.

The variables of type PhysDataType and LogDataType within GetFormatParameter are initialized with a series of typed constants (or STATIC variables in C), in which the necessary information for all supported formats is recorded. These constants, which are called DDPT_360, LOG_1200, or PHYS_720, can be identified quickly when looking through the listings.

Before the procedure copies the parameters to the passed variables, it checks to determine whether the format specified in the command line is a valid one for the drive. The procedure displays the results of this test to the caller as its return value, which is FALSE if drive and format aren't valid.

After these checks, program execution continues by calling DiskPrepare. This procedure uses BIOS function 18H.

Function 18H returns a pointer to the DDPT to the caller. The DDPT is part of the selected format. This pointer is ignored by the two programs, however, because a different DDPT is used by FormatGetParameter(). After DiskPrepare, the address of this DDPT is stored in the interrupt vector for interrupt 1EH. Remember the contents of this vector are first saved so the original DDPT address can be restored later.

Formatting then occurs using the PhysicalFormat function. The third parameter of the DOS command line indicates whether to verify the tracks. When formatting, PhysicalFormat uses the FormatTrack procedure to format one track at a time. FormatTrack calls the BIOS disk function 05H in a nested loop for tracks 0 to N; it formats side 0 first and then side 1 of each track. Obviously, it's also possible to format the entire first side and then the entire second side. However, this would take much longer because the read/write head would have to travel over the entire diskette twice. With this method, the drive is constantly switching between head 0 and head 1, but the formatting is performed much faster than moving the read/write arm from track to track.

After FormatTrack, PhysicalFormat calls the VerifyTrack procedure to determine the validity of the data (i.e., whether the contents of a sector and the corresponding CRC checksum match). This is performed only if FALSE is returned for the VERIFY parameter.

VerifyTrack, like FormatTrack and WriteTrack, which we haven't discussed yet, is simply a procedure name for the corresponding BIOS function. If the BIOS reports an error, this call is repeated several times before a "real" error indication is finally returned to the caller. The maximum number of attempts is determined by the MaxVersuch constant, which is defined at the beginning of the listings. By setting this constant to one, both versions of the program will frequently report an unsuccessful format because errors occur more often than you might think.

Now let's return to the main program. If the diskette was perfectly formatted with PhysicalFormat, then the last processing step begins. This step involves logically formatting the drive using LogicalFormat. As we mentioned, in this step the different data structures that DOS needs for managing files are written to the diskette. We discuss this in detail in Chapter 28.

One interesting structure is the boot sector, which must be written to the diskette if it is to contain the DOS operating system. The contents of the boot sector are defined at the beginning of the program in the BootMaske variable. You'll find the details about the data and the small machine language program in Chapter 28. But you should know the meaning of the BootMes variable, which immediately follows the boot sector. This variable contains the string that appears on the screen when the computer is booted. It's written to the diskette with the boot sector.

You can alter the contents of this string. For example, you can add your own name or the name of your company so it appears on the screen when you boot the computer from the diskette. However, remember the end of the sector is indicated by a byte with the value 00H.

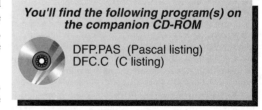

You'll find the following program(s) on the companion CD-ROM

DFP.PAS (Pascal listing)
DFC.C (C listing)

The end of LogicalFormat is essentially the end of program execution, because nothing happens in the main program except writing the status message.

Using BIOS To Access The Hard Drives

In this section we'll describe the BIOS functions for accessing hard drives. However, before we begin, we must warn you about experimenting with these functions. Unlike a floppy disk drive, in which you can insert an unused diskette for testing, a hard drive cannot be tested in this way. Using write and format functions carelessly can lead to irreparable data loss. Because of the structure DOS imposes on a hard drive, destroying one sector can cause all files and directories to disappear because DOS may no longer know where they are on the hard disk.

So, if you would like to "test" the BIOS functions, be sure to make a complete backup of your entire hard drive beforehand, or use another computer, if available. This is the only way you can avoid data loss, because even the most elaborate hard drive utility may not be able to help you.

The BIOS hard drive interrupt

As we mentioned, the hard drive shares interrupt 13H with the floppy disk drives. Although the functions for the hard drive and the floppy disk drives are identical, the BIOS controls the hard drive differently than the floppy disk drive. For this reason, the BIOS contains a module for controlling the hard drive and a separate one for controlling the floppy disk drives.

When interrupt 13H is called, the device number in the DL register determines whether a floppy or hard drive is being addressed. A value of 80H represents the first hard drive, while 81H represents the second hard drive. It's not possible to address more than two hard drives via the BIOS.

The functions of the hard drive BIOS have existed since the introduction of the XT. The original PC BIOS didn't have them. In 1981 no one thought of putting hard drives in microcomputers. When the AT and PS/2 model from IBM was introduced, some additional functions were added, as the following table shows:

Function	Task	Origin	Function	Task	Origin
00H	Reset	XT	0CH	Move read/write head	XT
01H	Read status	XT	0DH	Reset	XT
02H	Read	XT	0EH	Controller read test	only PS/2
03H	Write	XT	0FH	Controller write test	only PS/2
04H	Verify	XT	10H	Drive ready?	XT
05H	Format	XT	11H	Recalibrate drive	XT
08H	Check format	XT	12H	Controller RAM test	only PS/2
09H	Adapt to foreign drives	XT	13H	Drive test	only PS/2
0AH	Extended read	XT	14H	Controller diagnostic	XT
0BH	Extended write	XT	15H	Determine drive type	AT

Normal application programs don't usually access the hard drive through the BIOS. We'll describe only the most important functions in this section. You can find more information in the Appendix (located on the companion CD-ROM in which all the functions are described.

Status code

The hard drive functions use the carry flag to indicate an error. If the carry flag is set, then an error has occurred and the error status code is returned in the AH register.

The codes have the following meanings:

Error codes when calling BIOS Disk Interrupt 13h for accessing the hard drive			
Code	Meaning	Code	Meaning
00h	No error	10h	Read error
01h	Function number or drive not permitted	11h	Read error corrected by ECC
02h	Address not found	20h	Controller defect
04h	Addressed sector not found	40h	Search operation failed
05h	Error on controller reset	80h	Time out, unit not responding
07h	Error during controller initialization	AAh	Unit not ready
09h	DMA transmission error.Segment border exceeded.	CCh	Write error
0Ah	Defective sector		

When one of these error occurs (except for error 1), you should first reset the drive and retry the function. Usually, the operation will then be successful.

If error 11H is returned after a read function, the data isn't necessarily invalid. Actually, this status code indicates that a read error was detected, but was able to be corrected using an ECC (Error Correction Code) algorithm. This procedure is similar to the CRC procedure used by floppy disk drives. The individual bytes of a sector are calculated through a complicated mathematical formula. The resulting sum is written to the sector on the hard disk as four additional bytes. If a read error is detected, it can usually be corrected by using the ECC.

Using the hard drive functions

The hard drive functions also use registers for passing parameters. The function number is passed in the AH register. When the hard drive number must be identified, its value is passed in the DL register. The value 80H always represents the first hard drive, and 81H represents the second hard drive. The number of the read/write head and the side (0 or 1) are passed in the DH register.

The CH register specifies the cylinder number. Since you can represent only 256 cylinders with this 8-bit register and the hard drive of an XT has more than 306 cylinders, this register alone cannot specify the cylinder number. For this reason, bits 6 and 7 of the CL register are "appended" to the value in the CH register to determine the cylinder number. They form bits 8 and 9 of the cylinder number, so a maximum of 1024 cylinders (numbered 0 to 1023) can be addressed. Bits 0 to 5 of the CL register specify the sector number (1 to 17 per cylinder). If more than one sector is being accessed at the same time, the AL register specifies the number of sectors. In read and write operations you must also specify the address of a buffer, from which the data is written or to which the data are transferred. In this case, the ES register indicates the segment address and the BX register indicates the offset address of the buffer.

Resetting the hard drive controller

One function that doesn't require all the parameters is function 00H, which, like function 0DH, resets the controller. For example, after an error occurs, this function is routinely performed before the next data access. The only parameter needed is the hard drive number that is passed in the DL register.

Determining the status of the hard drive

Using function 01H, you can determine the status of the hard drive. Again, the drive number whose status is being checked is passed in the DL register.

Reading hard drive sectors

Function 02H reads one or more sectors of the hard drive. On each call to this function, you can read a maximum of 128 sectors. Perhaps you're wondering why the maximum is 128 instead of 256 sectors. The hard disk controller uses DMA capability to transfer data between the computer's memory and the hard drive. However, the DMA components can transfer a maximum of 64K of data at one time. This is equivalent to 128 sectors (64K = 128 sectors * 512 bytes/sector). Another restriction is the DMA components can transfer data only within a single memory segment. So, the read/write buffer is usually aligned to the start of a memory segment. Remember the ES:BX register pair point to the buffer. In this case, the ES register will point to the start of this segment and the BX register will have a zero offset.

When you use function 02H to read more than one sector per call, the sectors are read in the following order: First, the sectors in the specified cylinder and side are read in ascending order (by sector number). When the end of the cylinder is reached, the first sector on the same cylinder, but on the next head, is read. Sectors on the next cylinder aren't read until after the last head in the same cylinder is reached and there are sectors remaining to be read.

Writing hard drive sectors

Function 03H is used to write one or more sectors to the hard drive. This function is similar to function 02H except the data is written from the buffer to the hard drive. For a description of this function, refer to the one above.

Verifying hard drive sectors

Function 04H verifies the sectors of a cylinder. However, the data on the hard drive is compared with the ECC value instead of the data in memory (which is why it isn't necessary to specify a buffer address in ES:BX). The number of sectors to be verified is specified in the AL register.

Formatting the hard drive cylinders

A hard drive must be formatted before it can be used. Function 05H performs this task. This function is similar to the function for formatting a floppy diskette. The address of a buffer is passed in the ES:BX register pair. This buffer must be 512 bytes in size, although only the first 34 bytes are used.

The buffer consists of two one-byte entries for each of the 17 sectors to be formatted. The first byte indicates whether the sector is good or bad. Before calling this function, we assume that each sector is good. So we store a zero value here. The second byte is the logical sector number.

Bytes 1 and 2 of the table are used when the first physical sector of the cylinder is formatted. Bytes 3 and 4 are used when the second physical sector is formatted, etc. So, while the physical sequence is fixed, the logical sequence of sectors is defined by the two bytes of a sector specification in this table.

The most obvious way to format the hard drive is to assign a sector's physical sector number to each logical sector. However, a technique called sector interleaving is actually used to speed up hard disk performance. We'll discuss sector interleaving in more detail in the "Hard Drive Advancements" section later in this chapter.

The first byte of each table entry may contain the value 00H, which indicates the sector is good, or 80H, which indicates the sector is bad. During formatting, this byte is transferred to the sector marker that indicates that DOS shouldn't use this sector to store data.

Determining the hard drive parameters

Unlike floppy diskettes, hard drives don't have uniform characteristics. For some programs, it's important to know the hard drive's parameters. To do this, use function 08H to pass the hard drive number in the DL register.

After calling the function, the DL register contains the number of hard drives connected to the controller. The value returned may be 0, 1, or 2. The DH register contains the number of read/write heads. Since this value is relative to 0, a value of 7 means there are 8 heads. The number of cylinders is returned both in the CL register (bits 0-7) and the two upper bits of the CH register (bits 8 and 9). Again, this value is relative to 0. Finally, the number of sectors per track is returned in the lower 6 bits of the CH register. This specifies the number of sectors per track, but is relative to 1, not 0.

Initializing a "foreign" hard drive

The BIOS in each computer already contains the specifications for various hard drives. This makes it easy to select the hard drive specifications during SETUP. However, suppose the specifications for a particular hard drive aren't in the BIOS. There's another way to make the drive's specifications known to the BIOS. First a table containing the specifications is constructed. Then the address of the table is stored at interrupt 41H or interrupt 46H, depending on whether hard drive 0 or hard drive 1 is being initialized. The format of the table is predefined by BIOS and describes the characteristics of the hard drive.

Finally, function 09H, which initializes the controller with the new hard drive specifications, is called. The drive number (80H or 81H) is passed in the DL register. Usually the device driver provided by the hard drive manufacturer manages this function.

Extended hard drive sector read/write

Functions 0AH and 0BH are similar to the read and write functions 02H and 03H. However, one difference is that, in addition to the 512 bytes of data per sector that's transferred, the four ECC bytes at the end of each sector are also transferred. Since each sector is 516 bytes instead of 512 bytes, the maximum number of sectors that can be read or written at a time is 127 sectors, while functions 02H and 03H can handle 128 sectors.

Function 10H tests whether the hard drive, whose number is passed in the DL register, is ready to execute commands. If the carry flag is set to indicate the drive isn't ready, then the AH register will contain the error code.

Recalibrating the hard drive

Function 0BH is used to recalibrate the hard drive. After the function call, this function returns the error status along with the drive number in the DL register.

Self test of the hard drive controller

Function 14H is used to perform a self test. If the controller passes the test, the carry flag will be reset.

The final hard drive interrupt function is 15H, which is available only on ATs, not XTs. This interrupt returns the drive type. The drive number (80H or 81H) is passed in the DL register. If the drive isn't available, a value of 0 is returned in the AH register. A value of 1 or 2 indicates a floppy disk drive. A value of 3 indicates a hard drive. In this case, registers CX and DX contain the number of sectors on this hard drive. The two registers form a 32 bit number, with the CX register containing the high-order byte and the DX register containing the low-order byte.

Hard Drives And Their Controllers

The advancements in hard drive technology are related to four types of controllers: ST506, ESDI, SCSI, and IDE. The format, in which the data are saved on the hard drive, not only depends on the controller, but also on the data transfer rate between the computer and the hard drive.

The following table shows the maximum data transfer rates that are possible with the different controllers. However, these are theoretical maximum values that not only are seldom attained, but also are affected by other factors. Imagine a set of data on its way from the hard drive to be displayed on the screen (e.g., when you load a document into a word processor). In addition to the controller, the program must interface with many levels: the BIOS, the DOS, the application program, and perhaps one ore more TSRs.

Another factor that affects the data transfer rate is the speed of the bus. This limits the speed of hard drive controllers because at least the ISA bus still operates at 8 MHz, even though the speed of the CPU has already reached the 100 MHz limit. So any published values quickly diminish to about a fifth by the time the data actually appears.

Maximum data transfer rates of the various PC hard drive controllers			
Controller	Maximum Data Transfer Rate	Controller	Maximum Data Transfer Rate
ST506	1 Meg per second	IDE	4 Meg per second
ESDI	2.5 Meg per second	SCSI	5 Meg per second

Next, we'll introduce you to the various hard drive controllers, examine their structure, and describe their advantages and disadvantages. The role of the BIOS is also discussed.

ST506 controller

The first hard drives that were widely accepted in the PC world were developed for the ST506 controller and compatible controllers. As its name indicates, this controller originated from the Seagate company, which is an important hard drive manufacturer.

Even today, ST506 controllers are still the most widely used controllers, even though new hard drives usually are equipped with IDE controllers. Generally, hard drives designed for hookup to an ST506 controller are identified by the label "MFM/RLL". These letters refer to the two recording methods by which the controllers save data on the hard drive. Usually you can use DIP switches to set the format the controller uses. The RLL format is preferred because it provides higher hard drive capacity. (Refer to the "Recording Information On The Hard Drive" section in this chapter for more information.)

Because of its wide distribution, the ST506 controller has set different standards in hardware control systems, partly because the BIOS conforms to this controller type. The effects of this are evident today. For example, IDE and ESDI controllers are (and must be) compatible with ST506 controllers in various ways. We'll discuss this in more detail later.

The hardware

In the ST506 standard, the hard drive and controller are two separate components. The controller is on a separate card and occupies one of the PC's expansion slots.

A controller can usually manage two hard drives. Two types of cables connect the controller to each hard drive. Each hard drive connects to the controller with its own 20-pin data cable. If both hard drives are installed, they share the 34-pin control cable. The control cable sends electrical signals to the hard drive to select the desired read/write heads, search for the desired cylinder, etc. Data to be read from or written to the hard drive is transferred over the data cable in serial and analog mode.

The controller can convert the digital information on a cylinder into bit strings. The information on magnetic media exists as values of 0 or 1. The controller can reverse the digital values as needed; this process is called flux reversal.

The data transfer rate can be as high as 5 megabits/second using MFM recording and 7.5 megabits/second using RLL recording. Since the control information still must be "filtered out" from the stream of data, the effective transfer rate of useful data is considerably lower. Even so, MFM controllers can process .5 megabytes per second and RLL controller can even process 0.75 megabytes per second. However, usually these theoretical values ignore factors such as head select time, cylinder seek time, etc., and assume that you'll read contiguous sectors. We'll discuss this in more detail in the section on interleaving.

The higher transfer rate of RLL controllers is a result of a more efficient recording scheme. You'll see that more sectors can be written to each track using RLL. MFM drives can write 17 sectors on a track, but RLL drives can fit 26 sectors on each track. In both formats, the rotational speed of the drive is 3600 RPM.

When the XT first appeared, the only controller available was the ST506. As a result, the new hard drive functions of the ROM-BIOS were developed specifically for this controller. These hard drive functions have imposed rigid limitations on PC manufacturers. For example, the number of drives is limited to two, the maximum number of cylinders to 1204, the maximum number of sectors per track to 63, and the maximum number of heads to 16. Also, the sector size is fixed at 512 bytes. When combined with all the other factors, the maximum capacity of a drive is 504 Meg.

To overcome these limitations, some hard drive controllers "trick" the system into believing there are two hard drives, which are actually on the same drive. This makes it possible to have a hard drive with a capacity of up to 1 gigabyte. However, an ST506 controller is too slow for a drive with such enormous capacity. So, it isn't practical to connect such large hard drives to systems with ST506-type controllers. Because of this, the ST506-type controller will gradually disappear in the coming years.

ESDI controllers

The ESDI controller was developed after the ST506 controller. ESDI, which is an acronym for "Enhanced Small Devices Interface", is found in many IBM PS/2 models. This controller represents an advancement of the ST506 model. Generally, ESDI controllers are compatible with the ST506 and can be used in computers whose BIOS is programmed to support only ST506 controllers.

Unlike the ST506, ESDI doesn't transfer every flux reversal serially to the controller via the data line. Instead, part of the decoding logic, called the data separator, is already on the hard drive. The data separator prepares the data read from the hard drive and transfers only the useful data, in digital form, to the controller.

Because the controller and the data separator work in parallel, the transfer rate can be as high as 10 megabits/second. This represents only a doubling of the transfer rate of an MFM ST506 drive. However, this is accompanied by another performance enhancement. ESDI controllers usually have a sector buffer that makes an interleave factor of 1:1 possible. What does this mean? An ST506 drive with an interleave factor of six requires six full revolutions to transfer the contents of an entire track. With an interleave factor of three, this same drive still requires three full revolutions to transfer the contents of an entire track. However, an ESDI can perform the same task in a single revolution. This results in increasing the access speed by a factor of three to six.

Also, some ESDI systems can reach a transfer rate of 15, 20, and even 24 megabits per second. However, such controllers are rare and usually quite expensive. So most ESDI controllers work with 10 megabits.

The data separator isn't the only intelligent component on an ESDI system. An ESDI hard drive also stores information about its physical format and the addresses of defective sectors and can send this information to the controller. Then the controller can perform its own SETUP, which is a task that a user has to do with ST506 drives.

The BIOS and ESDI controllers

The hard drive information is then stored in the CMOS RAM of an AT. The BIOS must know the parameters of the hard drive and pass this information to the DOS device driver.

Because the ESDI controller can request this information from the hard drive, the information in the BIOS doesn't have to match the actual characteristics of the drive. Often this discrepancy cannot be avoided, because each BIOS knows only a limited number of hard drive types and their specifications.

You'll encounter problems on an ST506-type hard drive if the installed drive doesn't appear in the BIOS list. In this case, you must select a drive, from the list, whose specifications most closely match those of the installed drive. This often means "wasting" some of the drive capacity. You must select a BIOS entry for a drive with fewer cylinders, tracks, or heads. Otherwise the system might try to access sectors that don't even exist on the installed drive, which results in an error.

Another problem is when the BIOS doesn't have a hard drive type that works with the same number of sectors per track. Then you must select a BIOS entry for a drive with the next smallest sector size, which means wasting valuable sectors in every track on the drive and increasing the number of unused sectors to an undesirable level.

With ST506 drives, this isn't a problem because they only work with 17 or 26 sectors, depending on the recording method. However, ESDI drives have 34 or 36 sectors per track. So, if the BIOS contains entries for drives with only 26 sectors, then you might end up wasting one-third of your expensive hard drive capacity.

Fortunately, most ESDI controllers can avoid this problem. The BIOS entry for a drive with a slightly smaller capacity than the ESDI hard drive is selected during SETUP. Since ESDI hard drives can send their specifications to the ESDI controller, the controller knows the physical characteristics of the drive. Using a special feature called sector translation, the ESDI controller converts the BIOS logical drive specifications into the hard drive physical specifications. The conversion takes slightly longer, but ensures the ESDI hard drive can be used with almost any BIOS entry without wasting a lot of its capacity.

The ability to perform this conversion depends entirely on the ESDI controller. Some controllers support only certain BIOS entries, while others are more flexible and can accept any format. This is also an advantage if an ESDI drive encounters the limits imposed by the BIOS hard drive functions, for example, an ESDI drive with more than 1024 cylinders. Instead of wasting the cylinders above 1024, the controller simulates a greater number of sectors per track. Although the ESDI drive may have only 34 tracks per sector, it can pretend to have up to 63 tracks per sector. The ESDI controller then translates a logical cylinder/sector/head specification to the hard drive's physical specification.

SCSI controllers

The SCSI controller (pronounced "scuzzy") standard, isn't really a hard drive interface. Instead, it's a way to connect up to eight entirely different devices to a PC. Besides hard drives, you can connect tape backup streamers, CD-ROM drives, or scanners to a SCSI interface.

Unlike other hard drive controller standards, the SCSI (Small Computer System Interface) isn't found only in PCs, but also on many 68000 systems (Macintosh and Atari ST) and large workstations. One reason for its appeal is that you can easily couple and uncouple devices from the SCSI interface because the devices communicate with the controller through a bus that's separate from the PC bus.

Both the SCSI line specifications and the SCSI commands to control the devices are standardized. SCSI devices can be easily exchanged between different systems; only the SCSI controller must be matched to the host computer system.

The SCSI bus, which links different SCSI devices together, is usually a cable with an 80-pin plug. The bus allows 8-bit parallel data transfer. A new version, called SCSI2 allows 16-bit parallel data transfer.

Manufacturers of SCSI controllers like to tempt their customers by quoting data transfer rates of 4 or 5 Meg per second. Actually, these rates aren't possible. While the SCSI controller can handle these high data transfer rates, the hard drive connected to it cannot. So, you can expect a data transfer rate of between 1.5 and 2 Meg per second, unless you purchase an expensive EISA controller, which can manage 2.5 Meg per second.

SCSI drives continue the trend started by ESDI drives by integrating much of the control circuitry directly on the hard drive. Actually, this must be done with this system, because the controller must remain device-independent and not concern itself with the specific characteristics and features of a hard drive.

Shorter paths aren't the only advantage provided by the close proximity of the hard drive and its control circuitry. This also makes it easier to trick the controller into using a certain disk format that doesn't really exist. Like an ESDI controller, the SCSI controller asks the attached devices for its specification when the system starts and passes this information to the requester.

SCSI systems depend on their own built in BIOS. From a software standpoint, SCSI systems don't support the ST506 standard of the ROM-BIOS. The original functions of the BIOS Disk Interrupt are replaced by the SCSI BIOS. Unfortunately, the SCSI BIOS isn't useful in protected mode, in which "operating environments" such as Novell or OS/2 access the disk directly and often support only the ST506 standard. This requires a specific device driver, which may not be available for the particular operating environment. This is one of the biggest disadvantages of the SCSI interface.

However, if you have the required driver, the hard drive specifications are automatic. To install a new SCSI drive, simply connect it to the bus. The SCSI controller handles the rest by using the correct "driver ware".

IDE

The new star of hard drive controllers is the IDE controller (Intelligent Drive Electronics) interface. The IDE interface is found in almost every new PC. Its development started in 1984, when PC manufacturer Compaq asked Western Digital to develop an ST506-compatible controller that would fit on the hard drive to save space.

Using an IDE drive provides a hard drive and a controller in one. A single 40-pin cable combines the functions of a data cable and a control cable and connects the IDE drive directly to the system bus.

This is also where IDE drives get their nickname; sometimes they're called "AT Bus Drives". But IDE drives aren't limited to ATs with their 16 bit data buses. You can also use IDE drives on an 8-bit XT bus.

Many PCs have a connector for an IDE cable directly on the motherboard. With other PC's you must use a small expansion slot board, which then connects to the IDE cable.

Combining the drive and controller gives the IDE some of the same advantages of the SCSI controllers. Among these are the ability to emulate any drive format and track caching, in which the drive reads an entire track and keeps the data in an internal cache buffer until it's needed. IDE drives can operate with an interleave factor of 1:1, which provides faster access. IDE combines the advantages of the other three standards; it's flexible like SCSI, fast like ESDI, and is compatible to the ST506 standard so it can be connected to most PC systems easily.

Also, IDE drives have a very low power consumption, so they're ideal for laptops and notebooks.

Many IDE drives have special commands for working with laptops and notebooks. For example, these commands can put the notebook computer "to sleep", which minimizes power consumption. These commands are generally used in connection with special drivers or a BIOS that's adapted to work with IDE drives. From the BIOS' point of view, IDE drives behave like normal ST506 controllers, making it easy to integrate them into existing systems.

New standards are being defined for IDE drives. In the near future we'll most likely see new BIOS systems supporting IDE drives directly. Then PC makers can fully use the extended features offered by these drives, which go unused in many of today's systems.

From controller to memory

Regardless of the speed of the hard drive and the controller, the way in which the data is transferred by the controller to the memory determines the effective speed of a controller-hard drive combination. Four different methods can be used to do this:

- ➢ Programmed I/O (PIO)   ➢ Memory Mapped I/O
- ➢ DMA   ➢ Busmaster DMA

Programmed I/O

With programmed I/O, the different controller I/O ports manage both the drive commands and the transfer of the data between the controller and the main memory. If you use programmed I/O, you'll use the IN and OUT assembly language instructions. This means that every byte or word must be channeled through the CPU.

Here, the data transfer rate is limited by the speed of the PC bus and the performance of the CPU. While the ISA bus allows a maximum transfer rate of 5.33 Meg per second (16-bit rate), this rate is unattainable with any of today's CPUs. With fast 386es, 486es or Pentiums, the data transfer rate is limited to about 3 or 4 Meg and can be attained only with very fast and expensive hard drives.

Memory Mapped I/O

The CPU can process data from a disk controller even faster if it stores them in a fixed memory region. The segment located above the video RAM is generally used for this purpose. Data in a program's memory area can be transferred faster using MOV instructions. This is faster than accessing the I/O ports with IN and OUT.

Even by using memory mapped I/O, today's speedy CPUs can request data faster than the controller is capable of transferring. The controller can never reach the theoretical maximum value of 8 Meg per second. It can't even reach 5 to 6 Meg per second.

DMA

DMA (Direct Memory Access) transfer is more widely known than the first two methods. Using DMA, a device (hard drive, floppy disk drive, CD-ROM, etc.) can transfer data directly to the computer's memory. The CPU is bypassed. To use DMA, a program only needs to tell the DMA controller how many bytes should be transferred from one location to another. This makes DMA seem like the best method for transferring data.

However, the DMA controller in the PC is inflexible and slow. In fact, it's so slow that Programmed I/O is faster on 386 and higher systems. The DMA controller operates at 4 MHz on the AT or later systems even though it worked at 4.77 MHz on earlier PCs. So, DMA transfer is faster than Programmed I/O only on PCs. Using DMA, the data transfer rate is limited to about 2 Meg per second.

Therefore, the DMA method is no longer used on most modern hard drives, even though many hard drives do support this method in addition to Programmed I/O.

Busmaster DMA

Busmaster DMA is another form of direct memory access, but isn't related to the DMA circuitry on the motherboard of the computer. Using this method, the hard drive controller disconnects the CPU from the bus and transfers data to memory on its own using its own Busmaster DMA controller. Transfer rates of up to 8 Meg per second are possible. Unfortunately, this feature increases the price of the controller. Busmaster DMA is generally used only with very powerful SCSI controllers.

Protected mode

The methods of DMA transfer are limited to real mode programs. Without special intervention, DMA cannot be used in protected or virtual mode. How virtual memory management is performed by the CPUs memory management unit (MMU) is responsible for this limitation. The MMU maps a program's virtual memory addresses into real physical memory addresses.

A protected or virtual mode program doesn't realize this, because it's never aware of the physical addresses; it works only with virtual addresses. When this program wants to perform a DMA transfer, it passes a virtual address to the DMA chip. However, because the MMU isn't involved in the DMA transfer, it cannot map this virtual address into a physical address. As a result, the data is transferred to a different memory area. The system will soon crash because important memory areas are overwritten.

This is a characteristic of protected mode operating systems, such as Windows and OS/2. However, this also occurs in Virtual 86 mode using DOS if the EMM386.EXE device driver is used to emulate expanded memory. EMM386.EXE depends on the virtual memory management of the processor.

The solution is to "watch" the DMA controller. Do this in protected mode to control all the I/O ports. In Windows, for example, a virtual control monitor in the background is installed to watch the programming of the DMA controller via the BIOS or another program. This monitor converts the actual physical addresses before they are written to the register of the DMA controller.

Recording Information On The Hard Drive

To understand how information is written on a hard drive, you must first forget the concept of binary coding. Zeros and ones aren't stored on the magnetic surface of a hard drive. It's impossible to represent these two states as "magnetized" and "not magnetized".

Why isn't this possible? If you try to represent data as sequences of magnetized and non-magnetized particles, the read head of the hard drive wouldn't be able to keep the individual magnetic particles separate. So, it wouldn't be able to distinguish between three or five zeros.

One way to avoid this problem is by knowing the length of a magnetic particle and the elapsed time for each magnetic signal. In other words, you need a kind of clock that indicates, with each tick, that it's time for a new bit.

However, the constant period of time for a cycle cannot be clearly defined because of various factors. For example, the rotational speed of the hard drive may vary slightly. But a bigger factor is that a single magnetic particle can never be magnetized; only a group of magnetic particles, whose number isn't always constant, can be magnetized.

It is possible, however, to record flux reversals, which are short passages between non-magnetized particles and magnetized particles. The reversals in flux create an electrical pulse in the hard drive's read head. This pulse is then passed to the electronic circuitry, where it is used to decode the stored information as zeros and ones.

This coding and decoding of binary information has always been important to hardware developers The number of flux reversals that can be recorded per square inch on a hard drive is limited. This limit depends on the composition of the magnetic material, the gap of the read/write head, its sensitivity, etc. Anyone who can find ways to record more zeros and ones on the hard drive with an equal number of flux reversals will lead the competition in higher and higher disk capacities.

FM method

The simplest way to encode zeros and ones to a magnetic surface is to record a flux reversal for each one-bit and omit a flux reversal for each zero-bit. However, you'll encounter a problem when you want to record a long series of zeros. In this instance, you must omit many flux reversals to represent the string of zeros. This would confuse the controller that depends on flux reversals to keep in sync with the data on the hard drive.

To avoid this problem, a clock signal is written onto the drive along with the data. Using the FM method (Frequency Modulation) recording technique, a one-bit might be recorded as two consecutive flux reversals and a zero-bit recorded as a flux reversal followed by no flux reversal. In both cases, the initial flux reversal represents the timing signal. The data bit is then modulated "between" the timing signal (second flux reversal for one-bit and no flux reversal for zero-bit).

The FM method of recording

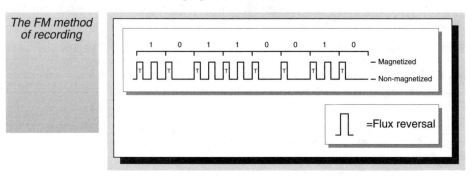

Although this method is simple and inexpensive, it has one major disadvantage. Each data bit requires two flux reversals, which reduces the potential disk capacity by half.

MFM method

To reduce the number of flux reversals of the FM method and thereby increase the density at which information can be recorded, another encoding technique is used. This technique is called MFM method (Modified FM). Basically, the data is encoded as follows:

Code table for the MFM	
Data bit value	Encoded as:
1	Flux reversal
0 following another 0-bit	Flux reversal followed by no flux reversal
0 following another 1-bit	No flux reversal followed by no flux reversal

With this method, the timing signal is also used to store data. Both zero-bits and one-bits are recorded using only a single flux reversal. Longer sequences of zeros and ones appear as a continuous sequence of flux reversals.

This encoding method requires improved control circuitry so the hard drive can synchronize with the normal sequence of timing flux reversals for longer sequences of zeros.

The only problem is when a one is followed by a zero, which requires a flux reversal to the normal timing position. The time between the flux reversal of the one and that of the zero amounts to only half the normal interval between two flux reversals. However, this won't work because the shortest interval between two flux reversals cannot be shorter; otherwise the electronic circuitry would no longer be able to keep up. Therefore, a flux reversal isn't stored for a zero that follows a one.

The next flux reversal comes after one and a half times the time for a flux change (bit combination 100b) or even after twice the time (bit combination 101b). The following illustration demonstrates this.

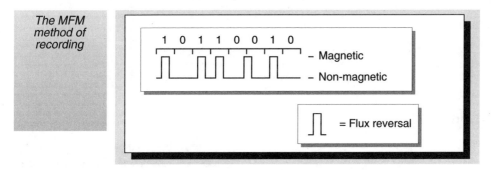

The MFM method of recording

1 0 1 1 0 0 1 0

– Magnetic
– Non-magnetic

⊓ = Flux reversal

RLL method

Another encoding method, called RLL method (Run Length Limited), packs up to 50 percent more information on the disk than MFM.

In RLL, ones are stored as flux reversals; zeros are stored as the absence of flux reversals. A timing signal isn't recorded. The hard drive circuitry itself supplies the timing reference. However, even with a very constant rotation of the hard drive and improvements in the read head and its electronic circuitry, this is possible only if there aren't too many zeros between two ones. With each zero, the time to the next flux reversal increases, and along with it, the possibility the hard drive controller will lose its beat.

However, the ones cannot follow each other too rapidly. Otherwise, the controller may not be able to keep pace.

RLL encoding method of recording

Byte to save or store

1 0 1 1 0 0 1 0

0 1 0 0 1 0 0 0 0 0 1 0 0 1 0 0   RLL-Code

⊓ = Flux reversal

Instead of encoding a single bit, the RLL method looks at and encodes a group of data bits. This group or bit string is from 2 to 4 bits in length. The new encoded string is twice as long as the original, but ensures the sequences of zeros aren't too long and the distances between ones don't become too short (and thereby overwork the circuitry). The 2,7 RLL encoding scheme is today's standard and is used in most modern hard drives. In the encoded string, a minimum of 2 and a maximum of 7 zeros will appear between two ones. This method increases the capacity of a drive by about 50 percent compared to MFM.

Another scheme is 3,9 RLL, which is called "advanced RLL", lets you fit even more information on the drive. With this method, the encoded scheme has a minimum of 3 and a maximum of 9 zeros between two ones.

The table on the right shows the encoding scheme for RLL 2.7. At first, you may think that a byte such as 00000001b cannot be encoded. However, don't forget that, on this level, you're working with sectors instead of single bytes. So, it's even possible to encode a byte, such as 00000001b, by including the bits of the following byte in the coding.

The only problem in coding occurs with the last byte of a sector because this method needs the following byte. This problem is solved by simply using a byte from the hard drive controller. The excess bits are simply truncated so the last byte of a sector is correctly decoded.

Code table for the RLL 2.7			
Bit pattern	Encoded as	Bit pattern	Encoded as
000	000100	11	1000
10	0100	011	001000
010	100100	001	00001000
0010	00100100		

Hard Drive Advancements

One of the remarkable achievements in PC computers has been the "smaller, faster, cheaper" advancements in hard drive technology. For instance:

➤ Access times in the top performance models have decreased from over thirty milliseconds to about ten milliseconds.

➤ Maximum storage capacities have increased by several hundred megabytes. Hard drives with a capacity of more than 1 gigabyte are now common.

➤ 1 Meg of hard drive capacity costs less than ten dollars.

The hard drive's performance and capabilities has increased because of the optimization in recording and playback techniques. In this section we'll discuss some of these techniques.

Interleaving and the interleave factor

Today hard drive controllers are so fast they can read an entire track even when only the data in a single sector is requested. So, when the data in the next sector is needed, the hard drive controller doesn't have to read the next sector. Instead, it can take the data from the controller's internal buffer. This significantly speeds up data access.

Most ST506 controllers have only an internal sector buffer (with a capacity to store the contents of exactly one sector), so only the newer controller types (SCSI, ESDI, and IDE) are track buffer compatible. Also, the sector buffer cannot be reused until the last byte of the previous sector is passed to the CPU. So, additional time is required until the next sector passes under the read head.

AT		XT	
Physical sectors	Logical sectors	Physical sectors	Logical sectors
1	1	1	1
2	7	2	4
3	13	3	7
4	2	4	10
5	8	5	13
6	14	6	16
7	3	7	2
8	9	8	5
9	15	9	8
10	4	10	11
11	10	11	14
12	16	12	17
13	5	13	3
14	11	14	6
15	17	15	9
16	6	16	12
17	12	17	15

The data in the subsequent sector cannot be read until the sector passes under the read head again; this requires almost an entire revolution of the hard drive. This process continues with each sector, noticeably reducing the speed of disk access. To minimize this delay, interleaving is used to spread the logical sectors across the track.

By interleaving the logical sectors, the controller has enough time to process and transfer the data in one sector before the next logical sector passes under the read head. This avoids the rotational delay of having to wait for a complete revolution before the sector can be read.

Interleaving is measured by the interleave factor. This value is the number of sectors by which the logical sector number was shifted, compared to the physical sector number. The original XT hard drive uses an interleave factor of 1:6, while the AT uses an interleave factor of 1:3. However, the interleave factor of the AT hard drive can be reduced to 1:2, which increases the access speed.

Today, interleave factors of 1:1 are common, which means there is no interleaving at all.

However, an interleave of 1:6 requires that five physical sectors be skipped before the next logical sector can be read. An interleave of 1:3 requests that two physical sectors be skipped. The table on the previous page shows the logical arrangement of sectors on a track with 17 sectors.

Despite the advantages of this method, the best interleave is actually no interleave at all. Without an interleave, an entire track be read within a hard drive revolution. However, two, three, or even more revolutions would be needed with interleaving, depending on the interleave factor.

Setting the interleave

Set the interleave in the "low-level-format" of the hard drive, which creates the address labels and sector numbers on the surface on an unused hard drive.

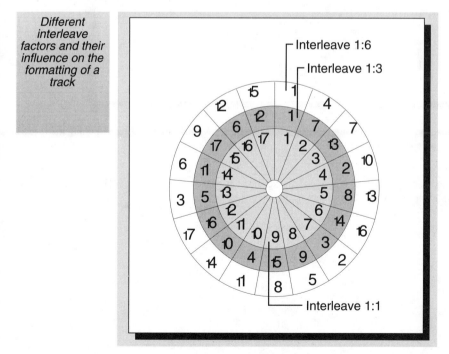

Different interleave factors and their influence on the formatting of a track

Because the logical sector number of a single sector is determined by the low-level-formatting program, it's possible to shift the sectors. Many hard disk utilities will prompt you for the desired interleave factor. If you select a "bad" value, your hard drive may slow down when loading programs or accessing files.

Even if you do select a "bad" interleave factor, you can still eliminate the problem later. You can use a program, such as the Norton Utilities, to do this. Such programs determine the optimum interleave factor and then execute the appropriate low-level-format for you. This usually takes just a few minutes.

You may think that this type of utility will lead to data loss because the program is "tampering" with the hard drive. However, as long as the program is error-free, you shouldn't loose any data. Since these programs work below DOS level, DOS is completely unaffected by the changes. Remember, DOS doesn't know the origin of a sector which it reads or writes. So, as long as the data are read before a track is reformatted and written back, DOS believes that nothing has changed.

Track and cylinder skewing

Carefully selecting an interleaving factor significantly increases hard disk performance. After the data from one track is read, data, which is in same cylinder but the following head, are usually accessed. As the controller switches the read/write head, the hard drive continues to rotate. After reading the last sector on the track, the first sector on the next head has already passed the read/write head. So you must wait almost an entire revolution.

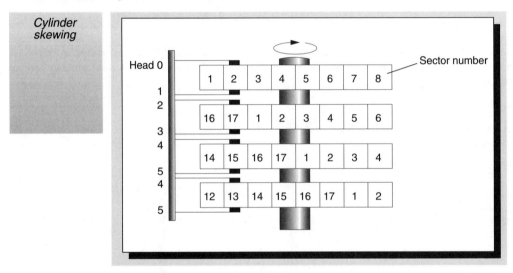

Cylinder skewing

To prevent this from happening, use cylinder skewing. All of the sectors on a track are shifted so, after switching to the next head, the first sector can be read without any rotational delay. You can set the cylinder skewing during the low-level-formatting of the drive.

In addition to cylinder skewing, there is also track skewing. This is similar to cylinder skewing, except that it considers the time needed by the drive to move the entire read/write arm to the next track.

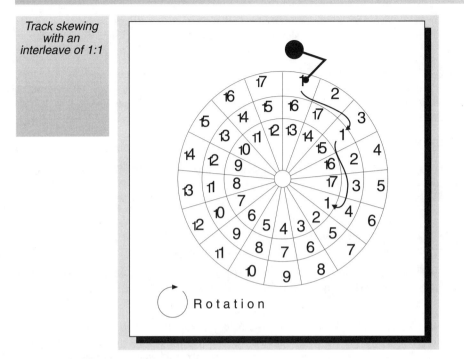

Track skewing with an interleave of 1:1

Rotation

Multiple zone recording

One way to increase the capacity of a hard drive is to format more sectors on the outer tracks. Since they have a larger circumference, the outer tracks have more space than the inner tracks. With ST506 controllers, the number of sectors per track was fixed and limited by the capacity of the innermost (shortest) track.

With modern SCSI and IDE disks, which only simulate the number of heads, tracks, and sectors, it's possible to format individual tracks with a different number of sectors. These controllers and drives translate a logical head, cylinder, and sector number to a physical head, cylinder, and sector number. So, it's possible to vary the number of sectors on outer tracks.

This places a greater demand on the controller circuitry and the read/write head. In the same (rotational) time, more sectors must be read or written to the outer tracks than on the inner track. So, while the length of the flux reversal decreases, the number of data bits to be read or written increases.

This can increase the capacity of a hard drive by between 20 and 50 percent compared to the usual, fixed sector per track arrangement.

Error correction

One important indicator of hard drive performance is its reliability. Impurities in the magnetic material are unavoidable and cause some sections of the hard drive to be unusable.

In the past, a list of defective sectors were printed on the hard drive case as they were detected by the manufacturer. During the low-level format, the user entered these sector numbers so the operating system would recognize these defective areas. Then the operating system would mark them as defective in the FAT (File Allocation Table) and avoid using them for storing data.

Newer hard drives, especially IDE models, no longer have a defective sector list. Either the sectors are already recorded on a separate data track by the manufacturer or they are recognized during the low-level format. These defective sectors are either skipped or replaced by other sectors from "alternate" areas. The tables that identify the defective sectors and their alternates are passed to the hard drive controller during initialization. When the hard drive controller tries to access a sector identified as defective, it can switch to the alternate sector. Although this slows access to such a sector, since there are very few defective sectors, this is hardly noticeable.

Many drives are also able to recognize defective sectors during read and write operations. This is the purpose of the ECC (Error Correction Code) that is automatically generated and saved with each sector. If an error is encountered during an operation, in many cases the data is reconstructed, an alternate sector is assigned, and the data is rewritten to this alternate sector. This feature is found in most of the IDE drives.

Other hard drive components

A hard drive contains more than just the data bit information. When a sector is formatted, an entire set of information is also written so the hard drive correctly recognizes and reads data. Although the format of this information is different depending on the controller, the information itself is the same (e.g., the cylinder number, the sector number, and the error correction code).

Each sector begins with a series of thirteen synchronization bytes with the value 00H (SYNC field). This bit pattern results in a constant series of flux reversals that help the controller synchronize itself to the sector.

Following this is the ID field, which identifies the sector. The cylinder, head, and sector numbers are recorded here (CH/S fields). This information starts with a special ID byte (ID field) and ends with a two byte error code that's used to check the validity of the information (CRCID field).

Next is a gap giving the controller a break before the start of the data field. The controller needs this break to read the information from the ID field to determine whether this is the desired sector. The gap also lets the controller resynchronize itself. The actual data field follows. The data field also has an ID byte (AM field) at the start, which is for identification. The 512 data bytes (DATA field) are next. The data field ends with two correction bytes (ECC-DATA field) the controller uses to determine whether the data is valid.

The sector ends with another gap to give the controller time to check the correction bytes. Here the gap contains bytes with the value 4EH. So the sector's total length is 570 bytes.

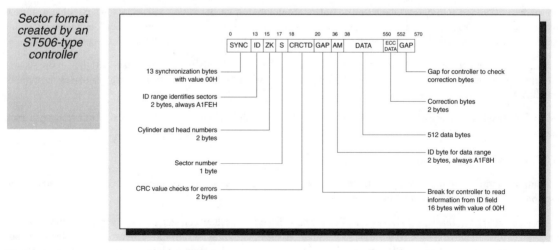

Sector format created by an ST506-type controller

Extra tracks

A hard drive also contains other "reserved" areas. For example, there are servo tracks, which are used by the hard drive's electronic circuitry to synchronize itself to the data clock. This is especially important when used with RLL controllers and drives.

Some drives also contain "reserved" or "alternate" tracks. These tracks are unknown even to the BIOS. The area on a reserved track is used as a replacement for defective sectors.

Finally, there is the park area. When the computer is switched off, the read/write heads "land" or settle on the surface of the park area. If the read/write head lands on a track containing data, that data might be destroyed or damaged. The park area contains no data and is a safe area that cannot be scratched or otherwise damaged by the read/write heads.

Access times

A hard drive's performance is measured by its access speed. Hardware manufacturers often claim their hard drives have access speeds of 10 or 30 milliseconds. This value represents the average seek time between two file accesses.

Most manufacturers also use track-to-track seek time and maximum seek time to express hard drive speed. The track-to-track seek time is the time needed to move the read/write head from one cylinder to the next. The maximum seek time is the time needed to move the read/write arm from the first cylinder to the last cylinder of the drive.

Although these factors have an important effect on how a hard drive accesses a file at the DOS level, there are other important factors. For example, a hard drive with extremely fast specification is useless unless the controller can keep pace with it. Also, a hard drive could be so fragmented the read/write arm is constantly jumping back and forth between different cylinders to access data. So, performance must also be measured according to the time that a read or write request spends at the various levels of the application program, at the DOS level with its device drivers, the BIOS, and any special hard drive drivers up to and including the programming of the hard drive controller.

To verify the performance data of a hard drive manufacturer, you can use a performance measuring program, such as SystemInfo from Norton Utilities or CORETEST from Core International.

Generally these programs measure a hard drive's data transfer rate by reading the largest possible data block from the hard drive. However, the size of this block is restricted to one complete cylinder, which means the read/write arm doesn't move during operation. We already know that ESDI, SCSI, and IDE controllers often "hide" the true specifications from the BIOS and instead translate the drive's cylinder, head, and sector values into physical ones. So, the results of these tests may not be accurate. A controller translation that results in a track change is also accompanied by a track-to-track delay, which distorts the result of the measurements.

When measuring the track-to-track seek time, you'll encounter a similar problem. To do this, read two sectors in adjacent tracks. However, the controller translation of these two sectors may not result in a track change, which produces an unrealistic zero track-to-track seek time.

Cache controllers and cache programs

The results of these measurements are especially suspicious when cache programs are used. At the software level, disk cache programs, such as SMARTDRV or PCKwik, can have a major effect on disk drive performance. These cache programs hook into the BIOS hard drive interrupt and intercept the read and write calls of the application programs and the device drivers of DOS.

When an application program wants to read data from a hard drive, the cache program intercepts the read request , passes the read request to the hard drive controller in the usual way, saves the data that was read in its cache buffer, and then passes the data back to the application program.

Depending on the size of the cache buffer, numerous sectors are read into and saved in the buffer. When the application wants to read more data, the cache program again intercepts the request and examines its buffers to see if the data is still in the cache. If it is, the data is immediately passed back to the application without another hard drive operation. As you can imagine, this speeds up access tremendously and can greatly affect the disk drive performance measurements.

In order to maintain accurate measurements, you can write a program to check the BIOS disk interrupt 13H. If it's still pointing to the ROM BIOS, then a cache program isn't active. If it's not, then you can request the user remove or disable the cache program until the measurements are completed.

Another type of disk cache is one that is part of the hard drive controller. This is a hardware disk cache and doesn't use any BIOS interrupts. Instead, the cacheing is performed at the hardware level and is invisible to normal performance measurement software.

Hard Drive Partitions

If you've ever installed a hard drive or added an operating system, such as XENIX or OS/2, then you've used the DOS FDISK command. This command is used to partition the hard drive. A hard drive must be partitioned when you want to logically divide the hard drive into separate volumes or when you want to install more than one operating system on the same hard drive.

Formatting process

To prepare a hard disk to be used by an operating system, you must perform three tasks.

First you must perform a low-level format. When you do this, you are organizing the drive into cylinders, tracks, and sectors by writing the appropriate address markers onto the drive surface. The address markers are later used by the controller to identify the specific sectors.

In the early days of the PC, the DOS DEBUG command was used to perform a low-level format. Today, low-level formatting is no longer complicated because most hard drive manufacturers provide programs that perform this task.

Partitioning the hard drive

Next, you must partition the hard drive. There are two reasons why this is necessary. First, it enables you to install multiple operating systems, such as DOS and XENIX, on a single drive. Partitioning a hard drive into separate areas lets each of the operating systems manage its disk space without the conflicts caused by different file structures.

The other reason for partitioning a hard drive is to be able to use the additional capacity of larger drives. The original XT had a hard drive with a 10 Meg capacity. Then drives with 40 and 80 Meg capacities appeared. Early versions of DOS were able to manage hard drive capacities of only 32 Meg. But this limitation was addressed by DOS 3.3. Now the 32 Meg maximum capacity applied only to a partition. DOS 3.3 allows one primary partition with a 32 Meg maximum and an extended partition that can be divided into as many as 23 logical devices (drives C: through Z:). Each of these logical devices can hold up to 32 Meg, which makes the entire hard drive capacity 768 Meg.

DOS 4.0 goes even farther, supporting drives with a maximum capacity up to 2 gigabytes. Nevertheless, many users continue to partition the hard drive into logical drives, because they would rather work with multiple drives than one large drive and several hundred or even several thousand files.

While the primary partition must be located within the first 32 Megs of the hard drive, the extended partition can be located anywhere. FDISK refers to these partitions as "PRI DOS" and "EXT DOS".

Partition sector

The partition sector is the structure that all versions of DOS use to define a hard drive's partitions. When you run the FDISK program for the first time, it creates the partition sector in the hard drive's first sector (cylinder 0, head 0, sector 1).

The BIOS first loads the partition sector, instead of the DOS boot sector, after the system is started or reset. The partition sector is loaded into memory at address 0000:7C00, if there are no diskettes in drive A:.

If the BIOS finds the values 55H, AAH, in the last two bytes of the partition sector's 512 total bytes, it considers the sector to be executable and starts executing the program at the first byte of the sector. Otherwise, the BIOS displays an error message and either starts ROM-BASIC or goes into a continuous loop, depending on the version of BIOS and the manufacturer.

Structure of the partition sector of a hard drive		
Addr.	**Contents**	**Type**
+000h	Partition code	Code
+1BEh	1.Entry in the partition table	16 BYTE
+1CEh	2.Entry in the partition table	16 BYTE
+1DEh	3.Entry in the partition table	16 BYTE
+1EEh	4.Entry in the partition table	16 BYTE
+1FEh	IDcode(AA55h),which identifies the partition sector as such	2 BYTE
Length: 1EH (30) bytes		

This program recognizes and starts the active partition's operating system. To do this, it must load the operating system's boot sector and pass control to the program within that boot sector. Since the later's program code must also be loaded at memory address 0000:7C00, the code from the partition sector is moved to the memory address 0000:0600 first, to make room for the boot sector.

Partition table

The program in the partition sector must be able to find the boot sector for the active partition. For this, it uses the partition table. This table is located at offset 1BEH of the partition sector.

Each entry in the partition table is 16 bytes. The table is located at the end of the partition sector, leaving enough room for 4 entries. So the number of partitions is limited to 4. To accommodate more than four partitions, some hard drive manufacturers use a special configuration program that relocates and enlarges the partition table and adapts the partition sector code to use this relocated table.

Sometimes the partition sector code is changed to allow you to boot any of the installed operating systems on the hard drive. This makes it easy to choose which of the operating systems should run when the computer is first started.

The partition table has the following layout:

Structure of an entry in the partition table		
Addr.	**Contents**	**Type**
+00h	Partition status 00h = inactive 80h = Boot-Partition	1 BYTE
+01h	Read/write head, with which the partition begins	1 BYTE
+02h	Sector and cylinder, with which the partition begins	1 WORD

Structure of an entry in the partition table		
Addr.	Contents	Type
+04h	Partition type 00h = Entry not allocated 01h = DOS with 12-Bit-FAT (primary Part.) 02h = XENIX 03h = XENIX 04h = DOS with 16-Bit-FAT (primary Part.) 05h = extended DOS-Partition (DOS 3.3) 06h = DOS-4.0 partition with more than 32 Meg DBh = Concurrent DOS Other codes possible combined with other operating systems or special driver software.	1 BYTE
+05h	Read/write head, with which the partition ends	1 BYTE
+06h	Sector and cylinder, with which the partition ends	1 WORD
+08h	Removal of first sector of the partition (Boot-sector) of partition sector in sectors	1 DWORD
+0Ch	Number of sectors in this partition	1 DWORD
Length: 10h (16 Bytes)		

Starting the boot partition

The first field of each partition table entry indicates whether a partition is active. A value of 00H indicates that partition isn't active; a value 80H indicates that partition is active and should be booted. If the partition sector program detects that more than one partition is active or that none of the partitions are active, it aborts the booting process, displays an error message, and waits in a continuous loop. You can exit this loop only by resetting.

When the partition sector program recognizes the active partition, is uses the next two fields to determine the location of this partition on the hard drive. The sector and cylinder numbers are expressed exactly as BIOS interrupt 13H (Diskette/Hard drive), including bits 6 and 7 of the sector number, which represent bits 8 and 9 of the cylinder number. At this point, BIOS interrupt 13H and its functions are the only way to access the hard drive. The DOS functions aren't available because DOS hasn't been booted yet.

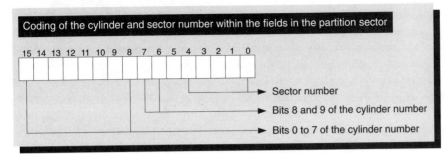

Coding of the cylinder and sector number within the fields in the partition sector

Other information in the partition table

The partition table also contains additional information. For example, each entry has a field that describes the operating system for that partition. The above figure shows the types that are supported.

In addition to the partition's starting sector, another field contains the partition's ending sector, expressed as cylinder, head, and sector numbers.

There are two additional fields for each table entry. The first is the total number of sectors within the partition. The last is the distance of a partition's boot sector from the partition sector, counted in sectors.

Remember the first partition on a drive usually begins in the first sector of track 0, head 1. In other words, almost an entire track is "wasted" because the partition sector occupies only one sector on track 0, head 0.

Structure of the extended partition under DOS

DOS 3.3 allows you to define one primary and one extended partition on a hard drive. FDISK builds the partition sector and partition table to identify the partitions, but doesn't write the program code into the partition sector.

The partition table has two entries. The first entry is for the first logical device of the extended partition and a partition type (value 1 or 4 that indicates a DOS partition with 12-bit or 16-bit FAT). The second entry is for the next logical device within the extended partition, is one exists.

To support other logical devices, this structure is repeated for each additional device. This results in a chained list that continues until the "partition type" field, in the second table entry of the partition table of the partition sector of an extended partition, contains has a zero value.

Examining the partition structure

You can use the FIXPARTP.PAS, FIXPARTC.C and FIXPARTB.BAS programs to examine the partition structures of a hard drive. FIXPARTP.PAS is written in Pascal and FIXPARTC.C in C. The programs display the contents of the partition sectors and the extended partitions (if there are any) from the hard drive. By default, they access the first hard drive, number 0, but you can also specify a different number (1, 2, 3, etc.) when running the programs to examine a different hard drive.

You'll find the following program(s) on the companion CD-ROM

FIXPARTP.PAS (Pascal listing)
FIXPARTC.C (C listing)
FIXPARTB.BAS (BASIC listing)

Chapter 15

Accessing And Programming The AT Realtime Clock

DOS uses the date and the time to timestamp files and to provide programs with the current date and time. Many BIOS functions are available to pass this information. Almost all ATs and higher end machines include battery operated realtime clocks. These clocks continue to run when the PC is switched off.

Reading The Date And Time From BIOS

BIOS interrupt 1AH addresses the various ROM-BIOS time functions. Although the PC and the PC/XT had only two of these functions, the AT and higher end models have eight functions that control the realtime clock (RTC). The AT realtime clock keeps time differently than the older PCs and PC/XTs, which used a software interrupt to perform this task. Before we discuss the BIOS time and date functions, let's look at the earlier method of time control in PC clocks.

Time measurement using timer interrupt 08H

The PC's timer chip (an Intel 8254 or a compatible chip) receives 1,193,180 signals per second from the heart of the system, which is an oscillating quartz crystal. After 65,536 of these signals, or about 18.2 times (18.20648193) a second, the chip calls interrupt 08H. The interrupt controller passes the call to the CPU. Interrupt 08H is called separately from the CPU frequency and takes its frequency from the vibrating quartz crystal.

After 18.2 occurrences, BIOS sends interrupt 08H to the ROM-BIOS. This increments a time counter. The current time can easily be calculated in seconds by reading this counter and dividing its value by 18.2. This value can then be converted into hours, minutes, and seconds.

Interrupt 08H also switches off the disk drive motors after a specific period of inactivity. This is done in conjunction with the BIOS interrupt 13H, through which a disk drive can be accessed. Since starting a disk drive motor is time-consuming, the motor remains on after receiving a BIOS disk function so it won't have to be restarted for the next disk operation.

After the interrupt interface has completed its tasks, it calls interrupt 1CH. Usually this interrupt carries an IRET instruction, which immediately returns program execution to the time interrupt interface. However, a program may define its own interface to use the cyclical time signal. This is useful for permanently displaying the current time on the screen, which is demonstrated by a TSR program in Chapter 35.

Timer interrupt 08H is the only way to measure time in PCs and PC/XTs. The AT and higher end computers contain realtime clocks with battery backup, which continue measure the time without a timer interrupt. The AT ROM-BIOS still manages the timer interrupt, however, to maintain downward software compatibility to the PC and PC/XT systems.

Function 00H: Get clock

Function number 00H obtains the current clock time. You can call this function by passing the number 00H to the AH register. The function loads the time into the CX and DX registers. These two registers combine to form a 32-bit counter value (CX contains the most significant 16 bits, while DX contains the least significant 16 bits). The BIOS timer increments this value by 1 each time interrupt 8H is called (18.2 times per second). The total value is the result of multiplying the contents of CX register by 65,536 and adding the contents of the DX register. Dividing this value by 18.2 returns the number of seconds elapsed, which can then be converted into minutes and hours.

The AT interprets time differently than the PC and XT. The PC/XT BIOS sets this counter to 0 during the system booting process. The value returned is the time passed since the computer was switched on (not the actual time). To obtain the time, the current time must be converted to the value corresponding to the counter, then passed to the BIOS (more on this later). The AT doesn't require this time value conversion because BIOS reads the actual time from the realtime clock during the system boot. It converts this time into a suitable timer value and then saves it. Reading the counter with the help of function 0 on the AT provides the current time.

Besides this counter, a value in the AL register indicates whether 24 hours have passed since the last reading. If the AL register contains a value other than 0, 24 hours have passed. This value doesn't indicate how many 24-hour periods have elapsed since the last reading.

If the conversion of time values into clock time is too complicated, function 2CH of DOS interrupt 21H can be used. This function simply reads and converts the current time using function 0 of interrupt 1AH. (See Chapter 22 for more information about function 2CH of DOS interrupt 1AH.)

Function 01H: *Set clock*

Function number 01H sets the current clock time. You can call this function by loading the number 1 into the AH register, the most significant 16 bits of the counter into the CX register, and the least significant 16 bits into the DX register. These two registers combine to form a 32-bit time value. If the conversion of the current time into a timer value is too complicated, function 2DH of DOS interrupt 21H can be used instead (see Chapter 24 for more information about function 2DH of DOS interrupt 21H.)

Functions for accessing the realtime clock

The following six functions are available only on the AT and higher end models. Although realtime clocks are also available for the PC and the PC/XT, they usually aren't supported by the computer's ROM-BIOS. So, unless the manufacturer also supplies a TSR program that implements the corresponding AT BIOS functions, calling these functions won't return any results on PCs and PC/XTs. When developing a program that accesses AT clock functions, test the model identification byte in F000:FFFE to ensure that the system is an AT or higher end machine (see Chapter 3 for more information about the model identification byte).

All six functions use BCD format for time and date indications. In this format, two characters are coded per byte; the higher number is coded in the higher nibble and the lower number in the lower nibble. All six functions use the carry flag following a return from the function call. If the carry flag is set, this indicates that the realtime clock is malfunctioning (e.g., from a dead battery). The called function couldn't be executed properly.

Function 02H: *Get current time*

Function 02H reads the realtime clock time. You can call the function by loading the function number (2) into the AH register. The current time is returned with the hour in the CH register, minutes in the CL register, and the seconds in the DH register.

Function 03H: *Set current time*

Function 03H sets the time on the realtime clock. You can call this function by loading the function number (3) into the AH register, the hour into the CH register, minutes into the CL register, and seconds into the DH register. The DL register indicates whether the "daylight savings time" option should be used. A 1 in the DL register selects daylight savings time, while 0 maintains standard time.

Functions 04H and 05H read and set the date stored in the realtime clock. Both functions use the century, year, month, and day as arguments. The day of the week (also administered by the realtime clock) doesn't apply to these functions. If you want to read the day of the week, you must directly access the realtime clock.

Function 04H: *Get current date*

Function 04H gets the current date from the realtime clock. You can call this function by loading the function number (4) into the AH register. The CH register contains the first two numbers of the year (the century). The CL register contains the last two numbers of the year (e.g., 88). The month is returned in the DH register and the day of the month in the DL register.

Function 05H: *Set current date*

Function 05H sets the current date in the realtime clock. You can call this function by loading the function number (5) into the AH register, either 19 decimal or 20 decimal into the CH register, the last two numbers of the year into the CL register (e.g., 89 decimal), the month into the DH register, and the day of the month into the DL register.

Function 06H: *Set alarm time*

Function 06H allows the user to set an alarm. Since only the hour, minute, and second can be indicated, the alarm time applies only to the current day. When the clock reaches the alarm time, the realtime clock calls a BIOS routine that in turn calls interrupt 4AH. A user routine can be installed under this interrupt to simulate the sound of an alarm clock. (You can program the routine to make other sounds.)

During the system initialization interrupt 4AH moves to a routine that contains only the IRET assembly language instruction. The IRET instruction forces the CPU to terminate the interrupt so that arriving at alarm time doesn't result in any action visible to the user. You can call this function by loading the function number (6) into the AH register, the alarm hour into the CH register, the alarm minute into the CL register, and the alarm second into the DH register.

Function 07H: *Reset alarm time*

Only one alarm time can be set. If this function is called while another alarm time is set or hasn't been reached yet, the carry flag is set after the function call. A new alarm time doesn't replace the old alarm time; the old time must be deleted first. You can call this function by loading the function number (7) into the AH register; no other parameters are required. This call clears the last alarm time so that a new alarm time can be programmed.

To call this function, place its function number in the AH register; no further arguments are required. This function call will then delete the current alarm time so a new alarm time may be set, if desired.

Reading And Setting The Realtime Clock

The AT and higher end models each have a battery operated realtime clock on the main circuit board. This clock is part of the Motorola MC-146818 processor, which contains 64 bytes of battery backup RAM. This RAM accepts clock data and system configuration data. It can be accessed through port addresses 70H to 7FH. However, the user needs only ports 70H and 71H.

Realtime clock registers

As the following table shows, the clock has sixteen important memory registers:

Realtime clock registers			
Reg.	Meaning	Reg.	Meaning
00H	Current second	08H	Month
01H	Alarm second	09H	Year
02H	Current minute	0AH	Clock status register A
03H	Alarm minute	0BH	Clock status register B
04H	Current hour	0CH	Clock status register C
05H	Alarm hour	0DH	Clock status register D
06H	Day of the week	32H	Century (19 or 20)
07H	Number of day		

Each time field (second, minute, hour) has a similar alarm field. With these alarm fields, a programmer can set the clock to trigger an interrupt at a particular time of the current day (more on this later).

Weekday

The day of the week provides the number of the current weekday. The value 1 represents Sunday, the value 2 represents Monday, 3 for Tuesday, etc.

Year

The year is counted relative to the century (the system assumes 1900). The value 87 in this field represents the year 1987.

The four status registers enable the user to program the clock.

Accessing the individual registers of the realtime clock

Since the registers are a part of the 64-byte RAM, you can access them like any other memory location. First load the number of the memory location to be accessed into the AL register. Then pass this value to port 70H using the OUT instruction. Since direct value output to a port is impossible, register AX is used for the output. The chip recognizes that an access to one of its memory locations occurred. Then either an OUT instruction writes to port 71H or an IN instruction reads the memory contents from port 71H.

The following instructions read or write a memory location in the realtime clock:

```
READ:                              WRITE:
    mov   al,Memory_location           mov   al,Memory_location
    out   70h, al                      out   70h,al
    in    al,71h                        mov   al,New_contents
                                       out   71h,al
```

Status register A

The four status registers are of particular interest to us because these registers are used for programming the clock. The following is a description of status register A:

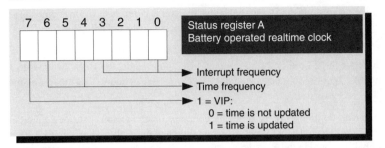

The ROM-BIOS set the two lower fields of these registers during the system boot. The interrupt frequency field has a default value of 0110b. This value results in an interrupt frequency of 1024 interrupts per second (i.e., an interrupt every 976,562 microseconds).

The contents of the time frequency field is 010b. This field triggers a time frequency of 32,768 KHz.

Bit 7 of the status register is used with these two fields. This bit indicates whether a second has just elapsed and increments the time fields (seconds, minutes, hours). If a second hasn't elapsed, this bit contains a 1. With this bit, you can read the individual time fields only when the time isn't being updated. Otherwise, a minute could pass and the second counter reset to 0 before the minute counter could be incremented. This could cause a time jump from 13:59:59 to 13:59:00, then the correct display of 14:00:01 one second later.

Status register B

Several clock parameters can be programmed through status register B:

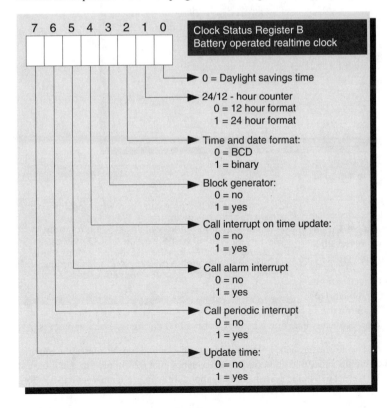

Some clock settings can be programmed through status register B. Bit 0 of status register B controls daylight savings time status. When this bit is set to 1, it indicates that daylight savings time is in effect. A value of 0 (the default value for this bit) indicates that standard time is in effect.

Bit 1 determines whether the clock should operate in 12-hour or 24-hour mode. In 12-hour mode, the clock switches to 1 o'clock after every 12 hours (midnight and noon). The 24-hour mode switches to 1 o'clock after 24 hours. This mode is active when you boot the system.

Bit 2 defines the format in which the time and date fields are stored. If this bit contains a 1, the various dates are stored in binary notation.The year (19)87 is coded as 01010111b in BCD format, which is switched on by the value 0 in bit 2. Two numbers are stored in every byte. The higher half is stored in the most significant four bits and the lower half is stored in the least significant four bits.

The number 87 in binary and BCD format

Binary

7	6	5	4	3	2	1	0	**Bit**
2^7	2^6	2^5	2^4	2^3	2^2	2^1	2^0	**Value**
0	1	0	1	0	1	1	1	

0+64+0+16+0 +4 +2 +1   = 87

BCD

7	6	5	4		3	2	1	0	**Bit**
2^3	2^2	2^1	2^0		2^3	2^2	2^1	2^0	**Value**
1	0	0	0		0	1	1	1	

8+0+0+0   = 8   0+4+2+1   = 7

8 * 10 = 80   +   7 * 1 = 7

80 + 7 = 87

Usually this bit contains a 0 and the numbers are stored in BCD format.

Bit 4 determines whether an interrupt should be called after the time (and date) update. This bit must contain a 1 if an interrupt should be called. The system suppresses this interrupt by setting this bit to 0 during the booting process.

Bit 5 can trigger an alarm. The clock reads the alarm time from locations 1, 3, and 5 (seconds, minutes, and hours) of clock RAM. When the alarm time is reached, an interrupt executes when bit 5 is set to 1. The system suppresses this interrupt when it sets bit 5 to 0 during the booting process.

NOTE

BIOS assumes BCD representation when performing the date function with interrupt 1AH. Programs that call these functions and obtain the information in binary format instead of the expected BCD may crash. The same applies to the 12-hour/24-hour time measurement, although a change to the 12-hour cycle wouldn't result in as serious consequences as the change in the date.

Bit 6 controls periodic interrupt calls when it is set to 1. The frequency of the interrupt calls depends on the interrupt frequency coded into bits 0-3 of status register A. Since the default value on bootup is a frequency of 1,024 kiloHertz, the interrupt triggers every 967,562 microseconds. Since bit 6 is set to 0 at the system start, an application program must set it to 1 before periodic interrupt calls can execute.

Bit 7 controls the periodic updating of the time and date, once every second. This bit is set to 0 when you boot the system so that the time constantly increments. Before entering a new date and time in the various memory locations, this bit should be set to 1 first to prevent the clock from changing the time immediately. Once you've entered all the necessary data, this bit can be reset and the time can continue updating.

RTC interrupt 70H

While discussing the bits in status register B, we've repeatedly referred to interrupt 70H. The realtime clock calls this interrupt under certain conditions. Even though there are several reasons for the clock to call an interrupt (alarm time, periodic interrupts, etc.), interrupt 70H is consistently called. This interrupt contains a BIOS routine that controls the two time functions in interrupt 15H, among other things.

Status register C

The routine uses status register C of the clock to determine the reason for the call. Only bits 4, 5, and 6 of this register are important to us at the moment. These bits correspond to the bits in status register B. For example, when you trigger the alarm interrupt (which can only occur if bit 5 in status register B was set), then bit 5 in status register C is also set to indicate that the alarm time has been reached.

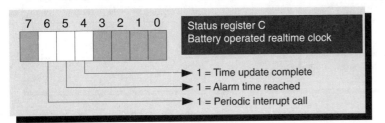

The first task of the routine that intercepts interrupt 70H is to read status register C. This routine then determines the reason for the interrupt call and reacts accordingly.

Status register D

Bit 7 is the only important bit in status register D. This bit indicates the status of the battery that maintains the data storage even when the PC's power supply is switched off. If this bit has the value 0, you should replace the battery because the present battery is dead or almost dead.

Some configuration data follows status register D.

Configuration Data And Battery Operated RAM

Besides the date and time information, the 64 battery backed memory registers also contain configuration data. Of the memory locations of various BIOS manufacturers, only those that are designated as unreserved contain the same information. Since all the other locations are used at the discretion of BIOS and hardware designers, these locations shouldn't be overwritten by a program.

Battery backed RAM registers			
Addr.	Content	Addr.	Content
0EH	Diagnostic byte (see below)	18H	High byte in K of an expansion board's main memory size
0FH	Status at system power-down	19H	Reserved
10H	Write to disk (see below)	2DH	Reserved
11H	Hard drive 1 type	2EH	Checksum high byte (memory locations 10H - 2DH)
12H	Hard drive 2 type	2FH	Checksum low byte (memory locations 10H - 2DH)
13H	Reserved	30H	Low byte in K of expansion memory size
14H	Configuration byte (see below)	31H	High byte in K of expansion memory size
15H	Low byte in K of hard drive main memory size	32H	First two century digits in BCD notation
16H	High byte in K of motherboard main memory size	33H-3FH	Reserved
17H	Low byte in K of an expansion board's main memory size		

Diagnostic byte (0EH)

The diagnostic byte documents various errors that may occur during the Power-On Self Test (POST).

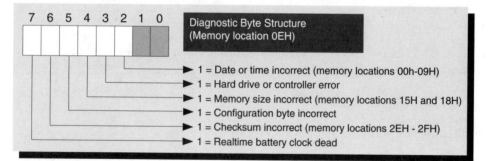

```
7 6 5 4 3 2 1 0    Diagnostic Byte Structure
                   (Memory location 0EH)

                   ► 1 = Date or time incorrect (memory locations 00h-09H)
                   ► 1 = Hard drive or controller error
                   ► 1 = Memory size incorrect (memory locations 15H and 18H)
                   ► 1 = Configuration byte incorrect
                   ► 1 = Checksum incorrect (memory locations 2EH - 2FH)
                   ► 1 = Realtime battery clock dead
```

Disk description (10H)

Memory address 10H of the battery backed RAM contains information identifying the first and the second disk drive formats (5.25-inch or 3.5-inch) and their capacities.

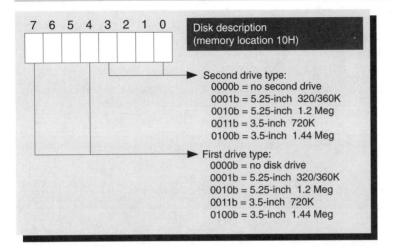

Disk description (memory location 10H)

Second drive type:
0000b = no second drive
0001b = 5.25-inch 320/360K
0010b = 5.25-inch 1.2 Meg
0011b = 3.5-inch 720K
0100b = 3.5-inch 1.44 Meg

First drive type:
0000b = no disk drive
0001b = 5.25-inch 320/360K
0010b = 5.25-inch 1.2 Meg
0011b = 3.5-inch 720K
0100b = 3.5-inch 1.44 Meg

Configuration byte (14H)

Memory address 14H of the battery backed RAM contains configuration data that specifies the number of disk drives, the video mode at system startup, and the availability of a math coprocessor.

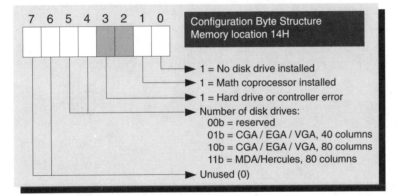

Configuration Byte Structure
Memory location 14H

1 = No disk drive installed
1 = Math coprocessor installed
1 = Hard drive or controller error
Number of disk drives:
00b = reserved
01b = CGA / EGA / VGA, 40 columns
10b = CGA / EGA / VGA, 80 columns
11b = MDA/Hercules, 80 columns
Unused (0)

Demonstration programs

The RTCB.BAS, RTCP.PAS and RTCC.C programs on the companion CD-ROM show how you can access the realtime clock from BASIC, Pascal, or C. Three routines perform most of the functions. The first routine reads a value from one of the clock's memory locations. The second routine places a value there. The third routine checks whether the clock is operating in binary mode or BCD mode, then reads a memory location in the clock, converting the contents of this location from BCD into binary if necessary. This routine is important for accessing all memory locations, containing information on date and time, that could be coded in BCD or in binary format.

The main program checks the battery on the clock. If there's power in the battery, the program calls two routines that, among other things, read the contents of the memory locations for the current date and current time from the clock. This data appears on the screen.

The main program doesn't access the routine for a description of memory locations. However, you can easily convert the program so the routine for the description of memory locations writes to the clock instead of reading date and time. This is only a suggestion; feel free to experiment.

You'll find the following program(s) on the companion CD-ROM

RTCB.BAS (BASIC listing)
RTCP.PAS (Pascal listing)
RTCC.C (C listing)

Chapter 16

System Configuration And Processor Types

Knowing the configuration configuration of a computer is often important. A program must frequently know the number of serial ports, the size of the RAM memory or whether a math coprocessor is present.

In this chapter we'll show you how to determine various configuration data with the help of two ROM-BIOS interrupts. You'll also learn how to determine the processor type and coprocessor type of a PC.

Determining The Configuration Using The BIOS

The ROM-BIOS has two interrupts for reading configuration information:

> ➢   Interrupt 11H

> ➢   Interrupt 12H

Each interrupt contains one function. With these interrupts you can obtain information about the hardware environment of a PC and determine the size of the RAM memory.

Unfortunately, even after using these interrupts, many of your questions will still be unanswered, as the following two sections will demonstrate.

Reading the hardware environment

Call BIOS interrupt 11H to obtain information about the hardware environment of a computer, the number of serial and parallel ports, disk drives and the DMA controller.

Unlike many other BIOS interrupts, the contents of the processor register are unimportant at the time this interrupt is called because a function number or any other argument isn't necessary. This interrupt consists of only a single function, which returns the desired information about the configuration in the AX register.

The following illustration shows the contents of the AX register after the function call represent a bit field. These fields provide information about various components of the hardware. However, this information is limited. Since this interrupt was introduced with the first PC and its original BIOS, it reflects the modest hardware environment that is typical of the early PCs.

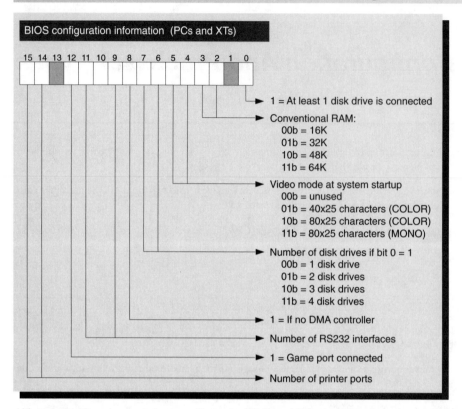

Although the bit assignment above applies to both PCs and XTs, it differs from the structure of the configuration word returned by the AT and its descendants. When the AT was introduced, this interrupt was revised to use the advancements in hardware technology and the improved PC equipment.

However, this interrupt doesn't provide important information, such as the processor type, the kind of keyboard, and the presence of a mouse or EMS memory. So, if you want to determine whether a mouse is present or what kind of video card is installed, refer to the appropriate chapters in this book.

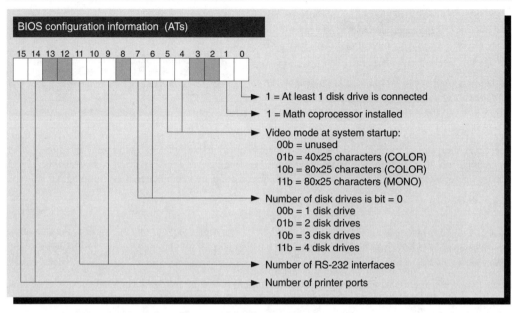

Don't use this function to prompt for the current video mode because it only specifies the video mode that was switched on when the system was running. You should use function 0FH of interrupt 10H, which returns the number of the current video mode.

We'll talk about a sample program which demonstrates how to use this interrupt later in this chapter.

Determining RAM configuration using the BIOS

Interrupt 11H, which hasn't changed since 1981, provides only the size of the RAM memory on the motherboard. However, calling interrupt 12H provides the size of the entire RAM memory. When the system boots up, the size of the RAM on the motherboard and any existing memory expansion boards are added up and saved. On PCs and XTs, this information is taken from the settings of the single DIP switches on each memory board, while on ATs the information is read from one of the 64 memory locations of the battery operated clock.

However, this method only determines the size of the RAM memory below the 1 megabyte boundary. This is sufficient for PCs and XTs because the address space of their processors is limited to 1 megabyte. So, they cannot have any additional RAM memory.

ATs and their descendants, however, don't fit into this category; they have processors capable of managing up to 16 megabytes of memory. On these computers you can install additional memory, which interrupt 12H cannot detect. So you should use function 88H of BIOS interrupt 15H instead. This function reads the size of the memory above the 1 megabyte boundary.

Like interrupt 11H, interrupt 12H doesn't expect any arguments in the various processor registers when you call it. It returns the memory size in the AX register as a factor of 1K (1024 bytes instead of 1000 bytes).

Demonstration programs

Three programs in BASIC, Pascal and C on the companion CD-ROM should demonstrate how to use the interrupts we just discussed. The three programs have the same structure and output the configuration data that can be determined by using BIOS interrupts 11H and 12H.

These programs first read the model identification byte in memory location F000:FFFE to determine whether the computer is a PC, XT, or AT. This information forms the foundation for the remaining procedures of the program.

Then interrupt 12H reads the size of the RAM memory on the motherboard and outputs this information. On ATs, the size of the RAM memory beyond the 1 megabyte boundary is determined with the help of function 88H of BIOS interrupt 15H.

After this information is output, the program calls interrupt 11H, which determines the configuration of the computer. The program's final task involves filtering the information from the various bit fields.

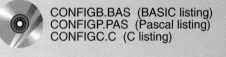

You'll find the following program(s) on the companion CD-ROM

CONFIGB.BAS　(BASIC listing)
CONFIGP.PAS　(Pascal listing)
CONFIGC.C　(C listing)

To keep the program as short as possible, we only used bits that are identical in both the configuration word of the PC/XT and the AT. For example, on ATs, the information about whether the computer has a mathematical coprocessor isn't used. This information isn't always reliable and the programs from the next section are much better at determining it.

Determining Processor And Coprocessor

Many programs are available which provide information about the configuration or layout of a PC. Besides the size of the RAM memory, the installed version of DOS, etc., you'll also learn which processor the computer uses and which coprocessor assists this processor.

This information can be very important, for example, when developing programs in high level languages because code generation can be adapted to a particular processor. Both the Microsoft C compilers and their Borland counterparts allow special code generation for the 8088, the 80286, or the 80386. This enables you to fully use the processor's capabilities and the command set. Generally this noticeably increases the performance of programs that work with large data sets.

One way you can use this capability is by compiling each of the processor types separately. Also, you can develop a program, which is used as a loader for the actual program, that prompts for the processor type after starting. Then it executes the particular program (of the three programs) that was compiled for the relevant processor. You can also do this with the numerical coprocessor.

However, now we must decide how to determine the installed processor. Unlike other configuration data, this cannot be determined by calling a BIOS or DOS function. Also, since there isn't a corresponding machine language command, which causes the processor to reveal its identity, you must use a complicated procedure that, according to statements of the hardware manufacturers, shouldn't even work.

This procedure involves a test that's based on how certain machine language commands are executed. Although the processors from the 8086 to the Pentium are software compatible, small changes were made in the logic of some commands during the development of this processor series. Since these changes are noticeable only in rare situations, a program developed for the 8088 will also run on all other processors of the Intel 80xxx series. So if you intentionally put the processor in this type of situation, you can establish the identity of the processor as a result of its behavior.

Since these differences are only noticeable on the machine language level, you can write such a test program only in machine language or assembly language. At the end of this chapter, this type of test routine is presented in the form of two assembly modules for linking to Pascal and C programs. We'll discuss how they operate and the differences between the individual processors in the following sections.

Determining the processor type

The test routine for determining the installed processor consists of several tests that can be used to differentiate the individual processor types. A test will run only if the preceding test fails.

Determining the processor type

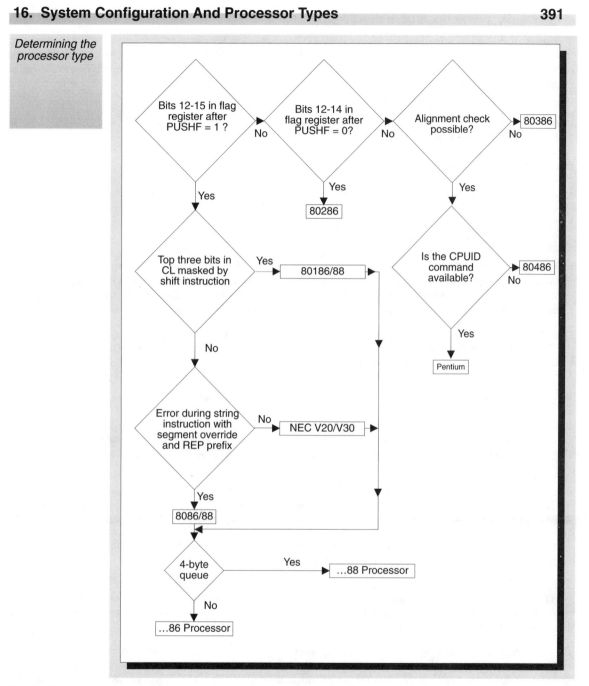

Varying layout of the flag register

The first test is based on the varying layout of the flag register on the different processors. Although the meaning of bits 0 to 11 are identical for all processors, bits 12 through 15 don't have a meaning until the 80286 (through the introduction of Protected Mode). The commands PUSHF (place contents of flag register on stack) and POPF (retrieve contents of flag register from stack) take this circumstance into account. These commands always set bits 12 to 15 of the flag register to 1 on all Intel processors up to the 80188. Beginning with the 80286, the processors behave differently.

The first test uses this by placing the value 0 on the stack and then using the POPF command to fetch it back to the flag register. Since there isn't a command for reading the contents of bits 12 through 15 in the flag register, the PUSHF command immediately places the flag register on the stack. However, this only happens so the POP AX command in the AX register can send for the flag register. It's easy to test the layout of bits 12 to 15 in the AX register. If all four bits are set, it cannot be a 80286 or any of its descendants, and the routine continues with the next test.

If all four bits aren't set, then the list of possible processors is limited to the 80286 and its descendants. Since the 80286 processes the POPF command differently than the 80386/80486, it's easy to distinguish the 80286 from its descendants. The entire procedure is repeated again, with the value 7000H, instead of 0, being placed on the stack. When the POPF command loads the flag register, it causes bits 12 to 14 to be set to 1.

However, if these bits no longer contain the value 1 when retrieving the flag register from the stack, the processor must be an 80286, which automatically sets these three bits to 0, unlike its successors. If this test indicates the processor is an 80286, the test routine ends.

Distinguishing the 80386 and 80486

If the processor isn't an 80286, you must determine whether it's an 80386 or an 80486. Again, you can use the flag register to do this because the 80486 has a new flag in the extended flag register EFlags. This flag, which is called "Alignment Check", is located at bit position 15. When this flag is set, the processor checks all memory accesses with the specified offset address. If the address isn't a multiple of four, the processor releases a special interrupt, called an Exception.

If the Alignment Check is operating, this will be the fate of the subsequent machine language command, for example, because it reads out the contents of memory location 102. Since 102 isn't a multiple of four, it isn't aligned. This also applies to memory location 77, which is addressed in the following command:

```
mov   al,[102]
shl   word ptr [77],3
```

Both of these commands would execute an alignment exception, which causes an exception handler to be executed the same way as an interrupt. The operating system usually intercepts this exception handler to acknowledge the misalignment. Depending on the user's judgment, the program can either abort or continue executing the command.

Access to memory on the 80486 is especially fast when the data to be processed is located at an offset address that's divisible by four. So, if an offset address isn't divisible by four, memory access on the 80486 takes a long time. To prevent this from happening, an operating system can enable the alignment check so it's aware of programs that access data which are misaligned during execution.

The operating system considers the release of the exception as an opportunity to send a warning message to the developer. In this way, the alignment check can help optimize programs for the 80486.

The results of the alignment check make it easy to distinguish between the 80386 and the 80486. Since the 80386 isn't familiar with the Alignment flag, it doesn't change its contents. So, you should first read and save the previous contents of the EFlags to reset the alignment bit. Then read the EFLags register again to check whether the contents of this flag have actually changed. If the contents have changed, you know that you're working with an 80486.

However, remember to set the Alignment flag back to its original value when you're finished. Since the EFlags register can be loaded and manipulated only from the stack, there are some other dangers. The following machine language commands demonstrate this process, which loads the EFlags register into the EAX register. This first command "pushes" the contents onto the stack so they can be "popped" into the AX register.

```
pushfd
pop eax
```

Although it isn't evident by looking at the two commands, memory is accessed twice because this is where the stack is located. If the alignment bit is already set when this command is executed, an exception is triggered if the stack pointer SP doesn't refer to an address that's divisible by four. However, this can easily be avoided by placing the following machine language command before the previous commands:

```
and esp,0FFFCh
```

This command simply sets the two bottom bits in the ESP register to 0, rounding off the stack pointer to the next address divisible by four. This type of processor test is usually executed within a subroutine. So, you should record the current contents of the stack pointer first so you can restore them later. Otherwise, at the end of the procedure, the stack pointer won't point to the return address of the caller, which was placed there when the subroutine was called. As a result, the program crashes.

Reading the SX versions

Although this test differentiates between 80386s and 80486s, it doesn't enable you to distinguish between the DX and SX versions of these processors. Also, no software programs distinguish between the 80386SX and the 80386DX.

However, it's possible to distinguish between the 80486SX and the 80486DX, even if only indirectly. The SX version of this processor doesn't have the mathematical coprocessor 80387, which is integrated in the DX version. Once you determine that you have an 80486 processor, you can easily determine whether the corresponding floating point commands are available. To do this, use a coprocessor test, which allows you to indicate the installed version of the processor.

However, just because floating point commands are supported doesn't mean that an 80486DX is present. It could also be an 80486SX that has a mathematical coprocessor. You can assume that you have an 80486SX only when you encounter an 80486 that doesn't support numerical operations of the floating point processor.

Differentiating between the 80486 and the Pentium

Regardless of whether you are dealing with an SX or a DX, after ruling out the possibility of the machine being an 80386, you cannot jump to the conclusion that you have an 80486. The misalignment flag is also supported by successors of the 486. This includes the Pentium. So, the final test must serve to differentiate between the 80486 and the Pentium.

You need to use a flag from EFLAG register again. This time we'll use bit 21. Since it was introduced with the Pentium, it's not available for the 80486. The Pentium and its successors use this bit to indicate their support for a new machine language command for CPU identification: The CPUID command.

To check if this flag exists, first call the EFLAGS register using the stack to the EAX register and note it in the ECX register. Then rotate the contents of bit 21 and write the new value back to the EFLAGS register using the stack. Now you can determine if you're using an 80486. All you have to do is use the stack to load back the EFLAGS register in the EAX register. Next, compare the new contents with the old contents stored in ECX. If the contents match, it means bit 21 could not be changed. This proves a 486 exists because it is possible to set this bit with the Pentium and its successors.

Distinguishing between 8086/8088 and 80186/80188

If the processor failed the first test, then the processor must be one of the four ancestors of the 80286. The following test determines whether the processor is an 80188 or 80186.

When these processors were introduced, the operation of the various shift commands (e.g., SHL and SHR) were changed to work in connection with the CL register as a shift counter. In the previous processors, the contents of the CL register specified the number of shifters in a range between 0 and 255. However, in the new processors the top three bits of the CL register are deleted before the shift, which limits the maximum number of shift operations. This makes sense because after 16 shifts of a word (17 if shifting by the carry flag), all bit positions contain the value 0. Additional shifting wastes valuable processor time, but no longer changes the value of the word.

The test considers this behavior by using the SHR command to shift the 0FFH value in the AL register by 21H positions to the right. If the processor is an 80188 or newer, it will first mask the upper 3 bits in the shift counter and then leave only a single shift of the 21H shifts.

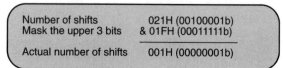

Number of shifts	021H (00100001b)
Mask the upper 3 bits	& 01FH (00011111b)
Actual number of shifts	001H (00000001b)

Unlike its predecessors, which actually shift the value FFH 21H times to the right, returning the value 0, the 80188 and 80186 return the value 7FH as a result. By examining the AL register after the shift, it's easy to determine whether the processor is an 80186 or 80188 (AL doesn't equal 0) or neither (AL equals 0).

Differentiating between 8086/8088 and NEC V20/NEC V30

If the processor didn't pass this test either, it must be an 8088, an 8086, or a clone from NEC. These clones, which are labeled V20 or V30, are the most common clones of the two Intel processors. They have the same command set as the Intel processors they're modeled after, but have a higher processing speed due to optimizations in the inner logic.

In addition to these improvements, the small error which occurred in some of the 8088 and 8086 processors, was eliminated in these processors. This error occurs if a hardware interrupt is triggered during the execution of a string command (e.g., LODS) in connection with the REP(eat) prefix and a segment override. After the interrupt ends, the command doesn't resume execution on some 8088 and 8086 processors. This is indicated by the fact the CX register, which functions as a cycle counter for this command, doesn't contain the value 0, as expected, after execution of the command.

The test program first loads the value 0FFFFH into the CX register and then executes the subsequent string command, with the REP prefix and segment override, 65,535 times. This process is time-consuming even for a fast processor. So, during one of the 65,535 executions of this command, a hardware interrupt will be triggered. In the case of the 8088 and 8086, the command isn't resumed and the remaining "loop runs" aren't executed. The test program uses the CX register to check this after the command is executed.

Reading the width of the data bus

The last test is for processors that are predecessors to the 80386. In this test, you determine whether the processor has an 8 bit or a 16 bit data bus. In other words, you're finally going to discover whether the identified processor is an 8088 or 8086, a V20 or V30, or an 80186 or 80188. Although you cannot use machine language commands to determine the width of the data bus, the length of the prefetch queue within the processor is related to this size.

The prefetch queue, which is located inside the processor, is responsible for loading the machine code of the subsequent commands into the processor while the current command is being executed. This can significantly increase the execution speed of the processor because the mechanism for filling the prefetch queue works parallel to the actual execution of the command. This allows the processor to access the next command immediately after one command ends. The processor doesn't have to worry about the address bus and data bus for loading the command.

As long as it doesn't use self-modified code, a program usually doesn't see the prefetch queue being filled. This refers to changes to the program code that were made by the program (e.g., by overwriting one machine language command in the code segment with another one from the program code). However, this isn't an unusual technique.

Problems occur with this method when commands, whose machine codes have already been loaded into the prefetch queue, are changed. This occurs when the command to be modified is very close to the command that's modifying it. For example, in the following code excerpt, an INC-CX command is replaced by an NOP command. The INC command is still executed because the two commands are so close to each other the modified INC command was already in the prefetch queue at the time of its execution.

```
        mov byte ptr cs:queue,Code NOP
queue:  inc dx
```

This procedure simplifies testing the length of the prefetch queue. With this information, you can also determine the width of the data bus. This is possible because processors with a 16 bit data bus have a 6 byte prefetch queue, while processors with an 8 bit data bus have 4 byte prefetch queues.

Test the length of the prefetch queue by using the STOSB (store string byte) string command to modify 3 bytes in the code segment. These three bytes appear immediately after the STOSB command. In this test, the bytes must be placed so they are already located within the queue on a processor with a 6 byte queue. This must be done so the processor doesn't notice this change to the program code. However, on a processor with a 4 byte queue, these commands are still outside the queue. So the changed commands are loaded and executed in their modified form the next time the queue is "filled up".

The program takes advantage of this because the INC DX command is among the modified commands. This command increments the contents of the DX register. Since this register receives the code of the determined processor within the test routine, it causes a switch to the next processor type. However, this happens only if this command is actually executed and if it's a processor with a 6 byte queue.

Since this always increases the processor code by 1 on xx86 processors, the processor codes within the test routine are chosen so the code for the corresponding xx88 processor is always followed by the code for the matching xx86 processor. For example, if processor code 4, for the 80188, is loaded into the DX register before the beginning of this test, then the processor code within this test is incremented by 1. The result is processor code 5, in the DX register, which is interpreted as a code for the 80186 by the test program.

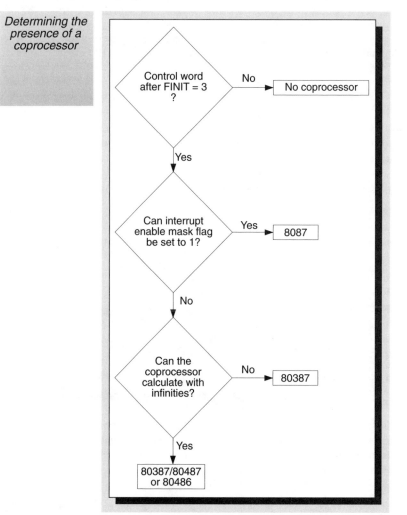

Determining the presence of a coprocessor

Coprocessor test

The installed coprocessor is also important although less than three percent of all computers have them. However, often just knowing that a mathematical coprocessor isn't installed is valuable information.

You can easily check whether a mathematical coprocessor is installed by using the machine language command FSTCW command. Before using this command, reset the coprocessor with the FINIT machine language command. FSTCW deposits the control word of the coprocessor into a specified variable and the hi byte of this register will always contain the value 3 after you reset the coprocessor. You'll immediately know whether there is a coprocessor because you won't be able to execute the FSTCW command and the value 3 won't be in the specified memory location unless you saved this value earlier.

Tests for determining the coprocessor

After discovering that your computer has a coprocessor, you must determine the type of coprocessor. Since the integrated coprocessor in the 80486 is identical to the 80387, you must simply distinguish between 8087, 80287, and 80387. This also applies to the 80487, which is simply a disguised 80486, in which the 80486 part has been switched off.

Differentiating between 8087 and 80287/80387

A flag, called Interrupt-Enable-Mask, in the control word differentiates the 8087 from the 80287 and 80387. In the 8087, this flag decides whether the coprocessor should trigger an interrupt upon receiving an invalid machine language command. Since the 80287 and 80387 use exceptions instead of interrupts, this flag is always set to zero on 80287/80387s and cannot be set to 1. You can check this by first loading the control word to set the flag to 0 and then using the FDISI machine language command to set the flag to 1. On an 80287/80387, this command won't have any effect. You can also confirm this by reading the control word and checking this flag.

Differentiating between an 80287 and 80387

If you don't have an 8087 coprocessor, this process becomes more complicated because flags can't be used to distinguish between them. However, the 80287 and 80387 processors differ in their ability to process infinite values, called infinities. To create an infinity within the test routine, divide one by zero. The result of this operation is duplicated, its sign reversed, and then two values are compared. Since switching the sign of infinity is possible only on the 80387, the two values will be different only on an 80387 coprocessor. Verify this by using the appropriate commands and then establish the identity of the coprocessor.

Demonstration programs

You can see how this theory works by reading the processor and its helper in two assembler modules, which were designed for linking to Pascal and C programs. These modules are called PROCPA.ASM and PROCCA.ASM; both of them contain two routines named GETPROC and GETCO. These routines represent functions that return a numeric value which characterizes the type of processor (GETPROC) or the type of coprocessor (GETCO).

The high level language programs PROCP.PAS and PROCC.C clearly illustrate this by using the return values of these functions as indexes in string arrays. The names of the various Intel processors and coprocessors are stored in these string arrays.

You'll find the following program(s) on the companion CD-ROM

PROCP.PAS (Pascal listing)
PROCPA.ASM (Assembler listing)
PROCC.C (C listing)
PROCCA.ASM (Assembler listing)

Accessing the 32 bit register

When you examine the assembler modules, which are identical, you'll notice the numerous DB commands in the GETPROC function. These commands represent the machine codes of the various commands used to distinguish between 80386 and 80486. This is where machine language commands of the 80386 and 80486, which rely on the extended 32 bit register of these processors (EAX, EBX etc.), are used. However, these commands can be used only if the assembler is informed, by the pseudo command .386, these commands are allowed.

Unfortunately this has an unpleasant side effect. The assembler gives the attribute "32-Bit" to the code segment and records this in the object file. The linker, which links the assembler module with the high level language model, doesn't approve of this because the various segments are no longer compatible. To avoid this conflict, the commands are specified directly in machine code so the assembler doesn't recognize them as enhanced 386 commands.

Chapter 17

A Brief History Of DOS

In this chapter we'll discuss the PC's operating system, which the PC loads from a floppy diskette or hard drive. This system is usually referred to as PC-DOS, MS-DOS, or simply DOS.

What is DOS?

Most users are familiar with only the user interface of DOS, which is used to run programs, format disks, etc. In the following sections, however, you'll view DOS from a different perspective.

Beneath the surface of DOS, many processes occur. DOS uses numerous routines (called functions) to accomplish its tasks. These functions are available to the user as well as to DOS. We'll discuss how these functions can be used in practical applications.

This chapter includes background information on the development of DOS, highlighting its origins in the CP/M operating system. You'll learn the differences between transient commands and resident commands, COM files and EXE files, and DOS file access. '

We'll also examine the data structures that act as the connecting link between the different DOS functions. These data structures make mass storage devices, such as floppy disks and hard drives, possible.

Finally, this chapter discusses each DOS function in detail and includes a brief look at DOS Version 5.0.

DOS Development

Let's begin our examination of DOS programming by studying DOS's history. DOS is an operating system that has been used for many years. Today, because of its long existence and compatibility requirements, DOS often contains more data than it actually needs.

For example, it's been almost ten years since DOS Version 2.0 was released. This version included FCB functions for performing file access. However, these functions are now considered obsolete by many developers, but DOS continues to support FCB functions, which occupy valuable space in the DOS kernel.

The story of DOS begins in the 1970s when Intel designed the 8086 microprocessor, which is the first generation of 16-bit microprocessors. In 1980, most microcomputers were 8-bit systems and the Intel 8080 and Zilog Z-80 processors were the microprocessors driving most micro systems. The PC was only a vision in the minds of developers, and the only microcomputer operating system available was CP/M 80, which was marketed by Digital Research Corporation.

*A visual history
of DOS*

August 1981	MS-DOS 1.0 PC-DOS 1.0	The first version for the first PC
March 1982	MS-DOS 1.25 PC-DOS 1.1	Supports double-sided 320K diskettes
March 1983	MS-DOS 2.0 PC-DOS 2.0	Introduced with XT. Supports UNIX-like hierarchical file system.
	PC-DOS 2.1	DOS for PC, Jr.
May 1983	MS-DOS 2.01	Version 2.0 extensions for international market (available from Microsoft).
October 1983	MS-DOS 2.11	Corrected errors and bugs in Version 2.01
	MS-DOS 2.25	Far East implementation of 2.11
August 1984	MS-DOS 3.0 PC-DOS 3.0	Introduced with AT. Supports 1.2 Meg disk drives and larger capacity hard drives.
March 1985	MS-DOS 3.1 PC-DOS 3.1	DOS with network capability.
December 1985	MS-DOS 3.2 PC-DOS 3.2	Supports 3.5-inch 720K disk drives
April 1987	MS-DOS 3.3 PC-DOS 3.3	Supports 3.5-inch 1.44 Meg disk drives. Offers simpler method of dividing larger hard drives into logical partitions.
July 1988	MS-DOS 4.0 PC-DOS 4.0	Supports hard drive partitions larger than 32 Megabytes. Supports EMS memory in properly equipped systems.
November 1988	MS-DOS 4.01 PC-DOS 4.01	Corrected errors found in Version 4.0.
June 1991	MS-DOS 5.0 PC-DOS 5.0	Occupies as little room as possible which leaves more room for the user's programs.
December 1993	MS-DOS 6.0	Includes DoubleSpace which is a hard drive compression program.
September 1994	PC-DOS 6.3	Includes Stacker, compression utilities, auto backup, anti-virus, memory optimizer and program scheduler.

Digital Research announced an operating system called CP/M-86 under development for the 8086. As of April 1980, the CP/M-86 operating system hadn't been released.

A programmer named Tim Paterson began developing a new operating system for the 8086. This operating system, originally called QDOS (Quick and Dirty Operating System) and later called 86-DOS was the basis for MS-DOS.

In 1980 a lot of software was available for CP/M-80 systems. The development of new software for an 8086 operating system would have required enormous expenses and effort. Paterson's goal was to allow easy conversion of existing software from CP/M-80 to the new operating system. He tried to include the functions and the most important data structures of the CP/M-80 operating system, while removing the weak points of CP/M-80. The finished product was an operating system that occupied 400 lines of assembler code, and, when assembled, required only 6K of memory. Programs developed for CP/M-80 could be converted to the 8086 easily. The new system was named 86-DOS.

Meanwhile, IBM was developing a 16-bit microcomputer. A company named Microsoft, known at the time for its BASIC interpreter for 8-bit systems, offered to develop an operating system for this microcomputer. IBM sent a prototype of the new computer to Microsoft, who bought the rights to Paterson's operating system and made some enhancements to 86-DOS. Even though Paterson participated in the project, the strict security provisions of IBM prevented him from seeing the machine for which he had developed an operating system. Despite this, the development work was completed in August 1981.

Version 1.0

The new operating system was released for the IBM PC under the name MS-DOS Version 1.0 (by Microsoft) and PC-DOS Version 1.0 (by IBM). Compared to current versions, MS-DOS 1.0 was a minimal system. It had only one root directory, in which the user kept all files. This version represented a compromise for Microsoft. They had relied heavily on CP/M-80 and needed to transfer existing programs quickly and easily. For instance, the filename structure (eight-character filename, three-character extension) was identical with CP/M-80. Also, the designation of the disk drives and the internal structure were very similar to the successful 8-bit operating system. MS-DOS Version 1.0 supported one or two disk drives (the IBM PC didn't support hard drives at the time) capable of single-sided, 160K disk format.

During this time, improvements were made to the hardware. These improvements included more RAM and faster disk drives. Microsoft decided to make DOS more hardware independent by removing the association between physical file length and logical file length.

In CP/M-80, every disk was divided into 128-byte units that could be accessed only as a whole. This is why you couldn't access individual bytes on the disk, which created a programming problem that shouldn't have existed anyway. DOS solved this problem by making logical and physical data length independent of one another. Also, functions were implemented to permit reading or writing of more than one data set of a file on a disk. By treating the input and output devices like files, hardware independence was achieved. These input and output devices were assigned their own names:

> CON   (Keyboard and display [CONsole])

> PRN   (Printer)

> AUX   (Serial interface [AUXiliary])

If, instead of a filename, you used one of these three names, the computer addressed the corresponding device instead of the disk drive. This also permitted redirecting input and output from the keyboard or screen to a file or other device.

Until this point, DOS supported only program files that loaded and executed from a fixed location in memory. Since this wasn't practical, MS-DOS Version 1.0 introduced a new program file type. This new file type had a file extension of .EXE instead of .COM. An .EXE file could be stored and executed from almost any memory location.

Two changes were made to the command processor, which is the part of the operating system that accepts commands from the user and controls the execution of these commands. The first change was to store the command processor in a separate file named COMMAND.COM. This allowed programmers to develop a customized command processor and link it to the system.

The second change was to divide the command processor into a resident and a transient portion. This approach was taken because early PC systems contained only a small amount of memory. The resident portion was written to be as small as possible. Many DOS commands were stored on disk and loaded and run only when required (hence the name transient). Examples of transient commands are DISKCOPY and FORMAT.

A major innovation that enabled MS-DOS Version 1.0 to surpass CP/M-80 was the introduction of the FAT (File Allocation Table (FAT)) on disk. Every entry in this table corresponds to a data area of 512 bytes (called a sector) on the disk. The FAT indicates whether the sector is allocated to a file or is still available.

The FAT has special significance in connection with the directory entry that exists for every file type. Besides the filename and other information, it also indicates the number of an entry in the FAT, which corresponds with the first sector of a file on the disk. This FAT entry points to another FAT entry, which indicates the next sector that was allocated to the file. The other FAT entries on a disk perform the same task.

Two additional features, which simplify working with the PC, were also developed:

The introduction of batch processing enabled the user to place several DOS commands into one file. When you -run this file (which has a file extension of .BAT), DOS executes the individual commands from this file as if you had entered the commands from the keyboard. This saves the user time because he/she doesn't have to enter frequently used groups of commands repeatedly.

The current date and time follow every filename. DOS includes this data to help the user determine the last time a file was modified.

In 1982, when IBM introduced a new PC, which used both sides of a disk for data storage, Microsoft released DOS Version 1.25 (called Version 1.1 by IBM) to support double-sided disk formatting.

Version 2.0

In March of 1983, IBM announced a new personal computer, called the PC XT. In addition to the floppy disk drive, this computer also had a hard drive (also called a fixed disk). The enormous capacity of this hard drive (10 megabytes) allowed the user to store several hundred files on one unit. However, this capacity also created some problems for the operating system. The main problem was that DOS could only handle one directory for each storage unit. It would be almost impossible for the hard drive user to maintain hundreds of files in a single directory. Microsoft had two ways to solve this problem: They could either borrow an idea from the CP/M-80 operating system, or borrow an idea from the UNIX operating system.

CP/M divided a hard drive into user areas, representing several individual disk drives that share the total storage on the hard drive. Each user area had one directory.

UNIX uses a hierarchical file system, in which each storage unit has a root directory. The root directory can contain both subdirectories and files, and each of these subdirectories can have subdirectories within them. This creates a directory tree whose trunk is the root directory and whose branches are represented by the individual subdirectories.

Microsoft chose the hierarchical file system, which has become a popular component of DOS. This was another step away from CP/M-80 and toward an efficient 16-bit operating system. When the hierarchical file system was introduced, the way DOS controlled files had to be changed. Before this time, file access was conducted through a file control block or File control block (FCB). This file control block had been introduced for compatibility with CP/M-80. The FCB contained important information about the name, size, and location of a file on disk. This CP/M wouldn't allow access to a file in another directory.

The DOS developers standardized file access through DOS functions. The access to a file occurs exclusively through the file handles. A handle is a numerical value passed to the program as soon as it opens a file through a DOS function. Although the FCBs weren't eliminated, programmers never encountered them because DOS took over the control block manipulation.

An important innovation was the introduction of installable installable device drivers. By using these drivers, a programmer could easily include different devices in DOS, such as an exotic hard drive, a mouse, or a tape drive. Version 2.0 introduced the display device driver ANSI.SYS, which gave the programmer flexibility in cursor positioning and color selection through DOS functions.

Background processing represented the first step toward multitasking. This allowed a program (e.g., PRINT.COM) to run unnoticed in the background, taking processor time only as needed, while another program ran in the foreground.

Version 2.0 added the option of formatting the individual tracks of a disk with nine sectors instead of eight. This increased the storage capacity of a single-sided disk from 160K to 180K, and the capacity of a double-sided disk from 320K to 360K.

Additions to Version 2.0

As Version 1.25 corrected bugs in Version 1.0, three Microsoft sub versions and one IBM custom version of 2.0 appeared on the market in the same year.

Version 2.01 supported international character sets, including the Kanji alphabet. Shortly after the release of Version 2.01, Version 2.11 appeared, correcting other small errors. This final version was the standard DOS until Version 3.0 was released.

IBM requested a DOS designed specifically for the IBM PCjr. This computer was IBM's attempt to succeed in the home computer market, which was dominated by Commodore and Atari in the early to mid 1980s. DOS Version 2.1, like the PCjr, quickly disappeared from the market. This marked the last time IBM and Microsoft didn't have similar DOS versions. Besides small differences between third party manufacturers (e.g., the inclusion or omission of EXE2BIN.EXE), the version numbers for the two companies are equivalent.

In 1985, after the release of Version 3.0, Version 2 was upgraded for the final time. Version 2.25 was designed specifically for users in the Far East, and supports foreign character sets, such as Kanji.

Version 3.0 and its descendants

Version 3.0, like Version 2.0, was developed for a new PC, called the IBM PC AT. This PC, which was released in August of 1984, supported a 20 megabyte hard drive, as well as the high-density 1.2 megabyte floppy disk drive. Many changes occurred in DOS's internal routines. Although these changes contribute to faster execution of certain operations, they are invisible to the programmer.

Within six months, Version 3.1 was released. This was the first time network support was available. Some new functions were added to implement networking.

Version 3.2 was released in 1985. This version of DOS supported 3.5" floppy diskettes with 720K capacity. This version was the standard for DOS implementations until the release of DOS Version 3.3 in April 1987.

In addition to being the most comprehensive DOS, Version 3.3 supported devices included on the IBM PS/2 systems and the 3.5" high-density floppy diskette format (1.44 megabytes). This version featured improved foreign language support, using code pages.

Version 3.3 also offered improved hard drive support by using partitioning. The user could split a hard drive into primary and secondary partitions, just as single disk drives can be divided into physical and logical drives. Extra driver software wasn't needed for this partitioning.

Most of the changes separating Version 3.0 from Version 2.0 are internal. These changes produce faster program execution, but are otherwise invisible to the user.

Version 4.0

DOS Version 4.0 appeared on the market in August 1988. Earlier, Microsoft released a new multiprocessing operating system called OS/2 multiprocessing operating system. Before OS/2, multiprocessing wasn't possible with MS-DOS.

The differences between DOS 4.0 and earlier versions of DOS were obvious. The line-oriented command line interpreter used by DOS Versions 3.3 and earlier was replaced with the DOS Shell (a graphical user interface). Also, user-defined menus were offered and applications, files, and directories could easily be selected with both the mouse and keyboard.

The changes that couldn't be seen were even more important. For instance, the operating system was adapted to the new hardware standards currently available on the market. However, as the operating system became more powerful, it also became more complex and required more memory. For example, earlier versions of DOS were limited to 640K of RAM and a 32 megabyte hard drive. However, DOS 4.0 handled the Expanded Memory System (EMS) following the LIM standard, normal RAM capacity up to 8 megabytes, and hard drives up to 2 gigabytes (2048 megabytes) capacity.

Unfortunately, DOS Version 4.0 was released before it could be completely tested. So, many users experienced unprovoked system crashes and loss of data. Microsoft released an improved update (Version 4.01) in November 1988, but most users simply returned to Version 3.3 and waited for a thoroughly-tested release.

Version 5.0

Microsoft initiated a vast beta test program before the release of DOS Version 5.0. Over 7,000 users and software developers worldwide installed, ran, and contributed feedback about DOS Version 5.0. The final version was released in June 1991.

Version 5.0 includes efficient RAM use, which leaves more user RAM for applications and TSR programs. Since device drivers and TSR programs can now be placed above the 640K barrier, this frees up even more user RAM.

Versions 6.0, 6.2 and 6.21

Version 6.0 doesn't feature any new innovations for your PC internally. The most important new enchancement is probably DoubleSpace. This program doubles the capacity of your hard drive. It's supported by a special software interface. You will find a description of this interface in Chapter 34.

One problem with Version 6.0 of DOS has concerned running DoubleSpace with certain hard drive configurations. The problem was that DoubleSpace would destroy the contents of some hard drives. Version 6.2 corrected this particular problem with DoubleSpace.

Meanwhile, Microsoft had a different problem with DoubleSpace: A software manufacturer named Stac won a lawsuit against Microsoft. Stac maintained their hard drive compression program called "Stacker" was released first and that Microsoft illegally used part of the Stac programming code. Microsoft was forced to remove DoubleSpace from the market and replace it with a new hard drive compression program. This new version is called DriveSpace and is part of DOS 6.22. It's bascially the same as the early version of DoubleSpace both in operation and in its programming interface.

A look back at DOS

In review, DOS Version 2.0 laid the groundwork for all subsequent releases of DOS. However, the most revolutionary improvements are yet to come, and may lie in graphical user interfaces, such as Windows and OS/2.

DR DOS

Since 1981, Digital Research has released alternative operating systems and graphical user interfaces. They released GEM, a graphic interface, which was quickly overshadowed by Microsoft Windows.

With DR DOS, Digital Research has captured part of the PC market. DR DOS's greatest feature is its compatibility with Microsoft products. Virtually everything we say about DOS in this book also applies to MS-/PC-DOS and DR DOS.

In 1993, Novell purchased Digital Research, so it no longer exists as a separate company. DR-DOS is now sold under the name of Novell DOS.

Chapter 18

Internal Structure Of DOS

In this chapter we'll discuss the internal structure of DOS and the booting process. Since these two items occur in everyday DOS programming, the programmer should understand what happens behind the scenes.

Components Of DOS

Several major components comprise DOS, each with a certain task within the system. The three most important components are the DOS-BIOS, the DOS kernel, and the command processor. Each appear in a separate file.

DOS-BIOS

DOS-BIOS is stored in a system file that appears under various names (IBMBIO.COM, IBMIO.SYS or IO.SYS). This file has the file attributes Hidden and Sys, which indicates that this system file doesn't appear when the DIR command is entered. The DOS-BIOS contains the device drivers for the following units:

```
CON    (Keyboard and Display)
PRN    (Printer)
AUX    (Serial Interface)
CLOCK  (Clock)
Disk drives and/or hard disks which have the drive specifiers A, B and C
```

If DOS wants to communicate with one of these, it accesses a device driver contained in this module, which in turn uses the routines of ROM-BIOS. The DOS-BIOS (i.e., the connection between individual device drivers and other hardware dependent routines) are the most hardware dependent components of the operating system and vary from one computer to another.

Don't confuse the device drivers in this module with the installable device drivers. The DOS-BIOS device drivers cannot be changed by the user.

DOS kernel

The DOS kernel in the IBMDOS.COM or MSDOS.SYS file is usually invisible to the user. It contains file access routine handles, character input and output, and more; it immediately follows the file IBMIO.SYS or IO.SYS. Both sets of files are assigned the SYSTEM, HIDDEN, and READ-ONLY file attributes. These attributes indicate that these files directly affect the system. So you can't view them or delete them by normal means.

These files contain the various DOS-API functions, which are called using interrupt 21H. The routines operate independent of the hardware and use the device drivers of DOS-BIOS for keyboard, screen, and disk access. The module can be used by different PCs without being limited to one machine. User programs can access these functions in the same way as the ROM-BIOS functions every function can be called with a software interrupt. The processor registers pass the function number and the parameters.

Command processor

Unlike the two modules we've described, the command processor is contained in the file named COMMAND.COM. It displays the "A>" or "C>" prompt on the screen, accepts user input, and controls input execution. Many users incorrectly think that the command processor is actually the operating system. Actually it's only a special program that executes under DOS control.

The command processor, also called a shell in programmer's terminology, actually consists of three modules: A resident portion, a transient portion, and the initialization routine.

The resident portion (the part that's always in the computer's memory) contains various routines called critical error handlers. These allow the computer to react to different events, such as pressing the [Ctrl][C] or [Ctrl][Break] keys or errors during communication with external devices (e.g., disk drives and printers). The latter causes the message:

```
Abort, Retry, Ignore
```

or

```
Abort, Retry, Fail
```

The transient portion contains code for displaying the (A>)Prompt prompt, reading user input from the keyboard, and executing the input. The name of this module is derived from the fact that the RAM memory where it's located is unprotected and can be overwritten under certain circumstances. When a program ends, control returns to the resident portion of the command processor. It executes a checksum program to determine whether the transient portion was overwritten by the application program. If it was, the resident portion reloads the transient portion.

The initialization portion loads during the booting process and initializes DOS. This part of the command processor will be examined in detail in the next chapter. When its job ends, it's no longer needed and the RAM memory it occupies can be overwritten by another program. The commands accepted by the transient portion of the command processor can be divided into three groups: internal commands, external commands and batch files.

Internal commands lie in the resident portion of the command processor. COPY, RENAME, and DIR are internal commands.

External commands must be loaded into memory from a diskette or hard disk as needed. FORMAT and CHKDSK are external commands.

After execution the command processor releases the memory used by these programs. This memory can then be used for other purposes.

Batch files

A batch file is a text file containing a series of DOS commands. When a batch file is started, a special interpreter in the transient portion of the command processor executes the batch file commands. Execution of batch file commands is the same as if the user entered them from the keyboard. An important batch file is the AUTOEXEC.BAT file, which executes immediately after DOS is first loaded.

Like all commands of a batch file, these commands are checked for internal commands, external commands, or calls to other batch files. If the first is true, the command executes immediately, since the code is already in memory (in the transient part of the command processor). If it's an external command or another batch file, the system searches the current directory for the command. If such a file doesn't exist in this directory, all directories specified in the PATH command are searched in sequence. During the search, only files with the .COM, .EXE, or .BAT extensions are examined.

Since the command processor cannot search for all three extensions simultaneously, it first searches for files with .COM extensions, then for .EXE files, and finally for .BAT files. If the search is unsuccessful, the screen displays an error message and the system waits for new input.

Booting DOS

The interaction between the DOS-BIOS, the kernel, and the command processor is most obvious when a program is in memory. However, the process of booting the system also calls these modules.

Searching for boot files

When a PC is switched on, the program contained in ROM begins executing. This ROM program is sometimes called the ROM-BIOS, POST (power on self test), resident diagnostics, or bootstrap ROM. It performs several tests on the hardware and memory and then starts to load the DOS.

First, the PC checks for a disk in the floppy disk drive. If a disk exists in the floppy disk drive, the PC checks the disk for the boot sector. If a disk isn't in the drive, the PC searches for a hard disk from which to boot DOS. If a hard disk doesn't exist, the PC displays an error message asking the user to insert a system disk.

The first sector on a bootable floppy disk or hard disk is called the boot sector. The program in the boot sector is read into memory and executes. First it checks for the presence of two files: IBMBIO.COM (sometimes called IO.SYS) and IBMDOS.COM (sometimes called MSDOS.SYS). A bootable floppy disk or hard disk must contain these two files or an error message is displayed. Next these program files are loaded into memory.

The program file IBMBIO.COM consists of two modules. The first contains the basic device drivers-keyboard, display, and disk. The second contains the initialization sequence for DOS. When the IBMBIO.COM program executes, it continues to initialize the system by moving the DOS kernal (loaded in the IBMDOS.COM program file) to the last available memory location.

The DOS kernal builds several important tables and data areas, and performs initialization procedures for individual device drivers that were loaded with the IBMBIO.COM program file.

Next, DOS searches the boot disk for a file named CONFIG.SYS. If this file is found, the commands contained in the file are executed. These commands add device drivers to DOS, allocate disk buffers and file control blocks for DOS, and initialize the standard input and output devices.

Finally, the command processor COMMAND.COM (or other shell specified in the CONFIG.SYS file) is loaded and control is passed to it. The booting process ends and the initialization routines remain as "garbage" data in memory until overwritten by another program.

Chapter 19

COM And EXE Programs

In addition to batch files, DOS also recognizes program files that have the .COM and .EXE file extensions. These extensions indicate these files have different properties and they are executable. These program types differ from others because of the way their program code is stored and the maximum program sizes that are allowed.

The differences between these program types aren't important to a programmer working in high level languages. The programmer only needs to know the program runs; the file format doesn't matter. Also, development packages, such as Turbo Pascal and QuickBASIC, create only EXE files. Some C compilers can produce COM programs using the TINY memory model, in which the combination of program code, data segment, and stack occupies 64K of RAM or less.

The only advantage COM programs have over EXE programs is their slightly smaller program size, which is often only a few hundred bytes.

The programmer working in a high level language doesn't have to worry about the formats and peculiarities of COM and EXE programs because the compiler handles this. However, this information is important to the programmer that's developing software in assembly language.

In this chapter we'll describe the structure and functions of these two program types.

Differences Between COM And EXE Programs

The COM program is basically a relic from the CP/M era, when RAM was minimal and programs weren't larger than 64K. In DOS, a COM program cannot be larger than 64K. An EXE program can be as large as the memory capacity available to DOS or even larger. (Instead of being loaded into memory, portions of the EXE program may be reserved for later use.)

In a COM program, the program code, data, and stack are stored in one 64K partition. All of the segment registers are set at the start of the program and remain fixed for the duration of the program execution. They point to the start of the 64K memory segment. However, the contents of the ES register may be changed because that register doesn't directly affect program execution.

Except for the ES registers, these values must also be stored during program execution. Program code in this segment can be addressed through the CS register, the data can be addressed through the DS register, and the stack can be addressed through the SS register. However, there are exceptions to the rule. For example, if you call a DOS function, which expects another segment address in the DS register, the DS register may be loaded with another value before the function call. Neither DOS nor the processor will object to this. After execution, the DS register must be reloaded with the COM program's segment address to make the global variables of the program or other data accessible.

Unlike COM files, a direct sequence doesn't exist for EXE file segments. Code, data, and the stack are stored in different segments according to size; they could be distributed over several segments. This distribution applies to larger, commercial programs (e.g., Microsoft Word), which contain program code consisting of several hundred kilobytes. So, during the execution of an EXE program, the various segment registers point to individual code, data, or stack segments instead of a general memory segment.

Regardless of the program type, DOS creates a data structure in memory called the Program Segment Prefix (PSP) before the program starts. (We'll discuss this in more detail later.) This data structure contains 256 bytes. It immediately precedes the program in memory, as shown in the following illustration:

Comparing COM and EXE programs in memory

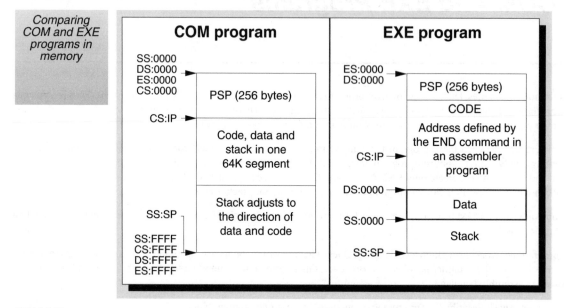

COM Programs

COM program files are stored on disk as an image copy of memory. Because of this, no further processing is needed during loading. So, COM programs load and start execution faster than EXE programs. Also, COM programs are usually more compact than EXE programs because other information, besides the program code and the initialized variables, are also stored there.

Although these items may have been important in the past, they are no longer significant. Programs have become so large that two or three hundred additional bytes no longer make that much difference in an EXE file. Also, computers have become so fast the speed advantage to loading a COM program has been reduced to a few milliseconds. Only a few dedicated assembly language programmers still use COM format when a program must be as compact as possible.

Microsoft and COM programs

Microsoft's COM program support is steadily decreasing. The Microsoft Assembler MASM assembles files as EXE programs. To convert these programs to COM programs, you need EXE2BIN, which is an important utility packaged with older versions of MS-DOS. MS-DOS 4.0 didn't contain EXE2BIN. The version check in all DOS programs ensured that copies of EXE2BIN, which were taken from older versions of MS-DOS, would not function under MS-DOS 4.0 or 4.01.

So, programmers who wanted to continue using EXE2BIN were forced to alter DOS's version check in order to make EXE2BIN compatible with MS-DOS.

Unlike the LINK program included with the Microsoft Assembler MASM, the Turbo Assembler from Borland International can create both EXE and COM programs.

When MS-DOS Version 5.0 was released, Microsoft again packaged EXE2BIN with DOS.

Registers during start of program

A COM program loads immediately following the PSP. Execution then begins at the first memory location following the PSP at offset 100H. For this reason, a COM program must begin with an executable instruction, even if it's only a jump instruction to the actual start of the program.

COM program memory limits

As we mentioned, a COM program can be only 64K (65,536 bytes). The PSP (256 bytes) and at least 1 word (2 bytes) for the stack must also be reserved. Even though the length of the COM program can never exceed 64K, DOS reserves the entire available RAM for a program. So, DOS cannot allocate additional memory and the COM program cannot call another program using the EXEC function. You can bypass this limitation by releasing the unused memory for other uses with a DOS function.

When control is given to the COM program, all segment registers point to the beginning of the PSP. Because of this, the beginning of the COM program (relative to the beginning of the PSP) is always at address 100H. The stack pointer points to the end of the 64K memory segment containing the COM program (usually FFFEH). During every subroutine call within the COM program, the stack is adjusted by 2 bytes in the direction towards the end of the program. The programmer is responsible for preventing the stack from growing and overwriting the program, which would cause a crash.

There are several ways to end a COM program and return control to DOS or the calling program:

If the program runs under DOS Version 1.0, it can be terminated by calling interrupt 21H function 0 or by calling interrupt 20H. It can also be terminated by using the RET (RETurn) assembler instruction. When this instruction executes, the program continues at the address at the top of the stack. Since the EXEC function stored the value 0 at this location before turning control over to the COM program, program execution continues at location CS:0 (the start of the PSP). Remember that this location contains the call for interrupt 20H, which terminates the program.

Since the odds of a DOS Version 1.0 user are quite low, use DOS function 4CH. Microsoft recommends this function for terminating programs for all subsequent versions of DOS. The terminating program can pass a numeric return code to the calling program. For example, a value of 0 may indicate the program executed successfully, while a non-zero value indicates an error occurred during execution.

Developing COM programs in assembly language

Now we'll discuss the details the assembly language programmer must handle when developing a COM program. If you're a high level programmer, you may want to skip this section because you don't have to worry about these details. The compiler or interpreter handles them for you.

We've mentioned that COM programs are stored on a diskette or hard drive as a direct image of the machine code. Also, instead of being placed at a fixed address by DOS, COM programs can be placed at any memory location divisible by 16. This placement means that COM programs cannot contain FAR calls or specific segment addresses. Only NEAR calls, which contain offset addresses but no segment address, are allowed. Because of this, commands always refer to the current segment in the CS, DS, ES, or SS registers instead of to a certain segment address.

COM programs cannot contain assembly language instructions, such as LDS or LES. The assembler and linker accept these instructions, but EXE2BIN will refuse to make the assembled EXE file into a COM file. This also applies to TLINK, the Turbo Linker.

You may load constants. For example, you can load the segment address of video RAM into a segment register. This is possible because a reference isn't made to the segments of the program, whose position is uncertain, until the actual start of the program.

Assembly language instructions such as the following aren't allowed because the MOV instruction reads the segment address of the program:

```
MOV   AX,SEG PROGRAM
MOV   DS,AX
```

The following instructions are allowed because a constant segment address is used for reference:

```
MOV   AX,0B000h
MOV   DS,AX
```

While the developer of a COM program is more limited in this instance than the developer of an EXE program, less work is required for the stack. Before the program is started, the stack is automatically placed at the end of the 64K COM segment by loading the SS register with the COM segment's address, and loading the SP register with the value 0FFFEH.

Before calling a COM program, DOS reserves all available memory for the program even though it normally uses only one 64K segment and indicates this by setting memory location 2 in the PSP. Usually the program terminates and the memory is made available to DOS again.

In some circumstances you may want to write a program that will remain resident after execution. However, DOS believes there isn't any memory available. This prevents other programs from loading and executing.

In other circumstances you may want to execute another program from this COM program using the EXEC function. Again, since DOS thinks that memory is unavailable, it won't allow the new program to run.

Both problems can be avoided by freeing up the unused memory.

> **You'll find the following program(s) on the companion CD-ROM**
>
> TESTCOM.ASM
> (Assembler listing)

There are two ways to do this. Release only the memory outside of the 64K COM segment or release memory outside of the 64K COM segment and any unused memory within the 64K COM segment. Although this creates more memory for other programs, it relocates the stack outside the protected COM segment memory. So, the stack can be overwritten by other programs. Because of this, the stack must be relocated to the end of the code segment before releasing the memory. Also, the size of the stack must be limited (usually 512 bytes is sufficient).

The TESTCOM.ASM sample program on the companion CD-ROM demonstrates how to develop a COM program. A small (init) routine relocates the stack to the end of the code segment after the start of the program and releases all remaining memory. Even when this program loads another program, it remains resident. This routine can be useful to applications and can be part of any COM program.

You can assemble this program with either MASM or TASM. You must assemble the source program using an assembler. Let's look at creating the program using the Microsoft assembler. First you assemble the code using MASM:

```
masm testcom;
```

After assembling the program, use the LINK program to create an EXE file:

```
link testcom;
```

When you execute LINK, the following message appears:

```
Warning: no stack segment
```

This message tells you what you already know: The program doesn't contain a stack segment, so it may not function correctly as an EXE file. Simply disregard this message.

If no other warnings or errors were indicated, you must convert the file to a COM file. The EXE2BIN program already mentioned performs this conversion using the following syntax:

```
exe2bin testcom.exe testcom.com
```

Now there may be two files named TESTCOM on the disk. Delete the one named TESTCOM.EXE; you want the TESTCOM.COM file. If all steps were performed correctly, the TESTCOM.COM program can be executed from DOS by simply typing "TESTCOM".

The following command set is required:

```
masm testcom;
link testcom;
exe2bin testcom.exe testcom.com
```

Borland's Turbo Assembler (TASM) and the TLINK linker perform the same task as MASM, LINK, and EXE2BIN, but in a slightly different manner. Assemble the TESTCOM.ASM file using TASM as follows:

```
tasm testcom
```

Use the following syntax for linking (this directly links the code to COM form):

```
tlink /t testcom
```

EXE Programs

EXE programs have an advantage over COM programs because they aren't limited to a maximum length of 64K for code, data and stack. However, these files are more complicated. This means that in addition to the program itself, other information must be stored in an EXE file.

Future versions of DOS may enable EXE programs to adapt to innovations, such as multitasking, because it's easier for DOS to estimate memory requirements for EXE programs than for COM programs.

EXE vs. COM

EXE programs contain separate segments for code, data, and stack that can be organized in any sequence. Unlike a COM program, an EXE program loads into memory from disk, undergoes processing by the EXEC function; and then finally begins execution. This is necessary because of the limitations already described for COM programs.

Instead of being limited to loading at a fixed memory location, EXE programs can load at any desired location in memory that's a multiple of 16. Since an EXE program can have several segments, FAR machine language instructions must be used. For example, a main program can be in one segment and call a subroutine in another segment. The segment address must be provided for this FAR instruction in addition to the offset for the routine to be called. The problem is the segment address may be different for every execution of the program. Consulting the CS register doesn't help because only the segment address of the current code segment, instead of the one to which the jump will be made, is stored there.

COM files avoid this problem because the program size is limited to 64K. So, FAR commands are unnecessary. EXE programs solve this problem in a more complex way. The LINK program places a data structure at the beginning of every EXE file that contains (in addition to other things) the addresses of all segments. It contains the addresses of all memory locations in which the segment address of a certain segment is stored during program execution. More specifically, these addresses indicate the addresses of the segment references within instructions. The assembly language code for a FAR jump consists of the following five bytes: the instruction code (one byte), the segment address (one word), and the offset address (one word). The words refer to the location of the jump.

If the EXEC function loads the EXE program, it knows the addresses where the various segments should be loaded. So, it can enter these values into the memory locations at the beginning of the EXE file. Because of this, more time elapses between the initial program call and when the program actually begins execution than for a COM program. The EXE program also occupies more memory than a COM program. The following table shows the structure of the header for an EXE file:

EXE file header		
Address	Contents	Type
00H	EXE program identifier (5A4DH)	1 word
02H	file length MOD 512	1 word
04H	file length DIV 512	1 word
06H	Number of segment addresses for passing	1 word
08H	Header size in paragraphs	1 word
0AH	Minimum number of paragraphs needed	1 word
0CH	Maximum number of paragraphs needed	1 word
0EH	Stack segment displacement	1 word
10H	SP register contents when program starts	1 word
12H	Checksum based on EXE file header	1 word
14H	IP register contents when program starts	1 word
16H	Start of code segment in EXE file	1 word
18H	Relocation table address in EXE file	1 word
1AH	Overlay number	1 word
1CH	Buffer memory	??
??H	Address of passing segment addresses (relocation table)	??
??H	Program code, data and stack segment	??

After the segment references within the EXE program have been resolved to the current addresses, the EXEC function sets the DS and the ES segment register to the beginning of the PSP, which also precedes all EXE programs in memory. Because of this, the EXE program can access the information contained in the PSP, such as the address of the environment block and the parameters contained in the command line (command tail). The stack address and the contents of the stack pointer are stored in the EXE file header and accessed from there. This also applies to the code segment address containing the first instructions of the program and the program counter. After the values have been assigned, the program execution begins.

To ensure compatibility with future DOS versions, an EXE program should terminate by calling interrupt 21H function 4CH.

RAM allocation

Obviously, memory must be available for the EXE program. The EXE loader determines the total program size based on the size of the individual segments of the EXE program. Then it can allocate this amount of memory and some additional memory immediately following the EXE program. The first two fields of the EXE program file header contain the minimum and maximum size of memory required in paragraphs (1-6 bytes).

First, the EXE loader tries to reserve the maximum number of paragraphs. If this isn't possible, the loader tries to reserve the remaining memory, which cannot be smaller than the minimum number of paragraphs. These fields are determined by the compiler or assembler, instead of the linker. The minimum is 0 and the maximum allowed is FFFFH. In most instances, this last number is unrealistic (it adds up to 1 megabyte) but reserves the entire memory for the EXE program.

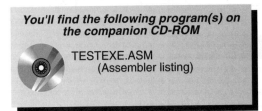

You'll find the following program(s) on the companion CD-ROM

TESTEXE.ASM
(Assembler listing)

Now we encounter the same problems as in COM programs. EXE files make poor resident programs, but an EXE program may need to call another program during execution. This is only possible if you first release the additional reserved memory. The following program contains a routine that reduces the reserved memory to a minimum.

The program uses separate code, data, and stack segments. You can use this program as a model for other EXE programs.

To create an EXE program, assemble it like a normal program with an assembler. Then link it with the LINK program. If the program doesn't contain errors, the LINK program creates an EXE file.

The following steps are used to prepare an EXE program from the assembly language source, named TESTEXE.ASM, using the MASM assembler:

```
masm testexe;
link testexe;
```

If you're using the Turbo Assembler TASM, the steps would be as follows:

```
tasm testexe
tlink testexe
```

If all these steps were executed correctly, the program TESTEXE.EXE can be started from the DOS level by typing "TESTEXE".

The PSP

We'll end this chapter by discussing the Program Segment Prefix (PSP) which DOS places before every EXE or COM program in memory. The PSP is a remnant of the CP/M era. It contains data DOS needs to manage the program to be executed. The PSP also stores information that's important to programmers, especially parameters supplied by the user when the program is called from the system prompt. While high level language compilers automatically read these parameters at the beginning of the program and write them to predefined global variables, the assembly language programmer must evaluate this information him/herself.

The following table shows the structure and fields of the PSP, many of which remain undocumented (or "reserved") by Microsoft. Most of these fields have been decoded, even though they are useless for practical programming.

Structure of the PSP		
Address	Contents	Type
00H	Interrupt 20H call	2 bytes
02H	Segment address of memory allocated for program	1 word
04H	Reserved	1 byte
05H	Interrupt 21H call	5 bytes
0AH	Copy of interrupt vector 23H	2 words
0EH	Copy of interrupt vector 23H	2 words
12H	Copy of interrupt vector 24H	2 words
16H	Reserved	22 bytes
2CH	Segment address of environment block	1 word
2EH	Reserved	46 bytes
5CH	FCB 1	16 bytes
6CH	FCB 2	16 bytes
80H	Number of characters in command line	1 byte
81H	Command line (CR-LF)	127 bytes

The PSP itself is always 256 bytes long and contains important information for DOS and the program to be executed.

Memory location 00H of the PSP contains a DOS function call to terminate a program. This function releases program memory and returns control to the command processor or the calling program. Memory location 05H of the PSP contains a DOS function call to interrupt 21H. Neither of these are used by DOS; they are remnants from the CP/M system.

Memory location 02H of the PSP contains the segment address to the end of the program. Memory location 0AH contains the previous contents of the program termination interrupt vector. Memory location 0EH contains the previous contents of the (Ctrl)(C) or (Ctrl)(Break) interrupt vector. Memory location 12H contains the previous contents of the critical error interrupt vector. For each of these memory locations, the program changes one of the corresponding vectors during execution; DOS can use the original vector if it detects an error.

Location 2CH contains the segment address of the environment block. The environment block contains information such as the current search path and the directory in which the COMMAND.COM command processor is located on disk.

Memory locations 5CH through 6CH contain a file control block (FCB). DOS doesn't use the FCB often because it doesn't support hierarchical files (paths) and is also a remnant from CP/M.

The string of parameters that are entered on the command line, following the program name is called the command tail. The command tail is copied to the parameter buffer in the PSP beginning at memory location 81H and its length is stored at memory location 80H. Any redirection parameters are eliminated from the command tail as it's copied to the parameter buffer. The program can examine the parameters in the parameter buffer to direct its execution.

The parameter buffer is also used by DOS as a disk transfer area (DTA) for transmitting data between the disk drive and memory. Most DOS programs do not use the DTA contained in the PSP because it's another remnant from CP/M.

Chapter 20

Character Input And Output From DOS

DOS input and output functions can address the keyboard, screen, printer, and serial interface. These functions can be divided into two types: Those carried over from the CP/M operating system and those borrowed from the UNIX operating system. While the two types of functions can be intermingled, to maintain consistency, we recommend using one type of function throughout a program.

The UNIX type functions use a file handle as an identifier to a device. Because of recent DOS trends to move closer to UNIX, you may want to give the handle functions precedence.

Handle Functions

The handle functions perform file access as well as character input to or output from a device. DOS recognizes the difference by examining the name assigned by the handle. If the handle is a device name, it addresses the device; otherwise it assumes that file access should occur. The table on the right lists the device names.

Device	Purpose
CON	Keyboard and screen
AUX	Serial Interface
PRN	Printer
NUL	Imaginary device (nothing happens on access)

Output and input go to and from the AUX, PRN, and NUL devices. For the device CON, output is sent to the screen and input is read from the keyboard.

When DOS passes control to a program, five handles are available for access to individual devices. These handles have values from 0 to 4 and represent the devices listed in the table to the right.

The following is a short example that demonstrates how to use this table.

Display error message

If a program wants to accept input from the user, this is indicated by the handle function 0 during the call because

Handle	Purpose
0	Standard input (CON)
1	Standard output (CON)
2	Standard output for error messages (CON)
3	Standard serial interface (AUX)
4	Standard printer (PRN)

the standard input device is addressed. Handle 0 normally represents the keyboard, permitting input from the user to the program. Since the user can redirect standard input, you can redirect input to originate from a file instead of the keyboard. This redirection remains hidden from the program.

Before we discuss these devices, you should be familiar with some functions used to access any device.

Function 40H of interrupt 21H sends data to a device. The function number (40H) is passed in the AH register and the handle is passed in the BX register. For example, to display an error message, the value 2 indicates the handle for displaying the error message (this device cannot be redirected, so handle 2 always addresses the console). The number of characters to be in the error message is passed in the CX register. The characters that constitute the message are stored sequentially in memory, whose segment address is stored in the DS register and offset address in the DX register.

Following the call to the function, the carry flag signals any error. If there's no error, the carry flag is reset and the AX register contains the number of characters that were displayed. If the AX register contains the value 0, then there was no more space available on the storage medium for the message. If the carry flag is set, the error message wasn't sent and an error code is indicated in the AX register. An error code of 5 indicates the device wasn't available. An error code of 6 indicates the handle wasn't opened.

Function 3FH of interrupt 21H reads character data from a device and is very similar to the previous function. Both functions have identical register usage. The function number is passed in the AX register and the handle in the BX register. The number of characters read is passed in the CX register and the memory address of the characters transferred are passed in the DS:DX register pair.

Following the call to the function, the carry flag also signals any error. Again, any error code is passed in the AX register. Error codes 5 and 6 have the same meaning as in function 40H. If the carry flag is reset, then the function executed successfully. The AX register then contains the number of characters read into the buffer. A value of 0 in the AX register indicates the data to be read should have come from a file but this file doesn't contain any more data.

As we mentioned, it's possible to redirect the input or output when accessing DOS. For example, a program that normally expects input from the keyboard can be made to accept the input from a file. So, to avoid having input or output redirected, you can open a new handle to a specific device. This handle ensures the transfer of data to or from the desired device takes place instead of to or from a redirected device.

Use function 3DH of interrupt 21H to open such a device.

The function number 3DH is passed in the AH register. The AL register contains 0 to enable reading from the device, 1 to enable writing to the device, and 2 for both reading and writing to the device. The name of the device is placed in memory whose address is passed in the DS:DX register pair. The names must be specified in uppercase characters so DOS can properly identify the device name. The last character of the string must be an end character (ASCII value 0).

Following the function calls, the status is indicated by the carry flag. A reset flag means the device was opened successfully and the handle number is passed back in the AX register. A set flag indicates an error and the AX register contains any error code.

The handle is closed using function 3EH of interrupt 21H. The function number is passed in the AH register and the handle number is passed in the BX register. The carry flag again indicates the status of the function call. A set carry flag indicates an error.

You can also close the predefined handles 0 through 4 using this function. But if you close handle 0 (the standard input device) you'll no longer be able to accept input from the keyboard.

Now let's examine the special characteristics of each device.

Keyboard

The keyboard can perform only read operations. The results of the read operations depend on the mode in which the device was addressed. Here DOS differentiates between raw and cooked. In the cooked mode DOS checks every character sent to or received from a device to determine whether it's a special control character. If DOS finds a special control character, it performs a certain action in response to the character. In raw mode, the individual characters are passed through unchecked and unmanipulated. DOS normally operates the device in cooked mode for character input and output. However, you can switch to raw mode within a program (see below).

The best way to illustrate the difference between cooked and raw mode is with an example of reading the keyboard. Suppose that 30 characters are read from the keyboard in cooked mode. As you enter the characters, DOS allows you to edit the input using several control keys. For example, `Ctrl` `C` and `Ctrl` `Break` abort the input. The `Ctrl` `S` keys temporarily halts the program until another key is pressed. The `Ctrl` `P` keys direct subsequent data from the screen to the printer (until `Ctrl` `P` is pressed again). The Backspace key removes the last character from the DOS buffer. If the Enter key is pressed, the first 30 characters (or all characters input up to now if there are less than 30) are copied from the DOS buffer into the input buffer of the program without the control characters.

In raw mode all characters entered (including control characters) are passed to the calling program without requiring the user to press the Enter key. After exactly 30 characters, control passes to the calling program, even if you pressed the Enter key as the second character of the input.

Screen

To display characters on the screen, handle 1 is usually addressed as the standard output device. Since this device can be redirected, output through this handle can pass to devices other than the screen. However, you cannot redirect the standard error output device (handle 2). So, error messages that pass through this handle always appear on the screen. This handle is recommended only for character display on the screen.

The screen is normally addressed in cooked mode; every character displayed on the screen is tested for the Ctrl C or the Ctrl Break control characters. Since this test slows down the screen output, changing to raw mode occasionally decreases program execution time.

Printer

Unlike the keyboard and screen, printer output cannot be redirected (at least not from the user level). An exception to this rule is redirecting output from a parallel printer to a serial printer. Characters ready to print can be sent to a buffer before they are sent to the printer. Handle 4 is used to address the standard printer. There are three standard printer devices LPT1, LPT2, and LPT3. Device PRN is synonymous with LPT1. When this handle is opened, the device name is specified as one of the three: LPT1, LPT2, or LPT3.

Serial interface

Much of the information that applies to the printer also applies to the serial interface. For example, serial input and output cannot be redirected to another device (e.g., from a serial printer to a parallel printer). The programmer can use the predefined handle 3 for serial access, through which you can address the standard serial interface (AUX).

Handle 3 is used to address the standard serial device. The two are named COM1 and COM2. A PC can have multiple serial interfaces. Only the first two (COM1 and COM2) are supported by DOS. Since the system doesn't know exactly which interface to access during AUX device access, you should open a new handle for access to the specific device.

Errors during read operations in DOS mode are returned to the serial interface in cooked mode. The number returned to the AX register won't match the number of characters actually read. We recommend that you operate the serial interface in raw mode, even if this mode ignores control characters, such as Ctrl C and EOF (end-of-file).

Traditional DOS Functions

The DOS functions for input and output aren't based on the handle oriented functions. If you use these functions you won't need to specify a handle, since each function pertains to a specific device. The various input and output devices and the way in which these functions work with them are listed later.

Keyboard

There are seven DOS functions for addressing the keyboard but they differ in many ways. For example, these functions respond differently to the Ctrl Break key. While some functions echo the characters on the screen, others don't.

You can use DOS functions 01H, 06H, 07H, and 08H to read a single keyboard character. The function number is passed in the AH register. Following the call, the character is returned in the AL register.

For DOS function 01H, DOS waits for a keypress if the keyboard buffer is empty. When this happens, the character is echoed on the screen. If the keyboard buffer isn't empty, a new character is fetched and returned to the calling program. DOS function

06H can be used for both character input and output. To input a character, a value of FFH is loaded into the DL register. Instead of waiting for a character to be input, this function immediately returns to the calling program. If the zero flag is set, a character wasn't read. If the zero flag is reset, a character was read and returned in the AL register. The character isn't echoed on the screen.

DOS functions 07H and 08H are used to read the keyboard similar to function 1. Both either fetch a character from the keyboard buffer or wait for a character to be entered at the keyboard. Neither echo the character to the screen. They differ because function 08H responds to Ctrl C but function 07H doesn't.

By using function 0BH, a program can determine whether one or more characters are in the keyboard buffer before calling any functions that read characters. After calling this function, the AL register contains 0 if the keyboard buffer is empty, and FFH if the keyboard buffer isn't empty.

DOS function 0CH is used to clear the keyboard buffer. After the buffer is cleared, the function, whose number was passed to function 0CH in the AL register, is automatically called.

DOS function 0AH is used to read a string of characters. Again, this function number is passed in the AH register. In addition, the memory address of a buffer for the character string is passed in the DS:DX register pair. This buffer is used to hold the character string. The first byte of the buffer indicates the maximum number of characters that may be contained in the buffer.

When this function is called, DOS reads up to the maximum number of characters and stores them in the buffer starting at the third byte. It reads until either the maximum number of characters is entered or the Enter key is pressed. The actual number of characters is stored in the second byte of the buffer. Extended key codes, which occupy two bytes each in the buffer, may be entered. The first byte of the pair (ASCII value 0) signifies that an extended key code follows. This means, for example, that for a maximum buffer size of 10 bytes, only five extended characters may be entered.

The following table illustrates how the various functions respond to Ctrl C or Ctrl Break and provides a quick overview of the individual functions for character input.

Function	Task	<Ctrl><C>	Echo
01H	Character input	yes	yes
06H	Direct character input	no	no
07H	Character input	no	no
08H	Character input	yes	no
0AH	Character string input	yes	no
0BH	Read input status	yes	no
0CH	Reset input buffer then input	varies	varies

Screen output

There are three DOS functions for character output.

DOS function 02H outputs a single character to the screen or standard output device. This character is passed to the DL register.

DOS function 06H, which is multipurpose, is also used to output a single character. The character is passed in the DL register. You can see the character, whose value is 255, cannot be output because this indicates the function must perform an input operation. Output using this function is faster than using function 02H because it doesn't test for the Ctrl C or Ctrl Break keys.

DOS function 09H is used for string output. Again, the function number is passed in the AH register. The address of the string is passed in the DS:DX register pair. The last character of the string is a dollar sign. Also, the following control codes are recognized:

Code	Character	Operation
07	Bell	Sounds a beep
08	Backspace	Erases preceding character and moves cursor left by one character
10	Linefeed	Moves cursor one line down (LF)
13	Carriage return	Moves cursor to the beginning of the current line (CR)

As with function 02H, this function also checks for Ctrl C or Ctrl Break.

Printer output functions

DOS function 05H is used to output a single character to the printer. If the printer is busy, this function waits until it's ready before returning control to the calling program. During this time, it will respond to the Ctrl C and Ctrl Break keys.

The function number is passed in the AH register. The character to output is passed in the DL register. The status of the printer isn't returned. Most programmers use the BIOS function instead of the DOS function for printer output because they can specify the exact printer device and determine the printer status using the BIOS version. Refer to Section 7.1 for more detailed information.

Serial interface functions

There are two DOS functions for communicating using a serial interface; one is used for input and one for output. Both functions respond to Ctrl C and Ctrl Break, but they don't return the status of the serial interface or recognize transmission errors.

DOS function 03H is used to input data from the serial interface. The character is returned in the AL register. Since the data isn't buffered, it can overrun the interface if the interface receives data faster than this function can handle it.

DOS function 04H is used to output data over the serial interface. The character to output is passed in the DL register. If the serial interface isn't ready to accept the data, this function waits until the serial interface is free.

Again, most programmers prefer to use the BIOS equivalent functions (see Chapter 3) to perform serial data transmission because of their complete data handling capabilities.

Toggling Between Raw And Cooked Modes

We mentioned that it's possible to switch a device from cooked mode to raw mode and then back again. The Pascal and C programs that follow demonstrate how to do this. They use the IOCTL functions which permit access to the DOS device drivers (see Chapter 27 for details on this routine). These routines act as interfaces between the DOS input/output functions and the hardware. The IOCTL functions in these programs tell the CON device driver (responsible for the keyboard and the display) whether it should operate in the cooked mode or in the raw mode.

To demonstrate how differently characters respond in the two modes, the programs switch the CON driver into raw mode first. Then this driver displays a sample string several times. Unlike cooked mode, pressing Ctrl C or Ctrl S in raw mode has no effect on stopping program execution or text display.

After the program finishes displaying the sample string, the driver switches to the cooked mode. The sample string is displayed again several times. When you press Ctrl C, the program stops (Turbo Pascal version). For the C version, you can press Ctrl C to stop the program or press Ctrl S to pause or continue the display.

Switching between the raw and the cooked mode doesn't occur directly through a function. First the device attribute of the driver is determined. This attribute contains certain information that identifies the driver and describes its method of operation. One bit in this word indicates whether the driver operates in raw or cooked mode. The programs set or reset this bit, depending on the mode you want running the driver.

You'll find the following program(s) on the companion CD-ROM

RAWCOOK.PAS (Pascal listing)
RAWCOOK.C (C listing)

DOS Filters

Filters are programs, routines or utilities that accept input and modify the data for output. Filters also perform these tasks on the operating system level. Characters are passed to these filters as input. Then the filters modify the characters and send them as output. This manipulation takes many forms. Filters can sort data, replace certain data with other data, encode data, or decode data.

DOS uses three basic filters:

> FIND   Searches input for a specified set of characters.

> SORT   Arranges text or data in order.

> MORE   Formats text display.

These filters perform simple redirection of standard input/output. They read characters from the standard input device, manipulate the characters as needed, then display them on the standard output device. Under DOS, the standard input device is the keyboard and the standard output device is the monitor. DOS Versions 2.0 and higher allow the user to redirect the standard input/output to files. So, depending on the standard input device selected, a filter can read characters from the keyboard or from a file. This is possible by using a filter along with one of the DOS handle functions for reading and writing. DOS provides the five handles listed in the table to the right.

0	Standard input	CON (Keyboard)
1	Standard output	CON (Screen)
2	Standard error output	CON (Screen)
3	Standard serial interface	AUX
4	Standard printer	PRN

If the user calls a program from the DOS level, the "<" character redirects input and the ">" character redirects output. In the following example, the input comes from the file IN.TXT instead of the keyboard. The output is written to the file OUT.TXT instead of the screen:

```
sort <in.txt >out.txt
```

SORT

After the user enters the previous command, DOS recognizes that a program named SORT should be called. Then it encounters the expression <IN.TXT, which redirects the standard input. This occurs by assigning the handle 0 (standard input, which formerly pointed to the keyboard) to the file IN.TXT. The expression >OUT.TXT resets handle 1 to the OUT.TXT file instead of the screen. The affected handle is first closed, and then the redirected file is opened.

Once the command processor finishes with the command line, it calls the SORT program by using the EXEC function (DOS function 4BH). Since the program called with the EXEC function has all the handles of the calling program available, the SORT program can input/output characters to handles 0 and 1. Where the characters originate isn't important to the program.

After the SORT program completes its work, it returns control to the command processor. The command processor resets the redirection and waits for further input from the user.

Pipes

The filter principle, as supported by DOS, becomes especially powerful through pipes. This is similar to a pipeline used for transporting oil or gas. DOS pipes have a similar function; they carry characters from one program to another and allow various programs to be connected to each other.

When this happens, characters output from one program to the standard output device can be read by another program from the standard input device. As in the redirection of the standard input/output, the two programs don't notice the pipelines. The difference between the two procedures is that under redirection of the standard input/output devices, data can be redirected to only one device or file, while the use of pipes allows data transfer to another program.

Combined filters

Pipes allow users to connect multiple filters. The pipe character | is inserted between the programs to be connected. For example, suppose that a text file named DEMO.TXT is sorted and then displayed on the screen in page format. Even though this task appears to be very complicated at first, it can be performed easily using the DOS filters SORT and MORE. SORT sorts the file and MORE displays the file on the screen in page format.

How can you tell the command processor to perform these tasks? First SORT is used. This filter is told to sort the file DEMO.TXT. The redirection of standard input can be used, as illustrated at the beginning of the chapter:

```
SORT <DEMO.TXT
```

After the user enters this command, SORT sorts the file DEMO.TXT and then displays the file on the screen. This display would be much easier to read in page format. Formatted output can be implemented by redirecting the output from SORT to a file (e.g., TEMP.TXT) and displaying this file using the MORE command. The following sequence of commands do this:

```
SORT <DEMO.TXT >TEMP.TXT
MORE <TEMP.TXT
```

You can use a pipe to connect the SORT filter and the MORE filter, which saves typing time. The following command line sends the output from SORT directly to MORE and immediately displays the sorted file in page format:

```
SORT <DEMO.TXT | MORE
```

Any number of filters can be connected using pipes. DOS always executes these pipelined filters from left to right. It sends the output from the first program as input to the second program, the second program's output as input to the third program, etc. The last program can again force the redirection of the output with the > character so the final result of the whole program or filter chain travels to a file or other device instead of the screen.

> **NOTE**
>
> DOS cannot send data from one filter directly to another because it would have to execute both filters simultaneously. However, the current version of DOS doesn't have multiprocessing capabilities. Instead, the following method is used. The input calls the first filter and redirects its output to a pipe file. After the first filter ends its processing, it calls the second filter but redirects its input to the pipe file to read in the output from the first filter. This principle applies to all filters. The pipe file is stored in the current working directory.

A Filter Demonstration Program

"Dump" is a computer term that refers to a way to display the contents of a file in ASCII characters and/or hexadecimal numbers. The following DUMP programs perform this task as a filter. As the contents are displayed in ASCII format, DUMP differentiates between normal ASCII characters (letters, numbers, etc.) and control characters, such as a carriage return, linefeed, etc. These control characters are displayed in mnemonic form (e.g., <CR> for carriage return and <LF> for linefeed). Although this DUMP filter has a fairly simple structure, it can be very useful for quickly examining a file's contents.

The structure of the DUMP program is typical for a filter. Since DUMP displays a maximum of nine ASCII characters and/or hexadecimal codes per line, it asks for nine characters by using the read function from the standard input device. If enough characters aren't available, it reads the available characters. DUMP places these characters in a buffer, then converts the characters into ASCII characters and hex codes. This buffer will accept a complete line of 78 characters. When the buffer processing is complete, the filter uses the handle to write to the standard output device. This process is repeated until no more characters can be read from the standard input device.

The following programs are written in Pascal, C and assembly language. Remember there isn't a BASIC version because, as an interpreted language, it isn't suitable for developing a filter that can be called from the DOS level. A BASIC compiler is needed for this task.

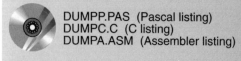

You'll find the following program(s) on the companion CD-ROM

DUMPP.PAS (Pascal listing)
DUMPC.C (C listing)
DUMPA.ASM (Assembler listing)

Chapter 21

File Management In DOS

The DOS file management functions are among the most basic available to the programmer. However, programmers using high level languages seldom access these DOS functions directly because the languages often have their own methods of file management. This chapter describes how the file functions are organized and how you can use them from higher level languages.

Two Sides Of DOS

The term "file management functions" refers to the functions used to manage files, such as creating, deleting, opening, closing, reading from, and writing to files. Operating systems such as DOS provide the programmer with functions for file management. For example, DOS provides functions that return special file information or rename a file.

One peculiarity of DOS is these functions exist in two forms because of the combined CP/M & UNIX compatibility. For every UNIX compatible file function, there is also a CP/M compatible file function. Versions 2.0 and up of DOS borrowed ideas from this UNIX compatibility.

FCB functions

The CP/M compatible functions are designated as FCB functions because they are based on a data structure called the FCB (File Control Block). DOS uses this data structure for storing information during file manipulation. The user must reserve space for the FCB within this program. The FCB permits access to the FCB functions which open, close, read from, and write to files.

Since the FCB functions were developed for compatibility with CP/M's functions, and since CP/M doesn't have a hierarchical file system, FCB functions don't support paths. As a result, FCB functions can only access files that are in the current directory.

The handle function concept

DOS Versions 2.0 and up support handle functions, which were first used in the UNIX environment. However, the UNIX compatible handle functions don't have the problems resulting from FCB functions. As the name suggests, a handle is used to identify the file to be accessed. DOS stores information about each open file in an area that is separate from the program.

No file structure differences

Remember the differences between these function groups are related to how these files are created, instead of their actual structures. Files created and edited using FCB functions can cause problems if subsequently accessed by handle functions and vice versa.

The most important fact to remember is to keep the two groups of functions separate when developing high level language programs. In the following sections, we'll take a closer look at each group of functions.

Handle Functions

It's easier for the programmer to access a file using the handle functions than using the FCB functions. With handle functions a programmer doesn't have to use a data structure for file access like the FCB functions do. Similar to the functions of the UNIX operating system, file access is performed using a filename. The filename is passed as an ASCII string when the file is opened or first created. This must be performed before the first write or read operation to the file. In addition to the filename, it may contain a device designator, a pathname, and a file extension. The ASCII string ends with the end character (ASCII code 0). After the file is opened, a numeric value called the handle is returned. Any further operations to this file are performed using this 16-bit handle. For a subsequent read or write operation, the handle, instead of the filename, is passed to the appropriate function.

For each open file, DOS saves certain information pertaining to that file. If the FCB functions are used, DOS saves the information in the FCB table within the program's memory block. When the handle functions are used, the information is stored in an area outside of the program's memory block in a table that is maintained by DOS. The number of open files is therefore limited by the amount of available table space. The amount of table space set aside by DOS is specified by the FILES parameter of the CONFIG.SYS file:

```
FILES = X
```

In DOS Version 3.0, this maximum is 255. If you change the maximum number of files in the CONFIG.SYS file, the change will not become effective until the next time DOS is booted.

```
FILES
```

While the FILES parameter (CONFIG.SYS) specifies the maximum number of open files for the entire operating system, DOS limits the number of open files to 20 per program. Since five handles are assigned to standard devices, such as the keyboard, monitor, and line printer, only 15 handles are available for the program. For example, if a program opens three files, DOS assigns three available File handles and reduces the number of additional available handles by three. If this program calls another program, the three files opened by the original program remain open. If the new program opens additional files, the remaining number of handles available is reduced even further.

Variable access length

Another difference from FCB functions lies in read and write functions. While FCB functions work with records of constant lengths, handle functions specify how many bytes should be read or written. This makes dynamic access to consecutive data records possible.

In addition to the standard read and write functions, there is also a file positioning function. This lets you specify an exact location within the file for the next data access. Knowing both a record number and the length of each data record allows you to specify the position to access a particular data record:

```
position = record_number * record_length
```

This function isn't used during sequential file access because DOS sets the file pointer during the opening or creation of a file to the first byte within the file. Each subsequent read or write operation moves the file pointer, by the number of bytes read, towards the end of the file so the next file access starts where the previous one ended.

The following table summarizes the handle functions. For a more detailed description of these functions, see Appendix D, which documents the DOS API functions.

You'll find additional information on the companion CD-ROM

Appendix D on the companion CD-ROM will give you a more detailed description of these handles. Appendix D also documents the DOS API functions.

Function	Operation	Function	Operation
3CH	Create file	57H/01H	Read/Write modifications & date/time of file
3DH	Open file	5AH	Create temporary file
3EH	Close file	5BH	Create new file
42H	Move file pointer/determine file size	5CH/00H	Protect file range against access (Version 3.0 and up)
43H	Read/Write file attribute	5CH/01H	Release protected file range (Version 3.0 and up)
56H	Rename file	6CH	Extended OPEN function (Version 4.0 and up)
57H/00H	Read/Write modifications & date/time of file		

Here are a few general rules to follow when using these functions:

1. Functions that expect a filename or the address of a filename as an argument (e.g., Create File and Open File) expect the segment address of the name in the DS register and the offset address in the DX register. If the function successfully returns a handle, it's returned in the AX register.

2. Functions that expect a handle as an argument expect to find it in the DX register. After the call, the carry flag indicates whether an error occurred during execution. If an error occurs, the carry flag is set and the error code is returned in the AX register.

3. Function 59H of DOS interrupt 21H returns very detailed information about errors that occur during disk operations. This function is available only in DOS Versions 3.0 and higher.

FCB Functions

As we discussed, DOS uses an FCB data structure for managing a file. The programmer can use this data structure to obtain information about a file or change information about a file. So, we'll examine the structure of an FCB before discussing the individual FCB functions. The FCB is a 37-byte data structure that can be subdivided into different data fields. The following figure illustrates these fields:

FCB 37-byte data structure		
Address	Contents	Type
+00H	Device name	1 byte
+01H	Filename	8 bytes
+09H	File mode	3 bytes
+0CH	Current block number	1 word
+0EH	Data record size	1 word
+10H	File size	2 words
+14H	Modification date	1 word
+16H	Modification time	1 word
+18H	Reserved	1 word
+20H	Current data record number	1 byte
+21H	Data record number for random access	2 words

Notice the name of the file is found beginning at offsets 01H through 0BH of the FCB. The byte at offset 0 is the device indicator, 0 is the current drive, 1 drive A, 2 drive B, etc.

The filename that begins at offset 1 is an ASCII string. It may not contain a pathname since it's limited to 8 characters. For this reason, the FCB functions can access only files in the current directory. Filenames shorter than eight characters are padded with spaces (ASCII code 32). The file extension, if any, occupies the next three bytes of the FCB. At offset 0CH of the FCB is the current number of the block for sequential file access. The two bytes at offset 0EH are the record size. The four bytes at offset 10H are the length of the file.

The date and time of the last modifications to the file are stored beginning at offset 14H of the FCB in encoded form.

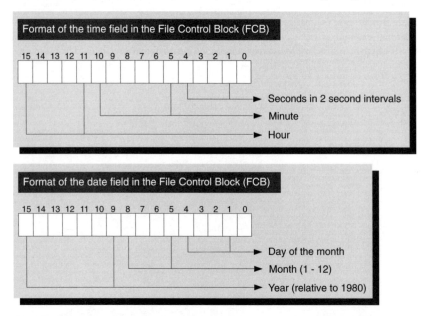

An eight-byte data area follows and is reserved for DOS (no user modifications allowed). The use of this area varies from one version of DOS to another.

Following this reserved data area is the current record number which is used with the current block number to simulate CP/M operations.

Random files

The last data field of the FCB is used for a type of access in which the data within the file may be retrieved or written in a non-sequential order. This field is four bytes long. If a record is equal to or larger than 64 bytes, only the first three bytes are used for indicating the current record number. All four bytes of this field are used for records smaller than 64 bytes.

Extended FCB

Besides a standard FCB, DOS also supports the extended FCB. Unlike normal FCBs, extended FCBs access files with special attributes, such as hidden files or system files. They also permit access to volume names and subdirectories (this doesn't mean that you can access files in other directories besides the current directory).

An extended FCB is similar to a standard FCB, but it's seven bytes larger. These seven bytes are located at the beginning of the data structure. So, all subsequent fields are displaced by seven bytes.

Extended FCB data structure		
Address	Contents	Type
+00H	FF	1 byte
+01H	Reserved(0)	5 bytes
+06H	File attribute	1 byte
+07H	Device name	1 byte
+08H	Filename	8 bytes
+10H	File extension	3 bytes
+13H	Current block number	1 word
+15H	File record size	1 word
+17H	File size	2 words
+1BH	Modification date	1 word
+1DH	Modification time	1 word
+1FH	Reserved	8 bytes
+27H	Current data record number	1 byte
+28H	Data record number	2 words

The first byte of an extended FCB always contains the value 255 and identifies this as an extended FCB. Since this address contains the device number in a normal FCB and therefore cannot contain the value 255, DOS can tell the difference between a normal and an extended FCB. The next five bytes are reserved exclusively for use by DOS. They shouldn't be changed. The seventh byte is a file attribute byte. Refer to the "Floppy Diskette And Hard Drive Structure" section of Chapter 14 for the details of the file attribute byte.

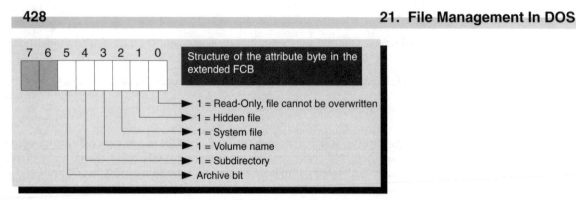

Now that you're familiar with the FCB structures, the next section focuses on using FCBs for accessing files.

FCB and file access

Before accessing a file, an FCB must be built in the program's memory area. The area can be reserved within the data segment of the program or by allocating additional memory using another DOS function (see Appendix D).

Although it's possible to write the data directly into the FCB, it is better to use one of the appropriate DOS functions to do this. For example, to set the filename in the FCB you can use DOS function 29H. The function number is passed in the AH register. The address of the FCB is passed in the ES:DI register pair. The address of the filename is passed in the DS:SI register pair. The filename is an ASCII string terminated by the end character (ASCII code 0). The AL register contains flags for converting the filename and are discussed in more detail in Appendix C.

Open FCB

After the FCB is properly formatted, the file can be opened or created using a DOS function. When this happens, DOS stores information about that file, such as the file size, date and time of file creation, etc., in the FCB. At this point the FCB is considered opened.

By default, the record length is set to 128 bytes when the FCB is opened. To override this record length, store the desired record length at offset 0EH of the FCB after it's opened. Otherwise, the default length will be used.

DTA

For record lengths greater than 128 bytes, the record buffer, also known as the DTA (Disk Transfer Area), must be moved to accommodate the longer record size. Usually DOS builds the DTA in the PSP (Program Segment Prefix). Accessing the file using the default DTA for a record length greater than 128 bytes would overwrite some of the other fields in the PSP.

The most convenient way to select a new DTA is to reserve the space in the program's data segment. To change the address of the DTA, use DOS function 1AH. The address of the new DTA is passed in the DS:DX register pair. Since DOS assumes that you've set aside an area large enough to accommodate your largest record length, you don't have to specify the new length.

File access

For sequential file access, processing begins at the first record in the file. DOS maintains a record pointer in the FCB to keep track of the current record within the file. Each time the file is accessed, DOS advances the pointer so the second, third, fourth, etc. record is processed sequentially.

For random file access, the records can be processed in any order. The position of each record relative to the beginning of the file determines its record number. This record number is then passed to DOS to access a specific record. The last field of the FCB is used to specify the record number to DOS.

It's also possible to change from sequential access mode to random access mode and vice versa, since processing depends on a specific DOS function to access the file. There are actually two sets of independent functions, one for sequential access and one for random functions.

The following table lists all the FCB functions of DOS interrupt 21H. A more detailed description of the functions is found in Appendix D which you'll find on the companion CD-ROM.

FCB functions of DOS interrupt 21H			
Function	Task	Function	Task
0FH	Open file	21H	Random Read (of record)
10H	Close file	22H	Random Write (of record)
13H	Delete file	23H	Determine file size
14H	Sequential read	24H	Set record number for random access
15H	Sequential write	27H	Random read (one or more records)
16H	Create file	28H	Random write (one or more records)
17H	Rename file	29H	Enter filename into FCB
1AH	Set DTA address		

The following are some basic rules about these functions:

Using the FCB functions, you can access several files, each with their own unique FCB. To tell DOS which file should be accessed, pass the address of the file's FCB in the DS:DX register pair.

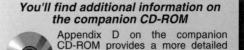

You'll find additional information on the companion CD-ROM

Appendix D on the companion CD-ROM provides a more detailed description of these functions.

Most of the functions return an error code in the AL register or the value zero if the function was successfully completed. For functions that open, close, create, or delete a file, a code of 255 is returned if an error occurs. The other functions return specific error codes. More detailed information about these errors can be determined by calling DOS function 59H but this is available only in DOS Versions 3.0 or later.

Handles-vs. FCBs

Now we'll briefly discuss the advantages and disadvantages of the individual functions. If you want to convert a program from the CP/M or UNIX operating systems into DOS, the choice will be easy. However, if you want to develop a new program under DOS, the following explanations should help you determine which set of functions to use.

Handles

There are two main advantages to using handle functions. The first is the ability to access a file in any subdirectory of the disk. The second is the handle functions aren't limited to the number of FCBs that can be stored in a program's memory space.

There are also several additional considerations. You can access the name of a disk drive only by using an FCB. When the FCB is opened, you can easily determine its file size and the date of the last modification. The handle functions automatically provide an area large enough to accommodate the records in the file.

As you can see, there are arguments for and against using either the FCB functions or the handle functions. For future versions of DOS, the handle functions will become more important and the importance of the FCB functions will diminish. This is reason enough to use the handle functions for your new program development.

Chapter 22

Accessing DOS Directories

Two groups of DOS functions are used to work with directories. The first group is used to manipulate the subdirectories and the second group is used to search for files on the mass storage devices.

DOS Version 2.0 introduced subdirectories. A mass storage device could be logically divided into smaller subdirectories, which could also be divided. This organization creates a directory tree.

Example of a directory tree

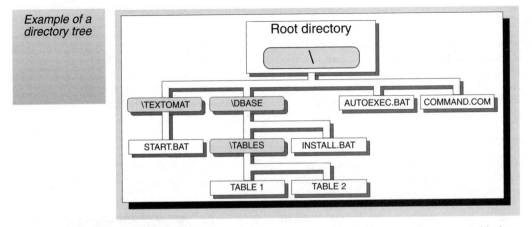

In this directory tree, the names and numbers of subdirectories are dynamic. There must be a way to add, change, and delete entries on the tree. Other functions must be available to set the current directory so a complete pathname isn't required for all file accesses. At the user level, the MD, RD and CD commands can be used to make a directory, remove a directory and change a current directory. These commands are performed internally with functions 39H, 3A and 3BH of DOS interrupt 21H.

All three functions use identical calling conventions. The function number is passed in the AH register. The address of the path is passed in the DS:DX register pair. The path is a string and may be a complete path designation, including a preceding drive letter followed by a colon (a device name) and terminated by ASCII code 0. If the device name is omitted, the current device is the default.

Following execution, the carry flag indicates the return code. If the carry flag is reset (0), then execution was successful. If the carry flag is set, then an error occurred and the error code is passed back in the AX register.

Function 39H creates or makes a new directory (Make Directory function). The name for the new directory is specified as the last element in the path. An error will be returned by the functions if one or more of the directories specified in the path doesn't exist, if the new directory name already exists, or if the maximum number of files in the root directory is exceeded.

Function 3AH deletes or removes a directory (Remove Directory function). An error will be returned by the function if the target directory isn't empty or the specified directory doesn't exist in the current path.

Function 3BH changes the current directory (Change Directory function). An error is returned if the directories named in the path don't actually exist.

Function 0EH sets the default disk drive. Besides the function number in the AH register, only the device code of the new current device must be passed in the DL register. Code 0 represents the device A, code 1 represents device B, code 2 represents device C, etc.

Directory specification

Before specifying the current directory using function 3BH, sometimes you must find the current directory. DOS provides function 47H for this purpose. Since it can return the path of the current directory for any device, the device number must be passed to the function. If this is the current device, the value 0 must be passed in the DL register. For all other devices, the value 1 must be passed for drive A, 2 for B, 3 for C, etc.

Besides the device code, the function must also have the address of a 64-byte buffer within the user program. The DS register contains the segment and the SI register contains the offset address of this buffer. After the function call, this buffer contains the path designation of the current directory, terminated with the end character (ASCII code 0). The path designation cannot be preceded by the device name or the \ character. If the current directory is the root directory, the buffer contains only the end character. If a device code unknown to DOS was passed during the function call, the carry flag is set and the AX register contains the error code 0FH.

Let's consider the functions for searching for one or more files in the current directory on the current device. Again you can see the connection between handle and FCB functions. Two function groups are used to search for files. The group of FCB functions limit the search to files in the current directory of a certain device, while handle functions allow you to search for files in any directories of any devices. The term "handle" functions isn't really appropriate for these functions because they aren't addressed with a handle. This designation originated with the introduction of subdirectories (and therefore the handle functions) in DOS Version 2.0. Version 1.0 offered only the FCB functions.

How the search function works

Although the handle and FCB functions have different capabilities, they are very similar. Both of them access functions called FindFirst and FindNext. FindFirst is called only once for each file because it initiates the search. This function expects the caller to pass the file's name and attribute (more on this later).

The search name can be conveyed as a filename with a path (e.g., C:\DOS\LETTER.DOC) or without a path (e.g., LETTER.TXT). Wildcard characters (* and ?) can be used to search for patterns instead of specific files. Similar to the DIR command used in DOS, FindFirst and FindNext can display all the files in a directory using these wildcards.

Regardless of the search name, FindFirst returns only the first filename found (if it exists in the indicated directory). This filename corresponds to the name or name pattern. All additional files can be found through subsequent calls of FindNext; with each call of this function, the next filename that fits the search pattern is returned.

Function	Assignment
11H	FindFirst (FCB)
12H	FindNext (FCB)
4EH	FindFirst (Handle)
4FH	FindNext (Handle)

The file attribute's role

The functions listed interact with the standard file attributes as assigned under DOS (see the table below for more information). The bits in the attribute byte specify different attributes. For example, when bit 4 is set, the directory entry is viewed as a subdirectory rather than a file. When bit 2 is set, this indicates that the file is hidden, and won't be visible when you call the DIR command from DOS.

After finding an entry, the attribute byte can be read for set attributes. Both FindFirst functions expect to receive a search attribute, which identifies the files to be found. These attributes don't include the read-only attribute or the archive bit. If the search attribute contains 0, all normal files are displayed whether their read-only and archive bits are set.

Directory entries that describe hidden files, system files, volume names, and subdirectories are treated differently. These are excluded from the file search if the corresponding bit in the search attribute isn't set. For example, if you set bit 4 in the search attribute, all subdirectories are returned as the result.

Attribute byte in file search		
Bit	Attribute	Meaning if set
00H	Read-only	File is read-only
01H	Hidden	File is hidden (invisible to DIR)
02H	System	File is part of operating system
03H	Volume label	Entry is volume label and not a file
04H	Subdirectory	Entry is a subdirectory and not a file
05H	Archive	Entry is a subdirectory and not a file
06H	Reserved	Reserved for later implementation
07H	Reserved	Reserved for later implementation

This method cannot exclude all normal files from the search in order to search exclusively for hidden files or subdirectories. However, you can evaluate the file attributes of the files that were found and only use the files that have the desired attribute flag set.

Searching For Files Using FCB Functions

This method of searching for files uses functions 11H and 12H. By using these functions, you can search for files with a fixed name or an extension. Function 11H finds the first file in the current directory. Function 12H finds any additional files. The FCBs are important because they mediate between the calling program and the two functions. Let's see how we can search for files in a directory:

First, the program must reserve space for two FCBs. This is done either by reserving memory in the data area of the program or by requesting memory from DOS using function 48H. The programmer can use either normal or extended FCBs, which are capable of searching for files with special attributes (system or hidden), volume names and subdirectories. The filename for which the search will be made is specified in one of the FCBs. DOS places the name of the file(s) that it finds in the other FCB. The two FCBs are identified by their names Search FCB and Found FCB.

The address of the Found FCB must be passed to DOS using function 1AH. When this function call occurs, the Found FCB becomes the new data transmission area (DTA). This area is important for these two functions as well as all other functions that transfer data between computer and disks. Therefore, function 2FH should determine the address of the current DTA before activating the new DTA. When the file search ends, the DTA can be restored to its original status using function 1AH.

After the DTA is set to the Found FCB, place the name of the file you're looking for into the Search FCB. For a more general search, you can use the wildcards * and ?. You can transfer the filename directly or transfer it using function 29H. If you want to search through all files, use the filename *.*. If an extended FCB is used, you may insert an additional value into the attribute field of the Search FCB to limit the search to files with only certain attributes (see the preceding pages of this chapter for more information on the various attributes).

This concludes the preliminary work. The file search can begin with the current directory. For this purpose, function 11H is called with the function number in the AH register, the segment address of the Search FCB in DS, and the offset address in the DX register. If the system finds a file with the indicated name, the AL register contains the value 0 after the function call. If the filename wasn't found, the AL register contains a value of 255.

The found filename and its attributes (if extended FCBs are used) can be read from the Found FCB. For additional searches, function 12H (not function 11H) is called. Function 12H's register contents during call and return are similar to function 11H. If it returns the value 255 in the AL register during one of the calls, the search has ended.

Demonstration programs

The FF.ASM program demonstrates FCB file searching by using FCB functions 11H and 12H. The assembled program is a COM program instead of an EXE program. FF represents FileFind because the program searches for a certain file, or a group of files, in all the directories of a drive. It shows that the FCB functions can be used for a file search in various directories by specifying the search directory as the current directory before the search begins.

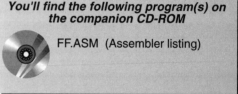

You'll find the following program(s) on the companion CD-ROM

FF.ASM (Assembler listing)

Call FF by using the following syntax:

```
ff [dr:]filename [+|-|=date]
```

Let's look at these parameters:

Parameter	Purpose
[dr:]	This represents the optional drive specifier. FF defaults to the current drive.
filename	This represents the filename or pattern you want to find. This parameter can include wildcards. If you type FF.ASM as the filename, FF will search for only the file FF.ASM. If you type *.ASM, FF searches for all files with ASM extensions, in all directories of the current drive.
+date	Lists files created or last modified after the specified date.
[-date]	Lists files created or last modified before the specified date.
[=date]	Lists files created or last modified on the specified date.

The following command finds all TXT files created after January 10, 1995:

```
ff *.txt +1-10-1995
```

Searching For Files Using Handle Functions

Working with handle functions is easier than working with the FCB functions. Two of these functions are used to search for the first file (the 4EH function) and subsequent files (the 4FH function). Both functions return the information to the DTA. Therefore, the DTA should be moved into an area accessible to the current program before calling either of these functions. This area must have at least 43 bytes available. As mentioned with the FCB functions, the DTA should be restored to its original address after the search ends.

During the call of the 4EH function, the function number is passed in the AH register, the attribute in the CX register, and the address of the file to be found in the DS:DX register pair. The filename is a series of ASCII characters followed by an end character (ASCII code 0). In addition to a device name, you may also add a complete path designation and the wildcard characters * and ?.

If a path isn't specified, DOS assumes that the search should be performed in the current directory of the indicated device. If a device isn't specified, the search continues on the current device. After the function call, the carry flag indicates whether a file was found. If the file couldn't be found, the carry flag is set and the AX register contains an error code. An error code of 2H is returned if the indicated path does not exist. If a file couldn't be found, an error code of 12H is returned. If the carry flag is reset, the DTA contains the information about the file that was found. The following table shows its structure:

DTA structure		
Address	Contents	Type
00H	Reserved for DOS	21 bytes
15H	Attribute of file found	1 byte
16H	Time of last modification	1 word
18H	Date of last modification	1 word
1AH	Low word of file size	1 word
1EH	High word of file size	12 bytes

Function 4FH performs any subsequent searches. The function number is passed in the AH register; additional parameters aren't necessary. The carry flag indicates whether the current directory contains any additional files that may apply to the search.

Demonstration programs

Two Pascal programs, two C language programs, and one BASIC program are listed. These dual implementations demonstrate how you can indirectly call DOS functions 4EH and 4FH. Many languages, such as Turbo Pascal, Microsoft C, and Turbo C, include FindFirst and FindNext functions in their libraries. These functions eliminate the need for direct calls to functions 4EH and 4 FH and also provide some other help for the programmer. (We'll discuss this in more detail later.)

QuickBasic contains only a rudimentary FILES command but not a library. The FILES command can display only the current directory's contents, without making this information available to the program. Direct calls to functions 4EH and 4FH are unavoidable in BASIC.

Program logic

All five programs are constructed according to the same basic framework. First the main program reads the command to determine which filenames should be displayed. If the program name was entered without parameters, the program defaults to the "*.*" wildcards. If the user entered a parameter after the program name, the program uses that as the pattern for file display. Entering more than one parameter ends the program and displays an error message.

The program passes the name of the file to be displayed and the attribute of the files to be displayed to the DIR function (or procedure). All the attributes are set to include volume name, subdirectories, system files, and hidden files. Although the attribute byte cannot be changed by the user, this byte setting can be altered from within the program code.

In the three programs, which directly communicate with functions 4EH and 4FH, the SetDTA procedure/function sets the DTA to a local data structure. SetDTA calls DOS function 1AH to move the DTA to the indicated address.

The data structure intended for the DTA exists in all three programs as type DirStruct. This structure represents a record in which the various fields are found by functions 4EH and 4FH. After DTA's initialization, the DIR procedure/function calls the ScreenDesign procedure/function. This routine creates a window on the screen, in which the directory will be displayed.

FindFirst begins the search, after which a loop continuously calls FindNext until no other files are found. The PrintData procedure/function displays these files on the screen. This procedure/function expects DirStruct as an argument, specifying where DOS stored information about the file. This information is decoded and displayed on the screen. The program and program listing for the DIRB.BAS BASIC version of this directory lister program is on the companion CD-ROM.

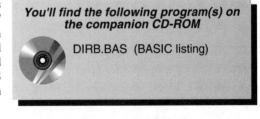

You'll find the following program(s) on the companion CD-ROM

DIRB.BAS (BASIC listing)

Direct calls to functions 4EH and 4FH in Pascal and C

The DIRP1.PAS and DIRC1.C Pascal and C programs perform direct calls to functions 4EH and 4FH. Predefined FINDFIRST and FINDNEXT procedures/functions aren't used.

Turbo Pascal includes a statement that easily defines any part of the screen as a window. The C language must use functions of BIOS

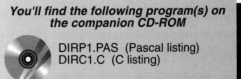

You'll find the following program(s) on the companion CD-ROM

DIRP1.PAS (Pascal listing)
DIRC1.C (C listing)

interrupt 10H to scroll the directory window up, one line at a time. The C program contains a function called PRINT. This function is similar to PRINTF() except that PRINT accepts the string's position on the screen and the color of the output. This display information can then be written directly to video RAM.

Using the predefined functions/procedures in Pascal and C

The DIRP2.PAS and DIRC2.C programs use the predefined FindFirst and FindNext functions from Turbo Pascal or the various C compilers supported by our example programs. This simplifies directory display because DTA positioning is bypassed.

Both programs use the 4EH and 4FH DOS functions, as well as a special data structure for storing file information. Turbo Pascal's SearchRec structure is defined in the DOS unit, along with FindFirst and FindNext. The DOS unit also defines various constants, which can be set with flags for controlling file attributes.

Unfortunately, the SearchRec structure combines the time and date fields into a long integer, which requires a little trick to divide the individual data elements. The DIRP2.PAS program demonstrates how this is done. Also, notice that FindFirst and FindNext in the Pascal version are procedures rather than functions. So, the program must check the DosError global variable after the function call to ensure that the file was found. After calling functions 4EH and 4FH, Turbo Pascal stores the contents of the AX register in DosError. If this variable contains 0, the file was found.

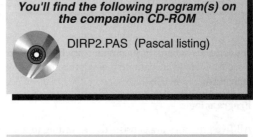

You'll find the following program(s) on the companion CD-ROM

DIRP2.PAS (Pascal listing)

The C program DIRC2.C encounters some problems because of differences between the Microsoft and Borland compiler libraries-especially those relating to DOS API interfaces. API is not yet enforced by ANSI standards, so compiler manufacturers can set their own standards for API. Thus, FindFirst and FindNext retain different names in the two different C compiler families, and operate using different data structures with different field names.

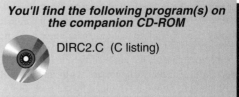

You'll find the following program(s) on the companion CD-ROM

DIRC2.C (C listing)

The DIRC2.C program can be compiled and linked by both compilers.
Macros include the device-dependent commands needed by the respective compilers.

Chapter 23

Date And Time

The AT realtime clock provides the date and time for BIOS routines and files. Four DOS functions, which have been available since the release of Version 1.0 of DOS, can be used to access time and date.

DOS and the AT realtime clock

In DOS Versions 3.2 and lower, these four functions passed information to and from DOS environmental variables. However, in DOS Versions 3.3 and higher, these functions passed the same information to and from the battery operated realtime clock. The time and date information is still available, even if the user switches off the computer. The time and date are passed using the BIOS functions described in Chapter 15.

DOS date and time functions	
Function	Task
2AH	Read date
2BH	Set date
2CH	Read time
2DH	Set time

This is also possible in older versions of DOS. However, the system must contain a built-in clock driver because DOS will communicate only with an onboard device driver named $CLOCK device driver.

Getting and setting the date

Functions 2AH and 2BH control the current date.

Function 2AH (get date):   *Get date*

Placing function number 2AH in the AH register returns the current date information in the processor registers listed in the table to the right.

Interrupt 21H, function 2AH

Function 2BH (set date):   *Set date*

Function 2BH places date information in the same registers used by function 2AH. This is useful for changing a creation or modification date in a file.

Output registers: Function 2AH	
Register	Contents
AL	Day of week*
CX	Year
DH	Month
DL	Day
*0=Sunday, 1=Monday, etc.	

The table below right shows that function 2BH requires the actual date (but not the day of the week). This is the only information DOS needs.

Remember that when working with this function, the earliest date allowed by the system is January 1, 1980 (01-01-1980). If an error occurs, check the AL register. If this register contains a value of 0, the data supplied in the other registers is valid. If the AL register contains a value of 255, the data couldn't be read.

Getting and setting the time

Functions 2CH and 2DH are similar to functions 2AH and 2BH, except that 2CH and 2DH handle time access.

Input registers: Function 2BH	
Register	Contents
AH	2BH
CX	Year
DH	Month
DL	Day

Function 2CH (get time):   *Get time*

Function 2CH reads the current time in the form shown in the following table. Place function number 2CH of DOS interrupt 21H in the AH register to read the following registers:

Output registers: Function 2CH	
Register	**Contents**
CH	Hour
CL	Minute
DH	Second
DL	Hundredths of a second

Function 2DH: **Set time**

Function 2DH sets the time. The AL register indicates whether the time is valid (e.g., a 36:48 setting generates a value of 255, which is an error).

Input registers: Function 2DH	
Registers	**Contents**
AH	2DH
CH	Hour
CL	Minute
DH	Second
DL	Hundredths of a second

BIOS or DOS?

You can use either BIOS or DOS to access time and date. Both methods have their advantages, and both methods are available on any given PC system. Which functions you access depends on your preferences.

Chapter 24

RAM Management

One of the basic tasks an operating system must perform is managing the RAM (Random Access Memory). This is where all the various system components (device drivers, TSR programs, applications, etc.) come together. Since each of these components needs some of the memory, DOS must ensure they work together. This prevents the components from overwriting each other and a single component from manipulating all the memory.

In this chapter we'll discuss the DOS memory management functions and how they work together to keep your RAM organized.

DOS RAM Management

The RAM management capabilities of DOS are based on the principle of using a DOS function to allocate a memory block of a pre-determined size. This memory block remains allocated to the program that requested it until it's freed by another DOS function. Then the block can be used by other programs.

The table on the right shows the four different functions for RAM management in DOS. The functions for allocating and freeing RAM are used by application programs, but they are also used by DOS itself in the form of EXEC loaders. When a program must be loaded and started, the EXEC loader reserves the RAM block, in which it will later load the program.

DOS functions for RAM management	
Function	Purpose
48	Allocate memory
49H	Free memory
4AH	Change size of a memory block
58H	Read/set memory management model

The amount of memory allocated depends on the type of program to be loaded. COM programs will reserve the entire RAM. The amount of memory required for an EXEC program is taken from the header of the EXE file. The EXEC loader can load the file only if a large enough block of RAM is available. If enough RAM cannot be found, the EXEC loader stops and displays the following error message:

```
Insufficient memory
```

Besides the EXEC loader, the application program itself can request memory from DOS. During execution, many programs will need more memory than they were given when they were initially loaded. This happens because they aren't able to determine the values of all variables or the sizes of all buffers at the time they are loaded. This information is usually determined by user input while the program is running.

Memory allocation with function 48H

If you're programming in a high level language, you don't have to worry about dynamic memory allocation. This is handled by the heap. However, assembler programmers must go to DOS when they need to allocate memory. This is done with function 48H. This function call requires the function number in the AH register and the size of the desired memory block in the BX register.

The size of the block is given in the number of paragraphs instead of the number of bytes. Since a paragraph consists of 16 bytes, allocated memory blocks will always be in multiples of 16 bytes. The smallest possible memory block that can be allocated is 16 bytes (BX = 1) and the largest is 1 Meg (BX = FFFFh).

However, requesting an entire megabyte from DOS isn't realistic because the processor doesn't even have that much RAM available in real mode. Actually, you cannot obtain 640K, 512K or even 400K from DOS because a large portion of RAM is used by the DOS programs and the DOS device drivers. TSR programs, which remain resident in memory (i.e, they don't free the memory allocated to them when they are started) also occupy a lot of memory.

Since DOS cannot always fulfill the requests it receives with function 48H, you must check the carry flag after the function call. If this flag is set, then the requested amount of RAM wasn't available. The BX register will then contain a value that corresponds to the actual amount of remaining RAM. This value is also given in paragraphs, so you must multiply it by 16 to obtain the number of bytes.

If the program can be run with this amount of memory, then function 48H is called again with this value in the BX register. All of the RAM that's still available will then be allocated to the program.

After this function call, the program will discover the carry flag isn't set. This means the AX register will contain the segment address of the memory block that DOS has reserved. This block is now completely under the control of the application for which it was allocated.

The application must always remember the size of the block. Depending on the amount of memory allocated, you may or may not be able to use the entire segment at the address returned by function 48H. For example, if you asked for only one paragraph, you'll have a memory block such as AX:0000 through AX:000F. This corresponds to only the first 16 bytes of the segment. If you asked for more paragraphs, the memory block will be correspondingly larger. It will always start at the segment address returned by the function and at offset address 0000H.

What happens if you request 4096 paragraphs? This corresponds to 64K, which would be the entire memory segment from AX:0000 through AX:FFFF. If you ask for more than 4096 paragraphs, the memory block will extend into the next segment.

In all cases, the application that now owns the memory block can address only the portion of the segment that belongs to it. Anything outside of this block may belong to another program or be allocated to another in the future. If two applications try to use the same part of the RAM, the system will usually crash.

Determining the amount of available RAM

Because of the way it works, function 48H can also be used to check the current amount of free RAM. This is the only DOS function that performs this task.

To force DOS to return the amount of free memory, we'll make a request that it can't possibly fulfill. We'll pass the value 0FFFFH in the BX register, thereby requesting a 1 megabyte memory block. Although it's impossible for DOS to allocate a block of this size, the function result in the BX register indicates the number of free paragraphs. From this value, we can easily calculate the number of free bytes remaining.

Releasing memory with function 49H

Once an allocated memory block is no longer needed, it must be released with function 49H. Before a program ends, all the memory allocated with function 48H must be released. Otherwise, the operating system will think that this memory is allocated to an application and other programs won't be able to use it. This can significantly reduce the amount of available memory and you may not be able to load the other programs you want to run. Only rebooting the computer can free this memory.

This function call requires the function number in the AH register and the segment address of the memory block to be freed in the ES register. This corresponds to the value that was returned to the AX register when the block was allocated with function 48H.

If the memory block was successfully released, function 49H returns with a cleared carry flag. DOS again has control of the memory block, which can be allocated to another application. If the function returns with the carry flag set, then the memory block couldn't be released because of an error. Various errors can cause this condition. The error code that describes what occurred is returned to the AX register.

An error code of 9 indicates that an incorrect segment address was given. This means that at the given address, a memory block allocated by this program wasn't found. It's possible the program did own a memory block at this address, but that it has already been freed with a previous call to function 49H. In this instance, you should determine whether you've inadvertently tried to free the same block twice.

Error code 7 indicates that a problem occurred within DOS's internal memory manager. The cause of this problem is usually a program that has tried to operate outside of its reserved memory blocks. If you encounter this error code, you should end your program and recommend a soft reboot to the user.

Changing the size of memory blocks

The third memory management function is function 4AH. This function changes the size of a previously allocated memory block. You can choose to make the block larger or smaller. However, you may not be able to increase the size of the block if there isn't enough memory.

To call function 4AH, pass the function number to the AH register and the segment address, of the memory block to change, to the ES register. The new size of the memory block is passed to the BX register. This value must be given in paragraphs. The contents of the registers after the function call will be the same as with function 48H. If the function fails due to lack of memory, it returns the maximum block size in the BX register. This is only important when increasing the size of a block. You should always be able to make a block smaller.

Where Does Memory Come From?

In DOS Versions up to 5.0, the memory that DOS allocates via function 48H always originates from the Transient Program Area (TPA). This refers to a region of memory that extends from the end of the resident DOS kernel at the beginning of the RAM all the way to the 640K limit. If a system has less than 640K, the TPA ends there. However, these systems are very rare today.

The RAM usually ends at the 640K limit. Beyond this limit is the memory reserved for video RAM, the ROM-BIOS and ROM expansions. The page frame of an EMS card is also stored in this memory region. Systems equipped with 1 Meg or more are usually configured with 640K of RAM below the 640K limit and the rest of the memory starts at the 1 Meg limit.

More memory with Upper Memory Blocks (UMBs)

Memory above the 1 Meg limit and memory between 640K and 1 Meg, cannot be directly addressed by DOS in real mode unless you're using DOS Version 5.0. This DOS version supports using Upper Memory Blocks (UMBs), which can be located anywhere above the 640K limit. The region from 640K to 1 Meg usually isn't completely occupied by the video RAM, the ROM-BIOS or other expansions. So, DOS 5.0 can use and allocate the unused regions as normal blocks of RAM.

Memory in the region between 640K and 1 Meg is extremely valuable to DOS programs, because it can be addressed in real mode. With DOS 5.0, a program cannot tell the difference between memory above and below 640K. As long as the memory doesn't extend beyond the 1 Meg limit, it's considered the same. Add UMB memory to your system with:

➢ The proper software configuration, such as a NEAT chip set, which creates RAM in the UMB region out of extended memory.

➢ A special UMB card that's equipped with its own RAM, which is then added to the UMB region of the system's addressable memory.

➢ Memory management programs that move extended memory to the UBM region, such as EMM386.EXE, 386Max, or QEMM.

The last option is becoming more popular since DOS 5.0 was introduced because this version includes the device driver for EMM386.EXE.

Upper memory blocks (UMBs) in the addressable memory of the PC	

```
FFFF:FFFF                          1 MByte
              BIOS
F000:0000
                              BIOS extensions
E000:0000  Space for
              UMBs          EMS page frame
D000:0000
                            Expansion cards
C000:0000  Video RAM
B000:0000  EGA / VGA
A000:0000




           Conventional RAM








0000:0000
```

The amount of memory available for UMBs depends on how much memory is occupied by video RAM, expansion cards and the ROM-BIOS. Many systems will have up to 260K available, while others may have less than 64K. Unlike RAM below 640K, this memory is often fragmented. So UMBs must make room wherever they can in the "holes" between 640K and 1 Meg.

Before DOS programs can use UMBs, either the command:

DOS=HIGH,UMB *or:* DOS=LOW,UMB

must be executed in the CONFIG.SYS file. After finding one of these commands, DOS looks for an XMS driver. DOS doesn't actually prepare the memory where the UMBs will be located. Instead, a device driver, such as EMM386.EXE (see above), performs this task. This is useful because different UMB cards have different ways of setting up the UMB memory. So, DOS can leave the setup to the driver that relates to the specific hardware. These drivers must adhere to the XMS standard. This standard defines how DOS allocates UMBs. So, DOS has control over all RAM allocation from the time the system is started.

Special DOS commands, such as DEVICEHIGH and LOADHIGH, are used to load device drivers or DOS programs into a UMB, as long as an appropriate one can be found. Since the UMB memory can be very fragmented, this may be difficult to do with larger programs. Enough memory may be available, but it's split into two or three separate regions in between the video RAM and the ROM-BIOS or something else. Because of this, small TSR programs and device drivers can easily be placed in UMB memory.

UMBs in routine memory management

UMB memory isn't used only when allocated by DOS programs or device drivers with DEVICEHIGH and LOADHIGH. UMBs are also included in routine memory management. This means that a call to function 48H can return a UMB. You can recognize a UMB by a segment address greater than A000H, which corresponds to the 640K limit.

Four subfunctions of DOS function 58H enable you to influence the way UMBs are included in routine memory management. The first two subfunctions, 00H and 01H, have been available since DOS Version 2.0. Subfunctions 02H and 03H were introduced with Version 5.0.

DOS function 58H Subfunctions	
Subfunction	Description
00H	Read memory model
01H	Set memory model
02H	Query UMB status
03H	Set UMB status

Subfunction 03H allows you to determine whether function 48H should consider using UMBs when allocating memory. This is useful for programs that must allocate a lot of additional memory after they're called.

Subfunction 03 is called with the function number 5803H in the AX register and either 0 or 1 in the BX register. A value of 1 indicates that UMBs will be included in memory allocation; 0 indicates that all memory will be allocated below the 640K limit.

Before making this function call, you should check the status of the UMB memory so you can restore it to its original condition after your program ends. Subfunction 02 will do this for you. This subfunction call only needs the function number 5802H in the AX register. After this function call, the AL register will contain a value of either 0 or 1. These values have the same meaning they have with subfunction 03H.

Remember these two subfunctions are only supported under DOS Versions 5.0 and higher and the DOS UMB command must be run in the CONFIG.SYS file for them to work properly. After calling either of these subfunctions, you should check the contents of the carry flag. If the carry flag is set, then one of the two conditions already described hasn't been met and UMBs cannot be supported. If you want to use UMBs in your program, try working with small memory blocks. You probably won't find a contiguous memory block of several hundred K in the UMB region. Instead, there will be numerous small blocks. So, you should request five 10K blocks instead of one 50K block, as long as your program algorithm will allow it.

Memory allocation models

Beginning with Version 2.0, DOS has allowed the use of various memory allocation models. The desired model is selected with subfunction 01H of function 58H. A memory allocation model refers to the way in which DOS searches for a free memory block. Three codes represent the three possibilities listed in the table on the right.

Code	Model
00H	Search low to high
01H	Search for the best fit
02H	Search high to low

Codes 00H and 02H are self-explanatory. These codes allow you to tell DOS to start the search for a memory block of the desired size starting either at the beginning or the end of the RAM. If the first free memory block that's found is at least the requested size, it's allocated.

"Search for the best fit" means that DOS will check the entire RAM for a free memory block that's either exactly the size requested or just a little larger. The idea behind this option is the RAM may be fragmented (e.g., if a TSR program frees some memory before it becomes resident). This leaves holes or "fragments" in the RAM. These fragments are usually very small.

If a program needs a small memory block, you can use this option to search for a memory fragment instead of simply using a small part of the first free memory block DOS finds. Subfunction 01 is used to set the memory allocation model. One of three codes previously listed must be passed in the BL register. In addition to the codes, bit 7 of the BL register is also important in DOS Versions 5.0 and up. This bit can be set or cleared regardless of the code that's used. The status of this bit determines whether the search for the next memory block should begin with the UMBs or in the TPA. To begin with the UMBs, this bit must be set to 1. This is only useful when you've already included UMBs with the proper call to subfunction 03H.

You can query the memory allocation model with subfunction 00H. The result of this function is returned to the AL register. With DOS 5.0 and up, remember to check the value of bit 7.

Viewing Memory Allocation

In this section, we'll discuss a program that enables you to display a graphic representation of RAM allocation on screen. The Pascal and C versions of this program are called MEMDEMOP.PAS and MEMDEMOC.C. Both perform the same task and are almost identical internally.

Both programs allow you to allocate, free and change the size of memory blocks using DOS functions 48H, 49H and 4AH. The location and size of the memory blocks are displayed on screen. Since the screen is too small for the entire TPA and all UMBs, the program is limited to monitoring two specific regions: a 160K region of the TPA and a 40K region from the UMBs.

The program limits itself to these regions by first allocating them as two consecutive blocks at the start of the program. Then the rest of the memory is allocated in 1K blocks so no free 1K blocks remain. We'll explain why 1K is used as the block size shortly.

In the next step, the two large memory blocks are freed again. This means these two regions now contain the only memory that isn't allocated. So, all memory will now be allocated from these regions, as long as 1K or more is requested. The program ensures that all requests for memory are in multiples of 1K.

The F1 and F3 function keys can be used to allocate and free memory (see the following illustration). When you press one of these keys, the program will then ask you with which block you want to work. Blocks are labeled within the program as A through Z (with no distinction between upper and lowercase). So, you can choose from a total of 26 blocks.

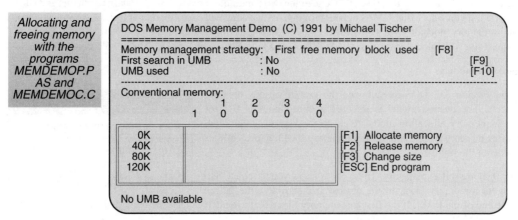

Allocating and freeing memory with the programs MEMDEMOP.P AS and MEMDEMOC.C

```
DOS Memory Management Demo  (C) 1991 by Michael Tischer
===============================================
Memory management strategy:  First  free memory  block  used     [F8]
First search in UMB          : No                                         [F9]
UMB used                     : No                                         [F10]
-----------------------------------------------------------------
Conventional memory:
                          1      2      3      4
                  1       0      0      0      0
   ┌─────────────┬────────────────────┬─────────────────────────┐
   │    0K       │                    │  [F1] Allocate memory    │
   │   40K       │                    │  [F2] Release memory     │
   │   80K       │                    │  [F3] Change size        │
   │  120K       │                    │  [ESC] End program       │
   └─────────────┴────────────────────┴─────────────────────────┘
   No UMB available
```

Enter the desired letter and press Enter. Remember the program will accept only those letters that haven't already been used when allocating a memory block. Only the letter of a memory block currently in use will be accepted if you want to free a memory block or change its size.

When you allocate a memory block or change the size of an existing memory block, you'll also be asked to enter the desired size in K. Enter a number and then press Enter.

After one of these operations, the program will redraw the screen to reflect the changes that you've made. The memory occupied by an allocated block is identified with the letter that was assigned to the block. Memory that hasn't been allocated appears empty. Each character represents 1K from the TPA or UMB region. This explains the values used for the scale.

The UMB window will appear on screen only if a 40K UMB was allocated at the start of the program. If this window isn't present, either UMBs aren't supported on the system or a 40K block wasn't available.

Memory allocation is interesting to watch when you experiment with the F1, F2 and F3 function keys. These keys control the way in which memory will be allocated and whether UMBs will be included. They act as toggle switches to switch the various modes on and off.

After switching the modes around, you can see how the next allocated memory block is placed either at the beginning or the end of the available memory in the TPA or UMB region.

To end the program, press the `Esc` key. This also frees all memory allocated by the program.

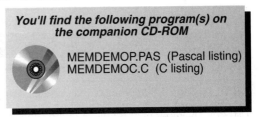
Behind The Scenes Of Memory Management

The acronym "MCB" in the program listings for the MEMDEMOP.PAS and MEMDEMOC.C programs is an abbreviation for Memory Control Block (MCBs). The MCBs are important in how DOS manages memory.

Managing allocated memory with Memory Control Blocks (MCBs)

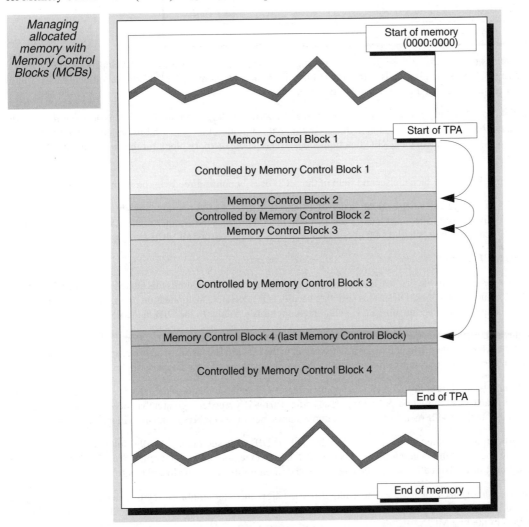

To manage memory blocks allocated with DOS function 48H, a Memory Control Block (MCB) is created for each allocated block. An MCB consists of 16 bytes. It always starts at an offset address that is divisible by 16 and it precedes the memory block it describes. The DOS memory management functions always work with the segment address of the allocated block, so the segment address of the corresponding MCB can be easily obtained by subtracting 1 from the segment address of the allocated block.

Structure of a Memory Control Blocks (MCB) in RAM		
Addr.	**Contents**	**Type**
+00h	ID ("Z" = last MCB, "M" = more to follow)	1 BYTE
+01h	Segment address of the corresponding PSP	1 WORD
+03h	Number of paragraphs in the allocated block	1 WORD
+05h	Unused	11 BYTE
+10h	The allocated memory block	x PARAG.
Length: 16 + the size of the allocated block		

The MCB contains three fields, as seen in the previous figure. Mark Zbikowski, one of the developers of MS-DOS, has immortalized himself by using his initials in the first field. If this field contains the letter "M", then additional MCBs follow this one. If it contains "Z", then this is the last MCB in memory.

The second field contains the segment address of the PSP for the corresponding program. This field is only significant if the allocated memory block is for the environment of a program. In this instance, this field establishes a link by pointing to the PSP. Before a program is loaded, the EXEC function allocates a separate memory block for the environment block of the program.

If the memory block is a PSP, then the second field of the MCB usually points directly to the memory block itself.

The third field is more important when evaluating the MCB. This field gives the size of the memory block in paragraphs. Since the next MCB follows directly after this memory block, this number represents the distance to the next MCB minus 1. In this way, each MCB indirectly points to the next one, which generates a linked list of all MCBs.

Accessing the MCB chain

You must know the address of the first MCB to access the entire MCB chain. DOS stores this address in an internal structure called the DOS Information Block (DIB). This structure usually isn't accessible to application programs. However, you can access it with the undocumented function 52H. This function returns a pointer to the DIB in the ES:BX register pair.

Curiously, this address points to the second field of the DIB instead of the first. However, the first field contains the address of the first MCB, which is what we're looking for. The pointer to the first MCB consists of an offset and segment address that occupies four bytes. So, we'll be able to find the desired information at the address ES:[BX-4].

This formula must be used carefully. You cannot simply subtract 4 from the contents of the BX register and end up with the desired address in all cases. This works only if the offset address in the BX register is greater than or equal to 4. If it's smaller, a negative number is the result. As the following example shows, negative numbers aren't used in memory addressing:

If the BX register returns a value of 0 as the offset address of the DIB, then subtracting 4 will result in the value 0FFFCH. In an arithmetic operation, this is correctly interpreted as -4, but as a memory address it points to 0FFFCH, which is at the end of the segment instead of before the given address. The desired information isn't located there.

The solution is to simply decrement the segment address by 1. This reduces the combined segment and offset address by 16. If you now add 12 to the offset address, this results in the original address minus 4, which takes us to the first field of the DIB and the address of the first MCB.

Demonstration program

➢   The number of the MCB

➢   The MCB's address in memory

> Address of the block managed by the MCB

> Contents of the ID field ("M" or "Z")

> Address of the corresponding PSP (regardless of whether it exists)

> Size of the corresponding memory block in paragraphs and bytes

Until DOS Version 3.0, the environment block contained only the previous information. Starting with Version 3.0, the name of the program, to which the environment block belongs, was added after the last environment string. The complete path is given with the program name.

The null byte after the last environment string and the start of the name string are separated by a word. Only if this word contains the value 0001H will the following program name and path be valid. The program name string also ends with a null byte.

An example of program output

To help interpreting the output of this program, we ran the C version on a computer and received the following results (your printout may appear slighty different). Each MCB is explained after the output.

```
MCBC (c) 1988, 91 by Michael Tischer

MCB number      = 1
MCB address     = 09C8:0000
Memory address= 09C9:0000
ID              = M
PSP address     = 0008:0000
Size            = 1554 paragraphs ( 24864 Byte )
Contents        = Unidentifiable as program or data


DUMP | 0123456789ABCDEF       00 01 02 03 04 05 06 07 08 09 0A 0B 0C 0D 0E 0F
-----+----------------------------------------------------------------------
0000 | n p  é! , $CLOCK        6E 01 70 00 08 80 21 00 2C 00 24 43 4C 4F 43 4B
0010 |      é                  20 06 03 80 02 1F 1D 1F 1E 1F 1E 1F 1F 1E 1F 1E
0020 |  .æ   .ö   -PSQR        1F 2E 89 1E 11 00 2E 8C 06 13 00 CB 50 53 51 52
0030 | WVU  ún  -> &Å]         57 56 55 1E 06 9C FC 0E 1F C4 3E 11 00 26 8A 5D
0040 |  é+ t!é+ tJ +u _        02 80 FB 04 74 21 80 FB 08 74 4A 0A DB 75 03 E9
---------------------------------------------------- Please press a key   ---
MCB number      = 2
MCB address     = 0FDB:0000
Memory address= 0FDC:0000
ID              = M
PSP address     = 0FDC:0000
Size            = 231 paragraphs ( 3696 Byte )
Contents        = PSP (with program following)
---------------------------------------------------- Please press a key   ---
MCB number      = 3
MCB address     = 10C3:0000
Memory address= 10C4:0000
ID              = M
PSP address     = 0000:0000
Size            = 3 paragraphs ( 48 Byte )
Contents        = Unidentifiable as program or data
```

```
DUMP  | 0123456789ABCDEF        00 01 02 03 04 05 06 07 08 09 0A 0B 0C 0D 0E 0F
------+-----------------------------------------------------------------------
0000  |         -    -·----     00 01 00 00 00 00 00 CB 00 00 00 FF FF FF FF FF
0010  | ---------------C        FF FF FF FF FF FF FF FF FF FF FF FF FF FF FF 43
0020  | :\AUTOEXEC.BAT          3A 5C 41 55 54 4F 45 58 45 43 2E 42 41 54 00 00
0030  | M_                      4D DC 0F 0A 00 00 00 00 00 00 00 00 00 00 00 00
0040  | COMSPEC=C:\COMMA        43 4F 4D 53 50 45 43 3D 43 3A 5C 43 4F 4D 4D 41
------------------------------------------------------- Please press a key  ---
MCB number    = 4
MCB address   = 10C7:0000
Memory address= 10C8:0000
ID            = M
PSP address   = 0FDC:0000
Size          = 10 paragraphs ( 160 Byte )
Contents      = Environment
Program name  = Unknown
Environment string
        COMSPEC=C:\COMMAND.COM
        PATH=C:\;C:\DOS;C:\BATCHES;E:\;D:\MSC\BIN
        INCLUDE=d:\msc\include
        LIB=d:\msc\lib
        TMP=d:\msc\tmp
        PROMPT=[$p]
------------------------------------------------------- Please press a key  ---
MCB number    = 5
MCB address   = 10D2:0000
Memory address= 10D3:0000
ID            = M
PSP address   = 10DD:0000
Size          = 9 paragraphs ( 144 Byte )
Contents      = Environment
Program name  = C:\DOS\KEYB.COM
Environment string
        COMSPEC=C:\COMMAND.COM
        PATH=C:\;C:\DOS;C:\BATCHES;E:\;D:\MSC\BIN
        INCLUDE=d:\msc\include
        LIB=d:\msc\lib
        TMP=d:\msc\tmp
------------------------------------------------------- Please press a key  ---
MCB number    = 6
MCB address   = 10DC:0000
Memory address= 10DD:0000
ID            = M
PSP address   = 10DD:0000
Size          = 341 paragraphs ( 5456 Byte )
Contents      = PSP (with program following)
------------------------------------------------------- Please press a key  ---
MCB number    = 7
MCB address   = 1232:0000
Memory address= 1233:0000
ID            = M
PSP address   = 123D:0000
Size          = 9 paragraphs ( 144 Byte )
```

```
Contents        = Environment
Program name    = C:\DOS\CED.COM
Environment string
          COMSPEC=C:\COMMAND.COM
          PATH=C:\;C:\DOS;C:\BATCHES;E:\;D:\MSC\BIN
          INCLUDE=d:\msc\include
          LIB=d:\msc\lib
          TMP=d:\msc\tmp
----------------------------------------------------- Please press a key   ---
MCB number      = 8
MCB address     = 123C:0000
Memory address= 123D:0000
ID              = M
PSP address     = 123D:0000
Size            = 1030 paragraphs ( 16480 Byte )
Contents        = PSP (with program following)
----------------------------------------------------- Please press a key   ---
MCB number      = 9
MCB address     = 1643:0000
Memory address= 1644:0000
ID              = M
PSP address     = 164E:0000
Size            = 9 paragraphs ( 144 Byte )
Contents        = Environment
Program name    = C:\DOS\CACHE-AT.COM
Environment string
          COMSPEC=C:\COMMAND.COM
          PATH=C:\;C:\DOS;C:\BATCHES;E:\;D:\MSC\BIN
          INCLUDE=d:\msc\include
          LIB=d:\msc\lib
          TMP=d:\msc\tmp
----------------------------------------------------- Please press a key   ---
MCB number      = 10
MCB address     = 164D:0000
Memory address= 164E:0000
ID              = M
PSP address     = 164E:0000
Size            = 1922 paragraphs ( 30752 Byte )
Contents        = PSP (with program following)
----------------------------------------------------- Please press a key   ---
MCB number      = 11
MCB address     = 1DD0:0000
Memory address= 1DD1:0000
ID              = M
PSP address     = 1DDC:0000
Size            = 10 paragraphs ( 160 Byte )
Contents        = Environment
Program name    = C:\DOS\KEYBUF.COM
Environment string
          COMSPEC=C:\COMMAND.COM
          PATH=C:\;C:\DOS;C:\BATCHES;E:\;D:\MSC\BIN
          INCLUDE=d:\msc\include
          LIB=d:\msc\lib
```

```
            TMP=d:\msc\tmp
            PROMPT=[$p]
------------------------------------------------------- Please press a key  ---
MCB number    = 12
MCB address   = 1DDB:0000
Memory address= 1DDC:0000
ID            = M
PSP address   = 1DDC:0000
Size          = 27 paragraphs ( 432 Byte )
Contents      = Unidentifiable as program or data

DUMP | 0123456789ABCDEF     00 01 02 03 04 05 06 07 08 09 0A 0B 0C 0D 0E 0F
-----+--------------------------------------------------------------------------
0000 |  M M M M M M M       00 4D 00 4D 00 4D 00 4D 00 4D 00 4D 00 4D 00 4D
0010 |  M M M M M M M       00 4D 00 4D 00 4D 00 4D 00 4D 00 4D 00 4D 00 4D
0020 | + 1 K K K K K        2B 1B 31 02 00 4B 00 4B 00 4B 00 4B 00 4B 00 4B
0030 |  K K K K K K K       00 4B 00 4B 00 4B 00 4B 00 4B 00 4B 00 4B 00 4B
0040 |  K K K K K K K       00 4B 00 4B 00 4B 00 4B 00 4B 00 4B 00 4B 00 4B
------------------------------------------------------- Please press a key  ---
MCB number    = 13
MCB address   = 1DF7:0000
Memory address= 1DF8:0000
ID            = M
PSP address   = 0FDC:0000
Size          = 4 paragraphs ( 64 Byte )
Contents      = PSP (with program following)
------------------------------------------------------- Please press a key  ---
MCB number    = 14
MCB address   = 1DFC:0000
Memory address= 1DFD:0000
ID            = M
PSP address   = 1E08:0000
Size          = 10 paragraphs ( 160 Byte )
Contents      = Environment
Program name  = D:\PCI\C\TC.EXE
Environment string
            COMSPEC=C:\COMMAND.COM
            PATH=C:\;C:\DOS;C:\BATCHES;E:\;D:\MSC\BIN
            INCLUDE=d:\msc\include
            LIB=d:\msc\lib
            TMP=d:\msc\tmp
            PROMPT=[$p]
------------------------------------------------------- Please press a key  ---
MCB number    = 15
MCB address   = 1E07:0000
Memory address= 1E08:0000
ID            = M
PSP address   = 1E08:0000
Size          = 16200 paragraphs ( 259200 Byte )
Contents      = PSP (with program following)
------------------------------------------------------- Please press a key  ---
MCB number    = 16
MCB address   = 5D50:0000
```

```
Memory address= 5D51:0000
ID              = M
PSP address     = 5D5C:0000
Size            = 10 paragraphs ( 160 Byte )
Contents        = Environment
Program name    = C:\TC\OBEX\MCBC.EXE
Environment string
                COMSPEC=C:\COMMAND.COM
                PATH=C:\;C:\DOS;C:\BATCHES;E:\;D:\MSC\BIN
                INCLUDE=d:\msc\include
                LIB=d:\msc\lib
                TMP=d:\msc\tmp
                PROMPT=[$p]
---------------------------------------------------- Please press a key   ---
MCB number      = 17
MCB address     = 5D5B:0000
Memory address= 5D5C:0000
ID              = M
PSP address     = 5D5C:0000
Size            = 4512 paragraphs ( 72192 Byte )
Contents        = PSP (with program following)
---------------------------------------------------- Please press a key   ---
MCB number      = 18
MCB address     = 6EFC:0000
Memory address= 6EFD:0000
ID              = Z
PSP address     = 0000:0000
Size            = 12547 paragraphs ( 200752 Byte )
Contents        = Unidentifiable as program or data

DUMP | 0123456789ABCDEF        00 01 02 03 04 05 06 07 08 09 0A 0B 0C 0D 0E 0F
-----+------------------------------------------------------------------------
0000 | H   6   % É   +         48 00 00 00 36 00 08 00 25 00 88 08 00 00 A8 00
0010 | (   v   --P   '         28 04 1E 00 76 00 17 00 FF FF 96 08 00 00 27 0C
0020 | H   Q   --P â .         48 1F 00 00 51 00 1E 00 FF FF 96 08 90 01 2E 05
0030 | HB  6   % P _ B         48 42 00 00 36 00 08 00 25 00 96 08 EC 01 42 00
0040 | ( ¦ v   --û   E         28 0D E3 00 76 00 17 00 FF FF A4 08 00 00 45 0C
---------------------------------------------------- Please press a key   ---
```

1   Although the program couldn't identify the first MCB (so the given PSP address isn't significant), the memory dump provides information about its contents. The first line of the ASCII dump contains the word "$CLOCK", which is the name of the DOS device driver for the internal clock.

As you might expect, this does look like a device driver. The first 18 bytes corresponds to the exact structure of a device driver header. However, this cannot be a permanently installed device driver from DOS because these are installed below the TPA (Transient Program Area) and don't require memory to be allocated for them.

So, this must be a driver that's installed with the DEVICE command from within the CONFIG.SYS file. The first device driver installed in our CONFIG.SYS file is "AT-UHR.SYS". This device uses the name "$CLOCK" as its device name.

This driver requires only a few kilobytes, but the allocated memory block is much larger than this. So, there must be more program code or data after this driver. By examining the five lines of the dump, we can see that all drivers that were installed with the DEVICE command can be found here. This means the first memory is already allocated by DOS during the boot procedure. It's given to all device drivers in the order in which they are named in the CONFIG.SYS file.

2   This memory block apparently contains a program. Since it's not preceded by an environment block that would provide the name of the program, we don't know which program this is. But from its location in the MCB chain and in RAM, we know that it was installed as a resident program shortly after the system was booted.

3   The contents of this memory block don't provide much information. Either it was allocated by a program for storing data at a later time, or it was simply left over after a memory block was freed.

4   This is obviously an environment block, but the corresponding program name is missing. 0FDC:0000 is given as the PSP address, which corresponds to the memory block managed by MCB 2. Since MCB 2 is a PSP and MCB 4 is an environment block, we can be almost certain these two blocks represent a program and its environment. Since the environment block doesn't have a program name associated with it, we can also conclude that this program wasn't started from the DOS command line or by a command in a BATCH file.

MCB 2 seems to represent the resident portion of the command processor COMMAND.COM, with the environment managed by MCB 4. This is confirmed by examining the program code in MCB 2 with a debugger.

5   This is the environment block for the program KEYB.COM, which enables us to work with the German keyboard. This program is started within our AUTOEXEC.BAT file using the command KEYB.GR. This is a resident program that remains in memory after it's installed.

6   The environment for KEYB.COM is in MCB 5 and the actual program is in MCB 6 (the PSP, meaning the program code and data). This is because the PSP address given in MCB 5 points to the memory block managed by MCB 6.

7, 8   These two blocks represent the environment and PSP for the CED.COM program, which is also started from within AUTOEXEC.BAT. This is also a memory resident program.

9, 10   Same as MCBs 7 and 8, except it's for the program CACHE-AT.COM.

11, 12   These blocks are for the program KEYBUF.COM (see Chapter 16). The environment block is clearly present, but the other block cannot be readily identified as the PSP. This is because this program uses (or rather misuses) a keyboard buffer as its PSP. So, the interrupt call at the start of the PSP is overwritten. This command identifies the PSP; without it the block cannot be identified as a block.

13   The program indicates that this block is occupied by a PSP. However, it must be only the beginning of a PSP, since this memory block is only 64 bytes and a PSP needs 256 bytes. This block was probably occupied by a PSP that wasn't completely overwritten after it was freed. So some of it still remains in memory.

14, 15   The program for outputting MCB contents was written in C, so we were in the Turbo C environment when we ran it. MCBs 14 and 15 therefore contain the environment and program code for Turbo C.

16, 17   To create this MCB memory dump, we compiled, linked, and executed the program MCBC within Turbo C. Executing this program also creates another process that starts Turbo C with the help of the EXEC loader. So, the block managed by MCBs 16 and 17 were allocated by the EXEC loader to run the program. After the program ends, they will be freed again.

18   The last memory block contains all the remaining memory that wasn't allocated at the time. This is about 200K of memory.

The MCBP.PAS, MCBC.C or MCBB.BAS demonstration program can be used to generate MCB dumps like the one we've described. The three versions are very similar. The BASIC version is slightly different because BASIC cannot use FAR pointers to query the memory. Instead, the PEEK and DEF SEG commands must be used (see Chapter 2 for more information).

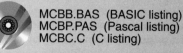

You'll find the following program(s) on the companion CD-ROM

MCBB.BAS (BASIC listing)
MCBP.PAS (Pascal listing)
MCBC.C   (C listing)

Chapter 25

The EXEC Function

We've briefly mentioned the EXEC function when discussing the command processor. We'll examine the EXEC function closesly and describe how it operates in this chapter.

Parent/child

The EXEC function is one of the many DOS functions that can be called with interrupt 21H (function 4BH). This function allows a parent program (main program) to call a child program (secondary program). The child program is loaded from a mass storage device into memory and then executes. If this child program doesn't become resident, the memory occupied by the child is released following program execution. The child program can also call another program that works with the parent program. This creates a type of program chaining that's limited only by the amount of available RAM.

One example of the EXEC function is the command processor. Using the EXEC function, the command processor executes user-specified programs and becomes the parent program. Some programs (such as Microsoft Word) permit the user to execute DOS commands from the main program using this function.

The parent program can pass parameters to the child program in the command line and can also pass parameters using the environment block. This program can also transfer information to the child program within the PSP. Since, like all executable programs, a PSP precedes the child program, information can be entered into the two FCBs within this PSP and made accessible to the child program.

Child program

When control is transferred to the child program, this program can access all the files and devices previously opened by the parent program (or one of the parent programs) with a handle function. This allows the child program to read information from a file or write information to a file whose handle is known (the child program doesn+t need to know the filename). This is only possible if the handle was passed by the parent program in one of the three methods we described or if the child program refers to one of the five handles, which are always open. These file accesses affect the file pointer. Since values aren't reset, these file accesses become -visible+ to the parent program when control returns to the parent program.

After the child program executes, control returns to the parent program and execution continues. To pass information (e.g., an error that occurred during the execution of the child program), the child program can pass a numeric value at the end of its execution. This can be done using DOS function 4CH, which terminates a program and returns a code to the parent program.

The communication between the parent and child programs works only if both programs agree on this return value. After control returns to the parent program, it can determine the code using function 4DH of interrupt 21H. To use function 4DH, only the function number is passed in the AH register. The code passed by the child program is returned to the calling (parent) program in the AL register.

Ending the child program

The contents of the AH register indicate how the child program terminated. The value 0 indicates a normal termination, while the value 1 indicates the child program terminated when the user pressed [Ctrl] [C] or [Ctrl] [Break]. If an error during access to a mass storage device forced the child program to terminate, a code of 2 is passed in the AH register. The value 3 indicates the child program terminated from a call to function 31H, or interrupt 27H; the child program then becomes resident in memory.

As we mentioned, the EXEC function can load the child program only if sufficient memory is available. While DOS can estimate the memory needed for EXE programs fairly accurately, it cannot do the same for COM programs. For COM programs, DOS reserves all unused memory. Because of this, a COM program cannot call another program with the EXEC function because DOS doesn't reserve any extra memory. This also applies to many EXE programs. If a call to a child program is necessary, the required memory space must be released from the calling program before the EXEC function is called (refer to the "Using BIOS To Access The Hard Drives" section in Chapter 14 for explanations on how to do this).

EXEC

If the EXEC function is called, the various parameters are loaded into the registers before calling interrupt 21H. Function number 4BH is passed in the AH register. A value of 0 or 3 is passed in the AL register. A value of 0 indicates the EXEC function will load and execute the program, while a value of 3 indicates the program is loaded as an overlay (without executing it). The address of the name of the program to be loaded or executed is passed in the DS:DX register pair and the address of the parameter block is passed in the ES:BX register pair.

The program name is specified as an ASCII string and ends with a null character (ASCII code 0). This name can include the device name and a complete path description. Its last element is the program name that, besides the name itself, must have either the .COM or .EXE extension. If the device name or path designation are omitted, the system searches for the program in the current directory of the current device. Since the EXEC function cannot execute a batch file directly, the program name that's passed cannot contain the .BAT extension.

Batch child

If a batch file must be executed, first the COMMAND.COM (command processor) file must be invoked. To indicate that a batch file should be executed, the parameter /c, followed by the name of the appropriate batch file, is added to the command line. Calling the command processor with the /c parameter also enables you to call any other program and even internal DOS commands, such as DIR.

Besides directly calling a program, it's also possible to specify program names without file extensions during a command processor call. The command processor searches for an EXE file, then a COM file, and finally a BAT file. If none of these files exist in the current directory, it searches all directories specified in the PATH command. This procedure isn't used during a direct program call without the addition of the command processor.

The directory that contains the command processor should be specified. If it isn't specified, it will be loaded from the path indicated by the COMSPEC environment string of the SET command.

Parameter blocks

Parameters can be passed to the command processor in the parameter block following the program name. These are the same parameters that are entered from the keyboard when the program is called. Later we'll see how these parameters affect the EXEC function. However, first we must discuss the parameter block's structure when the AL register contains the value 0.

The address for this block is passed to the EXEC function in the register pair ES:BX.

Field 1 indicates the segment address of the child program's environment block. This block doesn+t require an offset address because it always starts at a location divisible by 16. So, its offset address is always 0.

1	0- 1	Segment address: Environment block
2	2- 3	Offset address: Command parameter
3	4- 5	Segment address: Command parameter
4	6- 7	Offset address: First FCB
5	8- 9	Segment address: First FCB
6	10-11	Offset address: Second FCB
7	12-13	Segment address: Second FCB

Environment block

The command processor and other programs obtain information from the environment block. This is a series of ASCII character strings. This information can include paths for file searches. Each string has the following syntax, which ends in a null character (ASCII code 0):

```
Name = Parameter
```

The individual strings follow each other sequentially (i.e., the null character of one string is immediately followed by the first character of the next string). Environment blocks can have a maximum length of 32K.

The user can change the environment block by using the DOS SET and PATH commands. Programs that remain resident after execution are unaffected by any changes made to the environment block through these two DOS commands.

If the parent program wants to pass information to the child program using the environment block, it can either construct a new environment block or add the appropriate information to its own environment block. In the first instance, the segment address of the new environment block is specified in the first field of the parameter block. If the child program should have access to the environment block of the parent program, specify a value of 0 in this field. Before turning over control to the child program, the EXEC function stores the segment address of the environment block in the memory location at address 2CH of the child program's PSP.

If the child program must use a new environment block, it should contain at least 3 strings that are usually part of the environment block of the parent program and are important to the command processor:

```
COMSPEC = Parameter
PATH = Parameter
PROMPT = Parameter
```

If a child program modifies its environment block, the parent program's environment block remains unchanged after the child program completes its execution.

Fields 2 and 3 indicate the command parameters' address that is passed to the PSP of the program starting at address 80H. These fields must have the same structure in memory as expected by DOS in the PSP. The first byte indicates the number of command characters minus 1. This is followed by the command characters as normal ASCII codes. The command parameters terminate with a carriage return (ASCII code 13), which isn't included in the character count. For compatibility with COMMAND.COM, the first character in the string should be a space.

To call a batch program (called DO.BAT) using the command processor, the following command parameters must be specified as a string in memory:

```
DB 10," /C DO.BAT",13
```

The EXEC function copies the command parameters into the PSP of the program to be executed. It also removes all the parameters that would redirect the input or output, because a redirection of the standard input/output can only be performed by the parent program. The child program can still use input/output redirection if the standard input/output handles have been redirected by the parent program. (See Chapter 20 for more information and an example of this process.)

Fields 6, 7, 10, and 11 indicate two FCBs installed in the PSP at address 5CH or 6CH. If this isn't required, specify -1 (FFFFH) in these two fields. However, if this is needed for program execution, enter the first two command parameters in the two FCBs with DOS function 29H. Before passing control to the child program, the EXEC function copies these two FCBs into the PSP of the child program.

Although all the registers and the parameter block now have the required values, the EXEC function cannot be called yet. Since this function destroys the contents of all registers up to the CS and IP registers during execution, the contents of all the registers must be placed on the stack before this function is activated. Then the contents of the SS and SP registers must be stored within the code segment. Only then can interrupt 21H function 4BH be called to activate the EXEC function. After the EXEC function ends, the carry flag indicates whether the function executed normally. Before program execution can continue, the value of the SS and SP registers must be restored from the code segment. Then the contents of the other register can be restored again from the stack.

The EXEC function performs a different task when a value of 3 appears in the AL register. In this case, it loads a COM program or an EXE program into memory without executing. After the target program is loaded, control immediately returns to the calling program. Unlike subfunction 0, the program loads to a memory address indicated by the calling program instead of loading to any non-specific location. Since parameters aren't passed to the loaded program, the parameter block has a different structure during the call of subfunction 3 than during the call of subfunction 0:

Field	Byte	Purpose
1	0- 1	Segment address where overlay is located
2	2- 3	Relocation factor

Before the function is called, the segment address to which the program should be loaded is specified in the first field of the parameter block. If the calling program doesn't have enough memory available for loading the external program, it should request additional memory with one of the DOS memory management functions. The loaded program loads directly to the segment address indicated with the offset address 0 because a PSP doesn't precede the program.

Relocation

The relocation factor adjusts the segment address of the called program. Since this factor applies only to EXE programs (COM programs cannot have specific segment assignments), the relocation factor for COM programs should always equal 0. The relocation factor for EXE programs should indicate the segment address where the program will be loaded to conform to the program's segment assignments.

After the program is loaded, its routines are ready to be accessed. The routines of the loaded program should always be treated as subroutines (i.e., called with the machine language CALL instruction). It must always be a FAR type instruction although the loaded program may be located immediately after the calling program, but it can never have the same segment address.

The offset address for CALL is always 100H for a COM program because execution always starts immediately after the PSP at address 100H. However, this creates a problem. Subfunction 3 prevents the PSP from loading. So, the code segment of the COM program starts at address 0, instead of at the offset address 100H (relative to the load segment). Since all jump instructions and accesses to data within the COM program are relative to address 100H instead of address 0, you cannot execute a FAR CALL instruction with the address of the load segment as the segment address, and address 0 as the offset address. The segment address for the FAR CALL must indicate the address of the load segment minus 10H and the address 100H as the offset address.

If the COM program specifically acts as an overlay for another program, entry addresses other than address 100H are possible. In this case, only the offset address for the FAR CALL instruction changes. The segment address must remain 10H smaller than the address of the load segment.

EXEC and memory

The problem is different for EXE programs. If these programs are loaded for execution using subfunction 0, the EXEC function sets the code segment and the instruction pointer to the instruction that was declared as the first instruction in the assembler source. However, this address is unknown to the program that loaded the EXE program as an overlay. This problem can easily be solved by placing the first executable instruction in the EXE program at the beginning of the EXE program. This makes its offset address 0. The EXE program source must not be in the normal sequence with the stack first. In this case, the code segment must be the first segment in the source to ensure that it begins the EXE program.

The FAR CALL uses the address of the load segment as the segment address, and address 0 as the offset address.

Demonstration program

While BASIC, Pascal and C have commands or procedures to call a program from another program, assembly language routines must use DOS function 4BH. The EXEC.ASM program which you'll find on the companion CD-ROM is an example program that should help you understand this function.

The framework of the EXE program listed in Chapter 19 acts as the basis for this program. The EXEPRG procedure performs the actual work. This procedure calls the new program using function 4BH. Two strings, which contain the name of the program to be called and the necessary parameters, are passed to it. Both strings end with the null character (ASCII code 0). All the variables EXEPRG needs for execution are located in the code segment.

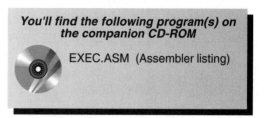

You'll find the following program(s) on the companion CD-ROM

EXEC.ASM (Assembler listing)

The advantage of this method is that, to use this routine, the lines from the code segment must be copied into only one of the application programs. After calling EXEPRG, the carry flag signals whether an error occurred. If true (carry flag=1), the AX register contains the error code as returned by the EXEC function of DOS. If the called program executed correctly, the carry flag is reset (0) and the termination code of the called program, as returned by DOS function 4DH, is returned by the AX register.

Within this program, EXEPRG displays the current directory using the command processor. The command processor defaults to the current directory of the current device.

Chapter 26

Ctrl Break *And Critical Error Interrupts*

In DOS, there are two ways to stop a program during execution. This occurs when the user presses Ctrl Break (Ctrl c) or when a critical error occurs during access to an external device (i.e., printer, hard drive, disk drive, etc.). Although the key combination that's used depends on the PC configuration, we'll use Ctrl Break in this section.

Ctrl Break

Pressing Ctrl Break to stop a program during execution can have serious consequences. After the user presses this key combination, DOS abruptly takes control from the program without allowing the program to perform any necessary "housekeeping". For example, files aren't closed properly, diverted interrupt vectors aren't reset, and allocated memory isn't released. This can result in data loss or a system crash.

To prevent this from happening, DOS calls interrupt 23H, which is also known as the <Ctrl><Break> interrupt. When a program is started, this interrupt points to a routine that causes the program to end. However, a program is able to select a routine of its own, which enables the program to maintain control of what occurs when the user presses <Ctrl><Break>.

However, the interrupt routine doesn't execute immediately. Instead, the break flag determines when this routine occurs. This flag can be set at the DOS prompt using the BREAK (ON/OFF) command from DOS, or with the help of DOS function 33H, subfunction 1. If the break flag is on, every time a function of DOS interrupt 21H is called, the keyboard buffer will be checked to see if either Ctrl Break or Ctrl C has been pressed. If the break flag is off, this check will be performed only when calling the DOS functions that access the standard input and output devices.

If this test finds the appropriate key combination, the processor registers are loaded with the values contained in the DOS function to be executed. Interrupt 23H is called only after this occurs.

If a program directs this interrupt to a routine of its own, several things may occur. For example, the program could display a window on the screen that asks whether the user wants to end the program. The program can also decide for itself whether the program should end.

Maintenance

If the program chooses to stop execution, some type of clean-up routine should be performed. This type of routine closes all open files, resets any changed interrupt pointers, and releases any allocated memory. After this, function 4CH can end the program without returning control to the interrupt 23H caller.

The IRET assembly language instruction must return control to DOS if Ctrl Break should be ignored. The program must then ensure that all processor registers contain the same values they had when interrupt 23H was invoked. Otherwise, the DOS function that was originally called cannot be performed without an error.

We'll demonstrate both of these methods in an example at the end of this section.

Critical error interrupt

Unlike the Ctrl Break interrupt, the critical error interrupt call usually isn't a reaction to something the user does intentionally. Instead, it's usually a reaction to an error that occurs when accessing an external device, such as a printer, disk drive, or hard disk. Although the user can correct the error in many cases (e.g., the printer isn't switched on), other errors can be caused by hardware failures that require repairs (e.g., read error while accessing the hard disk).

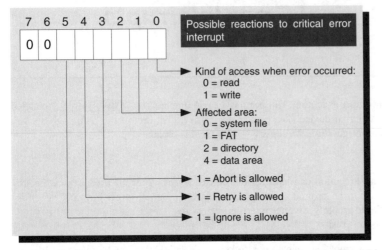

To make allowances for the various kinds of errors, the critical error interrupt (interrupt 24H) usually points to a DOS routine that displays the following or a similar message on the screen and waits for input from the user:

```
(A)bort (R)etry (I)gnore (F)ail
```

This clears the currently executing program from the screen. Similar to Ctrl Break, this interrupt ends the program abruptly. So, the files aren't properly closed, allocated memory isn't released, etc.

Installing an interrupt handler in a program to replace the DOS handler can help. DOS uses a processor register to pass this handler various information when it's called. This helps the interrupt handler locate the source of the error. Bit 7 in the AH register indicates either a floppy or hard disk access error (bit 7 off) or some other error (bit 7 on). The other bits give information about the reaction to possible error codes.

Also, the BP:SI register pair points to the head of the device driver that was being called when the error appeared. A detailed error code is contained in the lower 8 bits of the DI register and the contents of the upper 8 bits are undefined. This returns the following error codes:

Error codes passed to the critical error handler			
Code	Meaning	Code	Meaning
00h	Disk is write protected	07h	Unknown device type
01h	Access to an unknown device	08h	Sector not found
02h	Drive not ready	09h	Printer out of paper
03h	Unknown command	0Ah	Write error
04h	CRC error	0Bh	Read error
05h	Wrong data length	0Ch	General error
06h	Seek error		

When called, the critical error handler can respond by opening a window on the screen that asks the user to decide to ignore the error, retry the access, or abort the program. The last option can only instruct the interrupt to call DOS functions 01H to 0CH. This means the program ends abruptly, similar to pressing ⌈Ctrl⌉ ⌈Break⌉.

Although calling other DOS functions within the handler doesn't cause errors itself, the return to DOS causes a system crash. These handlers also aren't allowed to end a program by using DOS function 4CH. Instead, the handler must return to its caller with the help of the IRET command. With that, DOS expects a code in the AL register that will show it how to react to the error. It interprets the contents of the AL register as follows:

Output codes of a critical error handler	
Code	Meaning
00h	Ignore error
01h	Retry operation
02h	End program with interrupt 23H
03h	End function called with error (DOS 3.0 and up)

The last output code in the previous list represents the most sensible reaction to an error that can't be fixed by repeating the operation (e.g., when the printer must be switched on). The receipt of this code invokes the normal ending of the function call, in which the error occurred. The function then sets the carry flag to signal the error. While this makes a "critical" error and a "normal" error indistinguishable to the program, it's possible to distinguish them by setting a flag within the critical error handler.

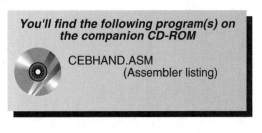

You'll find the following program(s) on the companion CD-ROM

CEBHAND.ASM
(Assembler listing)

Chapter 27

Device Drivers

The device driver is one of the most fascinating and most complicated, aspects of system programming. DOS uses device drivers to access external devices. Device drivers are short programs that provide support to a wide variety of devices, ranging from keyboards to CD-ROM drives. However, they are difficult to use because they can be programmed only in assembly language.

In this chapter, we'll show you how device drivers are structured under DOS. You'll also learn how to develop your own drivers. We've included source code for several functional drivers, which can also serve as the basis for your own, more complicated drivers.

Device Drivers Under DOS

A device driver is the part of the operating system that's responsible for controlling and communicating with the hardware. It represents the lowest level of an operating system and permits all other levels to work independently of the hardware. This is useful when adapting an operating system to various computers because the device drivers can be changed instead of the entire operating system.

In earlier operating systems, device drivers resided in the operating system code. This meant that changing or upgrading these routines to match new hardware was difficult, if not impossible. DOS Version 2.0 introduced a flexible concept of device drivers. This flexibility makes it possible for the user to adapt even the most exotic hard drives and EMS expansion cards to DOS.

A device driver consists of status information, which tells DOS what kind of driver it is and several software routines known as driver functions. These routines are responsible for tasks required by DOS to access the device the driver serves. For example, a hard drive device driver must contain functions for handling read, write and verify operations on sectors of the disk.

Custom drivers

Since communication between DOS and a device driver is based on relatively simple function calls and data structures, the assembly language programmer can develop a device driver to adapt any device to DOS. Unfortunately, device drivers cannot be programmed in a higher level language, as we mentioned earlier.

The rules for developing a COM program also apply when developing the code for a driver. Direct segment access isn't allowed. The difference is that a device driver starts at offset address 0H, instead of 100H. The end of this section explains the assembly language implementation in detail.

Name	Driver for
NUL	Null (imaginary) device
$CLOCK	Clock
CON	Console (keyboard and screen)
AUX	Serial port
PRN	Parallel port (printer)

Device drivers are installed by DOS during the boot process. They cannot be activated from the command line like normal EXE or COM programs. The drivers present in the DOS kernel are installed automatically during the boot process. These drivers are named $CLOCK device driver, CON device driver, AUX device driver and PRN device driver. In addition to these, drivers for the diskette drives and the hard disk will also be installed, if available.

The drivers are arranged sequentially in memory and connected to each other. If the user wants to install another driver, DOS must be informed using the CONFIG.SYS file. This text file contains the information that DOS needs for configuring the system. Contents of the CONFIG.SYS file are read and evaluated during the boot process after linking the standard drivers. If DOS finds the DEVICE= command, the driver described in that line is installed, based on the optional path.

ANSI.SYS

The following command sequence includes the ANSI.SYS driver, which is supplied with DOS. This driver makes enhanced character output and keyboard functions available:

```
DEVICE=ANSI.SYS
```

The new driver is added to the chain immediately after the NUL device driver (the first driver in the chain). The ANSI.SYS driver replaces the default CON driver. To ensure that all function calls for monitor or keyboard communication operate through ANSI.SYS, the ANSI.SYS driver is placed first in the device group and the CON driver is moved farther down the chain of devices. Since the operating system moves from link to link during the search, it finds the new CON driver (ANSI.SYS) first and uses it. So, the system ignores the old CON driver, as shown in the following illustration:

The driver chain before and after adding new CON driver

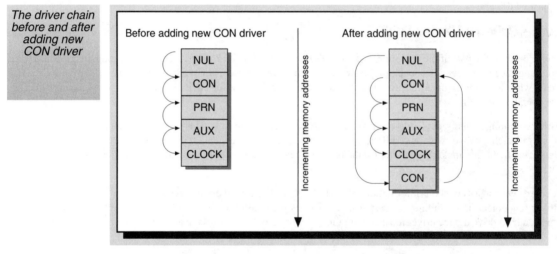

ASSIGN

Not all drivers can be replaced with new ones. The NUL driver is always the first driver in the chain. If you add a new NUL driver, the system ignores this driver and continues accessing the original NUL driver. This also applies to the drivers for floppy disk drives and hard drives. This occurs because disk drives have drive specifiers instead of names such as CON (e.g., A:). A new disk drive can be added to the system, but since DOS may assign it the name D:, it may not be addressed by all programs that want to access device A:.

This problem can be avoided by redirecting all device accesses using DOS's ASSIGN command. You can make the ASSIGN command part of the AUTOEXEC.BAT file. It executes after adding drivers and executing the CONFIG.SYS file. To redirect all accesses from drive A: (the first disk drive) to device D: (in this case, a new driver for a new disk drive), the AUTOEXEC.BAT file must contain the following command sequence:

```
ASSIGN A=D
```

The drivers for mass storage devices and the drivers, such as PRN, are handled differently. DOS has two kinds of device drivers:

➢   Character device drivers

➢   Block device drivers

Character device drivers

Let's start with character device drivers because they have a simple structure. Character device drivers transmit one byte for every function call. They communicate with devices, such as the keyboard, display, printer and modem. Since a device driver can service only one device, individual drivers for keyboard, display, printer, etc., exist in DOS after booting.

Character devices can operate in either cooked mode or raw mode.

Cooked mode

In cooked mode, the device driver reads characters from the device and performs a test for certain control characters. DOS then passes the character to an internal buffer. DOS also checks to determine whether any Enter, Ctrl P, Ctrl S or Ctrl C characters exist. If the system detects the Enter character, it ignores any further input from the device driver, even if the specified number of characters hasn't been read yet. Then the characters read are copied from the internal buffer to the buffer of the calling program. If characters are output in cooked mode, DOS tests for Ctrl C or Ctrl Break. If one of these combinations is detected, the currently running program stops. Pressing Ctrl S temporarily stops the program until the user presses any other key. Ctrl P redirects the output from the screen to the printer (PRN). Pressing Ctrl P a second time redirects the output from the printer back to the screen.

Raw mode

In raw mode, the device driver reads all characters without testing. If a program wants to read in 10 characters, it reads exactly 10 characters, even if the user presses the Enter key as the second character of the string. Raw mode transmits the characters directly to the calling program's buffer, instead of using an internal DOS buffer. During character output, raw mode doesn't test for Ctrl C or Ctrl Break.

DOS function 44H of interrupt 21H defines the mode of the character device driver (see the end of this section for a detailed description of this interrupt).

Block device drivers

Block device drivers usually communicate with mass storage devices, such as hard drives. Therefore, they simultaneously transmit a number of characters designated as a block. In some cases, a single call to a function transmits several blocks of data. The block sizes can differ depending on the mass storage device and within one particular mass storage device.

When DOS wants to access a storage medium with a block driver, DOS passes the number of the sector being addressed. The driver must then convert the logical sector number (counted starting from 0) to a physical address consisting of head, cylinder and sector numbers. The device driver selects the method used for converting logical sector numbers into physical sector addresses. It's only important that a unique, one-to-one relationship is maintained between logical and physical sectors. This means that a given logical sector uniquely identifies one and only one physical sector.

Unlike character device drivers, block device drivers can manage more than one device at a time. A single hard disk driver can work with two or more hard disks at once, for example. A block driver can also divide a mass storage device into several volumes, which is often done with hard disks.

Identifying devices managed by a driver

The drives managed by a block driver don't have device names or filenames. Instead, they use identifying letters such as A, B or C. The device letters are assigned by DOS and aren't selected by the driver. The letters DOS assigns are determined by the location of the block driver within the list of drivers. The first drive managed by a block driver receives the letter A, the second B and then C, etc.

Each of these devices must have a file allocation table (FAT) and a root directory. Block device drivers don't distinguish between cooked and raw modes. They always read and write the exact number of blocks unless an error is detected.

If a device driver supports several logical drives, these are assigned consecutive letters. For example, if a hard disk driver implements three logical drives and the first letter available is C, then the other two drives are assigned the letters D and E. The next block driver then begins with the letter F.

Device driver access

There are several ways to access a device driver. Character device drivers are accessed using the normal FCB or handle functions by simply indicating the name of a driver (e.g., CON: instead of a filename). A block device driver is accessed using the normal DOS functions (file, directory, etc.) by using the drive designator assigned by DOS during the boot process.

Functions 1H through CH of interrupt 21H invoke read and write operations in a device driver. There are also two other options for accessing device drivers, which we'll discuss shortly.

This can no longer be considered direct access, since various DOS functions are used to communicate between the driver and the device.

There are two other ways to communicate with device drivers. DOS function 44H, which is known as the IOCTL function (I/O control), is important to this communication. This function has many subfunctions, which we'll discuss in more detail later in this chapter.

Structure Of A Device Driver

Although the two types of device drivers differ in some important ways, they have similar structures. Each has a device header, a strategy routine and an interrupt routine (a different kind of interrupt from the ones we've discussed so far).

Device header

The device header appears at the beginning of each device driver and contains information that DOS needs for implementing the driver.

Device driver header		
Address	Contents	Type
00H	Offset address of next driver	1 word
02H	Segment address of next driver	1 word
04H	Device attribute	1 word
06H	Offset address of strategy routine	1 word
08H	Offset address of interrupt routine	1 word
0AH	Driver name (character driver) or number of devices (block driver)	8 bytes

Device driver header

The first field creates a link to the next device driver in the list. Once a driver is loaded, DOS enters the address of the next driver in this field. The programmer must initialize this field with the value -1 so that DOS will recognize the structure as a device driver.

Device attributes

The second field is a bit field that's used to describe the device driver. Bit 15 of this field tells DOS whether this is a block or a character driver. A value of 0 represents a block driver and 1 represents a character driver. The interpretation of all other bits in this field depends on the setting of bit 15. The following is the entire structure of this bit field:

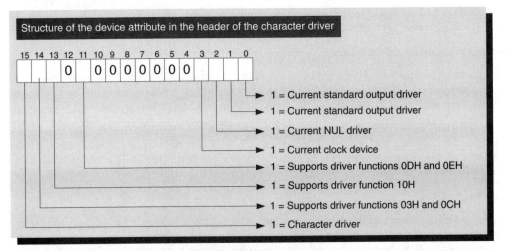

Structure of the device attribute in the header of the character driver

In the case of a character driver, bits 0 through 3 identify the driver (see the previous illustration). They indicate whether the new driver, instead of the CON driver, should be used for input and output or whether it should replace the NUL driver or the clock driver. If none of these bits are set, then the new driver doesn't replace any of the standard drivers.

The other bits indicate whether the driver supports various driver functions. To understand this, you must also know that DOS recognizes 15 different driver functions, all of which aren't automatically available to a driver. The optional functions 03H, 0CH, 0DH, 0EH and 10H must be explicitly requested by setting the corresponding bits. Some of these functions are available beginning only with DOS Version 3.1 and some aren't available until Version 5.0. You must be using the corresponding DOS version for the attribute bits to be properly recognized. We'll provide descriptions of these DOS driver functions later in this chapter.

Remember the values of these bits are valid only if bit 15 contains the value 1b, which indicates a character driver. These bits will have different meanings if it's a block driver.

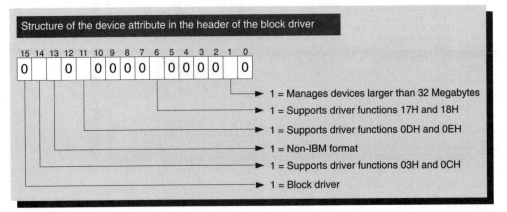

Structure of the device attribute in the header of the block driver

In addition to the bits that indicate which driver functions are supported, bit 1 is very important to block drivers. The feature indicated by this bit is supported in DOS Versions 4.0 and higher. If this bit is set, then the block driver is capable of supporting devices and partitions larger than 32 megabytes, which was made possible with the enlarged cluster size available starting with DOS 4.0.

With the 32 megabyte limit exceeded, the driver can no longer represent all the addressable sectors as 16-bit integers. This would allow for only 65,536 sectors, which, with a standard sector size of 512 bytes, corresponds to exactly 32 megabytes.

Device drivers with attribute bit 1 set expect sector numbers to be passed in another format so the sectors beyond the 32 megabyte limit can also be addressed. We'll provide more information about this when we discuss the driver functions.

Structure of the fields in the device driver header

Two fields that contain the offset addresses of the so-called strategy and interrupt routines follow the attributes field. DOS uses these routines to communicate with the driver. Only the offset addresses of these routines are required because device drivers, like COM programs, are limited to one segment. So, the explicit segment address isn't needed.

In the case of a character driver, the last field of the driver header contains the name of the device driver. If the name is less than the eight characters allowed in this field, the rest of the field must be filled with empty spaces (ASCII code 32). If the driver is a block driver, then this field contains the number of logical devices the driver supports. The other 7 bytes of this field should then be filled with the value 0.

Strategy and interrupt routines

DOS calls the strategy routine to initialize the driver before any function of the driver is called. An address is passed to this routine in the ES:BX register pair. This address points to a data structure that contains information about the operation to be performed and the corresponding data. The strategy routine doesn't execute these operations itself; it simply stores the address of the data block and gives control back to DOS. Then the driver interrupt routine is called and the operation is actually executed. We'll learn more about this later.

This mechanism frees DOS from having to know the address of every driver function. DOS can simply use the strategy and interrupt routines as an interface to the various driver functions. Therefore, the data block whose address is passed to the strategy routine will always also contain the number of the driver function that must be called. The data block always consists of at least 13 bytes. More bytes can be added, depending on the needs of the function being called. The following figure shows a typical structure for this data block. The first 13 bytes will appear with all function calls.

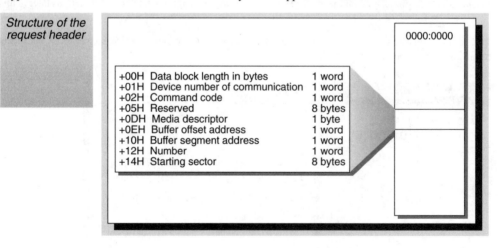

Structure of the request header

+00H	Data block length in bytes	1 word
+01H	Device number of communication	1 word
+02H	Command code	1 word
+05H	Reserved	8 bytes
+0DH	Media descriptor	1 byte
+0EH	Buffer offset address	1 word
+10H	Buffer segment address	1 word
+12H	Number	1 word
+14H	Starting sector	8 bytes

0000:0000

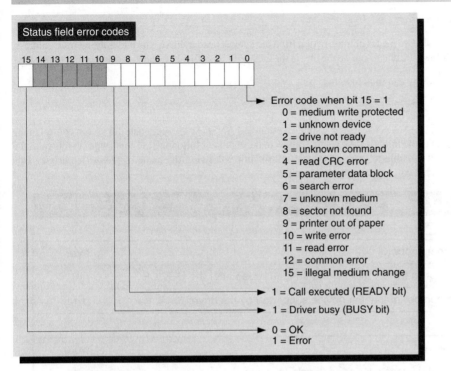

Status field error codes

```
15 14 13 12 11 10 9  8  7  6  5  4  3  2  1  0
```

Error code when bit 15 = 1
   0 = medium write protected
   1 = unknown device
   2 = drive not ready
   3 = unknown command
   4 = read CRC error
   5 = parameter data block
   6 = search error
   7 = unknown medium
   8 = sector not found
   9 = printer out of paper
   10 = write error
   11 = read error
   12 = common error
   15 = illegal medium change

1 = Call executed (READY bit)

1 = Driver busy (BUSY bit)

0 = OK
1 = Error

Device Driver Functions

Under DOS Version 2.0, any installable device driver must support 13 functions, numbered from 00H to 0CH, even if their only action consists of setting the DONE flag in the status word. DOS Versions 3.0, 4.0 and 5.0 include additional functions that can be supported, but aren't required. Some of these functions concern one of the two driver types, while others apply to both driver types (e.g., initialization). Unused functions must at least set the DONE flag of the status word. Let's look at the various functions in detail according to their function numbers.

Request header

Every function described here receives its arguments from the request header (whose address is passed by DOS to the strategy routine) and stores its "results" in the request header. Therefore, the offset address to the arguments, relative to the beginning of the request header, is passed to the specified function. These arguments are later transferred to variables. Besides this offset address, a flag indicates whether this information consists of a byte, word or PTR. The PTR data type represents a pointer to a buffer and consists of two adjacent words. The first word is the offset address of the buffer. The second word is the segment address of the buffer.

Function 00H: Driver Initialization

During the system boot procedure, DOS calls this function to initialize the device driver. This function can involve hardware initialization, setting various internal variables to their default values or the redirection of interrupts. Since the entire operating system hasn't been completely initialized at this point, the initialization routine can only call functions 01H through 0CH (character I/O) and 30H (DOS version number), 25H and 35H (get/set interrupt vector) of DOS interrupt 21H. These functions can be used to determine the DOS version number and to display a driver identification message on the screen. Even if the newly linked driver is a CON driver, the output to the display occurs through the old CON driver, because there are no new drivers linked into the system after the initialization routine is complete.

Initialization and the request header

The initialization routine can obtain two pieces of information from the request header. First, it provides the memory address, which contains the text that follows the equal sign on the line in the CONFIG.SYS file that loaded the driver into the system.

A typical line in a CONFIG.SYS file can look like this:

```
DEVICE=ANSI.SYS
```

In this instance, the device name is ANSI.SYS, which assigns the standard ANSI escape sequences for screen control to the PC. The memory address passed to the initialization routine points to the character following the equal sign (in this case, the A of ANSI.SYS). This makes it possible to store additional information following the name of the device driver. This information is ignored by DOS, but can be read by other routines.

Address	Contents	Type
Input parameters:		
Offset 2	Function number (0H)	byte
Offset 18	Address of character that follows the equal sign after the DEVICE	ptr
Offset 22	Device number of the first device supported by the driver (0=A,	byte
Returned parameters:		
Offset 3	Status word	word
Offset 13	Number of devices supported (block devices only)	byte
Offset 14	Address of first available memory location following the driver	ptr
Offset 18	Address of array containing BPB addresses (block devices only)	ptr

Logical device designation

The second item is only available under DOS Version 3.0 and higher and only if the driver is a b Block device driver. This is the letter designation of the first logical device of the driver. The value 0 represents A, 1 represents B, 2 represents C, etc.

The initialization routine must return four parameters to the calling DOS function. The first parameter is the status of the function (i.e., the indication of whether the function has executed properly). For a block device driver, the number of logical devices supported must also be passed. This information could also be obtained from the device driver's header, but is ignored by DOS.

The next parameter the device driver must pass to DOS is the highest memory address that it occupies or uses. This lets DOS know where the next device driver can be installed.

Remember, starting with DOS Version 5.0, drivers no longer have "unlimited" memory available to them. This DOS version allows you to load drivers into Upper Memory Blocks. Generally, there is less memory available there than in the TPA below the 640K limit. In Version 5.0, the "upper limit" address of the driver is loaded in the field where DOS normally would find the end address of the driver. The upper limit is the address in memory beyond which the driver may no longer allocate memory for itself. If this isn't sufficient for the driver, then it shouldn't even attempt to be installed.

BPB

If the driver is a block device driver, the last argument passed must be the address of an array that contains an entry for every logical device. This array contains the addresses of BIOS parameter blocks (BPBs). The address is passed as two words; the first word contains the offset and the second word contains the segment address of the array. The first two words within this table are the address for the first logical device supported. The next two words indicate the address for the second logical device, etc. The BPB is a data block containing information that describes a logical device. If all or some of the logical devices have the same format, all entries in the BPB address table can point to a single BPB.

Notice the last part of the BIOS parameter block, which is called the expanded BPB, is only required for block drivers that support partitions larger than 32 megabytes. This is only possible with DOS 4.0 or higher. To indicate that you want to manage partitions larger than 32 megabytes, set bit 1 in the driver attribute bit field. The total number of sectors and the number of reserved sectors in the normal BPB must be set to 0 and the corresponding fields in the expanded BPB must be loaded. These are 32 bit fields that can handle values greater than 65,535 (which is the limit for these fields in the normal BPB).

BIOS Parameter Block design		
+00H	Bytes per sector	1 word
+02H	Sectors per cluster	1 byte
+03H	Reserved sectors (including boot sectors)	1 word
+05H	Number of FATs	1 byte
+06H	Maximum number of entries in root directory	1 word
+08H	Total number of sectors	1 word
+0AH	Media descriptor	1 byte
+0BH	Number of sectors per FAT	1 word

Media descriptor byte	
Code	Medium
F0h	3.5-inch diskette, double-sided, 80 tracks, 18 sectors per track
	3.5-inch diskette, double-sided, 80 tracks, 36 sectors per track
F8h	Hard drive
F9h	5.25-inch diskette, double-sided, 80 tracks, 15 sectors per track
	3.5-inch diskette, double-sided, 80 tracks, 9 sectors per track
FAh	5.25-inch diskette, single-sided, 80 tracks, 8 sectors per track
	3.5-inch diskette, single-sided, 80 tracks, 8 sectors per track
FBh	5.25-inch diskette, double-sided, 80 tracks, 8 sectors per track
	3.5-inch diskette, double-sided, 80 tracks, 8 sectors per track
FCh	5.25-inch diskette, single-sided, 40 tracks, 9 sectors per track
FDh	5.25-inch diskette, single-sided, 40 tracks, 9 sectors per track
FEh	5.25-inch diskette, single-sided, 40 tracks, 8 sectors per track
FFh	5.25-inch diskette, single-sided, 40 tracks, 8 sectors per track

Starting with DOS Version 4.0, the function can also return an error flag to offset address 17H of the data block. If DOS finds a value other than 0 at this location after the function call, the message "CONFIG.SYS error in line xx" is displayed.

Function 01H: Media Check

This function is used only with a block device driver. A character device driver should simply set the DONE flag of the status word and exit. This function is used by DOS to determine whether the media (diskette) has changed. It's frequently used when examining a disk directory. If the disk medium wasn't changed since the last access, DOS still has this information in memory; otherwise DOS must reread the information from the media that delays the execution of the current task.

In some instances, as with floppy diskettes, the answer to the question is fairly complicated. Therefore, DOS permits function 1 to answer not only with "yes" and "no", but also with "don't know." The answer always affects further DOS activity.

If the media is unchanged, access to the media can occur immediately. If the media was changed, however, DOS closes all internal buffers related to the current logical device. This causes the loss of all data that should have been transmitted to the media. Then it calls function 2 of the current device driver and loads the FAT and the root directory.

If the media check function answers with "don't know," the additional steps taken by DOS depend on the status of the internal buffers related to the current logical device. If these internal buffers are empty, DOS assumes the media was changed and acts as if function 1 answered "yes." If the buffers contain data that should have been transmitted to the media, DOS assumes the media is intact and writes the data. If the media was indeed changed, the data written to a changed media may damage the new diskette's file structure.

Since subsequent processing depends on the response from the media check function, the driver should handle the response carefully. Before enabling the mechanism used by the function to respond, the function examines the parameters passed to it. If the driver supports several logical devices, the first parameter is the number of devices. Next is a media descriptor code. This code contains information about the type of media last used in the current logical device. Only devices that can handle several different formats can use this task (e.g., AT disk drives that can use both 360K and 1.2 megabyte diskette formats).

If the media check function determines the medium in a device is non-removable (e.g., a fixed disk), it can always respond "not changed". If, however, the device media can be changed (e.g., a disk), the correct response can only be determined with complex procedures. If these procedures aren't used, the response should be "don't know".

Address	Contents	Type
Input parameters:		
Offset 1	Device number	byte
Offset 2	Function number (1)	byte
Offset 13	Media descriptor byte	byte
Returned parameters:		
Offset 3	Status word	word
Offset 14	Was media changed? FFH = yes, 00H = don't know, 01H = no	byte
Offset 15	Address of buffer containing the previous volume name (only if device indicates a media change)	ptr

The following are the three procedures that provide fairly accurate results.

Since a device with changeable media has an opening and closing mechanism, the function should check to determine whether the media was removed. However, it cannot determine whether the removed media is identical to the newly inserted medium. If the media has a name, the function should read this name to determine whether the media was changed. This procedure only makes sense if every media has a unique name.

The disk drive procedure used by DOS is based on the fact that changing medium is time-consuming. DOS assumes that a user needs about two seconds to remove a diskette from a drive and insert a new diskette in the same drive. If two consecutive diskette accesses occur less than two seconds apart, DOS assumes the diskette wasn't changed. A byte in the data block is used to indicate changes. The value -1 (FFH) means "changed", 0 means "don't know" and 1 means "not changed".

If the media was changed, the device driver indicates this (bit 11 in the device attribute = 1); the address of a buffer must be passed to DOS Version 3 and higher, which contains the volume name of the previous media. This name must be stored there as an ASCII string and terminated with an end character (ASCII code 0).

Function 02H: Build BIOS Parameter Block (BPB)

This function is used only by block device drivers. A character device driver should just set the DONE flag of the status word and exit. DOS calls this function when the media check function determines the media was changed. This function returns a pointer to a new BPB for the media.

As you can see by the layout of the calling parameters, the device number media descriptor and a pointer to a buffer are passed to this function by DOS. If the device is a standard format (bit 13 of the device attribute =0), then the buffer contains the first sector of the FAT.

Starting with DOS Version 3.0, this function also reads and writes volume label names, because a call to function 01H must occur any time a device experiences a change of medium (bit 11 of the device attribute = 1).

Address	Contents	Type
Input parameters:		
Offset 1	Device number	byte
Offset 2	Function number (2)	byte
Offset 13	Media descriptor byte	byte
Offset 14	Address of a buffer containing the FAT (see above)	ptr
Returned parameters:		
Offset 3	Status word	word
Offset 18	Address of the BPB of addressed device	ptr

Function 03H: I/O Control Read

This function allows direct communication between a device driver and an application. This allows device drivers to implement additional logic not accessible from normal driver functions. It can only be called through function 44H of interrupt 21H if the IOCTL bit (bit 14), in the device attribute word in the device driver header, is set. Different parameters are passed to the function from a FAR pointer, depending on whether the driver is a character or a block device driver.

A character device driver is passed the number of characters to be transferred and the address of a buffer for the transfer of the data.

A block device driver is passed the device number, the media descriptor byte, the address of the buffer to be used for the data transfer, the pointer to the first sector to be read and the number of sectors to be read.

Address	Contents	Type
Input parameters:		
Offset 1	Device number (block devices only)	byte
Offset 2	Function number (3)	byte
Offset 13	Media descriptor byte (block devices only)	byte
Offset 14	Address of buffer into which data should be transmitted	ptr
Offset 18	Number of sectors to be read (block device) or number of characters to be read (character device)	word
Offset 20	First sector to be read (block devices only)	word
Returned parameters:		
Offset 3	Status word	word
Offset 18	Number of sectors read (block device) or number of characters read (character device)	word

Function 04H: Read

This function reads data from the device to a buffer specified in the calling parameter. If an error occurs while reading the data, the error status must be set. Also, the function must report the number of sectors or bytes that were successfully read. Simply reporting an error isn't sufficient.

Address	Contents	Type
Input parameters:		
Offset 1	Device number (block device only)	1 byte
Offset 2	Function number (4)	1 byte
Offset 13	Media descriptor byte (block device only)	1 byte
Offset 14	Address of buffer to which data should be read	1 ptr
Offset 18	Number of sectors to be read (block device) or	1 word
	Number of characters to be read (character device)	
Offset 20	First sector to be read (block device only)	1 word
Returned parameters:		
Offset 3 (word)	Status word	1 word
Offset 18 (word)	Number of sectors read (block device) or	1 word
	Number of characters read (character device)	
Offset 22 (ptr)	Pointer to volume ID on return of error 0FH (Version 3.0 and higher)	1 ptr

Block drivers have different methods of passing the sector number. The methods used depends on whether the driver is a 16-bit or a 32-bit driver. For 16-bit drivers, the sector number is stored in the data block as a word starting at offset address 14H. For 32-bit drivers, it is a dword starting at offset address 1AH. A 32-bit driver refers to a driver that can handle devices and partitions larger than 32 megabytes. This is indicated by setting bit 1 in the driver attribute bit field. In addition to this, the sector number at offset address 14H is set to FFFFH for 32-bit drivers to indicate the use of the 32-bit sector number at 1AH.

Function 05H: Non-destructive Read

This function is used by a character device driver to test for unread characters in the input buffer. A block device should set the DONE flag of the status word and exit.

DOS tests for additional characters using this function. If more characters exist, the busy bit must be cleared (set to 0) and the next character passed to DOS. The character that is passed remains in the buffer so that a subsequent call to a read function will return this same character. If additional characters don't exist, the busy bit must be set (set to 1).

Address	Contents	Type
Input parameters:		
Offset 2	Function number (5)	1 byte
Returned parameters:		
Offset 3	Status word	1 word
Offset 13	The character read	1 byte

Function 06H: Input Status

This function is used to determine whether a character is waiting to be read from the input buffer of a character device. A block device driver should set the DONE flag of the status word and exit.

If a character is waiting to be read from the input buffer, the busy bit is cleared (set to 0). If a character isn't in the input buffer, the busy bit is set (set to 1).

When a character is waiting to be read, the Input Status function (06H) resets the status word busy bit to 0 and returns the character to DOS. The character isn't removed from the buffer and is therefore non-destructive. This function is equivalent to reading one character ahead.

Address	Contents	Type
Input parameters:		
Offset 2	Function number (6)	1 byte
Returned parameters:		
Offset 3	Status word: 0 = Characters already in buffer 1 = Read request to physical device	1 word

Function 07H: Flush Input Buffers

This function clears the internal input buffers of a character device driver. Any characters read but not yet passed to DOS are lost when this function is used. A block device driver should set the DONE flag of the status word and exit.

Address	Contents	Type
Input parameters:		
Offset 2	Function number (7)	1 byte
Returned parameters:		
Offset 3	Status word	1 word

Function 08H: Write

This function transfers characters from a buffer to the current device. If an error occurs during transmission, the status word is used to indicate this error. Both block and character devices use this function.

The parameters used for this function depend on whether the driver is for a character or block device. Both pass a buffer address, from which a certain number of characters should be transferred. A character device driver is passed the number of bytes to be transferred in addition to this information.

A block driver is passed the number of sectors to transfer (not the number of characters), the number of the device to be addressed, its media descriptor and the address of the first sector on the medium.

If an error occurs writing the data, the error status must be set. Also, the function must report the number of sectors or bytes written successfully. Simply reporting an error isn't sufficient.

Address	Contents	Type
Input parameters:		
Offset 1	Device number (block drivers only)	1 byte
Offset 2	Function number (8)	1 byte
Offset 13	Media descriptor of device addressed (block device only)	1 byte
Offset 14	Address of the buffer containing data	1 ptr
Offset 18	Number of sectors to be written (block device) or	1 word
	Number of characters to be written (character device)	
Offset 20	First sector to be written (block device only)	1 word
Returned parameters:		
Offset 3	Status word	1 word
Offset 18	Number of sectors written (block device) or	1 word
	Number of characters written (character device)	
Offset 22	Pointer to volume ID on return of error 0FH (Version 3.0 up)	1 ptr

Function 09H: Write with Verify

This function is similar to function 08H, except the characters written are reread and verified.

Some devices, especially character devices, such as a monitor or a printer, don't require verification because either no errors occur during transmission (monitor) or the data cannot be verified (printer).

Address	Contents	Type
Input parameters:		
Offset 1	Device number (block drivers only)	1 byte
Offset 2	Function number (09H)	1 byte
Offset 13	Media descriptor of device addressed (block device only)	1 byte
Offset 14	Address of the buffer containing data	1 ptr
Offset 18	Number of sectors to be written (block device) or	1 word
	Number of characters to be written (character device)	
Offset 20	First sector to be written (block device only)	1 word
Returned parameters:		
Offset 3	Status word	1 word
Offset 18	Number of sectors written (block device)	1 word
	Number of characters written (character device)	
Offset 22	Pointer to volume ID on return of error 0FH (Version 3.0 up)	1 ptr

Function 0AH: Output Status

This function indicates whether the last write operation to a character device is completed. A block device should set the DONE flag in the status word and exit.

If the last write operation is complete, then the busy bit of the status word is cleared; otherwise the busy bit is set to 1.

Address	Contents	Type
Input parameters:		
Offset 2	Function number (0AH)	1 byte
Returned parameters:		
Offset 3	Status word: BUSY bit = 1 if the last character output hasn't been completed	1 word

Function 0BH: Flush Output Buffers

This function completely clears the output buffer even if it contains characters waiting for output. A block device should set the DONE flag on the status word and exit.

Address	Contents	Type
Input parameters:		
Offset 2	Function number (0BH)	1 byte
Returned parameters:		
Offset 3	Status word	1 word

Function 0CH: I/O Control Write

This function passes control information from the application program to the character or block device driver. It can only be called through function 44H of interrupt 21H, if the IOCTL; bit in the device attribute word in the device driver header is set. Different parameters are passed to the function, depending on whether the driver is a character or a block device driver.

A character device driver is passed the number of characters to be written and the address of the buffer from which these characters are transferred.

A block device driver is passed the device number (in case the driver services logical devices), the media descriptor byte, the address of the buffer from which the data is to be written, the number of the first sector to be written and the number of sectors to be written.

A character device driver returns the number of bytes written. A block device driver returns the number of sectors written.

Addr.	Contents	Type
Input parameters:		
Offset 1	Device number (block device only)	1 byte
Offset 2	Function number (0CH)	1 byte
Offset 13	Media descriptor of addressed device (block device only)	1 byte
Offset 14	Address of buffer from which data should be read	1 ptr
Offset 18	Number of sectors to be written (block device) or	1 word
	Number of characters to be written (character device)	
Offset 20	First sector to be written (block device only)	1 word
Returned parameters:		
Offset 3	Status word	1 word
Offset 18	Number of sectors written (block device) or	1 word
	Number of characters written (character device)	

The following four functions are supported by DOS Version 3.0 and higher.

Function 0DH: Open

This function can be used only if the OCR (Open/Close/RM) bit in the device attribute word in the device driver header is set. Its task differs, depending on whether it's a character or block driver.

A block driver uses this function every time a file is opened. This function determines how many open files exist on this device. Use this command carefully, since programs that access FCB function calls usually don't close open files. This problem can be avoided by assuming, during every media change, that no files remain open. For devices with non-changeable media (e.g., a hard drive), even this procedure may not help.

Within a character driver, this function can send an initialization string to the device before transmitting the data. This is helpful when used to communicate with the printer. The initialization string shouldn't be included in the driver, but can be called, for example, with the IOCTL function of interrupt 21H, which calls function 0CH of a driver to transmit it from an application program to the driver. The function can also be useful because it can prevent two processes (in a network or in multiprocessing) from both accessing the same device.

This function isn't called for the devices CON, PRN and AUX because these functions are always open.

Address	Contents	Type
Input parameters:		
Offset 1	Device number (block device only)	1 byte
Offset 2	Function number (0DH)	1 byte
Returned parameters:		
Offset 3	Status word	1 word

Function 0EH: Device Close

This function is the opposite of function 0DH. This function can only be addressed if the OCR bit in the device attribute word of the device driver header is set. Its task differs, depending on whether it's a character or block driver.

A block driver calls it after closing a file. This can be used to decrement a count of open files. Once all files on a device are closed, the driver should flush the buffers on removable media devices, because it's likely the user is about to remove the media.

A character driver can use this function to send some closing control information to a device after completing output. For a printer, this could be a formfeed. As in function 0DH, the string could be transmitted from an application using the IOCTL function.

Address	Contents	Type
Input parameters:		
Offset 1	Device number (block device only)	1 byte
Offset 2	Function number (0EH)	1 byte
Returned parameters:		
Offset 3	Status word	1 word

Function 0FH: Removable Media

This function indicates whether the media in a block device can be changed. This function is used only if the OCR bit in the device attribute word of the device driver is set. A character device driver should set the DONE flag in the status word and exit. If the media can be removed, the busy bit is cleared; otherwise it is set to 1.

Address	Contents	Type
Input parameters:		
Offset 1	Device number (block device only)	1 byte
Offset 2	Function number (0FH)	1 byte
Returned parameters:		
Offset 3	Status word: If the media can be removed, the busy bit must contain the value 0	1 word

Function 10H: Output Until Busy

This function transfers data from a buffer to an output device until the device is busy (i.e., can no longer accept more characters). Since this function is supported by character devices, a block device driver should set the DONE flag on the status word and exit.

This function works particularly well with print spoolers, through which files can be sent to a printer as a background activity while a program executes in the foreground. It's possible that not all the characters in the transfer request will be sent to a device during this function call. This usually isn't an error; it could be the result of the device becoming busy. The function is passed the number of characters to be transmitted as well as the buffer address. If, during transmission, the output device indicates that it can no longer accept additional characters, it indicates the number of characters successfully transferred and returns control to the device driver.

Address	Contents	Type
Input parameters:		
Offset 2	Function number (10H)	1 byte
Offset 14	Address of buffer from which data should be read	1 ptr
Offset 18	Number of characters to be read	1 word
Returned parameters:		
Offset 3	Status word	1 word
Offset 18	Number of characters written	1 word

The following functions are supported by DOS Version 4.0 and higher.

Function 17H: Get Logical Device

This optional function can only be used with block drivers. If a block driver contains this function, bit 6 of the device attribute bit field must be set so that DOS will know it's available. This function is only useful in conjunction with the DOS device driver DRIVER.SYS, which enables a diskette drive to use two different formats. This function is used to tell the caller which of the two formats is currently in use.

The device code isn't required as a parameter for this function. By definition, only one driver with a switchable disk drive is allowed within a system.

Address	Contents	Type
Input parameters:		
Offset 0	Number of bytes requested	1 byte
Offset 1	Device number (block devices only)	1 byte
Offset 2	Function number (17H)	1 byte
Returned parameters:		
Offset 3	Status word	1 word

Function 18H: Set Logical Device

This function is the opposite of function 17H. DOS uses it to tell the device driver the diskette drive it manages has another drive letter that can be addressed with a different diskette format.

Address	Contents	Type
Input parameters:		
Offset 0	Number of bytes requested	1 byte
Offset 1	Device number (block devices)	1 byte
Offset 2	Function number (18H)	1 byte
Returned parameters:		
Offset 3	Status word	1 word

Clock Drivers

The clock driver is a character device driver whose only function is to pass the date and time from DOS to an application. The clock driver can also have a different name (such as $CLOCK). This is possible because DOS identifies it by the fact that bit 2 in the device attribute word of the device driver header is set to 1, instead of by name. Bit 15 must also be set since the clock driver is a character device driver. Functions 2AH to 2DH of DOS interrupt 21H read the date and time and call the driver. A clock driver must support only functions 4, 8 and 0 (initialization). During the call of function 4 (reading), the date and time pass from the driver to DOS. DOS can set a new date and time with function 8. Both functions have the time and date passed in a buffer that is 6 bytes long.

The date format is unusual. Instead of passing the month, day and year separately, DOS passes the number of days elapsed since January 1, 1980 as a 16-bit number. A fairly complex formula converts this number into normal date format, taking leap years into account. The clock driver normally uses function 0 and 1 of the BIOS interrupt 1AH to read and set the time.

Clocks on AT models

AT and AT-compatible computers have a battery powered realtime clock. Functions 0 and 1 of interrupt 1AH use a software controlled time counter instead of the battery powered realtime clock. When the computer is rebooted, the date and time previously set with driver function 8 is cleared. You can use the clock driver to access the realtime clock using functions 2 and 5 of interrupt 1AH instead of function 0 and 1.

Passing date and time to a clock driver		
Address	Contents	Type
+ OOH	Number of days since January 1, 1980	1 word
+ O2H	Minutes	1 byte
+ O3H	Hour	1 byte
+ O4H	Hundredths of seconds	1 byte
+ O5H	Seconds	1 byte
Length: 6 bytes		

Device Driver Calls From DOS

Now that you're familiar with the functions of the different device drivers, you can develop your own personal device driver. The following steps are performed before and after calling a device driver function.

A chain of events begins when a DOS function, which handles input and output, is called using interrupt 21H. Calling one of these functions can, in turn, call a series of other functions and corresponding read and write operations.

Open

One example of this is when the Open function 3DH is called to open a file in a subdirectory. Before it can be opened, DOS must find the file. This may require a search of a set of directories instead of simply reading in the FAT. During each access of interrupt 21H, DOS determines which of the available device drivers should be used to read or write characters. When this happens, DOS sets aside an area in memory to store the information required by the device driver.

For files, DOS must convert the number of records to be processed into logical sector numbers. DOS then calls the strategy routine of the device driver, to which it passes the address of the newly created data block (request header). Then the interrupt routine of the driver, which stores all registers, is called. It isolates the function code of the requested function from the data block and starts to process the function.

If the addressed driver is a character device driver, the function only has to send the characters to the hardware or request the characters to be read.

Block devices

For a block device (e.g., a mass storage device such as a floppy or hard disk), the logical sector number must be converted into a physical address before a read or write access. The logical sector number is divided into a head, track and physical sector number.

After the read or write operation ends, the driver function must place a result code in the status field of the request header to be returned to the calling DOS function. Next, the contents of all registers are restored and control is returned to the calling DOS function, which, depending on the result of the driver function, sets or resets the carry flag and places any error code into the AX register. The interrupt function then returns control to the routine that called interrupt 21H.

Direct Device Driver Access: IOCTL

Now we'll discuss IOCTL in detail, because it offers an alternate method of communicating with the device driver. You can only use these functions if the IOCTL bit (bit 14) of the device attribute is set.

The IOCTL function itself is one of many functions addressable from DOS interrupt 21H. Its function number is 44H. Three groups of subfunctions are accessible:

> Device configuration

> Data transmission

> Driver status

The number of the desired subfunction is passed to the IOCTL function in the AL register. After the function call, the carry flag indicates whether the function executed correctly. A set carry flag indicates that an error occurred and the error code is located in the AX register.

Character device drivers status

The number of the desired subfunction is passed to the IOCTL function in the AL register. After the function call, the carry flag indicates whether the function executed correctly. A set carry flag indicates that an error occurred and the error code is located in the AX register.

Subfunctions 06H and 07H can determine the status of a character device driver. Subfunction 6 can determine if the device is able to receive data. Subfunction 7 can determine if the device can send data. The handle of this device is passed in the BX register.

If the device is ready, both functions 06H and 07H return the value FFH in the AL register.

Subfunction 02H reads control data from the character device driver. The handle is passed in the BX register and the number of bytes to be read is passed in the CX register. Also, the DS:DX register pair contain the address of the buffer into which the data will be read. If the carry flag is clear, then the function was successful and the AX register contains the number of characters read. If the carry flag is set, then there was an error and the AX register contains the error code.

Subfunction 03H writes control information from a buffer to the character device driver. Again, the handle is passed in the BX register, the number of bytes to be written in the CX register and the address of the buffer in the DS:DX register pair. The return codes are the same as for subfunction 02H. These two subfunctions are used to pass information between the application program and the device driver.

Block device driver status

Subfunctions 04H and 05H have the same task as subfunctions 2 and 3. However, they are used for block devices instead of character devices. Instead of passing the handle in register BX, you pass the drive code (0=A, 1=B, etc.) in the BL register.

Subfunction 0 is used to obtain device information for a specified handle. The subfunction number is passed in the AL register and the handle in the BX register. The function returns the device information word in the DX register.

For block devices:		For character devices:	
Bit(s)	Function	Bit(s)	Function
8-15	Reserved	15	Reserved
7	0 if a block device	14	1 if device supports IOCTL subfunctions
6	0 if file has been written		0 if device does not support IOCTL subfunctions
	1 if file has not been written	8-13	reserved
0-5	Drive code (0=A, B=1, etc.)	7	If a character device
		6	0 if end of file for input device
		5	0 if cooked mode
			1 if raw mode
		4	Reserved
		3	1 if clock device
		2	1 if NUL device
		1	1 if standard output device
		0	1 if standard input device

Cooked and raw modes

Subfunction 01H is used to set device information for a specified handle. This subfunction is often used to set the standard input device from cooked mode to raw mode or back.

Two final interrupts are sometimes used by block device drivers. These two interrupts, 25H and 26H, are used to read from and write to the disk drive. You can use these interrupts, for example, to process disks that were formatted using a "foreign" operating system.

The device number is passed in the AL register, the number of sectors to be transferred is passed in the CX register, the starting sector number to be transferred is passed in the DX register and the buffer is passed in the DS:BX register pair. The carry flag is clear if no errors occurred. If the carry flag is set, then the error code is returned in the AX register.

Starting with DOS 4.0, the operation of these two interrupts had to be changed because the 16-bit sector number in the DX register can only be used to address 65,535 sectors, which does not allow access beyond the 32 megabyte limit. Starting with

DOS 4.0, these interrupts are passed a pointer to a data block in the DS:BX register pair(see the illustration below). This allows access to larger volumes and partitions.

Also, the value -1 (FFFFH) must be passed in the CX register. This informs DOS the new parameters are being used and that it shouldn't search for parameters according to the old scheme. The old scheme can still be used for volumes larger than 32 megabytes as long as only sectors below the 32 megabyte limit are addressed.

Tips On Developing Device Drivers

When you're developing a device driver, problems occur when you test the new driver. First, a device driver must load into a memory location assigned to it by DOS, at an address unknown to the programmer. Also, a newly developed CON driver can't be tested using the DEBUG program, because DEBUG uses this driver for character input and output.

After you write the actual driver, you should write a short test program that calls the individual functions in the same way as DOS, but without having the driver installed as part of DOS. By doing this, everything executes under user control and the entire process can be corrected with a debugger. Remember, a new device driver (especially a block device driver) should be linked into the system only after it's been tested completely and proven to be error-free.

> **NOTE**
>
> When working with a hard drive, prepare a floppy system diskette before test booting the system from the hard drive with the new driver installed for the first time. If a small bug should exist in the new driver and the initialization routine hangs up, the booting process will not end and DOS will be out of control. In such a case, the only remedy is to reset the system and boot with a DOS diskette in the floppy disk drive. Once DOS loads, you can then access the hard drive and remove the new driver.

Driver Examples

This section describes a sample device driver for each of the three types of device drivers. This sample demonstrates the information you've read so far. We'll talk about an alternative console driver, a 160K RAM disk and a driver for a battery operated AT clock.

All these drivers must follow the same rules set for a COM program. They must comprise a single segment containing program code and driver data. No direct segment references can exist. Unlike a COM program, the device driver must begin at offset 0H (not 100H), because a PSP cannot exist in memory.

The first program is a character driver that corresponds exactly to the format of a normal console driver. The second program is a block device driver, which creates a 160K RAM disk. The final program is a DOS clock driver to support an AT computer realtime clock.

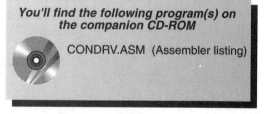

You'll find the following program(s) on the companion CD-ROM

CONDRV.ASM (Assembler listing)

The header of this driver describes a character device driver that handles both the standard input device (keyboard) and the standard output device (monitor). After linking it into the system, setting the two bits in the device attribute calls this driver on all function calls previously handled by the CON driver. Like any other driver, this driver has a strategy routine and an interrupt routine. The strategy routine stores the address of the data block in the variable DB_PTR.

The interrupt routine saves the contents of all registers that will be changed by it on the stack and obtains the routine number to be called from the data block. It then checks whether CONDRV supports this function. If it doesn't, it jumps directly to the end of the interrupt routine and sets the proper error code in the status field of the request header that was passed to the routine. Then it restores the registers that were saved on the stack and returns control to the calling DOS function.

For any of the functions that are supported by the device driver, the offset address of a routine to handle a particular function is determined from the table labeled FCT_TAB. Notice the routines named DUMMY and NO_SUP appear several times. DUMMY is for all functions that apply only to block device drives and, therefore, aren't used in this driver. The DUMMY routine clears the AX register and sets the BUSY bit in the status word. The NO_SUP routine handles any functions that cannot be used since the drive attribute for CONDRV doesn't support these functions.

The STORE_C routine can be accessed from the lower level routines in this driver. Its purpose is to store a character in the internal keyboard buffer of the driver. The driver really shouldn't have this buffer available since BIOS (whose functions are used by the driver to read characters from the keyboard) also has this type of buffer. The problem is the BIOS always returns two characters when pressing a key with extended codes (cursor keys, function keys, etc.). If the higher level functions of DOS only ask for one character at a time from CONDRV, the second character shouldn't be lost. Instead, it should be stored in a buffer and delivered to DOS by the read function on the next call. This is STORE_C's task.

Reading characters

The next routine is the READ function. It obtains the number of characters to be read from the request header passed by DOS. If it is 0, the routine is terminated immediately. If it isn't 0, then a loop, which executes once for every character read, starts. It first tests for characters still stored in the internal keyboard buffer. If characters are found, a character is passed to the buffer of the calling function. If an additional character exists in the keyboard buffer, function 0 of the BIOS keyboard interrupt 16H inputs a character from the keyboard. This character is also passed to the internal keyboard buffer. If it's an extended keycode, it's divided into two characters. The next step removes a character from the internal keyboard buffer and passes the character to the buffer of the calling function. The process repeats until all characters requested have been passed to DOS. Then the routine ends.

The higher level DOS functions also call the function named READ_P. It tests whether a character was entered from the keyboard. If not, it sets the BUSY bit in the status field of the request header passed by DOS and returns to the calling function. If a character was entered without having been read, the driver reads this character and passes it to the calling DOS function in the request header and resets the busy bit. The character remains in the keyboard buffer and on a subsequent call the read function, it's again passed to DOS. To test the availability of a character, the READ_P function uses function 1 of the BIOS keyboard interrupt 16H.

The function DEL_IN_B is also called by the higher level DOS functions. DEL_IN_B deletes the contents of the keyboard buffer. It removes characters from the buffer using function 0 of the BIOS keyboard interrupt until function 1 indicates that no more characters are available. This ends the function and it returns to the calling function after the BUSY bit is reset.

Writing characters

WRITE takes the number of characters from a buffer passed by DOS and displays the characters on the screen. This routine uses function 0EH of the BIOS video interrupt. Once all characters have been displayed, it sets the BUSY bit in the status field and ends the function. This function also executes when the higher level DOS functions call the Write and Verify functions.

Initialization

The last function, which is the initialization routine, is called first by DOS. Since CONDRV doesn't initialize variables and hardware, the routine simply enters the driver's ending address into the passed request header. The routine returns its own starting address since it will never be called again and is the end of the chain of drivers.

In its current form, the driver isn't very useful because it uses only those functions already available to the CON driver of DOS. It would be more practical if an enhanced driver, such as ANSI.SYS, was developed. An enhanced driver provides more control over the screen design. For example, it's possible that such a driver would have complete windowing capability, which could be accessed from any program, in any programming language.

The RAMDISK.ASM block device driver which you'll find on the companion CD-ROM creates a 160K RAM disk.

This driver is similar to the CONDRV driver. The biggest difference between the two lies in the functions that each supports.

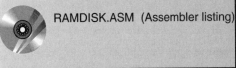

You'll find the following program(s) on the companion CD-ROM

RAMDISK.ASM (Assembler listing)

First, this routine finds the DOS version number using function 30H. If the version number is equal to or greater than 3, the request header passed by DOS contains the device designation of the RAM disk. The system reads the designation, changes it to a character and places the character into the installation message. DOS function 09H- is used to display this message on the screen.

Next, the program computes the ending address of the RAM disk. Since the actual data area of the RAM disk starts immediately after the last routine of this driver, 160K is added to the program's ending address. Also, the address of a variable (BPB_PTR) containing the address of the BIOS parameter block is passed to DOS. This variable describes the RAM disk's format. In this case, it tells DOS the RAM disk uses 512 bytes per sector. Each cluster consists of one sector and only one reserved sector (the boot sector) exists. In addition, only one FAT exists. Additional information indicates that a maximum of 64 entries can be made in the root directory and the RAM disk has 320 sectors available (160K of memory). The FAT occupies a single sector and the media descriptor byte FEH designates a diskette with one side and 40 tracks of 8 sectors each.

These parameters are then placed into the request header of DOS and the segment address of the data area of the RAM disk is calculated. (This information is needed by the driver itself instead of by DOS.)

The INIT routine

The RAM disk must now be formatted to create a boot sector, FAT and a root directory. Since these data structures are in the first sectors of the RAM disk, a normal INIT routine (which releases its memory to DOS), would overwrite itself with these data structures and would crash the system. This is why the initialization routine isn't at the end of the last routine of the driver, which would place it at the beginning of the RAM disk's data area.

The boot sector occupies the entire first sector of the RAM disk. However, only the first 15 words are copied into it because this is all DOS needs. The name "boot sector" is actually a misnomer here, because it's impossible to boot a system from a RAM disk.

The second sector of the RAM disk contains the FAT. The first two entries are the media descriptor byte and 0 in the subsequent entries. These zeros indicate unoccupied clusters (an empty RAM disk).

The last data structure is the root directory. It contains only the volume name.

Remaining routines

This concludes the work of the initialization routine and returns the system to the calling function. The remaining driver routines are explained in the order in which they appear.

The DUMMY routine performs the same task as the routine of the same name in the CONDRV driver.

The MED_TEST routine is found only in block device drivers. This routine informs DOS whether the medium was changed.

The next routine, GET_BPB, simply passes the addresses of the variables, which contain the address of the BPB of the RAM disk, to DOS, as the initialization routine had already done.

NO_REM allows DOS to sense whether the medium (the RAM disk) can be changed. You cannot change a RAM disk, so the program sets the BUSY bit in the status field.

The two most important functions of the driver perform read and write operations. As in CONDRV, the program calls Write and Verify instead of the normal Write function, since a data error cannot occur during RAM access. The routine itself does very little; it loads the value 0 into the BP register and jumps to the MOVE routine. The READ routine performs in a similar way, except that it loads a 1 into the BP register.

MOVE itself is an elementary routine for moving data. The BP register signals whether data is to move from the RAM disk to DOS or in the opposite direction. The routine receives all other data (the DOS buffer's address, the number of the sectors to be transferred and the first sector to be transferred) from the data block passed by DOS. See the comments in the MOVE routine for details of the procedure.

Changes

Obviously, this RAM disk can be enhanced. If you have enough unused memory, you can extend the size of the RAM disk to 360K. AT owners could make the RAM disk resident beyond the 1 megabyte boundary. In this case, the data transfer between DOS and the RAM disk would use function 87H of interrupt 15H.

The clock driver

This final sample driver directly accesses the battery powered clock of an AT computer. It's useful because when the DOS commands DATE and TIME are used, the date and time are passed directly to the battery powered realtime clock. Reading the date and time reads the information directly from the memory locations of the realtime clock.

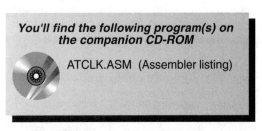

You'll find the following program(s) on the companion CD-ROM

ATCLK.ASM (Assembler listing)

The basic structure of this driver differs from the other drivers because it calls the individual functions directly, instead of through a table of their addresses. Since it only supports functions 00H, 04H and 08H, this driver can test the function numbers directly passed by DOS. If any other function occurs, it signals an error. Besides the INIT routine, which sets only the ending address of the driver like CONDRV, the driver also contains the Read Time and Date and Write Time and Date functions.

Time routine

The TIME routine is fairly simple. For reading the clock, the routine reads the time from the memory locations of the clock, converts the time from BCD to binary format and then passes the time to the DOS buffer. For setting the time, the reverse occurs: The routine reads the time from the DOS buffer, converts the code from binary to BCD format and writes the BCD code into the memory locations of the clock.

DOS uses the same format for indicating time as the clock: Hour, minute and seconds, each comprise one byte.

Date routine

The DATE routine is more complicated. While the clock stores day, month and year as one byte each, DOS encodes the date according to the number of days since January 1, 1980. This number must be converted into a date in the form of day, month and year as DOS writes the time and date. The opposite occurs when you call the Read function; the clock date must be converted into the number of days. Let's discuss how this is done.

The conversion routine begins with the year 1980. January 1, 1980 (called NUMDAYS from this point on) is equal to the value 0. The routine tests whether this year is less than the current year. If it is, the routine adds the number of days in this year to NUMDAYS, adding a day to compensate for each leap year. Then it increments the year and tests again for a smaller number than the current year. This loop repeats until it reaches the current year. The routine then computes the number of days in the current year's month of February and enters this month into a table that contains the number of days for each month.

In the next step, for every month less than the current month, the routine adds the number of days in this month to NUMDAYS. Once it reaches the current month, only the current days of the month are added to NUMDAYS. The end result is transferred to the DOS buffer and the routine terminates.

Converting to date format

Reverse this process to convert NUMDAYS into a date. The routine begins with the year 1980 and tests whether the number of days in this year is less than or equal to NUMDAYS. If this is the case, the year is incremented and the number of days in this year is subtracted from NUMDAYS. This loop is repeated until the number of days in a year is larger than NUMDAYS. The routine then computes the number of days in the current year's month of February and enters this month into the table of the months.

January starts another loop, which tests whether the number of days in the current month is less than or equal to NUMDAYS. If this is the case, the month increments and the routine subtracts the number of days from NUMDAYS. If the number of days in a month is larger than NUMDAYS, the loop ends. NUMDAYS must only be incremented enough to give the day of the month and complete the date.

The routine then converts the date to BCD format and enters the date in the memory locations of the clock.

EXE Programs As Device Drivers

Over the past few years, more device drivers have been developed as EXE files. This means that you can either install the driver from a DEVICE = command in your CONFIG.SYS file or you could install it directly from the DOS system prompt or a batch file. Even DOS has started to use this kind of device driver. The EMM386.EXE driver available in DOS Version 5.0 is an example of this type of device driver.

These programs aren't true device drivers. Actually they are TSR programs that function as device drivers. Like other driver programs, they can be installed with the CONFIG.SYS file when the system boots, so they don't have to compete for memory with other TSR programs.

These TSR drivers are character device drivers, which means that DOS doesn't assign drive letters to them. Their names are selected so they won't be confused with other files (e.g., EMMXXX0 for EMS drivers). Also, since they aren't intended to replace normal device drivers, they can only use one driver function (function 00H for initialization). This function must be supported so that DOS can properly install the TSR program as a driver.

Since you can't determine whether one of the other driver functions might be called, such a function call should be indicated as an error from the status flag.

The EXESYS.ASM demonstration program shows how this works. This program was written to be installed as a device driver or called as a normal EXE file. DOS isn't restricted to the ".SYS" file extension for device drivers, even though most driver program files use it. DOS can load any EXE file as a device driver, as long as it consists of only one segment and starts at address 00H in this segment with the standard driver header.

This can be done easily by including the following instruction at the start of the segment:

```
org 0h
```

The driver header follows this instruction. When the driver is installed, DOS will then be able to obtain the offset addresses of the strategy and interrupt routines and call them as with any other driver.

To run the program from the DOS command line, it must also have an entry point just like any other EXE file. This is easily done by inserting the name of a special initialization procedure (as would be found in a normal EXE program) after the END instruction at the end of the assembly language listing.

This way, the program will also be able to determine whether it was started as a device driver from CONFIG.SYS or from the DOS system prompt. The initialization procedure will only be called if the program is started from the command line. DOS will call the strategy and interrupt routines if the program is started from CONFIG.SYS.

But once you've installed a TSR program as a driver, why would you want to recall it? Doing this allows you to pass information to the driver by using command line parameters. This can easily be done with the IOCTL functions (DOS function 44H).

The EXESYS.ASM demonstration program contains all the basics for developing a driver that can be installed from CONFIG.SYS or called from the system prompt. This particular driver simply displays a message that indicates which method was used to start it. You can easily modify this program to perform more complicated driver operations.

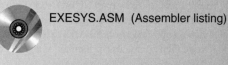

You'll find the following program(s) on the companion CD-ROM

EXESYS.ASM (Assembler listing)

CD-ROMs

After its introduction in the audio world, the compact disk was introduced to the PC market. A CD-ROM drive and a PC form an interesting combination. The compact disk (CD) medium itself is read-only, but 660 megabytes of data can be stored in the form of text, graphics, etc.

Many publications and references are currently available on CD-ROM, such as:

> Telephone directories

> Books in Print

> The Bible in various translations

> The English translation of Pravda

In addition, maps, photographic libraries, public domain program collections and medical databases are available in CD-ROM format. New titles are being published daily in this growing market.

Why CD-ROM?

The CD-ROM has a clear advantage over the printed medium. Once captured and digitized, information can be processed by a computer in whatever form the user needs. The possibilities appear to be limitless, considering how easy it is to read and compare information.

Another important advantage of CD-ROM is how easily data can be accessed. The user simply loads the driver software, presses a key or two and the information is displayed on the screen.

Currently, you can buy a PC-compatible CD-ROM player for $100 to 300. These players are available as either external or internal devices.

Interfacing

The PC's hardware can be easily interfaced to a CD-ROM player. However, the software may encounter some problems. This is understandable, since DOS was never intended to support these devices. In this section we'll show you how a CD-ROM drive, using the proper drivers and utility programs, can be accessed like a read-only floppy disk drive.

We've mentioned the device drivers act as mediators between the disk operating system and the external devices, such as monitor, printer, disk drives and hard disks. DOS differentiates between block device drivers and character device drivers. As a mass storage device capable of reading information in a block mode, a CD-ROM drive would normally be added to the rest of the system through a block driver. Here's where the problem begins: DOS makes a number of assumptions about block devices, but a CD-ROM drive cannot meet this criteria.

Memory limitations

In versions of DOS up to and including Version 3.3, the biggest obstacle to interfacing with a block driver was the 32 megabyte limit imposed on every volume designated as a block device. The second biggest obstacle is the lack of a file allocation table (FAT) on a CD-ROM. Instead of the FAT, the CD-ROM contains a form of data table into which the starting addresses of the various subdirectories and files are recorded. However, DOS still requires a FAT that it can read during driver initialization.

A character device driver works better for implementing a CD-ROM device driver because DOS doesn't make assumptions about the structure of the devices connected through character drivers. However, even character drivers have problems communicating with a CD-ROM drive, because they transmit characters one at a time instead of in groups of characters. Another disadvantage is the need for a name (e.g., CON) instead of a device designation. DOS must first see the CD-ROM driver as a character driver to DOS to prevent read accesses to a non-existent FAT. The CONFIG.SYS file supplies the name of the device during the system booting process.

Configuring the CD-ROM

The manufacturer usually includes CD-ROM driver software with the CD-ROM drive package. A driver of this type usually has a name such as SONY.SYS or HITACHI.SYS, depending on the manufacturer.

The CONFIG.SYS sequence that installs this driver can look something like this:

```
DEVICE=HITACHI.SYS /D:CDR1
```

The device driver selects the name CDR1 as the name of the CD-ROM drive.

After executing the initialization routine from DOS, the CD-ROM is treated as a block driver that has been enhanced with a few special functions supporting CD-ROMs. However, DOS still views the CD-ROM player as a character driver: DOS cannot view the CD-ROM's directory, nor can it directly access the files on the CD-ROM.

Driver software extensions

To overcome this obstacle, many CD-ROM players include a TSR (Terminate and Stay Resident) program, named MSCDEX (Microsoft CD-ROM Extension), in addition to the device driver software. This program must be called from within the AUTOEXEC.BAT file. The name of the CD driver can be passed to the program from the DOS prompt, as shown in the following example:

```
MSCDEX /D:CDR1
```

MSCDEX first opens this driver through the DOS OPEN function and provides it with a device designation. DOS assumes that MSCDEX is a device on a remote network, as supported by DOS in Version 3.1.

MSCDEX brings us closer to the solution, since DOS handles network devices as files containing more than 32 megabytes. These devices are accessed through redirection, rather than direct access from DOS. The resident portion of MSCDEX interfaces to the redirector and intercepts all calls to the redirector. If MSCDEX receives a call addressed to the CD-ROM drive, it adapts each instruction to a call applicable to the CD-ROM driver. This makes a perfect connection between DOS and the CD-ROM drive, while still allowing access to subdirectories and files at any time.

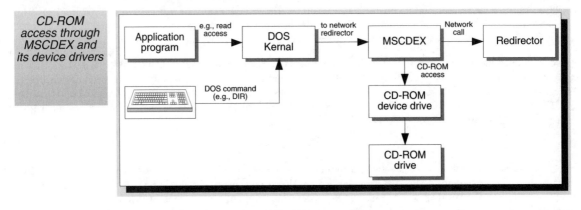

CD-ROM access through MSCDEX and its device drivers

Chapter 28

The DOS File System

The user doesn't see many of the tasks that DOS performs. This is why some users underestimate the complexity of DOS. For example, DOS requires many data structures for handling a mass storage device, although this is not always realized by the user. The file system must perform many steps before executing even small tasks, such as copying files or searching for a file on the hard drive.

Disk drives recognize tracks, sectors, and read/write heads instead of files and subdirectories. Therefore, DOS's file system addresses all available mass storage devices at both physical and logical levels. A file system of this type consists of a series of data structures, which describe the capacity and contents of a disk drive. In this chapter we'll discuss how the DOS file system is designed and how it works.

Basic Structure Of The File System

The volume is the basis of the DOS file system. From the user's viewpoint, DOS addresses mass storage devices as volumes. Each individual volume is assigned a letter. Floppy disk drives are identified by the letters A and B, while the letters C or D usually identify a hard drive. Although a hard drive can be divided into multiple volumes, a floppy disk drive can consist of only one volume.

DOS Versions 3.3 and lower limited volume size to a maximum of 32 megabytes. Therefore, any hard drives with capacities over 32 megabytes were divided into multiple volumes. In this chapter we explain how DOS Version 4.0 broke the 32 megabyte barrier.

Every DOS volume has its own structure, regardless of whether it's intended for diskettes or hard media. The size of the storage media isn't relevant to the structure because it only affects the number of individual data structures required to manage the volume.

Volume label names

Although not required, each volume can be assigned a vVolume label name when created. The DIR command lists volume label names when they're available. Each volume has its own root directory, which can contain multiple subdirectories and files. These subdirectories and files can be maintained and manipulated by using one or more of the interrupt 21H functions.

Sectors

DOS subdivides each volume into a series of sectors organized sequentially. Each sector contains a specific number of bytes (usually 512) and is assigned a consecutive logical sector number, beginning with sector 0. A 10 megabyte volume contains 20,480 sectors, consisting of logical sectors 0 to 20,479. DOS cannot control the physical arrangement of the sectors. This is controlled by the device driver, which mediates between the volume and DOS. The device driver's distribution of logical sectors (organized or not) is unimportant. It's only important the device driver clearly differentiates between logical and physical sectors.

Since DOS API function calls with interrupt 21H are directed to files instead of individual sectors, DOS converts these file accesses into sector accesses. To do this, DOS uses the volume's directory structure and a data structure known as the FAT (File Allocation Table).

The following table shows the basic structure of a mass storage device:

Mass storage devioce structure		
Sector number →	0	Manufacturer's name, device driver, boot routine
		First file allocation table (FAT)
		One or more copies of FAT
		Root directory with volume label names
		Data register for files and subdirectories

As we mentioned, every volume is divided into areas containing the various DOS data structures and individual files. The FORMAT command creates these data structures when you format a disk. Since the size of the individual areas can differ depending on the type of mass storage device (and the manufacturer), every volume contains a boot sector.

The Boot Sector

The boot sector contains all the information required to access the different areas and data structures. DOS creates this sector during disk formatting. Boot sectors always have the same structure and are always located in sector 0 so DOS can find and interpret it properly.

The following table on the right lists the layout of the boot sector.

The term "boot sector" is used because DOS "boots" (i.e., starts) from this sector. Since DOS usually isn't stored in permanent PC memory (ROM), it's loaded and started from disk. After you switch on the computer, the BIOS takes over system initialization. It loads physical sector 0 (not logical sector 0) of the floppy disk or hard drive into memory. Since device drivers aren't in memory, the BIOS checks physical sector 0 for information. It then loads the boot information from that sector. Once it completes its work, the BIOS starts execution at address 0.

The boot sector always contains an assembly language JUMP instruction at address 00H. Execution of the boot sector's program code begins at this address. After execution, the program continues at a location further into the boot sector. This instruction can be either a normal jump instruction or a "short jump." The field for this jump instruction is 3 bytes long, but a "short jump" only requires 2 bytes. Therefore, a NOP (No Operation) instruction always follows the "short jump" to fill in the extra byte. As its name suggests, this NOP instruction doesn't do anything.

Boot sector layout		
Address	Contents	Type
00H	Jump to boot routine (E9xxx or EBxx90)	3 bytes
03H	Manufacturer's name and version number	8 bytes
0BH	Bytes per sector	1 word
0DH	Sectors per cluster	1 byte
0EH	Number of reserved sectors	1 word
10H	Number of FATs	1 byte
11H	Number of entries in root directory	1 word
13H	Number of sectors in volume	1 word
15H	Media descriptor	1 byte
16H	Number of sectors per FAT	1 word
18H	Sectors per track	1 word
1AH	Number of read/write heads	1 word
1CH	Number of hidden sectors	1 word
1EH-1FFH	BOOT ROUTINE	

A series of fields, which contain certain information about the organization of the media, follow. The first field is 8 bytes long and contains the manufacturer's name, where the medium was formatted, as well as the DOS version number that performed the formatting. The field may also contain the name of a software manufacturer (e.g., if a program such as PCTools formatted the volume).

The next fields contain the physical format of the media (i.e., the number of bytes per sector, the number of sectors per track, etc.) and the size of the DOS data structures stored on the medium. The physical device information is needed when using the interrupt 13H BIOS functions. These fields are called the BIOS parameter block (BPB). DOS uses this information for various tasks.

> **NOTE**
>
> Some sources of undocumented DOS structures state the BPB is a parameter table, which can be accessed by using Get Service Data, instead of part of the boot sector. These sources imply the boot sector information is only part of the BPB.

Three additional fields, providing other volume information to the device driver, follow the BPB. However, these fields aren't used directly by DOS.

Bootstrap

Next is the bootstrap routine, to which the jump instruction branches at the beginning of this boot sector. This routine handles the loading and starting of DOS through the individual system components (see Chapter 3).

Several reserved sectors may follow the boot sector. These sectors can contain additional bootstrap code. The numbers of these sectors are recorded in the BPB in the field starting at offset address 0EH. This field terminates the boot sector; a 1 in this field indicates that additional reserved sectors don't follow the boot sector. This applies to most PCs, because no versions of DOS have required a bootstrap loader that cannot fit into the first boot sector.

The File Allocation Table (FAT)

DOS must know which sectors of the volume are still available before it can add new files or enlarge existing files. This information is contained in a data structure called the FAT (File Allocation Table), located immediately next to the media's reserved area. Each entry in the FAT corresponds to a certain number of logically contiguous sectors called clusters, on the media. Location 0DH of the boot sector specifies the number of sectors per cluster as part of the BIOS Parameter Block. Only powers of 2 (1, 2, 4, 8, etc.) are acceptable values. On an XT hard drive, this location contains the value 8 (8 consecutive sectors form a cluster). AT, 386, and 486 hard drives have only 4 sectors per cluster.

As the table on the right shows, the number of sectors comprising a cluster depends on the storage medium:

Despite the values in the previous table, a formatting utility, such as FORMAT, isn't limited to these cluster values. This applies particularly to volumes containing more than 32 megabytes. DOS Versions 4.0 and higher accommodate larger volumes by adding clusters. A volume larger than 32 megabytes quickly exceeds the 65,536 limit for clusters. So, the capacity of the file system can be extended at will, without changing the current structure, by including more sectors per cluster.

The following table (lower right) shows the clustering used by DOS Version 4.0 for volumes larger than 32 megabytes and up to 2 gigabytes.

This clustering allocates more memory to the last cluster of a file. This cluster is filled only when its size represents a multiple of the cluster size.

Sectors per cluster	
Device	Sectors per cluster
Single sided disk drive	1
Double sided disk drive	2
AT hard drive	4
XT hard drive	8

Volume and Cluster sizes of DOS 4.0					
Volume size (megabytes)	128	256	8K	16K	32K
Cluster size		2K	4K	8K	16K	32K
Sectors per cluster		4	8	16	32	64

File fragmentation

The idea of joining several sectors into a cluster is based on the logic used by DOS to write files to a medium. Instead of selecting adjoining sectors for file storage, DOS fragments (disassembles) the file so the various pieces can fit into the available sectors.

The following explains the reasons why DOS fragments the file. Users are constantly creating and deleting files. If you start with an empty volume, new files and their respective clusters are stored in sequence. However, when you delete a file, a gap may develop between two sectors. DOS doesn't adjust the clusters on a volume because this process requires too much time. This is especially true for larger volumes. So, DOS places new files in the gaps created when the older files were deleted. If the entire file could be stored in one of these gaps, it could be kept in one contiguous unit. However, this usually doesn't happen. As a result, DOS divides files and fits them into available gaps.

This process slows file access because the read/write head must be repositioned after almost every read function. To avoid an excessive disassembly of the file, DOS gathers several sequential sectors on the media into a cluster. This ensures that at least the sectors of a cluster contain a portion of a file. If DOS didn't use clusters, a file of 24 sectors could be stored in numerous sectors, which would require the read/write head to be positioned a maximum of 24 times to read the entire file. The cluster principle saves a lot of time, since a file comprised of 4 sectors per cluster is stored in 6 clusters and the read/write head must be repositioned only 6 times.

However, there is a problem with this process. Since a file is assigned at least one cluster, some storage space is wasted. Consider the AUTOEXEC.BAT file, which is usually no longer than 150 bytes. Normally, this file could be stored on a single sector (and still waste almost 400 bytes). However, AUTOEXEC.BAT occupies a cluster of 2048 bytes on an AT, which wastes more than 1.5K of hard drive space.

Disk optimizing programs, such as BeckerTools Disk Optimizer or DEFRAG in MS-DOS 6.x, solve this problem by re-organizing the medium and storing all the files in consecutive clusters.

The FAT layout

Now let's return to the file allocation table. The size of individual entries in the FAT under DOS Versions 1.0 and 2.0 is 12 bits. For DOS Versions 3.0 and up, the size of an entry in the FAT depends on the number of clusters. If a volume has more than 4,096 clusters, then each FAT entry is 16 bits; otherwise each FAT entry is 12 bits.

A 12-bit FAT permits control of 4,096 clusters, which corresponds to 4 sectors per cluster, providing a total of 8 megabytes. Although this amount could be expanded by adding more sectors to a cluster, such an expansion isn't recommended. Therefore, you'll find only 16-bit FATs on newer hard drives of 20 megabytes and up, thus allowing the 65,536 maximum of addressable clusters.

The number of bits per FAT entry must be determined before file access. The information in the BIOS parameter block is used for this purpose. The total number of sectors in the volume can be found starting at location 13H. Divide this number by the number of sectors per cluster to obtain the number of clusters in the volume.

The first two entries of the FAT are reserved and aren't related to the cluster assignment. Depending on the sizes of the individual entries, 24 bits (3 bytes) or 32 bits (4 bytes) can be available. The first byte contains the media descriptor, while the value 255 fills in the other bytes. The media descriptor, which is also stored in address 15H of the BPB, indicates the device the media uses (e.g., a diskette).

The following codes are possible:

Media descriptor codes		
Code	Device	Description
F0H	3.5" disk drive	2 sides, 80 tracks, 18 sectors per track
F8H	Hard drive	Varies
F9H	5.25" disk drive	2 sides, 80 tracks, 15 sectors per track
	3.5" disk drive	2 sides, 80 tracks, 9 sectors per track
FAH	5.25" disk drive	1 side, 80 tracks, 8 sectors per track
	3.5" disk drive	1 side, 80 tracks, 8 sectors per track
FBH	5.25" disk drive	2 sides, 80 tracks, 8 sectors per track
	3.5" disk drive	2 sides, 80 tracks, 8 sectors per track
FCH	5.25" disk drive	1 side, 40 tracks, 9 sectors per track
FDH	5.25" disk drive	2 sides, 40 tracks, 9 sectors per track
FEH	5.25" disk drive	1 side, 40 tracks, 8 sectors per track
FFH	5.25" disk drive	2 sides, 40 tracks, 8 sectors per track

Perhaps you're wondering why the individual entries of the FAT are 12 or 16 bits wide if all they do is show whether a cluster is occupied. This could have been done with one bit; the bit could contain 1 when the cluster is occupied and 0 if the cluster is available.

The entries in the FAT help mark the available clusters and identify the individual clusters containing a specific file. The directory entry of a file tells DOS which cluster holds the first sectors of a file. The number of this cluster corresponds to the number of the FAT entry belonging to it. In this entry is the number of the cluster containing the next sector of file data. This search continues until the last cluster of a file has been reached.

However, the cluster numbers refer to the beginning of the data structure rather than the beginning of the volume (more on this later). For example, assume the beginning of a file resides in the fourth cluster of the volume. You must read the fourth entry of the FAT to obtain the number of the next cluster containing the file, remembering that a FAT entry can be either 12-bit or 16-bit. This fourth entry contains the number of the next file cluster.

As the following illustration shows, a chain is formed in which the individual clusters assigned to a file can be located in the proper sequence. The logical number of each sector can be derived from the cluster number. DOS must send this logical number to the device driver before these sectors can be read or written by DOS. DOS device drivers operate at sector level rather than cluster level. To convert clusters to logical sectors, multiply the cluster number by the number of sectors per cluster.

*FAT entry and
file clusters*

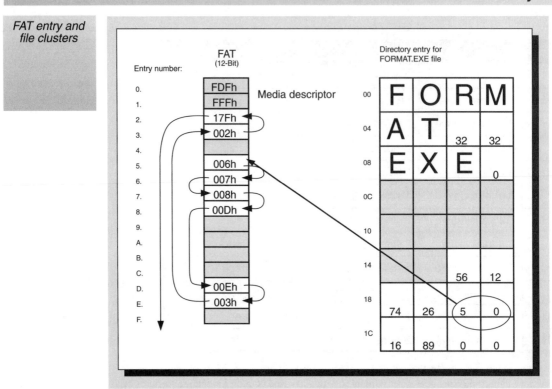

The FAT entry corresponding to the last cluster of a file must contain a special code that tells DOS the file ends here. A cluster number indicates this code, which is either greater than FF8H (12-bit) or greater than FFF8H (16-bit). However, the following tables show the meanings of the various FAT entries. For example, cluster numbers FF0H-FF6H (12-bit) or FFF0H-FFF6H (16-bit) indicate a reserved cluster (i.e., the root directory of a volume). The root directory has a fixed position and size, and the cluster can be independent rather than chained to the FAT.

Cluster codes FF7H (12-bit) and FFF7H (16-bit) also have special significance. These codes identify clusters whose sectors contain errors, ensuring that DOS doesn't write data to these bad clusters.

Cluster code 0H indicates unoccupied clusters, as well as the first cluster of the volume. Like the first cluster, code 0H represents no sectors, because it contains the volume's medium type. As you'll see later in this book, this is why the cluster number must be reduced by two when converting cluster numbers into sector numbers.

12-bit FAT cluster codes		16-bit FAT cluster codes	
Code	Meaning	Code	Meaning
000H	Cluster is available	0000H	Cluster is available
FF0H-FF6H	reserved cluster	FFF0H-FFF6	Reserved cluster
FF7H	Cluster damaged, not used	FFF7H	Cluster damaged, not used
FF8H-FFFH	Last file cluster	FFF8H-FFFF	Last file cluster
xxxH	Next file cluster	XXXXH	Next file cluster

Multiple copies of the FAT

The FAT's importance in the DOS file system becomes obvious when a virus or hardware error damages the FAT. All files and subdirectories are still available in principle. However, they remain inaccessible to the user because DOS can no longer gather the individual clusters into one unit.

DOS is designed so several identical copies of the FAT can be kept on a volume. The boot sector's offset address 10H contains the number of FATs. If DOS finds a medium of this type, it automatically updates all copies of the FAT and records this update in offset 10H while creating or deleting files. So, if one FAT is damaged, it can be replaced with another, which minimizes data loss.

The DOS CHKDSK command tests the various FATs to see if they are identical. If the primary FAT is damaged, CHKDSK replaces the damaged primary FAT with another FAT.

The Root Directory

Now let's look at the structure of a directory.

The root directory of a volume immediately follows the last copy of the FAT. This root directory (like all subdirectories) consists of 32-byte entries, in which information about individual files, subdirectories, and volume label names can be stored. The maximum number of entries in the root directory, and therefore its size, is stored in the BPB starting at address 11H. The FORMAT command specifies both the size number and the BPB. Before considering individual fields of this data structure, the table on the right provides an overview of a directory entry.

Directory entry layout		
Address	Contents	Type
00H	Filename (blanks padded with spaces)	8 bytes
08H	File extension (blanks padded with spaces)	3 bytes
0BH	File attribute	1 byte
0CH	Reserved	10 bytes
16H	Time of last change	1 word
18H	Date of last change	1 word
1AH	First cluster of file	1 word
1CH	File size	2 words

The first eight bytes usually contain the name of the current file. If the filename is shorter than eight characters, DOS fills the remaining characters with spaces (ASCII code 32).

If the directory entry doesn't contain information about a file, but the file is used in another way, the first byte of the filename (therefore the first byte of the directory entry) is identified by a special code (see the table on the right).

The second field contains the three character filename extension. If the extension is less than three characters long, DOS fills in the extra characters with blank spaces (ASCII code 32). The period between filename and extension is displayed by the DOS command DIR but isn't kept in the directory; DIR displays this character so the names are easier to read.

The first byte of the directory entry	
Code	Meaning
00H	Last directory entry
05H	First character of filename has ASCII code E5H
2EH	File applies to current directory
E5H	File deleted

The one-byte attribute field is next. As shown in the following figure, the individual bits of this field define certain attributes. The various attributes can be combined so a file (as in the IBMBIOS.COM file) can have the attributes READ_ONLY, SYSTEM, and HIDDEN.

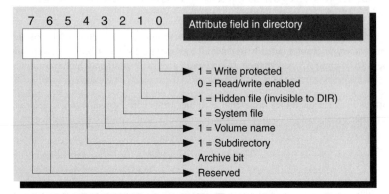

A reserved field follows the attribute field. DOS uses this field for internal operations, and some sources claim that Novell NetWare uses this bit for sharing data.

While the significance of bits 0 to 4 is easy to see, the significance of bit 5 needs additional explanation. The name archive bit comes from its use in making backup copies. Every time a file is created or modified, this bit is set to 1. If a program is used to backup this file, (for example the DOS BACKUP command), the archive bit is reset to 0. The next time the BACKUP command is used, it can determine, from the archive bit, whether this file has been modified since the last backup. If it still contains the value 0, the file doesn't have to be backed up again. If the archive bit contains a 1, the file was modified and should be backed up again.

The attributes volume label name and subdirectory will be discussed in more detail later. A reserved field, which DOS requires for internal operations, follows the attribute field. The time and date fields indicate when the file was last created or modified. Both are stored as words (2 bytes), but have special and different formats.

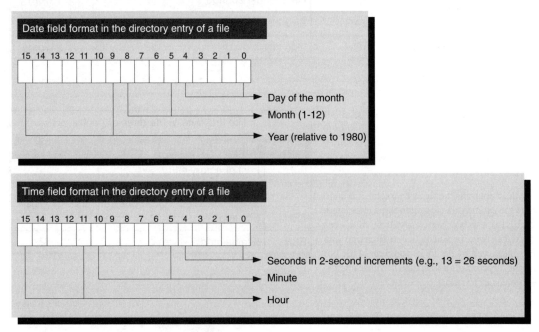

The next field shows the number of the cluster that contains the first data of the file. It also shows the number of the FAT containing the number of the next cluster assigned to the file. This field forms the beginning of a chain through which all the clusters assigned to a file can be retrieved.

The file size in bytes is stored in two words with the lower word stored first. Using a small formula and the two words, the file size can be calculated as follows:

```
File size = word1 + word2 * 65,536
```

Subdirectories

Both subdirectories and volume label names deserve special consideration. The volume label name can exist only in the root directory. It's indicated by bit 3 of the current directory entry's attribute field. The filename in a volume entry acts as the volume label name. Use the DOS commands DIR, VOL, and TREE to display the volume label name.

If bit 4 of the current directory's attribute field is set, then this entry is for a subdirectory. If bit 1 in this field is also set, the subdirectory can be addressed. However, this subdirectory isn't displayed when you execute the DIR command. For these entries, the filename and extension field contain the subdirectory name; the date and time field contain the time of its creation. The file length field is always 0. The field that usually indicates the first cluster of the file now indicates the cluster that contains the directory entries of this subdirectory. They have the same 32-byte structure as the entries in the root directory.

As in a normal file, the entry in the FAT corresponding to the subdirectory cluster points to the next cluster of the subdirectory. This is true as long as one cluster is enough for the directory of the subdirectory. This doesn't apply to the root directory, which extends through several sectors or clusters that follow each other logically. Also, the individual clusters of the root directory cannot be connected through the FAT, because the FAT only refers to the data area of the volume. This is the area that accepts files and subdirectories, but not the root directory.

The process previously described reveals that DOS separates the individual files in a storage unit according to their directories. Instead of storing the files of one directory in one area, DOS scatters the files across the storage medium.

When a subdirectory is created, two files are created with the names '.' and '..'. These files can be erased only when you remove the entire subdirectory. The first file points to the current subdirectory. Its cluster field contains the number of the first cluster of the current subdirectory. The second entry points to the parent directory located before the current directory in the directory tree. If the parent directory is the root directory, the cluster field contains the value 0. The path to the root directory can be traced back through this entry, since, as every subdirectory searches for its parent directory, it comes closer to the root directory.

Now let's return to our discussion of mass storage device structures. The file area follows the root directory. This area, which occupies the remaining storage area of the mass storage device, accepts the individual files and various subdirectories. There is an entry in the FAT corresponding to every cluster in this area. If a file is enlarged, DOS reserves a cluster that is still available to store the additional data of the file. The FAT entry of the last cluster, which previously indicated the end of the file, is changed to point to the new cluster. This in turn contains the new end character.

Both DOS Versions 1.0 and 2.0 search for unused clusters from the beginning. In DOS Versions 3.0 and higher, a more complicated search procedure is used to try to select an unused cluster near the other clusters comprising the file. This reduces the access time to the file. Conversely, when reducing file size or deleting a file, the FAT is updated to indicate the unused clusters are again available. They can be used again when a new file is created or expanded.

Let's begin at the point where DOS finds the first cluster or a file, and the FAT entry for the next cluster in the first cluster. We need to calculate the sector from this cluster.

1. Subtract 2 from the cluster number. The first two FAT entries contain the media descriptor, so FAT entry 2 is the actual zero cluster on the volume.

2. Multiply the cluster by the number of sectors per cluster. BIOS obtains this information from the BIOS Parameter Block loaded from the boot sector. The result relates to the first sector of the volume, instead of the first sector of the

data range (which is the result we want). You can compute the logical sector where the data range starts, also using information from the BIOS Parameter Block.

3. The boot sector, the FAT and its duplicates, and the root directory precede the volume's data range. The lengths of these ranges must be calculated and added together. Read the number of sectors reserved from offset address 0EH of the boot sector. Read the number of FAT sectors from offset address 16H of the boot sector, and multiply the number of FAT sectors by the number of FATs (found in address 10H), then add the total to the number of reserved sectors.

4. DOS also requires the number of sectors occupied by the root directory. This number is stored in the word beginning at offset 11H in the boot sector. Multiply this value by 32 (bytes per entry), and divide the result by 512 (bytes per sector). Add the result to the boot sector and FAT lengths to obtain the number of the first sector in the data range.

DOS performs this calculation only when booting, or when a medium has been changed (e.g, every time you change diskettes in a floppy disk drive).

Calculating the first sector of the data range

By adding the number of the first sector in the data range to the first sector number of the addressed file, you receive the logical sector number. DOS can then pass this logical sector number to the device driver for file access.

When DOS requires access to both the first cluster and subsequent clusters of the file, it must read those subsequent clusters from the FAT. These calculations vary depending on the widths of the FAT entries. Reading the next adjacent cluster is easy to do with a 16-bit FAT. Simply multiply the cluster number by 2 to find the next cluster. The result represents the offset address relative to the beginning of the FAT in memory, where the next cluster can be found.

If DOS is dealing with a 12-bit FAT, multiply the cluster number by 1.5. The whole number part of the product becomes the offset in the FAT. The word at this memory address is read. If the product is a whole number, the word read must be combined with a logical AND to 0FFFFH to obtain the number of the next cluster. If the product isn't a whole number, the AND is omitted and the word is shifted by 4 bits to the right (divided by 16).

DOS usually doesn't have to load the FAT into memory, because it permanently stores a copy of this data structure in memory to save execution time.

Now DOS knows the next cluster of the file. If you're using a 12-bit FAT, the next cluster lies in the range from FF8H to FFFH. If you're using a 16-bit FAT, the next cluster lies in the range from FFF8H to FFFFH. This process repeats until DOS finds the end of the file.

Diskette Formats

Diskettes require formats that specify the exact qualities of a volume. Non-DOS diskettes cannot be read by DOS unless a special device driver is available.

The following tables show the formats available for 3.5" diskettes:

3.5-inch disk formats					
Type	Density	Capacity	Tracks	Sector	DOS Version
DS DD	135 tpi	720K	80	9	3.2
DS HD	135 tpi	2.88 Mb	80	18	3.3

The following table shows the formats available for 5.25" diskettes:

5.25-inch disk formats					
Type	Density	Capacity	Tracks	Sector	DOS Version
SS SD	40 tpi	160K	40	8	1.0
SS SD	40 tpi	100K	40	9	2.0
DS SD	40 tpi	320K	40	8	1.1
DS SD	40 tpi	360K	40	9	2.0
DS HD	96 tpi	1.2 Mb	80	15	3.0

Chapter 29

The Multiplexer (Interrupt 27H)

Several DOS commands operate as TSR programs. This means they become memory resident when called and remain in the background until needed. These include the PRINT, ASSIGN, SHARE, APPEND, DOSKEY, etc. commands. These programs use interrupt 27H so they can be accessed once they've become memory resident. This interrupt is called the multiplexer. We'll explain in this chapter how the multiplexer works and which programs use the multiplexer.

How The Multiplexer Operates

Interrupt 27H is known as the multiplexer because it acts as a communications interface for all TSR programs instead of only one DOS program. After installing a TSR program in memory with an initial function call, it's often necessary to set specific parameters for the TSR or remove the TSR program from memory using DOS commands. These commands then use the multiplexer interrupt to address the memory resident TSR program.

However, it's also possible for application programs to use these calls to modify various resident DOS programs or determine whether they are currently active. For example, a network program requiring SHARE can determine whether this DOS program was loaded. If SHARE wasn't loaded, its startup is aborted and an error message is displayed.

TSR programs must ensure that more than one program can use interrupt 27H simultaneously. This is done in the following way:

Before a program uses the multiplexer (or MUX), it must assign itself an eight bit identification number. This number is known as the MUX code. The MUX codes 00H to BFH are reserved for various DOS programs and 0CH to FFH are reserved for application programs.

When this type of TSR program is loaded, it must install an interrupt handler for the multiplexer interrupt, in addition to the other interrupt handlers it may need. So, the program must redirect the interrupt 27H to its own routine, which replaces the previous interrupt handler. When a program activates the multiplexer interrupt, the program's interrupt handler is executed.

First this interrupt handler must determine whether its own program or one of the other programs, which is tied to the multiplexer, is being addressed. It examines the AH register, which should contain the MUX code of the program that's being addressed.

If it finds its own MUX code in this register, the interrupt handler simply reads the remaining processor registers that are important, executes its function, and returns to the caller program with an IRET machine language command.

The chain of MUX handlers

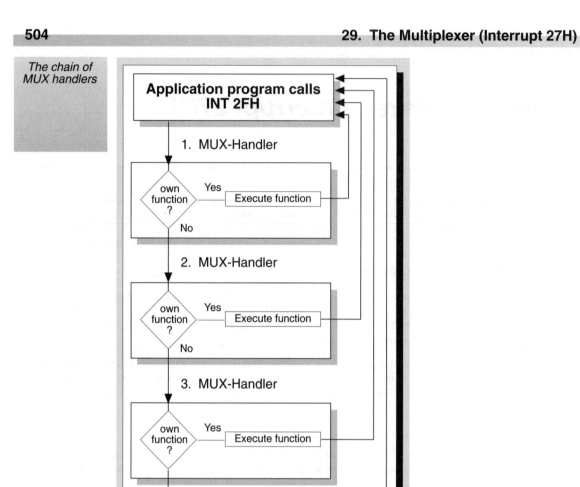

However, if the MUX code refers to a different TSR program, the interrupt handler cannot terminate its call and return. Instead, it must call the previous interrupt handler that it displaced upon its installation in the multiplexer. This means that a TSR program must note the address of the interrupt handler currently installed in the multiplexer before it can install its own handler.

Since each multiplexer interrupt handler checks the MUX code in this way, and calls the previous handler if the code isn't its own, the chain of interrupt handlers is passed until one of the handlers recognizes the code as its own. This handler then executes the appropriate function, instead of calling its predecessor. At the end of this chain is the first handler that was installed by BIOS when the system was booted. This handler is preceded only by the IRET machine language instruction.

Competition between multiplex handlers

This system works until two multiplex handlers use the same MUX code. When this happens, the more recent handler along this chain will identify the code as its own, and call the specified function. The "older" handler cannot be accessed.

This problem won't occur in DOS programs because Microsoft ensures that none of these programs use the same MUX code. However, if you develop your own TSR programs, it's possible that you'll use a code that's already in use by another program. However, there is a way to determine this at the start of your program.

Normally, each TSR program is stopped to run a function for the installation check. This function should be executed if, at the multiplexer call, the AH register contains the MUX code of the particular program and the value 00H is found in the AL register. If one of the installed handlers recognizes its own code, it must place a value that doesn't equal 00H (generally FFH) in the AL register.

However, if none of the resident handlers recognize the code as their own, it will be passed along the chain of interrupt handlers until it reaches the first handler that was installed. This handler consists of only an IRET instruction. If this is the case, the AL register will be returned unchanged. So, if the AL register still contains 0 after this check, then the specified MUX code isn't being used by an installed handler.

In Chapter 35 we'll demonstrate how the multiplexer interrupt is used with TSR programs.

How DOS Programs Use The Multiplexer

In this section we'll discuss how the multiplexer is used by various DOS programs and which functions these programs provide. For application programs, many people believe that only the PRINT command, which enables you to print text in the background, is useful. However, you'll see that this isn't really true.

DOS commands which work with the multiplexer

The following table shows the DOS commands which work with the multiplexer:

DOS commands which work with the multiplexer			
MUX code	DOS command	MUX code	DOS command
01H	PRINT	48H	DOSKEY
06H	ASSIGN	4AH	DBLSPACE.BIN
10H	SHARE	4DH	KEYB
1AH	ANSI.SYS	B0H	GRAFTABL
43H	HIMEM	B7H	APPEND

The functions of these individual DOS commands are listed and briefly explained below. You'll find detailed descriptions of their input and output parameters in Appendix E on the companion CD-ROM.

PRINT   MUX code 01H

The first DOS command to use the multiplexer was PRINT. The PRINT command uses this function to address its memory resident portion, to add files to the print queue list, to delete files from this list or to delete the list entirely.

Applications can also use this function when they need to execute long printing operations and don't want to monopolize the computer until the print operations are completed. Printers are normally slower than programs, which is why this function was introduced. To use PRINT, an application must "print" the desired output to a file and then add this file to the print queue. This can easily be done by using the PRINT function.

Function	Description
00H	Installation check
01H	Add file to queue
02H	Delete file from wait list
03H	Delete entire wait list
04H	Interrupt output and check status
05H	Resume output
06H	Check for printer

ASSIGN   *MUX code 06H*

SHARE   *MUX code 10H*

ANSI.SYS   *MUX code 1AH*

GRAFTABL   *MUX code B0H*

These commands support only function 00H, which is used for the installation check. If this function call returns the value FFH in register AL, that particular program has been installed. Refer to the previous table for the MUX code of each of these programs.

HIMEM.SYS   *MUX code 43H*

The device driver HIMEM.SYS, which is responsible for managing memory according to the XMS standard, provides two multiplexer functions. The first function, 00H, supports the installation check. It returns the value 80H when HIMEM.SYS is installed. However, unlike other corresponding functions, it returns the value FFH. The second function represents the access point to this device driver, through which the various XMS functions are accessed. In this instance, however, the multiplexer simply enables access to HIMEM.SYS.

Function	Description
00H	Installation check
10H	Obtain access to XMS function calls

For more information about these functions and HIMEM.SYS, refer to Chapter 12.

DOSKEY (Version 5.0 and later)   *MUX code 48H*

Since DOS 5.0, the memory resident program DOSKEY has permitted the storing and recalling of DOS command line entries, as well as the implementation of macros.

DOSKEY makes these functions available to applications, instead of only at the DOS command line. This is possible through multiplex functions. The MUX code of DOSKEY is 48H, and its two function numbers are 00H and 01H. As with other DOS commands, function 00H is used to check whether DOSKEY is installed. This function performs the usual installation check.

The second function can be used by an application program to ask DOSKEY to receive a command line from the user, in the same way as on the DOS command line. By using the cursor up and down keys, the user can move through previous DOS command line entries. New command lines entered with this function are also added to the list of entries stored by DOSKEY.

DBLSPACE.BIN   MUX code 4AH

DoubleSpace, the DOS 6 on-line hard drive compressor, offers ten functions to disk utilities through the multiplexer interrupt. Unlike other MUX interfaces, 11H must always be given as the function number in register AL, with the subfunction number placed in register BX.

Function	Description	Function	Description
00H	Return version information	06H	Deactivate DoubleSpace drive
01H	Scan drive map	07H	Establish storage space
02H	Switch drive ID	08H	Return information about CVF file fragmentation
05H	Link compressed drive	09H	Scan for maximum number of compressed drives

See Chapter 34 for more information about DoubleSpace.

KEYB   *MUX code ADH*

The KEYB.COM keyboard device driver supplies a total of four multiplex functions. They can be used to check the current KEYB version number, the current code page and the current country flag.

Function	Description
80H	Return version number
81H	Determine current code page
82H	Set country flag
83H	Return country flag

APPEND   *MUX code B7H*

Of the MUX codes used by the various DOS commands, the code used by APPEND carries the highest value. Although the function number sequence is slightly unconventional, these multiplex functions supply an application with all the functions offered to the user at the DOS command line.

Function	Description
00H	Installation check
02H	Check compatibility to DOS Version 5.0
04H	Return directory list
06H	Check operating mode
07H	Set operating mode
11H	Establish conversion to complete filename

Chapter 30

Network Programming

Over the last several years, networks have become an important part of using PCs. Networks were first used in large corporations, then in medium-sized companies, and now even in small private businesses. Most network systems can be purchased for several hundred dollars. As cheaper network cards become available, the cost of network systems will continue to decrease.

Because networks have become more popular, the demand for programs that support networking is steadily increasing. In this chapter will present the basics of network programming. Although we can't discuss network programming in detail in this book, you should have enough information to create your first network programs.

Basics Of Network Programming

Networks can be used for various purposes. Usually they connect individual PCs, called workstations, to a more powerful server. The server is usually a fast PC, equipped with a large amount of memory and disk capacity. The server allows these workstations to use its resources and perform various tasks. One of the most common tasks is file sharing, which allows files, which are stored and managed by the server, to be accessed by individual workstations.

File sharing is usually performed with database files. Since these files are essential to a business' operation, they must be accessed by several employees. A good example of this is a mail order inventory. With a network, several employees, working on separate workstations, can directly access the inventory, which is stored in a central database.

Generally, the file server is also used to store programs that can be called from individual workstations. This saves disk space on the workstation and minimizes installation work. Obviously it's requires less work and time to install a program once on the file server, than to install it on every workstation.

For example, Windows requires that certain files must be present on individual workstations, even if the main program has been installed on the file server. While the main Windows programs (WIN.COM, PROGMAN.EXE, etc.) can be located on the file server, each workstation needs its own WIN.INI and SYSTEM.INI files so each workstation can define its own environment.

However, even these files can be placed on the server by defining a private directory for each workstation or user. In this area, the private files of a given workstation can be stored without being modified by another workstation. A network operating system, which is the heart of any network system, manages these operations.

Besides making its storage media accessible to other workstations, the network file server can act as a print or communications server, giving workstations access to a printer, a modem, or even another network. These capabilities can significantly reduce equipment expenses, since they allow one printer to be used by many workstations.

Since the appearance of OS/2, SQL servers have become more popular. These servers operate under OS/2, which allows the network stations to access SQL (Structured Query Language) databases. SQL is a program-based language for accessing relational databases.

The SQL server not only manages the SQL databases, but also processes the queries directed to this database by individual workstations. For example, if a workstation queries a customer database for all addresses containing a zip code of 10000, the SQL server is responsible for screening and returning the appropriate records. This type of operation is often referred to as a remote procedure call, because the workstation is calling a procedure that's actually located in the SQL server.

The network operating system

Novell is the largest supplier of network operating systems. They offer a series of different NetWare versions. However, several other network operating system manufacturers, such as IBM, 3Com, an Banyan Vines, also produce both NetWare-compatible and independent systems.

A network operating system always consists of a server program, which manages the file server, and a workstation program, which manages each workstation and allows it to address the server. This software is usually supplied in the form of a device driver or a TSR program. Workstations must be able to use DOS as usual and must access the file server like a normal floppy diskette or hard drive. Because of this, the software is embedded deeply into DOS, which enables it to control how DOS manages files.

The network software intercepts all file operations and passes only local operations, which access the workstation's own disk space, to DOS. For example, if the server in a certain network is identified by the device letter "S", the network software would intercept "S:LETTER.TXT" and address this call to the server. So, files that are located on the server can be addressed from a workstation in the same way as local DOS files.

However, this doesn't mean that a workstation user automatically has access to all the information stored on the server hard disk. Since this information could total 1 gigabyte in size, this could be an enormous amount of information. Instead, a network administrator defines which directories and files can be accessed by a user or workstation. These access rights are often tied to passwords that must be entered with a workstations user's login.

Since many users can access the server simultaneously, the server is rarely operated under DOS, which would be too slow to process numerous simultaneous access requests. So, Novell NetWare supplies its own operating system. For instance, this is a system that runs in protected mode on the server and that doesn't need or work with DOS in any way. The server hard disk is managed by a special Novell file system, instead of under DOS. Even if the server could be booted on a DOS diskette, the hard disk still couldn't be accessed because DOS is unable to recognize the foreign disk format.

However, you don't need this information for network programming under DOS, unless you plan on developing tools for Novell NetWare, which is a completely different process. This also applies to network hardware, which you also won't be dealing with internally, regardless of whether you're using a Token-Ring network, an Ethernet, or an Arc-Net. The function interfaces that facilitate access to the server and communication between workstations are more important.

Function interfaces

Three function interfaces have established themselves as standards for the PC. These are rudimentary DOS functions that were introduced with DOS Version 3.0. They allow several workstations to access server files. These functions are supported by all popular network operating systems.

The IPX/SPX interface has been widely used because of Novell's large market share. This interface refers to the numerous functions that are available to a program running on a Novell NetWare workstation. These functions permit communication between workstations, which is vital for such things as E-mail or the remote operation of workstations.

NetBIOS interface, developed by IBM with its PC-LAN network operating system, works similarly. This interface is so widely used that Novell even offers a NetBIOS emulator for its Netware. This emulator transforms NetBIOS function calls into IPX/SPX functions. This is possible because both function interfaces were designed with the same operating principles. So, programs that have been written for NetBIOS can also run on Novell Netware systems. This is why we recommend NetBIOS for network programming, if you want to tackle such a task.

Peer to peer networking

Peer to peer networking has become very popular. With this type of networking, workstations can also act as servers. This technique is particularly suited for smaller operations, because purchasing a large and powerful server may be too expensive. In peer to peer networking, each workstation is equipped with a DOS supplement that allows the workstations to be accessed using standard DOS commands and file operations. Programs such as NetWare Lite by Novell and LANStatic by Microware use this technique.

Network Programming Under DOS

The two main DOS elements in network programming are DOS API functions and the SHARE program, which was introduced with DOS Version 3.0. This program implements the two DOS API functions, and, with their help, ensures that different programs don't interfere with one another while accessing files simultaneously. Often one program will run on several workstations simultaneously and store its files on the server, so these files can be accessed by the individual workstations simultaneously.

To illustrate this, we'll use an example of a large health club. Several employees use individual workstations to manage the reservations for courts and equipment. These workstations are connected to a server via a network, where a central file contains all the court reservations for the coming days and weeks. The workstations use a single program, which manages court reservations and rentals. As we'll see below, the simultaneous actions of these employees create several problems for the network. First, however, let's take another look at the SHARE program.

Checking for SHARE

Because SHARE is needed to work with DOS networking functions, any network program you write should determine whether SHARE is present at program startup. Remember that SHARE is completely integrated in DOS Versions 4.0, 5.0, and higher, so you can omit this check if you're absolutely certain that your program won't be running on earlier versions of DOS.

The SHARE test consists of only an interrupt call. Simply call the multiplexer function 1000H, since this is where the resident portion of SHARE is located. If this function call returns the value FFH in the AL register, you know that SHARE has been installed. We talk about the multiplexer in Chapter 29.

Record locking

The most important aspect of simultaneous file access by more than one workstation is record locking. To explain this concept, let's return to our example of the health club. The employees take court reservations from members over the phone. On their workstations, the employees check the availability of the courts for a particular date and time. This information is provided by a data file. Since the data file's records are only read, problems don't occur.

However, when one of these records must be changed, conflicts can occur. For example, this happens when one of the employees makes a reservation for a particular court. Since this reservation isn't recorded in the data file, this court still appears as available. So, it's possible that another employee will also make a reservation for the same court at the same time and date for another member. If the software isn't fast enough to display the previous record change before the second employee makes his or her reservation, the first reservation will be overwritten by the second.

Record locking is designed to prevent these type of situation. Under this principle, a program must first take possession of a record and lock it before the record can be changed in any way. Once this is done, another workstation cannot modify the record.

In our example, this would work as follows: when the first employee finds the record for the available court, he or she presses a special function key that informs the program that this court should be reserved. The program then locks the record, so the necessary changes can be made to the record. Once this has occurred, the other employees cannot access the record from their workstations as long as it remains locked.

The program responds to this access attempt by displaying a message, which indicates that this court is currently being reserved. However, the first member may cancel his/her reservation immediately after placing it. So, the workstation that's requesting access to the record shouldn't give up immediately. Instead, it should repeatedly try to access the record until it becomes available or until a certain time limit is reached.

Once the record becomes available, the second employee can determine whether the court has already been reserved by another member or whether it's still available. However, this works only if the record is unlocked as quickly as possible after the change has been made.

The following guidelines apply to the shared use of files and records by one or more programs on numerous workstations:

➢ Records must be locked before they are modified, so other programs or workstations cannot access them during that time.

➢ Records must be released immediately after they are modified, so they are available to other programs or workstations.

SHARE, in conjunction with the network operating system, ensures that locked records cannot be accessed from other sources by displaying an error message when these function calls occur.

Although this process may sound complicated, it's actually very simple. Records can be locked with a single DOS function, 5CH. This function requires the correct file handle and the offset address and length of the segment to be locked. Since files are often larger than 64K, these parameters are considered 32 bit values and are therefore shared by two processor registers. The upper 16 bits of the start offset are written to the CX register and the lower 16 bits to the DX register. The segment length is handled in the same way, by registers SI and DI.

So, although you're not dealing directly with records, locking them isn't very complicated. At a given record length, you can easily use the record number to calculate the correct start offset, and the segment length is already specified.

Since this function can also be used to unlock files, the AL register is used to indicate which operation the function should perform, either locking or unlocking the specified segment. It's also possible to lock more than one file segment with this function because many operations require more than one record to be locked at one time. This is necessary so other programs cannot access these records.

However, before a file or file segment can be locked, the file first must be opened. This is the only place you can obtain the handle the function needs to read from the BX register.

Register	Description
AH	5Ch
AL	Mode: 00 = Lock, 01 = Unlock
BX	File handle
CX:DX	Start offset in the source file as 32 Bit value
SI:DI	Segment (record) length as 32 Bit value
BU:	Parameters for function call 5Ch

File sharing

In addition to record locking, SHARE enables DOS to implement file locking, which prevents other programs and workstations from accessing a specific file. This option is activated by the DOS function 3DH, which is also used to open files in non-network situations. The only difference in network programming is that more information must be provided for this function in the AL register.

Parameters for function call 3Dh	
Register	Description
AH	3DH
AL	Access mode (see illustration on the next page)
DS:DX	Pointer to file name

As the following illustration shows, bits 4 through 6 define the operations other programs are allowed to perform on the specified file in a network setting. So, you can determine whether other programs can, for example, read, but not write to your file, or whether access should be completely denied while your program is using the file.

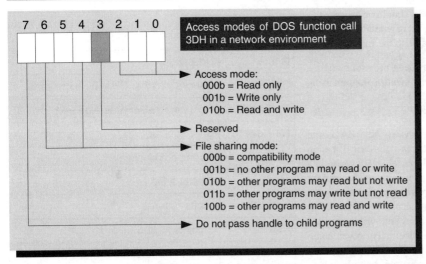

In this context, the lower three bits, which usually aren't significant in DOS programming, are important. These bits declare which operations a program will perform with a file upon opening it. A program using a READ file access mode when requesting access to an already open file, will be granted access to this file if the first program has released the file for READ operations through its file sharing mode.

So, in a network environment you shouldn't declare a READ and WRITE access mode if you only intend to read information from the file. Otherwise, you may be denied access to the file by a program that has already opened the file and denied WRITE access to other programs.

If a file access request with a given access mode doesn't succeed, function 3DH will return error code 5 (access denied). This error code is also used by the functions for reading and writing files when they are denied access to a file.

You've probably noticed the "compatibility mode" among the file sharing modes listed in the diagram above. This mode serves the same purpose as mode 001b; it doesn't allow other programs to read from and write to the specified file. However, instead of calling the normal error code 5 (access denied), the compatibility code calls the DOS critical error handler when another program attempts to access the locked file. When such an error occurs, DOS displays the following message on the screen:

```
Illegal SHARE operation while reading drive C
(A)bort, (R)etry, (F)ail
```

You shouldn't use this file sharing mode when other programs shouldn't access the locked file. Instead, use file sharing mode 001b.

An example of network programming

To demonstrate how to use DOS in network programming, we've developed two programs that use its file and record locking capabilities. You'll find the Pascal and C versions of these programs at the end of this chapter. A network isn't needed to use these programs; Windows 3.0 is sufficient. If you call SHARE prior to starting Windows 3.0, open several DOS boxes within Windows, and then start programs from these boxes, you can simulate any number of workstations.

You don't have to do this for the file locking programs (FLOCK.PAS and FLOCK.C) because these open a file twice from within the same program. This is the same as trying to open the file from a different program.

First, look at the two modules NETFILEP.PAS and NETFILEC.C, which provide the essential file access procedures for the two sample programs. Both of the programs use the same functions (or procedures) and constants. The difference between the two lies in the way the file, that should be accessed, is passed to these two programs. A list of available functions and procedures is listed in the table to the right.

Although the Pascal version has been programmed as a UNIT, you can integrate the C version into a program using #INCLUDE. So, compiling the module and defining a make or project file isn't necessary.

Similar to the Pascal commands ASSIGN, READ, and WRITE, the functions and procedures of the Pascal version accept a normal, standardized file variable. However, in a network environment, these commands cannot be used for accessing this type of a file, because they execute as soon as a file isn't open to read or write access. Because of this, special procedures for reading from and writing to files have been defined in the NETFILEP unit. However, using Turbo Pascal file variables is still useful because they provide the procedures with, for example, the length of individual records within the file. The file handle and access mode, which are otherwise entered by the REWRITE Pascal procedure, are also stored here.

In the C version, the file is represented by the following data structure, which should be passed, in the form of a variable, to the various functions in the NETFILEC.C module:

Procedures and functions provided by modules NETFILEP.PAS and NETFILEC.C.	
Name	Description
ShareInst	Checks whether SHARE is installed
NetErrorMs	Returns an error message text
NetRewrite	Creates a file
NetReset	Opens a specific file
NetClose	Closes a file
NetLock	Locks records
NetUnLock	Unlocks locked records
Is_NetWrite	Checks whether file may be written to
Is_NetRead	Checks whether file may be read from
Is_NetOpen	Checks whether file is open
NetWrite	Writes to file
NetRead	Reads from file
NetSeek	Sets data pointer

```
typedef struct { unsigned int Handle,   /
* File handle */

                          RecS,     /* Record size */
                          Mode;     /* Access mode */
                } NFILE;
```

The FLOCKP.PAS and FLOCKC.C programs illustrate how files are locked. First they ask the user for the access and file sharing modes for the two files that should be opened. However, the program actually opens only one file, named either FLOCKC.DAT or FLOCKP.DAT, depending on the program used. This file is then opened by two OPEN statements, so it can be addressed simultaneously over two handles. This simulates a network environment in which two programs are accessing the file simultaneously.

You'll find the following program(s) on the companion CD-ROM

NETFILEP.PAS (Pascal listing)
NETFILEC.C (C listing)

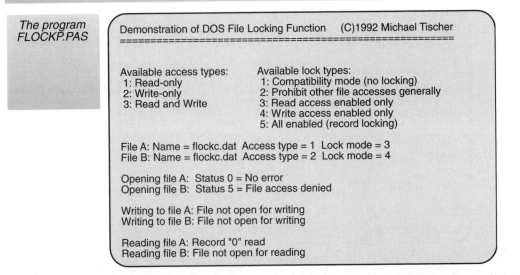

The program FLOCKP.PAS

```
Demonstration of DOS File Locking Function    (C)1992 Michael Tischer
========================================================

Available access types:     Available lock types:
  1: Read-only                1: Compatibility mode (no locking)
  2: Write-only               2: Prohibit other file accesses generally
  3: Read and Write           3: Read access enabled only
                              4: Write access enabled only
                              5: All enabled (record locking)

File A: Name = flockc.dat  Access type = 1  Lock mode = 3
File B: Name = flockc.dat  Access type = 2  Lock mode = 4

Opening file A:  Status 0 = No error
Opening file B:  Status 5 = File access denied

Writing to file A: File not open for writing
Writing to file B: File not open for writing

Reading file A: Record "0" read
Reading file B: File not open for reading
```

Upon opening these two handles, the DOS error messages are displayed on the screen. These handles are also used to execute write and read operations, the status of which is also displayed on the screen. After the handles have been opened, the text "AAAA" is written to the first handle, and the text "BBBB" is written to the second handle.

The file content is read through both handles in the next program step, and is then displayed on the screen. If the write access over the second handle was successful, the text "BBBB" will be displayed through both handles. This means the first text has been overwritten, assuming the first write attempt actually was successful. If both write access attempts failed, the file will be empty and two empty strings will appear on your screen. The last program step finally closes both handles.

These two programs are helpful because they can be used to test all different combinations of access and file sharing modes. However, some of them don't make sense and may lead to rather strange results. However, these results are similar to what sometimes occurs in a network environment.

Unlike the two FLOCK programs, the RELOCK programs (RELOCKP.PAS and RELOCKC.C) must either run on two network computers or within two separate DOS boxes under Windows. These programs lock specified records of the RELOCKP.DAT (Pascal version) or RELOCKC.DAT (C version) file. This file is created at the beginning of the program and is equipped with a total of 10 records, each containing 160 bytes. These records are assigned specific ASCII codes. The first record receives the ASCII code of the capital letter A, the second record the capital letter B, and the third the capital letter C, etc.

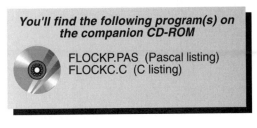

You'll find the following program(s) on the companion CD-ROM

FLOCKP.PAS (Pascal listing)
FLOCKC.C (C listing)

*The program
RECLOCK.PAS*

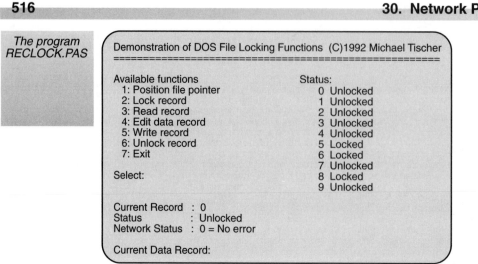

Demonstration of DOS File Locking Functions (C)1992 Michael Tischer
===

Available functions   Status:
   1: Position file pointer   0 Unlocked
   2: Lock record   1 Unlocked
   3: Read record   2 Unlocked
   4: Edit data record   3 Unlocked
   5: Write record   4 Unlocked
   6: Unlock record   5 Locked
   7: Exit   6 Locked
                                           7 Unlocked
Select: 8 Locked
                                           9 Unlocked

Current Record   : 0
Status   : Unlocked
Network Status   : 0 = No error

Current Data Record:

Both programs allow you to access different records, to read from and write to them, and, most importantly, to lock them. Currently locked records are indicated at the right side of the screen.

It may be interesting to lock several records from within the first program and then attempt to access these from the second program. DOS won't permit this access and will return error code 5, which displays an error message on your screen.

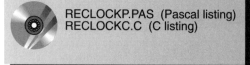

You'll find the following program(s) on the companion CD-ROM

RECLOCKP.PAS (Pascal listing)
RECLOCKC.C (C listing)

Chapter 31

DOS And Windows

Today anyone who produces DOS applications must expect that these applications will eventually be executed through Windows. Although Windows successfully simulates the DOS environment, there are certain things that DOS programs cannot do under Windows. So, if you're not careful, particularly with disk utilities, Windows may crash. TSR programs that access the DOS core deeply in order to shield themselves from other TSR programs will also cause problems.

In this chapter we'll discuss how a DOS application can detect the presence of Windows.

Sensing Windows

There isn't a single DOS function that indicates whether Windows is active, which version is active, and in which mode Windows is running. Multiple, unrelated functions must be called to provide this information.

The multiplex interrupt (interrupt 2FH) plays an important role in checking for Windows. Many resident DOS applications and utilities, such as SHARE and PRINT, use this interrupt to make their services available to other applications. Windows also assigns a few functions to this interrupt.

As the flowchart on the next page indicates, we begin by calling multiplex function 1600H, which is provided by Windows to specify the Windows operating mode. If another function wasn't linked to this function number in the multiplex interrupt, then the register settings will remain unchanged by the function call, and the AL register will remain set to 00H. This means that Windows 3.x is inactive. However, other tests must be performed to determine whether a different version of Windows is active.

If the AL register contains either 01H or FFH after the function call, Windows 2.x is active. Although the exact version is still unknown, this value indicates a running version of Windows.

If the AL register contains 80H, Windows 3.x is active in a mode other than enhanced mode.

If the AL register contains values other than 00H, 01H, 80H, or FFH, Windows 3.x (or even 4.x) is running in enhanced mode. The AL register value represents the major version number of the current Windows system, while the AH register value represents the minor version number.

Additional tests are needed to gather more information if the function call returned 00H or 80H. To determine whether Windows 3.x is active, use function 4680H, which links Windows 3.x to the multiplex interrupt. If this function returns the value 80H in the AL register, the function isn't even implemented and you can assume that no version of Windows is active.

The following flowchart illustrates how the Windows check should be performed. However, if you receive the value 00H, Windows 3 will be active. From there, all you need to do is determine the Windows operating mode. It can be running in either the standard or the real mode.

Algorithm for checking the Windows version and the operating mode

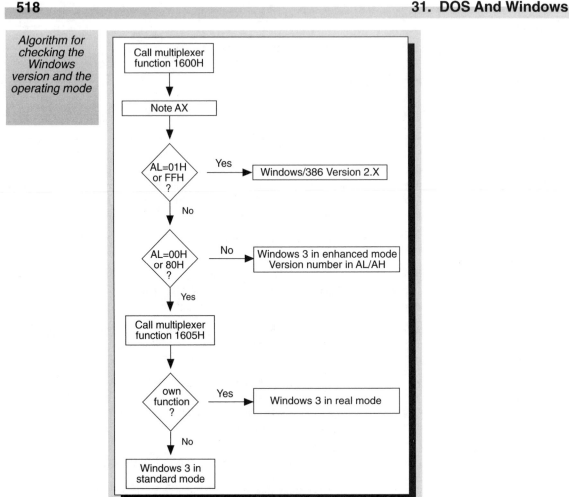

Function 1605H will help us determine the operating mode. This function switches Windows to standard mode from its current operating mode. If Windows is already in standard mode when function 1605H is called, this function will fail, placing 00H in the CX register to indicate this failure. Function 1606H switches Windows from standard mode into real mode. If Windows is already in real mode when function 1606H is called, this function will fail, placing 00H in the CX register to indicate this failure. Either function indicates the Windows 3.x operating mode, thus completing the test.

Demonstration programs

The WINDAB.BAS, WINDAP.PAS and WINDAC.C programs in BASIC, C, and Pascal implement the algorithm we've described. Each program contains a routine called WINDOWS, which returns constants named NO_WIN, WIN_386_X, WIN_REAL, WIN_STANDARD, or WIN_ENHANCED, depending on Windows status when the program is run. The programs will even tell you the exact version number if Windows 3.x is running in enhanced mode. For this, the function requires two integer variables (or in the case of the C implementation, the addresses of these variables) for storing the Windows version number.

You'll find the following program(s) on the companion CD-ROM

WINDAB.BAS (BASIC listing)
WINDAP.PAS (Pascal listing)
WINDAC.C (C listing)

Chapter 32

Maintaining Compatibility

We discuss three ways to access PC hardware in this book. You can either access available DOS or BIOS functions or develop new functions and routines for direct hardware control. Although this doesn't provide any advantages in mass storage device and keyboard access, special routines for screen display are often much faster and more efficient than BIOS and DOS routines that perform the same task.

We recommend using DOS functions for compatibility. To develop programs that run without problems on virtually any DOS computer, you must follow some rules for DOS function calls. To develop programs, under the current DOS versions, that should execute without problems under future versions of DOS, follow these suggestions:

➢ Use only DOS functions for screen and hardware access. Don't use BIOS or other hardware dependent functions.

➢ Display error messages on the standard error device (handle 2).

➢ Use Version 2 UNIX-compatible handle functions for file access. This ensures compatibility with future versions of DOS. If you must use old FCB functions for file or directory access (e.g., for special attributes), be sure no FCBs, which are already open, are opened and no FCBs, which are already closed, are closed.

➢ Check the DOS version number at the beginning of the program and end the program with an error message if it cannot execute under this version.

➢ Store as many constants as needed for program execution (e.g., the paths of programs and files to be loaded) within the environment block. Access these values from the environment block within the program.

➢ Release all memory not required by the program using the DOS functions. (This is especially important when working with COM programs.)

➢ If you need additional memory, request it using the proper DOS functions.

➢ Use the available DOS functions for interrupt vectors; don't directly access interrupt vectors. To change the contents of various interrupt vectors within a program, first save the old contents and restore them before the end of the program.

➢ Call one of the DOS functions (31H or 4CH) before the end of the program to pass a value to the calling program to signal whether the program was executed correctly. Avoid using the other functions for ending a program (interrupt 20H and function 0 of interrupt 21H).

➢ Use function 59H of interrupt 21H (available in DOS Versions 3.0 and higher) to localize error sources.

The table on the following page is an overview of the older DOS functions you should avoid and their replacements:

Old		New	
00H	End program	4CH	End Process
0FH	Open file	3DH	Open Handle
10H	Close file	3EH	Close handle
11H	Find first entry	4EH	Find first entry
12H	Find next entry	4FH	Find next entry
13H	Erase file	41H	Erase directory entry
14H	Sequential read	3FH	Read (through handle)
15H	Sequential writ	40H	Write (through handle)
16H	Created file	3CH	Created handle or
		5AH	Created temporary file or
		5BH	Created new file
17H	Rename file	56H	Rename directory entry
21H	Random access read	3FH	Read (through handle)
22H	Random access write	40H	Write (through handle)
23H	Sense file size	42H	Move file pointer
24H	Set data set number	42H	Move file pointer
26H	Create new PSP	4BH	Load and execute from file
27H	Random access read	3FH	Read (through handle)
28H	Random access write	40H	Write (through handle)

If you follow all these suggestions, your programs will execute on other computers and under future DOS versions with little or no modifications.

Chapter 33

Undocumented DOS Structures

Many reference books discuss undocumented information about DOS. Occasionally, we've found some DOS structures still undocumented, such as several DOS variables that contain extremely important information. In this chapter, we'll discuss some of these undocumented structures.

Documented And Undocumented Structures

DOS manages the operating storage media (RAM and mass storage) and programs that use multiple data structures. Some of these structures are thoroughly documented and have already been described in this book. These structures include:

> ➤ Program Segment Prefix (PSP), which precedes every program in memory

> ➤ File Control Blocks (FCBs), which control file access

> ➤ Memory Control Blocks (MCBs), which control RAM

> ➤ Structures in the header of a device driver

> ➤ Environment blocks, which contain information strings about every program in memory

> ➤ The many structures that DOS keeps in mass storage (boot sector, File Allocation Table [FAT], root directory, etc.)

There are also several undocumented structures. Until recently, only a few people knew of these structures because most technical manuals about DOS didn't describe them. The authors of many of these manuals believed these structures weren't needed for programming, and their coding would change in future versions of DOS. Actually, certain kinds of programming do depend on these structures and some applications couldn't be created without them.

Floppy disk and hard drive management utilities extensively use these undocumented structures. For example, if you examine Norton Utilities with a debugging application, you'd see how much this program accesses these structures.

A minor change in these undocumented structures occurred between DOS Version 3.3 and Version 4.0, but this is the first change since the introduction of DOS Version 2.0 in 1983. So, you probably won't find altered coding in the undocumented structures of subsequent DOS versions.

Knowing about these structures can be very useful when you're programming certain applications.

The DOS Info Block (DIB)

The DOS Info Block (DIB) is the key to accessing the most important DOS structures. This block contains pointers to several DOS structures and to other information. The DIB is useful to a program only if its address in memory is known. This address isn't in a fixed memory location, and cannot be obtained with any of the documented functions of DOS interrupt 21H. However, the undocumented function 52H can help locate this address. Calling function 52H returns the address of the DOS Info Block to the ES:BX register pair.

Unlike other DOS functions that retrieve pointers to a structure or data area, the contents of the ES:BX register pair point to the second, instead of the first, field within the DIB after the function call.

DIB structure

The first field in the DIB contains a pointer to the Memory Control Block (MCB) of the first allocated memory area.

Drive Parameter Block

The pointer in the second field of the DIB provides access to information that cannot be accessed in any other way. It points to the first Drive Parameter Block (DPB), which is a structure that DOS creates for all mass storage devices (floppy diskettes, hard drives, tape drives, etc.).

The first field of the DPB indicates the device to which the block belongs. 0 represents drive A, 1 represents B, 2 represents C, etc. The second field specifies the number of the subunit. To understand the meaning of this field, remember that access to the individual devices occurs through the device driver. DOS doesn't perform direct access to a disk drive or hard drive. So, DOS doesn't have to deal with the physical characteristics of a mass storage device. Instead, DOS calls a device driver, which acts as mediator between DOS and hardware.

Obviously, not every device has a separate device driver, since one device driver can support many devices. For example, the device driver built into DOS manages the floppy disk drives and the first available hard drive.

Since DOS configures a DPB for each device, a hard drive system automatically has 3 DPBs available. (A DPB is always configured for floppy disk drive B, even if only one floppy disk drive is actually available.)

Each device receives a number between 0 and the total number of devices minus 1, to help each driver identify the devices it manages. This is the number found in the subunit field.

The next field lists the number of bytes per sector. Under DOS, this is usually 512. After this is the interleave factor, which provides

DOS Info Block (DIB) structure		
Addr.	Contents	Type
-04H	Pointer to MCB	1 ptr
ES:BX	Pointer to first Drive Parameter Block (DPB)	1 ptr
+04H	Pointer to last DOS buffer	1 ptr
+08H	Pointer to clock driver (CLOCK)	1 ptr
+0CH	Pointer to console driver (CON)	1 ptr
+10H	Maximum sector length (based on connected drives)	1 word
+12H	Pointer to first DOS buffer	1 ptr
+16H	Pointer to path table	1 ptr
+1AH	Pointer to System File Table (SFT)	1 ptr
Length: 1EH (30) bytes		

Drive Parameter Block (DPB) structure		
Addr.	Contents	Type
+00H	Drive number or character (0 = A, 1 = B, etc.)	1 byte
+01H	Sub-unit of device driver for drive	1 byte
+02H	Bytes per sector	1 word
+04H	Interleave factor	1 byte
+05H	Sectors per cluster	1 byte
+06H	Reserved sectors (for boot sector)	1 word
+08H	Number of File Allocation Tables (FATs)	1 byte
+09H	Number of entries in root directory	1 word
+0BH	First occupied sector	1 word
+0DH	Last occupied cluster	1 word
+0FH	Sectors per FAT	1 byte
+10H	First data sector	1 word
+12H	Pointer to header (corresponding device driver)	1 ptr
+16H	Media descriptor	1 byte
+17H	Used flag (0FFH = Device not yet enabled)	1 byte
+18H	Pointer to next DPB (xxxx:FFFF = last DPB)	1 ptr
Length: 1CH (28) bytes		

the number of logical sectors displaced by physical sectors when the medium is formatted. This value can be 1 for floppy disk drives, 6 for the XT hard drive, and 3 for the AT hard drive. For floppy disk drives, this field can also have the value FEH if the disk in the drive hasn't been accessed. The value FEH indicates the interleave factor is currently unknown.

Several other fields are related to these two fields. We mentioned these fields when we discussed managing mass storage devices through DOS. Among other things, these fields describe the status and the size of the structures DOS created to manage mass storage devices. A pointer to the header of the device driver is located within these fields. DOS uses this pointer when accessing the device. Additional information can be obtained with this pointer since, for example, the driver attribute is listed in the header of the device driver.

Following this field is the media descriptor to which the Used flag is connected. As long as the device hasn't been accessed, this flag contains the value 0FFH. After the first access, it changes to 0 and remains unchanged until a system reset.

The DPB ends with a pointer that establishes communication with the next DPB. Since every DPB defines its end with such a pointer, a kind of chain is created, through which all DPBs can be reached. To signal the end of the chain, the offset address of this pointer in the last DPB contains the value 0FFFFH.

DPB access

When a program needs the information within the DPB, there are many ways to find the address of the desired DPB. One method is to follow the chain previously described by first determining the address of the DIB. This gives you the pointer to the first DPB, from which you can follow the chain until you reach the desired DPB.

However, there's a better method, which isn't as susceptible to changes within the DIB. This method involves two undocumented DOS functions, 1FH and 32H functions. Although these functions have been included in DOS since Version 2.0, they weren't documented by Microsoft. When called, both return a pointer to a DPB to the DS:BX register pair. While function 1FH always delivers a pointer to the DPB of the current disk drive, the address delivered by function 32H refers to the device whose number is passed to the function in the DL register at the time it's called (0 represents the current drive, 1 is drive A, 2 drive B etc.). Function 32H is much more flexible than function 1FH.

Using 1FH and 32H to access the various DPBs is also useful because it forces DOS to retrieve other information, such as the interleave factor and the media descriptor byte, which is determined for the disk drive only after the first access. If you get to the DPB through the pointer in the DIB block, the various fields may not have been initialized, and could contain the wrong values.

The DOS buffer

Besides the pointer to the first DPB, the DIB also contains the pointer to the first DOS buffer at address 12H. These DOS buffers store individual sectors, so the sectors don't have to be repeatedly loaded from disk. The DOS buffers are most effective when they're used to store disk sectors that are frequently needed by the currently running program. Besides the FAT, these sectors include the root directory and its subdirectories. The number of buffers can be defined by the user in the CONFIG.SYS file. If this number exceeds those needed for the FAT, root directory, and subdirectories, normal sectors can also be temporarily stored here. This is done so if they are called again in the near future, they can be taken directly from the buffer.

The individual sectors are linked together. This enables DOS to quickly check each buffer for the desired sector with each read operation.

As with DPBs, this occurs with the help of a pointer that appears at the start of every buffer. Also, the last buffer is reached when the offset address of the pointer contains the value 0FFFFH. After the field linking one buffer to the

DOS buffer structure		
Addr.	Contents	Type
+00H	Pointer to next DOS buffer	1 byte
+04H	Drive number (0 = A, 1 = B, etc.)	1 byte
+05H	Flags	1 byte
+06H	Sector number	1 word
+08H	Reserved	2 bytes
+0AH	Contents of buffered sector	512 bytes
Length: 210H (528) bytes		

next is the number of the drive where the buffered sector originates. The value is 0 for drive A, 1 for B, 2 for C, etc. Besides the drive number, the identification of a sector requires a sector number. This is located beginning at position 06H in the DOS buffer. The last field in the buffer header stores a pointer to the corresponding DPB, so DOS can obtain information about the device that loaded the buffered sector. Although this is the last field in the header of the DOS buffer, the buffered sector doesn't end immediately after this field. There are two more bytes which follow. The reason for this is the DOS code is written in machine language. So, when working with memory blocks, it's most efficient to have the buffered sector begin with an address that is divisible by 16.

The path table

The header of the DOS buffer isn't the last place we encounter the DPB. It appears again in the path table, which starts at address 16H in the DIB. This table contains the current path for each drive as well as a pointer to its DPB.

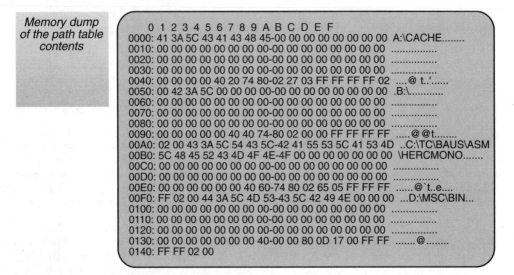

Memory dump of the path table contents

```
         0 1 2 3 4 5 6 7 8 9 A B C D E F
0000: 41 3A 5C 43 41 43 48 45-00 00 00 00 00 00 00 00   A:\CACHE........
0010: 00 00 00 00 00 00 00 00-00 00 00 00 00 00 00 00   ................
0020: 00 00 00 00 00 00 00 00-00 00 00 00 00 00 00 00   ................
0030: 00 00 00 00 00 00 00 00-00 00 00 00 00 00 00 00   ................
0040: 00 00 00 00 40 20 74 80-02 27 03 FF FF FF FF 02   ....@ t..'......
0050: 00 42 3A 5C 00 00 00 00-00 00 00 00 00 00 00 00   .B:\............
0060: 00 00 00 00 00 00 00 00-00 00 00 00 00 00 00 00   ................
0070: 00 00 00 00 00 00 00 00-00 00 00 00 00 00 00 00   ................
0080: 00 00 00 00 00 00 00 00-00 00 00 00 00 00 00 00   ................
0090: 00 00 00 00 00 40 40 74-80 02 00 00 FF FF FF FF   .....@@t........
00A0: 02 00 43 3A 5C 54 43 5C-42 41 55 53 5C 41 53 4D   ..C:\TC\BAUS\ASM
00B0: 5C 48 45 52 43 4D 4F 4E-4F 00 00 00 00 00 00 00   \HERCMONO.......
00C0: 00 00 00 00 00 00 00 00-00 00 00 00 00 00 00 00   ................
00D0: 00 00 00 00 00 00 00 00-00 00 00 00 00 00 00 00   ................
00E0: 00 00 00 00 00 40 60-74 80 02 65 05 FF FF FF FF   .....@`t..e....
00F0: FF 02 00 44 3A 5C 4D 53-43 5C 42 49 4E 00 00 00   ...D:\MSC\BIN...
0100: 00 00 00 00 00 00 00 00-00 00 00 00 00 00 00 00   ................
0110: 00 00 00 00 00 00 00 00-00 00 00 00 00 00 00 00   ................
0120: 00 00 00 00 00 00 00 00-00 00 00 00 00 00 00 00   ................
0130: 00 00 00 00 00 00 00 00-40 00 00 80 0D 17 00 FF FF   .......@........
0140: FF FF 02 00
```

As long as the LASTDRIVE command is in the system's configuration file, the table will have entries for drives A through the one specified by LASTDRIVE. If this command is missing, however, the table will have entries only for each device supported by the installed device driver. If you change the entries in this table, you can divert one drive to another. The JOIN and SUBST DOS commands also use this by manipulating the path table entry of the drive to be diverted.

Chapter 34

DOS 6.x

In 1993, Microsoft introduced the sixth version of DOS. Many users were surprised by how few of the promised features actually appeared in this version. For example, multitasking wasn't included. Instead, DoubleSpace and third-party memory support were added. In our opinion, DoubleSpace is the most important new feature of MS-DOS Version 6.

In this chapter, we'll discuss how DoubleSpace works and how it organizes information on a drive. We'll also discuss the DoubleSpace user interface. Then we'll explain the compression/decompression algorithms on which DoubleSpace is based, and show how you can use data compression and decompression capabilities in your own applications.

DoubleSpace

MS-DOS 6 includes an on-line disk compressor called DoubleSpace. Since similar products existed prior to DOS 6 (e.g., Stacker), DOS 6 provides for optimal integration of these components into the total system. Although the maximum performance is decreased by 10 percent, the hard drive capacity is almost doubled. For a history of DoubleSpace (and DoubleDrive) see Chapter 17.

First we'll examine some basic concepts of disk compression, then we'll look at the internal workings of DoubleSpace. You'll learn how DoubleSpace manages the compressed data and what DoubleSpace has to offer.

Data compression

There's nothing mysterious about data compression. Compressing files and directories produces an (apparent) expansion of available hard drive space. All compression programs, such as LHARC, Stacker, and DoubleSpace, condense data according to one of the following algorithms:

- ➤ Run Length Encoding (RLE)

- ➤ Huffman Coding

- ➤ Lempel-Ziv Compression, also known as LZW (Lempel-Ziv-Welsh).

There are several variations of these algorithms. However, each is based on a specific principle of data compression. All three processes have advantages and disadvantages regarding the amount of compression that's possible and the system resources needed for compression and decompression. Obviously resource utilization also affects the speed of compression and decompression, which, in turn, affects file access performance. However, an on-line compressor such as DoubleSpace provides a balanced relationship between degree of compression and performance.

The following descriptions of the various compression techniques should help explain why the developers at Microsoft decided to use the Lempel-Ziv process.

Run Length Encoding

Run Length Encoding is the simplest form of data compression. When compressing a file containing sequences of identical bytes, only the first byte of each sequence is stored, followed by the number of repetitions. These two bytes must be preceded by an ESC character. During unpacking the ESC character indicates that a repetitive sequence was encoded in this particular location.

Since the Escape character can also occur as a "normal" character in the file, additional precautions must be taken to ensure that this character isn't later interpreted as the start of a repetitive sequence. This doesn't affect the basic mechanism of Run Length Encoding, however.

The following illustration shows how a file is compressed using this method:

Compression with Run Length Encoding

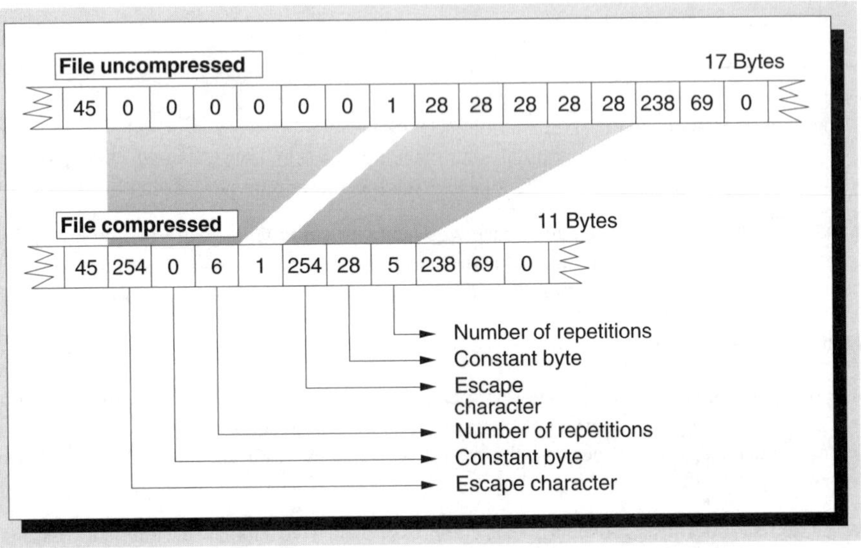

This type of data compression is especially suited to files containing numerous sequences of identical bytes, such as graphic files. Usually the greater the frequency of such sequences and the longer they are, the higher the degree of compression attained. The RLE process is relatively easy to implement, yet for large groups of differentiated files it yields the poorest results of all three algorithms. This is because it affects only constant byte sequences and leaves all other characters untouched.

Huffman coding

Huffman coding, named for the French mathematician Huffman, deviates from the commonly used standard in electronic data processing. Usually each character in a text or a file is represented by a constant number of bits (usually 8). However, with the Huffman method, the individual characters receive variable lengths.

The Huffman algorithm takes the file to be compressed and analyzes the frequencies with which various characters occur. Depending on these frequencies, the characters are then portrayed as bit sequences of varying lengths. The more frequently a character appears in the file, the shorter the bit sequence. As a result, some characters have bit lengths greater than eight. However, in the middle range of frequencies, lengths remain below eight, while the more frequently occurring characters are coded in far fewer than eight bits.

The actual process, once these bit sequences have been established and converted, is based on the creation of a binary tree, which contains the different characters and their frequencies. Since this is a relatively complicated procedure, we won't discuss it in detail here. The result of this process is that two bits are still needed for coding the most common characters, while longer bit sequences are needed for the less common characters. These sequences are usually longer than the original eight bits. However, a noticeable compression occurs relating to the common characters.

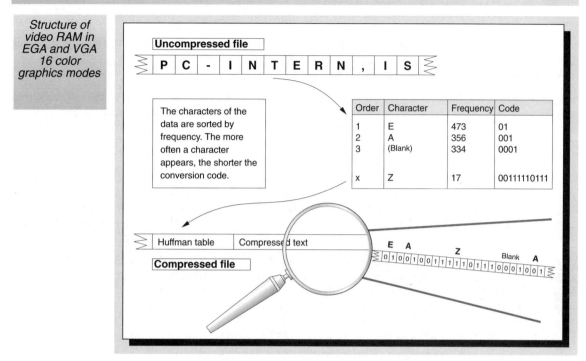

Structure of video RAM in EGA and VGA 16 color graphics modes

When comparing degrees of compression, the Huffman process is always superior to Run Length Encoding and in most cases superior to the LZ process. However, this depends on the contents of the file. The difference is smaller with the LZ process than with RLE. The Huffman process's disadvantage, as compared with the LZ process, lies in its complex conversions and the relative slowness of subsequent decompression. The file contents must be interpreted as bit sequences of varying lengths instead of as a group of 8-bit characters.

Lempel-Ziv process

Although the LZ process produces compression rates comparable to those of Huffman coding, it is much simpler and even has some similarities to Run Length Encoding. The focal point of this process is a search for repetitive sequences within a file. While Run Length Encoding looks only for sequences of the same byte, the LZ process checks the entire text.

For example, suppose the word "Miller" occurs in a file. The LZ algorithm searches for this word in the stored text. If it's found, a "match tag" is written into the file in place of the word. As a type of reverse-direction offset, the match tag indicates how many characters back one must go from the current location to the referenced character sequence, and how many characters should be taken from that point. In addition, the LZ process also incorporates Run Length Encoding for sequences of identical characters. The repeated character is written once to the file at its respective position and immediately after it's placed a match tag. Here the offset is 1 and the number equals the number of repetitions.

Of course this process is useful only if the match tag doesn't require more space than the text to which it refers. The version of the algorithm incorporated into DoubleSpace considers this and, depending on the type of file, achieves at least the following rates of compression (see the table on the right).

In this way, with a balanced mix of files, DoubleSpace can virtually double available hard drive capacity.

File type	Compression ratio
Program files	1.4:1
Texts, spreadsheets, databases	2:1
Graphics and other highly redundant files	3:1 or more

CVFs

To optimize the available hard drive capacity, DoubleSpace uses a CVF (Compressed Volume File). Usually this file, whose fixed size is determined when DoubleSpace is installed, occupies the majority of the storage space. The CVF includes both compressed files and all data structures needed for file upkeep.

With DoubleSpace, you can have more than one CVF file within a system. Each of these files is treated as a separate drive with its own drive identifier (i.e., virtual drives) and can occupy up to 512 Meg on the (uncompressed) hard drive. So, after compression, up to 1 gigabyte or more of files can be stored. The name "DBLSPACE.nnnh" is always assigned to this file; nnn is a sequential number. In converting an existing drive to a DoubleSpace drive, DoubleSpace always assigns the number "000" to the CVF file that is generated. Therefore, the file's name becomes "DBLSPACE.000."

When you start the system, this file isn't visible on drive C:. This occurs because what DOS states is drive C: is actually the contents of the CVF file; the original files from drive C: are stored as compressed files within the CVF file. However, the CVF file is accessible because the original drive C: now has drive identifier H:. When you look in the main directory of this drive, you'll see the file "DBLSPACE.000." You can also assign a device ID other than H:, as long you specifically define it during hard drive conversion.

While DoubleSpace sets up a slightly modified FAT system within the CVF file, the original drive (now H:) remains unchanged. Its structure and any files subsequently placed on it won't change. In particular, DoubleSpace leaves the DOS system files on the drive so the system can boot up as before from the hard drive. Actually, DoubleSpace is activated relatively late in the boot sequence. So, it isn't immediately available when the computer is switched on. The system first boots once using the normal FAT on drive C:. From the perspective of the C: drive, the CVF file looks like a completely normal file. To display the contents of drive H:, use the DIR H: /A:HS command. The following files will appear:

Use the DIR H: /A:HS command to display the contents of drive H:	Volume in Drive H is HOST_FOR_C Volume Serial Number is 1AAB-734F Directory of H:\

	IO SYS 40,767 03-10-93 6:00a
	MSDOS SYS 38,186 03-10-93 6:00a
	386SPART PAR 16,769,024 08-12-93 3:17p
	DBLSPACE BIN 51,288 03-10-93 6:00a
	DBLSPACE INI 91 06-30.93 10:37a
	DBLSPACE 000 295,322,624 08-12-93 3:16p
	    6 File(s) 312,221,980 bytes
	          111,099,904 bytes free

In addition to the DOS system files IO.SYS and MSDOS.SYS, and the CVF file DBLSPACE.000, three other files exist on this drive. One is the permanent Windows swap file (if installed), which for performance reasons should not be stored within a compressed drive. There are also two other DBLSPACE files required to set up the DoubleSpace drive at system startup (more on this later).

The following table summarizes the various DoubleSpace files:

Filename	Purpose
DBLSPACE.BIN	Enables access to compressed drives. This file is loaded while booting and executes even before DOS begins processing the CONFIG.SYS file.
DBLSPACE.EX	Sets up and maintains DoubleSpace drives.
DBLSPACE.HLP	Help file for DBLSPACE.EXE.
DBLSPACE.INF	Stores the DoubleSpace configuration.
DBLSPACE.INI	DoubleSpace configuration file for Windows.
DBLSPACE.WIN	Used only during installation to record information about the current Windows system.
DBLSPACE.SY	Device driver that determines the final location of the DBLSPACE.BIN program code and moves the code into upper memory when requested.
DBLSPACE.xxx	DoubleSpace CVF file containing a compressed drive.
DBLWIN.HLP	Help file for running DoubleSpace under Windows.

CVF file structure

To understand the structure of a CVF file, you must remember two requirements that existed when DoubleSpace was being developed and significantly influenced its development:

1. To utility programs, such as Norton's SpeedDisk and DirectorySort, a DoubleSpace drive must appear as a normal DOS drive.

2. The files stored on a DoubleSpace drive must always be compressed in blocks of fixed size, instead of compressed in their entirety.

The first requirement is related to compatibility, which is extremely important in DOS. So existing application programs and disk utilities can continue using DOS file access commands (especially interrupts 25H and 26H) to access DoubleSpace drives as well, the original FAT structure of such a drive must remain as close to intact as possible. Later you'll see that CVF files imitate the structure of a FAT volume, Although it's a slightly expanded and modified one.

Clustering compressed files

The second requirement is also clearly reflected in the CVF file structure. Based on the data compression techniques used in DoubleSpace, files shouldn't be compressed in their entirety. For example, to read in a record, a DOS program opens a file and positions the file pointer on the byte with offset 35,000. Under normal circumstances this operation, which eventually must be executed by the DOS file system, doesn't present a problem. As long as you don't have a virus-infected FAT, this byte will be found just where expected - 34,999 characters after the first byte in the file.

However, since the file exists in compressed form, DoubleSpace must first locate the byte within the framework of the compressed data. Because of the compression, the byte now located at the stated offset address may actually represent byte 48,000, 120,000, or any other byte in the system.

In this case, the only way to solve this problem is by completely decompressing the file, from the beginning of the file to the point at which 35,000 characters have been expanded. This process would be time-consuming. For this reason, DoubleSpace uses an alternate method of compressing files; it compresses in 8K blocks. For example, when accessing the byte with offset address 35,000 in the original (uncompressed) file, DoubleSpace can immediately find the block in which this byte is located. Although it must still decompress the entire block to reach the desired byte, all preceding blocks remain untouched.

This method of clustering of 8K blocks has both negative and positive effects on the quality of the compression. According to the LZW compression algorithm, references to already-encoded character strings are important.

One negative aspect is the references must always refer to the current 8K block, and can no longer access the file contents in their entirety. During file compression, the statistical midpoint will therefore contain fewer repeating sequences, resulting in less data being compressed through references, and lowering the degree of compression. However, it would take too long to search through the entire file for the current byte to be written, each time a reference is being created. In addition, the entire file would have to be kept in memory, which certainly isn't feasible either.

Also, too much space would be needed for the references themselves. After all, they must also contain the offset address for the character strings to which they refer. Within a closed 8K block, this offset address requires a maximum of 13 bits. Depending on its size, an entire file may require 24 bits or even 32. In the end, clustering of a compressed file into blocks of 8K each is the only practical way of ensuring the fastest and most efficient compression and decompression possible.

Now we'll return to CVF file structure. The term "cluster" is also used in connection with a FAT drive. Here the drive sectors are managed as clusters (groups) of 2, 4, 8, etc., instead of individually. In fact, the compressed 8K blocks form the basis of a DoubleSpace drive. These are the clusters that are maintained by the drive's File Allocation Table.

Differences from a normal FAT drive

In the following sections, we'll describe the various data structures within a CVF file. As you'll see, most of this information also applies to a normal DOS drive: A BIOS Parameter Block at the beginning of the drive, the boot sector, the FAT, the main directory, etc. However, two new data structures, called BitFAT and MDFAT, are also included.

These data structures are needed because the compressed 8K file clusters aren't meant to be stored in identically-sized areas on the disk. Depending on the degree of compression, such a cluster will rarely require 16 sectors (8K), which is a complete cluster. This happens only if the data wasn't compressed at all or only very slightly. On average, perhaps eight 512-byte sectors will be needed (50% compression). However, in all cases the number will range from a minimum of one (maximum compression) to a maximum of 16 (no compression).

While an 8K cluster on a normal FAT drive is always given 16 sectors and, therefore, exactly 8K, a DoubleSpace drive must be flexible. Therefore, instead of the usual 16 sectors, an 8K cluster is allotted only as many sectors as it still requires after compression. It is precisely in this way that sectors are saved; the additional sectors make the drive appear larger than its true size.

This is also the purpose of the two additional data structures; they reproduce, on the sector level, the cluster data from the normal FAT. Therefore, in the granularity of memory allocation, the sector is the most important unit (the cluster affects this granularity only superficially). In a certain sense, this undermines the concept of the cluster, although its existing structures are retained.

BitFAT

In this new scheme, the BitFAT acts as a type of free list, in which the still-free sectors within the CVF file are recorded. When a new 8K cluster must be written to the disk, DoubleSpace first looks here and searches for a corresponding number of free sectors. Usually it selects only adjacent sectors, so the cluster won't be scattered throughout the disk.

When allocating sectors, the corresponding entries in the BitFAT are marked as occupied. When they are later freed (by deleting the file belonging to them), they are designated as free.

MDFAT

Although the FAT cannot record the sectors in which an 8K cluster is ultimately stored, the normal FAT structure had to be retained. This led to the introduction of the MDFAT. According to their original design, FAT entries point to the cluster, in which the next portion of the current file resides. This operation isn't changed by the MDFAT. However, the relationship between the number of a FAT entry and the number of the cluster, in which the data is stored, is now invalid. In a normal FAT, the sectors of the cluster belonging to FAT entry 43 are also stored in cluster 43.

So, instead of actually accessing the cluster, on a DoubleSpace drive first you must examine the 43rd entry of the MDFAT. It is only here that you can determine in which sectors cluster 43 is stored within the CVF file, and how many sectors are required for this. We'll discuss the construction of an MDFAT entry in more detail in the following sections. The following illustration shows the link between directory, FAT, MDFAT and finally, the sectors in which a compressed 8K cluster is stored:

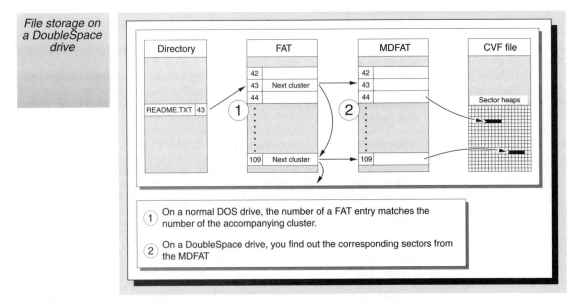

File storage on a DoubleSpace drive

Data structures in detail

Now that we've described the basic relationship between the various data structures in a CVF file, we'll discuss these structures in detail. You'll learn how the expanded BIOS Parameter Block and the MDFAT entries are constructed. As long as you're not planning to write programs that access these structures directly, these concepts should be easy to understand.

Data structure sequence

The following table shows the various data structures within a CVF file and their sizes. Note the sizes of the different structures and their starting points, relative to the beginning of the CVF file, depend on the size of the CVF file itself. Therefore, their positions must be determined during program runtime by reading the corresponding data from the expanded BIOS Parameter Block at the beginning of the CVF file.

All data structures, except for the sectors in the sector heap, aren't compressed. Therefore, they can be read without any special precautions.

Data structure	Sector offset	Size in sector	Description
MDBPB	0	1	Expanded BIOS Parameter Block (Microsoft DoubleSpace BIOS Parameter Block). This is a normal BIOS Parameter Block in the format used since MS-DOS 4.0, with several additional "DoubleSpace fields". Specifically, this is where the size of the CVF file is recorded, which determines the starting points and the sizes of the data structures that follow.
BitFAT	1	*	Contains one bit for each sector in the sector heap, set to either 0 or 1 depending on whether the corresponding sector is currently being used. The size of this data structure adapts itself to that of the sector heap and thus also to the size of the CVF file. Its maximum size is 128K with a CVF file of 512 Meg.
Reserved	*	1	Free sector for use with a future version of DoubleSpace.
MDFAT	*	*	This table of 4-byte entries reproduces the FAT-entry clusters onto the sectors from the sector heap. Its size depends on the size of the CVF file, consisting of a maximum of 256K with a CVF file of 512 Meg.
Reserved	*	31	A reserved area of 31 sectors for a future version of DoubleSpace.
Boot sector	*	1	The boot sector of the CVF drive representing a copy of the host drive. It is not used for booting, but is returned upon performing a read access on Sector 0 of the DoubleSpace drive (the normal location of the boot sector).
FAT	*	*	The FAT for the DoubleSpace drive, whose structure corresponds to that of a normal DOS FAT. Its size also depends on the size of the CVF file.
Main directory	*	32	A normal DOS main directory with the usual 32-byte directory entries.
Reserved	*	2	Two additional sectors for later use by DoubleSpace.
Sector heap	*	*	The sector storage location from which are obtained the sectors for storing the compressed clusters. It fills the rest of the CVF file until the end sectors are reached.
End sector	*	>=1*	Several sectors which close the CVF file.

* = Depends on the size of the CVF file and the length of the preceding data structures.

Expanded BIOS Parameter Block (MDBPB)

With the expanded BIOS Parameter Block in MDBPB format (Microsoft DoubleSpace BIOS Parameter Block), DoubleSpace defines the structure of the CVF file. Therefore, all structures within the CVF file can be located.

Up to the byte with offset 22H, the MDBPB's structure is identical to the normal BPB that's been used since DOS Version 4.0. Various fields are added to this standard BPB. In DoubleSpace these fields contain information about the size and construction of the CVF file.

The following table shows the structure of MDBPB:

Offset	Contents	Type
+00H	Branch instruction to boot-routine	3 bytes
+03H	Manufacturer and version number	8 bytes
+0BH	Bytes per sector	1 word
+0DH	Sectors per cluster	1 byte
+0EH	Number of reserved sectors	1 word
+10H	Number of File Allocation Tables (FAT)	1 byte
+11H	Number of entries in main directory (here always 512)	1 word
+13H	Number of sectors in volume	1 word
+15H	Media descriptor	1 byte
+16H	Number of sectors per FAT	1 word
+18H	Sectors per track	1 word
+1AH	Number of read/write heads	1 word
+1CH	Distance from first sector in the volume to the first sector on the storage medium	1 word
+1EH	Total number of sectors in volume	1 dword
DoubleSpace additions:		
+22H	First sector of the MDFAT	1 word
+24H	nlog2 of the number of bytes per sector	1 byte
+25H	Number of sectors preceding the DOS boot sector	1 word
+27H	First sector of main directory	1 word
+29H	First sector of sector heap	1 word
+2BH	Number of clusters (MDFAT entries) occupied by the DOS boot sector, the reserved area and the main directory	1 word
+2DH	Number of 2K pages in the BitFat	1 byte
+2EH	Reserved	1 word
+30H	nlog2 of the number of sectors per cluster	1 byte
+31H	Reserved	5 words
+3DH	FAT type (0 = 16-bit FAT, 1 = 12-bit FAT)	1 byte
+3EH	Maximum size of CVF file in megabytes (equals theword size of the host drive)	1
+40H-1FFH	Boot routine (not needed here)	449 bytes
Length: 512 bytes		

Using an existing CVF file as an example, you can see that usually much more space is reserved for the BitFAT, the MDFAT, and the normal FAT than is actually needed. So, enlarging the CVF file is a quick and easy process. Instead of having to move the entire sector heap to the back, which involves re-shuffling almost the entire CVF file, you must make only a few changes to the appropriate MDBPB fields.

In creating these data structures during setup of a DoubleSpace drive, DoubleSpace doesn't adapt itself to the CVF file size chosen by the user. Instead, it adapts itself to the size of the host drive. This is the maximum size to which the user can later expand the CVF file.

BitFAT

DoubleSpace uses the BitFAT to keep track of the sectors from the sector heap. The BitFAT is organized as a large bit array whose bits correspond to the various sectors. A bit-value set to 1 means the corresponding sector is being used, while 0 means the sector is free. Each word from the BitFAT corresponds to 16 sectors; bit 15 represents the first sector within this group, bit 14 represents the second, etc.

Unlike the other data structures, which are permanent, the BitFAT is recreated by DoubleSpace each time you start the system. The MDFAT serves as the basis for this operation.

MDFAT

The MDFAT acts as a link between the FAT and the sector heap. To access the sectors of a FAT entry, the entry corresponding to this FAT entry must first be read from the MDFAT. Each MDFAT entry encompass 4 bytes. The following table shows its structure and the inforamtion contained in the various bit groups within an MDFAT entry:

Bits 0 - 21	Start sector	Number of the first sector from the sector heap, in which the compressed cluster is stored. Successive sectors contain the remaining bytes of the compressed cluster.
Bits 22 - 25	Size of compressed cluster	Provides the number of sectors that were required for compressed storage of the cluster. The minimum is one sector while the maximum is 16. The values 1 to 16 are represented by 0 to 15, so the number 0 represents one sector.
Bits 26 - 29	Size of uncompressed cluster	Records the uncompressed size of the cluster, which is normally 16. The only exception is the last cluster of a file when the file size is not a multiple of the cluster size of 16 sectors. Here also the values from 1 to 16 are represented by the numbers 0 to 15. Therefore, most of the time this field contains the number 15, representing 16 sectors.
Bit 30	0 = Sector compressed 1 = Sector uncompressed	This flag shows whether the contents of the cluster were stored in compressed or uncompressed form. If, when compressing clusters, DoubleSpace doesn't save at least one sector, it forgoes the compression and stores the cluster as uncompressed.
Bit 31	0 = MDFAT entry unused 1 = MDFAT entry used	Shows whether the MDFAT entry is currently being used. This bit is maintained for DOS Undelete programs, which, when restoring files, mark the FAT clusters as again being used.
Total 32 bits		

Boot sector

The boot sector contains a 1:1 copy of the boot sector but doesn't actually boot the DoubleSpace drive. It's stored here only for compatibility reasons.

FAT

The File Allocation Table of a DoubleSpace drive acts just like a normal FAT that you would find on an uncompressed drive. However, unlike a normal drive, DoubleSpace maintains one FAT instead of two FATs. During read/write accesses by DOS programs, the second FAT is virtualized, so these programs don't notice the missing second FAT. Therefore, read accesses to the second FAT are rerouted to the first one while write accesses to the second FAT are ignored. Only write accesses to the first FAT are reflected in the FAT of a DoubleSpace drive.

Main directory

The structure of the main directory of a DoubleSpace drive is identical to that of an uncompressed drive. Here also the files and subdirectories stored in the main directory are represented by 32-byte entries. The main directory of a DoubleSpace drive contains space for 512 of these entries.

Sector heap

The sectors in the sector heap store the compressed files and subdirectories, which in this context are treated just like files. Sectors that contain compressed data always begin with a four-byte "tag", which describes how the data were compressed. For the standard DoubleSpace algorithm, the tag consists of the following bytes:

```
4DH 44H 00H 00H
```

Uncompressed sectors have no tag.

DoubleSpace and the boot process

So the user can address the compressed DoubleSpace drive in the same way as the original host drive, DoubleSpace is automatically started during the boot process. This occurs after loading and starting IO.SYS, which is one of the two core modules of DOS. At this point, all hardware tests have been executed, the active partition selected, and the boot sector contained therein loaded and started. In other words, DOS is on its way to taking control of the system.

Once IO.SYS is started, it begins by searching for the file DBLSPACE.BIN, which contains the program code for accessing compressed drives. If it finds the file in the main directory of the drive, it loads and executes the file. However, if the file is missing, IO.SYS follows its usual path of initializing the file system, completely oblivious to the possible existence of a DoubleSpace CVF file.

Once started, DBLSPACE.BIN first opens the initialization file DBLSPACE.INI, which lists the names of the CVF files on the drive and their future drive designations. DBLSPACE.BIN now mounts these CVF files (incorporates them as normal drives) into the DOS system. If DBLSPACE.BIN finds a CVF file with the number 000 (DBLSPACE.000), then this file's device ID is switched with that of the host drive, since DBLSPACE.000 always refers to the compressed contents of the host drive. The mounted drives from this moment on can be addressed, just like all other DOS drives, through their device IDs.

If DBLSPACE.BIN doesn't find a CVF file, it removes itself from memory and returns control to IO.SYS. This mechanism was included so you could also record on diskettes with the DBLSPACE.BIN file, without them actually being compressed.

After successfully mounting drives, the system continues as usual, processing the lines in the CONFIG.SYS file. Usually the kernel will arrive at the following line:

```
devicehigh=c:\dos\dblspace.sys /move
```

DoubleSpace inserts this line into CONFIG.SYS as part of its setup routine. Its function is to load DoubleSpace into upper memory (if available) so it no longer uses memory under 640K. The driver DBLSPACE.SYS's only purpose is to move the

DoubleSpace kernel from DBLSPACE.BIN into Upper Memory. So, by itself DBLSPACE.SYS isn't involved in disk access via DoubleSpace.

This second "initialization" of DoubleSpace is necessary because, when DBLSPACE.BIN executes, no upper memory exists. Upper memory only appears after HIMEM.SYS (a file called from CONFIG.SYS) accesses upper memory.

Since DoubleSpace anticipates this shift, DBLSPACE.BIN is placed at the top of low memory, immediately below the 640K limit. This ensures that, when it's later removed, a gap isn't left in lower memory and valuable memory wasted.

If a call for DBLSPACE.SYS is included within the CONFIG.SYS file, upon completing the processing of this file, DOS automatically takes over the task of shifting the program code from DBLSPACE.BIN into lower RAM (instead of into upper memory).

DoubleSpace and applications

In relation to DOS commands, DoubleSpace is completely transparent to the user. Similar to other storage devices, a DoubleSpace drive can be addressed via its respective drive designation. From there, you can execute the commands.

DoubleSpace is equally transparent at the level of application programs, although you must consider different types of disk access. At the topmost level, application programs access files and directories using DOS interrupt 21H functions. At some point during the "processing chain" that initiates the call to these functions, DoubleSpace also becomes part of the file system. Using the mechanism described earlier, it finds its way to the appropriate sector from the CVF file sector heap, in which the desired bytes are stored or should be stored. The data are then either compressed or decompressed, depending on the type of access.

The next level involves DOS interrupts 25H and 26H, with whose help DOS programs can directly read and write to individual sectors of a volume. While most application programs avoid these functions, they're basic for many DOS utilities and how they function. This especially applies to programs such as Norton's DirectorySort and defragmentation programs.

However, even to these programs, DoubleSpace provides the illusion of a normal DOS drive because it intercepts the two interrupts and converts the given sector numbers (via the MDFAT) to the sectors in which the respective information is actually stored or should be stored. Again, this also includes compression or decompression. The imitation goes so far that even DOS 5.0 defragmentation programs can be run under DOS 6 in combination with DoubleSpace. This occurs despite the fact that defragmentation is considered a very delicate operation.

In any case, there is not much to be gained from having such programs on a DoubleSpace drive, since they only re-combine the sectors of the file as they are defined in the FAT. They neglect to rearrange the various compressed cluster sectors in relation to their order in the sector heap. As children of the DOS 5 generation, these programs are completely unfamiliar with the sector heap. Therefore, on DoubleSpace drives we recommend installing the DEFRAG program included with DOS 6.2. This program takes the sector heap into consideration and restores order here as well.

DoubleSpace software interface

From the outside you can address DoubleSpace through a software interface, which depends mainly on an expansion of multiplexer interrupt 2FH. The eight functions address exclusively the requirements of disk utilities, and aren't intended for normal application programs. After all, DoubleSpace remains completely transparent to DOS programs, as long as they use the usual methods for accessing files, drives, and directories. Therefore, for normal application programs, a market doesn't exist for such a product.

The table on the right is an overview of the eight multiplexer functions of DoubleSpace:

Function	Description
00H	Obtain version information
01H	Scan drive map
02H	Switch drive ID
05H	Link compressed drive
06H	Deactivate a DoubleSpace drive
07H	Establish storage space
08H	Obtain information about CVF file fragmentation
09H	Scan number of compressed drives

All these functions must be called with the value 4A11H in the AX register and the function number in the BX Register. The code 4A11H acts as an identifier for DoubleSpace within the framework of the multiplexer interrupt. Also, all functions in the DL register await the device ID of the DoubleSpace drive currently to be addressed, where 0 stands for A:, 1 for B:, etc.

Function 0000H checks for the existence of DoubleSpace and obtains information about the drive designations used by DoubleSpace. This function call should precede all others, to ensure that DoubleSpace is resident in memory. It will also indicate whether DoubleSpace is in upper memory, or in conventional memory under 640K.

Function 0001H determines whether a particular drive is compressed and whether its drive identifier is genuine (i.e., not switched with the host drive). Function 0002H performs this drive identifier exchange, while function 0005H links drives. "Normal" DoubleSpace drives are linked automatically at system start, so this function is primarily designed for drivers governing interchangeable media. You can exchange any storage medium compressed by DoubleSpace and make it available to DoubleSpace in your system. In the opposite direction, Function 0006H provides a way for these programs to free a linked drive from DoubleSpace control, in which case it is no longer accessible under its previous device ID. It is not deleted however; its CVF file remains exactly as is.

Function 0007H determines the size of the sector heap within the CVF file and the maximum possible amount of compressed data. It doesn't indicate the maximum amount of data in uncompressed form, since this depends on the degree of compression, which you cannot predict for data that haven't been stored yet. This function also provides the number of sectors inside the sector heap.

Function 0008H offers some additional information of rather doubtful value, referring to CVF file fragmentation on the host drive. This function returns the same value as the MaxFileFragments setting in the DBLSPACE.INI configuration file. Similarly, Function 0009H is closely connected with another setting from this file. It returns the MaxRemovableDrives parameter setting. When DoubleSpace boots up, this function decides how many of a certain structure named DISK_UNIT DoubleSpace will create. One of these structures takes up 96 bytes and is required for the management of each active DoubleSpace drive.

In addition to the multiplexer functions, DoubleSpace offers two other functions, accessible from sub-function 04H of the DOS IOTCL function, rather than the multiplexer interrupt. The reason why these tasks are split up is simple. When you call functions through the multiplexer interrupt, DOS doesn't set the InDos flag, which enables reiterative calls to the function. In other words, while a multiplexer function is running, it can be called a second time by a TSR program or by another virtual DOS machine under Windows.

With the eight multiplexer functions, this potential for re-entry doesn't create a problem. However, this doesn't apply to the two IOCTL functions, since these relate to the internal caches that DoubleSpace maintains for temporary storage of cluster data and sectors from the MDFAT and BitFAT. Caches are always highly susceptible to re-entry problems.

In concrete terms, these two functions let you store the contents of the DoubleSpace caches onto disk, which is important if you want to exchange media or reset the system. For example, when a new drive is first installed, DoubleSpace can no longer write the contents of these caches onto the old one. That alone is bad enough, because data on the old drive can get lost. What's worse is that now the cache contents may be written to the new disk, which would guarantee even greater data losses from the new drive.

Therefore, any action, such as exchanging compressed media, must always be preceded by a call to one of the DoubleSpace IOCTL functions. The difference between them lies simply in the second simultaneously declares the cache contents invalid, while the first keeps them valid.

A detailed listing of all DoubleSpace multiplexer functions can be found in Appendix E on the companion CD-ROM. The two IOCTL functions are listed with the DOS API functions in Appendix D.

MRCI compression interface

DoubleSpace interacts closely with a software interface called MRCI (Microsoft Real-time Compression Interface). MRCI gives application programs, TSR programs and device drivers access to an MRCI server, which compresses and decompresses data blocks.

An MRCI server loads into memory as a component of DoubleSpace during bootup. Although DoubleSpace itself uses MRCI for compressing and decompressing data blocks, other programs can also access it. For example, the DOS 6 backup program uses the MRCI server to store backup data in compressed form. It is also used by the Flash File System. The Flash File System from Microsoft is used in combination with flash-memory cards conforming to the PCMCIA standard, which serve as substitutes for hard disks.

Microsoft Real-time Compression Format

The data here are compressed according to a fixed format, called Microsoft Real-time Compression Format, or MRCF. Following this format guarantees that data compressed on one MRCI server can be decompressed on another MRCI server.

The MRCF format results in a "loss-free" compression, which means there are no differences between the compressed data and the subsequently decompressed data. Although this seems only natural, it's precisely what distinguishes this type of compression from other processes, such as JPEG or MPEG, which "calculate away" data to a certain extent, to achieve higher compression rates. Such a thing never occurs with MRCI servers.

Hardware servers

MRCI servers can be implemented in hardware as well as software. Until now the DoubleSpace MRCI server has existed only as a software implementation. However, there is nothing to stand in the way of third-party manufacturers also offering a hardware version. The biggest advantage of a hardware implementation would be an increase in speed, since dedicated compression/decompression hardware could accomplish this task much faster than the CPU running the corresponding software. Hardware enhancements of this type are assigned to a fast bus so they can receive and transmit the data as quickly as possible. Therefore, the first hardware servers will probably be designed for the VL bus or the PCI bus.

Another advantage of hardware servers is an improved compression rate. Because a hardware server works faster than a software server, it can run through the data more often and look for further redundancies. Microsoft estimates that this will result in a 15 percent higher compression rate.

Last but not least, dedicated compression hardware can also enhance multitasking systems, such as Windows/NT. The CPU first assigns a compression/decompression job to the MRCI hardware server and, in the meantime, busies itself with another task. This allows for more efficient use of the resource processor, and a kind of multiprocessing results.

MRCI clients

While Microsoft will reveal the secrets of its MRCI server only to selected hardware manufacturers, the development of MRCI clients is open to all. MRCI clients are application programs, TSRs, or device drivers that use MRCI servers to compress or decompress data. The MRCI server can be used equally well by a terminal program compressing files to be transmitted, a program transmitting images over a network to various workstations, or a program compressing data for backup.

The remainder of this chapter is devoted to the software interface which the MRCI server makes available to MRCI clients. An MRCI server makes five different tasks available to an MRCI client, as shown in the following list. The names listed here have only symbolic meanings, since access to the MRCI server occurs through a single point of entry, instead of through specialized functions. For this point of entry, a constant must be passed to register AX to access the desired function.

Name	Purpose
MRCQuery	Obtains information about an installed MRCI server
MRCCompress	Compresses data block with standard compression
MRCDecompress	Decompresses data block
MRCMaxCompress	Compresses data block to maximum
MRCIncrementalDecompress	Incrementally decompresses data block

Establishing contact by MRCI client

An MRCI client must always call MRCQuery first, since it is only through this function that it gains entry into the MRCI server, through which it can then call the other functions. MRCQuery is called using multiplexer interrupt 2FH, whereby 4A12H must be placed in register AX as an MUX code for the MRCI server. To prove that it is a legitimate MRCI client, the ASCII codes for the character combination "MR" must be placed in register CX, and those codes for "CI" must be placed in register DX. The server transposes these character combinations, so register CX receives "IC" and register DX receives "RM."

Although at first this procedure may seem rather strange, it guarantees the MRCI client will be certain that it is dealing with an MRCI server. Any other program can engage the multiplexer interrupt under the code number 4A12H, yet none will answer the function call with precisely the same inversion of registers CH, CL, DH, and DL.

If this exchange didn't occur, then an MRCI server hasn't engaged the multiplexer interrupt. This means there is no MRCI software server in the system. However, this doesn't mean that a hardware server doesn't exist. This server enters the system through BIOS interrupt 1AH by using function B001H. Function B001H, newly developed by Microsoft, serves the same purpose as the multiplexer interrupt call, applying to registers CX and DX.

If this call is also unsuccessful, then an MRCI server doesn't exist in the system. However, if one of these two calls returns the desired combination in the register pair CX/DX, then the register pair ES:DI will contain the address of what is known as an MRCI info structure (see following table), which contains information about the MRCI server, its capabilities, and most importantly, the point of entry for calls to the various MRCI functions.

Offset	Meaning	Type
+00H	4-byte ASCII code with manufacturer name ("MSFT" for Microsoft)	4 bytes
+04H	Version number of MRCI server High byte contains main version number, low byte the sub-version number	1 word
+06H	MRCI version upon which server is based High byte contains main version number, low byte the sub-version number	1 word
+08H	MRCI server entry point for calling MRCI functions	1 var ptr
+0CH	Flag for server capabilities (see below)	1 word
+0EH	Hardware flag for server capabilities implemented through hardware	1 word
+10H	Maximum data block size that server can compress	1 word
Length: 18 bytes		

Bit 0 = Standard compression (1)
Bit 2 = Unused
Bit 4 = Unused
Bit 5 = Incremental decompression (32)
Bit 0 = Standard compression (1)
Bit 2 = Unused
Bit 4 = Unused
Total 16 bits

The two flags returned within the structure are identical in their makeup. The first flag indicates which functions are available overall, while the second flag indicates which of these are implemented through hardware. If a bit is set in the first flag and not in the hardware flag, then the corresponding function is available through the software and not the hardware.

While all MRCI servers support standard compression and decompression, this isn't true for maximum compression and incremental decompression. Maximum compression involves reducing the data even further than is possible with standard compression. However, doing this increases compression time. With incremental decompression, the idea is to decompress a compressed data block only up to a certain byte. This is useful when you need only a certain number of bytes instead of the entire data block. Instead of wasting time decompressing the entire block, with incremental decompression you can stop the unpacking of data at a certain byte and continue from that point later as desired. To determine whether each of these two functions is available, check the corresponding flags within the MRCI info structure.

One entry which you usually don't have to worry about is the maximum size of compressible data blocks. For MRCI servers, this always amounts to at least 8K, so for block sizes up to 8K checking the corresponding element within the data structure is unnecessary.

Calling the MRCI server functions

In the previous table, the various bits for the individual flags are purposely listed along with their order. Upon calling the MRCI server, these orders are the ones that must be given as a function code in register AX, as the entry point to the MRCI server. The MRCI server also looks in register CX for the value 0 or 1, depending on whether the client is a transient application program (0) or a resident system component (1), such as a TSR or device driver.

Furthermore, upon calling the MRCI server, it also awaits two FAR pointers in the register pairs ES:BX and DS:SI. ES:BX is for the pointer to the MRCI info block returned from the Query call, and DS:SI is for a pointer to an MRCI request block. Here the MRCI server obtains important information necessary for running the corresponding function (e.g., buffer addresses), where files to be compressed or decompressed are located. The following table gives the precise layout of this structure:

Offset	Contents	Type
+00H	FAR pointer to source buffer	1 var ptr
+04H	Length of source buffer in bytes	1 word
+06H	Reserved	1 word
+08H	FAR pointer to destination buffer	1 var ptr
+0CH	Length of destination buffer in bytes	1 word
+0EH	Block size for compressed data	1 word
+10H	Pointer for incremental decompression	1 var ptr
Length: 18 bytes		

The first four fields of the data structure describe the locations of the source and destination buffers in memory, as well as their length. During compression, data from the source buffer are compressed into the destination buffer (i.e., following a successful call to the function, the destination buffer contains a compressed version of the uncompressed data from the source buffer). The same happens with decompression, whereby the contents of the source buffer are decompressed into the destination buffer. The MRCI server requires that both buffers stay within their limits and, therefore, considers the given buffer sizes.

For the source buffer, the number of bytes to be compressed or decompressed is given during compression/decompression. The MRCI server uses this information to determine how much space is available in the destination buffer for the compressed or decompressed data. If there isn't enough space, the server function returns to the client with an error code. Therefore, there is no danger of overwriting the destination buffer. From the length of the destination buffer, you can also determine, following compression or decompression, the number of bytes in the compressed/decompressed data.

Offset 0EH (Block size for compressed data) applies only to data compression. This offset is designed to speed up the functioning of the MRCI server. Usually compressed data is stored in blocks of constant size. In DoubleSpace this is on the lowest level of the hard drive sector, which always contains 512 bytes. When compressing data, it's useless to carry the compression beyond 512 bytes, since you would still need the entire sector anyway. Even if you managed to squeeze the data into 300 or 200 bytes, as far as hard drive space is concerned it would make no difference. Therefore, the most practical method is stopping the compression at the 512-byte limit and saving the time that would otherwise have been used in continuing it.

Valid entries in this field are 1 to 32768. DoubleSpace sets the value to 512, but application programs can set it to 1 if they need a high degree of compression.

Server calls and Windows

The instruction code in AX, the type of application in CX, a pointer to the MRCI info block in ES:BX, and a pointer to the MRCI request block in DS:SI are needed to call an MRCI server function. However, first the program must enter a Windows Critical Section, for the case when the application is running in a virtual DOS machine under Windows in 386 Enhanced mode. Since true multitasking is being performed among these VMs, the MRCI server may be confronted with several function calls from different VMs simultaneously. The MRCI server can't handle this situation.

This problem is avoided by preceding the server call with entry into a Windows Critical Section. In a Critical Section of this type, only one VM or Windows application can exist at any given time. If another VM has already claimed this attribute, the call for entry into the Critical Section is held up until the other VM has left its Critical Section. The call for exiting a Critical Section is as important as the call for entering a Critical Section.

The entry code for a Critical Section and the subsequent exit code is precisely stipulated by Windows, and must be implemented in assembly language. The entry code is as follows:

```
Entry code     Exit code
push    ax     push    ax
mov     ax,8001h     mov     ax,8101h
int     2ah    int     2ah
pop     ax     pop     ax
```

If Windows isn't active these calls go into oblivion, since no special handler exists for these calls after interrupt 2AH. The program will continue execution, instead of crashing the system. Although there is no entry into a Critical Section, once Windows is inactive this doesn't matter anyway. Before calling a server function, TSR programs and device drivers must take control of the InDos flag. This is necessary to prevent a re-entrance of DOS (see Chapter 35 for information on TSR programming). Following a call to the MRCI server, a status value is returned in register AX. A value of 0 means the function was executed successfully, while all other values represent errors in accordance with the following table:

Code	Error
0	All OK
1	Incorrect function code
2	Server is busy
3	Destination buffer too small
4	Data cannot be compressed

Terminate And Stay Resident Programs

Since it was introduced, DOS has been criticized for its inability to handle multitasking (running more than one program simultaneously). Although OS/2 is capable of multitasking, it runs only on ATs or 80386-based computers. But TSR (Terminate and Stay Resident) programs can provide DOS machines with some of the advantages of multitasking. This type of program moves into the "background" once it's started, and becomes active when the user presses a particular key combination. The SideKick program produced by Borland International made TSR programs very popular.

Running a TSR program isn't true multitasking because only one program is actually running at any given time. However, by pressing a key, the user can immediately access useful tools, such as a calculator, calendar, or note pad. In addition to these applications, macro generators, screen layout utilities, and text editors are also available in TSR form.

Many TSR programs can even interact with the programs they interrupt and transfer data between the TSR and the interrupted program. An example is a TSR appointment book that inserts a page from its calendar in a file that's loaded into a currently running word processor. Although many different applications can be implemented with TSR programs, these programs share two characteristics:

➤ They operate in basically the same way

➤ They are based on similar programming concepts

In this chapter, we'll examine these two items and present simple implementations of TSR programs.

Before we begin, we must remind you that this involves very complex programming. So, to understand this material, you must know how things operate within the system. This especially applies to TSR programs, because, by their definition, they practically ignore the single-task nature of DOS, in which one program has access to all the system resources (RAM, screen, disk, etc.).

A TSR program must contend with many other elements of the system, such as the BIOS, DOS, the interrupted program, and even other TSR programs. Managing this is a difficult task, and can only be accomplished using assembly language. Of the available PC languages, only assembly language offers the ability to work at the lowest system level, the interrupt level. However, although it has this capability, assembly language is as flexible as high level languages for writing TSR applications, such as calculators or note pads. Because of this, we'll list two assembly language programs in this chapter. These programs will allow you to "convert" Turbo Pascal, Turbo C, and Microsoft C programs into TSR programs.

Activating A TSR Program

Let's begin by discussing how a TSR program is activated. To place our TSR program in the foreground immediately after we press a certain key combination (called the hotkey), we must install some sort of activation mechanism that's tied to the keyboard. We can use interrupts 09H and 16H, which are two system keyboard calls. Interrupt 16H is the BIOS keyboard interrupt, which programs use to read characters and keyboard status. If we use this interrupt, then our TSR program can only be activated when the main program is using interrupt 16H for keyboard input.

So, instead we should use interrupt 09H, which is called by the processor whenever a key is pressed or released. We can redirect this interrupt to our own routine, which can check to see whether the TSR program should be activated. Before it does this, the routine should call the old interrupt 09H handler. There are two reasons for this. The first reason is related to the task of interrupt 09H, which informs the system the keyboard needs the system's attention to transfer information about a key event. So, interrupt 09H usually points to a routine, within the ROM BIOS, that accepts and evaluates information from the keyboard. Specifically, it receives the code from the keyboard, converts it to an ASCII code, and then places this code in the BIOS's keyboard buffer. Since our TSR program neither wants nor is able to handle this job, we must call the original routine; otherwise keyboard input will be impossible.

The second reason has to do with the fact that other TSR programs may have been installed before ours. These routines would have redirected interrupt 09H to their own routines. Since our program is in front of these programs in the interrupt handler chain, their interrupt routines won't be called automatically if we don't call the old interrupt handler. So, we wouldn't be able to activate these TSR programs. Remember that when a TSR program is called using a redirected interrupt routine, it should always call the old interrupt handler before or after its own interrupt processing.

The call cannot be made with the INT assembly language instruction, because this would simply recall our own interrupt handler. Usually this leads to an infinite loop, a stack overflow, and, eventually, a system crash. To avoid this, we must save the address of the old interrupt handler when the TSR program is installed. We can then call the old interrupt handler with this stored address by using a FAR CALL instruction. To simulate calling this handler through the INT instruction, we must first place the contents of the flag register on the stack with the PUSHF instruction before the CALL.

Reading keys for TSR programs using interrupt 09H

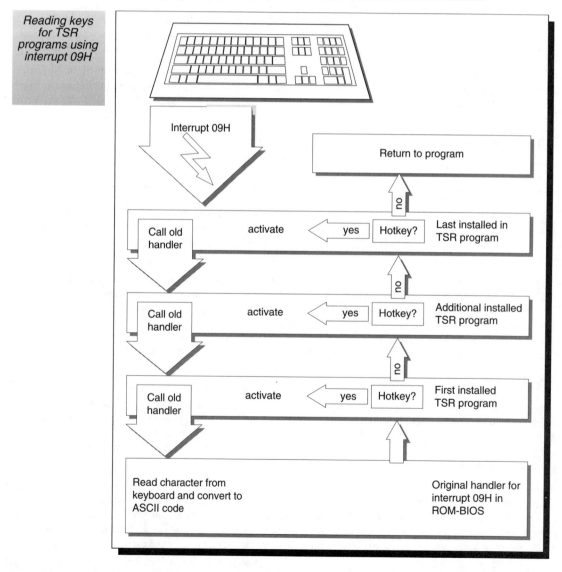

Following the interrupt handler call, the contents of port 60H are read. This port contains the scan code of the key most recently pressed (see Chapter 5 for more information on scan codes). The previous interrupt handler, which is called later, also reads the contents of this port to determine the scan code. When the new interrupt handler reads this port, the port's content remains unchanged, so when the old handler reads its contents later, the same value will be returned. This value remains constant until a new key is pressed.

From the contents of keyboard port 60H, the new TSR interrupt handler can determine whether the user has pressed its designated hotkey. However, this value will correspond to only part of the hotkey, since hotkeys are generally used as key combinations, often combining a letter or number with one or more modifier keys (Shift, Ctrl, Alt, etc.).

After the return from the interrupt handler, we can check to see whether the hotkey was pressed to activate the TSR. The BIOS keyboard status byte (BIOS variable address 0040:0017) indicates the status of the following keys:

- ➢ Right Shift key
- ➢ Ctrl key
- ➢ Num Lock key
- ➢ Caps Lock key
- ➢ Left Shift key
- ➢ Alt key
- ➢ Scroll Lock key
- ➢ Sys Req key (AT keyboard only)

If the appropriate keys are pressed, the user is trying to activate the TSR program. This is only possible if certain conditions are met, all of which are based on the fact the DOS is not re-entrant.

DOS

Since the TSR program can be activated from the keyboard at any time, regardless of the other processes in the system, it may interrupt a call to a DOS function. This may not lead to problems as long as the TSR program properly returns to the interrupted DOS function. However, a problem occurs when the TSR itself tries to call DOS functions, which is difficult to avoid when programming in a high level language. This demonstrates the problem of ..re-entry;. This refers to the ability of a system to allow multiple programs to call and execute its code at the same time. However, DOS is not re-entrant because it is a single-task system and assumes that DOS functions will be called in sequence, instead of in parallel.

Calling a DOS function from within a TSR program while another function is executing, leads to problems because the processor register SS:SP is loaded with the address of one of three DOS stacks when interrupt 21H is called. Which of the three stacks is used depends on the function group, to which the DOS function belongs, and cannot be determined by the caller. While the DOS function is being executed, it places temporary data, as well as the return address to the calling program, on this stack. If the execution of the function is then interrupted by the activation of a TSR program, which then calls a DOS function, DOS will again load register pair SS:SP with the starting address of an internal stack. If it's the same stack the interrupt function was using, each access to the stack will destroy the data of the other function call. The DOS function called by the TSR program will be executed properly, but the problem will occur when the TSR program ends and control returns to the interrupted DOS function. Since the contents of the stack have been changed in the meantime by other DOS calls, the DOS function will probably crash the system.

Bypassing re-entry

There are two ways to avoid these re-entry problems. You can either avoid calling DOS functions or allow the TSR program to be activated only if DOS functions aren't being executed. Since we've already ruled out the first option, we must use the second. DOS helps us by providing the INDOS flag, which is normally used only inside DOS but which is very useful to us as well. This flag is a counter that counts the nesting depth of DOS calls. If it contains the value 0, no DOS functions are currently being executed. The value 1 indicates the current execution of a DOS function. Under certain conditions, this counter can also contain larger values, such as when one DOS function calls another DOS function, which is allowed only in special cases.

Since there isn't a DOS function that can read the value of this flag, we must read the contents directly from memory. Since the address doesn't change after the system is booted, we can obtain the address when the TSR is installed and save it in a variable. DOS function 34H returns the address of the INDOS flag in register pair ES:BX.

This flag is read in the interrupt handler for interrupt 09H since it checks to see whether the hotkey was pressed, and allows the TSR program to be activated only if the INDOS flag contains the value 0. However, this doesn't completely solve our problem. It coordinates the activation of the TSR program with DOS function calls of the transient program being executed in the foreground, but it doesn't allow the TSR program to be called from the DOS user interface. Since the DOS command processor (COMMAND.COM) uses some DOS functions for printing the prompt and accepting input from the user, the INDOS flag always contains the value 1. In this instance, we can interrupt the executing DOS function, but we must ensure the INDOS flag contains the value 1, because a DOS function can be called from transient program or from the DOS command processor.

However, there is also a solution to this problem. It involves the fact the DOS is in a kind of a wait state when it's waiting for input from the user in the command processor. To avoid wasting any valuable processor time, it periodically calls interrupt 28H, which is responsible for short term activation of background processes, such as the print spooler (DOS PRINT command) and other tasks. If this interrupt is called, it's relatively safe to interrupt DOS and call the TSR program.

To use this procedure, a new handler for interrupt 28H is installed when the TSR program is installed. First it calls the old handler for this interrupt and then checks to see whether the hotkey has been pressed. If this has occurred, the TSR program can be activated, even if the INDOS flag isn't 0.

We still must add another restriction. The TSR program cannot even be activated with the handler for interrupt 09H if time-critical actions are being performed in the system.

Time-critical actions

These are actions which, for various reasons, cannot be interrupted because they must complete execution in a relatively short time. In the PC, this includes accesses to the floppy and hard disk, which at the lowest levels are controlled by BIOS interrupt 13H. If an access to these devices isn't completed by a certain time, the system can be seriously disrupted. A dramatic example of this is if the TSR program performs an access to these devices before another access, which is initiated by the interrupted program, has finished. Even if this doesn't crash the system, it will lead to data loss.

We can avoid this by installing a new interrupt handler for BIOS interrupt 13H. When this handler is called, it sets an internal flag that shows the BIOS disk interrupt is currently active. Then it calls the old interrupt handler, which performs the access to the floppy or hard disk. When it returns to the TSR handler, the flag is cleared, signaling the end of BIOS disk activity.

To prevent this interrupt handler from being interrupted, the other TSR interrupt handlers monitor this flag and will activate the TSR program only if the flag indicates the BIOS disk interrupt isn't active.

Delayed activation

Depending on the current DOS or BIOS operations, occasionally a TSR program may be unable to move into the foreground. Because of this, most TSR programs also install an interrupt handler for timer interrupt 08H. This interrupt handler can delay the start of the TSR. If the hotkey is recognized and the TSR program is unable to execute at that moment, a special flag is set within the keyboard interrupt handler.

This flag is then checked by the new timer interrupt handler, which is called 18.2 times a second if the current application hasn't changed the timer frequency. If the handler discovers the TSR program is waiting to be activated, and if DOS and BIOS have completed their operations, then the TSR program can be activated.

However, a time limit should be set for this delay. Otherwise, if the hotkey is pressed, and if DOS is currently executing a lengthy operation, the TSR program may only be activated after several seconds. If the length of this delay isn't limited, the user won't know whether the TSR program hasn't recognize the hotkey, or whether it's still waiting for an opportunity to start.

So, the flag that facilitates the delayed start of a TSR program also acts as a timekeeper. Its value decrements each time the timer interrupt is activated. When this value reaches 0, the interrupt handler stops trying to activate the TSR program. If the keyboard interrupt handler initializes this flag with a value of 6, for instance, then the maximum delay for the start of the TSR program consists of 6 timer interrupts, or about one third of a second. If the program cannot be activated within this time frame, the hotkey call has no effect.

Recursion

Since the hotkey can still be pressed after the TSR program has been activated, we must prevent the TSR program from being reactivated before it's finished. We can simply add another flag, which is checked before the TSR is activated. The TSR program sets this flag when it begins and clears it again just before it ends. If an interrupt handler determines that this flag is set, it will simply ignore the hotkey.

Once all these conditions have been met, we can activate the TSR program.

Context switch

The process of activating a TSR program is called a *context switch*. The program context or environment is the only information needed for operating the program. This includes such things as the contents of the processor registers, important operating system information, and the memory occupied by the program. We don't have to worry about the program memory in our context switch, however, since our TSR program is already marked as resident, which means the operating system won't give the memory it occupies to other programs.

The processor registers, especially the segment registers, must be loaded with the values the TSR program expects. These are saved in internal variables when the TSR program is installed. Since the contents of these and other registers will be changed by the TSR program, the contents of the registers must be saved because they belong to the context of the interrupted program and must be restored when it starts again.

This also applies to context dependent operating system information, which, for DOS, includes only the PSP (Program Segment Prefix) of the program and the DTA (Disk Transfer Area). The addresses of both structures must be determined and saved when the TSR program is installed so they can be reset when context is changed to the TSR program. Also, remember to save the addresses of the PSP and DTA of the interrupted program before the context change to the TSR program. There are DOS functions for setting and reading the address of the DTA (DOS functions 1AH and 2FH), but there are no corresponding documented functions for the PSP. DOS Version 3.0 includes function 62H, which returns the address of the current PSP, but has no function for setting the address. Undocumented functions for doing both exist in DOS 2.0: function 50H (set PSP address) and 51H (get PSP address). Both of these are used in our TSR demonstration program.

The TSR code must perform one final task. When the TSR program is activated using interrupt 28H, an active DOS function is interrupted. This function's stack shouldn't be disturbed. Generally we should take the top 64 words from the current stack and place them on the stack of the TSR program. This completes the context change to the TSR program, which means the TSR program can now be started.

At the moment, the TSR program can be viewed as a completely normal program which can call arbitrary DOS and BIOS functions. The only competitor left in the system is the foreground program. The TSR must ensure that it leaves both the foreground program and its screen undisturbed.

Saving the screen context

The tasks were exclusively handled in assembly language. However, the C or Pascal program comprising the TSR program itself can save the screen context. This screen context includes the current video mode, the cursor position, and the screen's contents. The contents of the color registers and other registers on the video card must also be saved, if any of these values are changed by the TSR program.

As we described in Chapter 4, the video mode can easily be determined with function 00H of BIOS video interrupt 16H. If the screen is in text mode (modes 0, 1, 2, 3, and 7), the TSR program must save the first 4000 bytes of video RAM. The video BIOS can be used for this or you can access the video RAM directly (see Chapter 4).

Saving the video mode becomes very complicated if a graphics mode is active, since the video RAM for EGA and VGA cards can be as large as 256K in some modes. If the TSR program interrupted a transient program, it may be impossible to allocate a large enough buffer to handle both programs.

This is why many TSR programs won't activate themselves from within graphics mode, and can only be used in text mode. Since PCs mostly use text mode, this isn't a major problem. Microsoft Windows¿, which operates only in graphics mode, is an exception. Since this program usually supports some mechanism for parallel execution of calculators, note pads, etc., TSR programs aren't very useful under Windows.

TSR Programs In Pascal And C

You must understand the information we just presented to completely comprehend the assembler modules TSRPA.PAS (for Pascal programs) and TSRCA.ASM (for C programs). Since both modules are based on the same basic principles and the differences between these programs are limited to the different conventions found in Pascal and C, we'll discuss only their structure.

Both assembly modules can install the TSR program upon the first program call from the DOS command line, and can reinstall the program upon a second call. They also offer a TSR program, being called from the DOS command line, the option of communicating with a memory-resident copy of the same program. This makes it possible, for example, to specify a new hotkey for the installed version, without having to remove the program from memory and then reinstall it. Other parameters can also be changed in this way, since any desired Pascal or C routine can be called within the memory-resident TSR program, as you'll see below.

Assembly language modules

To support the mentioned functions, the assembly module offers the high level language program seven procedures, which are listed in the table below.

Name	Description
TsrInit	Transforms the program into a TSR program, installs the interrupt handler, ends the program and installs it in memory.
TsrIsInst	Determines whether a copy of the program is already resident in memory.
TsrCanUninst	Determines whether the resident copy of the program may be uninstalled.
TsrUnInst	Removes a memory-resident copy of the program from memory.
TsrSetPtr	Sets a pointer to the address of the procedure that is to be called within the memory-resident copy of the program.
TsrCall	Calls the procedure identified by TsrSetPtr.
TsrSetHotkey	Sets the program's hotkey.

Checking the installation status

The high level language program must first call the TsrIsInst procedure to determine whether a copy of the program is already installed in memory as a TSR program. To do this, the procedure uses the DOS multiplex interrupt 2FH (MUX). This is possible because an interrupt handler for interrupt 2FH is also installed when a TSR program is loaded into memory.

This interrupt only responds to a very specific function, whose function number is determined when TsrIsInst is called. If it's called with another function number, the TSR program simply passes the call to the previous interrupt handler. The new MUX interrupt handler supports two functions as subfunctions of the specified function number, with the subfunction numbers AAh and BBh. The first subfunction is used to locate a resident version of the TSR program.

As is commonly the case with MUX functions, the function and subfunction numbers in registers AH and AL are simply swapped when the subfunction is called. However, if the TSR program isn't installed, this swap doesn't occur, because none of the previous MUX handlers recognize the function. The contents of the AX register are therefore returned unchanged.

In calling this MUX function, TsrIsInst can easily determine whether the program has already been installed. If this is the case, TsrIsInst also calls the second TSR program's second MUX function, which returns the resident program's segment address. This value is then stored in a variable within the TSR program. Like all other variables of the assembly module, this variable is stored in the module's code segment. This ensures the variables can also be addressed within the interrupt handler, even if the program's data segment cannot be accessed.

You now have enough information to understand how the two assembly language interfaces operate. The two programs are based on the principles we've outlined here; the differences between them reflect the different syntaxes of compiled C and Pascal programs. First, we'll concentrate on the similarities between the two programs.

Both programs assume the TSR program was installed by the first call from the DOS level and will be reinstalled on each new call. It's important to remember one general rule: a TSR program can be reinstalled only if no other TSR programs have been installed in the meantime. The LIFO (Last In, First Out) principle applies here, so the only way a TSR program can be reinstalled is if it was the last one to be installed, and if the corresponding interrupt vectors point to its interrupt handlers. If another TSR program was installed after it, the interrupt vectors point to its handlers.

To support this mechanism, the assembly language interface offers the high-level program three routines to install and later reinstall the TSR program. To decide whether the program should be installed or reinstalled, the first function should be called to determine whether the TSR program is already installed. This routine is passed an identification string, which will play an important role later when the program is installed. The routine looks for this ID string within the handler for interrupt 09H. If it finds the string, the TSR program is already installed and can be reinstalled.

If the ID string isn't found, the TSR program hasn't been installed, or another TSR program redirected the interrupt 09H vector in the meantime. The TSR program can then be installed with the help of the installation routine. This routine must receive the ID string used to detect whether the program has already been installed, the address of the high level routine that will be called when the TSR program is activated, and the hotkey value. The hotkey value is the bit pattern, in the BIOS keyboard flag, that will activate the TSR program and can be defined within the high level language program with the help of predefined constants.

The initialization routine first saves the addresses of the interrupt handlers for interrupts 09H, 13H and 28H. Then the data for the context of the high level program are read and saved in variables within the code segment, so they are available for the interrupt handler and for activation of the TSR program. In the next step, the new interrupt handlers for interrupts 09H, 13H, and 28H are installed. Finally, the number of paragraphs after the end of the program, which are to remain resident, must be calculated. Here the C and Pascal modules differ from each other. Information about this calculation can be found in the individual descriptions of the modules.

The actual installation is now complete and the program is terminated as resident. Notice the installation routine doesn't return to the high level language program, so all initialization, such as memory allocation or variable initialization, must be performed before the call to this routine.

If the installation test function of the assembly language module determines the program is already installed, it can be reinstalled with the help of another function. This function is passed the address of a routine in the high level language program, which will perform a "cleanup" of the program. This process includes releasing allocated memory and other tasks. If no such routine is to be called, the assembly language routine must be passed the value -1. Since the "cleanup" function is in the TSR program, instead of in the program that is performing the reinstallation, a context switch is necessary. Unlike activation of the TSR program and the corresponding interruption of the foreground program, this is from the program that is performing the reinstallation to the already installed TSR program. The reinstallation returns the redirected interrupt handlers to their old routines and releases the memory allocated by the TSR program.

In addition to these three functions, which are called from the high level language program, the assembler module contains some routines that may not be called by high level language programs. These include the interrupt handlers for interrupts 09H, 13H, and 28H as well as a routine that accomplishes the context switch to and from the TSR program.

Installation and setting the hotkey

The TSR program is usually installed after TsrIsInst has determined that a copy of the program hasn't been installed yet. The installation consists of two steps; the first step determines the program's hotkey using TsrSetHotkey. The program is then loaded into memory as a TSR program by the TsrInit function, and is, temporarily, terminated.

First, let's discuss TsrSetHotkey: The arguments used by this function are the two parameters that determine the hotkey. These are the bit mask for the modifier keys, and the scan code of the accompanying letter or number key. Both parameters can be constructed using constants presented at the beginning of the two programs in Pascal and C.

For the modifier keys, these parameters carry the names LSHIFT (left SHIFT key), RSHIFT (right SHIFT key), ALT, CTRL, etc. When the hotkey key combination must use more than one of these keys simultaneously, such as Ctrl+Alt with another key, they can be linked with a binary OR operator. This binary OR has the same effect for the user as the logical AND.

The constants for the keyboard scan codes all begin with the prefix SC_, which is then followed by the letter, number, or name of that key (for instance, SC_5, SC_X, or SC_SPACE). These constants can easily be found in both the Pascal and C program, since they are grouped into a large block. If your TSR program must be activated by a combination of only modifier keys, so no letter or number key must be pressed, you can use the SC_NOKEY constant.

Once the hotkey has been defined, TsrInit is called and transforms the program into a memory-resident TSR program. TsrInit also expects two arguments: the offset address of the actual TSR procedure and a value indicating the program's memory requirement. Since this parameter is handled differently in the Pascal and C assembly interfaces, we'll discus it in more detail later.

For now, simply remember the first parameter for TsrInit, which specifies the TSR procedure offset address, also determines the high level language procedure that is called when the TSR program is activated. This procedure embodies the actual purpose of the TSR program and is capable of utilizing all functions provided by the particular high level language that's used. It can even access files, read directories, and perform any other operation involving DOS functions. Once this procedure has been completed, the TSR program will again move to the background and clear the way for the previously interrupted program.

TsrInit's first task is to determine the addresses of interrupt handlers 08H, 09H, 13H, 28H, and 2Fh, and to store these addresses. Then the data required by the applicable high level language program are determined. These are also stored in variables within the code segment, so they'll be available to the interrupt handler as well as for activating the TSR program. Next, the new interrupt handlers for interrupts 08H, 09H, 13H, 28H, and 2FH are installed. The function number that was specified at the previous TsrIsInst call is assigned as the function number for MUX interrupt 2FH.

Before the program can be installed in memory by the DOS function 31H, the amount of memory or the number of paragraphs the program will need to remain resident after execution must be calculated. The Pascal and C versions perform this task differently. Below, we'll explain how the two programs perform this task.

This step completes the installation, and the program is terminated, but remains resident. Remember that once TsrInit has been called, the procedure doesn't return to the high level language program. Because of this, all tasks, such as memory allocation or the initialization of variables, must be completed before this procedure is called.

The high level language programs

The following programs in C and Pascal demonstrate the assembly language routines. First they determine whether the program is installed. On a new installation, a TSR routine is installed. You can activate the TSR by pressing both <Shift> keys. It stores the screen contents, then displays a message and asks the user to press a key. After this is done, the old screen contents are copied back and the execution of the interrupted program continues.

On a reinstallation, the assembly language reinstallation program calls a cleanup function in the TSR program. It prints the number of activations of the TSR program, which is set to zero when the TSR program is installed and incremented on each activation. This makes it clear the cleanup function is actually executed in the installed TSR program and not in the program that performs the reinstallation.

Removing TSR programs from memory

TSR programs are usually installed upon the first program call, and removed at the next call. So, if TsrIsInst determines, at the start of a program, that another copy is already resident, the resident copy must be removed.

For this, the TsrCanUninst function must be called. This function determines whether the program can be removed from memory because occasionally this won't be possible. This is the case when another TSR program has been installed since the original installation, because the second program also redirects the interrupt vectors of the timer, the keyboard, and other devices. This program, like other TSR programs, located the address of the first program's interrupt handler when it was first installed, and accesses these through its own handler. However, since the preceding handlers belong to the TSR program that must be uninstalled, these must also be removed. Since it isn't possible to inform the second program about removing these handlers, this action will inevitably result in a system crash.

Because of this, TsrCanUninst checks whether all redirected interrupts still point to the interrupt handler of the first copy of the TSR program, and responds with a corresponding TRUE or FALSE. Only when this function returns TRUE can the program call TsrUninst to remove the resident copy from memory.

For the uninstallation of a TSR program, the old interrupt handlers for interrupts 08H, 09H, 13H, 28H, and 2FH are restored. The memory occupied by the program is then released, so DOS can make it available to other programs. The program leaves no traces in memory.

Calling procedures in a resident TSR program

The possibility of utilizing procedures within the resident copy of the TSR program must be used when another copy is reinstalled. This is because even the high level language portion of a TSR program must frequently use operating resources (memory, interrupt vectors, files) that must be returned to the operating system once the program is removed from memory.

Since the segment address of the resident copy can easily be determined through the MUX handler, and since the offset address of the corresponding procedure is the same as that of the program that was just executed, it's possible to construct a FAR pointer identifying the procedure of the resident program that will be executed. The only prerequisite for this operation is the routine to be called is of the type VAR, and that can also be arranged.

However, there's a problem with this procedure. By calling this procedure directly, the context isn't switched to the resident copy of the program. So, the data segment of the new running program, and its PSP and DTA, remain active. This means the procedure being called couldn't access its variables stored in its data segment, because these belong to the copy of the program that was just called.

Therefore, a mediator must be used when calling a procedure within the resident copy so the context can be switched to that copy of the TSR program. The same mediator would switch the context back to the program being executed once the procedure has been completed.

This type of mediating procedure would only require the offset address of the procedure within the resident program that must be called. Although this works, it doesn't provide a way to pass arguments to the resident procedure and return arguments from this procedure.

To make the transmission of such arguments possible, another method of calling procedures within the resident program was selected. This method utilizes two procedures within the assembly interface: TsrSetPtr and TsrCall.

Of these two procedures, TsrSetPtr is called first. This procedure determines the address of the resident procedure that must be called and stores it in a variable of the assembly module. Then TsrCall is activated, which switches the context and uses the recorded address to call the desired resident procedure.

Again, the parameters that must be passed to and from the resident routine present an obstacle, because TsrCall must be declared within the high level language module. After all, the number and types of parameters required depends on the particular procedure that is being called. However, as you'll learn in the description of the Pascal and C programs, this problem can also be solved.

The interrupt handler

The interrupt handlers of the assembly interface operate according to the principles illustrated above. The most prominent of these handlers is the keyboard interrupt handler, which serves interrupt 09H. The coordination between this particular handler and the interrupt handlers for interrupts 08h (timer), 13h (BIOS disk), and 28h (DOS idle) is managed by three flags in the code segment of the assembly interface: in_bios, tsraktiv, and tsrnow.

Flags

The tsractive flag indicates whether the TSR program is currently active. It carries either the value 0 or 1. The same applies to inbios, which is incremented upon accessing handler INT 13H and is decreased upon leaving the handler. Since inbios, like all other flags, is initialized at 0, it carries the value 1 during an INT 13H call and then returns to 0. However, when another function of interrupt 13H calls the interrupt recursively, this flag is further incremented, increasing its value. However, it's important the flag carry the value 0 when no BIOS disk function is currently being executed. This indicates that at least this path is clear for the TSR program start.

The third flag, tsrnow, is set within the keyboard interrupt handler when the hotkey code has been detected and the TSR program currently cannot be activated, because of the reasons explained above. This flag is then checked by the timer and DOS idle interrupt handlers, to determine whether the TSR program is waiting to be executed.

The timer interrupt handler decreases the value of tsrnow with each call, so it will eventually reach 0 and the attempt to activate the program will be discontinued (since the user believes the program will never start).

Now let's discuss the code for the different interrupt handlers because it illustrates several interesting details of interrupt handler programming. We're particularly interested in the two handlers for timer interrupt 08H and keyboard interrupt 09H. Since the interrupt handlers of the assembly interfaces in both Pascal and C are identical, the discussion applies to both of these modules.

The timer interrupt handler

The following excerpt from the code of the assembly module contains the new interrupt handler for timer interrupt 08H.

The first command already checks the tsrnow flag. Interestingly, the command doesn't include a segment override (i.e., cmp cs:tsrnow,0), because this variable is found within the code segment. However, this override doesn't have to be included in the source code, because the assembler automatically includes it when the code is assembled into machine language. Also, an ASSUME command was used to indicate that only segment register CS is pointing to the code segment, and the contents of the DS register, as well as all other segment registers, are unknown.

```
assume cs:code, ds:nothing, es:nothing, ss:nothing
```

So, all interrupt handlers can access the different variables and flags of the assembly interface without having to explicitly specify a segment override. All of these have been stored in the code segment, so the data segment of the corresponding high level language program doesn't have to be continually loaded.

Now let's return to the timer interrupt. If the handler discovers, from the comparison of the tsrnow flag with 0, the TSR program isn't waiting to be activated (tsrnow = 0), it immediately jumps to label i8_end. There, the previous interrupt handler of the timer interrupt is called by the command:

```
jmp [int8_ptr]
```

Int8_ptr isn't a label, but rather a variable, in which the address of the previous interrupt handler was recorded at the installation of the TSR program using TsrInit. Since int8_ptr is a DWORD variable, the assembler knows that a FAR-JMP, instead of a NEAR-JMP, must be executed. After all, the previous handler is located in a different code segment than the currently active interrupt handler (belonging to the TSR program) and can be reached only in this way.

The IRET command found at the end of the old interrupt handler returns the execution to the program that was suspended by the call the TIMER interrupt handler. So, the jump to the old handler ends the execution of the new handler from within the assembly interface.

```
;-- New interrupt 08h handler (timer) ---------------------------

int08       proc var

            cmp   tsrnow,0         ;is TSR to be activated?
            je    i8_end           ;no, continue to new handler

            dec   tsrnow           ;yes, decrease incrementation flag

            ;-- TSR is to be activate, but is this possible? --------

            cmp   in_bios, 0       ;is BIOS disk interrupt currently active?
            jne   i8_end           ;YES--> cannot activate

            call  dosaktiv         ;may DOS be interrupted?
            je    i8_tsr           ;yes, call TSR

i8_end:     jmp   [int8_ptr]       ;jump to old handler

            ;-- activate TSR ------------------------------------------

i8_tsr:     mov   tsrnow,0         ;TSR is no longer waiting to activate
            mov   tsraktiv,1       ;TSR will activate shortly
            pushf                  ;simulate call of old handler using
            call  [int8_ptr]       ; INT 8h command
            call  start_tsr        ;start TSR program
            iret                   ;return to interrupted program

int08       endp
```

However, what happens when tsrnow isn't equal to 0, which indicates the TSR program is waiting to be activated? The value of this flag will then be decreased, so possibly even at the next call the TIMER interrupt handle the flag's value will have reached 0. At that point, the attempts to start the TSR program are discontinued so the program isn't activated after a several second delay.

Before that, however, the TSR program must be activated so the next step consists of testing whether this is possible. For this, the in_bios flag is first read. If this flag contains a value other than 0, then the timer interrupt has just interrupted a ROM BIOS disk operation in progress. In this case, the TSR program isn't activated and the execution jumps back to the old timer interrupt. If the flag's value is indeed 0, the INDOS flag is checked to test whether a DOS function has been interrupted during its execution.

For this check, the assembly procedure is called. This procedure simply reads the address of INDOS from a variable within the assembly module and then compares the value at this address (the INDOS flag) with 0. If this test indicates that DOS cannot be interrupted at this time (when INDOS > 1), execution returns to the old interrupt handler and the TSR program isn't activated.

If this test is passed as well, nothing can stop the TSR program from being activated. Before the actual start, however, the old interrupt handler of the timer interrupt must be executed. This handler plays an important role in time keeping and disk access. This handler also contains a machine language command that is very important to all interrupt handlers that are linked with hardware interrupts, specifically the following command:

`out 20h,20h`

This command informs the interrupt controller the interrupt's execution has been completed. The interrupt controller won't trigger hardware interrupts until this command is executed. This would not only mean that all further timer calls would drop out, so the PC's internal clock would freeze, but also the PC could receive no further keyboard input, since the keyboard interrupt 09H would be blocked.

The address stored in the variable int8_ptr is used to call the old interrupt handler. However, here a CALL command is used, so the CPU returns to the TSR program's new handler upon encountering the IRET command.

For this to occur, the contents of the flag register must be pushed onto the stack, using PUSHF, before CALL is executed. Usually CALL places only the return address on the stack, instead of the flag register, as is the case with an interrupt call. As a result of this, IRET would read part of its supposed return address from the flag register, and obtain the return address from the stack, which contains completely different information than was stored there earlier. This mixup results in a system crash.

Although the TSR program is started only after the old interrupt handler has been called, the tsrnow and tsractive flags are set to 0 and 1, respectively, before this point. Basically this indicates the TSR program is already active, and is therefore no longer waiting to be started. This is justified because the old handler informs the interrupt controller the execution of the interrupt has been completed (see above). This enables further interrupts to be processed while the timer interrupt handler is being executed. For example, a keyboard interrupt should be executed if the user pressed another key in the meantime.

If this keyboard input happened to be the program's hotkey, the TSR program would be activated again by the keyboard interrupt handler if tsractive wasn't already set to 1. This results in another unacceptable situation: the execution of the new timer interrupt handler could begin only after the TSR program has been terminated again, which means the program would start again immediately afterwards.

However, since the proper flags have been set before the old handler is called, the other interrupt handlers are unable to call the TSR program at that time. This ensures the problem we explained above doesn't occur.

Finally, start_tsr is called to activate the TSR program. This is an assembly procedure within the assembly module, which first secures the context of the current program that is being interrupted, sets the context of the TSR program, and then calls the TSR procedure that was specified in combination with TsrInit. After the TSR program has been completed, the context of the interrupted program is restored, and the procedure is ended.

Only then does the program execution return to the new timer interrupt handler, which finally returns to the interrupted program via IRET. Interestingly enough, the new timer handler is called repeatedly during execution of the TSR program, although its own execution basically hasn't been completed yet. However, this remains without consequence, providing the address of the original, interrupted program is still located on the stack upon the return from start_tsr. Also, to the system, the execution of the new timer interrupt was completed the moment the "out 20h,20h" was executed.

The keyboard interrupt handler

Much of what has been said about the timer interrupt handler also applies to the keyboard interrupt handler, serving interrupt 09H. Here, the AX register contents are first saved to the stack, since this register will be changed within the handler. Remember that once it's completed its execution, an interrupt handler cannot leave any of the processor registers changed. This didn't cause problems for the timer interrupt handler because it didn't change any registers. However, this must be considered for the keyboard interrupt handler.

In the next step, the contents of port 60H are read. The keyboard controller will store the scan code of the key, which the user pressed, in this port. The new keyboard handler must examine this scan code to identify the hotkey.

First, however, this new keyboard handler checks whether the TSR program is already active. If it is, all further tests can be skipped. The contents of the AX register are then pulled off the stack, and from label i9_end, the execution jumps directly to the old keyboard interrupt handler.

The same steps are taken when tsractive is 0 and tsrnow carries a value unequal to 0. This indicates the hotkey has already been detected and the TSR program is waiting for an opportunity to activate. So why detect the hotkey a second time?

This happens when the TSR program is neither active, nor waiting to be activated. Therefore, the hotkey scan code is first read from the variable sc_code. If the value contained in this variable is 128, a real hotkey hasn't been defined, and only the status of the modifier keys must be checked. In this case, the execution jumps to label i9_ks.

```
;-- New interrupt 09h handler (keyboard) --------------------------

int09        proc var

             push ax
             in   al,60h              ;read keyboard port

             cmp  tsraktiv,0          ;is the TSR program already active?
             jne  i9_end              ;YES: call old handler, then return

             cmp  tsrnow,0            ;is the TSR waiting for activation?
             jne  i9_end              ;YES: call old handler, then return

             ;-- test for hotkey ----------------------------------

             cmp  sc_code,128         ;is a scan code defined?
             je   i9_ks               ;No, check modifier {{?}} keys

             cmp  al,128              ;if yes, is it the release code?
             jae  i9_end              ;yes, but it is not the hotkey

             cmp  sc_code,al          ;make code, compare with key
             jne  i9_end              ;not correct, do not activate

i9_ks:       ;-- check modifier  key status       --------------------

             push ds
             mov  ax,040h             ;pull DS to the variable segment
             mov  ds,ax               ;of ROM-BIOS
             mov  ax,word ptr ds:[17h] ;get BIOS keyboard flag
             and  ax,key_mask         ;screen out non-hotkey bits
             cmp  ax,key_mask         ;are only hotkey bits remaining?
             pop  ds
             jne  i9_end              ;hotkey detected? NO --> return

             cmp  in_bios, 0          ;BIOS disk interrupt currently active?
             jne  i9_e1               ;YES --> cannot activate

             call dosaktiv            ;may DOS be interrupted?
             je   i9_tsr              ;yes, start TSR

i9_e1:       mov  tsrnow,TIME_OUT     ;TSR waiting to be activated

i9_end:      pop  ax                  ;get AX back
             jmp  [int9_ptr]          ;jump to old handler
```

```
i9_tsr:     mov     tsraktiv,1          ;TSR active (in a second)
            mov     tsrnow,0            ;no delayed start wanted
            pushf
            call    [int9_ptr]          ;call old handler
            pop     ax                  ;get AX back
            call    start_tsr           ;start TSR programs
            iret                        ;return to interrupted program

int09       endp
```

If a hotkey has been defined (sc_code not equal to 128), the scan code of the key that's been pressed is read from port 60H. If this code is larger than 128, it's identified as a release code, which indicates that a key has been released, instead of pressed. Since the pressing, instead of the releasing, of a key must start the TSR program, the key code isn't analyzed further. The execution then immediately jumps to the old handler.

Assuming that a key has been pressed, it's code is then compared with the value stored in sc_code. If these values don't match, the key is identified as not being the hotkey, and the execution jumps to the old keyboard interrupt handler. However, if the hotkey code matches the specified value, the status of the modifier keys must be checked.

With this, we've returned to label i9_ks, which was mentioned above. Here, the current modifier key status is read from the BIOS variable at address 0040h:0017h and compared with the value stored in key_mask. If the two values don't match, execution returns to the old keyboard interrupt handler, which then takes over the task of processing the keyboard input.

If this comparison determines the specified keys have been pressed, the TSR program must be activated. Before this can occur, you must check whether a BIOS disk interrupt or DOS API function is currently being executed. If any such function is currently active, the program isn't activated and execution returns to the old keyboard handler. However, before this jump, the tsrnow flag is set to the value specified by the TIME_OUT constant. This delay value gives the TSR program a chance to be activated during one of the next timer interrupt calls.

In the code listing provided, TIME_OUT is assigned the value 9, which corresponds to half of a second, since the timer interrupt is called 18.2 times each second. However, you may replace this value with one of your own values if you want to increase or decrease the maximum delay time in which the TSR program can be started after pressing the hotkey.

If DOS or BIOS functions aren't preventing the activation of the TSR program, it's necessary, as was the case with the timer handler, to call the old keyboard interrupt handler. Here again, the tsractive and tsrnow flags are initialized with appropriate values so no other interrupt handler will be able to activate the TSR program during this time. This then occurs automatically within the keyboard interrupt handler once the old handler is called.

The Pascal and C programs

Now we'll discuss the high level language programs, TSRP.PAS and TSRC.C, which demonstrate the use and function of the two assembly modules. Their structure is almost identical; they have several differences, which we'll discuss below. First, let's concentrate on the common characteristics of these two programs.

Upon program start, the ParamGetHotKey function evaluates any parameters entered on the command line. It accepts all parameters preceded by the prefix "/t" as hotkeys. This prefix may be followed either by the name of a modifier key (LSHIFT, RSHIFT, ALT, CTRL, etc.) or the scan code number of a particular key. This number must be entered as a decimal value.

To specify the left (Shift) and (Spacebar) as the hotkey key combination, the following two parameters must be entered:

```
/tlshift /t57
```

If <ALT> must be included in this hotkey, the following parameters would be required:

```
/tlshift /talt /t57
```

The order in which these parameters are entered isn't important.

ParamGetHotkey then stores the specified modifier key status and scan code in the two variables Keymask and ScCode, which are passed to the function for this purpose.

If, an error is discovered when the command line entry is evaluated, the program execution is stopped and a corresponding error message is displayed. If the parameters were entered correctly, the TsrIsInst function then checks whether the program has already been installed. Here, the function number through which the program's MUX handler can later be reached is also determined. Although the constant I2F_CODE specifies the function C4H for this, you can select another function. You must do this if you develop more than one TSR program using these assembly interfaces; otherwise these TSR programs would use the same MUX function and therefore conflict with one another.

However, you must be careful when selecting other MUX function numbers, since some of these may coincide with the function numbers of existing programs. However, you shouldn't use values smaller than C0H. Refer to Chapter 27 for more information about the DOS multiplexer.

If TsrIsInst indicates the program hasn't been installed yet, the values of KeyMasc and ScCode are checked to determine whether /t parameters were entered from the command line. If these parameters weren't entered, the variables will contain default values. In this case, the TsrSetHotkey assembly procedure will define a+_ as the hotkey key combination. If /t parameters have been entered, then TsrSetHotkey sets this specified hotkey combination.

At this point, the only remaining procedure to be executed is TsrInit, which transforms the program into a TSR program. The high level language procedure TSR is thereby specified as the TSR procedure. We'll discuss this in more detail later.

If TsrIsInst indicates the program has already been installed, then the following action depends on the original user input. If a hotkey was specified at the program call, TsrSetHotkey will install the specified key combination as the updated hotkey in the resident program, then the program is ended without performing a new installation. However, if a hotkey wasn't specified, TsrCanUninst is first used to check whether the resident copy may be deactivated. If it can, TsrUninst is called to remove the resident copy from memory.

Before the TSR program is uninstalled, however, a high level language routine named endFCT (in C) or EndTPrc (in Pascal) is called. This routine frees the program's internal resources and displays a message indicating the number of times the TSR program was activated.

This number is defined by the global variable ATimes, which is incremented each time the TSR program is activated. This is done in the program's TSR procedure named Tsr. Before the TSR program is removed, then, the keyboard buffer is emptied to remove the hotkey, the screen of the previously interrupted program is saved, and a message asking the user to press any key is displayed. As soon as the user has done this, the screen of the interrupted program is restored, and the TSR program procedure ends. Then the execution of the previous program resumes.

The C implementation

Since TSR programs should use as little memory as possible, the assembly language interface was developed to be linked with the smallest C memory model (the small model). In both Microsoft and Turbo C compilers, the program code and data are placed in two separate segments, each of which cannot be larger than 64K. The data includes global and static data as well as the stack and the heap. As the following figures show, Turbo C and Microsoft C use different memory organization, despite their similarities. In Turbo C the stack is placed behind the heap and moves from the end of the data segment to the end of the heap and in Microsoft C the stack is between the global data and the heap.

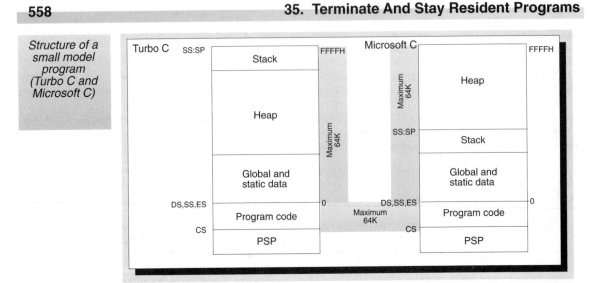

Structure of a small model program (Turbo C and Microsoft C)

If this organization doesn't affect the assembly language interface, we could allocate the entire 64K of the data segment resident in memory in addition to the program code. However, since this would waste a lot of memory and TSR programs should use as little memory as possible, only the part of the data segment that is actually needed should be marked as resident by the assembly language module.

The size of this memory area depends on the size of the data (or objects) that will be allocated on the heap by the functions calloc() and malloc(). You must guess this size and pass it to the initialization routine so the end of the required memory in the data segment can be calculated.

This mechanism allows you to use the heap functions normally within the TSR program. Unfortunately, this applies only to the Turbo C compiler. Microsoft C uses an allocation algorithm that assumes that all the memory to the end of the data segment is available. So, allocating heap storage should be avoided within a TSR program compiled with Microsoft C. You should allocate the buffers and variables required when the TSR program is initialized or place the required objects in global variables. The example C program allocates the two buffers it needs in the main() function and then places the addresses of the buffers in global variables.

There is something else you should be aware of when using Turbo C. Since the stack grows from the end of the 64K data segment to the heap, it finds itself outside the program when parts of the data segment are released again, and in an area of memory that DOS may give to other programs. To avoid problems with this, the assembly language module places the stack immediately after the heap, giving it 512 bytes of space. This should be sufficient for most applications, but may lead to problems if you use large objects (such as arrays) as local variables or pass them to other functions via the stack. In this case, you should enlarge the stack by setting the constant TC_STACK in the assembly language module to a larger value.

Because of this differentiated use of the stack, TsrInit must be informed whether the program has been developed using a Microsoft or a Borland compiler. However, since this is managed from within the C program with constants that are defined through conditional preprocessor instructions, you don't need to worry about this operation.

Such functions are also used by GetHeapEnd, which is called from the assembly module by TsrInit. It supplies the assembly module with a FAR pointer to the end of the occupied heap. With Borland compilers, this information can be gathered through the library function SBRK, which is also the case in MSC up to Version 6.0 and in QuickC up to Version 2.5. However, in current versions, this function is no longer supported. So, the library function _heapwalk must be used to search the stack for the last occupied heap block.

The way in which the C version of the program calls functions within the resident copy of the program is also interesting. As we mentioned in the description of the assembly module, the assembler procedure TsrSetPtr must first be called. This procedure receives the address of the procedure that must be executed and stores it. The stored address is later accessed by TsrCall when this function is called.

In the C version of the assembly module, TsrSetPtr then directly returns a pointer to TsrCall. The advantage of this is the desired function can be called directly using the result of TsrSetPtr. However, this requires a CAST operation to secure the compiler's cooperation. Let's take a closer look at this operation.

At the start of the C module, two types of function pointers, OAFP and SHKFP, are defined. Of these two, OAFP points to all function types that don't require arguments, and therefore also don't return function results. SHKFP, however, has been tailored specifically to meet then requirements of the TsrSetHotkey assembler procedure.

```
typedef void (*OAFP)(void);
typedef void (*SHKFP)( WORD Keymask, BYTE ScCode );
```

The following expression is used to call TsrSetHotkey using TsrSetPtr:

```
(*(SHKFP) TsrSetPtr(TsrSetHotkey))( Keymask, ScCode );
```

This expression first calls TsrSetPts, in which the address of TsrSetHotkey is passed, as one of its arguments, in the form of a FAR pointer. Actually, this operation requires only a NEAR pointer, since the segment address of the resident copy must later be used as the segment address anyway. However, the various functions that are called in this way must be FAR so they can be called out of other code segments. To avoid the compiler error message following the otherwise impending transformation of a FAR pointer to a NEAR pointer, TsrSetPtr receives the FAR address of the desired function and processes only its offset address.

TsrSetPtr then returns the address of TsrCall as a NEAR pointer. However, in casting the pointer, the expression from above determines that this pointer is of type SHKFP. This is the only technique where the desired parameters can be entered so the compiler will copy them to the stack without any interjections. TsrCall is finally called by referencing the pointer cast in this way.

Therefore, when TsrCall is executed, it finds the arguments, which are actually intended for the function that will be called, located on the stack. These arguments must be copied to the stack of the resident copy of the TSR program, since we must switch to this stack before this function can be called. This is because most C compilers generate code under the assumption the segment register DS point to the same memory segment as register SS. If the stack wasn't switched, this assumption wouldn't be true, and the function couldn't be executed properly.

Therefore, if you want to use the same technique for calling functions in a resident copy of your TSR program, you'll need to follow these two steps:

1. Define a function pointer type that emulates a function with arguments that are also required by the actual function you want to call.

2. Pass the address of this function to TsrSetPts, cast the function result in a previously defined pointer, and call the function using the required arguments.

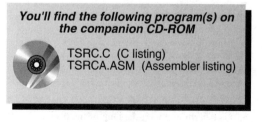

You'll find the following program(s) on the companion CD-ROM

TSRC.C (C listing)
TSRCA.ASM (Assembler listing)

The Pascal implementation

Turbo Pascal offers only one memory model, unlike the various C compilers. The organization of this model is well suited to TSR programs.

The following illustration shows the program code and the required routines from the various units and the runtime library follow the PSP. After these are the predefined constants, the global data, and the stack segment. While the size of these program components are set at compilation and cannot be changed after the program is loaded into memory, this doesn't apply to the size of the heap, which follows the stack segment. When new objects are created with the NEW command, the heap grows toward the end of memory.

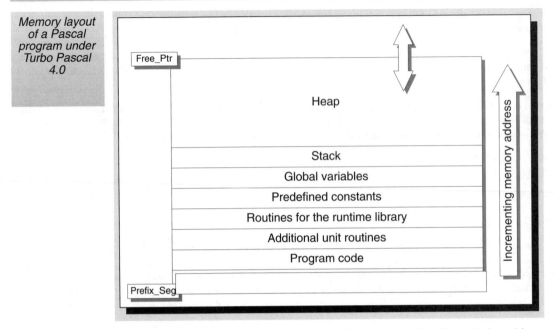

Memory layout of a Pascal program under Turbo Pascal 4.0

Free_Ptr

Heap

Stack

Global variables

Predefined constants

Routines for the runtime library

Additional unit routines

Program code

Prefix_Seg

Incrementing memory address

Unlike C compilers, Turbo Pascal allow you to set the maximum size of the heap, as well as the stack size, with a compiler directive inside the source code. This is the $M directive, which must be passed the following parameters:

```
{$M stack size, minimum heap size, maximum heap size}
```

All specifications are in bytes, so the directive:

```
{$M 2048, 0, 5000}
```

results in a 2K stack and a maximum 5000 byte heap. If no such directive is found in a program, the heap isn't limited and it can grow to the end of main memory. This would have devastating results for a TSR program, because the entire memory must be reserved for the TSR program and there would be no memory left for additional programs. But with the $M directive placed at the beginning of the program, we can set the maximum size of the program in memory and the number of paragraphs that must remain resident after the program is terminated.

Turbo Pascal also allows the number of paragraphs to be reserved to be calculated from the Pascal program, which eliminates the complicated calculation in the assembly language interface. In a C program, important data needed for this calculation (segment addresses of the PSP and data segment, and size of the heap) are available only at the assembly language level, but Turbo Pascal places this information in normal variables, which are available to a Pascal program in the form of pointers. For our purposes, we need the starting address of the PSP and the end of the heap, since they mark the start and end of the TSR program in memory.

The figure shows the segment address of the PSP is found in the variable PrefixSeg, while the end of the heap (up to Version 6.0) is determined with the help of the pointer variable FreePtr. This variable doesn't point directly to the end of the heap, but the segment portion of this pointer contains the end address of the heap minus $1000. This information is used within the TSR program in the ResPara procedure, which calculates the number of paragraphs to remain resident after the installation of the TSR. Version 6.0 changes this; the HeapEnd pointer directly indicates the end of the heap.

The procedure ResPara within the TSR program uses this information by utilizing these variables to calculate the number of paragraphs the TSR program will occupy while remaining resident in memory. Through the help of conditional compiling, either the HeapPtr or the HeapEnd pointer can then be accessed for this purpose, depending on the Turbo Pascal version used.

However, the procedures, within the resident program, that will be executed must be of the type FAR. Unfortunately, calling these functions isn't as simple here as in the C version, since Turbo Pascal doesn't permit the casting of function pointers. Because of this, TsrSetPtr doesn't return a result upon its call, and the calls of TsrSetPtr and TsrCall cannot be combined.

However, in the Pascal version, it's also necessary to declare code pointers that depict the procedures and functions that will be called, and particularly their arguments. As you can see in the following listing of TSRP.PAS, these pointers are called WoAPrcK and SHKPrcK. WoAPrcK is a pointer to a procedure that doesn't require any arguments, while SHKPrc is specifically designed to serve the TsrSetHotkey procedure.

```
type WoAPrcK  = procedure;                   { Procedure without arguments }
     SHKPrcK = procedure( KeyMask : word;               { TsrSetHotkey }
                          ScCode  : byte );
     PPtrT   = record         { Union for creating the procedure pointer }
                 case integer of
                    1 : ( WoAPrc : WoAPrcK  );
                    2 : ( SHKPrc : SHKPrcK );
               end;

const Call : PPtrT = ( WoAPrc : TsrCall );
```

These types are collected in a variant record that contains an entry for each of these types. Here these entries have been named WoAPrc for WoAPrcK and SHKPrc for SHKPrcK. A global variable named Call has been declared for calling the functions that are associated with these types. The WoAPrc component of this variable is initialized as a pointer to the TsrCall procedure.

This variable can then be used to call the desired procedure or function, providing its offset address is first passed to TsrSetPtr. This is illustrated by the following two program lines. At the TsrSetPtr function call, TsrSetHotkey is specified as the procedure that will be executed. TsrCall is then called together with the arguments for TsrSetHotkey.

```
TsrSetPtr(ofs(TsrSetHotKey));
Call.SHKPrc( Keymask, ScCode );
```

This approach works because, by employing the SHKPrc component of Call, the compiler assumes that such a procedure is actually being called. Actually, however, TsrCall is being executed. In respect to the stack, this function has it easier than its C counterpart.

The reason for this is that Turbo Pascal programs don't expect the data segment to correspond to the stack segment. So, the stack of the currently running program can remain active, even when a procedure or function within the resident copy of the program is being called.

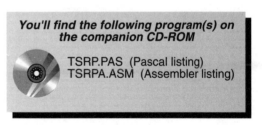

You'll find the following program(s) on the companion CD-ROM

TSRP.PAS (Pascal listing)
TSRPA.ASM (Assembler listing)

A Few Tips

In this chapter we've demonstrated how easily TSR programs can be developed, even in high level languages, by simply placing the core procedures in assembler modules and linking these with high level language modules. However, TSR programming is still a complicated task.

So, we recommend using several techniques that are suitable for TSR programs. First develop the program as a normal program that can be compiled from DOS, or an integrated development environment, and executed.

You should also try to reduce the number of changes needed to convert the program to a TSR program. To do this, you should also develop an initialization procedure, as well as the actual TSR procedure, which will be called when the hotkey is activated. However, unlike the final TSR program, these procedures should still be called from within the main program procedure (or function) so their execution doesn't depend on the hotkey yet.

In this way, you can completely develop and test the program. Once you're satisfied with the results and have found all its bugs, you can convert it to a TSR program. Correcting all errors prior to this is particularly important, since it's almost impossible to detect errors once the conversion has occurred, even through the use of a debugger.

The actual conversion into a TSR program is actually rather simple. You only need to integrate the assembly module with the program, and to call the appropriate functions from the assembler module. The two sample programs illustrate the logistics of this operation in detail, and all necessary function calls can be found within the main program.

Chapter 36

Protected Mode, DOS Extensions, DPMI/VCPI

Recently, 80286 Protected mode has been making headway into the world of DOS. However, DOS is a Real mode operating system. So, it cannot use Protected mode.

This is also true for the ROM-BIOS of a PC, which is also intended for Real mode operation. ROM-BIOS crashes when the first BIOS call is made after switching to Protected mode.

The 80386 and i486 demonstrate their true power in Protected mode. Many software developers have been searching for a back door to make Protected mode usable with DOS. This has resulted in the creation of EMS emulators, memory management programs, DOS extensions, and multitaskers. These utilities run DOS as a Protected mode operating system. In this chapter we'll explain how Protected mode works and how it can be distinguished from Real mode.

Protected Mode

Protected mode was introduced in 1982, when the 80286 microprocessor was introduced. It was originally developed for multitasking operating systems. However, since DOS is based on the older Real mode and would have to be completely rewritten to use Protected mode on Intel processors, it cannot use this mode.

Nearly ten years passed before Protected mode could actually be used. This occurred with the introduction of the 32-bit version of Windows and OS/2 Version 2.0. Previously, temporary solutions, such as the standard and enhanced modes used with Windows 3, were used.

Characteristics of multitasking operating systems

To understand the various characteristics of Protected mode, we must study how these characteristics are applied. This involves the structure and requirements of multitasking operating systems and how they are related to the capabilities of the underlying processors. Protected mode was developed to interact with this type of operating system.

The most obvious characteristic of multitasking operating systems is their ability to run several programs or tasks simultaneously. Not only do different programs run simultaneously, but often separate executable files within these programs also run.

One example of this is a word processing program that formats a file and sends it to the printer while you continue entering text. These two tasks run concurrently within a single program. When executing programs concurrently in a multitasking environment, both tasks must be able to coexist in memory. Each task assumes that it's the only one controlling the computer. The tasks must operate in unison, while the operating system itself must be protected from the programs and their various tasks. This is why the name "Protected mode" was chosen.

Processor requirements for a multitasking environment

A multitasking environment must meet the following criteria:

1. Mutual protection of tasks and the operating system from overwriting areas of memory.

2. Support during task switching, particularly when restoring the executable state of a task.

3.   Privileged status for the operating system when executing specific assembly language instructions and operations.

4.   Support during the setup of virtual memory management.

We'll discuss how tasks and the memory areas are protected from each other later. However, remember that this is the first requirement imposed on an operating system.

Task switching support

The simultaneous execution of multiple programs in a multitasking environment is usually an illusion. Theoretically, true multitasking exists only when the hardware contains several processors, performing several tasks in parallel. Actually, usually only one processor is available at any given time. So, multitasking normally means that several tasks are sharing processor time, with each task using the processor for only a fraction of a second.

For example, suppose that a very slow system is running three tasks concurrently. The first task executes for a third of a second, then the second task executes for a third of a second, then the third task executes for a third of a second. Then the cycle repeats.

This is called *preemptive multitasking* and follows the principle of *time slicing*. The time slicing process is based on an abrupt intrusion into task execution. After a specific period of time, the operating system simply stops executing the current task and continues with another task. This procedure must be transparent to the interrupted task. The task being interrupted cannot prepare for this interruption, because it can occur at any moment.

The operating system is responsible for ensuring that program execution continues without interruption between tasks. System resources (i.e., memory, files being processed, and processor registers), must remain unchanged by the task switch. Maintaining system integrity following an interruption can be managed through software, although task switching speeds up if the processor manages this assignment.

Finally, the illusion of parallel execution occurs only when switching between tasks is repeated many times per second. However, this switching wastes a lot of processor time and doesn't help task execution. So, support for task switching is the second requirement imposed on a processor with a multitasking capability.

Operating system privileges

The third requirement is the operating system must have certain privileges; priority must be given to certain assembly language instructions, while task execution remains on hold. These instructions include those involving task switching and those that influence the processor's operating mode.

Suppose that a task simply switched the processor from Protected mode to Real mode. This probably wouldn't result in a system crash, just as overwriting some areas of memory wouldn't cause a crash. However, data and other programs could be corrupted. The operating system is responsible for correcting these errors or, if a correction isn't possible, ending the offending program and removing it from memory. Other programs should remain undisturbed.

Virtual memory

The processor should help the operating system manage virtual memory. Memory requirements increase with the number and complexity of the programs being executed simultaneously. Often the memory requirements exceed the amount of physical memory that's available. The operating system should allow programs access to more memory than actually exists, by using virtual memory.

The memory areas that aren't needed by the current task can be moved to the hard drive until they are needed again. The processor supports the capacity to determine which memory is needed and which isn't.

Now let's see how these requirements are actually used. We'll look at Protected modes on the 80286, 80386, and i486. The latter two Protected modes are downwardly compatible with the 80286, but include significant improvements. You'll see how efficient and how complicated programming in this mode can be.

Unfortunately, all Intel processors work in Protected mode more slowly than in Real mode. In the following sections we'll explain why this occurs.

80286 Protected mode

Anyone familiar with assembler programming in Real mode under DOS, but who hasn't worked in Protected mode, often asks how the differences between the two modes affect the processor. If the processor suddenly no longer recognizes such familiar instructions as JMP, PUSH, or MOV in Protected mode, you may be wondering whether the processor then recognizes new instructions. Some programmers also fear that since they are confronted with a different processor, programming concepts used in Real mode no longer apply.

However, this isn't true. Instructions used in Real mode are also used in Protected mode; only a few new instructions have been added. However, the assembly language programmer barely notices many of the instructions. These include memory addressing, such as loading of segment addresses in the segment register, and the creation and coding of FAR pointers within JMP instructions and subroutine calls.

80286 registers

The register complement of the 80286 was expanded from the 8086 instruction set, as shown in the following diagram. Although these new registers are also available to the programmer in Real mode, they have no meaning. Some of the registers, such as GDTR, LDTR, and IDTR, must be loaded before switching to Protected mode, because the system relies on these registers. We'll discuss the meaning of these registers below.

The 80286 registers in Protected mode

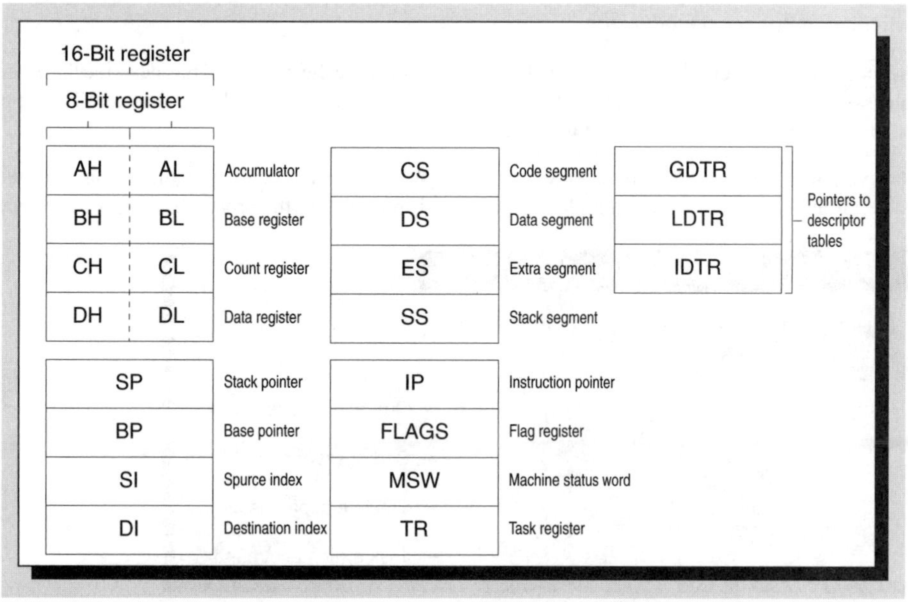

16-Bit register				
8-Bit register				
AH : AL	Accumulator	CS	Code segment	GDTR
BH : BL	Base register	DS	Data segment	LDTR
CH : CL	Count register	ES	Extra segment	IDTR
DH : DL	Data register	SS	Stack segment	
SP	Stack pointer	IP	Instruction pointer	
BP	Base pointer	FLAGS	Flag register	
SI	Spurce index	MSW	Machine status word	
DI	Destination index	TR	Task register	

Pointers to descriptor tables

The Protected mode uses the flag register in almost the same way as Real mode. Existing flag positions remain unchanged, but Protected mode adds two new flags (IOPL and NT). Both flags are discussed in detail later in this section.

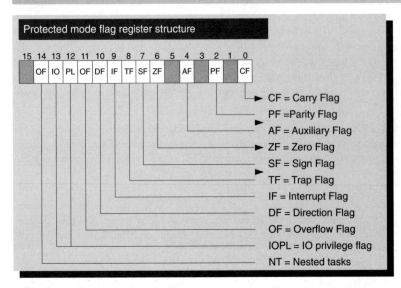

Protected mode flag register structure

Switching to Protected mode

The machine status word (MSW) is a type of flag register because the individual bits describe the processor status. The 80286 processor uses only the lower four bits of the 16 available bits. Bits 1, 2, and 3 (MP, EM, and TS) support a math coprocessor and aren't important in the context of this chapter.

However, bit 0 (PE) is the key to the Protected mode. When the processor is initialized, this bit is set to 0, which places the processor in Real mode. If a program loads the value 1 into this bit, the processor returns to Protected mode.

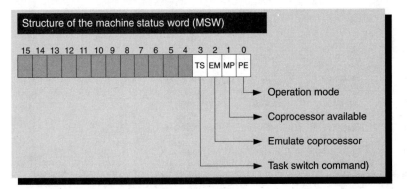

Structure of the machine status word (MSW)

Unfortunately, resetting this bit doesn't automatically return the 80286 to Real mode. Eventually DOS programs, such as DOS extensions or EMS simulators, always reach a point where they must switch back to Real mode, when enables the user to continue working under DOS.

Complicated procedures are needed to do this because the 80286 doesn't have an instruction for resetting the PE bit in the machine status word. Usually the ROM-BIOS must be initialized, which clears all RAM. Various tricks must be used to prevent this from happening.

It's unknown why the 80286 isn't able to restore Real mode. However, switching the processor back to Real mode from Protected mode is possible. Unfortunately this process is time-consuming and requires some elaborate precautions.

The task register (TR) manages, and switches between, the various tasks (more on this later).

Memory management in Protected mode

Real mode offers one megabyte of address space. Within this address space, you can load any memory segment address between 0000H and FFFFH into one of the four segment registers. Now, suppose that you enter the resident portion of COMMAND.COM, then delete some variables in the BIOS variable range, or change a few entries in the interrupt vector table. The computer will promptly reset.

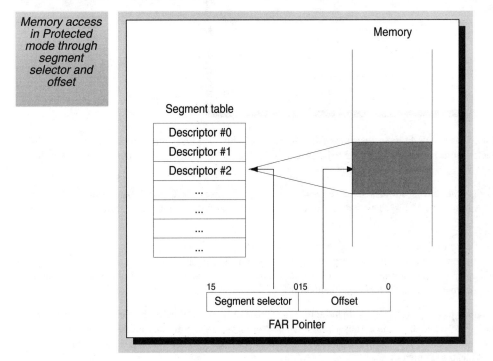

Memory access in Protected mode through segment selector and offset

If you do the same thing in Protected mode, or even load the wrong segment address, the computer reacts differently. Instead of a crash or reset, an exception occurs (more on this later). The operating system maintains control of program execution and the offending program ends.

This protection is possible because, even though Protected mode segment addresses contain 16 bits, additional segment addresses aren't created. Instead, segment selectors are used. This results in an index pointing to a segment table describing the various memory segments. This table is similar to a large array of segment descriptors that tells the processor the base address of the segment. The offset address, indicated by the FAR pointer, is added to this address to obtain the address of the memory location in question. Unlike the segment address in Real mode, this base address isn't multiplied. It's possible for memory segments in Protected mode to begin with the memory address desired, not merely at addresses divisible by 16.

The descriptor table in Protected mode provides a link between a virtual address (segment selector:offset) and a linear address (base address comprising the segment descriptor + offset). In the 80286, the linear address and physical address are identical (i.e., the actual memory location to which access is ultimately gained). The 80386 and 80486 addressing is coded to permit the physical address to be determined initially by this new transformation. We'll discuss this in greater detail later.

The above description doesn't show the structure of the segment descriptor within the descriptor table. There is more information stored here than just the starting address of the segment in question. The following chart shows the exact structure of a segment descriptor in Protected mode.

Structure of a segment descriptor

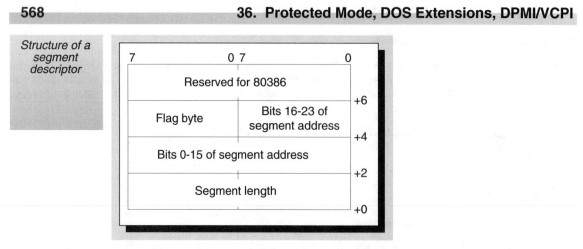

A segment descriptor consists of eight bytes distributed among various fields. The first byte is the segment length. Unlike Real mode, the Protected mode segments don't have to be exactly 64K. The first field in the segment descriptor specifies the length of the segment (between one byte and 64K).

The next three bytes yield the starting address of the segment in memory. The use of three bytes expands the address width from the 20 bits of Real mode to 24 bits. This also enlarges the physically addressable memory from 1 megabyte to 16 megabytes.

The fact the location of a segment is coded in the segment descriptor instead of in the FAR pointers, which provides access to this segment, helps implement an efficient memory management system. The parallel execution of multiple programs is characterized by the continual allocation and release of memory ranges. This causes memory fragmentation. Constantly shifting these memory segments minimizes this fragmentation.

In Real mode, all references to such a segment within the appropriate program must be adjusted. However, in Protected mode, the segment must be displaced and the segment descriptor must be redirected to the new base address. Now it's possible to continue to use the original segment selector in the various references to the segment, even though the segment now resides at an entirely different location in memory.

Following the base address of the segment, within the segment descriptor, is the byte with the various flags that we'll discuss shortly. The last field contains a word reserved for the 80386 and its successors. This field always contains the value 0 for the 80286. This will also be discussed in more detail later in Section 33.1.3 (Mode Programming of the 80386 and i486).

Various segment types

Protected mode recognizes three different segment types: data segments, code segments, and system segments. Although data segments can be described and read, program code cannot be executed here. However, code segments can be executed, but cannot be read or described. The third type, system segments, describes different types of segments, all of which apply to Protected mode.

Besides the segment type, additional segment attributes are recorded in the flag byte. The meanings of these attributes depend partially on the segment type. A special bit determines whether the contents of a code segment may at least be read. In a data segment, the corresponding bit can be used to block write access to this segment, which makes the block's contents "read only".

Regardless of the type of the segment, the flag byte contains a presence bit that helps program virtual memory management. Whenever the operating system moves a segment to disk, it must set this bit to 0 to signal an error to the processor when it next accesses a memory location in this segment. An operating system routine reloads the segment into memory before program execution continues.

The access bit is also important. The processor sets this bit to 1 on each segment access. When virtual memory management must decide which segments should be removed from memory because additional room is needed, preference can be given to those segments not recently accessed (those with their access bits set to 0).

Privilege levels

The processor in Protected mode recognizes four different privilege levels for separate programs. These privilege levels specify the execution of various assembly language instructions, and govern access to memory segments. They are designated with numbers 0 through 3 (privilege level 0 is highest, 3 is lowest).

If you only had to distinguish between applications and the operating system, two privilege levels would obviously be sufficient. However, an operating system is usually divided into components that contain different privileges. The highest privileges (level 0) are used by the operating system kernel, which watches over memory management and task switching.

Privilege level 1 is granted to the various operating system services called by programs and operating system utilities. These include file management functions, routines for screen output, and printer control utilities.

Privilege level 2 is reserved for operating system extensions that rely on the system services of privilege level 1. In the OS/2 operating system, these include the SQL server and the LAN manager.

Privilege level 3 is for various programs that run under operating system control. Since these programs execute on a lower privilege level than the operating system, they can be controlled by the operating system (but not vice versa). Privilege level arrangement can be viewed as a series of concentric circles, as presented in the following illustration. The innermost circle, the heart of the system, is the kernel of the operating system. As they proceed outward from privilege 0, the privileges diminish as they approach program and user level.

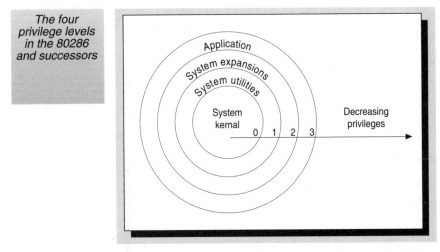

The four privilege levels in the 80286 and successors

The various privilege levels are important for accessing memory in other segments and transferring program execution to other segments. A program must be prevented from accessing the memory segment of the operating system kernel, or from transferring executions to just any location within another segment without the actual specification of a destination point in a specific routine.

So, the processor compares the privilege levels before accessing memory and signals an error whenever a task tries to access a segment of higher priority. The segment selectors and the segment descriptors contain information on their respective privilege levels.

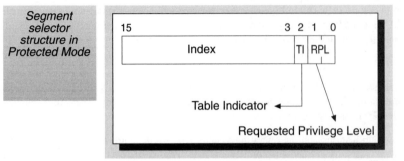

As you can see in the illustration above, the Requested Privilege Level (RPL) is recorded in the low order two bits of each segment selector. The processor also uses two other privilege information sources, the Current Privilege Level (CPL) and the Descriptor Privilege Level (DPL). The privilege entries do the following:

DPL

The privilege level of a segment, which is recorded in bits 5 and 6 in the flag byte of a segment descriptor.

CPL

The privilege level of the current task. It's determined from the segment descriptor describing the current code segment. The selector of this segment descriptor is found in the CS register.

RPL

The privilege level that is recorded within a selector. It always corresponds to the privilege level of the segment to which the selector points. Hence, RPL = DPL of the segment addressed.

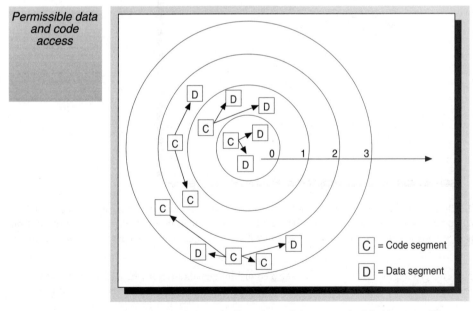

Data and code accesses (jump instructions and subroutine calls) are permissible if:

```
CPL = DPL
```

In other words, the current code segment is on the same privilege level as the code or data segment addressed. If the two privilege levels happen to be different, other rules will apply, depending on the type of access that will be used by the processor as the basis for determining the validity of an access attempt.

Data access

For data access, this simple rule applies:

```
CPL <= DPL,
```

This means that a task cannot access a data segment on a higher level than itself. It's impossible for an application to access the data segments of the operating system, but the operating system can send data to the application in a buffer.

This rule applies when a selector is loaded into a data segment in one of the segment registers (DS or ES). If one of the protection rules is violated, the processor stops program execution by returning an exception and calls an operating system routine that handles this error.

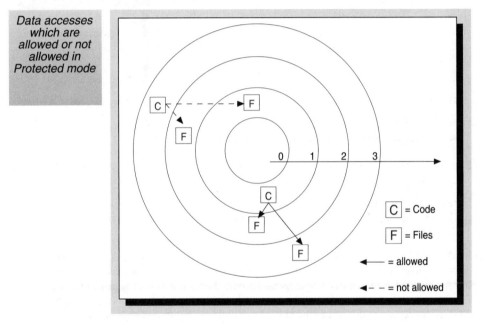

Data accesses which are allowed or not allowed in Protected mode

Code accesses and gates

The processor is even more restrictive with code accesses, which is the transfer of program execution by a JMP or CALL instruction. These are only permitted if the segment to which the jump is made is on the same privilege level as the caller. This prevents uncontrolled calls to code on another privilege level. You may be wondering how an application can invoke operating system services, which are on a higher privilege level, while it's on a lower privilege level.

The gates created especially for this purpose provides a solution to this problem. These are special segment descriptors (system descriptors) that occupy eight bytes like any other descriptor and are located in the descriptor table. But, unlike code and data segment descriptors, they don't define a memory segment. Instead, they define a point of entry into a routine whose code segment can be on a higher privilege level than that of the caller.

This segment is defined in the form of an entirely normal selector within the CALL gate descriptor, which must be an executable code segment. Not only the code segment in question is recorded here, but also the offset (i.e., the point of entry into the desired routine). This makes it impossible to jump to just any address within the code segment. Otherwise, it would be extremely easy to drop into the middle of a routine or an assembler instruction.

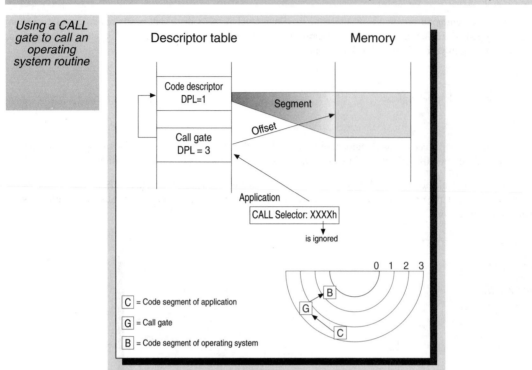

Using a CALL gate to call an operating system routine

Because the offset address is recorded in the call gate, it loses its significance within the actual CALL instruction and is ignored. Only the selector for access to the call gate is used. However, you must still follow the privilege rules.

In this case, the CALL gate is treated like a data segment and can only be addressed if its DPL carries the same or a lower (numerically higher) level than the caller (CPL <= DPL). So, the operating system must position its CALL gates at level 3 if its use throughout all privilege levels is also to be permitted to applications.

An operating system provides CALL gates to each program so they can call various system functions. The contents of these CALL gates (the address of the routine called) is unknown to the program, although its segment selector is supplied by the operating system. Another interesting feature is the conforming segments. In this case, we're concerned with normal coding segments, which are characterized as conforming segments by a special bit in the flag register of its segment descriptor. A characteristic feature of this code segment is the accommodation of its privilege level to that of its caller.

For example, if an application calls an operating system function, accommodated in a conforming segment, the program code contained in the latter is automatically executed at the level of the application (3) instead of at the privilege level of the operating system (0). This makes sense in various situations where the operating function must be viewed as an extension of the application and should not enjoy higher privileges.

Local and global descriptor tables

So far we've been considering only those descriptor tables in which the processor stores the descriptor of the appropriate segment. Actually, in Protected mode, it's possible to set up as many as 8193 descriptor tables:one global and 8192 local.

However, only two descriptor tables are active at a time: the global and a local. Each task is assigned its own local descriptor table. When tasks are switched, a change is made to the descriptor table of the new task. The two descriptor tables are assigned the names global descriptor table (GDT) and local descriptor table (LDT). They are the registers that expanded the 80286 over the 8086.

It's only possible to load these registers from the operating system using the LGDT (Load global descriptor table) and LLDT (Load local descriptor table) instructions. Whenever a task calls these instructions, which do not carry privilege 0, an exception, which automatically stops execution, is issued and a routine is called in the system kernel.

Execution of the LGDT instruction loads the physical address of the global descriptor table and its length into the GDTR register. The length entry enables the processor to determine the number of descriptors in this table (length / 8) and is able to rapidly recognize an attempt to access nonexistent descriptors. If the global descriptor table contains only 34 entries, each selector, whose index component exceeds the value 33, is invalid because the descriptors are numbered starting with 0.

Whether a selector addresses the global or the local descriptor table is determined by the TI bit. If it contains a 0, the global descriptor is referenced; a one refers to the local descriptor.

Usually an application will access its local descriptor table where the operating system stores the descriptors of all code and data segments of the task in question. However, the CALL gates for calling the operating system functions aren't located here. Storing information about the CALL gates, which can sometimes number into the hundreds, in each local description table would simply take up too much memory.

The global descriptor table contains not only the CALL gates of operating system functions, but also the code and data segment of the operating system, as well as various other system descriptors. Included among these are the descriptors of the memory segments containing the local descriptor tables. Unlike the GDTR register, which contains the physical address of the global descriptor table, the LDTR register contains only one selector that must point to an LDT descriptor in the LDT descriptor table. So, it's very easy to install a new local descriptor table when switching tasks. It's only necessary to load the LDTR register with the selector of the new local descriptor table.

Virtual address space size

When calculating the size of the virtual address space:Size of, it's necessary to multiply the maximum number of descriptors by the maximum segment size of 64K. To do this, first you must know the number of descriptors that can fit in the global descriptor table and in the various local descriptor tables. For both tables the size is 8192. There are two reasons for this.

First, local and global descriptor tables affect segments. In the 80286, segments cannot be larger than 64K. It's impossible to store more than 8192 descriptors in 64K because each descriptor occupies 8 bytes.

Also, you cannot address more than 8192 descriptors in the global or local descriptor table because the descriptor number within a selector is coded with only 13 bits. So, only numbers between 0 and 8192 can be accessed.

For example, suppose the global descriptor table contains 8192 descriptors of local descriptor tables, each of them containing in turn 8192 descriptors of 64K code or data segments. The virtual memory capacity would be:

```
8192 * 8192 * 64K = 1 gigabyte
```

which can be addressed (theoretically) only by an efficient virtual memory management system.

Accessing a descriptor

Although the linkage between selectors and descriptors and between the global and local descriptor tables may be complicated, you'll rarely encounter it in application programming. Simply avoid conflict between the selectors.

Essentially, the values used by an application come directly or indirectly from the operating system. An application cannot directly access the local descriptor table or the global descriptor table. Also, it cannot expand this table with new descriptors, or alter existing descriptors. This is solely the task of the operating system kernel, running at privilege level 0. The various instructions needed to manipulate this table can be found at this privilege level.

The operating system also supplies the local descriptor table with the various segment descriptors it needs to receive program code and data when an application is being loaded. 64K segments aren't set up automatically. Only that amount of memory, which is actually required by the segment in question, is released. If the application, because of an application error, seeks access to data or program code beyond the segment end, execution of the program is immediately interrupted by an exception, and an operating system routine is called to handle the error.

Even with the establishment of the various segments and the associated descriptors, reference must be made to these segments within the program, as shown by the following sequence of instructions from an assembler program:

```
MOV AX, segment data
MOV DS, AX
```

In a C program, to transfer a FAR pointer of a function in code segment to a different function, the desired segment selector must be available. In this case, we're concerned with the selector of a code segment, instead of a data segment. The situation in both cases is the same.

In this respect, a multitasking operating system functions almost the same as DOS: The head of the EXE file contains the addresses of the instructions within the program code, or of the variables from the constant data segment within which the various program and data segments are referenced. This table allows the loading function of the operating system to write the selectors of the addressed segments directly into the program code or the variables in question. Operating system calls will probably be handled in the same way, except that a CALL gate selector is required.

Some operating system functions return selectors as function results, especially the functions from the memory management area. These functions can be treated as a component part of a FAR pointer, like normal segment addresses. You can avoid manipulating this presumed segment address, which is frequently required in DOS programming. Manipulating this presumed address could create a selector pointing to an entirely different, or even nonexistent, descriptor.

The RPL field is important to the interaction between the operating system and application selectors. The preceding section indicated the privilege level of a task is always recorded in the RPL field of a selector by the task in possession of this selector (RPL = CPL).

It's possible to load any value into this field. However, when assigning selectors, the operating system will always enter the privilege level of the respective task into the RPL field of the selector transferred.

If such a selector is later transferred to an operating system function, permitting the latter to access a buffer, the high privilege level of the function shouldn't be used. Instead, this access should be executed at the privilege level of the caller, which prevents the latter from accessing data levels on all four privilege levels via the operating system function.

So, in these instances, the RPL field in the selector is set for the privilege check and points to the privilege level of the caller instead of to the privilege level of the operating system.

Shadow registers

When the various memory segments are addressed using selectors as pointers to segment descriptors (instead of their physical addresses), you can no longer address physical addresses in the segment register, as we demonstrated earlier. The processor must address the respective descriptor in the global or local descriptor table using a segment register selector, and from that determine the position and length of the segment in question. If the processor tried to do this in the case of each instruction, in whose execution one of the segment registers is involved, too much time would be wasted.

The data on the physical address of a segment and its length are loaded, when a segment register is loaded, into a shadow register. A shadow register exists for each segment register. Besides the visible 16-bit selector, each of the four segment register contains an additional invisible part that is 48 bits wide. This applies to the GDTR, LDTR, and IDTR registers, but these shadow registers manage different data.

Loading the shadow registers and the associated validity and privilege checks account for slower execution of all instructions affecting the content of the segment registers. For example, only two clock cycles are needed to execute the following instruction in Real mode:

```
MOV DS, AX
```

The same instruction line in Protected mode requires 18 clock cycles. This doesn't significantly affect execution speed when these instructions are rarely encountered within an application. However, this usually isn't the case, especially with high level language programs that are compiled using memory models with FAR pointers. For example, in C all memory models except SMALL and TINY use FAR pointers. The restriction of memory segments to 64K frequently makes any other procedure in Real mode impossible.

Aliasing

Data cannot be written into a code segment and the content of a data segment cannot be read by two tasks, whose code segments have different privileges. These are two of the many protection rules designed to ensure that a multitasking operating system runs smoothly.

However, there are other situations, in which these protection rules don't apply. For example, how can the operating system load the program code into an application segment, in which its contents may not be written? How can two tasks on different privilege levels gain access to the same data segment? In these situations, a mechanism known as aliasing circumvents the protection rules of the processor.

Although the processor controls access to a memory segment through its descriptor, it cannot prevent several descriptors from being entered in one or more different descriptor tables for the same memory range. So, it's possible that a memory range, which is already identified by a descriptor as a code segment, will be described partially or entirely as a data segment. The second descriptor is called an alias because it permits addressing a range in memory under another "name."

This makes it possible not only to load program code into a data segment, but to solve the problem of common memory usage. You can then set data segment descriptors in the task's LDT to duplicate the privilege level of the task. This duplicate then accesses the data segment using the descriptor.

Aliasing is useful whenever you must bypass the protection mechanisms of the processor. However, it can also cause several problems. So, the operating system uses aliases only in very special situations.

Hardware access

You can also restrict hardware access by using I/O ports. The INS and OUTS instructions (80286 extensions of the IN and OUT instructions) can be privileged.

The IOPL (I/O Privilege Level) bits in the flag register are responsible for this privileging. They indicate the privilege level a task must have before the task can execute the named assembler instructions. If both of these bits contain the value 1, only tasks on the 0 and 1 levels of privilege may execute this instruction. If they are executed from levels 2 or 3, the processor launches an exception, which activates an operating system routine.

This mechanism is only useful if the right to alter the contents of the IOPL bits isn't limited to the various applications. Conceding these rights could give applications the power to take over I/O execution themselves. Changing the flag register isn't difficult; simply push the desired contents onto the stack and execute the POPF instruction.

The 80286 developers made slight changes to the way the POPF instruction works. Although the POPF instruction can still be used at all privilege levels for setting the various flags in the flag register, this doesn't apply to the two IOPL bits. POPF changes the IOPL bits only when the calling task is executed on privilege level 0. This prevents normal applications from influencing the IOPL bits.

Task switching

The task register (TR) and the task state segments (TSS) support rapid task switching in Protected mode. These registers control memory ranges and comprise 44 bytes, which store the contents of all processor registers when a task is interrupted.

Also, a pointer to the task state segment of the previously active task is stored. This enables the processor to easily return to this task. As with all memory segments, each task state segment possesses a descriptor, which must be accommodated in the global descriptor table. However, this is a special system descriptor that points to the location and size of its segment like a normal descriptor.

This descriptor is referenced by the TR register, which contains the selector for the descriptor of the current task. In the case of a task switch, the contents of the processor registers can be stored immediately in its task state segment.

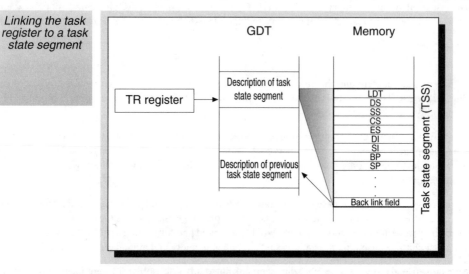

Linking the task register to a task state segment

A task switch can occur in several ways; usually a FAR JMP or FAR CALL instruction is used. In this type of instruction, an offset address must be indicated in addition to a selector. However, only the selector is important for the task switch, which is similar to a function call by using CALL gate. The offset address is essentially ignored.

This selector can be either the selector of a TSS descriptor from the GDT or the selector of a task gate. Similar to the CALL gate already described, such a gate serves as an intermediary and represents a system descriptor that can be accommodated either in the global or one of the local descriptor tables. The only significant data it contains is the selector of the TSS descriptor from the GDT, which identifies the new task.

Following the task gate route, the processor arrives at the required descriptor of the task state segment from the global descriptor table. The task change can be completed with its help; the former contents of the TR register are processed first (i.e., the pointer to the descriptor of the current task state segment).

This segment initially contains the current contents of the processor registers. The TR register is loaded with the TSS selector of the new task. In any case, the former content of the TR register is only stored briefly to permit it to be entered in the back link field of the new task state segment.

The processor contents stored here are loaded from the new task state segment. Because the CS and IP registers are also included among the secured registers, program execution continues at the exact location where the new task was interrupted.

If the operating system wants to set and start a new task, it will first set up a TSS descriptor in the GDT and use it to establish a task state segment for this task. Because the task wasn't active yet, the memory locations for the processor registers inside the new TSS must be initialized manually. The segment registers, the stack pointer, and the IP register are especially important. The starting address of the new task is established by CS:IP register pair. Program execution is then transferred to the new task by means of a FAR JMP with the selector of the TSS.

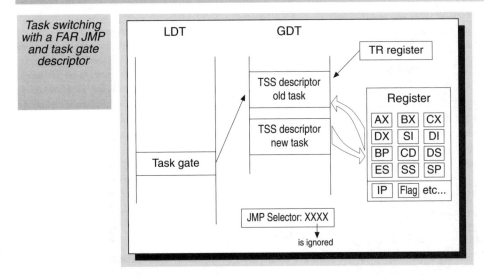

Task switching with a FAR JMP and task gate descriptor

Interrupts and exceptions

Interrupts are handled differently in Protected mode than in Real mode. The processor still recognizes 256 different interrupts, and still interacts between an interrupt and its interrupt handler, but the Real mode interrupt vector table no longer applies.

The solution is the Interrupt Descriptor Table (IDT), which is structured like a global or local descriptor table. Its starting address is stored in physical memory, and its length in the IDTR processor register. Access to this register in Protected mode is reserved for the operating system kernel, and this access executes on privilege level 0.

Unlike Real mode, an application isn't able to influence interrupt execution. This is an important prerequisite for a stable multitasking system. Under DOS, many TSR problems are caused as a result of the free accessibility to the interrupt vector table.

If an interrupt is triggered over the INTR processor line by an external device, or as the result of an INT assembler instruction, the processor enters the interrupt vector as an index into the interrupt descriptor table and reads the corresponding descriptor. This can be either an interrupt or a trap gate, since their structures are very similar. Both contain a selector and an offset address.

The selector serves as the access key to a code segment descriptor in the global or local descriptor table. The processor notifies the code segment containing the interrupt handler for the triggered interrupt. The offset, however, serves as the point of entry into this code segment, thus representing the start address of the interrupt handler within this code segment.

The difference between an interrupt and a trap gate consists of the association with the interrupt flag in the interrupt register. In Real mode, further interrupts usually cannot be called immediately after calling one interrupt, because the processor automatically sets this flag to 0 until returning to the interrupted program.

The processor proceeds in much the same way with an interrupt call through an interrupt gate. However, if it encounters a trap gate, the interrupt flag in the flag register isn't deleted. This makes it possible to trigger additional interrupts even during execution of the interrupt handler.

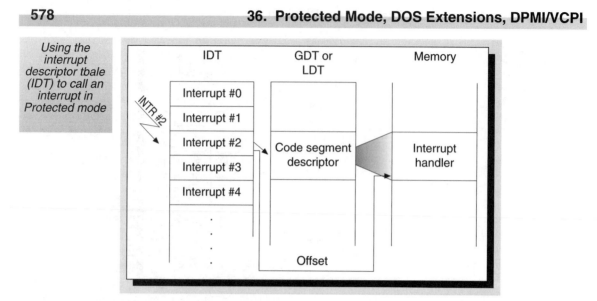

Exceptions are essentially interrupts, except they are directly called by the processor if an error occurs during the execution of an instruction. A reason for this could be infringement of privilege rights during access to memory segments or the specification of addresses following the end of the segment in question.

The processor recognizes interrupt requests from the interrupt controller, but only between the execution of two instructions. So, exceptions are triggered in the middle of the execution of a instruction. Once the error has been handled and removed by the exception handler of the operating system, the execution of the program must begin anew. The exceptions of the 80286 control occupy interrupts 0H through 10H. They are shown in the following table. Depending on the exception, the processor pushes data onto the stack before calling the exception handler, which more closely specifies the cause of the exception.

No.	Meaning	No.	Meaning
\multicolumn{4}{Exceptions in Protected Mode}
0	Division error	8	Double error
1	Single step	9	Coprocessor segment overflow
2	NMI (memory error)	10	Invalid Task Status Segment
3	Break point	11	Segment not available
4	Break caused by INTO	12	Stack error
5	Break caused by BOUND	13	Invalid segment access
6	Unknown command code	16	Coprocessor error
7	Coprocessor not available		

By programming for the Protected mode of the 80286 or one of its successors, you leave the world of 8086 compatibility. Here's a short list of the most important new instructions. These instructions may also be used in Real mode.

Op code	Definition
BOUND	Checks whether the contents of a register is within a specified range.
ENTER	Creates the stack frame and temporary storage required by many high level languages by copying function parameters onto the stack and reserving memory for local variables.
INS	Transfers data from a specified I/O port into a memory operand pointed to by the ES segment register and DI/EDI (the destination index register) and updates the index to prepare for the next transfer.
LEAVE	Counterpart to ENTER, but reverses the action of the ENTER instruction. Deletes the transferred function parameters and the local variables from the stack.
OUTS	Transfers data from a memory operand pointed to by the source index register to the specified I/O port and updates the index to prepare for the next transfer.
PUSHA	Saves the 16-bit or 32-bit general registers on the stack.
POPA	Restores registers from the stack.

The instructions from the following table aren't suitable for Protected mode programming because you must provide your own operating system services. All these instructions are privileged and may only be executed on privilege level 0. This makes them accessible in Real mode and are treated by the processor like a task with the privilege level 0.

Op code	Definition
ARPL	Checks and tests the privilege level of a code segment.
LAR	Loads the access rights byte of a descriptor.
LGDT	Loads the address and the length of the global descriptor table in the GDT register.
LIDT	Loads the address and the length of the interrupt descriptor into the IDT register.
LLDT	Loads the local descriptor table register.
LMSW	Loads the machine status word from the source operand.
LSL	Load segment limit.
LTR	Loads the task register (TR).
SGDT	Stores the contents of the GDT register.
SIDT	Stores the contents of the IDT register.
SLDT	Stores the contents of the LDT register.
SMSW	Stores the machine status word.
STR	Stores the contents of the task register TR.
VERR	Verifies a segment for reading.
VERW	Verifies a segment for writing.

Protected mode on the 80386 and 80486

Protected mode operation on the 80386 and i486 processors changes only slightly from that of the 80286. However, a few new concepts were included that shouldn't be used by a multitasking operating system. These include the paging of 4K memory blocks (vital to virtual memory management) and locking out individual I/O ports. These extensions are discussed in the following sections.

The Real mode changes are more important in these processors, especially the availability of 32-bit registers and the changes to the instruction set to accommodate the new register width. We'll start with an overview of the 80386 and i486's register complement, and how it affects Protected mode.

The 80386 and 80486 registers

The introduction of the 80386 marked the start of the 32-bit processor age. This is evident in the processor's register structure, since most registers have a 32-bit width. The AX, BX, CX, DX, DI, SI, and BP registers are still six bits wide. However, these 16 bits form part of an expanded 32-bit register, representing the low word of the 32-bit register. These 32-bit registers are named EAX, EBX, ECX, etc. The E represents extended.

The register complement of the 80386 and i486 (no floating-point registers)

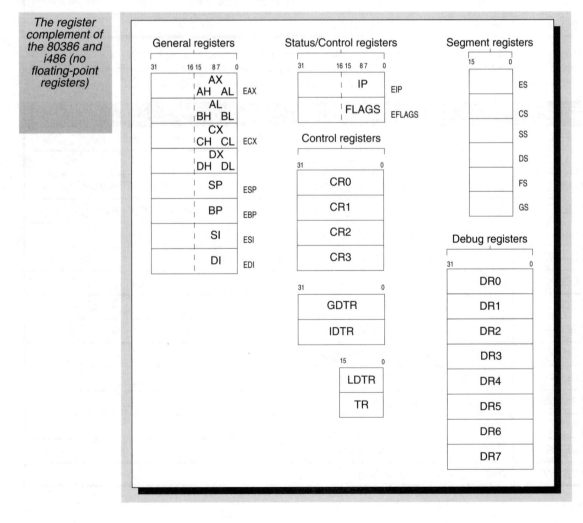

The 8-bit registers (AH, AL, BH, BL, etc.,) are still available, but the upper 16 bits of the E registers cannot be divided into two 8-bit registers. The number of available 8-bit registers remains unchanged, maintaining downward compatibility with the earlier 80xxx chips.

Instructions, such as MOV, SHL, ADD, etc., apply to 8-bit, 16-bit, and 32-bit registers alike. The 80386 and its successors use this to achieve higher speed, especially when processing dwords (long in C and LongInt in Pascal).

The illustration on the previous page shows both wider registers than the 80286 and new registers. Notice the FS and GS registers. These two new segment registers can be used for memory access just like the ES register. As before, DS still acts as the default register for accessing data, and CS actsas the default register for program execution.

Like the 80286, the various segment registers in 80386 Real mode mirror the segment addresses of the segments addressed. While in Protected mode, they accept selectors for segment descriptor access from the local or global descriptor table.

The GDTR, LDTR, IDTR, and TR registers, which are used for memory management and task control, also remain the same. These registers can only access the operating system kernel on privilege level 0.

Four 32-bit control registers have been added: CR0, CR1, CR2, and CR3. These control registers are reserved for the operating system kernel (more on this later).

The 80386 includes eight debug registers called DR0 through DR7. These registers allow you to set four different break points that can be triggered at any point in a program (e.g., when execution reaches a specific instruction, when a read access occurs, or when a write access occurs). So, the 80386 presents software debugging options that were only possible with expensive hardware extensions.

Larger segments

The general registers (AX, BX, CX and DX) and the index registers (DI, SI, BP and SP) are all 32-bit registers in the 80386. The segment length was also expanded to 32 bits. This means a segment now has the capacity to hold up to 4 gigabytes (232), without changing the segment descriptor size from that of the 80286. The Intel developers had reserved a word at the end of the descriptor for the 80286 and its successors.

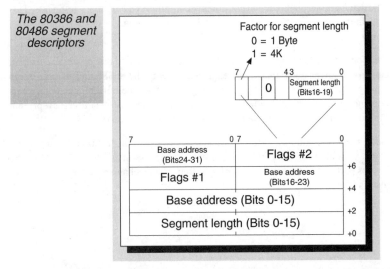

The 80386 and 80486 segment descriptors

As you can see, so far the structure of the descriptor in the 80286 is identical to the more advanced 80386 and i486 processors. However, the seventh byte of the descriptor contains an extension of the flag register in the 80386 and i486. The lower four bits are used as bits 16 through 19 of the segment length. This produces a segment length of 20 bits and permits a segment to be expanded to only 1 megabyte, instead of 4 gigabytes, as we metnioned.

At this point, the granularity flag is used. This flag occupies bit 7 of this second flag byte and specifies whether the segment length must be taken as a factor of one byte or 4K (212). In the latter case, the indicated segment length must be multiplied by 4K, which is equivalent to a shift of 12 bit positions to the left. This expands the segment length, however, to 32 bits, which results in the previously stated maximum length of 4 gigabytes.

The segment's base address is expanded to 32 bits. Although the lower 24 bits are found in their traditional locations, bits 24 through 31 are located in the last byte of the descriptor. The 32-bit base addresses and length data extend the linear address space in the 80386 and i486 to 4 gigabytes, and the virtual address space to 64 terabytes (246).

The 512K memory chips (4 megabits) are becoming more affordable. Eight of these are usually combined into a single inline memory module (or SIMM) with a capacity of 4 megabytes. The 4 gigabyte goal is still off by the factor 210 (1024). Assuming that a new generation of chips is developed every two years, we may not reach this level for another 20 years. This doesn't include trying to develop manufacturing standards. So, there's not much need to widen the address register to 64 bits.

By expanding the offset address to 24 bits, FAR pointers in 80386 and i486 Protected mode contain six bytes instead of four: two for the segment selector and four for the offset address.

Paging and virtual memory management

Virtual memory management can be implemented with the 80286, because each segment descriptor contains a flag indicating the presence of the segment in memory. If the processor encounters a missing segment during processing, it automatically triggers an exception. The operating system interprets the exception as a request to load the segment.

This is the best way to implement virtual memory management. The memory blocks to be moved in and out are always various lengths. They are always complete segments that (in the 80286) can have a length between 1 byte and 64K. However, only a portion of the segment may be needed, and this segment can be removed in the next instant when another task is executed. In each case, the entire segment must be unloaded, then reloaded. Also, the size of the unloading file (or swap file) steadily increases.

Now, imagine that you want the system to unload segment B. However, there's no space left in the swap file because of segment A, which was just reloaded into memory. Fragmentation also occurs in RAM because the various loaded and unloaded segments are different sizes. The virtual memory management continually compresses the memory segments. This occurs transparently, without interfering with the various programs (the segment descriptor changes, instead of the segment selector). This process is still time-consuming.

These problems are solved if the sizes of the blocks to be loaded and unloaded are kept constant, and this process is inserted after the segmentation process. This places it on a lower level and in makes it transparent. The 80386 and its successors implement a paging mechanism to solve this problem. The paging is based on a group of 4K memory blocks. When this mechanism is disabled, the linear addresses resulting from the dissolution of segment selectors and offset addresses represent physical addresses, just as in the 80286, and these addresses can actually be accessed by the processor.

Once paging is enabled, the *page table* models the linear addresses after physical addresses (i.e., the linear addresses are no longer identical to physical addresses). If we view this in executing a single memory access instruction, this slows the execution speed. However, if we think of this as part of a multitasking operating system, the mechanism is very efficient for implementing a virtual memory management system.

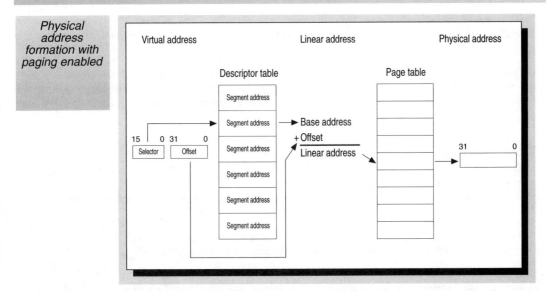

Physical address formation with paging enabled

Using constant memory blocks does more than simply manage the swap file. It also prevents the swap file from continually increasing. Memory can be allocated in 4K pages, instead of the entire 1 gigabyte segment.

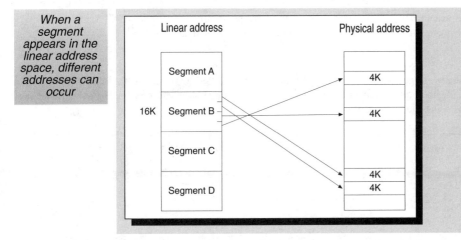

When a segment appears in the linear address space, different addresses can occur

Memory compression is also no longer needed, because the blocks can be merged into any linear memory address by using the page table. The four blocks of a 16K memory segment can be stored at entirely different physical addresses to form a continuous memory block within the linear address space, and can be addressed by an application.

What appears in the linear address space to be a continuous segment, can occupy entirely different addresses in the physical address space.

Page tables

The PG bit in control register 0 (CR0) is responsible for activating the paging mechanism. Normally this bit is set to 0. Linear addresses are modeled directly on physical addresses. So, paging doesn't occur. However, if this bit is set to 1 within the Protected mode, the linear addresses are converted by the page table.

The size of each page is 4K. Each page begins at a physical address divisible by 4K. The 4 gigabyte (232) linear address space of the 80386 and i486 is divided into 220 different pages, each containing 212 bytes (4K). The calculation is correct because 220*212 again yields 232.

The specification of 4K limits makes it possible for the lower 12 bits of a linear address to be incorporated directly into the physical address. They represent a type of offset in the respective page. The upper 20 bits of the linear address indicates the number of the page containing the memory location addressed. They are considered to be an index in the page table, from which the physical base index of the respective page can be taken.

The entries in the page table are respectively 32 bits wide. Only 20 bits are actually needed for the base address, which must begin at a physical memory location divisible by 4K. The lower 12 bits is 0 in each case. The lower 12 bits contain various flags for the virtual memory management system. For example, the flags indicate whether the page is currently present in memory or must first be loaded from the swap file. Only the upper 20 bits from the page table entry are used to form the physical address. They are complemented by the 12 lower bits of the linear address, which are used unchanged.

Actually, the entire process is more complicated. The page table with its 220 entries of four bytes each would otherwise use the entire four megabytes. This would mean throwing away several megabytes of valuable memory since only 1024 entries and 4K of memory are actually required for the page table with four megabytes of RAM installed.

An entry in the page table must be made available to the processor for each page in the linear address space. This considers instances, in which a false address is swapped into a segment descriptor, which results in the formation of a linear address, for which no entry was established in the page table. However, this can't be recognized by the processor. Unlike the global and local descriptor table, no length data is recorded for the page table.

The processor will read the presumed page table entry, although the corresponding memory location will contain an arbitrary data or code segment. The processor will then create one or more random physical addresses.

Dividing the page table

The page table is divided into two stages. The page directory handles several smaller page tables. As the following illustration shows, the upper 10 bits of the linear address constitute the index in the page directory, which consists of 1024 entries. Since each entry contains 32 bits, this table uses 4K of memory.

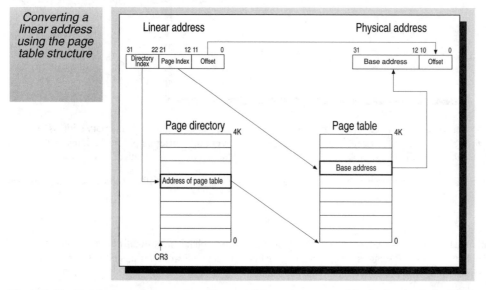

Converting a linear address using the page table structure

The individual entries are pointers to the addresses of the various page tables in the physical address space. This is where the processor first learns the address of a page. The entry number used in the respective page table for calculating the address is produced from bits 12 through 21 of the linear address, and is divided into two parts: a 10-bit index for the page directory and a 10-bit index for the page table in question. The page directory and each page table contains the addresses of 1024 pages and occupies 4K of memory.

Because of the page table structure, each entry within the page directory occupies a four megabyte range within the linear address space. The advantage of this is that during initialization of the operating system only a page directory and a page table, to control the first four megabytes of memory, must be established. In the beginning more than four megabytes isn't required.

The operating system consistently divides this memory sequentially, instead of arbitrarily throughout the linear address space. The total assigned memory appears in the first four megabytes, controlled by the page table indicated by the first entry in the page directory. All other entries in the page directory can initially be marked invalid by setting special flags in the lower 20 bits. Setting these special flags instructs the processor to trigger exceptions (more on this later).

Once memory requirements exceed the four megabyte limit, the system must create a new page table, and store its address in the second entry of the page directory. For every four megabytes of memory, only 4K is needed in the page table, which is less than the four megabytes in a continuous page table for all the pages in the linear address space.

The page directory's address must be passed to the processor, along with the addresses of the page tables. The CR3 register contains the physical address of this data structure.

The CR2 register plays a subordinate role in the paging mechanism. When a paging error triggers an exception, the processor places the address to be converted in the CR2 register.

Structure of a page table entry

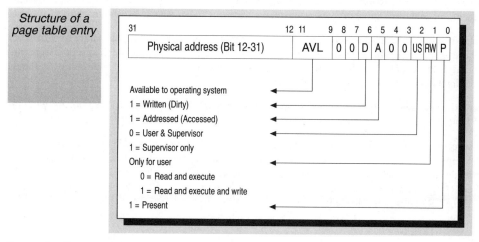

Page unloading strategies

The virtual memory management system performs its duties by using various flags in the lower 20 bits of the page table entries. The Present flag (bit zero of the page table entry) must be set to 0 by the operating system if a page was unloaded. The processor then triggers an exception when this page is accessed, enabling the operating system to take control of program execution and load the page. The Present flag must then be reset to 1, or the processor will again cause an exception on the next access.

The Dirty bit and the Accessed bit are also useful in virtual memory management. The Accessed bit is automatically set to 1 by the processor before accessing the page of a page table entry. This flag is even set to 1 if only one of the total of 1024 pages in a directory entry is addressed.

Because this flag is set only to 1 by the processor, and never to 0, the virtual memory management system can use it for marking addressed pages. It must set this bit to 0 after loading, or after establishing a page. The Accessed bit can then be used to test whether this page was already addressed.

This information is very helpful when space in physical memory is limited, which making it necessary to shift pages into the swap file. Then it's possible to give priority to recently addressed and immediately needed pages.

There are also reasons why the pages just addressed should be unloaded. Supporters of this theory argue these pages were already in the queue, while the others are only to be addressed in the next instant. A further criterion for this decision is supplied by the Dirty bit, which is set to 1 only when write accesses occur. Reading this bit makes it possible to distinguish altered pages from unaltered pages. Priority should be given to unaltered pages during unloading because they are retained in their original form in the swap file, and will have to be reloaded again later. With proper planning, some execution time can be saved.

Protective mechanisms

The remaining flags in the page table entries constitute a protective mechanism, similar to the one found at the linear address level.

Distinctions are made between supervisor and user code, instead of between four privilege levels. All tasks carrying privilege levels 0, 1, or 2, which can thus be part of the operating system, have supervisor code authority. Tasks from privilege level 3 are designated as user codes.

If a page's user/supervisor flag is set, which indicates a supervisor page, user tasks are generally denied access to this page and create an exception. However, if this flag isn't set, access is open both to user tasks as well as supervisor tasks.

The Read/Write flag determines access to user tasks. If this flag contains a 0 value, the page in question may be read and executed, but not written. If it contains a value of 1, the page allows writing. Errors generate exceptions in this case also.

Converting a linear address into a physical address is time-consuming, particularly when loading page tables from memory. The 80386 and its successors have a built-in cache to store the page table entries that were just loaded. This cache is frequently called a translation lookaside buffer (TLB). In the 80386 and i486, this buffer stores the last 32 page table entries. Although only 120K are covered, Intel maintains that this cache is 98% effective.

Although this cache may be very helpful for the conversion rate, like all caches it has problems. These problems will most likely occur if a page table entry's contents change in memory, but the change isn't reflected in the cache.

In the 80386 and its successors, software must maintain the integrity of the translation lookaside buffers. The processor doesn't handle this task. However, the processor does provide a simple mechanism that can help the cache contents up to the point where they can be declared invalid, which allows the individual entries to be gradually reloaded into the cache. This consists of loading the CR3 register with the starting address of the page directory. Its starting address is changed, the cache is declared invalid, and the CR3 register is reloaded:

```
MOV AX,CR3
MOV CR3,AX
```

This keeps the translation lookaside buffer clear. However, the paging mechanism shouldn't be used globally for all tasks. Instead, it should only be switched on for individual tasks and suppressed for others. It's possible to set or delete the paging flag in the CR0 register or even load the CR3 directory with the start address of a page directory (or of several page directories) with each task switch.

Selective I/O port blocking

The 80386 and its successors have a slightly different approach than the 80286 for determining whether an I/O port may be addressed by a task.

Although only the IOPL flag in the flag register and the privilege level of the task in question count in the 80286, it's now possible to set up an I/O permission bitmap in the task state segment of a task. This bitmap is a large bit array with up to 216 entries. Provisions are made for all 65536 possible ports to be tested as a group, to determine whether a basic access without reference to privilege level will be possible, or whether a test via the IOPL flag should occur. The value 0 indicates free access; 1 represents the IOPL test.

The starting offset within the task page segment isn't fixed, but can be selected by the operating system. It must be specified at offset address 66H in the task state segment, which, in the 80386, has grown to at least 102 bytes because of the expanded processor registers.

From this starting address and the length of the task state segment stored in the descriptor, the processor determines the size of the bit array. The ports, which are no longer covered by the bit array, are subject to the IOPL test.

If the offset address of the bit array is larger than or equal to the segment length, there won't be a bit array and the IOPL test is executed. If more room is left between the offset address and the segment length than the maximum length of 8K, all ports will be covered by the array. If none of these conditions are met, the interval between the end of the task state segment and the start of the bit array is calculated and this value is multiplied by 8 to determine the number of ports represented in it.

More flexible addressing modes

The types of addressing were also significantly expanded with the introduction of the 80386. All general registers are viewed as base and index registers, both in Real mode and Protected mode, instead of only certain combinations of the SI, DI, and BP registers. Also, it's possible to multiply an index register by a factor of 2, 4, or 8 to permit rapid access to word, dword, or qword arrays. A constant 8-bit or 32-bit offset can be added, as the following illustration shows:

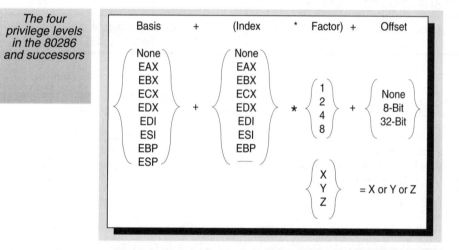

The four privilege levels in the 80286 and successors

The 80386 and i486 processors include the ability to accommodate data and variables, according to their size in memory, to word, dword, or qword limits. Otherwise, access will last significantly longer because several read and write accesses are needed to compose the operands.

New instructions

As with the 80286, the 80386 was also extended by a few instructions or operation modes for instructions already familiar to programmers. These changes are for non-privileged instructions. System instructions on the 0 privilege level don't have any changes.

The following table provides an overview of the new options hidden in the 80386 instruction set:

BT,BTC,BTR,BTS	Instructions for testing and setting bits in registers and variables.
BSF,BSR	Instructions for scanning bits in registers and variables.
LSS,LFS,LGS	Loads one of the segment registers: SS, FS, or GS.
Jxx 32-bit	Conditional jump instruction (JC, JA, JBE, etc.) with 32-bit displacement.
MOVSX,MOVZX	MOV instruction with automatic expansion of the prefix or setting the remainder register to 0.
MOV DRx,Reg	Load one of the debug registers.
MOV Reg,DRx	Load a register with one of the debug registers.
MOV CRx,Reg	Load the control register.
MOV Reg,CRx	Loads a registers with the control register.
SHRD,SHLD	Shifts DWORDS left or right.
SETxx	Loads one of the various 8-bit registers with an indicated value, if the condition of the instruction is met. Functions like a combination of CMP, Jxx, and MOV.

Virtual-86 mode

Virtual-86 mode (V86) mode was created as a compromise between Real mode and Protected mode. Many EMS emulators (e.g., Microsoft Corporation's EMM386.SYS) and multitasking environments (e.g., DesqView/386) use V86.

When a system operates in V86 mode, the computer is running in Real mode, while retaining the background memory management, task management, and privilege rules found in Protected mode. When you run a program in V86 mode, it runs like an independent V86 task, while the Protected mode mechanisms remain hidden. The program sees only its one megabyte address space, which is addressed according to the standard rules of Real mode:

```
segment_address * 16 + offset_address
```

From the V86 task's point of view, we're concerned with ordinary segment addresses instead of selectors, as in Protected mode. A program can load any value into one of the segment registers without having to worry about an exception occurring.

The processor issues an exception for a V86 task if it uses one of the 80386's 32-bit address modes to generate an offset address outside the 64K segment limit. All the 80386 and i486 address types are available for a V86 task, including the use of 32-bit registers and offsets, with segments larger than 64K as the exception.

V86 mode is used for executing normal DOS programs that rarely access the expanded capabilities of the 80386 and its successors. Only linear addresses exist in V86 mode because of the lack of selectors or descriptor tables. So, the one megabyte address space of a task is patterned after the first megabyte of physical RAM, as long as paging is disabled. If paging is enabled, it's possible for the address space of a V86 task to accommodate itself using the page directory and the necessary page table in any range in physical memory.

While a task is executed in V86 mode, it's possible for other tasks to be active not only in V86 mode. Protected mode is available both in the 80286 compatible 16-bit version, and in the 32-bit version of the 80386 and i486. These modes are generally used by a virtual control monitor, which controls the execution of the DOS program in V86 mode in the background, giving it the feel of a normal DOS machine. In the subsections on EMS emulators and multitaskers, we'll discuss how this occurs.

Protected mode also handles the interrupts and exceptions triggered by a V86 task. The processor switches to Protected mode and the interrupt or exception handlers are called using the associated gate in the interrupt descriptor table. The V86 task isn't responsible for the initialization of this table and preparing the interrupt and exception handlers. This is controlled by the virtual control monitor running the task.

Switching to V86 mode

There are several ways to switch from Protected mode to the V86 mode with the 80386 and its successors. The most common method is task switching through a task gate. The operating mode, in which the new task is executed, is controlled by the VM flag from the EFLAGS register, which is loaded from the task gate segment of the new task during the task change. If this flag is set, the program runs in V86 mode. If the flag isn't set, normal Protected mode is used.

Earlier we described how a new task can be "launched" by generating a task state segment, using an associated task gate and its call. In V86 mode, you can simply initialize the VM flag within the task state segment with a 1 to begin task execution in V86 mode.

V86 tasks always run on the lowest privilege level (3). All instructions with any sort of influence on the content of the interrupt or VM flags within the EFLAGS register (PUSHF, POPF, INIT, IRET, CLI and STI) are subject to the IOPL test and may be executed only if a value of 3 is in the IOPL flag. This prevents V86 tasks from acquiring the capacity to switch into Protected mode.

It's also possible to control changes in the interrupt flag. DOS programs have a tendency to delete this flag for a certain time interval to suppress INTR requests. This usually isn't a good practice for a virtual control monitor. During the time the INTR request is suppressed, interrupt requests for other tasks get backed up and cannot be processed quickly enough.

Exceptions are generally triggered from the IOPL for all attempts to access the EFLAGS register. Changes to the addressed flags are prevented.

Permanently calling these exception handlers slows down program execution. It's recommended that "safe" DOS programs be supplied with IOPL 3. In V86 mode, the instructions IN, OUT, INS, and OUTS aren't privileged, as they are in Protected mode. Before executing such an instruction, the processor requests the I/O permission bitmap from the task state segment of the task in question to selectively block or release individual ports. Accessing a blocked port generates an exception and the virtual control monitor gains control of program execution. This gives it the ability to virtualize certain ports. We'll look at this process in more detail in the section on multitaskers.

As you can see, V86 mode supplies the means for executing DOS programs, even in multitasking operations. The following section explains how this is done.

Protected Mode Utilities

The V86 mode, which we described in the previous section, is mainly suitable for developing Protected mode DOS utilities. It's possible to develop a monitor program that runs in Protected mode, but controls one (or more) virtual machines in V86 mode. This provides DOS with an "assistant", which controls all the steps without being noticeable. The following two sections show what happens when V86 mode is combined with DOS.

EMS Emulators and memory management programs

There are EMS (Expanded Memory Specification) simulators for systems ranging from the 8086 to the i486. These simulators are responsible for making expanded memory available according to the LIM (Lotus-Intel-Microsoft) specification. The various types of EMS emulators operate according to different principles, depending on the Intel processor for which they were designed.

The prerequisites for these utilities and their effectiveness have improved with each generation of processor. All of these utilities make the LIM specification available, but often the EMS memory is still inaccessible. Using an EMS emulator is hardly worthwhile for 8086 processors because it uses the available EMS memory on a hard drive file and also unloads there. This process is too time-consuming. The EMS window, with its 64K, must be located in RAM below the 640K limit (conventional memory). This means that you'll lose valuable main memory. EMS emulators for the 8086 aren't very useful.

However, there's a difference when considering the 80286. Although it's possible to take the simulated EMS memory from the hard drive, you shouldn't do this. Instead, you should use the extended memory above the 1 megabyte limit. This memory area is available on almost any AT. The EMS emulator uses this as expanded memory by copying memory from extended memory into the EMS page frame with a special BIOS function.

In any case, you must locate the page frame below the 640K limit. When EMS memory is frequently used, you should install an EMS expansion card, even in 80286 computers. However, many ATs (especially those with the NEAT BIOS chip set) can configure extended memory as expanded memory.

The introduction of the 80386 finally permitted EMS emulators to achieve a significant breakthrough. Various performance characteristics of this processor were designed specifically for EMS emulators. The basis for making expanded memory available is the extended memory above the 1 megabyte limit. However, unlike the 80286, in this case, the memory doesn't have to be copied into a page frame.

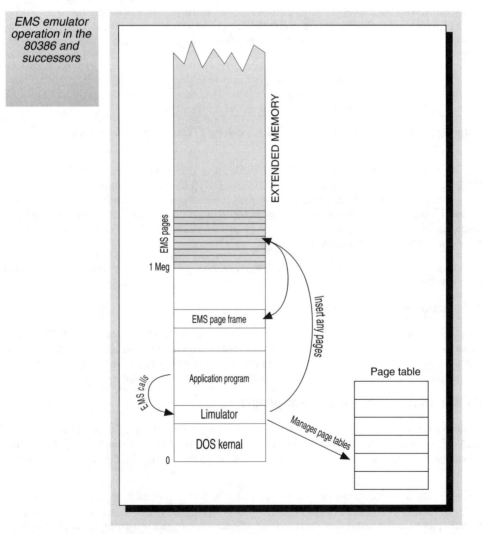

EMS emulator operation in the 80386 and successors

The 80386 and its successors provide an efficient paging method. This method makes it easy to model extended memory in the EMS page frame and use the area between 640K and 1 megabyte, even when physical memory doesn't exist there. That's how efficient memory management programs like 386-To-The-Max, QEMM386, and EMM386 perform this task.

However, one small problem remains. In Real mode, from which DOS programs request and use EMS memory, you cannot use 80386 paging. You must use the V86 mode, which means the EMS emulator must be switched into V86 mode at the very start, then continue in the background as the virtual control monitor. We'll discuss this in more detail in the section on multitaskers.

Memory management programs

Memory management programs, such as 386-To-The-Max or QEMM386, generally make access to extended memory available for EMS emulators and the XMS (eXtended Memory Specification) interface. They also provide an option for loading TSR programs, device drivers, and parts of DOS above the 640K limit, which creates more space in conventional RAM. These programs and drivers are loaded, using the page table, into memory ranges between the 640K and the 1 gigabyte limits, without actually being present there.

The main trick is to determine which parts of this memory range are unused by hardware or other software, rather than to program the page tables.

Multitaskers

Recently PCs have reached the performance levels of mainframe workstations. Because of this, many DOS users are demanding more advanced features, especially multitasking. Actually, many users are more concerned with being able to switch between programs, than with multitasking.

Programs that make task switching possible are available for all types of PCs. One of the most popular programs is DesqView from Quarterdeck. However, the Task Swapper available in the DOS 5.0 Shell has been giving DesqView some competition. DesqView/386 and Windows 3 bring true multitasking to the DOS world. Both systems permit parallel execution of multiple DOS programs and can display output in separate screen windows.

These multitaskers, which are a type of operating system that's grafted onto DOS, can run other operating systems besides DOS. Since we're concerned about system programming, we won't discuss these systems in detail. Instead, we'll examine a system programming problem called "hardware virtualizing". The V86 mode has been extremely important to the solution to this problem.

Virtualizing hardware presents the illusion of an independent PC to any program executed in a multitasking environment. DOS programs are inhospitable to other programs, writing directly to video RAM or programming the interrupt controller to reserve all available memory for themselves.

Hardware virtualization

The screen is one example of the basic problems that can occur in multitasking. Usually, each DOS program can assume that it can access the entire 80x25 text screen. However, multitasking provides a window smaller than the screen for each program. The multitasker places the output from each program into a buffer and displays a part of the buffer in the window assigned to the respective program.

To display all program output, the multitasker shifts the window contents. This displays other parts of the virtual screen. The virtual screen may also be expanded to use the entire physical screen, similar to Windows.

Intercepting video RAM access

Now that we know what happens from the user's perspective, let's see what goes on behind the scenes and how the multitasker handles the output from different programs.

Problems shouldn't occur as long as the program sends output to the screen using ROM-BIOS video functions. The multitasker simply redirects the ROM-BIOS video interrupt to its own function. The multitasker's function stores the characters in the virtual screen (the internal buffer mentioned above), instead of writing the characters directly to the screen. The multitasker then passes the characters to the respective program window.

The functions in the multitasker handler intercept DOS video functions and high level language commands, such as PRINT, printf(), and WriteLn(), as well as ROM-BIOS functions.

Suppose the program doesn't support any of these options, and directly accesses video RAM (like most DOS based applications). Systems based on the 8086/8088 or 80286 processors can't be used because they don't provide an option for direct memory access. However, the V86 mode's paging mechanism allows you to control the memory access in 80386 and higher processors.

You may remember from the section on the 80386's paging mechanism the linear address space is modeled on the physical address space using the page table. This page table is vital to the multitasker. All DOS applications must be given the illusion they're operating in the first megabyte of memory, regardless of their physical locations in memory.

The paging mechanism also contributes to virtual screen management. The Present bit is part of this virtual management. This bit is part of the flag saved with each entry in one of the page tables.

If the Present bit is unset during page access, the processor assumes the page currently doesn't exist in memory. An exception, which passes program control to the operating system, occurs. After program control is redirected, the page loads. The exception call occurs regardless of whether virtual memory is implemented.

A multitasker takes advantage of the exception by marking the pages, which correspond to video RAM, as not present. Each video RAM access calls the exception routine of the multitasker, which stores the video RAM access. The multitasker then places the byte (or word) to be displayed in the appropriate program's virtual screen for later display.

Actually, this procedure saves us from having to redirect the video BIOS function. The video RAM directly receives the data, which inadvertently calls the multitasker's exception handler. Since this requires a lot of microprocessor time, a multitasker usually reroutes video BIOS for its own use. By using the procedure we just explained, we can protect both video RAM and other memory ranges from access. This also applies to individual memory locations and entire 4K pages.

Since the offset address of the access is always transmitted to the exception handler of the multitasker, it's even possible to protect ranges smaller than 4K. If the exception handler determines the memory location lies outside the range to be protected, it sets the Present bit to 1, executes the memory access, and changes the Present bit to 0.

I/O access interception

Hardware ports must also be handled if they're accessed simultaneously by DOS applications under multitasker control. Let's return to our screen output example. Think of how a video card changes to graphics mode or selects another color palette. The multitasker notices such changes through the I/O permission bitmap in Protected mode (see the "Protected Mode" section in this chapter for more information). This bitmap is always active in V86 mode and offers the multitasker the option of protecting ports from program access.

If a program tries to control of one of these ports, an exception occurs, notifying the multitasker. Windows Enhanced mode uses this method when a DOS window in V86 mode calls the DMA controller during disk access. Paging doesn't help; the addresses are viewed as true physical addresses. So, Windows must intercept each access to this chip within the DOS window and convert the specified physical addresses into their real physical addresses before passing them to the DMA chip.

The V86 mode, the paging mechanism, and the I/O permission bitmap can solve many of the other problems facing multitaskers. However, the conflict that occurs in Protected mode between multitaskers and DOS extensions cannot be solved by any of them. If you start a program, which was developed using a DOS extension, from a multitasker, accessing the program in Protected mode isn't possible and accessing the program from V86 mode will run it on the lowest privilege level.

The DPMI and VCPI software intercepts provide a solution to this problem (see the "DPMI And VCPI" section in this chapter).

DOS Extensions

Memory must accommodate data and program code in extended memory, but this memory area must be kept separate. This is a typical situation in Real mode under DOS. Software drivers, such as EMS or XMS, grant access to more memory for data. However, this usually involves compatibility problems that require program reconfiguration. For years, software developers have been demanding options that enable DOS programs to use extended memory just like conventional RAM.

DOS extensions make these options available. These are development tools that are available from various software developers and are designed to work with specific compilers. Standard C compilers and other languages (e.g., Turbo Pascal) provide DOS extensions. In this section, we'll discuss DOS extensions and how they are used in the C language.

DOS extensions must be specially adapted to the compiler because they interact with the executable code generated by the compiler. DOS extensions attempt to permit DOS program execution in Protected mode on 80286, 80386, or i486 processors. A program running in Protected mode can access all of RAM, instead of only the 640K specified by DOS.

How a DOS extension works

A short definition of how a DOS extension works is: Run a program in Protected mode and revert to Real mode before making DOS or BIOS calls. You can change code in an EXE file to run it in Protected mode, but this doesn't apply to DOS or ROM-BIOS. This presents some problems, as you'll soon see.

DOS extensions operate according to a fairly simple principle, but with a twist. DOS extensions include various tools that apply to the standard compiler (e.g., Microsoft C 5.1 or 6.0). First, a new starting address for the program is passed, followed by the program code of the DOS extension.

The DOS extension built into the program copies the program into extended memory without executing it. Next, while still in Real mode, a global descriptor table appears, containing code and data segment descriptions of the program. The data needed for this is obtained from the OBJ file, which was generated by the compiler when the program was created.

The sequence in which the various segment descriptors are entered was established during program creation. The various segment references from the data and code segment were already selector entries that couldn't be changed. Adjusting segment references, such as with a DOS loader, isn't necessary when loading a Real mode program. The segment addresses are already defined in the segment descriptors and can no longer be changed.

The program is almost ready to run, although it still needs an interrupt descriptor table and the interrupt handlers used for calling DOS and BIOS functions. Once these are installed, the program can execute in Protected mode. The DOS extension switches the processor into the Protected mode and starts the program. While the program is active, the DOS extension runs in the background above various DOS and BIOS functions (more on this later).

If the program ends in the usual way (i.e., DOS function 4CH), the DOS extension regains control of program execution. It releases memory and reverts to Real mode, thus returning to DOS level. The user receives no indication that Protected mode is being used.

DOS extensions for the 80286, 80386, and i486

DOS extensions can be divided into two areas: DOS extensions for the 80286 and DOS extensions for the 80386 and i486. The second group uses the full capabilities of the 80386 processor and its successors, and achieves higher execution speeds than the 80286 could handle. To fully use the 80386/i486 extension, the source code of your program must be changed. However, an 80286 extension may not require source changes (more on this later).

The Demands of Protected mode

A DOS program in Protected mode first confronts changes to memory management, which is characterized by selectors, segment descriptors and descriptor tables. Segment addresses and constant 64K segments don't exist. The DOS extension solved most of this problem by accessing the compiler generated code before calling the program.

The DOS program encounters problems if it must execute DOS or BIOS calls, or trigger external device interrupts. None of these were designed to be executed in Protected mode. So, calling them would crash the system when loading the first segment address into one of the segment registers.

Many programmers insist their programs don't contain DOS or BIOS calls because they are designed to run under the XYZ system. However, even if a program doesn't directly call DOS or BIOS functions, many indirect calls still exist. If you use high level language statements and functions for screen display, file management, or reading the keyboard, these statements and functions are still DOS or BIOS calls at their lowest levels.

Now, let's see what happens if a software interrupt or the keyboard calls a BIOS or DOS function (e.g., a hardware interrupt) during execution. The DOS extension assumes control of program execution because it placed its interrupt handler in the interrupt descriptor table before the program started. The DOS extension provides its own interrupts to replace the DOS interrupts (20H, 21H, 24H, etc.), the BIOS interrupts (10H, 11H, 12H, 13H, 14H, 15H, 16H, etc.), and the hardware interrupts (08H, 09H, 0AH, etc.).

The IRQ0 to IRQ7 interrupt sources usually trigger the same interrupts as the various Protected mode exceptions (interrupts 08H through 0FH). Most DOS extensions reprogram the interrupt controller to redirect hardware interrupts IRQ0 through IRQ7 to other interrupts. This keeps hardware interrupts and exceptions separate.

Let's return to the DOS extension's interrupt handlers as they are executed from Protected mode. These interrupt handlers are responsible for reverting to Real mode, calling the original interrupt handler from the interrupt vector table, then returning to Protected mode. The return to Protected mode indicates the end of the interrupt handler execution, after which the program can continue running. This momentary switch into Real mode remains completely transparent to the program itself.

Switching between Protected mode and Real mode is time-consuming. This is especially true with the 80286, which directly supports only the switch from Real mode into Protected mode (returning to Real mode takes some effort). A modern AT with a clock speed of 16 MHz makes about 2000 loops from Real mode to Protected mode and back in a single second. An 80386 with a clock speed of 20 MHz makes nearly 9000 loops. This occurs because of the clock speed and the ease with which the 80386 returns to Real mode from Protected mode.

Both these numbers seem small when compared to the hundreds of thousands of assembly language instructions executed by a processor every second. However, fewer calls to DOS, BIOS, and hardware interrupts occur than you might think, especially in programs that access large quantities of data rather than interact with the user. These data access programs are good candidates for DOS extensions, because the standard 640K of RAM just isn't sufficient. So, the time loss between Real and Protected mode is minimal.

Transferring buffer addresses

Switching from Protected mode to Real mode doesn't affect many interrupt functions, especially interrupt 21H and its DOS functions. These functions expect parameters in the various processor registers and also frequently store data in these registers. The DOS extension's interrupt handler could pass this information to the original DOS interrupt handler unchanged, following the transition to Real mode, but a system crash would result. A crash will most likely occur when a call is made to a DOS function, which expects a buffer address as a parameter. This also applies to many DOS functions.

Before the DOS function call, the program loads the buffer address into the register provided. However, when the DOS function is called, the function finds a selector instead of the segment address it expected to find. Remember the selector and segment address don't correspond. The DOS function might access segment 104H, although what was actually intended was selector 104H (and any segment above the 1 megabyte limit).

The DOS extension converts the indicated Protected mode buffer references into segment references before calling the DOS function. However, a look at the associated global or local descriptor table reveals additional problems. The table provides a 24-bit or 32-bit base address, but no 16-bit segment address. The Protected mode address is rarely converted into a normal segment address, because the program and its buffers are beyond the 1 megabyte barrier, and beyond the reach of the Real mode functions of DOS.

Before the function call, the DOS extension must copy the transmitted buffer contents into its own temporary buffer, allocated below the 1 megabyte limit. This process must be repeated after the function call, in reverse order. If DOS changed the content of this buffer, these changes must be passed to the function caller. This means the contents of the temporary buffer must be copied back to the original Protected mode buffer.

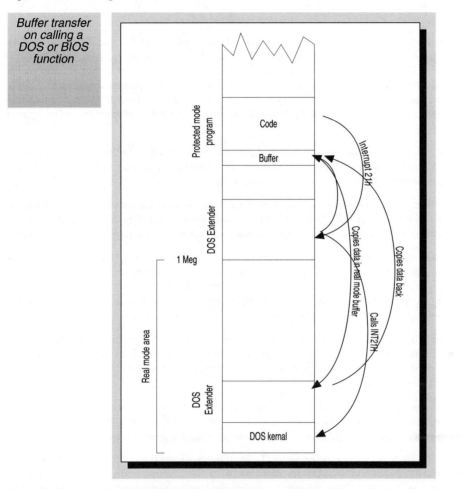

Buffer transfer on calling a DOS or BIOS function

Transferring the contents of buffers is time-consuming, especially when accessing files that contain large data blocks. However, this is actually where the recopying process barely matters because copying a buffer using a REPMOSW instruction takes less time than accessing an external storage medium.

As described, the DOS extension masks the various DOS functions and BIOS interrupts that can be called by an application. TSRs and other system extensions that alter functions have done this for years in DOS. Copying data between Real mode and Protected mode buffers involves a lot of work and also takes time, but this isn't the biggest problem confronting the developers of DOS extensions.

Not all DOS functions expect a buffer address. The transition takes place in different buffers and the buffer length isn't consistently coded. The DOS extension must have an intimate knowledge of DOS functions, treating each function separately.

The biggest problem occurs when an application uses undocumented DOS functions. The DOS extension may not recognize the registers, and may not be able to change to Real mode buffers. So, you should avoid calling undocumented DOS functions.

Similar problems arise with other, more frequently used software interfaces, such as the Microsoft Mouse Interface (interrupt 33H) and the NetBIOS functions (interrupt 5CH). If the DOS extension doesn't support these functions, the programmer must convert the selectors into segment addresses and the copying buffers. However, it's possible to use a few functions that are specifically provided by the DOS extension for this job.

Memory management

The DOS extension must act as a replacement for these functions, rather than simply an extension of the functions. This applies to memory management functions that usually control memory ranges below the 640K barrier. Almost all programs, even those produced by high level language compilers, use these functions to allocate memory for their own use. DOS never gives them more memory than is available up to the 640K barrier. If it did, most programs would use the memory immediately because it lies below the 1 megabyte limit and is addressable from Real mode. A program created with DOS extensions should be able to use all RAM. The program needs a way to identify the various memory ranges using selectors instead of segment addresses.

This is reason enough for a DOS extension to take over memory management instead of calling DOS memory management functions. These functions can then tell the program how much memory is still available, up to a complete megabyte. The number of free 16-byte paragraphs in BX limit that amount to one megabyte.

The next step is for the program to request the necessary memory, probably as far as the upper limit determined by the previous function call. The DOS extension may allocate one megabyte, then this memory is accessed by the appropriate selector. Because most programs make multiple memory requests for different purposes, this may make all physical memory available.

However, a problem occurs when you make memory ranges greater than 64K available. If the program code was written for an 80286 or one of its successors, it will work exclusively with 16-bit registers and, consequently, only 64K segments. When running through larger memory ranges, the program will occasionally be forced to increase the segment address to get past the first 64K of such a memory range. However, Protected mode prohibits segment address arithmetic, because new selectors, which point to entirely different memory ranges, are then created.

Making memory segments larger than 64K available in the 80286 creates problems for the DOS extension because a segment cannot accept more than 64K. Creating a larger memory block forces the DOS extension to access several segments and enter multiple segment descriptors in the global or local descriptor table. In turn, these descriptors require more selectors, which the DOS function doesn't return to its caller.

So that memory segments containing more than 64K can be allocated and accessed, in the case of the 80286, the interaction between a program and the DOS extension is read. This goes beyond the normal calling of a DOS function. We'll see how this actually works later in this section.

The absolute reference to specific segments also causes problems. Think of the interrupt vector table (segment 0000H), the BIOS variable range (segment 0040H), and the video RAM (segments A000H, B000H and B800H) that are addressed directly by many programs. The DOS extension can specify its own segment descriptors, with numbers identical to the corresponding segment addresses, although the video segments will cause some additional problems.

You must extend the global or local descriptor table, as needed, to B800 + 1 entries. This allows the video segment to be modeled by the descriptor with the number B800H. The descriptor table will exceed 360K, but most of the entries remain unused because no DOS extension needs B800H different segments for program execution.

DOS extensions form the cited segments using segment descriptors, which are appended to the original end of the descriptor table in question, and include an index with no relationship to the modeled memory segment. The DOS extension makes this selector available to its program functions. The memory segments can then be accessed easily.

DOS Extensions for the 80286

It's generally true that DOS extensions for 80386 and i486 result in more efficient programs than DOS extensions for the 80286. However, the 80286 extension simplifies porting programs.

In fact, porting with one of the best known of the 286 DOS extensions, DOS/16M from Rational Systems, is even restricted to recompilation under the Large memory model and subsequent attachment of the DOS extension. DOS/16M allows you to easily change a program for execution on a DOS machine that may have caused "insufficient memory" messages. After adding DOS/16M, the program can access more memory than before. This works as long as the developer follows the rules, especially in segment address interaction.

Creating a Protected mode program with DOS/16M

Program creation isn't very different for the compiler. The program is compiled in the Large memory mode to execute all data and code pointers as FAR pointers. So, data and code can exceed the 64K limit.

The OBJ file is initially still an ordinary Real mode program. The linking process combines the program, C libraries, and DOS extension object modules. These give the program a new starting routine and replace the various C compiler library routines with the extension's own routines. Memory is also allocated for the later attachment of the descriptor tables. The new starting routine ensures that program execution immediately terminates if the program is run on an 8086 system, or if insufficient extended memory exists. The resulting EXE file cannot run in Real Mode or protected mode. It must be sent through a conversion program named MAKEPM, which converts the EXE file into an EXP file. MAKEPM configures the segment addresses to the physical location of the segments in memory.

Remember that a Protected mode program requires selectors instead of segment addresses. MAKEPM replaces the various segment addresses with selector numbers. The sequence of these selector numbers indicates which segment descriptors will be entered in the descriptor table when the program starts. After MAKEPM processing, the file won't start from DOS. It must be run through a special loader. This loader loads the segments from the EXE file, places them in memory and stores their locations in the global descriptor table.

Two programs are needed: the loader from the DOS extension and the EXP program. Most DOS extensions include utilities that incorporate the loader into the EXP file. The DOS/16M utility is named SLICE, and creates an ordinary EXE file that can be started from DOS.

Altered library functions

Creating a Protected mode program is an interesting task because a Real mode compiler, such as Microsoft C or Turbo C, acts as the point of departure. There is only a slight difference between Real mode and Protected mode assembly language, if you overlook the selectors. Selectors are the same size as segment addresses, are stored in the same way, are processed by the same instructions, follow the same limits, and can be generated by a "postprocessor" like MAKEPM without accessing the actual program code.

However, the compiler library functions are changed dramatically when they're linked to the program code. Although a few functions remain intact, most are changed to avoid conflicts with the Protected mode rules. Among these are functions that change the program code, which is usually done under DOS for interrupt functions such as int() and int86x(). Other examples are the functions that handle segment arithmetic.

The malloc() function also changes. This is important to remember when porting C programs. Malloc() controls memory allocation in the C language, which is performed dynamically using the heap. Unlike the old malloc() function, the version included in DOS extensions can relinquish all extended memory to a program. In doing so, mallo() returns the selector and offset address of the allocated memory range.

Since the malloc() function controls memory allocation, the DOS functions aren't used here.

Detecting pointer errors

Any program that extensively uses pointers will most likely encounter pointer errors. This is especially true for C programs; most crashes and errors in C code occur because of pointers that miss the intended memory object. If we assume that a single object was allocated using malloc(), such pointer errors can be easily detected from within Protected mode. The malloc() function specifies a new segment and a respective segment descriptor. This segment descriptor contains the size of the object as requested from the caller. If a pointer shoots past this segment, or accepts an invalid segment number, an exception occurs.

However, it's almost impossible to implement this procedure because the global descriptor table can accept only 8191 descriptors, many of which are also needed for other memory segments. Frequently using malloc() quickly fills the global descriptor table. It soon becomes impossible to allocate the remaining memory to the program. Although you could create a supplemental local descriptor table containing another 8192 segments, most DOS extensions rely exclusively on the global descriptor table.

Malloc() is forced to pack several memory ranges into a segment that increases with each call. Once the segment is full, or a requested memory block no longer fits, the next memory segment is established by appending a new descriptor to the global descriptor table. Different memory objects thereby share the same selector, even if their offset addresses are different. Problems occur only if a program wants to allocate more than 64K at the same time. The malloc() function in Real mode already allows this.

Despite the 64K limitation, it is fascinating how easily the data memory of an application can be expanded by changing the malloc() function. In the Real mode version, most C programs call malloc() until this function can allocate no more memory. Since Protected mode permits more memory, the process of allocating memory takes longer. This is the basis for the portability of normal C programs with an 80286 DOS extension.

It's still impossible to manage memory blocks larger than 64K, even though the DOS extensions offer special functions to handle this. For managing larger memory blocks, these functions simply create more sectors, one for each 64K segment. Obviously, it's impossible to run through such allocated memory ranges with normal pointer arithmetic. Instead, you must use special functions, which automatically switch to the previous or subsequent selector when a pointer approaches or overruns an offset part.

Additional options with the 80386

We've mentioned that programs created for the 80386 with a DOS extension execute more rapidly than those converted into a Protected mode program using an 80286 DOS extension. Now we'll learn why this happens.

DOS Extensions for the 80386

DOS extensions for the 80386 let you develop faster and more efficient Protected mode applications than you could with a DOS extension designed for the 80286. There are several reasons for this, all of which involve the number 32. The 80386 is a 32-bit processor; this fact is important to high level language compilers:

➢ Segments can contain up to 4 gigabytes. This makes it possible to eliminate juggling multiple code and data segments.

➢ 32-bit integers can be accommodated in a single register and processed by a single instruction.

➢ String instructions for copying, traversing, and processing memory ranges can operate on a dword basis, resulting in higher execution speed.

The following are other reasons why the 80386's abilities are better than the 80286's abilities:

➢ The paging mechanism lets the DOS extension provide the Protected mode program with virtual memory management that's transparent to the program. There are no memory restrictions.

➢ The addressing possibilities are expanded. Each register can now be used as an index register and multiplied automatically by a factor of 2, 4, or 8. This accelerates array access and gives the compiler the option of retaining more local variables permanently in registers.

➢ The instruction set is expanded by the addition of efficient instructions for processing bit arrays. The compiler can use these instructions for processing bit fields and arrays for a dramatic increase in speed.

➢ Certain long distance jumps are also possible. Previously these could be made only by combining several instructions, which made the resulting program code larger and slower.

These options cannot be used with normal DOS compilers, which seldom support the 80286's expanded instruction set. Also, since pointer offsets are 32-bit instead of 16-bit, portability problems occur when using pointers.

The flat model

DOS compilers don't support the memory model used in most authentic 80386 compilers. This flat model is responsible for even greater increases in the execution speed of Protected mode programs. This model represents programs that consist of only two parts: a code segment housing all the program code and a data segment containing all constants and variables. The TINY model in DOS is similar, although the size of both segments is restricted to 4K. The 80386 flat model's segments combined can be up to 4 gigabytes in length, which is more memory than most of us may ever need.

Since the flat model uses NEAR pointers, faster execution is guaranteed. An offset address is needed, but a segment selector isn't necessary. The data offset address is found in the DS register, and the program code is in the CS register. The offset address occupies 32 bits. The flat model eliminates constant loading and reloading of the segment registers, as well as pointer arithmetic. So you can increment and decrement pointers like normal numerical words (dwords) without having to worry about changes in the selector.

Version 2.0 of OS/2 uses the flat model. Speed was one reason for this choice. The other involved portability. DOS extensions for the 80386 are frequently used for porting large programs from UNIX (programs used for mathematical or statistical applications). In UNIX, however, memory segmentation is unknown and porting through a UNIX-compatible memory model is clearly simplified.

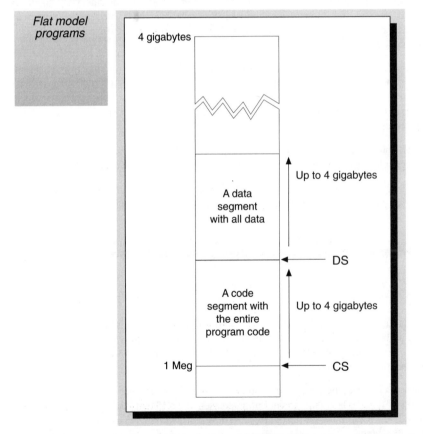

Flat model programs

The compiler itself was often carried over from the UNIX side by using a DOS extension. UNIX compilers frequently have features that overshadow their DOS counterparts. However, uses these features requires knowledge of the program, a lot of programming effort (resulting in large amounts of source code), and much compiler memory. The best known 386 compilers are the C386 compiler from MetaWare and the Watcom C/386 compiler by Watcom, Inc.

The best known DOS extension for the 80386 is the 386 DOS extension from Phar Lap. It works with both C386 and Watcom C/386. Its operation is barely different than the techniques described in conjunction with the DOS extensions for the 80286. DOS and BIOS calls in 80386 DOS extensions are frequently executed in V86 mode instead of in Real mode.

Calling DOS functions

Something has changed in DOS function emulation. The buffers, whose addresses must be given to many DOS functions, lie beyond the first 64K in the data segment of a 386 Protected mode program. So, these buffers cannot be reached by a 16-bit address, as DOS functions expect. Therefore, emulated DOS functions use 32-bit offset addresses and the expanded part of the register in question for the upper 16 bits.

Let's look at an example. DOS function 09H displays a string on the standard output device. To do this, it expects to find the address of the string to be entered in the DS:DX register pair. However, the emulated DOS function uses DS:EDX to process an offset address beyond the 64K limit. The DOS extension accepts the contents of the indicated buffer, but copies it into a temporary buffer below the 640K barrier. There the offset address is less than 64K, and the original DOS function is called, as usual, with the buffer address in DS:DX. The register expansion described here is used in both buffer address transfer and the handling of variable length data (e.g., in file functions).

The number of bytes to be processed are taken from the ECX rather than the CX register. Because the original DOS functions can only process 64K at one time, the DOS extension automatically divides its call into several 64K blocks. This repeats as needed, until the number of characters indicated was read or written. This is only one example of various functions that formerly processed 16-bit data, but can now accept 32-bit values.

Let's examine the Phar Lap DOS extension mentioned above. This extension can be used with another product from Phar Lap, 386|VMM. This virtual memory management system makes almost unlimited (virtual) memory available to a Protected mode program. All memory barriers are gone, even though loading and reloading memory takes some time and thus affects performance. We recommend that you use this extension for programs that definitely require more memory than is available in most of the computers of the targeted user group.

IBM Interleaf Publisher has also earned notoriety. This highly developed publishing system comes from UNIX. Before Phar Lap, it required a minimum of six megabytes of RAM; after Phar Lap it requires only two megabytes of RAM.

Utilizing a virtual memory management system should be an integral part of program development. For example, anyone allocating an eight megabyte array, which is constantly being accessed from one end to the other, should realize that this array is going to slow program execution.

DOS programmers must gradually learn how to work with 386 compilers because INT variables are now 32 bits wide instead of 16 bits. If you still want to work with 16-bit integers, you must use the SHORT type. Many functions (such as malloc()) were expanded.

DPMI and VCPI

The old saying, "Too many cooks spoil the soup," also applies to Protected mode. Resource conflicts in Protected mode are similar to the cooperation or dissension between cooks. Protected mode utilities fight between two resources: extended memory and the processor's Protected mode. Each utility thinks it has all of extended memory available, and each utility believes that it can select the processor's operating mode.

A central authority doesn't exist to assume control of these operations. So, we find ourselves back in the world of DOS, where concepts like extended memory and Protected mode are unknown. For this reason, the different cooks cannot prevent one another from acting. Nor can EMS emulators prevent the startup of programs developed with a DOS extension, or switch the processor into virtual 86 mode for multitasking.

The solution to this problem is important to system programmers, but not to the average user. From the user's viewpoint, he/she bought the 386 version of a program, and now must determine whether the program will work with the onboard memory management utility. The memory management utility is necessary because it keeps the RAM from filling with device drivers. However, the program refuses to work in multitasking operations.

Some progress has been made since the early days of Protected mode utilities. The participating software manufacturers defined software interfaces to ensure the peaceful coexistence of the various Protected mode utilities in the system. Two standards resulted: the somewhat older Virtual Control Programming Interface (VCPI), which is used in some DOS extensions and memory management programs, and the more recent DOS Protected Mode Interface (DPMI) used by Microsoft in Windows 3.

If we compare the two, DPMI easily wins. Although it's still too early to have found its niche in DOS extensions and other Protected mode utilities, DPMI seems more advanced than VCPI.

Discussing these interfaces in detail would exceed the scope of this book. So, in the following subsections we'll provide some general information about each interface and discuss the mechanisms used to keep DOS alive artificially.

VCPI

The VCPI interface was introduced in 1989 by a group of software firms under the leadership of Phar Lap (manufacturer of DOS extensions) and Quarterdeck (manufacturer of DESQView and QEMM). VCPI addresses the problems arising from the coexistence of DOS extensions, multitaskers, and memory management programs when these are run on an 80386 or i486 machine. The 80286 plays no role in this specification.

The problem begins with installing a memory management program supplying the PC with virtual EMS memory. To use the paging properties of the processor, the DOS engine is switched into V86 mode and restricted to privilege level 3. If an application developed with a DOS extension is started on this plane from a multitasker, it won't be able to switch the processor into Protected mode or to install any sort of descriptor table. The processor's protective mechanisms perform this task.

These programs have the option with VCPI of switching into Protected mode and offer peaceful coexistence in extended memory. Most known memory management programs (QUEMM, 386-To-The-Max, etc.) support VCPI like the Phar Lap DOS extensions and the Quarterdeck DESQView multitasking environment. Newer versions of DOS, starting with DOS 5.0, also offer VCPI support which gives the EMM386.SYS device driver the job of providing access to the upper memory blocks.

Programmers developing an application with a DOS extension, or designing software for use under DESQView, rarely encounter the VCPI interface. The DOS extension or the DESQView API handles this. This interface is only important to programs that want to use Protected mode but don't have access to these utilities.

Client and server

If you work with networks, the terms client and server may already be familiar to you. These terms have somewhat different meanings under VCPI.

Server designates the application made available by the VCPI functions for use by the various clients. Under VCPI, the server is always a memory management program (e.g., EMM386.EXE), because these programs are installed by the CONFIG.SYS file on booting the system, and are present even before the first call to a DOS extension or multitasking environment.

The installed VCPI uses DOS extensions and multitaskers as clients located through the memory management system. A DOS extension or multitasker could work just as well as a server, though memory management programs are only active from the time the computer is started until it is reset. The other Protected mode utilities don't immediately assume this. Also, whatever utility gets there first has first priority, which favors the memory management programs.

VCPI services

The VCPI server provides a total of 13 different services to its clients, covering the ranges in which conflicts between the various Protected mode utilities can occur:

> ➤ Three functions dedicated to VCPI initialization.

> ➤ Four functions for rudimentary extended memory management.

> ➤ Three functions for access to CR0 (the first control register) and the processor's debug registers.

> ➢ Two functions for driving the interrupt controller.

> ➢ One function for toggling between V86 mode and Protected mode.

These functions were implemented as an extension of the EMS memory manager. Each memory management program must also make the EMS function interface available for EMS support. The point of departure is Version 4.0 of the LIM standard. The various functions can be called from EMS interrupt 67H, all functions carrying the function number DEH.

The VCPI is specified by a function code in the AL register ranging from 00H to 0CH. The client receives the result of the function call in the AH register, which is common in most EMS functions. A value of 0 indicates OK, and all other values indicate an error.

You can call interrupt 67H only from within Real mode or V86 mode. In Protected mode, the processor no longer uses the normal interrupt vector table, in which the pointer to the EMS handler is marked. Communication between the client and the server must be introduced in V86 mode by various function calls, which also give the client access to the server in Protected mode.

Initializing a client-server link

VCPI functions can only be used if a VCPI server is available. A potential client must first check for the presence of a VCPI server. This means the client must determine whether an EMS driver is available at all (see Chapter 12).

Next, an EMS page must be called using the normal EMS functions. This is done because many EMS emulators leave the computer in Real mode when no EMS memory is requested. It's only possible to recognize many EMS emulators as VCPI servers after switching to V86 mode. The EMS page must remain allocated until the end of the program to prevent the EMS emulator from returning to Real mode and switching off its VCPI services.

Function 00H checks for EMS emulator support of the VCPI interface. Placing DE00H in the AX register returns 00H in the AH register if proper support is available, and 84H in the AH register if only the normal EMS interface is supported. The BX register receives the VCPI version, with the version number in BH and the subversion number in BL.

Function 01H receives the VCPI interface. This is a relatively complex function, and can be understood only against the background of memory management in Protected mode.

Using the page tables

The VCPI server and the client running in Protected mode don't have descriptor tables. They have complete control over the GDTR, LDTR, IDTR, and TR registers. This doesn't cause conflicts because the descriptor tables contain linear addresses instead of physical addresses. They first come into play through the page tables by using the EMS emulator. EMS emulator operation is based on the use of the paging mechanism.

The VCPI client must use the paging mechanism, and may not model linear addresses directly on physical addresses by switching it off.

There's a good reason for this. Although the VCPI server and client may use the same (linear) addresses in their linear address segment, this is impossible in the physical address space. Doing so would mean using common physical memory ranges, and mutually overwriting each other in memory. Dividing the physical address space means either using a single page table structure for server and client (and leaving the CR3 register constantly unchanged) or partially working with identical page tables.

This last option is handled by VCPI. The VCPI client must initiate its work with the interface by calling VCPI function 01H, which will fill its page table. This call must be made in Real mode, before switching into Protected mode. On calling the ES:DI register pair, the VCPI client must pass the physical address of a 4K range in memory, which it will use later as its first page table to the server, for modeling the first 4K of linear memory in physical memory.

The page directory, whose first entry to this page table must be denied, must be configured by the client before switching into Protected mode. The future page table is initialized by the server so the first 256 entries, which model the first megabyte of the linear address space on the physical address space, produce a 1:1 ratio between linear and physical address space. This means the client accesses the first megabyte of the physical address space using the first megabyte of its linear address space, the ROM-BIOS (which can access the video RAM), and conventional DOS memory.

This is how the VCPI server operates. It enables the use of this range for the exchange of data between client and server. However, the VCPI server can image further linear memory on physical memory with the aid of the indicated page table. VCPI function 01H returns the offset of the first entry in the page table in the DI register. From this address, the client can insert its own page table entries.

The length of the previously defined page table entries can be determined from the original offset address extracted from the value in the DI register. Because each entry takes up four bytes, the result of dividing the length by 4 is the number of pages already modeled, and the index of the next free page. Multiplying this index by 4K results in the first free address in the linear address space. This is important when allocating memory (more on this later).

Function 01H expects a pointer in the DS:SI register pair. Starting with this memory location, the server allocates three segment descriptors with a total size of 24 bytes, which the client must later add to its global descriptor table. It can copy the three descriptors for this purpose at any positions within its GDT, or reposition the GDT by the size of the memory range entered in DS:SI. It must also mark its position within the GDT and its index. This information will be used later as a selector to this first entry.

That describes the code segment by which the client is able to access the EMS functions of the server in Protected mode. However, here we're dealing with only one code segment instead of a CALL gate, so an offset address for the server call is needed. This is returned to the caller of function 01H, in the BX register.

Calling the server must be done using a FAR instruction referring to the selector of the server code segment. This indicates the value returned from the BX register as the offset address.

VCPI memory management

A VCPI client can usually assume the VCPI server has taken control of all available memory for itself and is to remain free. This memory is probably reserved for a RAM disk, a cache program, or something similar.

Calling BIOS interrupt 15H or the XMS interface is ordinarily useless to extended memory. Memory can only be requested by the VCPI client in Protected mode using the VCPI server, if you overlook the small fragment which the program is able to gain control of by using DOS functions, while still in Real (V86) mode.

VCPI memory management is based on the 4K pages the 80386 and its successors control by paging. Memory can be allocated and released in multiples of 4K. All four VCPI functions can be called in both V86 mode and Protected mode. This doesn't apply to all VCPI functions.

Function 02H determines the physical address of the highest page yielded by the VCPI server. Pass the value DE02H to the AX register. A value of 0H returned in the AH register indicates the call was successful. The required information will then be found in the EDX register.

Use this information carefully. Many VCPI servers produce the address of that last possible page instead of the address of the last physically available page. The result can be that function 02H will always return the value FFF000H (last page before the 16 megabyte limit), and not 3FF000H, if the computer has four megabytes of RAM.

You should avoid using function 02H. Instead, call function 03H. This function returns the number of pages available in the EDX register. This page number total can then be requested using function 04H, but only under certain circumstances.

With each call, function 04H returns the physical address of the required page if the value in the AH register is 00H. Any other value points to an error in page allocation and proceeds with an undefined value in the EDX register.

The VCPI client must do two things to access this memory:

➤ It must establish a segment descriptor in its global or local memory descriptor table to address the allocated memory using a segment. The segment can contain more than 4K if several pages must be combined.

➤ It must make an entry in the memory table by which the 4K from the linear address space can be modeled on their physical address. Naturally, the linear address recorded in the segment descriptor will be important. It determines the position of the associated entry in the page table. Because a page table was already established for the first four megabytes (it must be returned by function 01H), a linear address within the first four megabytes should be chosen. Don't forget the VCPI server, when calling function 01H, has already made some entries in the page table to image at least the first megabyte of the linear address space. The first free linear address and the index in the page table can be calculated, as we previously explained.

Function 05H frees pages if the VCPI client no longer needs them, but the client may no longer access them, even though this would seem to be possible through its page table. Besides the function number, the function expects the physical page address in the EDX register.

VCPI and EMS memory

Memory can also be requested by the VCPI client from the normal EMS functions by using a multiple of 16K. Access to these EMS pages occurs by focusing them in a page frame below the one megabyte barrier. VCPI function 06H returns the physical address of a 4K page below the one megabyte barrier. You can also discover memory ranges not normally occupied by RAM, which can be used by the memory management program through the page table. DOS Version 5.0 also uses this backfilling process for accessing the upper memory blocks.

The number of the requested page is placed in the CX register after the call to function 06H. This is returned by dividing the linear address by 4096, which is the same as rotating this address 12 bits to the right. Calling the function returns the physical address of the memory page at this address in the EDX register.

If the content of the EDX register is identical to the returned CX value multiplied by 4096, no alien memory is being used at the address in question. The linear address of this 4K page is different from its physical address. You cannot request the entire one megabyte address space in this manner, especially for those ranges occupied by the ROM-BIOS or BIOS extensions. In these cases, the function 06H returns error code 8BH in the AH register. Otherwise, a value of 00H in the AH register indicates no error.

Accessing debug and status registers

It's possible, at least in V86 mode, to access the various debug registers because the privilege level 3 is active. VCPI functions 08H and 09H read from and write to the various debug registers from V86 mode. These registers aren't very useful to a normal program, but are extremely useful to Borland's Turbo Debugger, which also uses the VCPI interface.

These two functions process all eight debug registers. The register contents are passed to a buffer to which the ES:DI register points when calling the function. Because each debug register occupies 32 bits, this buffer must have room for 32 bits. DR0 is stored in the first dword of the buffer, DR1 in the second, etc. Function 08H copies the debug register contents into the buffer, while function 09H loads them from the buffer.

Function 07H, which returns the contents of the CR0 status register in the EBX register, appears as an anachronism. Although the current operating mode and the paging mechanism status can be determined through this register, it's also returned by the nonprivileged SMSW instruction which loads the content of this register into another processor register or a memory location.

Intercepting and setting interrupt vectors

Earlier in this chapter, we recommended reprogramming the first interrupt controller for V86 mode exceptions. If you don't reprogram, hardware interrupts IRQ0 through IRQ7 encounter many exceptions.

VCPI function 0AH returns the base interrupt of the first interrupt controller in the BX register, and the base interrupt of the second interrupt controller in the CX register. If the two controllers no longer contain their default values (08H and 70H), the VCPI server has already rerouted these interrupts. Further rerouting is then strictly forbidden.

If the interrupt controller hasn't already been changed, it is possible to reprogram the first and second interrupt controllers. Of course, access to the two controllers must be done after all interrupts have been switched off.

VCPI function 0BH notifies the VCPI server about the reprogramming. This function must be called by the client before the interrupt flag is reset. Like function 0AH, the base address of the first interrupt controller must be entered in the BX register and the second in the CX register.

Changing the operating mode

One of the most important services of the VCPI server is the controlled transition from V86 mode into Protected mode and back to V86 mode. VCPI function 0CH performs this task.

This function can be called from V86 mode using the normal EMS interrupt. In Protected mode, function 0CH is accessible only through the code segment and the offset address returned by the VCPI server on calling VCPI function 01H. When calling this function from V86 mode, the linear address of a data structure, whose structure is shown in the following table, is expected in the ESI register. The following values are loaded into the various system registers:

Data structure for switching from V86 mode to Protected mode after calling VCPI function 0CH		
Function	Meaning	Type
00H	CR3 (Starting address of page directory)	dword
04H	Linear address of variables under dword one megabyte limit, containing the FAR pointer for the GDTR register	fword
08H	Linear address of variables under dword one megabyte limit, containing the FAR pointer for the IDTR register	
0CH	Selector for the LDTR register	word
0EH	Selector for the TR register	word
10H	Point of entry into the program code after switching into Protected mode with selector and 32 bit-offset address	fword

It's very important that this data structure be established beneath the one megabyte barrier. Only in this range are the address spaces of the VCPI server and its clients identical, as noted in connection with VCPI function 01H. The CR3 function is loaded with the value provided in the first step after calling this function. The page tables of the VCPI server are no longer valid; the page tables of the client are used instead. The server can now read data only from the coincident ranges, from the range below one megabyte.

Next, the GDTR register is loaded. The global descriptor table is referenced and may be anywhere in the address space of the VCPI client. This table must have been previously initialized in V86 mode and it's assumed the VCPI function was also previously called.

Now the LDT, IDTR, and TR registers are loaded and finally the switch to Protected mode is made. All interrupts are still blocked at this point and should remain so. Of the six segment registers, only the CS register is loaded with a valid selector at this time. It's time to set up the program's own stack and load the DS, ES, FS, and GS registers with valid selectors. Only then may the interrupt lines again be opened. If an interrupt does happen to occur before the segment register is loaded, invalid selectors will be loaded. The processor will trigger an exception. Returning to V86 mode is effected by function 0CH, but this time with entirely different register loading.

However, as the starting point, it's again necessary to obtain the code segment selector and the offset address returned by function 01H.

Before calling function 0CH, the VCPI client must establish a data structure in physical RAM below the one megabyte limit. The values which the VCPI server is to enter after switching into V86 mode are stored there. Using the entries for CS:EIP, the memory address is established for program execution in V86 mode. SS:ESP describe the new location of the stack.

Remember the values for the various segment registers do not concern selectors, but base addresses (physical address divided by 16), as is normal in Real mode and V86 mode. Should the program in V86 mode not have been developed especially for the 80386 or its successors, any values can be specified for the FS and GS registers because they aren't important to program execution.

Although only one word is required for the various segment registers, two words are used in the data structure shown below. The respective segment address is entered in the first word, while the second word remains unused.

Data structure for switching from Protected mode to V86 mode after calling VCPI function 0CH					
Func	Meaning	Type	Func	Meaning	Type
00H	Reserved	dword	18H	SS after switching into V86 mode	dword
08H	EIP after switching into V86 mode	dword	1CH	ES after switching into V86 mode	dword
0CH	CS after switching into V86 mode	dword	20H	DS after switching into V86 mode	dword
10H	Reserved for EFLAGS register	dword	24H	FS after switching into V86 mode	dword
14H	ESP after switching into V86 mode	dword	28H	GS after switching into V86 mode	dword

For the VCPI server to access the above table after calling function 0CH, its linear address must be transferred to the SS:ESP register pair. It's also necessary for the client to load the DS register with a selector to a data segment descriptor which it has itself entered in its global or local descriptor table before calling the function. This descriptor must contain the base address 0 and have a size of one megabyte.

After switching into V86 mode, the content of the normal registers (EBX, ECX, etc.) is retained. Only the content of the EAX register has been changed and is undefined. The Protected mode registers GDTR, LDTR, etc. have again been loaded by the VCPI server with the addresses or the selectors of its descriptor tables; but that doesn't in any way affect a program in V86 mode.

DPMI

The DOS Protected Mode Interface (DPMI) wasn't originally created as a general standard for collaboration between multitaskers and other Protected mode utilities. Instead, it initially appeared during the development of Windows 3.0 as an in-house product used for enabling the execution of Windows applications in extended memory. For unknown reasons, Microsoft decided to publish and expand this interface. A DPMI committee met in early 1990. The members of this group include Microsoft, Borland, Intel, Eclipse, IBM, Lotus, Phar Lap, Quarterdeck, and Rational Systems. Since many of these companies are VCPI supporters, we can assume the DOS extenders, multitaskers, and memory management programs of these manufacturers will also support both DPMI (DOS Protected Mode Interface) and VCPI in the future.

Differences from VCPI

Microsoft's marketing strength and the popularity of Windows are the principal driving forces behind this committee. The DPMI specification is superior to VCPI, in both concept and execution. DMPI is simply "cleaner" and more generic than VCPI.

DPMI covers the entire spectrum of services required by DOS programs in Protected mode for peaceful coexistence with other Protected mode programs. These include:

➢ Managing descriptor tables of a protected mode program

➢ Management and allocation of extended memory

➢ Management of interrupts and exceptions

➢ Communication with Real mode programs and interrupt handlers

➢ Access to various processor registers

➢ DMA virtualization

These services show that DPMI clients must relinquish much of their Protected mode rights to the DPMI host. Unless the programs cooperate, this is impossible. The processor ensures that clients will use the services in this way. Unlike the VCPI server, the DPMI host runs on a higher privilege level than its client, giving it control of all clients and their activities. The lack of such protection was one of Microsoft's greatest complaints against the VCPI interface.

Clients and hosts

DPMI uses the term hosts instead of servers. The two words mean basically the same thing, and the change was probably intended to separate DMPI from the old client-server model. Despite this name change, DPMI has a host (program) which makes the DPMI services available to clients. However, DPMI has only one host, which is Microsoft Windows. Windows 3.X supports DPMI Specification Version 0.9 (the version the DPMI Committee released to the public). Version 1.0 was recently released, and has a few differences from Version 0.9 (more on this later).

16-bit or 32-bit DPMI

Unlike VCPI, DPMI was conceived for the 80286, even though Windows 3.0 doesn't support the 80286. Remember that DPMI becomes active in Windows enhanced mode, which is only available on 80386 or higher systems. As 80286 machines become less important, it isn't likely that an 80286 DPMI host will be released.

Because of the 80286 support, DPMI hosts exist in 16-bit and 32-bit versions. 16-bit hosts are designed for execution on 80286 computers, and support 64K memory segments. A 32-bit DPMI host works with 32-bit memory segments (up to four gigabytes) and the resulting flat model. So, a host of this type runs only on a computer with 80386/i486 processors.

The target group

Like VCPI, DPMI is aimed primarily at the developers of DOS extenders and memory management programs. They should take advantage of the services of this interface to enable their Protected mode programs to run without difficulty even under a multitasking environment like Windows 3. The first DOS extenders that use them are already available on the market. Such a DOS extender, or the program generated by it, must also be able to function as DPMI host. If the program is started namely from the DOS prompt, without another DPMI host having been activated first, it must make these services available itself.

Execution on a virtual machine

The DPMI host always runs its clients on a virtual machine (VM), such as the DOS screen under Windows. A VM can run more than one DPMI client. For example, the memory management program can use the DPMI host services in a Windows DOS screen, and a program using a DOS extender can also be started from the DOS screen. As part of a virtual machine, the various programs in Real mode thereby divide up an address space, emulating a one megabyte DOS machine plus HMA. Multitasking between the various clients within a VM is possible between the various VMs. Then Windows can run several DOS programs in various DOS screens simultaneously. This becomes possible using preemptive multitasking, where the DPMI host interrupts program execution in a VM after a time to continue running a program on the next VM.

This occurs automatically when a time slice ends, although it's possible for clients to support this procedure by reporting they aren't busy, using the interrupt 2FH, function 1680H call. Once this happens, the DPMI host can pass execution on to the next VM, without the need to waste valuable processor time.

The biggest difference between Version 0.9 and Version 1.0 lies in management of the virtual machine. Under Version 0.9, all clients share a local descriptor table (LDT) and an interrupt descriptor table (IDT) within the VM. Clients can gain access to other memory segments (and perhaps other clients) by using the descriptors. The DPMI host cannot prevent this. However, this makes simultaneous execution of 16-bit and 32-bit clients impossible, because their respective segments cannot be merged into a single descriptor table.

DPMI Version 1.0 assigns each client its own LDT and IDT within a VM, which causes difficulties, especially in Windows. Many DOS Protected mode programs, which previously ran perfectly in Windows Protected mode from the DOS screen, are designed for the use of a common LDT with other programs, and require rewriting. Perhaps this why the Windows DPMI host continues to support only Version 0.9.

DPMI outputs and functions

The DPMI interface covers a series of output ranges. We'll provide a brief outline of these ranges, then list the most important data in more detail. We selected DPMI Version 0.9 as our standard.

Only 13 different functions process the local descriptor table of the client and the segment descriptors contained there. This is quite different from VCPI, where the processing of these descriptor tables remains in the hands of the client, thus leaving the system open to many types of problems. Remember, though, that some DPMI functions still leave a few openings with potential for mayhem.

Each task under DPMI can access its own local descriptor table, kept separate from global descriptor tables. Global descriptor tables are reserved exclusively for the DPMI host.

DPMI supports three different memory management function groups:

1. The first group allocates and accesses conventional memory below the one megabyte barrier. As we explained in the section on DOS extenders, Protected mode programs require this memory when calling DOS functions that expect to find data in buffers.

2. The second group handles extended memory. Memory blocks can be requested, freed, or altered.

3. The third group handles virtual memory. The 80286's lack of a paging mechanism makes this group unavailable on 80286 machines. This group includes functions for page maintenance, such as locking a page to prevent removal from memory.

A fourth group calls Real mode routines and interrupt handlers from Protected mode. By calling DOS or BIOS functions, the DPMI host saves its client a lot of work. However, you can also call a Protected mode routine from a Protected mode interrupt handler using callbacks.

The DPMI specification also includes functions supporting the debug register in the 80386 and its successors, for requesting and setting Real mode or Protected mode interrupt handlers, for blocking hardware interrupt releases, and for initializing a client and switching into Protected mode.

The following tables summarize the various services offered to the DPMI client by the DPMI host.

Interrupt 2FH call in Real mode	
1680H	Client unoccupied, pass on program execution
1686H	Query operating mode (also Protected mode)
1687H	Query DPMI availability status

Interrupt 31H call in Protected mode

LDT memory management

0000H	Allocate LDT segment descriptor	0007H	Establish segment base address
0001H	Release LDT segment descriptor	0008H	Establish segment length
0002H	Image Real mode segment on segment descriptor	0009H	Establish access rights/segment type
0003H	Query increment for selector	000AH	Create alias for a code segment
0004H	Block removal of segment	000BH	Query segment descriptor
0005H	Permit segment removal	000CH	Load segment descriptor
0006H	Query base address of segment	000DH	Request specific selector

DOS memory access

0100H	Request DOS memory	0102H	Change size of a memory block
0101H	Release DOS memory		

Interrupt and exception management

0200H	Return address of a real mode interrupt handler	0205H	Install protected mode interrupt handler
0201H	Set real mode interrupt handler	0900H	Block virtual interrupt flag
0202H	Query address of an exception handler	0901H	Release virtual interrupt flag
0203H	Install exception handler	0902H	Query virtual interrupt flag
0204H	Query address of a protected mode interrupt handler		

Calling real mode routines

0300H	Simulate Real mode interrupt	0303H	Create callback
0301H	Call Real mode routine	0304H	Return callback
0302H	Call Real mode routine		

Miscellaneous functions

0400H	Query version number		

Functions for accessing extended memory

0500H	Request memory use data	0503H	Change size of memory block
0501H	Allocate memory in extended memory	0800H	Convert physical address into linear address
0502H	Release memory block		

Interrupt 31H call in Protected mode (continued)			
Functions for managing interrupts and exceptions			
0600H	Protect memory range from removal		
Unlock memory region			
0602H	Unlock Real mode memory region	0702H	Privilege memory region during removal
0603H	Relock Real mode memory region	0703H	Mark memory range as overwriteable
0604H	Query page size		
Support for the debug registers of the 80386 and successors			
0B00H	Define breakpoint	0B02H	Get breakpoint status
0B01H	Delete breakpoint	0B03H	Reset breakpoint status

Client initialization and switching into Protected mode

DPMI calls begin with querying the DPMI host. The services cannot be accessed until this query occurs. The query must occur in Real mode (after the potential client starts at the DOS level).

So you must use function 1678H, which the DPMI host clicks into the DOS multiplexer interrupt 2FH during initialization. If it returns a 0 value in the AX register following its call, a DPMI host is installed. Status data on the DPMI host is then found in the other processor registers. For example, bit 0 of the BX register indicates whether the DPMI host is 16-bit or 32-bit. If bit 0 = 0, the DPMI host is 32-bit.

However, the CL register indicates the processor type and the DX register indicates the version number of the DPMI host. The information in the SI register is also very important. SI conveys the memory block size in paragraphs required by the DPMI host for management tasks. The client must allocate this block size before the switch to Protected mode can occur.

The switch itself occurs through a routine whose address is returned in the ES:DI register pair once the multiplexer function is called. A jump must be made to this address using a FARCALL assembly language instruction. The segment address of the memory block made available to the DPMI host is placed in the ES register. If the DPMI routine called from ES:DI returns with the carry flag set, the program remains in Real mode because the switch to Protected mode failed for a reason not described in detail. But if the carry flag is unset, the program moves into Protected mode and can then call all DPMI services from interrupt 31H. Remember that most DPMI functions trigger an error during execution by setting the carry flag, but return no special error code beyond that. This, too, is a point of departure for future DPMI expansions.

Even after switching into protected mode, the program is still obviously below the 640K barrier. However it runs in an entirely normal manner, because the existing segment addresses in CS, DE, and SS were replaced by selectors. They point to memory segments of 64K each, whose segment descriptors were automatically established by the DPMI host. The selectors in DS and SS are identical, if the two segments were already coinciding in Real mode.

Aside from that, ES points to a segment descriptor describing the PSP of the program and records 100H bytes as the segment length. GS and FS, if present, are also loaded with the value 0.

After the successful switch into Protected mode, a DOS extender, for example, will attempt to load the program it created into extended memory from the hard drive, to run it there. However, to do this, it must first allocate extended memory from the DPMI host and enter (or cause the entry of) the associated segment descriptors in its local descriptor table (more on this later).

Calling DOS interrupt 21H, function 4CH from within Protected mode ends execution of the Protected mode program. The DPMI host then switches back to Real mode automatically, removes the original Real mode program (the loader) from memory, and returns to the normal DOS prompt.

Managing the client's local descriptor table

Since it has 14 functions, the local descriptor table can be difficult to manage. You'll rarely use these functions because the memory management area of the DPMI simply divides extended memory into memory blocks, but doesn't specify segment descriptors for them. The client is responsible for this. Also, the client cannot access its descriptor table directly for reasons of privilege. Instead, the client must use the DMPI host functions.

Function 0000H lets the client request one or more segment descriptors in its local descriptor table. In this context, the word "request" means the host establishes a desired number of data segment descriptors in the local descriptor table, each descriptor being first supplied with the starting address 0 and a corresponding length. Only additional DPMI calls allow the client to specify the desired starting address, segment length, and type, in case the client requires code segment descriptors instead of data. As the result, function 0000H returns a selector to the created segment descriptor. If several segment descriptors were requested, their numbers can be determined by addition of the value returned by function 0003H. Because of the complicated structure of selectors, you shouldn't assume, however, that it's always necessary to increment the returned selector by the value 1 to determine the following selectors one by one.

Before ending the program, all the selectors requested in this manner must be returned. Function 0001H performs this task for one sector.

If you want to address a memory segment beneath the one megabyte barrier while in protected mode, you'll need a segment descriptor and an associated selector. Passing the Real mode segment address to function 0002H produces a segment descriptor for a 64K data segment. This segment returns to this descriptor. A segment descriptor taken over by the client using function 0000H or 0002H can be modified with the help of functions 0007H, 0008H, and 0009H. These let you specify the starting address, the segment length, access rights, etc. Regarding the segment length and starting address, the client must ensure that memory segments that aren't allocated yet or allocated memory segments that are covered by several, overlapping segment descriptors aren't accessed. The functions named simply aren't responsible for tests of this sort. This is the back door we mentioned earlier.

These data can be read using the LSL (Load Segment Limit) and LAR (Load Access Rights) instructions, or function 0006H can return the base address of a segment.

Function 000BH can read a segment descriptor. Function 000CH loads a complete segment descriptor into a buffer. The DPMI ensures the client isn't granted a priority higher than 3.

Function 000AH generates a corresponding data segment descriptor for a specific code segment. This descriptor contains the starting address and code segment length, returning a selector.

Extended memory allocation

Functions 0500H, 0501H, 0502H, and 0503H manage and allocate extended memory. Function 0500H returns status data. This data includes free memory available and swap file size on a virtual memory management system.

Function 0501H allocates extended memory. After the function call, the BX:CX register pair contains the extent of the requested memory range available. Because the DPMI system is divided internally into 4K blocks due to virtual memory management (nearly always implemented in the case of a 32-bit host), we recommend that you request blocks in multiples of 4K. If the call was successful, the BX:CX register pair receives the linear address of the allocated memory block. The SI:DI register pair receives a handle required for further block processing by the various DPMI functions.

Once the client takes possession of the memory block by calling function 501H, the block is still inaccessible. First, the client lacks the associated segment descriptor mentioned earlier. Function 0000H must be called to allocate the block, then fill the block with the transmitted starting address and the known length.

The client now has the option of subdividing the required memory range into several contiguous segments. This is useful because DPMI doesn't have a type of "garbage collection" working in the background to combine memory blocks automatically that have become free to form larger units. A DPMI client should allocate all the memory required using function 501H.

Function 0502H returns a memory block from extended memory. The handle returned by this function identifies the memory block for the DPMI host (very important).

Function 0503H changes a previously allocated memory block. The block's size (not its contents) is changed by this function, which passes the memory block's handle and its new size. If the call was successful, the new starting address is returned along with a new handle (if needed). If the memory block was in fact moved, the client is then responsible for bringing the start into agreement with the segment or segments created for gaining access to the memory block.

DOS memory allocation

Functions 0100H, 0101H, and 0102H allocate and manage DOS memory. These functions are similar to standard DOS functions 48H, 49H, and 4AH. Unlike the extended memory functions, these functions create a segment for access to the memory block allocated immediately, making it unnecessary for the client to perform the same task.

Function 0100H requests the DOS memory. It requires the size, in paragraphs, of the desired range. If the call was successful, the function returns the selector to the allocated block's segment descriptor selector. Function 0101H releases the DOS block requested by function 0100H.

Function 0102H lets you change the size of a memory block. Pass the selector in the DX register, and the new memory block size (in paragraphs) in the BX register.

DOS memory blocks are needed by DOS extenders, in particular, when DOS function calls issue from Protected mode, which results in the transfer of data into buffers. This is frequently the case when accessing files.

Virtual memory management

Functions 0600H, 0601H, 0602H, 0603H, and 0604H manage virtual memory. These functions are implemented only with 32-bit hosts (the 80286 doesn't have page tables or virtual memory management). These functions lock and unlock memory ranges. Function 0600H locks the specified memory range from removal. This prohibits the removal of interrupt handlers. Function 0601H unlocks locked memory ranges.

Functions 0602H and 0603H target RAM below the one megabyte barrier, which was allocated using function 0100H. Function 0602H unlocks pages for removal, and function 0603H locks pages. As the last function in this group, function 0604H returns the size of a page to the caller.

Interrupt handling and calling Real mode routines

Interrupt handling, particularly the reaction to hardware interrupts, represents one of the greatest difficulties in the Real mode programming of DOS extenders and other Protected mode utilities. How should a program react if an interrupt, normally available in Real mode, occurs in Protected mode? VCPI leaves this question to the programmer, but DPMI offers various solutions. Before we discuss these functions, however, let's briefly look at the concepts behind them.

First, no problems exist in DPMI between the various exceptions and the hardware interrupts IRQ0 through IRQ7. The host reprograms the first interrupt controller in each case. The lower privilege level of the client keeps the client from doing the same thing.

The DPMI host also ensures that all hardware interrupts land in Protected mode, even if they occurred during program execution in Real mode or V86 mode.

The DPMI standard handler initially receives control over program execution, passing control to the first client that has recorded a handler for this interrupt through an appropriate DPMI function.

If it returns to the caller through an IRET assembly language instruction, this is completed during interrupt handling. The interrupt handlers of the other clients are no longer used. So, the existing handler should be queried with an appropriate DPMI function before installing a hardware interrupt handler, and called within its own interrupt routine.

When all interrupt handlers operate according to this scheme, the result is a sort of chain, with every interrupt handler getting its due time. Each DMPI client can protect itself against the release of hardware interrupts with certain functions. The DPMI host maintains a virtual interrupt flag for each client. This flag, which is stored in the Flag or EFlag register, ensures that no hardware interrupts can reach one client, while allowing passage to another client.

The situation changes with software interrupts triggered in Real mode. Only three of these interrupts reach protected mode, if the client makes corresponding handlers available: the BIOS timer interrupt (1CH), the [Ctrl][C] interrupt (23H), and the critical error interrupt (24H).

But software interrupts can also be triggered in Protected mode when, for example, a DOS extender enters an INT instruction in assembly language. If no DPMI client specified an interrupt handler for the respective interrupt, such a software interrupt results in a switch to Real mode, execution of the interrupt, and a subsequent switch back to Protected mode.

There's a problem with this switching. These functions generally receive data from the processor registers. There's no problem in the general registers, but the contents of the segment registers are destroyed during the shift into Real mode because they contain selectors instead of segment addresses. Because of this, DOS extenders break into the various software interrupts and convert the selectors in the segment registers into segment addresses while still in Protected mode, before passing the interrupt on to Real mode.

DPMI interrupt handling

Six different functions manage Real mode interrupt handlers, Protected mode interrupt handlers, and exception handlers. These functions, number 0200H through 0205H, install handlers, query handlers, and release handlers.

Also, the DPMI host uses function 0300H to simulate a Real mode interrupt from within Protected mode. The Protected mode software interrupt handlers intercept the various software interrupts (BIOS, DOS, etc.), check the indicated function number, and, on the basis of this data, convert the pointers returned in processor registers into Real mode format after previously copying the data addressed into a DOS buffer below the one megabyte barrier.

Functions 0301H and 0302H call Real mode routines residing below the one megabyte limit. Function 0301H ends with the VAR RET assembly language instruction, while function 0302H ends with the IRET instruction.

You can also simulate a Protected mode routine from within Real mode. For example, the mouse driver can allow a routine call when the mouse moves or button status changes. The routine must be performed in Real mode, but in certain cases, the mouse event should be readable from the context of a Protected mode program.

The DPMI host uses function 0303H for creating a callback. This callbacks is a short routine created independently in RAM by the DPMI host. When the callback is called, the desired Protected mode routine executes, if the switch to Protected mode has occurred.

Functions 0900H, 0901H, and 0902H manage the virtual interrupt flags, protecting your program from unauthorized hardware interrupts.

Access to debug registers

To permit each DPMI client to access the debug registers of the 80386 and its successors, the DPMI host centralizes register access in four different functions. Each client can install its own breakpoints (sometimes called watchpoints) whose addresses are loaded by the DPMI host into the processor's debug registers, as soon as the client reaches execution.

Function 0B00H defines a breakpoint. The function requires the parameters needed to configure the debug register: the linear address of the breakpoint, its size (bytes, word, or dword), and its type (read, write, or execute memory location). It then returns a breakpoint handle, as long as too many break points weren't installed or an invalid parameter wasn't indicated on calling the function.

Function 0B01H deletes a previously defined breakpoint. The function requires the handle of the defined breakpoint (function 0B00H returned this handle).

Function 0B02H queries the status of a breakpoint. This indicates whether the breakpoint was triggered. Function 0B03H resets breakpoint status, which permits execution of the next breakpoint.

Then you learn whether the break point was already triggered. The corresponding flag can then be reset with function 0B03H so a new execution of the breakpoint can be detected.

Chapter 37

CD-ROM And Its Technology

Today's most popular storage medium is the CD-ROM. Already several major computer manufacturers deliver only CD-ROM equipped PCs. CD-ROM titles which are available today number in the thousands, whereas these numbered in the hundreds only two years ago.

Developers have been adapting many hard drive based software applications to run on the CD-ROM drives. Some applications take advantage of the easy distribution method offered by CD-ROMs while other applications take advantage of the huge amount of storage space and special properties the CD-ROM offers over conventional drives.

In this chapter we'll talk about the structure of a CD-ROM and the different CD formats. We'll take you from the smallest bit all the way to the directory structure. You'll learn how to use software to link CD-ROM drives to a DOS system and how to control the drives directly using the appropriate drivers.

CD Formats

To understand the technology of CD-ROMs there's a few basic questions that we can first answer. For example, how are the individual bit sequences stored on the CD and how are they combined into logical blocks? What about the file system which groups the blocks into files and records information about the stored files in directories? We'll answer these questions in this chapter.

When talking about CD formats our starting point is the Red Book. The Red Book was published by Sony and Philips, the inventors of the CD, in 1982. This book is a detailed technical specification that describes the format of the audio CD in all its parts.

Other CD formats are based on the audio CD format and are specified by other books. For obvious reasons, these are known as the "Rainbow Books". The Yellow Book is concerned with the CD-ROM format, the Green Book contains the format for CD-I and the Orange Book describes the format for recordable CDs and the Photo-CD. However, all these formats are based on the Red Book.

The physical format

We'll start with the physical format which is identical for all types of CDs. Regardless of whether a CD is to be used for audio or data, the platter is 4.75 inches in diameter and 1.2 millimeters thick. The hole in the center of the CD has a diameter of 15 millimeters. The CD has a reflective layer of aluminum which is coated by a protective layer of clear paint.

*Dimensions and
structure of a
CD*

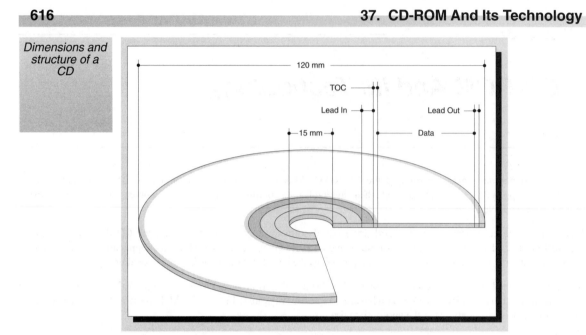

When the CD is manufactured, the information to be stored on the CD is pressed into the layer of aluminum in the form of pits (indentations) and lands (elevations) which represent the individual bits. The pits and lands are arranged along a single spiral which covers the entire CD, winding from the inside to the outside. Unlike records, CDs start at the inner edge instead of the outer edge.

Because the pits are only 0.6 micron wide (a micron is the equivalent of one millionth of a meter), the path this spiral are separated by a microscopically small distance of only 1.6 micron. The track density is almost 16,000 tracks per inch (TPI). Compare this to the 135 TPI on a 3.5-inch HD diskette.

*Pits and lands
located on a
CD-ROM*

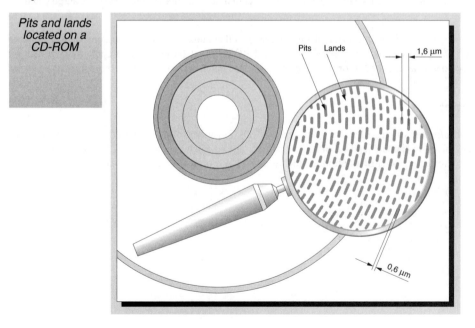

If this spiral were stretched out in a straight line it would be approximately 3.75 miles (6 kilometers) long. It also includes no fewer than 2 billion pits. Naturally, the laser beam that reads these pits and lands must be correspondingly small. The scanning beam is approximately one micron in diameter which makes it only a little larger than the wavelength of the light that forms its beam.

Organization of a CD

The recordable surface of a CD is divided into the following three sections:

➤ The lead-in

➤ The data area

➤ The lead-out

The lead-in occupies the first four millimeters of the CD's inner edge and contains a type of table of contents. The lead-in is followed by the data area, which can occupy up to 33 millimeters, depending on how much data is on the CD. Finally, the lead-out range marks the end of the data. It follows immediately after the data area and is approximately 1 millimeter wide.

CAV and CLV methods of storing data

The two methods of storing data on rotating mass storage systems are called CAV (Constant Angular Velocity) and CLV (Constant Linear Velocity). Both names refer to the rotation speed of the storage medium.

Hard drives and diskettes that are divided into individual tracks and sectors follow the CAV principle. This is based on constant angular velocity. Regardless of where the read/write head is located above the medium, the medium always rotates below the read/write head at a constant speed. If the read/write head is above a track at the inner edge of the medium, it travels a much shorter course than it would over an outer track. Today's hard drives take advantage of this factor by packing more sectors into the larger areas of the outer tracks.

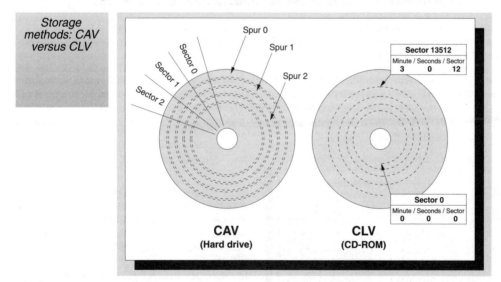

Storage methods: CAV versus CLV

Perhaps the most important difference between the CAV method and the CLV procedure is the rotation speed. The rotation speed of the medium doesn't change with CAV. This is true regardless of the read/write head location. The opposite is true with the CLV method used by CDs. The read/write head for CLV always travels a constant distance in a specific unit of time regardless of whether the head is at the inner or outer edge of the CD. However, the rotation speed must be changed based on the position of the head (rotation speed = angular velocity).

Therefore, the rotation speed of the drive increases as the head moves from the inner edge of the medium to its outer edge. This is one of the reasons why a CD-ROM drive has significantly slower access times than a hard drive. It must constantly change its rotation speed. The time to speed up and to slow down becomes significant. Also, it's much more difficult to find a sector along a 3.75 mile long spiral than it is to find the same sector on a medium which is neatly organized into tracks and sectors.

Storage of bits and bytes

Since all the data on a disc is represented in a single continuous spiral, you might think of it as a data channel. On a CD, the bits are referred to as 'channel bits'. The transition from a land to a pit or the transition from a pit to a land is used to represent binary 1. Land and pits are used to represent binary 0. The length of a land or the length of a pit determines how many binary 0's are represented. This is the same procedure used to record data on magnetic storage devices like hard drives. The only difference is that magnetic flux change replaces the pits and lands.

A sequence of zeros and ones using pits and lands

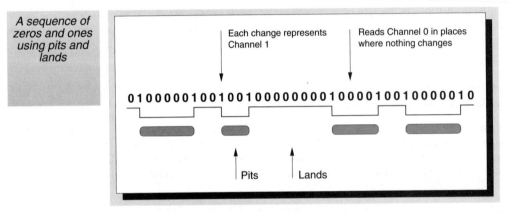

Due to technical limitations, the minimum length of either a land or a pit is 3 bits; the maximum length is 11 bits. From this you can see there's a problem trying to represent two consecutive 1 bits when the technical limitations require no less than two and no more than 10 binary 0's between transitions.

Using this scheme, it isn't possible to represent all combinations of 0 and 1. Instead a scheme called EFM is used. EFM stands for Eight-to-Fourteen-Modulation. Using EFM, a byte that is to be stored is converted from its normal eight bits into 14 channel bits. The sequence of channel 0 and channel 1 within these bits is set by a simple conversion table which is part of the control unit of every CD-ROM drive. The codes within the EFM table are chosen so they avoid two adjacent channel 1 bits and stay within the maximum length of 11 channel 0 bits.

Par of the EFM table (EFM = Eight-To-Fourteen-Modulation)

Byte		EFM-Code
Dec	Binary	
0	00000000	01001000100000
1	00000001	10000100000000
2	00000010	10010001000000
3	00000011	10001000100000
4	00000100	01000100000000
5	00000101	00000100010000
6	00000110	00010000100000
7	00000111	00100100000000
8	00001000	01001001000000
9	00001001	10000001000000
10	00001010	10010001000000

However, even conversion by EFM table doesn't consider the separation of individual bytes. When the first byte ends in a channel 1 and therefore changes from pit to land (or vice versa), the next byte cannot again start with such a change, because there is no room between the two. Therefore, each byte with its 14 channel bits is extended by three additional channel bits called *merge bits*. Merge bits separate the bytes from each other and increase the number of channel bits to 17 per byte.

Frames

Now let move onto the smallest contiguous information block of a CD. This is called the *frame*. A frame includes 24 bytes (each having 17 channel bits). Other information is added, which establishes the frame as a data block. This block begins with a sync pattern, a specific pattern of 27 channel bits which indicate the beginning of a new frame to the drive. This is followed by a control byte and then the 24 bytes of actual data. Finally, an additional 8 bytes for error detection and error correction, (again each having 17 channel bits) are appended to the frame. From the table on the right, you can see that there are 588 channel bits per frame:

Channel bits	Sync pattern
27	Control byte
1 * 17	Data
24 * 17	Error correction & error detection
8 * 17	588 Channel bits per frame

Sectors

At the next level, 98 frames comprise one sector. The following illustration shows that a sector consists of 3,234 bytes. A total of 2,352 of these bytes are available as usable data and the remaining 882 bytes consist of the data for error correction and detection and 98 control bytes. All audio CDs are based on this original CD-DA format.

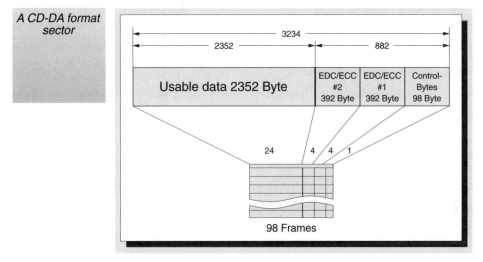

A CD-DA format sector

This format is for the CD-DA format (CD Digital Audio) for audio tracks. Knowing that a CD audio player reads 75 of these sectors per second, we can draw some important conclusion about the operation and data transfer rates of a CD system. A CD player works with a scanning rate/frequency of 44.1 KHz, 16-bit samples and 2 channels, you can see that this the throughput is 1,411,200 bits per second (44100x16x2). This equals 18,816 bits per 1/75 second, which again equals the 2,352 bytes of usable data that a sector can store according to CD-DA format.

Sectors are played back in a specific time. Addressing the data on a CD is based on time units in the format: minutes/seconds/sector. For example, the time unit for the fifteenth sector of the third second in the 13th playing minute of the CD is 13/03/15.

Subchannels

Above we found that each frame contains a byte of control information. This is called the *control* or *subcode byte*. Taken together from all of the frames in a sector, there are a total of 98 subcode bytes.

The individual bits of each subcode byte are identified by the letters P through W. The first bit is named P, the second Q, and so on. A subchannel results by associating all bits in the same position of the subcode bytes in successive frames. The data stream consisting of the first bits of the 98 subcode bytes in a sector is called the P-channel. The sequence of data made up of the second bits is called the Q-channel. The six bits R through W are combined to make a single R-through-W subchannel.

Subchannel P indicates whether music or computer data is found in a sector.

Subchannel Q contains timing information. This may be either the absolute time measured from the start of the CD (ATime) or the relative track time measured from the start of the track (RTime). In the lead-in areas of the disc, 72 bits of the Subchannel Q contain the table of contents, while the remaining 26 bits are used for synchronization and error correction.

Illustration of the subchannels

The R-through-W subchannel contains data for synchronization and error correction.

Storage capacity

The storage capacity of a CD-ROM is determined by the number of sectors. CD-ROM storage capacity ranges from 500 Meg to 680 Meg. This depends on the amount of surface area used to press the disc. Originally some of the surface area was left unused because the CD duplicators had problems pressing the outer 5 millimeters of a CD-ROM. As a result, storage capacity was limited to 550 Meg. As manufacturing techniques improved, the full surface area was used yielding the maximum capacity of a CD-ROM can be used with 682 Meg.

Error correction

There are 2 x 392 bytes of error correction information stored in each sector. The contents of this information is defined by an algorithm specified in the Red Book. This proven algorithm is used at hardware level for error free transfer of sectors with all audio CD players and CD-ROM drives. It is based on a widely used technique called the "Reed-Solomon-Code". The code was slightly modified for CD-ROMs and called Cross Interleaved Reed-Solomon Code (or simply, CIRC).

Using CIRC, the error rate is kept to about one in 10^8 bits. In other terms, for every 100 million bits of information read, only one bit will not be detected as an error nor corrected. Someone listening to an audio CD will barely notice such an error due to the rapid sequence of sectors in 1/75 second cycle. However, this error rate is still too high for computer users where any defective bit in the program code or critical data can lead to a disaster. To insure a higher level or error-free data throughput, the format for a CD-ROM is different than the Red Book format.

CD-ROM formats

The format for CD-ROM discs is specified in the Yellow Book. The Yellow Book is based on the Red Book and builds on the standards for audio CDs, creating a standard reference for the storage of computer data on the same size discs used for audio CDs.

The following illustration shows the Yellow Book format differs from the CD-DA format in the amount of data that can be stored in each sector. To decrease the likelihood of errors, the Yellow Book specifies additional error detection and correction information be added to each sector. The amount of usable data is reduced to 2,048 bytes (2K) per sector instead of the 2,352 bytes for the CD-DA format. Most programmer's would agree that 2K is an easier number of bytes to work with.

CD-ROM format: Mode 1 and Mode 2

		3234						
	2352					882		
SYNC	Header	User data 2048 Byte	EDC	free	ECC	EDC/ECC #2	EDC/ECC #1	Control-Bytes
12 Byte	4 Byte		4 Byte	8 Byte	276 Byte	392 Byte	392 Byte	98 Byte

CD-ROM / Mode 1

		3234			
	2352			882	
SYNC	Header	User data 2336 Byte	EDC/ECC #2	EDC/ECC #1	Control-Bytes
12 Byte	4 Byte		392 Byte	392 Byte	98 Byte

CD-ROM / Mode 2

You'll see from the above illustration that the Yellow Book defines two CD-ROM formats - Mode 1 and Mode 2. Data written in Mode 2 doesn't use the additional error detection and correction information. Mode 2 sectors should be used only for data that isn't critical An example of this type of data are graphic images that are overlaid on the screen for a short time. Remember the basic error detection and correction methods are still used with Mode 2 data, so the chance of an error are still quite low. But using Mode 2, additional data can be packed into a sector. In practice, very few CD-ROMs are written using Mode 2.

One advantage of Mode 2 sectors is that the transfer rate of a drive is increased - even if only slightly. If 75 Mode 1 sectors are read per second, the effective transfer rate is 75 * 2K = 150K per second. With Mode 2 sectors, this increases to 75 * 2,336 bytes / 1,024 bytes per K = 171K per second. Double, triple and quad speed drives are able to transfer more data.

Both sector formats have 12 synchronization bytes at the start of the sector and a 4-byte header. It identifies the sector number and type of sector in Red Book. Mode 0 denotes an empty sector filled exclusively with zeros.

XA format

Today's CD-ROM drives also use a format which has become a defacto standard for CD-ROM multimedia titles. This format is called the XA format (also called the CD-ROM XA) developed by Sony and Philips with Microsoft in 1989. A revised XA format, called "eXtended Architecture" (XA) was announced in 1991. Until recently, only few users have been manufactured using this format. CD-ROM/XA is closely connected with CD-I format, which Philips developed for its CD interactive system.

CD-ROM Sector Header, Mode 1 or 2		
Offset	Contents	Type
00h	Sector address: Minute	1 BYTE
01h	Sector address: Second	1 BYTE
02h	Sector address: Sector	1 BYTE
03h	Type of sector	1 BYTE
	0 = Mode 0	
	1 = Mode 1	
	2 = Mode 2	

The XA standard was developed to solve a typical problem for multimedia applications. To display text on the screen while a video runs and music plays in the background, an application must simultaneously process three data streams from three different files. Furthermore, the application must do this in real time. However, since only one CPU is available, it must repeatedly work with small amounts of data representing text, audio output and video display. This means the CPU must download a piece of the file with the text, then a piece from the file with the audio and finally a piece from the file with the video in rapid succession. If these files are in stored on the CD in different locations, the read head must constantly move from one file to the next. When you consider the slow seek times of a CD-ROM drive, the colorful world of multimedia can quickly collapse. The video becomes jerky, the sound distorted and the text no longer matches the image.

The important feature of the XA standard is its ability interleave sectors. Using interleaving the CPU is able to read the required text, video and audio without moving the read head. The sectors are nested with the file. For example, three text sectors start a sequence. These are followed by four video sectors and then three audio sectors. This repeats itself until all three data streams are completed.

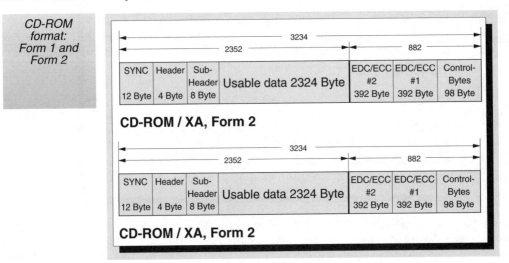

CD-ROM format: Form 1 and Form 2

There are two different sector format for CD-ROM XA: Form 1 and Form 2. Both are similar to Mode 1 of CD-ROM format, but differ slightly at the start of the sector, where the usable data is stored.

Subheader of CD-ROM XA Sector, Form 1 or 2		
Offset	Contents	Type
00h	File number for interleaving 0 = no interleaving	1 BYTE
01h	Channel number for audio data	1 BYTE
02h	XA flag	1 BYTE
03h	Coding flag for audio or video data	1 BYTE (0 with data sectors)
04h-07h	Duplicate of bytes 00h to 03h	4 BYTES

Both Form 1 and Form 2 use the eight unused bytes of CD-ROM Mode 1 between the data for error detection (EDC) and error correction (ECC). These bytes are shifted with XA to the beginning of the sector, where they form a subheader. The subheader contains additional information, for example, information for interleaving, which contrasts XA format from normal CD-ROM format.

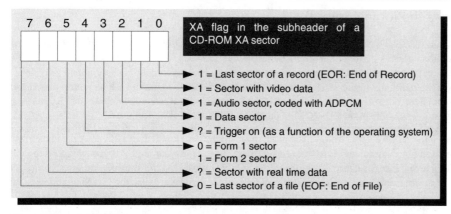

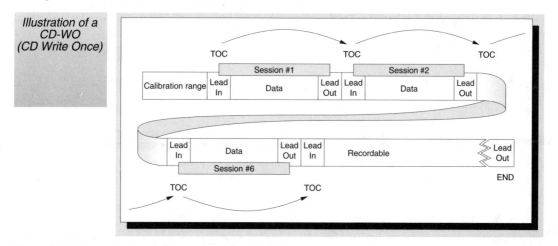

Photo CD and CD-WO

The Photo CD belongs to a class called CD-WO, an acronym for CD-Write Once. You may also hear another term for Photo CDs - term CD-R. CD-R is an acronym for CD-Recordable. The special feature of Photo CDs is that you can write to this type of CD more than once. This standard is described in the Orange Book (the latest book in the "Rainbow Series") published in 1990.

Recordable CDs are immediately recognizable because they're gold colored. In contrast, read-only CDs are silver colored. The reason recordable CDs are gold is to achieve a higher reflection level. Instead of the pits and lands, beneath the gold layer is an organic chemical compound, whose reflective properties can be changed by the laser to simulate pits or lands. This technique also allows standard CD-ROM drives to also read recordable CDs.

Since a CD-WO can be recorded more than once, it must have a different structure than a standard CD-ROM. While the beginning of a standard CD-ROM is identified by a lead-in, the lead-in of a CD-WO is preceded by two other areas used to align the laser along the writable portion of the media.

Each time you record data on a CD-WO you create a session. During a session the lead-in, the data area and the lead-out are written to the media. The table of contents (TOC) to the information in the data area is written to part of the lead-in.

During a following session, the recording after the lead-out of the preceding session. The new volume is written, again composed of a lead-in, a data area and a lead-out. Because the lead-ins are linked by their TOCs, a drive can move from volume to volume (in other words from session to session) gathering the entire contents of the CD-WO.

High Sierra represents the logical format

So far we've talked only about the physical format of the CD-ROM. But for most applications, it's more pertinent to talk about the logical format - files and directories. A peripheral manufacturer can choose to use its own logical format for their CD-ROM drive. But doing so requires proprietary drivers for each operating system. This severely limits the compatibility of CD among users. This is the problem that many in this industry were trying to avoid in 1985 when various representatives of software and hardware manufacturers met to discuss the HSG format. This format is used today for computer CD-ROMs used on PCs and many UNIX systems. The companion CD-ROM to this book follows the HSG format.

The HSG derives its name from the "High Sierra Group". The participants in the development of HSG took the name from their first meeting place, the High Sierra Hotel and Casino in Lake Tahoe, Nevada. A year later this group's released their recommendation, called "Volume and File Structure of Compact Read-Only Optical Disk for Information Interchange". It was standardized by the ISO (International Standards Organization). It has since then been called the ISO Standard 9660, or simply "ISO 9660".

Although the ISO standard accepted 99.5% of the HSG proposal, there are a few slight differences. The most notable difference is in the structure of the directory entries. This is why some talk about HSG format, others talk about ISO-9660 and still others yet talk about HSG/ISO-9660; they all refer to the same standard.

We'll summarize the most important concepts from the ISO specification on the following pages. Anyone who wants to access CD-ROM files from DOS will not need to understand these concepts since CD-ROMs are now standard mass storage devices and are easily accessed just like a hard drive. However, anyone who wants to access the hardware driver of a CD-ROM drive, for example to begin playback of audio tracks, must be familiar with these concepts.

Logical sectors

The HSG format defines the logical sector. The size of the HSG logical sector is 2,048 bytes (2K). Each sector has a unique number called a Logical Sector Number (LSN). The first addressable LSN is the number 0 and corresponds to the physical sector at the Red Book address 00:02:00. Therefore, the first 150 physical sectors, which form the first two seconds of a CD, are not accessible at the logical format level. At the same time, this gives us the conversion formula between Red Book addresses (mm:ss:ff) and LSN:

```
LSN(mm:ss:ff) = (mm * 60 + ss) * 75 - 150
```

Logical blocks

To be able to access the components of a logical sector easier and to allow for smaller subdivisions, HSG subdivides a logical sector into several logical blocks. Logical blocks (LBN) can be 512 bytes, 1,024 bytes or 2,048 bytes in size. LBNs are also addressed by numbers. Let's use a logical block size of 512 for this example. Here, LBN 0 represents the first logical block in the first physical sector, 1 represents the second, 2 for the third and 3 for the fourth. Logical block 4 is then at the beginning of the second physical sector.

Logical sectors and Logical blocks

Files and file names

HSG files are stored as a continuous sequence of logical blocks called an "extent". Therefore, you won't find a FAT (File Allocation Table) on a CD-ROM. By knowing the beginning of a file and its length, you also know all of the LBNs in which the file is stored. Because files on a CD-ROM cannot be deleted, there is no need to fill "freed up" space with fragments of new files (the purpose of a FAT on a hard or floppy drive). Additionally, HSG provides the somewhat exotic option of having files extend over several CDs. This option however, is not supported by DOS.

HSG/ISO-9960 defines the rules for filenames. This is one of the few areas where ISO and HSG differ. HSG filenames follow the Microsoft specifications: 8 character filenames followed by a period followed by a 3 character extension. A filename may contain only uppercase characters A-Z, numerals 0-9 and the underscore "_".ISO filenames are closer to UNIX specifications. A filename can have up to 31 characters with or without a separating period. The filename can be followed by a semicolon, which identifies an optional version number. Due to the long filenames, ISO CDs aren't compatible for DOS users.

Directories and subdirectories

An ISO CD contains a root directory for structuring the stored files. The root directory can have subdirectories. In turn, these subdirectories can have subdirectories, resulting in the tree structure you are familiar with from DOS and UNIX. The only restriction is that maximum number of directory levels is eight.

The root directory and all of its subdirectories are stored as files. The "directory files" can be arranged between all other files anywhere on the CD.

Offset	HSG Field	Type	Meaning	ISO Field	Type
+00h	len_dr	1 BYTE	Length of directory entries in bytes	=	
+01h	XAR_len	1 BYTE	Number of logical sectors reserved for XAR	=	
+02h	loc_extendl	1 DWORD	first logical block of the file in Intel format (Start block number)	=	
+06h	loc_extendM	1 DWORD	ditto in Motorola format	=	
+0Ah	data_lenl	1 DWORD	File length in bytes in Intel format	=	
+0Eh	data_lenM	1 DWORD	ditto in Motorola format	=	
+12h	record_time	6 BYTE	Date and time of the file	record_time	7 BYTE
+18h	file_flags_hsg	1 BYTE	HSG file flags	-	
+19h	Reserved	1 BYTE		file_flags_iso	1 BYTE
+1Ah	il_size	1 BYTE	Number of contiguous sectors for interleave (0=all)	=	
+1Bh	il_skip	1 BYTE	Number of sectors that must be skipped after an interleave block (dividing sectors)	=	
+1Ch	VSSNI	1 WORD	Volume number in Intel format	=	
+1Eh	VSSNM	1 WORD	ditto in Motorola format	=	
+20h	len_fi	1 BYTE	Length of file name	=	
+21h	file_id	n BYTE	File name as a string, length specified in len_fi (up to 32 characters)	=	
+21h+n	padding	1 BYTE	Fill byte, when the next field wouldn't start at an even memory address otherwise	=	
	sys_data	n Byte	Any additional information, from whose length the length of the file name (len_fi), the length of the fixed fields and the total length of the directory entry (len_dr) can be calculated (system data)	=	

You'll note the directory entries for ISO and HSG are identical except for the time field and a connecting flag byte.

Also note that several fields appear twice: once with the suffix I and once with the suffix M. This points to a compatibility problem between Intel and Motorola systems. On Intel systems values larger than 8-bits are arranged low order first, followed by high order. On Motorola systems, the order is reversed. In this table, all 16-bit and 32-bit values appear twice: once in Intel format (I suffix) and once in Motorola format (M suffix). This allows the operating system to use the data with the appropriate format for the processor on which the operating system runs.

On the physical level, the CD-ROM XA sector format manages the requirement for interleaving files, On a logical level, the directory entry manages this task. The two fields il_size and il_skip indicate how many logical sectors of a file follow one another and how many logical sectors must be skipped until the next block follows with the continuous sectors of the file.

One recommendation is to place no more than 40 files in a directory. By limiting the number of entries in a directory, you'll be able to find a file as quickly as possible. Because so many directory entries fit into a logical sector you'll only need to read the first sector of a directory to find the desired file.

Path table

The standard file system intersperses directory names and filenames. It's a simple and efficient technique but becomes quite involved, especially when searching for files in deeply nested subdirectories. In this case, there may be many directory names to search and read until you find the directory with the desired filename entry. Since the CD-ROM drive has a relatively slow seek times the filename search time increases.

The path table was developed as a way to circumvent the subdirectory problem. The path table contains the names of all the directories and subdirectories on a CD. It also contains the logical sector number at which the subdirectory file begins. By keeping this table in memory, you need only read one sector to determine the address of a file assuming that the directory entry of the file is located in the first sector of the directory data.

Illustration of the path table

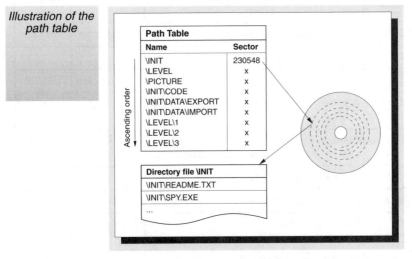

Because the path table contains 32-bit integers representing logical sector numbers, there are two copies of the path table on a CD-ROM. One copy has values in the Intel format and the other in Motorola format.

Extended Attribute Records (XAR)

Another interesting feature is eXtended Attribute Records (XAR). These records give the creator of a file the option of saving as much information about a file as he/she wants, forming the basis of an object-oriented file system. For example, you can keep track of who created the file, whether it expires at a specific time because the data is no longer current and so on.

This information is not saved in the directory entry of a file. Instead it's written to the first logical sector of the file. This prevents the information from needlessly filling up the directory space. The application program or the operating system can then determine how many XAR sectors to skip until the "actual" file begins.

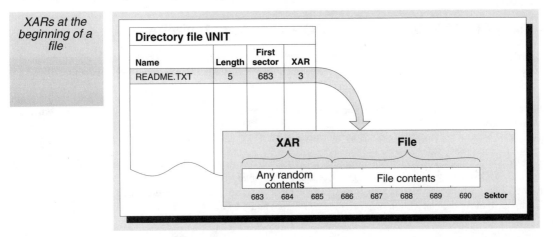

XARs at the beginning of a file

In addition to the user definable attributes, HSG also provides some predefined XAR attributes, for example, a user identification, access rights, information about the structure of the records stored in the file and much more. However, these attributes are not applicable under DOS because DOS basically ignores XAR entries.

Volumes

Like the other mass storage systems, another level exists above the level of files and directories on the CD. This level is called the volume. A volume is formed by all the files and directories stored on a CD. HSG describes a volume format based on two components: A system area and a data area. The system area occupies the first 16 logical sectors of a CD (LSN 0 to LSN 15). Its use is not defined and is reserved for the operating system under which the CD is to be used. For example, you could place a boot sector here if you wanted to boot from the CD.

Volume Descriptors (VD) precede the data area of a volume. HSG defines 5 different volume descriptors. Each one describes a different aspect of the medium, but all them fill one complete logical sector. Of the five different VDs, only the "standard volume descriptor" must be present, all the rest are optional. However, you won't find a field with the number of VDs. Instead, a Volume Sequence Terminator indicates the end of the VD.

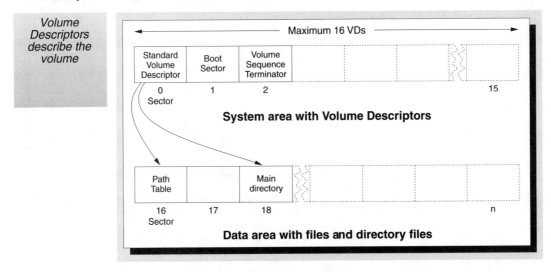

Volume Descriptors describe the volume

The most important information contained in a standard volume descriptor is the address of the directory file with the root directory and the address of the path table. The names of the copyright file and the abstract file are also listed. These files are in the root directory. The copyright file gives information about the author of the CD while the abstract file gives information about the CD's contents.

Integrating CD-ROM Drives Into A DOS/Windows Environment

The best hardware is useless if you cannot easily access it from the operating system. DOS uses device drivers which can also be used to access CD-ROM drives under Windows. One problem arose when Microsoft was developing the first drivers for CD-ROM drives under DOS. This new media didn't fit in with the previous concept of device drivers.

CD-ROMs are based on the High Sierra format, not on the standard file allocation table format used by DOS. The High Sierra format doesn't recognize the FAT nor any other data structures that DOS uses. At the time the High Sierra format was announced, DOS 3.0 was the current operating system version. DOS 3.0 had a maximum storage capacity of 32 Meg.

This precluded the developers from implementing the CD-ROM driver as a DOS block device. Instead they decided to implement it as a DOS character device. Character drivers follow the same structure as block drivers but cannot be addressed by drive letters like A:, B:, etc., which is the advantage of block drivers. So, another piece of code had to be inserted ahead of the CD driver to make the connection between the DOS kernel and the CD driver. This code is the MSCDEX driver.

MSCDEX

Every PC system which includes a CD-ROM drive also uses the MSCDEX driver. MSCDEX is started from the AUTOEXEC.BAT file. After it is loaded, you can then address the CD-ROM drive using a normal device label (usually D:). Not only is MSCDEX a TSR program but it also attaches itself to the "redirector", a part of the DOS kernel responsible for linking network drives. MSCDEX manages to simulate the existence of a network drive to DOS through the redirector, which in reality is a CD-ROM drive. The only responsibility of the DOS kernel is to provide a device letter to MSCDEX. From then on, this will be the name of the device under DOS. The device letter is usually D: depending on the number of other device drivers and network drives installed in the system.

The DOS kernel handles all accesses to a network drive by delegating them to the redirector. MSCDEX waits there to intercept these accesses. However, MSCDEX doesn't address the CD drive itself, but instead, manages the access through the appropriate device driver.

From outward appearances, this is a character driver, but it is a special kind of character driver that performs the functions that MSCDEX requires for access to the drive. More about this later in the chapter.

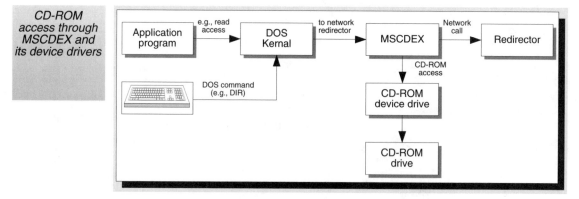

CD-ROM access through MSCDEX and its device drivers

In addition to starting MSCDEX from the AUTOEXEC.BAT file, you have to load the CD-ROM device driver in the CONFIG.SYS file. In fact, you can install several different CD-ROM drivers if you're using CD-ROM drives from various manufacturers. Because a CD-ROM driver depends on the hardware and the interface of the CD-ROM drive, it's usually able to handle multiple drives from "their own" manufacturer, but not drives from other manufacturers.

Until now, the separation of function between MSCDEX and the device driver has worked perfectly: MSCDEX is hardware independent and is isolated from the differences among the various drives by the CD-ROM drivers. This is why manufacturers can supply the same MSCDEX for installation of a drive. However, the actual CD-ROM drivers are hardware dependent. The manufacturer of the drive has to supply the appropriate drivers.

Connecting MSCDEX and the device drivers

One critical area is connecting MSCDEX and the device driver when the PC system is booting. Being part of the AUTOEXEC.BAT file, MSCDEX isn't loaded until after the CD-ROM device drivers are been loaded from the CONFIG.SYS file. Each CD-ROM driver must have a specific name for MSCDEX to recognize it. A name such as MSCD00x (where x represents a number) is often used so that you can add a different driver which can be identified by another name. The complete name is specified by the user when the driver is started from the CONFIG.SYS file. This applies to all drivers whether it be a Sony, NEC, Philips, Hitachi or SoundBlaster CD drive. Here's an example:

```
device=SBCD.SYS /P:200 /D:MSCD001
```

Although this approach may at first seem a little awkward and complicated, it's necessary to maintain the functional separation between the hardware dependent components and the hardware independent components.

Programming considerations

After you've installed the drivers and MSCDEX, you can access the CD-ROM drive just like a normal DOS drive. Not only is the drive available at DOS level, where "DIR D:" is enough to display the root directory of the CD-ROM to the screen. The D: drive is now a normal drive on the level of the DOS API (Application Program Interface), and can be used with all the functions for opening and reading files and directories. The corresponding functions of DOS interrupt 21h are available to the programmer without restrictions. However, the nature of the medium prevents all types of write accesses unless you have a CD-ROM recorder.

The unique character of a CD-ROM drive is, to a large extent, hidden from view at the DOS API level. But these unique functions are available. For example, MSCDEX has functions to access the "copyright files" and "abstract files" which are only found on a CD-ROM. But MSCDEX doesn't have a function to playback audio CDs. Because MSCDEX has limited abilities, you'll have to write a device driver to be able to perform all of the operations that are built into the hardware.

Accessing The CD Using The MSCDEX API

MSCDEX is one of the "MUX handlers" (see Chapter 29) which DOS uses with the PRINT, DOSKEY and APPEND commands. MSCDEX also attaches itself to DOS interrupt 2Fh. Calling this interrupt is called with a value of 15H in the AH register is passed onto MSCDEX which then handles the call.

There are several versions (1.0 to 1.1, 2.0, 2.1 and 2.2) of MSCDEX. The APIs listed in the following table is based on Version 2.2 of MSCDEX. A total of 15 functions are defined.

Function Subroutine AX		Task	MSCDEX from Version
AH	AL		
15h	00h	Get number of CD-ROM drives.	1.0
15h	01h	Get CD-ROM driver list	1.0
15h	02h	Get copyright filename	1.0
15h	03h	Get abstract filename	1.0
15h	04h	Get bibliographic filename	1.0
15h	05h	Read volume table of contents	1.0
15h	06h	Reserved	1.0
15h	07h	Reserved	1.0
15h	08h	Read sectors	1.0
15h	09h	Write sectors	1.0
15h	0Ah	Reserved	1.0
15h	0Bh	CD-ROM drive check	2.0
15h	0Ch	Get MSCDEX version number	2.0
15h	0Dh	Get CD-ROM units	2.0
15h	0Eh/ 00h	Get volume descriptor preference	2.0
15h	0Eh/ 01h	Set volume descriptor preference	2.0
15h	0Fh	Read directory entry	2.0
15h	10h	Send device request	2.1

Calling a function from the MSCDEX API

When you call one of the MSCDEX function, you'll use the processor registers as follows:

AL   Number of the function to be performed

CX   For functions that expect a drive letter of the CD-ROM drive to be accessed. 0 represents A:, 1 represents B:, etc.

ES:BX   For functions that expect a pointer to a buffer they are passed in this register pair in the form of FAR pointers.

DX   For functions that require a specific number of sectors, this is passed in DX.

DI:SI   For functions that require a sector number, this is passed as a 32 bit integer in the register pair DI:SI. DI contains the high-order 16-bits (the Hi-Word) and SI contains the low-order 16-bits (the Lo-Word).

Carry flag   Indicates an error following a call to one of the MSCDEX functions.

AL   Error code if carry flag is not zero

The complete listing and description of these functions are in Appendix E. These functions are commonly known as the multiplexor functions. The following discussions describe some of the practical uses for the MSCDEX functions.

Checking for a CD-ROM drive

Before calling any MSCDEX function, you should first make certain that MSCDEX is actually installed and its API is available. MSCDEX function 0 is used to check the installation. This function returns the number of CD-ROM drives that MSCDEX is able to address in the BX register.

One way to proceed is to zero the BX register and then call function 0.. If BX still contains zero, then MSCDEX has not been properly installed. It MSCDEX was available, then BX would contain a value of at least one. If not, you can save yourself the trouble of all other MSCDEX calls, because it isn't installed, and most likely a CD-ROM drive is not installed either.

Interrupt 2Fh, MUX Code 15h, Function 00h	MSCDEX Version 1.0 and above
Get the number of CD-ROM drives	

Use this function to determine the number of installed CD-ROM drives. You can also use this function to check whether MSCDEX is installed.

Input	AH = 15h
	AL = 00h
Output	BX = Number of managed CD-ROM drives
	CX = Drive label for the first CD-ROM drive (0=A:, 1=B:, etc.)

Remarks:

You should call this function before all other MSCDEX functions to ensure that MSCDEX is installed. To do this, load the value 0 in the BX register before calling the function and check whether BX still contains 0 after the function call. If BX still contains 0, MSCDEX cannot be used since no CD-ROM drive are present.

Although it's possible to determine the drive labels of the CD-ROM drives after the function call from the combination of BX and CX, we recommend using the 0Dh function if an MSCDEX driver in Version 2.0 or above is available. There's no guarantee that consecutive drive labels will be assigned to the installed CD-ROM drives, especially on networks. For example, the first CD-ROM drive might be D:, followed by the network drive E:, with the second CD-ROM drive getting the drive label of F:. Since you can't determine this information from function 00h, use function 0Dh.

Version number

Because the MSCDEX API has changed several times, you should make certain you have a version of MSCDEX that supports the desired function before you call it. Use MSCDEX function 0Ch (introduced in Version 2.0) for this purpose. This function returns the whole number portion of the version number in the BH register, and the decimal portion of the version number in the BL register. For example, BH = 2 and BL =20 would mean version 2.20.

However, since this function became available with Version 2.0, make certain you don't have Version 1.x of the MSCDEX driver before calling it. To do this, simply load the BX register with a value of 0 before calling the function and then check the register's contents. If the register still contains 0 after the function call, you won't be able to call function 0Ch, because your MSCDEX driver is Version 1.x.

Interrupt 2Fh, MUX Code 15h, Function 0Ch	MSCDEX Version 2.0 and above
Query MSCDEX version number	

Call this function to determine the version number of the installed MSCDEX driver.

Input	AH = 15h
	AL = 0Ch

Output	BH = the whole number portion of the version number (1, 2, etc.)
	BL = the decimal portion of the version number, e.g., 10 for 1.10 or 2.10

Remarks:

Call this function before calling function 00h to make certain the MSCDEX is actually installed.

Because this function is not available until MSCDEX Version 2.0, the BX register should be loaded with a value of 0 prior to calling the function. If you still encounter this value after the function call, it means the function could not be executed and you have Version 1.x of an MSCDEX driver.

Determining the drive letters

To access a CD-ROM drive using MSCDEX, you need to know its drive letter. Function 0 returns this information in the CX register. If BX contains 2 and CX contains 3, it means the current system has 2 drives (BX) that can be addressed using drive labels D: (CX) and E:. However, there's a little catch to this equation, especially when network drives are involved. MSCDEX can't always assign consecutive drive labels in such cases, e.g., because E: may already be reserved for a network drive. In the situation we just described, MSCDEX would call the first CD-ROM drive D:, but the second one would not be E:, instead, it would be F:.

Unfortunately, this cannot be handled by function 0 because it is from Version 1.0 of the MSCDEX specification. At the time, developers either didn't recognize this problem or simply ignored it. A newer function, 0Dh, was introduced in Version 2.0 to solve this problem. In addition to the function number in ES:BX, it also expects a pointer to an array that can be a maximum of 26 bytes in size. The function writes the drive labels of the CD-ROM drives addressable using MSCDEX in this array. In the worst case scenario, all 26 drive labels would represent CD-ROM drives. While this is almost impossible, you will know the actual number of drives from a previous call for function 0. Only the first n entries in the array are filled in by the function.

Interrupt 2Fh, MUX Code 15h, Function 0Dh   **MSCDEX Version 2.0 and above**
  Get CD-ROM drives

This function provides the caller with the exact drive labels for the CD-ROM drives managed by MSCDEX. It is preferable to function 00h, because it doesn't assume that all CD-ROM drives will have consecutive drive letters.

Input	AH = 15h
	AL = 0Dh
	ES:BX = FAR pointer to a buffer in which the drive labels of the CD-ROM drives are entered.

Output	ES:BX = FAR pointer to buffer with corresponding data

Remarks:

The buffer must provide one byte for each connected CD-ROM drive. The drive label for the CD-ROM is entered in this byte, with 0 standing for A:, 1 for B:, etc. If the buffer is to be dynamically allocated during program execution, use function 00h to determine the number of CD-ROM drives beforehand, because precisely one buffer entry is required for each CD-ROM drive. On the other hand, if the buffer is statically allocated, you have to figure on the "worst case scenario", providing one entry for each of the maximum 26 CD-ROM drives (from A: to Z:).

If you want to know whether a drive is a CD-ROM drive, simply pass the drive label in the CX-register to MSCDEX function 0Bh. If the drive is actually a CD-ROM drive, a non-zero value will be returned in the AX-register.

Interrupt 2Fh, MUX Code 15h, Function 0Bh	MSCDEX Version 2.0 and above
Query CD-ROM drive	

Use this function to determine whether the given drive is a CD-ROM drive being managed by MSCDEX.

Input	AH = 15h
	AL = 0Bh
	CX = Drive label for the CD-ROM drive to be accessed (0=A:, 1=B:, etc.)
Output	AX = 0: not a CD-ROM drive
	<> 0 : is a CD-ROM drive
	BX = ADADh

Remarks:

After calling the function, you must first inspect the contents of the BX register to determine whether the function call was really handled by MSCDEX and not some other MUX handler. If the BX register contains the MSCDEX signature ADADh, then the contents of AX indicate whether the specified drive is a CD-ROM drive.

Reading and writing

The original task of a drive is to read and write data. Functions 08h and 09h embody these tasks for MSCDEX. The two functions correspond to DOS interrupts 25h and 26h, which are used for absolute reading and writing of sectors from and to storage media. At this level, MSCDEX works with 2K sectors, not files and directories. However, you can only write these sectors if the device is a CD-ROM recorder, which will probably be the case only rarely.

To access files and directories, you won't need to use these functions. You can use these functions, for example, when you want to "dump" the contents of specific CD-ROM sectors or copy areas of a CD-ROM.

Interrupt 2Fh, MUX Code 15h, Function 08h	MSCDEX Version 1.0 and above
Read sectors	

This function corresponds to interrupt 25h which is used to read sectors from any drive. Unlike interrupt 25h, this function can be sent only to a CD-ROM drive.

Input	AH = 15h
	AL = 08h
	CX = Drive label for CD-ROM drive to be accessed (0=A:, 1=B:, etc.)
	SI:DI = Number of the first sector
	DX = Number of sectors to be read
	ES:BX = FAR pointer to a buffer for the sectors that are read
Output	Carry flag = 0: OK

      = 1 : Error, in this case

      AL = 15: invalid drive specified or

      21: drive not ready

Remarks:

Each sector 2,048 bytes, so the buffer must be large enough to accommodate 2,048 bytes per sector.

The number of the first sector to read is coded as a 32-bit value in SI and DI. SI contains the high-order 16-bits (the Hi-Word) while DI contains the low-order 16-bits (the Lo-Word).

Interrupt 2Fh, MUX Code 15h, Function 09h	**MSCDEX Version 1.0 and above**
Write sectors	

This function can be used only for CD-ROM recorders since a standard CD-ROM drive is read-only. The function corresponds to interrupt 26h, which is used to write sectors to any drive. Unlike interrupt 26h, this function can only be sent to CD-ROM drives.

Input   AH = 15h

            AL = 09h

            CX = Drive label for CD-ROM drive to be accessed (0=A:, 1=B:, etc.)

            SI:DI = Number of first sector

            DX = Number of sectors to be written

            ES:BX = FAR pointer to buffer containing the data to be written.

Output   Carry flag = 0: OK.

                    = 1 : Error, in this case

            AL = 15: invalid drive specified or

                 21: Drive not ready

Remarks:

The buffer contains 2048 bytes for each sector to be written to the CD-ROM.

The number of the first sector to be written is coded as a 32-bit value in SI and DI. SI contains the high-order 16 bits (the Hi-Word), while DI contains the low-order 16 bits (the Lo-Word).

CD-ROM-specific information

The High-Sierra standard allows three special files to be stored on a CD-ROM. These three files are called the "copyright file", "abstract file" and "bibliographic document file". Although not every CD includes these three files, you can determine if the names of these files are contained on the current CD with functions 02h, 03h and 04h. If these files are present, the function returns the filename, which is always contained in the root directory of the CD. These files are recorded there as a normal file and can be opened and read using the usual functions for accessing files.

Interrupt 2Fh, MUX Code 15h, Function 02h	MSCDEX Version 1.0 and above
Get name of copyright file	

A CD-ROM may contain a "copyright file" which gives information about the author of the CD. Use this function to determine the name of this file.

Input	AH = 15h
	AL = 02h
	CX = Drive label for the CD-ROM drive to be accessed (0=A:, 1=B:, etc.)
	ES:BX = FAR pointer to the buffer that will contain the filename
Output	Carry flag = 0: OK
	= 1 : Error, in this case
	AL = 15: invalid drive specified

Remarks:

The buffer should be 38 bytes in length, although the filename of the copyright file for HSG CDs is limited to 8 characters for the name and 3 characters for the extension, thus taking on the conventional form of "nnnnnnnn.eee". The name is written to the buffer as an ASCIIZ string, so is ended by a zero byte. The filename does not contain a path, since the file is assumed to be located in the root directory of the CD-ROM.

If a blank string is returned, the CD-ROM does not contain a copyright file.

Interrupt 2Fh, MUX Code 15h, Function 03h	MSCDEX Version 1.0 and above
Get name of abstract file	

A CD-ROM may contain an "abstract file" with a brief summary of the CD's contents. Use this function to determine the name of this file.

Input	AH = 15h
	AL = 03h
	CX = Drive label for the CD-ROM drive to be accessed (0=A:, 1=B:, etc.)
	ES:BX = FAR pointer to the buffer that will contain the filename
Output	Carry flag = 0: OK
	= 1 : Error, in this case
	AL = 15: invalid drive specified

Remarks:

The buffer should be 38 bytes in length, although the filename of the abstract file for HSG CDs is limited to 8 characters for the name and 3 characters for the extension, thus taking on the conventional form of "nnnnnnnn.eee". The name is written to the buffer as an ASCIIZ string, so is ended by a zero byte. The filename does not contain a path, since the file is assumed to be located in the root directory of the CD-ROM.

If a blank string is returned, the CD-ROM does not contain an abstract file.

Interrupt 2Fh, MUX Code 15h, Function 04h	MSCDEX Version 1.0 and above
Get name of bibliographic documentation file	

A CD-ROM may contain a "bibliographic documentation file", which gives information about the sources of the information stored on the CD. Use this function to determine the name of this file.

Input	AH = 15h
	AL = 04h
	CX = Drive label for CD-ROM drive to be accessed (0=A:, 1=B:, etc.)
	ES:BX = FAR pointer to the buffer that will contain the filename.
Output	Carry flag = 0: o.k.
	= 1 : Error, in this case
	AL = 15: invalid drive specified

Remarks:

The buffer should be 38 bytes in length, although the filename of the copyright file for HSG CDs is limited to 8 characters for the name and 3 characters for the extension, thus taking on the conventional form of "nnnnnnnn.eee". The name is written to the buffer as an ASCIIZ string, so is ended by a zero byte. The filename does not contain a path, since the file is assumed to be located in the root directory of the CD-ROM.

If a blank string is returned, the CD-ROM does not contain a bibliographic documentation file.

HSG CD-ROM contains a VTOC, or volume table of contents. The VTOC is a type of table of contents with status information about the CD. It fills a complete 2K sector and is read by using MSCDEX function 05h.

Interrupt 2Fh, MUX Code 15h, Function 05h	MSCDEX Version 1.0 and above
Read VTOC	

Use this function to read the VTOC of a CD-ROM.

Input	AH = 15h
	AL = 05h
	CX = Drive label for CD-ROM drive to be accessed (0=A:, 1=B:, etc.)
	DX = Number of volume whose VTOC is to be read.
	ES:BX = FAR pointer to 2K buffer for VTOC
Output	Carry flag = 0: o.k., in this case
	= 1 : Error, in this case
	AX = 1 : Read VTOC
	00ffh : no more volumes, so no more VTOCs to read (terminator)

AL = 15: invalid drive specified or

21: Drive not ready

Remarks:

The buffer must be 2,048 in length to accommodate the volume table of contents.

Most CD-ROMs contain only one volume, so they also have just one VTOC. Multisession CDs such as Photo CD's or CD-MOs contains multiple VTOCs.

Accessing the CD-ROM using drivers

When MSCDEX functions won't do the trick, you can try switching to the functions of the CD-ROM device driver. Although we'll show how this is done in the next section, you should use the MSCDEX function introduced in Version 2.1 that was created especially for this purpose, function 10h. You only need to pass the function the drive label as well as a pointer to the normal data block which must be present for each call of a DOS driver function. The important advantage to this function is that it uses the specified drive label to find the driver responsible for the drive as well as uses subunit code. Since a CD-ROM driver can manage several drives at the same time, a numerical value in the form of subunit code is passed to the driver to select the desired drive. This is another task that function 10h handles for the caller.

Interrupt 2Fh, MUX Code 15h, Function 10h	MSCDEX Version 2.1 and above
Send request to device driver	

Use this function to send a request to the device driver for the CD-ROM drive without having to know the address of the device driver and the subunit code for the CD-ROM drive.

Input	AH = 15h
	AL = 10h
	CX = Drive label for CD-ROM drive to be accessed (0=A:, 1=B:, etc.)
	ES:BX = FAR pointer to buffer with request for device driver

Output	None

Remarks:

Microsoft recommends using this function to communicate with the device driver of a CD-ROM drive because it gives the programmer the option of addressing a device driver without knowing its address and the subunit code of the drive. When you call this function, MSCDEX automatically puts this information in the device request block which is passed and determines the appropriate device driver from the drive label.

If you want to bypass this call, MSCDEX can return the addresses of the individual drivers and the matching subunit code. Use MSCDEX function 01h to perform this task.

Interrupt 2Fh, MUX Code 15h, Function 01h	MSCDEX Version 1.0 and above
Get information about CD-ROM driver	

Returns information about the various device drivers installed for the CD-ROM drives. Using this information, you can bypass MSCDEX to access the individual device drivers directly.

Input	AH = 15h
	AL = 01h
	ES:BX = FAR pointer to buffer for the returned information

Output	none

Remarks:

Each entry in the buffer requires 5 bytes. If the buffer is dynamically allocated during program execution you should determine the number of CD-ROM drives beforehand using function 00h, because each CD-ROM drive requires exactly one buffer entry. On the other hand, if the buffer is statically allocated, you can use the "worst case scenario", and provide an entry for each of the possible 26 CD-ROM drives (from A: to Z:).

The individual entries of the buffer include a FAR pointer to the start of the appropriate device driver and the subunit code. The subunit code is required because a device driver is able of handling several CD-ROM drives, although the drives usually come from the same manufacturer. When you call the driver, you have to specify the subunit code to differentiate between the different drives.

Offset	Contents	Type	
00h	Sub-Unit-Code	1 BYTE	for first CD-ROM drive
01h	FAR pointer to head of appropriate device driver	1 DWORD	
05h	Sub-Unit-Code	1 BYTE	for second CD-ROM drive
06h	FAR pointer to head of appropriate device driver	1 DWORD	
0Ah	Sub-Unit-Code	1 BYTE	for third CD-ROM drive
0Bh	FAR pointer to head of appropriate device driver	1 DWORD	
etc.			

Accessing The CD Using The CD-ROM Driver

MSCDEX doesn't access a CD-ROM drive directly, but instead passes its requests onto the appropriate CD-ROM driver.

The following table lists the functions which the device drivers must support under DOS. From a technical viewpoint, a CD-ROM driver is a character driver. In practice it the driver does not have to implement all of these functions.

For a simple CD-ROM driver, the functions that are checked in the first column, "CD-ROM Driver", are sufficient. Several functions with function numbers greater than or equal to 80h fall into this category. These functions have been specially tailored to the requirements of MSCDEX and are unknown to normal device drivers under DOS.

In addition to simple CD-ROM drivers that can only access data CDs, DOS also recognizes extended CD-ROM drivers that support additional functions such as playback of audio tracks. Above all, CD-ROM drives that operate with sound cards have the ability to playback normal audio CDs. The device driver supports this ability using the appropriate functions.

A third category of functions are those which are used for CD-ROM recorders. Besides the functions of a normal CD-ROM driver, these drivers must also have functions for mastering or cutting a CD. There are only three functions of this type.

	Driver functions that must be supported by different types of CD-ROM drivers			
Fct	Name/Task	CD-ROM driver	Extended CD-ROM driver	Driver for CD-ROM writer
00h	INIT Initialization of driver	░░░		
01h	MEDIA CHECK Check disk/media change			
02h	BUILD BPB Create Bios Parameter Block			
03h	IOCTL INPUT Direct read	░░░		
04h	INPUT Read			
05h	NONDESTRUCTIVE INPUT Read character without removing it			
06h	INPUT STATUS Check input status			
07h	INPUT FLUSH Erase input buffer			
08h	OUTPUT Write			
09h	OUTPUT WITH VERIFY Write with verify			
0Ah	OUTPUT STATUS Check output status			
0Bh	OUTPUT FLUSH Empty output buffer			░░░
0Ch	IOCTL OUTPUT Direct write	░░░		
0Dh	DEVICE OPEN Open device	░░░		
0Eh	DEVICE CLOSE Close device	░░░		
0Fh	REMOVABLE MEDIA Removable media?			
10h	OUTPUT UNTIL BUSY Output until busy			
17h	GET LOGICAL DEVICE Get logical device			
18h	GET LOGICAL DEVICE Set logical device			

Fct	Name/Task	CD-ROM driver	Extended CD-ROM driver	Driver for CD-ROM writer
\multicolumn{5}{Driver functions that must be supported by different types of CD-ROM drivers (Continued)}
80h	READ LONG — Read sectors	■		
81h	Reserved			
82h	READ LONG PREFETCH — Read ahead	■		
83h	SEEK — Find sector	■		
84h	PLAY AUDIO — Play audio		■	
85h	STOP AUDIO — Stop audio		■	
86h	WRITE LONG — Write sectors			■
87h	WRITE LONG VERIFY — Write sectors with verification			■
88h	RESUME AUDIO — Resume audio playback		■	

The device header

Like any other DOS device driver, a CD-ROM device driver begins with the device header. This header is located at offset address 0000h of the memory segment into which the driver was loaded. The device header has the normal structure of a DOS device driver except for the two fields at the end of the header. The only unusual feature about the device header is the driver name must read MSCD00x, with x standing for a number. This is the only way MSCDEX can later recognize that the driver is a CD-ROM device driver for which it is responsible.

Address	Contents	Type
\multicolumn{3}{The header of a CD-ROM device driver}
+00h	FAR pointer to next driver	1 PTR
+04h	Device attribute	1 WORD
+06h	Offset address of the strategy routine within the driver segment	1 WORD
+08h	Offset address of interrupt routine within driver segment	1 WORD
+0Ah	Driver name (MSCD00x) filled with up to 8 spaces	8 BYTE
+12h	Reserved	1 WORD
+14h	Drive letter for first CD-ROM drive of this driver (0=A:, 1=B: etc.)	1 BYTE
+15h	Number of CD-ROM drives managed by the driver	1 BYTE

The last two fields can be important to a program. You can determine the number of CD-ROM drives managed by the driver and determine the drive label for the first of these drives.

From the device attribute which is stored as part of the device header, it is evident the driver is passing itself off as a character driver to the system. The attribute has the typical structure of device attributes, with the individual flags accepting the following values:

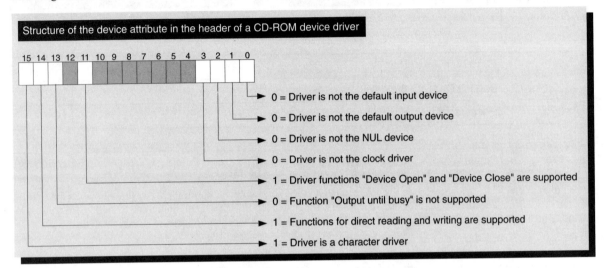

Structure of the device attribute in the header of a CD-ROM device driver

15 14 13 12 11 10 9 8 7 6 5 4 3 2 1 0

- 0 = Driver is not the default input device
- 0 = Driver is not the default output device
- 0 = Driver is not the NUL device
- 0 = Driver is not the clock driver
- 1 = Driver functions "Device Open" and "Device Close" are supported
- 0 = Function "Output until busy" is not supported
- 1 = Functions for direct reading and writing are supported
- 1 = Driver is a character driver

Calling a driver function

All driver functions are available to programs and utilities, except for driver function 00h, which can only be called once when you are loading a driver. Whenever possible, call the driver through MSCDEX function 10h, which is designed especially for this purpose. Function 10h handles various tasks which you would otherwise have to perform yourself if you call the driver function directly:

1. Determines the address of the device header (e.g., using MSCDEX function 01h)

2. Calls the strategy routine of the driver from its address in the device header, passing FAR pointer to ES:BX with the parameters of the function call (the parameter data block).

3. Calls the interrupt routine of the driver from its address in the device header.

Calling MSCDEX function 10h doesn't relieve you of the task of organizing the parameter data block. This structure is your way of communicating with the various driver functions. In this respect, a CD-ROM driver is no different than an ordinary DOS device driver.

MSCDEX function 10h also determines the subunit code which tells the driver which of the CD-ROM drives to access within the function call. Programmers who want to call a driver function on their own must enter this information in the parameter data block manually before calling the strategy routine. The information must be entered in the form of a byte at offset address +02h.

The structure and size of the parameter data block itself varies depending on function, and must be allocated n memory by the user prior to calling the function.

The offsets for the function number and the status word are fixed within the parameter data block. The status word returns information about the success or failure of the function following the call. The function number is always specified at offset address 01h in the parameter block. The status word is always returned at offset 03h of parameter block. If you have worked with other device drivers under DOS, then you'll already be familiar with this, because nothing has changed for CD-ROM drivers.

A typical parameter data block will look like the following:

Input and output parameters in the parameter data block when calling function 03h of a CD-ROM driver		
Address	Contents	Type
Input parameters		
+01h	Function number (03h)	1 BYTE
+02h	Subunit Code for the drive	1 BYTE
+0Eh	Pointer to data structure with additional information	1 PTR
Output parameter		
+03h	Status Word	1 WORD

A program should always begin by calling driver function 0Dh. This function informs the driver that another caller is using one of its functions so it can prepare for subsequent calls. The first function The program should end by calling driver function 0Eh which lets the driver know that it has finished processing. Driver function 0Eh 'closes' the driver to the program.

Status word

The status word tells the user whether the desired function was completed properly. If the highest-order bit is set after the function call, an error has occurred, whose meaning can be taken from the error code in bits 0 to 7.

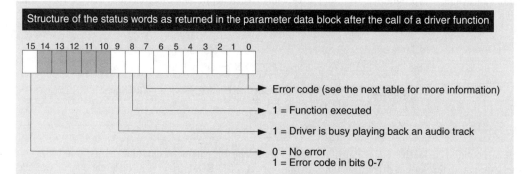

Structure of the status words as returned in the parameter data block after the call of a driver function

00h	Write access not possible	07h	Medium type unknown (wrong CD-ROM format)
01h	Unknown drive	08h	Sector not found
02h	Drive not ready (CD not inserted)	0Ah	Write error
03h	Unknown function/function not supported	0Bh	Read error
04h	CRC error	0Ch	General error
05h	Parameter data block wrong length	0Eh	Medium not inserted
06h	Seek error	0Fh	Invalid disk change

When the driver is used for audio playback, bit 9 is used for a special purpose. This is the BUSY bit. When this bit is set, the drive is busy playing an audio track. In this situation, all function calls which result in the movement of the read head are stopped with an error code until the track has finished playing. The BUSY bit is then cleared and the driver is again ready to accept function calls that move the read head.

Querying and setting status information

A frequently called driver function is 03h for direct reading. It returns status information that affect the driver, the CD-ROM drive and the inserted CD. For example, you can query the status of the drive or the current position of the read head. For audio, this function returns information about the number of individual tracks, their length and the total playing time of the CD. You can also use driver function 03h to query the CD's universal product code. This is a unique code of 13 BCD numbers that are also printed on the CD jacket. It is used as a bar code for identifying the CD at scanner cash registers.

Because of its uniqueness, some CD player software make use the UPC code. Many CD player software programs can catalog your CD albums by letting you type the title and then automatically saves both the title and UPC code in a database. The next time the user inserts the CD, the CD player software can automatically display the CD's title because it recognizes the UPC code.

Function 0Ch (direct write) is the counterpart of function 03h. Not only can you make various settings to the driver with this function, you can also perform such elementary tasks as ejecting a CD from the drive. This gives a program immediate control over the drive, something you cannot achieve with MSCDEX functions.

Playing audio tracks

An operation that you cannot perform through MSCDEX is to start the playback of audio tracks. Most CD-ROM drives have audio playback capability, particularly the drives bundled with sound cards. Besides the drive interface cable, a three or five pin cable usually connects the audio output of the CD-ROM drive to the audio input line of the sound card. The audio signals are then played through the speakers connected to the sound card.

During audio playback, MSCDEX is not involved. You can control the playback through driver functions 84h, 85h and 88h, which were especially introduced for this purpose. Before the first call you should obtain the drive status using driver function 03h. Then you can determine whether the driver is capable of audio playback and, if so, whether it has the appropriate functions.

CD-ROM device driver functions

The following pages list the 15 different functions that a CD-ROM driver, depending on what type it is and the CD-ROM drive itself, must support.

INIT	**Initialization (00h)**

Like an ordinary driver, the initialization function of a CD-ROM driver is only called once (during initialization of the driver). Even in the case of a CD-ROM driver, it's the DOS kernel, not MSCDEX, that first calls this function. Because the driver must pass itself off as a character driver to DOS, the value 0 is returned for the number of supported devices, as DOS expects from a character driver.

Input and output parameters when calling function 00h of a CD-ROM driver		
Address	Contents	Type
Input parameters		
+02h	Function number (00h)	1 BYTE
+0Eh	Maximum end address of the driver (DOS 5.0 and above)	1 PTR
+12h	Address of character that follows the equals sign after the DEVICE command in the CONFIG.SYS file	1 PTR
Output parameters		
+03h	Status Word	1 WORD
+0Dh	Number of supported devices, must be set to 0	1 BYTE
+0Eh	Address of first free byte after the driver	1 PTR
+16h	Drive label, must be set to 0 for MSCDEX	1 BYTE

Besides the normal initialization functions of a device driver, the CD-ROM driver must also place the device name in the device header during execution of the initialization function. MSCDEX, which won't be active until later, expects the name "MSCDEX00x" in the device header so it can recognize the driver as one of its own. The x represents a consecutive number that helps differentiate between the different CD-ROM device drivers in the system. The device drivers take these numbers (or the entire driver name) from the DEVICE= line in the CONFIG.SYS. This is the command line that loads the device drivers into memory. For example, here's a device driver for CD-ROM drives connected to a SoundBlaster card.

```
device=SBCD.SYS /P:220 /D:MSCD001
```

So it's the task of the initialization function to filter this name from the DEVICE= line and place it in the device header, where it must be filled with up to eight spaces.

IOCTL INPUT   Read (03h)

This function returns certain status information. The information reflects different facets of the current drive status. The caller determines which information is to be returned.

Input and output parameters when calling function 03h of a CD-ROM driver		
Address	Contents	Type
Input parameters		
+01h	Function number (03h)	1 BYTE
+02h	Subunit code for the drive	1 BYTE
+0Eh	Pointer to data structure with additional information	1 PTR
Output parameter		
+03h	Status Word	1 WORD

The caller passes a pointer to a data structure at offset address 0Eh in the parameter data block. The driver function infers the type of information that is to be returned from the data structure. The first byte of this data structure contains the code for the desired information. The byte serves as a type of subfunction number for the CD-ROM driver. The CD-ROM driver returns the desired information in the default sequence to the caller following this byte. The size of the buffer is determined by the subfunction and the parameters the subfunction returns.

If the driver does not know the specified subfunction number or it is not supported, it returns error code 3 for "Unknown Command" in the status word. If the driver can return the desired information, but is unable to do so at the time of the call, it returns error code 2 for "Drive Not Ready" in the status word.

The following subfunctions are available.

Subfunctions of function 03h of a CD-ROM driver					
Code	Meaning	Buffer size/BYTE	Code	Meaning	Buffer size/BYTE
0	Get address of device header	5	8	Request size of current volume	5
1	Get position of read head	6	9	Request information about disk change	2
2	Reserved	-	10	Request information about audio CD	7
3	Return error information	-	11	Request information about audio track	7
4	Get information about audio channels	9	12	Request Audio-Q-Channel	11
5	Request drive information	130	13	Request Audio-Sub-Channel	13
6	Request drive status	5	14	Request UPC (Universal Product Code)	11
7	Get sector size	4	15	Request status of audio playback	11

Subfunction 0   **Get address of device header**

Use this subfunction to determine the address of the device header. Other programs wanting to inspect the device header can also use the subfunction.

Data block for executing subfunction 0 of function 03h of a CD-ROM driver.		
Address	Contents	Type
To be loaded by caller		
+00h	Subfunction number (00h)	1 BYTE
To be loaded by the subfunction		
+01h	FAR pointer to device header	1 PTR

Subfunction 1   **Get position of read head**

Use this subfunction to determine the current position of the read head in HSG or Red Book format. Although the device driver is free to choose either format, it must signal the format in the data block of the subfunction using a corresponding flag.

Data block for execution of subfunction 1 of function 03h of a CD-ROM driver.		
Address	Contents	Type
To be loaded by caller		
+00h	Subfunction number (01h)	1 BYTE
To be loaded by subfunction		
+01h	Format (0 = HSG, 1 = Red Book)	1 BYTE
+02h	Position of read head as logical block number in HSG format or as a unit of minutes/seconds/frames in Red Book format	1 DWORD

Subfunction 3	**Return error information**

This subfunction is designated for future use. The structure of the returned error information is not defined. As a result, CD-ROM drivers don't have to implement this function.

Data block for executing subfunction 3 of function 03h of a CD-ROM driver.		
Address	Contents	Type
To be loaded by caller		
+00h	Subfunction number (03h)	1 BYTE
To be loaded by subfunction		
+01h	undetermined array with error information	variable

Subfunction 4	**Get information about audio channels**

Use this subfunction to request information about how the input channels are assigned to output channels as well as the volume of the output channels.

Data block for executing subfunction 4 of function 03h of a CD-ROM driver.		
Address	Contents	Type
To be loaded by caller		
+00h	Subfunction number (04h)	1 BYTE
To be loaded by subfunction		
+01h	Input channel (0 - 3) for output channel 0	1 BYTE
+02h	Volume for output channel 0 (0 - 0FFh)	1 BYTE
+03h	Input channel (0 - 3) for output channel 1	1 BYTE
+04h	Volume for output channel 1 (0 - 0FFh)	1 BYTE
+05h	Input channel (0 - 3) for output channel 2	1 BYTE
+06h	Volume for output channel 2 (0 - 0FFh)	1 BYTE
+07h	Input channel (0 - 3) for output channel 3	1 BYTE
+08h	Volume for output channel 3 (0 - 0FFh)	1 BYTE

Subfunction 5   **Request drive information**

This subfunction is reserved for use by the CD-ROM manufacturer. It allows up to 128 bytes of data to be read from the CD-ROM drive. This forms a type of communications channel between the drive and its firmware. This subfunction is not intended for use by users.

Data block for executing subfunction 5 of function 03h of a CD-ROM driver.		
Address	Contents	Type
To be loaded by caller		
+00h	Subfunction number (05h)	1 BYTE
To be loaded by subfunction		
+01h	Number of returned bytes (maximum 128)	1 BYTE
+02h	Buffer for transmission of information	max. 128 Byte

Subfunction 6   **Request drive status**

Use this subfunction to determine the current drive status and the capabilities of the drive.

Data block for execution of subfunction 6 of function 03h of a CD-ROM driver.		
Address	Contents	Type
To be loaded by caller		
+00h	Subfunction number (06h)	1 BYTE
To be loaded by subfunction		
+01h	Drive status	1 DWORD

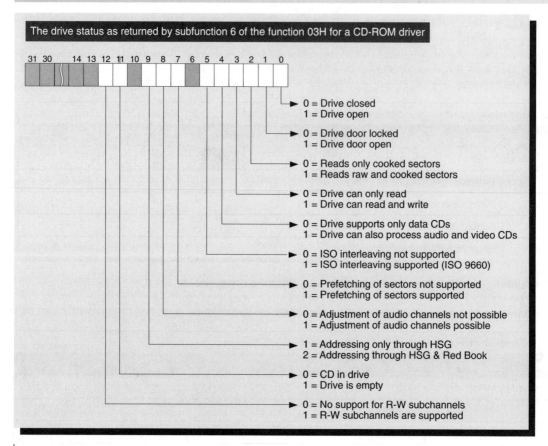

The drive status as returned by subfunction 6 of the function 03H for a CD-ROM driver

0 = Drive closed
1 = Drive open

0 = Drive door locked
1 = Drive door open

0 = Reads only cooked sectors
1 = Reads raw and cooked sectors

0 = Drive can only read
1 = Drive can read and write

0 = Drive supports only data CDs
1 = Drive can also process audio and video CDs

0 = ISO interleaving not supported
1 = ISO interleaving supported (ISO 9660)

0 = Prefetching of sectors not supported
1 = Prefetching of sectors supported

0 = Adjustment of audio channels not possible
1 = Adjustment of audio channels possible

1 = Addressing only through HSG
2 = Addressing through HSG & Red Book

0 = CD in drive
1 = Drive is empty

0 = No support for R-W subchannels
1 = R-W subchannels are supported

Subfunction 7   **Get sector size**

Use this subfunction to determine the sector size, either in raw or cooked mode.

Address	Contents	Type
Data block for execution of subfunction 7 of function 03h of a CD-ROM driver.		
To be loaded by caller		
+00h	Subfunction number (07h)	1 BYTE
+01h	Read mode (0 = raw, 1 = cooked)	1 BYTE
To be loaded by subfunction		
+02h	Sector size in specified mode in bytes	1 DWORD

Raw sectors take up 2352 bytes on a CD-ROM, and contain correction and control information in addition to usable data. Cooked sectors contain only pure usable data and comprise 2048 bytes (2K).

Subfunction 8	Request size of current volume

Use this subfunction to determine the size of the current volume on the CD. The subfunction gets its information by calculating the corresponding sector number at the position of the Lead-Out-Track, as recorded in the TOC (table of contents). Here is the conversion formula for converting the Red Book start position of the Lead-Out-Track to the HSG sector number:

```
(Minute * 60 * 75) + (Second * 75) + Frame.
```

Data block for execution of subfunction 8 of function 03h of a CD-ROM driver.		
Address	**Contents**	**Type**
To be loaded by caller		
+00h	Subfunction number (08h)	1 BYTE
To be loaded by subfunction		
+01h	Size of volume in sectors	1 DWORD

Subfunction 9	Request information about disk change

Use this subfunction to determine whether the CD in the drive has been changed since the last time you called this subfunction. This subfunction is preferable to driver function 1 (media check) which performs the same task but is not implemented with CD-ROM device drivers.

Data block for execution of subfunction 9 of function 03h of a CD-ROM driver.		
Address	**Contents**	**Type**
To be loaded by caller		
+00h	Subfunction number (09h)	1 BYTE
To be loaded by subfunction		
+01h	Status -1 : CD has been changed 0 : The driver doesn't know whether a change has taken place 1 : CD has not been changed	1 BYTE

Subfunction 10	Request information about Audio CD

Use this subfunction to determine the number of the first and last tracks, resulting in the number of tracks on the CD as well. The subfunction also returns the address of the Lead-Out-Track in Red Book format. This represents the total playing time of the CD.

Data block for execution of subfunction 10 of function 03h of a CD-ROM driver		
Address	Contents	Type
To be loaded by caller		
+00h	Subfunction number (0Ah)	1 BYTE
To be loaded by subfunction		
+01h	Number of first track	1 BYTE
+02h	Number of last track	1 BYTE
+03h	Beginning of Lead-Out-Track in Red Book format (playing time)	1 DWORD

Subfunction 11	Request information about audio track

Use this subfunction to determine the beginning of a track and status information about the track. The caller must also pass the number of the desired track in the buffer before calling the subfunction.

Data block for execution of subfunction 11 of function 03h of a CD-ROM driver.		
Address	Contents	Type
To be loaded by caller		
+00h	Subfunction number (0Bh)	1 BYTE
+01h	Number of the track	1 BYTE
To be loaded by subfunction		
+02h	Start of track in Red Book format	1 DWORD
+06h	Status information about track (Hi-Nibble CONTROL, Lo-Nibble ADR)	1 BYTE

The following codes apply to the status information, with bit 5 (x) serving as a copy bit, 0 = "digital copy allowed" and 1 = "digital copy not allowed". This code does not effect the ability of a PC to read the corresponding track, storing the information in digital format and then duplicating it. Instead, the code indicates to audio devices whether duplication of the track is allowed.

Status information about an audio track as returned by subfunction 11 of function 03h of a CD-ROM driver		
Code CONTROL	ADR	Meaning
00x0	0000b	Track contains 2 audio channels without Pre-Emphasis
00x1	0000b	2 audio channels with Pre-Emphasis
10x0	0000b	Track contains 4 audio channels without Pre-Emphasis
10x1	0000b	4 audio channels with Pre-Emphasis
01x0	0000b	Not an audio track, but a data track

Subfunction 12	Request audio Q-Sub-Channel

Use this subfunction during playback of audio tracks to get information about the current position of the read head both within the current track and in relation to the entire CD. Status information about the current track is also output. All the information comes from the Q-Sub-Channel of the CD, which is continuously read during playback.

Data block for execution of subfunction 12 of function 03h of a CD-ROM driver.		
Address	Contents	Type
To be loaded by caller		
+00h	Subfunction number (0Ch)	1 BYTE
To be loaded by subfunction		
+01h	Status information as with subfunction 11 (CONTROL and ADR bytes)	1 BYTE
+02h	Track number as BCD-Value, when ADR = 1, conversion to binary format takes place	1 BYTE
+03h	Current index as BCD-Value (POINT)	1 BYTE
+04h	Minute within the current track	1 BYTE
+05h	Second within the current track	1 BYTE
+06h	Frame within the current track	1 BYTE
+07h	0 (Reserved)	1 BYTE
+08h	Minute within total playing time	1 BYTE
+09h	Second within total playing time	1 BYTE
+0Ah	Frame within total playing time	1 BYTE

Subfunction 13	Request audio sub-channel

Use this subfunction to read the R-W subchannels, i.e., the low-order 6 bits from the subchannel of several sequential frames. This results in 96 bytes per sector that contain the subchannel information. Allocation of this subfunction by a CD-ROM device driver is optional and is indicated by bit 12 in the attribute of the device driver.

Data block for execution of subfunction 13 of function 03h of a CD-ROM driver.		
Address	Contents	Type
To be loaded by caller		
+00h	Subfunction number (0Dh)	1 BYTE
+01h	Number of first frame whose subchannel is to be read in Red Book format	1 DWORD
+05h	FAR pointer to buffer in which the subchannel information is to be placed	1 PTR
+09h	Number of frames to be read (sector number)	1 DWORD

Subfunction 14	Request UPC

Use this subfunction to read the universal product code, a 13 digit number that identifies the CD. This number is also printed on the CD jacket in the form of a bar code (for scanner cash registers). This code is recorded in the Q subchannel of a mode 2 frame.

Data block for execution of subfunction 14 of function 03h of a CD-ROM driver.		
Address	Contents	Type
To be loaded by caller		
+00h	Subfunction number (0Eh)	1 BYTE
To be loaded by subfunction		
+01h	CONTROL/ADR-Flag	1 BYTE
+02h	UPC/EAN-Code	7 BYTE
+09h	0	1 BYTE
+0Ah	Reserved	1 BYTE

A value of 0 is returned in the CONTROL and ADR bytes, if the CD does not contain a UPC. Otherwise, the UPC is present as a BCD number, with each of the 7 bytes containing two BCD digits. The last digit, i.e., the low-order nibble in the seventh byte, is always 0.

Subfunction 15	Request status of audio playback

Use this subfunction during playback of audio CDs, to determine the current status of the playback. Among this information is a pause flag and the start and end position for the next RESUME command.

Data block for execution of subfunction 15 of function 03h of a CD-ROM driver.		
Address	Contents	Type
To be loaded by caller		
+00h	Subfunction number (0Fh)	1 BYTE
To be loaded by subfunction		
+01h	Audio status with bit 0 as pause flag Bit 0 = 0 : Pause not active 　　　　 1 : Pause active	
+03h	Start position for next RESUME command as Red Book address	1 DWORD
+07h	End position for next RESUME command as Red Book address	1 DWORD

INPUT FLUSH	Erase input buffer (07h)

Use this function to erase all its input buffers, cancel any requests not yet processed and any driver calls.

Input and output parameters when calling function 07h of a CD-ROM driver		
Address	Contents	Type
Input parameters		
+01h	Function number (07h)	1 BYTE
+02h	Subunit code for the drive	1 BYTE
Output parameter		
+03h	Status Word	1 WORD

OUTPUT FLUSH   **Empty output buffer (0Bh)**

Use this function to write all unwritten output buffers to the CD. This driver must refer to a CD-ROM recorder.

Input and output parameters when calling function 0Bh of a CD-ROM driver		
Address	Contents	Type
Input parameters		
+01h	Function number (0Bh)	1 BYTE
+02h	Subunit code for the drive	1 BYTE
Output parameter		
+03h	Status Word	1 WORD

IOCTL OUTPUT   **Write (0Ch)**

This function lets you specify various settings for CD-ROM device driver. For example, you can open and close the drive door and eject the CD.

Input and output parameters when calling function 0Ch of a CD-ROM driver		
Address	Contents	Type
Input parameters		
+01h	Function number (0Ch)	1 BYTE
+02h	Subunit code for the drive	1 BYTE
+0Eh	Pointer to data structure with additional information	1 PTR
Output parameter		
+03h	Status Word	1 WORD

Like the Read driver function, the caller must pass a pointer to a data structure at offset address 0Eh in the parameter data block. The driver function determines the type of setting to be made from this data structure. The first byte of this data structure must contain the code for the desired settings, as a type of subfunction number. Depending on the subfunction, the caller must add various additional information to this byte so the parameter data block describes the function call completely.

The following subfunctions are available:

Subfunctions of function 0Ch of a CD-ROM device driver		
Code	Meaning	Buffer size/BYTE
0	Eject CD-ROM	1
1	Lock/unlock drive door	2
2	Reset drive	1
3	Set audio channels	9
4	Send control information directly to drive	variable
5	Close door	1

Subfunction 0   Eject CD-ROM

Use this subfunction to eject the inserted CD, unlocking the drive door at the same time.

Data block for execution of subfunction 0 of function 0Ch of a CD-ROM driver.		
Address	Contents	Type
To be loaded by caller		
+00h	Subfunction number (00h)	1 BYTE

Subfunction 1   Lock/unlock drive door

Use this function to lock or unlock the drive door. Locking the door is required for playing the CD and unlocking it is required for removing the CD. Not all drives are physically able to lock the door. Nevertheless, this subfunction must also be called with these drives.

Data block for execution of subfunction 1 of function 0Ch of a CD-ROM driver.		
Address	Contents	Type
To be loaded by caller		
+00h	Subfunction number (01h)	1 BYTE
+01h	0 = unlock, 1 = lock	1 BYTE

Subfunction 2   Reset drive

Use this subfunction after an error to reset and reinitialize the drive.

Data block for execution of subfunction 2 of function 0Ch of a CD-ROM driver.		
Address	Contents	Type
To be loaded by caller		
+00h	Subfunction number (02h)	1 BYTE

Subfunction 3 — Set audio channels

Use this subfunction to set the audio channels. You can set the current assignment between the four input and output channels as well as the volume of the output channels.

Address	Contents	Type
Data block for execution of subfunction 3 of function 0Ch of a CD-ROM driver.		
Address	Contents	Type
To be loaded by caller		
+00h	Subfunction number (03h)	1 BYTE
+01h	Input channel (0 - 3) for output channel 0	1 BYTE
+02h	Volume for output channel 0 (0 - 0FFh)	1 BYTE
+03h	Input channel (0 - 3) for output channel 1	1 BYTE
+04h	Volume for output channel 1 (0 - 0FFh)	1 BYTE
+05h	Input channel (0 - 3) for output channel 2	1 BYTE
+06h	Volume for output channel 2 (0 - 0FFh)	1 BYTE
+07h	Input channel (0 - 3) for output channel 3	1 BYTE
+08h	Volume for output channel 3 (0 - 0FFh)	1 BYTE

Not all drives are capable of setting the volume of the various channels to the precision in the range of 0 to 255. With these drives, the driver has the task of reproducing the specified value in one of the drive's possible settings. In the simplest case 0 means channel off and 255 means "maximum volume".

Channel 0 represents the left output and 1 represents the right output, while 2 and 3 stand for the two "Prime outputs" which make quadrophonic sound possible. Output channel 2 represents the left prime channel, while 3 represents the right channel. Drivers whose drive only recognizes the two normal stereo outputs simply ignore the settings for channels 2 and 3.

Subfunction 4 — Send control information directly to drive

This subfunction is reserved for communication between the firmware of a CD-ROM drive (utilities, for example) and the drive. The subfunction creates a communications channel through which the firmware can directly control the drive.

Address	Contents	Type
Data block for execution of subfunction 4 of function 0Ch of a CD-ROM driver.		
Address	Contents	Type
To be loaded by caller		
+00h	Subfunction number (04h)	1 BYTE
+01h	Any data	variable

Subfunction 5 — Close door

Use this subfunction to close the door automatically on a drive with that capability.

Data block for execution of subfunction 5 of function 0Ch of a CD-ROM driver.		
Address	Contents	Type
To be loaded by caller		
+00h	Subfunction number (05h)	1 BYTE

DEVICE OPEN   Open device (0Dh)

Use this function to notify the CD-ROM driver that it intends to use CD-ROM driver functions.

Input and output parameters when calling function 0Dh of a CD-ROM driver		
Address	Contents	Type
Input parameters		
+01h	Function number (0Dh)	1 BYTE
+02h	Subunit code for the drive	1 BYTE
Output parameter		
+03h	Status Word	1 WORD

DEVICE CLOSE   Close Device (0Eh)

Use this function to notify the CD-ROM driver that it has completed using the CD-ROM driver functions.

Input and output parameters when calling function 0Eh of a CD-ROM driver		
Address	Contents	Type
Input parameters		
+01h	Function number (0Eh)	1 BYTE
+02h	Subunit code for the drive	1 BYTE
Output parameter		
+03h	Status Word	1 WORD

READ LONG   Read sectors (80h)

Use this function to read sectors of the CD directly from the CD-ROM device driver, with both Red Book addressing and HSG being supported. You can request the sectors as cooked sectors with the pure 2048 bytes of usable data, or as raw sectors. If you request raw sectors, 2352 bytes must be reserved for each sector in the buffer. This is because the driver function will then copy the sync and header bytes and the EDC bytes to the buffer in addition to the user data. If a driver cannot return part of the control data, it pads the corresponding portion of the sector contents with NULL bytes so the rest of the sector layout does not shift.

Input and output parameters when calling function 80h of a CD-ROM driver		
Address	Contents	Type
Input parameters		
+01h	Function number (80h)	1 BYTE
+02h	Subunit code for the drive	1 BYTE
+0Dh	Addressing mode 0 = HSG, 1 = Red Book	1 BYTE
+0Eh	FAR pointer to buffer for receiving read sectors	1 PTR
+12h	Number of sectors to be read	1 WORD
+14h	First sector to be read	1 DWORD
+18h	Read mode 0 = Cooked (2048 bytes), 1 = Raw (2352 bytes)	1 BYTE
+19h	Interleave Size	1 BYTE
+1Ah	Interleave Skip	1 BYTE
Output parameter		
+03h	Status Word	1 WORD

The two interleave parameters are specified only if the driver supports reading in interleave mode. In this case, Interleave Size represents the number of contiguous sectors and Interleave Skip represents the number of sectors that have to be skipped to get to the next part of the file.

READ LONG PREFETCH	Read ahead (82h)

This function was introduced to increase the performance of CD-ROM drives. Operating systems use this function (in our case, the operating system is MSCDEX) to have the driver read pre-determined sectors that will probably be needed soon. For example, it makes sense to use Read Long Prefetch when a large directory occupies contiguous sectors or when a program reads a file from CD-ROM step by step. In such situations, MSCDEX is able to guess which sectors will be needed soon.

Before MSCDEX passes the read sectors on to the operating system or program, it can use this driver function to read the next sectors. This is a method of getting around the relatively slow access times of a CD-ROM drive, because when the guess turns out to be right, the driver will have already placed the desired sectors in a type of internal cache and can return them immediately. At the very least, the driver will have performed a seek on the specified sector so that access can take place more quickly.

Input and output parameters when calling function 82h of a CD-ROM driver		
Address	Contents	Type
Input parameters		
+01h	Function number (82h)	1 BYTE
+02h	Subunit code for the drive	1 BYTE
+0Dh	Addressing mode 0 = HSG, 1 = Red Book	1 BYTE
+12h	Number of sectors to be read	1 WORD
+14h	First sector to be read	1 DWORD
+18h	Read mode 0 = Cooked (2048 bytes), 1 = Raw (2352 bytes)	1 BYTE
+19h	Interleave Size	1 BYTE
+1Ah	Interleave Skip	1 BYTE
Output parameter		
+03h	Status Word	1 WORD

The data to be passed during the call for the driver is identical to the data of driver function 80h, except for the missing buffer address. A buffer address isn't required, since this function returns no data. Instead it's a notification to the driver than a read operation is imminent. The driver will relinquish control to the caller immediately. The driver can then prepare for the expected read access in the background while the user is performing other programming tasks.

SEEK   **Find sector (83h)**

Use this function to move the read head of the CD-ROM drive to the specified sector thereby eliminating the seek time for a subsequent read access to this sector. The driver will relinquish control to the caller immediately. The driver can then perform the seek to the desired sector in the background while the user is performing other programming tasks.

Input and output parameters when calling function 83h of a CD-ROM driver		
Address	Contents	Type
Input parameters		
+01h	Function number (83h)	1 BYTE
+02h	Subunit code for the drive	1 BYTE
+0Dh	Addressing mode 0 = HSG, 1 = Red Book	1 BYTE
+14h	Sought sector	1 DWORD
Output parameter		
+03h	Status Word	1 WORD

PLAY AUDIO   Play audio (84h)

Use this function to start the playback of an audio track. The function doesn't operate at track level, but rather at sector level, so the address of a track must be determined beforehand. You use subfunction 11 of driver function 3 (Read) for this purpose. By specifying a sector address, playback can also be started in the middle of the track.

The driver returns to the caller immediately after playback starts and continues playback in the background until the specified ending address is reached. The function uses the Busy bit in the status word to indicate that the driver is in play mode and therefore cannot accept any read or seek operations. A driver that doesn't support playback of audio CDs simply ignores this function call and doesn't set the Busy bit.

If a program wants to wait until the driver finishes playback, it is advisable to use permanent polling of the audio status using subfunction 15 of driver function 3 (Read). Subfunction 15 returns the corresponding information.

Input and output parameters when calling function 84h of a CD-ROM driver		
Address	Contents	Type
Input parameters		
+01h	Function number (84h)	1 BYTE
+02h	Subunit code for the drive	1 BYTE
+0Dh	Addressing mode 0 = HSG, 1 = Red Book	1 BYTE
+0Eh	First sector to be played	1 DWORD
+12h	Number of sectors to be played	1 DWORD
Output parameter		
+03h	Status Word	1 WORD

STOP AUDIO   Stop audio (85h)

Use this function to stop audio playback. If this function is called while the drive is in pause mode, only the start and end positions for the next RESUME command are reset (see driver function 3, subfunction 15).

Input and output parameters when calling function 85h of a CD-ROM driver		
Address	Contents	Type
Input parameters		
+01h	Function number (85h)	1 BYTE
+02h	Subunit code for the drive	1 BYTE
Output parameter		
+03h	Status Word	1 WORD

WRITE LONG   Write sectors (86h)

Use this function to write individual sectors to a CD-ROM recorder. This function allows for various sector format, although the specification requires that the drive support only Mode 1. The other formats are optional.

Input and output parameters when calling function 86h of a CD-ROM driver		
Address	Contents	Type
Input parameters		
+01h	Function number (86h)	1 BYTE
+02h	Subunit code for the drive	1 BYTE
+0Dh	Addressing mode 0 = HSG, 1 = Red Book	1 BYTE
+0Eh	FAR pointer to buffer with sectors	1 PTR
+12h	Number of sectors to be written	1 WORD
+14h	First sector to be written	1 DWORD
+18h	Write mode 0 = Mode 0 1 = Mode 1 2 = Mode 2 Form 1 3 = Mode 2 Form 2	1 BYTE
+19h	Interleave Size	1 BYTE
+1Ah	Interleave Skip	1 BYTE
Output parameter		
+03h	Status Word	1 WORD

Depending on the write mode, the data to be written has varying lengths. In Mode 0, the buffer is ignored since the sectors will be filled with null values. In Mode 1 and Mode 2 Form 1 the buffer contains 2,048 bytes of data per sector written. In Mode 2 Form 2 the buffer contains 2,336 bytes of data per sector.

WRITE LONG VERIFY   Write sectors with verification (87h)

Use this function to write and verify individual sectors to a CD-ROM recorder. The parameters for this function are identical to Write Long (86h) driver function except that the data is verified immediately following the write operation. The results of the verification are returned in the status word. A write error leaves an appropriate error message in the status word.

RESUME AUDIO   Resume audio playback (88h)

Use this function to resume playback after playback has been stopped by function 85h.

Input and output parameters when calling function 88h of a CD-ROM driver		
Address	Contents	Type
Input parameters		
+01h	Function number (88h)	1 BYTE
+02h	Subunit code for the drive	1 BYTE
Output parameter		
+03h	Status Word	1 WORD

Program Examples

So you can see some of these functions in action, we've written a module named CDUTIL.C which contains wrapper functions for all MSCDEX and driver functions. CDUTIL includes the CDUTIL.H header file, in which all constants and types required for working with the functions of CDUTIL.C are declared. The following tables give you an overview of the available functions, arranged by task area.

Functions for converting between the various addressing modes	
Function	**Task**
Time2Frame	Converts time to number of frames
Time2HSG	Converts time to HSG address
Time2REDBOOK	Converts time to REDBOOK address
FrameTime	Splits number of frames into minute, second, frame
REDBOOK2Time	Splits REDBOOK address into minute, second, frame
HSG2Time	Splits HSG address into minute, second, frame
REDBOOK2HSG	Convert REDBOOK address to HSG address
HSG2REDBOOK	Convert HSG address to REDBOOK address

Functions for calling MSCDEX functions	
Function	**Task**
MSCDEX_GetNumberOfDriveLetters	Get number of supported drives
MSCDEX_Installed	MSCDEX installation check
MSCDEX_GetCDRomDriveDeviceList	Get information about drive letters
MSCDEX_GetCopyrightFilename	Get name of copyright file
MSCDEX_GetAbstractFilename	Get name of abstract file
MSCDEX_GetBibDocFilename	Get name of BibDoc file
MSCDEX_ReadVTOC	Read Volume Table of Contents (VTOC)
MSCDEX_AbsoluteRead	Read data from sector(s)
MSCDEX_AbsoluteWrite	Write data to sector(s)
MSCDEX200_CDRomDriveCheck	Is drive a CD-ROM drive?
MSCDEX200_GetVersion	Get MSCDEX version
MSCDEX200_GetCDromDriveLetters	Get all CD-ROM drive letters
MSCDEX200_GetVDPreference	Get Volume Descriptor Preference
MSCDEX200_SetVDPreference	Set Volume Descriptor Preference

Functions for calling MSCDEX functions (Continued)	
Function	**Task**
MSCDEX200_GetDirectoryEntry	Read directory entry of a file
MSCDEX210_SendDeviceRequest	Send device request to device, Version 2.1 and above
MSCDEX_SendDeviceRequest	Send device request to device prior to Version 2.1
MSCDEX_ReadWriteReq	Run MSCDEX-IOCTLI_READ/WRITE request
_CallStrategy	Send device request to device driver

Functions for calling driver functions	
Function	**Task**
cd_IsError	Does status word describe an error?
cd_GetReqHdrError	Get error code
cd_IsReqHdrBusy	Device still busy?
cd_IsReqHdrDone	Last device command completely processed?
cd_GetDeviceHeaderAdress	Get address of device header
cd_GetLocationOfHead	Get location of (read)/write head
cd_GetAudioChannelInfo	Get assignment of input channels to output channels
cd_ReadDriveBytes	Read drive bytes
cd_GetDevStat	Read device status (drive status)
cd_GetSectorSize	Get size of a sector
cd_GetVolumeSize	Get number of sectors of a CD
cd_GetMediaChanged	CD changed?
cd_GetAudioDiskInfo	Get number of titles (songs, tracks)
cd_GetAudioTrackInfo	Get information about a title
cd_IsDataTrack	Is Track an audio track or a data track?
cd_GetTrackLen	Get size of a track.
cd_QueryAudioChannel	Query time information from Q-Sub-Channel
cd_GetAudioSubChannelInfo	Get information about audio subchannels
cd_GetUPCode	Get universal product code (UPC)
cd_GetAudioStatusInfo	Get current audio status
cd_Eject	Open tray
cd_CloseTray	Close tray
cd_LockDoor	Lock/unlock door

Functions for calling driver functions (Continued)	
Function	**Task**
cd_Reset	Reset drive
cd_SetAudioChannelInfo	Set assignment between CD channels and output channels
cd_WriteDriveBytes	Writes drive data
cd_PlayAudio	Play audio track
cd_StopAudio	Stop audio playback
cd_ResumeAudio	Resume audio playback
cd_Seek	Find sector
cd_ReadLong	Read sectors
cd_ReadLongPrefetch	Prepare to read sectors
cd_WriteLong	Write sectors
cd_WriteLongVerify	Write with verify
cd_FastForward	Fast forward current music output 2 seconds

Functions for outputting information to screen	
Function	**Task**
cd_PrintDiskTracks	Display all titles and playing times
cd_PrintActPlay	Display playing times and title of current track
cd_PrintSektor	Dump sector contents onto screen
cd_PrintDirEntry	Decode directory entry
cd_PrintDevStat	Output device status
cd_PrintUPCode	Output UPC as BCD number

We recommend that you use CDROM.C as an example of working with functions from CDUTIL.C. CDROM is a program that lets you display diverse information about CDs. With CDROM you can output the number of tracks and their duration, the directory entries of the files and the contents of sectors. Also, you can also use this utility to play audio tracks (if your CD-ROM drive has this capability).

You can set all the functions from the command line when you call the program, for example

```
CDROM D: -UPC
```

displays the universal product code of the inserted CD. If you call the program without any switches/parameters, it displays a listing of the different options on the screen.

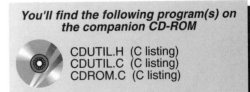

You'll find the following program(s) on the companion CD-ROM

CDUTIL.H (C listing)
CDUTIL.C (C listing)
CDROM.C (C listing)

Chapter 38

Sound Blaster Compatible Cards

Early multimedia was synonymous with sound cards. Today's multimedia is much more, but sound cards remain a very important part of the equation. One of the main reasons for popularity of sound cards in the late 1980s were computer games. These games removed the "business machine" stigma attached to the PC. Today, sound cards are everywhere.

There are many different makes and style of sound cards. However, as with other classes of peripherals, sound cards standards quickly evolved so programmers weren't forced to write for an unlimited number of different sound cards. The name for this standard is the same as the name of the most popular sound card: Sound Blaster. Creative Labs, the manufacturer of the Sound Blaster, developed a card with good features, ease of installation and reasonable priced. By dominating the early sound card market their card became the standard.

Most sound cards today are "Sound Blaster compatible". This chapter discusses these cards.

The Family Of Sound Blaster Cards

Sound Blaster cards from a few years ago are unlike the cards of today. Like most peripherals, new features, improvements and upgrades have been added to the Sound Blaster cards. These features cover three major functional areas:

➤ Generating synthetic sound. This task is performed by the Yamaha OPL chip found in Sound Blaster cards, and many other compatibles. This chip produces up to 11 voices which you can play back simultaneously. With skillful programming, this chip can coax a veritable fireworks of sound from your PC.

There have been four different versions of the OPL chip, Version 1, 2, 3, and finally Version 4. Version 2 that is still considered to be the standard for Sound Blaster compatibility.

➤ Sampling sound. This task is performed by a "Digital Sound Processor" (DSP) found in Sound Blaster cards. The DSP is manufactured by Creative Labs and also licensed to other manufacturers. In sampling, analog signals from a CD, stereo equipment or a microphone are recorded and saved onto a storage device for later playback.

➤ Mixing sound. A mixer controls the volume of the various sound sources and combines them.

Blaster environment variable

Regardless of the different capabilities of the various cards in the Sound Blaster family, all Sound Blaster cards use the "Blaster environment variable", which is defined in the AUTOEXEC.BAT file. If you have a Sound Blaster card installed in your computer, there's a command line in your AUTOEXEC.BAT file that look similar to this:

```
SET BLASTER=A220 I5 D1 H5 P330 T6
```

This environment variable contains all the important information about the port address of the installed sound card, the interrupt being used, the DMA channel and more. Programs that access the Sound Blaster card usually query this environment variable so they can determine the parameters for accessing the sound card. The components of this environment variable specify the following information:

Parameters of the Blaster environment variable	
Parameter	Meaning
A	base port address of the card
I	interrupt number used
D	8-bit DMA channel
H	16-bit DMA channel, for cards supporting 16-bit DMA transfer
M	base port address of Sound Blaster Mixer
P	MIDI port
T	Sound Blaster card identification (1 = early versions of Sound Blaster, 3 = Sound Blaster 2.0, 6 = Sound Blaster 16)

One piece of information the variable does not disclose is the exact type of Sound Blaster card installed. However, by knowing the base address, it's relatively easy to determine this information, as we'll see shortly.

As you evaluate the environment variable, keep in mind the sequence of parameters may change. The A and I parameters are mandatory. The sample programs in later sections contain routines that analyze the environment variable.

This chapter is made of many sections, but they're all centered around the most important aspects of Sound Blaster cards: synthetic sound generation using FM synthesis, sampling using the digital sound processor of the card, and controlling the mixer and speech output.

We've omitted MIDI which is available on only a few Sound Blaster cards. Creative Labs does provide library routines for performing many of the tasks. However, most of the examples here involve direct programming of the card and introduce you to some custom libraries. While there is still a certain compatibility between cards from different manufacturers on a hardware level, there is no such thing on a driver level. Since there is no Sound Blaster standard on this level, we have given preference to direct programming.

FM Synthesis

Frequency modulation, also called FM or FM synthesis, is the most common form of synthetic sound production using PC sound cards. Like all procedures for synthetic sound production, the goal of FM synthesis is to reproduce the signal progression of natural voices and instruments as true to the original as possible. Therefore, to understand this procedure, you must first look closely at the physical nature of sound.

The physical nature of sounds and frequency modulation

We can "see" sounds generated by a guitar, a piano or a trumpet by using an oscilloscope. The oscilloscope displays sounds as oscillations or vibrations whose path follows a type of sine curve. Such a sine curve is characterized by constant highs and lows over time. It begins with a continuous vibration of the sound carrier, for example a guitar string as it is struck. The string vibrates depending on how hard it is plucked by the player. However, it always vibrates at its characteristic speed, or "frequency". It's this frequency which determines the pitch. For example, the concert pitch of A has a frequency of 400 Hertz (1 Hertz = 1 oscillation per second).

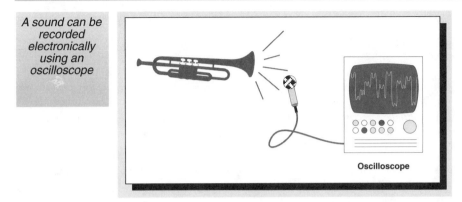

A sound can be recorded electronically using an oscilloscope

Oscilloscope

The frequency produced is predetermined by the tautness, or tension of the string. The guitar player can modify this frequency by turning the guitar peg to tighten or loosen the string. Anyone who has ever held a guitar in their hands is familiar with this effect. The more you tighten the string, the higher the pitch it generates because the string vibrates more frequently. With an electronic recording, this effect is expressed by a higher frequency, i.e., a faster sequence of highs and lows in the sine curve.

However, frequency is not the only factor which determines the appearance of the sine curve. The force with which the string is struck determines the intensity of the highs and lows of the sine curve. The force determines the amplitude of the vibration. Frequency and amplitude, then, are the deciding attributes of a sound. Therefore, from a mathematical standpoint, you can represent the frequency rate of a sound with the following formula (where pi = 3.14):

```
f(t) = Amplitude * Sine(Frequency * t * 2 pi)
```

with t representing the time in s (seconds). The factor 2 pi must be used because the sine function is a radian measure. This requires conversion between the argument t and the radian measure. Because a sine function always returns a value between 1 and -1, the amplitude in this formula provides the maximum and minimum value of the function result.

Sound production is, of course, more complicated in practice than in theory. The sound pattern of a natural instrument is much more complex because several sine waves usually overlap. Moreover, the amplitude doesn't remain constant during the progression of the sound, but instead, builds up first, only to slowly decrease, which the listener perceives as the sound fading away.

Still, it is true that you can produce sounds using a simple sine generator, even if the sounds are relatively simple. Daily life is full of such sounds. The dial tone of the telephone, the buzzing of an alarm clock or the beeping of the microwave oven are just a few examples.

Although a simple sine generator can't imitate the complex sound pattern of a guitar or a trumpet, such sine generators are the only resources available to the Sound Blaster and other sound cards. Sine generators are relatively easy to implement and can be found in other areas inside a PC, for example in the timer chip and in the battery-backed real-time clock.

The principal of frequency modulation

Frequency modulation is a technique for creating complex sound patterns. Intuitively, you might think the output of several sine generators are simply combined to make the sounds. However in practice, the sine generators are arranged so the output signal of one generator also becomes the input signal of a second generator. The first generator is termed the modulator, while the second one is called the carrier.

Here's what it looks like mathematically:

```
f(t) = Amplitude2 * Sin(Frequency2 * t  * 2 pi + (Amplitude1 * Sin(Frequency1 * t * 2pi))
pi = p = 3.14...
```

```
Amplitude2: Carrier
Amplitude1: Modulator
Frequency1: Modulator
Frequency2: Carrier
```

This function says the carrier (*Amplitude2*) varies between *-Amplitude1* and *+Amplitude1* over time *t*. This means that sin(t+1) does not necessarily follow sin(t), but depending on the values of *Frequency* and *Amplitude* of the first Modulator, may be sin(t-5) or sin(t+100).

The following illustration shows that you can generate very diverse signal patterns which are more similar to the natural signal progression of an instrument than are possible by simply adding two sine generators.

Various Signal Progressions generated by frequency modulation

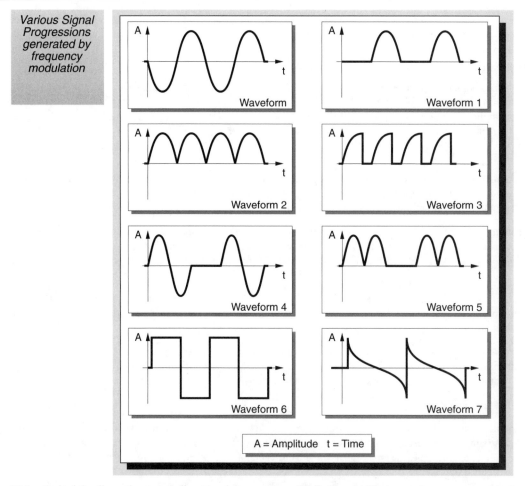

We've limited the discussion to coupling two sine generators. While it's possible to couple more generators to create more complex signal progressions, two is a practical limit. Here's why. The Yamaha OPL2 chip used in many sound cards has a two generator limit. A successor, the Yamaha OPL3, couples up to four sine generators, but the chip isn't found in many cards and isn't considered a Sound Blaster standard. So for the remainder of this chapter, we'll focus on the OPL2. Yamaha refers to the sine generators as operator cells.

Making sound with operator cells and channels

An operator cell is the lowest level of sound generation. The OPL chip has eighteen such cells. Two cells - a carrier and a modulator - are used to generate one voice. Therefore nine different voices can be played simultaneously.

A channel is the next higher level of sound generation. Two operator cells are paired to make one channel.

In addition to the standard mode of nine voices, the OPL has a second mode of operation with six different voices (using twelve cells) and five percussion instruments (using the additional six cells).

Which of the two modes you choose depends on your requirements. If you want to play a drum or other percussion instrument, you can use the second mode. On the other hand, the nine voice mode is preferable for playing classical music. We'll see how to select between modes shortly.

The Sound Blaster Pro sound card contains two OPL chips for a total of 36 cells. This means there are a total of 18 channels. To program the different chips, use a separate port address and output channel. While the first of the two chips is located at the original port address and becomes the left output channel of the Sound Blaster Pro card, the second chip is found at a different address and becomes the right output channel. Programming the two chips are identical except for the port address. We'll only mention that to be Sound Blaster compatible, you may want to limit yourself in programming only one of the OPL chips.

Next we'll describe the parameters of an operator cell. Experimenting with the different settings is the best way to understand the significance of the parameters. At the end of this chapter, we'll present a program for interactively testing and hearing the results of various parameter settings.

The cell envelope

From the guitar string example, we know that generating sound is more than just turning it on. On the contrary, a sound slowly builds until it reaches its greatest volume (amplitude). The volume remains at this level for a specific time, depending on the instrument, before fading. For example, the sound from a flute fades immediately, whereas the sound from a bell continues for several seconds, even though it rings more softly.

The *envelope* describes a voice's sound progression characteristics. Four parameters are used to specify the envelope for a voice: attack, decay, sustain and release.

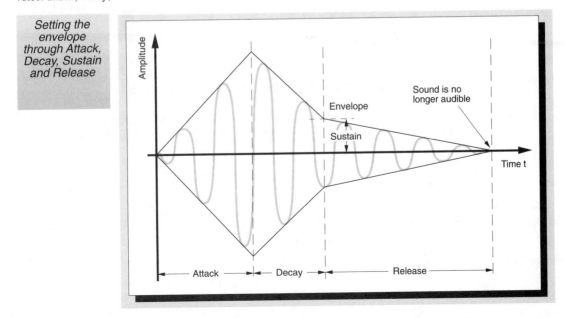

Setting the envelope through Attack, Decay, Sustain and Release

These parameters are collectively referred to as ADSR. For a sound card channel, you any of the ADSR parameters can be set to values from 0 to 15.

The *attack* parameter is responsible for the first phase of sound generation. It specifies how quickly the sound reaches its full volume or amplitude. An attack parameter of zero represents a very gradual increase. An attack parameter of 15 means the sound immediately rises to maximum.

The other parameters describe the other three phases of sound generation. These specify how quickly the sound fades away and falls from the maximum amplitude to a zero amplitude.

Different envelopes through different settings of attack, decay, sustain and release

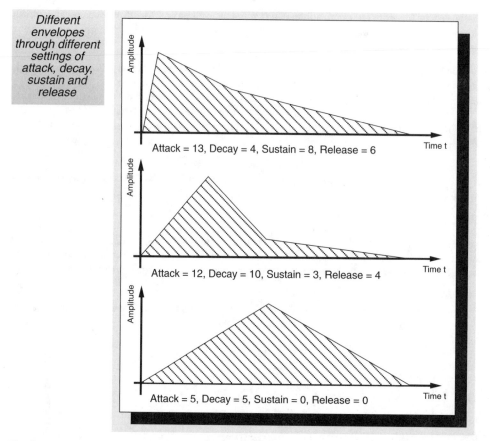

Attack = 13, Decay = 4, Sustain = 8, Release = 6

Attack = 12, Decay = 10, Sustain = 3, Release = 4

Attack = 5, Decay = 5, Sustain = 0, Release = 0

The *decay* parameter specifies the amount of time for the sound to fall from its maximum to the level specified by the *sustain* parameter. The greater the decay value, the faster the level falls to sustain level. A decay value of zero means the level falls quite slowly, while a value of 15 causes the level to drop almost immediately.

The *sustain* parameter specifies the amplitude level at which the transition between decay and release takes place. The sustain parameter refers to the relationship between maximum and zero amplitude. The greater the value, the shorter the decay phase.

The *release* parameter specifies the amount of time for the sound to fade. The greater the value, the faster the sound disappears. While a sound may no longer be heard at the end of the release phase (because the amplitude has reached the value 0), the generator cells nevertheless continues to operate. We'll discuss this again shortly.

A second envelope type is the continuous envelope.

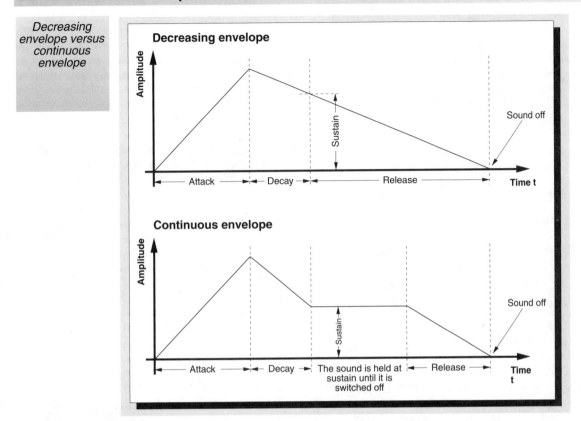

Decreasing envelope versus continuous envelope

A continuous envelope is also defined by the attack, decay, sustain and release parameters. However it differs from a decreasing envelope, described above, in one important way - the programmer can sustain the sound as long as he wishes.

Like a decreasing envelope, you specify the duration of the attack and decay phases for the continuous envelope using the parameters for these variables. The OPL chip holds the sound at a constant amplitude in the sustain phase until the program switches off the sound through the appropriate channel. Only then does the sound move to the release phase and fade away.

The envelope you choose depends on the instrument you're simulating. With string instruments and all other instruments that fade by themselves, use the decreasing envelope. After all, there is no way with this envelope to determine the duration of the sound after making it. However, it's a different story with wind instruments, for example, which can hold their sounds until the musician runs out of breath or the program ends. Therefore, we recommend using the continuous envelope with this type of instrument.

When you use the decreasing envelope, you also have the option of setting automatic envelope reduction for high notes. This allows you to vary the sound for pianos and other stringed instruments, for example, where the high notes fade faster than the low notes.

The mute factor

The *mute factor* lets you lower the amplitude of an operator cell when you want one voice to be softer than the others. You can choose a setting between 0 and 63 according to following formula:

```
Mute = mute factor * 0.75 dB      (where dB is Decibel measurement)
```

The multiplication factor

Use the *multiplication factor* to set the frequency ratio between the modulator and the carrier operator cells. While the frequency of the two cells can be different depending on the pitch of the desired tone, the ratio between modulator and carrier frequency for a given instrument is always the same. This is what gives an instrument its own characteristic timbre and is the reason the frequency is set for a channel, not for a generator cell. The frequency at which the cell oscillates is a result of multiplying the channel frequency by the multiplication factor of the cell.

The multiplication factor for a cell can be a value between 0 and 15. This value is multiplied by the frequency of the channel according to the table on the right. For example, the channel frequency with a setting of 0 would be cut in half.

The multiplication factor determines the frequency of a cell			
Multiplication factor	Frequency factor	Multiplication factor	Frequency factor
0	0.5	8	8
1	1	9	9
2	2	10	10
3	3	11	10
4	4	12	12
5	5	13	12
6	6	14	15
7	7	15	15

To set an uneven ratio between the modulator and the carrier, e.g., 5:7, you must set a multiplication factor of 5 for the modulator and a multiplication factor of 7 for the carrier. However, the channel frequency compared with the actual desired frequency on the carrier must then be divided by 7. The OPL chip doesn't make the conversion, instead, the program must perform the computations.

High mute

With the piano and other stringed instruments, the deeper the tone the louder the sound. The softer sounds appear closer to the end of the scale. Therefore, the OPL chip provides the option to mute notes in relation to their pitch. A setting of 0 to 3 according to the table on the bottom right defines high mute.

Setting options for high mute	
Value	High mute
0	None
1	3 dB per octave
2	1.5 dB per octave
3	6 dB per octave

Tremolo and vibrato

The OPL has two additional features that are often found on home organs. These are tremolo and vibrato. These sound effects can be turned on or off for each operator cell.

When tremolo is turned on, the sound volume rises and falls continuously at a frequency of 3.7 Hz. The volume level can be changed by either 1dB or 4.8 dB.

When vibrato is turned on, the frequency of the generator cell is varied. For a cell frequency of 6.4 Hz, the frequency is increased by either 7% or 14% and then lowered. You can use vibrato to create a siren effect.

Waveform

A cell can be programmed to generate a waveform different from the normal sine wave. As Type 1, the generator cells continuously produce a zero level in the negative phase of the sine wave. As Type 2, the absolute value of the sine wave is continuously output. Type 3 is similar to Type 2, except the signal is shortened to zero in the falling phase of the wave. By varying the waveforms, it's possible to generate a completely different set of voices even though the other parameters remain constant.

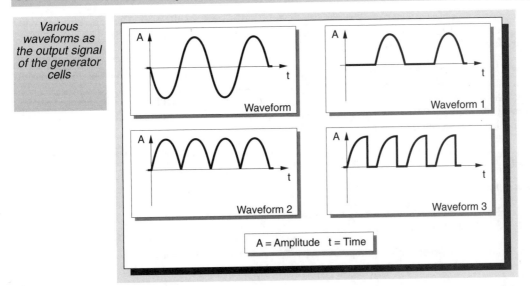

Various waveforms as the output signal of the generator cells

Waveform

Waveform 1

Waveform 2

Waveform 3

A = Amplitude   t = Time

Setting the generator cells

The OPL chip has about 120 different registers. These registers are used to set the operator cells, the channels and other characteristics for sound generation. Because the chip is a separate component of the sound card and the number of registers is rather large, not all registers appear in the I/O address range of the sound card. Instead, you communicate with the internal registers through the OPL's address and data register. These later two are accessible through the I/O ports.

➢ Ports 388h and 389h
  To access the registers of the OPL chip, use ports 388h and 389h. These ports, first popularized by the AdLib card, are used by almost all sound cards that contain the OPL chip.

➢ First two ports of the Sound Blaster card, i.e., base address +0 and base address +1.
  Accessing the OPL chip through 388h and 389h has become the preferred method for programming the sound card.

Accessing the OPL - address and data registers

To access any of the OPL's internal registers, follow this procedure. Write the number of the OPL register to the address port of the OPL chip: either port 388h or the SB-base address + 0.

The OPL needs 3.3 microseconds to enable access to one of its internal registers. Therefore a machine language program may require a slight delay loop. One way to avoid this problem is to immediately read the port after writing to it. This insures the OPL has cleared the internal path to the desired register.

Now you can write to the internal register, by writing the desired data value to either port 389h or the SB-base address + 1. The OPL needs 23 microseconds to complete to write operation to the internal register. You'll have to consider in your programming tasks.

So writing to the internal registers is easy. However, there is no way to read the contents of the OPL registers. This limitation poses a few programming challenges especially for registers that are used to specify settings as a group of bits. For example, register 60h, is used to specify the attack and decay parameters of the envelope for generator cell 0. Since there is no way to read the contents of a register, how do you change one parameter without changing the other one?

One technique for handling this is to use "shadow RAM". With this method, the contents of the registers are held in an array. The OPL which has about 120 registers whose addresses are scattered over an address range from 0 to 255. By allocating 256 bytes, we can use call on a common routine to access the real registers. Let's call this routine SB_Write.

To keep things in sync, all accesses the OPL registers must be passed to the SB_Write function. This is because SB_Write not only writes the value to the desired register, but also copies the value to the shadow array. The shadow array now contains an accessible copy of the register contents.

To change single bits in a register, you simply have to read out the current contents from the shadow array, modify the bits in question and then use SB_Write to output the new contents to the OPL chip which then saves the contents in the shadow array. To ensure the shadow array actually represents the current contents of the various OPL registers at program start, you usually initialize all the registers and the entire array with the value zero. This suppresses sound generation and resets the OPL chip, since the defaults for all OPL settings are zero.

The sample programs at the end of this chapter give you a demonstration of how all of this works. However, right now let's get back to setting the operator cells.

The operator cell settings

The following table lists the five base registers for setting the various parameters of the operator cells. Some of these registers hold several parameters. We'll describe their structure in later.

The addresses specified in the table apply only to operator cell 0. For other cells, you must add an offset to each address, which results from the second table. By adding the offset, you get the number of the register used to set the desired parameter for a specific cell.

The base register for setting the cells	
Base register	**Contents**
20h	Multiplication factor, Envelope reduction and type, Vibrato, Tremolo
40h	Mute factor, High mute
60h	Envelope: Attack, Decay
80h	Envelope: Sustain, Release
E0h	Waveform

Offsets for the different registers used to set the generator cells			
Operator cell	Offset	Operator cell	Offset
0	00h	9	0Bh
1	01h	10	0Ch
2	02h	11	0Dh
3	03h	12	10h
4	04h	13	11h
5	05h	14	12h
6	08h	15	13h
7	09H	16	14h
8	0Ah	17	15h

Notice the offset for operator cell 10 is 0Ch. To set the attack and decay envelope parameters for this cell, add offset 0Ch to the base address 60h of this register. This yields register 6Ch, in which the desired setting is written.

To determine the offset for a cell, create a static array within the program in which the offsets of the individual operator cells are stored. To access one of these cells, use the cell number as the index into the array, which gives you the required offset address. Then add the offset address to the base address for the cell.

The following five illustrations show the interrelationship between registers and operator cells:

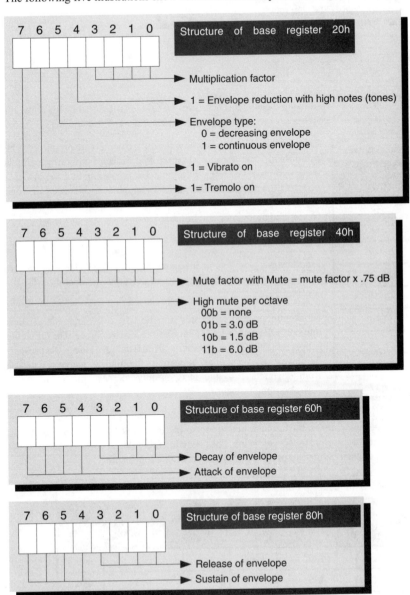

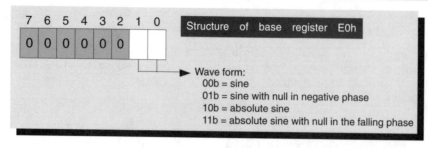

7	6	5	4	3	2	1	0
0	0	0	0	0	0		

Structure of base register E0h

Wave form:
00b = sine
01b = sine with null in negative phase
10b = absolute sine
11b = absolute sine with null in the falling phase

Setting the channels

Earlier we said that two operator cells are paired to make a single channel. Therefore, the OPL's 18 generator cells allow for up to nine channels. This means that up to nine different voices can be programmed independent of one another.

Organization of the operator cells and channels		
Channel	Operator cell - Modulator	Operator cell - Carrier
0	0	3
1	1	4
2	2	5
3	6	9
4	7	10
5	8	11
6	12	15
7	13	16
8	14	17

The table on the left shows how the OPL channels are organized. The relationship between a channel and its two operator cells is predetermined. To program the channels, create a static array in which you store the numbers of the carrier and modulator operator cell. Then use the channel number as an index into the array to determine the carrier and modulator cell numbers.

The Channel parameters

Five different parameters can be set for each channel. These parameters define the tone to be generated and the mode of operation for the operator cells.

Block number and frequency are the first two parameters. Block number is the octave from which a note is to be played. The OPL chip supports eight octaves, numbered from 0 to 7. A value of 0 represents the lowest octave, while 7 represents the highest octave. To switch from one octave to the next, simply increase the value in the corresponding register.

Frequency is set in relation to the current block number or octave. Although an octave consists of only twelve harmonic tones, the frequency can be set to values between 0 and 1023. This means the resolution of the OPL chip far exceeds that of a normal music keyboard. The following table shows corresponding values of frequency and harmonic tones. Other frequency values are permissible if you want to experiment.

Settings for the frequency parameter of a channel								
Tone	Value for frequency parameter	Freq (Hz)	Tone	Value for frequency parameter	Freq (Hz)	Tone	Value for frequency parameter	Freq (Hz)
C#	363	277.2	F	458	349.2	A	577	440.0
D	385	293.7	F#	485	370.0	B	611	466.2
D#	408	311.1	G	514	392.0	H	647	493.9
E	432	329.6	G#	544	415.3	C	686	523.3

Another parameter specifies the type of connection between the two operator cells of a channel. One type of connection is the coupling of two cells as described earlier which is the basis of FM synthesis. Another type of connection is to combine the output of two cells through addition. This generates two overlapping oscillations which can generate some interesting voices and effects.

Still another parameter tells the modulator operator cell to add a portion of its output signal back to the input. A value between 0 and 7 determines the intensity of the feedback. The default value of zero disables feedback. Because the effect of this feedback is quite difficult to describe, we simply recommend that you experiment with this parameter. A good starting point is to use the sample program at the end of this section.

A final parameter tells the channel to either start or stop an operation. The next section shows you how to set the various parameters using the registers of the OPL chip.

Setting the channel parameters

Like the operator cells, the channel parameters are also set using different base registers, to which an offset must be added for the desired channel. Unlike operator cells, you don't have to look up the offset in a table, because the channel number itself is the offset. To program channel 7, simply add 7 to the base address of the appropriate channel registers.

The five different channel parameters are contained in three base registers with addresses A0h, B0h and C0h. The frequency parameter is contained in two registers, since ten bits are required to represent its range (0-1023).

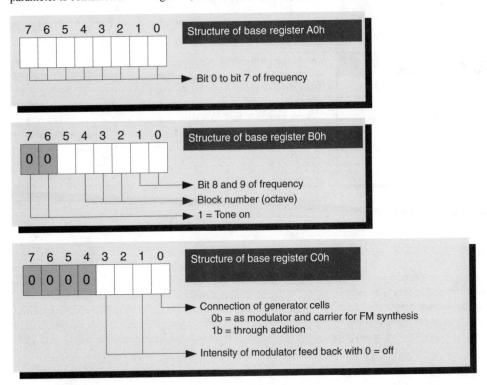

Percussion mode

In addition to the default mode with nine independent voices (channels), the OPL chip has a second mode in which only six independent voices are available. However, five percussion instruments are also available. Most games with sound accompaniment operate in this mode because the percussion instruments provide the necessary effects. Therefore, the limited number of voices isn't a problem. Register 0BDh, bit 5 switches between percussion and nine voice modes.

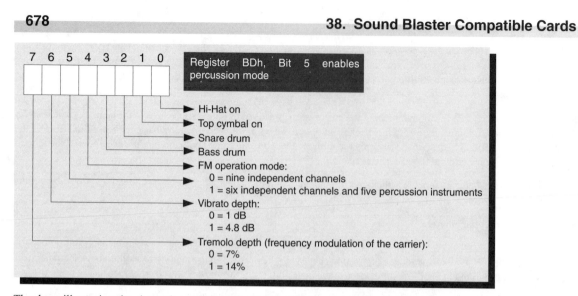

The above illustration also shows that register BDh also specifies the settings for the tremolo and vibrato depth. These values affect all generator cells that have tremolo or vibrato enabled. For now, let's return to percussion mode.

Percussion Mode instrument, operator cells and channels		
Instrument	Operator cell	Channel
Bass Drum	12 + 15	6
Hi Hat	13	7
Tom Tom	14	8
Snare Drum	16	7
Top Cymba1	7	8

The table on the left shows the interrelationship between the percussion mode instruments and cells.

The channel and operator cell assignments have not changed compared to standard mode. One slight difference is that, except for the bass drum, two operator cells share a single channel. To enable sound generation of the percussion instruments you must set the appropriate bit in register 0BDh, rather than enabling the channel. In fact, the on/off bit in the channel register for the percussion instruments must also be set to zero; otherwise, the percussion instruments will remain silent.

Since two percussion instruments share a channel, only one block number and one frequency register are available for both instruments. As a result, the two percussion instruments of a channel will play in the same pitch, provided they are played at the same time. The multiplication factor of the operator cell allows for varied tuning.

FM Programming

All this information about the various registers provides only a theoretical description of how the OPL operates. To really learn how it works, you'll have to experiment and see how the different register contents affect the sound generation. The FM program, at the end of this section, lets you interactively set many of the registers and use a keyboard to elicit sound from the card. If you take the time to experiment with FM, you'll quickly develop a feeling for the numerous ways that you can influence the sound card. FM works with Sound Blaster and other compatible cards containing an OPL chip at ports 388h and 389h.

FM itself includes only the code for interacting with the user. Two other modules, SBUTIL and FMUTIL, control the sound card. Any program can use the include files for these modules (SBUTIL.C or FMUTIL.C) to use the functions contained in them. The SBUTIL module is used often in this chapter since it contains some very basic routines for programming Sound Blaster cards. FMUTIL is intended specially for programming the OPL chip.

Functions in module SBUTIL	
Function	Task
sb_GetEnviron	Initialize SB_base structure using the SB environment variables
sb_Print	Display SB_base structure
sb_LoadDriver	Load Sound Blaster driver into memory
sb_UnloadDriver	Remove Sound Blaster driver from memory

SB_base structure listed in the table for the sb_getEnviron and sb_Print functions refers to the data structure of the same name in the SBUTIL.H include file. Calling sb_GetEnviron, initializes the structure with the important parameters about the installed Sound Blaster card. All the functions in SBUTIL and FMUTIL that directly access a register of the Sound Blaster card reference the port address of the sound card from this data structure. Therefore, you must call sb_GetEnviron before the other two modules. FMUTIL is given this information by fm_SetBase.

Functions in module FMUTIL	
Function	Task
fm_SetBase	Provide routines with an initialized SB_base structure
fm_Write	Write value in an OPL register
fm_WriteBit	Set or Clear a bit in OPL register
Reset_Card	Reset all OPL registers
fm_GetChannel	Get channel number of an oscillator
fm_GetModulator	Get modulator number of a channel
fm_GetCarrier	Get oscillator number of a channel
fm_SetOscillator	Sets all the parameters of an operator cell
fm_SetModulator	Sets all the parameters of the modulator
fm_SetCarrier	Sets all the parameters of a carrier
fm_SetChannel	Sets all the parameters of a channel
fm_PlayChannel	Switch channel on or off
fm_SetCard	Set tremolo and vibrato depth for all channels
fm_PollTime	Time delay
fm_PlayHiHat	Switches hi hat on or off
fm_PlayTopCymb	Switches top cymbal on or off
fm_PlayTomTom	Switches tom tom on or off
fm_PlaySnareDru	Switches snare drum on or off
fm_PlayBassDru	Switches bass drum on or off
fm_PercussionMo	Switches between nine channel mode and percussion mode

FMUTIL contains functions for controlling all aspects of FM synthesis. FMUTIL uses a shadow array (Mirror array variable) to keep track of the current OPL register contents.. However, remember the reliability of this array is assured only if you use the FMUTIL functions fm_Write and fm_WriteBit to change the various OPL registers.

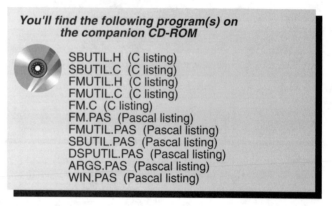

You'll find the following program(s) on the companion CD-ROM

SBUTIL.H (C listing)
SBUTIL.C (C listing)
FMUTIL.H (C listing)
FMUTIL.C (C listing)
FM.C (C listing)
FM.PAS (Pascal listing)
FMUTIL.PAS (Pascal listing)
SBUTIL.PAS (Pascal listing)
DSPUTIL.PAS (Pascal listing)
ARGS.PAS (Pascal listing)
WIN.PAS (Pascal listing)

Sampling

Sampling is a method of recording analog sounds by converting them into a series of digital pulses. You can record these analog sounds through a microphone or from stereo equipment for example, and save the sequences of pulses on your hard drive. At a later time you can replay the recording without a decrease in audio quality. Sampling is the same technique that is used to record audio CDs in a sound studio.

Basically, sampling is a high quality digital to analog or analog to digital conversion. During recording, the sound card receives the analog sound signal and converts it into digital "samples". Recording is therefore an analog to digital conversion. When you play back the sample, the digital data stream of the sample is converted back into an analog signal.

Samples of signals

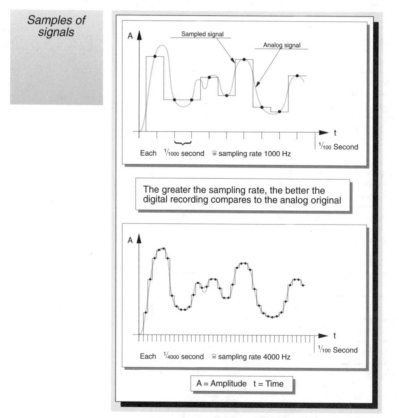

How well the results of this analog to digital conversion match the original analog signal depends on the sample frequency and its resolution. Ideally, the analog signal is sampled infinitely. Of course this is impossible and would require an infinite amount of disk space. Instead, a specified number of samples are taken per second. At continuous intervals the current analog signal is converted to a digital value. The more frequently this happens and the shorter the intervals between single samples, the higher the recording quality. For audio CDs, the sampling rate is 44.1 KHz. This means that 44,100 samples per second are taken.

In addition to the sample frequency, the resolution of the sample determines the quality of digital recordings. Resolution is the range of values used to represent the analog sound signal on a digital scale. For audio CD's, sound is recorded at a level of 16-bits. So it's possible to differentiate between 65,536 signal intensities. If a lower resolution is used (for example, 8-bit resolution) then the width is 256 times smaller, a value which your ears can clearly detect.

Sampling lets you record any natural sounds. You can edit the sounds with appropriate software tools. You can then send the sounds to other programs such as games. You can record many more sounds and much more realistic ones than are possible using a synthesizer such as the OPL. This is an overriding advantage of sampling compared to synthetic sound production.

One of the drawbacks of sampling is that digitized sound requires a large amount of disk space. For example, one second of CD quality music requires about 170K; ten seconds requires 1.7 Meg and a minute requires about 10 Meg of disk space. A complete CD with 72 minutes of music needs 600 Meg

With these large storage requirements, the CD-ROM is the only practical way to distribute software that uses large amounts of sampled sound.. But even with CDs, it's still necessary to find ways to reduce the volume of data, for example, by reducing the sampling frequency. Doing this is usually acceptable because many sounds are still realistic even when recorded at much lower sampling rates. The rule-of-thumb minimum is 12 KHz; at this level, the human ear can clearly distinguish the loss of sound quality.

Next we'll discuss how to record and playback sound using the Digital Sound Processor (DSP) on the Sound Blaster card.

DSP Basics

All Sound Blaster cards have a built-in digital sound processor. First some background information.

The various DSP versions

With each new generation of Sound Blaster card, its digital sound processor has become more powerful. In fact, you can identify the different Sound Blaster cards by knowing which version of DSP it uses. Later, we'll see how you can determine which version of DSP is on a card from a program.

The following table lists the cards and DSP versions in the Sound Blaster family:

SB Card	DSP version
SB 1.5	1.xx - 2.00
SBMCV (Sound Blaster for the MicroChannel)	1.xx - 2.00
SB 2.0	2.01+
SBPRO	3.xx
SBPRO MCV (Sound Blaster Pro for the MicroChannel)	3.xx
SB 16	4.xx
SB 16 with ASP (Advanced Signal Processor)	4.xx

The DSP first appeared with the Sound Blaster and Sound Blaster 1.5 (both are now called Sound Blaster 1.5). These cards have various versions of the DSP versions including Version 1.xx and Version 2.0. From a programmer's viewpoint, there are no differences among the various 1.xx versions. This is also true with Versions 3.xx and 4.xx.

DSP Version 2.01, used in the Sound Blaster 2.0 card, features a "High Speed mode". Version 3.xx also has this "High Speed mode". However, this feature is missing from DSP Version 4.

The Sound Blaster Pro card uses DSP Version 3. The SB 16 and its upgrades use the current version, DSP Version 4.xx.

The main differences among the various versions of the DSP chip is sampling speed and bit depth. Speed refers to the number of samples that can be recorded or played back per second. Bit depth refers to the resolution of the sample - the range of values used to represent the original analog signal on a digital scale. A higher resolution yields a higher quality reproduction.

In abbreviated terms, the quality of an audio CD is "16-bit, stereo, 44.1 KHz". This means the original is recorded by sampling 44,100 time per second, using 16-bit values to represent the original analog signal intensity; two channels are recorded simultaneously - the left and right channels. This amounts to a data rate of 170K per second (44,100 samples per second * 2 bytes per sample * 2 channels).

The following tables compare the quality levels for the different DSPs:

Sampling rates of different DSPs for output				
DSP Version	Mono/Stereo	High-Speed	Data Format	Sampling Rate
All DSPs	Mono		8-bit/4-bit ADPCM*	4000-12000 Hz
	Mono		8-bit/3-bit ADPCM	4000-13000 Hz
	Mono		8-bit/2-bit ADPCM	4000-11000 Hz
1.xx and 2.00	Mono		8-bit	4000-23000 Hz
2.01+	Mono		8-bit	4000-23000 Hz
	Mono	Yes	8-bit	23000-44100 Hz
3.xx	Mono		8-bit	4000-23000 Hz
	Mono	Yes	8-bit	23000-44100 Hz
	Stereo	Yes	8-bit	11025-22050 Hz
4.xx	Mono		8-bit	5000-44100 Hz
	Mono		16-bit	5000-44100 Hz
	Stereo		8-bit	5000-44100 Hz
	Stereo		16-bit	5000-44100 Hz

Sampling rates of different DSPs during recording				
DSP Version	Mono/Stereo	High-Speed	Data Format	Sampling Rate
1.xx and 2.00	Mono		8-bit	4000-13000 Hz
2.01+	Mono		8-bit	4000-13000 Hz
	Mono	Yes	8-bit	13000-15000 Hz
3.xx	Mono		8-bit	4000-23000 Hz
	Mono	Yes	8-bit	23000-44100 Hz
	Stereo	Yes	8-bit	11025-22050 Hz
4.xx	Mono		8-bit	5000-44100 Hz
	Mono		16-bit	5000-44100 Hz
	Stereo		8-bit	5000-44100 Hz
	Stereo		16-bit	5000-44100 Hz

High speed mode in DSP versions 2.01+ and 3.xx uses a higher sampling rate than earlier versions. But as mentioned, this feature was removed in DSP Version 4 which attains CD quality reproduction without this mode.

DSP transfer modes

The DSP chip supports five different modes of operation. In one mode, the DSP operates using a polling technique. For the other four modes, the DSP operates in conjunction with the DMA controller. The advantage of the four DMA modes is the data can be transferred in the background while the CPU performs other tasks. When the data transfer is complete, the DSP signals the CPU using an interrupt.

Here's a summary of the five different modes:

Direct mode

In direct mode, the DSP operates by polling. Data is passed to or from the DSP, one byte at a time, by a program. The sampling rate is determined by the speed at which the program runs. The samples are limited to eight-bit unsigned values. To achieve a constant sampling rate, the data is passed to or from the DSP using an interrupt routine that is tied to the timer.

An advantage of direct mode is its ease of programming. Since you don't have to interface with the DMA controller, writing code for direct mode is quick and dirty. A disadvantage of direct mode is that it cannot achieve anywhere near the sampling rates possible using the other DMA modes. In fact, the sampling rate is limited to about 15,000 Hz which limits the quality.

Single cycle DMA mode

In single cycle mode, the DMA controller handles the data transfer between the DSP and RAM. Both the DMA controller and the DSP are programmed separately for each sample block transferred. Based on the type of DMA controller, a block can be a maximum of 64K or 128K. The entire data block must fit within a single 64K memory page (or within one 128K memory page while using a 16-bit DMA channel). After the transfer is complete, the DSP triggers an interrupt. As its name suggest, this mode is used to transfer a single sample block between RAM and DSP.

As with the other DMA modes, the DSP can process 8-bit samples, 16-bit samples and ADPCM samples.

Auto initialize DMA mode

Auto initialize mode can handle the high data rates needed for CD-audio quality - 16-bit stereo samples at 44.1 KHz.. This mode takes advantage of the DMA controller's ability to initialize itself with the original starting address and block length after a block transfer (Auto-Init-Mode). This makes it possible to edit samples of almost any length. The technique used to manage Auto initialize DMA mode is commonly called "double buffering". Once the DSP is in auto initialize DMA mode, there are two ways to halt the data transfer:

➤ By sending the DSP a command for executing a single cycle DMA mode transfer. The DSP completes the current block transfer and then perform the single cycle DMA mode transfer.

➤ By sending the DSP a command to exit auto initialize mode. Here too, the DSP completes the current block transfer and then exits auto initialize DMA mode.

High speed DMA mode

To reach higher sampling rates than can be achieved with auto initialize DMA mode, you can use high speed DMA mode found in DSP Versions 2.01+ and 3.xx. High speed DMA mode can perform both single cycle DMA transfers and auto initialize DMA transfers (for 8-bit mono and stereo samples only).

The one drawback of high speed DMA mode is that this mode can only be terminated by reset after the transfer is complete. Because this mode is supported only by DSP versions 2.01+ and 3.XX, it's not very commonly used. Beginning with version 4, this mode isn't needed since the new DSP chip is capable sampling at a 44.1 KHz rate in auto initialize DMA mode.

ADPCM DMA mode

Earlier we touched on the tremendous volumes of data produced by sampling. To reduce the amount of data you can compress it. One compression technique called ADPCM (Adaptive Delta Pulse Code Modulation), records the difference between samples rather than the value of each sample. Sound Blaster cards using DSP Version 1 can playback samples that have been compressed using the ADPCM.

The Sound Blaster card recognizes these ADPCM formats: 8/4, 8/3 and 8/2. Format 8/4 uses four bits to specify the difference from the previous sample. Therefore two samples can be packed into a single byte which reduces the space requirements of the sample block in half. The limitation is the change compared to the previous sample can only range between -7 and +7, since four bits are available and one is used for the sign, leaving three bits for the difference. Sample data containing larger changes cannot be compressed perfectly with ADPCM 8/4.

Different DSP operating modes of the Sound Blaster family					
	DSP Version				
Mode	1.xx	2.00	2.01+	3.xx	4.xx
8-bit mono single cycle					
8-bit mono auto initialize					
8-bit mono ADPCM single cycle					
8-bit mono ADPCM auto initialize					
8-bit mono high speed single cycle					
8-bit mono high speed auto initialize					
8-bit stereo high speed single cycle					
8-bit stereo high speed auto initialize					
8-bit/16 bit mono single cycle					
8-bit/16 bit mono auto initialize					
8-bit/16 bit stereo single cycle					
8-bit/16 bit stereo auto initialize					

For higher compression, you can use ADPCM formats 8/3 and 8/2. With these, however, the differences between the sampling values must be even lower, because only 3 (8/3 mode) or 2 bits (8/2 mode) remain to record the difference between samples.

The three ADPCM formats are used only for 8-bit samples. Unless you're using a SB 16 card with ASP, you cannot directly record using the ADPCM formats. Creative Labs hasn't released the exact specifications for ADPCM samples, so there is no easy way to convert raw, uncompressed recordings into ADPCM formatted recordings.

Transfer modes supported by the different DSPs

The table above lists the transfer modes which are available to the different versions of DSP. Notice that CD quality recording with 16-bit samples is possible with DSP Version 4.xx (found in Sound Blaster 16).

DSP and DMA controller interaction

In the different DMA transfer modes, the DMA controller and the DSP work hand in hand. For example, when recording, the DSP receives the analog signals from a sound source, converts them into digital samples, and then transfers them to a buffer in RAM with the help of the DMA controller. Because of the limitations of the DMA controller, the transfer buffer must be located in the first Meg of RAM and cannot exceed a 64K page limit.

Conversely, when playing samples, the DMA controller transfers the data to the DSP from a buffer in RAM. The DSP converts the sample data into analog signals and passes the signals to the Sound Blaster card amplifier. From there, the signals are head as sound through a set of headphones or speakers.

The interaction between the DMA controller and the DSP is controlled by the sampling software. The software must first program the DMA controller before recording or playing back the sample. The settings for the Sound Blaster card's DMA channel are found in the BLASTER environment variable. The D parameter is the channel number for 8-bit transfer; the H parameter is the channel number for 16-bit transfer. Remember, 16-bit transfer is a feature of the Sound Blaster 16 with a DSP Version 4.xx.

Next the software specifies the starting address of the transfer buffer and the block length for the DMA controller. To perform auto initialize DMA mode transfers, you must also switch the DMA controller channel to auto init mode. The DMA controller is ready to go.

Now on to the DSP side. The DSP needs several items of information. One is the sampling frequency; a second is the length of the data to be transferred from memory to the DSP or from the DSP to memory; a third is the source of the sound samples or the destination for the sound output. Now the software sends a special command to the DSP to start the recording or playback of the samples.

After processing the last sample, the DSP triggers an interrupt informing the sampling software the transfer is complete. The interrupt is again found in the BLASTER environment variable as parameter I. As a rule, the sampling software provides its own interrupt handler for the interrupt, which can recognize this event and then continue working.

Shortly, we'll discuss the details of programming the DSP. First, we'll look double buffering, a technique which lets you capture or play back samples of nearly any length.

Double buffering

Double buffering is a software technique which "converts a PC into a DAT drive". You can use double buffering (sometimes called ping-pong buffering) to record samples from any sound source onto the hard drive or to play back prerecorded samples previously recorded on the hard drive. To use this technique, first allocate a DMA buffer. Recall that a DMA buffer has a maximum size of 64K and is located within a 64K memory page.

During recording, the samples are transferred from the DSP to this buffer. During playback, the samples are transferred from this buffer to the DSP. Prior to either recording or playback, the DMA controller is programmed with the starting address, the length of the block and to operate in auto init mode. Each time the buffer is filled (during capture) or emptied (during playback), the operation is repeated. Once started, the DMA controller repeats the operation over and over.

With double buffering, the DSP is programmed to transfer only half of the length of the block. During recording, the DSP fills only one-half of the buffer with sampled data and then triggers an interrupt. The interrupt handler sets an internal flag and then commands the DSP to write additional sampled data to the second half of the buffer and completes its task.

During playback, the DSP reads and plays the data from the first half of the buffer and then triggers an interrupt. The interrupt handler sets an internal flag and commands the DSP to read additional data from the buffer and is finished. Since the DMA controller was not reprogrammed, only half of the transfer has been complete. Therefore the controller continues from the point where it left off - at the first byte of the second half of the buffer.

While the DSP reads from or writes to the second half-buffer in the background, critical work is taking place in the main program. Since the start of sampling, the program has been looping continuously. This purpose of the loop is to check the flag set by the interrupt handler. If set, then the DSP has jumped from the first half-buffer second half-buffer. For recording, the program writes the completed half-buffer to the sample file. For playback, the program loads the next half-buffer with the next block of data from the sample file.

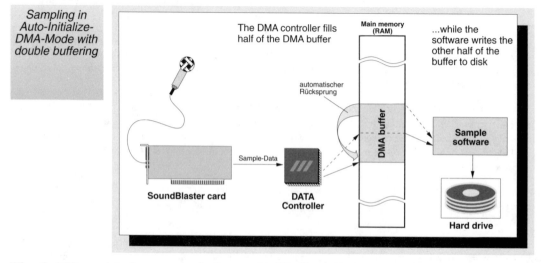

Sampling in Auto-Initialize-DMA-Mode with double buffering

When the DSP completes the processing for the second half-buffer, the DMA controller jumps back to the beginning of the buffer to repeat the next transfer from the first half-buffer again. This ensures the program can always reload or save the half-buffer which the DSP is not processing and the DSP can move from one half-buffer to the other half-buffer without being disturbed. So, the DSP and DMA controller access the first and second half-buffers alternately.

Of course this method assumes the main program runs fast enough to reload or save the idle half-buffer before the DMA controller returns again to the beginning of this same half-buffer. On systems with a 486 processor, this is no problem provided the modules and subroutines are programmed intelligently. The program at the end of this section and on the companion CD-ROM uses this technique.

Sample data structure

The DSP writes the sample data to RAM in a specific format. This same format is used later to play back the samples. The exact sequence of the samples depends on whether the samples are recorded in mono or stereo and whether the samples are 8- bit or 16-bit.

The DSP can handle both unsigned and signed values. 8-bit samples are unsigned while 16-bit samples can be either signed or unsigned. An unsigned sample is recorded as a positive number. An 8-bit unsigned value ranges from 0 to 255 (00h to ffh); a 16-bit unsigned value ranges from 0 to 65,535. A 16-bit signed value ranges from -32,768 to +32,767 (-8000h to 7FFFh).

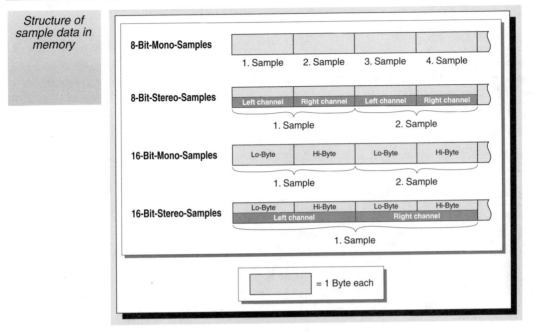

Structure of sample data in memory

Accessing the DSP

DSP ports				
Port	Name	Read	Write	Purpose
+06h	Reset			Resets the DSP.
+0Ah	Read Data			Reads data from the DSP.
+0Ch	Write Command / Data			Writes commands and data to DSP.
+0Ch	Write Buffer status			Indicates whether DSP is ready to receive commands or data.
+0Eh	Read Buffer status			Indicates whether data can be read from the DSP.

The table above lists the five different registers that control the DSP. Their addresses are relative to the base address of the Sound Blaster card.

Sending data and commands to the DSP

The assembly language OUT instruction sends commands and their parameters to the DSP. However, you cannot write to the port unless the Write-Buffer status port is empty. If the DSP is still processing a previous command, the status port contains the last command or data value. Reading the Write-Buffer status port to determine if bit 7 is set. If so, the DSP is still busy. You can then loop until the Write-Buffer status port is clear. Only then should you send the next command or data to the DSP.

The assembly language code looks as follows:

```
          mov     dx,SbPortBase       ;Load port address of SB card
          add     dl,0Ch              ;Offset for Write Buffer Status
Wait:     in      al,dx               ;Read the Write Buffer Status Reg
          test    al,80h              ;Check bit 7
          jne     Wait                ; If not 0, then one more pass
```

```
;--- DSP is now ready to receive the next instruction
         mov      al,CommandByte      ;Load DSP command
         out      dx,al               ;and output
```

Several DSP commands require parameters. Both the command code and the parameters are passed to the DSP through the port. The command code is always sent first. Then the parameters are transferred to the DSP one at a time, in a predetermined order depending on the command. Here again, you must wait for the DSP to tell you its ready to accept the next byte using the Write-Buffer status port.

Reading data from the DSP

Reading data is similar to the writing to the DSP. In this case, the Read-Buffer status register is used to signal when the requested data is ready. The difference is that ready is indicated when bit 7 of this register is 1, not zero.

In assembly language, the code looks like this:

```
         mov      dx,SbPortBase    ;Load port address of SB card
         add      dl,0Eh            ;Offset for Read Buffer Status
Wait:    in       al,dx            ;Read the Read Buffer Status Reg
         test     al,80h            ;Check bit 7
         je       Wait             ;If not 1, then one more pass((blank line paragraph))
;--- DSP is now ready to accept the next command
         sub      dl,4             ;from Read Buf Status Reg. to
                                          ;Read Data Register
         in       al,dx            ;Read the Read Data Register
```

DSP reset

A program should always begin by resetting the DSP. This resets all the internal registers and also returns information as to whether a Sound Blaster card and a DSP are actually located at the specified port address.

Here are the steps for doing this:

1. Write the value 1 to the Reset port.

2. Wait at least three microseconds (the DSP requires this long to respond).

3. Write the value 0 to the Reset port.

4. The byte sequence 0 and 1, tells the DSP to perform a reset. When complete, and the Read-Buffer status register goes to 1, the DSP writes the value 0AAh to the Read-Buffer status port. Since you still don't know at this time whether a DSP is actually present, you should include a time out loop; otherwise you may be waiting a very long time.

The assembly language code for reset looks like this:

```
;--- first send 1 to reset port --------------------
         mov      dx,SbPortBase  ;load port address of SB card
         add      dl,6            ;Offset for reset port
         mov      al,1
         out      dx,al   ;--- give DSP so time time
                          ;--- Loop 256 times
         sub      al,al          ;Set AL to 0
DspLoop1: dec     al             ;Decrement AL
         jne      DspLoop1       ;not 0, then loop again

         out      dx,al          ;send second byte (0) to DSP
```

```
;--- wait for Read Buffer Status Register to -
;--- indicate availability of a byte
            xor       cx,cx          ;maximum 65536 loops
            add       dl,8           ;from reset port to Read Buffer status register
DspLoop2:   in        al,dx          ;read Read Buffer status register
            test      al,80h         ;test bit 7
            jne       ByteAvail      ;if set, then byte available
            loop      DspLoop2       ;if not, then next loop run
            jmp       NoDSP          ;if there's still no byte after 65536 runs

ByteAvail:  ;--- a byte is available at Read data port --
            sub       dl,4           ;from Read Buffer Status to Read Data
            in        al,dx          ;read out Read data register
            cmp       al,0AAh        ;the DSP must answer with 0aah
            jne       NoDSP          ;if not, then no DSP present

;--- if the processor comes here, a DSP is present
            jmp       DSPFound
NoDSP:      ;--- could not find DSP, continue error processing
```

Handling interrupts

The Read Buffer status register plays an important part in handling DSP interrupts. If the DSP triggers an interrupt following the processing of a sample block, the interrupt handler must indicate to the DSP that it received the interrupt. Before DSP Version 4.xx, reading the Read Buffer status register was sufficient for this purpose.

Beginning with DSP Version 4.xx, you must first check the source of the interrupt. Unlike earlier versions, completed 8-bit and 16-bit transfers can trigger interrupts with DSP Version 4.xx. Also, both 8-bit and 16-bit transfers share an interrupt and an interrupt handler. Therefore, the interrupt handler must first read register 82h of the Sound Blaster mixer, to find out what activity triggered the interrupt.

Like the OPL's internal registers, the mixer registers are addressed through separate address and data ports. The number of the desired mixer register is written to the address port; then its contents can be read or data written to that register through the data port.

The mixer's address and data ports are relative to the base address of the Sound Blaster card as follows:

```
Mixer address port = Sound Blaster base address + 4
Mixer data port = Sound Blaster base address + 5
```

Writing a value of 82h to the mixer address port and then reading the mixer data port, returns the contents of the Sound Blaster card's interrupt status register. The contents is as follows (found only on Sound Blaster cards with DSP Version 4.xx and above):

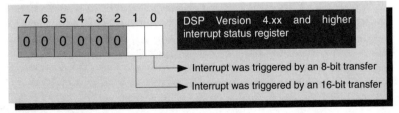

To acknowledge that an 8-bit transfer, the interrupt handler should read the port at offset 0Eh. To acknowledge a 16-bit transfer interrupt, the interrupt handler should read the port at offset 0Fh. This is the only way the DSP receives confirmation the interrupt was processed by the interrupt handler.

The following assembly language code demonstrates the confirmation by the interrupt handler:

```
;--- first read mixer register 82h ------------
;---(Interrupt Status Register)
            mov       dx,SbPortBase   ;load port address of SB card
            add       dl,4            ;Offset for mixer address port
            mov       al,82h          ;identify the interrupt status register
            out       dx,al           ;write to mixer address port
            inc       dl              ;DX now at mixer data port
            in        al,dx           ;read contents of interrupt status register
                                      ;from mixer data port

            add       dl,9            ;DX now at Read Buffer status reg.
            test      al,2            ;test whether 16-bit interrupt
            jne       SbInt16         ;set, then 16-bit

;--- it's an 8-bit interrupt
            in        al,dx           ;read Read Buffer status register,
                                      ;to confirm to DSP
            jmp       Irqendwo        ;continue

;--- it's a 16-bit interrupt
SbInt16:    inc d                     ;DX on/to register with offset 0Fh
            in  al,dx                 ;read register to confirm to DSP

Irqendwo:                                      ; continue IRQ processing
```

The Sound Blaster interrupt is a hardware interrupt. Therefore, the interrupt handler will have to send an EOI command to the interrupt controller before returning to the interrupted program, i.e., before executing the IRET instruction. Otherwise, subsequent interrupts will be blocked. For more information on interrupts and interrupt controller, refer to Chapter 4.

DSP Commands

Most of the 40 DSP commands date back to Version 1.0. Half of these commands read and write the sample data. The other half perform housekeeping tasks such as switching on and off the DSP-amplifier connection or returning the DSP version number.

The following table summarizes these commands. Following the tables, are practical examples of some of the most important commands. Following the examples is a command reference describing all the commands in detail.

Listing of DSP commands by function group

The following commands are available beginning with DSP Version 1.xx.

Command type	Code	Command
8-bit direct mode commands	10h	output an 8-bit sample in direct mode
	20h	input an 8-bit sample in direct mode
Set sample frequency	40h	Set sample frequency
8-bit single cycle DMA mode commands	14h	8-bit single cycle DMA output
	24h	8-bit single cycle DMA input
	16h	8/2 bit ADPCM single cycle DMA output
	17h	8/2 bit ADPCM single cycle DMA output with reference byte
	74h	8/4 bit ADPCM single cycle DMA output
	75h	8/4 bit ADPCM single cycle DMA output with reference byte
	76h	8/3 bit ADPCM single cycle DMA output
	77h	8/3 bit ADPCM single cycle DMA output with reference byte
8-bit control commands	D0h	Pause 8-bit DMA transfer
	D4h	Continue 8-bit DMA transfer
Control speakers	D1h	Switch on speaker
	D3h	Switch off speaker
Miscellaneous	80h	Pause input briefly
	E1h	Get version number of DSP

The following commands are available beginning with DSP Version 2.0.

Command type	Code	Command
8-bit auto init DMA mode commands	1Ch	8-bit auto init DMA output
	2Ch	8-bit auto init DMA input
	1Fh	8/2 bit ADPCM auto init DMA output with reference byte
	7Dh	8/4 bit ADPCM auto init DMA output with reference byte
	7Fh	8/3 bit ADPCM auto init DMA output with reference byte
	DAh	Terminate 8-bit sample auto init DMA transfer
Set block transfer size	48h	Set block length for auto init and high speed DMA transfers
Control speakers	D8h	Get status of speaker

The following commands are available for DSP Version 2.01+ and 3.xx only.

Command type	Code	Command
8-bit high speed mode commands	90h	8-bit high speed auto init DMA output
	98h	8-bit high speed auto init DMA input
	91h	8-bit high speed single cycle DMA output
	99h	8-bit high speed single cycle DMA input

The following commands are only available for DSPs of Version 3.xx only:

Command type	Code	Command
Set Mono/Stereo input	A0h	Set input mode to Mono
	A8h	Set input mode to Stereo

The following commands are available for DSP Version 4.xx and higher.

Command type	Code	Command
Set sampling frequency	41h	Set sampling frequency for output
	42h	Set sampling frequency for input
Input and output 8-bit samples	Cxh	8-bit samples DMA input/output
Input and output 16-bit samples	Bxh	16-bit samples DMA input/output
	D5h	Pause 16-bit sample DMA transfer
	D6h	Continue 16-bit sample DMA transfer
	D9h	Terminate 16-bit sample auto init DMA transfer

Determining the DSP version

The E1h command is used to determine the version number of a DSP. To do this, read the Read Data register twice in succession after writing this command code. The DSP main version number is returned as the first byte, and the DSP subversion number is returned as the second byte. The version number helps you determine which type of Sound Blaster card is installed.

Setting the sampling rate/sampling frequency

Before sampling begins, you must first set the sampling rate which is a function of the sampling frequency. To set the sampling rate, use DSP command 40h. In addition to the command code, you must also pass the desired sampling rate to the DSP. The rate is set according to the following formula:

```
rate = 65536 - (256000000/(Channels * Sampling frequency))
```

where   Channels = 1 for mono sampling

or

               Channels = 2 for stereo sampling

The most significant byte of the result is passed to the DSP; the least significant byte is discarded.

For DSP Versions 4.xx and higher, there are two additional commands for setting the sampling rate. These commands 41h and 42h are easier to use since the argument does not have to be converted as above. Both commands 41h and 42h are identical in syntax but one is for capturing samples and the other for playback of samples. Command 41h is used to set the sampling frequency for input (capture); command 42h is used for output (playback). With both commands, write the desired sample frequency in hertz to the Write command data port: first the most significant byte and then the least significant byte. It doesn't matter whether you are sampling in mono or stereo.

Setting the transfer length

Besides the sampling rate, you must also specify the transfer length so the DSP knows how many samples to capture or playback before triggering an interrupt. Depending on the type of sampling mode, you can set the transfer length separately using command 48h (for all auto init and high speed DMA modes) or specify it as part of the sampling command itself (for all single cycle DMA modes).

After writing command code 48h, you then write the least followed by the most significant byte of the transfer length. Recall the DSP expects the transfer length less one. To transfer 4K (1000h), specify a length of 0FFFh.

Switching the speaker on and off

Switching the speakers on or off refers to the connection between the DSP and the Sound Blaster amplifier. The speaker is switched on (DSP command D1h) to playback sample data or switched off (DSP command D3h) to capture sample data.

DSP Version 4.xx Commands

With DSP Version 4.xx, the Cxh and Bxh commands are used to capture and playback samples. The Cxh commands are for 8-bit samples and the Bxh commands for 16-bit samples. The x in both commands is a variable parameter; the lower nibble of the command code is defined by the desired mode of operation.

First, we'll have a look at Bxh. The complete command code is composed of a bit field whose upper four bits are always Bh, and whose lower four bits define a specific operation. The following illustration defines these operations:

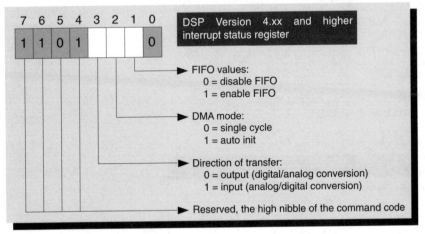

Bit 3 specifies either input (capture) or output (playback) operation.

Bit 2 specifies whether single cycle or auto init DMA mode is used.

Bit 1 specifies whether FIFO (a small internal buffer of the DSP) is disabled or enabled. With high sampling frequencies, you should enable FIFO; otherwise, when a higher priority DMA channel interferes with the DMA controller during data transfer, you can easily lose sample data.

For example, BAh (10111010b) specifies capturing 16-bit samples in single cycle mode with the FIFO enabled. B4h specifies playing back 16-bit samples in auto init mode without FIFO disabled.

To start an operation, first write the command code to the DSP. A second byte is then written containing two other parameters: the recording format (unsigned or signed) and the number of channels (mono or stereo).

The following illustration shows the structure of this byte:

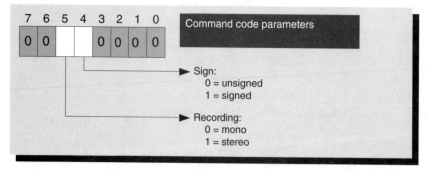

Finally a 16-bit value is written that specifies the number of 16-bit samples (not bytes) -1. The value is sent least significant followed by most significant byte. The DSP command Cxh is the same except that it applies to 8-bit samples. The command code for Cxh is determined by the same three bit fields describing the Bxh command. However, the last 16-bit parameter specifies the number of 8-bit samples.

Before recording or playing back samples, first set the sampling rate. Use DSP command 41h to play back samples or command 42h to capture samples. With both commands, a 16-bit value follows the command code, specifying the sample frequency in Hertz. Values between 5,000 and 44,100 are permissible. It doesn't matter whether you are sampling in mono or stereo. Send the most significant byte of the sampling rate to the DSP first, followed by the least significant byte.

Before sampling, program the DMA controller with the starting address and number of sample bytes (Cxh) or sample words (Bx). Remember that 16-bit samples use a different DMA channel than 8-bit samples. After the desired number of samples have been captured or played, the DSP triggers an interrupt. If auto init DMA mode was selected, you can terminate this mode within the interrupt routine by using the DAh command for 8-bit samples and D9h for 16-bit samples.

8-bit Mono, Single Cycle DMA mode

Eight different commands are available for capturing and playing back 8-bit sample in single cycle DMA mode. They're all programmed similarly, so we'll describe them together.

DSP commands for 8-bit Mono, Single Cycle DMA mode	
Command Code	Task
14h	8-bit single cycle DMA output
24h	8-bit single cycle DMA input
16h	8/2 bit ADPCM single cycle DMA output
17h	8/2 bit ADPCM single cycle DMA output with reference byte
74h	8/4 bit ADPCM single cycle DMA output
75h	8/4 bit ADPCM single cycle DMA output with reference byte
76h	8/3 bit ADPCM single cycle DMA output
77h	8/3 bit ADPCM single cycle DMA output with reference byte

First, switch on the speaker. Command D1h switches the speaker on so you can playback the samples. Command D3h switches the speaker off so you can capture samples. Next set the sample frequency, using command 40h.

Now program the DMA controller by setting the starting memory address and block length. An interrupt handler must be activated to deal with the transferred data. To begin recording or playback of the samples, use one of the commands from the table followed by the transfer length parameter. This parameter is sent as two bytes: the least followed by most significant byte. Following the transfer, the DSP triggers an interrupt.

After you've completed a recording or playback, you must disconnect the DSP from amplifier using command D3h. Now the operation is considered finished.

8-bit Mono, Auto Init DMA mode

Five different commands are available for capturing and playing back 8-bit samples in auto init DMA mode. These commands are similar to single cycle DMA mode except that a separate command is used to terminate the operation.

DSP commands for 8-bit Mono, Auto Init DMA mode	
Command Code	Task
1Ch	8-bit auto init DMA output
1Fh	8/2 bit ADPCM auto init DMA output with reference byte
2Ch	8-bit auto init DMA input
7Dh	8/4 bit ADPCM auto init DMA output with reference byte
7Fh	8/3 bit ADPCM auto init DMA output with reference byte

8-bit mono, High Speed Single Cycle DMA mode

DSP Version 3.xx features a high speed DMA mode to allow higher sampling rates. Two additional commands are used to record and play back 8-bit samples in the single cycle version of this mode.

DSP commands for 8-bit Mono, Auto Init DMA mode	
Command Code	Task
91h	8-bit high speed single cycle DMA output
99h	8-bit high speed single cycle DMA input

These two commands are similar to commands 14h and 24h. However, when high speed mode is complete, you must reset the DSP. Only then will the DSP be able to accept new commands.

8-bit Mono, High Speed Auto Init DMA mode

DSP Version 3.xx also includes two commands for recording and playing back samples in high speed auto init DMA mode.

DSP commands for 8-bit Mono, Auto Init DMA mode	
Command code	Task
90h	8-bit high speed auto init DMA output
98h	8-bit high speed auto init DMA input

These two commands are similar to commands 1Ch and 2Ch. However, when high speed mode is complete, you must reset the DSP. Only then will the DSP be able to accept new commands.

8-bit Stereo, High Speed Single Cycle DMA mode

DSP Version 3.xx also features stereo recording and playback. While this is a desirable feature, it's also more time-consuming to program. Sampling is started using commands 91h and 99h, described above. However, both before and after you send the above commands, you must perform certain other operations, which we'll describe.

DSP commands for 8-bit Mono, Auto Init DMA mode	
Command code	Task
91h	8-bit high speed single cycle DMA output
99h	8-bit high speed single cycle DMA input

For recording, first disconnect the speakers using DSP command D3h. Then switch to DSP stereo mode using command A8h.

For playback, connect the speaker using command D1h. Next set bit 2 in mixer register 0Eh. Now transfer one byte containing the value 80h. For this, first program the DMA controller for the address of the single byte and a transfer length of one, then issue the DSP single cycle transfer command 14h, also specifying 1 byte as the transfer length.

There are a few more preparation for both recording and playback of the stereo samples. Set the DMA controller for the address of the transfer buffer and block length. Next set the sampling frequency using command 40h. Now back to the mixer. For playback the mixer register is 0Eh and for recording the mixer register is 0Ch. Read and save the contents of the respective register. Then set bit 5 and rewrite the contents back to the register. This activates the input or output filter.

Finally start the sampling operation by first setting the transfer length using command 48h followed by either command 99h (record) or 91h (playback). When the block has been processed, an interrupt is triggered.

You can then perform additional stereo sample operations from within the interrupt handler. Simply program the DMA controller and issue DSP command 99h or 91h. It isn't necessary to perform the other operations again, such as accessing the mixer.

When the stereo operations are complete, you'll have to undo these settings. Restore the previous contents of mixer register 0Ch or 0Eh which you already saved.

Switch the DSP back to mono mode. For recording, return the DSP to mono mode simply by issuing command A0h. For playback, clear bit 1 in mixer register 0Eh. Finally, disconnect the speaker to conclude the whole operation. You'll probably discover that recording or playing back stereo samples using DSP Version 3.xx requires a lot of effort.

8-bit Stereo, High Speed Auto Init DMA mode

These commands are similar to the auto init DMA mode commands. The major difference is that a transfer using high speed auto init DMA mode can be terminated only by resetting the DSP. Otherwise, the procedure is every bit as complicated as the procedure for previous high speed single cycle DMA mode.

DSP commands for 8-bit stereo, High Speed Auto Init DMA mode	
Command code	Task
90h	8-Bit High Speed Auto Init DMA output
98h	8-Bit High Speed Auto Init DMA input

DSP command reference

DSP commands by command code		DSP commands by command code	
10h	8-bit sample Direct Mode output	80h	Pause input
14h	8-bit Single Cycle DMA output	90h	8-bit High Speed Auto Init DMA output
16h	8/2 bit ADPCM Single Cycle DMA output	91h	8-bit High Speed Single Cycle DMA output
17h	8/2 bit ADPCM Single Cycle DMA output with reference byte	98h	8-bit High Speed Auto Init DMA input
1Ch	8 bit Auto Init DMA output	99h	8-bit High Speed Single Cycle DMA input
1Fh	8/2 bit ADPCM Auto Init DMA output with reference byte	A0h	Set input mode to mono
20h	8-bit Direct Mode input	A8h	Set input mode to stereo
24h	8-bit Single Cycle DMA input	Bxh	16-bit DMA input/output
2Ch	8-bit Auto Init DMA input	Cxh	8-bit DMA input/output
40h	Set sample frequency	D0h	Pause 8-bit DMA transfer
41h	Set sample frequency for output	D1h	Switch speaker on
42h	Set sample frequency for input	D3h	Switch speaker off
48h	Set block length for Auto Init and High-Speed DMA transfers	D4h	Continue 8-bit DMA transfer
74h	8/4 Bit ADPCM Single Cycle DMA output	D5h	Pause 16-bit DMA transfer
75h	8/4 Bit ADPCM Single Cycle DMA output with reference byte	D6h	Continue 16-bit DMA transfer
76h	8/3 Bit ADPCM Single Cycle DMA output	D8h	Get status of speaker
77h	8/3 Bit ADPCM Single Cycle DMA output with reference byte	D9h	Conclude 16-bit Auto Init DMA transfer
7Dh	8/4 Bit ADPCM Auto-Init DMA output with reference byte	DAh	Conclude 8-bit Auto Init DMA transfer
7Fh	8/3 Bit ADPCM Auto-Init DMA output with reference byte	E1h	Get version number of DSP

DSP Commands in detail

10h	**8-bit Direct Mode Output**

Output   10h   Command code

bSample   sample byte to be output

Output an 8-bit sample through the DSP. The frequency at which this command is executed determines the sampling rate.

Available	1.xx	2.0	2.01+	3.xx	4.xx
	●	●	●	●	●

14h	8-bit Single Cycle DMA Output

Output	14h	Command code
	lo(Length-1)	Low-byte of block length - 1
	hi(Length-1)	High-byte of block length - 1

Output a block of 8-bit samples using Single Cycle DMA mode through the DSP. Before using this command, set the sample frequency and program the DMA controller with the starting address and block length. When using this command, specify block length - 1.

Available

1.xx	2.0	2.01+	3.xx	4.xx
●	●	●	●	●

16h	8/2 bit ADPCM Single Cycle DMA Output

Output	16h	Command code
	lo(Length-1)	Low-byte of block length - 1
	hi(Length-1)	High-byte of block length - 1

Output a block of 8/2 bit ADPCM samples using Single Cycle DMA mode through the DSP. Before using this command, set the sample frequency and program the DMA controller with the starting address and block length. When using this command, specify the block length - 1. This command is used to output the second and all subsequent 8/2 bit ADPCM sample blocks. Output the first block using command 17h.

Available

1.xx	2.0	2.01+	3.xx	4.xx
●	●	●	●	●

17h	8/2 bit ADPCM Single Cycle DMA Output with reference byte

Output	17h	Command code
	lo(Length-1)	Low-byte of block length - 1
	hi(Length-1)	High-byte of block length - 1

Output a block of 8/2 bit ADPCM samples using Single Cycle DMA mode through the DSP. Before using this command, set the sample frequency and program the DMA controller with the starting address and the block length. The first byte of the block is a normal 8-bit sample, not an ADPCM compressed sample. Subsequent blocks are output using command 16h.

Available

1.xx	2.0	2.01+	3.xx	4.xx
●	●	●	●	●

1Ch	8-Bit Auto Init DMA Output

Output	1Ch	Command code

Output a block of 8-bit samples using Auto Init DMA mode through the DSP. Before using this command, set the sample frequency and program the DMA controller with the starting address and block length and set the DSP block length using command 48h.

Two commands can be used to terminate an Auto Init operation. Use either command DAh to terminate Auto Init mode or command 14h to return to Single Cycle mode.

Use command D0h to pause Auto Init mode. Use command D4h to resume processing following the pause.

Available	1.xx	2.0	2.01+	3.xx	4.xx
		●	●	●	●

1Fh	**8/2 bit ADPCM Auto Init DMA Output with reference byte**

Output	1Fh	Command code

Output a block of 8/2 bit ADPCM samples using Auto Init DMA mode through the DSP. Before using this command, set the sample frequency, program the DMA controller with the starting address and block length and set the DSP block length using command 48h. The first byte of the data block contains the reference byte

Two commands can be used to terminate an Auto Init operation. Use either command DAh to terminate Auto Init mode or command 16h to return to Single Cycle 8/2 bit ADPCM mode.

Use command D0h to pause Auto Init mode. Use command D4h to resume processing following the pause.

Available	1.xx	2.0	2.01+	3.xx	4.xx
		●	●	●	●

20h	**8-bit Direct Mode Input**

Output	20h	Command code

Input an 8-bit sample through the DSP. The sample byte is read from the DSP Read -Data port. The frequency at which this command is executed determines the sampling rate.

Available	1.xx	2.0	2.01+	3.xx	4.xx
	●	●	●	●	●

24h	**8-bit Single Cycle DMA Input**

Output	24h	Command code
	lo(Length-1)	low-byte of block length - 1
	hi(Length-1)	high-byte of block length - 1

Input a block of 8-bit samples using Single Cycle DMA mode through the DSP. Before using this command, set the sample frequency and program the DMA controller with the starting address and block length. When using this command, specify the block length - 1.

Available	1.xx	2.0	2.01+	3.xx	4.xx
	●	●	●	●	●

2Ch   8-bit Auto Init DMA Input

Output	2Ch	Command code

Input a block of 8-bit samples using Auto Init DMA mode through the DSP. Before using this command, set the sample frequency, program the DMA controller with the starting address and block length, and set the DMA block length using command 48h.

Two commands can be used to terminate an Auto Init operation. Use either command DAh to terminate Auto Init mode or command 24h to return to Single Cycle DMA mode.

Use command D0h to pause Auto Init mode. Use command D4h to resume processing following the pause.

Available

1.xx	2.0	2.01+	3.xx	4.xx
	●	●	●	●

40h   Set sample frequency

Output	40h	Command code
	hi(time constant)	most significant byte of time constant

Use one of these formula is used to calculate the time constant for a desired *sample frequency*:

```
16 Bit:  time constant = 65536 - (256000000/(Channels * Sample frequency)),
 8 Bit:  time constant =  256 - (1000000/(Channels*Sample frequency)),
```

where *channels* = 1 for mono;

= 2 for stereo

Only the most significant (high)byte of the resulting value is passed to the DSP by this command. For DSP Version 4.xx, you can set the sample frequency using commands 41h and 42h.

Available

1.xx	2.0	2.01+	3.xx	4.xx
●	●	●	●	●

41h   Set Output Sample Frequency

Output	41h	Command code
	hi(Sample frequency)	high-byte of sample frequency
	lo(Sample frequency)	low-byte of sample frequency

This DSP 4.xx command sets the sample frequency for Single Cycle and Auto Init DMA output transfers. The sample frequency may range between 5,000 and 45,000 (Hertz). This command is for either mono or stereo modes.

Available

1.xx	2.0	2.01+	3.xx	4.xx
				●

42h — Set Input Sample Frequency

Output	41h	Command code
	hi(Sampling frequency)	high-byte of sampling frequency
	lo(Sampling frequency)	low-byte of sampling frequency

This DSP 4.xx command sets the sample frequency for Single Cycle and Auto Init DMA input transfers. The sample frequency may range between 5,000 and 45,000 (Hertz). This command is for either mono or stereo modes.

Available	1.xx	2.0	2.01+	3.xx	4.xx
					●

48h — Set Auto Init and High Speed DMA Block Length

Output	48h	Command code
	hi(BlockLength-1)	high-byte of block length in bytes - 1
	lo(BlockLength-1)	low-byte of block length in bytes - 1

This command sets the block length in bytes for subsequent Auto Init and High Speed DMA transfers. An interrupt is triggered after this amount of data is transferred.

Available	1.xx	2.0	2.01+	3.xx	4.xx
		●	●	●	●

74h — 8/4 bit ADPCM-Single Cycle DMA Output

Output	74h	Command code
	lo(Length-1)	low-byte of block length - 1
	hi(Length-1)	high-byte of block length - 1

Output a block of 8/4 bit ADPCM samples using Single Cycle DMA mode through the DSP. Before using this command, set the sample frequency and program the DMA controller with the starting address and block length. When using this command, specify block length - 1. This command is used to output the second and all subsequent 8/4 bit ADPCM sample blocks. Output the first block using command 75h.

Available	1.xx	2.0	2.01+	3.xx	4.xx
	●	●	●	●	●

75h — 8/4 bit ADPCM Single Cycle DMA Output with reference byte

Output	75h	Command code
	lo(Length-1)	low-byte of block length - 1
	hi(Length-1)	high-byte of block length - 1

Output a block of 8/4 bit ADPCM samples using Single Cycle DMA mode through the DSP. Before using this command, set the sample frequency and program the DMA controller with the starting address and block length. The first byte of the block is a normal 8-bit sample, not an ADPCM compressed sample. Subsequent blocks are output using command 74h.

Available

1.xx	2.0	2.01+	3.xx	4.xx
●	●	●	●	●

76h   8/3 bit ADPCM Single Cycle DMA Output

Output	76h	Command code
	lo(Length-1)	low-byte of block length - 1
	hi(Length-1)	high-byte of block length - 1

Output a blcok of 8/3 bit ADPCM samples using Single Cycle DMA mode through the DSP. Before using this command, set the sample frequency and program the DMA controller with the starting address and the block length. When using this command specify block length - 1. This command is used to output the second and all subsequent 8/3 bit ADPCM sample blocks. Output the first block using command 77h.

Available

1.xx	2.0	2.01+	3.xx	4.xx
●	●	●	●	●

77h   8/3 bit ADPCM Single Cycle DMA Output with reference byte

Output	77h	Command code
	lo(Length-1)	low-byte of block length - 1
	hi(Length-1)	high-byte of block length - 1

Output a block of 8/3 bit ADPCM samples using Single Cycle DMA mode through the DSP. Before using this command, set the sample frequency and program the DMA controller with the starting address and the block length. The first byte of the block is a normal 8-bit sample, not an ADPCM compressed sample. Subsequent blocks are output using command 76h.

Available

1.xx	2.0	2.01+	3.xx	4.xx
●	●	●	●	●

7Dh   8/4 bit ADPCM-Auto-Init DMA Output with reference byte

Output	7Dh	Command code

Output a block of 8/4 bit ADPCM samples to the DSP using Auto Init DMA mode through the DSP. Before using this command, set the sample frequency, program the DMA controller with the starting address and block length and set the DSP block length using command 48h. The first byte of the data block contains the reference byte

Two commands can be used to terminate an Auto Init operation. Use either command DAh to terminate Auto Init mode or command 74h to return to Single Cycle 8/4 bit ADPCM output mode.

Use command D0h to pause Auto Init mode. Use command D4h to resume processing following the pause.

Available	1.xx	2.0	2.01+	3.xx	4.xx
		●	●	●	●

7Fh	**8/3 bit ADPCM Auto Init DMA Output with reference byte**

Output   7Fh   Command code

Output a block of 8/3 bit ADPCM samples using Auto Init DMA mode through the DSP. Before using this command, set the sample frequency, program the DMA controller with the starting address and block length, and set the DSP block length using command 48h. The first byte of the data block contains the reference byte

Two commands can be used to terminate an Auto Init operation. Use either command DAh to terminate Auto Init mode or command 76h to return to Single Cycle 8/3 bit ADPCM output mode.

Use command D0h to pause Auto Init mode. Use command D4h to resume processing following the pause.

Available	1.xx	2.0	2.01+	3.xx	4.xx
		●	●	●	●

80h	**Pause Input**

Output   80h   Command code

         lo(PauseDuration - 1)   low-byte of duration of pause - 1

         hi(PauseDuration - 1)   high-byte of duration of pause - 1

Temporarily pause (halt) the transfer started using Single Cycle or Auto Init DMA input. The duration of the pause is relative to the sample frequency set by command 40h. After this period of time has passed, the transfer resumes.

Available	1.xx	2.0	2.01+	3.xx	4.xx
	●	●	●	●	●

90h	**8-bit High Speed Auto Init DMA Output**

Output   90h   Command code

Output a block of 8-bit samples using High Speed Auto Init DMA mode through the DSP. Before using this command, set the sample frequency, program the DMA controller with the starting address and block length and set the DSP block length using command 48h.

To terminate High Speed Auto Init mode, you must reset the DSP.

Available	1.xx	2.0	2.01+	3.xx	4.xx
			●	●	

91h   8-bit High Speed Single Cycle DMA Output

Output	91h	Command code

Output a block of 8-bit samples using Single Cycle High Speed DMA mode through the DSP. Before using this command, set the sample frequency, program the DMA controller with the starting address and block length and set the DSP block length using command 48h.

Available

1.xx	2.0	2.01+	3.xx	4.xx
		●	●	

98h   8-bit High Speed Auto Init DMA Input

Output	98h	Command code

Input a block of 8-bit samples in High Speed Auto Init DMA mode through the DSP. Before using this command, set the sample frequency, program the DMA controller with the starting address and block length and set the DSP block length using command 48h

To terminate High Speed Auto Init mode, you must reset the DSP.

Available

1.xx	2.0	2.01+	3.xx	4.xx
		●	●	

99h   8-bit High-Speed-Single-Cycle DMA input

Output	91h	Command code

Input a block of 8-bit samples using Single Cycle High Speed DMA mode through the DSP. Before using this command, set the sample frequency, program the DMA controller with the starting address and block length and set the DSP block length using command 48h

Available

1.xx	2.0	2.01+	3.xx	4.xx
		●	●	

A0h   Set Input mode to Mono

Output	A0h	Command code

Set the DSP input mode to mono. This is the default setting.

Available

1.xx	2.0	2.01+	3.xx	4.xx
			●	

A8h   Set Input mode to Stereo

Output	A8h	Command code

Set the DSP input mode to stereo. Reset this mode to mono when recording is complete.

Since this command is not available after DSP Version 4.xx, use command Bxh instead.

Available	1.xx	2.0	2.01+	3.xx	4.xx
				●	

Bxh   **16-bit DMA Input/Output**

Output	Bxh	Command code
	Operation mode	see below
	lo(Samples-1)	low-byte of number of 16-bit samples - 1
	hi(Samples-1)	high-byte of number of 16-bit samples - 1

For DSP Version 4.xx, input or output a 16-bit sample block. The complete command code varies depending on the transfer direction, the selected DMA mode and usage of the FIFO buffer. The command code has the following structure:

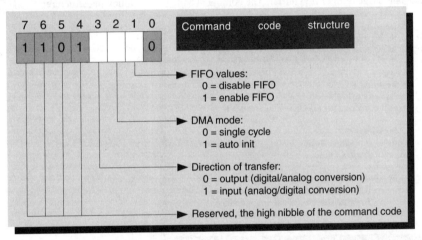

The operation mode contains two bit fields that specify whether to sample in mono or stereo and also whether the samples are unsigned or signed. Using unsigned values, the smallest measurable signal amplitude corresponds to the value 0h; using signed values, this corresponds to 8000h (-1).

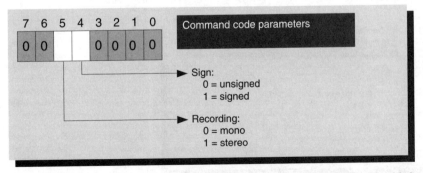

Before using this command, set the sample frequency, program the DMA controller with the starting address and block length and set the DSP block length using command 48h.

For an Auto Init DMA transfer, you can terminate this mode by using command D9h to terminate Auto Init mode or command Bxh again with bit 2=0 (Single Cycle).

Use command D5h to pause Auto Init mode. Use command D6h to resume processing following the pause.

Available

1.xx	2.0	2.01+	3.xx	4.xx
				●

Cxh	8-Bit DMA Input/Output

Output	Cxh	Command code
	Operation mode	see below
	lo(Samples-1)	low-byte of number of 8-bit samples - 1
	hi(Samples-1)	high-byte of number of 8-bit samples - 1

For DSP Version 4.xx, input or output an 8-bit sample block. The complete command code varies depending on the transfer direction, the selected DMA mode and usage of the FIFO buffer. The command code has the following structure:

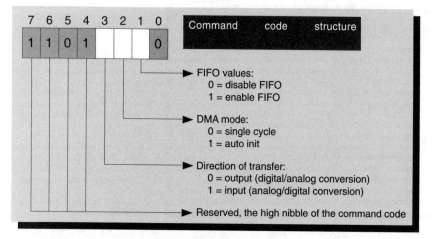

The operation mode contains two bit fields that specify whether to sample in mono or stereo and also whether the samples are unsigned or signed. Using unsigned values, the smallest measurable signal amplitude corresponds to the value 0h; using signed values, this corresponds to 80h (-1).

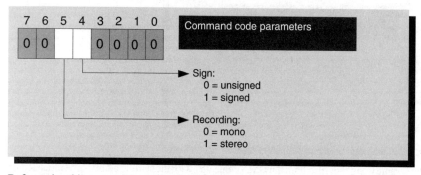

Before using this command, set the sample frequency, program the DMA controller with the starting address and block length and set the DSP block length using command 48h.

For an Auto Init DMA transfer, you can terminate this mode by using command DAh to terminate Auto Init mode or command Cxh again with bit 2=0 (Single Cycle).

Use command D0h to pause Auto Init mode. Use command D4h to resume processing following the pause.

Available	1.xx	2.0	2.01+	3.xx	4.xx
					●

D0h   8-Bit DMA Input/Output

Output	D0h	Command code

Temporarily pause (halt) an 8-bit DMA transfer started in Single Cycle or Auto Init DMA mode. Use command D4h to resume the transfer.

Available	1.xx	2.0	2.01+	3.xx	4.xx
	●	●	●	●	●

D1h   Switch Speaker On

Output	D1h	Command code

Connect the DSP to the amplifier on the Sound Blaster card. This command is discontinued, starting with DSP Version 4.xx.

Available	1.xx	2.0	2.01+	3.xx	4.xx
	●	●	●	●	●

D3h   Switch Speaker Off

Output	D1h	Command code

Disconnect the DSP from the amplifier on the Sound Blaster card. This command is discontinued, starting with DSP Version 4.xx.

Available	1.xx	2.0	2.01+	3.xx	4.xx
	●	●	●	●	●

D4h   Resume 8-bit DMA transfer

Output	D4h	Command code

Resume the 8-bit DMA transfer that has been paused by command D0h

Available	1.xx	2.0	2.01+	3.xx	4.xx
	●	●	●	●	●

D5h	Pause 16-bit sample DMA transfer

Output	D5h	Command code

Temporarily pause (halt) a 16-bit DMA transfer started by the Bxh command. Use command D6h to resume the transfer.

Available	1.xx	2.0	2.01+	3.xx	4.xx
					●

D6h	Resume 16-bit DMA transfer

Output	D5h	Command code

Resume the 16-bit DMA transfer that has been paused by command D5h

Available	1.xx	2.0	2.01+	3.xx	4.xx
					●

D8h	Get Speaker Status

Output	D8h	Command code

Returns the status of the DSP connection to the Sound Blaster card amplifier. After writing this command code, read the Read-Data port. A value of 0FFh (-1) means they are connected; a value of zero manes they are not connected.

Available	1.xx	2.0	2.01+	3.xx	4.xx
		●	●	●	●

D9h	Terminate 16-bit Auto Init DMA transfer

Output	D9h	Command code

Terminate the 16-bit Auto Init DMA transfer initiated by command Bxh. The current transfer is allowed to complete before the operation is terminated.

Available	1.xx	2.0	2.01+	3.xx	4.xx
					●

DAh	Terminate 8-bit Auto Init DMA transfer

Output	DAh	Command code

Terminate the 8-bit Auto Init DMA transfer initiated by command Cxh. The current transfer is allowed to complete before the operation is terminated.

Available	1.xx	2.0	2.01+	3.xx	4.xx
					●

E1h	Get DSP Version number

Output	E1h	Command code

Returns the DSP version number. After writing this command code, read the Read-Data register twice. The first byte is the DSP main version number; the second byte is the DSP subversion number. Use the version number to determine what kind of Sound Blaster card is installed.

Available

1.xx	2.0	2.01+	3.xx	4.xx
●	●	●	●	●

Hard drive recording in practice

You'll find the following program(s) on the companion CD-ROM

DSPUTIL.H (C listing)
DSP.C (C listing)
ARGS.PAS (Pascal listing)
SBUTIL.PAS (Pascal listing)
MIXUTIL.PAS (Pascal listing)
DSP.PAS (Pascal listing)
DSPUTIL.PAS (Pascal listing)
DMAUTIL.PAS (Pascal listing)

The Mixer

The mixer controls the volume of the individual input and output sources, specifies how the sources are to be connected and enables the sample input signals.

Since different DSPs are used on various Sound Blaster cards, the mixers used on these cards in the Sound Blaster family are also different. There are three types of mixers:

1. CT1335 - This is a relatively primitive mixer; used primarily on the Sound Blaster 2.0 with CD-ROM drive expansion board.

2. CT1345 - A more advanced mixer; found on Sound Blaster Pro cards.

3. CT1745 - A more powerful mixer; introduced on Sound Blaster 16.

The features of the mixers vary from primitive to powerful. The mixer settings affect the combination of different inputs and outputs, the provision of filters for noise reduction and the sound card's resolution capacity relative to the volume of a sound source or an output signal. The greater the resolution capacity, the more different input levels are possible for the different sources.

Controlling the mixer

The mixer registers are addressed through separate address and data ports. The number of the desired mixer register is written to the address port, then its contents can be read from or data written to that register through the data port. The mixer's address and data ports are at offsets to the Sound Blaster card base address as follows:

```
Mixer Address Port = Sound Blaster Base Address + 4
Mixer Data Port = Sound Blaster Base Address + 5
```

Unlike the OPL chip, after writing the desired register number to the mixer address port, you can immediately read from or write to the register.

This assembly language code shows you how to write to one of the mixer's registers:

mov	dx,SbPortBasiS	;Load port address of SB card
add	dl,04h	;Offset for mixer address port
mov	al,MixRegNr	;Number of desired mixer register
out	dx,a	;Send to mixer address port
inc	d	;Set access to mixer data port
mov	al,NewWord	;load new value for register
out	dx,A	;and write to mixer data port

The following shows you how to read the contents of one of the mixer's registers:

mov	dx,SbPortBasis	;Load port address of SB card
add	dl,04h	;Offset of mixer address port
mov	al,MixRegNr	;Number of desired mixer register
out	dx,a	;Send to mixer address port
inc	d	;Set access to mixer data port
in	al,dx	;and read mixer registers

In the following descriptions, you'll notice the function of many of the register bits is undefined. Creative Labs warns you to not make assumptions about the contents of the reserved bits when accessing these registers and suggests the following procedures:

1. To test the contents of a register: read and then mask out the undefined bits.

2.. To modify the contents of a register: read the register contents; set or reset only those bits that require changing; rewrite the entire register contents.

3. To protect the mixer environment: a program that changes the mixer registers should initially read and save the register contents and later restore the register contents before ending

CT1335 mixer

The CT1335 mixer has five registers. These registers control the various output sources. It also lets you set the volume for Line-In, MIDI, CD and Microphone.

The CT1335 Mixer	Register	Bit 7	Bit 6	Bit 5	Bit 4	Bit 3	Bit 2	Bit 1	Bit 0
	00h	Mixer-Reset							
	02h					Master-Volume			
	06h					MIDI-Volume			
	08h					CD-Volume			
	0Ah					Voice-Volume			

Register 00h   **Mixer Reset**

To reset the mixer, write any value to this register. Reset restores the default register contents.

Register 02h   **Master Volume**

To set a master volume level, write a value from 0 to 7 to this register. This value changes the volume level from -46 to 0 decibels in increments of about 4 decibels. The default is 4, for -11 decibels.

Register 06h   **MIDI Volume**

Same as register 02h, but for MIDI.

Register 08h   **CD Volume**

Same as register 02, but for CD except the default is 0, for -46 decibels.

Register 0Ah   **Voice Volume**

To set a voice volume, write a value from 0 to 3 to this register. This value changes the volume level from -46 decibels to 0 decibels in increments of about 7 decibels. The default is 0, for -46 decibels.

CT1345 Mixer

The CT1345 mixer has separate volume controls for the left and right stereo channels and lets you select the input source to feed to the DSP for sampling. It also contains an input and output filter for noise suppression.

The 1345 Mixer

Register	Bit 7	Bit 6	Bit 5	Bit 4	Bit 3	Bit 2	Bit 1	Bit 0
00h	Mixer-Reset							
04h	Voice-Volume left				Voice--Volume right			
0Ah						Microphone Volume		
0Ch			Input-Filter		Low-Pass-Filter	Sample source		
0Eh			Output-Filter				Stereo-Switch	
22h	Master-Volume left				Master-Volume right			
26h	FM--Volume left				FM-Volume right			
28h	CD--Volume left			·	CD-Volume right			
2Eh	Line--Volume left				Line-Volume right			

Register 00h   **Mixer Reset**

To reset the mixer, write any value to this register. Reset restores the default register contents.

Register 04h   **Voice Volume Left & Right (Values 0-15)**

Register 0Ah, Bits 0-2   **Microphone Volume**

To set a microphone volume level, write a value from 0 to 7 to this register. This value changes the volume level from -46 to 0 decibels in increments of about 6 decibels. The default is 0, for -46 decibels.

Register 0Ch, Bits 1-2	**Input Source**

00b   Microphone (Default)

01b   CD

10b   Microphone

11b   Line In

Register 0Ch, Bit 3	**Set Input Filter**

Specifies the range of the input filter, if register 0Ch, Bit 5 is set. If register 0Eh, Bit 5 is set, it becomes an output filter.

0b   3.2 Khz Low Pass Filter (Default)

1b   8.8 Khz Low Pass Filter (High Filter)

Register 0Ch, Bit 5	**Activate Input Filter**

0b   Low Pass Input Filter is active (Default)

1b   Low Pass Input Filter is inactive

Register 0Eh, Bit 1	**Stereo Switch**

Enable mono or stereo output.

0b   Mono output (Default)

1b   Stereo output

Register 0Eh, Bit 5	**Activate Output Filter**

0b   Low Pass Output Filter is active (Default)

1b   Low Pass Output Filter is inactive

Register 22h	**Master Volume Left & Right (Values 0-15)**

Register 26h	**FM Volume Left & Right**

To set the Master or FM volume level, write a value from 0 to 15 to one of these registers. This value changes the volume level from -46 to 0 decibels in increments of about 4 decibels. The default is 4, for -11 decibels.

Register 28h	**CD Volume Left & Right (Values 0-15)**

Register 2Eh	**Line Volume Left & Right (Values 0-15)**

To set the CD or Line volume level, write a value from 0 to 15 to one of these registers. This value changes the volume level from -46 to 0 decibels in increments of about 4 decibels. The default is 0, for -46 decibels.

The low pass filters are used to attenuate high-frequency sounds during recording to achieve a better recording quality. The 3.2 KHz filter is recommended for mono samples with sampling rates less than 18 Khz, while the 8.8 KHz filter is recommended for mono samples with sampling rates between 18 Khz and 36 Khz.

Disable both filters for all stereo sampling and for mono sampling at a sampling rate greater than 36 Khz.

CT1745 Mixer

The CT1745 mixer is the top of the line mixer in the Sound Blaster line. The large number of registers is an indication of this mixer's capabilities.

The CT1745 Mixer

Register	Bit 7	Bit 6	Bit 5	Bit 4	Bit 3	Bit 2	Bit 1	Bit 0
00h	Mixer-Reset							
04h	Voice-Volume left				Voice-Volume right			
0Ah					Microphone--Volume			
22h	Master-Volume left				Master-Volume right			
26h	FM-Volume left				FM-Volume right			
28h	CD-Volume left				CD-Volume right			
2Eh	Line-Volume left				Line-Volume right			
30h	Master-Volume left							
31h	Master-Volume right							
32h	Voice-Volume left							
33h	Voice-Volume right							
34h	MIDI-Volume left							
35h	MIDI-Volume right							
36h	CD-Volume left							
37h	CD-Volume right							
38h	Line-Volume left							
39h	Line-Volume right							
3Ah	Mikrofon-Volume							
3Bh	PC-Loudspeaker Volume							
3Ch				Line left	Line right	CD left	CD right	Microphone
3Dh		MIDI left	MIDI right	Line left	Line right	CD left	CD right	Microphone
3Eh		MIDI left	MIDI right	Line left	Line right	CD left	CD right	Microphone
3Fh	Input Preamplifier left							
40h	Input Preamplifier right							
41h	Output Preamplifier left							
42h	Output Preamplifier right							
43h								AGC
44h	Treble left							
45h	Treble right							
46h	Bass left							
47h	Bass right							

The CT1745 has any new features. For example, the resolution of the individual volume registers is finer. Several output sources can be mixed into the output signal. Several input sources can be mixed into the input signal. Finally, the treble and bass settings are individually adjustable for the left and right output channels. The CT1745 lacks the filter bits of the CT1345, since the new mixer uses dynamic signal filtering.

Register 00h	Mixer Reset

To reset the mixer, write any value to this register. Reset restores the default register contents.

Register 04h	Voice Volume Left & Right

Register 0Ah	Microphone Volume

To set the Microphone volume level, write a value from 0 to 7 to one of this register. This value changes the volume level from -42 to 0 decibels in increments of about 6 decibels. The default is 0, for -42 decibels.

Register 0Ah is for compatibility with the previous mixers. You can also set the microphone volume using register 3Ah which offers finer resolution.

Register 22h	Master Volume Left & Right

Register 26h	FM Volume Left & Right

To set the Master or FM volume level, write a value from 0 to 15 to one of these registers. This value changes the volume level from -60 to 0 decibels in increments of about 4 decibels. The default is 12, for -12 decibels.

Registers 22h and 26h are for compatibility with the previous mixers. You can also set the volumes using registers 30h to 3Ah which offers finer resolution.

Register 28h	CD Volume Left & Right

Register 2Eh	Line Volume Left & Right

To set the CD and Line volume levels, write a value from 0 to 15 to these register. This value changes the volume level from -60 to 0 decibels in increments of about 4 decibels. The default is 0, for -60 decibels.

Registers 28H and 2Eh are for compatibility with the previous mixers. You can also set the line volume using registers 30h to 3Ah which offers finer resolution.

Register 30h/31h	FM Volume Left & Right

Register 2h/33h	Voice Volume Left & Right

Register 34h/35h	MIDI Volume Left & Right

To set any of these volume levels, write a value from 0 to 31 to these register. This value changes the volume level from -62 to 0 decibels in increments of about 2 decibels. The default is 24, for -14 decibels.

Register 36h/37h	CD Volume Left & Right

Register 38h/39h	Line Volume Left & Right

Register 3Ah	Microphone Volume Left & Right

To set any of these volume levels, write a value from 0 to 31 to these register. This value changes the volume level from -62 to 0 decibels in increments of about 2 decibels. The default is 24, for -14 decibels.

Register 3Bh — PC Speaker Volume

To set the speaker volume level, write a value from 0 to 3 to this register. This value changes the volume level from -18 to 0 decibels in increments of about 6 decibels. The default is 0, for -18 decibels.

Register 3Ch — Output Mixer

To connect a source to the output signal, set the respective bit.

Register 3Dh — Left channel Input Mixer

To connect a source to the left input signal, set the respective bit.

Mono recordings are sampled from this channel. For mono recordings from a stereo device, map both channels to this left input channel using registers 3Dh and 3Eh.

Register 3Eh — Right channel Input Mixer

To connect a source to the right input signal, set the respective bit.

Register 3Fh/40h — Input Preamplifier Left & Right

Register 41h/42h — Output Preamplifier Left & Right

To set the preamplifier volume levels, write a value from 0 to 3 to one of these registers. This value changes the volume level from -18 to 0 decibels in increments of about 6 decibels. The default is 0, for 0 decibels.

Register 43h, Bit 0 — Automatic Microphone Preamplifier (AGC)

0   = AGC on

1   = Preamplifier fixed at 20 dB

Register 44h/45h — Treble Left & Right

Register 46h/47h — Bass Left & Right

To set the treble or bass levels, write a value from 0 to 15 to one of these registers. This value changes the level from -14 to +14 decibels in increments of about 2 decibels. The default is 8, for 0 decibels.

Programming the mixers

In the following table, module MIXUTIL contains functions to query and set the mixer registers. As you read through following table, you'll see that we've differentiate between functions for accessing the CT1335 mixer (mix_...), the CT1345 mixer (mix3_...) and the CT1745 mixer (mix4_...).

MIXUTIL functions	
Function	Task
mix_SetBase	Set port address of Sound Blaster card
mix_Write	Send byte to mixer register
mix_Read	Read byte from mixer register
mix_Reset	Reset mixer
mix3_SetADCFilter	Switch ADC filter on or off
mix3_GetADCFilter	Get status of ADC filter
mix3_SetDACFilter	Switch DAC filter on or off
mix3_GetDACFilter	Get status of DAC filter
...	
...	
mix3_SetDACStereo	Switch stereo playback (DAC) on or off
mix3_GetDACStereo	Get status of stereo playback
mix3_SetADDACLowPass	Set low pass filter for recording
mix3_GetADDACLowPass	Get low pass filter being used
mix3_PrepareForStereo	Mixer for stereo recording/playback
mix3_RestoreFromStereo	Restore mixer to old state
mix3_SetVolume	Set output volume
mix3_GetVolume	Get output volume
mix3_SetADCSource	Set recording source
mix3_GetADCSource	Get current recording source
mix4_PrepareForMonoADC	Prepare mixer for mono recording
mix4_RestoreFromMonoADC	Restore mixer state
mix4_SetVolume	Set output volume of a mixer source
mix4_GetVolume	Get output volume
mix4_SetADCSource	Set recording source for left ADC
mix4_SetADCSourceR	Set recording source for right ADC
mix4_GetADCSource	Get recording source for left ADC
mix4_GetADCSourceR	Get recording source for right ADC
mix4_SetOUTSource	Set output(playback) source
mix4_GetOUTSource	Get output source
mix4_SetADCGain	Set recording preamplifier

MIXUTIL functions	
Function	Task
mix4_GetADCGain	Get recording preamplifier settings
mix4_SetOUTGain	Set output preamplifier
mix4_GetOUTGain	Get output preamplifier settings
mix4_SetAGC	Set/clear automatic gain control
mix4_GetAGC	Get automatic gain control
mix4_SetTreble	Set treble
mix4_GetTreble	Get treble setting
mix4_SetBass	Set bass
mix4_GetBass	Get bass setting

Program MIX demonstrates the use of these functions. Run the MIX program using the appropriate switches to set the desired mixer registers. Run this program without a switch, MIXUTIL.C to display the syntax on screen.

You'll find the following program(s) on the companion CD-ROM

MIXUTIL.C (C listing)
MIX.C (C listing)
MIX.PAS (Pascal listing)
SBUTIL.PAS (Pascal listing)
DSPUTIL.PAS (Pascal listing)
ARGS.PAS (Pascal listing)
MIXUTIL.PAS (Pascal listing)
IRQUTIL.PAS (Pascal listing)

Speech Output

A talking machine is a particularly fascinating idea to many people. Some still consider this to be pure "science fiction" but digitized speech has been around for several years. Two early computers, the Apple II and the Commodore 64, both had speech capabilities for converting text to speech. The Sound Blaster card too, has speech capabilities.

One problem in digitized speech output is the amount of disk space required for the data..

The quality of speech output is related to the number of recognizable phoneme sequences. After all, an A in front of an H sounds much different than an A following an S, and an S at the end of a word can easily turn into a Z ("Bees"), while at the beginning of a word it actually sounds like ESS. Quality speech output recognizes these differences.

In this section, you'll see that digitized speech from the Sound Blaster is easy to use.

The architecture of the Text-To-Speech Engine

To use the Sound Blaster speech output, these drivers are needed: CTTS.DRV, SBTALKER.EXE and BLASTER.DRV. When you run the Sound Blaster install, these files are copied to your hard drive, so they should be ready to use.

The following shows the role of these drivers in generating speech.

SBTALKER, the actual speech module, is a TSR (terminate and stay resident) program. Usually, you run this program immediately before you are to perform any speech output. Alternatively, you can start this program from within another program (use the DOS Exec function - see Chapter.25).

SBTALKER accesses the Sound Blaster card through driver BLASTER.DRV. This driver is in the same directory as SBTALKER (usually C:\SBTALKER). The installation program also places a batch file there named SBTALK.BAT which has only one line:

```
SBTALKER /dBLASTER
```

This line run the SBTALKER program. The /d switch (d represents driver) is the name of the environment variable containing the Sound Blaster hardware settings. If you call SBTALKER from a program, don't forget to specify this /d switch.

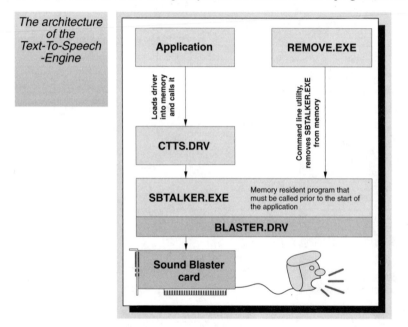

The architecture of the Text-To-Speech -Engine

Since SBTALKER is a TSR program that resides in memory, you may want to remove it from memory when you end your program. The REMOVE.EXE program in this same directory performs this function.

Loading the driver and calling the driver functions

SBTALKER contains all the functions necessary for speech output. However, another driver, CTTS.DRV links your talking program to SBTALKER. Your program load this driver into memory before outputting speech.

SBUTIL, already introduced to you, contains two functions for this purpose: sb_LoadDriver and sb_UnloadDriver.

sb_LoadDriver requires the filename of the driver as its only argument. With this information, it determines the driver size, allocates a sufficient amount of RAM and loads the driver in the allocated memory segment. It also assures the driver begins at a paragraph boundary (an address that is divisible by 16), a prerequisite for smooth operation of the driver.

The following section describes the different driver functions. After the descriptions of the driver functions, we'll describe the CTTS module which contains high-level language functions for using all these driver functions.

Function 0	**Get Version Number**

Returns CTTS driver version number

Input	BX	=	0

Output	AH = Main version number
	A = Subversion number

Function 1	**Get Blaster environment variable**

Returns the contents of the Blaster environment variable containing the Sound Blaster hardware settings

Input	BX = 1
	ES:DI = FAR pointer to an ASCIIZ string containing the Blaster environment variable. The string has to start after the equals sign, so the text "BLASTER=" does not appear in the string.

Output	AX = 0: OK
	1: Error, ES:DI is NULL or pointing at a blank string
	2: Error, invalid settings in string

This must be the first called function in a program that uses this driver.

Function 2	**Initialize CTTS driver**

Initialize the CTTS driver. This must be the second called function in a program that uses this driver.

Input	BX = 2

Output	AX = 0: OK
	<> 0: Error

Before this function can be called, function 1 must be successfully called.

Function 3	**End driver**

Informs the driver that no additional driver functions will be called.

Input	BX = 3

Output	None

This function does not remove itself from memory. To call other driver functions afterwards, you must initialize the driver again with functions 1 and 2.

Function 4   Set speech output parameters

Set various parameters for speech output. Among these parameters are the sex of the voice, the pitch, volume and speech tempo.

Input	BX = 4

A = Sex: 0 = male or 1 = female*

AH = Register, 0 = low and 1 = high

D = Volume 0 thru 9. The default is 5.

DH = Pitch 0 thru 9. The default is 5.

C = Speech tempo 0 thru 9. The default is 5.

Output	None

* ignores specification of AL = 1 female.

Function 5   Speech Output

Start text to speech conversion

Input	BX = 5

ES:DI = FAR pointer to ASCIIZ string containing text to be converted.

Output	AX = 0: OK, text conversion completed

1: Error, specified string is blank

2: Error, string is too long

Sample programs

The CTTS program contains wrapper functions for all the Sound Blaster driver functions. You can add the CTTS.H include file to your programs so they can access the CTTS functions.

Functions from the CTTS module	
Function	**Task**
ctts_GetDrvVer	Get driver version number
ctts_GetEnvSettings	Return the BLASTER environment variable
ctts_Init	Initialize driver
ctts_SetSpeechParam	Set speech parameters
ctts_Terminate	Uninstall driver
ctts_Say	Convert text to speech

Program VOICE has examples of using the CTTS functions. VOICE is a command line utility for "speaking sentences" through the Sound Blaster card. For example, you could use the following call:

```
voice "this is your Sound Blaster talking"
```

VOICE also accepts the various speech parameters for gender, volume etc. Run VOICE without parameters to display the command's syntax on screen. You'll have to call SBTALKER before starting VOICE. Also make sure the CTTS driver is in the same directory as VOICE.

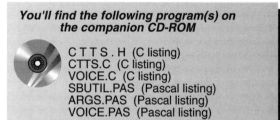

You'll find the following program(s) on the companion CD-ROM

C T T S . H (C listing)
CTTS.C (C listing)
VOICE.C (C listing)
SBUTIL.PAS (Pascal listing)
ARGS.PAS (Pascal listing)
VOICE.PAS (Pascal listing)

Index

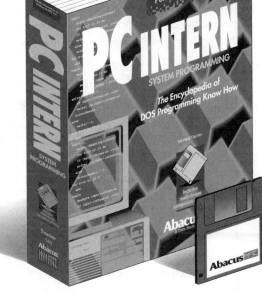

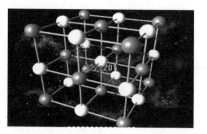

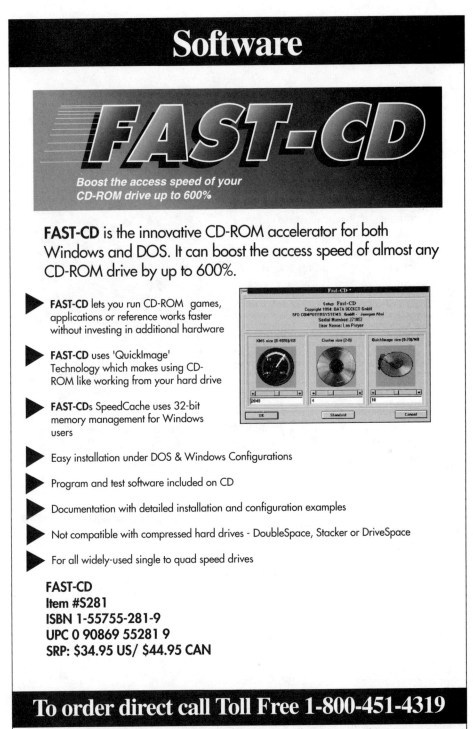

The PC Video Book

The PC Video Book teaches you the fundamentals of video technology and the hardware for creating your own videos on the PC. Quickly learn how to put credits in videos, how to adjust video color and write it back to the tape, and much more. It's the complete guide to video production including- video planning, digitizing, editing, changing color, adding effects, titles, and credits, etc. From the fundamentals of video technology to creating your own video productions- this book offers valuable tips, concrete shopping suggestions, and helpful explanations.

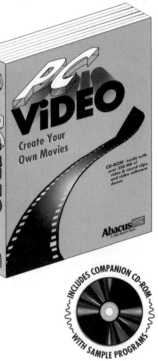

The book includes:
- Video production step-by-step
- Frame grabbing for desktop video
- Using Video for Windows
- File formats: AVI, FLC, FLI, DIB, WAV, PCM
- Creating and recording animations
- Capturing video and sound
- Choosing and connecting VCRs, camcorders and other hardware
- Editing video and sound clips

On the CD-ROM are hundreds of megabytes of digitized material (videos, images, sounds), which can be tried out and used in multimedia applications.

Authors: Kerstin Eisenkolb & Helge Weickardt
Order Item: #B265
ISBN: 1-55755-265-7
Suggested retail price: $34.95 US / $44.95 CAN includes CD-ROM

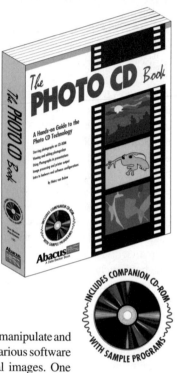

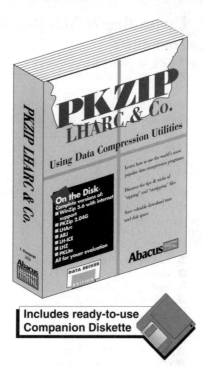

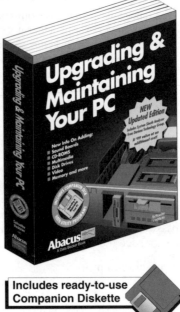

The Companion CD-ROM

PC Intern is *THE* Encyclopedia of DOS Programming Know How. We've included a CD-ROM containing the complete text of the **PC Intern** book, including all the source code and programs we talk about in the book. To view the book on the CD-ROM you must install Adobe Acrobat Reader 2.0 for Windows on your computer.

The Adobe™ Acrobat Reader 2.0 for Windows™ software gives you instant access to documents in their original form, independent of computer platform. By using the Acrobat Reader™, you can view, navigate, print selected files and present Portable Document Format (PDF) files.

System Requirements

- ➤ 386- or 486-based personal computer (486 or higher recommended)
- ➤ Microsoft Windows 3.1 or greater
- ➤ 4 Meg hard drive space and 4 Meg application RAM

Why a companion CD-ROM?

As you look through this copy of **PC Intern**, you'll quickly notice that it includes dozens of assembly language, BASIC, the C language and Pascal programs and routines. However, it would take the average user weeks to type in the listings accurately (there is over three megabytes' worth of program listings in this book).

The companion CD-ROM saves you time because now you won't have to type in the dozens of program listings we talk about in **PC Intern**. The program listings include the actual source codes in QuickBASIC, Turbo Pascal, assembly language, and C (almost all the C source codes are compatible from Turbo C++ and Microsoft C 6.00). For those BASIC, Pascal, and C codes that require separate assembly language modules, the companion CD-ROM has assembler source code and assembled object code for easy compilation.

The program files on this companion CD-ROM demonstrate general interrupt calls, video card access, keyboard operation, disk drive access, parallel port control, mouse support, joystick, support, extended and expanded memory, COM and EXE files, networking, sound, TSRs, and much more.

PLEASE NOTE: We do not include Microsoft QuickBASIC, the Microsoft Macro Assembler (MASM), Turbo C++, Microsoft C Version 6.00 with this book/CD-ROM package. We recommend that you contact Microsoft Corporation and Borland International for information on purchasing these quality program development tools.

Installing Acrobat Reader

Follow these steps to install Acrobat Reader 2.0 on your hard drive (Installation requires approximately 2 Meg of free hard drive space). Insert the CD-ROM in your drive and load Windows. From the Windows Program Manager, choose Run from the File menu. Next, type the following:

```
[drive]:\acroread.exe
```

and press Enter.

Then simply follow the instructions and prompts which appear on your screen.

Double click the Acrobat Reader icon to load it. After the Acrobat Reader is loaded, go to **File/Open...** and select either MAINFILE.PDF to view/read the **PC Intern** book *or* select PRG_MAIN.PDF to view the program pages.

Files And Directories On The Companion CD-ROM

You'll find the following files and directories on the companion CD-ROM:

PCINTERN Root Directory includes the following:

> README.TXT   > MAINFILE.PDF (the TOC)

> PRG_MAIN.PDF   > PROGLST.PDF

> ACROREAD.EXE

The directories include the following:

BOOKFILE   Contains all the Chapters in PC INTERN in portable document files.

ASM   Contains the PDF files and all the stand alone assembly language programs we talk about in the book, ready for assembly using the Microsoft Macro Assembler MASM. These programs include device drivers, a keyboard character dumper, a file finder, a macro key installer, a printer character converter, general examples of COM and EXE files, a sound program and three video display programs.

BAS   Contains the PDF files and all the BASIC programs we talk about in the book. These programs, which you can run using Microsoft QuickBASIC 4.5, include a general interrupt demonstration, a PC configuration reader, a directory reader, a joystick support program, four keyboard support programs, a memory control block reader, a real-time clock reader, hard drive configuration reader, and a program that checks whether Microsoft Windows exists in memory. PLEASE NOTE: These programs will not run under QBASIC, packaged with MS-DOS Version 5.0, BASICA, or GW-BASIC.

C   Contains the PDF files and all C language programs, assembly language modules, and assembled object codes we talk about in the book, ready for compiling with Microsoft C Version 6.00 or Borland's Turbo C++. Where applicable, special instructions for compiling are included at the beginning of each source code. These programs include a general interrupt demonstration, a PC configuration reader, a directory reader, a joystick support program, a mouse support program, four keyboard support programs, a memory control block reader, a real-time clock reader, hard drive configuration reader, a series of video programs for MDA, CGA, Hercules Graphics Card, EGA, VGA and Super VGA, sprite demonstrations, and a program for checking for the existence of Microsoft Windows in memory.

PAS   Contains the PDF files and all Pascal programs, assembly language modules, and assembled object codes, ready for compiling with Turbo Pascal Version 6.0. These programs include a general interrupt demonstration, a PC configuration reader, a directory reader, a joystick support program, a mouse support program, four keyboard support programs, a memory control block reader, a real-time clock reader, hard drive configuration reader, a series of video programs for MDA, CGA, Hercules Graphics Card, EGA, VGA and Super VGA, sprite demonstrations, and a program for checking for the existence of Microsoft Windows in memory.

EXE   Contains all the executable programs.

PRGS   Contains all the source code and programs for PC INTERN

Thank you for purchasing PC Intern and we hope you find it to valuable addition to your library.

Abacus Editorial Staff